INSTRUCTOR'S EDITION

Marketing Dynamics

FOURTH EDITION

◊DECA inside

PRECISION EXAMS

Brenda Clark, EdD
Retired CTE Director
Jenison High School
Jenison, Michigan

Cynthia Gendall Basteri, EdD
Grants Coordinator
Marketing Coordinator Emeritus
Tewksbury Public Schools
Tewksbury, Massachusetts

Chris Gassen, MBA, CFA
Faircourt Valuation Investments
Grosse Pointe Woods, Michigan

Michelle Walker, PhD
Founder
Trebla Consulting, LLC
McLean, Virginia

Publisher
The Goodheart-Willcox Company, Inc.
Tinley Park, IL
www.g-w.com

Copyright © 2019

by

The Goodheart-Willcox Company, Inc.

Previous editions copyright 2014, 2010, 2006.

All rights reserved. No part of this work may be reproduced, stored, or transmitted in any form or by any electronic or mechanical means, including information storage and retrieval systems, without the prior written permission of
The Goodheart-Willcox Company, Inc.

Manufactured in the United States of America.

ISBN 978-1-63126-630-0

1 2 3 4 5 6 7 8 9 – 19 – 22 21 20 19 18 17

The Goodheart-Willcox Company, Inc. Brand Disclaimer: Brand names, company names, and illustrations for products and services included in this text are provided for educational purposes only and do not represent or imply endorsement or recommendation by the author or the publisher.

The Goodheart-Willcox Company, Inc. Safety Notice: The reader is expressly advised to carefully read, understand, and apply all safety precautions and warnings described in this book or that might also be indicated in undertaking the activities and exercises described herein to minimize risk of personal injury or injury to others. Common sense and good judgment should also be exercised and applied to help avoid all potential hazards. The reader should always refer to the appropriate manufacturer's technical information, directions, and recommendations; then proceed with care to follow specific equipment operating instructions. The reader should understand these notices and cautions are not exhaustive.

The publisher makes no warranty or representation whatsoever, either expressed or implied, including but not limited to equipment, procedures, and applications described or referred to herein, their quality, performance, merchantability, or fitness for a particular purpose. The publisher assumes no responsibility for any changes, errors, or omissions in this book. The publisher specifically disclaims any liability whatsoever, including any direct, indirect, incidental, consequential, special, or exemplary damages resulting, in whole or in part, from the reader's use or reliance upon the information, instructions, procedures, warnings, cautions, applications, or other matter contained in this book. The publisher assumes no responsibility for the activities of the reader.

The Goodheart-Willcox Company, Inc. Internet Disclaimer: The Internet resources and listings in this Goodheart-Willcox Publisher product are provided solely as a convenience to you. These resources and listings were reviewed at the time of publication to provide you with accurate, safe, and appropriate information. Goodheart-Willcox Publisher has no control over the referenced websites and, due to the dynamic nature of the Internet, is not responsible or liable for the content, products, or performance of links to other websites or resources. Goodheart-Willcox Publisher makes no representation, either expressed or implied, regarding the content of these websites, and such references do not constitute an endorsement or recommendation of the information or content presented. It is your responsibility to take all protective measures to guard against inappropriate content, viruses, or other destructive elements.

Cover image: Julien Tromeur/Shutterstock.com

Instructor's Edition Contents

Instructional Strategies............ IE-4

Learning and Working in a Changing World — IE-4
Helping Students Develop Critical-Thinking Skills IE-4
Helping Students Develop Problem-Solving and Decision-Making Skills..... IE-4
Helping Students Recognize and Value Diversity............................ IE-5

Differentiated Learning — IE-5
English Language Learners............. IE-5
Learning Styles and Multiple Intelligences .. IE-6
    Learning Styles IE-6
    Multiple Intelligences............. IE-6

Best Practices for Using Mobile Devices in the Classroom — IE-7
Safety IE-7
Appropriate Usage..................... IE-7
Access..................................... IE-7
Parents IE-7

Reading Strategies — IE-7
Active Reading in the Student Text IE-10
    Before Reading................. IE-10
    During Reading................. IE-10
    After Reading IE-10
Reading to Improve Vocabulary Comprehension..................... IE-11

Portfolio Development — IE-12

Incorporating the Career Clusters — IE-12
Career Planning..................... IE-12
Career Pathways IE-13
Programs of Study.................. IE-13

Incorporating Career and Technical Student Organizations — IE-13
DECA®............................... IE-13
Competitive Events IE-13
Advisor's Role IE-13
CTSOs Officially Recognized by the US Department of Education......... IE-14

Curriculum Sequencing — IE-15
Eighteen-Week Course Schedule IE-15
Thirty-Six-Week Course Schedule IE-16

Student Performance — IE-18
Formative Assessment IE-18
Summative Assessment IE-18
Performance Assessment IE-18
College and Career Readiness Portfolio Assessment.................... IE-18

Answer Keys IE-19

Instructional Strategies

Learning and Working in a Changing World

Your students will be entering a rapidly changing workplace—not only in the area of technology, but also in the diverse nature of the workforce. Today's workforce is made up of people who represent many different views, experiences, and backgrounds. The workforce is aging, too, as the ranks of mature workers swell. Because of these trends, young workers must learn how to interact with a variety of people who are considerably unlike them.

Helping Students Develop Critical-Thinking Skills

As today's students leave their classrooms behind, they will face a world of complexity and change. They are likely to work in several career areas and hold many different jobs. Young people must develop a base of knowledge and be prepared to solve complex problems, make difficult decisions, and assess ethical implications. In other words, students must be able to use critical-thinking skills. These skills are often referred to as the higher-order thinking skills. Benjamin Bloom listed these as:

- *analysis*—breaking down material into its component parts so its organizational structure may be understood;
- *synthesis*—putting parts together to form a new whole; and
- *evaluation*—judging the value of material for a given purpose.

In a broader perspective, students must be able to use reflective thinking to decide what to believe and do. According to Robert Ennis, students should be able to:

- define and clarify problems, issues, conclusions, reasons, and assumptions;
- judge the credibility, relevance, and consistency of information; and
- infer or solve problems and draw reasonable conclusions.

Critical thinking goes beyond memorizing or recalling information. Critical thinking cannot occur in a vacuum; it requires individuals to apply what they know about the subject matter. Critical thinking requires students to use their common sense and experience. It may involve controversy, too.

Critical thinking also requires creative thinking to construct all the reasonable alternatives, consequences, influencing factors, and supporting arguments. Unusual ideas are valued and perspectives outside the obvious are sought.

Finally, the teaching of critical thinking does not require exotic and highly unusual classroom approaches. Complex thought processes can be incorporated in ordinary, basic activities, such as reading, writing, and listening, if the activities are carefully planned and skillfully executed.

Help your students develop their analytical and judgment skills and to go beyond what they see on the surface. Rather than allowing students to blindly accept what they read or hear, encourage them to examine ideas in ways that show respect for others' opinions and different perspectives. Encourage students to think about points raised by others. Ask them to evaluate how new ideas relate to their attitudes about various subjects.

Helping Students Develop Problem-Solving and Decision-Making Skills

An important aspect in the development of critical-thinking skills is learning how to solve problems and make decisions. Some very important decisions lie ahead for your students, particularly those related to their future education and career choices.

Simulation games and role-playing allow students to practice solving problems and making decisions under nonthreatening circumstances. Role-playing allows students to examine the feelings of others as well as their own. It can help them learn effective ways to react or cope when confronted with similar situations in real life.

Helping Students Recognize and Value Diversity

Appreciating and understanding diversity is an ongoing process. The earlier and more frequently young people are exposed to diversity, the better able they will be to bridge cultural differences. If your students are exposed to different cultures within your classroom, the process of understanding cultural differences can begin. This is the best preparation for success in a diverse society. In addition, instructors have found the following strategies helpful for teaching diversity.

- Actively promote a spirit of openness, consideration, respect, and tolerance in the classroom.
- Use a variety of teaching styles and assessment strategies.
- Use cooperative learning activities whenever possible and make sure group roles are rotated so everyone has leadership opportunities.
- When grouping students, make sure the composition of each group is as diverse as possible with regard to gender, race, and nationality.
- Make sure one group's opinions do not dominate class discussions.
- If a student makes a sexist, racist, or other offensive comment, ask the student to rephrase the comment in a manner that will not offend other class members and remind students that offensive statements and behavior are inappropriate.
- If a difficult classroom situation arises involving a diversity issue, ask for a time-out and have everyone write down thoughts and opinions about the incident, which allows everyone to calm down as you plan a response.
- Arrange for guest speakers who represent diversity in gender, age, and ethnicity.
- Have students change seats occasionally throughout the course and introduce themselves to their new "neighbors" so they become acquainted with all of their classmates.
- Several times during the course, ask students to make anonymous, written evaluations of the class, reporting any problems that may not be obvious.

Differentiated Learning

Each of your students has unique learning needs based on his or her individual abilities. In addition, your students have diverse backgrounds, interests, and learning styles. By using differentiated instruction techniques, you can help your students achieve specific learning goals and maximize their potential in the classroom. The strategies you use to differentiate instruction will, of course, depend on the specific learning needs of your students.

The following sections offer research-based strategies and techniques for differentiating instruction for the English language learner, as well as for students with different learning styles.

English Language Learners

English language learners (ELLs) are students who have limited proficiency in speaking, interpreting, reading, and/or writing the English language. Generally, English is their second language. ELL students may be quite capable academically, but they lack the language skills necessary for satisfactory completion of some classroom assignments. Perhaps they have difficulty interpreting verbal or written language. Or perhaps they struggle to comprehend abstract concepts expressed in English and need additional examples to reinforce those in the text.

ELL students with moderate English proficiency can benefit from enrollment in career education courses and make significant contributions to student discussion. Limited English proficiency is little or no barrier to working as photographers, videographers, designers, business managers, distribution managers, artists, and any number of other vital positions in the workforce. They should be afforded the opportunity to contribute from their strengths while addressing their language limitations. Their varied perspectives and experiences enrich coverage.

Experiences in a career-education course will give ELL students a rich language experience, association with many English-proficient peers, confidence in the developing language ability, and an insight into American democracy not available elsewhere.

The following general strategies can be used to help ELL students succeed in your classroom.

- Use a slow but natural rate of speech. Speak clearly, use shorter sentences, and repeat concepts in several different ways.
- When possible, use pictures, photos, and charts.
- Write key terms on the board. Point to the words as you say them. Utilize the glossary in the text and activities on the companion website to reinforce these terms. Take time to review them and frequently check for understanding.

- Corrections should be limited and appropriate. Avoid correcting ELL students' grammar or usage errors in front of the class. The resulting embarrassment may cause them to become inhibited and, therefore, reluctant to participate in classroom discussions.
- Whenever possible, give honest praise and positive feedback through your voice tones and visual articulation.
- Allow students to use their native language to grapple with difficult or abstract content and tasks. Encourage collaboration with other bilingual students.
- Integrate students' cultural backgrounds into class discussions. Honor the contributions their cultural perspectives bring to your publication and the extent to which they can bring the eyes and ears of their community to your work.
- Provide for additional time for ELL students to use additional drafts, revisions, and copy editing in classroom assignments. With support and time, their work can be brought to near the same standard as their peers.
- Use cooperative learning during which students have opportunities to practice expressing ideas without risking language errors in front of the entire class.

Learning Styles and Multiple Intelligences

Educators and researchers are continually analyzing the complex factors that affect learning and achievement. The desire and the push to improve education are ongoing.

One of the biggest concerns today is how to help *all* students, not just most, learn effectively. More educators than ever before recognize that each student is an individual. While the majority of students can function in regular classes, many fail at a basic level to achieve their full potential (see Figure IE-1 for strategies specific to students of different abilities). When instructors better understand the differences in how students learn, they can teach in ways that maximize learning for more students. Information about learning styles and multiple intelligences can provide insight into such differences.

Learning Styles

People learn in different ways. There is no single right way to learn. Learning styles are the methods that individuals prefer and find most effective for processing and absorbing information. Some people are visual learners who learn best by seeing. Auditory learners learn most easily by hearing or listening to information. Those who learn best by performing hands-on or physical activities are called kinesthetic-tactile learners. Most people learn in all three ways, but one style is often dominant.

The existence of different learning styles is an important concept for instructors. When instructors recognize that students learn effectively in different ways, they can plan their lessons to allow for different modes of learning. Knowing how each student learns best allows instructors to help individual students. In addition, when instructors know their own preferred learning style, they can ensure that they do not emphasize only that style in their teaching or favor students with a similar style. The characteristics of the three learning styles, along with learning strategies that typically work best for each type of learner, are shown in Figure IE-2.

Visual Learners Visual learners learn best when they can see the information to be learned. When presented with a spoken math problem, a visual learner often responds by saying, "Wait a minute; let me write it down." Seeing the problem on paper is a key to comprehending and processing it.

Auditory Learners Can you sit in a class and, without taking notes or looking at the board or a computer screen, learn by simply listening? Do you find it easy to remember spoken directions? Auditory learners learn best when they hear information. Although lecturing is generally considered the least effective teaching method, auditory learners get the most from lectures. Auditory learners often say, "Can you explain that to me?" They find information presented orally easiest to understand and remember.

Kinesthetic-Tactile Learners Kinesthetic-tactile learners learn best by doing or through hands-on activity. *Kinesthetic* refers to bodily movement. *Tactile* refers to touch. These learners often say, "Let me play around with it for a while." A kinesthetic-tactile learner would find it hard to sit still during a lecture. Reading a chapter in the text might be punctuated with breaks. Studying with others, particularly other students with a similar learning style, might be helpful.

Multiple Intelligences

The term *intelligence* is often used to mean learning ability. In the 1980s, Howard Gardner of Harvard University published his theory of multiple intelligences. His research and observations led him to the idea that individuals have a broad range of types of intelligence, each to a varying degree.

Gardner identified nine different types of intelligence. **Figure IE-3** provides an overview of characteristics, strengths, and learning styles associated with each type of intelligence; however, the list is still evolving. Gardner believes that each person possesses multiple intelligences, but with greater strengths in certain areas.

Schools typically focus on just a few of these types of intelligence. If a student has strong logical intelligence, he or she may earn high grades in math. However, students are not often graded directly on strong interpersonal skills or dramatic abilities, for example.

Gardner's work has prompted many schools and instructors to adopt a broader view of intelligence. They have found that by using activities that draw upon the different types of intelligence, students learn more, all areas of intelligence improve, and behavioral problems are reduced.

Best Practices for Using Mobile Devices in the Classroom

If used appropriately, mobile devices, such as smartphones and tablets, can be valuable teaching tools. Instructors should reinforce appropriate electronics usage with students before using these devices in class, including sharing information on mobile safety and expectations for using mobile devices in class. Following are some guidelines to help you with this discussion.

Safety

Explain that mobile activities (including all forms of communication such as pictures, texts, and online posts) are part of a student's digital footprint. Students should understand their digital footprints have a long-term impact, and may even be part of a background check in the future when they apply to college or for jobs. Remind students that communication on a mobile device is not private and is part of their permanent online identities.

Encourage students to know their mobile plans. Students may know all of the features of their mobile devices, but may not know what they are being charged to use these features. You should encourage students to take time to know their plans and what they are being charged to access the Internet and use the features of their devices.

Appropriate Usage

If you are allowing students to use their mobile devices in the classroom, you may want to outline guidelines for usage. Examples of some of these guidelines include the following.

- Students may only use the devices in the classroom for educational purposes with permission under the guidance of the instructor.
- All devices should be turned off until students are told to turn them on.
- All devices must be on vibrate or silent mode at all times.
- All devices should be left on the corner of students' desks or at the front of the classroom until they are ready to be used.

You may want to encourage students' involvement in creating classroom rules for mobile device use and have students sign a contract agreeing to these rules.

Access

Alternatives should exist for students who do not have access to mobile devices, such as using cooperative learning, differentiating assignments based on device functions, or using alternative methods to access the content. For those who do not have access to a mobile device, the content is available on the G-W Learning companion website for this text at www.g-wlearning.com. This website can be accessed from any Internet-connected computer.

Parents

Parents might also be included in the discussion on using mobile devices in the classroom. Consider sending home a letter letting parents know what a powerful instructional tool a mobile device can be and your plans to include such devices in the classroom.

Reading Strategies

One way to help students succeed in any class is to teach them strategies for active reading. Active reading is increased involvement with a text while reading. Students who are active readers might, for example, take a moment to speculate about what they will encounter before they begin to read; they might pause during reading to take

Teaching Strategies for Various Abilities

	Learning Disabilities*	Cognitive Disabilities*	Behavioral and Emotional Disabilities*
Description	Students with learning disabilities (LD) have neurological disorders that interfere with their ability to store, process, or produce information, creating a *gap* between ability and performance. These students are generally of average or above average intelligence. Examples of learning disabilities are distractibility, spatial problems, and reading comprehension problems.	Students with cognitive disabilities (also known as intellectual disabilities) have limitations in their intellectual functioning compared with others their age. They may have difficulty remembering, associating and classifying information, reasoning, problem solving, and making judgments. They may also have difficulties with such adaptive behavior as daily living activities and developing occupational skills.	Students with these disabilities exhibit undesirable behaviors or emotions that may, over time, adversely affect educational performance. The inability to learn cannot be explained by intellectual, social, or health factors. Such students may be inattentive, withdrawn, timid, restless, defiant, impatient, unhappy, fearful, unreflective, lack initiative, have negative feelings and actions, and blame others.
Teaching Strategies	• Assist students in getting organized. • Give short oral directions. • Use drill exercises. • Give prompt cues during student performance. • Provide computers with specialized software (that checks spelling and grammar and/or recognizes speech) to students with poor writing and reading skills. • Break assignments into small segments and assign only one segment at a time. • Demonstrate skills and have students model them. • Give prompt feedback. • Use continuous assessment to mark students' daily progress. • Prepare materials at varying levels of ability. • Shorten the number of items on exercises, tests, and quizzes. • Provide more hands-on activities.	• Use concrete examples to introduce concepts. • Make learning activities consistent. • Use repetition and drills spread over time. • Provide work folders for daily assignments. • Use behavior management techniques, such as behavior modification, in the area of adaptive behavior. • Encourage students to function independently. • Give students extra time to both ask and answer questions while giving hints to answers. • Give simple directions and read them over with students. • Use objective test items and hands-on activities because students generally have poor writing skills and difficulty with sentence structure and spelling.	• Call students' names or ask them questions when you see their attention wandering. • Call on students randomly rather than in a predictable sequence. • Move around the room frequently. • Improve students' self-esteem by giving them tasks they can perform well, increasing the number of successful achievement experiences. • Decrease the length of time for each activity. • Use hands-on activities instead of using words and abstract symbols. • Decrease the size of the group so each student can actively participate. • Make verbal instructions clear, short, and to the point.

Figure IE-1

*We appreciate the assistance of Dr. Debra O. Parker, North Carolina Central University, with this section.

Academically Gifted	Physical Disabilities
Students who are academically gifted are capable of high performance as a result of general intellectual ability, specific academic aptitude, and/or creative or productive thinking. Such students have a vast fund of general knowledge and high levels of vocabulary, memory, abstract word knowledge, and abstract reasoning.	Includes individuals who have physical, mobility, visual, speech, hearing (deaf, hard-of-hearing), or health (cystic fibrosis, epilepsy) impairments. Strategies will depend on the specific disability.

Description

- Provide ample opportunities for creative behavior.
- Make assignments that call for original work, independent learning, critical thinking, problem solving, and experimentation.
- Show appreciation for creative efforts.
- Respect unusual questions, ideas, and solutions these students provide.
- Encourage students to test their ideas.
- Provide opportunities and give credit for self-initiated learning.
- Avoid overly detailed supervision and too much reliance on prescribed curricula.
- Allow time for reflection.
- Resist immediate and constant evaluation. This causes students to be afraid to use their creativity.
- Avoid comparisons with other students, which imply subtle pressure to conform.

- Seat students with visual and hearing impairments near the front of the classroom. Speak clearly and say out loud what you are writing on the board.
- To reduce the risk of injury in lab settings, ask students about any conditions that could affect their ability to learn or perform.
- Rearrange lab equipment or the classroom and make necessary modifications to accommodate any disability.
- Investigate and utilize assistive technology devices that can improve students' functional capabilities.
- Discuss solutions or modifications with the student who has experience with overcoming his or her disability and may have suggestions you may not have considered.
- Provide an opportunity for the student to test classroom modifications before utilizing them in class.
- Ask advice from special education teachers, the school nurse, or physical therapist.
- Plan barrier-free field trips that include all students.

Teaching Strategies

Figure IE-1 *(Continued)*

Learning Styles

Learning Styles	Visual	Auditory	Kinesthetic-Tactile
Characteristics	• Prefers written and visual materials • Remembers details of how things look • Takes detailed notes • Often distracted by movement • Doodles • Prefers written directions	• Prefers to listen to information • Sounds and songs stimulate memory • Takes incomplete notes • Often distracted by sounds or talking • Prefers oral directions	• Prefers to learn by doing • Remembers how things were done • May not take notes • Often distracted by movement • Finds it difficult to sit still • Prefers directions with examples
Learning Strategies	• Reading • Photos, diagrams, charts • PowerPoint presentations • Films, television • Flashcards	• Lectures, explanations • Discussions • Listening to recordings • Films, television • Reading aloud • Repeating information	• Demonstrations • Hands-on activities • Models • Projects • Field trips • Dramatizing • Labs, experiments • Singing, clapping • Games

Figure IE-2

notes on interesting, important, or confusing topics; or they might pause to evaluate material that they have just read.

Active Reading in the Student Text

Marketing Dynamics engages students in active reading. The text features an abundance of critical-thinking questions and activities that encourage students to engage with the text. This level of student involvement in the material promotes heightened conceptual understanding and retention. Following a plan that focuses on preparing students before reading, how they engage with and absorb material during reading, and evaluate and apply what they have learned after reading, the text supports active reading and sets students up for success in the course.

Before Reading

Each chapter in the text begins with a Reading Prep activity that encourages students to practice active reading strategies as they progress through the chapter. Following the Reading Prep is a list of Learning Objectives and Key Terms. Presenting this material before the student begins each chapter serves as a primer for what they will encounter later in the chapter. Familiarizing themselves with the key terms before they begin reading will make these important concepts stand out when students encounter the topics in the text.

Each section within a chapter begins with an Essential Question. These questions are designed to provoke thoughtful discussions about the content. This helps students better understand the material and how it applies to their lives.

During Reading

It is important to encourage students to pause at intervals throughout each chapter and lesson so they can think about what they have just read. This strategy aids in both comprehension and retention. Check Your Understanding questions located in the Section Review at the end of each section allow students to examine what they have learned, while giving them an opportunity to digest and, if necessary, revisit the material. In addition, these questions also give instructors an opportunity to gauge understanding.

After Reading

Each chapter in the text concludes with a Review and Assessment. This includes a summary of each section within the chapter. Review Your Knowledge questions can be used to engage students and assess their conceptual

Gardner's Multiple Intelligences

Type of Intelligence	Strengths	Student Characteristics	Preferred Learning Activities
Logical-Mathematical	Good with logical problems and math	Performs well in math and science, abstract thinking, classifying	Strategy games, experiments, math problems, logic exercises, problem solving
Spatial	Good at visualizing	Has artistic skills, imagination, can think in three dimensions	Drawing, picturing, making models, seeing patterns, visual puzzles
Bodily-Kinesthetic	Good with movement, hands-on activities	Coordinated, athletic, may like art, crafts, or building	Drama, dance, crafts, experiments
Linguistic	Good with words	Has good written or oral communication skills and large vocabulary, learns languages easily	Reading, storytelling, writing, note taking, summarizing, word puzzles
Musical	Good with rhythm and sound patterns	Understands rhythm, tone, sings or hums to self, emotionally sensitive	Music, auditory activities, those requiring emotional sensitivity
Intrapersonal	Good analyzer of self, own strengths and weaknesses	Reflective, goal-oriented, instinctive, makes good personal decisions	Journaling, reflection exercises, self-paced work, personal projects
Interpersonal	Good with communication	Communicates well, leadership, sensitive to others, understands others, resolves conflicts	Group activities, discussions, group projects
Naturalistic	In tune with and analyzes environment	Observes, classifies, visualizes	Collections, observations, journaling, creating charts
Existentialist	Good at asking philosophical questions	Learns best through seeing the "big picture" of human existence	Interactive communication tools, such as email, teleconferencing

Figure IE-3

understanding while stimulating factual recall of terms and concepts. The Apply Your Knowledge activities found in the review challenge students to think critically about what they have learned and to apply this to simulated or real-life situations.

Students also have opportunities to reinforce their understanding of key concepts and terms through activities developed around the four modes of communication (listening, speaking, reading, and writing) and basic math skills.

Reading to Improve Vocabulary Comprehension

Each chapter contains key terms that are defined in the text. The glossary at the end of the text contains the definitions of all key terms in the text.

When students struggle with the meaning of a particular word, they may use certain strategies to decipher its meaning. One way for students to make sense of a challenging word is through context, the examination of clues in surrounding words or sentences. To help them decipher the meaning of a word they do not know, students can ask themselves the following question: Is the word being compared to something else in the text? If, for example, students are familiar with the object or idea to which the word is being compared, that knowledge may help them decipher the meaning of the unknown word. A cause-and-effect relationship illustrated in the text can also help students understand the meaning of a term.

If examination of contextual clues does not help students decipher the definition of a particular term, you might recommend that they revisit the term itself. In doing so, students can ask themselves the following questions: Is this word similar to one that I have seen before? Do I recognize any of the word parts? By examining root words, combining forms, prefixes, and suffixes—the elements that make up words— students often can use the definitions of individual parts to arrive at a general definition of the whole.

Portfolio Development

A portfolio is a selection of related materials compiled as evidence of an individual's skills, talents, or experiences. Methods of collection, as well as selection and storage of materials, are addressed in the Portfolio Development activities that appear at the end of each chapter. The completed portfolio can be used by the student to apply for a paying job or a volunteer position as well as admission to a college program of study.

The process of collecting and evaluating items to be included in the portfolio is a course-long, project-based activity. The portfolio rubric, included in the Instructor Resources, can be used to evaluate the students' work. It is suggested to distribute copies of the rubric to students before they begin the portfolio activities. This will prepare them for the expectations of the project and how they will be evaluated.

Incorporating the Career Clusters

In the mid-1990s, a project called Building Linkages began development, led by the Office of Vocational and Adult Education (OVAE). Building Linkages was funded in partnership by the US Departments of Labor and Education. The goal of the project was to create a reliable set of standards for the integration of academics with workplace skills. Another goal was to show how higher levels of skills and knowledge lead to higher positions. Eventually the organization of the project emerged as career clusters, and The States' Career Clusters Initiative was launched in 2001. The career clusters are now accessed through the Career Technical Education (CTE) website.

In total, there are 16 Career Clusters in the National Career Clusters Framework. Depending on the business and industry environment, many states adapt a Career Cluster to reflect the state's educational objectives, standards, and economic development practices. Within the 16 Career Clusters, there are 79 different career pathways.

In each cluster, four levels of knowledge and skills exist, ranging from broad to specific. *Foundational Academic Expectations* are the academic requirements specific to the student's state. *Essential Knowledge and Skills* apply to all levels of careers in all clusters. *Cluster (Foundation) Knowledge and Skills* are the highest level of skills and knowledge within a given cluster and apply to all pathways within the cluster. *Pathway Knowledge and Skills* list the skills necessary for a career subgroup within a cluster. All levels promote employability, academic, and technical skills.

Career Planning

Students should not expect that the right job will simply "come along." People who make no career plans usually find themselves left with jobs no one else wants or no jobs at all. Instead, students should investigate what resources are needed to achieve a goal and map out a plan. What can be done now, next semester, next year, and so on to improve the chances of successfully entering the career of choice?

Having a career means an individual will hold several occupations related by a common skill, purpose, or interest over a lifetime. A career is a series of related occupations that show progression in a field of work. The term "job" is commonly used to mean occupation. Strictly speaking, a job is a task, while an occupation is paid employment that involves handling one or more jobs. A career is followed by a worker over a span of several years. The worker may enter the field doing one job well, learn to do others, and eventually supervise others. As workers move from one job to the next, they will gain new skills and knowledge.

Career Clusters are groups of occupations or career specialties that are similar or related to one another. The occupations within a cluster require a set of common knowledge and skills for career success. The 16 clusters were developed by state partnerships among educators, employers, and professional groups. The purpose of the clusters is to prepare students to transition from school to a rewarding career in an era of changing workplace demands.

Career Pathways

To help narrow career options, each career cluster is further divided into career pathways. These subgroups often require additional and more specialized knowledge and skills.

Knowing the relationship between careers in a given pathway is helpful when researching information about careers. The skills required for different occupations in a similar field may overlap somewhat. Preparing for more than one career in a related field allows more flexibility when searching for employment. If an individual cannot find the exact position desired, skills will be needed by other occupations in the same pathway. The more students learn about related careers now, the more easily they will be able to adapt to changes in an occupation later.

Programs of Study

Since occupations in a career pathway require similar knowledge and skills, they also require similar programs of study. A program of study is the sequence of instruction used to prepare students for occupations in a given career pathway. The program includes classroom instruction, cocurricular activities such as student organizations, and other learning experiences including worksite and service learning.

Customizing a program of study for an individual learner's needs and interests results in a personal plan of study. A plan of study will help prepare a study for the career direction chosen. The first step is taking the appropriate classes in high school and participating in related organizations.

Once the foundation has been laid, students should seek out programs that address their career interests. It is possible that some high school classes can count toward college credit. A plan of study does not expire with high school. Students should update their plans at least yearly, but more often if plans change.

Incorporating Career and Technical Student Organizations

The purpose of career and technical student organizations (CTSOs) is to help students acquire knowledge and skills in career and technical areas as well as leadership skills and experience. CTSOs achieve these goals by enlisting instructor-advisors to organize and lead local chapters in their schools. Support for instructor-advisors and their chapters is often coordinated through each state's education department. The chapters elect officers and establish a program of work. The program of work can include a variety of activities, such as community service, cocurricular projects, and competition preparation. Student achievement in specified areas is recognized with certificates or public acknowledgment through awards ceremonies.

DECA® Emerging Leaders

At the beginning of each chapter in the textbook, there is a DECA® Emerging Leaders activity. DECA® is a national association for students of marketing. The learning activity begins with identification of the career cluster, instructional area, and performance indicators associated with the activity content. Performance indicators are specific work-based skills and knowledge that identify what an employee must know or be able to do in order to achieve a performance element in an instructional area. Performance indicators define performance elements.

DECA® Emerging Leaders provides first-hand opportunity for students to explore learning activities to prepare for college and careers. Engagement in rigorous project-based learning activities will help develop creative solutions with practical outcomes. Completion of these learning activities provides realistic insight into industry. Students discover what it means to become an academically prepared, community-oriented, professionally responsible, and experienced leader through DECA®.

Competitive Events

Competitive events are a main feature of most CTSOs. The CTSO develops events that enable students to showcase how well they have mastered the learning of specific content and the use of decision-making, problem-solving, and leadership skills. Each CTSO has its own list of competitive events and activities. Members develop career and leadership skills even though they may not participate in or win competitions.

Advisor's Role

Preparing students for competitions takes much time and commitment, often beyond the traditional school day. Dedication to this process, however, does have its rewards. You see your students develop complex skills and grow in their roles as leaders and team members. Their ultimate goal is to become competent, successful members of the workforce.

Once you and your students commit to participating in one or more competitions, much responsibility is involved in your role as advisor. If this is a new experience for you or your school, there are some important first steps to take. They include, but are not limited to, the following.

- Obtain membership and competition requirements from organizations that sponsor the competitions, such as DECA.
- Meet with school administrators to gain permission to start a CTSO or gain support for an existing chapter and contact advisory committee members to build support in the school and community.
- Identify competitions that best meet the needs of your students.
- Make sure local, state, and national membership requirements are met.
- Learn where state meetings and competitions are held and attend them.
- Research application or competition deadlines and plan accordingly.
- Build parent support for competitive events by emphasizing that through competition, students enhance their workplace skills and may also receive recognition awards and, in some cases, scholarships, if they win at state and national levels.

CTSOs offer a wide variety of activities that can be adapted to almost any school and classroom situation. If you would like more information, visit the websites of the individual CTSOs.

CTSOs Officially Recognized by the US Department of Education

BPA
Business Professionals of America
www.bpa.org

DECA®
An Association of Marketing Students
www.deca.org

Educators Rising
www.educatorsrising.org

FBLA/PBL
Future Business Leaders of America—Phi Beta Lambda
www.fbla-pbl.org

FCCLA
Family, Career and Community Leaders of America
www.fcclainc.org

FFA
National Future Farmers of America
www.ffa.org

HOSA
Health Occupations Students of America
www.hosa.org

SkillsUSA
www.skillsusa.org

TSA
Technology Student Association
www.tsaweb.org

Curriculum Sequencing

The following program planning guide suggests a way to schedule the chapters of *Marketing Dynamics* for either an eighteen-week or a thirty-six-week course schedule. Incorporate activities from the Instructor Resources, Student Workbook, and Instructor's Presentations for PowerPoint® to provide variety during extended class periods.

Eighteen-Week Course Schedule

Week 1	Page
Chapter 1 Introduction to Marketing	4
Section 1.1 Marketing Defined	6
Section 1.2 Marketing Basics	9
Chapter 2 Marketing Plan	20
Section 2.1 Researching a Marketing Plan	22
Section 2.2 Developing a Marketing Plan	27
Week 2	
Chapter 3 Business Basics	36
Section 3.1 Business Defined	38
Section 3.2 Laws and Regulations	43
Chapter 4 Ethics and Social Responsibility	52
Section 4.1 Ethics	54
Section 4.2 Social Responsibility	59
Week 3	
Chapter 5 Economic Principles	70
Section 5.1 Introduction to Economics	72
Section 5.2 Economic Systems and Market Forces	78
Chapter 6 Economic Activity	88
Section 6.1 Economic Measurement	90
Section 6.2 Government and the Economy	99
Chapter 7 Global Trade	106
Section 7.1 Global Business Environment	108
Section 7.2 Global Marketplace	113
Week 4	
Chapter 8 Marketing Research	126
Section 8.1 Marketing-Research Data	128
Section 8.2 Conducting Marketing Research	138
Week 5	
Chapter 9 Targeting a Market	146
Section 9.1 Identify the Market	148
Section 9.2 Evaluate the Competition	156
Week 6	
Chapter 10 Understanding the Customer	166
Section 10.1 B2C Customers	168
Section 10.2 B2B Customers	175
Section 10.3 Credit Basics	180

Week 7	
Chapter 11 Product	192
Section 11.1 Product	194
Section 11.2 New-Product Development Process	201
Week 8	
Chapter 12 Branding	214
Section 12.1 Product Branding	216
Section 12.2 Brand Identity and Protection	221
Week 9	
Chapter 13 Price	232
Section 13.1 Importance of Price	234
Section 13.2 Price Influencers	238
Chapter 14 Pricing Product	248
Section 14.1 Pricing Strategies	250
Section 14.2 Governmental Influence on Pricing	254
Week 10	
Chapter 15 Place	264
Section 15.1 Channels of Distribution	266
Section 15.2 Supply Chain	274
Chapter 16 Purchasing and Inventory Control	284
Section 16.1 Purchasing	286
Section 16.2 Inventory Control	293
Week 11	
Chapter 17 Promotion	306
Section 17.1 Promotion Basics	308
Section 17.2 Types of Promotion	315
Week 12	
Chapter 18 Advertising	324
Section 18.1 Advertising Basics	326
Section 18.2 Developing an Advertising Campaign	334
Week 13	
Chapter 19 Visual Merchandising	344
Section 19.1 Visual Merchandising	346
Section 19.2 Display	351

Thirty-Six-Week Course Schedule

Week 1	Page
Chapter 1 Introduction to Marketing	4
Section 1.1 Marketing Defined	6
Section 1.2 Marketing Basics	9
Week 2	
Chapter 2 Marketing Plan	20
Section 2.1 Researching a Marketing Plan	22
Section 2.2 Developing a Marketing Plan	27
Week 3	
Chapter 3 Business Basics	36
Section 3.1 Business Defined	38
Section 3.2 Laws and Regulations	43
Week 4	
Chapter 4 Ethics and Social Responsibility	52
Section 4.1 Ethics	54
Section 4.2 Social Responsibility	59
Week 5	
Chapter 5 Economic Principles	70
Section 5.1 Introduction to Economics	72
Section 5.2 Economic Systems and Market Forces	78
Week 6	
Chapter 6 Economic Activity	88
Section 6.1 Economic Measurement	90
Section 6.2 Government and the Economy	99
Week 7	
Chapter 7 Global Trade	106
Section 7.1 Global Business Environment	108
Section 7.2 Global Marketplace	113
Week 8	
Chapter 8 Marketing Research	126
Section 8.1 Marketing-Research Data	128
Week 9	
Section 8.2 Conducting Marketing Research	138
Week 10	
Chapter 9 Targeting a Market	146
Section 9.1 Identify the Market	148
Week 11	
Section 9.2 Evaluate the Competition	156
Week 12	
Chapter 10 Understanding the Customer	166
Section 10.1 B2C Customers	168

Week 14	
Chapter 20 Personal Selling	362
Section 20.1 Role of Sales	364
Section 20.2 Selling	368
Section 20.3 Customer Service	380
Week 15	
Chapter 21 Marketing Management	390
Section 21.1 Management	392
Section 21.2 Financial Management	396
Chapter 22 Soft Skills	404
Section 22.1 Skills for Managers	406
Section 22.2 Teams in the Workplace	414
Chapter 23 Communication in the Workplace	422
Section 23.1 Communication Basics	424
Section 23.2 Communication Skills	430
Week 16	
Chapter 24 Entrepreneurship	448
Section 24.1 Becoming an Entrepreneur	450
Section 24.2 Starting a Business	457
Chapter 25 Risk Management	466
Section 25.1 Identify Risk	468
Section 25.2 Manage Risk	472
Chapter 26 Business Funding	480
Section 26.1 Options for Funding	482
Section 26.2 Apply for Financing	490
Week 17	
Chapter 27 Planning for Success	500
Section 27.1 Career Investigation and Planning	502
Section 27.2 Preparing for Your Education	515
Week 18	
Chapter 28 Preparing for Your Career	528
Section 28.1 Finding and Applying for Employment	530
Section 28.2 Interviewing and the Employment Process	540
Chapter 29 Digital Citizenship	552
Section 29.1 Communicating in a Digital Society	554
Section 29.2 Internet Use in the Workplace	560

Week 13
Section 10.2 B2B Customers	175
Section 10.3 Credit Basics	180

Week 14
Chapter 11 Product	192
Section 11.1 Product	194

Week 15
Section 11.2 New-Product Development Process	201

Week 16
Chapter 12 Branding	214
Section 12.1 Product Branding	216
Section 12.2 Brand Identity and Protection	221

Week 17
Chapter 13 Price	232
Section 13.1 Importance of Price	234

Week 18
Section 13.2 Price Influencers	238

Week 19
Chapter 14 Pricing Product	248
Section 14.1 Pricing Strategies	250
Section 14.2 Governmental Influence on Pricing	254

Week 20
Chapter 15 Place	264
Section 15.1 Channels of Distribution	266
Section 15.2 Supply Chain	274

Week 21
Chapter 16 Purchasing and Inventory Control	284
Section 16.1 Purchasing	286
Section 16.2 Inventory Control	293

Week 22
Chapter 17 Promotion	306
Section 17.1 Promotion Basics	308
Section 17.2 Types of Promotion	315

Week 23
Chapter 18 Advertising	324
Section 18.1 Advertising Basics	326

Week 24
Section 18.2 Developing an Advertising Campaign	334

Week 25
Chapter 19 Visual Merchandising	344
Section 19.1 Visual Merchandising	346
Section 19.2 Display	351

Week 26
Chapter 20 Personal Selling	362
Section 20.1 Role of Sales	364

Week 27
Section 20.2 Selling	368
Section 20.3 Customer Service	380

Week 28
Chapter 21 Marketing Management	390
Section 21.1 Management	392
Section 21.2 Financial Management	396

Week 29
Chapter 22 Soft Skills	404
Section 22.1 Skills for Managers	406
Section 22.2 Teams in the Workplace	414

Week 30
Chapter 23 Communication in the Workplace	422
Section 23.1 Communication Basics	424
Section 23.2 Communication Skills	430

Week 31
Chapter 24 Entrepreneurship	448
Section 24.1 Becoming an Entrepreneur	450
Section 24.2 Starting a Business	457

Week 32
Chapter 25 Risk Management	466
Section 25.1 Identify Risk	468
Section 25.2 Manage Risk	472

Week 33
Chapter 26 Business Funding	480
Section 26.1 Options for Funding	482
Section 26.2 Apply for Financing	490

Week 34
Chapter 27 Planning for Success	500
Section 27.1 Career Investigation and Planning	502
Section 27.2 Preparing for Your Education	515

Week 35
Chapter 28 Preparing for Your Career	528
Section 28.1 Finding and Applying for Employment	530
Section 28.2 Interviewing and the Employment Process	540

Week 36
Chapter 29 Digital Citizenship	552
Section 29.1 Communicating in a Digital Society	554
Section 29.2 Internet Use in the Workplace	560

Student Performance

Various assessment techniques are incorporated throughout the *Marketing Dynamics* textbook to aid in student learning. Suggestions for using these features with the teaching package are provided as follows.

Each chapter of *Marketing Dynamics* includes a variety of methods for assessing your students' performance. *Formative assessment* is used to measure student progress in understanding the concepts, while *summative assessment* can be used to measure the extent to which they have mastered the concepts. *Performance assessment* can be used to measure student progress based on a given rubric.

Formative Assessment

Formative assessment takes place often and is ongoing throughout a course. The many comprehension strategies used throughout the text can be used as formative assessment techniques. They measure students' grasp of the concepts as well as their abilities to internalize the skills and apply them to new situations. Many formative assessments can be completed as groups because the main focus is on the learning that is taking place and student self-assessment. Formative assessment includes:
- review activities at the end of each section; and
- end-of-chapter activities.

Summative Assessment

The ExamView® Assessment Suite has traditionally been used for summative assessment. This method of evaluation is good to use when assigning grades. The text also contains end-of-chapter summative assessments.

Performance Assessment

When assigning students some of the projects from the text that you plan to use as either formative or summative assessment, a rubric can be helpful for measuring student achievement. A rubric consists of a set of criteria that includes specific descriptors or standards that can be used to arrive at performance scores for students. A point value is given for each set of descriptors, leading to a range of possible points to be assigned, usually from one to five. The criteria can also be weighted. This method of assessment reduces the guesswork involved in grading, leading to fair and consistent scoring. The standards clearly indicate to students the various levels of mastery of a task. Students are even able to assess their own achievement based on the criteria.

When using rubrics, students should see the criteria at the beginning of the assignment. They can then focus their efforts on what needs to be done to reach a certain level of performance or quality of project. Therefore, they have a clear understanding of your expectations of achievement.

Though you will want to design many of your own rubrics, generic ones can be found in the Instructor Resources. They are designed to assess:
- individual participation;
- individual reports; and
- group participation.

These rubrics allow you to assess a student's performance and arrive at a performance score. Students can see what levels they have surpassed and what levels they can still strive to reach.

College and Career Readiness Portfolio Assessment

A portfolio is a selection of related materials compiled as evidence of an individual's skills, talents, or experiences. Methods of collection, as well as selection and storage of materials, are addressed in the Portfolio Development activities that appear at the end of each chapter. Students can use their completed portfolio to apply for a job, community volunteer program, or admission to a college program of study.

The process of collecting and evaluating items to be included in the portfolio is a course-long, project-based activity. The portfolio rubric, found in the Instructor Resources, can be used to evaluate the students' work. It is suggested that copies of the rubric be distributed to students before they begin the portfolio activities. This will prepare them for the expectations of the project and how they will be evaluated.

Goodheart-Willcox Welcomes Your Comments

We welcome your comments or suggestions regarding *Marketing Dynamics* and its supplements. Please send any comments you may have to the editor by visiting our website at www.g-w.com or writing to:
Editorial Director—BMC
Goodheart-Willcox Publisher
18604 West Creek Drive
Tinley Park, IL 60477-6243

Answer Keys

Chapter 1 Introduction to Marketing

You Do the Math: Basic Math
1. The number of hats for sale in the store is 215.
   293 − 43 − 96 − 28 − 61 + 48 + 60 + 18 + 24 = 215
2. There is 1.716 in³ of liquid in the flask.
   1 cubic centimeter = 0.06 cubic inches
   28.6 cubic centimeters × 0.06 cubic inches = 1.716 cubic inches
3. 10.8% of the e-mails generated responses.
   1,022 responses ÷ 9,500 e-mails = .10757 rounded to .1076
4. The restaurant must order 321 pounds of flour for the week.
   356 biscuits per day × 7 days = 2,492 biscuits per week
   0.045 pounds of flour per biscuit × 2,492 biscuits per week = 112.14 pounds of flour per week
   48 loaves of bread per day × 7 days = 336 loaves per week
   0.62 pounds of flour per loaf × 336 loaves per week = 208.32 pounds of flour per week
   112.14 pounds of flour per week + 208.32 pounds of flour per week = 320.46 pounds of flour per week.

Section 1.1 Review
1. The goal of marketing is to meet customer needs and wants with products they can and will buy.
2. A good is a physical item that can be touched. A service is an action that is done for you.
3. Marketing professional.
4. As a consumer, you need to make informed decisions about the products you buy. Knowledge about marketing will help you understand how businesses influence your purchasing decisions.
5. (Any) Job searching, applying for college, volunteering, and asking for a promotion.
Answers to Build Your Vocabulary terms are key term definitions and can be found in the glossary.

Section 1.2 Review
1. The three elements of the marketing concept are customer satisfaction, total company approach, and profit.
2. Product, price, place, and promotion.
3. Activities in market planning include (any) identifying the target market, determining appropriate marketing strategies, setting a marketing budget, and using metrics to measure budget effectiveness.
4. Adding value means enhancing a feature or service to inspire a customer to purchase.
5. Marketing helps to create a positive cycle of economic growth by persuading people to buy goods and services. When customers are spending more, businesses sell more products and increase profits, helping the state of the economy. Marketing positions account for a large portion of all jobs in the United States.
Answers to Build Your Vocabulary terms are key term definitions and can be found in the glossary.

Review Your Knowledge
1. Marketing consists of dynamic activities that identify, anticipate, and satisfy customer demand while making a profit. These activities help to tell the story of the company, the brand, the person, or the idea. The goal of marketing is to meet customer needs and wants with products they can and will buy.
2. A marketing professional is a person who helps determine the marketing needs of a company, develops and implements marketing plans, and focuses on customer satisfaction.
3. Learning about marketing will make you a better consumer. As a consumer, you need to make informed decisions about the products you buy. Knowledge about marketing will help you understand how businesses influence your purchasing decisions. Learning about marketing will make you a better employee. You can become a more valuable worker by understanding marketing functions and how to work with a marketing team. Learning about marketing also helps you learn how to market yourself, which means selling your talents and abilities. Learning about marketing can influence your career path.
4. The marketing concept is an approach to business that focuses on satisfying customers while achieving profit goals for the company. The three elements of the marketing concept are customer satisfaction, total company approach, and profit. These three elements overlap and work together.
5. The marketing mix is the strategy for using the elements of product, price, place, and promotion. Products include goods, services, and ideas. Price

is the amount of money requested or exchanged for a product. Place refers to activities involved in getting a product or service to the end users. Promotion is the process of communicating with potential customers in an effort to influence their buying behavior.
6. The keys to creating a successful marketing mix are choosing the right product; selling it at the right price; making it available at the right place; and promoting it in a way that will reach the target customers.
7. The seven functions of marketing are: channel management; marketing-information management; market planning; pricing; product/service management; promotion; and selling.
8. Form utility is the characteristic added when a business changes the form of something to make it more useful. Place utility is the characteristic added when products are available at convenient places. Time utility is the characteristic added when products are made available at the times that customers need and want them. Information utility is the characteristic added when marketing provides information about a product to a customer. Possession utility is the characteristic added when it becomes easier for a customer to acquire a product.
9. Marketing provides information to educate consumers to enable those who are purchasing products to make educated decisions. Marketing stimulates competition to create more and better products at competitive prices. Marketing helps to create a positive cycle of economic growth by persuading people to buy goods and services. Marketing activities help to identify new business opportunities.
10. Marketing helps to create a positive cycle of economic growth by persuading people to buy goods and services. When customers are spending more, businesses sell more products and increase profits, helping the state of the economy. Marketing positions account for a large portion of all jobs in the United States. Jobs are vital to the success of any community. Businesses are aware of the importance of their standing in the community. When an economy grows, more people are employed. More purchases are made and businesses can help their communities more.

Apply Your Knowledge

Student answers will vary for Apply Your Knowledge questions.

Apply Your Math Skills

1. The airline made $18,240.
$114 \times 160 = \$18,240$
2. Benny will ask for $382.50.
First repair:
$\$75 + (3 \times \$25) =$
$\$75 + \$75 = \$150$
Second repair:
$\$75 + (1 \times \$25) + \$20 =$
$\$75 + \$25 + \$20 = \$120$
Third repair:
$\$75 + (1.5 \times \$25) =$
$\$75 + \$37.50 = \$112.50$
$\$150 + \$120 + \$112.50 = \$382.50$

Chapter 2 Marketing Plan

You Do the Math: Order of Operations

1. −8
$8 - (4 \times 3) + 2^3 \div 2 =$
$8 - 12 + 2^3 \div 2 =$
$8 - 12 + 8 \div 2 =$
$8 - 12 + 4 =$
$8 - 16 = -8$
2. 211
$11^2 + (45 \times 2) =$
$11^2 + 90 =$
$121 + 90 = 211$
3. 4
$3 + 4 - 27 \div 9 =$
$3 + 4 - 3 =$
$7 - 3 = 4$

Section 2.1 Review

1. In a small company, there may only be one marketing manager who creates the plan for the entire company. Large companies generally have multiple marketing managers who are responsible for individual product lines. Each marketing manager completes a plan for his or her product line.
2. A SWOT analysis identifies strengths, weaknesses, opportunities, and threats the business faces.
3. This process identifies potential opportunities and threats to a company's business plans and strategies.
4. Target markets have four characteristics: clearly defined wants and needs that the business can meet; money to buy the product;

willingness and ability to buy the product; and enough customers to be profitable.
5. In a competitive analysis, competitors are listed with their physical locations, product lines, pricing, and market share. From this information, marketers can determine how the company will compete with others to gain its share of sales in the market.

Answers to Build Your Vocabulary terms are key term definitions and can be found in the glossary.

Section 2.2 Review

1. An executive summary provides the overview of the marketing plan by highlighting the critical points in the plan. The goal is to provide a snapshot that will entice the reader to review the entire document.
2. Two components of the analysis section are market analysis and sales analysis.
3. Marketing goals are simple and clear statements of the results to be accomplished through marketing efforts.
4. Product strategies are the decisions made about what products a business should sell. Price strategies are the business decisions about pricing and how prices are set to make a profit. Place strategies are the decisions about how and where the products are produced, acquired, shipped, and sold to customers. Promotion strategies are decisions about which selling, advertising, sales promotions, and public relations activities to use in the promotional mix.
5. Three components of an action plan include a time line, budget, and metrics.

Answers to Build Your Vocabulary terms are key term definitions and can be found in the glossary.

Review Your Knowledge

1. A marketing plan is a document describing business and marketing goals and the strategies and tactics that will be used to achieve them.
2. A situation analysis is a snapshot of the environment in which a business has been operating over a given period of time, usually the last 12 to 16 months. It evaluates internal and external environments as they relate to marketing and sales. A SWOT analysis is an internal analysis that identifies company strengths, weaknesses, opportunities, and threats the business faces. An environmental scan is an analysis of the external factors that affect the success of business.
3. A target market is the specific group of customers at which a company aims its products and services. These are the people whose wants and needs are fulfilled by the products a business offers. They are the people most likely to buy the goods or services.
4. In order for a company to achieve sales goals, it may need to take business away from the competition.
5. Market size is the total sales per year for a specific product held by all the competing businesses. Market share is the percentage of total sales in a market that is held by one business. Market potential is the maximum number of customers and amount of sales that can be generated from a specific segment in a defined time period.
6. The opening section of a marketing plan is usually divided into Executive Summary and Business Description subsections.
7. The analysis section of the marketing plan provides detailed information about the market and sales analyses that have been performed. This detail is necessary to understand the environment in which the business is operating and the goals to be met. This section includes Market Analysis and Sales Analysis subsections.
8. The best opportunities for making new and repeat sales should be clearly defined. This information comes from market research and sales team feedback and includes opportunities to take business away from competitors, new geographic areas, and other potential sales sources.
9. Marketing strategies are the decisions made to execute the marketing plan and meet the goals of the business. These strategies outline the who, what, where, and how of the marketing process. They include establishing marketing goals, identifying the target market, defining components of the marketing mix, and defining the product positioning.
10. The action plan is a list of the marketing tactics with detailed plans to execute each tactic. An action plan ensures the marketing efforts remain on track and funds are spent wisely. Three components of an action plan include a time line, budget, and metrics to evaluate the effectiveness of campaigns.

Apply Your Knowledge
Student answers will vary for Apply Your Knowledge questions.

Apply Your Math Skills
1. Elaine's marketing budget will be $22,500.
   $150,000 × .15 = $22,500
2. The new marketing budget will increase by $440,000.
   $22,000,000 × 7% = $1,540,000
   $22,000,000 × 9% = $1,980,000
   $1,980,000 − $1,540,000 = $440,000

Chapter 3 Business Basics

You Do the Math: Number Sense
1. The total is $93.
   First, add $10 + $40 + $30 = $80
   Then, add $6 + $2 + $5 = $13
   Finally, combine these two sums to find the answer: $80 + $13 = $93
2. The total cost is $26,500.
   First, add $10,000 + $3,000 + $12,000 = $25,000
   Then, add $800 + $200 + $500 = $1,500
   Finally, combine these two sums to find the answer: $25,000 + $1,500 = $26,500

Section 3.1 Review
1. Profit is the difference between the income earned and expenses incurred by a business during a specific period of time.
2. Businesses using the marketing concept understand that building a strong base of satisfied customers leads to healthy profits. Satisfied customers are repeat customers and repeat customers ensure higher sales.
3. Stability, recognizability, divisibility, portability, and durability.
4. The functions of business are production, finance, marketing, and management.
5. A sole proprietorship is a business owned by one person. A partnership is the relationship between two or more people who join to create a business.

Answers to Build Your Vocabulary terms are key term definitions and can be found in the glossary.

Section 3.2 Review
1. Federal Trade Commission (FTC) is a federal agency that was created to protect consumers and promote business competition.
2. (Any) Children's products, endorsements, environmental marketing, health claims, made in USA claims, online advertising and marketing, and telemarketing.
3. (Any) US Department of Labor (DOL), Equal Employment Opportunity Commission (EEOC), and Occupational Safety and Health Administration (OSHA).
4. Antitrust, bankruptcy, and securities laws protect the financial interests of businesses and individual investors.
5. (Any) The right to safety; the right to be informed; the right to choose; the right to be heard; the right to satisfaction of basic needs; the right to redress; the right to education; and the right to a healthful environment.

Answers to Build Your Vocabulary terms are key term definitions and can be found in the glossary.

Review Your Knowledge
1. Business is the term for all of the activities involved in developing and exchanging goods and services. Business includes manufacturing, construction, mining, wholesaling, retailing, and farming. A business sells products, but it also manages people, makes financial decisions, and decides what and how much needs to be produced. Businesses using the marketing concept understand that building a strong base of satisfied customers leads to healthy profits. Satisfying customers successfully over the long term benefits businesses. Business provides most of the goods and services that you use every day. It also employs people in exchange for paying wages.
2. *Profit* is the difference between the income earned and expenses incurred by a business during a specific period of time. Businesses using the marketing concept understand that building a strong base of satisfied customers leads to healthy profits. Satisfied customers are repeat customers and repeat customers ensure higher sales. Companies using the marketing concept treat all contact with customers as a chance to market the business. Customer satisfaction is the goal of all employees, and leads to business success in the long term. Different departments of the business, such as production, finance, and management, share information with the marketing team to help the company succeed.
3. Money is anything of value that is accepted in return for goods or services. Money makes it easier to do business and exchange goods and

services. In our economy, money serves three functions: medium of exchange, unit of value, and store of value.
4. Business plays a role in society by providing products, creating markets, and generating economic benefits.
5. The production function is responsible for creating goods and services. The finance function of business includes all activities involving money. Marketing is the function of business that focuses on the customer. The management function of business controls and makes decisions about a business.
6. Three main forms of business organization are sole proprietorship, partnership, and corporation. A sole proprietorship is a business owned by one person. A partnership is the relationship between two or more people who join to create a business. A corporation is a business that is legally separate from its owners and has most of the legal rights of an actual person. Most corporations are for-profit businesses. A nonprofit organization is an entity that exists to serve some public purpose.
7. The Federal Trade Commission (FTC) is a federal agency that was created to protect consumers and promote business competition. The FTC develops and enforces laws related to advertising and marketing that all businesses must follow. Additional rules may apply to some specialized products or services.
8. Employment and labor laws cover everything from preventing discrimination and harassment in the workplace, ensuring employee safety, enforcing wage and hour laws, and monitoring workers' compensation regulations.
9. Finance laws exist to ensure fair competition and to protect the financial interests of companies and individual investors. Antitrust, bankruptcy, and securities laws protect the financial interests of businesses and individual investors.
10. The federal government provides protections through consumer-protection laws. These laws are designed to hold companies accountable for providing safe products, honest marketing practices, and documentation that is not fraudulent.

Apply Your Knowledge
Student answers will vary for Apply Your Knowledge questions.

Apply Your Math Skills
1. Ahmet owns 52 percent. Brandon owns 37 percent. Christy owns 11 percent.
$35,000 + $24,500 + $7,500 = $67,000 total invested
$35,000 ÷ $67,000 = .52 → 52%
$24,500 ÷ $67,000 = .365 → 37%
$7,500 ÷ $67,000 = .11 → 11%
2. Elliot makes $14,898 per year.
52 weeks per year × 40 hours per week = 2,080 hours per year
$19,864 per year ÷ 2,080 hours per year = $9.55 per hour
$9.55 per hour × 30 hours per week × 52 weeks = $14,898 per year

Chapter 4 Ethics and Social Responsibility

You Do the Math: Percentages
1. The percentage of waste that was recycled was 34 percent.
89 million tons ÷ 258 million tons = 0.34
0.34 × 100 = 34%
2. The amount of paper thrown away was 69.66 million tons. (70 million tons rounded)
258 million tons × 0.27 = 69.66 million tons
3. The amount of metal recycled was 8.01 million tons. (8 million tons rounded)
89 million tons × 0.09 = 8.01 million tons
4. The percentage of waste that was landfilled is 53 percent.
136 million tons ÷ 258 million tons = .527
0.53 × 100 = 53%

Section 4.1 Review
1. Two ways a company might convey its expectations for acceptable employee behavior are with a code of conduct and a code of ethics.
2. Workplace bullying is the repeated mistreatment of another person using verbal abuse, threats, or any other action that prevents a person from doing his or her job without fear.
3. Stated codes of ethics generally address relationships and interactions of the business with employees, customers, suppliers, investors, creditors, competitors, and community.
4. (Any) American Marketing Association (AMA), Better Business Bureau (BBB).
5. Advertising must be truthful and nondeceptive. Advertisers must have evidence to back up their claims. Advertisements cannot be unfair.

Answers to Build Your Vocabulary terms are key term definitions and can be found in the glossary.

Section 4.2 Review

1. Examples of these actions include philanthropy, supporting the local economy, and protecting the environment.
2. A socially responsible business makes an effort to conduct business locally and use local resources whenever possible. It is good business practice to hire people from the community.
3. Many items used in daily business operations can be recycled, such as paper, printer cartridges, and plastic. Businesses can make small changes in their daily operations that will make an impact in sustainability efforts. Environmentally friendly products or components can be used both in business operations and for product packaging. Businesses can offer customers reusable shopping bags, reuse cardboard boxes when shipping products, and use environmentally-safe cleaning products in the maintenance of their facilities.
4. The Environmental Protection Agency (EPA) offers information and resources about environmental protection, sustainable business practices, and environmental law. Companies looking to implement green practices can contact the EPA for guidance.
5. Businesses benefit by increasing customer loyalty and possibly gaining new customers as a result of their cause marketing activities.

Answers to Build Your Vocabulary terms are key term definitions and can be found in the glossary.

Review Your Knowledge

1. Business ethics are the rules for professional conduct and integrity in all areas of business. Two ways a company might convey its expectations for acceptable employee behavior are with a code of conduct and a code of ethics.
2. The goal of a code of ethics is to establish a value system for the company that enables employees to make sound ethical decisions.
3. The American Marketing Association (AMA) is a professional organization that sets the standards for ethical behavior in the marketing industry.
4. If a company or employee acts unethically, it can have long-lasting effects on the success of the business. Business is lost when customers do not trust a company or do not approve of its business practices and choose to buy products from a competitor.
5. Ethical practices must also be adhered to, including customer privacy, honest marketing information, fair pricing, and ethical selling practices.
6. Corporate social responsibility (CSR) is the actions a business takes to further social good. These are actions that go beyond the profit interests and legal requirements of a business. CSR is important because it can make a difference in a community, improve relations with clients or customers, and create goodwill. Goodwill creates customer loyalty, earns the trust of the community, and is vitally important to success in business.
7. Philanthropic activities are most effective when they align with the existing goods or services that a business offers.
8. (Student answers may vary, but should be similar to the following.) Sustainable business practices include conserving natural resources, reducing pollution, and recycling. Many items used in daily business operations can be recycled, such as paper, printer cartridges, and plastic. Businesses can make small changes in their daily operations that will make an impact in sustainability efforts. Environmentally friendly products or components can be used both in business operations and for product packaging. Businesses can offer customers reusable shopping bags, reuse cardboard boxes when shipping products, and use environmentally-safe cleaning products in the maintenance of their facilities.
9. Socially responsible marketing is a belief that a company's marketing approach should consider the benefit to and betterment of society as a whole. Examples include green marketing and cause marketing.
10. Nonprofit organizations benefit financially, through increased public awareness, or both.

Apply Your Knowledge

Student answers will vary for Apply Your Knowledge questions.

Apply Your Math Skills

1. The animal welfare charity will receive $360.
   12 × $20 = $240
   $240 × .50 = $120
   $120 + $240 = $360

2. The volunteer work cost the company $460.25 in wages.
7 × $13.00 = $91.00
7 × $15.25 = $106.75
7 × $18.50 = $129.50
7 × $19.00 = $133.00
$91.00 + $106.75 + $129.50 + $133.00 = $460.25

Chapter 5 Economic Principles

You Do the Math: Interpreting Line Graphs
1. July.
2. March.
3. Sales increased by $4,000.
   $16,000 − $10,000 = $4,000
4. Increase.

Section 5.1 Review
1. Macroeconomics studies human behavior and choices that relate to the entire economy of a nation. Microeconomics studies human behavior and choices that relate to the economic decisions of individuals and businesses.
2. Land, labor, capital, and entrepreneurship.
3. Scarcity develops when demand is higher than the available resources.
4. Scarce resources limit the quantity of goods and services produced. This means decisions must be made about which goods or services will be created.
5. Define the decision to be made. Explore all alternatives. Choose the best alternative. Act on the decision. Evaluate the solution or decision.

Answers to Build Your Vocabulary terms are key term definitions and can be found in the glossary.

Section 5.2 Review
1. Private property, profit, economic freedom, voluntary exchange, and competition.
2. The price, demand, and availability of a product or service.
3. Supply is the quantity of goods available for purchase. Demand is the quantity of goods that consumers want to purchase.
4. Profit is the difference between the income earned and expenses incurred by a business during a specific period of time.
5. Competition is the action taken by two or more businesses attempting to attract the same customers.

Answers to Build Your Vocabulary terms are key term definitions and can be found in the glossary.

Review Your Knowledge
1. Economics is a science that examines how goods and services are produced, sold, and used. It involves how people, governments, and businesses make choices about using limited resources to satisfy unlimited wants.
2. Land includes all of a nation's natural resources. Labor is the work performed by people in businesses. As a factor of production, capital is all of the tools and machinery used to produce goods or provide services. Entrepreneurship is the willingness and ability to start a new business.
3. Transportation infrastructure includes highways, bridges, railroads, public transportation, seaports, and airports. Utility infrastructure includes sanitation systems, electric power plants, water systems, and telecommunications services.
4. The economic problem states that human wants are unlimited, while resources are limited, or scarce. Scarce resources limit the quantity of goods and services produced. This means that decisions must be made about which goods or services will be created.
5. Individuals make economic decisions based on what is most valuable to them.
6. A traditional economy is one in which economic decisions are based on a society's values, culture, and customs. In a command economy, the government makes all the economic decisions for its citizens. A market economy is one in which individuals and businesses are free to make their own economic decisions with limited government involvement. In a mixed economy, both the government and individuals make decisions about economic resources.
7. Private property means that individuals have the right to own property. Profit means that individuals and businesses have the right to make a profit. Economic freedom means that individuals are free to make their own economic decisions. They can decide what to

IE-25

buy, when to buy, and how to use what they have bought. Voluntary exchange means that individuals have the right to buy and sell in a marketplace where prices are freely set by the forces of supply and demand. Competition means that businesses can compete to sell goods and services and decide what to produce, how to produce, and for whom to produce.
8. When businesses are intently focused on profit, other facets of the business environment and greater society can become problematic issues. Pollution levels can rise due to unregulated manufacturing activity; consumer and worker safety may become a low priority to businesses; unfair business practices can become common; and critical aspects of the economy's infrastructure may be neglected.
9. Market forces are economic factors that affect the price, demand, and availability of a product or service. In a free-enterprise system, the decisions related to market forces result in the production of the best goods and services at the most attractive prices. Market forces include supply and demand, the profit motive, and competition. The principle of supply and demand is critical to business because it determines the price of goods and services. Supply is the quantity of goods available for purchase. Demand is the quantity of goods that consumers want to purchase. Profit motive is the reason people take the risk to start and expand businesses. Profit is the difference between the income earned and expenses incurred by a business during a specific period of time. Competition is the action taken by two or more businesses attempting to attract the same customers.
10. Higher demand results in higher prices, and lower demand results in lower prices. An increase in the supply of a product often lowers prices. When the supply of a product decreases, the price usually increases.

Apply Your Knowledge

Student answers will vary for Apply Your Knowledge questions.

Apply Your Math Skills

1. 200
2. $3.00
3. Student answers will vary.
4. Student answers will vary.

Chapter 6 Economic Activity

You Do the Math: Types of Numbers

1. 5.87 + 4.956 + 2.011 + 4 = 16.837
2. 34 + 9 − 127 + 783 = 699
3. 112.058 + 2.1 + 93.237 = 207.395
4. 987 + 705 + 827 + 4 = 2,523
5. 73 + 8 − 12 = 69

Section 6.1 Review

1. A healthy economy is one that is experiencing growth through high productivity, a high rate of employment, and stable prices in the market.
2. The most significant effect of inflation is that it reduces the purchasing power of money.
3. Per capita GDP is the GDP of a nation divided by its population. It shows the amount of economic output for each person in the country.
4. If every person who is willing and able to work has a job, the economy would be at full employment.
5. Lagging indicators.

Answers to Build Your Vocabulary terms are key term definitions and can be found in the glossary.

Section 6.2 Review

1. Monopolistic competition.
2. Price competition is when a lower price is the main reason for customers to buy from one business over another. Nonprice competition is when strategies other than price are used to attract customers.
3. The government takes a role to manage the economy. This is done through fiscal and monetary policies.
4. Fiscal policy and monetary policy.
5. (Any) Sherman Antitrust Act, Clayton Antitrust Act, and Federal Trade Commission Act.

Answers to Build Your Vocabulary terms are key term definitions and can be found in the glossary.

Review Your Knowledge

1. Gross domestic product (GDP), inflation, interest rates, unemployment rate, and the stock and bond markets.
2. Consumer spending includes everything people buy for personal use, such as food, clothing, cars, medical care, and recreation. It is considered to be an economic indicator because the rate of consumer spending is linked to the health of the economy. When consumer spending is high, economic growth

is often strong. If consumer spending is low, the economy tends to be weak.
3. Price stability means that prices are changing either very slowly or not at all, at an inflation rate of about zero percent to three percent. Price stability is usually considered good for the economy because lower inflation leads to lower interest rates, making borrowing money less expensive. It also makes financial planning easier because wages tend to be better to keep up with prices.
4. Expansion is a period when the economy is growing and the GDP is rising. The peak marks the end of expansion and is the highest point in the business cycle. Recession is a period of significant decline in the total output, income, employment, and trade in an economy. A trough is the lowest stage of a business cycle and marks the end of a recession.
5. A leading indicator is one that changes before a change in economic activity. A lagging indicator is one that changes after a change in economic activity. A coincident indicator is one that changes at the same time as changes in economic activity.
6. A monopoly is a market structure with one business that has complete control of a market's entire supply of a product. An oligopoly is a market structure with a small number of businesses selling the same or similar products. Monopolistic competition is a large number of businesses selling similar, but not the same, products and at different prices. This is also known as imperfect competition. Perfect competition is characterized by a large number of businesses selling the same product at the same prices.
7. Specific roles the government plays in the operation of our economy include managing the economy, providing public goods and services, providing a legal framework, promoting competition, and correcting for externalities.
8. The Federal Reserve System is the central bank of the United States. It carries out the nation's monetary policy "to promote effectively the goals of maximum employment, stable prices, and moderate long-term interest rates." The Fed looks at many economic indicators to evaluate the condition of the economy. When the economy is slow or weak, it may take action to increase the money supply and lower interest rates. If the economy is growing too fast, the Federal Reserve can take action to slow the economy and avoid inflation.
9. Antitrust laws promote fair trade and competition among businesses. These laws have been established to prevent monopolies and unfair pricing and business practices. Antitrust laws attempt to ensure that markets are open and fair.
10. Student examples will vary, but should be similar to the following. Emissions from a factory can be harmful to those living close to the business. It can cause problems for those who inhale the fumes.

Apply Your Knowledge
Student answers will vary for Apply Your Knowledge questions.

Apply Your Math Skills
1. The economic growth rate was 2.6 percent.
   [($19.5 trillion − $19.0 trillion) ÷ $19.0 trillion] × 100 = 2.6% economic growth rate
2. The economic growth between the two years will be 5.1 percent.
   [($20.5 trillion − $19.5 trillion) ÷ $19.5 trillion] × 100 = 5.1% economic growth rate

Chapter 7 Global Trade

You Do the Math: Currency Conversion
1. A. The books cost $29.57 in US dollars.
      £17.98 ÷ .60797 = $29.57
   B. The total cost of the purchase including shipping is $45.97 in US dollars.
      £9.97 ÷ .60797 = $16.40
      $16.40 + $29.57 = $45.97
2. The cost of the circuit boards in rupees is ₹231,000.
   $3,500 × 66 = ₹231,000

Section 7.1 Review
1. The terms global trade and international trade are sometimes used interchangeably. However, there is a slight difference. Global means the world, such as global economy. International trade is the buying and selling of goods and services between two or more specific nations rather than all nations in the world.
2. Exchange rates are needed because currencies have different values.
3. Weakened.
4. (Any) Trade barrier, embargo, trade sanction, tariff, quota.

5. The World Trade Organization (WTO).
Answers to Build Your Vocabulary terms are key term definitions and can be found in the glossary.

Section 7.2 Review
1. Identifying a target market and handling problems related to communication, shipping, and legal issues.
2. The licensor earns revenue, often for little or no extra work. The licensee gets product into the market quickly.
3. Political, economic, social, and technological factors.
4. Product adaptations customize existing products to the local tastes, expectations, buying habits, and customs of a foreign market.
5. Standardization is applying consistent promotion strategies to the marketing of a product regardless of the specific market. Adaptation is changing the marketing strategies to meet the preferences and demands of customers in a specific market.

Answers to Build Your Vocabulary terms are key term definitions and can be found in the glossary.

Review Your Knowledge
1. International trade is the buying and selling of goods and services between two or more specific nations rather than all nations in the world. Nations engage in international trade because most countries do not have the factors of production needed to produce all the goods and services needed by their population. The available land, labor, capital, and entrepreneurship vary by country. Trading the goods and services produced by each country's businesses allows more of the needs and wants of consumers to be met. This has created a global dependency in which countries depend on each other for products.
2. When businesses, individuals, or governments in the same country buy and sell goods to one another, they use the same currency. Most countries have their own currencies and typically only accept their own currency for business exchanges. This can become complicated because the value of each country's currency is different when compared to other currencies. Factors that affect the way a nation's currency functions in the global market include the foreign exchange rate and the currency value.
3. (Any) Political stability or instability in the world, nations changing their laws, nations in dispute with other nations, and economic conditions, such as interest rates.
4. There are several types of trade barriers, including embargos, tariffs, and quotas. An embargo is a governmental order that prohibits trade with a foreign country. A tariff is a governmental tax on imported goods. A quota is a limit on the amount of a product imported into a country during a specific period of time.
5. Trade policy, trade regulations, and trade agreements are ways in which governments play a role in international trade.
6. There are various ways that a domestic business can enter a global market. These include exports and imports, licensing, franchising, starting a joint venture, expanding a company into a multinational, and contract manufacturing.
7. Exporting presents certain challenges for a business. Identifying a target market, overcoming communication issues and time differences, and understanding laws and regulations are examples of struggles that are encountered. Importing also presents business challenges. Products imported into the United States must meet the same governmental standards as domestically produced ones. In addition, there can be quotas set by the United States to control how much product is brought in from other countries. An important disadvantage in contract manufacturing is that outsourcing manufacturing to foreign countries causes domestic jobs to be lost.
8. Before completing a marketing plan, a review of the external environment that the business will face should be completed. An environmental scan is an analysis of the external factors that affect the success of business. This process identifies potential opportunities and threats to a company's business plans and strategies.
9. Political structure is an important external factor for conducting global business. Traditional, command, market, and mixed economies each function differently. The type of economic system may require changes to the business and marketing plans in order for the business to be successful in a foreign country. Culture is the shared beliefs, customs, practices, and social behavior of a particular group or nation. It affects how people think, work, interact, and communicate with others. The cultural beliefs and values of potential customers in a market

affect how they make economic decisions and set economic goals. Cultures vary widely in terms of their beliefs and values.
10. Global marketing consists of dynamic activities that identify, anticipate, and satisfy customer demand for product in countries worldwide while making a profit for the business. It involves making decisions about the four Ps for a specific product or group of products. Standardization is applying consistent promotion strategies for marketing a product. Using a standardization strategy saves the business money by avoiding costs related to the promotion campaigns. Adaptation is changing the marketing strategies to meet the preferences and demands of customers in a specific market. This strategy considers the local culture and economy that affect customers in the market.

Apply Your Knowledge
Student answers will vary for Apply Your Knowledge questions.

Apply Your Math Skills
1.

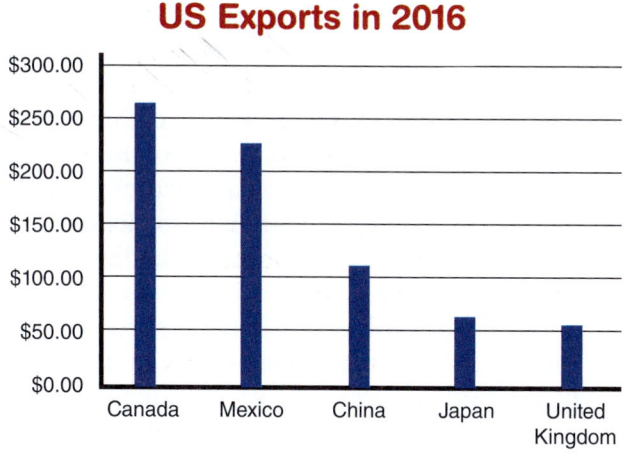

US Exports in 2016

(bar chart showing exports by country: Canada ~$265, Mexico ~$225, China ~$110, Japan ~$60, United Kingdom ~$55)

2.

Amount of Sales

(line graph showing sales from 2010 to 2016, rising from near $0 to about $130,000)

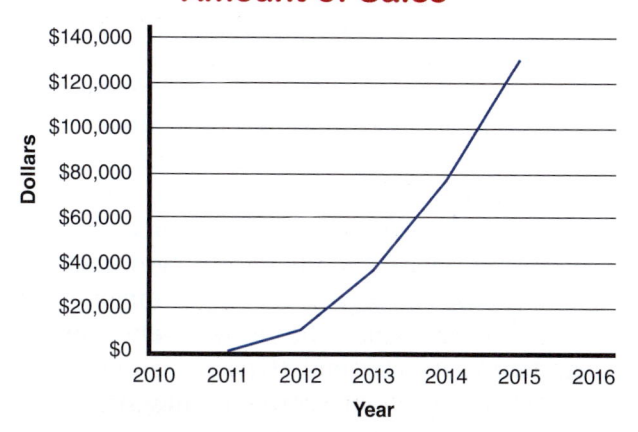

Chapter 8 Marketing Research

You Do the Math: Margin of Error
1. The lowest percentage of households that can be assumed to make this purchase within the next year is 37.6 percent.
   45.6 percent − 8 percent = 37.6 percent
2. The maximum weekly expenses should be $12,355.35.
   $12,054 × 2.5 percent = maximum weekly expenses
   $12,054 × .025 = $301.35
   $12,054 + $301.35 = $12,355.35
3. The range of percentages of families that will drive at least 500 miles is 69 percent to 78.2 percent.
   73.6 percent − 4.6 percent = 69 percent
   73.6 percent + 4.6 percent = 78.2 percent

Section 8.1 Review
1. Marketing-information management (MIM) is the marketing function that involves gathering and analyzing information about markets, customers, industry trends, new technology, and competing businesses. It also includes making sure the right people in an organization get the information needed to make good business decisions.
2. Primary data is beneficial to researchers because it is information they have personally collected and evaluated. Researchers can design their data-collection methods to meet their needs. The research can be tailored to a specific target market. Secondary data are usually easier to find and less expensive than primary data.
3. The sample size is the number of people in the research sample.
4. Fads are very popular for a short time and die out quickly. Trends develop over a long period of time and affect large numbers of people.
5. The information stored in a company's MkIS can help target offers to customers based on products they have already purchased. In doing this, customers feel like the company knows them and what they want or need.
Answers to Build Your Vocabulary terms are key term definitions and can be found in the glossary.

Section 8.2 Review
1. Informal research may take place with little or no planning, such as a casual conversation with customers in a store. Formal research

IE-29

involves a strategy, requires planning, and follows the formal research process.
2. All research begins by identifying the problem and defining it.
3. Analyzing involves studying the data for patterns, organizing the information into graphs and charts, and making comparisons with previous studies. Analysis may be done manually or by using a software program. After the data is analyzed, it may be presented in various formats. The format chosen will depend on the type of information to be presented and on the needs of those receiving the information.
4. Research results that are wrong lead to poor business decisions.
5. Marketing research may be unreliable for a number of reasons, including problems with the research sample, question structure, data analysis, or reporting errors.

Answers to Build Your Vocabulary terms are key term definitions and can be found in the glossary.

Review Your Knowledge

1. Marketing research produces various data about customers, competition, products, and the industry. The data help businesses define their target markets, learn about the needs and wants of their customers, and investigate what motivates people to buy. It also helps identify the competition, learn about new business opportunities, and answer many other important business questions.
2. The difference between primary and secondary data is availability. Primary data are pieces of information collected directly by an individual or organization for its own use. Secondary data are information, statistics, or other data that someone has collected for other reasons, but anyone can use it.
3. (Any) Using the observation method, a researcher watches people or situations and accurately records data while remaining unbiased. An interview is a formal meeting between two or more people to obtain insight into the thoughts and opinions of people about a product or business. A survey is a set of questions posed to a group of people to determine how that group thinks, feels, or acts. Survey data can be collected through an in-person survey, over the telephone, by mail, or electronically. A diary is a written record of the thoughts, activities, or plans of the writer during a given period of time. Researchers typically use diaries to study how people use their time and spend their money. In the experiment method, a researcher sets up two situations that differ in only one variable. Results from the two experiment situations can then be compared.
4. (Any) Government sources: federal, state, and local governmental agencies; market-research sources: research firms, state and local chambers of commerce; academic sources: universities, community colleges, and local libraries; trade associations: association websites and industry publications; and the Internet: competitors' websites and sites ending in .gov or .edu.
5. A marketing trend is a pattern of change in consumer behavior that leads to changes in the marketing mix. Trend research often combines research on customers, competition, and possible opportunities. This information is important to businesses because it helps them adjust product, price, place, and promotion to meet new trends. Successful marketers notice trends early and help their businesses offer products to meet new wants or needs. Social trends are the patterns of change in society as a whole. Demographic trends are changes the size of different segments of the population. Product trends are changes in current product features or new products being developed.
6. The system provides marketing intelligence so decisions can be made and problems solved.
7. 1. Define the problem: Ask the questions for which answers are needed. 2. Conduct background research: Learn as much as possible about the problem that has been defined. 3. State a hypothesis: Write a statement that can be tested and proved to be either true or false through marketing research. 4. Develop a research plan: Develop a plan to test the hypothesis and produce a desired outcome using primary or secondary research. 5. Collect the data: Individuals collect the primary or secondary data. 6. Analyze the data: Analyzing data makes it useful and involves studying the data for patterns, organizing the information into graphs and charts, and making comparisons with previous studies. 7. Draw conclusions and make recommendations: Research conclusions are based on data analysis

that confirm or disprove the hypothesis. Marketing researchers usually write the results, conclusions, and recommendations in a formal report. 8. Follow up: The final step in the marketing research process is to follow up to determine if the recommendations from the research were implemented.

8. Data mining is searching through large amounts of digital data to find useful patterns or trends. It is used in the process of analyzing raw data gathered from marketing research.
9. Research conclusions are based on data analysis. The research hypothesis will be confirmed or disproved by the analyzed data. If disproved, the process typically starts over with a different hypothesis. If the research confirms the hypothesis, the business may decide to move forward with the researched marketing activity.
10. Marketing research may be unreliable for a number of reasons, including problems with the research sample, question structure, data analysis, or reporting errors. A number of errors may come from using a poor research sample. The sample size may be too small. The sample may include people who are not in the targeted market, or the wrong target market may have been used. Question structure errors occur when order bias happens. Order bias is the skewing of results caused by the order in which questions are placed in a survey. This happens if answer choices for questions are not rotated among all surveys given. Questions using vague or misleading language, do not stay on topic, or assume certain knowledge may also skew results. Data errors occur when analysis is performed incorrectly, such as simple math errors or a misunderstanding of the information by the person analyzing the data. Reporting errors, such as leaving out crucial data, grammar and sentence structure, or incorrect visuals, can create incomplete or inaccurate research results.

Apply Your Knowledge

Student answers will vary for Apply Your Knowledge questions.

Apply Your Math Skills

1. Sophia needs to survey at least 1,750 people.
   35 ÷ .02 = 1,750
2. There will be four people in each focus group.
   32 ÷ 4 = 8
3. The total number of participants who would buy the cereal is 20.
   32 focus-group participants ÷ 2 = 16 participants per marketing strategy
   16 participants × .75 = 12 participants
   16 participants × .50 = 8 participants
   12 + 8 = 20

Chapter 9 Targeting a Market

You Do the Math: Mean, Median, and Mode

1. The mean is $3.36.
   $3.49 + $3.67 + $3.52 + $3.58 + $2.56 = $16.82
   $16.82 ÷ 5 = $3.36
2. A. The mode is $105.
   B. The mean is $102.50.
   $75 + $99 + $99 + $105 + $105 + $105 + $116 + $116 = $820
   $820 ÷ 8 = $102.50

Section 9.1 Review

1. When using mass marketing tools, everyone in the larger group gets the same promotional message. This saves time and money because all people receive the same, single promotional message. The main disadvantage to mass marketing is that it ignores differences among customers. Sending everyone the same message may prove to be inefficient, miss the best customer, and waste marketing funds.
2. An accurately identified target market has clearly defined wants and needs that the business can meet, enough money to buy the product, is willing and able to buy the product, and there are enough customers in the target market to be profitable.
3. Segmenting the market can help in accurately identifying a target market. The people in a target market are a company's most likely customers.
4. Age is a common segmentation variable because people of different ages have different needs and wants. The period of history in which a group of people grew up in also has a major effect on their attitudes, wants, and needs.
5. Accurate customer profiles help determine the best promotional strategies. By knowing who is most interested in a company's products, promotional dollars can be used wisely. Instead of hoping that mass marketing efforts

will reach likely customers, the good or service can be promoted specifically to those within the target markets.

Answers to Build Your Vocabulary terms are key term definitions and can be found in the glossary.

Section 9.2 Review

1. A competitive advantage based on factors other than price is called nonprice competition.
2. A unique selling proposition (USP) is a statement summarizing the special features or benefits of a product or business. Its purpose is to convince the customer that their product is the only one that can satisfy their needs.
3. After gathering information about the competition, competitive advantages should be evaluated. A marketing manager must know what the competition is offering and their pricing models, as well as product features and benefits. Information about price, features, benefits, and other information about each company is recorded in the analysis.
4. A SWOT analysis lists company strengths, weaknesses, opportunities, and threats faced by the business. It can help determine marketing and product development strategies.
5. (company sales ÷ total sales in market) × 100 = percent market share

Answers to Build Your Vocabulary terms are key term definitions and can be found in the glossary.

Review Your Knowledge

1. In the world of marketing, a market is all the people and organizations that might purchase a product. Markets are the focus of all marketing efforts. Markets include the particular types of customers most likely to buy certain goods or services. It is these groups that companies want to reach in order to increase sales, earn profits, and stay in business.
2. Mass marketing uses one marketing mix of product, price, place, and promotion for a market. Mass marketing ignores differences among customers. The market is viewed as one large group. It assumes that everyone has exactly the same wants and needs for the product. The advantage of mass marketing is that it saves time and money because all people receive the same, single promotional message. A disadvantage is that mass marketing ignores differences among customers. Sending everyone the same message may prove to be inefficient, miss the best customer, and waste marketing funds. A target market is the specific group of customers at which a company aims its goods and services. These are the people most likely to buy the goods or services a business offers. Accurately identifying target market customers supports the 80/20 rule of business which states 80 percent of a business' sales come from 20 percent of its customers. Identifying the target market can save money in the budget when marketing dollars are spent focusing on customers who are most likely to buy, rather than a larger group of people who may or may not be interested.
3. Market segmentation is the process of dividing a large market into smaller groups. Segmenting the market can help in accurately selecting a target market. This can also save money in the budget when marketing dollars are spent focusing on customers who are most likely to buy rather than a larger group of people who may or may not be interested.
4. The variables used for market segmentation are geographic, demographic, psychographic, and behavioral. Segmenting a market based on where customers live is called geographic segmentation and includes region, climate, and population density. Demographic segmentation is dividing the market of potential customers by their personal statistics, including age, gender, income, ethnicity, education level, occupation, marital status, and family size. Psychographic segmentation is dividing the market by certain preferences or lifestyle choices, such as values, attitudes, activities, and interests. Behavioral segmentation divides a market by the relationships between customers and a good or service. These include benefits sought, usage rate, buying status, brand loyalty, and special occasions.
5. Once marketers have divided a market into segments, the segments are analyzed to determine which have the most sales potential. A customer profile is a detailed description of the typical consumer in a market segment. Accurate customer profiles help determine the best promotional strategies. This allows goods or services to be promoted specifically to those within the target markets.
6. There are two types of competitors: direct and indirect. Direct competitors are companies that sell identical or very similar goods or services. Indirect competitors offer different, but similar, goods or services that meet customer needs.

The products sold by a company's indirect competitors might be acceptable substitutes for the company's products.
7. Businesses use price and nonprice competition to gain a competitive advantage. Price competition occurs when a lower price is the main reason for customers to buy from one business over another. For businesses competing on price, the focus is to make more sales by offering the lowest prices. A competitive advantage based on factors other than price is called nonprice competition. Some businesses choose to provide notably better service or exclusive brands to beat their competition. Nonprice competition may also focus more on the features and benefits of a product, rather than the price. Nonprice features of a business may include extended hours, gift wrapping, or custom orders.
8. Components of a market analysis are a competitive analysis, a SWOT analysis, and an environmental scan.
9. Product positioning is the process used to influence the customer's perception of a brand or product in relation to the competition. It is a marketing strategy that focuses on influencing the perception of a product in the minds of consumers.
10. The sales analysis begins with reviewing current and past sales. An important part of analyzing sales is to determine what the market potential is available in the current environment. Market potential is the maximum number of customers and amount of sales that can be generated from a specific segment in a defined time period. Determining the market potential will confirm that sales can be generated from the group of customers in the identified market segment. If the market potential exists, the business will forecast its portion of the market share in comparison to its competitors. Market share is useful for comparing the companies within a market to each other and showing the relationships among the companies.

Apply Your Knowledge
Student answers will vary for Apply Your Knowledge questions.

Apply Your Math Skills
1. There are 240 customers responsible for 80 percent of the restaurant's sales.
Convert 20% to .20 for the calculation
1,200 × .20 = 240 customers

2. The market share of Jason's Italian Restaurant is 17.5 percent.
($945,000 ÷ $5,400,000) × 100 = 17.5

Chapter 10 Understanding the Customer

You Do the Math: Rounding
1. The mean price of Jenny's weekly lunch is $7.00.
$5.67 + $5.67 + $5.67 + $6.79 + $6.79 + $7.94 + $8.50 + $8.50 = $55.53
$55.53 ÷ 8 = $6.94.
2. A. $2
$75 ÷ 48 = $1.56
Round $1.56 up to $2.
B. $3
$189 ÷ 56 = $3.38
Round $3.38 down to $3.
C. $1
$84 ÷ 96 = $.88
Round $0.88 to $1.

Section 10.1 Review
1. People will buy products to meet needs at the bottom of the pyramid before buying products to meet higher needs.
2. Family, friends, classmates, and other groups to which an individual belongs make up his or her social environment. Culture is a strong influence that affects many aspects of life and often shapes an individual's social environment. The ethnic group, geographic location, and social class in which people grow up also contribute to their cultural influences.
3. To motivate is to provide the internal push that results in action.
4. At this stage, consumers draw on past experiences and may ask for recommendations from those within their reference groups. Many consumers conduct product research on the Internet, through store advertisements, and by reading product reviews.
5. Large, expensive products tend to require quite a bit of research and planning. Smaller, less expensive products usually require little research and planning before the purchase. Some consumers have a more difficult time making decisions than others. Often, these consumers take much longer researching their first purchase of a product.

Answers to Build Your Vocabulary terms are key term definitions and can be found in the glossary.

Section 10.2 Review

1. The business-to-business market can be split into five categories: producers, resellers, service businesses, governments, and institutions.
2. Common variables used to segment business customers are by industry, business size, and business needs.
3. Business customers use the products they buy either to make new products, resell to customers, or to operate the business.
4. Relationship selling focuses on building long-term relationships with customers.
5. Often, something occurs to make a buyer less satisfied with a product or vendor he or she has been using. A modified purchase is a decision to buy a familiar product that needs some changes or modifications.

Answers to Build Your Vocabulary terms are key term definitions and can be found in the glossary.

Section 10.3 Review

1. Credit is an agreement or contract to receive goods or services before actually paying for them.
2. Secured loans require collateral, which is an asset pledged to guarantee the loan will be repaid. If the loan is not repaid, the asset can be taken by the creditor and sold to recover the cost of the loan.
3. Offering credit through credit cards, installment loans, or trade credit can create a steady income for the business. Another reward of extending credit to customers is building customer loyalty.
4. A credit report provides the following information about a credit applicant: number and types of credit accounts and indicates any that are past due; how promptly credit cards statements and loans were paid off in full; on-time payment of other bills, such as rent, taxes, or utilities; current total outstanding debts; and amount of available credit on credit cards and home equity loans.
5. The three Cs of credit are character, capacity, and capital.

Answers to Build Your Vocabulary terms are key term definitions and can be found in the glossary.

Review Your Knowledge

1. Maslow's Hierarchy of Needs states that unsatisfied needs motivate people to act. People tend to fulfill physical needs before others that are less critical for survival. When physical needs are met, people look to fulfill needs for security, love and acceptance, esteem, and self-actualization. Many marketers use Maslow's theory to develop products that fulfill certain needs. They also focus promotions on how their products meet those needs.
2. Common factors that influence consumer buying include social environment, situational influences, personal factors, and psychological influences. Family, friends, classmates, other social groups, and culture make up your social environment. Situational influences come from the environment and can affect buying choices. Personal factors are the qualities that make each person unique, including age, gender, and ethnicity. Psychological influences come from within a person and explain why a person has certain needs and wants.
3. A buying motive is the reason a consumer seeks and buys a good or service. Consumer buying motives can be categorized as emotional, rational, and patronage. Emotional buying motives are based on emotions, feelings, and social needs. Rational buying motives follow logical reasoning. For example, if you are hungry, you seek food because buying food is logical when you are hungry. Patronage buying motives are based on features of a specific store or product, such as consumers who are loyal to a certain product brand.
4. The consumer decision-making process is a series of steps people take in making buying decisions. Typically, this is a five-step process that includes awareness of a need or problem, an information search, review of the purchase options, make the purchase decision, and evaluate the purchase.
5. The four levels of consumer buying decisions are impulse, routine, limited, and extensive. Impulse buying decisions are made without any research or planning. Routine buying decisions are made quickly with little thought and usually involve products with which the consumer has experience or prefers. Limited buying decisions require some amount of research and planning because the products are unfamiliar to or not frequently purchased by the consumer. An extensive buying decision involves a great deal of research and planning and is usually made when buying higher-priced items.
6. Influences in B2B buying decisions can be grouped into three categories: internal, external, and

situational. Internal influences are motivators that come from within the business and include the structure, goals, and management team of a company. External influences are motivators from outside the business and include business competition, new technology, and product trends. Situational influences come from the environment in which the business exists and may include the economy, political environment, and business regulations or laws.

7. The levels of B2B buying decisions are new purchases, repeat purchases, and modified purchases. A new purchase requires a great deal of research and thought. Repeat-purchase decisions occur when the buyer is satisfied with the product, vendor, and terms of sale. A modified purchase involves a familiar product that needs some changes or modifications.

8. Credit is an agreement or contract to receive goods or services before actually paying for them. The debtor-creditor relationship is a legal relationship based on good faith that both parties will uphold their end of the agreement. Marketers view credit as a customer convenience and benefit. However, issuing credit to customers has a direct impact on pricing. There are multiple costs involved when businesses extend or accept credit. Consumer credit is credit given to individual consumers by a retail business. Trade credit is granting a line of credit to another business for a short period of time to purchase its goods and services.

9. When credit is extended to customers, rewards include generation of sales, customers often buy more with credit, and the business builds customer loyalty. Credit risk is the potential for financial loss due to credit not being repaid. When extending credit to business customers or consumers, there is always the possibility that some customers will be unable to pay their debt. Customers that fail to pay bills on time may create a cash-flow problem for the business that extended the credit.

10. When granting credit to customers, it is important to establish a credit process that reduces risk. Having a credit policy in place can help guide the process of extending credit. Customers should complete an application that provides credit history, work history, and other information necessary to qualify for credit. Order a credit report to evaluate the credit history and financial behavior of a business or individual. Evaluate the credit worthiness of each applicant based on the three Cs of credit. Keep track of when amounts owed to a company by its customers, the accounts receivable, are due or overdue.

Apply Your Knowledge
Student answers will vary for Apply Your Knowledge questions.

Apply Your Math Skills
1. Consumers spent the most money on food eaten at home in Year C.
2. Consumers spent the most money on food eaten away from home in Year D.
3. The largest gap between the home and away amounts occurred in Year C.
   Year A: $3,838 − $2,620 = $1,218
   Year B: $3,921 − $2,678 = $1,243
   Year C: $3,977 − $2,625 = $1,352
   Year D: $3,971 − $2,787 = $1,184

Chapter 11 Product

You Do the Math: Word Problems
1. Henry should request $274.56 for the rest of the week.
   (total cost of gas + total cost of tolls) × number of days remaining = total petty cash needed for the rest of the week
   $61.24 total gas cost in one day × 4 more days = $244.96 remaining weekly gas cost
   $7.40 daily tolls × 4 more days = $29.60 remaining weekly toll cost
   $244.96 + $29.60 = $274.56
2. There can be 11 cartons of catalogs on the palette.
   150 maximum pounds per palette ÷ 12.6 pounds per carton = number of cartons per palette
   150 ÷ 12.6 = 11.9 cartons per palette
3. The supervisor should add 4 researchers to the project.
   78 interviews completed ÷ 6 researchers = 13 interviews completed in half of the work day
   13 interviews per researcher × 2 = 26 interviews completed per researcher per day
   26 interviews per researcher per day × 5 days = 130 interviews per researcher per week
   130 interviews per researcher per week × 6 researchers = 780 interviews per week
   1,200 − 780 = 420 outstanding interviews
   420 outstanding interviews ÷ 26 interviews completed per researcher per day = 16 researcher-days

16 researcher-days ÷ 4 remaining days = 4

Section 11.1 Review

1. Services are different from goods in four important ways. Services are intangible, inseparable, variable, and perishable.
2. (Any three) Raw materials, processed materials, component parts, major equipment, office equipment and supplies, and business services.
3. A warranty is a written document that states the quality of a product with a promise to correct certain problems that might occur. The warranty promises that the manufacturer will replace or repair faulty items. A guarantee is a promise that a product has a certain quality or will perform in a specific way. A guarantee typically has certain terms or conditions, such as a set period of time or following the intended use of a product.
4. The various forms of protection may be intended to protect the product, the user, or both.
5. Product managers work closely with accounting, sales teams, and the advertising department or ad agency.

Answers to Build Your Vocabulary terms are key term definitions and can be found in the glossary.

Section 11.2 Review

1. Because genuinely new products are risky, many companies choose to develop variations on currently or previously successful products. These variations should improve the function of the existing product. Such products become improved and revised versions of the originals and are advertised as such.
2. Marketing plays an important role in new-product development, including research, product testing, and creating the promotional strategies.
3. Product ideas are usually the result of trend research, observation, customer feedback, and brainstorming.
4. Awareness of the life cycle stage of their products helps businesses develop effective marketing-mix strategies.
5. During the introduction and growth stages, prices are often higher because the product is new, there is little or no competition, and the business needs to recoup development costs. During the maturity stage, prices are often lowered because there is more competition. During the decline stage, prices are often at their lowest to stimulate slow sales.

Answers to Build Your Vocabulary terms are key term definitions and can be found in the glossary.

Review Your Knowledge

1. A product is a good, service, or idea that is bought and sold. Product is the primary *P* of the marketing mix because it is the first element of the marketing mix to be decided. If a business does not have a product to sell, the other elements of the marketing mix are not needed.
2. In the B2C market, consumer products are those sold to consumers for their personal use. The basic categories of consumer products are convenience goods, shopping goods, and specialty goods. In the B2B market, business products are items sold to businesses for use in their operations. Business products categories are raw materials, processed materials, component parts, major equipment, office equipment and supplies, and business services.
3. Product planning is the process of making decisions about features and benefits that will help make a product successful and managing the product throughout its life cycle. These decisions help businesses determine how to distinguish their products from others. The first decision made by any business is to select which product mix it will offer. A product mix is all the goods and services that a business sells. The next decision is to focus on the product elements. All products have certain elements that may be changed to meet customer needs, including product features, usage, and protection. Understanding these elements can enable a business to more effectively fulfill the marketing concept of attaining customer satisfaction.
4. A product mix is all the goods and services that a business sells. Small businesses may only sell a few products, while large corporations can offer thousands of different products. Usually, the product mix consists of goods and services that relate to each other in some way.
5. Product/service management determines which products a business should offer to meet customer needs. It manages the development, marketing, and sale of a product or products.
6. A new product is different in some way from existing products. The difference between new and existing products may be minor or major. There are six categories of new products: new-to-the-world products, minor

product variations, new product lines, additions to existing product lines, repositioned existing products, and less expensive version of current product.
7. The new-product development process generally follows seven steps: idea generation, idea screening, business analysis, product design, test marketing, commercialization, and evaluation.
8. A service business usually goes through a period during which the details of providing a new service are planned. Training the service providers must also be completed before the business opens. Depending on the service, a physical location is chosen and the business may perform trial runs.
9. The product life cycle has four stages. The introduction stage is the time when a new product is first brought to the market. The growth stage is the period in which product sales increase rapidly. As the product becomes more successful, competitors enter the market. The maturity stage occurs when product sales are stable. Sales are no longer increasing quickly, nor are they decreasing. In the decline stage, product sales begin to decrease. If sales decline rapidly, the company may stop making or selling the product.
10. Frequent review of products to determine their life cycle stages is necessary to determine which products a business should offer, as well as how to market them. Knowing the life cycle stage of their products helps marketers develop effective marketing-mix strategies. This affects the product, price, place, and promotion of a specific good or service.

Apply Your Knowledge

Student answers will vary for Apply Your Knowledge questions.

Apply Your Math Skills

1. There were 14 negative reviews.
   280 × 5% = number of negative reviews
   280 × 0.05 = 14 negative reviews
2. 85% of customers surveyed were satisfied
   255 ÷ 300 = percent of customers that were satisfied
   255 ÷ 300 = 0.85
   0.85 × 100 = 85% of customers surveyed were satisfied

Chapter 12 Branding

You Do the Math: Problem Solving and Reasoning

1. No. The problem does not say what the weight of a smartphone or its packaging is.
2. No. The problem does not say how much each item costs individually.
3. No. The problem does not say how many miles per gallon Lana's car has.

Section 12.1 Review

1. The tangible elements of a brand are its name, graphic design elements, packaging, and tagline or slogan. These are the brand elements that can be seen and heard. Intangible elements of a brand include the implied promise of the brand, consistency of the brand, and customer perceptions of the brand image. Intangible elements are hard to measure because they cannot be seen or heard.
2. The function of label information is to verify facts about the product, such as contents, nutritional information, and weight. Some packaging and labeling contain safety precautions and directions to prevent injury to the user.
3. The perceptions of brand image are formed in three ways: personal experience, hearing the experiences of others, and how a brand is promoted.
4. National, private label, and generic.
5. National brands are probably the most familiar to consumers because they are carried by many large and small retail stores.

Answers to Build Your Vocabulary terms are key term definitions and can be found in the glossary.

Section 12.2 Review

1. The key to a unique brand is creating products and promotions that appeal to the needs and wants of the target market.
2. One way to accomplish this goal is to align the brand with a positive message. Many companies visibly participate in community and charitable events. Some large corporations buy the naming rights for sports stadiums, convention centers, and other public places to show their support for a community.
3. Extending a brand creates new marketing opportunities, which can lead to higher sales and profit for the company. Customers who were not interested in the brand before might be interested in the new products. However,

brand extension does come with risks. This practice may cause the brand to appear stretched too thin. Using the brand on too many products or products that are unrelated to the original can cause the brand to lose customer appeal. In addition, if a brand is extended to a new product and that product fails, the entire brand could suffer.
4. A trademark protects taglines, names, graphics, symbols, or any unique method used to identify a product or company. A service mark is similar to a trademark, but it identifies a service rather than a product.
5. Once a trademark or service mark has been registered, the symbol ® can be used with the mark. These symbols notify the public that the creator claims exclusive rights to the brand and its use.

Answers to Build Your Vocabulary terms are key term definitions and can be found in the glossary.

Review Your Knowledge

1. Brands are created through both tangible and intangible elements. The tangible elements of a brand are its name, graphic design elements, packaging, and tagline or slogan. These are the elements that can be seen and heard. Intangible elements of a brand include the implied promise of the brand, consistency of the brand, and customer perceptions of the brand image. Examples include customer expectations, their feelings about the brand, and their direct interactions with it.
2. The brand promise is what consumers get when they purchase a good or service from a brand. A brand is the promise made to consumers that may or may not be included in the graphics or tagline. Consumers develop expectations for a brand based on how it is promoted and priced.
3. There are three types of product brands: national, private label, and generic. A national brand is one created by a manufacturer for its own products. Private-label brands are products owned by and created specifically for large retailers. Private-label products are only sold by one retailer. A generic brand is a consumer product that lacks a widely recognized name or logo. Generic brands are not advertised, and it is not immediately obvious who manufactured them.
4. A consumer product that lacks a widely-recognized name or logo is a generic brand. Generic brands are not advertised and it is not immediately obvious who manufactured them. Without the additional cost of product promotions, generic brands can cost up to 50 percent less than similar brand-name products. This is different from national and private-label brands, which aim to create widely-recognized logos, brand names, and promotions.
5. Brand identity is the way in which a business wants to be perceived by customers. The true power of a brand lies in its ability to influence purchasing behavior. Branding efforts should create a unique brand identity, contribute to the positive image of the brand, and inspire brand loyalty and repeat sales. In developing a unique brand identity, businesses create products and promotions that appeal to the needs and wants of the target market. Aligning the brand with a positive message helps brands to be perceived in a positive light to keep sales up. Brand loyalty occurs when a good, service, or business consistently meets customer needs and expectations.
6. Branding efforts should create a unique brand identity, contribute to the positive image of the brand, and inspire brand loyalty and repeat sales.
7. Brand extension is the practice of using an established brand name on different products in a product mix. Co-branding combines the products of one or more manufacturers in the creation of a product. Brand licensing is the practice of leasing a brand name for use by another business under the specifications of an agreement.
8. Certain intellectual-property laws protect the unique phrases, symbols, and designs associated with brands. Trademarks and service marks do not protect the product itself from theft; however, they protect the ways in which the product is identified. Many companies also choose to protect their brands by registering them with the United States Patent and Trademark Office (USPTO). Once a trademark or service mark has been registered, the symbol ® can be used with the mark to notify the public that the creator claims exclusive rights to the brand and its use.
9. The symbols ™ for trademark and ℠ for service mark.
10. When a brand name becomes a generic name, the brand no longer has legal trademark protection and can be used by anyone.

Apply Your Knowledge
Student answers will vary for Apply Your Knowledge questions.

Apply Your Math Skills
1. Curtis saved $25.00.
   $4.50 \times 10 = $45.00
   $7.00 \times 10 = $70.00
   $70.00 − $45.00 = $25.00 saved
2. The percentage of revenue attributed to generic brands is 15%.
   $450,000 ÷ $3,000,000 = 0.15
   0.15 × 100 = 15%

Chapter 13 Price

You Do the Math: Exponents
1. Susan will have $11,180.00 at the end of the term. Answers may vary slightly due to rounding.
   FV = PV × (1 + r)^n
   FV = $10,000 × (1 + .0378)^3
   FV = $10,000 × (1.118)
   FV = $11,180.00
2. $3,850.00 in interest will have been paid by the end of the loan. Answers may vary slightly due to rounding.
   FV = PV × (1 + r)^n
   FV = $25,000 × (1 + .029)^5
   FV = $25,000 × (1.154)
   FV = $28,850
   $28,850 − $25,000 = $3,850.00 in interest
3. The third option offers the lowest total amount of interest paid. Answers may vary slightly due to rounding.
   First option:
   FV = PV × (1 + r)^n
   FV = $36,575 × (1 + .049)^4
   FV = $36,575 × (1.211)
   FV = $44,292.33
   $44,292.33 − $36,575 = $7,717.33 in interest
   Second option:
   FV = PV × (1 + r)^n
   FV = $36,575 × (1 + .019)^5
   FV = $36,575 × (1.10)
   FV = $40,232.50
   $40,232.50 − $36,575 = $3,657.50 in interest
   Third option:
   FV = PV × (1 + r)^n
   FV = $36,575 × (1 + .009)^6
   FV = $36,575 × (1.055)
   FV = $38,586.63
   $38,586.63 − $36,575 = $2,011.63 in interest

Section 13.1 Review
1. The pricing function of marketing handles all activities involved in setting acceptable prices for product.
2. The price must cover the costs of producing and selling the product; should generate the desired level of profit for the business; and must be what customers are willing to pay for the product.
3. Pricing objectives typically fall under one of two categories: maximize sales or maximize profit.
4. net profit after taxes ÷ total assets = ROI
5. $$\frac{\text{cost} \times \text{number of units}}{\text{selling price}} = \text{break-even point}$$

Answers to Build Your Vocabulary terms are key term definitions and can be found in the glossary.

Section 13.2 Review
1. Elastic demand means that the higher the price of a product the lower the demand. Inelastic demand means that the sale of the product is not influenced by the price. People will buy no matter what the price is.
2. (cost × percentage of markup) + cost = base price
3. cost × 2 = base price
4. The price may be set above, below, or at the competitor's price, depending on the pricing objective. To effectively use a competition-based pricing strategy, marketers monitor the prices of competitors often and propose price adjustments as necessary.
5. Premium quality is the highest level of quality available in products. Moderate quality is the middle range of product quality. Value quality is an adequate level of product quality.

Answers to Build Your Vocabulary terms are key term definitions and can be found in the glossary.

Review Your Knowledge
1. As one of the four Ps of marketing, price is the amount of money requested or exchanged for a product. As a function of marketing, businesses set prices that will help the company increase sales and profits.
2. Two categories of pricing objectives are to maximize sales and maximize profits. Maximizing sales is a pricing objective based on offering the lowest price possible to get the largest number of customers to buy a product. This can be accomplished by increasing

market share and establishing volume pricing. Maximizing profit is a pricing objective that means generating as much revenue as possible in relation to total cost. A business charges the highest price customers will pay before that the price exceeds the value for customers.
3. When demand is high and the supply is low, marketers usually raise prices. Customers are willing to pay higher prices for products they really want. When demand is low and supply is high, marketers usually lower prices to increase sales. Customers are often more willing to buy a product when the price is low. The higher the price, the lower the demand.
4. Equilibrium is the point at which the supply equals the demand for the product.
5. Some products have both elastic and inelastic demand depending on the situation. For example, perhaps you drive a car to school every day. If the price of gasoline doubles, you may choose to decrease your demand for gasoline by carpooling with other students. In this case, your demand for gasoline is elastic because you have options. You can car pool instead of buying gas yourself. However, suppose that you are driving on a limited-access highway and notice that your fuel gauge is on empty. You need gas in order to reach your destination and will pay the high price. In this case, your demand for gasoline is inelastic because it is a necessity.
6. There are expenses related to the creation, marketing, and distribution of all products. In addition, there are many costs related to the daily operations of a business. These costs influence the price that is set for that product because a profit is made only after all of the expenses are paid. Pricing strategically is a balancing act because both profit and sales goals are important. In order to make a profit, prices must be set high enough to cover the costs. However, if the product is priced too high, customers and sales may be lost. If the price is set too low, the costs related to the products may not be covered, which means the company could lose money.
7. Researching the product pricing of competitors is an important step in remaining competitive in the market. Marketers understand that price may be the deciding factor for a customer when making a purchase. If the competition offers lower prices, a customer may buy from the competitor because price was the deciding factor. If a business wants to maintain market share, it must be aware of competitor pricing and decide what pricing strategy to use.
8. Customers have different perceptions when making a purchase and may perceive price to be an indicator of the quality of a product. Sometimes, customers believe that a higher price means a better-quality product, but that is not always the case.
9. Customers also look for non-price factors that may influence the price of a product. Special services, extended warranties, and other non-price issues can convince a customer not to pay a higher price for added amenities.
10. The stage in the product life cycle affects the pricing of a product. During the introduction stage, the price of a brand-new product is often high. During the growth stage, more competitors enter the market, and the price of a high-priced, new product usually falls. During the maturity and decline phases of a product, prices are usually lowered even further.

Apply Your Knowledge

Student answers will vary for Apply Your Knowledge questions.

Apply Your Math Skills

1. Method C, dollar-markup pricing with a $4 markup, gives Emma the highest price.
    A. ($3 × .5) + $3 = base price
        $1.50 + $3 = $4.50 base price
    B. $3 × 2 = $6 base price
    C. $3 + $4 = $7 base price
2. The return on investment for each jar of honey sold is 133%.
    $7 − $3 = $4 profit
    $4 ÷ $3 = 1.33
    1.33 × 100 = 133%
3. Emma must sell 120 jars of honey in order to break even.

    $$\frac{\$3 \times 280}{\$7} = \text{break-even point}$$

    $$\frac{\$840}{\$7} = \text{break-even point}$$

    120 = break-even point

Chapter 14 Pricing Product

You Do the Math: Multiplication

1. Sunbeam Cycles offers a better deal.
   $265 × .06 = $15.90
   $265 + $15.90 = $280.90 for the bicycle from Sunbeam Cycles.
   $220 × .06 = $13.20
   $220 + $13.20 = $233.20
   $233.20 + $25 = $258.20
   $258.20 + $35 = $293.20 for the bicycle from Express Bikes.
2. A. Store A:
      $5.50 ÷ 2 = $2.75 per pair
      Store B:
      $3.50 × .25 = $.87
      $3.50 - $.87 = $2.63 per pair
      Store C:
      $5.00 ÷ 2 = $2.50 per pair
   B. Store C has the lowest price per pair because you can get two pairs for the price of one, essentially paying $2.50 per pair.
   C. Store A has the highest price per pair at $2.75 per pair.

Section 14.1 Review

1. In product mix pricing, marketers choose to balance the overall profit of an entire product mix by applying different pricing strategies to individual lines. This is so the entire product mix can hit a profit goal rather than specific lines reaching individual goals.
2. It is based on the assumption that some customers buy on emotions.
3. (Any) Odd pricing; buy one, get one (BOGO) pricing.
4. A cash discount is a percentage deducted from the total invoice amount that is offered to encourage a customer to pay a bill early.
5. A promotional discount is given to businesses that agree to advertise or promote a manufacturer's product.

Answers to Build Your Vocabulary terms are key term definitions and can be found in the glossary.

Section 14.2 Review

1. Price-fixing occurs when a group of competitors agree to set the price for a specific product, which is usually high. Predatory pricing is setting very low prices to remove competition.
2. A monopoly usually sets high, unfair prices that hurt consumers and can interfere with the workings of a market economy.
3. Sales-below-cost (SBC) laws ban loss-leader pricing.
4. Price ceilings are maximum prices set by the government when it thinks certain products are being priced too high. The government may believe that consumers need some help to purchase the products. Price ceilings on some products are often set during times when there may be shortages that could drive prices unreasonably high.
5. Producers.

Answers to Build Your Vocabulary terms are key term definitions and can be found in the glossary.

Review Your Knowledge

1. Three examples of product mix pricing strategies are price lining, captive pricing, and bundling.
2. Bundling benefits the customer by saving him or her money, and it benefits the store by selling two items instead of one.
3. Common B2C psychological pricing includes odd, even, prestige, and BOGO.
4. (Any) Even pricing, prestige pricing.
5. The most popular B2B discount pricing strategies marketers use are cash discount, quantity discount, trade discount, promotional discount, and seasonal discount.
6. Cash discounts encourage customers to pay their bill early, which helps with the cash flow of the business.
7. A trade discount is not applied in the same way as other traditional discounts. It is actually the way that manufacturers quote prices to wholesalers and retailers. The MSRP is often used as a list price. The manufacturer then offers the wholesaler or retailer a percentage off the list price.
8. (Any) Buying goods this far in advance allows them to take advantage of lower prices. Seasonal discounts help manufacturers plan production and reduce inventory.
9. Bait and switch, price-fixing, price discrimination, deceptive pricing, predatory pricing, price gouging, monopolies, unit pricing, and sales-below-cost (SBC) laws.
10. Price ceilings are maximum prices set by the government when it thinks certain products are being priced too high. Price floors are minimum prices set by the government for certain goods and services that it thinks are being priced too low.

Apply Your Knowledge
Student answers will vary for Apply Your Knowledge questions.

Apply Your Math Skills
1. Brand A has the lowest unit price at $0.04 per ounce.
   Brand A
   $7.88 ÷ 210 ounces = $0.04 per ounce
   Brand B
   100-ounce bottle × 2 bottles per package = 200 ounces of cleaner
   $11.18 ÷ 200 ounces = $0.06 per ounce
   Brand C
   100-ounce bottle × 2 bottles per package = 200 ounces of cleaner
   $9.83 ÷ 200 ounces = $0.05 per ounce
2. Cody will pay $644.95 if he accepts the terms of the cash discount.
   5% → 0.05
   $678.90 total × 0.05 = $33.95 discount
   $678.90 total − $33.95 discount = $644.95 due with cash discount.

Chapter 15 Place

You Do the Math: Measurement Reasoning
1. The shipping container can fit 864 boxes inside.
   Volume = length × width × height
   Volume of container = 6 × 18 × 8 = 864 ft^3
   Volume of box = 1 × 2 × .5
   (Have to convert 6 inches to feet: 6 ÷ 12 = .5 feet)
   Volume of box = 1 × 2 × .5 = 1 ft^3
   864 ft^3 ÷ 1 ft^3 = 864 boxes
2. The height of the box is 6.4 in.
   Volume = length × width × height
   161.28 in^3 = 3.5 in × 7.2 in × height
   161.28 in^3 = 25.2 in^2 × height
   161.28 in^3 ÷ 25.2 in^2 = 6.4 in
3. The area of the base of the cylinder is 28.85 ft^2.
   Volume = height × area of base
   122.6 ft^3 = 4.25 ft. × area of base
   122.6 ft^3 ÷ 4.25 ft. = 28.84705 rounded to 28.85 ft^2

Section 15.1 Review
1. A major part in the decision of place is selecting the channel of distribution.
2. There are several types of intermediaries, including wholesalers, retailers, and agents.
3. Wholesalers are sometimes categorized as merchant wholesalers or manufacturer's sales branches.
4. Some producers do not want to assume the responsibility of selling or shipping products. Those producers contract with an agent to handle their goods after production.
5. Standards may include prompt delivery, cooperative advertising, meeting sales quotas, service quality, treatment of lost or damaged goods, and overall satisfaction.

Answers to Build Your Vocabulary terms are key term definitions and can be found in the glossary.

Section 15.2 Review
1. It makes products available where needed, correctly fills orders, and provides on-time delivery.
2. The goal is to utilize the best distribution services for the lowest cost. Efficient distribution services help to keep customer prices lower.
3. If a business does not have enough storage space within its facility, it will need to rent, lease, or build space. Businesses may also use wholesalers to store products until they are needed.
4. (Any) Streamlined inventories; lower operating costs; timely product availability; and increased customer satisfaction.
5. Distribution can be a challenge as other countries may not have the same quality of transportation infrastructure, including roads and airports, that is needed. In less-developed countries, basic infrastructure services may be inadequate, such as electricity, telephone services, and Internet connectivity.

Answers to Build Your Vocabulary terms are key term definitions and can be found in the glossary.

Review Your Knowledge
1. Place refers to the activities involved in getting a good or service to the end user. It involves determining when, where, and how products get to customers. Place is also known as distribution. A major part in the decision of place is selecting the channel of distribution. Channel members are the organizations that help move product from its origination to the consumer. Channel members include producers and intermediaries.
2. The transactional function is typically the sales and marketing activities for the business. The logistics function is physically moving products from the manufacturers to distributors, retailers, or end users. The

facilitating function is the final part of the supply chain. This involves the actual selling of the product or service to the end users.
3. Distribution channels can be direct or indirect. A direct channel is the path of selling goods or services directly from a producer or manufacturer to end users without using intermediaries. There are three channels of indirect distribution for consumer goods. They include a retailer, wholesaler, or agent/broker channels. There are three channels of indirect distribution for industrial goods in the B2B market. These channels include industrial distributor, agent/broker, and agent/broker industrial distributor.
4. The result of channel conflict is that the manufacturer, intermediaries, and retailers may end up competing with one another for the same product sales.
5. To manage the channel of distribution and maintain efficiencies, the channel members must be selected, motivated, and evaluated.
6. There are six main methods of transportation. These transportation methods are road, rail, air, water, pipeline, and digital.
7. Products need protection from weather, theft, and damage. Retail and manufacturing businesses need areas to store physical inventory.
8. A supply chain is the businesses, people, and activities involved in turning raw materials into products and delivering them to end users. When a business controls the supply chain, it can recognize efficiencies in time, process, and money. Supply chain management is coordinating the events happening throughout the supply chain. Several factors should be considered before deciding which channel of distribution to use: the target market, distribution requirements of the product itself, impact of distribution cost on final price, and level of distribution used.
9. Intensive distribution is when product is placed in every potential sales situation possible. Selective distribution is selecting only certain places that the manufacturer or wholesaler wants a product to be sold. Exclusive distribution occurs when there is only one distributor of products in a market area.
10. Companies that buy, sell, or distribute products globally can have more complex, or different, place decisions than those that only sell domestically. There are legal and political issues that must be considered when operating a business globally. In addition, before distributing products to foreign markets, a business plan should be created. There are many product, price, place, and promotion issues that must be addressed. Distribution can be a challenge as other countries may not have the same quality of transportation infrastructure, including roads and airports, that is needed. In less-developed countries, basic infrastructure services may be inadequate, such as electricity, telephone services, and Internet connectivity.

Apply Your Knowledge

Student answers will vary for Apply Your Knowledge questions.

Apply Your Math Skills

1. The production company generates $7.99 profit on each DVD.
   $19.99 − $12.00 = $7.99
2. The production company generates $9.99 profit on each Blu-ray.
   $21.99 − $12.00 = $9.99
3. The production company generates $4.99 profit on each digital download.
   $16.99 − $12.00 = $4.99

Chapter 16 Purchasing and Inventory Control

You Do the Math: Unit Conversion

1. The carton weighs 41.6 pounds.
   18.7 kilograms ÷ 0.45 = 41.6 pounds
2. −17.8° Celsius must be written on the label.
   Celsius = [(Fahrenheit − 32) × 5] ÷ 9
   Celsius = [(0° − 32) × 5] ÷ 9
   Celsius = [(−32°) × 5] ÷ 9
   Celsius = −160° ÷ 9
   Celsius = −17.8°
3. Luis should order 100 millimeters of rod.
   1 inch = 25.4 millimeters
   0.3 feet × 12 inches/foot = 3.6 inches
   3.6 inches × 25.4 millimeters/inch = 91.44 millimeters

Section 16.1 Review

1. Purchasing agents buy goods and services the company needs internally to operate its business. The goods purchased are not resold

to customers; rather, they are used within the organization.
2. They purchase products that the business will not use, but resell to customers.
3. The bidding process is a series of steps the buyer takes to obtain the best price for a purchase.
4. Negotiating a purchase involves getting a good price and payment schedule for the goods as well as timely delivery. It also includes confirming quality and value as well as scale discounts.
5. FOB shipping point means that the buyer is responsible and pays for shipping. FOB destination point means the seller is responsible until the shipment reaches the buyer. The seller pays the shipping.
Answers to Build Your Vocabulary terms are key term definitions and can be found in the glossary.

Section 16.2 Review

1. Lead time is the total time it takes from placing an order until it is received.
2. (Any) Capital costs; handling costs; storage costs; inventory-risk costs; and inventory insurance costs.
3. It is important to conduct a physical inventory once or twice a year.
4.
$$\frac{\text{cost of goods sold}}{\text{average inventory value}} = \text{turnover rate}$$
5. To discourage theft, closed circuit television and video security systems may be installed. Sensing devices placed on merchandise, ringing alarms, and security guards also help to prevent theft. The obvious presence of security measures cuts down on stealing.
Answers to Build Your Vocabulary terms are key term definitions and can be found in the glossary.

Review Your Knowledge

1. There are two types of organizational buyers: purchasing agents and buyers. Purchasing agents buy goods and services the company needs internally to operate its business. The goods purchased are not resold to customers; rather, they are used within the organization. Wholesale and retail buyers purchase goods for the sole purpose of reselling them to customers. They purchase products that the business will not use, but resell to customers.
2. Identify inventory needs, identify vendors, initiate bidding process, negotiate the purchase, award the contract, receive the order, pay the invoice, and evaluate the vendor.
3. Organizations do not automatically choose the lowest-priced bid. A bid includes a combination of goods and services. The buyer will choose the bid that provides the best combination of goods and services for the price. In other words, the buyer decides which bid provides the best value for the company. The decision on bids may require written approval by more than one person in the company.
4. When a shipment of goods is received, it includes a packing slip that lists the contents of the package. The person receiving the shipment verifies the contents by comparing items to the packing slip. The confirmation process ensures that everything received also agrees with the PO. After receiving and inspecting the shipment, the details are recorded on a receiving record and filed for future use. Once goods are received and checked, they are usually marked with tickets or UPC codes.
5. Managing inventory correctly is one key factor in keeping costs down while maintaining enough products on hand for maximum sales. Inventory management is ordering the goods, receiving them into stock on arrival, and paying the supplier or vendor. It also includes managing the costs of shipping, storage, and other tasks while keeping the costs associated with the inventory low. Inventory management is usually the responsibility of the supply chain manager. When managing inventory, there are three factors that need to be considered: lead time; stock needs; and carrying costs.
6. There are three primary types of retail inventory-control systems: perpetual, periodic, and just-in-time. A perpetual inventory-control system is a method of counting inventory that shows the quantity on hand at all times. There are two types of perpetual inventory systems: manual and computerized. In a manual perpetual inventory-control system, the inventory is calculated by physically counting and recording individual items. While manual systems have their place, most businesses use a computerized inventory-control system for more control and information. Inventory software programs track incoming inventory and sales. A periodic inventory-control system involves taking a physical count of merchandise at regular periods, such as weekly

or monthly. The just-in-time (JIT) inventory-control system keeps a minimal amount of production materials or sales inventory on hand at all times.
7. For a JIT system to be successful, each company in the supply chain must coordinate each activity and be flexible when necessary.
8. A business needs to determine the correct amount of money to invest in inventory each year. Sales forecasting based on previous sales history helps businesses plan for upcoming inventory needs. It is usually done a year in advance. Most businesses then review actual weekly sales and adjust the sales projections, which will also impact inventory orders. Many businesses use the 80/20 rule to forecast sales to have enough inventory on hand.
9. The productive inventory is the 20 percent of the inventory that produces the most sales.
10. The difference between the perpetual inventory and the actual physical inventory is called inventory shrinkage. There are many causes for inventory shrinkage, including data input errors, product damage, and theft. Internal theft is committed by employees of a store, a supplier, or a delivery company. It is the source of most inventory shrinkage. External theft is stealing by people who are not employed or otherwise associated with the retailer.

Apply Your Knowledge

Student answers will vary for Apply Your Knowledge questions.

Apply Your Math Skills

1. The turnover rate of the business is 2.53.

    $$\frac{\$480,000}{\$190,000} = 2.53$$

2. The turnover rate of the business is 4.26.

    $$\frac{\$64,000}{\$15,000} = 4.26$$

Chapter 17 Promotion

You Do the Math: Statistical Reasoning

1. Qualitative data: attractive, blue, smooth finish. Quantitative data: 5 inches wide, weighs 14 ounces

2. Qualitative data: pleasant, helpful. Quantitative data: 17 representatives, seven technicians total (five certified technicians and two master technicians)
3. Student answers will vary.

Section 17.1 Review

1. A product promotion promotes specific products. An institutional promotion is promoting the company rather than its products.
2. The promotional mix is a combination of the elements of advertising, sales promotion, public relations, and personal selling used to reach the customer in the target market. Promotion strategies involve choosing the best promotional mix for the budget.
3. Examples of participatory marketing include e-mail campaigns, social media, videos, and blogs.
4. Attention: getting customers to look at the product or promotion is the first step. Interest: customers must be interested in the business or product to make a purchase. Desire: the promotion should encourage customers to sample, use, or touch the product. Action: the promotion should explain exactly how, where, and when the product can be bought.
5. Metrics are standards of measurement that determine the effectiveness of a promotion. Answers to Build Your Vocabulary terms are key term definitions and can be found in the glossary.

Section 17.2 Review

1. Advertising can be the key part of the promotional mix as it provides information about the features and benefits of a product, including prices and descriptions.
2. A call to action is a statement or request that urges the customer to do something in response to a promotion.
3. Sponsorships are another way marketers can help reach business goals at a trade show. A sponsorship is the support of an activity, usually financial, that can help a business meet its goals. Sponsorships send the message that the business cares and supports customers and the organization. They can create positive brand recognition as well as goodwill.
4. Some communication channels used in PR include press releases, press kits, and press conferences.

5. Companies that sell equipment and raw materials to manufacturers are involved in B2B sales. Manufacturers that sell finished products to retailers are involved in B2B sales. Answers to Build Your Vocabulary terms are key term definitions and can be found in the glossary.

Review Your Knowledge

1. Promotion is one of the four Ps of marketing. It is the process of communicating with potential customers in an effort to influence their behavior or beliefs. Businesses are interested in influencing a customer's buying behavior by promoting the price of a product, its features and benefits, and the place where it is offered. Promotion is considered marketing communication, which is broadly described as communications from an organization to its customers and the public. It is the most visible part of marketing.
2. Integrated marketing communications (IMC), participatory marketing, push promotional concept, and pull promotional concept.
3. Promotion has three goals: to inform, persuade, or remind people about the business or its products. Promotions that inform tell people something they want or need to know to make decisions. Persuasion is the use of logic to change a belief or get people to take a certain action. The end goal of most promotions is to persuade people to buy a product. Promotions that remind are created to keep the product on a person's mind.
4. The coordination of marketing communications to achieve a specific goal is a promotional campaign. It is also called a promotional plan. Promotional plans are designed to encourage customers to buy. Each element of the promotional mix is focused on attracting customer attention, interest, desire, and action. Included in a promotional plan is a detailed list of goals, dates, and other activities that are carefully researched and documented. This serves as a guideline to make sure the business can reach its goals effectively.
5. Advertising is any nonpersonal communication paid for by an identified sponsor. Direct marketing is a type of advertising sent directly to individual customers without the use of a third party. Sales promotion is the efforts used to encourage customers to buy a product as soon as possible. Public relations (PR) consists of the marketing activities promoting goodwill between a company and the public. Personal selling is any direct contact between a salesperson and a customer.
6. Print media, such as newspapers, magazines, and directories; broadcast media, such as television and radio; outdoor media, such as billboards and transit media; and Internet advertising.
7. Direct marketing is a type of advertising sent directly to individual customers without the use of a third party. It includes marketing pieces such as brochures, coupons, flyers, e-mail, and post cards. Direct marketing is a common and popular form of advertising used by marketers. It has a distinct advantage in that it can be tracked because it is sent to individual addresses. Direct marketing includes a call to action as part of the message. Success can be measured when the customer actually reads the message and responds in some form.
8. Sales promotion is the efforts used to encourage customers to buy a product as soon as possible. A sales promotion can include coupons, rebates, promotional items, samples, loyalty programs, contests and sweepstakes, trade shows, and displays.
9. Public relations (PR) consists of the marketing activities promoting goodwill between a company and the public. Proactive public relations is when the company presents itself in a positive manner to build an image. Reactive public relations is used to counteract a negative public perception about the company.
10. Personal selling is any direct contact between a salesperson and a customer. Business-to-consumer (B2C) selling is selling to consumers. Business-to-business selling (B2B) is a business selling to another business.

Apply Your Knowledge

Student answers will vary for Apply Your Knowledge questions.

Apply Your Math Skills

1. Sasha's Threads spent $1,350 on Internet advertisements; $900 on print advertisements; $450 on promotional items; and $300 on a charitable donation as proactive PR.
$3,000 × .30 = $900 on print advertisements
$3,000 × .45 = $1,350 on Internet advertisements

$3,000 × .15 = $450 on promotional items
$3,000 × .10 = $300 on a charitable donation as proactive PR
2. The coupon was redeemed by 4 percent of potential customers who received it.
80 ÷ 2,000 = 0.04 → 4%

Chapter 18 Advertising

You Do the Math: Fundamental Counting Principle

1. There are 1,260 total combinations.
   3 × 14 × 2 × 5 × 3 = 1,260
2. There are 120 different packages available.
   3 × 5 × 2 × 4 = 120
3. There are 108 possible combinations.
   4 × 3 × 9 = 108

Section 18.1 Review

1. The main purposes of advertising are to persuade customers to buy a product or accept an idea, inform customers about products, or remind them to take action.
2. False advertising is overstating the features and benefits of goods or services or making false claims about them. False advertising is both unethical and illegal.
3. The most expensive form of advertising is television because it reaches the most people.
4. Before conducting an e-mail campaign, marketers should read and understand the 2004 CAN-SPAM Act.
5. In all types of media, the cost increases depending on the amount of exposure, or number of impressions, the ad will get. Reach is the total number of people exposed to the ad during a given time. Frequency refers to the number of times an ad will be shown to an audience. Cost per thousand (CPM) refers to the cost of an advertisement per one thousand impressions. Circulation is the number of copies distributed to subscribers in a defined time period. Prime time refers to the hours during which broadcast media consumption is at its peak. Running broadcast advertisements during prime time is more expensive than during other hours of the day.
   Answers to Build Your Vocabulary terms are key term definitions and can be found in the glossary.

Section 18.2 Review

1. Concepting is the creative concept process of looking at the big picture and brainstorming what the campaign should look like.
2. The unique selling proposition (USP) is a statement of how the products, brand, or company are better than the competition. It explains why the customer should purchase products from your company rather than another company.
3. The aspect of an advertisement that grabs attention is often called the hook.
4. Choosing typography includes decisions about typeface, size, and weight.
5. Graphics include typography, art, and layout.
   Answers to Build Your Vocabulary terms are key term definitions and can be found in the glossary.

Review Your Knowledge

1. Advertising is one element of the promotional mix. It is any nonpersonal communication paid for by an identified sponsor. Advertising is a daily influence in our lives. Advertising can change people's beliefs and attitudes about products and help them make buying decisions. The main purposes of advertising are to persuade customers to buy a product or accept an idea, inform customers about products, or remind them to take action.
2. (Any) Inform consumers and businesses about product choices; encourage consumers to seek a higher standard of living; stimulate competition among businesses so they offer better products at lower prices; help increase employment needed to keep up with demand for advertised products; encourage acceptance of new and innovative products; provide revenue to pay for broadcast programming and print vehicles; and help people learn about health and social issues.
3. Advertising must be truthful and nondeceptive. Advertisers must have evidence to back up their claims. Advertisements cannot be unfair.
4. Advertising makes its way to an audience through various types of media, including print media, outdoor media, broadcast media, and the Internet. Newspapers, magazines, and directories are print media. Two common forms of outdoor advertising media are billboards and transit promotion. There are two forms of broadcast media: television

and radio. Internet advertising includes online advertising, e-mail campaigns, and social media.
5. These include the cost of creating the advertisement, cost of placement, and lead time.
6. An advertising campaign is a coordinated series of related advertisements with a single idea or theme. The advertising campaign is one piece of the overall promotional campaign. Large companies usually have advertising teams that create the various elements in the promotional mix. Some companies use an advertising agency to create promotions. An advertising agency is a firm that creates advertisements, commercials, and other parts of promotional campaigns for its clients.
7. Steps for creating successful advertising campaigns are to set the goals, establish a budget, brainstorm the creative concept, write the message, select the media, and evaluate the results.
8. (Any) Reach, frequency.
9. Headline, copy, graphics, and signature.
10. Creates intrigue, appeals to the senses, sounds newsworthy, and uses action words.

Apply Your Knowledge

Student answers will vary for Apply Your Knowledge questions.

Apply Your Math Skills

1. The total cost of the radio commercial is $3,000.
   $500 air time per station × 4 stations = $2,000 air time
   $2,000 air time + $1,000 production = $3,000 total
2. The total cost of the SEO is $6,600.
   $300 per month for SEO × 12 months = $3,600
   $3,600 for SEO service + $3,000 for website configuration = $6,600 total
3. Hero's Sandwich Shoppe is paying the advertising agency $9,600 total.
   $3,000 for radio commercial + $6,600 for SEO = $9,600 total

Chapter 19: Visual Merchandising

You Do the Math: Area

1. The area of the parking lot is 9,375 ft^2.
   Area = length × width
   75 feet × 125 feet = 9,375 ft^2
2. The area of the living room is 391 ft^2.
   Area = length × width
   17 feet × 23 feet = 391 ft^2
3. Need to purchase 10 sheets of plywood.
   Area = length × width
   Area of room: 12 ft. × 25 ft. = 300 ft^2
   Area of plywood: 4 ft. × 8 ft. = 32 ft^2
   Sheets needed = total area of room ÷ area of one sheet of plywood
   300 ÷ 32 = 9.375 sheets of plywood
4. The volume of paint in each bucket is 2,712.96 in^3.
   Volume = area of the base × height
   2 feet = 24 inches
   Height = 24 inches
   Radius = diameter ÷ 2 = 12 in ÷ 2 = 6 in
   Area of base = 3.14 × radius^2 = 3.14 × (6 in)^2 = 113.04 in^2
   Volume = area of base × height = 113.04 in^2 × 24 in = 2,712.96 in^3

Section 19.1 Review

1. Displays are designed to excite customers, motivate their interest in the merchandise, and entice them to buy.
2. (Any) Bargain, casual, discount, expensive, sophisticated, trendy, upscale, and youthful.
3. (Any) Store sign or logo, marquee, display windows, entrances, outdoor lighting, landscaping, and the building itself.
4. Selling area, sales support area, storage space, and customer comfort space.
5. (Any) Point-of-purchase (POP), open, closed, and architectural displays, plus store decorations.

Answers to Build Your Vocabulary terms are key term definitions and can be found in the glossary.

Section 19.2 Review

1. The ultimate goal of visual merchandising is to entice a customer to buy the merchandise.
2. Hue, value, and intensity.
3. Formal balance means that you have an object on one side of the line, and another object of equal size the same distance from the line on the other side.
4. The first step in display development is to select the merchandise that will be featured. The merchandise should be eye-catching or notable in some way.
5. Dirty, messy displays can ruin the image of a store. To maintain a good image, a display must be kept clean and orderly.

Answers to Build Your Vocabulary terms are key term definitions and can be found in the glossary.

Review Your Knowledge

1. Visual merchandising is the process of creating floor plans and displays to attract customer attention and encourage purchases. It is often used as the sales promotion element of the promotional mix, especially in the B2C market. Visual merchandising attracts customers and invites them to examine merchandise more closely. Visual merchandising helps to define the image of the store. Visual merchandising is used primarily in retail situations and at trade shows. Visual merchandising is also important for other types of businesses, such as service businesses, manufacturers, and wholesalers.
2. Store image is created through the location, design, and décor of a business.
3. Store exterior, store layout, store interior, and interior displays.
4. Display windows are used to show a selection of merchandise available in the store. These displays often have a theme, such as a season or holiday, to attract customers' interest. Merchandise featured in the display is usually at eye level so people walking past the store will see it, and hopefully be inspired to make a purchase.
5. Elements of design include color, line, shape, texture, light, and motion.
6. A color has three distinct qualities: hue, value, and intensity.
7. The principles of design are guidelines that can help the elements of design be used effectively. The principles of design include emphasis, movement, balance, and proportion. Emphasis is drawing the attention of the viewer to the most important part of a display. Movement refers to the way the design guides viewer eyes over an item or display. Balance refers to the way items are placed around an imaginary centerline. Proportion refers to the size and space relationship of all items in a display to each other and to the whole display.
8. Elements of design are the building blocks that can be manipulated to create a visual effect. Successful displays often use the elements of design in new and creative ways. The principles of design are guidelines that can help the elements of design be used effectively.
9. The first step to develop a visual display is to set goals the display will hopefully accomplish. Next, select the merchandise that will be featured. Then, determine the type of display. The display theme is chosen next. Then, the display is evaluated to measure its effectiveness. Finally, maintain the display.
10. (Any) Check at least once a day to make sure the display looks as clean, crisp, and fresh as when it was first completed. Clean the floor, table, props, and merchandise regularly. Replace any merchandise that has been removed or damaged. If merchandise has been moved, put it back where it belongs. Check lights and replace as necessary.

Apply Your Knowledge

Student answers will vary for Apply Your Knowledge questions.

Apply Your Math Skills

1. The hooks should be placed 16 inches apart.
2. The signs should be hung 12 feet apart.

Chapter 20 Personal Selling

You Do the Math: Slope

1. The lines are parallel.
   $1 \div 2 = .5$
   $6 \div 12 = .5$
2. The rise is 4 and the run is 12.
3. Hill A is steeper.
   Hill A: $8 \div 4 = 2$
   Hill B: $8 \div 6 = 1.3$

Section 20.1 Review

1. Selling adds value to a business because it includes all personal communication with customers. The scope of selling activities includes helping customers in a store, making sales presentations or product demonstrations, and providing customer service. Selling is a valuable function of marketing.
2. (Any) Field sales, industrial sales, organizational sales, governmental sales, or institutional sales.
3. Most B2C sales are made by a salesperson in the place of business, such as a retail store.
4. External customers are the people and businesses who purchase product from an organization. Internal customers are the coworkers within the business with whom each employee works and collaborates.
5. The sales team is the first line of contact with a customer.

Answers to Build Your Vocabulary terms are key term definitions and can be found in the glossary.

Section 20.2 Review
1. The preapproach tasks include understanding company selling policies, participating in product training, and learning how to identify potential customers.
2. (Any) Customers visiting a trade show may ask for someone to contact them about more information. People who visit a website or call customer support may ask for a salesperson to call them. A dedicated sales staff may generate leads. Lists of names of potential customers can be purchased.
3. Service approach, greeting approach, and merchandise approach.
4. This is where desire is created for the product.
5. Sales tax is calculated by multiplying the sales price by the tax rate.
   sales price × sales tax rate percentage = sales tax
   Answers to Build Your Vocabulary terms are key term definitions and can be found in the glossary.

Section 20.3 Review
1. Marketing plays an important role by providing product information and training to the customer support team.
2. Online support is convenient for customers because they can find answers when they are needed.
3. This information may be useful to the product development team to help create better products.
4. One advantage to this type of customer support is the responses are immediate so problems can usually be solved quickly.
5. If a customer service representative is unable to resolve a customer issue, the call will probably be transferred to a supervisor. A supervisor may have more options to offer the customer a solution.
   Answers to Build Your Vocabulary terms are key term definitions and can be found in the glossary.

Review Your Knowledge
1. A salesperson adds value to the promotional mix. Personal selling provides information that a marketing brochure or website cannot provide. A salesperson can persuade a customer to make a decision about how to meet a need or want. Customers can give feedback that helps product development meet customer needs. People like personal contact when making a buying decision. While other parts of the promotional mix are important, personal contact is at the top of the customer list.
2. Business-to-business (B2B) and business-to-consumer (B2C). There are typically two types of sales positions for B2B sales, inside sales and outside sales. An inside salesperson communicates with customers via phone or e-mail from inside the company's place of business. The salesperson typically does not have face-to-face contact with a customer. An outside salesperson visits with the customer at his or her place of business. Some communication will be via phone or e-mail, but the primary contact is face-to-face and relationship selling.
3. People who are successful in sales must have excellent work habits and be goal oriented. Strong ethics of honesty, integrity, and confidentiality are important for successful long-term relationships that lead to repeat sales. Sales positions are generally independent and require minimal day-to-day supervision, requiring that salespeople are responsible. In addition, working in sales requires that a person have excellent customer-service skills. It also requires that a person be able to make presentations that are clear, concise, and persuasive.
4. The preapproach consists of tasks that are performed before contact is made with a customer. These tasks include understanding company selling policies, participating in product training, and learning how to identify potential customers. Product training is the first step to becoming successful in a sales role. A salesperson must understand the product and be confident so customer questions can be answered accurately. Sales training is generally a joint effort of the sales and marketing teams. The next step in the preapproach stage of selling is identifying potential customers. A lead is a potential customer. For a salesperson in a retail situation, potential customers may walk in the store. However, for salespeople who need to call on customers, they must start with a list of contacts.
5. Approach the customer; determine the customer's needs; present the product; answer questions or objections; close the sale; follow-up after the sale.
6. In B2B sales transactions, a salesperson will request the billing department to create an invoice to be sent to the customer. Most B2B customers pay invoices by check or credit card. B2C sales transactions usually transpire in a

retail situation. These sales are completed by the use of cash, credit cards, or debit cards.
7. For lost sales, it is necessary to evaluate exactly what happened and why. Customer feedback may provide reasons why the purchase was not made. Feedback from coworkers or supervisors on the execution of the sales process may also be helpful. An impartial observer may be able to point out something that went wrong in the sales process. The most important thing to remember is that keeping a good attitude is important to do well in a sales career. Rejection is part of the process. Learning from experiences, both good and bad, will help close future sales.
8. While customer service is provided by all employees, an organized customer support team is usually a part of the sales and marketing team. The customer support team consists of the employees who assist customers, take orders, or answer questions coming into the company via phone or website.
9. (Any) Frequently asked questions (FAQ) pages; e-mail support; product tracking; online chat; social media; discussion boards.
10. Handling customer complaints appropriately is a courtesy that encourages repeat business. When customers feel like their voice was heard and their problems were resolved, they often continue to give the company their business.

Apply Your Knowledge

Student answers will vary for Apply Your Knowledge questions.

Apply Your Math Skills

1. The total cost of the new office furniture is $5,813.76.
(6 × $339) + (2 × $275) + (8 × $190) + (8 × $149) = sales price
$2,034 + $550 + $1,520 + $1,192 = $5,296 sales price
$5,296 sales price × .06 tax rate = $317.76 tax
$5,296 sales price + $317.76 tax + $200 shipping and assembly = $5,813.76
2. The total cost of the Hernandezes' new furniture is $2,178.84.
$999 + (2 × $100) + $215 + $500 = sales price
$999 + $200 + $215 + $500 = $1,914 sales price
$1,914 sales price × .06 tax rate = $114.84
$1,914 sales price + $114.84 tax + $150 shipping and assembly = $2,178.84

Chapter 21 Marketing Management

You Do the Math: Algebraic Reasoning

1. $25 - x$ = remaining money
2. $2.37 \times x$ inches = total price
3. $350 \div x$ = payment amount

Section 21.1 Review

1. Management is the process of controlling and making decisions about the business.
2. There are three levels of management: upper, middle, and supervisory.
3. Operational planning.
4. The chain of command is the structure in a company from the highest to the lowest levels of authority.
5. A management style is how a person leads a team.

Answers to Build Your Vocabulary terms are key term definitions and can be found in the glossary.

Section 21.2 Review

1. previous-year sales dollars + forecasted sales-increase dollars = forecasted sales-dollar goal
2. previous-year sales dollars × sales-increase factor percentage = forecasted sales-increase dollars
3. A budget is a financial plan for a fixed period of time that reflects anticipated revenue and shows how it will be allocated in the operation of the business.
4. Assets are property or items of value owned by a business. Liabilities are the debts of a business.
5. A positive result is referred to as net income or profit.

Answers to Build Your Vocabulary terms are key term definitions and can be found in the glossary.

Review Your Knowledge

1. A manager is an employee who directs the work of others and is responsible for carrying out the goals of a department. Management is the process of controlling and making decisions about the business. Managers are responsible for making sure that all marketing tasks are completed. One task is to create and execute the marketing plan. Another task is to train individual team members to perform

IE-51

specific job duties. Still another is to monitor the performance of individual team members.
2. The five elements are plan, organize, staff, lead, and control.
3. Strategic planning is setting long-term marketing goals for the company. Tactical planning is setting short-term marketing goals for the company. Operational planning is setting day-to-day goals for the company.
4. Most businesses create an organizational chart to show the chain of command. An organizational chart is a diagram of employee positions showing how the positions interact within the chain of command.
5. In the democratic management style, the leader encourages team members to participate and share ideas equally. In the autocratic management style, the leader makes all decisions without input from others. The consulting management style is a combination of the democratic and autocratic styles. The manager makes the final decision, but only after considering input from the employees. In the laissez-faire management style, a manager allows employees to make their own decisions about how to complete tasks.
6. Financial planning is the process of setting financial goals and developing methods for reaching them. Most businesses set yearly goals and develop plans to achieve those goals. One of the most important goals is usually to earn a specific amount of revenue. The sales and marketing teams work with senior management to help define specific revenue goals for the company. By evaluating past performance, future performance can be predicted. A sales forecast helps define actions that the sales and marketing team will put into motion to meet those revenue goals. In order to remain profitable, it is important for a company to constantly monitor its sales forecasts and make changes as necessary.
7. External factors are those things that are beyond company control, such as the economy or political events. Internal factors are events such as changes in the distribution channel or labor problems.
8. A budget is a financial plan for a fixed period of time. The budget reflects anticipated revenue and shows how it will be allocated in the operation of the business. Budgets are often used during financial planning. Typically, each department in a company has a yearly budget, and the company has an overall budget. Budgets can be prepared for one month, one quarter, six months, or one year.
9. Two of the main financial reports used in business are the balance sheet and the income statement. A balance sheet is a financial report that reports the assets, liabilities, and owner's equity. An income statement is a financial report that shows the revenue and expenses for a business during a specific period of time.
10. assets = liabilities + owners' equity

Apply Your Knowledge
Student answers will vary for Apply Your Knowledge questions.

Apply Your Math Skills
1. The expected amount of sales increase in dollars is $7,011.
$46,740 × .15 = $7,011
2. The sales forecast for next year is $53,751.
$46,740 + $7,011 = $53,751

Chapter 22 Soft Skills
You Do the Math:
Solution Accuracy
1. No. The reported sales figure is too high by $0.02.
387 × 27.48/unit = $10,634.76
2. No. His car actually gets 37.1 miles to the gallon.
687 ÷ 18.5 = 37.1 miles/gallon
3. No. The finance charge will be $0.66. Answer may vary slightly due to rounding.
$FV = PV × (1 + r)^n$
r = interest rate, n = percent of a year. FV = future value, PV = present value
$FV = \$43.87 × (1+.197)^{1/12}$
FV = $43.87 × (1.015)
FV = $44.53
$44.53 − $43.87 = $0.66

Section 22.1 Review
1. Professionalism, positive attitude, respectfulness, trustworthiness, and etiquette. (May also include soft skills listed in Figure 22-1.)
2. Perseverance is continued effort to achieve a goal despite difficulties.
3. Time-management skills help people be efficient, meet deadlines, and keep appointments.

4. Two types of critical thinking are deductive reasoning and inductive reasoning.
5. A kickback is an amount of money given to someone in return for providing help in a business deal.

Answers to Build Your Vocabulary terms are key term definitions and can be found in the glossary.

Section 22.2 Review

1. In a functional team, each member has basically the same skills and qualifications. In a cross-functional team, the members have different skills.
2. Leaders influence others and inspire excellence. They are assertive, which means to be self-assured and confident. Leading others requires that an individual take charge and get a job done.
3. Conflict resolution requires that each party involved exhibits self-control. This means each person directs his or her feelings and reactions toward a desirable result that is socially acceptable. Yelling or losing emotional control will not be helpful in resolving an issue. Listening to each other without interruption is necessary to resolve the conflict. Speaking clearly and in a calm manner is required to keep the communication lines open.
4. Consensus building is a way to solve a problem and resolve conflicts by coming to a decision that all stakeholders can live with.
5. Formal methods of conflict resolution, such as negotiation, may be required in extenuating circumstances. Recall that negotiation is when individuals come together in an attempt to reach an agreement. Negotiation requires that each party is willing to compromise by giving something up and meeting the other party in the middle. Mediation is sometimes necessary during negotiation.

Answers to Build Your Vocabulary terms are key term definitions and can be found in the glossary.

Review Your Knowledge

1. Soft skills are skills used to help an individual find a job, perform in the workplace, and gain success in a job or career.
2. Employers expect professionalism in their employees so that positive, effective workplace relationships can evolve. This includes relationships with peers, supervisors, and customers.
3. Time management, problem solving, critical thinking, and stress management.
4. Procrastination is the delay of doing something that should be done immediately. Procrastination can become a serious barrier to work success when it results in missed deadlines or substandard work. It is best to start assigned tasks right away. The longer you put off a task, the more anxious and worried you are likely to become.
5. Avoid: Stay away from the source of the stress on purpose. Alter: Change your behavior in order to change the situations that cause stress. Adapt: Modify your standards or expectations in order to adapt to the source of the stress. Accept: Some stressors cannot be avoided, altered, or adapted to, and must be accepted as they are.
6. Ethical behavior refers to actions that adhere to a person's ethical standards. Examples of ethical behavior include respecting diversity, keeping proprietary information confidential, avoiding conflicts of interest, and avoiding participation in insider trading.
7. A team consists of two or more people working together to achieve a common goal. There are two basic types of teams: functional and cross-functional. In a functional team, each member has basically the same skills and qualifications. The purpose of a functional team is to come together for a specific purpose. In a cross-functional team, the members have different skills. A cross-functional team is often brought together to solve a specific problem.
8. Leadership, collaboration, and conflict resolution are some of the skills that contribute to a successful team. Leadership is the ability of a person to guide others to a goal. Leaders influence others and inspire excellence. They are assertive, which means to be self-assured and confident. Leading others requires that an individual take charge and get a job done. Leadership skills are necessary for success in the workplace. Teams must be able to collaborate in order to be successful. Collaboration is working with others to achieve a common goal. Successful collaboration includes cooperation, sharing ideas and responsibilities, and compromising when necessary. It is important for members of a collaborative team to express their ideas. The entire team benefits from everyone sharing his or her unique perspective. Conflict-resolution

skills are important to team success. When people work together, there is likely to be some conflict. Conflicts can be positive when people disagree in a respectful manner and learn from the disagreements. Conflict resolution is the process of recognizing and resolving disputes.

9. Constructive criticism is giving well-reasoned opinions about the ideas or work of others. Destructive criticism is a judgment given with the intention of harming or offending someone. This behavior is unproductive for the workplace.
10. During the majority-rules process, the winners may be happy, but the losers may be very unhappy and could undermine management's efforts to resolve the issue at hand. The goal of building a consensus is to have all stakeholders agree on a unanimous solution.

Apply Your Knowledge

Student answers will vary for Apply Your Knowledge questions.

Apply Your Math Skills

1. Total sales for March were $21,643.
   $5,280 + $3,260 + $4,752 + $283 + $6,770 + $1,298 = $21,643
2. The store made a profit of $1,965 in March.
   $21,643 − $19,678 = $1,965

Chapter 23 Communication in the Workplace

You Do the Math: Using a Calculator

There is $240.50 in the account.
$250 + $25 + $120 = $395
$395 − $25 − $8.50 − $98 − $20 − $3 = $240.50

Section 23.1 Review

1. Sender, message, channel, receiver, translation, feedback.
2. Peer-to-peer communication is often informal and progresses naturally. In contrast, presentation-style communication requires preparation and practice.
3. Eye contact occurs when two people look directly into each other's eyes.
4. A sending barrier can occur when the sender says or does something that causes the receiver to stop listening. A receiving barrier can occur when the receiver says or does something that causes the sender's message not to be received.
5. Ethical communication is applying ethics to make sure all communication is honest and respectful.

Answers to Build Your Vocabulary terms are key term definitions and can be found in the glossary.

Section 23.2 Review

1. (Any) Promotions, reports, and business correspondence including letters, e-mail, and memos.
2. Tone of speech refers to the feeling conveyed to the receiver from the way words are spoken.
3. (Any) Placing a telephone call; leaving a voice mail message; receiving telephone calls; introducing yourself; introducing others; introducing speakers; leading a meeting.
4. Hearing is a physical process. Listening is an intellectual process that combines hearing with evaluation.
5. An essential part of reading is comprehension. It is important to comprehend what is being read. Active reading is processing the words, phrases, and sentences you read.

Answers to Build Your Vocabulary terms are key term definitions and can be found in the glossary.

Review Your Knowledge

1. *Communication* is sending and receiving messages that convey information, ideas, feelings, and beliefs.
2. Inform: a message that informs provides information or education. Persuade: a message that persuades attempts to change the behavior of the receiver. Instruct: a message that instructs others attempts to provide direction or guidance. Make a request: a message that makes a request, asks a question, or for an action to occur. Respond to a request: alternative to making a request, there will be times that you must respond to a request that has been made of you.
3. Communication is generally classified as four different types. It includes written, visual, verbal, and nonverbal communication.
4. A barrier is anything that prevents clear, effective communication. Barriers can arise from many situations in the workplace. Barriers may occur in all types of communication. A sending barrier can occur when the sender says or does something

that causes the receiver to stop listening. A receiving barrier can occur when the receiver says or does something that causes the sender's message not to be received.
5. Ethical communication is applying ethics to make sure all communication is honest and respectful. It is every employee's responsibility to maintain ethical behavior in communication that represents his or her employer.
6. Marketing managers write marketing plans, promotion pieces, and many other forms of communication in the course of a day. These communications represent the company. The ability to write clear, concise, and well-written messages is a necessary soft skill for marketing careers.
7. The journalistic approach to writing is asking who, what, where, when, why, and how questions.
8. Telephone calls, including placing a call, leaving a voice mail message, and receiving telephone calls; making introductions, including introducing yourself, introducing others, and introducing speakers; and leading a meeting.
9. Listening skills are the ability of an individual to not only hear what a person says, but also understand the message. Listening is required for all positive communication.
10. Have a purpose; skim, scan, or read for detail; focus on the words; read for meaning.

Apply Your Knowledge

Student answers will vary for Apply Your Knowledge questions.

Apply Your Math Skills

1. The manager will need $3,108 for six employees to attend the seminar.
$200 + $168 + $150 = $518
$518 × 6 = $3,108
2. The manager did not budget enough money and is short by $251.66.
203 miles × $0.535 = $108.61
$108.61 × 6 = $651.66
$651.66 − $400 = $251.66

Chapter 24 Entrepreneurship

You Do the Math: Probability

1. The probability of receiving a 25 percent discount is one in four (1/4), or 25 percent.
1 discount / 4 possibilities = 25 percent

2. The probability of a patient not having the flu is 80 in 100 (80/100), or 80 percent.
20 flu patients / 100 patients total
100 − 20 = 80
80 non-flu patients / 100 patients total = 80 percent
3. The probability of a customer buying shoes in a color other than blue is 58 in 100 (58/100), or 58 percent.
42 blue pairs / 100 pairs sold
100 − 42 = 58
58 not blue shoes / 100 pairs sold = 58 percent
4. The probability that a customer will purchase groceries is 60 in 122 (60/122), or 49.2 percent. Answers may vary slightly due to rounding.
47 + 13 + 62 = 122 total customers
47 + 13 = 60 customers who bought groceries
60 ÷ 122 = 0.4918 rounded to 0.492

Section 24.1 Review

1. (Any) Being your own boss. Taking advantage of your earning potential. Enjoying your career. Making a difference in the world.
2. The five Ps of entrepreneurship are passion, perseverance, persistence, planning, and problem solving.
3. Sole proprietorship, partnership, and corporation.
4. Many counties and states require sole proprietors to apply for a DBA license before starting a new business. A DBA license, or a doing business as license, is needed to register a business under a name other than the name of the business owner. In some states, a DBA license is known as a fictitious name registration.
5. Limited liability company (LLC) and limited liability partnership (LLP).

Answers to Build Your Vocabulary terms are key term definitions and can be found in the glossary.

Section 24.2 Review

1. Business opportunities are ideas that have potential to become successful commercial ventures.
2. Successful entrepreneurs and businesses conduct some form of feasibility analysis, often called a feasibility study, before starting a new business. The analysis helps determine if their new product idea is worth pursuing. This requires some research to determine whether customers will buy the product and if

investors would be likely to fund the business. Feasibility studies must be based on reality, not theory.
3. There are many advantages to buying an existing business. The business already has customers, employees, a location, business equipment, and working business operations. An existing business also has records that describe its financial history. In addition, the person selling the business may be willing to act as a consultant to help you get started.
4. The franchise agreement includes the rules and standards that the buyer, or franchisee, must follow in running the franchised business. The franchisee owns the franchise business, but is legally connected to the franchisor by the franchise agreement. A franchise agreement also states the franchise fee.
5. Title page, table of contents, executive summary, business description, market evaluation, operations, financial plan, conclusion, bibliography, appendices.

Answers to Build Your Vocabulary terms are key term definitions and can be found in the glossary.

Review Your Knowledge

1. An entrepreneur is a person who starts a new business. Entrepreneurship is taking on both the risks and responsibilities of starting a new business. The reasons for starting a business include being your own boss, taking advantage of your earning potential, enjoying your career, and making a difference in the world. Risks of entrepreneurship can include being responsible for the success or failure of the business, working long hours, and risking personal finances.
2. Personality traits include the five Ps of entrepreneurship: passion, perseverance, persistence, planning, and problem solving. Many entrepreneurial skills can be learned at school. Others are learned through life experiences. These include communication, math, business, computers, and soft skills including problem solving and decision making.
3. A sole proprietorship is a business owned by one person. A sole proprietor is the person who owns the business and is personally responsible for all its debts. He or she has total responsibility for the business and receives all the profits. A partnership is the relationship between two or more people who join to create a business. Each person involved in owning a partnership is called a partner. The partners share the legal and financial responsibilities as well as the profits. A corporation is a business that is legally separate from its owners and has most of the legal rights of an actual person. It is the most complicated form of ownership. As a legal entity, a corporation can perform all business activities. A corporation can buy and own property, run a business, manufacture products, earn money, pay taxes, sue, and be sued. A corporation can even buy businesses and other corporations.
4. A general partnership is a business structure in which all partners have unlimited liability. The personal assets of each partner, including savings, investments, and homes, can be used to pay off the debts of the business. In a limited partnership (LP), there is one managing partner and at least one limited partner. Limited partners have limited liability. Limited liability means that a partner or owner cannot lose more than the amount originally invested by that person. They are not personally liable for the debts of the business.
5. In some types of corporations, both the individual stockholders and the corporation's profits are taxed. This is called double taxation and is seen as a disadvantage to many business founders.
6. Before starting a new business, entrepreneurs must go through a discovery process and then determine if the new business is feasible. In its simplest form, the entrepreneurial discovery process is the process of finding a need for a product. The entrepreneurial discovery process consists of two parts: the recognition of a need or want that is not being met and the willingness to take advantage of the opportunity. Successful entrepreneurs and businesses conduct some form of feasibility analysis, often called a feasibility study, before starting a new business. The analysis helps determine if their new product idea is worth pursuing.
7. Start a new business, purchase an existing business, purchase a franchise.
8. A business plan is a written document that describes a new business, how it will operate, and how it will make a profit. A business plan is a required part of a business loan application. Writing a business plan is also a valuable planning tool. Researching and writing a

business plan will help you figure out how to start and run your business successfully. Creating a thorough business plan will also identify the risks of the business so you can overcome them.
9. The executive summary should present the key points in a way that makes the reader excited about your business and its potential for success. The executive summary is the first thing that the lenders will read. If they are not impressed with the summary, they might not bother to read the rest of the business plan.
10. The financial plan describes how you plan to fund the business and expect to make a profit. First, present the start-up costs. Next, describe how you will get the money to cover the start-up costs. Include how much of your own money you plan to use and the amount and sources of any loans. When discussing the loans, explain how you will repay them. Also, present anticipated sales and profits. This section will include many financial documents, such as budgets, cash flow analysis, profit and loss statement, and balance sheet.

Apply Your Knowledge

Student answers will vary for Apply Your Knowledge questions.

Apply Your Math Skills

1. Marius had the highest profit in Year 3.
2. The business lost money in Year 4.
3. Marius had the largest gain in income in Year 3.
   Year 2: $37,000 – $34,300 = $2,700
   Year 3: $42,500 – $37,000 = $5,500
   Year 4: $36,500 – $42,500 = –$6,000
   Year 5: $41,000 – $36,500 = $4,500
4. Year 1: $34,300 – $30,000 = $4,300
   Year 2: $37,000 – $30,000 = $7,000
   Year 3: $42,500 – $30,000 = $12,500
   Year 4: $36,500 – $30,000 = $6,500
   Year 5: $41,000 – $30,000 = $11,000
5. Marius would make an income of $12,500 income if his predictions are correct.
   $30,000 + $3,000 = $33,000 in business expenses
   $41,000 + $4,500 = $45,500 in profit
   $45,500 profit – $33,000 expenses = $12,500 income

Chapter 25 Risk Management

You Do the Math: Problem Solving and Reasoning

1. Scott will pay $500 because of his deductible. The insurance companies will pay $2,500.
   Total cost – deductible = total insurance payment
   $3,000 – $500 = $2,500
2. Angela's new annual premium is $1,590.
   $1500 × 1.06 = $1,590
   Angela will pay $7.50 more each month.
   $1,500 ÷ 12 = $125
   $1,500 × .06 = $90
   $1,500 + $90 = $1,590
   $1,590 ÷ 12 = $132.50
   $132.50 – $125 = $7.50
3. Ahmed's new premium will be $1,606.07.
   $1,889.50 × .15 = $283.43
   $1,889.50 – $283.43 = $1,606.07

Section 25.1 Review

1. Business risk is the possibility of loss or injury that might occur in a business.
2. (Any) Controllable or uncontrollable; speculative or pure.
3. A liability risk is one that has the possibility of losing money or other property as a result of legal proceedings.
4. Accidents, theft, and fraud.
5. (Any) Shoplifting, burglary, robbery.
   Answers to Build Your Vocabulary terms are key term definitions and can be found in the glossary.

Section 25.2 Review

1. Avoid, reduce, transfer, and assume.
2. Risks can be avoided by taking steps to eliminate the risk.
3. Occupational Safety and Health Administration (OSHA).
4. Emergency procedures are a series of actions taken to minimize risks in the event of an emergency. These procedures describe what to do in case of fires or other disasters. A major component of emergency procedures is an evacuation plan to safely get every person out of the building if necessary.
5. A business may self-insure by saving money to cover some risks should they happen.
   Answers to Build Your Vocabulary terms are key term definitions and can be found in the glossary.

Review Your Knowledge
1. A risk is the possibility of loss, damage, or injury. A controllable risk is one that cannot be avoided, but can be minimized by purchasing insurance or implementing a risk management plan. Uncontrollable risk is a situation that cannot be predicted or covered by purchasing insurance.
2. A speculative risk carries with it the chance of a profit or loss. A pure risk is the threat of loss with no chance for profit.
3. Natural risk is a situation caused by acts of nature. Economic risk is a situation that occurs when the economy suffers due to negative business conditions in the United States or the world. Market risk is the potential that the target market for new products or services is much less than originally thought. Human risk is a negative situation caused by human actions.
4. Economic risk and market risk.
5. (Any) Vendor theft, bad checks, expired or stolen credit cards, counterfeit money, data fraud.
6. Risk management is the process of measuring risk and finding ways to minimize or manage loss. Businesses and individuals are liable for their risks. Individuals and businesses handle potential liability by assessing the risks. Risk assessment is the process of analyzing a situation for possible risks. Risk assessments should be done on a regular basis as risks may change over time.
7. Risks can be avoided by taking steps to eliminate the risk altogether. Risks can also be reduced by creating a plan to minimize risks that cannot be totally avoided.
8. Structural security consists of security features in a building, such as lights, alarms, locks, and computerized security systems.
9. Many risks can be transferred by purchasing insurance to cover different risk events.
10. To assume the risk means to make financial preparations for the possibility of future loss.

Apply Your Knowledge
Student answers will vary for Apply Your Knowledge questions.

Apply Your Math Skills
1. The monthly cost of this insurance policy is $42.50 per month.
   $510 ÷ 12 months = $42.50 per month
2. The new insurance policies will cost a total of $840 together.
   $25 per month × 12 months = $300 per year
   $45 per month × 12 months = $540 per year
   $300 + $540 = $840

Chapter 26 Business Funding

You Do the Math: Interpreting Circle Graphs
1. 17 percent
2. 12 percent
3. Rent and savings are both 25 percent each.
4. Four percent more is spent on gasoline.
   21 percent − 17 percent = 4 percent

Section 26.1 Review
1. Bartering is the exchange of products or services for other products or services. No money changes hands.
2. (Any) Personal funds, family and friends, partners, angel investors, venture capitalists.
3. A fixed expense is an expense that remains the same every month. A variable expense is an expense that can change on a monthly basis.
4. Expect everything to cost twice as much and take twice as long as you think it will.
5. The break-even point is the amount of revenue a business must generate in order to equal its expenses. It is only after the break-even point is reached that profits are earned.

Answers to Build Your Vocabulary terms are key term definitions and can be found in the glossary.

Section 26.2 Review
1. (Any) Loan application; résumé; signed personal financial statements; sound business plan; DBA, licenses, and registrations required to conduct business; partnership agreement or Articles of Incorporation; copies of supplier contracts; franchise agreement; commercial lease; personal and business income tax returns for the previous three years; one year of personal and business bank statements.
2. The five Cs of banking include character, cash flow, capital, collateral, and conditions.
3. Lenders need to see evidence that the new business will make enough money to repay the loan in a timely manner.

4. The two main sections of a pro forma income statement are projected revenue and projected expenses.
5. Fixed assets are the items of value that may take time to sell. Liquid assets are cash or the items a business owns that can be easily turned into cash.

Answers to Build Your Vocabulary terms are key term definitions and can be found in the glossary.

Review Your Knowledge

1. Bootstrapping is cutting all unnecessary expenses and operating on as little cash as possible. Some ways to bootstrap are use free resources, use personal assets, negotiate, monitor expenses, and barter.
2. SCORE, the SBA, and state websites offer advice and other resources at no charge. Social media is also a free resource to use as a marketing tool.
3. Two common sources of financing are equity financing and debt financing. Equity financing is raising money for a business in exchange for a percentage of the ownership. Debt financing is borrowing money for business purposes.
4. (Any) Banks and credit unions, peer-to-peer lending, SBA-assisted loans, retirement accounts, family and friends, and trade credit.
5. New business owners must plan for a number of things before actually opening the doors. It is important for owners to project the start-up costs and operating expenses, budget for owner cash withdrawal, and price their products or services correctly.
6. All lenders require the completion of a loan application. The application will ask for detailed information. Education, experience, past jobs, current debt, and the business projections all help the lender evaluate your application. When applying for equity or debt financing, applicants are asked to provide documentation proving they are good credit risks. It is important for all owners to provide résumés. All business loan programs require a sound business plan be submitted with the loan application. Most business loan programs require applicants to submit personal and, if possible, business income tax returns for the previous three years. Many loan programs also require one year of personal and business bank statements. Collateral requirements vary greatly, often depending on the requested loan amount and degree of risk. When applying for a business loan, lenders evaluate applicants based on the five Cs of banking: character, cash flow, capital, collateral, and conditions.
7. Lenders want to know that a business can generate enough cash flow to repay the loan on time. Sometimes, lenders ask for a cosigner on the loan. A cosigner is a person who signs a loan with the applicant and takes on equal responsibility for repaying it. The cosigner usually has a better-established financial history than the primary applicant.
8. A pro forma cash flow statement reports the anticipated flow of cash into and out of the business. A pro forma income statement projects the financial progress of the business. The pro forma balance sheet reports the assets, liabilities, and owner's equity for a proposed business.
9. If the business projects receiving more cash from sales than is spent on expenses, the cash flow is positive.
10. Short-term liabilities are those expected to be paid within the current year. Long-term liabilities are debts that extend beyond the current year.

Apply Your Knowledge

Student answers will vary for Apply Your Knowledge questions.

Apply Your Math Skills

1. Jeremiah's expected net cash flow for August is $1,240.
$3,000 − $500 − $825 − $60 − $300 − $75 = $1,240
2. Jeremiah's net cash flow for September is $140.
$1,500 − $250 − $825 − $60 − $150 − $75 = $140
3. Jeremiah's new expected net cash flow would be $1,565 for August and would be $465 for September.
$825 − $500 = $325
$1,240 + $325 = $1,565
$140 + $325 = $465

Chapter 27 Planning for Success

You Do the Math: Functions

1. Discrete function.
2. Discrete function.
3. Continuous function.
4. Continuous function.

Section 27.1 Review

1. A job is the work a person does regularly in order to earn money. A career, on the other hand, is a series of related jobs in the same profession.
2. The first step is setting SMART career goals. The second step is conducting a self-assessment. The third step is creating a career plan that will lead you to achieve your goals.
3. (Any) Aptitudes, talents, abilities, values, work values, interests, and personal traits.
4. The goal of CTSOs is to help students acquire knowledge and skills in different career and technical areas.
5. Entry-level jobs require the least amount of education and experience.

Answers to Build Your Vocabulary terms are key term definitions and can be found in the glossary.

Section 27.2 Review

1. (Any) High school, postsecondary, graduate, postgraduate.
2. (Any) Occupational training, internships, apprenticeships, and military service.
3. Doing so can ensure that the education you receive will be well worth the investments of both time and money.
4. (Any) Search using the term *college access* plus the name of your state. If you have already been thinking about a specific school, visit its official website to learn about admission requirements and to find out what financial help might be available to you. The US Department of Education, the College Board, and the National College Access Network have websites that include a wealth of information about college access. Talk to your family, friends, and guidance counselor for information to begin planning for college.
5. Free Application for Federal Student Aid (FAFSA).

Answers to Build Your Vocabulary terms are key term definitions and can be found in the glossary.

Review Your Knowledge

1. A job is the work a person does regularly in order to earn money. A career, on the other hand, is a series of related jobs in the same profession. A career is a position for which you prepare by attending school or completing specialized training. Over time, a job can turn into a career. Getting a job is often a short-term goal. Building a career is a long-term goal.
2. Entry level, career level, specialist level, supervisory level, and executive level.
3. Making a career plan now points you in a direction that enables you to gain experience and expertise in a particular area. As a teen, if you know yourself well and form a good plan, your future career will have a solid foundation. As you pursue a specific career goal through planning, you learn a great deal about yourself and the career. You might also discover that the career is not right for you. You will not have wasted your time pursuing the career, though. You will have gathered important information about yourself and the world of work to develop your next career goal and plan.
4. A self-assessment is conducted by examining your aptitudes, abilities, values, interests, and personal traits. You can write down what you learn about yourself in a journal to help you analyze your findings. Then, you can make decisions based on what you learned. In addition, you will change and grow as you learn more about the world of work and yourself. You can use your journal to record and monitor these changes. This information can provide the basis for future decisions.
5. (Any) CTSOs, informational interviews, on-the-job experience, and employment trends.
6. Your educational needs will depend on your career interests and goals. Early career planning can help you make decisions about your education. Investigating the opportunities and costs of future education, training, and certification is an investment in your future. Education, training, and certification have a direct effect on income and career potential. Certain positions may require additional training in order to advance career potential.
7. Students enrolled in this program take classes just like other college students. The program is considered an elective. However, students also receive basic military and officer training.
8. (Any) Academic reputation; faculty; acceptance standards; graduation statistics; and other considerations, such as where you plan to live, interests and hobbies, job opportunities, and the campus.
9. College access refers to building awareness about college opportunities, providing guidance regarding college admissions, and identifying ways to pay for college. College access includes

access to many types of postsecondary institutions. Attending a postsecondary school to further your education can be a critical step in your career plan. However, preparing to go to college can present challenges to students and families, both academically and financially. The sooner you begin planning, the better. It is never too early.
10. (Any) Grant, scholarship, work-study program, need-based award.

Apply Your Knowledge

Student answers will vary for Apply Your Knowledge questions.

Apply Your Math Skills

1. Wesley's tuition and books at the state university will cost $134,872. Wesley's tuition and books at the private college will cost $260,880.
   $32,518 for state tuition + $1,200 for books = $33,718
   $33,718 per year × 4 years = $134,872
   $64,020 for private tuition + $1,200 for books = $65,220
   $65,220 per year × 4 years = $260,880
2. Bella will need an additional $22,000 for her tuition this year.
   $1,750 per credit hour × 12 credits per semester = $21,000 per semester
   $21,000 per semester × 2 semesters = $42,000 per year
   $42,000 per year – $10,000 from parents – $10,000 scholarship = $22,000

Chapter 28 Preparing for Your Career

You Do the Math: Multiplication

1. Shelia's gross pay is $516.
   $12 × 40 = $480 regular pay
   1.5 × $12 = $18 overtime hourly wage
   42 – 40 = 2 hours of overtime
   $18 × 2 = $36 overtime wages
   $480 + $36 = $516 gross pay
2. The total fee is $2.15.
   2% becomes .02
   $24.76 × .02 = $0.50
   $52.76 × .02 = $1.06
   $29.35 × .02 = $0.59
   $0.50 + $1.06 + $0.59 = $2.15
3. 8.5% becomes 0.085   7% becomes 0.07

   A. You would pay $12.75 in sales tax in your home area, but save $2.25 by shopping in the other county.
      $150 × 0.085 = $12.75
      $150 × 0.07 = $10.50
      $12.75 – $10.50 = $2.25
   B. You would pay $2.55 in sales tax in your home area, but save $0.45 by shopping in the other county.
      $30 × 0.085 = $2.55
      $30 × 0.07 = $2.10
      $2.55 – $2.10 = $0.45
   C. You would pay $0.17 in sales tax in your home area, but save $0.03 by shopping in the other county.
      $2 × 0.085 = $0.17
      $2 × 0.07 = $0.14
      $0.17 – $0.14 = $0.03

Section 28.1 Review

1. First, make sure that you are the right product. Next, think about the marketing concept. Finally, actively market yourself to the employer.
2. Online job boards are websites that host job postings for employers and allow applicants to apply for jobs.
3. A résumé is a document that profiles a person's career goals, education, and work history. Think of a résumé as a snapshot that shows who you are and why you would be an asset as an employee. A résumé is the first impression that potential employers will have of you.
4. The body of the cover message is where to demonstrate your positive work behaviors and qualities that make you employable. This may include illustrating your ambition, determination, and skills. Examine the job description for the position and identify the positive traits and skills the employer seeks. Then, focus on these traits and skills. Explain why you are qualified and how your traits, skills, and experience make you the best candidate for the job.
5. The process of applying for employment typically involves completing a job application form along with submitting a résumé and cover message.

Answers to Build Your Vocabulary terms are key term definitions and can be found in the glossary.

Section 28.2 Review

1. The purpose of the interview for the employer is to decide which candidate will be the best for the job.
2. If you want employers to look further into your qualifications, you must impress them at your first meeting. Appropriate appearance and behavior are very important when interviewing.
3. Hypothetical questions require a candidate to imagine a situation and describe how he or she would act. Frequent topics of hypothetical questions relate to working with and getting along with coworkers. Behavioral questions are questions that draw on an individual's previous experiences and decisions. Your answers to these types of questions indicate past behavior, which may be used to predict future behavior and success in a position.
4. (Any) Form I-9 Employment Eligibility Verification, Form W-4 Employee's Withholding Allowance Certificate, and benefits forms.
5. To give notice means to notify a supervisor of the intention to leave a job. Usually, this is done by writing a letter of resignation.

Answers to Build Your Vocabulary terms are key term definitions and can be found in the glossary.

Review Your Knowledge

1. First, make sure that you are the right product. *Self-awareness* is a sense of being aware of one's feelings, behaviors, needs, and other elements that make up the whole person. In order to promote yourself to an employer, you must be aware of who you are. Analyze whether you meet the requirements for the positions you seek. Match your skills, talents, and other qualities with the needs of the right employer. Next, think about the marketing concept. When you apply for a job, think in terms of what you can do for the employer. Finally, actively market yourself to the employer. You have to launch an organized promotional campaign. Make sure you are appropriately packaged. Everything about the way you dress, speak, and act should be targeted toward the position you are seeking.
2. The most common ways of finding job leads are using online resources such as job boards, social media, and company websites; networking; and newspapers. Other potential places include career and college placement offices, and job fairs. Want ads appear in a variety of places.
3. Personal fact sheet, résumé, cover message, references list, and portfolio.
4. Names and addresses of all schools attended and dates of attendance, skills, honors, activities, hobbies, and interests. It should also include detailed information about your work or volunteer experience, such as name and address of employers, dates of employment, supervisor's name, salary, and job duties.
5. The application process usually consists of completing a job application form along with submitting a résumé and cover message. Some employment opportunities may also require the submission of a portfolio.
6. Applying online and applying in person.
7. When preparing for a job interview, learn as much as you can about the position and the company. Make sure you know where the interview will take place and exactly how to get there. Find out how long it will take to get there. Know the name and title of the person who will interview you. Call the day before to confirm the time and place. Prepare a few sentences of introduction. Practice speaking slowly and clearly. Practice your handshake. Before the interview, try to anticipate questions the interviewer is likely to ask you. It is a good idea to prepare a list of questions to ask the interviewer about the position, the job responsibilities, and the company.
8. Your response to such questions might be as follows: "Please explain how that relates to the job," or "I would rather not answer personal questions."
9. The employer will complete an employment verification using the information on your application or résumé. Another important part of the employment process is a background check. Many employers use Internet search engines, such as Google, to search for your name. Employers may also check social networking websites, such as Facebook and Twitter. If an employer decides to offer you a position after the interview process and employment verification, someone will contact you with an official offer of employment. Be sure to evaluate the offer before making a decision. The first day on the job, you will spend a considerable amount of time in the human

resources department completing necessary forms for your employment. Come prepared with the personal information required for the many forms you will need to complete.
10. Most businesses require that you give at least a *two-week notice* before leaving a job. Usually, this is done by writing a letter of resignation. The letter of resignation should express appreciation for the time you have spent with the company, express regrets about leaving, and give the date of your last day on the job. This letter should be addressed to your supervisor. Then, take the letter with you when you tell your supervisor that you are leaving. Politely explain why you are leaving the company, express appropriate appreciation, and leave the letter with your supervisor.

Apply Your Knowledge

Student answers will vary for Apply Your Knowledge questions.

Apply Your Math Skills

1. Marketing manager
2. $61.90
3. $9.28
4. $23,530

Chapter 29 Digital Citizenship

You Do the Math: Units

1. No. The correct equation is total sales dollars ÷ total reps.
2. No. The correct equation is pounds per box ÷ pounds per product.
   65 pounds per box ÷ 1.3 pounds per product = 50 products per box
3. The final unit is square feet per second (ft^2/sec).
   12.8 feet × 3.6 feet = 46.08 ft^2
   46.08 ft^2 ÷ 7.6 seconds = 6.06 ft^2/sec

Section 29.1 Review

1. Digital citizenship is the standard of appropriate behavior when using technology to communicate. Good digital citizenship focuses on using technology in a positive manner rather than using it for negative or illegal purposes. People who participate in the digital society have a legal responsibility for their online actions, whether those actions are ethical or unethical.
2. Cyberbullying is using the Internet to harass or threaten an individual. It is using social media, text messages, or e-mails to harass or scare a person with hurtful words or pictures. Even though a victim of cyberbullying cannot be physically seen or touched by the bully, this does not mean the person cannot be harmed by his or her actions.
3. Plagiarism is claiming another person's material as your own, which is both unethical and illegal. Piracy is the illegal copying or downloading of software, files, or other protected material, including images, movies, and music.
4. A licensing agreement is a contract that gives one party permission to market or produce the good or service owned by another party.
5. Article I: Individual Rights; Article II: Individual Responsibilities; Article III: Rights of Educational Institutions; and Article IV: Institutional Responsibilities.

Answers to Build Your Vocabulary terms are key term definitions and can be found in the glossary.

Section 29.2 Review

1. Most companies have an established acceptable use policy. An acceptable use policy is a set of rules that explains what is and is not acceptable use of company-owned and company-operated equipment and networks. Employees are typically made aware of acceptable use policies during training, before they are allowed access to the company's computers and network.
2. The s stands for secure.
3. Spyware is software that spies on a computer. Spyware can capture private information, such as e-mail messages, usernames, passwords, bank account information, and credit card information. A software virus is a computer program designed to negatively impact a computer system by infecting other files. A virus may destroy data on the computer, cause programs to malfunction, bring harm to a network, or steal information.
4. To protect your mobile device from use by a thief, create a password to lock it. Have the number of your mobile device in a safe place so that if the unexpected happens, you can contact your service provider.
5. If a virus invades your computer or the hard disk crashes, it may be too late to retrieve your files and computer programs.

Answers to Build Your Vocabulary terms are key term definitions and can be found in the glossary.

Review Your Knowledge

1. Digital communication is the exchange of information through electronic means. Digital communication is composed of digital literacy and digital citizenship. Digital literacy is the ability to use technology to locate, evaluate, communicate, and create information. Digital citizenship is the standard of appropriate behavior when using technology to communicate.
2. (Any two) Using a computer or mobile device, including the mouse, keyboard, icons, and folders. Using software and applications to complete tasks, such as word processing and creating spreadsheets, tables, and databases. Using the Internet to conduct searches, use e-mail, and register on a website. Communicating online, including sharing photos and videos, using social media networks, and learning to be an informed digital citizen. Helping children learn to be responsible and make informed decisions online.
3. Intellectual property is something that comes from a person's mind, such as an idea, invention, or process. Intellectual property laws protect a person's or a company's inventions, artistic works, and other intellectual property.
4. Fair use doctrine allows individuals to use copyrighted works without permission in limited situations under very strict guidelines.
5. The Electronic User's Bill of Rights details the rights and responsibilities of both individuals and institutions regarding the treatment of digital information. The articles are not legally binding, but contain guidelines for the appropriate use of digital information. The articles in the Electronic User's Bill of Rights are: Article I: Individual Rights; Article II: Individual Responsibilities; Article III: Rights of Educational Institutions; and Article IV: Institutional Responsibilities.
6. Most companies have an established acceptable use policy. An acceptable use policy is a set of rules that explains what is and is not acceptable use of company-owned and company-operated equipment and networks. Employees are typically made aware of acceptable use policies during training, before they are allowed access to the company's computers and network. Many companies and schools use filters that prevent unauthorized Internet surfing or visiting selected websites, such as Facebook, during working hours. Employers are legally allowed to censor information that employees read on the Internet during work hours.
7. One way is to prevent them from being accepted by the browser. Most Internet browsers allow the user to set a preference to never accept cookies. Another way to protect your computer is to delete cookies on a regular basis. Still another way to remove cookies is to run a disk cleanup utility.
8. The most common form of phishing is sending a fake e-mail to a group of people. The e-mail message looks like it is from a legitimate source, such as an employment agency. The e-mail asks for certain information, such as a social security number or bank account information, or it provides a link to a web page. The linked web page looks real, but its sole purpose it to collect private information that is then used to commit fraud.
9. Ways you can practice digital security for yourself and your employer include using common sense, avoiding identity theft, and creating a security plan.
10. An important part of a security plan is backing up the data on your computer. If a virus invades your computer or the hard disk crashes, it may be too late to retrieve your files and computer programs.

Apply Your Knowledge

Student answers will vary for Apply Your Knowledge questions.

Apply Your Math Skills

1. Antivirus B is cheaper to purchase for two years of virus protection.
   Antivirus A:
   $7.49 per month × 24 months = $179.76
   Antivirus B:
   $79.99 per year × 2 years = $159.98
2. 79% of Alexandria's credit card bill is for charges that she did not make.
   $48.75 + $74.80 + $376.30 + $94.55 = $594.40 total charges
   $594.40 – $48.75 – $74.80 = $470.85 in fraudulent charges
   $470.85 ÷ 594.40 = 0.792 or 79%

G-W PUBLISHER

FOURTH EDITION
Marketing Dynamics

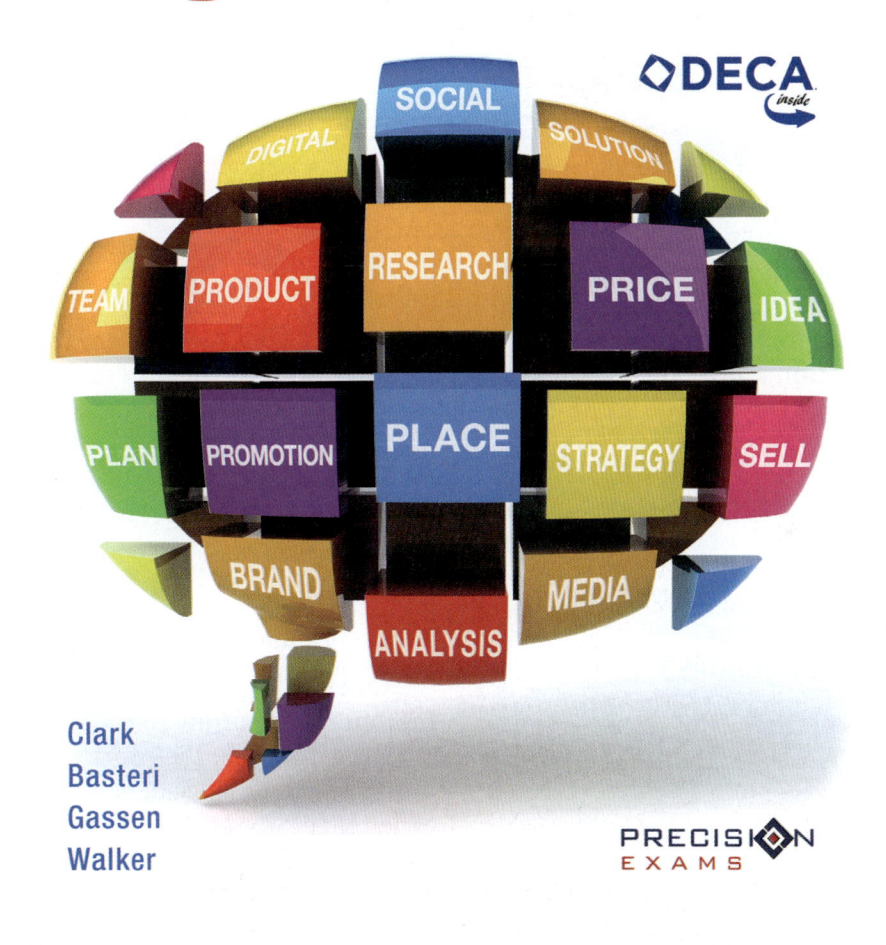

DECA inside

SOCIAL • SOLUTION • DIGITAL • TEAM • PRODUCT • RESEARCH • PRICE • IDEA • PLAN • PROMOTION • PLACE • STRATEGY • SELL • BRAND • MEDIA • ANALYSIS

Clark
Basteri
Gassen
Walker

PRECISION EXAMS

Learn how the four Ps of marketing—product, place, price, and promotion—are all around you.

Prepare for Your Future

Marketing is all around us. Marketing influences how we think, what we buy, and even the careers we choose. *Marketing Dynamics* will help guide you in understanding how marketing will affect your decisions as a consumer, as well as a career you might choose.

Marketing creates eye-catchers. Merriam-Webster defines an *eye-catcher* as "something that arrests the eye." To illustrate how marketing *arrests* the eye of the consumer, each unit opens with an example of a business that used a clever eye-catcher to gain attention. These features will have you thinking about other eye-catchers you see every day.

Marketing Standards are important to the presentation of content. Each unit opener identifies which of the seven specific marketing core functions are presented in that unit. These are the marketing core functions as identified by the MBA Research and Curriculum Center.

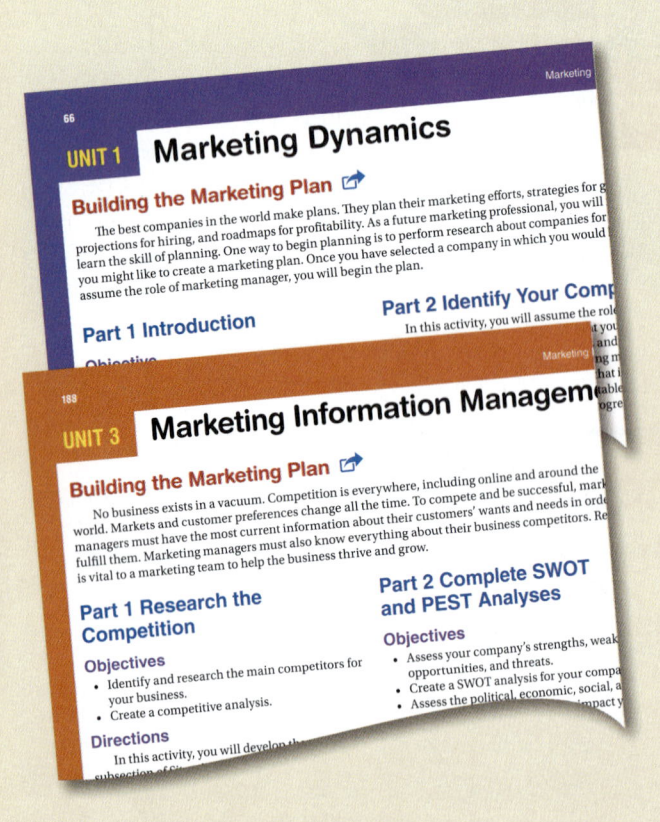

One of the goals of a marketing course is for you to learn how to write a marketing plan. Ongoing **Building the Marketing Plan** activities provide a project-based, hands-on learning experience. Starting at the end of Unit 1, you will begin writing a marketing plan for a business you select. By the end of the text, you will have completed your own unique marketing plan. The Building the Marketing Plan project addresses these 21st Century learning skills:
- creativity and innovation;
- critical thinking and problem solving; and
- communication and collaboration.

Creating a marketing plan takes work. To make your experience easier, activity files are provided on the G-W Learning companion website to guide you through the marketing plan project.

Amplify Your Learning

Content is presented in an easy-to-comprehend and relevant format. Activities relate to everyday learning to enable you to experience real-life communication situations and challenges.

- Each chapter opens with a **pretest** and concludes with a **posttest**. The pretest will help you evaluate your prior knowledge of the chapter content. The posttest will help you evaluate what you have learned after studying the chapter.
- The **Essential Question** at the beginning of each section will engage you as you uncover the important points presented in the content.
- **DECA Emerging Leaders** features provide first-hand opportunities to explore learning activities that will help prepare you for college and career. Discover what it means to become an academically prepared, community-oriented, professionally responsible, and experienced leader through DECA®.

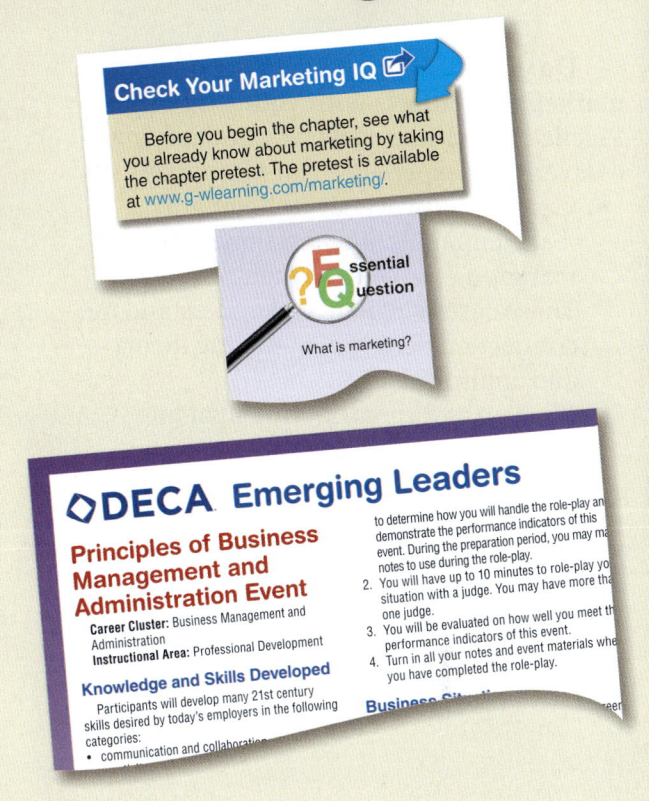

It is all about getting ready for college and career. College and career readiness activities address literacy skills to help prepare you for the real world.

- English/Language Arts standards for reading, writing, speaking, and listening are incorporated in **Reading Prep** activities, as well as in end-of-chapter **Communication Skills** applications. These provide ways for you to demonstrate the literacy skills you have mastered.
- **Portfolio Development** activities provide guidance to create a personal portfolio for use when exploring volunteer, education and training, and career opportunities.
- Research skills are critical for success in college and career. **Internet Research** activities at the end of each chapter provide opportunities to put them to work.

Maximize the Impact

Do you ever wonder how the world of marketing connects with your life? Practical activities relate everyday learning to enable you to experience real-life marketing.

- **Case in Point** scenarios highlight real companies and how they apply marketing concepts to their businesses. These cases will help you understand the connection between marketing theory and application.
- **Marketing Ethics** offers insight into ethical issues that arise for marketing professionals and tips on how to make ethical decisions.
- **Green Marketing** shares information for marketers on best business practices for the environment. 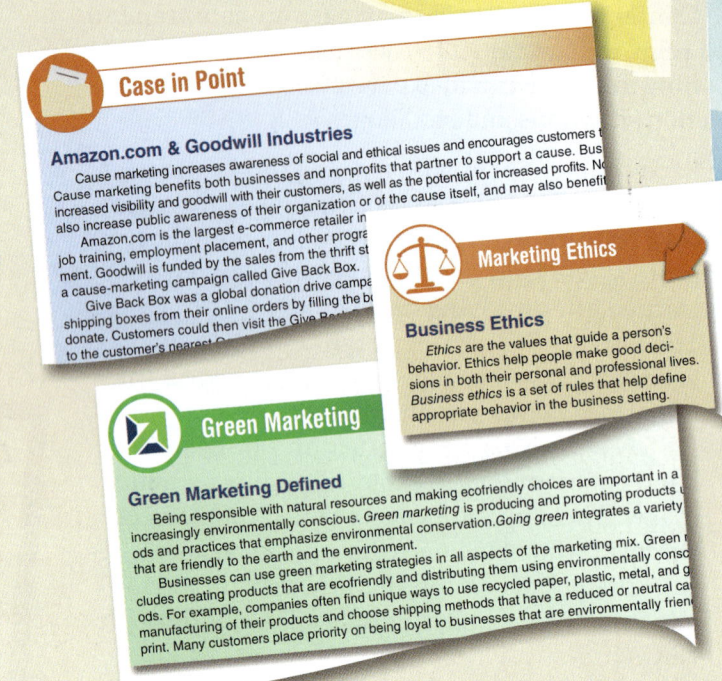 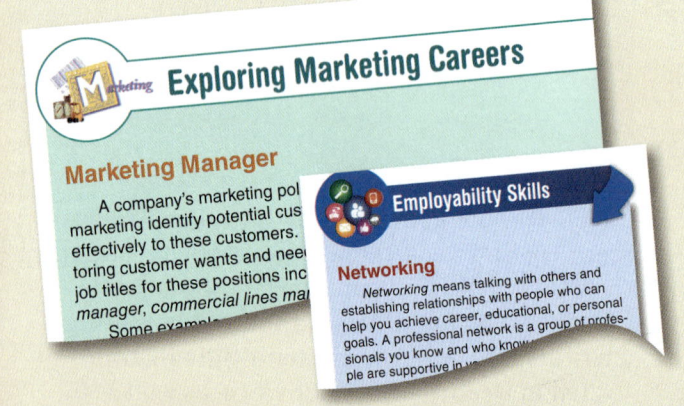
- **Exploring Marketing Careers** features present information about potential career opportunities in the Marketing career cluster. By studying these, you can explore career possibilities for your future.
- **Employability Skills** features review essential soft skills for success in the workplace.
- **Social Media** features explore how companies can use social media as a marketing tool.
- **You Do the Math** activities focus on skills that are important to your understanding of mathematics concepts.

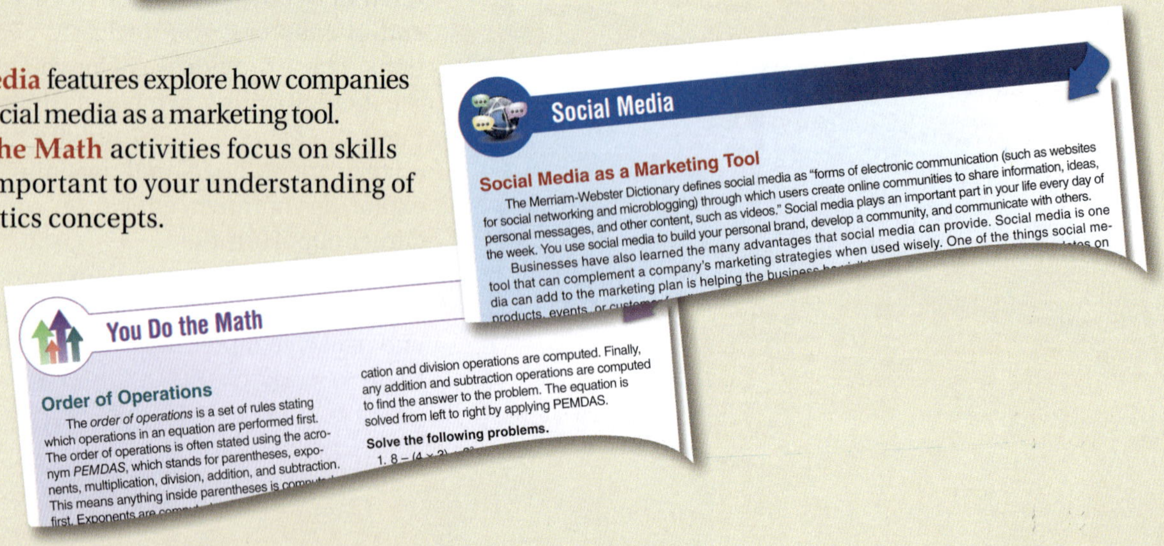

Case in Point
Amazon.com & Goodwill Industries
Cause marketing increases awareness of social and ethical issues and encourages customers to... Cause marketing benefits both businesses and nonprofits that partner to support a cause. Businesses increased visibility and goodwill with their customers, as well as the potential for increased profits. Nonprofits also increase public awareness of their organization or of the cause itself, and may also benefit...
Amazon.com is the largest e-commerce retailer in... job training, employment placement, and other progra... ment. Goodwill is funded by the sales from the thrift st... a cause-marketing campaign called Give Back Box.
Give Back Box was a global donation drive campa... shipping boxes from their online orders by filling the b... donate. Customers could then visit the Give B... to the customer's nearest G...

Marketing Ethics
Business Ethics
Ethics are the values that guide a person's behavior. Ethics help people make good decisions in both their personal and professional lives. *Business ethics* is a set of rules that help define appropriate behavior in the business setting.

Green Marketing
Green Marketing Defined
Being responsible with natural resources and making ecofriendly choices are important in a... increasingly environmentally conscious. *Green marketing* is producing and promoting products u... ods and practices that emphasize environmental conservation. *Going green* integrates a variety... that are friendly to the earth and the environment.
Businesses can use green marketing strategies in all aspects of the marketing mix. Green... cludes creating products that are ecofriendly and distributing them using environmentally conso... ducts. For example, companies often find unique ways to use recycled paper, plastic, metal, and g... manufacturing of their products and choose shipping methods that have a reduced or neutral ca... print. Many customers place priority on being loyal to businesses that are environmentally frien...

Exploring Marketing Careers
Marketing Manager
A company's marketing pol... marketing identify potential cus... effectively to these customers.... toring customer wants and nee... job titles for these positions inc... *manager, commercial lines ma...* Some example...

Employability Skills
Networking
Networking means talking with others and establishing relationships with people who can help you achieve career, educational, or personal goals. A professional network is a group of professionals you know and who know... ple are supportive in...

Social Media
Social Media as a Marketing Tool
The Merriam-Webster Dictionary defines social media as "forms of electronic communication (such as websites for social networking and microblogging) through which users create online communities to share information, ideas, personal messages, and other content, such as videos." Social media plays an important part in your life every day of the week. You use social media to build your personal brand, develop a community, and communicate with others.
Businesses have also learned the many advantages that social media can provide. Social media is one tool that can complement a company's marketing strategies when used wisely. One of the things social media can add to the marketing plan is helping the business... products, events, or custom...

You Do the Math
Order of Operations
The *order of operations* is a set of rules stating which operations in an equation are performed first. The order of operations is often stated using the acronym PEMDAS, which stands for parentheses, exponents, multiplication, division, addition, and subtraction. This means anything inside parentheses is compu... first. Exponents are c... cation and division operations are computed. Finally, any addition and subtraction operations are computed to find the answer to the problem. The equation is solved from left to right by applying PEMDAS.

Solve the following problems.
1. $8 - (4 \times 3)...$

Assess Your Progress

It is important to assess what you learn as you progress through the textbook. Multiple opportunities are provided to confirm learning as you explore the content. *Formative assessment* includes the following:

- **Check Your Understanding** questions at the end of each section of the chapter provide an opportunity to review what you have learned before moving on to additional content.
- **Build Your Vocabulary** activities review the key terms presented in each section. By completing these activities, you will be able to demonstrate your understanding of marketing terms.
- **Review Your Knowledge** questions cover basic concepts presented in the chapter so you can evaluate your understanding of the material.
- **Apply Your Knowledge** questions challenge you to relate what you learned in the chapter with your own ideas, experiences, and goals.
- **Apply Your Math Skills** problems relate basic math skills to the concepts covered in the chapter.
- The **Math Skills Handbook** provides a quick reference for basic math functions. This information will help clarify math used in marketing as it is presented in the chapters.
- **Communication Skills** activities provide ways for you to demonstrate the literacy and career-readiness skills you have mastered.
- **Teamwork** activities encourage a collaborative experience to interact with other students in a productive manner.

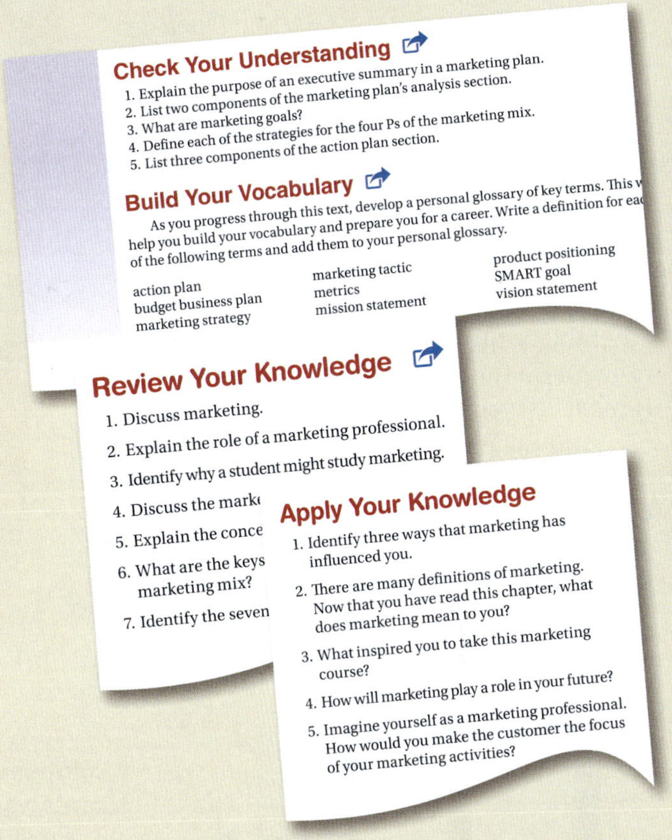

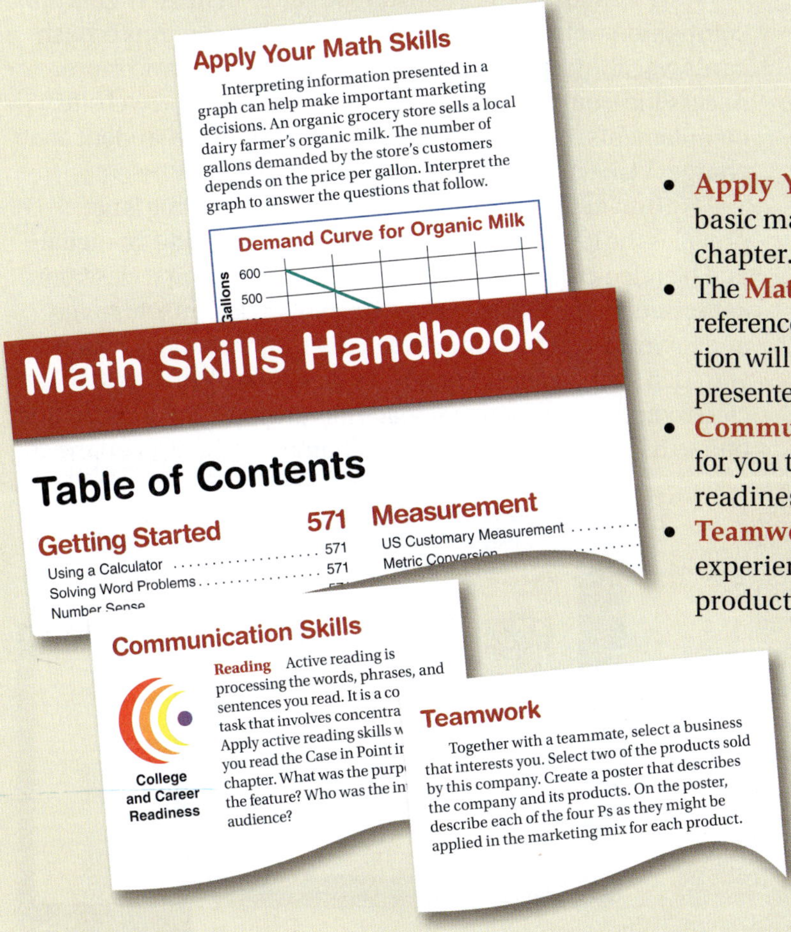

Check Your Understanding
1. Explain the purpose of an executive summary in a marketing plan.
2. List two components of the marketing plan's analysis section.
3. What are marketing goals?
4. Define each of the strategies for the four Ps of the marketing mix.
5. List three components of the action plan section.

Build Your Vocabulary
As you progress through this text, develop a personal glossary of key terms. This will help you build your vocabulary and prepare you for a career. Write a definition for each of the following terms and add them to your personal glossary.

action plan
budget business plan
marketing strategy
marketing tactic
metrics
mission statement
product positioning
SMART goal
vision statement

Review Your Knowledge
1. Discuss marketing.
2. Explain the role of a marketing professional.
3. Identify why a student might study marketing.
4. Discuss the mark...
5. Explain the conce...
6. What are the keys... marketing mix?
7. Identify the seven...

Apply Your Knowledge
1. Identify three ways that marketing has influenced you.
2. There are many definitions of marketing. Now that you have read this chapter, what does marketing mean to you?
3. What inspired you to take this marketing course?
4. How will marketing play a role in your future?
5. Imagine yourself as a marketing professional. How would you make the customer the focus of your marketing activities?

Apply Your Math Skills
Interpreting information presented in a graph can help make important marketing decisions. An organic grocery store sells a local dairy farmer's organic milk. The number of gallons demanded by the store's customers depends on the price per gallon. Interpret the graph to answer the questions that follow.

Demand Curve for Organic Milk

Math Skills Handbook

Table of Contents

Getting Started
Using a Calculator
Solving Word Problems
Number Sense

571 Measurement
571 US Customary Measurement
571 Metric Conversion

Communication Skills
Reading Active reading is processing the words, phrases, and sentences you read. It is a co... task that involves concentra... Apply active reading skills w... you read the Case in Point in... chapter. What was the purp... the feature? Who was the in... audience?

College and Career Readiness

Teamwork
Together with a teammate, select a business that interests you. Select two of the products sold by this company. Create a poster that describes the company and its products. On the poster, describe each of the four Ps as they might be applied in the marketing mix for each product.

Student Resources

Student Textbook *Marketing Dynamics* introduces the basic concepts of marketing, including the four Ps of product, place, price, and promotion. By studying this comprehensive text, students will explore the framework needed to become a marketing professional.

Online Textbook The online text is accessible through any Internet-enabled device, including computers, smartphones, and tablets. Students can study in the classroom or on the go—whenever or wherever it is most convenient.

Student Workbook The *Marketing Dynamics* student workbook reinforces the concepts in the text and provides enrichment activities to improve students' understanding of mathematics and leadership.

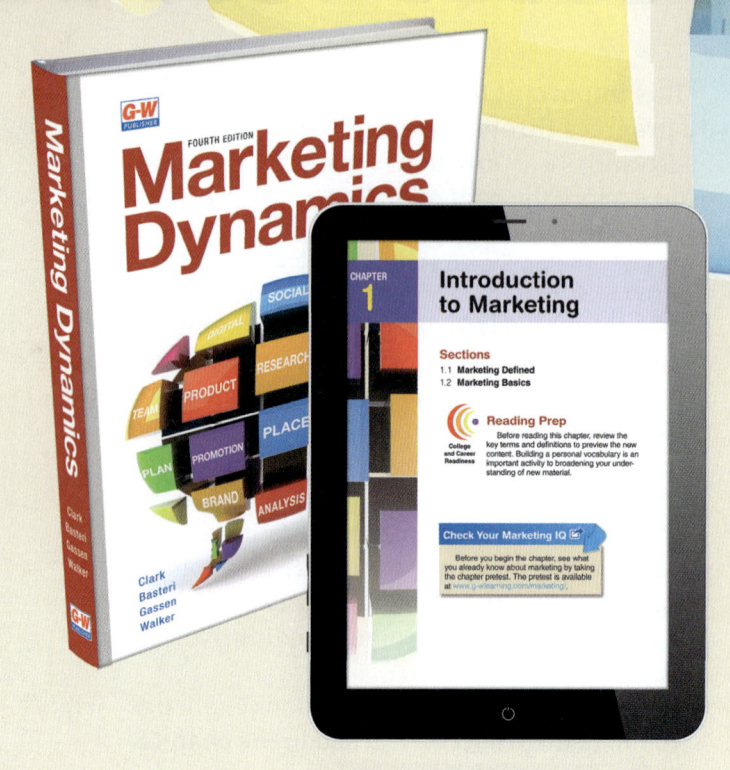

G-W Learning Companion Website The G-W Learning companion website is a study reference that contains e-flash cards, vocabulary exercises, interactive quizzes, and more. Accessible from any digital device, the companion website complements the textbook and is available to the student at no charge. Visit www.g-wlearning.com/marketing/.

Online Learning Suite The Online Learning Suite provides the foundation of instruction and learning for digital and blended classrooms. An easy-to-manage shared classroom subscription makes it a hassle-free solution for both students and instructors. An online student text and workbook, along with rich supplemental content, brings digital learning to the classroom. All instructional materials are found on a convenient online bookshelf and accessible at home, at school, or on the go.

Online Learning Suite/Student Textbook Bundle Looking for a blended solution? Goodheart-Willcox offers the Online Learning Suite bundled with the printed text in one easy-to-access package. Students have the flexibility to use the printed text, the Online Learning Suite, or a combination of both components to meet their individual learning styles. The convenient packaging makes managing and accessing content easy and efficient.

Instructor Resources

Instructor's Edition of Student Textbook The Instructor's Edition of *Marketing Dynamics* contains the full student text plus additional pages rich with resources to help successfully plan and teach this course.

Instructor's Resource CD One resource provides instructors with time-saving preparation tools such as answer keys, rubrics, lesson plans, correlation charts to standards, and other teaching aids.

Instructor's Presentations for PowerPoint® The Instructor's Presentations for PowerPoint® help teach and visually reinforce the key concepts from each chapter.

ExamView® Assessment Suite The ExamView® Assessment Suite allows the quick and easy creation of printable tests from a test bank of hundreds of questions. Tests you create may be published for LAN-based testing or be packaged for online testing using WebCT, Blackboard, or ANGEL. The ExamView® software products are compatible with interactive whiteboard technology.

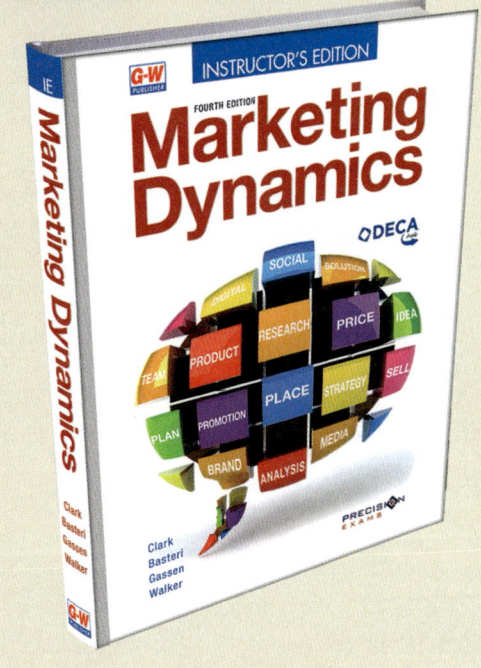

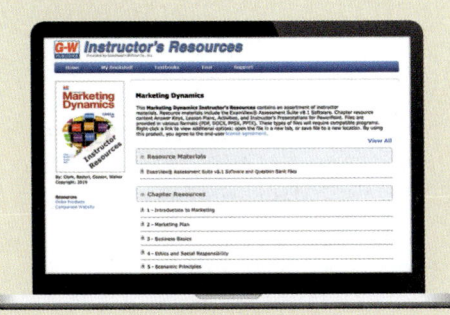

Online Instructor Resources Online Instructor Resources provide all the support needed to make preparation and classroom instruction easier than ever. Resources include answer keys, lesson plans, Instructor Presentations for PowerPoint®, ExamView® Assessment Suite, and more. Online Instructor Resources are available as a subscription and can be accessed at school or at home.

G-W Integrated Learning Solution

For the Student:
Student Textbook (print)
Student Workbook (print)
G-W Learning Companion Website (free)
Online Learning Suite (subscription)
Online Learning Suite/Student Textbook Bundle

For the Instructor:
Instructor's Edition of Student Textbook (print)
Instructor's Presentations for PowerPoint® (CD)
ExamView® Assessment Suite (CD)
Instructor Resources (CD)
Online Instructor Resources (subscription)

FOURTH EDITION

Marketing Dynamics

◇DECA inside

Brenda Clark, EdD
Retired CTE Director
Jenison High School
Jenison, Michigan

Cynthia Gendall Basteri, EdD
Grants Coordinator
Marketing Coordinator Emeritus
Tewksbury Public Schools
Tewksbury, Massachusetts

PRECISION
EXAMS

Chris Gassen, MBA, CFA
Faircourt Valuation Investments
Grosse Pointe Woods, Michigan

Michelle Walker, PhD
Founder
Trebla Consulting, LLC
McLean, Virginia

Publisher
The Goodheart-Willcox Company, Inc.
Tinley Park, IL
www.g-w.com

Copyright © 2019

by

The Goodheart-Willcox Company, Inc.

Previous editions copyright 2014, 2010, 2006.

All rights reserved. No part of this work may be reproduced, stored, or transmitted in
any form or by any electronic or mechanical means, including information storage and
retrieval systems, without the prior written permission of
The Goodheart-Willcox Company, Inc.

Manufactured in the United States of America.

ISBN 978-1-63126-625-6

1 2 3 4 5 6 7 8 9 – 19 – 22 21 20 19 18 17

The Goodheart-Willcox Company, Inc. Brand Disclaimer: Brand names, company names, and illustrations for products and services included in this text are provided for educational purposes only and do not represent or imply endorsement or recommendation by the author or the publisher.

The Goodheart-Willcox Company, Inc. Safety Notice: The reader is expressly advised to carefully read, understand, and apply all safety precautions and warnings described in this book or that might also be indicated in undertaking the activities and exercises described herein to minimize risk of personal injury or injury to others. Common sense and good judgment should also be exercised and applied to help avoid all potential hazards. The reader should always refer to the appropriate manufacturer's technical information, directions, and recommendations; then proceed with care to follow specific equipment operating instructions. The reader should understand these notices and cautions are not exhaustive.

The publisher makes no warranty or representation whatsoever, either expressed or implied, including but not limited to equipment, procedures, and applications described or referred to herein, their quality, performance, merchantability, or fitness for a particular purpose. The publisher assumes no responsibility for any changes, errors, or omissions in this book. The publisher specifically disclaims any liability whatsoever, including any direct, indirect, incidental, consequential, special, or exemplary damages resulting, in whole or in part, from the reader's use or reliance upon the information, instructions, procedures, warnings, cautions, applications, or other matter contained in this book. The publisher assumes no responsibility for the activities of the reader.

The Goodheart-Willcox Company, Inc. Internet Disclaimer: The Internet resources and listings in this Goodheart-Willcox Publisher product are provided solely as a convenience to you. These resources and listings were reviewed at the time of publication to provide you with accurate, safe, and appropriate information. Goodheart-Willcox Publisher has no control over the referenced websites and, due to the dynamic nature of the Internet, is not responsible or liable for the content, products, or performance of links to other websites or resources. Goodheart-Willcox Publisher makes no representation, either expressed or implied, regarding the content of these websites, and such references do not constitute an endorsement or recommendation of the information or content presented. It is your responsibility to take all protective measures to guard against inappropriate content, viruses, or other destructive elements.

Cover image: Julien Tromeur/Shutterstock.com

Introduction

Take a look around—you are surrounded by marketing messages. No matter where you look, you will probably see or hear a message that was strategically placed by a marketer to get your attention. Marketing is all around you and affects almost everything you do.

Marketing Dynamics will help guide you in understanding how marketing will affect your personal decisions as a consumer, as well as the career you might choose. You will learn about the four Ps of marketing—product, place, price, and promotion—as well as how research is conducted and applied to make solid business decisions.

One of the major goals of this text is for you to create your own marketing plan. Each unit ends with a project-based activity called Building the Marketing Plan that is designed to lead you through the creation of a unique marketing plan. A template is available on the G-W Learning companion website to assist in the completion of this project.

DECA Emerging Leaders features will expand your professional knowledge base and help you prepare for competitive events. In addition, you will learn how to prepare for college and career by perfecting your soft skills and learning the importance of ethics in business. Portfolio Development activities will guide you in the creation of a portfolio to use as you pursue volunteer, education and training, or career opportunities.

Marketing Dynamics provides an opportunity for you to maximize and refine your knowledge. As you explore and discover marketing concepts, you will learn life-long skills that will follow you wherever your interests may lead.

About the Authors

Brenda Clark is a retired CTE director, marketing instructor, SBE advisor, and DECA advisor for Jenison, Michigan, Public Schools. She was named Marketing Teacher of the Year at state and national levels. She is a consultant for the MBA Research and Curriculum Center. Clark is also a coauthor of *Entrepreneurship* and *Principles of Business, Marketing, and Finance*. Clark's program was named Business of the Year by the Jenison Chamber of Commerce. Two of her marketing department's school-based enterprises were awarded Gold Certification in 2010 and 2013, respectively. She earned a bachelor degree in marketing education, a master degree in educational leadership, and an EdD in educational leadership with a concentration in career and technical education from Western Michigan University. She currently serves on the DECA Competitive Events Task Force.

Cynthia Gendall Basteri, EdD, is a retired high school math and marketing teacher who served as a DECA competitive events coordinator at the district, state, and international levels. Currently, Basteri is the grants coordinator for Tewksbury Public Schools in Tewksbury, Massachusetts. She also oversees all the school year and summer credit recovery programs at the middle school and high school levels in Tewksbury. She continues to update the curriculum in all content areas to reflect current state and national standards.

Chris Gassen is the principal of an investment firm and formerly an equity mutual fund manager, financial analyst, accountant, and college instructor. Gassen writes educational materials and business valuations. He holds a master of business administration degree with a concentration in finance from Indiana University and a bachelor of science degree in management from Oakland University. He is a Chartered Financial Analyst (CFA) and served as a grader for the national CFA exam.

Michelle Walker is the owner of Trebla Consulting, LLC. Prior to founding Trebla Consulting, Michelle was director of education at DECA Inc., where she used diverse professional development engagement strategies to expand and strengthen the performance of 5,900 teachers and managers in the high school and collegiate divisions. She previously worked with a variety of education, nonprofit and private organizations including Texas Education Agency, University of North Texas, and Walker Consulting. Walker has a doctor of philosophy degree in applied technology, training, and development from the University of North Texas. She also taught marketing education and was a DECA advisor in the Dallas Independent School District.

Reviewers

The authors and publisher wish to thank the following industry and teaching professionals for their valuable input into the development of the fourth edition of *Marketing Dynamics*.

Richard T. Austin
Marketing Teacher/DECA Advisor
Livonia Churchill High School
Livonia, Michigan

Willene M. Biere
Business Academy Director
Canyon Springs High School
Moreno Valley, California

Faith Davenport
Marketing Teacher
Mill Creek High School/Gwinnett County Public Schools
Hoschton, Georgia

Marlena Dixon
Marketing Teacher
Stewarts Creek High School
Smyrna, Tennessee

Dawn Eisenhardt
Business Teacher
Cherokee High School
Marlton, New Jersey

Dwionne R. Freeman, EdD
CTAE Coordinator
Atlanta Public Schools
Atlanta, Georgia

Joy C. Gornto
Marketing Teacher and DECA Advisor
Alcoa High School
Alcoa, Tennessee

Madge L. Gregg
Business Education Teacher
Hoover High School
Hoover, Alabama

Julie Hutto
Business and Technology Teacher
Bleckley County High School
Cochran, Georgia

Phyleshia Jackson-Jones
Director
VyStar Academy of Business & Finance
Jean Ribault Senior High School
Jacksonville, Florida

Myla Lowrance
Brand Marketing Team Lead
PennWell Corporation
Houston, Texas

Angela Norris McGregor
Business Education Teacher
Irmo High School
Irmo, South Carolina

Dr. Carol Lynn S. Nute
Teacher/DECA Advisor (Lead)
River Bluff High School
Lexington, South Carolina

Shelley Pewitt, NBCT
Work Based Learning (Cooperative Education)/DECA Advisor
Hoover High School
Hoover, Alabama

Kari F. Roach
Business Department Chairperson and Teacher
Hobart High School
Hobart, Indiana

April L. Smith
CTE Teacher and Marketing Professional
Millbrook High School/Owner at The KinZac Group
Raleigh, North Carolina

v

Dr. Anjanette M. Stewart
CTAE Teacher
Sol C. Johnson High School/Savannah-Chatham
　Public School System
Savannah, Georgia

Tresa Warner, MBA
Academy Director, iMAGination Inc. Academy of
　Marketing and Graphic Design
Lake Region High School
Eagle Lake, Florida

Linda Wilson
Teacher of Marketing/Business Education
Sandia High School
Albuquerque, New Mexico

Ashley Wood
Marketing Teacher
Chatham Charter School
Siler City, North Carolina

Grant Wood
Business Teacher
Lubbock-Copper High School
Lubbock, Texas

Precision Exams Certification

　Goodheart-Willcox is pleased to partner with Precision Exams by correlating *Marketing Dynamics* to the Standards, Objectives, and Indicators for Precision Exams Marketing, Introduction; Marketing I; and Marketing II exams. Precision Exams were created in concert with industry and subject matter experts to match real-world job skills and marketplace demands. Students who pass the exam and performance portion of the exam can earn a Career Skills Certification™. To see how *Marketing Dynamics* correlates to the Precision Exam Standards, please visit www.g-w.com/marketing-dynamics-2019/ and click on the Correlations tab. For more information on Precision Exams, please visit www.precisionexams.com.

I earned a CAREER SKILLS™ Certificate in Marketing. You can earn one, too!

Ask your instructor how you can earn a CAREER SKILLS™ Certificate for your résumé.

800.470.1215　　PRECISION EXAMS　　precisionexams.com

Brief Contents

Unit 1
Marketing Dynamics 2
- Chapter 1 Introduction to Marketing 4
- Chapter 2 Marketing Plan 20
- Chapter 3 Business Basics 36
- Chapter 4 Ethics and Social Responsibility 52

Unit 2
Economics 68
- Chapter 5 Economic Principles 70
- Chapter 6 Economic Activity 88
- Chapter 7 Global Trade 106

Unit 3
Marketing-Information Management 124
- Chapter 8 Marketing Research 126
- Chapter 9 Targeting a Market 146
- Chapter 10 Understanding the Customer . . . 166

Unit 4
Product 190
- Chapter 11 Product 192
- Chapter 12 Branding 214

Unit 5
Price 230
- Chapter 13 Price 232
- Chapter 14 Pricing Product 248

Unit 6
Place 262
- Chapter 15 Place 264
- Chapter 16 Purchasing and Inventory Control 284

Unit 7
Promotion 304
- Chapter 17 Promotion 306
- Chapter 18 Advertising 324
- Chapter 19 Visual Merchandising 344
- Chapter 20 Personal Selling 362

Unit 8
Management 388
- Chapter 21 Marketing Management 390
- Chapter 22 Soft Skills 404
- Chapter 23 Communication in the Workplace 422

Unit 9
Entrepreneurship 446
- Chapter 24 Entrepreneurship 448
- Chapter 25 Risk Management 466
- Chapter 26 Business Funding 480

Unit 10
Preparing for a Career 498
- Chapter 27 Planning for Success 500
- Chapter 28 Preparing for Your Career 528
- Chapter 29 Digital Citizenship 552

Contents

Unit 1
Marketing Dynamics 2

Chapter 1 Introduction to Marketing....... 4
   Section 1.1 Marketing Defined.......... 6
   Section 1.2 Marketing Basics 9
   Chapter 1 Review and Assessment...... 17
Chapter 2 Marketing Plan 20
   Section 2.1 Researching a Marketing Plan... 22
   Section 2.2 Developing a Marketing Plan ... 27
   Chapter 2 Review and Assessment...... 33
Chapter 3 Business Basics 36
   Section 3.1 Business Defined 38
   Section 3.2 Laws and Regulations 43
   Chapter 3 Review and Assessment...... 49
Chapter 4 Ethics and Social Responsibility .. 52
   Section 4.1 Ethics 54
   Section 4.2 Social Responsibility 59
   Chapter 4 Review and Assessment...... 63
Building the Marketing Plan............. 66

Unit 2
Economics 68

Chapter 5 Economic Principles 70
   Section 5.1 Introduction to Economics.... 72
   Section 5.2 Economic Systems and
      Market Forces 78
   Chapter 5 Review and Assessment...... 85
Chapter 6 Economic Activity 88
   Section 6.1 Economic Measurement..... 90
   Section 6.2 Government and the Economy...99
   Chapter 6 Review and Assessment..... 103
Chapter 7 Global Trade 106
   Section 7.1 Global Business Environment....108
   Section 7.2 Global Marketplace......... 113
   Chapter 7 Review and Assessment..... 120
Building the Marketing Plan............. 123

Unit 3
Marketing-Information Management 124

Chapter 8 Marketing Research 126
   Section 8.1 Marketing-Research Data... 128
   Section 8.2 Conducting Marketing
      Research 138
   Chapter 8 Review and Assessment..... 143
Chapter 9 Targeting a Market 146
   Section 9.1 Identify the Market 148
   Section 9.2 Evaluate the Competition ... 156
   Chapter 9 Review and Assessment..... 163
Chapter 10 Understanding the Customer... 166
   Section 10.1 B2C Customers........... 168
   Section 10.2 B2B Customers........... 175
   Section 10.3 Credit Basics............ 180
   Chapter 10 Review and Assessment.... 184
Building the Marketing Plan............. 188

Unit 4
Product 190

Chapter 11 Product 192
   Section 11.1 Product 194
   Section 11.2 New-Product Development
      Process 201
   Chapter 11 Review and Assessment.... 211
Chapter 12 Branding 214
   Section 12.1 Product Branding 216
   Section 12.2 Brand Identity and
      Protection..................... 221
   Chapter 12 Review and Assessment.... 226
Building the Marketing Plan............. 229

Unit 5
Price 230

Chapter 13 Price 232
   Section 13.1 Importance of Price....... 234
   Section 13.2 Price Influencers......... 238
   Chapter 13 Review and Assessment.... 245
Chapter 14 Pricing Product 248
   Section 14.1 Pricing Strategies 250

Section 14.2 Governmental Influence
on Pricing. 254
Chapter 14 Review and Assessment. . . . 258
Building the Marketing Plan. 261

Unit 6
Place 262

Chapter 15 Place. 264
Section 15.1 Channels of Distribution . . . 266
Section 15.2 Supply Chain 274
Chapter 15 Review and Assessment. . . . 281
Chapter 16 Purchasing and Inventory
Control. 284
Section 16.1 Purchasing 286
Section 16.2 Inventory Control 293
Chapter 16 Review and Assessment. . . . 300
Building the Marketing Plan. 303

Unit 7
Promotion 304

Chapter 17 Promotion 306
Section 17.1 Promotion Basics. 308
Section 17.2 Types of Promotion 315
Chapter 17 Review and Assessment. . . . 321
Chapter 18 Advertising 324
Section 18.1 Advertising Basics. 326
Section 18.2 Creating an Advertising
Campaign 334
Chapter 18 Review and Assessment. . . . 341
Chapter 19 Visual Merchandising 344
Section 19.1 Visual Merchandising 346
Section 19.2 Display 351
Chapter 19 Review and Assessment. . . . 359
Chapter 20 Personal Selling 362
Section 20.1 Role of Sales. 364
Section 20.2 Selling. 368
Section 20.3 Customer Service 380
Chapter 20 Review and Assessment. . . . 383
Building the Marketing Plan. 386

Unit 8
Management 388

Chapter 21 Marketing Management 390
Section 21.1 Management. 392
Section 21.2 Financial Management . . . 396
Chapter 21 Review and Assessment. . . . 401
Chapter 22 Soft Skills 404
Section 22.1 Skills for Managers 406
Section 22.2 Teams in the Workplace 414
Chapter 22 Review and Assessment. . . . 419
Chapter 23 Communication in the
Workplace 422
Section 23.1 Communication Basics 424
Section 23.2 Communication Skills 430
Chapter 23 Review and Assessment. . . . 441
Building the Marketing Plan. 445

Unit 9
Entrepreneurship 446

Chapter 24 Entrepreneurship. 448
Section 24.1 Becoming an Entrepreneur. . . 450
Section 24.2 Starting a Business. 457
Chapter 24 Review and Assessment. . . . 463
Chapter 25 Risk Management. 466
Section 25.1 Identify Risk 468
Section 25.2 Manage Risk. 472
Chapter 25 Review and Assessment. . . . 477
Chapter 26 Business Funding 480
Section 26.1 Options for Funding 482
Section 26.2 Apply for Financing. 490
Chapter 26 Review and Assessment. . . . 494
Building the Marketing Plan. 497

Unit 10
Preparing for a Career 498

Chapter 27 Planning for Success 500
Section 27.1 Career Investigation
and Planning 502
Section 27.2 Preparing for Your
Education. 515
Chapter 27 Review and Assessment. . . . 525
Chapter 28 Preparing for Your Career 528
Section 28.1 Finding and Applying for
Employment. 530
Section 28.2 Interviewing and the
Employment Process. 540
Chapter 28 Review and Assessment. . . . 549
Chapter 29 Digital Citizenship 552
Section 29.1 Communicating in a
Digital Society 554
Section 29.2 Internet Use in the
Workplace 560
Chapter 29 Review and Assessment. . . . 565
Building the Marketing Plan. 568

Math Skills Handbook. 570
Glossary. 586
Index. 607

Features

Case in Point

Eataly	7
Zappos	28
Cuisinart	41
Amazon.com & Goodwill Industries	61
Amtrak	74
Hyundai	100
Mattel, Inc.	114
Global Public-Private Partnership for Handwashing	131
Spanish Television	153
UPS	178
L.L. Bean	197
M&M's® and State Farm	218
Microsoft	237
Dollar Tree	251
Amazon Prime Air	276
Target	287
T-Mobile	317
Airbnb	335
Apple	347
IBM	369
Enterprise Holdings	395
Cisco	409
Fisher-Price	426
method®	453
Gillinder Glass	473
Warby Parker	484
Walt Disney	504
TaskRabbit	533
Hyatt	556

Employability Skills

Soft Skills	15
Professional Image	25
Professionalism	43
Etiquette	60
Self-Management Skills	76
Emotional Control	92
Resilience	112
Protocol	133
Positive Attitude	150
Self-Confidence	174
Self-Esteem	202
Humility	219
Self-Awareness	239
Workspaces	253
Polite Language	269
Prompt Response	297
Networking	313
Inside Voice	329
Workspace Etiquette	357
Workplace Attire	371
Respect	396
Telephone Etiquette	413
Listening	431
Personal Space	454
Paralanguage	475
Shared Workspaces	485
Punctuality	512
Out-of-Office Notice	535
Prompt Response	560

Exploring Marketing Careers

Marketing Manager	10
Sales Manager	47
Telemarketer	79
Customer Service	115
Market Analyst	149
Product Manager	199
Trade Show Manager	235
Supply Chain Manager	278
Advertising and Promotions Manager	316
Graphic Designer	355
Community Affairs	397

Copywriter 427
Outside Sales Representative 474
Interactive Media Specialist 518
Webmaster 561

Green Marketing

Green Marketing Defined 31
Environmental Protection Agency 58
Greenwashing 94
Lifestyles of Health and Sustainability 130
Benefit Corporation 182
Sustainable Packaging 222
Carbon Footprints 252
Ecofriendly Purchasing 289
Ecofriendly Marketing Premiums 336
Customer Incentives 373
Green Team 415
Sustainability Training 456
Paper Consumption 488
Green Job Search 537

Marketing Ethics

Business Ethics 10
Code of Ethics 46
Integrity 75
Sourcing 110
Responsible CRM 152
Proprietary Information 195
Going Out of Business Sale 241
Collusion 267
Truth-in-Advertising Laws 312
Ethical Sales Messages 358
Expense Accounts 397
Communication 438
Tax Returns 476
Copyrights 506
Online Merchandise 557

Social Media

Social Media as a Marketing Tool 29
Social-Media Marketing (SMM) 60
SMM Terms 101
Content Marketing 136
SMM Goals 172
Social-Media Analytics 224
Social-Media Dashboards 257
Facebook 298
Twitter 327
YouTube 378
LinkedIn 416
Blogs 461
Hashtags 487
Ethical Social Media Use 532

You Do the Math

Basic Math 13
Order of Operations 32
Number Sense 44
Percentages 55
Interpreting Line Graphs 84
Types of Numbers 97
Currency Conversion 116
Margin of Error 139
Mean, Median, and Mode 160
Rounding 177
Word Problems 206
Problem Solving and Reasoning 220
Exponents 243
Multiplication 256
Measurement Reasoning 272
Unit Conversion 295
Statistical Reasoning 319
Fundamental Counting Principle 339
Area 349
Slope 377
Algebraic Reasoning 399
Solution Accuracy 408
Using a Calculator 439
Probability 458
Problem Solving and Reasoning 470
Interpreting Circle Graphs 489
Functions 507
Multiplication 547
Units 563

UNIT 1
Marketing Dynamics

Chapters

1. **Introduction to Marketing**
2. **Marketing Plan**
3. **Business Basics**
4. **Ethics and Social Responsibility**

While studying, look for the activity icon for:
- Building the Marketing Plan activity files
- Pretests and posttests
- Vocabulary terms with e-flash cards and matching activities
- Self-assessment

These activities can be accessed at www.g-wlearning.com/marketing/.

Developing a Vision

Exploring career opportunities is an important step. The choices are endless. In this text, you will have an opportunity to investigate career choices for becoming a marketing professional. Unit 1 introduces you to the basics of marketing and business. This will be the foundation for learning about the marketing profession.

One of the most important tasks a marketing professional will perform is to create a marketing plan. In this unit, you will learn the basics for creating a marketing plan. You will also learn about the importance of ethics and social responsibility in marketing. Exploring these concepts will help you expand your knowledge of the business world.

Marketing Core Functions Covered in This Unit

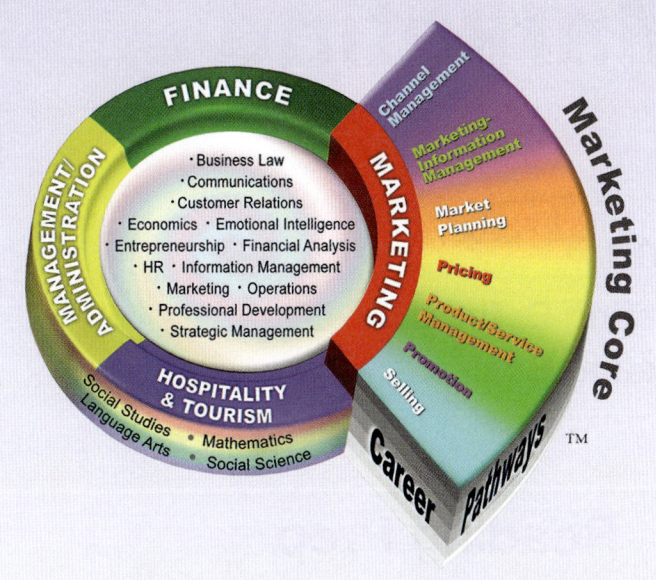

Functions of Marketing

- Channel management
- Marketing-information management
- Market planning
- Pricing
- Product/service management
- Promotion
- Selling

Copyright MBA Research, Columbus, Ohio. Used with permission.

EYE-CATCHER

Marketing Matters

You are surrounded by marketing messages. Sometimes, you may not even realize it. Times Square in New York City is a perfect example of marketing strategies that reach over 174 million people each year. While Times Square is less than *one* percent of New York City's total area, revenue from these advertisements account for *ten* percent of the money generated in the entire city. For many pedestrians, the bright lights of the electronic billboards function as much as entertainment as they do advertising. People who pass by may not even be aware that the message is capturing their attention.

Christian Mueller/Shutterstock.com

CHAPTER 1

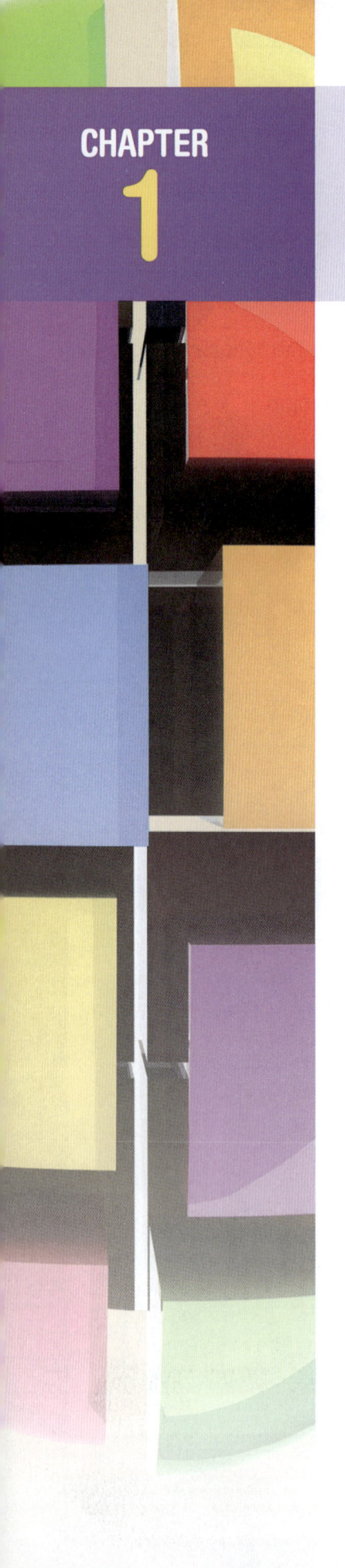

Introduction to Marketing

Sections

1.1 **Marketing Defined**
1.2 **Marketing Basics**

College and Career Readiness

Reading Prep
Before reading this chapter, review the key terms and definitions to preview the new content. Building a personal vocabulary is an important activity to broadening your understanding of new material.

Check Your Marketing IQ
Before you begin the chapter, see what you already know about marketing by taking the chapter pretest. The pretest is available at www.g-wlearning.com/marketing/.

◇DECA Emerging Leaders

Introduction

This learning activity, *DECA Emerging Leaders*, is designed for you to become familiar with DECA activities and connect them to chapter content. Where appropriate, the learning activity begins with identification of the career cluster, instructional area, and performance indicators associated with the activity content. Performance indicators are specific work-based skills and knowledge that identify what an employee must know or be able to do in order to achieve a performance element in an instructional area. Performance indicators define performance elements.

Career Cluster: Marketing
Instructional Area: Professional Development

Performance Indicators

- Explain marketing and its importance in a global economy.
- Explain career opportunities in marketing management.
- Assess the services of professional organizations in marketing.
- Employ career-advancement strategies in marketing.

Purpose

Designed for DECA members, this activity enables student members to better understand opportunities available through DECA in marketing, finance, hospitality, and management.

DECA's Comprehensive Learning Program consists of all DECA activities by category and supports programs of study in the four career clusters.

- **College, Business, and Educational Partnerships** provide scholarships, classroom presentations and career guidance, internships, work experience, and community service activities.
- **Competitive Events Program** provides authentic situations relating to current business practices.
- **DECA Direct Magazine** is a full-color international publication featuring articles on career development in leadership; community service; and professionalism.
- **Educational Conferences** provide targeted, highly focused learning experiences for members and advisors while connecting with corporate professionals.
- **Emerging Leader Series** strives to empower DECA members to provide effective leadership through goal setting, consensus building, and project implementation.
- **Global Entrepreneurship Week (GEW)** engages millions of young people around the world each November to embrace innovation, imagination, creativity, and problem solving.
- **School-Based Enterprises** reinforce and enhance career preparation.
- **Social Media Correspondent Program** creates conversation among chapters and shares best practices and ideas.
- **Video Challenges** provide classroom activities that challenge members to apply highly engaging, relevant learning activities from their seats in the classroom.

Procedure

1. DECA members should become familiar with the organization and its diverse learning activities. Use the following activities to learn about DECA, identify membership benefits, and apply DECA's connection to college and career preparation.
2. The information will be presented to you through the navigation of the DECA website. Visit the DECA website at www.deca.org to become familiar with the activities and opportunities available to you as a student and DECA member. Find the page for High School Programs and review the Comprehensive Learning Program.

Critical Thinking

1. Review the components of DECA's Comprehensive Learning Program.
2. Which activities enhance your career or personal goals? How do they help you achieve your career and personal goals?
3. Select two activities about which you wish to learn more and discuss them with your instructor.

Visit www.deca.org for more information.

Published by DECA Inc. Copyright © by DECA Inc. No part of this publication may be reproduced for resale without written permission from the publisher. Printed in the United States of America.

Section 1.1

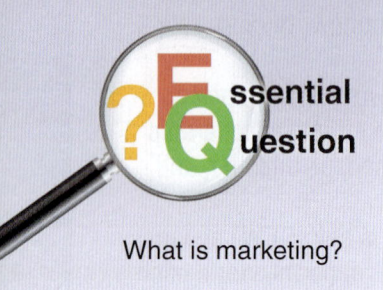

Essential Question
What is marketing?

Marketing Defined

Learning Objectives

LO 1.1-1   Discuss marketing.
LO 1.1-2   Identify why a student might study marketing.

Key Terms

marketing
need
want
product
good
service
idea
marketing professional
consumer

Marketing Is More Than an Advertisement

When you hear the term *marketing*, what goes through your mind? When asked this question, most people respond that marketing is advertising. Think of an advertisement you saw today or yesterday. What story did the advertisement tell? What impression did it leave on you? Did you think the advertisement was marketing? If you did, then you were correct. However, marketing is much more than just an advertisement.

Marketing consists of dynamic activities that identify, anticipate, and satisfy customer demand while making a profit. These activities help to tell the story of the company, the brand, the person, or the idea. The goal of marketing is to meet customer needs and wants with products they can and will buy. A **need** is something necessary for survival, such as food, clothing, and shelter. A **want** is something that a person desires, but could live without.

A **product** is a good, service, or idea. A **good** is a physical item that can be touched. A **service** is an action that is done for you, usually for a fee. An **idea** is a concept, cause, issue, image, or philosophy.

Marketing takes on both the risks and responsibilities of getting others to buy products. Activities involved in marketing include:

dcwcreations/Shutterstock.com

Marketing is more than just an advertisement. It tells a story about a company, person, brand, or idea. *What stories does marketing tell?*

- determining what type of research about customers is needed;
- deciding how to get products to customers;
- pricing, promoting, and selling the products; and
- deciding how to manage data and information.

There are many experts who express their ideas about the definition of marketing. These all have similar themes that revolve around selling products, connecting with customers, and satisfying customers' needs. A few examples of these definitions are as follows.

- Marketing is "to find out what your customers want and then give it to them," from Tim Cohn, marketing consultant.
- Marketing is "a way to connect what products and services you have to offer with customers who want and need such products and services," from Trish Green, Executive Vice President, Head of Marketing, Student Funding Group, LLC.
- The job of marketing is "to sell lots of stuff and make lots of money," from Sergio Zyman, former Chief Marketing Officer of The Coca-Cola Company.
- "Marketing is getting someone who has a need to know, like, and trust you," from John Jantsch, author of *Duct Tape Marketing*.

To fully define someone involved in marketing today, a broad term and definition is needed. A **marketing professional** is a person who helps determine the marketing needs of a company, develops and implements marketing plans, and focuses on customer satisfaction. In a small business, a marketing professional might also be the owner or a manager. In most large companies, marketing professionals usually work together as a marketing team.

LO 1.1-2 Why Study Marketing?

Marketing is global. No matter where you go or what you do, marketing will impact the decisions you make about what to buy, where to travel on vacation, and even what you eat for lunch today.

Learning about marketing will make you a better consumer. A **consumer** is a customer who buys a product for his or her own use. As a consumer, you need to make informed decisions about the products you buy. Knowledge about marketing will help you understand how businesses influence your purchasing decisions. Marketing includes the products businesses offer, the prices charged, and other information to help you make wise purchasing decisions.

Learning about marketing helps you learn how to market yourself. Marketing is not just for selling products, but for selling your talents and abilities as well. Whether you are job searching, applying for college, volunteering, or asking for a promotion, marketing can help prepare you for your future.

Case in Point

Eataly

The marketing concept is an approach to business that focuses on satisfying customer needs and wants while achieving profit goals for the company. Eataly is an example of a company that is completely focused on its customers and making sure they have an enjoyable experience at Eataly stores.

Eataly is a unique business with locations around the world. Each store is modeled after an open-air European market. The stores have a fresh market as well as multiple Italian eateries and cafés under one roof. The fresh market displays signage informing customers about each product, including its Italian history. Each of the Eataly restaurants uses ingredients sold in the fresh market.

Customers enjoy learning about what they are eating. Being able to shop for the food that is served in the restaurant is a unique touch customers cannot resist. Eataly also offers cooking classes at *La Scuola di Eataly*, or The School of Eataly, in Italian pastas, sauces, desserts, and more. To continue the experience after customers leave, cooking tips and recipes are available through social media and e-mail newsletters. Eataly separates itself from the competition by providing customers with unique products and information all in one convenient location.

A marketing professional helps determine the marketing needs of a company. *What aspects of a marketing career interest you?*

marketing will make you a better employee in any job field. Many people in a company will perform their job duties, but they often do not know the company's vision and what it wants to achieve. You can become a more valuable worker by understanding marketing functions and how to work with the company's marketing team.

Learning about marketing can influence your career path. You may have been talking all of your life about what you want to be when you grow up. Now the time is here, and you are making career plans. It is an exciting time in your life. There are many marketing careers you could pursue, including marketing manager, sales professional, market researching, buyer, or logistics professional. No matter what your talents are, there is a marketing career that will probably fit.

Later chapters will explore marketing careers in more depth. As you progress through the text, think about your personal connection with marketing. There may be a career waiting for you.

In the competitive working environment in the United States, employers look for workers who will add value to the business. Learning about

Section 1.1 Review

Check Your Understanding

1. What is the goal of marketing?
2. Explain the difference between a good and a service.
3. What is the broad term applied to a person who works in marketing?
4. How does learning about marketing make a person a better consumer?
5. Provide an example of a situation in which a person might need to market himself or herself.

Build Your Vocabulary

As you progress through this text, develop a personal glossary of key terms. This will help you build your vocabulary and prepare you for a career. Write a definition for each of the following terms and add them to your personal glossary.

consumer
good
idea
marketing
marketing professional

need
product
service
want

Section 1.2

Marketing Basics

Essential Question

Why is marketing necessary for business success?

Learning Objectives

LO 1.2-1   Discuss the marketing concept.
LO 1.2-2   Explain the marketing mix.
LO 1.2-3   Identify the seven functions of marketing.
LO 1.2-4   Define *economic utility*.
LO 1.2-5   Describe benefits of marketing.

Key Terms

marketing concept
market
business-to-consumer (B2C) market
business-to-business (B2B) market
target market
profit
marketing mix
price
place
promotion
promotional mix
channel
channel management
marketing-information management (MIM)
market planning
pricing
product/service management
selling
utility

Marketing Concept

LO 1.2-1

Marketing focuses on customers in order to meet their needs and wants. The **marketing concept** is an approach to business that focuses on satisfying customer needs and wants while achieving profit goals for the company. The three elements of the marketing concept are customer satisfaction, total company approach, and profit. These three elements overlap and work together, as illustrated in Figure 1-1.

Marketing is about building relationships between buyers and sellers. A long-term relationship leads to customers who are more satisfied and loyal to the business. Research has shown that it is less costly to keep a current customer than to attract a new one. Developing and maintaining relationships with customers is not only cost efficient, it is a good business practice.

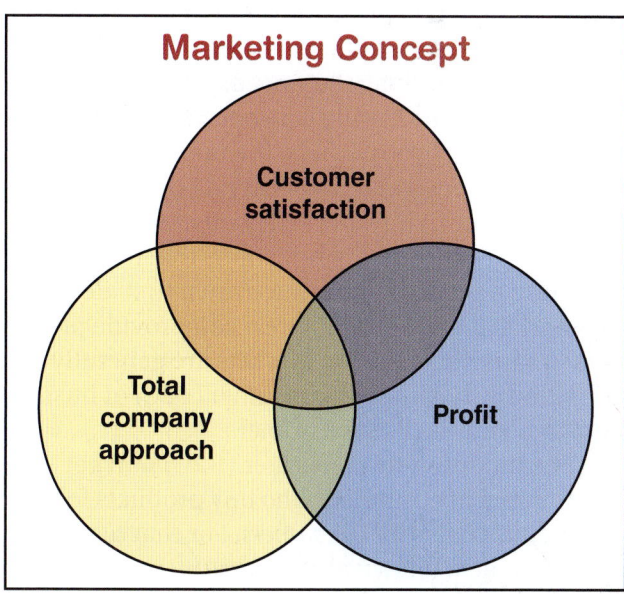

Goodheart-Willcox Publisher

Figure 1-1 The marketing concept is an approach to business that focuses on satisfying customer needs and wants while achieving profit goals for the company.

Exploring Marketing Careers

Marketing Manager

A company's marketing policies play a large role in the products or services it offers. People who work in marketing identify potential customers and develop strategies to market the company's products or services effectively to these customers. In addition, marketing professionals help keep the company on track by monitoring customer wants and needs and suggesting new products or services to satisfy those needs. Typical job titles for these positions include *marketing manager*, *marketing director*, *marketing coordinator*, *brand manager*, *commercial lines manager*, and *market development manager*.

Some examples of tasks that marketing professionals perform include:
- Coordinate marketing activities and policies to promote the company's products or services
- Develop marketing and pricing strategies
- Perform market research and analysis
- Coordinate or participate in promotional activities and trade shows to showcase the company's products or services

Marketing professionals need a strong background in sales and marketing strategy, as well as in principles of customer service and employee management. They need a solid knowledge of the English language, business and management principles, and media production and communication. Marketing professionals must also be able to think creatively and use critical thinking skills to solve problems. A bachelor's degree in marketing, advertising, communications, or a related field is required. Management positions generally require one to five years of work experience. For more information, access the *Occupational Outlook Handbook* online.

Customer Satisfaction

Customer satisfaction is the degree to which customers are pleased with a company's products. One of the ways it can be measured is by the number of repeat customers. The marketing concept benefits customers because the business is focused on meeting their needs.

Before the marketing concept can be implemented to satisfy customers, the market must be identified. A **market** is anywhere a buyer and a seller convene to buy and sell goods. It also refers to all the people and organizations that might purchase a product. A business must first identify the market it will serve before it can provide products to satisfy customers. Markets are generally classified as business to consumer (B2C) or business to business (B2B) customers.

- The **business-to-consumer (B2C) market** consists of customers who buy products for their own use, or *consumers*. For that reason, B2C is also known as the *consumer market*.
- The **business-to-business (B2B) market** consists of customers who buy products for use in a business rather than for personal use. These customers are called *clients* in the business market. The market also includes governmental agencies and other organizations.

Market identification is the process of identifying existing or potential customers as business to consumer (B2C) or business to business (B2B) customers. Each type of customer has specific needs and wants.

The B2C and B2B markets are large and it is necessary to target specific customers within those segments. A **target market** is the specific group of customers whose needs and wants a company will focus on satisfying. For example, a target

Marketing Ethics

Business Ethics

Ethics are the values that guide a person's behavior. Ethics help people make good decisions in both their personal and professional lives. *Business ethics* is a set of rules that help define appropriate behavior in the business setting.

Students are a target market for companies that sell school supplies. *In what ways do you think you might belong to a target market?*

market in B2C could be teens ages 16–18 who live in the southern United States. A target market in B2B could be governmental agencies located in Chicago, Illinois, that purchase tablet computers. Each of these target markets would be approached in a unique way to meet their specific needs.

Total Company Approach

Businesses using the marketing concept integrate the total company in the goal of customer satisfaction. Employees in production, finance, marketing, and management must work together as a team to achieve that goal.

Marketing-oriented companies believe that every interaction with a customer should be viewed as a marketing opportunity. This means every person in the business, from the delivery people to the technical support staff, has a goal of satisfying their customers. By sharing information about customers with production, finance, and management departments, marketing helps an entire business focus on customer satisfaction goals.

Profit

Profit is the difference between the income earned and expenses incurred by a business during a specific period of time. Businesses using the marketing concept understand that building a strong base of satisfied customers leads to healthy profits. Satisfied customers are repeat customers and repeat customers ensure higher sales. Satisfying customers successfully over the long term benefits businesses.

Successful businesses need more than just marketing. Marketing is just one piece of the puzzle. In order to understand marketing, it is necessary to understand the basic concepts of business. Business concepts are covered in Chapter 3.

LO 1.2-2 Marketing Mix

For each product that a company markets, a plan is developed called the marketing mix. The **marketing mix** is the strategy for using the elements of product, price, place, and promotion, as shown in Figure 1-2. Product, price, place, and promotion are known as the *four Ps of marketing*.

A marketing mix can be developed for a single product, a group of products, or an entire business. One marketing mix usually does not meet the needs of all customers. The keys to creating a successful marketing mix are:
- choosing the right product;
- selling it at the right price;
- making it available at the right place; and
- promoting it in a way that will reach the target customers.

Figure 1-2 The marketing mix is the strategy for using the elements of product, price, place, and promotion.

Product

Product may be the most important of the four Ps because without it, there are no sales. Price, place, and promotion relate directly to the product. Products include goods, services, and ideas. Examples of goods include laptops, boots, and cars. Examples of services include a haircut, a concert, and medical care. Examples of ideas include *contribute to a charity*, *buckle up for safety*, or *vote for this candidate*. Image has become a very important product. Marketers sell the image of goods and services, a business itself, and people.

Price

Price is the amount of money requested or exchanged for a product. A business can set prices at any level. However, if the price is too high, customers might not buy the product. If the price is too low, the business might not take in enough money to cover expenses necessary to make a profit. Determining the right price is a difficult task. There is no one formula for setting price. The goal of the business is to charge the exact amount a customer is willing to pay for an item. Setting the best price is important for both business success and customer satisfaction.

Place

In marketing, **place** refers to activities involved in getting a product or service to the end users. Place is also known as *distribution*. Physical distribution activities include shipping, order processing, inventory warehousing or storage, and stocking of goods.

Place decisions involve determining when, where, and how products get to customers. Place includes decisions about where to locate manufacturing plants, warehouses, and stores. It also involves making decisions about whether to have a physical store or an online store. Businesses try to make products available to customers at convenient times and places.

Promotion

Promotion is the process of communicating with potential customers in an effort to influence their buying behavior. It includes telling people about the price of the product and the place where it is offered. If customers do not know that a product exists, they cannot buy it. If customers do not know where to find a product, they will not be able to buy it.

Promotion is the most visible part of marketing. The **promotional mix** is a combination of the elements used in a promotional campaign and includes personal selling, advertising, sales promotion, and public relations. For example, a salesperson delivers promotional messages when he or she helps a customer to learn more about the product before making a purchase. Advertising delivers paid promotional messages on television, the radio, mobile apps, the Internet, video games, and through many other formats.

Functions of Marketing
LO 1.2-3

Marketing consists of hundreds of activities, and they can be organized in many different ways. *Function* is a general word for a category of activities. There are seven functions of marketing, as shown in the marketing core in Figure 1-3:
- channel management;
- marketing-information management (MIM);
- market planning;
- pricing;
- product/service management;
- promotion; and
- selling.

In a small company, these functions might be performed by one or two people. In a large corporation, each function might have its own department.

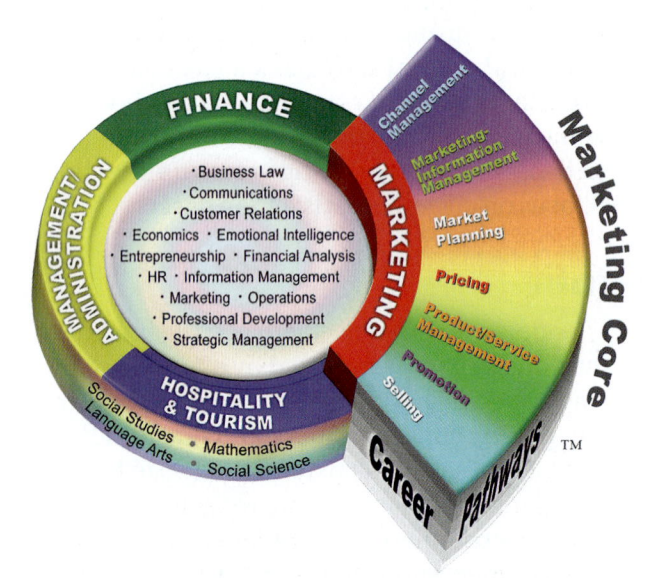

Copyright MBA Research, Columbus, Ohio. Used with permission.

Figure 1-3 There are seven functions of marketing.

Channel Management

A **channel** is a route a product takes from a producer to a customer. The **channel management** function is handling the activities involved in getting products through the different routes from producers to customers. These may include managing the methods used to transport and store goods, deciding where products are sold, finding sources for products, on-time delivery, and transferring product ownership. A channel can be as simple as a farmer having a roadside stand. It can also be as complicated as a product sold in 20 different countries that is built from parts produced in 17 different countries.

Marketing-Information Management (MIM)

The **marketing-information management (MIM)** function is gathering and analyzing information about markets, customers, industry trends, new technology, and competing businesses. It also includes making sure the right people in an organization get the information needed to make business decisions. MIM is also called *marketing research*. Activities might include developing surveys, analyzing survey results, preparing recommendations, and meeting with customers. If you have ever completed a survey for a store, research company, or political campaign, you have participated in marketing-information management.

Market Planning

The **market planning** function is analyzing the potential of different marketplaces in order to create strategies to target a specific market. Activities in market planning include identifying the target market, determining appropriate marketing strategies, setting a marketing budget, and using metrics to measure budget effectiveness.

Pricing

The **pricing** function is all the activities involved in setting prices for products. This includes researching and analyzing pricing of competitors. It also involves using financial information to set prices that cover costs and allow the business to make a profit, as well as adjust prices when conditions change. The price of the product also depends on what the customer is willing to pay. Pricing directly affects the profit of any business.

You Do the Math

Basic Math

Mathematics is an educational discipline that is used extensively in many other educational disciplines. Science, business, economics, accounting, engineering, and many other areas feature mathematics as an integral part of the discipline. For example, accountants must use math to calculate balance sheets, marketers must use math to forecast sales, engineers must use math to calculate loads, and economists must use math to calculate the gross domestic product.

Solve the following problems.

1. A store manager must calculate the total number of winter hats available to sell in the store from a starting number of 293. In the past month, the store sold 43 blue hats, 96 black hats, 28 red hats, and 61 pink hats. The store received a shipment of 48 blue hats, 60 black hats, 18 red hats, and 24 pink hats. How many total hats does the store have for sale?
2. The volume of liquid in a packaged product must be converted from cubic centimeters to cubic inches. One cubic centimeter is equal to 0.06 cubic inches, and the product's package contains 28.6 cubic centimeters of liquid. How many cubic inches of liquid are in the package?
3. A marketing manager must calculate the response rate for the latest e-mail marketing campaign. Over the course of the campaign, the marketing department sent 9,500 e-mails. The company received 1,022 responses from the promotional e-mail. What percentage of e-mails generated responses?
4. A restaurant must calculate how much flour to order for the week. Each day the restaurant sells 356 biscuits and 48 loaves of bread. One biscuit requires 0.045 pounds of flour and each loaf of bread requires 0.62 pounds of flour. How many pounds of flour must be ordered for the week (seven days)?

Product/Service Management

The **product/service management** function is determining which products a business should offer to meet customer needs. Activities can include developing a new product or service or improving a current one. In retail, product/service management includes deciding which products to carry or services to offer. Other decisions are about which brands, quantities, colors, sizes, features, or options to offer. One shoe store might sell many brands and styles of shoes, including athletic, dress, and casual shoes, as well as boots for children and adults. Another shoe store might focus on children's shoes or athletic shoes.

Promotion

Communicating with potential customers in an effort to influence their behavior is *promotion*. All communication from an organization to its customers and the public can be considered promotion. The promotional mix has four activities: personal selling, advertising, sales promotion, and public relations. For example, helping a customer in your school store choose a sweatshirt, posting promotional messages on Twitter, offering a discount if a customer shows an event ticket stub, or sending out a press release about the grand opening of a store are all promotional activities.

Selling

Selling is all personal communications with customers. Selling activities include helping customers in a store, making sales or product demonstrations, and providing any form of customer service. Personal selling is done most often in business sales and for large-ticket items in retail settings. For example, if you know someone who is in the market for a new car, that person will most likely talk with a salesperson as they are shopping for the new car.

Economic Utility

One of the major tasks of marketing is to provide economic utility. *Utility* means usefulness. In an economics context, **utility** is the characteristics of a product that satisfy human wants and needs. The process of adding utility is often referred to as adding value. *Adding value* means enhancing a feature or service to inspire a customer to purchase. There are five types of utility. Examples of each type are shown in Figure 1-4.

Form Utility

Form utility is the characteristic added when a business changes the form of something to make it more useful. The main job of the production is to add form utility. For example, an auto manufacturer turns steel, plastic, fabric, and glass into an automobile. In a service business, the performance of the service itself provides the utility. Marketing influences the creation of products in a business.

Place Utility

Place utility is the characteristic added when products are available at convenient places. For example, people often need to get cash when they are not near the bank. Financial institutions provide place utility through automated teller machines (ATMs) at convenient places, such as a supermarket or airport. Marketing guides business in adding place utilities.

tanuha2001/Shutterstock.com

Product/service management includes deciding which brands, quantities, colors, sizes, features, or options to offer. *How do you think a business makes these decisions?*

Utility Examples	
Form	Any manufacturing process
Place	Convenience stores
Time	Daily newspaper delivery
Information	Product advertising
Possession	Credit cards

Goodheart-Willcox Publisher

Figure 1-4 Each type of utility adds value to a product.

Time Utility

Time utility is the characteristic added when products are made available at the times that customers need and want them. For example, banks used to close at 4:00 p.m. and were never open on Saturdays. Many people who needed to do business at the bank were working during the time that banks were open. To provide time utility, most banks now stay open later, are open on Saturday mornings, or offer online banking 24 hours a day. Marketing research helps provide the data to make decisions about time utility.

Information Utility

Information utility is the characteristic added when marketing provides information about a product to a customer. A major part of information utility is telling the customer about products and where to buy them. Websites provide information utility by describing products and giving purchase opportunities. Advertising and other promotions provide information utility as well. Product information also includes providing directions or instructions, such as through owner manuals.

Possession Utility

Possession utility is the characteristic added when it becomes easier for a customer to acquire a product. Possession utility includes offering various kinds of credit. For example, you need a car to get to work, but you do not have enough money to pay for it. The car dealer provides possession utility by helping you arrange for a loan. The loan enables you to take possession and use the car while you are still paying for it.

Benefits of Marketing
LO 1.2-5

In today's world of information overload, it is often difficult to get the attention of customers. Marketing efforts can target the best customers, research how to improve a product, and find new ways to sell it. Without marketing, companies cannot grow and business profits would decline because there would be fewer sales. Workers would lose their jobs, and many businesses might close.

Marketing efforts help businesses sell more products and increase profits. When customers are spending more, companies are willing to invest more. They can expand a current business or start new ones. Marketing helps to create a positive cycle of economic growth.

> **Employability Skills**
>
> **Soft Skills**
>
> *Soft skills* are the skills used to communicate and work well with others. They are considered essential employability skills, which are skills that help an individual find a job, perform well in the workplace, and gain success in a job or career. Soft skills are also known as *people skills*.

Provides Information

Marketing provides information to educate consumers. Information about products enable customers to make educated decisions about purchases. For example, detailed labeling can provide information to the consumer to help make wise purchasing decisions. Green packaging encourages environmental protection. Educational material, such as nutrition labels, encourages healthy eating and can lead to improved standards of living.

Stimulates Competition

Marketing stimulates competition to create more and better products at competitive prices. Today's customers want products when, where, and how they want them. Customers have access to more information in one day than the generation before them had in one week. Instant information and the ability to shop around the world results in more products being available from many sources.

Improves the Economy

Marketing helps to create a positive cycle of economic growth by persuading people to buy goods and services. When customers are spending more, businesses sell more products and increase profits, helping the state of the economy.

Marketing positions account for a large portion of all jobs in the United States. Jobs are vital to the success of any community. Businesses are aware of the importance of their standing in the community. When an economy grows, more people are employed. More purchases are made and businesses can grow and help their communities more.

Identifies New Business Opportunities

Marketing activities help to identify new business opportunities. New products have been developed because market research showed the need for a change to an existing product or an entirely new product.

Marketing activities help to establish a brand and create loyal customers. It would be hard for a company to have loyal customers if marketing did not exist. Customers learn to trust and depend on certain businesses to meet their needs. People are more likely to buy from companies they know and trust.

Radu Bercan /Shutterstock.com

Part of information utility is providing instructions, such as these assembly instructions for a LEGO® Brand product. *How has a company provided information utility for you?*

Section 1.2 Review

Check Your Understanding

1. List three elements of the marketing concept.
2. Name the four elements of the marketing mix.
3. Provide examples of activities in the market planning function.
4. What does it mean to add value?
5. How does marketing improve the economy?

Build Your Vocabulary

As you progress through this text, develop a personal glossary of key terms. This will help you build your vocabulary and prepare you for a career. Write a definition for each of the following terms and add them to your personal glossary.

business-to-business (B2B) market
business-to-consumer (B2C) market
channel
channel management
market
marketing concept
marketing-information management (MIM)
marketing mix
market planning
place
price
pricing
product/service management
profit
promotion
promotional mix
selling
target market
utility

CHAPTER 1 Review and Assessment

Chapter Summary

Section 1.1 Marketing Defined

LO 1.1-1 Discuss marketing.
Marketing consists of dynamic activities that identify, anticipate, and satisfy customer demand while making a profit. The goal of marketing is to meet customer needs and wants with products they can and will buy. A marketing professional is a person who determines the marketing needs of a company, develops and implements marketing plans, and focuses on customer satisfaction.

LO 1.1-2 Identify why a student might study marketing.
Learning about marketing will make a student a better consumer and will help him or her learn how to sell his or her talents and abilities. It will also make a student a better employee who understands a company's vision. Learning about marketing can influence a career path because there is a marketing career that will probably fit a student's talents.

Section 1.2 Marketing Basics

LO 1.2-1 Discuss the marketing concept.
The marketing concept is an approach to business that focuses on satisfying customers while achieving profit goals for the company. The three elements of the marketing concept are customer satisfaction, total company approach, and profit.

LO 1.2-2 Explain the marketing mix.
The marketing mix is the strategy for using the elements of product, price, place, and promotion, known as the four Ps of marketing. Products include goods, services, and ideas. Price is the amount of money requested or exchanged for a product. Place involves getting a product to the end users. Promotion is communicating with potential customers to influence their buying behavior.

LO 1.2-3 Identify the seven functions of marketing.
There are seven functions of marketing: channel management, marketing-information management (MIM), market planning, pricing, product/service management, promotion, and selling.

LO 1.2-4 Define *economic utility*.
Utility is the characteristics of a product that satisfies human wants and needs. There are five types of utility: form, place, time, information, and possession.

LO 1.2-5 Describe benefits of marketing.
Marketing provides information to educate consumers and enable them to make educated decisions. Marketing stimulates competition to create more and better products at competitive prices. Marketing also helps create a positive cycle of economic growth by persuading people to buy goods and services. It also helps identify new business opportunities.

Check Your Marketing IQ

Now that you have completed the chapter, see what you have learned about marketing by taking the chapter posttest. The posttest is available at www.g-wlearning.com/marketing/.

Review Your Knowledge

1. Discuss marketing.
2. Explain the role of a marketing professional.
3. Identify why a student might study marketing.
4. Discuss the marketing concept.
5. Explain the concept of the marketing mix.
6. What are the keys to creating a successful marketing mix?
7. Identify the seven functions of marketing.

8. Explain different forms of economic utility.
9. Describe benefits of marketing.
10. How does marketing impact the economy?

Apply Your Knowledge

1. Identify three ways that marketing has influenced you.
2. There are many definitions of marketing. Now that you have read this chapter, what does marketing mean to you?
3. What inspired you to take this marketing course?
4. How will marketing play a role in your future?
5. Imagine yourself as a marketing professional. How would you make the customer the focus of your marketing activities?
6. How can you use the marketing concept to promote the school store or a CTSO?
7. In this text, you will be creating a marketing plan for a business you select. Make a list of several goods, services, or ideas that you would consider as the focus of a marketing plan.
8. Based on the last question, identify the customer for your chosen marketing product.
9. List three instances of marketing providing information that informed a purchasing decision of yours.
10. How has marketing influenced the economy of the area in which you live?

Apply Your Math Skills

Math skills will be important to a successful marketing career. Apply your math skills to solve the following problems.

1. Marcy purchased an airplane ticket to visit a college in another state. There were 159 other passengers on the plane. Each individual's ticket cost $114. How much money did the airline make on ticket sales for this flight?
2. Benny purchased a dishwasher from a department store for $600. The appliance has required repairs three times in six months. The repair company charged $75 for each service visit in addition to a rate of $25 per hour. The first service call took 3 hours. The second service call took 1 hour and required a new part which cost $20. The third service call took 1.5 hours. Benny is going to write a letter to the manufacturer of the dishwasher asking to be reimbursed for the cost of the repairs. How much money will he ask for?

Communication Skills

Reading Active reading is processing the words, phrases, and sentences you read. It is a complex task that involves concentration. Apply active reading skills while you read the Case in Point in this chapter. What was the purpose of the feature? Who was the intended audience?

Writing Write one or two paragraphs that clearly and accurately describe the concept of marketing as you interpret it. Select, organize, and analyze information to support your thoughts and ideas.

Speaking Impromptu speaking is talking without advance notice to plan what will be said. Engage in an impromptu conversation with a classmate about the functions of marketing. Express your thoughts and ideas clearly and persuasively. Build on the ideas of your conversation partner.

Internet Research

Definition of Marketing Conduct an Internet search for *definition of marketing*. After reading a number of different results, write your own definition of marketing.

Marketing Associations There are professional organizations that can help you become a marketing professional. Conduct Internet research on professional marketing associations. Select one that interests you and report how this organization can help a student learn more about a career in marketing.

Customer Service Conduct an Internet search for *best customer service in the United States*. Review the top companies listed in the search results. What practices make them the best? Determine whether there are any common themes among these companies. Write a paragraph about what makes these companies stand out for their customer service.

Teamwork

Together with a teammate, select a business that interests you. Select two of the products sold by this company. Create a poster that describes the company and its products. On the poster, describe each of the four Ps as they might be applied in the marketing mix for each product.

Portfolio Development

College and Career Readiness

Portfolio Overview When you apply for a job, community service, or college, you will need to tell others why you are qualified for the position. To support your qualifications, you will need to create a portfolio. A *portfolio* is a selection of related materials that you collect and organize to show your qualifications, skills, and talents to support a career or personal goal. For example, a certificate that shows you have completed lifeguard and first-aid training could help you get a job at a local pool as a lifeguard. An essay you wrote about protecting native plants could show that you are serious about ecofriendly efforts and help you get a volunteer position at a park. A transcript of your school grades could help show that you are qualified for college. A portfolio is a *living document*, which means it should be reviewed and updated on a regular basis.

Artists and other communication professionals have historically presented portfolios of their creative work when seeking jobs or admission to educational institutions. However, portfolios are now used in many professions.

Two formats of portfolios commonly used are print portfolios and digital portfolios. A digital portfolio may also be called an *e-portfolio*.

1. Use the Internet to search for *print portfolio* and *digital portfolio*. Read articles about each type of portfolio.
2. In your own words, compare and contrast a print portfolio with a digital one.

CHAPTER 2

Marketing Plan

Sections

2.1 **Researching a Marketing Plan**
2.2 **Developing a Marketing Plan**

Reading Prep

College and Career Readiness

Before reading this chapter, look at the chapter title. What can you predict will be presented?

Check Your Marketing IQ

Before you begin the chapter, see what you already know about marketing by taking the chapter pretest. The pretest is available at www.g-wlearning.com/marketing/.

◆DECA Emerging Leaders

Business Administration Core

Career Cluster: Marketing
Instructional Area: Emotional Intelligence

Performance Indicators
- Demonstrate responsible behavior.
- Demonstrate honesty and integrity.
- Demonstrate ethical work habits.
- Describe legal issues affecting businesses.

Purpose

Designed for DECA members, this activity helps individuals to understand opportunities available through DECA in marketing, finance, hospitality, and management.

DECA's Comprehensive Learning Program consists of all DECA activities by category and support programs of study in the four career clusters.

- **College, Business, and Educational Partnerships** provide scholarships, classroom presentations and career guidance, internships, work experience, and community service activities.
- **Competitive Events Program** provides authentic situations relating to current business practices.
- **DECA Direct Magazine** is a full-color international publication featuring articles on career development in leadership; community service; and professionalism.
- **Educational Conferences** provide targeted, highly focused learning experiences for members and advisors while connecting with corporate professionals.
- **Emerging Leader Series** strives to empower DECA members to provide effective leadership through goal setting, consensus building, and project implementation.
- **Global Entrepreneurship Week (GEW)** engages millions of young people around the world each November to embrace innovation, imagination, and creativity.
- **School-Based Enterprises** reinforce and enhance career preparation.
- **Social Media Correspondent Program** creates conversation among chapters and shares best practices and ideas.
- **Video Challenges** provide classroom activities that challenge members to apply highly engaging, relevant learning activities from their seats in the classroom.

Procedure

1. DECA members should become familiar with the organization and its diverse learning activities. Use the following activities to learn about DECA, identify membership benefits, and apply DECA's connection to college and career preparation. One way to learn about business culture is to become familiar with the company.
2. The information will be presented to you through the navigation of the DECA website. Visit the DECA website at www.deca.org to become familiar with the activities and opportunities available to you as a student and DECA member. Find the page for Partners and review the list of businesses that partner with DECA. Business partners include corporations, foundations, and associations that provide classroom presentations and career guidance, community service activities, internships and work experience, and scholarships.

Critical Thinking

1. Select three companies you wish to learn about based on your career goals.
2. For the companies you select, click on the website link and research the following: core values, corporate and social responsibilities, social policies, and history.
3. Record the information you discovered. Keep the information for use as you make college and career decisions.
4. What conclusions can you draw about the companies as it relates to their ethical behavior and social responsibility?
5. Find at least two classmates who researched the same DECA college and business partners. Compare your findings.

Visit www.deca.org for more information.

Published by DECA Inc. Copyright © by DECA Inc. No part of this publication may be reproduced for resale without written permission from the publisher. Printed in the United States of America.

Section 2.1

Essential Question

Why does a business need a marketing plan?

Researching a Marketing Plan

Learning Objectives

LO 2.1-1 State the purpose of a marketing plan.
LO 2.1-2 Define *situation analysis* and identify its components.
LO 2.1-3 Explain a target market.
LO 2.1-4 Describe a competitive analysis.

Key Terms

marketing plan
situation analysis
SWOT analysis
environmental scan
PEST analysis
market segmentation
competition
competitive analysis
market size
market share
market potential

LO 2.1-1 Marketing Plan

Benjamin Franklin once said, "If you fail to plan, you are planning to fail." This is true in both your personal and professional lives. In your personal life, you have probably made plans for a trip with friends or tried to organize an activity for a larger group. Without a plan, it probably never happened. Similarly, successful marketing efforts take time, money, and planning.

A **marketing plan** is a document that describes business and marketing goals and the strategies and tactics that will be used to achieve them. One way to understand a marketing plan is to think of the document as a set of travel plans. The marketing goals are *where* you plan to travel, such as to Ireland, Asia, or the East Coast. The marketing strategies are *how* to get to the destination, such as flying, taking a

A marketing plan describes business and marketing goals and the strategies and tactics that will be used to achieve them. *How does detailed planning contribute to success?*

Pepsco Studio/Shutterstock.com

train, or driving. The marketing tactics are the specific *paths* taken to reach the final destination, such as highways and roads.

The market planning function is responsible for creating an actionable marketing plan and is written by a marketing manager. In a small company, there may only be one marketing manager who creates the plan for the entire company. Large companies generally have multiple marketing managers who are responsible for individual product lines. Each marketing manager completes a plan for his or her product line.

Preparing a marketing plan takes time and research. Marketers spend many months gathering information about the past performance of the company. They then analyze how marketing could influence future company performance. As research is conducted, resources that are used should be documented. A *bibliography* lists all the sources used as resources to develop the marketing plan. A bibliography is shown in Figure 2-1. Resources might include interviews, books, periodicals, websites, and other information gathered for the plan. The bibliography should be created when the writing process begins so that each source can be added as it is used.

Marketing plans are usually written a year in advance of being implemented. They can, and should, be modified throughout the year to address market changes or take advantage of new opportunities. Established companies generally have a set format that outlines the components that are included in a marketing plan. However, if a format is not established, there are many professional organizations, such as the American Marketing Association (AMA), that provide templates free of charge.

Marketing plans are read by company executives, shareholders, and select members of the sales, marketing, and product development teams. If the company is seeking additional funding from outside sources, the marketing plan will accompany the request for funding. This is the opportunity to show how marketing can help drive future sales and profits for the company.

As you progress through this text, you will be writing your own marketing plan. The template you will use is shown in Figure 2-2.

Marketing Plan

Title Page
Table of Contents
  I. Executive Summary
  II. Business Description
      A. Overview
      B. Vision Statement
      C. Mission Statement
      D. Company Goals
  III. Market Analysis
      A. SWOT Analysis
      B. Environmental Scan (PEST Analysis)
      C. Competitive Analysis
  IV. Sales Analysis
      A. Sales History and Projection
      B. Best Opportunities
      C. Sales Goals
  V. Marketing Strategies
      A. Marketing Goals
      B. Target Market
      C. Marketing Mix
          1. Product Strategies
          2. Price Strategies
          3. Place Strategies
          4. Promotion Strategies
      D. Product Positioning
  VI. Action Plan
      A. Timeline
      B. Budget
      C. Metrics
  VII. Bibliography
  VIII. Appendices

Goodheart-Willcox Publisher

Figure 2-2 A marketing plan usually includes each of the elements listed in this outline.

Bibliography

"Employment Situation Summary." Bureau of Labor Statistics. United States Department of Labor. April 7, 2017.
https://www.bls.gov/news.release/empsit.nr0.htm

McCarthy, Alison. "News App Usage Rises Worldwide." eMarketer. February 7, 2017. https://www.emarketer.com/Article/News-App-Usage-Rises-Worldwide/1015151

Wallace, Tracey. "Ecommerce Trends in 2017: 135 Statistics About Online Selling." *The BigCommerce Blog*. April 13, 2017.
https://www.bigcommerce.com/blog/ecommerce-trends/

Goodheart-Willcox Publisher

Figure 2-1 The bibliography is an important record of the information sources used to write the marketing plan.

Situation Analysis

To properly prepare a marketing plan, the environment in which the business operates must be evaluated. A business cannot determine where to go or how to get there without knowing where it has been. A **situation analysis** is a snapshot of the environment in which a business has been operating over a given period of time, usually the last 12 to 16 months. The situation analysis evaluates internal and external environments as they relate to marketing and sales.

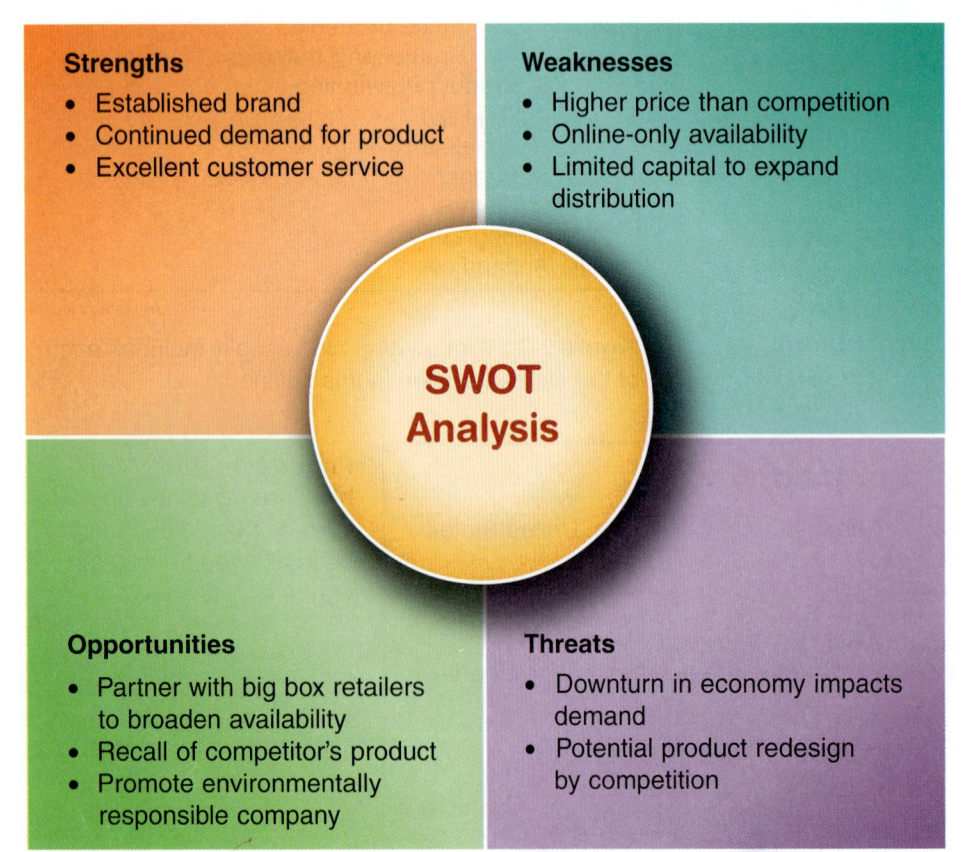

SWOT Analysis

A **SWOT analysis** identifies strengths, weaknesses, opportunities, and threats the business faces. It is an internal analysis that helps to explain why the company's product is different or better than those offered by the competition.
- *Strengths* are internal factors that give a company a competitive advantage.
- *Weaknesses* are internal factors that place a company at a disadvantage relative to competitors.
- *Opportunities* are external factors that provide chances for a company to increase profits.
- *Threats* are external factors, such as the economy, that can potentially jeopardize a company's growth or ability to make profits.

For example, a SWOT analysis looks at whether the business offers a wider variety, better prices, or better sizing than the competitors. A SWOT analysis can be presented similar to the format in Figure 2-3.

Environmental Scan

A review should be completed of the external environment that the business will encounter. An **environmental scan** is an analysis of the external factors that affect the success of business.

One way to complete an environmental scan is to conduct a **PEST analysis**, which is an evaluation of the political, economic, social, and technological factors in a certain market or geographic region that may impact the success of a business. This process identifies potential opportunities and threats to a company's business plans and strategies.
- *Political factors* affect the stability of the government and the success of the businesses that operate within it.

Strengths
- Established brand
- Continued demand for product
- Excellent customer service

Weaknesses
- Higher price than competition
- Online-only availability
- Limited capital to expand distribution

Opportunities
- Partner with big box retailers to broaden availability
- Recall of competitor's product
- Promote environmentally responsible company

Threats
- Downturn in economy impacts demand
- Potential product redesign by competition

Figure 2-3 A SWOT analysis identifies strengths, weaknesses, opportunities, and threats the business faces.

Goodheart-Willcox Publisher

- *Economic factors* affect the ability of consumers to purchase products, as well as the cost of doing business.
- *Social factors* are the cultural aspects within a business environment and the personal qualities of its customers, such as age, gender, income, ethnicity, education level, occupation, marital status, and family size.
- *Technological factors* affect the ease with which a business can operate within a market or region, as well as the level of productivity possible once the business is in operation.

A PEST analysis can be presented in a format similar to the one in Figure 2-4.

Target Market
LO 2.1-3

Research must be completed in order to accurately define the customer. A *target market* is the specific group of customers at which a company aims its products and services. These are the people whose wants and needs are fulfilled by the products a business offers. They are also the people most likely to buy the goods or services. Target markets have four characteristics:

- clearly defined wants and needs the business can meet;
- money to buy the product;
- willingness and ability to buy the product; and
- enough customers to be profitable.

Depending on the products a company offers, it may be wise to segment the target market. The process of dividing a large market into smaller groups is called **market segmentation**. A *market segment* is the smaller group of people, businesses, or

Employability Skills

Professional Image

An *image* is the perception others have of a person based on that person's dress, behavior, and speech. It is what people remember about a person from business, professional, and even social interactions. A *professional image* is the image an individual projects in the professional world. A positive professional image projects honesty, skill, courtesy, and respect for others.

Political
- Changes in state and federal government leadership
- Trade regulations
- Employment laws and regulations

Economic
- Stability of the economy
- Interest rates and availability of financing
- Costs of business resources

Social
- Lifestyle trends
- Population growth rates
- Cultural influences

Technological
- Up-to-date communication technology infrastructure
- Market expectations of technology integration
- Emerging technologies

PEST Analysis

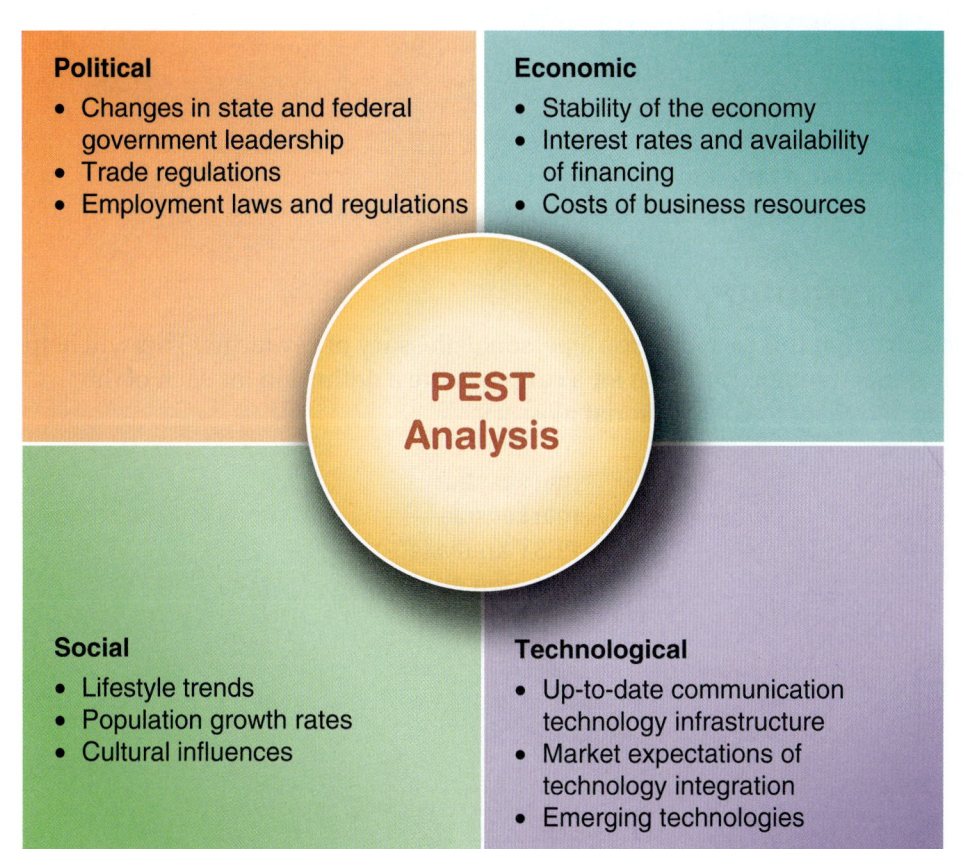

Figure 2-4 A PEST analysis is an evaluation of the political, economic, social, and technological factors in a certain market or geographic region that may impact the success of a business.

Goodheart-Willcox Publisher

organizations with common characteristics or needs. The market may be segmented by lifestyle factors, habits, demographics, or another set of factors unique to the business. Market segments eventually become target markets for various products or businesses. By breaking the market into segments, messages can be targeted to specific groups. The way in which the message is delivered to each group may also change.

LO 2.1-4 Competitive Analysis

Understanding the competition is part of marketing research. **Competition** is two or more businesses attempting to attract the same customers. One of the most important parts of the marketing plan is the section that describes other businesses competing for customers. In order for a company to achieve sales goals, it may need to take business away from the competition. The sales team will be helpful in providing information about competitors.

A **competitive analysis** is a tool used to compare the strengths and weaknesses of a product or company that competes with a business. In the analysis, competitors are listed with their physical locations, product lines, pricing, and market share. These grids are used to analyze the strengths and weaknesses of the competition. From this information, marketers can determine how the company will compete with others to gain its share of sales in the market.

Learning about the competition includes estimating the portion of the market that each competitor holds. **Market size** is the total sales per year for a specific product held by all the competing businesses. **Market share** is the percentage of total sales in a market that is held by one business. **Market potential** is the maximum number of customers and amount of sales that can be generated from a specific segment in a defined time period.

Section 2.1 Review

Check Your Understanding

1. Who is responsible for writing the marketing plan?
2. What are the components of a SWOT analysis?
3. What information does a PEST analysis identify?
4. List the characteristics of a target market.
5. List examples of information included in a competitive analysis.

Build Your Vocabulary

As you progress through this text, develop a personal glossary of key terms. This will help you build your vocabulary and prepare you for a career. Write a definition for each of the following terms and add them to your personal glossary.

competition
competitive analysis
environmental scan
marketing plan
market potential
market segmentation

market share
market size
PEST analysis
situation analysis
SWOT analysis

Section 2.2

Developing a Marketing Plan

Essential Question
How does a marketing manager develop a marketing plan?

Learning Objectives

LO 2.2-1 Identify components of the opening section of a marketing plan.
LO 2.2-2 Describe the analysis section of a marketing plan.
LO 2.2-3 Discuss marketing strategy.
LO 2.2-4 State the purpose of the action plan for a marketing plan.

Key Terms

business plan
vision statement
mission statement
SMART goal
marketing strategy
product positioning
action plan
marketing tactic
budget
metrics

LO 2.2-1 Opening Section

The opening section of a marketing plan provides an overview and a snapshot of the business with information from the business plan. This section is usually divided into Executive Summary and Business Description subsections.

Executive Summary

A marketing plan usually begins with an executive summary. An *executive summary* provides an overview by highlighting the critical points in the plan. The goal is to provide a snapshot that will entice the reader to review the entire document. Even though the executive summary is the beginning of the marketing plan, it should be written last. The executive summary should be kept short, to the point, and not more than two pages in length.

Business Description

The business description presents an overview of the business as outlined in the business plan. A **business plan** is a written document that describes a business,

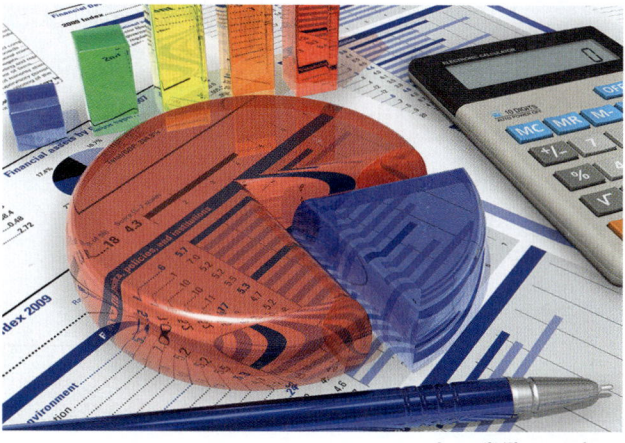

Scanrail1/Shutterstock.com

To properly prepare a marketing plan, the environment in which the business operates must be evaluated. *How might the business environment impact marketing activities?*

how it operates, and how it makes a profit. This information may be condensed, but anything created by company executives should not be edited or changed.

In the business description section, the product is described and the business is identified as an online business, a brick-and-mortar store, or a combination. The vision statement, mission

Copyright Goodheart-Willcox Co., Inc.

statement, and company goals will also be stated. This information shows how the marketing plan aligns with the overall direction of the business.

Vision Statement

A **vision statement** is what the business aspires to accomplish. The vision statement is like looking into a crystal ball and seeing the future of the company. One example of a vision statement is, "To become the safest, most customer-focused manufacturer in the world." A good vision statement should inspire employees and help drive the business.

Mission Statement

The **mission statement** is the company message to customers about why the business exists. It describes the business, identifies the customers, and shows how the business adds value. One example of a mission statement is, "Providing the most fuel-efficient cars to help you save money and the environment."

Company Goals

Company goals project where the business should be this year and up to five years in the future. These goals lay the foundation for revenue projections. They are written by the executive team and are found in the business plan or annual report.

Analysis Section

The analysis section details information about market and sales analyses that have been performed. This detail is necessary to understand both the environment in which the business is operating and the business goals to be met. This section includes Market Analysis and Sales Analysis subsections.

TORWAISTUDIO/Shutterstock.com

A marketing plan can be viewed as a set of travel plans. *Why do you think goal setting is important in marketing?*

Market Analysis

The information gathered through the SWOT, environmental scan, and competitive analyses is described here. Charts may be included to describe and illustrate the content. If the charts are brief, they can be embedded in the copy. If they are lengthy, they can be included in the *appendices* with an in-text reference noting where they can be found. The appendices may also include financial projections, data about the target market or competitors, and other documents that support the plan. These documents should be arranged in a logical order and listed in the table of contents under the Appendices section.

Case in Point

Zappos

Zappos is an online shoe and clothing retailer that is well known for its variety of products and excellent service. It is a billion-dollar entity with a marketing plan to continue growing every year.

Marketing strategies are the decisions made to execute the marketing plan and meet the goals of the business. Zappos has a defined marketing strategy that has helped make it a successful business. Their strategy is a basic premise focused on customer recommendations, mostly via social media, and of the great customer experience of buying clothing and shoes on the website.

Marketing tactics are the specific activities implemented to carry out the marketing strategies. Zappos limits its marketing dollar investment to low-cost tactics, including search engine marketing that uses brand names or styles of shoes. This supports the Zappos customer experience by making it easy for the customer to find the product desired. Other low-cost tactics used by Zappos are free shipping and easy returns, which encourage customers to buy again and again. Their marketing strategy is a grass-roots example of customer focus and the success that it can bring.

Social Media

Social Media as a Marketing Tool

The Merriam-Webster Dictionary defines social media as "forms of electronic communication (such as websites for social networking and microblogging) through which users create online communities to share information, ideas, personal messages, and other content, such as videos." Social media plays an important part in your life every day of the week. You use social media to build your personal brand, develop a community, and communicate with others.

Businesses have also learned the many advantages that social media can provide. Social media is one tool that can complement a company's marketing strategies when used wisely. One of the things social media can add to the marketing plan is helping the business be visible. By communicating regular updates on products, events, or customer feedback, a company can help keep its brand in front of customers.

Sales Analysis

The sales analysis section will help determine future sales goals. Before sales goals can be created, however, it is necessary to analyze sales history, make sales forecasts, and evaluate the best sales opportunities.

Sales History and Projections

To create a marketing plan for a specific product or product line, the previous sales by year, up to five years, will be reviewed. The market share is also noted. These numbers are analyzed and future sales projections are made. *Sales projections*, or *forecasts*, are the dollars and units of product the company wants to achieve. The sales and executive teams create these forecasts. Sales forecasts are typically made for a minimum of one year and from three to five years in the future.

Best Opportunities

The best opportunities for making new and repeat sales should be clearly defined. This information comes from market research and sales team feedback. The marketing team works with the sales team by assisting them to identify opportunities, such as identifying the top ten sales opportunities that will be pursued in the upcoming year. Opportunities to take business away from competitors, expand in new geographic areas, and other potential sales sources are also identified.

Sales Goals

Sales goals are written based on sales history, sales projections, and best opportunities. The goals identify where new and repeat sales can be generated and at what levels. Customer targets or geographic regions are defined.

For goals to be as effective as possible, they should be written as SMART goals. A **SMART goal** is one that is specific, measurable, attainable, realistic, and timely, as shown in Figure 2-5.
- *Specific.* A goal should be specific and straightforward.
- *Measurable.* Progress toward a goal should be measurable.
- *Attainable.* A goal needs to be attainable.
- *Realistic.* A goal must be realistic.
- *Timely.* A goal should have a starting point and an ending point.

LO 2.2-3 Marketing Strategies Section

Marketing strategies are the decisions made to execute the marketing plan and meet the goals of

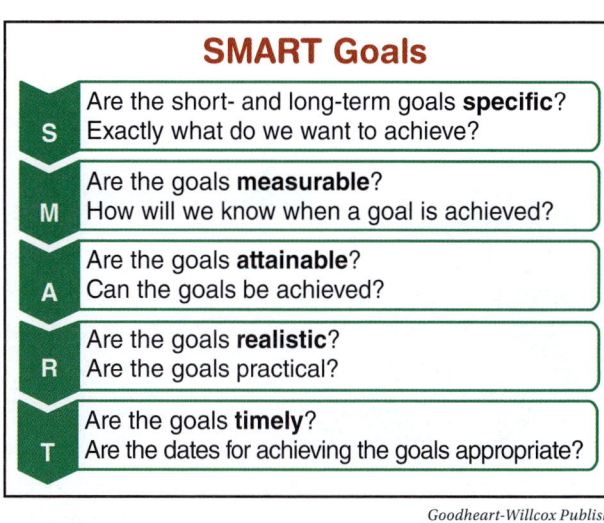

SMART Goals

S	Are the short- and long-term goals **specific**? Exactly what do we want to achieve?
M	Are the goals **measurable**? How will we know when a goal is achieved?
A	Are the goals **attainable**? Can the goals be achieved?
R	Are the goals **realistic**? Are the goals practical?
T	Are the goals **timely**? Are the dates for achieving the goals appropriate?

Goodheart-Willcox Publisher

Figure 2-5 SMART goals are specific, measurable, attainable, realistic, and timely.

the business. These strategies outline the *who, what, where,* and *how* of the marketing process. They include establishing marketing goals, identifying the target market, and defining components of the marketing mix. The product positioning can then be defined.

Marketing Goals

Marketing goals are simple and clear statements of the results to be accomplished through marketing efforts. These goals can be specific, such as a target end-of-year sales figure or a percentage increase in number of customers. They can also be stated in broader terms, as in achieving a high level of customer satisfaction. Marketing goals should be realistic, measurable, and should support the business goals. The marketing goals provide big-picture direction for the efforts of the marketing team. They should clearly state the intended results of the marketing strategies and provide direction for the marketing team.

Target Market

The information gained from research on the target market is recorded in this section of the marketing plan. One of the most important decisions a marketer makes is correctly choosing the best target market. Selecting the wrong target market means the business loses an opportunity for success in a different one.

Many businesses select more than one target market. However, each one selected must meet the four characteristics of a target market. If these characteristics are not met, the business will probably not meet its sales goals.

Marketing Mix

In Chapter 1, you learned about the four Ps that make up the marketing mix: product, price, place, and promotion. Decisions about the marketing mix are the basis of a marketing plan. Those decisions provide the important framework for choosing specific marketing strategies and tactics to implement the plan.

Product Strategies

Product strategies are the decisions made about which products a business should sell. Product strategies can include decisions on quantities, sizes, packaging, warranties, brand names, image, and design. In an established company, these decisions may already be in place.

Price Strategies

Price strategies are the business decisions about pricing and how prices are set to make a profit. The marketing plan covers price points, percentage of annual sales, and expected profit by product. Evaluating how prices compare to the competition is also part of developing a price strategy. Pricing policies affect company image.

Place Strategies

Place strategies are the decisions about how and where products are produced, acquired, shipped, and sold to customers. The sales team is a good source of information to help make some of the place decisions because they are in direct contact with the customers. Place strategies involve not only a physical location, but how goods or services are distributed. Is the product offered online, internationally, locally, or through other stores?

Promotion Strategies

Promotion strategies are decisions about which selling, advertising, sales promotions, and public relations activities to use in the promotional mix. The *promotional mix* is a combination of the elements used in a promotional campaign. A promotional mix can include any or all of the promotional elements shown in Figure 2-6.

Promotion decisions also include who will handle specific promotions and public relations efforts. Large companies may have a communications team that works with the marketing team to help create the advertising and sales pieces. However, in many companies, the marketing manager may be responsible for all promotion strategies. For both current and new products, it is important to describe the benefits as they relate to how the product will make life better for the customer.

dean bertoncelj/Shutterstock.com

Product strategies are the decisions made about which products a business should sell. *How does the target market affect product strategies?*

Chapter 2 Marketing Plan 31

Green Marketing

Green Marketing Defined

Being responsible with natural resources and making ecofriendly choices are important in a world that is increasingly environmentally conscious. *Green marketing* is producing and promoting products using methods and practices that emphasize environmental conservation. *Going green* integrates a variety of activities that are friendly to the earth and the environment.

Businesses can use green marketing strategies in all aspects of the marketing mix. Green marketing includes creating products that are ecofriendly and distributing them using environmentally conscious methods. For example, companies often find unique ways to use recycled paper, plastic, metal, and glass in the manufacturing of their products and choose shipping methods that have a reduced or neutral carbon footprint. Many customers place priority on being loyal to businesses that are environmentally friendly.

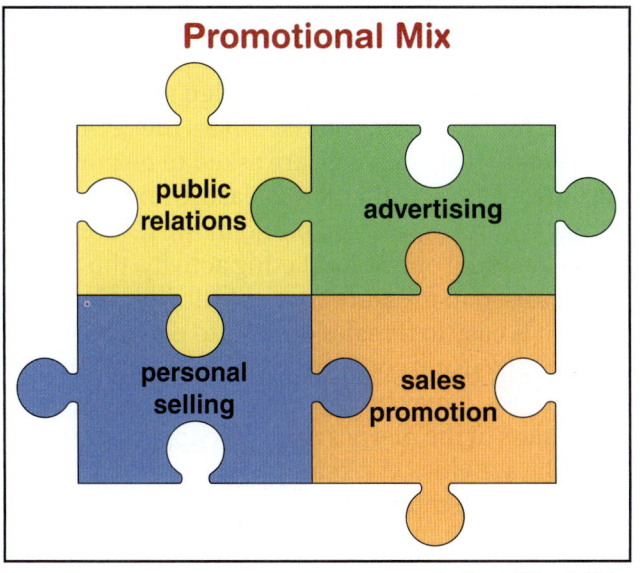

Promotional Mix

- public relations
- advertising
- personal selling
- sales promotion

Goodheart-Willcox Publisher

Figure 2-6 The pieces of the promotional mix fit together to form a promotional campaign.

Product Positioning

Product positioning is the process used to influence the customer's perception of a brand or product in relation to the competition. Marketers use the components of the marketing mix—product, price, place, and promotion—to uniquely identify what the company offers in terms of goods and services. The goal is to *position* the product as better than the competition in some specific way. For example, Geico Insurance positions itself as, "More than just car insurance." This positioning statement informs the consumer that the product, insurance, is available to protect other assets in addition to automobiles. It implies that the offering is different or better than the competition.

LO 2.2-4 Action Plan Section

The **action plan** is a list of the marketing tactics with details about how to execute each tactic. **Marketing tactics** are the specific activities implemented to carry out the marketing strategies. Every marketing strategy will have a set of tactics designed to accomplish it. As an example, for the strategy *price products at or below the competition*, tactics might include the following.

- Monitor online competition prices every Monday.
- Monitor sales, advertising, and coupons in the local weekend papers.
- Meet with the vice president every Tuesday to review competitive pricing information.
- Reset prices as needed.

A strong marketing plan includes an action plan to ensure the marketing efforts remain on track and funds are spent wisely. Three components of an action plan include a timeline, budget, and metrics.

Timeline

The timeline lists when each activity starts, where it happens or runs, end date, and the person responsible. A timeline keeps the marketing team on track and moves the plan forward. A spreadsheet can be beneficial when creating a timeline.

Budget

A **budget** is a financial plan for a fixed period of time that reflects anticipated revenue and shows how it will be allocated in the operation of the business.

Copyright Goodheart-Willcox Co., Inc.

You Do the Math

Order of Operations

The *order of operations* is a set of rules stating which operations in an equation are performed first. The order of operations is often stated using the acronym *PEMDAS*, which stands for parentheses, exponents, multiplication, division, addition, and subtraction. This means anything inside parentheses is computed first. Exponents are computed next. Then, any multiplication and division operations are computed. Finally, any addition and subtraction operations are computed to find the answer to the problem. The equation is solved from left to right by applying PEMDAS.

Solve the following problems.
1. $8 - (4 \times 3) + 2^3 \div 2 =$
2. $11^2 + (45 \times 2) =$
3. $3 + 4 - 27 \div 9 =$

Most businesses base the overall marketing budget on a percentage of sales generated for the company or other factors related to sales. A detailed budget shows the costs to implement the planned marketing tactics and promotional activities. Some tactics may include several sets of costs. Once again, a spreadsheet is helpful in creating and tracking the budget. List each marketing activity and its related cost.

Metrics

Metrics are standards of measurement. Marketing is an expensive part of operating a business. The company executives expect a system to measure marketing effectiveness in order to justify the expense. Metrics should be created for campaigns to determine the success rate of each related action.

Hard metrics are standards that can be measured, such as the click-through rates of an e-mail campaign. A minimum number of clicks can be established to determine the successfulness of the campaign.

Soft metrics are standards that are not easily measured. For example, a campaign may be created for brand awareness. Unless the recipients of the marketing message are asked to respond in some way, it is difficult to measure how many people will recognize the brand in the future.

Depending on the marketing activity, the metrics used to measure success will differ. In some cases, it is easy to tie sales directly to marketing activities by using coupons or electronic offer codes. Other times, it may be harder to track direct sales. Regardless of the metrics used, it is important to track the activities of all campaigns to determine if they are worth repeating.

Section 2.2 Review

Check Your Understanding

1. Explain the purpose of an executive summary in a marketing plan.
2. List two components of the marketing plan's analysis section.
3. What are marketing goals?
4. Define each of the strategies for the four Ps of the marketing mix.
5. List three components of the action plan section.

Build Your Vocabulary

As you progress through this text, develop a personal glossary of key terms. This will help you build your vocabulary and prepare you for a career. Write a definition for each of the following terms and add them to your personal glossary.

action plan	marketing tactic	product positioning
budget	metrics	SMART goal
business plan	mission statement	vision statement
marketing strategy		

CHAPTER 2 Review and Assessment

Chapter Summary

Section 2.1 Researching a Marketing Plan

LO 2.1-1 State the purpose of a marketing plan.
A marketing plan is a document that describes business and marketing goals and the strategies and tactics that will be used to achieve them. The market planning function is responsible for creating an actionable marketing plan designed to achieve business goals.

LO 2.1-2 Define *situation analysis* and identify its components.
The situation analysis evaluates internal and external environments as they relate to marketing and sales. A SWOT analysis identifies company strengths, weaknesses, opportunities, and threats the business faces. An environmental scan is an analysis of the external factors that affect the success of business.

LO 2.1-3 Explain a target market.
A target market is the specific group of customers at which a company aims its products and services. These are the people whose wants and needs are fulfilled by the products a business offers. They are the people most likely to buy the goods or services.

LO 2.1-4 Describe a competitive analysis.
A competitive analysis is used to compare the strengths and weaknesses of a product or company that competes with a business. This information helps marketers determine how the company will compete to gain its share of sales in the market.

Section 2.2 Developing a Marketing Plan

LO 2.2-1 Identify components of the opening section of a marketing plan.
The opening section provides an overview and a snapshot of the business with information from the business plan. This section is usually divided into Executive Summary and Business Description subsections.

LO 2.2-2 Describe the analysis section of the marketing plan.
The analysis section provides detailed information about the market and sales analyses that have been performed. This detail is necessary to understand both the environment in which the business is operating and the business goals to be met.

LO 2.2-3 Discuss marketing strategy.
Marketing strategies are the decisions made to execute the marketing plan and meet the goals of the business. They include establishing goals, identifying the target market, defining components of the marketing mix, and defining the product positioning.

LO 2.2-4 State the purpose of the action plan for a marketing plan.
The action plan is a list of the marketing tactics with detailed plans to execute each tactic. It ensures the marketing efforts remain on track and funds are spent wisely. Three components of an action plan include a timeline, budget, and metrics.

Check Your Marketing IQ

Now that you have completed the chapter, see what you have learned about marketing by taking the chapter posttest. The posttest is available at www.g-wlearning.com/marketing/.

Review Your Knowledge

1. State the purpose of a marketing plan.
2. Define *situation analysis* and identify its components.
3. Explain a target market.

4. Why is it important to research competing businesses?
5. What factors can be used to estimate the portion of a market that each competitor holds?
6. Identify the components of the opening section of a marketing plan.
7. Describe the analysis section of a marketing plan.
8. Explain the best sales opportunities information included in the analysis section.
9. Discuss marketing strategy.
10. State the purpose of an action plan for a marketing plan.

Apply Your Knowledge

1. List three topics you will need to research when writing your marketing plan.
2. Choose a local company with which you are familiar. Brainstorm what each of the four Ps of the marketing mix might be for that business.
3. Think about students at your school as a target market. What types of promotions appeal to students at your school the most?
4. Create a Venn diagram to compare two local businesses. Write the name of one local company as the heading for the first circle. Identify a competitor for that business as the heading for the second circle. In the first circle, list the strengths and attributes of the first business. In the second circle, list those of its competitor. In the center, list what the two businesses have in common.
5. Conduct a SWOT analysis for your school-based enterprise or for another local company.
6. Failure to conduct research is one of the reasons some marketing plans fail. List the ways you would research your idea for a marketing plan. How can you ensure that your plan will not fail?
7. The bibliography lists all of the resources used to develop the marketing plan. Make a list of resources you think would be useful when conducting research for your marketing plan.
8. The ideas that you explored in question one may be a starting place for the marketing plan you will be writing. Write a letter or e-mail to one or two businesses to request information about their marketing plans and what research they conducted. Explain why you chose those businesses.
9. Identify political, economic, social, and technological factors that affect the business you select for your marketing plan.
10. Choose a promotion or advertisement for a local business. How do you think the business tracks activity related to the promotion or advertisement? In your opinion, how could the business measure the success of the promotion or advertisement?

Apply Your Math Skills

Many businesses base the overall marketing budget on a percentage of company sales. Using this method, marketing budgets vary depending on the size of the business. Apply your math skills to solve the following problems.

1. Elaine opened a new specialty gift store. As a new business, she does not have an established sales figure to use in determining a marketing budget. She was advised to use 15 percent of her projected sales on marketing. Elaine's business plan projects sales in her first year to be $150,000.00. What should her marketing budget be?
2. A small grocery chain has been in business for many years and is established within the communities served by its stores. The company has been successful with the marketing budget set at 7 percent of its annual sales, which average $22 million. However, the company has new competitors in several communities and plans to increase the marketing budget to 9 percent. How much will the marketing budget increase in dollars?

Communication Skills

Reading There are many marketing terms listed in bold as key terms in this chapter. There are other terms that are italicized. Make a list of the italicized terms and add them to your personal glossary.

Writing Generate your own ideas to support the need and importance of conducting an environmental scan as part of the marketing plan. Write an argument to support your reasoning.

Listening Hearing is a physical process. Listening combines hearing with evaluation. Listen carefully to your instructor as the marketing plan material of this chapter is presented. Take notes about the main points. Then, organize the key information that you heard. What points would you reiterate if you were presenting the chapter?

Internet Research

Marketing Plans Numerous marketing plan templates can be found on the Internet. Conduct an Internet search using the term *marketing plan templates*. Compare the templates you find online with the one you will use in this text. Examine the common elements of each. Compare and contrast the section names within the different documents. Identify the marketing objectives outlined in each plan.

Metrics Marketing metrics are used to track and evaluate marketing activities. Conduct an Internet search for *marketing metrics*. Create a list of four common marketing metrics that companies use to evaluate the effectiveness of their marketing strategies. Write a brief summary of what each metric on your list measures.

Marketing Tactics Conduct an Internet search for the term *marketing tactics*. Make a list of five tactics that the experts consider to be cutting edge. What advice would you give your fellow classmates on how to write effective marketing tactics to support marketing strategies?

Teamwork

Working with a partner, make a list of ten memorable product positioning statements that are popular today, similar to the Geico example in the chapter. Next, involve your classmates by writing each statement on a piece of paper and drop in a box. Have a student pick a folded paper out of the box, read the statement, and see if he or she can identify the product that the statement represents. What did you learn about product positioning from this experience?

Portfolio Development

Types of Porfolios Artists and other communication professionals have historically presented portfolios of their creative work when seeking jobs or admission to educational institutions. However, portfolios are now used for many reasons. It is helpful to identify which type is appropriate for the industry in which you are applying for a position. Examples of types of portfolios are as follows.

- *Documentation portfolio.* Demonstrate past and ongoing successes in academics or professional work performances.
- *Process portfolio.* Show growth and accomplishments in skilled work or academics with the inclusion of personal reflections in the form of commentaries, blog posts, or similar.
- *Professional portfolio.* Exhibit accomplishments related to a career or profession, including proof of valuable job-specific skills, training programs completed, and other work-related accomplishments.
- *Showcase portfolio.* Document grades, awards, and milestones, as well as artistic works and public speaking events.
- *Hybrid portfolio.* Combine multiple portfolio types and include feedback from professional third parties.

1. Research the different types of portfolios mentioned here, as well as any others that may be appropriate for your goals.
2. Select the type of portfolio to create to match your career goals.

CHAPTER 3
Business Basics

Sections

3.1 **Business Defined**

3.2 **Laws and Regulations**

Reading Prep

College and Career Readiness

Before reading this chapter, go to the end of the chapter and read the summary. The chapter summary highlights important information that was presented in the chapter. Did this help you prepare to understand the content?

Check Your Marketing IQ

Before you begin the chapter, see what you already know about marketing by taking the chapter pretest. The pretest is available at www.g-wlearning.com/marketing/.

◆DECA Emerging Leaders

College and Career Connection

Career Cluster: Business Administration Core
Instructional Area: Financial Analysis

Performance Indicator
- Explain types of business ownership.

Purpose

Designed for DECA members, this activity enables student members to better understand opportunities available through DECA in marketing, finance, hospitality, and management.

DECA's Comprehensive Learning Program consists of all DECA activities by category and support programs of study in the four career clusters.

- **College, Business, and Educational Partnerships** provide scholarships, classroom presentations and career guidance, internships, work experience, and community service activities.
- **Competitive Events Program** provides authentic situations relating to current business practices.
- ***DECA Direct* Magazine** is a full-color international publication featuring articles on career development in leadership; community service; and professionalism.
- **Educational Conferences** provide targeted, highly focused learning experiences for members and advisors while connecting with corporate professionals.
- **Emerging Leader Series** strives to empower DECA members to provide effective leadership through goal setting, consensus building, and project implementation.
- **Global Entrepreneurship Week (GEW)** engages millions of young people around the world each November to embrace innovation, imagination, and creativity.
- **School-Based Enterprises** reinforce and enhance career preparation.
- **Social Media Correspondent Program** creates conversation among chapters and shares best practices and ideas.
- **Video Challenges** provide classroom activities that challenge members to apply highly engaging, relevant learning activities from their seats in the classroom.

Procedure

1. DECA members should become familiar with the organization and its diverse learning activities. Use the following activities to learn about DECA, identify membership benefits, and apply DECA's connection to college and career preparation.
2. The information will be presented to you through the navigation of the DECA website. Visit the DECA website at www.deca.org to become familiar with the activities and opportunities available to you as a student and DECA member. Select the tab that says *High School*. Then select *High School Programs* and click on *Competitive Events*.
3. Review the event descriptions, guidelines, and sample events for Business Operations Research Events and Entrepreneurship Events.

Critical Thinking

1. List the type of business ownership that relates to each event. Explain why the type of business ownership is appropriate for the event.
2. Which events allow team participants? Which events are for an individual participant? What do *team participants* and *individual participant* mean?
3. Which functions of business appear to be addressed in each event?
4. Which of the Business Operations Research Events and Entrepreneurship Events do you find interesting? How will the event support your career goals?
5. Share with your class how participating in a DECA competitive event enhances your college and career preparation.

Visit www.deca.org for more information.

Published by DECA Inc. Copyright © by DECA Inc. No part of this publication may be reproduced for resale without written permission from the publisher. Printed in the United States of America.

Section 3.1

Business Defined

Learning Objectives

LO 3.1-1 Discuss the term *business*.
LO 3.1-2 Explain the functions of money in society.
LO 3.1-3 Define the functions of business.
LO 3.1-4 Identify forms of business ownership.

Key Terms

business
money
medium of exchange
unit of value
store of value
time value of money
production
producer
manufacturer
management
manager
sole proprietorship
partnership
corporation
nonprofit organization

Essential Question: What is the role of business in society?

LO 3.1-1 Business

In order to understanding marketing, you first need to understand the basic concepts of business. **Business** is the term for all of the activities involved in developing and exchanging goods and services. Business includes manufacturing, construction, mining, wholesaling, retailing, and farming. A business sells products, but it also manages people, makes financial decisions, and decides what and how much needs to be produced.

Profit is the difference between the income earned and expenses incurred by a business during a specific period of time. Businesses using the marketing concept understand that building a strong base of satisfied customers leads to healthy profits. Companies using the marketing concept treat all contact with customers as a chance to market the business. Customer satisfaction is the goal of all employees, and leads to business success in the long term. Different departments of the business, such as production, finance,

Roman Tiraspolsky/Shutterstock.com

Trader Joe's is a business that sells products, manages employees, makes financial decisions, and decides what needs to be produced. *What do you think of when you hear "business"?*

and management, share information with the marketing team to help the company succeed.

Business provides most of the goods and services that you use every day. It also employs

38　　Copyright Goodheart-Willcox Co., Inc.

Chapter 3 Business Basics

people in exchange for wages. A *wage* is money earned for working. People use the wages they earn to buy what they need.

LO 3.1-2 Money

Money is anything of value that is accepted in return for goods or services. Another word for money is *currency*. Coin or paper money represents different values of money. In ancient times, people exchanged goods for other goods. The exchange of one good or service for another good or service is called *bartering*. Bartering can be very difficult, time-consuming, and sometimes unsuccessful. To solve problems with bartering, money was created.

Money makes it easier to do business and exchange goods and services. In our economy, money serves three functions: medium of exchange, unit of value, and store of value, as shown in Figure 3-1.

- A **medium of exchange** is an item that is accepted in exchange for goods and services. Money is a convenient tool for trading. It is the basis of our economy.
- A **unit of value** is a common measure of what something is worth or what something costs. Each country has its own unit of value, or currency. In the United States, everyone knows what a dollar is and how much it is worth. Using money as a unit of value is an easy way to place a price on an item or service.
- A **store of value** is something that can be saved or stored and used at a later date. An item that holds its value over a period of time is said to have a good store of value. Currency is fairly stable. However, it can lose some of its purchasing power.

To be useful and meaningful in an economy, money must have the following properties.

- *Stability*. The value of money must be stable over time in order for it to be widely accepted. People in an economy are confident to use and accept money that has a consistent value.
- *Recognizability*. Money must be immediately recognizable. The US dollar is the most widely recognized currency around the world.
- *Divisibility*. There must be a way to divide money into smaller units. In US currency, paper and coin money allow dollars to be divided into smaller units.
- *Portability*. To make purchases, people must be able to carry money with them. Therefore, money must be easily portable.
- *Durability*. Physical money is handled many times by many people and machines. It needs to be strong and last a long time. US bills are made out of a special blend of cotton and linen rather than paper. US coins are made with a blend of metals.

Money is worth more today than the same amount would be in the future. The **time value of money** is the idea that money decreases in value over time. Money received or earned today can be invested or put in a savings account to earn interest.

LO 3.1-3 Functions of Business

Business plays a role in society by providing products, creating markets, and generating economic benefits. Businesses perform many activities or functions. The functions of business are production, finance, marketing, and

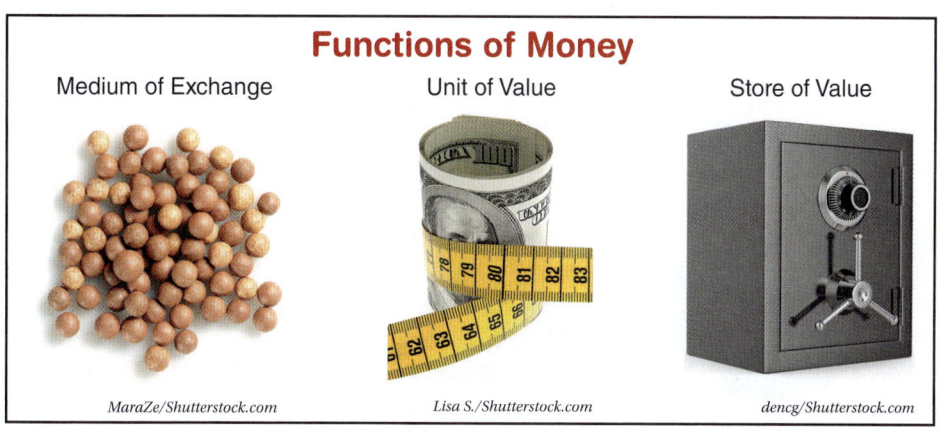

Functions of Money

Medium of Exchange   Unit of Value   Store of Value

MaraZe/Shutterstock.com   *Lisa S./Shutterstock.com*   *dencg/Shutterstock.com*

Figure 3-1 Money serves three functions in the economy.

Goodheart-Willcox Publisher

Medium of exchange means that money is accepted in exchange for goods and services. *Which of the three functions of money do you think is the most important?*

management, as shown in Figure 3-2. Businesses using the marketing concept integrate the total company and its functions in the goal of customer satisfaction. Employees in production, finance, marketing, and management must work together to achieve that goal.

Production

Production is any activity related to making a product, which can be a good, a service, or an idea. The *production* function is responsible for creating goods and services. A **producer** is a business that creates goods and services. Production includes farming, mining, and construction. A **manufacturer** is a type of producer that uses raw materials from other producers and converts them into finished goods.

Finance

The *finance* function of business includes all activities involving money. Businesses receive money in the form of customer payments. In turn, they pay for raw materials, services, employee wages, and taxes. Sometimes businesses borrow money from financial institutions, like banks.

Figure 3-2 The four functions of business must work together to create a successful, profitable company.

Four Functions of Business

Production
Making goods, services, ideas

Finance
Activities related to money

Marketing
Activities focusing on the customer

Management
Planning, coordinating, and monitoring

Case in Point

Cuisinart

Consumers have a right to safety and a right to be informed about the products they purchase. While most people generally assume the products they buy are safe, there are often times when the opposite is discovered to be true.

Businesses have a social and legal responsibility to inform consumers when a product has been found to no longer be safe and to inform them about how those products can be repaired or replaced. Cuisinart voluntarily recalled its food processors due to a faulty blade, even though the defect was discovered during the busy holiday cooking season. The blade was prone to cracking when in use, resulting in bits of broken metal in food being processed. The recall affected 22 models of food processors sold over almost two decades—an estimated eight million products. Luckily, Cuisinart received only 69 reports of consumers with defective products.

To protect consumers, recall information was posted on Cuisinart's social media pages. Cuisinart also created a dedicated web page with information on the recall and instructions on how to request a replacement blade. The food processors were placed on the recalled products list maintained by the US government. Cuisinart demonstrated compliance and accountability for providing safe products, honest marketing practices, and truthful documentation.

An important part of the finance function is planning. The people who work in finance are often responsible for developing budgets. A *budget* is a financial plan for a fixed period of time that reflects anticipated revenue and shows how it will be allocated in the operation of the business. A budget helps the business make sure it has enough money to cover expenses. It also helps the business understand whether it is handling its money wisely and making a profit. If a business decides to take a loan, the financing function plans for the repayment of the loan.

Accounting is one part of finance. Accounting keeps track of all money that enters or leaves the business. It pays bills and receives payments.

Marketing

Marketing is the dynamic activities that identify, anticipate, and satisfy customer demand while making a profit. Marketing is the function of business that focuses on the customer. Marketing professionals are responsible for helping the entire business focus on the needs and wants of customers. The marketing function includes learning about customers, developing products, and pricing them for sale. Marketing activities then promote and sell the products to those customers. Marketing activities also follow up to find out how satisfied customers are with their products.

Management

The **management** function of business controls and makes decisions about a business. It includes all of the activities required to plan, coordinate, and monitor a business. A **manager** is an employee who directs the work of others and is responsible for carrying out the goals of the department. A manager makes decisions, implements plans, and controls. Managers look at the big picture and lead workers to make changes to

Albert Karimov/Shutterstock.com

A manufacturer uses raw materials from other producers and converts them into finished goods, such as plastic bottles for water. *Why do you think manufacturers need marketing?*

Levels of Management

Level	Function
Top-level	Control and oversee entire business
Middle-level	Execute business plans, act as intermediary between top-level and first-level managers
First-level	Focus on controlling everyday tasks

Goodheart-Willcox Publisher

Figure 3-3 There are three levels of management. A company may or may not have all three levels, as it depends on the size of the organization.

improve the business. They also hire, train, and supervise employees. There are three levels of management, as shown in Figure 3-3.

Business Ownership
LO 3.1-4

There are three main forms of business ownership. They are sole proprietorship, partnership, and corporation. As a marketing professional, you may find yourself working for one of these business types.

- A **sole proprietorship** is a business owned by one person. That person makes all the decisions and receives all the profits from the business. It is the simplest form of business to start and own.
- A **partnership** is the relationship between two or more people who join to create a business. Each partner contributes to the business. They may contribute money, property, labor, or expertise to the business.
- A **corporation** is a business that is legally separate from its owners and has most of the legal rights of an actual person. The goal of a for-profit corporation is to make a profit for the owners. Most corporations are for-profit businesses.

A **nonprofit organization** is an entity that exists to serve some public purpose. Nonprofit corporations are also called *nonprofits* or *not-for-profit organizations*.

Section 3.1 Review

Check Your Understanding

1. What is profit?
2. How is the marketing concept related to business profit?
3. Name the properties of money.
4. What are the functions of business?
5. What is the difference between a sole proprietorship and a partnership?

Build Your Vocabulary

As you progress through this text, develop a personal glossary of key terms. This will help you build your vocabulary and prepare you for a career. Write a definition for each of the following terms and add them to your personal glossary.

business
corporation
management
manager
manufacturer
medium of exchange
money
nonprofit organization
partnership
producer
production
sole proprietorship
store of value
time value of money
unit of value

Section 3.2

Laws and Regulations

Essential Question

Why are laws for business needed in our economy?

Learning Objectives

LO 3.2-1 Describe the role the FTC plays in advertising and marketing law.
LO 3.2-2 Identify protections provided by employment and labor law.
LO 3.2-3 Define the purpose of finance law.
LO 3.2-4 Explain consumer protection laws.

Key Terms

Federal Trade Commission (FTC)
false advertising
endorsement
telemarketing
antitrust laws
monopoly
bankruptcy

Advertising and Marketing Law

LO 3.2-1

The *Federal Trade Commission Act* was passed in 1914 and created the Federal Trade Commission. The **Federal Trade Commission (FTC)** is a federal agency that was created to protect consumers and promote business competition. The FTC develops and enforces laws related to advertising and marketing that all businesses must follow.

Under these laws, claims in advertisements must be truthful, cannot be deceptive or unfair, and must be evidence-based. **False advertising** is overstating the features and benefits of products or services or making false claims about them. Misrepresenting information, intentionally or unintentionally, can lead to lawsuits, loss of customers, or loss of jobs.

For some specialized products or services, additional rules may apply. Examples of areas covered by advertising and marketing law include children's products, endorsements, environmental marketing, health claims, made in the USA claims, online advertising and marketing, and telemarketing.

Children's Products

Businesses that advertise directly to children or market child-related products to their parents must comply with truth-in-advertising standards. The *Children's Online Privacy Protection Act (COPPA)* imposes requirements on websites and online services regarding the personal information collected about children who are under the age of 13. It also restricts how companies can use that information.

Endorsements

An **endorsement** is an advertising message that a person, business, or other organization is paid by another party to give. The purpose of an endorsement is for consumers to believe that the

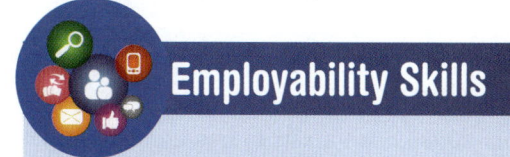

Employability Skills

Professionalism

Professionalism is the act of exhibiting appropriate character, judgment, and behavior by a person who is trained to perform a job. It is a person's conduct while at work or representing an employer. Professionalism extends to every job, career, and industry. It means conducting oneself in a manner that exhibits responsibility, integrity, and excellence.

Environmental Marketing

A company's claim about environmental responsibility or product energy efficiency and any related "green" claims must be truthful and verifiable. This applies to ecofriendly business practices, product components and packaging, and statements of energy efficiency. The FTC-issued *Green Guides* help businesses ensure that the claims made in promotions are true and substantiated.

Health Claims

Companies must have solid proof to support health-related advertising claims. Under federal law, health claims made in product advertisements must be backed by scientific evidence. This is especially true for businesses that market food, over-the-counter drugs, dietary supplements, contact lenses, and other health-related products.

Made in USA Claims

Products marketed as "Made in the USA" must disclose which materials, ingredients, or components were made in the United States. Companies that choose to make claims about the amount of US content need to know the guidelines set in the FTC's *Enforcement Policy Statement on US Origin Claims*.

Online Advertising and Marketing

When advertising online, there are rules and guidelines that protect consumers. These also

Leonard Zhukovsky/Shutterstock.com

Michael Phelps is a famous Olympic athlete who endorses the Under Armour brand. *What impact do you think celebrity endorsements have on product sales?*

advertising message reflects the opinions of the person who is paid to give it. A famous example of an endorsement is Jessica Simpson's endorsement of Proactiv skincare products. Businesses that use endorsements to market products must meet the standards of the FTC Act and the FTC's *Guides Concerning Use of Endorsements and Testimonials in Advertising*. Standards that define endorsements and how they can be used are updated regularly.

You Do the Math

Number Sense

Number sense is an ability to use and understand numbers to make judgments and solve problems. For example, suppose you want to add three basketball scores: 35, 21, and 18.

First, add 30 + 20 + 10 = 60.
Then, add 5 + 1 + 8 = 14.
Finally, combine these two sums to find the answer: 60 + 14 = 74.

Solve the following problems.

1. Micah wants to purchase several items of clothing. He is not sure he has enough money to buy the items he wants. His budget is $95 before tax. The prices of each of the three items are $16, $42, and $35. How can he figure the total cost of the three items without using a calculator?

2. A business owner is looking at making several improvements to her facility. New office furniture is going to cost $10,800. Installing new light fixtures is going to cost $3,200. Resurfacing the parking lot will cost $12,500. How can she figure the total cost of the business improvements without using a calculator?

help businesses by maintaining the credibility of the Internet as a marketing medium. In addition, truth-in-advertising standards apply when selling computers, software, apps, or other products or services related to the Internet.

Telemarketing

Telemarketing is personal selling done over the telephone. The FTC's *Telemarketing Sales Rule* helps protect consumers from fraudulent telemarketing calls. This rule also gives them certain protections under the *National Do Not Call Registry*, which allows consumers to opt out of telemarketing sales calls. Companies also need to be familiar with rules banning most forms of robocalling. *Robocalling* is using a computerized automatic dialing device to deliver a prerecorded sales message when someone answers.

LO 3.2-2 Employment and Labor Law

All businesses in the United States are required to protect employees and treat them fairly. Employment and labor laws cover many topics, such as preventing discrimination and harassment in the workplace, ensuring employee safety, enforcing wage and hour laws, and monitoring workers' compensation regulations. Examples of laws that protect employees in the United States are shown in Figure 3-4.

The *US Department of Labor (DOL)* enforces workplace laws and regulations. The DOL works with many other governmental agencies to protect employees. The *Equal Employment Opportunity Commission (EEOC)* protects the civil rights of employees in the workplace. These rights include nondiscrimination based on factors such as gender and race. The *Occupational Safety and Health Administration (OSHA)* sets and enforces workplace safety standards. OSHA performs inspections to ensure workplaces are safe and healthy for employees, handles safety complaints, and investigates workplace accidents.

LO 3.2-3 Finance Law

Finance laws exist to ensure fair competition and to protect the financial interests of companies and investors. Antitrust, bankruptcy, and securities laws protect the financial interests of businesses and individual investors. Examples of business finance regulations are described in Figure 3-5.

The FTC's *Bureau of Competition* was established to promote fair competition and is responsible for enforcing the antitrust laws. **Antitrust laws** promote fair trade, open markets, and competition among businesses. Antitrust laws prevent companies from forming a monopoly. A **monopoly** occurs when one business has complete control of a market's entire supply of goods or services. The *Sherman Antitrust Act* and *Clayton Antitrust Act* have been used effectively to prevent monopolies and price-fixing. Businesses can refer to the FTC for information on how antitrust laws work.

Employment and Labor Laws

Fair Labor Standards Act (1938)	Establishes the minimum wage, overtime pay, record-keeping, and youth employment standards
Equal Pay Act (1963)	Employers cannot pay different wages to men and women if they perform equal work in the same workplace
Title VII of the Civil Rights Act (1964)	Employers cannot discriminate based on the race, color, religion, national origin, or gender of an individual
Age Discrimination in Employment Act (1967)	Employers cannot discriminate against people who are age 40 and older based on age
Title I of the Americans with Disabilities Act (1990)	Employers cannot discriminate against a qualified person with a disability and must make reasonable accommodations for known physical or mental limitations of an otherwise qualified individual
Family and Medical Leave Act (1993)	Requires that eligible employees be allowed to take unpaid, job-protected leave for specified family and medical reasons
The Genetic Information Nondiscrimination Act of 2008	Employers cannot discriminate against employees or applicants because of genetic information, such as information about any disease, disorder, or condition of an individual's family members

Goodheart-Willcox Publisher

Figure 3-4 All businesses in the United States are required to observe employment and labor laws.

Marketing Ethics

Code of Ethics

Most businesses establish a code of ethics that all employees must follow. A *code of ethics* dictates how business should be conducted. It outlines acceptable behavior when interacting with managers, coworkers, suppliers, and customers. Some companies post their code of ethics on their websites so customers and clients can be aware of how they conduct business.

Bankruptcy is a legal process that allows a company to reorganize or go out of business when it runs out of funding. While no company ever wants to file for bankruptcy, there are laws in place that will allow for it under certain conditions. *Bankruptcy laws* apply to the handling of business debts when a business is no longer profitable. The FTC distributes information for businesses about bankruptcy options, the process, and the tax consequences.

Securities include stocks and other financial investments. Businesses that sell publicly traded securities must comply with certain financial laws and reporting obligations. *Securities laws* regulate businesses that have publicly traded stocks and bonds. These laws are enforced by the *US Securities and Exchange Commission (SEC)*, which regulates corporations that are publicly traded. These regulations include preparing documentation for the SEC to review and complying with the Sarbanes-Oxley Act. In 2002, a number of accounting frauds at major corporations led to the US Congress passing the *Sarbanes-Oxley Act*, which requires open and honest business accounting and reporting practices. The accounting scandals, which included Enron and WorldCom, cost investors billions of dollars. The act was passed to prevent companies from fraudulent accounting practices that would mislead investors as to the strength of a company. Businesses that do not accurately report the use of company funds commit an unethical and illegal act. The SEC website includes informational resources for businesses.

LO 3.2-4 Consumer Protection

Customers typically assume the products they buy are safe. They rely on the seller or the producer to ensure that products are safe to use as directed. However, companies that neglect product safety may put the well-being of customers at risk. For example, children's toys that have sharp edges, toxic paint, or small parts that can be easily swallowed have caused serious injuries. Companies that know their products are unsafe

Business Finance Regulations	
Truth in Lending Act (1968)	Requires the disclosure of terms and costs on all consumer credit agreements and in advertisements for credit plans
Fair Credit Reporting Act (1970)	Regulates the collection of credit information and who can access consumer credit reports
Electronic Fund Transfer Act (1978)	Protects consumers who use electronic fund transfer (EFT) services, including ATMs, point-of-sale terminals, automated bill-payment arrangements, and remote banking programs
Electronic Signatures in Global and National Commerce Act (2000)	Allows electronic signatures to be used for interstate and international commerce transactions that require written signatures
Sarbanes-Oxley Act (2002)	Prevents companies from fraudulent accounting practices that would mislead investors as to the strength of a company
Securities laws	Body of laws that regulate businesses that have publicly traded stocks and bonds
Bankruptcy laws	Body of laws that apply to the handling of business debts when a business is no longer profitable

Figure 3-5 These laws protect the financial interests of businesses and individual investors.

Goodheart-Willcox Publisher

Exploring Marketing Careers

Sales Manager

A company's sales force is its point of contact with potential customers. A sales manager hires, trains, and directs salespeople to achieve the company's sales goals. Sales managers establish sales territories and quotas for sales representatives, monitor sales potential and inventory requirements, and analyze sales statistics. In larger companies, the sales manager may report to a regional or national sales manager. In smaller companies, the sales manager reports directly to the company executives. Other typical job titles for a sales manager include *director of sales*, *sales supervisor*, *sales executive*, and *store manager*.

Some examples of tasks that sales managers perform include:
- Hire and train local sales representatives
- Monitor customer preferences to help focus the efforts of sales representatives
- Prepare sales budgets
- Complete performance evaluations of local sales representatives
- Resolve customer complaints as needed

Sales managers must be able to manage and motivate employees effectively to maximize each individual's potential. They should understand the principles and methods of selling and marketing. In addition, they should be familiar with all of the products offered for sale by the company, as well as those offered by the competition. Many jobs in this field require a bachelor degree, as well as considerable experience or on-the-job training. For more information, access the *Occupational Outlook Handbook* online.

---

but choose to sell them anyway are acting unethically. Depending on the situation, they may be also breaking the law.

The federal government provides protections through *consumer protection laws*. These laws are designed to hold companies accountable for providing safe products, honest marketing practices, and truthful documentation.

In 1962, President John F. Kennedy addressed the Congress and outlined four basic consumer rights. Since 1962, four more rights have been added. The marketing concept directs businesses to focus on customer satisfaction. One way to do this is for businesses to respect the Consumer Bill of Rights and treat customers ethically. The eight rights of consumers are:
- the right to safety;
- the right to be informed;
- the right to choose;
- the right to be heard;
- the right to satisfaction of basic needs;
- the right to redress;
- the right to education; and
- the right to a healthful environment.

The FTC's *Bureau of Consumer Protection* works to stop unfair, deceptive, and fraudulent businesses practices. It collects and investigates consumer complaints, takes legal action against businesses and individuals that violate the law, and provides educational resources for both consumers and businesses. The efforts of this bureau are distributed among eight divisions, shown in Figure 3-6, which monitor businesses to make sure that consumers are protected and laws are followed.

In addition, the *Consumer Product Safety Act* established the *Consumer Product Safety Commission (CPSC)* in 1972. The purpose of the CPSC is to protect the public against unreasonable risks associated with consumer products. CPSC works to reduce the risk of injuries and deaths from consumer products by:
- issuing and enforcing mandatory safety standards;
- developing voluntary safety standards for an industry;
- banning products if standards would not adequately protect people;
- recalling products and arranging for their repair, replacement, or refund;
- researching potential product hazards; and
- informing and educating consumers about product safety issues.

The US *Food and Drug Administration (FDA)* is the governmental agency responsible for protecting the health of consumers by ensuring the safety of food, medicine and medical devices, and cosmetics,

FTC's Bureau of Consumer Protection	
Division	**Description**
Advertising Practices	Protects consumers from unfair and deceptive advertising practices; also oversees the marketing of alcohol, tobacco, and violent entertainment
Consumer and Business Education	Provides information to businesses so they can follow the laws, and to consumers so they can make good decisions about purchases
Consumer Response and Operations	Collects, monitors, and analyzes data to assist law enforcement and provide education on consumer protection
Enforcement	Litigates civil actions, enforces court orders in federal cases, and works with law enforcement agencies to uphold consumer-protection laws
Financial Practices	Provides honest and fair transactions in debt collection, credit card practices, financial institution practices, loans, and leases
Litigation Technology and Analysis	Assists with legal work for the FTC by collaborating with attorneys and helping to manage investigations
Marketing Practices	Handles consumer fraud by businesses using illegal marketing practices
Privacy & Identity Protection	Oversees consumer privacy, credit reporting, identity theft, and information security

Figure 3-6 The FTC's Bureau of Consumer Protection is divided into eight divisions that work together to stop unfair, deceptive, and fraudulent business practices.

Goodheart-Willcox Publisher

among others. The FDA assures that these products are safe to consume and properly labeled. Companies who wish to manufacture products regulated by the FDA can look to the FDA's *Basics for Industry* guides.

Many state and federal laws have been enacted to increase consumer protection and honor consumer rights. These laws are designed to protect consumers, employees, and businesses from poorly constructed or dangerous products, illegal pricing practices, and illegal hiring practices, to name a few.

Section 3.2 Review

Check Your Understanding

1. List two reasons for which the Federal Trade Commission (FTC) was created.
2. Name one type of specialized product for which additional advertising or marketing rules apply.
3. Cite two governmental organizations that enforce workplace laws and regulations.
4. What types of laws protect the financial interests of businesses and individual investors?
5. List examples of consumer rights.

Build Your Vocabulary

As you progress through this text, develop a personal glossary of key terms. This will help you build your vocabulary and prepare you for a career. Write a definition for each of the following terms and add them to your personal glossary.

antitrust laws
bankruptcy
endorsement
false advertising
Federal Trade Commission (FTC)
monopoly
telemarketing

CHAPTER 3 Review and Assessment

Chapter Summary

Section 3.1 Business Defined

LO 3.1-1 Discuss the term *business*.
Business is all of the activities involved in developing and exchanging goods and services. Businesses using the marketing concept understand that building a strong base of satisfied customers leads to healthy profits. Business also provides most of the goods and services that individuals use every day and employs people in exchange for wages.

LO 3.1-2 Explain the functions of money in society.
Money serves three functions: medium of exchange, unit of value, and store of value. To be useful and meaningful in an economy, money must have stability, recognizability, divisibility, portability, and durability.

LO 3.1-3 Define the functions of business.
The functions of business are production, finance, marketing, and management. Production is responsible for creating goods and services. Finance includes all activities involving money. Marketing that focuses on the customer. controls and makes decisions about a business.

LO 3.1-4 Identify forms of business ownership.
Three main forms of business organization are sole proprietorship, partnership, and corporation. A sole proprietorship is owned by one person. A partnership is two or more people who join to create a business. A corporation is legally separate from its owners and has most of the legal rights of an actual person.

Section 3.2 Laws and Regulations

LO 3.2-1 Describe the role the FTC plays in advertising and marketing law.
The Federal Trade Commission (FTC) is a federal agency that was created to protect consumers and promote business competition. The FTC develops and enforces laws related to advertising and marketing that all businesses must follow.

LO 3.2-2 Identify protections provided by employment and labor law.
All businesses in the United States are required to protect employees and treat them fairly. Employment and labor laws cover many topics, such as preventing discrimination and harassment in the workplace, ensuring employee safety, enforcing wage and hour laws, and monitoring workers' compensation regulations.

LO 3.2-3 Define the purpose of finance law.
Finance laws exist to ensure fair competition and to protect the financial interests of companies and individual investors. Antitrust, bankruptcy, and securities laws protect the financial interests of businesses and individual investors.

LO 3.2-4 Explain consumer protection laws.
The federal government provides protections through consumer-protection laws. These laws are designed to hold companies accountable for providing safe products, honest marketing practices, and documentation that is not fraudulent.

Check Your Marketing IQ

Now that you have completed the chapter, see what you have learned about marketing by taking the chapter posttest. The posttest is available at www.g-wlearning.com/marketing/.

Review Your Knowledge

1. Discuss the term *business*.
2. Discuss profit and its relationship to the marketing concept.
3. Explain the functions of money in society.
4. Define the role of business in society.
5. Define the functions of business.
6. Identify and explain forms of business ownership.
7. Describe the role the FTC plays in advertising and marketing law.
8. Identify protections provided by employment and labor law.
9. Define the purpose of finance law.
10. Explain consumer-protection laws.

Apply Your Knowledge

1. At the end of this unit, you will begin writing a marketing plan. Consider a type of business that you might select for this project. What products does this business sell?
2. Which type of ownership does the company you selected in question 1 have?
3. Does the business you selected sell products in the business or consumer market?
4. Is the business you selected a producer, reseller, or service provider?
5. How does business fulfill the marketing concept of satisfying the customer? List three ways in which the business you selected might do this.
6. Recall a time a marketing claim caused you to doubt its truthfulness. Describe the claim and explain why you thought it might not be true.
7. Select one of the business finance regulations described in Figure 3-5 and explain how this regulation could impact the business for which you will write a marketing plan.
8. Select one of the laws or regulations described in this chapter. How would marketing be affected if this law were not in place?
9. Create a three-column chart. In the first column, list four laws or regulations that apply to marketing. In the second column, describe what each law covers. In the third column, explain how you can ensure that your marketing activities abide by the law or regulation listed.
10. Review the eight items listed in the Consumer Bill of Rights. Describe how the business you selected will support these rights for its customers.

Apply Your Math Skills

Math skills are important to successfully operating a business. Apply your math skills to solve the following problems.

1. Ahmet, Brandon, and Christy are three friends who have decided to open a business as a partnership. Their ownership percentages are based on their individual investment in the company. Ahmet invested the most, providing $35,000. Brandon invested $24,500. Christy invested $7,500. Based on their investments in the business, what are the ownership percentages for each person?
2. Farm Supply Co. is a retail business covered by the Equal Pay Act, which states that employers cannot pay different wages to men and women who perform equal work. Dominique and Elliot are cashiers at this company who make the same hourly wage. Dominique works 40 hours per week and makes $19,864 per year (for 52 weeks). Elliot works 30 hours per week. How much does Elliot make per year?

Communication Skills

Reading The ability to read and interpret information is an important workplace skill. As a consumer, it is important that you understand your consumer rights. Read the Consumer Bill of Rights section in this chapter. Interpret how each of these rights influences consumer behavior.

College and Career Readiness

Writing Writing style is the way in which a writer uses language to convey an idea. Select a page or pages of notes you have taken during class. Evaluate your writing style and the relevance, quality, and depth of the information.

Speaking Developing effective communication skills requires that individuals be able to participate in and contribute to discussions. As your instructor lectures on this chapter, contribute thoughtful, relevant comments when participation is invited. Ask questions when necessary to help determine or clarify the meaning of the topics discussed during the lesson.

Internet Research

Basic Business Concepts Conduct an Internet search for *basic business concepts*. Make notes on the concepts that you believe are important to marketing.

Made in the USA Products marketed as "Made in the USA" must disclose which materials, ingredients, or components were made in the United States. Companies that choose to make claims about the amount of US-made content need to understand the guidelines set by the FTC. Visit the website of the FTC and search for *Made in the USA* using the website's search function. Read the information about the guidelines that must be followed to use this claim. Create a brief outline of the information.

Lemon Laws Lemon laws are consumer protection laws specific to the automobile industry. Using the Internet, research *lemon laws*. What events led to their creation? How have they changed the ways companies can conduct business? Describe how this change in the law impacted customers. Document the sources of your research.

Teamwork

Working with your team, make a list of three current legal issues related to business that have been in the news. Indicate if the legal issues involve the owner, employees, or other individuals. Discuss the business laws that may have been violated in each of the three situations.

Portfolio Development

College and Career Readiness

Objective Before you begin collecting information for your portfolio, write an objective for the finished product. An *objective* is a complete sentence or two that states what you want to accomplish.

The language in your objective should be clear and specific. Include enough details so you can easily judge when it is accomplished. Consider this objective: "I will try to get into college." Such an objective is too general. A better, more detailed objective might read: "I will get accepted into the communications program at one of my top three colleges of choice." Creating a clear objective is a good starting point for beginning to work on your portfolio.

1. Decide the purpose of the portfolio you are creating, such as short-term employment, career, community service, or college application.
2. Set a timeline to finish the final product.
3. Write an objective for your portfolio.

CHAPTER 4
Ethics and Social Responsibility

Sections

4.1 **Ethics**
4.2 **Social Responsibility**

Reading Prep

College and Career Readiness

Before reading this chapter, go to the Review Your Knowledge section at the end of the chapter and read the questions. This exercise will prepare you for the content that will be presented in this chapter. Review questions at the end of the chapter to serve as a self-assessment to help you evaluate your comprehension of the material.

Check Your Marketing IQ

Before you begin the chapter, see what you already know about marketing by taking the chapter pretest. The pretest is available at www.g-wlearning.com/marketing/.

DECA Emerging Leaders

Principles of Business Management and Administration Event

Career Cluster: Business Management and Administration
Instructional Area: Professional Development

Knowledge and Skills Developed

Participants will develop many 21st century skills desired by today's employers in the following categories:

- communication and collaboration
- creativity and innovation
- critical thinking and problem solving
- flexibility and adaptability
- information literacy
- initiative and self-direction
- leadership and responsibility
- productivity and accountability
- social and cross-cultural skills

Performance Indicators

- Explain the need for innovative skills.
- Describe techniques for obtaining work experience.
- Analyze employer expectations in the business environment.
- Explain employment opportunities in business.

Purpose

Designed for first-year DECA members who are enrolled in introductory-level principles of marketing/business courses, the event measures the student's proficiency in those knowledge and skills identified by career practitioners as common academic and technical content in business management and administration. This event consists of a 100-question, multiple-choice, business administration core exam and a business situation role-play with a business executive. Participants are not informed in advance of the performance indicators to be evaluated.

Procedure

1. The event will be presented to you through your reading of these instructions, including the Performance Indicators and Business Situation. You will have up to 10 minutes to review this information to determine how you will handle the role-play and demonstrate the performance indicators of this event. During the preparation period, you may make notes to use during the role-play.
2. You will have up to 10 minutes to role-play your situation with a judge. You may have more than one judge.
3. You will be evaluated on how well you meet the performance indicators of this event.
4. Turn in all your notes and event materials when you have completed the role-play.

Business Situation

You are to assume the role of Director of Career Services at State Business College. The newly appointed **Vice President of Student Development (judge)** has complained to you that career services in most colleges are ineffective and there is limited importance in helping students at the point of graduation. You must explain to the vice president (judge) the need and importance of assisting students nearing graduation with their professional skills to secure employment in the field.

You must explain the common requirements and skills needed for securing employment in the business field, along with characteristics employers look for when hiring. You should also suggest to the vice president (judge) methods for finding career opportunities and benefits for State Business College when graduates from the college are successfully employed in the business field.

You will meet with the vice president (judge) in the vice president's workspace. The vice president (judge) will begin the role-play by greeting you and asking to hear your understanding of career services. After you have provided your explanation and have answered the vice president's (judge's) questions, he or she will conclude the interview by thanking you for your presentation.

Critical Thinking

1. What role does a student's academic history play in securing employment?
2. Once a job is secured, why is ongoing education important?

Visit www.deca.org for more information.

Section 4.1

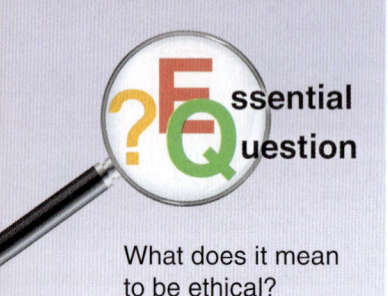

Essential Question
What does it mean to be ethical?

Ethics

Learning Objectives

LO 4.1-1 Summarize the concept of business ethics.
LO 4.1-2 State examples of ethical marketing practices.

Key Terms

ethics
morals
business ethics
code of conduct
code of ethics
customer relationship management (CRM)
spam

LO 4.1-1 Business Ethics

Ethics are the set of moral values that guide a person's behavior. **Morals** are an individual's ideas of what is right and wrong. Ethics help people determine the most appropriate behavior for situations in both their personal and professional lives.

Businesses expect their employees to perform in an ethical manner. **Business ethics** are the rules for professional conduct and integrity in all areas of business. Business ethics help guide management and employees to make correct decisions for a company.

Most businesses adopt clear guidelines for the ethical behavior expected from their employees in the workplace. Two ways a company might convey its expectations for acceptable employee behavior are with a code of conduct and a code of ethics.

Code of Conduct

A **code of conduct** is a document that identifies the manner in which employees should behave while at work or when representing the company.

Roman Tiraspolsky/Shutterstock.com

Wells Fargo was cited for unethical behavior after opening millions of accounts for customers without their knowledge. *What is your impression of a company that conducts business in an unethical manner?*

To discourage unethical behavior in the workplace, some businesses provide a set of employee guidelines with clear definitions of right and wrong actions. The following list contains examples of actions that are not tolerated and warrant

54 Copyright Goodheart-Willcox Co., Inc.

immediate termination of employment. These may be listed in codes of conduct.
- Purposeful falsification or causing the falsification of any time, attendance, personnel, business, financial, or other records of the company will be grounds for dismissal.
- Disorderly conduct during work time or on company property, including fighting, threatening, yelling at, or otherwise abusing or harassing a coworker by word or act or serious horseplay involving or having the potential for personal injury will be grounds for suspension.
- Possession of weapons on company property, during company events, or while conducting company business will be grounds for dismissal.

Workplace bullying is a serious example of conduct that is unacceptable in the workplace and may be a part of a code of conduct. *Workplace bullying* is the repeated mistreatment of another person using verbal abuse, threats, or any other action that prevents a person from doing his or her job without fear. Such behavior can escalate to a point that endangers an individual's well-being and instills fear of bodily harm.

Code of Ethics

A **code of ethics** is a document that dictates how business should be conducted. It may also be referred to as a *statement of ethics*. Its goal is to establish a value system for the company that enables employees to make sound ethical

SpeedKingz/Shutterstock.com

Any action that prevents a person from doing his or her job without fear is workplace bullying. *When have you witnessed bullying?*

decisions. For example, some businesses do not allow their employees to accept gifts from clients. A written code of ethics is illustrated in Figure 4-1.

Stated codes of ethics generally address relationships and interactions of the business with employees, customers, suppliers, investors, creditors, competitors, and community. Business codes of ethics frequently relate to issues such as fair treatment of employees, teamwork, competition, and conflicts of interest. Other issues may include use of business resources and assets, confidentiality, working with suppliers, and environmental concerns.

You Do the Math

Percentages

A percentage is a part of 100 and is the same as a fraction or decimal. For example, 15 percent is the same as 15 ÷ 100, which is .15. To calculate the percentage of a number, change the percentage to a decimal and multiply by the number. For example:

15 percent of 200 = 15 ÷ 100 × 200 = 30

or

.15 × 200 = 30

Solve the following problems.

1. In a recent year, Americans generated 258 million tons of municipal waste. However, 89 million tons was recycled. What is the percentage of waste recycled?
2. Of the 258 million tons of waste generated, 27 percent was paper. How much paper was thrown away in million tons?
3. Of the 89 million tons of waste that was recycled, 9 percent was metal. How much metal was recycled in million tons?
4. In the same year, of the 258 million tons of waste generated, 136 million tons ended up in a landfill. What is the percentage of waste that was landfilled?

Figure 4-1 This code of ethics excerpt defines a company's expectations of integrity and respect from its employees.

Yours in Retro
CODE OF ETHICS

Yours in Retro is committed to putting customers first and being responsible members of the community. Yours in Retro will create meaningful work, protect the environment, be socially responsible, produce a solid return for our owners and employees, and provide an important service to society.

Integrity
Integrity is at the core of everything we do at Yours in Retro. We are an honest, ethical, and trustworthy organization. Integrity is the foundation of our relationship with our clients, our communities, and each other. We will never record hours not worked or bill a client for hours that were not spent directly on tasks for the client's project.

Respect
Respect is the foundation of any good relationship. Discrimination or harassment based on age, race, ethnicity, gender, or any other legally protected status is not tolerated.

Goodheart-Willcox Publisher

Respected companies regulate themselves by voluntarily adhering to ethical behavior. The *American Marketing Association (AMA)* is a professional organization that sets the standards for ethical behavior in the marketing industry. Another professional organization that businesses can voluntarily join is the Better Business Bureau (BBB). When a business joins the BBB, it agrees to follow the BBB Business Partner Code of Conduct. When a business joins a professional organization, such as the AMA or BBB, the company is agreeing to abide by its ethical standards. Membership in professional organizations is also a way companies can promote their ethical behavior.

Ethical Marketing Practices
LO 4.1-2

Customers willingly purchase from companies they trust and perceive to act ethically. On the other hand, if a company or employee acts unethically, it can have long-lasting effects on the success of the business. Business is lost when customers do not trust a company or do not approve of its business practices. These customers might choose to buy products from a competitor. This hurts a business both in the short and long term. Those who are responsible for marketing must abide by marketing laws, as explained in Chapter 3. Ethical practices including customer privacy, honest marketing information, fair pricing, and ethical selling must also be adhered to.

Customer Privacy

Customers have the right to expect a company to keep their personal information confidential. Businesses that collect customer information may not sell it or abuse it by sending customers unwanted communications. Additionally, companies must guard against hackers accessing business data files and e-mails to steal confidential information. Businesses are expected to protect customers by keeping their private information secure. Customers should be notified if information has been stolen.

Most businesses use a system to manage data related to their customer relationships. **Customer relationship management (CRM)** is a system to track contact information and other information for current and potential customers. All CRM information should be considered private. CRM systems are used for marketing and sales purposes.

Marketing Information

The advertising efforts of a business should not intentionally mislead customers. The information conveyed through promotional material

must be factual and accurate. Advertising pieces must follow federal guidelines set by the *Federal Trade Commission (FTC)*. Under the *Federal Trade Commission Act*, federal law states the following:
- Advertising must be truthful and nondeceptive.
- Advertisers must have evidence to back up their claims.
- Advertisements cannot be unfair.

False advertising is overstating the features and benefits of goods or services or making false claims about them. False advertising is both unethical and illegal. Businesses that misrepresent their products or services risk losing customers, at the very least.

It is unethical to send spam when promoting a business using electronic communication. **Spam** is electronic messages sent in bulk to people who did not give a company permission to e-mail them. Sending spam can reflect poorly on a company and irritate current and potential customers. Marketing efforts should include sending e-mails only to customers who have given the company permission to do so.

Pricing

It is both unethical and illegal for businesses to engage in unfair pricing practices. The pricing practices shown in Figure 4-2 are both harmful to consumers and illegal. Businesses that use unfair pricing practices are breaking laws in addition to being unethical. Unfair pricing practices are usually reported to authorities by unhappy customers. The best-case scenario for these businesses is that sales and profits are decreased. In the worst-case scenario, owners may have to pay costly fines and the company may go out of business.

State and federal laws regulate pricing to prevent unfair pricing policies and practices used by some businesses. For example, more than half of the United States have laws that

Carlos Yudica/Shutterstock.com

Advertising claims, like the ones shown on these products, must be truthful and nondeceptive. *How do advertising claims on a product label influence your purchasing decisions?*

Unfair Pricing Practices	
Bait and switch	Advertising one product with the intent of persuading customers to buy a more expensive item when they arrive in the store
Deceptive pricing	Pricing products in such a way as to intentionally mislead a customer
Predatory pricing	Setting very low prices to drive competition from the market
Price discrimination	Selling the same product to different customers at different prices based on the personal characteristics of customers
Price gouging	Raising prices on certain kinds of goods to an excessively high level during an emergency or period of unusually high demand
Price-fixing	Group of competitors agreeing to a set price for a specific product, which can be high or low

Figure 4-2 Unfair pricing practices are harmful to consumers and are often illegal.

Goodheart-Willcox Publisher

Green Marketing

Environmental Protection Agency

The US Environmental Protection Agency (EPA) is a governmental organization with a mission to protect human health and the environment. The EPA is a rich resource of information on environmental issues, such as pollution, climate change, protecting wildlife, and hazardous waste disposal.

The EPA also publishes information on environmental laws and regulations by business sector. It is important for businesses to do their part to protect the environment. *Green businesses* lead by example and educate their employees, and often customers, on sustainable practices, reducing waste, and lowering energy consumption. Visit the EPA's website to learn more.

---

protect consumers from price-gouging practices. The government also prevents the formation of monopolies, which interfere with the workings of a market economy. If one company has all of the business in a market, it could set unfair prices due to lack of competition. Some US states have their own laws against additional pricing practices. However, there are no federal laws banning these practices. They are enforced at the state level.

Selling

Ethical selling practices are important for the success of a company. Many businesses address the following issues related to selling.

- It is illegal to accept or pay bribes for the purpose of closing a sale or obtaining business licenses.
- High-pressure selling is not illegal, but many customers perceive it as unethical.
- It is unethical to accept gifts from suppliers in exchange for the promise to continue buying from them.

Section 4.1 Review

Check Your Understanding

1. State two ways a company might convey its expectations for acceptable employee behavior
2. Define *workplace bullying*.
3. What do codes of ethics typically address?
4. Name a professional organization that sets standards for ethical behavior.
5. List the tenets of the Federal Trade Commission Act.

Build Your Vocabulary

As you progress through this text, develop a personal glossary of key terms. This will help you build your vocabulary and prepare you for a career. Write a definition for each of the following terms and add them to your personal glossary.

business ethics
code of conduct
code of ethics
customer relationship management (CRM)
ethics
morals
spam

Section 4.2

Social Responsibility

Essential Question

How can acting in a socially responsible manner benefit a business?

Learning Objectives

LO 4.2-1 Explain the importance of corporate social responsibility.
LO 4.2-2 Identify socially responsible marketing activities.

Key Terms

social responsibility
corporate social responsibility (CSR)
goodwill
philanthropy
sustainability
recycling
socially responsible marketing
green marketing
cause marketing

Corporate Social Responsibility

LO 4.2-1

Social responsibility is behaving with sensitivity toward social, economic, and environmental issues. It includes a duty to help others and to improve society in general. **Corporate social responsibility (CSR)** is the actions a business takes to further social good. These are actions that go beyond the profit interests and legal requirements of a business.

CSR is important because it can make a difference in a community, improve relations with clients or customers, and create goodwill. **Goodwill** is the advantage a business has due to its positive reputation. Goodwill creates customer loyalty, earns the trust of the community, and is vitally important to success in business.

There are many actions a business can take to demonstrate CSR. Examples of these actions include philanthropy, supporting the local economy, and protecting the environment.

Philanthropy

Philanthropy is promoting the welfare of others, usually through donating time, property, or money. Philanthropic activities are most effective when they align with the existing goods or services that a business offers. For example, employees at an advertising agency could volunteer to help a nonprofit organization develop a marketing plan.

ESB Professional/Shutterstock.com

Philanthropy is promoting the welfare of others through donating time, property, or money. *What philanthropic activities do you think would be the most helpful in your community?*

Employability Skills

Etiquette
Etiquette is the art of using good manners in any situation. *Professional etiquette* is applying the rules of good manners in the workplace and in other work-related situations.

Local Economy

There is an economic aspect of social responsibility that goes beyond volunteering time or donating money. A socially responsible business makes an effort to conduct business locally and use local resources whenever possible. It is a good business practice to hire people from the community. When local citizens are employed, they have more economic resources to purchase goods and services from all types of businesses in the community.

Environment

Social responsibility includes respect for the environment. Protecting the environment is important because it impacts society as a whole.

Many socially responsible businesses attempt to implement environmentally sustainable business practices. **Sustainability** is creating and maintaining conditions under which humans and nature can coexist both now and in the future. Sustainable use of natural resources meets current needs without depleting resources and reducing the ability to meet future needs.

Sustainable business practices include conserving natural resources, reducing pollution, and recycling. **Recycling** is the reprocessing of resources so they can be used again. Many items used in daily business operations can be recycled, such as paper, printer cartridges, and plastic. Businesses can make small changes in their daily operations that will make an impact in sustainability efforts. Environmentally friendly products or components can be used both in business operations and for product packaging. Businesses can offer customers reusable shopping bags, reuse cardboard boxes when shipping products, and use environmentally safe cleaning products in the maintenance of their facilities.

LO 4.2-2 Socially Responsible Marketing

Socially responsible marketing is a belief that a company's marketing approach should consider the benefit to and betterment of society as a whole. Marketing professionals are expected to act ethically and follow the laws related to marketing activities. However, socially responsible marketing takes a broader view of marketing activities. It considers the impact of marketing activities and how marketing can make life better for customers. Examples include green marketing and cause marketing.

Social Media

Social-Media Marketing (SMM)
Social-media marketing (SMM) is the use of social media as a part of the marketing plan to convince consumers to buy product, help build brand recognition, and increase the customer base. For SMM to be effective, the message must be *sticky*, meaning that it will hold the attention of the user. The message must be brief, relevant, and interesting. It works on the premise that the user will stay on the website long enough to perform the desired action before leaving the site, such as make a purchase or share the information with someone else.

A goal of social media marketing is to create messages so interesting or compelling that the reader shares it with friends, coworkers, or family. It relies on *viral marketing*, or buzz marketing, which is passing on information to others through electronic means.

Green Marketing

Green marketing is producing and promoting products using methods and practices that emphasize environmental conservation. Businesses that employ green marketing make environmentally conscious decisions in every aspect of the marketing mix, from product offerings to sustainable distribution strategies.

Governmental resources are available to help businesses identify and implement green practices. The *Environmental Protection Agency (EPA)* offers information and resources about environmental protection, sustainable business practices, and environmental law. Companies looking to implement green practices can contact the EPA for guidance. The EPA also provides information about environmental-compliance rules and regulations, which vary by business sector.

digitalreflections/Shutterstock.com

Kohl's promotes its social responsibility by informing customers when a store has been built or modified to be environmentally friendly. *When have you observed green marketing?*

Cause Marketing

Cause marketing is a type of marketing in which a for-profit business and a nonprofit organization or charity work together for mutual benefit. Businesses typically choose a cause that is relevant to their products, important to customers, and can impact the community. For example, a pet supply business may choose to promote and support the efforts of a local animal rescue organization. This cause is relevant to the products of the business, its customers, and the local community.

This marketing strategy can be used to increase awareness of certain issues and encourage customers to take action. A business may advertise that it donates a percentage of its profits, hold in-store fund-raising events, or simply provide information to educate customers about a particular cause or organization. In doing this, the nonprofit benefits financially, through increased public awareness, or both.

Case in Point

Amazon.com & Goodwill Industries

Cause marketing increases awareness of social and ethical issues and encourages customers to take action. Cause marketing benefits both businesses and nonprofits that partner to support a cause. Businesses gain increased visibility and goodwill with their customers, as well as the potential for increased profits. Nonprofits can also increase public awareness of their organization or of the cause itself, and may also benefit financially.

Amazon.com is the largest e-commerce retailer in the world. Goodwill Industries is a nonprofit that offers job training, employment placement, and other programs for people who have challenges finding employment. Goodwill is funded by the sales from the thrift stores it operates. These two organizations partnered in a cause-marketing campaign called Give Back Box.

Give Back Box was a global donation drive campaign that invited Amazon.com customers to reuse the shipping boxes from their online orders by filling the box with clothing and household goods they wished to donate. Customers could then visit the Give Back Box website to print a free shipping label to send the box to the customer's nearest Goodwill donation center. Give Back Box made donating goods simple, easy, and convenient for the consumer. This cause marketing campaign demonstrated the commitments made by both Amazon.com and Goodwill Industries to social and environmental issues.

Cause marketing demonstrates a company's commitment to ethical and social issues. This can have a powerful effect on consumers. Many consumers place a priority on patronizing businesses that display social awareness, including environmentally friendly practices, charitable giving, and supporting community activities. Businesses benefit by increasing customer loyalty and possibly gaining new customers as a result of their cause marketing activities.

Section 4.2 Review

Check Your Understanding

1. List examples of actions a business can take to demonstrate CSR.
2. How can a business support the local economy?
3. What are some ways a company can recycle?
4. Where can businesses get help in identifying and implementing green practices?
5. How do businesses benefit from cause marketing?

Build Your Vocabulary

As you progress through this text, develop a personal glossary of key terms. This will help you build your vocabulary and prepare you for a career. Write a definition for each of the following terms and add them to your personal glossary.

cause marketing
corporate social responsibility (CSR)
goodwill
green marketing
philanthropy
recycling
social responsibility
socially responsible marketing
sustainability

CHAPTER 4 Review and Assessment

Chapter Summary

Section 4.1 Ethics

LO 4.1-1 Summarize the concept of business ethics.
Business ethics are the rules for professional conduct and integrity in all areas of business. Two ways a company might convey its expectations for acceptable employee behavior are with a code of conduct and a code of ethics.

LO 4.1-2 State examples of ethical marketing practices.
There are many examples of ethical marketing practices. These include customer privacy, honest marketing information, fair pricing, and ethical selling practices.

Section 4.2 Social Responsibility

LO 4.2-1 Explain the importance of corporate social responsibility.
Corporate social responsibility (CSR) is the actions a business takes to further social good. It can make a difference in a community, improve relations with clients or customers, and create goodwill. Goodwill creates customer loyalty, earns the trust of the community, and is vitally important to success in business.

LO 4.2-2 Identify socially responsible marketing activities.
Socially responsible marketing is a belief that a company's marketing approach should consider the benefit to and betterment of society as a whole. Examples include green marketing and cause marketing.

Check Your Marketing IQ

Now that you have completed the chapter, see what you have learned about marketing by taking the chapter posttest. The posttest is available at www.g-wlearning.com/marketing/.

Review Your Knowledge

1. Summarize the concept of business ethics.
2. What is the goal of a code of ethics?
3. What is the role of the American Marketing Association?
4. Explain the effect of unethical behavior on a business.
5. State examples of ethical marketing practices.
6. Explain the importance of corporate social responsibility (CSR).
7. When are the philanthropic activities of a business most effective?
8. Cite examples of sustainable business practices.
9. Identify examples of socially responsible marketing activities.
10. How do nonprofit organizations benefit from cause marketing?

Apply Your Knowledge

1. As a marketing professional, which ethical issues do you think will be most important for your career? List and explain your reasoning for each.
2. Having a personal code of ethics will be important as you prepare for a marketing career. Write a summary describing the important topics that you will include in your personal code of ethics.
3. Why do you think a business would require a marketer to sign a confidentiality agreement?
4. Customers have the right to expect a company to keep their personal information confidential. What confidential customer

Copyright Goodheart-Willcox Co., Inc.

information might a marketing professional possess?

5. Marketing professionals are in the position of setting prices for products sold to other businesses. Describe your ethical obligations as a marketing professional in pricing products.
6. Describe your personal level of social responsibility, including regular behaviors and related actions you take.
7. A tornado has struck your town. The business for which you work already supports a number of charities in the area. Should the company react and assist with the disaster? Explain your answer.
8. You would like to incorporate the value of being socially responsible into your marketing career. List and describe three activities that you can implement to increase a company's level of responsibility to the local community.
9. Look around your community and select a company that you think is socially responsible. What is this business doing to support the community?
10. Brainstorm ideas of ways in which a business could become more environmentally friendly. Create a list of ten ideas.

Apply Your Math Skills

Corporate social responsibility actions make a difference in a community and create goodwill. Many companies demonstrate social responsibility by donating money and time to local charities. Apply your math skills to solve the following problems.

1. Kieran donated $20 per month to an animal welfare charity for the last 12 months. He works for a company that matches the charitable donations made by employees at 50 percent of the total employee donation. How much will the animal welfare charity receive from Kieran and his employer?
2. The Brand It, Inc. company provides employees paid time off to perform volunteer work. Four employees took advantage of this benefit and worked 7 hours at a local food pantry. The hourly wages of each employee were as follows: $13.00 per hour, $15.25 per hour, $18.50 per hour, and $19.00 per hour. How much did the volunteer work cost the company in wages?

Communication Skills

College and Career Readiness

Reading *Reading for detail* involves reading all words and phrases, considering their meanings, and determining how they combine with other elements to convey ideas. Using this approach, read the first section this chapter. Consider the way the words are used by the author in each paragraph. After you have finished, determine if you have obtained grasp of the content by reading for detail.

Writing Schools often have a code of conduct that applies to the conduct and ethical behavior of students. This may include an honor code, behavior policy, and other policies. Write a summary of your school's code of conduct as it applies to student behavior. Explain how students benefit from each of the policies you identified. Describe the impact of these policies on the school community as a whole.

Listening Informative listening is the process of listening to gain specific information from the speaker. Interview a person who is responsible for the recycling program in a household, business, or other organization. Make notes as the policies are described. Evaluate the speaker's point of view and reasoning. Did you listen closely enough to write accurate facts?

Internet Research

American Marketing Association Using the Internet, visit the website of the American Marketing Association (AMA). Use the website's search function to locate the AMA's Statement of Ethics. Read the Preamble, Ethical Norms, and Ethical Values. How might this information impact your role as a marketing professional in the future?

Ethical Business Behavior Use Internet resources to locate an example of a business that behaved unethically. Determine the *who*, *what*, *where*, *when*, and *why* of the situation. Write a short paragraph to summarize the long-lasting effects of the unethical behavior on the business.

Workplace Bullying Workplace bullying is a growing problem for workers and employers. Conduct an Internet search for *workplace bullying*. After you have reviewed several articles, describe how you would coach a coworker to identify if he or she is being bullied. Next, outline steps you would suggest taking to approach the employer about the issue.

Teamwork

Working with your team, create a code of ethics for your classroom. Use various resources as inspiration, such as the AMA Statement of Ethics or your school's student handbook, if desired. Brainstorm the possible ethical issues that may arise in a classroom situation and address how they should be handled in your statement. Share your team's code of ethics with the rest of the class.

Portfolio Development

Checklist Once you have written your portfolio objective, consider how you will achieve it. It is helpful to have a checklist of components that will be included in your portfolio. The checklist will be used to record ideas for documents and other items that you might include. Starting with a checklist will help you brainstorm ideas that you want to pursue. The elements that you select to include in your portfolio will reflect your portfolio's purpose. For example, if you are seeking acceptance into art school, create a portfolio that includes your best artwork.

College and Career Readiness

1. Ask your instructor for a checklist. If one is not provided, use the Internet and research Student Portfolio checklists. Find an example that works for your purpose.
2. Create a checklist. This will be your roadmap for your portfolio.

UNIT 1 Marketing Dynamics

Building the Marketing Plan

The best companies in the world make plans. They plan their marketing efforts, strategies for growth, projections for hiring, and roadmaps for profitability. As a future marketing professional, you will need to learn the skill of planning. One way to begin planning is to perform research about companies for which you might like to create a marketing plan. Once you have selected a company in which you would like to assume the role of marketing manager, you will begin the plan.

Part 1 Introduction

Objective
- Review the marketing plan template.

Directions
In this textbook, you will be exploring the world of marketing. As you learn about marketing and progress through the chapters, you will write a marketing plan. Step one of the process is to become acquainted with the marketing plan template you will use. Access the *Marketing Dynamics* companion website at www.g-wlearning.com/marketing/. Complete the activity file as indicated in the following instructions.

1. **Marketing Plan Template** Download the activity file called Marketing Plan Template. Preview each section of the template in this file. To become familiar with the marketing plan format, read the instructions and questions that will guide you in the writing process. As you progress through the chapters, you will be directed to complete each section. Keep in mind that the sections you complete in each activity may not be in the order listed in the document.

2. Ask your instructor where to save your documents. This could be on the school's network or a flash drive of your own. Save the marketing plan template as your own document to use for creating your Marketing Plan. Save the document as FirstnameLastname_MktPlan.docx (i.e., JohnSmith_MktPlan.docx).

Part 2 Identify Your Company

In this activity, you will assume the role of marketing manager for a company that you select. You will research potential companies and select one for which you will act as a marketing manager. Spend time now selecting a company that interests you and for which you will feel comfortable playing the marketing manager role. As you progress through this text, it will be your assignment to create a Marketing Plan for your company.

Objectives
- Identify a company for which you will assume the role as marketing manager.
- Create a title page for your Marketing Plan.
- Write a business description for your business.
- Gather information about the target market of your business.

Directions

1. **Unit Activity 1-1—Research Company** Identify a company for which you will write a marketing plan. You will also perform research to find the business plan for the company you have chosen. Much information found in the business plan will be helpful when completing the marketing plan.

2. Open the Marketing Plan document you saved in Part 1. Locate the Title Page of the Marketing Plan. Complete the Title Page using the information you gathered in Activity 1-1. Key your company name, product line, and your name. Leave the date blank until the Marketing Plan is completed. As you progress through this text, you will be directed to complete each section.

3. Locate the Business Description section of the Marketing Plan. Based on information in the business plan, give an overview of the business. This section describes the product and identifies the type of business. Then, list the vision statement, mission statement, and company goals. This will be a short section, no longer than one page. It is permissible to condense this information. However, it is not acceptable to rewrite or recreate it.

4. Locate the Marketing Strategies section of the Marketing Plan. Begin writing the Target Market subsection. You will learn more details about target markets later in this text. For this exercise, record information about the customer to whom the business sells. This information can be found in the Target Market section of your company's business plan. Write as much information about the targeted customer as is available in the business plan. You will continue adding to this section as the marketing plan develops.

5. Use the suggestions and questions listed in the template to help you generate ideas. Delete the instructions and questions when you are finished recording your responses. Proofread your document and correct any errors in keyboarding, spelling, and grammar.

6. Save your document.

UNIT 2: Economics

Chapters

5 **Economic Principles**
6 **Economic Activity**
7 **Global Trade**

While studying, look for the activity icon for:
- Building the Marketing Plan activity files
- Pretests and posttests
- Vocabulary terms with e-flash cards and matching activities
- Self-assessment

These activities can be accessed at www.g-wlearning.com/marketing/.

Developing a Vision

Take a look around you. The state of our economy is in the news every day. Economics plays an important role in today's business. Successful marketers know how to use economic information and apply it to marketing strategies. Marketing a product in slow economic conditions may be difficult. Or, it may present opportunities. Understanding the marketing concept and how to apply it in both good and bad conditions is crucial.

Marketing is global. Trade barriers are disappearing, and communication is improving. Opportunities to take products to other parts of the world exist. It is an exciting time to be a marketer.

Marketing Core Functions Covered in This Unit

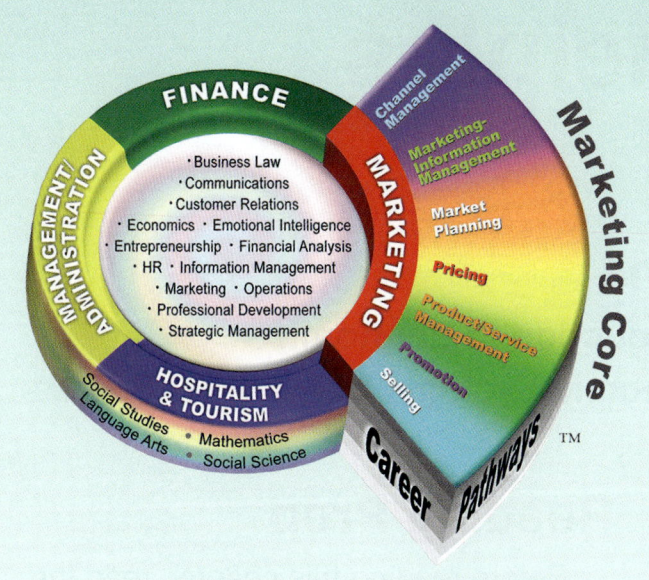

Functions of Marketing

- Channel management
- Marketing-information management
- Market planning
- Pricing
- Product/service management

Copyright MBA Research, Columbus, Ohio. Used with permission.

EYE-CATCHER

Marketing Matters

The economy can have a direct impact on a company's marketing strategy. For example, when the economy is slow, sales may also be slow. This is a time when marketing is needed more than ever to maintain a customer base and keep sales from slipping further. One inexpensive marketing strategy that can be used to encourage customers to keep buying products is a customer loyalty program that rewards customers for making frequent purchases. One common example of this is an airline frequent flyer program. By incentivizing customers to continue patronizing the business when money is tight, those same customers may be there when the economy improves.

Nadalina/Shutterstock.com

CHAPTER 5

Economic Principles

Sections

5.1 **Introduction to Economics**
5.2 **Economic Systems and Market Forces**

Reading Prep

College and Career Readiness

Before reading this chapter, read the opening pages for this unit and review the chapter titles. These can help prepare you for the topics that will be presented in the unit. What do the opening pages for the unit tell you about what you will be learning?

Check Your Marketing IQ

Before you begin the chapter, see what you already know about marketing by taking the chapter pretest. The pretest is available at www.g-wlearning.com/marketing/.

DECA Emerging Leaders

Sports and Entertainment Marketing Team Decision-Making Event, Part 1

Career Cluster: Marketing
Instructional Area: Economics

Knowledge and Skills Developed

Participants will develop many 21st century skills desired by today's employers in the following categories:
- communication and collaboration
- creativity and innovation
- critical thinking and problem solving
- flexibility and adaptability
- information literacy
- initiative and self-direction
- leadership and responsibility
- productivity and accountability
- social and cross-cultural skills

Specific Performance Indicators

- Explain the concept of economic resources.
- Explain the principles of supply and demand.
- Discuss the global environment in which businesses operate.
- Identify factors affecting a business's profit.
- Explain factors affecting pricing decisions.
- Describe factors used by businesses to position corporate brands.
- Demonstrate connections between company actions and results.

Purpose

Designed for a team of two DECA members, the event measures the team's ability to explain core business concepts in a case-study format through a role-play. This event consists of a 100-question, multiple-choice, cluster exam for each team member and a decision-making case study situation. The Team Decision-Making Event provides an opportunity for participants to analyze one element or a combination of elements essential to the effective operation of a business in the specific career area presented as a case study.

For the purposes of this text, you will be presented with the material for this event in two parts. Part 1 presents the knowledge and skills assessed and an overview of the event's purpose and procedure. Part 2 presents the remaining procedures and the event situation.

Procedure, Part 1

1. For Part 1 in this text, read both sets of performance indicators. Discuss these with your team members.
2. If there are any questions, ask your instructor to clarify.

Critical Thinking

1. What is the significance of performance indicators while preparing for the event?
2. What is your team's strategy to effectively communicate your response to the performance indicators?

Visit www.deca.org for more information.

Published by DECA Inc. Copyright © by DECA Inc. No part of this publication may be reproduced for resale without written permission from the publisher. Printed in the United States of America.

Section 5.1

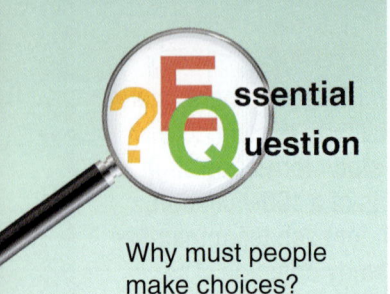

Introduction to Economics

Essential Question
Why must people make choices?

Learning Objectives

LO 5.1-1 Explain the concept of economics.
LO 5.1-2 Describe the factors of production.
LO 5.1-3 Explain the economic problem.

Key Terms

economics
macroeconomics
microeconomics
factors of production
labor
productivity
capital
capital goods
infrastructure
technology
entrepreneurship
scarcity
trade-off
opportunity cost
systematic decision-making

LO 5.1-1 Economics

Economics is a science that examines how goods and services are produced, sold, and used. It examines how people, governments, and businesses make choices about using limited resources to satisfy unlimited wants. The study of economics is divided into two branches: macroeconomics and microeconomics.

Macroeconomics

Macroeconomics is the branch of economics that studies human behavior and choices that relate to the entire economy of a nation. The prefix *macro* means *large*. Macroeconomics looks at the entire economy as a whole. It concentrates on a nation's system of producing and distributing goods. This includes the study of broad factors, such as the total output and growth of an economy, inflation, and unemployment. Macroeconomics also studies economic cycles and how the government tries to manage the economy through policies related to spending, taxes, and the money supply.

Microeconomics

Microeconomics is the branch of economics that studies human behavior and choices that relate to the economic decisions of individuals and businesses. The prefix *micro* means *small*. It focuses on such things as how individuals decide

Maridav/Shutterstock.com

Economics examines how people, governments, and businesses make choices about using limited resources to satisfy unlimited wants. *What economic choices have you made recently?*

how to spend and invest their money. It also studies how businesses try to earn profits and compete against each other.

Factors of Production
LO 5.1-2

Factors of production are the economic resources a nation uses to make goods and supply services for its population. The factors of production are land, labor, capital, and entrepreneurship.

Think about goods that you use often, such as athletic shoes. Many economic resources were used to create them: cotton, rubber, shoe-fabricating machines, people operating the machines, and a business owner. These resources represent the four factors of production: land, labor, capital, and entrepreneurship, as shown in Figure 5-1. In this example, cotton and rubber represent the land resource.

Workers provide the labor. The shoe-fabricating machines are the capital. The business owner represents entrepreneurship by organizing the other three economic resources to operate the business.

Land

Land includes all of a nation's natural resources. *Natural resources* are raw materials found in nature. These include soil, water, minerals, plants, and animals. Every good produced uses natural resources in some form. Many natural resources are scarce and take a very long time to replenish.

Natural resources are not equally distributed among nations. Even developed nations like the United States have limited natural resources. Some are found only in certain parts of the world. For example, South Africa has mines producing great quantities of diamonds and other gemstones. While the United States is rich in minerals like coal, lead, and zinc, it does not have any profitable diamond mines.

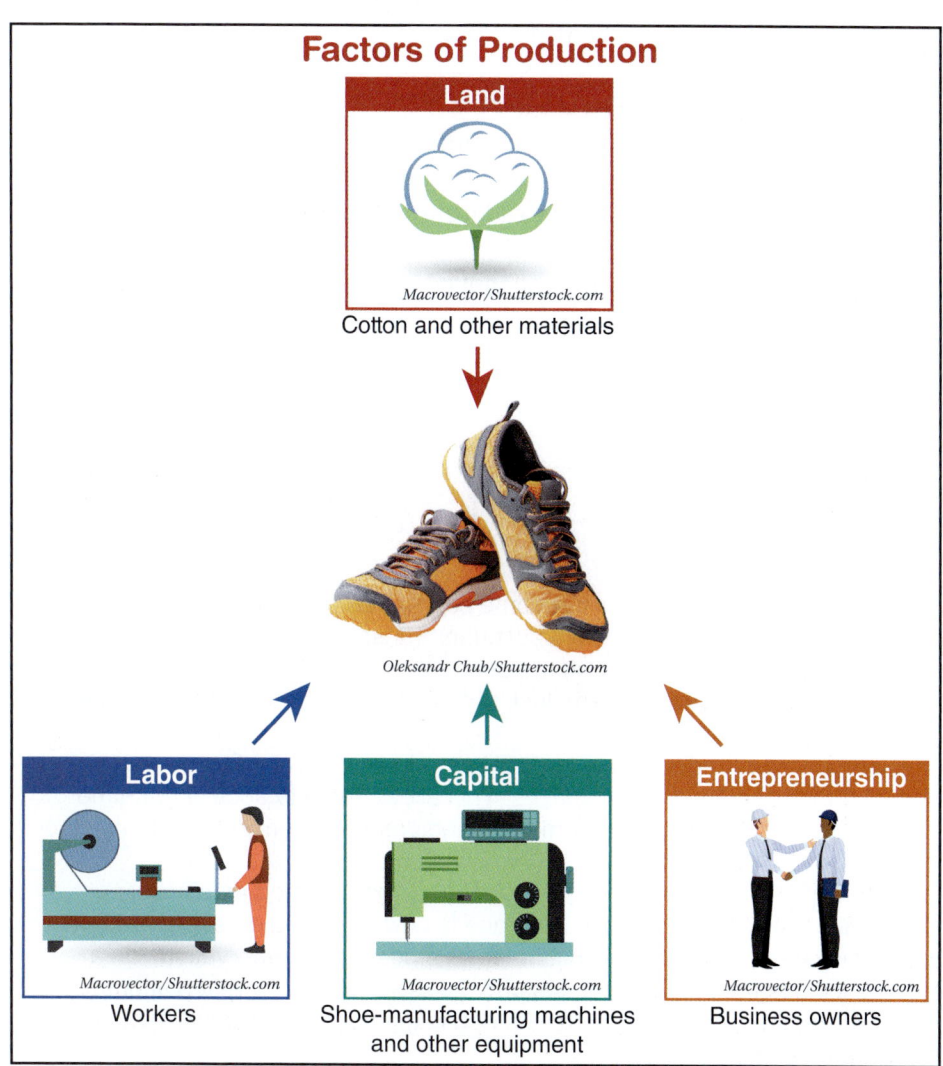

Figure 5-1 Production of athletic shoes requires land, labor, capital, and entrepreneurship.

The size of a nation can also affect the quantity of a nation's available natural resources. For example, Japan is four percent the size of the United States. Therefore, it has much fewer natural resources and relies heavily on imports for these materials.

Labor

Labor is the work performed by people in businesses. Another term for labor is *human resources*.

Productivity is the amount of work a person can do in a specific amount of time, usually an hour. A nation can make up for a lack of natural resources if its people are very productive. Because Japan is a geographically small country, it has proportionately few natural resources. However, it has the world's third-largest economy. This is because Japanese workers in their largest industries, automobile and electronics manufacturing, are highly skilled and very productive.

Capital

As a factor of production, **capital** is all the tools and machinery used to produce goods or provide services. **Capital goods** are those products businesses use to produce other goods. Capital goods are used to make final products, which are then sold to consumers. For example, a shoe-fabricating machine is a capital good because its only purpose is to make shoes. The shoes are the final product. Consumers do not buy capital goods, they buy final products.

Delmas Lehman/Shutterstock.com

Transportation infrastructure includes highways, seaports, airports, and bridges, like the Sunshine Skyway Bridge in Florida. What forms of infrastructure exist in your community?

Infrastructure

Infrastructure is considered a form of capital. **Infrastructure** consists of the transportation systems and utilities necessary in a modern economy. Infrastructure is usually large and cannot be moved from place to place.

Case in Point

Amtrak

In a world where wireless communication technology has become part of everyday life, key components of Amtrak's operations had been left behind. The railway passenger transportation company relied on a paper-based ticketing system in use since the 1800s. Amtrak transports over 30 million passengers each year. Customers voiced frustration about the inefficient system, lack of flexibility, and absence of real-time travel information.

Amtrak responded to their customers by upgrading many of their operational systems. Conductors now have smartphones that connect with the company's databases. This allows them to access real-time passenger manifests to verify seat availability, as well as enter maintenance requests that can be completed at the next station on the line.

To improve the customer experience, Amtrak added on-board Wi-Fi and implemented an eTicketing system. The eTicketing system was piloted on select routes in 2011 and is now accepted on every Amtrak route. Passengers can purchase tickets online and print them at home or present their reservations on a mobile device. Additional online tools include train status updates and the ability to modify reservations. Amtrak integrated technology to meet customer demand, which resulted in greater customer satisfaction, improved customer experience, and more efficient operations.

Marketing Ethics

Integrity

Integrity is defined as the honesty of a person's actions. Integrity and ethics go hand-in-hand in both personal and professional lives. As a leader, a marketing manager helps to establish the reputation of the business. Displaying integrity helps create a positive culture within the business, as well as a positive impression with customers and the community.

Infrastructure provides the foundation on which modern industry is built. *Transportation infrastructure* includes highways, bridges, railroads, public transportation, seaports, and airports. *Utility infrastructure* includes sanitation systems, power plants, water systems, and telecommunications services. Some infrastructure, such as power plants and railroads, is often built and operated by private companies. Other infrastructure, like highways, bridges, and airports, is most often built and operated by the government.

Imagine you are looking for a place to build a factory. You have a choice between two areas. One area has excellent infrastructure. It is close to major highways, railroads, and power plants. The other area has poor highway access and is very far from rail service. Where would you want to build your new factory? Your answer will likely be in the area with the better infrastructure.

Technology

Another form of capital as a factor of production is technology. **Technology** is the use of science to invent useful things or to solve problems. Countries can use early technology or advanced technology. The type of technology used has a major impact on an economy.

Early technology includes the six simple machines: lever, wedge, inclined plane, screw, pulley, and wheel and axle. Machines powered by people or animals are also examples of early technology. Early technology brought about great improvements in productivity during ancient times. However, in modern times, countries that only use early technology struggle to meet the basic needs of food and shelter for citizens.

Advanced technology includes industrial and digital technologies. *Industrial technology* is powered by steam and fuel combustion. For example, automobiles and jets are powered by fuel combustion, as are many factories. *Digital technology* uses electricity to control data. Examples include computers, smartphones, and the Internet. Countries using advanced technologies produce more goods and services than those using early technology.

Entrepreneurship

The final factor of production is entrepreneurship. **Entrepreneurship** is the willingness and ability to start a new business. Entrepreneurs organize the other three factors of production to produce a good or service and earn a profit. They are able to take financial and personal risks necessary to start and run a business.

From a small store to a large manufacturer, all businesses are started by entrepreneurs. For example, the entrepreneur Steve Jobs cofounded Apple, Inc. It became one of the most successful corporations in the world. The number and quality of entrepreneurs in a country have a major impact on an economy.

LO 5.1-3 Economic Problem

All economic resources are limited. Individuals, businesses, and governments must constantly make choices about how to use limited resources to satisfy unlimited needs and wants. The *economic problem* states that human wants are unlimited, while resources are limited, as illustrated in Figure 5-2. **Scarcity** develops when demand is higher than the available resources.

Scarce resources limit the quantity of goods and services produced. This means decisions must be made about which goods or services will be created. The problem of scarcity leads to three

Limited Resources → Scarcity ← Unlimited Wants
↓
Economic Problem

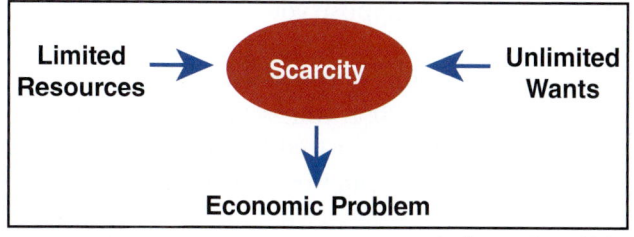

Goodheart-Willcox Publisher

Figure 5-2 The economic problem states that wants are unlimited, while resources are limited.

Three Economic Questions

Economic Question	Related Questions	Examples
What should be produced and how much?	Which goods, services, and ideas should we produce? How much of each product should we produce?	Should we produce consumer products or weapons for the military? Should we grow crops or raise cattle? Should we explore outer space or research a cure for cancer?
How should resources be allocated in production?	Who should produce each type of product? How shall we use our natural resources? What production techniques should be used?	Who should be a doctor and who should be a farmer? Should we generate electricity from coal, oil, or nuclear power? Should natural areas be preserved or used for mining? Should people or computers calculate the payroll?
For whom are the goods and services produced?	How will the nation decide who gets each product? How should products be distributed?	Should the rich get all the products they want? Should the head of the government get whatever he or she wants? How should the nation provide for the poor? How should the country ration scarce resources in times of crisis?

Figure 5-3 Economic systems develop around the way each country answers the three basic economic questions.

Goodheart-Willcox Publisher

important economic questions every nation must answer, shown in Figure 5-3.
- What should be produced and how much?
- How should resources be allocated in production?
- For whom are the goods and services produced?

Scarcity forces choices to be made. Every economic decision has a cost. Choosing one option means giving up other options that may have been available. A **trade-off** is when something is given up in order to gain something else. When a trade-off occurs, an opportunity cost is created. **Opportunity cost** is the value of the next-best option that was not selected. *Value* is the relative worth of something.

For example, suppose you have two hours of free time. You can watch television or go to work and earn $20. If you choose to watch television, you will not earn $20. If you go to work, you will miss your favorite show. In this situation, the opportunity cost of watching television is $20; however, if you choose to work, the opportunity cost is missing your favorite television show. You make the decision by deciding which one is more valuable to you.

Individuals make economic decisions based on what is most valuable to them. Nations also have many economic needs and wants, but resources are limited. As a result, nations have to make economic choices with bigger opportunity costs.

When making economic decisions, a systematic decision-making process can help identify

Employability Skills

Self-Management Skills

Self-management skills are the skills that enable an individual to control and make the best use of his or her time and abilities. They are important because they facilitate productivity, help ensure employee success, and provide assurance for an employer that the employee will help the business meet its goals. An individual has complete control over the development and use of self-management skills. Some important self-management skills are emotional control, problem-solving, time management, and goal-setting.

the best option. **Systematic decision-making** is a process of choosing an option after evaluating the available information and weighing the costs and benefits of the alternatives. A systematic decision-making process can be used by both businesses and individuals. The process involves five steps, as shown in the chart in Figure 5-4.

1. *Define the decision to be made.* Have a clear understanding of the end goal. For a business, it may be to offer a new product or change the image of the business. For an individual, it may be a purchasing decision or how to cut expenses.
2. *Explore all alternatives.* Analyze the options available. What is the benefit of each option? What is the disadvantage of each? What is the financial cost of each option?
3. *Choose the best alternative.* After considering all alternatives, decide which option is best. The decision may be a single option or a combination of several options.
4. *Act on the decision.* Carry out the plan.
5. *Evaluate the solution or decision.* Evaluate how effective the choice is in reaching the end goal. Did the plan work? How can it be improved? The evaluation process can help an individual or business stay on track and make better decisions in the future. Evaluation is an ongoing process.

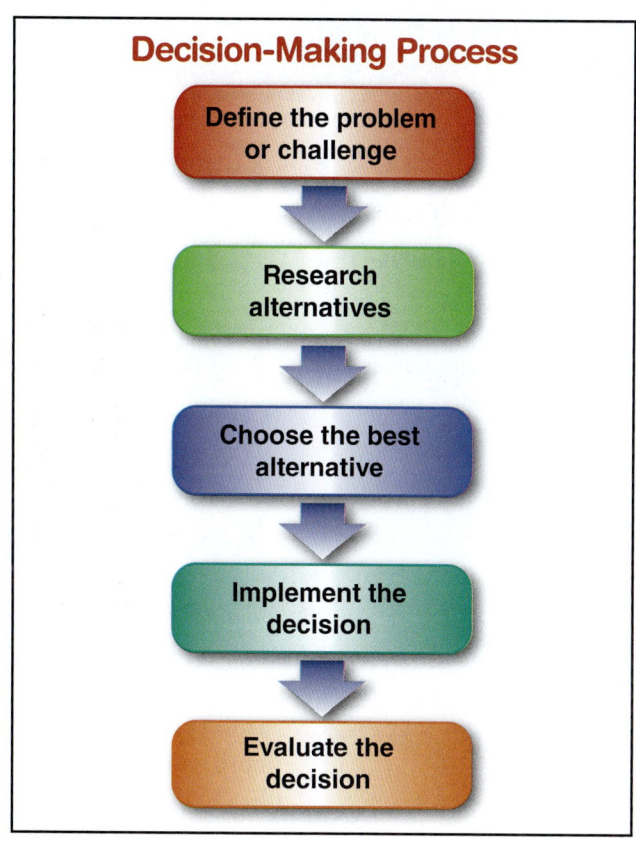

Decision-Making Process

- Define the problem or challenge
- Research alternatives
- Choose the best alternative
- Implement the decision
- Evaluate the decision

Goodheart-Willcox Publisher

Figure 5-4 A systematic decision-making process can be helpful when making economic decisions.

Section 5.1 Review

Check Your Understanding

1. What is the difference between macroeconomics and microeconomics?
2. Identify the factors of production.
3. What causes scarcity to develop?
4. What is the result of scarcity?
5. List the steps in the decision-making process.

Build Your Vocabulary

As you progress through this text, develop a personal glossary of key terms. This will help you build your vocabulary and prepare you for a career. Write a definition for each of the following terms and add them to your personal glossary.

capital
capital goods
economics
entrepreneurship
factors of production
infrastructure
labor
macroeconomics

microeconomics
opportunity cost
productivity
scarcity
systematic decision-making
technology
trade-off

Section 5.2

Economic Systems and Market Forces

Essential Question: Who should control an economy?

Learning Objectives

LO 5.2-1 Define four economic systems.
LO 5.2-2 Describe market forces in a free-enterprise system.

Key Terms

economic system
economic input
economic output
traditional economy
command economy
market economy
mixed economy
market forces
law of supply and demand
equilibrium

Economic Systems

LO 5.2-1

A *system* is a way to manage, control, or organize something that follows a set of rules. For example, a computer system consists of input, a production mechanism, and output. The information or data keyed into the computer is the input. The production mechanism includes the computer hard drive, software programs, and the printer. The output is the physical or electronic document produced. Figure 5-5 shows simple examples of systems.

An **economic system** is an organized way in which a nation chooses to use its limited resources to create goods and services that answer the three economic questions.

- What should we produce?
- How should we produce it?
- For whom should it be produced?

Economic systems also have input, production mechanisms, and output. **Economic input** includes the resources used to make products. **Economic output** is all the goods and services produced by an economic system during a specific time. A nation's economic system develops around the way it deals with scarcity.

Economists classify economic systems as being a traditional, command, or market economy. However, many economies today are mixed. Mixed economies have elements of both command and market economies.

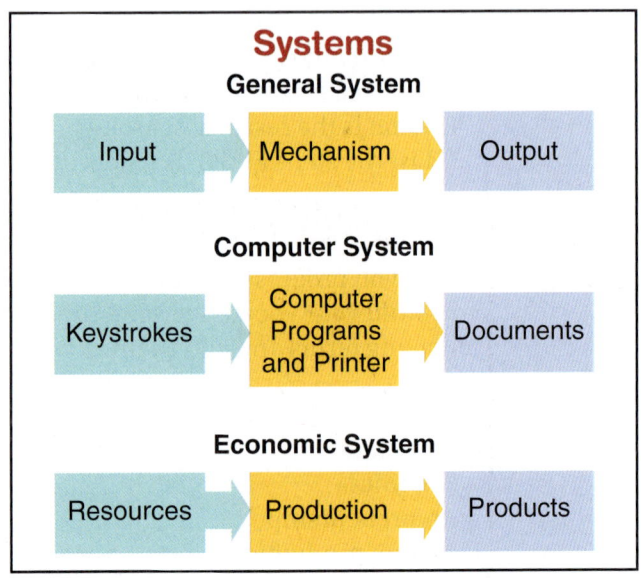

Systems

General System
Input → Mechanism → Output

Computer System
Keystrokes → Computer Programs and Printer → Documents

Economic System
Resources → Production → Products

Goodheart-Willcox Publisher

Figure 5-5 An economic system turns resources into products.

Traditional Economy

Tradition is a way of thinking, behaving, or acting that has been used by a group of people for a long period of time. A **traditional economy** is one in which economic decisions are based primarily on a society's values, culture, and customs. Elders of the society usually make economic decisions for the group based on tradition. Traditional economies existed early in human history. They are still found today in underdeveloped nations. These economies answer the three economic questions quite differently from other economic systems.

- *What to produce?* Most citizens in a traditional economy have just enough to survive. Food, shelter, and clothing are produced to support the survival of the population. They rely heavily upon the natural resources around them.
- *How to produce it?* Countries with traditional economies typically have large rural populations that rely on farming and hunting activities to produce the products required to meet basic needs. There is usually little to no manufacturing in this type of economy. Any tools or equipment used are typically basic and made using techniques handed down from ancestors.

Sasin Tipchai/Shutterstock.com

Most citizens in a traditional economy produce enough to support the survival of the population. *Why do you think traditional economies still exist?*

Exploring Marketing Careers

Telemarketer

Telemarketing, or personal selling done over the telephone, is a sales tool used by some companies as an alternative to more expensive marketing techniques. Charities also use telemarketing techniques to request donations. The two main types of telemarketers are those who place calls to potential customers, and those who answer calls from customers who are responding to advertisements. Other typical job titles for telemarketers include *telephone sales representative (TSR)*, *telesales specialist*, and *telemarketing sales representative*.

Some examples of tasks that telemarketers perform include:
- Research names and telephone numbers of potential customers from directories, magazine reply cards, and lists purchased from other organizations
- Call businesses or individuals to solicit sales or to request donations for charitable causes
- Read prepared "sales talks" from scripts that describe the products or services they are selling
- Input customer information, including payment information, into computerized ordering systems
- Answer telephone calls from potential customers who are responding to advertisements to "call this number"

Telemarketers need a good understanding of sales and marketing methods and strategies. They should have good speaking skills, including good diction and clear pronunciation, as well as a pleasing speaking voice. Because telemarketers sometimes encounter unpleasant responses, they should have an even temperament and be able to remain calm and pleasant at all times. Many telemarketing jobs require a high school diploma. For more information, access the *Occupational Outlook Handbook* online.

- *For whom should it be produced?* People in traditional economies develop strong community relationships, which help them meet their basic needs. Most people trade or barter for goods and services they cannot produce on their own. To *barter* is to exchange one good or service for another good or service. For example, a farmer may trade grain with a hunter for meat.

Command Economy

In a **command economy**, the government makes all the economic decisions for its citizens. A command economy is also called a *centrally planned economy* because a central government makes all decisions. Command economies are found in communist and socialist societies. The nations of North Korea and Cuba are current examples. In this type of economic system, the government is in charge of answering the three economic questions.

- *What to produce?* In command economies, the government owns and controls all the factors of production. It decides what and how much will be produced and sets the prices of goods and services. Citizens give up much individual freedom in a command economy.
- *How to produce it?* The government owns all the factors of production, so it also decides how goods and services are produced. This means that the government in a command economy controls all the business activities and quantity of goods and services within the economy. In some instances, it also determines the jobs for its citizens and how much they are paid.
- *For whom should it be produced?* Ideally, the government in a command economy tries to give all citizens an equal share of the limited resources and meet their basic needs. It also tries to provide education, medical care, and housing to everyone in the nation.

A command economy is usually far too large and complex for a government to control all of a nation's resources. As a result, these economic systems have historically failed to meet the needs of their citizens. Common problems are inefficiencies, product shortages, and poverty. Some command economies have moved to allow more individual freedoms to try to correct these problems.

Market Economy

A **market economy** is one in which individuals and businesses are free to make their own economic decisions with limited governmental involvement. It is also known as *free enterprise*, *private enterprise*, a *consumer economy*, or *capitalism*. The characteristics of free enterprise are shown in Figure 5-6 and are considered advantages of this type of system. They include the following.

- *Private property.* Individuals have the right to own property.
- *Profit.* Individuals and businesses have the right to make a profit.
- *Economic freedom.* Individuals are free to make their own economic decisions. They can decide what to buy, when to buy, and how to use what they have bought.
- *Voluntary exchange.* Individuals have the right to buy and sell in a marketplace where prices are freely set by the forces of supply and demand.

Monkey Business Images/Shutterstock.com

Individuals can make their own decisions with limited governmental involvement in a market economy.
Which characteristic of a market economy is most important to you?

Characteristics of Free Enterprise

[Diagram showing Free Enterprise System at center with arrows pointing to: Private Property, Profit, Economic Freedom, Voluntary Exchange, Competition]

Goodheart-Willcox Publisher

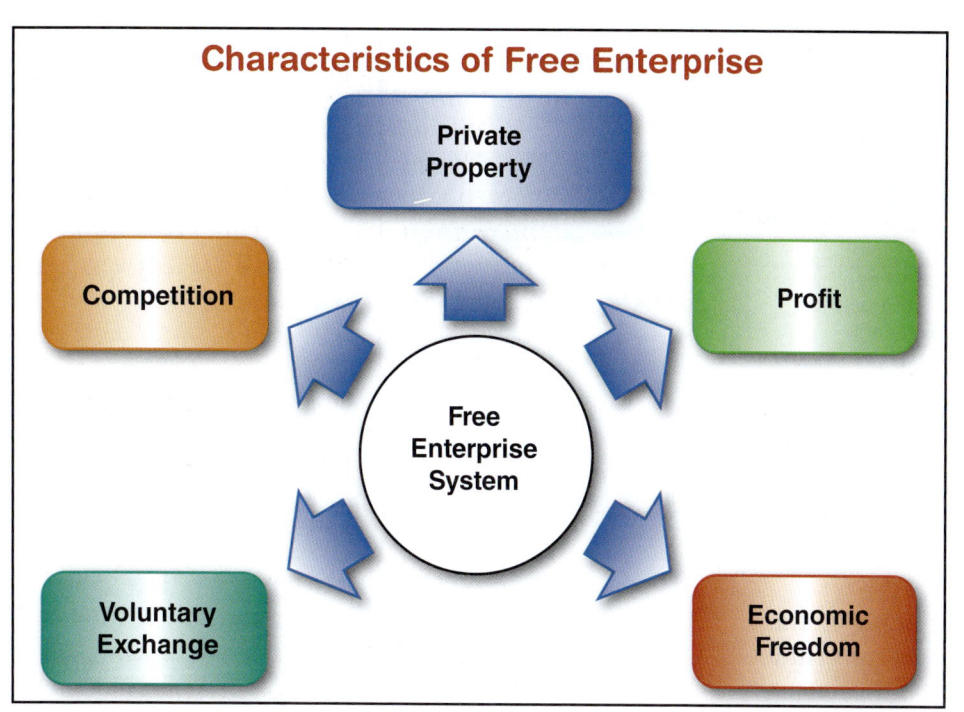

Figure 5-6 The characteristics of a free-enterprise system enable consumers to make decisions.

- *Competition.* Businesses can compete to sell goods and services and decide how to answer the three economic questions.

A free-enterprise system has some disadvantages. When businesses are focused only on profit, other problems for society can arise.
- Pollution levels can rise due to unregulated manufacturing activity.
- Consumer and worker safety may become a low priority to businesses.
- Unfair business practices can become common.
- Critical aspects of the economy's infrastructure may be neglected, such as public roads, law enforcement, and national defense.

To address and correct some of these disadvantages, a certain level of government involvement is needed in these economies. This involvement typically leads to the development of a mixed economy.

A market economy answers the three economic questions in the following ways.
- *What to produce?* In a market economy, consumers determine what should be produced through their buying decisions in the marketplace. Consumers determine prices by how much they are willing to pay for various items. Businesses respond by producing what consumers demand at a price they are willing to pay.
- *How to produce it?* Businesses determine how goods and services are produced. This freedom motivates businesses to efficiently produce the goods and services that people want in order to be competitive and earn a profit.
- *For whom should it be produced?* Goods and services are available in the marketplace to anyone who wishes to purchase them. Consumers in a market economy freely choose what and how much to buy based on how much money they have.

Mixed Economy

In a **mixed economy**, both the government and individuals make decisions about economic resources. Many economies are mixed, having elements of both command and market economies. The economy of the United States is based on free enterprise, but also has governmental involvement. The degree of governmental involvement in mixed economies varies from one economy to another.

It can be helpful to look at modern economies as being on a continuum, as shown in Figure 5-7. On the left side of the continuum is the pure command economy. On the right side of the continuum is the pure market economy. The economies of different nations fall at different points

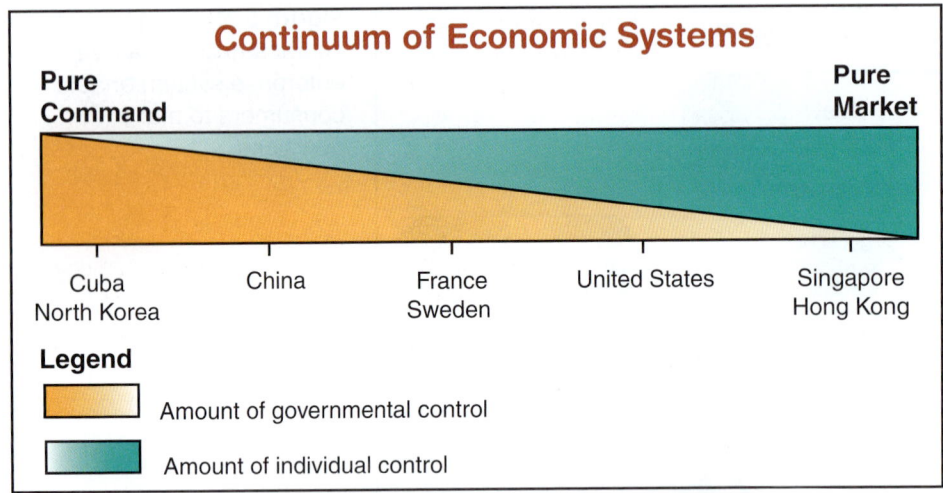

Figure 5-7 The amount of individual and governmental control changes across the continuum.

Continuum of Economic Systems

Pure Command — Cuba, North Korea; China; France, Sweden; United States; Singapore, Hong Kong — Pure Market

Legend:
- Amount of governmental control
- Amount of individual control

Goodheart-Willcox Publisher

between the two extremes depending on the amount of control exercised by the government.

LO 5.2-2 Market Forces

Market forces are economic factors that affect the price, demand, and availability of a product or service. In a free-enterprise system, the decisions related to market forces result in the production of the best goods and services at the most attractive prices. Market forces include supply and demand, the profit motive, and competition.

Supply and Demand

The principle of supply and demand is critical to business because it determines the price of goods and services. *Supply* is the quantity of goods available for purchase. *Demand* is the quantity of goods that consumers want to purchase. The **law of supply and demand** says that the price of a product is determined by the relationship between the supply of a product and the demand for the product.

Generally, higher demand results in higher prices, and lower demand results in lower prices. An increase in the supply of a product often lowers prices. When the supply of a product decreases, the price usually increases. **Equilibrium** is the point at which the supply equals the demand for a product. The price, known as the *market price*, is determined at equilibrium.

The law of supply and demand can be illustrated with a supply and demand curve, which is plotted on the graph in Figure 5-8. A *graph* depicts information through the use of lines, bars, or other symbols. This graph shows the relationship between the price of a product (*Y*-axis) and the quantity of goods supplied (*X*-axis). The *supply curve* shows that producers are willing to supply a greater quantity of goods at greater prices. The

wavebreakmedia/Shutterstock.com

Changes in attitudes toward healthy living have resulted in a growing demand for organic, local food products. *What changes in product demand have you witnessed in your lifetime?*

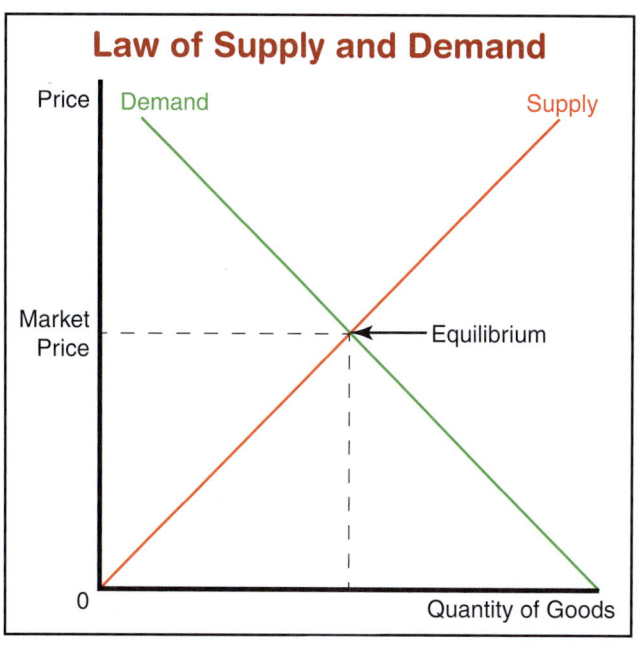

Law of Supply and Demand

Figure 5-8 A supply and demand curve shows the relationship between the quantity of goods producers are willing to supply and the quantity customers are willing to buy.

demand curve shows that consumers are willing to buy fewer goods at higher prices. The point at which the demand and supply curves intersect shows the market price at which the quantity supplied equals the quantity demanded.

Prices can change quickly when the forces of supply and demand react to changes in the economy. When the economy is strong, many consumers have more money to spend. They demand more products to satisfy their wants. If the demand for a product becomes greater than the available supply, a *shortage* develops. In this case, consumers compete to buy the available supply, which forces the price up.

When the economy weakens, consumers typically have less money to spend and they demand fewer products. If the demand for a product becomes less than the available supply, a *surplus* develops. In this case, sellers compete to sell the available supply, which forces the price down.

Prices play a critical function in our economy by helping to efficiently allocate resources and reduce shortages and surpluses. When prices rise, there is a natural incentive for supply to increase and demand to fall. This helps reduce the shortage. When prices fall, the natural incentive is for supply to fall and demand to increase, which helps reduce the surplus.

Demand can be influenced by changes in society. For example, many people today are more concerned about living healthier lifestyles than people were several decades ago. The result is a greater and growing demand for products like fitness equipment, all-natural products, and foods with high nutritional value.

Profit Motive

Profit is a powerful market force. *Profit* is the difference between the income earned and expenses incurred by a business during a specific period of time. The following is the formula to determine profit.

sales – expenses = profit

Suppose the sales of a business totaled $426,000 last year. In order to make those sales, the *expenses*, or costs, of producing and selling the product were $374,000. These costs included rent, utilities, raw materials, maintenance, salaries, and marketing. The profit is $52,000.

$426,000 sales – $374,000 expenses = $52,000 profit

Profit motive is the reason people take the risk to start and expand businesses. Even though many people create businesses for personal satisfaction, independence, and other advantages, profit is the driving force. Profits are increased by increasing sales or reducing expenses.

Competition

Competition among businesses is an important factor in a free-enterprise system. *Competition* is the action taken by two or more businesses attempting to attract the same customers. Because consumers have the freedom to choose the products and services they buy, businesses must work to win each consumer's business.

You Do the Math

Interpreting Line Graphs

A *graph* depicts information through the use of lines, bars, or other symbols. Many times, it is easier to understand the data if they are shown in a graphical form instead of a numerical form in a table. A line graph organizes information on vertical and horizontal axes. Data are graphed as a continuous line. Line graphs are often used to show trends over a period of time.

Solve the following problems using the line graph.
1. Of the five months shown, which month has the highest sales?
2. Of the five months shown, which month has the lowest sales?
3. How much did sales increase between May and June?
4. Based on the overall trend shown in the graph, will sales increase or decrease in the month of August?

Section 5.2 Review

Check Your Understanding

1. List five characteristics of a free-enterprise system.
2. What do market forces affect?
3. Define *supply* and *demand*.
4. What is profit?
5. Define *competition*.

Build Your Vocabulary

As you progress through this text, develop a personal glossary of key terms. This will help you build your vocabulary and prepare you for a career. Write a definition for each of the following terms and add them to your personal glossary.

command economy
economic input
economic output
economic system
equilibrium
law of supply and demand
market economy
market forces
mixed economy
traditional economy

CHAPTER 5 Review and Assessment

Chapter Summary

Section 5.1 Introduction to Economics

LO 5.1-1 Explain the concept of economics.
Economics examines how goods and services are produced, sold, and used. Individuals, businesses, and governments must decide how to use limited economic resources to meet their needs. The study of economics is often classified as macroeconomics and microeconomics.

LO 5.1-2 Describe the factors of production.
The factors of production are land, labor, capital, and entrepreneurship. These factors are used to produce goods and services that meet the wants and needs of individuals, businesses, and governments.

LO 5.1-3 Explain the economic problem.
Scarce resources limit the quantity of goods and services produced in any economic system. Scarcity leads to three important economic questions every nation must answer: What should be produced and how much? How should resources be allocated in production? For whom are the goods and services produced?

Section 5.2 Economic Systems and Market Forces

LO 5.2-1 Define four economic systems.
A nation's economic system is the way in which the nation chooses to use its resources to create goods and services. Economists classify economic systems as being a traditional, command, market, or mixed.

LO 5.2-2 Describe market forces in a free-enterprise system.
Market forces are economic factors that affect the price, demand, and availability of a product or service. Market forces include supply and demand, profit motive, and competition.

Check Your Marketing IQ

Now that you have completed the chapter, see what you have learned about marketing by taking the chapter posttest. The posttest is available at www.g-wlearning.com/marketing/.

Review Your Knowledge

1. Explain the concept of economics.
2. Describe the factors of production.
3. Cite two examples of infrastructure.
4. Explain the economic problem.
5. How do individuals make economic decisions?
6. Define four economic systems.
7. List and explain characteristics of a free-enterprise system.
8. List and explain examples of disadvantages of a free-enterprise system.
9. Describe market forces in a free-enterprise system.
10. Explain how supply and demand affect price.

Apply Your Knowledge

1. You selected a business for which you will be writing a marketing plan. How can an understanding of economics help a marketing manager develop a viable marketing plan?
2. Identify the factors of production that will impact the marketing activities of the business you have selected.
3. Scarcity leads to three important economic questions every nation must answer: What should be produced and how much? How should resources be allocated in production? For whom are the goods and services produced? Answer these questions for the business you have chosen.

4. How might scarcity impact the marketing decisions of a company?
5. Identify a decision to be made that is related to the marketing plan you will be writing. Describe how the systematic decision-making process might be used to solve the problem.
6. Why would it be helpful for a marketing manager to have information about the opportunity costs of potential customers?
7. Would a marketing manager be needed more in a command economy or a market economy? Briefly explain.
8. Explain the principles of supply and demand and how they apply to the business for which you are writing a marketing plan.
9. How will the market forces of supply and demand, profit motive, and competition influence your marketing plan?
10. How do you think the free-enterprise system benefits the marketing activities of a business?

Apply Your Math Skills

Interpreting information presented in a graph can help make important marketing decisions. An organic grocery store sells a local dairy farmer's organic milk. The number of gallons demanded by the store's customers depends on the price per gallon. Interpret the graph to answer the questions that follow.

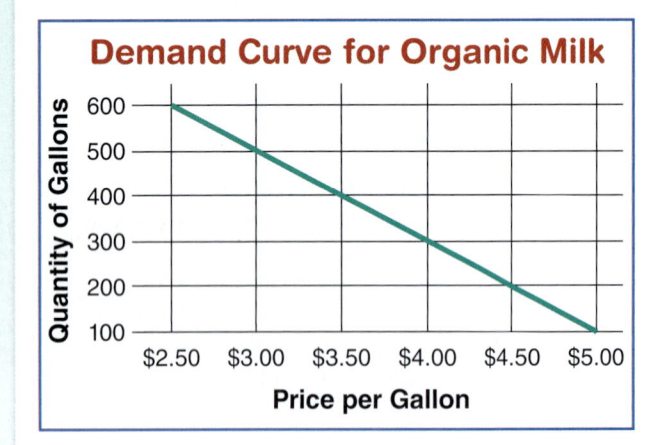

Demand Curve for Organic Milk

1. How many gallons of milk are bought when the price is $4.50?
2. Below what price will the number of gallons purchased exceed 500?
3. What does the demand curve for organic milk reveal?
4. How might a marketing manager use this information in a marketing plan?

Communication Skills

College and Career Readiness

Reading Rhetoric is the art of effectively speaking or writing to persuade someone. After you have read the chapter, reflect on the content you read. What was the writer's purpose for communicating the information in this chapter? Analyze how the author used rhetoric to advance this purpose.

Writing Compare and contrast how the various economic systems (traditional, market, command) answer the three basic economic questions: What should we produce? How should we produce it? For whom should we produce it? Develop and strengthen your ideas as needed by planning, revising, and editing your writing.

Speaking Select three of your classmates to participate in a discussion panel. Acting as the team leader, assign each person to a specific task, such as timekeeper, recorder, etc. Discuss the concept of the economic problem. Keep the panel on task and promote democratic discussion. The recorder should make notes of important information that was discussed. The notes should be edited and a final document created for distribution to the class.

Internet Research

Factors of Production Search the Internet to find the three industries in your state that generate the most revenue. What is the most important factor of production to each of these industries: land, labor, capital, or entrepreneurship? Describe whether your state is well-suited to provide these resources.

Recycling Natural Resources Using the Internet, research the recycling efforts of countries with different economic systems. Find examples of recycling efforts in at least two different economic systems. How do the citizens of these countries use and conserve natural resources?

Scarcity Use the Internet to research the factors of production of a country in which you are interested. Write several paragraphs to discuss how scarcity and factors of production require the nation to make economic choices.

Economic Systems Use Internet resources to identify a country with a traditional economy, a country with a command economy, and a country with a market economy. Explore how the type of economic system affects private ownership and the role of government in each economy.

Teamwork

Together with a partner, explain and discuss each of the characteristics of a free-enterprise system. Have one partner argue for the claim that private ownership, competition, risk, and the profit motive benefit society. Have the other partner argue against these ideas. Cite evidence to develop original claims and counterclaims.

Portfolio Development

College and Career Readiness

Hard Copy Organization As you collect material for your portfolio, you will need an effective strategy to keep the items clean, safe, and organized for assembly at the appropriate time. Structure and organization is important when working on an ongoing project that includes multiple pieces. A large manila envelope works well to keep hard copies of documents, photos, awards, and other items safe. A three-ring binder with sleeves is another good way to store your materials.

Plan to keep similar items together and label the categories. For example, store sample documents that illustrate your writing or technology skills together. Use notes clipped to the documents to identify each item and state why it is included in the portfolio. For example, a note might say, "Newsletter that illustrates desktop publishing skills."

1. Select a method for storing hard copy items you will be collecting.
2. Create a master spreadsheet to use as a tracking tool for the components of your portfolio. You may list each document alphabetically, by category, date, or other convention that helps you keep track of each document that you are including.
3. Record the name of each item and the date that you stored it.

CHAPTER 6

Economic Activity

Sections

6.1 **Economic Measurement**
6.2 **Government and the Economy**

Reading Prep

College and Career Readiness

Before reading this chapter, flip through the pages and make notes of the major headings. Compare these headings to the objectives. What did you discover? How will this help you prepare to read new material?

Check Your Marketing IQ

Before you begin the chapter, see what you already know about marketing by taking the chapter pretest. The pretest is available at www.g-wlearning.com/marketing/.

DECA Emerging Leaders

Sports and Entertainment Marketing Team Decision-Making Event, Part 2

Career Cluster: Marketing
Instructional Area: Economics

Procedure, Part 2

1. In the previous chapter, you studied the performance indicators for this event.
2. The event will be presented to you through your reading of the Knowledge and Skills Developed, Specific Performance Indicators, and Case Study Situation. You will have up to 30 minutes to review this information and prepare your presentation. You may make notes to use during your presentation.
3. Teams will meet with the judge for a **15-minute** presentation. The team will spend no more than 10 minutes at the beginning of the interview describing the team's analysis of the situation given. Both members of the team must participate in the presentation. The judge will spend the remaining 5 minutes questioning the participants. Each participant must respond to at least one question posed by the judge.
4. Turn in all your notes and event materials when you have completed the event.

Case Study Situation

You are to assume the roles of merchandise managers for Deluxe Linens, a popular brand of luxury bath towels. The **marketing manager (judge)** has asked your team to decide the best way the company should respond to rising cotton prices.

Deluxe Linens was introduced 15 years ago when the economy was soaring and consumers had much more disposable income. The company sells luxury bath towels made from 100 percent cotton that are known for superior softness and absorbency. Deluxe Linens bath towels are sold in department stores and are moderately priced.

In the last year, continuous bad weather has resulted in smaller cotton crops overseas. Since all textiles worldwide are made from the same cotton crops, all textile companies are competing for the small supply of cotton. This has created a steady increase in cotton prices. Before the year is over, prices for cotton will be more than double the usual price.

Deluxe Linens cannot afford to pay the steep prices for cotton and still sell the merchandise at moderate prices. The marketing manager has come up with two possible solutions to the rise in cotton prices and wants you to determine which is the best option for Deluxe Linens. You can raise the price of Deluxe Linens' bath towels or switch to a less-expensive cotton blend.

Your team will explain which solution you have chosen and the reasoning for the choice to the marketing manager (judge) in a meeting to take place in the marketing manager's office. The marketing manager will begin the meeting by greeting you and asking to hear your ideas. After you have explained your solution and reasoning and have answered the marketing manager's questions, the marketing manager (judge) will conclude the meeting by thanking you for your work.

Critical Thinking

1. How does the present economy affect a company's sales strategy?
2. What other option should the marketing manager (judge) consider in response to the rising prices?

Visit www.deca.org for more information.

Section 6.1

Economic Measurement

Essential Question

What can past economic data reveal about the future?

Learning Objectives

LO 6.1-1 Identify common indicators used to measure economic activity.
LO 6.1-2 Describe the four stages of the business cycle.
LO 6.1-3 Explain three classifications of economic indicators.

Key Terms

gross domestic product (GDP)
standard of living
inflation
inflation rate
consumer price index (CPI)
deflation
interest
interest rate
labor force
unemployment rate
specialization
stock market
business cycle
expansion
peak
recession
depression
trough

LO 6.1-1 Economic Indicators

Economic activity is the production, distribution, and consumption of products. The market forces of supply and demand, the profit motive, and competition influence the economic activity of individuals, businesses, and governments. Businesses respond to these market forces by deciding which goods and services to produce, how much to produce, and at what price. These economic decisions have a direct impact on the activity and health of the economy. A *healthy economy* is one that is experiencing growth through high productivity, a high rate of employment, and stable prices in the market.

The strength of the economy can be measured using certain economic indicators. An *indicator* is a sign that shows the condition or existence of something. Indicators enable individuals, businesses, and governments to make wise economic decisions.

Some of the most widely followed indicators of the economy include gross domestic product (GDP), inflation, interest rates, labor, and the stock and bond markets.

Gross Domestic Product

Gross domestic product (GDP) is the market value of all final products produced in a country during a specific time period. It is also known as *economic output*. GDP is measured in dollars and is one of the most closely followed economic indicators. GDP is used by the president and Congress to prepare the federal budget. It is used by companies when preparing business plans and sales forecasts. Financial institutions also use GDP as an indicator of economic activity, which can affect consumer interest rates.

Per capita GDP is the GDP of a nation divided by its population. It shows the amount of economic output for each person in the country. When per capita GDP is high, there is more economic output per person. When per capita GDP is low, there is less economic output per person. This may indicate the economy is suffering.

Per capita GDP is one way to measure a country's standard of living. **Standard of living** refers to the financial well-being of the average person in a country. One of the goals of a government is to increase the standard of living for its citizens.

Measuring the standard of living with per capita GDP has some drawbacks. Per capita GDP does not consider quality-of-life factors, such as health, safety, environmental concerns, and political freedom. These factors are important, but are difficult to measure.

Measuring GDP

One way to measure GDP is to add together the total amounts of money spent in the economy in each of the following categories: consumer spending, business spending, government spending, and net exports. These four categories are shown in the graph in Figure 6-1.

Consumer spending includes everything people buy for personal use, such as food, clothing, cars, medical care, and entertainment. It is considered an economic indicator because the rate of consumer spending is linked to the health of the economy. When consumer spending is high, economic growth is often strong. If consumer spending is low, the economy tends to be weak.

Business spending includes all purchases made for capital goods and construction. These may include factories, machines, and warehouses. Business spending is also called *investment spending*.

Government spending includes spending by national, state, and local governments. The government spends on projects and services, such as national defense, police and fire protection, roads, and many social programs.

Net exports are a country's exports minus imports. If a country imports more goods and services than it exports, it is spending more on trade than it is earning.

supergenijalac/Shutterstock.com

Business spending includes all purchases made for capital goods, such as factories, machines, and warehouses. *How does business spending contribute to the overall economy?*

Growth Rate of GDP

GDP changes over time, as referenced in the graph in Figure 6-2. The *economic growth rate* shows the amount and direction of the change in

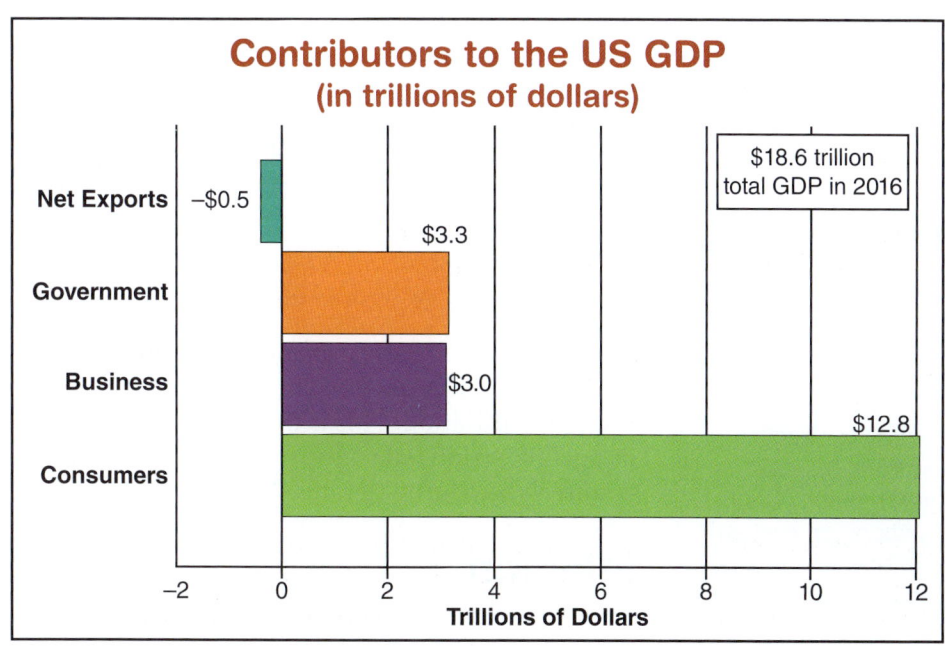

Contributors to the US GDP
(in trillions of dollars)

- Net Exports: −$0.5
- Government: $3.3
- Business: $3.0
- Consumers: $12.8

$18.6 trillion total GDP in 2016

Source: US Bureau of Economic Analysis; Goodheart-Willcox Publisher

Figure 6-1 The GDP includes consumer, business, and government spending, as well as net exports.

Percent Change in US GDP

Figure 6-2 The GDP changes from year to year. It can rise, fall, or be negative, depending on consumer, business, and government spending for that year.

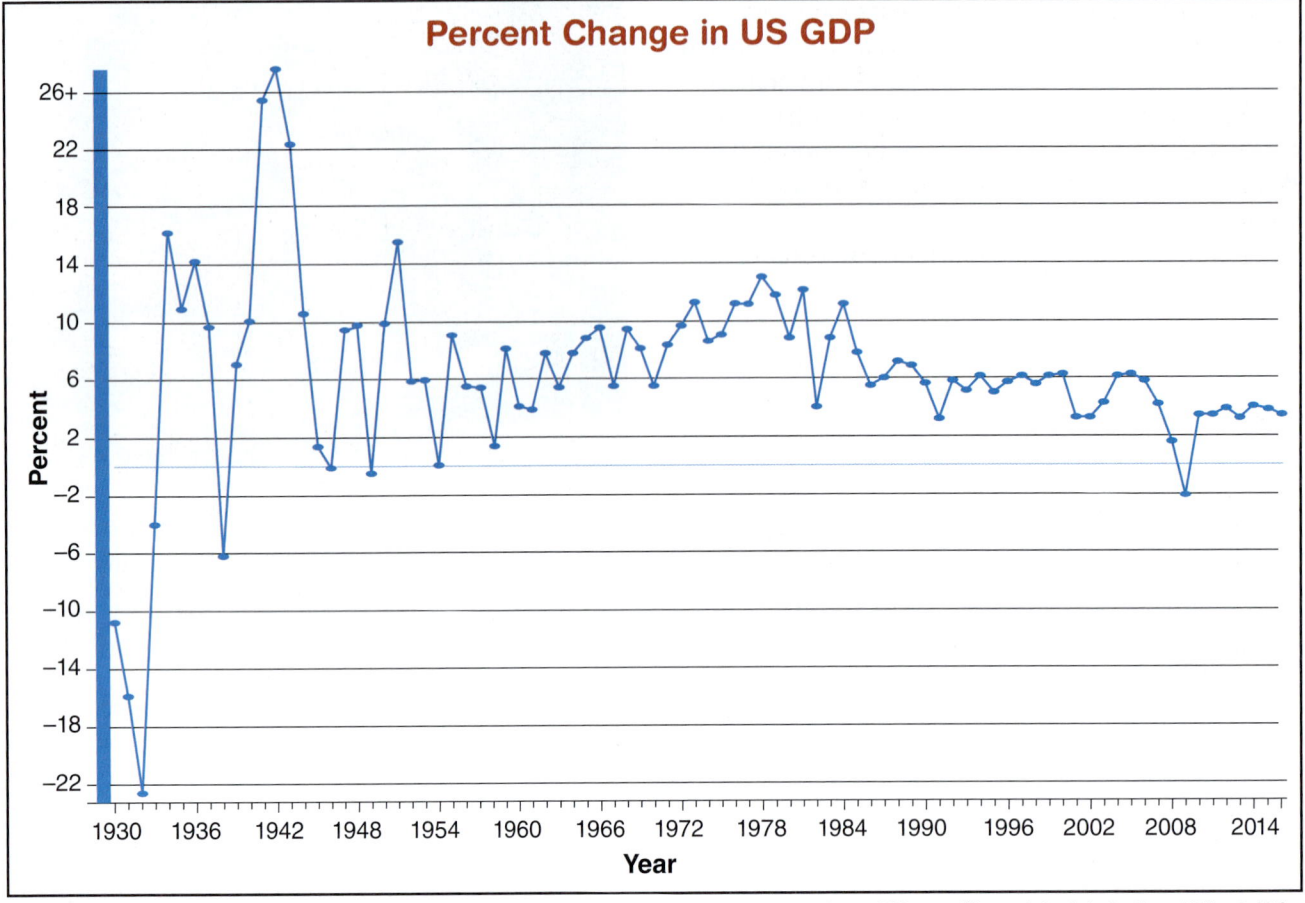

Source: US Bureau of Economic Analysis; Goodheart-Willcox Publisher

GDP for a specific time period, such as a quarter or year. When GDP is rising, the economy is growing. When GDP growth is above average, it indicates a strong economy. When the rate of GDP growth is below average, it is a sign that the economy is weakening. Sometimes economic growth turns negative and GDP falls, which can indicate a recession.

The formula for growth rate of the economy, which is a rate of change, is as follows.

[(GDP for time 2 − GDP for time 1) ÷ GDP time 1] × 100 = economic growth rate

For example, GDP was $18.6 trillion for 2016 and $18.0 trillion for 2015. The growth rate in 2016 was 3.3 percent.

[($18.6 trillion − $18.0 trillion) ÷ $18.0 trillion] × 100 = 3.3% economic growth rate

In the United States, economic growth has averaged about three percent a year since 1929, excluding inflation. This is the range of growth for many industrialized countries. Many fast-growing countries have growth rates that are higher.

Inflation

Inflation is the general rise in prices throughout an economy. The most significant

Employability Skills

Emotional Control

Emotional control is the process of directing one's feelings and reactions toward a desirable result that is socially acceptable. The lack of emotional control in a workplace situation can cost an individual his or her job. Learning how to manage emotions helps a person think logically and act appropriately.

effect of inflation is that it reduces the purchasing power of money. **Inflation rate** is calculated as the rate of change in prices over a period of time, usually monthly or yearly, and expressed as a percent. The economic impact of inflation can be significant because it affects business costs and consumer spending.

When inflation is at an average or lower rate, prices are stable. *Price stability* is when the prices of products in the marketplace are changing very slowly or not all. This is reflected as an inflation rate of about zero to three percent. Price stability is usually considered good for the economy because lower inflation leads to lower interest rates, which makes borrowing money less expensive. Price stability also makes financial planning easier because wages tend to keep up with prices better.

In contrast, economic problems begin when inflation rates increase to four percent or higher. High inflation leads to higher interest rates, which make borrowing money more expensive. It also disrupts the financial planning of workers because prices rise faster than wages. High inflation generally adds uncertainty to an economy.

There are several indicators of inflation, but the consumer price index is the most widely used. The **consumer price index (CPI)** is a measure of the average change in the prices paid by consumers for typical consumer goods and services over time. The CPI is compiled by the US Bureau of Labor Statistics.

Inflation can be divided into four levels: low to average, high, severe, and hyperinflation, as shown in Figure 6-3. Each level is based on the inflation rate. Severe inflation is also called *double-digit inflation*. Inflation in the United States has averaged around three percent annually over the past 100 years. *Hyperinflation* is an extremely rapid, out-of-control rise in inflation. A country's currency is severely devalued by hyperinflation. The United States has never experienced hyperinflation.

Deflation is a general decline in prices throughout an economy. It is the opposite of inflation. This situation usually occurs when the economy is very weak. The last time there was significant deflation in the United States was during the Great Depression in the 1930s.

Levels of Inflation

Level	Inflation Rate	Effect on Economy
Low to average	0% to 3%	Good. Economy and prices are stable.
High	4% to 9%	Some problems. Prices begin rising faster than wages. Purchasing power falls.
Severe (double-digit)	10% or higher	Economic problems increase. Purchasing power falls more quickly.
Hyper-inflation	Over 1,000%	Occurs rarely, but destroys the value of money and the economy. One of the most well-known instances of hyperinflation occurred in Germany after World War I.

Goodheart-Willcox Publisher

Figure 6-3 The terms for inflation levels are usually applied to changes that occur on a month-to-month or year-to-year basis.

borrowed. Many different interest rates can be found in an economy because there are many different borrowers, lenders, and types of loans. Borrowers can be consumers, businesses, and governmental agencies. Lenders include banks, finance companies, and investors. Loans are made in the form of home mortgages, auto loans, student loans, business loans, and for other purposes.

The interest rate on a loan is determined by the forces of supply and demand. An increase in demand to borrow money tends to increase interest rates. Interest rates usually decrease when the demand for loans falls. As a result, interest rates typically rise when the economy is strong and there is more demand to borrow money to buy various goods and services. Interest rates often decline when the economy is weak and there is less demand to borrow money.

An increase in the supply of money available for lending may also lower interest rates. The supply is influenced by the amount of money that is saved in an economy and made available for loans. The government can change the supply of money to influence interest rates.

Interest Rates

Interest is the amount a borrower pays to a lender for a loan. An **interest rate** represents the cost of a loan and is expressed as a percent of the amount

Labor

All the people in a nation who are capable of working and want to work are called the **labor force**. It does not include children, individuals who

All people in a nation who are capable of working and want to work are included in the labor force. *Who of your family and friends is a part of the labor force?*

are retired, or people who choose not to work. The total labor force includes civilian workers as well as those who are in the military.

Labor is important in an economy. Without labor, goods and services would not be available. Those who provide labor receive wages. Workers spend their wages on goods and services, which supports businesses and economic activity.

Unemployment Rate

The civilian labor force is divided into two categories: employed and unemployed. *Employed* includes everyone who is working. *Unemployed* includes those who do not have a job, but are actively looking for one. The **unemployment rate** is the percentage of the civilian labor force that is unemployed.

If every person who is willing and able to work has a job, the economy would be at *full employment*. Interestingly, even when the economy is considered to be at full employment, the unemployment rate is still about four percent. This is because there are always people who are not working for many different reasons. They may be entering or reentering the workforce or may be between jobs.

An unemployment rate between four and five percent indicates a healthy economy. An unemployment rate above this level indicates a weakening economy because it means businesses are not hiring or are eliminating part of their labor force. Higher levels of unemployment cause consumer spending to weaken, which reduces the rate of economic growth.

Productivity

Productivity is a measure of a worker's production in a specific amount of time, such as an hour, a day, or a week. The more a worker produces in the amount of time specified, the higher his or her productivity. Higher productivity means more products can be produced at the same cost, often in a shorter amount of time. It also means fewer workers are needed, so employers have lower costs. This, in turn, generally results in more profit. More profit enables companies to reinvest more money in their businesses.

Productivity can also lead to a higher standard of living for consumers. When the selection of products is greater, individuals have more choices when making purchase decisions.

Green Marketing

Greenwashing

Many companies promote their environmentally friendly products and initiatives. However, some companies that promote themselves as green businesses do not actually follow environmentally conscious practices. This type of deception is called *greenwashing*. Businesses that implement greenwashing marketing tactics intend to benefit from the positive image of being an environmentally friendly company without the expense of implementing green initiatives.

The Federal Trade Commission issued the *Green Guides* to address the public need of validating eco-friendly claims. The publication provides guidance for marketers, including general principles that apply to all environmental marketing claims, understanding how consumers interpret particular claims, how companies can substantiate claims, and how marketers can avoid deceiving consumers.

ESB Professional/Shutterstock.com

When the selection of products is greater, individuals have more choices. *How do you think product selection is related to a nation's standard of living?*

Businesses are always looking for ways to increase productivity that will also increase profitability. One way to increase productivity is to increase efficiency through specialization. **Specialization** is focusing on the production of specific goods so more products can be produced with the same amount of labor. Specialization is often centered on the factors of production. Nations typically specialize in products for which they have the resources and talent to produce. Trying to produce all the products to meet all the needs of every consumer is not always efficient or profitable.

Specialization can also apply to labor. Henry Ford was one of the first to apply specialization in his company by using the assembly line. Before the assembly line, ten Ford workers produced ten cars in a day. With an assembly line, each worker specialized in one-tenth of the car's assembly. Work was much more efficient, and the same ten workers produced thirty cars in a day.

Stock and Bond Markets

The **stock market** is a system and marketplace for buying and selling stocks. A *stock* represents the right of ownership in a corporation. Ownership of a corporation is divided into *shares*. Each share represents a partial ownership. Buying partial ownership in a corporation is a form of investment. People who buy shares of stock in a company are called *stockholders* or *shareholders*.

When the value of the stock market increases, it indicates the value of businesses is rising. Investors make decisions based on their expectations of economic growth and profits for a corporation. As a result, they often buy stock when they think the economy will get stronger. This sends the value of the stock market higher.

A falling stock market means the market value of businesses is falling. Investors tend to sell stocks when they think the economy will get weaker. This sends the value of the stock market lower.

The values in stock markets continually go up and down and do not always reflect the actual state of an economy. History has shown that stock markets tend to peak right before a downturn in the economy. However, nobody really knows when a market has reached its peak. As a result, many investors are surprised when stock markets fall.

A *bond* is a certificate of debt issued by an organization or government. Corporations and governments issue bonds to borrow large amounts of money. The bonds are sold to investors, who are essentially the lenders to corporations and governments. Bondholders are paid interest for the use of their money.

Bonds can be traded in a market among investors after they are issued. *Trading* means to buy or sell. There are markets for various corporate and government bonds. The largest market is for bonds issued by the US government. The interest rates in the bond markets can change every day. Rising rates tend to reflect a stronger economy. Lower rates tend to reflect a weaker economy.

LO 6.1-2 Business Cycle

The economy of the United States has been very successful and experienced growth over many years. However, the economy does not grow at the same rate each year. In some years, the economy and GDP grow by more than the average amount. At other times, they grow less than the average amount or may even decline. These alternating periods of expansion and contraction in the economy are called the **business cycle**.

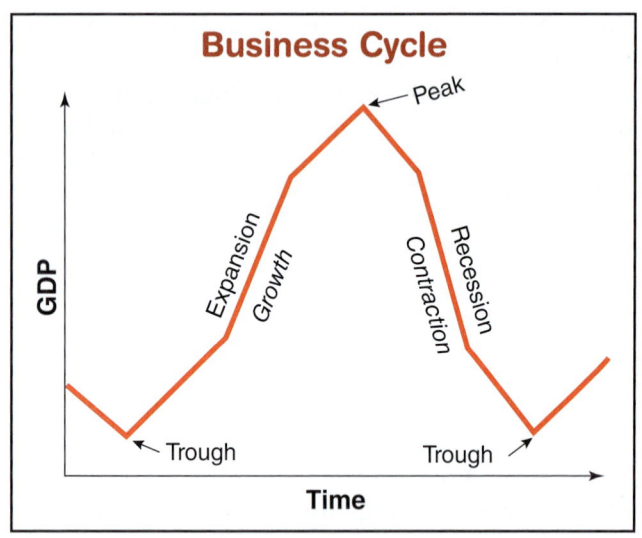

Business Cycle

Figure 6-4 A single business cycle includes all the economic activity from the beginning of one trough to the next.

There are four stages of the business cycle: expansion, peak, recession, and trough. Each stage can vary in length. The graph in Figure 6-4 illustrates the cyclical movement in our economy. Understanding these stages helps individuals, businesses, and governments make better economic decisions.

Expansion

Economic **expansion** is a period in which the economy is growing and the GDP is rising. It usually begins with an increase in consumer demand for goods and services. Businesses react to expansion by increasing production and hiring more workers. During an expansion, wages also begin to increase. More workers and higher wages produce an even greater demand for goods and services. Inflation tends to increase during periods of economic expansion because increased consumer demand forces prices to rise. Many individuals and businesses prosper during periods of expansion. *Prosperity* is a time period of growth and financial well-being. The expansion phase impacts the economy by fueling widespread growth in many parts of the country.

Peak

The **peak** is the highest point in the business cycle and marks the end of expansion. At this point, consumer demand for goods and services starts to slow. Businesses react by reducing production and workers. Wage growth tends to slow or stop. Overall economic growth slows. Economic expansion may end for a reason that is obvious. One example of this is the Great Recession of 2008, which started with a financial crisis and housing market collapse. Other times, the reason for the end of expansion is not clear.

Recession

Recession follows a peak in the business cycle. **Recession** is a period of significant decline in the total output, income, employment, and trade in an economy. It usually lasts from twelve to eighteen months, but may be less. The recession phase impacts the economy by causing a widespread *contraction*, or decline, in many parts of the country. The inflation rate tends to decline during a recession. Falling consumer demand forces many businesses to lower prices. In addition, wages fall as businesses cut back on hiring.

A period of economic contraction that is severe and lasts a long time is called a **depression**. The last period of depression in the United States was from 1929 to 1940. During this time, many banks failed, unemployment reached over 20 percent, many people lost their homes, and there was widespread poverty. The causes of the Great Depression are still debated by economists. However, some reasons include the crash of stock prices, a decline in business spending, and a reduction in the money supply.

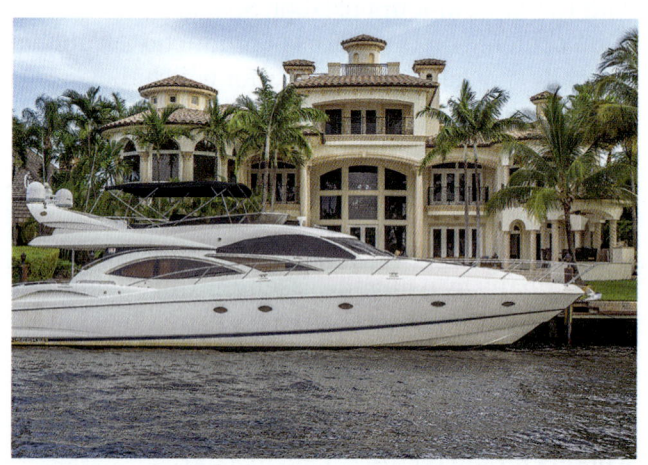

During economic expansion, the economy is growing and consumer demand for goods increases. *What are other signs of prosperity during periods of economic expansion?*

Trough

A **trough** is the lowest stage of a business cycle and marks the end of a recession. The period of expansion that follows a trough is called *economic recovery*. The reasons a recession comes to an end are not always clear. However, the economy begins to grow again and is fueled by increased consumer demand for goods and services. The business cycle continues again into another period of expansion.

Economic Indicators and the Business Cycle
LO 6.1-3

Economic indicators can provide information about which stage of the business cycle an economy is in and the stage that is coming next. This information can be valuable when making marketing decisions.

The relationship between different economic indicators and the business cycle is not always the same. As a result, indicators are commonly classified as being leading, lagging, or coincident.
- A *leading indicator* is one that changes *before* a change in economic activity.
- A *lagging indicator* is one that changes *after* a change in economic activity.
- A *coincident indicator* is one that changes *at the same time* as a change in economic activity.

Some important indicators that are widely used when analyzing the business cycle include GDP, inflation rate, unemployment rate, and the stock market.

GDP

GDP is a coincident indicator of economic activity. When GDP is rising and the growth rate is increasing, it is a sign of economic expansion. Recall that the average growth rate of real GDP has been about three percent over the long term. When GDP is growing faster than average, the economy is strong. The economy is weakening when the rate of GDP growth is declining and falling below average. When GDP growth turns negative, it signals a recession.

Inflation Rate

The inflation rate is also considered a coincident indicator of economic activity. The inflation rate generally tends to rise during an economic expansion. This happens because increased consumer demand forces prices higher. In addition, more hiring during an expansion also tends to increase overall wages. Conversely, the inflation rate generally tends to decline during a recession. This is because consumer demand falls, which tends to lower prices. In addition, workforce cuts during a contraction also tend to decrease overall wages.

Unemployment Rate

The unemployment rate is a lagging indicator of economic activity. An economic expansion usually begins with rising consumer demand for goods and services. Businesses then respond by increasing production and eventually hiring more workers. The unemployment rate declines, but not until after the expansion has been underway for around six to nine months. During a recession, the

---

You Do the Math

Types of Numbers

An effective marketing manager realizes that information needed to make strategic decisions involves understanding numbers. *Real numbers* are all whole and fractional or decimal numbers on a continuous number line. *Whole numbers* are numbers with no fractional or decimal portion. *Decimals* are numbers with digits to the right of the decimal point.

To add a positive number, move to the right on the number line. To subtract a positive number, move to the left on the number line.

Solve the following problems.
1. 5.87 + 4.956 + 2.011 + 4 =
2. 34 + 9 − 127 + 783 =
3. 112.058 + 2.1 + 93.237 =
4. 987 + 705 + 827 + 4 =
5. 73 + 8 − 12 =

unemployment rate rises, but not until after the contraction has started and been underway for a while.

This lagging relationship was evident during the Great Recession. Real GDP declined in the first quarter of 2008, but the unemployment rate remained steady at about five percent during that period. The unemployment rate eventually increased to 5.4 percent in the second quarter of 2008. It continued to rise and eventually peaked at 10 percent. However, the peak occurred in October 2009, about four months after the recession had ended, according to the National Bureau of Economic Research (NBER).

Stock Market

The stock market is considered by many to be a leading indicator of economic activity. This is because investors make decisions based on what they believe will happen in the future. As a result, changing stock prices reflect expectations for changes in economic activity. Many believe a rising stock market will lead an economic expansion and a falling stock market will lead a contraction.

This leading relationship was also evident during the Great Recession. The stock market reached a peak in late October 2007. It began to decline a few months before the recession actually started. The stock market eventually dropped over 40 percent. It troughed in early March 2009, and then started recovering about three months before the recession ended.

Robert Lucian Crusitu/Shutterstock.com

The stock market is considered by many to be a *leading indicator* of economic activity. *What do you know about the stock market?*

Section 6.1 Review

Check Your Understanding

1. What is a healthy economy?
2. State the most significant effect of rising inflation.
3. What is per capita GDP and what does it show?
4. What is meant by *full employment*?
5. Name the type of economic indicator that changes *after* a change in economic activity.

Build Your Vocabulary

As you progress through this text, develop a personal glossary of key terms. This will help you build your vocabulary and prepare you for a career. Write a definition for each of the following terms and add them to your personal glossary.

business cycle
consumer price index (CPI)
deflation
depression
expansion
gross domestic product (GDP)
inflation
inflation rate
interest

interest rate
labor force
peak
recession
specialization
standard of living
stock market
trough
unemployment rate

Section 6.2

Government and the Economy

Essential Question

Why do governments exist in our society?

Learning Objectives

LO 6.2-1 Describe four basic market structures.
LO 6.2-2 Identify the role of government in the US economy.

Key Terms

market structure
monopoly
oligopoly
monopolistic competition
perfect competition
price competition
nonprice competition

fiscal policy
monetary policy
Federal Reserve System
money supply
price-fixing
collusion
externality

LO 6.2-1 Market Structure

Market structure is how a market is organized based on the number of businesses competing for sales in an industry. Competition is a critical force in a free-enterprise system. As shown in Figure 6-5, there are four basic market structures that represent varying degrees of competition.

- A **monopoly** is a market structure with one business that has complete control of a market's entire supply of a product.
- An **oligopoly** is a market structure with a small number of businesses selling the same or similar products.
- **Monopolistic competition** is a large number of businesses selling similar, but not the same, products and at different prices. This is also known as *imperfect competition*.
- **Perfect competition** is characterized by a large number of businesses selling the same product at the same prices.

Most businesses operate in a market structure of monopolistic competition. Each business competes for customers using price or nonprice competition.

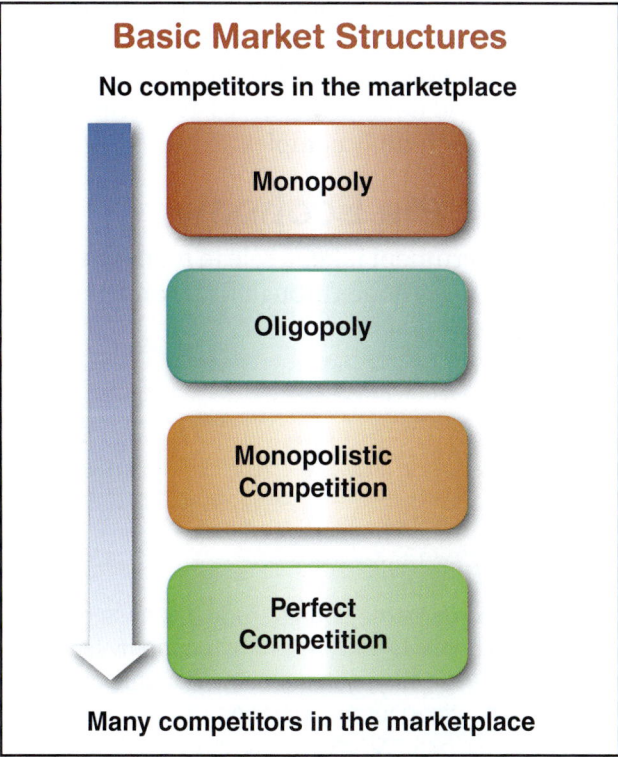

Basic Market Structures

No competitors in the marketplace

- Monopoly
- Oligopoly
- Monopolistic Competition
- Perfect Competition

Many competitors in the marketplace

Goodheart-Willcox Publisher

Figure 6-5 Four basic market structures represent various levels of competition in an economy.

Copyright Goodheart-Willcox Co., Inc.

99

Price competition is when a lower price is the main reason for customers to buy from one business over another. Although lowering prices may attract more customers, it could also reduce total profit. **Nonprice competition** is when strategies other than price are used to attract customers. These might include things like better quality or customer service or more convenience.

Role of Government in the US Economy
LO 6.2-2

Even a free-enterprise system needs government involvement to function efficiently. First, the government acts as a *regulator*. It creates and enforces laws that protect liberties and private property rights. It also provides political stability.

Second, the government acts as a *provider*. It makes goods and services available for the public's benefit in various areas, such as safety, education, and welfare programs. Examples of specific roles the government plays in the operation of our economy include:
- manage the economy;
- provide public goods and services;
- provide a legal framework;
- promote competition; and
- correct for externalities.

Governmental policies are intended to help a free-enterprise system operate in an efficient manner. However, these policies are difficult to implement and not always successful because the economy is incredibly complex.

Manage the Economy

The government takes a role to manage the economy. This is done through fiscal and monetary policies.

holbox/Shutterstock.com

As a *regulator*, the government creates and enforces laws. *In what ways does the government regulate aspects of your life?*

Fiscal Policy

Fiscal policy is the tax spending decisions made by the president and Congress. The government often uses fiscal policies to boost the economy when it is weak. Fiscal policy may also be used to reduce the extreme highs and lows of the business cycle. For example, the government may choose to lower taxes during an economic contraction. This would give people more money to spend and may reduce the impact of a sharp fall in the economy. However, consumers and businesses may choose to save the money from lower taxes instead of spending it. Fiscal policy is the decision made by the government, but the action taken by the people can be unpredictable.

Monetary Policy

Monetary policy is policy that regulates the supply of money and interest rates by a central bank in an economy. The **Federal Reserve System** is the central bank of the United States, created

Case in Point

Hyundai

Marketing professionals study business cycles to help determine strategies to which consumers will react in a positive way. When the economy is stable, consumers are more willing to spend more money. When the economy is in a slump, though, consumers may not be willing or able to spend. However, businesses must continue generating revenue through all business cycles.

Hyundai Motor Company is a good example of how a business can generate sales in a slow economy by using creative marketing techniques. The auto industry suffered losses during the Great Recession. To keep sales moving during this slow economic period, Hyundai introduced an innovative sales program. The company advertised that buyers could purchase a new car and return the vehicle within a year if they lost their jobs—with no questions asked. Through a consumer-oriented marketing program, Hyundai strengthened its image and kept sales stable.

by Congress in 1913. It carries out the nation's monetary policy "to promote effectively the goals of maximum employment, stable prices, and moderate long-term interest rates." The Federal Reserve, also called the *Fed*, looks at many economic indicators to evaluate the condition of the economy.

When the economy is slow or weak, the Fed may take action to increase the money supply and lower interest rates. **Money supply** is the total money circulating at any one time in a country. It includes both cash and money in the bank. Lower interest rates make borrowing money easier, which may encourage consumers and businesses to spend more. When more money is spent, the economy grows faster.

If the economy is growing too fast, the Federal Reserve can take action to slow the economy and avoid inflation. When the demand for goods and services grows faster than the supply, inflation can increase. Higher interest rates make borrowing money more expensive. As a result, individuals and businesses become more cautious about spending, and demand is reduced.

Provide Public Goods and Services

The government provides certain public goods and services that are available to everyone in the economy. Governmental agencies collect taxes to pay for these goods and services. Public education is an example of a public service provided by the government. A nation benefits when its population is well educated. This can result in a society that is generally more productive and stable. However, education is expensive. If private schools were the only options, few people could afford the cost of education. Other public services include construction and maintenance of roads, police and fire protection, postal services, and public parks.

The main motives in a market economy are money and profit. People who have money can buy what they need and want. However, people with little money may struggle to meet basic needs. The government has developed social programs to offer goods and services to citizens in need. Medicare and Social Security are among the largest social programs that benefit retirees and the disabled. Unemployment compensation provides some money to workers who have lost their jobs. The Federal Emergency Management Agency (FEMA) provides relief to victims of disasters, such as hurricanes and earthquakes. There are many other programs at the federal, state, and local levels.

Provide a Legal Framework

A legal framework is necessary for a market economy to function. Laws are needed to define and enforce property rights and provide for public safety. They establish boundaries and define acceptable behavior. They help protect individuals and businesses from dishonest business practices. Laws are made and enforced at all levels of government. Criminal laws define conduct that threatens public safety and outlines punishment for such acts. Civil laws define conduct between individuals in situations such as contracts and property.

Social Media

SMM Terms

There are many SMM terms that are necessary for a marketer to know and understand. The list is always growing, so it is important to stay current. Some examples are:
- OLA: online advertising
- engagement rate: measure of social media users interacting with your social media
- PTAT: people talking about this
- trending: a word or topic that is popular at any given minute
- impression: how many times a post has been displayed
- CTA: call to action
- conversion rate: how many people are acting on the call to action

Keeping on top of new terms and learning the proper way to use social media is a priority for social-media marketing.

Federal Antitrust Laws	
Sherman Antitrust Act (1890)	This act supports fair commerce and trade by making the formation of monopolies and agreements to practice price fixing illegal. Violations of this act are punishable as criminal felonies.
Clayton Antitrust Act (1914)	This act helps prevent the formation of monopolies that will reduce competition. Businesses planning a merger or acquisition must notify the Department of Justice Antitrust Division and the Federal Trade Commission.
Federal Trade Commission Act (1914)	This act prohibits unfair competition in interstate commerce. It also created the Federal Trade Commission to oversee related business activity.

Source: US Department of Justice; Goodheart-Willcox Publisher

Figure 6-6 Federal antitrust laws are enforced by departments of the federal government. Individual states also enforce their own antitrust laws.

Promote Competition

The United States has laws to ensure that markets are competitive, open, and fair. *Antitrust laws* promote fair trade, open markets, and competition among businesses. These laws have been established to prevent monopolies and unfair pricing and business practices. **Price-fixing** occurs when two or more businesses in an industry agree to sell the same product or service at a set price. This practice eliminates price competition. When two or more businesses work together to remove their competition, set prices, and control distribution, it is called **collusion**.

There are three major federal antitrust laws: Sherman Antitrust Act, Clayton Antitrust Act, and Federal Trade Commission Act. These three laws are shown in Figure 6-6. The US Department of Justice and the Federal Trade Commission enforce antitrust laws in the US economy.

Correct for Externalities

An **externality** is something that is not directly connected to an economic activity, but that affects people. For example, emissions from a factory can be harmful to those living close to the business. It can cause problems for those who inhale the fumes. Controlling emissions is not an economic activity. However, the government can impose fines and taxes on industries to reduce this type of externality.

Section 6.2 Review

Check Your Understanding

1. Which market structure is characterized by a large number of businesses selling similar, but not the same, products and at different prices?
2. Distinguish between price and nonprice competition.
3. How does the government manage the economy?
4. What two major policies are used by the government to manage the economy?
5. Name one antitrust law.

Build Your Vocabulary

As you progress through this text, develop a personal glossary of key terms. This will help you build your vocabulary and prepare you for a career. Write a definition for each of the following terms and add them to your personal glossary.

- collusion
- externality
- Federal Reserve System
- fiscal policy
- market structure
- monetary policy
- money supply
- monopolistic competition
- monopoly
- nonprice competition
- oligopoly
- perfect competition
- price competition
- price-fixing

CHAPTER 6 Review and Assessment

Chapter Summary

Section 6.1 Economic Measurement

LO 6.1-1 Identify common indicators used to measure economic activity.
Various economic measurements are used to analyze the economy. They include gross domestic product (GDP), inflation, interest rates, unemployment rate, and the stock and bond markets.

LO 6.1-2 Describe the four stages of the business cycle.
Alternating periods of expansion and contraction in the economy are called the business cycle. Expansion is when the economy is growing and the GDP is rising. Peak marks the end of expansion and is the highest point in the cycle. Recession is a significant decline in the economy. A trough is the lowest stage of the cycle and marks the end of a recession.

LO 6.1-3 Explain three classifications of economic indicators.
Economic indicators can provide information about which stage of the business cycle an economy is in and the stage that is coming next. A leading indicator changes before a change in economic activity. A lagging indicator changes after a change in economic activity. A coincident indicator changes at the same time as changes in economic activity.

Section 6.2 Government and the Economy

LO 6.2-1 Describe four basic market structures.
Market structure is how businesses are organized in an industry to compete for sales and profit. Four basic market structures represent varying degrees of competition. A monopoly is the least competitive structure, followed by oligopoly, monopolistic competition, and perfect competition.

LO 6.2-2 Identify the role of government in the US economy.
The government acts as both a regulator and provider of public goods and services to help our free-enterprise system operate in an efficient manner. The government manages the economy, provides public goods and services, provides a legal framework, promotes competition, and corrects for externalities.

Check Your Marketing IQ

Now that you have completed the chapter, see what you have learned about marketing by taking the chapter posttest. The posttest is available at www.g-wlearning.com/marketing/.

Review Your Knowledge

1. Identify common indicators used to measure economic activity.
2. Interpret the measure of consumer spending as an economic indicator.
3. Describe the concept of price stability as an economic measure.
4. Describe the four stages of the business cycle.
5. Explain three classifications of economic indicators.
6. Describe four basic market structures.
7. Identify the role of government in the US economy.
8. Describe the role of the Federal Reserve System.
9. What is the purpose of antitrust laws?
10. Provide an example of an externality.

Apply Your Knowledge

1. Identify examples of economic measurements used to analyze the economy. How do these measurements relate to the marketing process for the marketing plan you are writing?
2. How can the current GDP be useful information for a marketing manager?
3. How might the inflation rate influence your decision to market a product? Consider both high and low inflation.
4. How might your marketing plan for a product be impacted during a period of high inflation, when costs are increasing rapidly?
5. Do you think it is a better strategy to increase profits by increasing productivity or decreasing expenses? Briefly explain.
6. How might your marketing strategy differ if you try to increase sales by encouraging current customers to buy more, instead of attracting new customers?
7. Create a graphic illustration of the business cycle that includes each stage using the information in this chapter as a basis. Describe the condition of the economy during each stage of the business cycle. Cite examples of how the business for which you are creating a marketing plan might benefit during each phase.
8. Explain how marketing strategies differ in the recession phase of a business cycle instead of the expansion phase. Then, explain how marketing strategies differ in the expansion phase versus the recession phase.
9. Provide five nonprice examples of ways the business you have chosen can compete for customers in the marketplace.
10. Discuss the importance of public goods and services on your local economy. How might these affect your decisions for marketing a product?

Apply Your Math Skills

When making marketing decisions that impact the business, the economic growth rate is useful for planning purposes. Use the formula for economic growth rate to perform the calculations that follow.

[(GDP for time 2 − GDP for time 1) ÷ GDP time 1] × 100 = economic growth rate

1. Assume GDP was $19.5 trillion in a recent year. It was $19.0 trillion the year before. What was the economic growth rate?
2. Suppose GDP grows to $20.5 trillion, compared to $19.5 trillion. What will be the economic growth between these two years?

Communication Skills

College and Career Readiness

Reading Analyze the quality of the illustrations presented in this chapter. Is the information coherent? Is concrete evidence presented? Note any changes you would make to specific figures.

Writing To become career ready, it is important to learn how to communicate clearly and effectively using reasoning. Using the information in this chapter, write a summary of your assessment of the role of government in a free-enterprise system.

Listening Active listening is fully participating as you process what a person says. Active listeners know when to comment and when to remain silent. Use active listening skills while your instructor presents this chapter. Participate in the discussion by making relevant comments when appropriate and build on the instructor's ideas by asking related questions.

Internet Research

Economic Indicators Search the Internet for the current information on GDP, standard of living, inflation rate, interest rate, unemployment rate, productivity, stock market reports, and CPI in the United States. What do these figures indicate about the overall economic health of US markets? Explain how these economic indicators are used in a market economy by businesses, government, and individuals for business analysis and marketing decisions.

Role of Government in the Free-Enterprise System Using the Internet, research the *role of government in the free-enterprise system*. How does the information you learned in this chapter help support your research?

Federal Worker Protection Use online resources to identify a federal regulatory agency or law that was developed to protect workers. Summarize the events that led to the creation of this agency or law. Include your thoughts on how the existence of this agency or law might impact both domestic and foreign trade.

Teamwork

Together with your team, discuss how businesses, governments, and individuals are connected. Determine the relationship between these entities in the current economic climate of your state and country. Make notes on the key points your team discusses.

Portfolio Development

College and Career Readiness

Digital Presentation Options Before you begin collecting items for a digital portfolio, you will need to decide how you are going to present the final product. This will dictate file naming conventions and file structure. There are many creative ways to present a digital portfolio.

One option is to create an electronic presentation with slides for each item. The slides could have links to documents, videos, graphics, or sound files.

Websites are another option for presenting a digital portfolio. You could create a personal website to host the files and have a main page with links to various sections. Each section page could have links to pages with your documents, videos, graphics, or sound files. (Be sure you read and understand the user agreement for any site on which you place your materials.)

Another option is to place the files on a CD. The method you choose should allow the viewer to easily navigate and find items.

1. Establish the types of technology that are available for you to create a digital portfolio. Will you have access to cameras or studios? Do you have the level of skill to create a website?
2. Decide the type of presentation you will use. Research what will be needed to create the final portfolio product.

CHAPTER 7

Global Trade

Sections

7.1 **Global Business Environment**
7.2 **Global Marketplace**

Reading Prep

College and Career Readiness

As you read this chapter, determine the author's point of view or purpose. What aspects of the text help establish this purpose or point of view?

Check Your Marketing IQ

Before you begin the chapter, see what you already know about marketing by taking the chapter pretest. The pretest is available at www.g-wlearning.com/marketing/.

DECA Emerging Leaders

Principles of Hospitality and Tourism Event

Career Cluster: Hospitality and Tourism
Instructional Area: Human Resources Management/Professional Development

Knowledge and Skills Developed

Participants will develop many 21st century skills desired by today's employers in the following categories:
- communication and collaboration
- creativity and innovation
- critical thinking and problem solving
- flexibility and adaptability
- information literacy
- initiative and self-direction
- leadership and responsibility
- productivity and accountability
- social and cross-cultural skills

Performance Indicators

- Discuss the nature of human resources management.
- Assess personal interests and skills needed for success in business.
- Orient new employees.
- Analyze employer expectations in the business environment.

Purpose

Designed for first-year DECA members who are enrolled in introductory-level principles of marketing/business courses, the event measures the student's proficiency in those knowledge and skills identified by career practitioners as common academic and technical content in hospitality and tourism. This event consists of a 100-question, multiple-choice, business administration core exam and a business situation. Participants are not informed in advance of the performance indicators to be evaluated.

Procedure

1. The event will be presented to you through your reading of these instructions, including the performance indicators and business situation. You will have ten minutes to review this information to determine how you will perform the task and demonstrate the performance indicators of this event. During the preparation period, you may make notes to use during the business situation.
2. You will have up to ten minutes to role-play your situation with a judge. You may have more than one judge.
3. You will be evaluated on how well you meet the performance indicators of this event.
4. Turn in all your notes and event materials when you have completed the role-play.

Business Situation

You are to assume the role of a human resources department full-time employee at the Majestic Hotel, a family-oriented hotel chain. You have worked at the Majestic Hotel for several years and have the knowledge and understanding of the importance of human resources management and professional development.

Majestic Hotel is currently experiencing an extremely high turnover of employees. This turnover is causing a significant decrease in hotel profits and employee morale. A **new manager (judge)** has just been hired and you have been asked to explain the importance of staff growth and development in order to increase productivity and employee satisfaction.

The new manager (judge) wants you to explain why human resources management and professional development are important to the success and profitability of a business. Your presentation should also address the additional performance indicators listed on the first page of this event.

You will discuss customer relations with the new manager (judge) in the Majestic Hotel general manager's office. The new manager (judge) will begin the role-play by greeting you and asking you to explain your knowledge and understanding of the importance of human resources management and professional development to the success and profitability of a business. Following your explanation, the new manager (judge) will ask you additional questions.

Critical Thinking

1. What is the value of employee orientation?
2. What are several ways to reward employee loyalty?
3. What are several current employment trends in the hospitality and tourism industry?

Visit www.deca.org for more information.

Published by DECA Inc. Copyright © by DECA Inc. No part of this publication may be reproduced for resale without written permission from the publisher. Printed in the United States of America.

Section 7.1

Global Business Environment

Essential Question

How are you connected to the global economy?

Learning Objectives

LO 7.1-1 Cite reasons nations engage in international trade.
LO 7.1-2 Discuss currency in the global marketplace.
LO 7.1-3 Identify ways governments play a role in international business.

Key Terms

globalization
international trade
absolute advantage
comparative advantage
export
import
balance of trade
balance of payments
foreign exchange rate
floating currency

trade policy
protectionism
trade barrier
embargo
trade sanction
tariff
quota
trade agreement
trading bloc

LO 7.1-1 Globalization

Globalization is the connection made among nations worldwide when economies freely move goods, labor, and money across borders. The global environment in which businesses operate includes modern technology that allows communication to flow easily around the world. It has created opportunities for nations to connect by opening new markets, creating jobs, and developing political relationships.

The terms *global trade* and *international trade* are sometimes used interchangeably. However, there is a slight difference. *Global* means the world, such as *global economy*. **International trade** is the buying and selling of goods and services between two or more specific nations rather than all nations in the world. For example, an *international treaty* is signed by specific countries rather than all the countries in the world.

The United States has an absolute advantage in wheat production over many countries. *How might a country's absolute advantages impact business opportunities in that country?*

Nations engage in international trade because most countries do not have enough factors of production to produce all the goods and services needed by their population. The available land, labor, capital, and entrepreneurship vary by country. Trading goods and services produced by each country's businesses allows more needs and wants to be met.

An **absolute advantage** exists when a country can produce goods more efficiently and at a lower cost than another country. The United States has an absolute advantage over Costa Rica in the production of wheat. Costa Rica has an absolute advantage over the United States in the production of bananas. The United States can benefit from trading wheat for bananas.

A **comparative advantage** exists when a country specializes in products that it can produce efficiently. For example, the United States might be very efficient at producing both aircraft and certain items of clothing. However, producing aircraft might be much more profitable. As a result, the United States can benefit by specializing in aircraft production and buying clothing from another country.

International trade takes place through exporting and importing. An **export** is a product that is produced within a country's borders and sold in another country. An **import** is a product that is brought into a country from outside its borders. Figure 7-1 shows US exports to the top ten foreign markets in 2016. Exporting and importing has a created a *global dependency*. This means countries depend on each other for products.

All countries measure and record the economic exchanges that take place with all other trading countries. The **balance of trade** is the difference between a nation's exports and its imports. A nation that has more exports than imports has a positive balance of trade, or a *trade surplus*. When a nation imports more products than it exports, the result is a negative balance of trade, or a *trade deficit*.

The **balance of payments** is the total amount of money that comes in to a country, minus the total amount of money that goes out for a specific period of time. This includes all the goods and services a country imports and exports, as well as all the country's international financial transactions. Financial transactions include investments in stocks, real estate, and international companies. It also includes tourism. A country has a *positive* balance of payments when more money comes into the country than leaves it. If more money leaves a country than comes into it, a *negative* balance of payments is created.

LO 7.1-2 Currency

Currency is money. When businesses, individuals, or governments in the same country buy and sell goods to one another, they use the same currency. Most countries have a unique currency and typically will only accept this currency for business exchanges. For example, a US business that buys from Europe needs to exchange dollars for euros to complete the financial transaction. This can become complicated because the value of each country's currency is different when compared to other currencies. Factors that affect the way a nation's currency functions in the global market include the foreign exchange rate and the currency value.

The **foreign exchange rate** is the cost to convert one currency into another. Exchange rates are needed because currencies have different values. For example, the value of one US dollar (USD) is not equal to one British pound (GBP). The exchange rate helps determine how much in British pounds is needed to equal one US dollar. Figure 7-2 shows examples of five foreign currency exchange rates.

When buying and selling products in countries that use different currencies, it is important to understand the value of the foreign currencies.

United States Exports in 2016

Country/Region	Export Dollar Amount (billions)	Percent of Total US International Exports
Canada	$ 266.8	18.3%
Mexico	231.0	15.9
China	115.8	8.0
Japan	63.3	4.4
United Kingdom	55.4	3.8
Germany	49.4	3.4
South Korea	42.3	2.9
Netherlands	40.3	2.8
Hong Kong	34.9	2.4
Belgium	32.3	2.2
World Total	**$1,454.6**	**100.0%**

Source: U.S. Department of Commerce, Census Bureau, Economic Indicator Division; Goodheart-Willcox Publisher

Figure 7-1 The data in this chart reflects US exports to the top ten foreign markets in 2016.

Most countries have a unique currency and will only accept their own currency for business exchanges. *Why do you think different countries developed unique currencies?*

James L. Davidson/Shutterstock.com

The *foreign exchange market (FOREX)* is a financial marketplace for buying and selling the currencies of different countries. It works like a stock market for foreign currencies.

The exchange rate of currency is often considered to be an indicator of the economy's health. The rates can be influenced by many factors:
- political stability or instability in the world
- nations changing their laws
- nations in dispute with other nations
- economic conditions, such as interest rates

Today, most currencies are floating. A **floating currency** is one with an exchange rate that is set by the market forces of supply and demand in the foreign exchange market. Exchange rates can vary from day to day and even hour to hour. This fluctuation in exchange rates can make financial exchanges complicated.

The US dollar is a floating currency. It can strengthen or weaken against other currencies.

Sometimes, the value of a foreign currency declines in US dollars. When this happens, it means the value of the US dollar has *strengthened*. A stronger dollar can buy more imports. However, exports then become more expensive to foreign buyers. When the value of foreign currency increases in US dollars, it means the value of the US dollar has *weakened*. A weaker dollar can buy fewer imports. However, exports then become less expensive to foreign buyers.

LO 7.1-3 Role of Government in International Trade

Governments regulate many aspects of international trade for various reasons. Most governments try to protect domestic companies from foreign competitors. They may also want to put pressure on foreign governments for political reasons. Trade policy, trade regulations, and trade agreements are ways in which governments play a role in international trade.

Marketing Ethics

Sourcing

Ethical businesses try to purchase raw materials or goods from reputable foreign suppliers whose products are manufactured in sustainable and environmentally safe conditions. They also look for suppliers who treat their employees well. However, sourcing products overseas in an ethical manner is often challenging because other countries have standards that are different from those in the United States.

Currency Exchange Rates (Value per USD)

Currency	December 31, 2014	December 31, 2015	December 31, 2016
British Pound (GBP)	£0.64	£0.68	£0.81
Canadian Dollar (CAD)	$1.16	$1.38	$1.34
European Union Euro (EUR)	€0.82	€0.92	€0.95
Japanese Yen (JPY)	¥119.76	¥120.31	¥116.97
Mexican Peso (MXN)	$14.74	$17.25	$20.27

Source: Board of Governors of the Federal Reserve System; Goodheart-Willcox Publisher

Figure 7-2 The value of foreign currencies tends to fluctuate over time.

Trade Policy

Trade policy is the body of laws related to the exchange of goods and services for international trade. Most governments believe that fair and open trade among nations benefits everyone. Governments are constantly negotiating trade terms with one another. Disagreements among governments are often related to access to markets. Trade disputes may arise over certain policies and practices. This can create an unfair advantage or disadvantage for at least one of the trading partners.

Trade Regulations

The nature of trade regulations is to promote fair competition and honest business practices in the global marketplace. Trade regulations may be used to prevent hazardous products from entering a country. They are also used to put political pressure on foreign governments and protect domestic businesses from foreign competitors. **Protectionism** is a policy of protecting a country's domestic industries by enforcing trade regulations on foreign competitors. Methods used in protectionism are trade barriers such as tariffs, quotas, and other regulations. Protectionist policies can work against the goal of free trade.

Governmental policies that regulate trade can restrict or discourage import activity through trade barriers. A **trade barrier** is any governmental action taken to control or limit the amount of imports. There are several types of trade barriers, including embargos, tariffs, and quotas.

An **embargo** is a governmental order that prohibits trade with a foreign country. A *total embargo* is the most severe trade restriction. A **trade sanction** is an embargo that affects only certain goods. For example, trade sanctions can prohibit the import of a specific product for public health reasons.

A **tariff** is a governmental tax on imported goods. A tariff may also be called a *duty, customs duty*, or *import duty*. There are two reasons governments impose tariffs: revenue and protection. Tariffs generate revenue for the government because the tax is paid on each related product. Imposing tariffs also protects domestic businesses. The additional tax makes imported products more expensive for consumers than competing products available from domestic businesses.

A **quota** is a limit on the amount of a product imported into a country during a specific period of time. For example, the United States has quotas on sugar, some textiles, tuna, beef, certain dairy products, and peanuts. Import quotas are meant to protect domestic producers by limiting foreign competition.

Governments use import regulations to protect the health and safety of citizens from dangerous imported products. The United States has laws controlling hazardous materials, firearms, and drugs coming into the country. There are also laws regulating plants, animals, and food that may bring pests or diseases into the country. Endangered plant and animal species and products made from them are banned under the US Endangered Species Act.

Trade Agreements

The United States has trade agreements and partnerships with many individual nations and regions around the world. A **trade agreement** is a document listing the conditions and terms for importing and exporting products between countries. The goal of trade agreements is to create economic benefits and opportunities for all participating nations by allowing free trade and investing across their borders.

The *World Trade Organization (WTO)* is a global organization that negotiates trade agreements and enforces a system of trade rules for its member countries. It is composed of over 160 nations around the world that have signed the WTO's international commerce agreements. These

monticello/Shutterstock.com

Laws regulate the import of plants, animals, and food that may bring pests or diseases into the country. *What consequences may result from importing a product that introduces pests or diseases?*

agreements outline the rights and responsibilities of member nations that engage in international trade with each other. In addition, the WTO handles trade-related disputes that arise between members. Most countries that engage in international trade belong to the WTO.

The *North American Free Trade Agreement (NAFTA)* is a trade agreement between the United States, Canada, and Mexico that was established in 1994. The agreement lowered trade barriers and opened markets among the three countries. Trade has increased dramatically among the three nations since NAFTA went into effect. Canada and Mexico are top trading partners of the United States.

A **trading bloc** is a group of countries that has joined together to trade as if they were a single country. A trading bloc is usually a free-trade zone, as well. A *free-trade zone* is a group of countries that have reduced or eliminated trade barriers among themselves.

The *European Union (EU)* is a major trading bloc and free-trade zone in the modern global economy. It currently consists of 28 countries in Europe and is the largest trade sector in the world. The EU has one of the largest GDPs and is the largest importer and exporter of goods and services. Many of the EU countries share the euro as the common currency. The main trading partners of the EU include the United States, China, Switzerland, and Russia.

Employability Skills

Resilience

Resilience is a person's ability to cope with and recover from change or adversity. Resilient people are able to aptly handle challenges in one aspect of their lives while not letting it affect other aspects. They can bounce back even when they feel as if they have been knocked down.

Section 7.1 Review

Check Your Understanding

1. What is the difference between global trade and international trade?
2. Why are exchange rates needed?
3. When the value of a foreign currency increases in US dollars, has the US dollar strengthened or weakened?
4. List examples of trade regulations.
5. Which organization regulates international free-trade practices on a global scale?

Build Your Vocabulary

As you progress through this text, develop a personal glossary of key terms. This will help you build your vocabulary and prepare you for a career. Write a definition for each of the following terms and add them to your personal glossary.

absolute advantage	international trade
balance of payments	protectionism
balance of trade	quota
comparative advantage	tariff
embargo	trade agreement
export	trade barrier
floating currency	trade policy
foreign exchange rate	trade sanction
globalization	trading bloc
import	

Section 7.2

Essential Question
How does the place in which you live impact what you buy?

Global Marketplace

Learning Objectives

LO 7.2-1 Identify ways businesses can enter the global market.
LO 7.2-2 Discuss the importance of an environmental scan.
LO 7.2-3 Describe global marketing strategies.

Key Terms

licensing
franchise
joint venture
multinational corporation
offshoring
contract manufacturing

demographics
culture
diversity
global marketing
standardization
adaptation

LO 7.2-1 Engaging in Global Business

There are various ways a company can enter the global market and conduct business in foreign countries. These include exporting and importing, as well as other opportunities for international expansion.

Exports and Imports

Exporting products to foreign markets can benefit businesses and the overall economy. Companies can realize potential new markets and increase their profits. Creating products for export also generates jobs. These jobs mean employment for the citizens of the origin country, as well as new tax dollars for that country. The positive ripple effect is felt throughout that country's economy.

Exporting also presents challenges for companies. These include identifying a target market and handling problems related to communication, shipping, and legal issues. However, these obstacles can often be overcome with careful planning. Export advice and assistance is available to US businesses from governmental agencies such as the US Department of Commerce.

Importing is another way a domestic company can increase sales potential. This presents the opportunity to introduce a new or different product to the domestic market. For example, a food

EvrenKalinbacak/Shutterstock.com

Both importing and exporting products can increase the sales potential of a business. *In what ways does the expansion of global business benefit the average consumer?*

Copyright Goodheart-Willcox Co., Inc. 113

company might increase its sales by importing a pasta sauce from Italy that is new to US customers.

Importing also presents business challenges. Imports must meet the same US standards as domestic products. For example, food and drugs must comply with standards of the US Food and Drug Administration. In addition, imports can be restricted by trade quotas set by the United States. Importers often hire specialists known as *customs brokers* to handle the legal requirements of foreign trade.

Licensing

Licensing is when a business sells the right to manufacture its products or use its trademark. Licensing involves selling the rights in exchange for a fee, also known as a royalty. A *royalty* is an amount of money paid to the original creator of something, such as a company brand. The company that sells the license is the *licensor*. The buyer of the license is the *licensee*.

An example of a licensing agreement is when Walt Disney entered the Japanese market as the licensor of Tokyo Disneyland. The amusement park carried the Disney name but was built and operated by Oriental Land Company.

Licensing can benefit both parties. The licensor earns revenue, often for little or no extra work. The licensee gets product into the market quickly. However, there are potential problems that arise when licensing. Examples are improper use of the trademark or product and failure to deliver the material or property to the licensee.

Franchising

A **franchise** is the right to sell a company's goods or services in a specific area in return for royalty fees. The *franchisor* is the parent company that owns the chain and the brand. The *franchisee* is the company that buys the rights to use the brand.

Franchising enables the franchisee to enter a market where the product or service is already known. The franchisor provides standards and procedures to get the company organized and in operation. However, buying a franchise can be expensive and maintaining established franchise standards can be challenging.

photopixel/Shutterstock.com

One way a company can enter the global market is to become a part of a franchise business, such as Marriott. *How do franchises support the expansion of global business?*

Case in Point

Mattel, Inc.

A company has many decisions to make when planning to go global. These include the culture of the potential market and marketability of the product it wants to sell. Mattel, Inc. decided to capitalize on decades of success in the United States with the Barbie doll and enter the Chinese market. The company built a flagship Barbie store in Shanghai with six floors draped in Barbie's signature pink color. The store also displayed the largest collection of Barbie dolls and related products in the world. In order to attract both young girls and adult women, the store featured a hair and nail salon, customized Barbie dolls, a restaurant and tea lounge, and other unique amenities.

Mattel made a large investment to enter the Chinese market, but the company miscalculated the recognition of their product and the Barbie brand in China. While popularity of Barbie products has remained strong for generations in the United States, Barbie was not widely popular in China and customers did not associate any meaning with the brand. In addition, because Mattel did not source the Barbie products sold in the store from China, many of the products were expensive. Chinese consumers did not hold Barbie as a cultural icon and did not want to pay high-end prices for Barbie-branded merchandise. To many, Barbie dolls were just a toy. Because of these mistakes in marketing strategy, Barbie Shanghai closed after less than two years, costing Mattel tens of millions of dollars.

Exploring Marketing Careers

Customer Service

No matter how hard a company works to provide excellent quality in its products or services, customers will occasionally have questions or complaints. How the company handles these can have a huge effect on the success of the company—for better or worse. People who work in customer service are a company's interface or connection with its customers. Typical job titles for these positions include *customer service representative*, *customer service specialist*, *hub associate*, *account service representative*, and *call center representative*.

Some examples of tasks that customer service professionals perform include:
- Provide product or service information to customers in person or by telephone
- Keep records of customer comments and complaints and actions taken to resolve the issues
- Solve customer complaints by exchanging merchandise, offering a refund, or making adjustments to charges
- Refer unresolved issues to the appropriate department for further research
- Recheck to make sure customers' problems have been solved

People skills are of utmost importance for customer service professionals. They must be active listeners, giving their full attention to what the customer is saying. They also must have the ability to speak well and persuasively. They use critical thinking to negotiate solutions that work for the customer and the company. Most customer service positions require a high school diploma and up to a year of on-the-job training. Prior experience in working with the public is also helpful. For more information, access the *Occupational Outlook Handbook* online.

Joint Venture

A **joint venture** is a partnership of two or more companies that work together for a specific business purpose. Each company remains independent but they share the profits or losses. Joint ventures may be formed between two domestic businesses, or between a domestic and foreign company. Some countries do not allow a foreign business to enter unless it has a joint venture with a domestic company.

An example of an international joint venture is Campbell Soup Company forming a joint venture with local companies in Japan and Malaysia. This enabled Campbell Soup to enter foreign markets without assuming all the risk.

Multinationals

A **multinational corporation** is a business that operates in more than one country. Multinational corporations often have their corporate headquarters in one country and divisions of the business in another country, or located *offshore*. **Offshoring** is moving sections of a business to another country. General Motors and Johnson & Johnson are examples of multinational corporations.

Contract Manufacturing

Contract manufacturing is transferring production work to another company. This is also known as *outsourcing*. Companies outsource production to avoid capital expenditures, reduce costs, or improve product quality. Many companies outsource work to foreign companies because the operating costs in other countries are lower. This can include the manufacture or assembly of final products or parts. Unfortunately, foreign outsourcing results in lost domestic jobs.

Global Environmental Scan

LO 7.2-2

Before completing a marketing plan, a review of the external environment that the business will encounter should be completed. An *environmental scan* is an analysis of the external factors that affect the success of business. One way to complete an environmental scan is to use a *PEST analysis*, which is an evaluation of the political, economic, social, and technological factors in a certain market or geographic region that may impact the success of a business. This process identifies potential opportunities and threats to a company's business plans and strategies.

The process is also applied to global business strategies. A *global environmental scan* should be completed before the marketing plan is written. A business will face many similar issues for conducting global business as they encounter with their domestic business.

Political Factors

Political structure is an important external factor for conducting global business. Traditional, command, market, and mixed economies each function differently. The type of economic system may require changes to the business and marketing plans in order for the business to be successful in a foreign country.

The level of stability in a country's government affects the success of businesses that operate within it. Stability also impacts the willingness and ability of consumers to purchase products. Many situations can lead to political instability in a country, such as military conflicts, changes in political leadership, and poor economic conditions.

Laws relating to trade regulation and taxation have a significant impact on businesses. Trade regulations determine the extent to which a company can engage in business within certain markets. A country's tax policy affects the potential success of a business expanding overseas. Some countries have tax policies created to attract foreign businesses, while the tax laws of other countries make it more difficult for a business to be successful.

Economic Factors

Economic factors affect the ability of consumers to purchase products, as well as the cost of doing business. Examples of economic factors to consider include exchange rate, infrastructure, cost of labor, standard of living, and economic indicators.

Foreign Exchange Rate

The way a nation's currency functions in the global market affects the operation and profitability of a business. When the US dollar strengthens against a foreign currency, US products become more expensive and less attractive to foreign buyers. When the US dollar weakens against a foreign currency, US products become less expensive and more attractive to foreign buyers.

Infrastructure

Infrastructure consists of the transportation systems and utilities necessary in a modern economy. It is considered a type of capital and is a factor of production. Countries with an up-to-date and stable infrastructure have reliable access to basic necessities, such as clean water, electricity, fuel, and waste removal. They also have access to the transportation, shipping, and communication infrastructure required to conduct business. This can include airports, highways, railways, telephone systems, and Internet services.

Labor

There are many issues related to a country's labor force that can impact the success of conducting

You Do the Math

Currency Conversion

When conducting global business, it is necessary to understand currency conversion. To determine currency exchange, you can use one of the many currency converters found on the Internet.

Solve the following problems.
1. You want to buy two books published only in the UK. The prices of the books are listed in British pounds (GBP or £). The cost of the books is £17.98. The current exchange rate is $1.00 = £0.60797.
   A. What is the cost of the books in US dollars? (Round to the nearest cent.)
   B. Shipping from the UK is £9.97. What is the total cost of your purchase including shipping in US dollars?
2. A manufacturer of small home appliances needs to purchase $3,500 worth of circuit boards from a supplier located in India. The supplier's prices are listed in Indian rupees (INR or ₹). The current exchange rate is $1.00 = ₹66.00. What is the cost of the circuit boards in rupees?

business abroad. Each country has unique labor laws that determine who can work, the standard number of days and hours of work, and minimum rates of pay. The standard of acceptable working conditions also varies from country to country.

The education and skill level of a country's labor force determines the type of work it is able to do and its overall productivity. For example, countries with a highly educated population have a large pool of workers who are qualified to work in the fields of technology, science, and medicine. The workforce of other countries may be very skilled at efficiently manufacturing consumer goods for an affordable price. Work that requires a higher level of education will cost a business more in labor.

Standard of Living

Standard of living refers to the financial well-being of the average person in a country. The standard of living of people within an economy affects their demand for products, as well as how they go about fulfilling their needs and wants. Businesses evaluate standard of living to determine which products to offer in the market, as well as the potential for earning profits. For example, a furniture company identifies a market where a large portion of the population lives in smaller, efficiency-style housing. Expansive wall units for entertainment systems, oversized sectional couches, and large bedroom sets would not sell in this market due to the standard of living. To be profitable, the company would need to offer smaller-scaled furniture in the market.

Economic Indicators

The strength of the economy can be measured using certain common economic indicators. Some of the most widely followed indicators of the economy include gross domestic product (GDP), inflation, interest rates, unemployment rate, and the stock and bond markets. These are discussed in detail in Chapter 6.

Social Factors

Social factors refer to the demographic and cultural aspects within a business environment. **Demographics** are the qualities of a specific group of people including age, gender, income, ethnicity, education level, occupation, marital status, and family size. Demographic information is used to target a market in a foreign country, just as it is in a business's home country.

Everything/Shutterstock.com

Culture is the shared beliefs, customs, practices, and social behavior of a particular group or nation. *Why is it important for a business to consider culture when considering conducting business in a foreign country?*

Culture is the shared beliefs, customs, practices, and social behavior of a particular group or nation. It affects how people think, work, interact, and communicate with others. **Diversity** is the different backgrounds, cultures, or demographics and includes age, race, nationality, gender, mental ability, physical ability, and other qualities that make an individual unique.

The cultural beliefs and values of potential customers in a market affect how they make economic decisions and set economic goals. Cultures vary widely in terms of their beliefs and values. Examples are as follows:

- attitude toward spending, saving, and borrowing money;
- degree to which religious beliefs affect the use of money;
- influence of family in financial decision making;
- role of the individual in society;
- traditional values related to money; and
- value of independence and entrepreneurship.

Culture also influences people's political preferences, such as how involved the government should be in economic issues. The attitudes of potential customers toward topics such as health, environmental issues, and how leisure time should be spent can have a significant impact on whether a product is successful.

Social factors include the customs and expected behaviors related to carrying out business activities, such as meetings, financial transactions, developing business relationships, and other business functions. Social and business etiquette may differ in foreign countries. For example, in some countries it is customary to bring a gift to the host of a business meeting. In others, this would be an awkward and uncomfortable gesture.

Technological Factors

Technological factors affect the ease with which a business can operate within a country and the level of productivity possible once the business is in operation. Infrastructure for telephone systems, cellular phone service, Internet connectivity, broadcast media, and transportation are all included in the technological factors a business should evaluate.

Technology also impacts the array of products offered within a country's market and the cost of the products for both businesses to produce and for customers to purchase. The level of technology used in production often determines the productivity level of a company.

Global Marketing Strategies

Global marketing consists of dynamic activities that identify, anticipate, and satisfy customer demand for product in countries worldwide while making a profit for the business. Many companies sell products that can be profitable on a global scale when the correct marketing strategies are applied.

Marketing is important in the global economy because it can help increase international trade. When businesses participate in international trade, they generate competition within the global economy. The competing businesses conduct marketing activities that promote a variety of products at competitive prices for consumers around the world. Successful global marketing can result in profitable businesses, which support international trade activities and the global economy.

Global marketing, similar to marketing domestically, starts with the marketing mix. As you recall, the *marketing mix* is the strategy for using elements of the product, price, place and promotion. It involves making decisions about the four Ps for a specific product or group of products.

Product

Some businesses have products that are suitable for both domestic and global sales. The product can be sold in both markets without any changes. A good example is Head & Shoulders shampoo manufactured by Procter & Gamble. The same product is sold globally.

Other products can be sold globally if changes are made. *Product adaptations* customize existing products to the local tastes, expectations, buying habits, and customs of a foreign market. They can be accomplished by changing the ingredients or materials used, the quantity packaged, certain components or functions, or even the name of the product itself.

For example, areas of Africa that have electrical supply grids often experience power surges and outages. Samsung Electronics adapted their LED televisions for the instability of the region's power supply by adding functionality that allows the television to operate on both AC and DC power. The televisions can be powered by the AC electrical supply from household outlets and DC electrical supply from other power sources, such as solar cells and batteries.

Price

Determining the selling price of a product for global markets can be challenging. As with pricing for the domestic market, many factors have to be taken into consideration. If the product is exported, many costs must be considered. If the product is made in the country in which it is sold, the cost to produce it could be more or less than exporting. Global markets may be more price-sensitive than the domestic market and profit margins may be less. Much planning and research is necessary when determining pricing strategies.

Place

Place decisions involve determining when, where, and how products get to customers. It involves distribution strategies to get the product to the consumer. Distributing to foreign countries involves a vast and well-planned supply chain. A *supply chain* is the businesses, people, and activities involved in turning raw materials into products and delivering them to the end users.

Promotion

Standardization is applying consistent promotion strategies to the marketing of a product regardless of the specific market. One product and one message create a uniform perception of the brand. Using a standardization strategy saves the business

Microsoft applies consistent promotional strategies to the marketing of its products regardless of the specific market. *How might consistent promotional strategies contribute to a company's image?*

testing/Shutterstock.com

money by avoiding costs related to the promotion campaigns. A good example of standardization is Microsoft. No matter where the product is sold, marketing standardization is applied.

However, for many companies, a standardized global strategy does not address the differences in culture, distinct preferences, and other unique characteristics among customers in various foreign markets. Ignoring these factors may make products less appealing or completely unappealing to global market customers. This can put the profits of a company in jeopardy.

In marketing, **adaptation** is changing the marketing strategies to meet the preferences and demands of customers in a specific market. This strategy considers the local culture and economy that affect customers in the market. The goal of the adaptation strategy to is to make an existing product appeal to a new market.

Adaptation modifies strategies and elements of promotion to align with the regulations, culture, and social expectations of a local market. This includes using graphics, packaging, slogans, and advertisements that are acceptable and appealing in a foreign market. For example, television advertising directed at children is prohibited in Sweden and Norway. When planning promotional activities in these markets, businesses must ensure that the message and appeal of the promotions are directed at adults.

Adaptation also includes changes made to conform to local laws and regulations. This may include using the local language on packaging, pricing in the local currency, stating contents in local units of measure, and product warning and instruction requirements.

Section 7.2 Review

Check Your Understanding

1. What types of challenges do businesses face when exporting?
2. How does licensing benefit both the licensor and the licensee?
3. When conducting a global environmental scan, what four factors should be evaluated?
4. What are product adaptations?
5. Explain the difference between standardization and adaptation strategies.

Build Your Vocabulary

As you progress through this text, develop a personal glossary of key terms. This will help you build your vocabulary and prepare you for a career. Write a definition for each of the following terms and add them to your personal glossary.

adaptation
contract manufacturing
culture
demographics
diversity
franchise

global marketing
joint venture
licensing
multinational corporation
offshoring
standardization

CHAPTER 7 Review and Assessment

Chapter Summary

Section 7.1 Global Business Environment

LO 7.1-1 Cite reasons nations engage in international trade.
Nations engage in international trade because most countries do not have the factors of production needed to produce all the goods and services needed by their population. International trade allows more of the needs and wants of consumers to be met.

LO 7.1-2 Discuss currency in the global marketplace.
The value of a country's currency is different when compared to other currencies. Factors that affect the way a nation's currency functions in the global market include the foreign exchange rate and the currency value. The exchange rate of currency is often considered to be an indicator of the economy's health.

LO 7.1-3 Identify ways governments play a role in international business.
Trade policy, trade regulations, and trade agreements are ways in which governments play a role in international trade. Governmental policies can restrict or discourage import activity through trade barriers such as embargos, tariffs, and quotas. The goal of trade agreements is to create economic benefits and opportunities by allowing free trade and investing across their borders.

Section 7.2 Global Marketplace

LO 7.2-1 Identify ways businesses can enter the global market.
A domestic business can enter a global market in various ways. Exporting and importing are obvious ways of conducting international business. Licensing, franchising, joint ventures, multinationals, and contract manufacturing may also provide a company with growth opportunities in global markets.

LO 7.2-2 Discuss the importance of an environmental scan.
An environmental scan is an analysis of the external factors that affect the success of business, including potential political, economic, social, and technological opportunities and threats to a company's business plans and strategies.

LO 7.2-3 Describe global marketing strategies.
Global marketing consists of dynamic activities that identify, anticipate, and satisfy customer demand for product in countries worldwide while making a profit for the business. It involves making decisions about the four Ps for a specific product or group of products.

Check Your Marketing IQ

Now that you have completed the chapter, see what you have learned about marketing by taking the chapter posttest. The posttest is available at www.g-wlearning.com/marketing/.

Review Your Knowledge

1. Cite reasons nations engage in international trade.
2. Discuss currency in the global marketplace.
3. Provide an example of factors that can affect the exchange rate of currency.
4. Identify examples of barriers to trade.
5. Identify ways governments play a role in international business.
6. Identify ways businesses can enter the global market.
7. Explain struggles encountered by companies engaging in exporting, importing, and contract manufacturing.
8. Discuss the importance of an environmental scan.

9. Explain how culture and political structure affect international trade.
10. Describe global marketing strategies.

Apply Your Knowledge

1. How might diversity and cultural differences in the global marketplace impact the marketing plan for the company you selected?

2. Explain the impact of imports and exports on the US economy. How might your company benefit? Are there negative aspects to your company participating in importing or exporting activities? Write several paragraphs to explain your answers.

3. Assume your marketing plan will include global marketing strategies. Outline items to evaluate in an environmental scan in order to create a successful global marketing plan.

4. In order to develop global marketing strategies, you will need to determine the marketing mix for your product that will be marketed internationally. Describe each of the four Ps of your product's marketing mix as they apply to the global marketplace.

5. Assume the company you selected will be expanding its business operations through exporting. Identify potential strategies to include in your marketing plan for entering the global market through exporting.

6. Describe how the foreign exchange rate can affect the buying power of the US dollar and your business..

7. A US company makes furniture and uses large amounts of exotic woods. How will quotas on imported wood affect the price of the product and the marketing plan?

8. A restaurant chain that specializes in Stromboli sandwiches is considering opening restaurants in a foreign country. However, the company discovered that Stromboli sandwiches are virtually unknown there. Identify a potential advantage and disadvantage of expanding into this new market.

9. The management team of the business you selected is considering entering the global market. What strategy or strategies would you recommend for this company to enter the global market: exporting, importing, licensing, franchising, joint venture, expanding to a multinational, or contract manufacturing? Explain the pros and cons of the option(s) you choose to recommend.

10. Describe potential barriers to communication that can occur when conducting international business. How can your company prepare itself for intercultural communication?

Apply Your Math Skills

An important component of a global marketing plan is to show statistical evidence of the factors that can lead to success. Communicating marketing facts and figures using visuals is typically more meaningful and engaging for meeting participants. Apply your math skills to solve the following problems.

1. On a sheet of paper, draw a bar graph that shows the amount of exports for each of the top five countries in 2016. Use the data from Figure 7-1. List the top five countries on the horizontal axis and the dollar amount (in billions) on the vertical axis.

2. Your company had the following sales in Canada over these five years:
   2013: $0
   2014: $10,000
   2015: $35,000
   2016: $75,000
   2017: $130,000

   On a sheet of paper, draw a line graph to show the growth in sales. List sales on the vertical axis and the years on the horizontal axis.

Communication Skills

Listening Practice active listening skills while listening to a broadcast business report on the radio, on television, or podcast. Select a single story about foreign or domestic trade and its importance in a global economy. As you are listening, take notes on important points that you hear.

College and Career Readiness

When you are finished, review your notes and conclude whether you were an active listener.

Writing Generate ideas that relate to the importance of accurate information. Make a list of reasons you would provide a business owner when explaining why it is important to have accurate exchange rates when conducting business with a foreign company. After your list is complete, write a paragraph summarizing your reasoning.

Speaking The cultural beliefs and values of potential customers in a market affect how they make economic decisions and set economic goals. Prepare a brief speech that summarizes your viewpoint about this statement. Present the information clearly, concisely, and logically so the audience can follow your line of reasoning, organization, and the development of your ideas.

Internet Research

Global Currencies Select three countries whose currency you desire to research. Next, locate a currency conversion calculator online. Determine how much each type of currency is worth in US dollars. In which countries is the dollar worth more than it is in the United States? In what countries is it worth less?

Protectionism Perform online research about *US protectionism*. Cite a recent example from the news in which US protectionism has been critiqued, defended, or referenced. Compose an original argument for or against US protectionism. Support your position with evidence. Are there any sanctions affecting a given industry or country that you would recommend be removed or kept in place?

Product Adaptations Identify a product that could be adapted for the market in a foreign country. How would the product need to be adapted in order to be successful in this new market? Use online resources to help identify what features may need to be added, removed, or changed.

Teamwork

Working with your team, discuss the benefits nations derive from forming trade agreements and trade blocs such as NAFTA, WTO, and the EU. Explain whether you think these benefits flow equitably to all countries involved.

Portfolio Development

Digital File Formats A portfolio will contain documents you have created electronically, as well as documents in hard copy format that will be digitized. It will be necessary to choose file formats to be used for both types of documents. Before you begin, consider the technology you might use for creating and scanning documents. You will need access to desktop publishing software, scanners, cameras, and other digital equipment or software.

For documents that you create, consider using the default file format to save the files. For example, you could save letters and essays created in Microsoft Word in DOCx format. You could save worksheets created in Microsoft Excel in XLSx format. For presentations that include graphics or video, confirm the file formats necessary for each item. Use the appropriate formats as you create the documents.

Hard copy items will need to be converted to digital format, or *digitized*. Portable document format, or PDF, is a good choice for scanned documents.

Another option is to save all documents as PDF files. Keep in mind that the person reviewing your digital portfolio will need programs that can open these formats to view your files. Having all of the files in the same format can make viewing them easier for others who need to review your portfolio.

1. Decide the strategy you will use for saving documents. Make note of where the technology is available for your use, such as your home computer or the school lab.
2. Document any special instructions needed to use the software or equipment. This will save time when you are ready to create or save files.

UNIT 2 Economics

Building the Marketing Plan

As a famous philosopher said, "A journey of a thousand miles begins with a single step." The first step of your journey as a marketing professional is your marketing plan. You will make many revisions to the plan as you proceed through the text. Remember, there are no right or wrong answers to any of the activities that you complete. You have reviewed the parts of the marketing plan and are now ready to begin writing your own plan. Keep in mind that you are writing a draft as you complete each section of your marketing plan. You will revise each section or subsection multiple times as you conduct more research and learn more about your business and industry.

Economic Conditions

Objectives

- Evaluate current economic conditions and the impact on your business.
- Explore the impact of inflation on your business.

Directions

In this activity, you will begin developing the Market Analysis section of the marketing plan. The Market Analysis is a snapshot of the environment in which a business has been operating over a given time, usually the last 12 to 16 months.

Access the *Marketing Dynamics* companion website at www.g-wlearning.com/marketing/. Download the activity file as indicated in the following instructions.

1. **Unit Activity 2-1—Research Economic Conditions** In this activity, you will examine the current economic conditions of the country or region in which the business operates, inflation rate, and business cycles.

2. Open your saved marketing plan document.

3. Locate the Market Analysis section of the plan. In your role as a marketing manager for the company you selected, how do you think the current economic conditions would influence the marketing of your product or business? Assume your role as the marketing manager and provide information about the state of the economy and its impact on the business. Complete the introduction for this section.

4. How does inflation impact the marketing of your product or business? As marketing manager, provide information about the current inflation rate and its impact on the business. Continue adding information to the introduction for this section.

5. How does the current business cycle impact the marketing of the product that your business offers? As marketing manager, provide information about the current business cycle and its impact on your business.

6. Use the suggestions and questions listed to help you generate ideas. Delete the instructions and questions when you are finished recording your responses. Proofread your document and correct any errors in keyboarding, spelling, and grammar.

7. Save your document.

UNIT 3
Marketing-Information Management

Chapters
8 Marketing Research
9 Targeting a Market
10 Understanding the Customer

While studying, look for the activity icon for:
- Building the Marketing Plan activity files
- Pretests and posttests
- Vocabulary terms with e-flash cards and matching activities
- Self-assessment

These activities can be accessed at www.g-wlearning.com/marketing/.

Developing a Vision

Customer demand and competition are driving factors in the marketplace. Consumer buying habits change daily. New competition for customer dollars makes a business work harder. A business must take an objective look at the market through the eyes of the buyer as well as the competition. Consumer preferences and competitive information are learned through market research.

Research also forces marketing to be efficient and target the correct audience. Understanding the customer is the key to marketing success. Is your target business-to-consumer (B2C) customers? Or is your target business-to-business (B2B) customers? Focused marketing helps businesses meet their sales and profit goals.

Marketing Core Functions Covered in This Unit

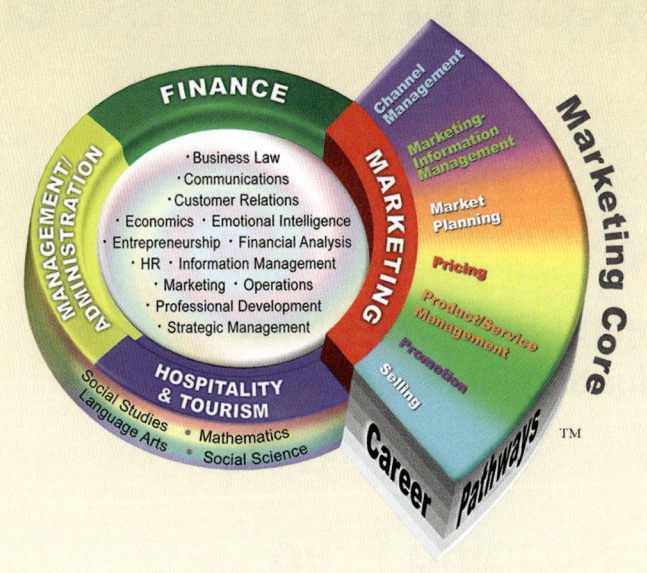

Functions of Marketing

- Marketing-information management
- Market planning
- Pricing

Copyright MBA Research, Columbus, Ohio. Used with permission.

EYE-CATCHER

Marketing Matters

It makes sense that the best way to make a profit is through the marketing concept, or customer satisfaction. Satisfying the needs and wants of target-market customers leads to customer satisfaction. Logically, the businesses that do a better job of meeting those needs will sell more than the competition.

Research companies help businesses make decisions about the products that customers want. The Nielsen Company has been the leader in measuring and analyzing consumer behavior since the 1930s. Today, Nielsen surveys consumers in more than 100 countries, including over 250,000 household panelists.

360b/Shutterstock.com

CHAPTER 8

Marketing Research

Sections

8.1 **Marketing-Research Data**
8.2 **Conducting Marketing Research**

Reading Prep

College and Career Readiness

Before you begin reading this chapter, try to find a quiet place with no distractions. Make sure your chair is comfortable and the lighting is adequate.

Check Your Marketing IQ

Before you begin the chapter, see what you already know about marketing by taking the chapter pretest. The pretest is available at www.g-wlearning.com/marketing/.

◆DECA Emerging Leaders

Principles of Marketing Event

Career Cluster: Marketing
Instructional Area: Information Management

Performance Indicators
- Assess information needs.
- Demonstrate basic database applications.
- Obtain needed information efficiently.
- Store information for future use.

Purpose
Designed for first-year DECA members who are enrolled in introductory-level principles of marketing/business courses, the event measures students' proficiency in those knowledge and skills identified by career practitioners as common academic and technical content in marketing. This event consists of a 100-question, multiple-choice, business administration core exam and a business situation role-play with a business executive. Participants are not informed in advance of the performance indicators to be evaluated.

Procedure
1. The event will be presented to you through your reading of these instructions, including the Performance Indicators and Business Situation. You will have 10 minutes to review this information to determine how you will handle the business situation and demonstrate the performance indicators of this event. During the preparation period, you may make notes to use during the role-play situation.
2. You will have up to 10 minutes to interact with a judge and explain the designated concepts. You may have more than one judge.
3. You will be evaluated on how well you meet the performance indicators of this event.
4. Turn in all your notes and event materials when you have completed the role-play.

Business Situation
You are to assume the role of marketing employee at the national headquarters of Project Smile, a non-profit business dedicated to providing cleft lip and palate repair to children whose families are unable to afford the corrective surgery. You are responsible for soliciting and acknowledging monetary donations from the general public. The **marketing manager (judge)** has invited you to a face-to-face meeting to measure your knowledge and understanding of an aspect of the business. The marketing manager (judge) wants to make sure you understand the role that the donor database plays in the business's ability to raise the necessary funds.

In the first part of your meeting, you will assess the information needs of the business as it relates to soliciting and acknowledging donations. In addition, you must explain how database management can facilitate the information needs of the business and how this produces accurate business records and provides for proper customer receipts. Your presentation should also address the additional performance indicators listed on the first page of this event. Following your explanation, the marketing manager (judge) will ask you to respond to additional questions.

The meeting will take place in the marketing manager's (judge's) office. The marketing manager (judge) will begin the meeting by greeting you and asking to hear your ideas on how proper operation of the donor database can help to raise the funds needed by the business. After you have provided your explanation and have answered the marketing manager's (judge's) questions, the marketing manager (judge) will conclude the meeting by thanking you for your presentation.

Critical Thinking
1. How will the marketing manager (judge) use the information obtained in the meeting?
2. What are you to do in the first part of your meeting?
3. What is the relationship between the performance indicators identified and your presentation with the marketing manager (judge)?
4. Match information in the role-play with each performance indicator.
5. What is one question the marketing manager (judge) may ask about information management at Project Smile? How will you respond?

Visit www.deca.org for more information.

Published by DECA Inc. Copyright © by DECA Inc. No part of this publication may be reproduced for resale without written permission from the publisher. Printed in the United States of America.

Section 8.1

Marketing-Research Data

Essential Question

What is the role of data in marketing research?

Learning Objectives

LO 8.1-1 Identify two types of data gathered through marketing research.
LO 8.1-2 Discuss trend research.
LO 8.1-3 Explain the purpose of a marketing-information system.

Key Terms

marketing research
data
database
primary data
representative sampling
qualitative data
quantitative data
focus group
survey
variable
secondary data
marketing trend
social trend
marketing-information system (MkIS)
database marketing

LO 8.1-1 Marketing Research

Marketing research is gathering and analyzing information to help make sound marketing decisions. The information gained through marketing research is used by businesses to define target markets, learn about the needs and wants of customers, and understand what motivates people to buy. Research helps identify the competition, learn about new business opportunities, and answer many other important business questions. Information provided by marketing research is also known as *market intelligence* because it helps a business gain a competitive edge.

Marketing research is also called marketing-information management (MIM). *Marketing-information management (MIM)* is the marketing function that involves gathering and analyzing information about markets, customers, industry trends, new technology, and competing businesses. It also includes making sure the right people in an organization get the information needed to make business decisions.

After research is complete, the results are used in the marketing planning function. A marketing plan should refer to the research that helped form the goals, strategies, and tactics described in the plan. Conducting marketing research helps businesses develop strategies to reach their target customers. The *marketing concept* focuses on

Creativa Images/Shutterstock.com

The marketing function that involves gathering and analyzing information about markets, customers, industry trends, new technology, and competing businesses is marketing-information management (MIM). *Why is MIM important?*

satisfying customers as the means of achieving profit goals. Meeting the needs and wants of target-market customers leads to customer satisfaction. Logically, businesses that do a better job of meeting customer needs will sell more than their competitors.

Marketing research produces various data about customers, competitors, products, and the industry. **Data** are pieces of information gained through research. To be useable by businesses and marketers, the data must be organized. A **database** is an organized collection of data in digital form. Many businesses collect data and contact information about their current customers and store the information in a *customer database*. Some companies also develop databases specifically for information about potential customers.

A *marketing research database* contains the results of marketing research. There are two types of data collected through marketing research: primary and secondary.

Primary Data

Primary data are pieces of information collected directly by an individual or organization. To collect primary data, marketers conduct primary research. *Primary research* is conducted first-hand by a researcher. Large businesses often conduct primary research to collect their own data. Businesses might also hire marketing research firms to conduct the research if they do not have in-house researchers or if the project is large. Marketing research is a big business. Some of the larger marketing research companies include The Nielsen Company, J.D. Power and Associates, Gallup, and Yankelovich.

Primary data is beneficial to researchers because it is information they have personally collected and evaluated. Researchers can design their data-collection methods to meet their needs. The research can be tailored to a specific target market. However, primary data is also the most expensive to collect because the costs of conducting a research study fall to the business or person performing it.

Primary research must be performed properly in order for the data to be accurate. For example, it is important to ensure that the right people are asked the right questions. A **representative sampling** is a group that includes a cross section of the entire population that is targeted. *Population* is the number of people who live within a defined area, such as a nation, geographic region, or market. The responses collected from a smaller group of people within the target market reflect those of the larger population. However, the sample size must be large enough for the results to be valid. The *sample size* is the number of people in the research sample. As an example, many national surveys use 1,000 people to get useful information about national attitudes and opinions. The people who choose samples and analyze results are statisticians and marketing researchers.

Primary data collected is categorized as either qualitative or quantitative, as shown in Figure 8-1.

A representative sampling includes a cross section of the entire targeted population. *Why is sample size an important factor in a representative sampling?*

g-stockstudio/Shutterstock.com

Differences between Qualitative and Quantitative Data

Senior Class Survey: Qualitative Data Questions	Senior Class Survey: Quantitative Data Questions
Why do you think it is important to be community-minded?	Do you participate in community activities?
How do you show your school spirit?	Do you attend school events and functions?
What is the next step for you after graduation? Why did you choose that path?	After graduation, are you: A. heading to college? B. entering the workforce? C. enlisting in the military?

Goodheart-Willcox Publisher

Figure 8-1 Qualitative and quantitative data are useful for different reasons.

Qualitative data provides insight into what people think about a topic. This comes from research questions that require judgment instead of simple "yes" or "no" answers. **Quantitative data** are facts and figures from which conclusions can be drawn. An example of quantitative data is the number of customers who answered questions after using a product. The most common ways to collect primary data are through observations, interviews, surveys, diaries, and experiments.

Observation

Using the observation method, a researcher watches people or situations and records facts. Designing marketing research to use the observation method is most appropriate when consumer behavior is the central research issue. The key to getting accurate information through observation is to make sure subjects do not know they are being observed. Their behaviors must be real and not influenced by the observer.

For example, a business may want to test its window displays. Using the observation method, a researcher could sit in front of the store and observe reactions to the displays. Data collected might include the number of people who:
- walked by;
- looked at the store windows;
- entered the store; or
- left with purchases.

Another form of observation many companies use is the secret shopper. A *secret shopper* is a person hired by a company to visit its place of business and observe the quality of service. Secret shoppers may also buy products to interact with and test the staff. The employees do not know which customers, if any, are secret shoppers. Secret shoppers report their experiences in writing to the business, including both good service and any problems.

When observation is used, objectivity is important. To have *objectivity* is to be free of personal feelings, prejudices, or interpretations.

Green Marketing

Lifestyles of Health and Sustainability

A prominent marketing trend that continues to grow is the preference for healthful and sustainable products. Lifestyles of Health and Sustainability (LOHAS) is a group of consumers that actively seek out goods and services that support healthy, eco-friendly, and sustainable lifestyles.

LOHAS consumers demand products that are not only high quality, but also have a low impact on the environment. They prefer organic, locally grown food, as well as organic or all-natural personal-care and household products. These consumers are very conscious of fuel and energy efficiency in the products they buy, such as vehicles, electronics, and appliances. The growth and strength of the LOHAS trend has influenced the products offered by businesses in every market.

The observer needs to accurately record data and remain unbiased. When enlisting the assistance of others, providing a standard checklist or form to each observer can help ensure that consistent data is recorded.

Interview

An *interview* is a formal meeting between two or more people to obtain certain information. Designing marketing research to use the interview method is most appropriate when the central research issue requires insight into the thoughts and opinions of people about a product or business. When interviews are conducted with a group of people, it is called a focus group. A **focus group** is a group of people brought together to discuss a specific topic. Focus groups usually consist of six to nine people. Participants are almost always paid for their time. A focus group is run by one person who asks questions and keeps the group on the topic. The activity of focus groups is often recorded on video. Participants may also be watched in real time by others from behind a one-way mirror. Focus groups are useful for gaining information based on how people in the group interact with each other.

One-on-one interviews can be used to gather the same type of information collected in a focus group. Depending on the topic, individual interviews might yield better information. Some respondents are more likely to give straightforward answers in a one-on-one interview rather than in a group of people.

Monkey Business Images/Shutterstock.com

A focus group is brought together to discuss a specific topic. *How do you think a focus group might be useful when conducting marketing research?*

Survey

A **survey** is a set of questions posed to a group of people to determine how that group thinks, feels, or acts. Surveys are often used to obtain quantitative data. Designing marketing research to use the survey method is most appropriate when the central research issue involves gathering facts and figures about a group of consumers. A questionnaire is given to each person to answer individually, without discussion among others in the group. Data can be collected through an in-person survey, over the telephone, by mail, or electronically. Electronic survey methods are most common.

Case in Point

Global Public-Private Partnership for Handwashing

Market research is important to the success of many different types of organizations. The Global Public-Private Partnership for Handwashing (PPPHW) is a coalition of national and international organizations that work to promote handwashing with soap as a regular personal hygiene habit to prevent diseases and infections, such as diarrhea and cholera, that plague many third-world countries.

In order to ensure the best possible success of their efforts, the PPPHW actively conducts market research to learn about the habits and thoughts of people in a particular region. What do they consider to be dirty? How many people are aware of the benefits of handwashing compared to how many people actually practice handwashing? What are the standard handwashing practices in health care and food preparation? Having this information helps the PPPHW target their activities to have the greatest impact. For example, research in a remote area of Africa revealed that handwashing behavior was deterred by both limited water supply and lack of handwashing facilities. To address these obstacles, the PPPHW developed water-efficient and economical handwashing stations that could be installed almost anywhere. The PPPHW uses market research to improve public health and the standard of living for people around the world.

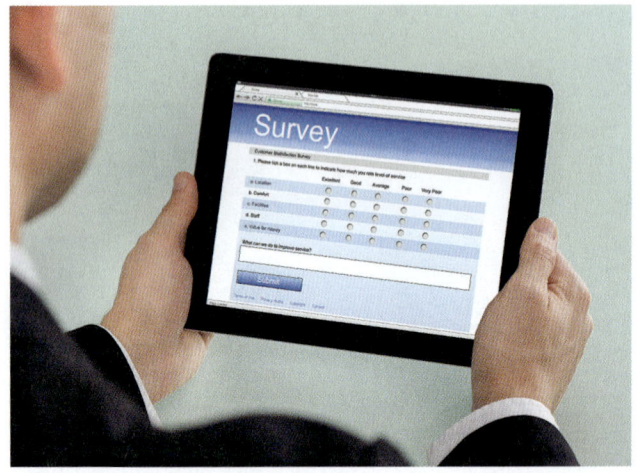

A survey is used to determine how a group of people thinks, feels, or acts. *Why do you think surveys are more useful for obtaining quantitative, rather than qualitative, data?*

The success of a survey depends on identifying a representative sampling. Surveys conducted by professionals, such as political polls, use complex formulas and methods to identify an appropriate representative sampling. A business can use company data to identify groups that represent a subset of respondents, such as customers or employees.

A written survey is highly structured and contains multiple items for response. Some considerations before deciding to use a written survey include the following:

- What is the best method for getting information?
- Who is the target audience?
- How many people should receive the survey to get an adequate number of responses?
- How will a representative sampling be selected?

When writing a survey, it is important to develop questions in a format that encourages responses. See Figure 8-2 for suggestions.

When a survey is distributed, state its purpose, a plan for the responses, and a deadline for responses. Participants must understand their time is respected and that timely responses are important to the success of the survey. In some cases, an incentive can be used to increase the number of surveys returned. Common incentives include a gift, a copy of the final report, or some other motivational item.

Participants should be assured that the survey is anonymous and their contact information will not be used in any way. If a survey is conducted via email, the document should be created in a way that can easily be returned. If an online survey tool is used, a hyperlink should be included for participants to easily click, access, and complete the survey. Each online survey service provider has guidelines that should be followed.

Creating a Survey

- **Create questions that are easy to answer.** Questions should have a choice of answers, such as yes/no, multiple choice, or agree/disagree/strongly agree/strongly disagree. These are known as *closed-ended questions*. They make it easy for the responder to give an answer and for the marketer to evaluate responses.
- **Write objective questions.** Questions should not lead respondents to a particular answer, as biased questions produce biased data.
- **Put the questions in a logical sequence.** Questions should be in sequence and, when possible, items should be grouped and have headings.
- **Keep the survey short.** A survey should be short. If there are too many questions, the respondent may not take the time to complete the survey.
- **Include space for comments.** The best information may come from unstructured responses.

Figure 8-2 A written survey is highly structured and contains multiple items for response.

Diary

A *diary* is a written record of the thoughts, activities, or plans of the writer during a given period of time. Market researchers use diaries in much the same way. Designing marketing research to use the diary method is most appropriate when the central research issue involves learning about the activities of consumers. Researchers typically use diaries to study how people use their time and spend their money. Diaries can use open-response format, forced-choice format, or a combination of both.

An *open-response format* allows respondents to write whatever they want about their experiences. It allows people to give more feedback. Open-response format diaries take a long time to analyze, which makes them a costly option for data collection.

A *forced-choice format* is more like a multiple-choice test, where only one answer can be chosen from several options. This type of diary is easier to

Using Diaries in Market Research	
Advantages	**Disadvantages**
• Ability to collect sensitive information that a participant may not provide in an interview • Greater reliability because participants are not asked to recall information • Supplements other research methods	• Expensive method of research • Overly conscientious participants may write too much • Large dropout rate, about 40 percent, immediately after the initial interview • Inaccurate participant responses

Figure 8-3 Using diaries as a research method has both advantages and disadvantages.

Goodheart-Willcox Publisher

analyze than open-response, but provides much less feedback. Diaries offer a number of advantages and disadvantages, as shown in Figure 8-3.

Experiment

An *experiment* is a procedure performed in a controlled environment in order to test or discover something. Designing marketing research to use the experiment method is most appropriate when the central research issue involves testing a variable. A **variable** is something that changes or can be changed. In the experiment method, a researcher sets up two situations that differ in only one variable. Results from the two experiment situations can then be compared.

When testing window displays of a business, for example, a researcher might count the number of people passing by and how many people enter the store for a specific number of days. The store then changes the window display. The new window display is the variable. The researcher again counts the number of people passing by and how many people enter the store. Analyzing this data might show if the number of people entering the store was influenced by the different window display.

Taste tests are common product experiments in which researchers may simultaneously use observation, survey, and experiment methods. Using a combination of methods in conjunction with each other can result in the most valid primary research data.

Secondary Data

Secondary data are information, statistics, or other type of data that already exists. Someone has already collected the information, but others can use it. For that reason, secondary data is usually easier to find and less expensive to obtain than primary data. However, for secondary data to be useful, it should relate to the research topic and be timely. In general, secondary data older than five years is not useful.

If the data already exists, there is no need to go through the time and expense of collecting primary data. To collect secondary data, marketers conduct secondary research. *Secondary research* is searching data already assembled and recorded by someone else. Resources for secondary data can include internal and external sources.

Internal sources of secondary data are reports, spreadsheets, and databases compiled within a business. Every business collects internal data in many forms that can be used for different purposes. The data include sales records, customer databases, financial statements, and marketing records. Internal business records are the best place to start when learning about current customers and their buying behaviors.

External sources of secondary data are any accessible source of secondary data outside of a business. There are many external sources available for reliable secondary data. Examples include governmental sources, market-research sources, academic sources, trade associations, and the Internet.

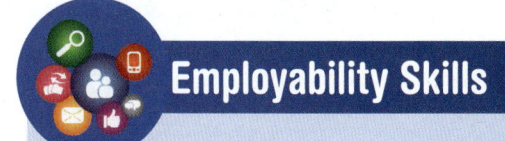

Employability Skills

Protocol

Protocol is a set of customs and rules that explains appropriate conduct or procedures in formal situations. *Business protocol* refers to the customs and rules found in the professional world. Many aspects of business protocol are not in written format and therefore must be learned from experience.

wavebreakmedia/Shutterstock.com

Secondary data are information, statistics, or other type of data that already exist. *What sources of secondary data have you used?*

Governmental Sources

Federal, state, and local governments collect an enormous amount of data. Information can easily be found about the economy, industries, and the population. Some of the many governmental agencies that can be data resources are shown in Figure 8-4.

Market-Research Sources

Many companies collect data that can be used by others for marketing-research purposes. Some may be available at no or low cost on the companies' websites. Research firms, such as Dun & Bradstreet, collect market data to sell to other businesses. Getting market-research data through a research firm may be costly, but typically not as costly as independently conducting and analyzing primary research.

State and local chambers of commerce are also good sources for free secondary data. A *chamber of commerce* is a group of businesses whose main purpose is to encourage local business development. They can often provide current information about other area businesses and the local economy.

Academic Sources

Universities, community colleges, and local libraries are great resources for secondary data. Colleges and their libraries can help marketers find databases and research done by the schools. Most universities also have small-business organizations on campus that provide secondary data. Local community libraries house books, business directories, magazines, journals, newsletters, newspapers, and other free resources.

Trade Associations

A *trade association* is an organization of people in a specific type of business or industry. The members of a trade association work together to help each other succeed. Information from a trade

Federal Governmental Data Sources	
Agency	**Data Available**
FedWorld	Online locator service for a comprehensive inventory of information disseminated by the US federal government
International Trade Administration	Data about US industries, exports, imports, and trade analysis
US Bureau of Economic Analysis	Economic data related to economic growth, regional economic development, inter-industry relationships, and the nation's position in the world economy
US Bureau of Labor Statistics	Measures and reports labor market activity, working conditions, and price changes in the US economy
US Census Bureau	Source of quality data about the nation's people and economy
US Department of Commerce	Data from all related bureaus, including economic, population, international trade, business development, and telecommunications information
US Federal Reserve	Innovative research on a broad range of topics in economics and finance

Figure 8-4 Secondary research gathered from governmental sources is generally reliable.

Goodheart-Willcox Publisher

association may be free to anyone, or may be free only to members. Depending on the source, sometimes it is available for a fee.

Some information can also appear on association websites. For example, the National Grocers Association posts results from various surveys on its website. Businesses can compare themselves to others of similar size and location by using trade association data.

Industry publications, also called *trade journals*, are magazines or newsletters focusing on a specific industry. Many trade associations publish trade journals. The journals usually cover a wide range of topics that are of interest to those within the industry. One example of a trade journal is the National Retail Federation (NRF) publication, *STORES Magazine*.

Internet

Using various Internet search engines can add a great deal of efficiency to the marketing-research process. Information can be learned about the competition, their marketing mixes, and promotions by viewing competitors' websites. Internet sources used for research purposes should be verified. Open-source websites and business websites ending in .com or .net may or may not have correct information. More trustworthy sites tend to be those ending in .gov or .edu.

LO 8.1-2 Trend Research

A major goal of marketing research is to identify business opportunities that support growth. One way to do this is to look for new trends. In general, a *trend* is an emerging pattern of change. Trends tend to be long lasting.

A **marketing trend** is a pattern of change in consumer behavior that leads to changes in the marketing mix. Trend research often combines research on customers, competition, and possible opportunities. This information is important to businesses because it helps them adjust product, price, place, and promotion to meet new trends.

A number of marketing firms specialize in researching and predicting trends. Faith Popcorn and her company, BrainReserve, is one of the best-known trend researchers. BrainReserve has successfully predicted some major trends before they happened. For example, it predicted the fast growth of social media and consumer demand for fresh, locally grown foods.

Trends develop over a long period of time and affect large numbers of people. They are different from fads. A *fad* is something that is very popular for a short time and dies out quickly. Examples of fads include selfie sticks, planking, and various fad diets.

There are many types of trends that can be seen in society. However, marketers are particularly interested in social, demographic, and product trends. Successful marketers notice trends early and help their businesses offer products to meet new wants or needs.

Social Trends

Social trends are the patterns of change in society as a whole. Social trends often lead to changes in consumer behavior. One of the major social trends of the 21st century is the availability and integration of technology into our daily lives. This led to development of smartphone apps that are used every day by millions of consumers for scheduling, shopping, health tracking, reading books, listening to music, and many other tasks.

Demographic Trends

Demographics are the qualities of a specific group of people, such as age, gender, and income. *Demographic trends* are changes in the size of different segments of the population. Marketers are interested in demographic trends because they often bring

Production Perig/Shutterstock.com

A fad is something that is very popular for a short time and dies out quickly, such as selfie sticks. *What fads have you seen come and go?*

changes in product preferences. Businesses looking to grow are interested in recent demographic trends.

One trend is the increase in the population over age 65. As the Baby Boomer generation ages, this group of people has time, money, and possible health concerns. Travel, health care, and financial services companies are finding new, stable markets for their products and services in this demographic.

Product Trends

Product trends are changes in current product features or new products being developed. Marketers must know product trends to meet customer needs. For example, the trend in electronic devices is toward interactive, wearable designs. This means consumers are buying more Bluetooth products that can be worn as wristbands or watches.

Marketing-Information System (MkIS)

LO 8.1-3

Researchers analyze raw data to draw conclusions and help make informed decisions. A **marketing-information system (MkIS)** is the organized system of gathering, sorting, analyzing, evaluating, distributing, and storing information for marketing purposes. Examples of these activities are shown in Figure 8-5. Data are constantly gathered and updated from both internal and external sources. The system provides marketing intelligence so decisions can be made and problems solved.

Some marketing-information systems are complex, while others are simple, such as a database. Each business decides which system best meets their needs. Company records, competitor information, and customer databases are part of many MkIS.

Database marketing consists of gathering, storing, and using customer data for marketing

Marketing-Information System Activities

Activity	Examples
Gather	Input customer contact information, customer purchases, and primary product research data
Sort	Sort data by customer zip codes, products purchased, and purchase months
Analyze	Determine how many customers bought the products during each month by zip code
Evaluate	Update current product and marketing mixes based on analysis; shift budgets to increase personalized marketing efforts
Distribute	Send all MkIS data and reports to mid-level managers and above for decision-making purposes
Store	Store all data for future planning, decision-making, and comparison

Goodheart-Willcox Publisher

Figure 8-5 A marketing-information system (MkIS) is the organized system of gathering, sorting, analyzing, evaluating, and distributing information for marketing purposes.

Social Media

Content Marketing

Content marketing is the process of creating online material that generates interest in content or information rather than the brand or the business. Customers are interested in information that helps their lives become easier, better, or makes them feel good. They may or may not be interested in the company, brand, or product. Rather, the interest may be to learn something or be entertained.

Content marketing is just one strategy used in social-media marketing where the focus is on content. It is not about the "hard sell" of a product, but for providing content to gain the interest of the customer. The use of blogs, podcasts, and videos are examples of vehicles that can be used to educate or inform customers about a product. The end goal is for customers to be impressed with the information they learned and look to the business for future purchases.

directly to customers based on their histories. Database marketing makes customer relationship management (CRM) easier and more effective. CRM databases can help build stronger customer relationships by allowing companies to monitor certain activities and target customers.

For example, some companies store credit card purchase information in their MkIS. This information helps target customers based on products they have already purchased. In doing this, customers feel like the company knows them and what they want or need.

Section 8.1 Review

Check Your Understanding

1. What is marketing-information management (MIM)?
2. What are the benefits of using primary data and secondary data?
3. What is sample size?
4. How are trends different from fads?
5. How is a marketing-information system (MkIS) used in customer relationship management?

Build Your Vocabulary

As you progress through this text, develop a personal glossary of key terms. This will help you build your vocabulary and prepare you for a career. Write a definition for each of the following terms and add them to your personal glossary.

data
database
database marketing
focus group
marketing-information system (MkIS)
marketing research
marketing trend
primary data
qualitative data
quantitative data
representative sampling
secondary data
social trend
survey
variable

Section 8.2

Conducting Marketing Research

Essential Question

Why is accuracy important for marketing research?

Learning Objectives

LO 8.2-1 Identify steps in the marketing-research process.
LO 8.2-2 Describe reasons why marketing research may be unreliable.

Key Terms

hypothesis
raw data
data mining
table
graph
chart
reliability
validity
order bias

Marketing-Research Process

LO 8.2-1

Marketers collect many types of research data. This may include data about new opportunities, potential customers, trends, competition, pricing, or other areas that can help a business make product and promotion decisions. Data can be gathered in both formal and informal ways. Both methods can help businesses understand what customers really want and need.

Informal research may take place with little or no planning. For example, the owner of a gift shop might walk around her store and talk with customers. She can learn what customers think of the store's products and services. If she notices that sales are down, the owner may start asking customers questions about the products and what they are buying instead.

Formal research involves a strategy and requires planning. For example, a business may develop and distribute a survey to current clients or hold a focus group to test a new product. The formal research process follows eight steps and is very similar to the scientific method of research.

1. Define the problem.
2. Conduct background research.
3. State a hypothesis.
4. Develop a research plan.
5. Collect the data.
6. Analyze the data.
7. Draw conclusions and make recommendations.
8. Follow up.

Define the Problem

All research begins by identifying the problem and defining it. The first step is to ask the questions for which answers are needed. For example, questions might include the following:

- How is the competition promoting its products?
- What goods or services will make the business more competitive?
- What are the demographics of the best customers?

138 Copyright Goodheart-Willcox Co., Inc.

You Do the Math

Margin of Error

The *margin of error* is an allowance permitted to account for changes in circumstances or miscalculations. Margin of error is commonly seen in surveys used in marketing research. For example, a marketing-research survey may compare the percentage of consumers favoring one brand of pasta sauce over another. These surveys almost always state a margin of error, such as ±3 percent. In this case, the margin of error means the stated percentages may be 3 percent too high or too low.

Solve the following problems.
1. A market survey revealed that 45.6 percent of American households will purchase a new television in the next year. The survey has a margin of error of ±8 percent. When estimating how many televisions will be sold, what is the *lowest* percentage of households that can be assumed to make this purchase within the next year?
2. A business calculated its weekly expenses as $12,054 with a margin of error of ±2.5 percent. What is the *maximum* the weekly expenses should be?
3. A hotel chain conducted a survey of families planning to take a vacation over the upcoming holiday weekend. The survey results state that 73.6 percent will drive at least 500 miles. The margin of error is ±4.6 percent. Allowing for the margin of error, what is the range of percentages of families that will drive at least 500 miles?

A written statement should be created that precisely defines the problem before research begins. Then, the problem or situation can be analyzed.

Part of the analyzing process is to review material that is already on hand about the problem. Talking to other people within the company may reveal others who have experience with a similar problem or situation. Using the company CRM system may provide the answer or solution needed. In some situations, the problem may be solved before any further research begins.

Conduct Background Research

It is important to learn as much as possible about the problem that has been defined. Personal interviews with current and potential customers can be helpful. Research should be gathered through multiple sources in order to gain information about the competition and industry, as well as to understand the marketing challenge.

State a Hypothesis

A **hypothesis** is a statement that can be tested and proved to be either true or false. A hypothesis is always stated in the positive. For example, if you are marketing clothing, the hypothesis might be: "Customers buy Superstar-brand clothes because Superstar clothing makes them feel trendy." It is a good idea to test the hypothesis before creating a marketing plan based on it. Research will either confirm or disprove a hypothesis. Plans can then be changed if the hypothesis does not test well.

Develop a Research Plan

A research plan is necessary to test the hypothesis and produce a desired outcome. A plan must be in place to accommodate the requirement of quantitative data, qualitative data, or both. If primary research is to be used, research instruments must be chosen and designed. When the situation requires outside research firms, budgets must be developed to accommodate the costs. Some situations require secondary research. If secondary research will be used, the type of data needed and where it can be found should be identified.

Collect the Data

Depending on the research plan, the actual data collection may be done by internal marketing employees or by hiring an external firm. This step will require training for the people who are doing the research. If it is primary research, the people

Section 8.2 Review

Check Your Understanding

1. What is the difference between informal research and formal research?
2. How does all research begin?
3. What is involved in the process of analyzing and presenting data?
4. What is one of the dangers of flawed marketing research?
5. Identify reasons that marketing research may be unreliable.

Build Your Vocabulary

As you progress through this text, develop a personal glossary of key terms. This will help you build your vocabulary and prepare you for a career. Write a definition for each of the following terms and add them to your personal glossary.

chart
data mining
graph
hypothesis
order bias

raw data
reliability
table
validity

CHAPTER 8 Review and Assessment

Chapter Summary

Section 8.1 Marketing-Research Data

LO 8.1-1 Identify two types of data gathered through marketing research.
Two types of data collected through marketing research are primary and secondary data. Primary data are collected directly by an individual or organization. Secondary data are information, statistics, or other data collected for other reasons.

LO 8.1-2 Discuss trend research.
A marketing trend is a pattern of change in consumer behavior that leads to changes in the marketing mix. Trend research often combines research on customers, competition, and possible opportunities. Marketers are interested in identifying social, demographic, and product trends to offer products to meet new wants or needs.

LO 8.1-3 Explain the purpose of a marketing-information system.
A marketing-information system (MkIS) is the organized system of gathering, sorting, analyzing, evaluating, distributing, and storing information for marketing purposes. Database marketing using MkIS data makes customer relationship management (CRM) easier and more effective.

Section 8.2 Conducting Marketing Research

LO 8.2-1 Identify steps in the marketing research process.
The formal marketing research process consists of eight steps. They are: define the problem; conduct background research; state a hypothesis; develop a research plan; collect the data; analyze the data; draw conclusions and make recommendations; and follow up.

LO 8.2-2 Describe reasons why marketing research may be unreliable.
The results of any research are only as good as the research process. Marketing research may be unreliable for a number of reasons, including problems with the research sample, question structure, data analysis, or reporting errors.

Check Your Marketing IQ

Now that you have completed the chapter, see what you have learned about marketing by taking the chapter posttest. The posttest is available at www.g-wlearning.com/marketing/.

Review Your Knowledge

1. Describe how businesses use marketing-research data.
2. What is the difference between primary and secondary data?
3. Identify and describe methods of collecting primary data.
4. List external sources available for reliable secondary data. Provide an example of each.
5. Discuss the use of trend research.
6. What does a marketing-information system (MkIS) provide?
7. List and describe the steps in the marketing-research process.
8. How is data mining used in the marketing-research process?
9. How do marketers draw conclusions from marketing-research data?
10. Summarize reasons why marketing research may be unreliable.

Apply Your Knowledge

1. You identified a company for which you are creating a marketing plan. Explain why you will need primary or secondary data to market products for the company you have selected.
2. Describe the difference between qualitative and quantitative data. Explain how each type of data would benefit your marketing plan.
3. Where would you search for secondary data about the products you are marketing for your selected business?
4. Which methods would you use to conduct informal research about customers for your product?
5. Assume you determined primary data is needed to help the development team create a relevant product for the business. Analyze each method of conducting primary marketing research: observations, interviews, surveys, diaries, and experiments. How can each method help your company gain a competitive edge? Evaluate the design of the marketing-research methods and decide which is appropriate for the research problems or issues related to the product or business you are marketing.
6. What kind of research do you think your competitors are conducting? Explain why you think so.
7. Explain the nature and scope of the marketing-information management function that will be implemented to support your marketing plan.
8. Assume your company is creating a new customer database. Identify the types of data that should be included and monitored to help make marketing decisions.
9. What product trends will you have to address in your marketing plan?
10. What steps could you take to ensure your research is reliable?

Apply Your Math Skills

Sophia is a marketing manager for a company that produces breakfast cereal. She is getting ready to conduct a marketing-research project. Apply your math skills to solve the following problems.

1. Sophia is preparing a survey about breakfast cereal preferences. She will need at least 35 responses. She knows from previous surveys to expect a response rate of 2 percent. How many people must she survey in order to ensure 35 responses?
2. Sophia is going to conduct four focus groups to generate feedback about the taste of a new breakfast cereal. She has received a list of 32 people who participate in the focus groups from a marketing-research firm. How many people will participate in each focus group?
3. Half the focus groups were given a breakfast cereal marketed as *all natural* and *made with whole grains*. In these groups, 75 percent of the participants said they would buy the cereal. The other half were given the same cereal marketed as being *great tasting* and *a cereal your children will love*. In this group, 50 percent of the participants said they would buy the cereal. What is the total number of participants who said they would buy the cereal?

Communication Skills

Reading Imagery is descriptive language that indicates how something looks, feels, smells, sounds, or tastes. After you read this chapter, find an example of how the author used imagery to appeal to the five senses. Analyze the presentation of the material. Why did you think this appealed to the senses? How did this explanation create imagery? Describe how it influenced your mood.

Writing To become career-ready, it will be important to learn how to communicate clearly and effectively using reason. Write several paragraphs that clearly communicate your opinion on the importance of marketing research. Consider your audience as you prepare the information.

Listening When a person speaks literally, he or she means exactly what the words indicate. Ask a classmate to verbally summarize one of the topics presented in this chapter. Listen carefully to the statements he or she makes. Did your classmate speak literally?

Internet Research

Demographics Marketers are interested in demographic trends because they often bring changes in consumer preferences. Visit the website of the US Census Bureau American Fact-Finder to find demographic information specific to your state. What useful demographic information is provided? Explain how this information could be helpful in identifying the preferences of a market.

Effective Surveys Using the Internet, conduct a search for the phrase *how to write effective survey questions*. Research types of questions that are the most effective for gathering data. What question-writing tips did you come across? Summarize the information you learned in one to two paragraphs.

Limitations of Market Research The results of market research are only as good as the research itself. Conduct an Internet search for *limitations of market research*. Read several articles on the topic. Based on the information you have read, write a brief summary of how the limitations of market research can impact your research plans.

Teamwork

Work with your team to develop a checklist that could be used to observe reactions of people passing by a retail window display. The checklist should provide information for the observers so that each observes, interprets, and communicates the same data. The observation technique is successful only when the same criteria are used by everyone on the research team.

Portfolio Development

College and Career Readiness

File Structure After you have chosen a file format for your documents, determine a strategy for storing and organizing the materials. The file structure for storing digital documents is similar to storing hard copy documents.

First, you need a place to store each item. Ask your instructor where to save your documents. This could be on the school's network or a flash drive of your own. Next, decide how to organize related files into categories. For example, *Certificates* might be the name of a folder with subfolders for *Community Service Certificates* and *School Certificates*. The names for folders and files should be descriptive but not too long.

1. Decide on the file structure for your documents.
2. Create folders and subfolders on the school's network drive or flash drive on which you will save your files.

CHAPTER 9

Targeting a Market

Sections

9.1 **Identify the Market**
9.2 **Evaluate the Competition**

Reading Prep

College and Career Readiness

Before reading this chapter, read the objectives for each of the two sections. Keep these in mind as you read. Focus on the structure of the author's writing. Was the information presented in a way that was clear and engaging?

Check Your Marketing IQ

Before you begin the chapter, see what you already know about marketing by taking the chapter pretest. The pretest is available at www.g-wlearning.com/marketing/.

◇DECA Emerging Leaders

Creative Marketing Project, Part 1

Career Cluster and **Instructional Area** are not identified for this event.

Knowledge and Skills Developed

The chapter representatives will demonstrate knowledge and skills needed to address the components of the project as described in the content outline and evaluation forms. Participants will develop many 21st century skills desired by today's employers in the following categories:
- communication and collaboration
- creativity and innovation
- critical thinking and problem solving
- flexibility and adaptability
- information literacy
- initiative and self-direction
- leadership and responsibility
- media literacy
- productivity and accountability
- social and cross-cultural skills

Purpose

Designed for one to three chapter representatives, the project is a research study in the marketing field, planned, conducted, and reported by a DECA chapter, the use of which will measurably improve the marketing activities of an individual company, a group of companies (such as a shopping mall), an organization, a club, or the business community. All chapter members are encouraged to participate. The project may begin at any time after the close of the previous chartered association conference and run to the beginning of the next chartered association conference.

Procedure, Part 1

1. For Part 1 in this text, read the skills developed and purpose of the event. Discuss these with your chapter members.
2. The written document will account for 60 points, and the oral presentation will account for the remaining 40 of the total 100 points.
3. The body of the written entry must be limited to 30 numbered pages, including the appendix (if an appendix is attached), but excluding the title page and the table of contents.
4. The Written Event Statement of Assurances must be signed and submitted with the entry. Do not include it in the page numbering.
5. Prior to the presentation, the judge will evaluate the written portion of the entry. The major emphasis of the written entry is on the content. Drawings, illustrations, and graphic presentations (where allowed) will be judged for clarity.
6. The chapter representatives will present the project to the judge in a 15-minute presentation worth 40 points.
7. If there are any questions, ask your instructor to clarify.

Critical Thinking

1. How can your chapter benefit from participating in this project?
2. What strategy will be used to identify the chapter representatives?

Visit www.deca.org for more information.

Published by DECA Inc. Copyright © by DECA Inc. No part of this publication may be reproduced for resale without written permission from the publisher. Printed in the United States of America.

Section 9.1

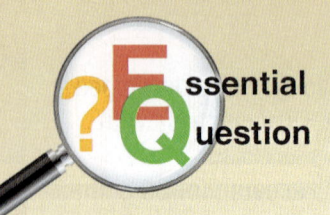

Identify the Market

Essential Question

What might people in a target market have in common?

Learning Objectives

LO 9.1-1 Differentiate between mass marketing and target marketing.
LO 9.1-2 Define variables used for market segmentation.
LO 9.1-3 Explain the importance of a customer profile.

Key Terms

mass market
niche market
geographic segmentation
demographic segmentation
generation
disposable income
discretionary income
psychographics
psychographic segmentation
values
attitude
Likert scale
behavioral segmentation
usage rate
buying status
customer profile

LO 9.1-1 Market

The term *market* can mean a number of different things. In the world of marketing, a *market* is all the people and organizations that might purchase a product. Markets are the focus of all marketing efforts. Markets can be large or small, broad or narrow. What they all have in common is the inclusion of particular types of customers most likely to buy certain goods or services. This includes the groups of people that companies want to reach in order to increase sales, earn profits, and stay in business.

Mass Market

A **mass market** is the overall group of people who might buy a good or service. Products that appeal to nearly everyone have mass markets. For example, everyone who wants a car and can afford to buy one is part of the mass market for cars. This means the mass market for cars is nearly everyone old enough to drive and who has a source of income.

Mass marketing uses one marketing mix of product, price, place, and promotion for a market. Mass marketing ignores differences among customers. The market is viewed as one large group. Everyone is assumed to have exactly the same wants and needs for the product. When using mass marketing tools, such as television, everyone in the larger group gets the same promotional message.

The advantage of mass marketing is that it saves time and money because all people receive the same promotional message. A disadvantage is that mass marketing ignores differences among customers. The market assumes that everyone has exactly the same wants and needs for a product.

However, customers are unique. There are many groups of customers with differing wants and needs. Sending everyone the same message may prove to be inefficient, miss the best customer, and waste marketing funds.

Target Market

The opposite of a mass market is a target market. A *target market* is the specific group of customers whose needs and wants a company will

Exploring Marketing Careers

Market Analyst

A profitable product or service is one that customers want to buy. Companies rely on market analysts to find out what products or services people want and how much they are willing to pay for them. Market analysts research market conditions, including public interest, potential competitors, current sales, and prices. Their information helps company executives make decisions about which products or services to offer. Typical job titles for these positions include *market analyst*, *market research analyst*, *market research consultant*, and *business development specialist*.

Some examples of tasks that market analysts perform include:
- Gather information about selected products and product ideas
- Analyze data about customer preferences and buying habits to identify potential markets
- Monitor related industries and businesses
- Forecast trends in sales and marketing

Market analysts need to be able to analyze large amounts of data to find trends and other information so company executives can make good product decisions. They must evaluate not only the data, but also the reliability of the data sources. A strong background in statistics is necessary, as well as the ability to use information-retrieval software. A bachelor degree is required for about 70 percent of the jobs in this field. For more information, access the *Occupational Outlook Handbook* online.

---

focus on satisfying. These are the people at whom a company aims to sell its goods and services. They are also the people most likely to buy the products. An accurately identified target market meets these four criteria:
- clearly defined wants and needs that the business can meet;
- enough money to buy the product;
- willingness and ability to buy the product; and
- includes enough customers to be profitable.

Consumer markets are diverse. Marketing professionals spend much time, effort, and money determining the best markets for the products or businesses they promote. They do not want to waste marketing dollars on an audience who does not want or need their products. Target marketing uses unique marketing mixes of product, price, place, and promotion for a product. Marketing budgets and energy are used where sales are most likely to happen, which is in the target market.

For example, the target markets for specific cars are different from the mass market for cars. Can you imagine a car manufacturer making one car that would meet the needs of every person in the mass market? Think about the many different needs customers have for their cars. One group wants a sports car for enjoyment driving. Another group wants a minivan to hold a team of kids and all their sports gear. Yet another group wants a pickup truck for business purposes. In other words, the mass market consists of many customer groups with different needs, wants, and product preferences.

A business may have more than one target market. Correctly choosing the best target market is one of the most important decisions made by marketing. In fact, selecting the wrong target market means the business loses an opportunity for success in the right market. This also means the business will probably not meet its sales goals.

LO 9.1-2 Market Segmentation

Target marketing can be challenging. If the target market turns out to be too small, there may not be enough customers to make a profit. If the wrong target market is chosen, the opportunity to make a profit from a different market is lost. *Market segmentation* is the process of dividing a large market into smaller groups. Segmenting the market can help in accurately identifying a target market.

The people in a target market are a company's most likely customers. Accurately identifying target market customers supports the 80/20 rule of business. The *80/20 rule* is a basic guideline that states 80 percent of the sales for a business comes from 20 percent of its customers. This can also save money in the budget when marketing dollars are spent focusing on customers who are most likely to buy rather than a larger group of people who may or may not be interested.

Research has found that customers in the same market segments have similar buying patterns and behaviors. This creates an advantage because the promotion can be customized for the people receiving it. However, targeting certain market segments can also be a disadvantage because the promotion pieces may require more time to focus the message on what the market segment wants. It may also cost more money to get contact information for a small segment of the market rather than sending the promotion out to the mass market.

A **niche market** is a portion of a market segment that is very narrow and specific. For example, the market for high-performance, exotic sports cars is a specific portion, or niche, of the sports car target market. Niche markets are often identified by businesses looking for customers whose needs or wants are not being met. Niche markets can be small or large, but they are very specific and can be very profitable.

The segments of a market are determined by certain variables. The variables used for market segmentation are geographic, demographic, psychographic, and behavioral. Within those groups, customer types can be refined even further by using additional variables.

Geographic Segmentation

Customer product needs can vary based on where they live. Segmenting a market based on where customers live is **geographic segmentation**. This also includes how far customers will travel to make purchases or conduct business. Customers can be segmented by region, climate, or population density.

Region

Customers in one region often need different products from those in other areas. For example, people in countries who drive on the right side of the road must have cars with steering wheels on the left side of the vehicle. Vehicles sold in countries where people drive on the left side must have steering wheels on the right. Therefore, a company producing cars for the global market would segment it by countries needing left-side and right-side steering wheels.

> **Employability Skills**
>
> **Positive Attitude**
> Professionals exhibit a positive attitude in their job performance and workplace interactions. *Attitude* is how personal thoughts or feelings affect a person's outward behavior. It is a combination of how you feel, what you think, and what you do. Attitude is how an individual sees himself or herself, as well as how he or she perceives others.

Climate

Climate has a large impact on what customers need. Customers who live in climates where it never gets colder than 60°F (15.5°C) do not need thick, warm coats. Customers who live in areas where the average winter temperature is 20°F (–6.7°C) do need warmer coats. Therefore, a coat manufacturer might segment its market based on average winter temperatures.

Population Density

Customers may be grouped according to the population density of the area in which they live. These geographic segments are *urban*, *suburban*, and *rural*. If a product appeals to people working on a ranch, the target market may be rural. If a product appeals to people who live in larger cities, the target market is likely urban.

Demographic Segmentation

Demographics are the qualities, such as age, gender, and income, of a specific group of people. **Demographic segmentation** is dividing the market of potential customers by their personal statistics. The United States conducts a population census every ten years. A *census* is a count of the people in a country made by the government on a regular basis. Some of the census data collected includes age, gender, income, ethnicity, education level, occupation, marital status, and family size. The governmental agency that performs the census is the *US Census Bureau*.

Age

Age is a common segmentation variable because people of different ages have different needs and wants. For example, babies require special food. To meet the need of this age group, a number of companies specialize in making baby food. Clothing is another area affected by the age of the target market. Different age groups often like or want different products.

An important age variable is generation. A **generation** is a group of people who were born and lived during the same time period. People within the same generation are often called *cohorts*. Common generational categories are listed in Figure 9-1. A *multigenerational population* is made up of people who represent multiple age groups and generations.

The period of history in which a group of people grew up has a major effect on their attitudes, wants, and needs. For example, people in Generation Z have a high interest in electronic products, information technology, and on-demand buying.

One of the largest generations is Generation Y, also called the *Millennial* generation. These people were born between 1981 and 2000 and came of age at the turn of the 21st century. The number of Americans in this generation is estimated to be over 80 million. Millennial consumers have been influenced by the September 11th attacks, the Great Recession, and the digital revolution. The *digital revolution* is the continuing expansion of technical, economic, and cultural changes resulting from advances in computer technology. The shared experiences of a generation affect not only their attitudes and perspectives, but also the product demands of the people within each generation.

Gender

Customers are often grouped by gender because men and women tend to have different needs and wants. Certain goods and services are preferred by men, by women, or by both genders. For example, spa services are more popular with women, while more men buy hand tools. However, if a company is selling hand tools or spa services,

Generations

Generation	Born Between	Common Traits
Greatest Generation	1901–1926	• Loyal • Moralistic • Team players
Silent Generation	1927–1945	• Cautious • Disciplined • Tendency to conform
Baby Boomers	1946–1964	• Ambitious • Hardworking • Multitaskers
Generation X	1965–1980	• Pragmatic • Self-sufficient • Skeptical
Millennials (Generation Y)	1981–2000	• Confident and social • Technologically savvy • Validation seekers
Generation Z	2001 and beyond	• Raised with technology • Independent and entrepreneurial • Influenced by trends

Goodheart-Willcox Publisher

Figure 9-1 A generation is a group of people born during a certain time in history.

Generation Z is made up of people born in 2001 and beyond. *What characteristics do you think you share with others in your generation?*

Ollyy/Shutterstock.com

Marketing Ethics

Responsible CRM

Marketing uses customer relationship management (CRM) software in which contact information is recorded about each customer. This information has been given to the company by the customer for its specific use. It is unethical and irresponsible for a marketer to sell this information to another company unless every single customer has given permission to have his or her information sold.

this does not mean it should ignore women or men as potential customers. In fact, there is a market for hand tools targeted at women, just as there is a market for men's spa services.

Income

People with similar income levels often buy similar types of products. The two categories of income in which marketers are interested in are disposable and discretionary.

Disposable income is the take-home pay a person has available to spend. Usually, disposable income is used for the necessities of life, such as food, clothing, shelter, and transportation.

Discretionary income is the remaining take-home pay after life necessities are paid for. Discretionary income is the money people can spend at their *discretion*, or however they want. Discretionary income is often spent on wants instead of needs, such as entertainment, vacations, and dining out.

Ethnicity

The United States is composed of people from many ethnic backgrounds. The needs for products may vary with ethnic heritage. People of the same ethnic background may have similar preferences, which can lead to similar buying patterns for several types of goods and services. Preferences in certain foods, types of entertainment, and clothing styles might be more prevalent with specific ethnic groups and not with others.

Education Level

Education level is another way to segment a market. A person with a high school education may have very different wants or needs than someone with a bachelor degree. Somebody with a bachelor degree may have very different wants or needs than someone with a doctoral degree.

Occupation

People in certain jobs often have similar wants or needs based on their job type. The terms blue collar and white collar are commonly used in describing types of jobs. *Blue collar* generally refers to a job that involves physical labor in which a person typically wears work clothes or protective gear. *White collar* usually refers to a job in an office environment in which workers primarily use mental abilities and knowledge acquired in higher education. A person's job may affect his or her buying behavior.

Marital Status

Common marital status categories are married, single, widowed, and divorced. Marital status can influence purchases, such as houses, vacations, and food. A single person, for example, may purchase a smaller house and travel more often than a married couple.

Family Size

Marketing research has shown that the needs and wants of a one-person household differ from households with multiple people. As a result, marketers often segment the market based on family size. For example, many convenience food manufacturers have developed both family-size and single-serving packaging to meet the needs of various household sizes.

Psychographic Segmentation

Psychographics are data about the preferences or choices of a group of people. Customers have psychological and emotional characteristics that affect their buying habits. **Psychographic segmentation** is dividing the market by certain preferences or lifestyle choices. When targeting markets, it is crucial to know psychographic characteristics that affect purchases, such as values, attitudes, activities, and interests. Psychographic information about target markets is very useful when planning a marketing mix.

Values and Attitudes

Customers can be segmented by their values and attitudes. **Values** are the principles and beliefs that an individual considers important. An **attitude** is how a person feels about something. For example, customers who feel fashionable clothing is important may shop at high-end, name-brand stores. However, customers who place a higher importance on saving money may be more likely to shop at discount stores. Customers who value the environment may choose to buy a hybrid vehicle over a high-performance sports car.

Consumer values, attitudes, and lifestyles can be difficult to measure. In order to group people in this way, marketing researchers can conduct surveys. One well-known consumer-behavior research tool is the VALS™ survey. This survey was developed by the Strategic Business Insights (SBI) research company. It asks respondents to rate statements using a Likert scale. A **Likert scale**, pronounced "LICK-ert," asks survey respondents how strongly they agree or disagree with a given statement. The dozens of statements in the survey are designed to measure the attitudes, interests, and opinions of survey takers. The following statements are from the VALS™ survey.

- "I follow the latest trends and fashions."
- "I would rather make something than buy it."
- "I consider myself an intellectual."

After taking the survey, each person is assigned a VALS™ type based on his or her responses to statements measuring their resources and innovation plus their ideals, achievements, and self-expression. The eight VALS™ types are as follows:

- Innovators
- Thinkers
- Believers
- Achievers
- Strivers
- Experiencers
- Makers
- Survivors

According to SBI, each of the VALS™ types has specific characteristics and behaviors. For example, the Achievers are concerned about status, have a mid-level income, buy premium products, and watch an average amount of television. Survivors are concerned with safety, have a lower income, tend to be loyal, and watch an above-average amount of television.

The VALS™ survey results show what motivates people to buy. Results can also predict different consumer buying behaviors. These results can be quite useful when businesses make marketing decisions.

Activities and Interests

People who like the same activities or have the same interests or hobbies tend to have similar buying patterns. Activities and interests can include sports, hobbies, traveling, or attending cultural events, to name a few. For example, the market segment of people who enjoy basketball tend to buy basketball-related items and attend basketball games.

Behavioral Segmentation

Customers differ in how they use products. **Behavioral segmentation** divides a market by the relationships between customers and a good or service. Behavioral variables include benefits sought, usage rate, buying status, and brand loyalty.

Case in Point

Spanish Television

Demographics are important when targeting a market. By dividing larger markets into smaller, more targeted markets, companies can better meet the needs of those customers and earn a profit. Recent research shows the need for Hispanic media is growing rapidly in the United States. The US Census Bureau reveals that the Hispanic population has increased by more than 40 percent in the last century. The US Latino population is made up of American-born Latinos and immigrants.

This mix of generations looks for Spanish-language programming that preserves their culture and incorporates some aspects of American culture. Latinos want quality entertainment and news programs. They also want a variety of programming choices. Media providers have jumped at the opportunity to appeal to the Hispanic target market. Telemundo, Univision, and Fox offer Spanish television programming, some with English subtitles. The media providers are constantly researching the audience to determine which type of shows are preferred. This growing Latino market is inspiring competition for quality amongst the media providers.

Benefits Sought

Many customers choose the same products, but often for entirely different reasons. One customer may want a computer with high processing capabilities for gaming. A second customer may want a computer with a large amount of RAM to edit videos. A third customer may only want a computer to check e-mail and social media. All of these customers are buying a computer, but each seeks a different benefit from the product.

Usage Rate

The **usage rate** is how often a customer buys or uses a good or service. Usage rates are classified as heavy, moderate, light, and nonuser.
- A *heavy usage rate* means the person buys the product often.
- A *moderate usage rate* falls somewhere between heavy and light.
- A *light usage rate* means the person rarely buys the product.
- A *nonuser usage rate* means the person never buys the product.

Marketers send different messages to people based on how often they buy the product.

Buying Status

Buying status describes when a customer will buy a good or service. The most common categories are potential, first-time, occasional, and regular.
- A *potential customer* is one who has not bought the product, but is thinking about it.
- A *first-time customer* is one who has bought the product once.
- An *occasional customer* is one who rarely buys the product.
- A *regular customer* is one who buys the product often or on a predictable basis.

Marketing messages can vary depending on a customer's buying status.

Brand Loyalty

Loyal customers are generally the source of most sales for a business. Following the 80/20 rule, 80 percent of total sales for many businesses tend to come from 20 percent of the customers. As a result, marketers often segment the market based on degree of loyalty. For example, airlines have frequent-flyer programs to reward customers who often fly on that airline. These programs give customers free tickets or other merchandise after flying a certain number of miles with an airline. Many businesses, both large and small, use loyalty programs to increase sales.

LO 9.1-3 Customer Profile

Once marketers have divided a market into segments, they choose which segments to target for marketing purposes. The segments are analyzed to determine which ones have the most sales potential. One or more segments are selected and a customer profile is created for each segment. A **customer profile** is a detailed description of the typical consumer in a market segment. The profile includes geographic, demographic, psychographic, and behavioral characteristics about the typical customer. An example of a customer profile is shown in Figure 9-2.

For example, some businesses may decide to sell luxury items that appeal to people with high incomes and specific values. Marketing research can determine which areas of the country have the highest average incomes. It can also determine other traits of the people likely to buy luxury goods, such as their attitudes, values, occupations, or education level. The customer profile developed for luxury items would reflect all of these variables.

Accurate customer profiles help determine the best promotional strategies. By knowing who is most interested in a company's products, promotional dollars can be used wisely. Instead of hoping that mass marketing efforts will reach likely customers, the good or service can be promoted specifically to those within the target markets.

Customer Profile: Video Gamer

Demographics
Age: 16–35 years old
Gender: Male and female
Income: $25,000–$90,000
Ethnicity: Any
Education level: Any
Occupation: Any
Marital status: Any
Family size: Any

Psychographics
Values: Entertainment, social interaction with friends and family, accomplishment
Attitudes: Video games are a way to connect and spend time with other people. Playing together promotes teamwork and communication. Video games provide mental stimulation or education. Money spent on video games is a better value than other forms of entertainment.
Interests: Movies, social media, sports, technology, television

Behavioral
Benefits sought: Entertainment, value, social connection
Usage rate: Light to heavy usage
Buying status: Occasional to regular customers

pikselstock/Shutterstock.com
Goodheart-Willcox Publisher

Figure 9-2 A customer profile lists demographic, psychographic, and behavioral characteristics about consumers in the market segment.

Section 9.1 Review

Check Your Understanding

1. List an advantage and a disadvantage of mass marketing.
2. Identify four criteria that an accurately identified target market meets.
3. Why is market segmentation important?
4. How do various generations influence marketing activities?
5. Explain how accurate customer profiles can help lead to marketing success.

Build Your Vocabulary

As you progress through this text, develop a personal glossary of key terms. This will help you build your vocabulary and prepare you for a career. Write a definition for each of the following terms and add them to your personal glossary.

attitude
behavioral segmentation
buying status
customer profile
demographic segmentation
discretionary income
disposable income
generation
geographic segmentation
Likert scale
mass market
niche market
psychographics
psychographic segmentation
usage rate
values

Section 9.2

Evaluate the Competition

Essential Question

How does competition for customers influence a marketing plan?

Learning Objectives

LO 9.2-1 Identify types of competition that a business encounters.
LO 9.2-2 Identify components of a market analysis.
LO 9.2-3 Define *product positioning*.
LO 9.2-4 Discuss steps taken to create a sales analysis.

Key Terms

direct competitor
indirect competitor
feature
benefit
unique selling proposition (USP)
trade show
competitive advantage
repositioning
market-share leader

Competition (LO 9.2-1)

Knowing exactly what the competition is doing helps marketers make decisions about how to market their products or companies. Identifying competitors helps in market planning efforts, which is one of the functions of marketing. Competition is either direct or indirect. It is also based on price and nonprice factors.

Direct or Indirect Competition

Direct competitors are companies that sell identical or very similar goods or services. For example, if your business provides carpet cleaning services, the other businesses that provide the same services compete directly with yours.

Indirect competitors offer different, but similar, goods or services that meet customer needs. The products sold by a company's indirect competitors might be acceptable substitutes for the products that a specific company sells. For example, all of the businesses that offer entertainment options within a community are indirect competitors. There may be a movie theater, miniature golf course, laser tag arena, and arcade in a town. Each of these businesses competes indirectly for the same customers.

Pieter Beens/Shutterstock.com

Direct competitors are companies that sell identical or very similar goods or services. *What products or companies can you name that are in direct competition with each other?*

156 Copyright Goodheart-Willcox Co., Inc.

Price or Nonprice Competition

Price competition occurs when a lower price is the main reason for customers to buy from one business over another. The focus of businesses engaged in price competition is to make more sales by offering the lowest prices. For example, many gas stations compete through their pricing. Customers often make their fuel-buying decisions based on price alone. However, some consumers may think it is not worth driving around to find the lowest price.

Although price is important, many companies, especially smaller ones, cannot afford to compete using price alone. A competitive advantage based on factors other than price is called *nonprice competition*. Some businesses choose to provide notably better service or exclusive brands to beat their competition. For example, the department store Nordstrom is known for its excellent customer service, which is a great advantage for the retailer's customers.

Nonprice competition may also focus more on the features and benefits of a product, rather than the price. **Features** are facts about a product. **Benefits** are the traits of a product that serve as an advantage for the customer. A **unique selling proposition (USP)** is a statement that summarizes the special features or benefits of a product or business. Its purpose is to convince the customer that their product is the only one that can satisfy their needs. An example of a USP might be, "Our conditioning shampoo makes your hair shiny and manageable in half the time." The feature is that the shampoo has a conditioner. The benefit is gaining shiny, manageable hair in half the time. The consumer knows right away why he or she should use the product.

Nonprice features of a business may include extended hours, gift wrapping, or custom orders. The benefits of these services are that they save time and are convenient.

LO 9.2-2 Market Analysis

A *market analysis* is the process of gathering information on the market in which a business is competing. A market analysis is completed as a part of the process of developing a marketing plan. However, it should be updated regularly so that a business can evaluate its sales, products, and promotions compared to current competition in the market. By completing and evaluating a competitive analysis, a SWOT analysis, and an environmental scan, the business can better position itself in the marketplace.

Competitive Analysis

A marketing manager must know what the competition is offering and their pricing models, as well as product features and benefits. In other words, the marketing mix for the competition must be identified. A *competitive analysis* is a tool used to compare the strengths and weaknesses of a product or company with its competitors.

Just like sports teams study their competition, it is important for businesses to analyze their competitors. This helps them learn the best way to compete with each one. Marketers first need to know what products competitors are selling and at what prices. They also need to determine the features and benefits of competing products and how they are sold. It is also important to monitor the promotions of the competition. In other words, marketers need to know the competition's marketing mix to be able to compete with them.

There are many ways to find information about competitors, including websites, competitor's products, trade shows, and the company's sales team.

- *Websites*. Competitor websites are a good source for information about their products and social media comments that discuss customer strategies.

Jonathan Weiss/Shutterstock.com

Nordstrom is known for its excellent customer service, which is an example of nonprice competition.
Why would a marketing plan include strategies for nonprice competition?

- *Competitor's product.* One of the most efficient ways to evaluate a competitor's product is to buy it. After a product is obtained, the price and packaging can be reviewed as well as its features and benefits.
- *Trade shows.* A **trade show** is a large gathering of businesses for the purpose of displaying products for sale. A great number and variety of businesses typically attend trade shows. The competition will probably have catalogs, brochures, marketing pieces, and other information available at their exhibits. Listening to customers interacting with the competition can provide valuable information.
- *Sales team.* A company's sales team is one of the most important sources of competitive information. Sales people develop relationships with their customers and will likely hear comments about the competition's products and sales strategies.

It is important to make ethical decisions when investigating the competition. The tactics used should not put customers in an uncomfortable position to provide you with information about a competitor.

Each company uses its own format for this analysis. An example is shown in Figure 9-3. The analysis can be completed by first identifying the names of the primary competitors. Information about price, features, benefits, and other information about each company is recorded in the analysis. Once the analysis is complete, it can be used to evaluate each competitor and determine if they pose a threat to take business from the company and why. A competitive analysis is an important component of a marketing plan.

A trade show is a great way to find information about the competition. How does information about the competition help marketing efforts?

After the competitive analysis is complete, information about the competition can help a business develop strategies necessary to maintain its current market share or take away business from the competition. Through evaluation of the competition, a business can analyze its own company's goods or services and determine where it excels or lacks in features and benefits.

The **competitive advantage** of a product or business is offering better value, features, or service than the competition. The competitive advantage is the answer to the question: "Why will customers want to buy the product from *this* business instead of from a competitor?" Having an advantage over competitors tends to increase sales, which is necessary for most companies to make a profit.

Competitive Analysis

Variables	Your Company	Competing Company A	Competing Company B	Competing Company C
Price	$28–$50	$40–$100	$30–$60	$20–$80
Sizes	S–XL	S–XL	S–XXL	XS–XXL
Designers	Well known	High end	Knockoff	Well known and knockoff
Monogramming	Yes	Yes	No	No
Special order	No	Yes	No	Yes
Continental US shipping	$0	$4–$6	$5.00 flat fee	$2.99–$4.99
Physical stores	Yes	Yes	No	No

Goodheart-Willcox Publisher

Figure 9-3 A competitive analysis is a tool used to compare the strengths and weaknesses of a product or company with its competitors.

SWOT Analysis

As you will recall, a *SWOT analysis* lists company strengths, weaknesses, opportunities, and threats faced by the business.
- *Strengths* are internal factors that give a company a competitive advantage.
- *Weaknesses* are internal factors that place a company at a disadvantage relative to competitors.
- *Opportunities* are external factors that provide chances for a company to increase profits.
- *Threats* are external factors, such as the economy, that can potentially jeopardize a company's growth or ability to make profits.

A SWOT analysis helps determine marketing and product development strategies. An example of a SWOT analysis is shown in Figure 9-4.

Environmental Scan

Recall that an *environmental scan* is an analysis of the external factors that affect the success of business. A *PEST analysis* is a type of environmental scan that evaluates the political, economic, social, and technological factors that may impact the success of a business.
- *Political factors* affect the stability of the government and the success of the businesses that operate within it.
- *Economic factors* affect the ability of consumers to purchase products, as well as the cost of doing business.
- *Social factors* are the cultural aspects within a business environment and the personal qualities of its customers, such as age, gender, income, ethnicity, education level, occupation, marital status, and family size.
- *Technological factors* affect the ease with which a business can operate within a market or region, as well as the level of productivity possible once the business is in operation.

Conducting a PEST analysis helps identify potential opportunities and threats to a company's business plans and strategies. An example of a PEST analysis is shown in Figure 9-5.

SWOT Analysis

Strengths	Weaknesses	Opportunities	Threats
• Well-known designers • Competitive pricing • Monogramming option • Free shipping to continental United States	• Designers do not offer XS or XXL • Cannot take special orders • Lacking promotional plan • Current inventory is limited	• Find designers offering XS and XXL • Take special orders • Partner with local organizations for increased brand presence • Expand product line to offer more customization options	• Continued growth of on-line retail clothing stores • Rumored that Company A will also go into lower-priced market • Designer knockoffs sold by Companies B and C are priced competitively

Goodheart-Willcox Publisher

Figure 9-4 A SWOT analysis lists company strengths, weaknesses, opportunities, and threats faced by the business.

PEST Analysis

Political	Economic	Social	Technological
• Local, state, and national governments currently stable • Country not engaged in military conflict • Presidential election coming up	• Value of US dollar is rising • International suppliers are raising prices in response to US dollar rising • Unemployment is down, meaning target customer has more discretionary money to spend	• Casual clothing styles are currently trendy • Fashion trends have changed, making a new set of colors popular for clothing • Holiday shopping season is a few months away	• New website design is needed • E-commerce interface is slow and needs updating • International suppliers often report delays due to machines needing repair

Goodheart-Willcox Publisher

Figure 9-5 A PEST analysis is a type of environmental scan that evaluates the political, economic, social, and technological factors that may impact the success of a business.

LO 9.2-3 Product Positioning

Evaluating competitive advantages helps in deciding how to present the product, or position the product, in a way that appeals to the target market. *Product positioning* is the process used to influence the customer's perception of a brand or product in relation to the competition. It is a marketing strategy that focuses on influencing the perception of a product in the minds of consumers. To do this, a company determines the needs and wants of its customers and positions its product to be appealing.

For example, Southwest Airlines positions themselves as the low-cost airline with no hidden or unexpected fees. This product positioning is supported by the company's Transfarency campaign: "Low fares. Nothing to hide. That's Transfarency." In this case, Southwest identified that airline customers wanted reasonable, honest, straightforward pricing without unexpected or hidden fees. The company's marketing team positioned the product to satisfy customers in their market.

Products are commonly positioned using features and benefits, price and quality, and competitive positioning.

- *Features and benefits.* Products may be positioned based on key features and benefits that a product offers the customer. Promotions based on features and benefits highlight a unique attribute of the product and emphasize its value to customers.
- *Price and quality.* Businesses may position their products on the basis of price, which often is seen as an indication of quality. The high price of a product can be used to emphasize high quality, prestige, or luxury. A low-priced product can be positioned as a good value or budget-conscious product, but may be perceived to be lower in quality.
- *Competitive positioning.* Businesses regularly evaluate their competition in order to keep a competitive advantage. In promotions based on competitive positioning, a company may directly compare its product to that of a competitor. Many cell phone carriers use competitive positioning in their promotions by showing maps that compare coverage areas or graphics that illustrate the service reliability of competing carriers.

Repositioning is changing the marketing strategy used to influence consumer perception of a product in comparison to the competition with the goal of increasing sales. There are instances in which the original positioning strategy failed and adjustments become necessary.

GongTo/Shutterstock.com

Southwest Airlines positions itself as an affordable option for cost-conscious consumers. *How do you think product positioning influences customers?*

You Do the Math

Mean, Median, and Mode

There are three measures of the center of a data set. The *mean* is the average of all values in the data set. Mean is calculated by adding all values and dividing that sum by the total number of values. The *median* is the middle number in a data set. To find the median, the numbers must be listed in numerical order. The *mode* is the value that occurs most frequently in the data set.

Solve the following problems.
1. A recent survey of gasoline prices for a region reported these prices per gallon: $3.49, $3.67, $3.52, $3.58, and $2.56. What is the mean price per gallon?
2. An online electronics retailer sold merchandise at the following prices during one hour: $99, $105, $75, $116, $99, $105, $105, and $116.
   A. What is the mode price?
   B. What is the mean price?

Chapter 9   Targeting a Market

A feature of this road bicycle is its titanium frame, which provides the benefit of a lighter weight for faster speed. When have you purchased a product to obtain the benefits of owning it?

Radu Razvan/Shutterstock.com

LO 9.2-4   Sales Analysis

After the market segment has been identified and market analysis completed, a sales analysis can be performed. A sales analysis helps a business forecast future sales.

The sales analysis begins with reviewing current and past sales. A business typically evaluates number of units sold and dollars generated in sales for the current year and up to five previous years. By evaluating current and past sales, conclusions can be made about whether sales are increasing or decreasing. Businesses can identify any trends that may affect the profitability of the company. This helps the sales team create sales goals for the current year.

An important part of analyzing sales is to determine what market potential is available in the current environment. *Market potential* is the maximum number of customers and amount of sales that can be generated from a specific segment in a defined time period. Determining the market potential will confirm that sales can be generated from the group of customers in the identified market segment. It must be verified that the marketing decisions made will be profitable before moving forward with the marketing plan.

If market potential exists, the business will forecast its portion of the market share in comparison to its competitors. *Market share* is the percentage of the total sales that one business has in a specific market. Market share is based on the size of the market. *Market size* is the total sales per year for a specific product held by all the competition. Sales can be measured in a number of ways, such as in dollars or number of items sold.

Most businesses look at market share in terms of total sales dollars. The market share formula is as follows.

(company sales ÷ total sales in market) × 100 = percent market share

An example of calculating market share is shown in Figure 9-6. For example, assume the market size for granola bars is $100 million. This means that in one year, total sales of granola bars equal $100 million. Three companies make them.

- General Foods, a big company, sells $75 million of granola bars each year; its market share is 75 percent.
- Country Choice, a medium company, sells $20 million; its market share is 20 percent.
- Grainy Snacks, a small company, sells $5 million; its market share is 5 percent.

Calculating Market Share

Formula

$$\frac{\text{company sales}}{\text{total sales in market}} \times 100 = \text{percent market share}$$

Data

Total Sales in Market = $100 million
General Foods Sales = $75 million
Country Choice Sales = $20 million
Grainy Snacks Sales = $5 million

General Foods

$$\frac{\$75 \text{ million}}{\$100 \text{ million}} \times 100 = 75\%$$

Country Choice

$$\frac{\$20 \text{ million}}{\$100 \text{ million}} \times 100 = 20\%$$

Grainy Snacks

$$\frac{\$5 \text{ million}}{\$100 \text{ million}} \times 100 = 5\%$$

Goodheart-Willcox Publisher

Figure 9-6   This simplified example shows how market share is calculated.

Market share is useful for comparing the companies within a market to each other and showing the relationships among the companies, as shown in Figure 9-7. **Market-share leaders** are the companies with the largest combined market share. Some research shows that market-share leaders are more profitable and successful than companies with smaller market shares. For example, the two market-share leaders in the previous example, General Foods and Country Choice, have a 95 percent market share when combined. A business goal of many companies is to increase market share, which makes it a marketing goal as well.

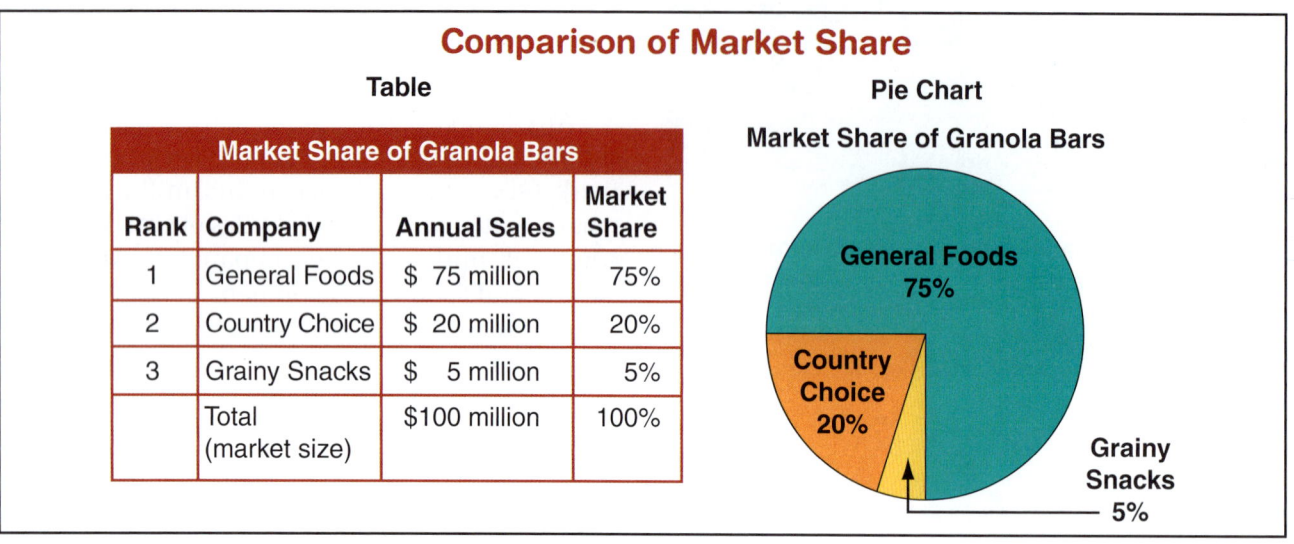

Comparison of Market Share

Table — Market Share of Granola Bars

Rank	Company	Annual Sales	Market Share
1	General Foods	$ 75 million	75%
2	Country Choice	$ 20 million	20%
3	Grainy Snacks	$ 5 million	5%
	Total (market size)	$100 million	100%

Pie Chart — Market Share of Granola Bars
- General Foods 75%
- Country Choice 20%
- Grainy Snacks 5%

Goodheart-Willcox Publisher

Figure 9-7 Market share can be shown as tables or charts that illustrate the competitive relationship of companies within a market.

Section 9.2 Review

Check Your Understanding

1. What is nonprice competition?
2. What is a unique selling proposition (USP)?
3. List examples of information that is evaluated for a competitive analysis.
4. How does a SWOT analysis contribute to a market analysis?
5. State the market share formula.

Build Your Vocabulary

As you progress through this text, develop a personal glossary of key terms. This will help you build your vocabulary and prepare you for a career. Write a definition for each of the following terms and add them to your personal glossary.

- benefit
- competitive advantage
- direct competitor
- feature
- indirect competitor
- market-share leader
- repositioning
- trade show
- unique selling proposition (USP)

CHAPTER 9 Review and Assessment

Chapter Summary

Section 9.1 Identify the Market

LO 9.1-1 Differentiate between mass marketing and target marketing.
A mass market is the overall market or group of people who might buy a good or service. A target market is the specific group of customers at which a company aims its goods and services.

LO 9.1-2 Define variables used for market segmentation.
Market segmentation is the process of dividing a large market into smaller groups, which can help in accurately selecting a target market. Segmenting a market based on where customers live is geographic segmentation. Demographic segmentation is dividing the market of potential customers by their personal statistics. Psychographic segmentation is dividing the market by certain preferences or lifestyle choices. Behavioral segmentation divides a market by the relationships between customers and a good or service.

LO 9.1-3 Explain the importance of a customer profile.
A customer profile is a detailed description of the typical consumer in a market segment. Accurate customer profiles help determine the best promotional strategies. This allows goods or services to be promoted specifically to those within the target markets.

Section 9.2 Evaluate the Competition

LO 9.2-1 Identify types of competition that a business encounters.
Direct competitors are companies that sell identical or very similar goods or services. Indirect competitors offer different, but similar, goods or services that meet customer needs. Price competition occurs when a lower price is the main reason for customers to buy from one business over another. Nonprice competition is a competitive advantage based on factors other than price.

LO 9.2-2 Identify components of a market analysis.
A market analysis is the process of gathering information on the market in which a business is competing and is completed as a part of the process of developing a marketing plan. Market analysis includes a competitive analysis, SWOT analysis, and environmental scan.

LO 9.2-3 Define *product positioning*.
Product positioning is the process used to influence the customer's perception of a brand or product in relation to the competition. It is a marketing strategy that focuses on influencing the perception of a product in the minds of consumers.

LO 9.2-4 Discuss steps taken to create a sales analysis.
The sales analysis begins with reviewing current and past sales and determines the market potential. Determining the market potential will confirm that sales can be generated from the group of customers in the identified market segment. If the market potential exists, the business will forecast its portion of the market share in comparison to its competitors.

Check Your Marketing IQ

Now that you have completed the chapter, see what you have learned about marketing by taking the chapter posttest. The posttest is available at www.g-wlearning.com/marketing/.

Review Your Knowledge

1. Explain how the concept of a market applies to marketing products.
2. Differentiate between mass marketing and target marketing.
3. Explain the concept of market segmentation.
4. Define variables used for market segmentation.
5. Explain the importance of a customer profile.
6. Identify types of competition that a business encounters.
7. Differentiate between price and nonprice competition.
8. Identify the components of a market analysis.
9. Define *product positioning*.
10. Discuss steps taken to create a sales analysis.

Apply Your Knowledge

1. In an earlier chapter, you identified the business for which you are creating a marketing plan. Describe the mass market for the products sold by this business.
2. Identify a potential niche market for the products you will be marketing.
3. Describe the target market for the marketing plan you are writing. Which demographic, geographic, psychographic, and behavioral factors will you use to identify the target market?
4. Summarize the wants or needs fulfilled by the products you are marketing.
5. List three direct competitors and three indirect competitors that you will evaluate for your marketing plan.
6. List and describe three competitive advantages of the products you will market.
7. Describe nonprice competition factors for the products included in your marketing plan.
8. Write a unique selling proposition (USP) for the products included in your marketing plan.
9. List three strengths and three weaknesses of the products you will market.
10. Create a competitive analysis by evaluating the competition you will encounter in the market.

Apply Your Math Skills

The 80/20 rule and the market share formula can both be helpful when evaluating the marketing opportunities for a business. Apply your math skills to solve the following problems.

1. Jason's Italian Restaurant recently ran a promotion to gather customer data. After the promotion, Jason compiled a database of current restaurant customers with 1,200 entries. Following the 80/20 rule, how many of his customers are responsible for 80 percent of the restaurant's sales?
2. The total market size for Italian restaurants in a suburban city is $5,400,000. Jason's Italian Restaurant makes $945,000 per year in sales. Use the market share formula to calculate the market share of this restaurant.

Communication Skills

Reading After you read this chapter, analyze how the author unfolds a series of ideas, including the order in which the points are made, how they are introduced and developed, and the connections drawn between them.

Writing Write a narrative to develop the steps you would take in identifying a target market. Focus on your writing style and tone while selecting the right words to express your thoughts. Use well-chosen details and structure the events in a logical sequence.

Speaking Many situations will require you to persuade a listener. When you persuade, you convince a person to take a course of action or adopt a viewpoint you propose. Marketing messages attempt to persuade and change the behavior of customers. Write a persuasive message about why mass marketing is a waste of money. Deliver your message to a classmate. Ask your classmate for feedback on whether your persuasive message was successful.

Internet Research

Generational Cohorts Select one of the generations in Figure 9-1 that interests you and conduct Internet research on your selection. Identify common characteristics about this group, as well as any alternative names for it. What significant historical events shaped this generation and in what ways? How do you think this shaped or shapes their buying preferences?

VALS™ Survey Using the Internet, navigate to the Strategic Business Insights VALS™ Survey website. Follow the prompts on the website to take the VALS™ Survey. What is your VALS™ type: Innovator, Thinker, Believer, Achiever, Striver, Experiencer, Maker, or Survivor? Did your result surprise you? Conduct further Internet research to learn what your type says about your buying preferences.

Targeting a Market Use the Internet to locate recent examples of mass marketing used to market a product. Select an example that interests you. How might the mass market for this product be segmented using geographic, demographic, psychographic, and behavioral segmentation? Why do you think the company chose to use a mass marketing strategy instead of a target marketing strategy?

Teamwork

Working in a team, choose a product that all team members know well. Collaborate to create a customer profile using geographic, demographic, psychographic, and behavioral variables for market segmentation. Describe the experience of creating a customer profile and the amount of work that is required.

Portfolio Development

College and Career Readiness

Certificates Exhibiting certificates you have received in your portfolio reflects your accomplishments. For example, a certificate might show that you have completed a training class. Another one might show that you can key at a certain speed.

Include any certificates that show tasks completed or your skills or talents. Remember that this is an ongoing project. Plan to update when you have new certificates to add.

1. Scan the certificates that will be in your portfolio.
2. Name the files appropriately and save in a folder or subfolder.
3. Place the hard-copy certificates in a container for future reference.
4. Record these documents on your master spreadsheet that you started earlier to record hard-copy items. You may list each document alphabetically, by category, date, or other convention that helps you keep track of each document that you are including.

CHAPTER 10

Understanding the Customer

Sections

10.1 **B2C Customers**
10.2 **B2B Customers**
10.3 **Credit Basics**

College and Career Readiness

Reading Prep

As you read this chapter, stop at the Section Reviews and take time to answer the Check Your Understanding questions. Were you able to answer them without referring to the chapter content?

Check Your Marketing IQ

Before you begin the chapter, see what you already know about marketing by taking the chapter pretest. The pretest is available at www.g-wlearning.com/marketing/.

DECA Emerging Leaders

Creative Marketing Project, Part 2

Career Cluster and **Instructional Area** are not identified for this event.

Procedure, Part 2

1. In the previous chapter, you studied the developed skills and procedures for this event.
2. The presentation begins immediately after the introduction of the chapter representatives to the judge by the adult assistant. Each chapter representative must take part in the presentation.
3. The oral presentation may be a maximum **15 minutes** in length, including time for the judge's questions.
4. The judge will evaluate the presentation, focusing on the effectiveness of public speaking and presentation skills and how well the chapter representatives respond to questions that the judge may ask during the presentation.
5. The chapter representatives may use the following items during the oral presentation.
   - Not more than three (3) standard-sized posters not to exceed 22 1/2 inches by 30 1/2 inches each. Participants may use both sides of the posters, but all attachments must fit within the poster dimensions.
   - One (1) standard-sized presentation display board not to exceed 36 1/2 inches by 48 1/2 inches.
   - One (1) desktop flip chart presentation easel that is 12 inches by 10 inches (dimensions of the page).
   - One (1) personal laptop computer.
   - Cell phones, smartphones, iPods, MP3 players, iPads, tablets, or any type of a handheld, information-sharing device will be allowed in written events *if* applicable to the presentation.
   - Sound, as long as the volume is kept at a conversational level.
6. Only visual aids that can be easily carried to the presentation by the actual chapter representatives will be permitted, and the chapter representatives themselves must set up the visuals. No set-up time will be allowed. Chapter representatives must furnish their own materials and equipment. No electrical power will be supplied.
7. Materials appropriate to the situation may be handed to or left with judges in all competitive events. Items of monetary value may be handed to but may not be left with judges. Items such as flyers, brochures, pamphlets, and business cards may be handed to or left with the judge. No food or drinks are allowed.
8. If any of these rules are violated, the adult assistant must be notified by the judge.

Project

This project might concern itself with finding new markets for local products, promoting the community's resources, increasing the trading area of facilities, increasing sales, increasing employment, providing better shopping facilities, or solving problems or challenges affecting the marketing process, etc.

Critical Thinking

1. What problem will your chapter select?
2. What is the rationale for selecting the problem?

Visit www.deca.org for more information.

Published by DECA Inc. Copyright © by DECA Inc. No part of this publication may be reproduced for resale without written permission from the publisher. Printed in the United States of America.

Section 10.1

B2C Customers

Essential Question

What motivates consumers to buy a product?

Learning Objectives

LO 10.1-1 Explain how a hierarchy of needs impacts consumer buying behavior.
LO 10.1-2 Describe common factors that influence consumer buying.
LO 10.1-3 Define categories of consumer buying motives.
LO 10.1-4 Summarize steps in the consumer decision-making process.
LO 10.1-5 Describe each level of consumer buying decisions.

Key Terms

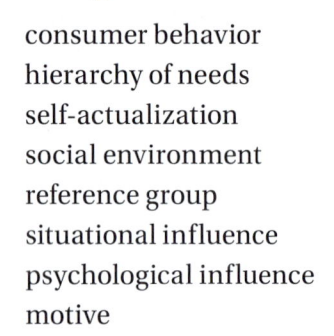

consumer behavior
hierarchy of needs
self-actualization
social environment
reference group
situational influence
psychological influence
motive
buying motive
consumer decision-making process
value
impulse buying decision
routine buying decision
limited buying decision
extensive buying decision

LO 10.1-1 Consumer Buying Behavior

Businesses that sell to consumers as their primary market are called *business-to-consumer (B2C)* companies. Marketing professionals who work for B2C companies need to understand *why* people buy and use their products in order to create the ideal marketing mix. They study **consumer behavior**, which is the behavior and actions taken by people to satisfy their needs and wants, including what they buy.

In the 1950s, psychologist Abraham Maslow was trying to understand why people behave the way they do. He developed a theory that is now referred to as *Maslow's Hierarchy of Needs*. Maslow's theory states that unsatisfied needs motivate people to act. However, not all needs are equal. There is a **hierarchy of needs**, or an order in which certain needs are satisfied before others. Maslow noticed that people tend to fulfill physical needs before others that are less critical for survival. After physical needs, the needs for security, love and acceptance, esteem, and self-actualization are fulfilled, in that order. Maslow presented this hierarchy of needs in pyramid form, as shown in Figure 10-1.

According to Maslow, the strongest needs are physical. These needs must be met in order to survive, such as having enough air, water, and food. The next level of need is for security. People need to be safe from physical harm and have financial security. After security are the needs for love and acceptance, which are also called *social needs*. People need to feel accepted by others and be part of a group. The next level of need is for esteem. People need to feel self-confident and have the respect of others. The last level of need is for self-actualization. **Self-actualization** is the expression of a person's true self through reaching personal goals and helping others.

Maslow's Hierarchy of Needs can be applied to explain human behavior as it relates to buying behavior. People will buy products to meet needs at the bottom of the pyramid before buying products to meet higher needs. For example, if a person is hungry, he or she will seek food before any other product. This

Maslow's Hierarchy of Needs

Self-Actualization
All needs have been fulfilled to some degree

Esteem
Need to be liked and respected

Love and Acceptance
Need for support, assurance, praise, acceptance

Security
Need to feel safe in surroundings

Physical Needs
Need for air, water, food, clothing, shelter

Goodheart-Willcox Publisher

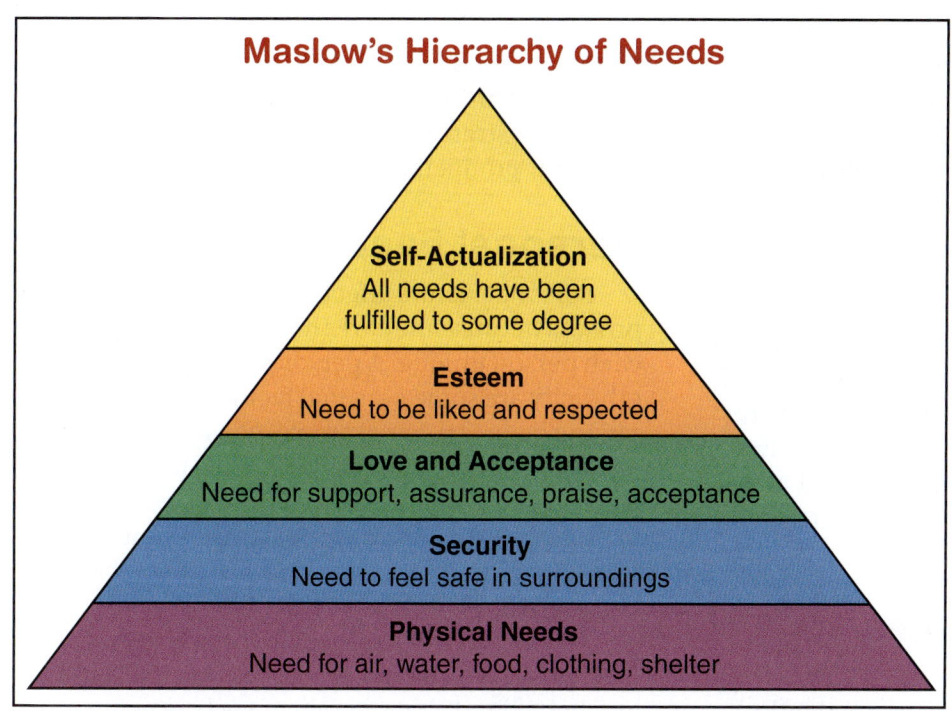

Figure 10-1 Abraham Maslow believed physical needs must be met before all other needs and wants.

need is partly the reason why so many shopping malls have food courts. People will not be interested in buying other products when they are hungry.

People may not always be aware of all their needs but usually know their wants. For example, a person may want a certain brand of clothing. The underlying need might be acceptance by peers who also wear that clothing brand. Marketers can use their understanding of different customer needs to increase sales. They can develop products and promotions to satisfy needs customers are aware of and the ones of which they are not aware.

From a marketing viewpoint, the lower levels of the pyramid have the largest markets. Everyone needs to eat, but not all people focus on their self-actualization needs. Many marketers use Maslow's theory to develop products that fulfill certain needs. They also focus promotions on how their products meet those needs. For example, digital devices meet several needs, including safety, acceptance, and esteem. Promotions for digital devices focus on how the products easily keep people connected, up-to-date, and safe anyplace in the world.

Consumer Buying Influences
LO 10.1-2

Many factors can influence consumer buying behavior, especially since every consumer is different. By performing marketing research, companies can learn what influences consumers in their target markets. Common factors that influence consumer buying include social environment, situational influences, personal factors, and psychological influences.

Social Environment

Social environment is the aggregate of the groups that make up the surroundings in which people live and interact. Family, friends, classmates, and other groups to which an individual belongs make up his or her social environment. Culture is a strong influence that affects many aspects of life and often shapes an individual's social environment. The ethnic group, geographic location, and social class in which people grow up also contribute to their cultural influences. The culture with which consumers are most familiar often shapes their attitudes about products, credit, and shopping.

Within a social environment are reference groups. A **reference group** is a specific group of people that influences our attitudes, beliefs, and behavior. Most people identify with one or more reference groups. The football team is an example of a reference group for some high school students.

Reference groups are classified as normative or comparative. A *normative reference group* is one that directly influences an individual, such as family or peers. Family is one of the major influences on all consumers. The adults in a family, particularly parents and grandparents, pass on their values, religion, and behaviors to their children. Family also influences the buying behavior of children. In addition, friends are very influential to many people because of the human need for acceptance and esteem.

A *comparative reference group* is one to which a person compares him or herself, such as celebrities or political leaders. For example, some people compare themselves to a specific celebrity by wearing the same clothing, participating in the same leisure activities, or driving the same automobile. By patterning one's appearance or activities after a celebrity, the person believes he or she is a part of the same reference group.

Situational Influences

Situational influences are the influences that come from the environment. Situational influences that can affect buying choices include the weather, store location, time of day, and current sales promotions. The mood, physical health, and available finances of a buyer at the time of a potential purchase are also situational influences. For example, perhaps you need more paper for your printer, but it is raining and you do not have transportation. That situation may help you decide to put off buying the printer paper. However, if you have a 25 percent discount coupon that expires the next day, you may find a way to make the purchase.

indira's work/Shutterstock.com

Situational influences come from the environment and can affect buying choices, such as weather. *When have situational influences affected your buying decisions?*

It is important for marketers to understand how situational influences affect consumer behavior. This information helps in developing marketing strategies that increase the likelihood that their products will be purchased.

Personal Factors

Personal factors affect the consumer buying process because they are the qualities that make each person unique. A person's age, gender, and ethnicity are some personal factors that influence buying behavior. For example, consider the differences in buying decisions between a middle-aged woman and a teenaged boy. The needs and wants of these two consumers are quite different based on their age and gender, which will affect their buying behavior.

Personality also influences buying behaviors. *Personality* is reflected in a variety of emotional and behavioral characteristics, such as being energetic, shy, competitive, cheerful, ambitious, or stubborn. Your personality affects the image of yourself that you portray to others, which affects what you buy. For example, if you are competitive and participate in team sports, you are likely to buy athletic clothing and equipment. Your personality often influences your outward appearance, activities, and interests.

Psychological Influences

Psychological influences are those that come from within a person and explain why a person has certain needs and wants. Examples of psychological influences include a person's image of himself or herself, the desire to being accepted by peers, or the need to manage stress.

Marketers and researchers work hard to learn why some people buy certain products, while other people do not. Understanding the psychological influences of consumers is helpful when creating promotions and while working with potential customers.

LO 10.1-3 Consumer Buying Motives

A **motive** is an internal push that causes a person to act. The strongest motives are based on the most pressing needs or wants. To *motivate* is to provide the internal push that results in action. A **buying motive**

is the reason a consumer seeks and buys a good or service. Consumer buying motives can be categorized as emotional, rational, and patronage.
- *Emotional buying motives* are based on emotions, feelings, and social needs. For example, a person who wants to be accepted by his or her peers may buy the same brand of jeans.
- *Rational buying motives* follow logical reasoning. For example, buying food is logical when you are hungry.
- *Patronage buying motives* are based on features of a specific store or product, such as consumers who are loyal to a certain product brand.

Examples of these buying motives are shown in Figure 10-2.

The human mind usually transforms needs into wants. For example, any type of food, including simple bread and water, can satisfy hunger. However, most people turn the need for food to satisfy hunger into the want for a certain food. With so many food choices, hunger can be satisfied in thousands of different ways. In the modern consumer market, many products are available to satisfy a single need.

When there is a choice between products, marketers want to know what motivates consumers to choose one product over another. For example, you may want a car to satisfy the need for transportation to and from work. What motivates you to pick one car over another? In addition to providing basic transportation, a certain make and model may also impress your friends. In this case, purchasing the car that would meet your transportation needs and impress your friends is motivated by rational, emotional, and patronage motives.

Consumer Buying Motives

Buying Motives	Examples
Emotional motives	Friendship, respect, acceptance, appreciation, love, prestige, thrill seeking, recognition, enjoyment, socialization
Rational motives	Maintain health and well-being, fulfill a need, save money, use a dependable product
Patronage motives	Location, reputation for reliability and quality, image, brand, service

Goodheart-Willcox Publisher

Figure 10-2 A buying motive is the reason a consumer seeks and buys a good or service.

Consumer Decision-Making Process

Awareness of need or problem
↓
Information search
↓
Review options
↓
Make purchase decision
↓
Evaluate purchase

Goodheart-Willcox Publisher

Figure 10-3 The consumer decision-making process is a series of steps people take when making buying decisions.

Consumer Decision-Making Process

LO 10.1-4

The **consumer decision-making process** is a series of steps people take when making buying decisions. Typically, this is a five-step process, as shown in Figure 10-3. Depending on the individual consumer and what he or she is buying, the time each of the steps takes can vary. In some cases, one or more steps may even be skipped. However, some form of each step is considered by most consumers before, during, and after a purchase.

Awareness of Need or Problem

The first step in the consumer decision-making process is to define the need to be fulfilled or problem to be addressed. If there were no problems or unanswered questions, a decision would be unnecessary. Consumers first become aware of a problem when there is a need or want to be satisfied. For example, winter is coming and you realize your old coat no longer fits. To fulfill this need, you must buy a new coat.

Information Search

Next, the search for information on how to fulfill the need begins. At this stage, consumers draw on past experiences and may ask for recommendations from those within their reference groups. Many consumers conduct product research on the Internet, through store advertisements, and by reading product reviews. If the risk of buying the wrong product is low, then the search for information usually takes a short amount of time.

In the winter coat example, you may use every form of information research to make the best coat-purchase decision. This may be because the risk of buying the wrong coat is high: coats are expensive, they come in many different styles, you will wear it often, you want the right brand, and it may need to last several years.

Review Options

After product information is gathered, all the purchase options are reviewed. A number of things are considered in this step. The price, value, brand, features, and benefits of each purchase option are weighed against each other. **Value** is the relative worth of something. Consumers may tie value to price and brand. For example, perhaps you found four options for a new winter coat. When evaluating each one, you might consider whether it is a good value for the price. You may be willing to spend more on a name brand that your friends also wear. Or, you may prefer certain features, such as a hood, inside pockets, or fleece lining.

ESB Professional/Shutterstock.com

The consumer decision-making process includes reviewing purchase options. *How does the consumer decision-making process influence your personal buying decisions?*

Social Media

SMM Goals

Social-media marketing goals should be established as part of the promotions strategy in the marketing plan. They should be written as SMART goals in order to give direction and be effective. There are specific goals that a business will establish, examples of which are:
- drive sales
- establish brand identity
- generate customer leads
- promote public relations
- research customer needs

By aligning social-media plans with the marketing and business goals, you will be able to focus on the priorities. Selecting one to two manageable goals that can be successfully accomplished is better than taking on multiple goals that can be difficult to reach.

Make the Purchase Decision

Once a product is chosen, the consumer then decides where and when to buy it. Consumers may look for the best price, which determines where the item will be purchased. Or, consumers may decide to postpone the purchase to a later date, perhaps for financial reasons. There may be other external factors that impact where and when purchases are made. For example, if you started looking for a winter coat in the summer, prices may be lower than in the fall. Local stores may not carry the coat you want and you must buy it online. Or, you may choose to wait until the coat goes on sale.

Evaluate the Purchase

After a purchase, consumers compare the recent purchase with earlier ones. Every situation is different, but each consumer has certain expectations of the shopping experience. The recent purchase may match, beat, or fall below those expectations. Consumers may like or dislike the product, store, or service they received. Good business owners and marketers make sure customers are satisfied with a purchase because it ensures repeat business. For example, perhaps the coat you bought was poorly made and the zipper broke after only a few wears. When you returned it to the store, the manager apologized and gave you a new coat of your choosing. In this situation, your evaluation of the store would be positive, but you are unlikely to buy that brand of clothing again.

Consumer Buying Decisions

LO 10.1-5

Some purchases require more research and thought than others. The level of a buying decision varies both with the individual consumer and what he or she seeks to purchase. Large, expensive products tend to require quite a bit of research and planning. Smaller, less expensive products usually require little research and planning before the purchase.

Some consumers have a more difficult time making decisions than others. Often, these consumers take much longer researching their first purchase of a product. After they become familiar with the product, it becomes easier to make subsequent purchases of it. There are four levels of buying decisions: impulse, routine, limited, and extensive, as shown in Figure 10-4.

Impulse Buying Decisions

A purchase made without any planning or research is called an **impulse buying decision**. For example, you are waiting in the checkout line at a grocery store. A display of key chains, including one with your name on it, is on the counter. You put a key chain in your cart without giving it a second thought. You did not consciously plan to buy it, but the urge to buy a key chain with your name on it suddenly became powerful. You did not use any steps in the decision-making process to buy that product. Marketers often place product displays near checkout counters to encourage impulse purchases.

Routine Buying Decisions

A **routine buying decision** is a purchase made quickly and with little thought. For example, you may not think about the decision to buy shampoo very much. You might go into the store, locate the brand you use, and buy it. Routine buying decisions are made when the consumer has experience with a product or prefers a certain brand. Products purchased routinely include groceries, cosmetics, cleaning products, and other inexpensive items.

Levels of Consumer Buying Decisions	
Level	Activity
Impulse	No prior planning; spur of the moment purchase
Routine	Little thought or planning; familiar products purchased often
Limited	Some research and planning; unfamiliar or infrequently purchased products
Extensive	A great deal of research, time, and planning; typically expensive products

Figure 10-4 Some consumer buying decisions involve little planning and no research, while others may involve a great deal of thought and research.

Goodheart-Willcox Publisher

Employability Skills

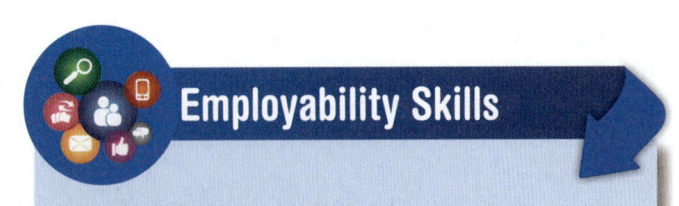

Self-Confidence

Self-confidence is being certain and secure about one's own abilities and judgment. People with self-confidence believe in their ability to perform or make something positive happen in a situation. These individuals know what they are good at doing and how to best use their abilities to achieve goals.

Sometimes, expensive items are also purchased in a routine way. For example, if you usually buy a specific brand of contact lenses, the buying decision is routine.

Limited Buying Decisions

A **limited buying decision** is one requiring some amount of research and planning. This type of decision is made when buying unfamiliar products or those only bought occasionally. For example, suppose you need to buy a blender and you have never bought one before. It is not an expensive purchase, but you want to buy the best blender available for the amount of money you have to spend. Therefore, you research blenders on the Internet and read *Consumer Reports* magazine. You list the product options with their features and prices. After that, you choose the best blender for the price and buy it. You just made a limited buying decision.

Extensive Buying Decisions

An **extensive buying decision** involves a great deal of research and planning. It is usually made when buying higher-priced items. For example, imagine you are ready to buy your first car. This purchase will have a major impact on your daily life, safety, and finances. You will analyze your budget to determine how much you can afford to spend. You may have to start planning for this purchase a year or more to save for a down payment. You may conduct Internet research, visit many car dealerships, and test-drive a number of cars. If you decide on a used car, you should plan to have a mechanic inspect the car before buying it. You will also need to research and purchase auto insurance. All of the activities described in buying your first car are examples of an extensive buying decision.

Section 10.1 Review

Check Your Understanding

1. How can Maslow's Hierarchy of Needs be applied to buying behavior?
2. What groups make up a person's social environment?
3. What does *motivate* mean?
4. How do consumers search for information when making a buying decision?
5. Explain why the level of a buying decision varies with both the individual consumer and what he or she seeks to purchase.

Build Your Vocabulary

As you progress through this text, develop a personal glossary of key terms. This will help you build your vocabulary and prepare you for a career. Write a definition for each of the following terms and add them to your personal glossary.

buying motive
consumer behavior
consumer decision-making process
extensive buying decision
hierarchy of needs
impulse buying decision
limited buying decision
motive
psychological influence
reference group
routine buying decision
self-actualization
situational influence
social environment
value

Section 10.2

B2B Customers

Essential Question: What factors motivate business customers to make purchases?

Learning Objectives

LO 10.2-1 Identify common variables used to segment businesses in the B2B market.
LO 10.2-2 Describe common factors that influence business-customer buying.
LO 10.2-3 Describe levels of buying decisions made by business customers.

Key Terms

producer
reseller
service business
government market
institution
North American Industry Classification System (NAICS)
internal influence
external influence

Segmenting the B2B Market

LO 10.2-1

Businesses that sell primarily to other businesses are called *business-to-business (B2B)* companies. B2B companies focus on meeting the needs of businesses. Examples include Cisco Systems Inc. technology solutions and Maersk Line shipping. These companies provide products and services to other businesses. There are some companies, such as Staples and FedEx, that sell to both B2C and B2B markets. However, most companies sell to one market or the other. Overall, the needs and buying behaviors of business customers are different from those of consumers. The business-to-business market can be split into five categories: producers, resellers, service businesses, governments, and institutions.

- A **producer** creates goods and services. Producers buy raw materials and equipment, which they use to make products and product components. They are also called *manufacturers*.
- A **reseller** buys finished products to resell to consumers. Retail stores are a common type of reseller. Both producers and resellers may also buy distribution and warehousing services.
- A **service business** provides services. In the B2B market, services might include leasing companies and law firms. Service businesses may need to buy very specific products to operate their businesses, such as cars, equipment, or tuxedos to rent.
- The **government market** includes national, state, and local governmental offices and agencies. They buy a wide variety of goods, from airplanes to office supplies and computers. Governments also buy services, such as building maintenance services and group medical insurance.
- An **institution** is an established public or private organization. Examples of these include schools, hospitals, museums, and charities, such as United Way and the American Cancer Society. Much like the government, institutions also buy a wide variety of goods and services.

In some ways, targeting business-market segments is similar to targeting consumer-market segments. Variables are used to segment the customers, and then a customer profile is created. B2B marketers use customer profiles to determine the best marketing mix. Common variables used to segment business customers are by industry, business size, and business needs.

Industry

Businesses are classified by industry using NAICS codes. The **North American Industry Classification System (NAICS)** is a numerical system used to classify businesses and collect economic statistics. Figure 10-5 lists the major industrial categories in NAICS (pronounced nākes).

This system was developed by the United States, Canada, and Mexico for trade purposes. Marketers use the unique NAICS codes to identify different business market segments. More information on NAICS is available through the US Census Bureau.

Business Size

The size of a business customer may be determined by its annual revenue, number of employees, or number of locations. For a marketer, the size of a business customer impacts the methods used for promotion and making contact. Business customers that are large may have vast

NAICS Business Classifications	
11	Agriculture, Forestry, Fishing and Hunting
21	Mining, Quarrying, and Oil and Gas Extraction
22	Utilities
23	Construction
31–33	Manufacturing
42	Wholesale Trade
44–45	Retail Trade
48–49	Transportation and Warehousing
51	Information
52	Finance and Insurance
53	Real Estate Rental and Leasing
54	Professional, Scientific, and Technical Services
55	Management of Companies and Enterprises
56	Administrative and Support and Waste Management and Remediation Services
61	Educational Services
62	Health Care and Social Assistance
71	Arts, Entertainment, and Recreation
72	Accommodation and Food Services
81	Other Services (except Public Administration)
92	Public Administration

Goodheart-Willcox Publisher

Figure 10-5 Each major NAICS category is subdivided into smaller, more specific categories.

organizational structures with many departments involved in purchasing decisions. In this case, a considerable amount of time may be spent marketing to and communicating with people in various departments in order to win their business. In small companies, the person or people involved in purchasing decisions may be easier to identify and directly market to and communicate with.

Business Needs

Business customers vary in the way they use products, especially raw materials and product components. Business customers use the products they buy either to make new products, resell to customers, or to operate the business. B2B marketers target sales efforts to companies with similar uses for their products, even when not in the same business category.

Syda Productions/Shutterstock.com

A hair salon is an example of a service business. *What are examples of services that you buy on a regular basis?*

Make New Products

Many businesses buy products to make new products. These types of businesses are often referred to as *producers* or *manufacturers*. Producers buy raw materials and other goods from suppliers to form them into different goods for the consumer market. For example, a company that makes water bottles must buy sheets or pellets of plastic from a plastic supplier. It then forms the plastic into different bottle designs and sells the goods to retailers.

Resell to Customers

Retail businesses buy finished goods to sell to their consumers. Most retailers buy goods from other businesses called *vendors*. Retail stores then resell those goods to make a profit. These goods are the *inventory* of the retail stores. For example, sporting goods stores buy water bottles from suppliers to sell to consumers who use them.

Operate the Business

Every business needs goods and services to run the business. Most businesses buy equipment and office supplies they need to operate. For example, an accounting firm buys ten computers for its accountants. Those computers are used to operate the business; they are not sold by the business. The product of the accounting firm is accounting services.

Business-Customer Buying Influences

LO 10.2-2

The needs of an organization are the primary influencer of B2B buying decisions. However, there may be additional influences on product purchases. These influences can be grouped into three categories: internal, external, and situational.

Internal Influences

Internal influences are motivators or change factors that come from within the business itself. These include the structure, goals, and management team of a company. For example, one company might have a president who values innovation. That company may be willing to use new vendors or develop new products. Another company might have a president who does not like change. That president would be less likely to approve the purchase of new products from new vendors.

External Influences

External influences are motivators or change factors from outside the business. These include business competition, new technology, and product trends. For example, if a competitor comes out with a new product, a business might decide to create a similar one. This means the business will

---

You Do the Math

Rounding

Many times, you will not need as precise a number as a calculation provides. For example, when working with decimals, especially multiplication and division operations, the final answer may have several more decimal places than you need.

To round a number, locate the value place to which you want to round. Then, look at the digit to the right of this place. If the digit to the right is 5 or greater, add 1 to the value place to which you are rounding. If the digit to the right is less than 5, do nothing to the value place to which you are rounding.

Solve the following problems.

1. Jenny works at the mall every Saturday. She bought a meal in the food court during her shift every week for two months. She paid the following prices: $5.67, $8.50, $6.79, $5.67, $7.94, $6.79, $5.67, $8.50. What was the mean price of Jenny's weekly lunch rounded to the nearest dollar?
2. A buyer for a small grocery store purchased the following quantities of inventory to resell to consumers. Calculate the price paid per item. Round your answer to the nearest dollar.
   A. 48 boxes of cereal for $75
   B. 56 jars of pickles for $189
   C. 96 cartons of eggs for $84

need new goods, materials, and services to develop that product.

Situational Influences

Situational influences are influences that come from the environment in which the business exists. These include the economy, political environment, and regulations or laws. Analyzing situational influences is the same as conducting a *PEST analysis*. For example, if the economy is strong, a business might be more likely to expand. An expanding business will buy more goods and services. In a poor economy, sales may decrease, so business purchases will also decrease.

Business-Customer Buying Decisions

LO 10.2-3

Business customers have very different buying needs and motives than consumers. A typical consumer buys goods or services to use personally and typically in a quantity or size that can be stored in the home. However, a business buys products to manufacture new products, resell, or use for its operations. Businesses usually buy in greater volume than the average consumer. For example, resellers in the food industry may buy very large amounts of tomatoes from farmers to resell to grocery stores and restaurants.

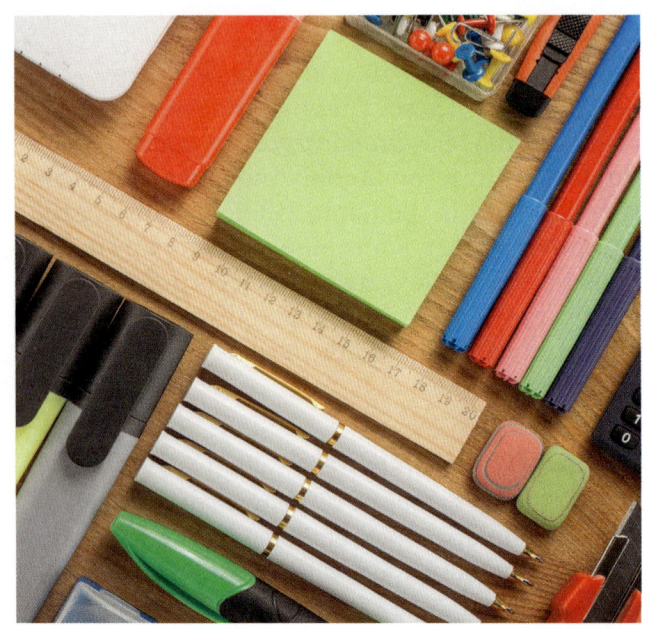

slava17/Shutterstock.com

A repeat purchase is a buying decision that requires little research and thought, such as office supplies. *What other examples of repeat purchases can you identify that a business might make?*

A B2B sale may take a long time to close and is often based on relationship selling. *Relationship selling* focuses on building long-term relationships with customers. The salesperson may have only a few customers. Like B2C buying, some B2B purchases can be made on the Internet and may be made from international companies.

Case in Point

UPS

The marketing concept plays an important role in every business, especially for businesses that have been around for generations. Satisfying the customer is the number one priority for any successful business.

UPS began as a messenger service in 1907 and is now the largest package delivery company in the world. Countless individuals, businesses, and organizations use UPS to send and receive packages all over the globe. As the global marketplace expands and connects a growing number of buyers and sellers, new delivery service companies have emerged. UPS needed a strategy to keep the company visible in an increasingly competitive market.

In 2015, UPS launched a new marketing campaign that targeted B2B customers. The United Problem Solvers™ campaign promotes the company's expertise in logistics and distribution to solve problems for business customers, from small businesses to large corporations. The campaign communicates the company's ability to help businesses in various industries achieve their goals. UPS offers solutions for supply chains, global shipments and customs, and proactive planning with a network of more than 400,000 UPS employees around the world ready to help solve business problems. The United Problem Solvers™ campaign helped customers understand that UPS can meet their growing needs and allowed the company to remain ahead of its competition.

Businesses have levels of buying decisions similar to the levels of consumer buying decisions previously presented. However, there is generally no impulse buying in the business market. The levels of B2B buying decisions are new purchases, repeat purchases, and modified purchases.

New Purchase

A *new purchase* is a decision to buy a new product that requires a great deal of research and thought. New purchases are challenging, as the business does not have experience in making that particular buying decision. The business will probably create product specifications outlining exactly what the business expects for this new product. This is similar to the extensive buying decisions of consumers.

Repeat Purchase

Many businesses purchase the same items on a regular basis. A *repeat purchase* is a buying decision that requires little research and thought. For example, a computer manufacturing business continues to renew a long-standing vendor contract for computer parts. Repeat-purchase decisions occur when the buyer is satisfied with the product, vendor, and terms of sale. This is similar to the routine buying decisions of consumers.

Modified Purchase

Sometimes, something occurs to make a buyer less satisfied with a product or vendor he or she has been using. A *modified purchase* is a decision to buy a familiar product that needs some changes or modifications. The current vendor, as well as other vendors, may be given an opportunity to supply the modified product. This is similar to the limited buying decisions of consumers.

Section 10.2 Review

Check Your Understanding

1. The B2B market can be split into five categories. What are they?
2. Identify common variables used to segment businesses in the B2B market.
3. How do business customers use the products they buy?
4. What is relationship selling?
5. Why might a business make a modified purchase?

Build Your Vocabulary

As you progress through this text, develop a personal glossary of key terms. This will help you build your vocabulary and prepare you for a career. Write a definition for each of the following terms and add them to your personal glossary.

external influence
government market
institution
internal influence
North American Industry Classification System (NAICS)
producer
reseller
service business

Section 10.3

Credit Basics

Learning Objectives

LO 10.3-1 Explain the role of credit.
LO 10.3-2 Identify the rewards and risks of extending credit.
LO 10.3-3 Describe ways to reduce credit risk.

Key Terms

credit
debtor
creditor
consumer credit
installment loan
trade credit
customer loyalty
credit risk
collection agency
credit report
credit bureau
accounts receivable
accounts receivable aging report

Essential Question: Why do businesses extend credit to customers?

Credit

Credit is an agreement or contract to receive goods or services before actually paying for them. The **debtor** is the individual or business who owes money for goods or services received. The **creditor** is the individual or business to whom money is owed for goods or services provided.

The *debtor-creditor relationship* is a legal relationship existing between the two parties. This relationship is based on good faith that both parties will uphold their end of the agreement. The debtor must repay the creditor based on the terms of the agreement. This relationship can be enforced by law because it is a contract. In addition, the US government has a number of laws that protect consumers who attempt to get credit or who already have it, as shown in Figure 10-6.

US Consumer Credit Laws	
Truth in Lending Act (1968)	Requires businesses and financial institutions to disclose all costs and charges related to consumer credit agreements
Fair Credit Reporting Act (1970)	Gives consumers the right to receive a copy of their credit reports and to dispute inaccurate information it may contain
Fair Credit Billing Act (1974)	Protects consumers from billing errors and provides outlets to challenge incorrect statement
Equal Opportunity Act (1975)	Protects consumers from discrimination based on sex, marital status, race, national origin, religion, or age
Fair Debt Collection Practices Act (1977)	Establishes legal protection against abusive debt-collection practices
Credit Card Accountability, Responsibility, and Disclosure Act (2009)	Makes the rates and fees of credit cards more transparent and prohibits unfair practices related to credit card rates and fees

Goodheart-Willcox Publisher

Figure 10-6 A number of laws protect US consumers who use or want to use credit.

Consumer Credit

Consumer credit is credit granted to an individual consumer by a retail business. Consumer credit can be in the form of a loan or credit card.

If a business sells big-ticket items, like appliances or cars, consumer credit may be offered in the form of an installment loan. An **installment loan** is a loan for a specific amount of money that is repaid in regular payments, or *installments*, with interest until the loan is paid in full. Installment loans are also called *secured loans*. Secured loans require *collateral*, which is an asset pledged to guarantee the loan will be repaid. If the loan is not repaid, the asset can be taken by the creditor and sold to recover the cost of the loan.

Some businesses extend credit by accepting debit or credit cards from their customers. Businesses such as Macy's or Target issue *proprietary credit cards*. These are cards that can be used only in the store that offers the card. Some businesses prefer to accept *bank cards*, such as MasterCard and Visa. An advantage of accepting these cards is that the responsibility for collecting the money owed is transferred from the retailer to the bank. The bank provides a *financial service* by collecting the money owed for the sale directly from the customer and then pays the business. This service is *not* free for the retailer or the customer. For the retailer, the bank adds a service charge to each purchase made on one of its debit or credit cards. For the customer, he or she must pay monthly interest on unpaid balances to the bank that issued the credit card.

Trade Credit

Trade credit is granting a line of credit to a business for a short period of time to purchase its goods and services. Trade credit is often used by established businesses. The line of credit is generally extended for 30 or 60 days. This means that the purchase is interest free for 30 or 60 days. Full payment is expected at the end of the time period. If the bill is paid in full by the specified date, no interest is charged. However, if the bill is not paid or not paid in full by the specified date, interest charges begin to accumulate. Due dates for trade credit repayment must be carefully monitored to maintain adequate cash flow and avoid interest charges.

LO 10.3-2 Rewards and Risks of Extending Credit

When credit is extended to customers, there are obvious rewards. However, while there are many rewards to offering consumer or trade credit, there are also risks. If customers fail to pay a bill on time, it may cause a cash-flow problem for the business.

Rewards

The most obvious reward is the generation of sales. Research shows that people will often spend more when using credit than if they are paying with cash. Offering credit through installment loans, credit cards, or trade credit can create a steady income for the business.

Another reward of extending credit to customers is building customer loyalty. **Customer loyalty** is the continued and regular patronage of a business even when there are other places to purchase the same or similar products. There are many reasons customers are loyal to a business, but one of them is convenience. Customers appreciate using credit cards for in-store or Internet purchases.

Risks

Credit risk is the potential for financial loss due to credit not being repaid. When extending trade credit to business customers or installment loans to consumers, there is always the possibility that some will be unable to pay their debts. Customers who fail to pay bills on time may create a cash-flow problem for the business that extended the credit.

It may be necessary for the creditor to incur the costs of hiring a collection agency when customers do not pay their debts. A **collection agency** is a company that collects past-due bills for a fee. Businesses may also attempt to get payment for

Jacob Lund/Shutterstock.com

Some businesses extend credit by accepting debit or credit cards from their customers. *What do you know about credit?*

Green Marketing

Benefit Corporation

A *benefit corporation*, sometimes called a *B corporation*, is a for-profit corporation that maximizes the positive impact its business operations have on the environment and society while minimizing any negative impact. Traditionally, corporations put company profit above all other goals. B corporations break the mold by using their economic power for the benefit of all people, not just corporate shareholders. B corporations promise to conduct business as if other people and places matter, and pledge not to allow harm to result from their business practices.

B corporations exist in the United States and around the world. Environmentally conscious consumers often seek out B corporations, which include Patagonia and Etsy. These consumers want to know their dollars are going to companies that are active in improving the world and society.

---

debts under a certain amount of money through small claims court, depending on the state. However, collecting bad debts creates additional expenses for the business. In turn, this decreases profitability.

LO 10.3-3 Reducing Credit Risk

Businesses view credit as a customer convenience and benefit. Each business must decide if extending credit to customers is a wise business decision. Some businesses choose to only accept cash or checks to avoid the transaction fees associated with credit. When granting credit to customers, it is important to establish a credit process that reduces risk.

Create a Credit Policy

Having a credit policy in place can help guide the process of extending credit. Credit policies vary by the type of credit extended to both businesses and individual customers.

Before extending credit, a business should write clear directions and explanations for the staff regarding policies for extending credit to customers. Dollar figures should be established for the amount of credit that can be extended for installment loans and trade credit. Credit limits and guidelines are typically set based on how much credit the business can afford to extend. Most importantly, when extending credit, the cash flow of the business should be monitored.

Customer guidelines that include specific terms of repayment, interest rates, late fees, penalties, and actions for nonpayment should be set. The business should include a policy in these guidelines that employees ask for customer identification when accepting credit cards. This can help avoid credit card fraud.

Require a Credit Application

It is important to check the financial backgrounds of customers desiring credit when providing credit through installment loans or with a proprietary credit card. Customers should complete a credit application that provides credit history, work history, and other information necessary to qualify for credit. Depending on the loan amount or trade credit extended, the business may also request financial statements that show net worth and financial status. Bank statements are also commonly requested.

Obtain a Credit Report

Before a business extends credit, the credit history of an applicant should be checked. A credit history may provide information about his or her likelihood of repaying the credit. A **credit report** is a record of a business' or person's credit history and financial behavior. The report provides this information about an applicant:

- the number and types of credit accounts and whether any are past due;
- how promptly credit card statements and loans were paid off in full;
- on-time payment of other bills, such as rent, taxes, or utilities;
- current total outstanding debts; and
- amount of available credit on credit cards and home equity loans.

Credit reports are issued by credit bureaus. A **credit bureau** is a private firm that maintains consumer-credit data and provides credit

Minerva Studio/Shutterstock.com

Character means an individual or business has a good record of paying bills and repaying debt on time. *How would you describe your character?*

information to businesses for a fee. There are three national credit-reporting agencies: Equifax, Experian, and TransUnion LLC.

Evaluate the Information

Once information is obtained about the customer, the credit worthiness of the applicant is evaluated based on the *three Cs of credit*.
- *Character*. The individual or business has a good record of paying bills and repaying debt on time.
- *Capacity*. The individual has a stable employment history or the business has consistent earnings.
- *Capital*. The individual has a positive net worth.

Customers approved for credit should receive a copy of the credit policies of the business. This is necessary so the customer knows his or her responsibilities in repaying the credit. Included may be a payment schedule, interest rate, and late payment penalties. The *Truth in Lending Act* requires that businesses convey all information on the credit terms and costs to customers before the first transaction. If the customer is *not* approved for credit, businesses must convey that message as well.

Manage Accounts Receivable

One very important financial-management task for a business is to keep track of when the accounts receivable are due or overdue. The **accounts receivable** are the amounts owed to a company by its customers. This activity is critical to keeping cash flow at a level that allows a business to pay its own bills and remain open. Customers who are late making payments should be sent reminders urging them to pay.

An **accounts receivable aging report** shows when accounts receivables are due, as well as the length of time accounts have been outstanding. An aging report typically shows receivables as current, 30 days, 60 days, 90 days, and 120 days and over. The purpose of an aging report is to indicate which receivables are more urgent to collect because they have been past due for a longer period of time.

Section 10.3 Review

Check Your Understanding

1. What is credit?
2. Why is collateral required for secured loans?
3. What is an example of a risk involved with extending credit?
4. List the information that is provided on a credit report.
5. What are the three Cs of credit?

Build Your Vocabulary

As you progress through this text, develop a personal glossary of key terms. This will help you build your vocabulary and prepare you for a career. Write a definition for each of the following terms and add them to your personal glossary.

accounts receivable
accounts receivable aging report
collection agency
consumer credit
credit
credit bureau
creditor
credit report
credit risk
customer loyalty
debtor
installment loan
trade credit

CHAPTER 10 Review and Assessment

Chapter Summary

Section 10.1 B2C Customers

LO 10.1-1 Explain how a hierarchy of needs impacts consumer buying behavior.
Maslow's Hierarchy of Needs states that unsatisfied needs motivate people to act. People tend to fulfill physical needs before those less critical for survival. Maslow's theory is used in marketing to develop products that fulfill certain needs and wants.

LO 10.1-2 Describe common factors that influence consumer buying.
Common factors that influence consumer buying include social environment, situational influences, personal factors, and psychological influences. Family, friends, classmates, other social groups, and culture make up an individual's social environment. Situational influences come from the environment. Personal factors are the qualities that make each person unique. Psychological influences explain why a person has certain needs and wants.

LO 10.1-3 Define categories of consumer buying motives.
A buying motive is the reason a consumer seeks and buys a good or service. Consumer buying motives can be categorized as emotional, rational, and patronage. Emotional buying motives are based on emotions, feelings, and social needs. Rational buying motives follow logical reasoning. Patronage buying motives are based on features of a specific store or product.

LO 10.1-4 Summarize steps in the consumer decision-making process.
The consumer decision-making process is a series of steps followed when making buying decisions. This is a five-step process that includes awareness of a need or problem, an information search, review of the purchase options, make the purchase decision, and evaluate the purchase.

LO 10.1-5 Describe each level of consumer buying decisions.
The four levels of buying decisions are impulse, routine, limited, and extensive. A purchase made without any planning or research is called an impulse buying decision. A routine buying decision is a purchase made quickly and with little thought. A limited buying decision requires some research and planning. An extensive buying decision involves a great deal of research and planning.

Section 10.2 B2B Customers

LO 10.2-1 Identify common variables used to segment businesses in the B2B market.
Common variables used to segment business customers are by industry, business size, and business needs. Businesses are classified by industry using NAICS codes. The size of a business customer may be determined by its annual revenue, number of employees, or number of locations. Business customers vary in the way they use products, such as to make new products, resell to customers, or to operate the business.

LO 10.2-2 Describe common factors that influence business-customer buying.
Influences in B2B buying decisions can be grouped into three categories: internal, external, and situational. Internal influences include the structure, goals, and management team of a company. External influences include business competition, new technology, and product trends. Situational influences come from the environment in which the business exists and may include the economy, political environment, and business regulations or laws.

LO 10.2-3 Describe levels of buying decisions made by business customers.
The levels of B2B buying decisions are new purchases, repeat purchases, and modified purchases. A new purchase requires a great deal of research and thought. Repeat-purchase decisions occur when the buyer

is satisfied with the product, vendor, and terms of sale. A modified purchase involves a familiar product that needs modifications.

Section 10.3 Credit Basics

LO 10.3-1 Explain the role of credit.
Credit is an agreement or contract to receive goods or services before actually paying for them. The debtor-creditor relationship is a legal relationship based on good faith that both parties will uphold their end of the agreement. Consumer credit is credit given to individual consumers by a retail business. Trade credit is granting a line of credit to a business for a short period of time to purchase its goods and services.

LO 10.3-2 Identify the rewards and risks of extending credit.
There are many rewards to a business for extending credit to customers. Offering credit can create a steady income for the business and build customer loyalty. Credit risk is the potential for financial loss due to credit not being repaid. When extending credit to customers, there is always the possibility that some will be unable to pay their debt. Customers that fail to pay bills on time may create a cash-flow problem for the business that extended the credit.

LO 10.3-3 Describe ways to reduce credit risk.
When granting credit to customers, it is important to establish a credit process that reduces risk. Having a credit policy in place can help guide the process of extending credit. Businesses should require customers to complete a credit application. Then their credit history should be reviewed, and credit worthiness evaluated based on the three Cs of credit.

Check Your Marketing IQ

Now that you have completed the chapter, see what you have learned about marketing by taking the chapter posttest. The posttest is available at www.g-wlearning.com/marketing/.

Review Your Knowledge

1. Explain how a hierarchy of needs impacts consumer buying behavior.
2. Describe common factors that influence B2C buying.
3. Define categories of consumer buying motives.
4. Identify the steps in the consumer decision-making process.
5. Describe each level of consumer buying decisions.
6. Describe common factors that influence B2B buying.
7. Describe levels of buying decisions made by B2B customers.
8. Explain the role of credit.
9. Identify the rewards and risks of extending credit.
10. Describe ways to reduce credit risk.

Apply Your Knowledge

1. In an earlier chapter, you identified the product for which you are creating a marketing plan. As a marketing manager, how do you plan to turn customer needs and wants into buying motives for your product?
2. Consider the product you are marketing. How would you define the reference group that influences the majority of your target market?
3. Create a flowchart for the consumer decision-making process that your customers might use. Provide details about how a typical customer in your target market might act for each step.
4. Consider the level of buying decisions that customers will use for the product you are marketing. Explain how you will provide customers with the information they need to make their buying decision.

5. Explain how routine buying decisions by customers influence your marketing plans.

6. The business market can be grouped into five categories: producers, resellers, service businesses, governments, and institutions. Assume your marketing plan includes strategies for selling into the business market. Describe the segment of business into which you will be marketing your product.

7. Assume your company sells in the B2B market. Describe how you would use market segmentation to develop a customer profile. How will segmenting the market contribute to successful marketing?

8. Select one of the US consumer-credit laws described in Figure 10-6 and explain how this law might impact the business for which you are writing a marketing plan.

9. Write a credit policy that could be used to explain the types and purposes of consumer and business credit that would be extended by your company.

10. Do you think offering credit provides enough benefits to both the customer and business to justify the cost? Explain your position.

Apply Your Math Skills

During a recent four-year period, overall consumer spending in the economy increased. The graph shows the average annual expenditure for food at home versus away from home during this period. Interpret the graph to answer the questions that follow.

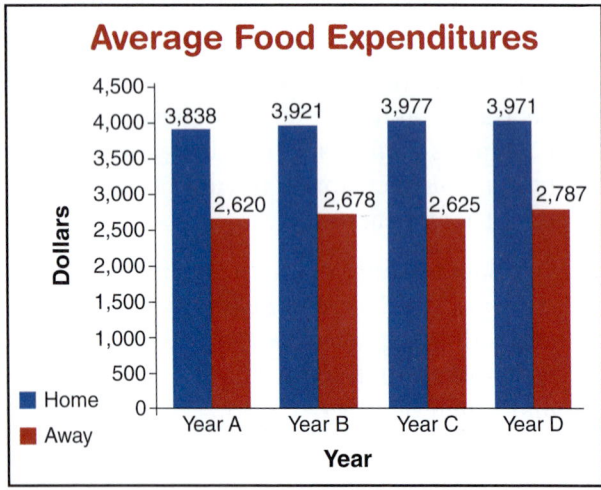

1. In what year did consumers spend the most money on food eaten at home?
2. In what year did consumers spend the most money on food eaten away from home?
3. In what year did the largest gap between the home and away amounts occur?

Average Food Expenditures

Year	Home	Away
Year A	3,838	2,620
Year B	3,921	2,678
Year C	3,977	2,625
Year D	3,971	2,787

Source: US Bureau of Labor Statistics; Goodheart-Willcox Publisher

Communication Skills

Reading In order to retain information that you read, it is necessary to focus and read with a purpose. The Employability Skills feature in this chapter discusses self-confidence. Read the feature with the intention of focusing on each word that is written. After you have finished, close the book. Can you remember what you read?

Writing Create a Venn diagram to show the relationships of new purchases, repeat purchases, and modified purchases. Where do the circles overlap? What do you think this overlap signifies?

Listening Listen to product advertisements on the radio and television as you go about your day. How might the messages you hear influence you to make a buying decision? Analyze the social, situational, personal, and psychological factors that might influence whether you buy these products.

Internet Research

Impulse Buying Conduct an Internet search for the phrase *psychology of impulse buying* and select one or two articles on the topic. Read the articles in detail, making notes as you read. Cite reasons people make impulsive purchases and list possible consequences of impulsive buying behavior.

Consumer Reports Use the Internet to navigate to the website of *Consumer Reports* magazine. Select a product that interests you, such as tablet computers, cars, or hair dryers. Use the information available on the website to research the product as if you were making a buying decision. How do you think this information would impact the different buying influences and motives of consumers?

NAICS Codes Search the website of the US Census Bureau for information on the North American Industry Classification System. Find the NAICS code that applies to the business for which you are writing a marketing plan. Identify two ways that marketers could use the information in promoting their products or businesses.

Credit Policies Research the topic of *business credit policies* on the Internet. Summarize your findings in a paragraph and describe the precautions a business should take when extending credit to customers.

Teamwork

Working in a team, create a list of ten businesses that sell products to both consumers and businesses. Indicate any differences in price, availability, or other product features that are specific to the B2B or B2C market. What strategies were common for both markets?

Portfolio Development

College and Career Readiness

Academic Work Academic information is important to include in a portfolio in order to show your accomplishments in school. Include items related to your schoolwork that support your portfolio objective. These items might be report cards, honor roll reports, or diplomas that show programs you completed.

1. Create a Microsoft Word document that lists the items you will be including in this section. Use the heading "Academic Work" on the document along with your name.

2. Scan hard-copy documents related to your schoolwork, such as report cards, to serve as samples. Place each document in an appropriate folder.

3. Place the hard copy documents in the container for future reference.

4. Update your spreadsheet.

UNIT 3 — Marketing Information Management

Building the Marketing Plan

No business exists in a vacuum. Competition is everywhere, including online and around the world. Markets and customer preferences change all the time. To compete and be successful, marketing managers must have the most current information about their customers' wants and needs in order to fulfill them. Marketing managers must also know everything about their business competitors. Research is vital to a marketing team to help the business thrive and grow.

Part 1 Research the Competition

Objectives
- Identify and research the main competitors for your business.
- Create a competitive analysis.

Directions
In this activity, you will develop the subsection of Situation Analysis that addresses your competition. Access the *Marketing Dynamics* companion website at www.g-wlearning.com/marketing/. Download the activity files as indicated in the following instructions.

1. **Unit Activity 3-1—Competition Research** As marketing manager for your company, it is important to recognize the competition. Complete this activity to research your company's competition.

2. **Unit Activity 3-2—Competitive Analysis** Use this document to create a competitive analysis grid that will be included in the Appendix of your Marketing Plan.

3. Open your saved Marketing Plan document.

4. Locate the Marketing Analysis section, then the Competitive Analysis subsection. Make notes on the research you did for the competition, and refer the reader to the Appendix for the competitive analysis.

5. Save your document.

Part 2 Complete SWOT and PEST Analyses

Objectives
- Assess your company's strengths, weaknesses, opportunities, and threats.
- Create a SWOT analysis for your company.
- Assess the political, economic, social, and technological factors that may impact your company.
- Create a PEST analysis for your company.

Directions
In this activity, you will assess your business as it compares to the competition to continue creating the Situation Analysis. Access the *Marketing Dynamics* companion website at www.g-wlearning.com/marketing/. Download the activity files as indicated in the following instructions.

1. **Unit Activity 3-3—Company Assessment** Complete research about your company that is necessary to create a SWOT analysis.

2. **Unit Activity 3-4—SWOT Analysis** Use this document to create a SWOT analysis that will be included in the Appendix of your marketing plan. Refer back to the research you completed in Activity 3-3 to complete the analysis.

3. **Unit Activity 3-5—Environmental Scan** Complete research about the environment in which your company is operating that is necessary to create a PEST analysis.

4. **Unit Activity 3-6—PEST Analysis** Use this document to create a PEST analysis that will be included in the Appendix of your marketing plan. Refer back to the research you completed in Unit Activities 2-1 and 3-5 (as well as

optional Unit Activity 2-2, if completed) to complete the analysis.

5. **Unit Activity 3-7—Global Environmental Scan** In the future, your product may be sold internationally. Conduct a global environmental scan to evaluate the political, economic, social, and technological factors that could affect the marketing of your product.

6. Open your saved marketing plan document.

7. Locate the Market Analysis section, and then the Competition Analysis subsection. Make notes on the research you did and refer the reader to the Appendix for the SWOT and PEST analyses.

8. Use the suggestions and questions listed in the marketing plan template to help you generate ideas. Delete the instructions and questions when you are finished recording your responses. Proofread your document and correct any errors in keyboarding, spelling, and grammar.

9. Save your document.

Part 3 Determine the Target Market

Objective
- Identify the target market for your company's products.

Directions
In this activity, you will conduct research to determine who is most likely to purchase your products, known as your target market(s). Access the *Marketing Dynamics* companion website at www.g-wlearning.com/marketing/. Download the activity file as indicated in the following instructions.

1. **Unit Activity 3-8—Target Market Analysis** Based on the products and services of your company, define your target market. Who are the people or businesses most likely to buy from your business?

2. Open your saved marketing plan document.

3. Locate the Marketing Strategies section, then the Target Market subsection. Make notes on the research you completed for the target market, and refer the reader to the Appendix for the target market analysis.

4. Use the suggestions and questions listed in the marketing plan template to help you generate ideas. Delete the instructions and questions when you are finished recording your responses. Proofread your document and correct any errors in keyboarding, spelling, and grammar.

5. Save your document.

Part 4 Complete a Customer Profile

Objective
- Define a typical customer within your target market to create a customer profile.

Directions
Information about your target market's needs and product preferences is very important to any marketing plan. In this activity, you will create a customer profile representative of the target market for your business. Access the *Marketing Dynamics* companion website at www.g-wlearning.com/marketing/. Download the activity file as indicated in the following instructions.

1. **Unit Activity 3-9—Customer Profile** Use this document to create a customer profile containing as much information as possible about your typical target-market customer, including product preferences.

2. Open your saved marketing plan document.

3. Locate the Marketing Strategies section, then the Target Market subsection. Make notes on the research you completed, and refer the reader to the Appendix for the customer profile.

4. Use the suggestions and questions listed in the marketing plan template to help you generate ideas. Delete the instructions and questions when you are finished recording your responses. Proofread your document and correct any errors in keyboarding, spelling, and grammar.

5. Save your document.

UNIT 4 Product

Chapters
11 **Product**
12 **Branding**

While studying, look for the activity icon for:
- Building the Marketing Plan activity files
- Pretests and posttests
- Vocabulary terms with e-flash cards and matching activities
- Self-assessment

These activities can be accessed at www.g-wlearning.com/marketing/.

Developing a Vision

Product is the heart of any business. A marketer would not have a job if product did not exist. Product is the starting point for the marketing mix.

Price, place, and promotion only happen because a business has a product or service to sell. New offerings are important for a business to remain competitive. By reviewing the life cycle of current products, it can be determined what is needed to sustain profits and generate growth.

However, marketing decisions do not end there. Success depends on customer recognition and awareness. Branding is how a marketer distinguishes products in the marketplace. Creating a branding strategy can determine the success or failure for a business.

Marketing Core Functions Covered in This Unit

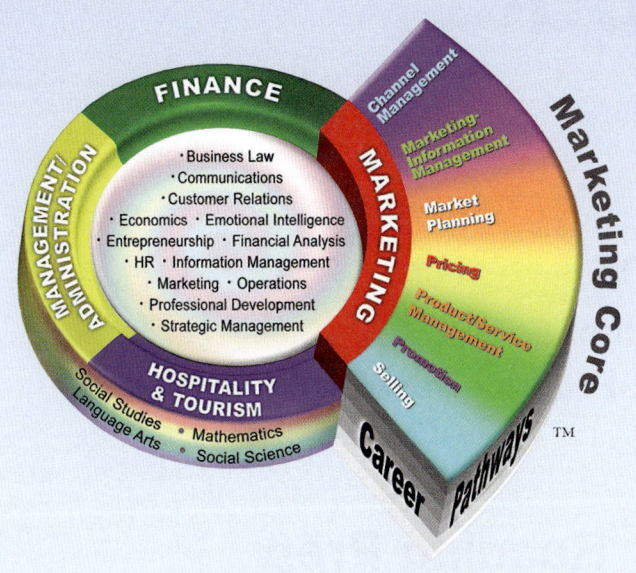

Functions of Marketing

- Market planning
- Product/service management
- Promotion

Copyright MBA Research, Columbus, Ohio. Used with permission.

EYE-CATCHER

Marketing Matters

To marketers, *product* can mean a consumer good, business service, brand, store, person, or even a website. Product is anything with an identity that needs attention brought to it through marketing efforts. For example, Macy's is a department store chain that sells many thousands of products. However, Macy's is also a product with its own logo and brand identity. Here, the marketers for Macy's flagship store in New York City are positioning it as *the world's largest store*.

pio3/Shutterstock.com

CHAPTER 11 Product

Sections

11.1 **Product**
11.2 **New-Product Development Process**

Reading Prep

College and Career Readiness

Before reading the chapter, skim the material by reading the first sentence of each paragraph. Use this information to create an outline for the chapter before you read it.

Check Your Marketing IQ

Before you begin the chapter, see what you already know about marketing by taking the chapter pretest. The pretest is available at www.g-wlearning.com/marketing/.

DECA Emerging Leaders

Buying and Merchandising Team Decision-Making Event, Part 1

Career Cluster: Marketing
Instructional Area: Product/Service Management Promotion

Knowledge and Skills Developed

Participants will develop many 21st century skills desired by today's employers in the following categories:
- communication and collaboration
- creativity and innovation
- critical thinking and problem solving
- flexibility and adaptability
- information literacy
- initiative and self-direction
- leadership and responsibility
- productivity and accountability
- social and cross-cultural skills

Specific Performance Indicators

- Describe factors used by marketers to position products.
- Explain the nature of product/service branding.
- Describe the use of grades and standards in marketing.
- Explain the nature of a promotional plan.
- Coordinate activities in the promotional mix.
- Explain the role of promotion as a marketing function.
- Demonstrate connections between company actions and results.

Purpose

Designed for a team of two DECA members, the event measures the team's ability to explain core business concepts in the format of a case study in a role-play. This event consists of a 100-question, multiple-choice, cluster exam for each team member and a decision-making case study situation. The Team Decision-Making Event provides an opportunity for participants to analyze one or a combination of elements essential to the effective operation of a business in the specific career area presented as a case study.

For the purposes of this text, you will be presented with the material for this event in two parts. Part 1 presents the knowledge and skills assessed and an overview of the event's purpose and procedure. Part 2 presents the remaining procedures and the event situation.

Procedure, Part 1

1. For Part 1 in this text, read both sets of performance indicators. Discuss these with your team members.
2. If there are any questions, ask your instructor to clarify.

Critical Thinking

1. Explain the relationship between the specific performance indicators and the case study situation.
2. Discuss with your team member how you will incorporate the performance indicators in your presentation.

Visit www.deca.org for more information.

Published by DECA Inc. Copyright © by DECA Inc. No part of this publication may be reproduced for resale without written permission from the publisher. Printed in the United States of America.

Section 11.1

Product

Essential Question: What is a product?

Learning Objectives

LO 11.1-1 Define product as one primary *P* of the marketing mix.
LO 11.1-2 Discuss the difference between products for the B2C and B2B markets.
LO 11.1-3 Describe product planning.
LO 11.1-4 Define the goal of product/service management.

Key Terms

product planning
product mix
product line
product width
product item
product depth
product mix strategy
warranty
guarantee
packaging
product manager
category manager

LO 11.1-1 What Is Product?

A *product* is a good, service, or idea that is bought and sold. Businesses sell products to satisfy customer needs. Product is the primary *P* of the marketing mix because it is the first element of the marketing mix to be decided. Other marketing mix decisions about price, place, and promotion are based on the product decision. If a business does not have a product to sell, the other elements of the marketing mix are not needed. Collectively, goods and services are called *products*. Goods are physical items. Services are activities performed by others.

Services are considered products, but they are different from goods in four important ways. Services are intangible, inseparable, variable, and perishable.

- *Intangible* is something that cannot be touched. Services cannot be experienced before they are purchased.
- *Inseparable* is the inability of items to be separated from each other. A service cannot be separated from the person who performs it. For example, a computer repair does not exist until a technician performs the service on the equipment. Because services are inseparable from their providers, customers often think of the service and the service provider as one and the same.
- *Variable* is the ability to be changed. A service is almost always unique and is rarely repeated in exactly the same way for each customer.
- *Perishable* is the likelihood of something to disappear or be destroyed if not stored properly. This means that services cannot be stored for later use.

Many products are combinations of both goods and services. Imagine having dinner in a restaurant. What is the product of that restaurant? Is it a good or a service? Actually, it is both. The food itself is a tangible good. The restaurant atmosphere, food preparation, and table service are services for which you pay.

Products can be seen as being on a *continuum*, or a range, as shown in Figure 11-1. On the left end, the products are pure goods. On the right end, the products are pure services, such as tutoring. In between are the products with varying combinations of goods and services.

Good-Service Continuum

Pure Goods — Pure Services

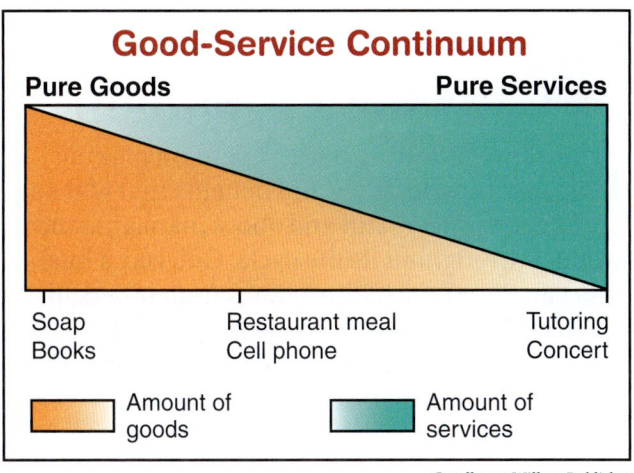

Soap, Books | Restaurant meal, Cell phone | Tutoring, Concert

■ Amount of goods   ■ Amount of services

Goodheart-Willcox Publisher

Figure 11-1 Many products are a combination of goods and services.

Consumer and Business Products
LO 11.1-2

As you recall, two types of customers that are served by a business are business-to-consumer (B2C) and business-to-business (B2B). The B2C market consists of customers who buy products for their own use, or *consumers*. The B2B market consists of customers who buy products for use in a business rather than for personal use. These customers are called *clients* in the business market. The market also includes governmental agencies and other organizations. Each type of customer has specific product needs.

Africa Studio/Shutterstock.com

Consumer products, such as furniture, are sold to consumers for their personal use. *When have you or your family purchased consumer goods?*

Consumer Products

In the B2C market, *consumer products* are those sold to consumers for their personal use. Three basic categories of consumer products are convenience goods, shopping goods, and specialty goods.

- *Convenience goods* are bought often and with little effort. These goods are typically for immediate use. Convenience goods include most grocery items and gasoline.
- *Shopping goods* are usually purchased after making the effort to compare price, quality, and style in more than one store. Shopping goods are purchased less often than convenience goods. They include more expensive, durable items, such as appliances and furniture.
- *Specialty goods* are unique items that consumers are willing to spend considerable time, effort, and money to buy. Examples include unique sports cars and rare antiques. Specialty goods have the smallest target markets because fewer people have the time, money, or desire to expend the effort to find unique goods.

The amount and variety of goods and services a business makes available to consumers must be broad enough to meet their needs and wants. Otherwise, customers will go elsewhere to shop.

Business Products

In the B2B market, *business products* are items sold to businesses for use in their operations. Business products tend to fall into one of six categories: raw materials, processed materials, component

---

Marketing Ethics

Proprietary Information

Proprietary information, sometimes referred to as *trade secrets*, is information specific to a company that it wishes to keep confidential. Product formulas, financial information, or manufacturing processes are examples of proprietary information. It is unethical to share proprietary information with people outside the company, even friends and family. Some companies require employees to sign nondisclosure agreements to keep information secret.

Raw materials become part of a manufactured product, such as plastic pellets that are melted and turned into other products. *What other examples of raw materials can you name?*

parts, major equipment, office equipment and supplies, and business services.

- *Raw materials* are natural or man-made materials that become part of a manufactured product. Raw materials include wood, plastic pellets, metal, and other substances. They are sold to manufacturers for different uses.
- *Processed materials* are used in the manufacturing of another product. Their use or presence may not be readily identifiable in the finished product. Examples of processed materials include food additives and industrial glue. These are sold to product manufacturers.
- *Component parts* are assembled pieces that become a part of a finished product. Component parts are manufactured items, such as computer chips, tires, and switches. They are sold to companies that produce final products, such as car and computer manufacturers.
- *Major equipment* is large machines and other equipment used for production purposes, such as furnaces, cranes, and conveyors. Manufacturing companies of all sizes and types need different equipment.
- *Office equipment and supplies* are products for basic office needs. These may include computers, calculators, paper, pens, and other office items. All businesses need these products.
- *Business services* are the tasks necessary to keep a business operating. Examples of business services include building maintenance, equipment repair, and accounting.

The needs of an organization are the primary motivating force of B2B buying decisions.

Product Planning

Product planning is the process of making decisions about features and benefits that will help a product be successful and about managing the product throughout its life cycle. One way a business can distinguish its products from others in the market is to focus on the features and benefits, including packaging, labeling, and branding, that will entice consumers to buy the product.

Decisions made in the product-planning process consider the target-customer profile and how to distinguish the product from others in the market. Product planning includes decisions about the product mix, as well as product elements such as features, usage, and protection.

Product Mix

A **product mix** is all the goods and services a business sells. Small businesses may only sell a few products, while large corporations can offer thousands of different products. Usually, the product mix consists of goods and services that relate to each other in some way. For example, the product mix for a local stationery store may include specialty paper, greeting cards, pens, and custom invitation printing.

Products are generally organized into product lines. A **product line** is a group of closely related products within the product mix. For example, a sporting goods store may sell several different lines

A product line is a group of closely related products within the product mix. These Apple watches are a specific item in a product line of watches. *What other items might be in this product line?*

of tennis racquets, such as child and adult sizes. The **product width** is the number of product lines a company offers.

A **product item** is the specific model, color, or size of products in a line. For example, the product items in a sporting goods store include the different styles, colors, and sizes of athletic shoes. Perhaps the store has five identical, size-ten running shoes. They are not considered different items, but the quantity (five) of one item (size-ten running shoes). **Product depth** is the number of product items within a product line.

Recall that *product strategy* is all the decisions made about a given product. The first decision made by a business is to select which products will be offered in the product mix. The **product mix strategy** is the process of planning which goods or services the business will support. Some businesses offer only one good or service, such as carpet cleaning or furnace repair. However, many businesses sell more than one type of product.

Product Elements

All products have certain elements that may be changed to meet customer needs. These elements can be organized into three categories: features, usage, and protection. Understanding these elements can enable a business to more effectively fulfill the marketing concept of attaining customer satisfaction.

Features

A *feature* is a fact about a good or service. For example, a feature of a tablet computer as a *good* is the size of its display screen. A *service* feature for the tablet can be technical support or data services.

An *optional feature*, or *option*, is a feature that can be added to a product by customer request. Many products have a basic design and customers can choose to add various features. For example, options on an automobile might include a sunroof or leather seats. Options allow consumers to customize products to their specific needs and wants.

Extended product features apply after the sale of a good or service. Examples of these are warranties, guarantees, delivery, and installation.

A **warranty** is a written document that states the quality of a product with a promise to correct certain problems that might occur. The warranty promises the manufacturer will replace or repair faulty items. Depending on the product offered, companies may offer various types of warranties, such as the following.

- A *full warranty* covers the repair or replacement of a product in its entirety due to any defect during the specified warranty period.
- A *limited warranty* covers only specified parts or types of defects for a product. There may be certain conditions that apply to limited

Case in Point

L.L. Bean

Listening to the customer is an important marketing task. Customer input about new products usually leads to business success. L.L. Bean is a retail company well known for listening to its customers. It has a process for interviewing product users and performs follow-up meetings for user feedback. The company's policy of 100% Satisfaction Guaranteed was established by its founder, Leon Leonwood Bean, and continues to be a cornerstone of operations.

To test product quality and performance, L.L. Bean has a team of 1,300 independent field testers who personally test products under various conditions and report results to the company. The company also has its own independent lab for testing and revising products until they meet the most stringent standards. Products continue to be tested, even while they are in the marketplace, to ensure the highest quality. The goal of 100 percent satisfaction does not stop there. Customer service is also considered an extremely important component of the business. Employees are trained to provide outstanding customer service whether on the telephone, via online chat, in person, or through social media. In fact, the Customer Satisfaction Department operates 24 hours a day, 365 days a year. In the words of L.L. Bean president Steve Smith, "Our commitment to superior customer service is the very foundation of our brand."

warranties. For example, the warranty may cover the cost of a part that needs to be replaced but not the cost of professionally installing the replacement part.

- An *extended warranty* is an agreement to extend coverage of a product beyond the initial warranty period. Customers usually pay for an extended warranty for a set period of time. The terms of coverage in an extended warranty may be different from the coverage provided in the original product warranty.

A **guarantee** is a promise that a product has a certain quality or will perform in a specific way. A guarantee is similar to a warranty but is not a written document. A guarantee typically has certain terms or conditions, such as a set period of time or following the intended use of a product. For example, a business that provides a money-back satisfaction guarantee on its products typically includes a time restriction, often 30 days after purchase.

Many businesses that sell large items, such as appliances and furniture, offer delivery service to their customers. Offering to deliver the product after the sale is an extended product feature that is a convenience for many customers. It also contributes to customer satisfaction.

Installation is the act or process of putting a good in a certain place and preparing it for use. Installation is a service offered with many large or complex products. Products that require installation include heating and air conditioning systems, carpeting, plumbing fixtures, and landscaping, to name a few. Although some customers prefer to install their own goods, many want an expert to install goods for them.

Usage

Usage means the way something is used. Many goods are designed to be assembled, installed, or used in a specific way. Businesses make decisions about how to help customers use the product correctly. If customers do not know how to properly use a product, they might become frustrated and dissatisfied. They may return the product or just never buy it again. Product usage includes the available instructions, training, and technical support.

Instructions are steps that must be carried out in a specific order to successfully complete a task. Some products with instructions include furniture needing assembly, electronic devices, and software. Simple products may include one sheet of assembly instruction. Complex products often include instructions in the form of an owner's manual or user's guide.

Training is focused instruction provided on a specific topic or task. The use or maintenance of a product may not be easily understood by all customers. Providing training helps customers make the best use of a product and may foster a sense of loyalty to the company. Some companies provide classes or seminars to help customers learn to use their products. Computer software companies and home improvement supply stores often provide such classes. For example, in-person training sessions are offered at many Apple stores for the various products they sell to consumers.

Technical support includes the people and resources available to help customers with usage problems. Many everyday products, such as appliances and home security systems, have an integrated computer that directs their functions. These products can develop problems from time to time in both the computerized parts of the products and the functional parts. Many companies selling such products offer technical support.

Protection

Protection is a broad category that includes safety inspections, packaging, and product maintenance and repair services. The various forms of protection may be intended to protect the product, the user, or both.

marketinggraphics/Shutterstock.com

A promise that a product has a certain quality or will perform in a specific way is a guarantee. *Why do consumers look for product guarantees?*

Safety Inspections The safety features of products may influence consumer buying decisions. Most manufacturers work diligently to verify product safety through quality-control checks during the manufacturing process. In addition, certain laws establish safety standards for some products. Special governmental agencies may be involved in setting and enforcing safety standards for certain products. For example, the National Highway Traffic Safety Administration (NHTSA) regulates safety standards for automobiles. Automobile manufacturers must meet minimum safety standards before their products are sold.

Packaging **Packaging** protects products until customers are ready to use them. Some items, such as fresh food products, require special packaging to keep them fresh and healthy. Many fragile products, such as glassware and electronics, must be carefully packaged to prevent damage. The packaging of consumer products is often designed to make them easier to stack or display. It may also protect the product from theft. For example, small items are often placed in large or bulky packages to make it harder for shoplifters to hide them.

Maintenance and Repair Services Complex machinery, vehicles, and other equipment often require regular maintenance to remain in safe, working order. The availability and cost of maintenance and repair services can affect customer buying decisions. Customers in the B2C and B2B markets may make purchases based on services available from the vendor.

Zvonimir Atletic/Shutterstock.com

Packaging protects fragile products, such as eggs, until customers are ready to use them. *How do companies decide what kind of packaging to use for product protection?*

LO 11.1-4 Product/Service Management

One of the functions of marketing is product/service management. *Product/service management* determines which products a business should offer to meet customer needs. It manages the development,

Exploring Marketing Careers

Product Manager

Retail stores such as department stores, clothing shops, and electronics superstores offer a large variety of products and usually several different brands of each product as well. Who decides which products the store will carry? A product manager investigates new products, analyzes buying trends, and—for current products—reviews sales records to determine how profitable each product is likely to be. Based on this information, the product manager buys products for resale to the store's customers. Typical job titles for a product manager include *buyer*, *merchandiser*, *merchandise manager*, *purchasing manager*, and *procurement specialist*.

Some examples of tasks that product managers perform include:
- Use spreadsheet software to organize, locate, and analyze sales figures on products in inventory
- Meet with sales personnel to get information about customer wants and needs
- Analyze sales records and trends to determine how much of each product to purchase
- Negotiate prices and discounts in order to purchase the selected products
- Set markups and selling prices for the products

Product managers must be able to analyze product performance based on financial figures. They also need good negotiation skills in order to get the best prices and terms for the products they buy. Most jobs in this field require an associate degree or equivalent training in a vocational school, but on-the-job training may be substituted for these. For more information, access the *Occupational Outlook Handbook* online.

Copyright Goodheart-Willcox Co., Inc.

marketing, and sale of a product. Successful businesses constantly review their product mixes to determine if they are meeting market demands. Companies may choose to change the product mix by adding, changing, or removing products.

A **product manager** is a marketing professional who guides the selection of products and oversees the marketing and sales of those products. The product manager is one part of the team responsible for company profits. A **category manager** performs the same functions as a product manager but is responsible for an entire category of products.

Product managers work closely with many areas in a company to make sure profit goals are met. For example, they may get constant updates from accounting on the profits or losses for each product. Product managers help the sales team learn how to sell products to different markets. They help prepare product sales forecasts and monitor inventory levels.

Since part of managing products is driving successful promotions, product managers also work closely with the advertising department or an outside ad agency. Underlying all these functions, product managers need current and accurate marketing research based on the right variables. It is the research that justifies a large capital investment to develop any new products that are needed.

Section 11.1 Review

Check Your Understanding

1. In what ways are services different from goods?
2. Provide three examples of business product categories.
3. How do product warranties and guarantees provide quality assurances for customers?
4. What is the purpose of protection features of products?
5. List examples of departments within a company that a product manger collaborates with when carrying out product/service management tasks.

Build Your Vocabulary

As you progress through this text, develop a personal glossary of key terms. This will help you build your vocabulary and prepare you for a career. Write a definition for each of the following terms and add them to your personal glossary.

category manager
guarantee
packaging
product depth
product item
product line
product manager
product mix
product mix strategy
product planning
product width
warranty

Section 11.2

New-Product Development Process

Essential Question

How is a new product idea developed?

Learning Objectives

LO 11.2-1 Explain new product.
LO 11.2-2 Identify the steps in new-product development.
LO 11.2-3 Describe the stages of the product life cycle.

Key Terms

new product
repackaging
product obsolescence
image
brand
prototype
trial run
test marketing
virtual test markets
reverse engineering
product life cycle
introduction stage
growth stage
maturity stage
saturated market
decline stage

LO 11.2-1 New Product

A **new product** is a product that is different in some way from existing products. Technology has changed the way the world works, and there are many genuinely new products in the marketplace. However, even a small change to an existing product can be considered a new product. The difference between new and existing products may be minor or major. There are six categories of new products.

- *New-to-the-world products* are new inventions or products with never-seen-before technology.
- *Minor product variations* are improved and revised versions of existing products.
- *New product lines* are created when an established company adds a product line to enter an existing market.
- *Additions to existing product lines* are used to add depth to existing product lines in order to support the product mix and sales.
- *Repositioned existing products* are existing products that are marketed in a new way.
- *Less-expensive versions of current products* are developed using less-expensive manufacturing materials or methods to reduce the cost and lower the consumer price.

New products often replace products at the end of their life cycles. Genuinely new products are either new inventions or products with never-seen-before technology. Consumers may not even know how the products work. The marketing strategy for *new-to-the-world products* is to explain what they are, how they work, and why people should buy them. The cost and risk of developing truly new products is high. However, when a new-to-the-world product is successful, the rewards can be great. Often, new products are developed to meet a specific need, such as the polio vaccine or a shampoo to reduce dandruff. Others are developed to meet a new want, such as faster computers or smartwatches with Bluetooth connectivity.

Because genuinely new products are risky, many companies choose to develop variations on currently or previously successful products. These variations should improve the function of the existing product. Such products become *improved* and *revised* versions of the originals and are advertised as such. For example, Procter & Gamble regularly uses the marketing strategy of introducing new and improved versions of its products. Tide, a popular Procter & Gamble laundry detergent, introduced a new version of their laundry detergent called Tide purclean™. This liquid detergent is advertised as a sustainable, ecofriendly option created with alternative energy sources. Laundry detergent is not a new product, but Tide purclean™ is a new product. Tide introduced a revised version of the product that could compete with other all-natural, ecofriendly laundry detergents.

Repositioning is changing the marketing strategy used to influence consumer perception of a product in comparison to the competition with the goal of increasing sales. Marketing an existing product in a new way can create a new position in the minds of customers. Many existing products can be valuable for uses other than the originally intended one. A classic example of successful repositioning is Kleenex. The thin paper tissues were developed in 1924 as a disposable towel for removing makeup. However, by 1926, customer feedback showed that most people were using the product to blow their noses. Kleenex began advertising the product as a disposable handkerchief and product sales doubled.

Repackaging, or using new packaging on an existing product, is another common way to create a new product. The product stays the same, but the packaging is changed to make it more efficient or attractive. For example, the dairy company Daisy® Brand introduced sour cream in a squeezable pouch in 2015. The new packaging allows for easy, drip-free dispensing of the product. It

Sheila Fitzgerald/Shutterstock.com

Repackaging is a common way to create a new product. This single-serve cereal container offers customers a different buying option. *When have you seen repackaging as a marketing strategy?*

also eliminates the need to wash a spoon after dispensing sour cream. Daisy® Brand determined the majority of consumers used sour cream as a topping and repackaged their existing product to meet this need. The squeezable pouch design makes it easier to use the product as a topping on other foods, while still allowing it to be measured for recipes. Products created to meet a real need have a better chance of success than products whose usefulness must be sold as much as the product itself.

Each year, over 25,000 new consumer products hit the market. More than 75 percent of these new products fail. New products fail for many reasons. One of the main reasons for a failed product is the lack of planning and research. The product did not meet a market need, was unappealing, or a better product came out at the same time. Some well-known failed products include the Sony Betamax, Microsoft's Zune, and the Newton computer from Apple.

Another reason for product failure is product obsolescence. **Product obsolescence** occurs when a product becomes outdated. This is common for electronic products. Technology changes quickly and some newer products are considered outdated as soon as the next advancement in technology is available.

A failed product can be very costly. For example, a large corporation might invest $20

Employability Skills

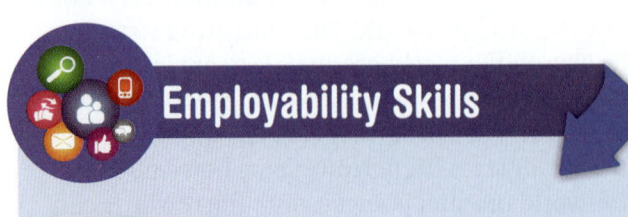

Self-Esteem

Self-esteem is how an individual feels about his or her value as a person. It is your sense of self-worth and how you see yourself when you look in the mirror. The more comfortable you are with yourself as a person, the more self-confidence you will exhibit.

Product obsolescence occurs when a product becomes outdated, like this typewriter. *Can you name other products that have become obsolete in your lifetime?*

million to develop, produce, advertise, and introduce a new product. If the product fails, most of that investment is lost. In some cases, product failure can ruin a business.

LO 11.2-2 New-Product Development

Identifying the best products to meet target-market needs sounds simple. However, much thought and planning is necessary before making final product decisions. Marketing plays an important role in new-product development, including research, product testing, and creating promotional strategies. Marketing, along with the sales team, is the all-important direct link between a company and its customers.

Marketing research is critical to planning and developing new products to meet customer needs and wants. A new product must also be able to fulfill company profit goals. Marketing research is necessary to make sure introducing a new good or service is the best business decision. There are two questions that must be answered during the new-product development process.

1. Will the target-market customers buy the product?
2. Can the company produce and sell the product profitably?

Many large companies hire marketing-research firms that specialize in trend research and new product ideas. For example, trend research shows that Americans want more healthy choices when dining out. For this reason, many restaurants have added more entrée salads and other heart-healthy choices to their menus. Trend research does not always have to be formal or expensive, though. Marketers can conduct their own secondary research to identify the latest trends within their industries.

Customer input and feedback is critical for companies that follow the marketing concept. The sales team is also a great source for new product ideas because they are in constant contact with customers. Salespeople hear customers' ideas, their unmet needs, complaints, and suggestions about how to improve products. Some companies have a formal process for salespeople to submit product ideas.

The new-product development process generally follows seven steps, as shown in Figure 11-2.
- Idea generation
- Idea screening
- Business analysis
- Product design
- Test marketing
- Commercialization
- Evaluation

Customer feedback is critical for companies that follow the marketing concept. *Why do you think companies ask consumers to rate products?*

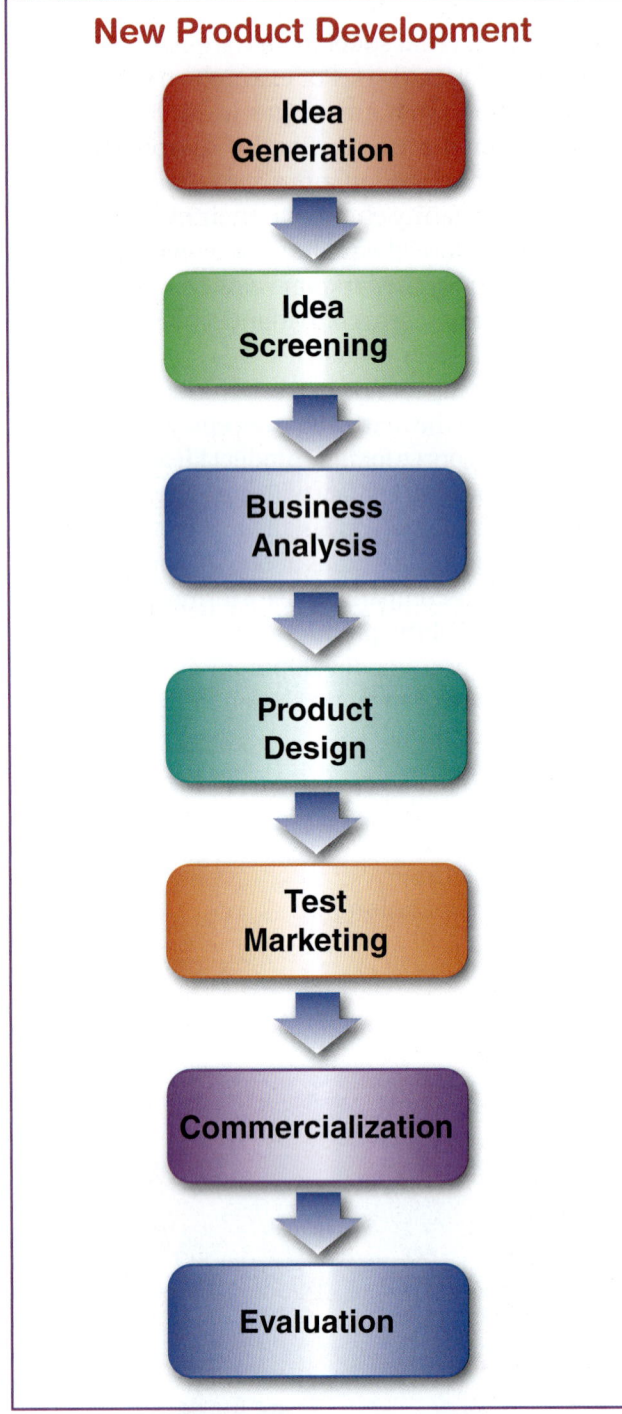

New Product Development

- Idea Generation
- Idea Screening
- Business Analysis
- Product Design
- Test Marketing
- Commercialization
- Evaluation

Goodheart-Willcox Publisher

Figure 11-2 There are seven common steps in the process of developing a new product.

Idea Generation

New product ideas may be prompted by alterations to an existing product, new technology, a design that meets a new need, or many other factors. Product ideas are usually the result of trend research, observation, customer feedback, and brainstorming.

Tracking trends in consumer and market activity can lead to product ideas. Many large companies hire marketing research firms that specialize in *trend research* and new product ideas. However, organizations may choose to conduct their own research to identify the latest trends within an industry.

Observation is a common source of product ideas. Observing people and activities within the business environment may reveal unfilled customer needs. Finding a way to fulfill a need often leads to a new product idea.

Customer feedback is critical for companies that follow the marketing concept. Customer ideas, unmet needs, complaints, and suggestions for product improvement provide important information for new-product development. For example, Uber built real-time customer feedback functionality into their ride request app to make customer feedback as simple and accessible as possible.

Brainstorming is a creative process that focuses on new product ideas. Bringing people together with different experiences, skills, and backgrounds can generate ideas and new ways of looking at a product.

Idea Screening

Once a list of new product ideas is generated, it must be reviewed. The goal of idea screening is to choose the best and, hopefully, most profitable ideas. This is the time to conduct primary and secondary research to learn if the product will meet customer needs and wants. It is important to screen ideas before the company makes a large investment to develop and produce a new product.

During idea screening, new product ideas are evaluated from the customer's viewpoint. Sending surveys or holding focus groups can help discover if the new product will meet customer needs and wants.

Business Analysis

A business analysis of a new product idea looks at the projected costs and forecasts of product sales. Does the company have the necessary people, expertise, equipment, and money to develop and promote the new product? Even a nonprofit organization must determine whether it can afford a new product.

Analysis includes researching the cost of revising a current product or bringing a new product to market. Market research should help

DeymosHR/Shutterstock.com

A brand is the name, term, or design that sets a product or business apart from its competition. Abercrombie & Fitch is an example of a well-known brand. *How many brands can you name?*

determine if the product can generate enough sales to cover costs and make the desired profit. All companies create a detailed financial analysis of each new product plan.

A new product must also align with the company image and goals. An **image** is the idea that people have about someone or something. Many companies choose to develop a specific image through their brand, which marketers help to create. A **brand** is a name, term, or design that sets a product or business apart from its competition. For example, Jaguar has the image of a company that builds luxury sports sedans. A truck would not fit the Jaguar brand.

New products should also meet company goals. For example, Jaguar had a goal to expand its market by appealing to a more price-conscious group of consumers. To meet this goal, Jaguar could have considered creating a new line of less-expensive vehicles, such as trucks. However, the Jaguar brand is associated with luxury sedans, and trucks do not fall into that category. To expand its market, Jaguar instead developed the X-Type, a less-expensive version of its premium luxury car.

Product Design

After proving the new product meets a need in the market and company profit goals, the next step is designing the product. This is the stage in which the product idea becomes a reality. During the design phase, details of how to produce the product are planned. Determining the product brand is also part of the design phase. The name, image, logo, slogan, and packaging of the good or service is usually created at this stage.

In the development of goods, numerous product designs are completed and evaluated. In the development of new services, the new services are usually tried out on a few potential customers.

Goods

A **prototype** is a working model of a new product for testing purposes. Product designers experiment with the prototype to determine if it performs as expected. Any problems found are fixed before full-scale production. Prototypes are especially important for products with moving parts.

For example, Toyota had a goal to develop a new car that used much less gas and saved natural resources. To accomplish that goal, Toyota engineers developed an entirely new hybrid engine: one powered by both gas and electricity. This meant the engine delivered more miles per gallon (mpg) and used far less fuel than other cars. The design team built a prototype and tested it for performance and safety before full-scale production. Toyota's first hybrid car, the Prius, was very successful and remains a best seller in its vehicle class.

VanderWolf Images/Shutterstock.com

Engineers for Toyota built a prototype of the popular Prius before making it widely available to consumers. *How might a prototype help lead to the success of a new product?*

You Do the Math

Word Problems

Problems needing to be solved mathematically are not always presented in the "language" of math. Usually, the mathematical concepts within the word problem must be identified first. Then, an appropriate mathematical expression can be determined to solve the problem.

Solve the following problems.
1. While driving his sales route the first day of his five-day workweek, Henry noticed that he filled the gas tank twice: once with 8.3 gallons and once with 7.9 gallons. The total cost of these two fill-ups was $61.24. He also had to pay $7.40 in tolls that day. How much petty cash should Henry request for the rest of the week?
2. A shipping carton contains 128 product catalogs. The dimensions of the shipping carton are 11 inches by 17 inches by 16 inches. The weight of the carton is 12.6 pounds. A shipping pallet can hold a maximum of 150 pounds. How many cartons of catalogs can be placed on the pallet?
3. A marketing research supervisor notices that six researchers have completed 78 consumer interviews before lunch on Monday. The company wants 1,200 consumer interviews completed by the end of the day on Friday. How many additional researchers must be added to the project in order to complete all the interviews required?

Businesses also use prototypes to get customer feedback before a final design is chosen. Large companies may create several prototypes for a single product, each with different features. Researchers may have focus groups test the different prototypes, including customers within the target market. Responses from product testers help businesses determine which prototype and features will sell the best. Creating prototypes can be expensive, however. To save money, a product manager may choose to create a prototype of only one of the designs that market research suggests will sell best. Once the prototype is researched and approved, the product can go into full production.

Services

A service business usually goes through a period during which the details of providing a new service are planned. Training the service providers is also an important step to complete before the business opens. Depending on the service, a physical location is chosen and the business may perform trial runs. A **trial run** consists of testing the service on a few select customers to make sure that everything runs smoothly. A trial run is like a dress rehearsal for a business. For example, a new restaurant might start serving meals to small groups before the grand opening to work out any problems in food preparation, timing, and service.

Test Marketing

Due to the expense and potential risk of failure, many companies do not immediately produce a new product in large numbers. This is especially true for products that will be sold on the national or global level. **Test marketing** is the process of introducing a new product to a small portion of the target market to learn how it will sell. Test marketing can test the entire marketing mix, which includes product, place, price, and promotion.

Customer responses in the test market help the research and development team solve unexpected problems. Test marketing may also determine whether the product should be produced on the mass level. For example, Peoria, Illinois has long been a test-market city for many new products. It is seen as a representative population of the overall Midwestern market, and the media prices for advertising are inexpensive. Over the years, companies such as Hellman's and Google have tested new goods and services in Peoria.

An alternative to using traditional test marketing methods is to evaluate products in virtual test markets. **Virtual test markets** are computer simulations of products and shopping environments. A test market simulation is created to reflect an actual retail setting and a realistic depiction of product offerings. Participants can enter the virtual shopping environment, browse through the store, and inspect products. Marketers monitor customer behavior in the virtual environment to evaluate interaction with and responses to the test product. The use of technology may encourage many target market customers to participate. Once the virtual test market has been developed, it can be distributed using a URL link sent by e-mail.

While test marketing products can save money by identifying and resolving problems before production, it can have a downside. There is the risk that competitors can buy your product and copy it through reverse engineering. **Reverse engineering** is taking apart an object to see how it was made, usually in order to produce something similar. Some companies reverse engineer existing products to copy or enhance them without the expense of developing their own products. They may be able to produce a better product before the test market product is finalized and available for purchase.

Commercialization

The *introduction stage* of the product life cycle is also called *commercialization*. The goal of commercialization is to bring attention to a product and, hopefully, create demand for it. Activity in this stage begins before a product is available in the marketplace. Management chooses a release date to make the new product available for sale and promotional campaigns start before the product is released. Marketing focuses heavily on promotions that explain the new product and its benefits. In addition, the production and shipping functions must have the product ready for shipment and in the stores by the release date.

For example, the seventh Harry Potter book, *Harry Potter and the Deathly Hallows*, was set for release at 12:01 a.m. on July 21, 2007. The book publisher, Scholastic, Inc., had to make sure the books were printed and delivered to thousands of stores before the release date. Anticipation and promotion of the book started months earlier when the release date was announced. Many bookstores planned parties for the release date of the book, and it set a record for preorders. At midnight on July 21, 2007, 12 million copies of the book went on sale. More copies of *Harry Potter and the Deathly Hallows* were sold on the first day of release than any other book previously had.

Often, new products are introduced at industry trade shows to monitor customer response. A *trade show* is a large gathering of businesses for the purpose of displaying products for sale. There are trade shows for every industry and type of B2C product. For example, the annual North American International Auto Show (NAIAS) is held in Detroit. Since 1989, over 1,300 new vehicles have been introduced at the NAIAS.

There are also trade shows for B2B products. For example, the National Retail Federation (NRF) holds an annual convention called Retail's BIG Show. Manufacturers introduce retailers to every kind of new product.

Evaluation

All businesses, including institutions and governments, need to know if their products are successful. It is important to evaluate both new and existing products often. The success of a product is based on how well it met the sales and other goals established for the product during the business analysis. The marketing team shares in the responsibility of determining the success of products.

Anton_Ivanov/Shutterstock.com

Commercialization of each *Harry Potter* book in the series created high demand for the products. *How does marketing affect the demand for a new product?*

Product Life Cycle

LO 11.2-3

The **product life cycle** is the stages a product or a product category goes through from its beginning to end. The complete life cycle of a product can be long or short. For example, certain products, such as computers or cell phones, can have a short life cycle due to rapidly changing technology. Depending on the product, the length of each stage within the life cycle also varies.

Stages of the Product Life Cycle

Businesses are always reviewing the stages of a product's life cycle because marketing efforts differ in each stage. Figure 11-3 illustrates the four stages of the product life cycle: introduction, growth, maturity, and decline.

Introduction Stage

The **introduction stage** is the time when a new product is first brought to the market. Usually, very few people know about the product. At this stage in the life cycle, marketing focuses heavily on promotions explaining the new product and its benefits. Sales tend to be low until more people learn about why they should buy the product. Profits are also lower in the introduction stage due to low sales and higher costs.

Production costs for a new product tend to be higher because until demand increases, fewer units are produced. In addition, the company has already invested a large amount of money on market research, product development, production, and promotion. It is expected that the investment will be recovered as the product begins to sell. Profits tend to rise later in the product life cycle due to increased sales and decreased production costs.

Growth Stage

The **growth stage** is the period in which product sales increase rapidly. To keep product sales high, new models of the product may be introduced. Modifications may also be made to the product to keep customers interested or meet new needs.

As the product becomes more successful, competitors may enter the market. This means there are many companies competing for customers. During the growth stage, marketers focus on promotions distinguishing their brands from the competition. They also use strategies to build brand loyalty.

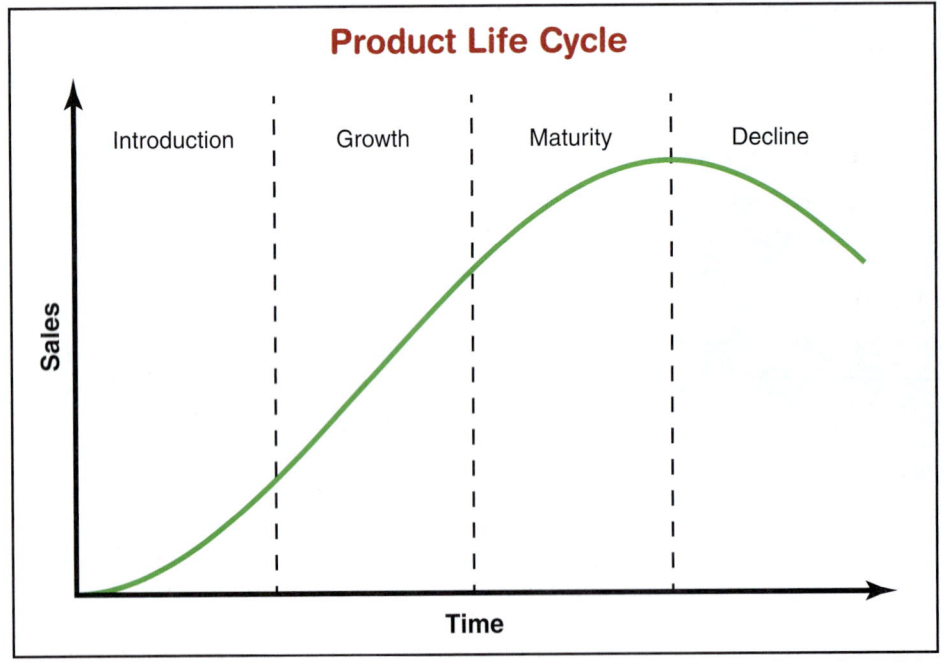

Figure 11-3 A product life cycle is based on the overall industry sales of that product over time.

Goodheart-Willcox Publisher

Maturity Stage

The **maturity stage** occurs when product sales are stable. During this stage, competition for customers is intense. Sales are no longer increasing quickly, nor are they decreasing. Maturity can happen when the market becomes saturated with a product or when a newer, better product is introduced to fill the consumer's needs. A **saturated market** is one in which most of the potential customers who need, want, and can afford a product have bought it. At this stage, businesses look for new ways a product could be used or try to identify new markets for the product to avoid losing revenue.

Decline Stage

Mature products eventually enter the **decline stage** in which product sales begin to decrease. If sales decline rapidly, the company may stop making or selling the product. Decline often occurs when a new technology is growing rapidly, so the older products become obsolete quickly.

Deciding whether a product is truly at the end of its life cycle can be tricky. A decline in sales does not always mean the product is in the decline stage. For example, in an economic recession, sales for expensive products like video game systems may decline quickly because consumers need to save money. However, that does not mean that the video game systems are at the end of the life cycle.

Impact on the Marketing Mix

The *product/service management* marketing function determines which products a business should offer, as well as how to market them. Frequently reviewing products to determine their life cycle stages is part of this marketing function. Some businesses choose to offer products that are in a specific life cycle stage. For example, discount stores may buy a large amount of discontinued products at the end of the product life cycle. Because the life cycle for these products is nearly over, the business can buy them for an extremely low price. Due to the low cost, the business can still make a profit when reselling the goods at discount-store prices.

After a product completes its life cycle, a new product or service may be needed to replace lost revenue. Awareness of the product life cycle stage helps businesses develop effective marketing-mix strategies. This affects the product, price, place, and promotion of a specific good or service.

Product

As a business matures, the market needs and wants may change. The product mix may need adjustment to remain competitive. One option to keep sales from declining is to develop new uses for the current product. A classic example is Arm & Hammer baking soda. The original use for baking soda was as an ingredient in homemade baked goods. As fewer people baked at home, baking soda sales declined. Through market research, Arm & Hammer found that some customers were using baking soda to deodorize refrigerators, clean rugs, and brush their teeth. Arm & Hammer began to market its baking soda as an essential cleaning product, and sales rose. Arm & Hammer now sells products, such as toothpaste and laundry detergent, with baking soda as the differentiating feature.

Price

Different pricing strategies are used at varying stages of the product life cycle. For example, during introduction and growth, prices are often higher because the product is new and there is no competition. In addition, the business needs to recoup its development costs. During the maturity stage, prices are often lowered because there is more competition, which forces competitive pricing strategies. During the decline stage, prices are often at their lowest to stimulate slow sales.

Place

To prevent declining sales in a maturity stage, businesses can search for new markets that need or want the product. This search may lead businesses to expand into the global market. Or, they may look for a new delivery system, such as through the Internet.

Promotion

Promotions and the marketing message change throughout the life cycle of a product. During the introduction stage, promotions inform customers about the new product, explain its benefits, and persuade them to buy. During the growth and maturity stages, increased competition forces promotions to make the case for customers to choose one seller or brand over another. During the decline stage, promotions often focus on low prices to increase sales.

Section 11.2 Review

Check Your Understanding

1. Why do companies develop variations on currently or previously successful products?
2. What is the role of marketing in new-product development?
3. Identify ways new product ideas are generated.
4. Why do businesses need to be aware of a product's stage in its life cycle?
5. How do the stages of the product life cycle impact product pricing?

Build Your Vocabulary

As you progress through this text, develop a personal glossary of key terms. This will help you build your vocabulary and prepare you for a career. Write a definition for each of the following terms and add them to your personal glossary.

brand	product obsolescence
decline stage	prototype
growth stage	repackaging
image	reverse engineering
introduction stage	saturated market
maturity stage	test marketing
new product	trial run
product life cycle	virtual test markets

Chapter 11 Review and Assessment

Chapter Summary

Section 11.1 Product

LO 11.1-1 Define product as one primary *P* of the marketing mix.
Product is the primary *P* of the marketing mix because it is the first element of the marketing mix to be decided. If a business does not have a product to sell, the other elements of the marketing mix are not needed.

LO 11.1-2 Discuss the difference between products for the B2C and B2B markets.
B2C products are sold to consumers for their personal use. The basic categories of consumer products are convenience goods, shopping goods, and specialty goods. B2B products are items sold to businesses for use in their operations. Business products categories are raw materials, processed materials, component parts, major equipment, office equipment and supplies, and business services.

LO 11.1-3 Describe product planning.
Product planning is the process of making decisions about features and benefits that will help make a product successful and managing the product throughout its life cycle. These decisions help businesses determine how to distinguish their products from others.

LO 11-1.4 Define the goal of product/service management.
Product/service management determines which products a business should offer to meet customer needs. It manages the development, marketing, and sale of a product or products.

Section 11.2 New-Product Development Process

LO 11.2-1 Explain new product.
A new product is different in some way from existing products. There are six categories of new products: new-to-the-world products, minor product variations, new product lines, addition to existing product lines, repositioned existing products, and less expensive versions of current products.

LO 11.2-2 Identify the steps in new-product development.
Marketing research is critical to planning and developing new products. The new-product development process generally follows seven steps: idea generation, idea screening, business analysis, product design, test marketing, commercialization, and evaluation.

LO 11.2-3 Describe the stages of the product life cycle.
The stages a product or a product category goes through from its beginning to end is the product life cycle. The introduction stage is when a new product is first brought to the market. The growth stage is when product sales increase rapidly and competitors enter the market. The maturity stage occurs when product sales are stable. In the decline stage, product sales begin to decrease.

Check Your Marketing IQ

Now that you have completed the chapter, see what you have learned about marketing by taking the chapter posttest. The posttest is available at www.g-wlearning.com/marketing/.

Review Your Knowledge

1. Define product as one primary *P* of the marketing mix.
2. Discuss the difference between products for the B2C and B2B markets.
3. Describe product planning.
4. Explain the concept of product mix.
5. What is the goal of product/service management?
6. Explain new products.
7. Identify the steps in new-product development.

8. Explain how service businesses design their products.
9. Describe the stages of the product life cycle.
10. How does the life cycle of a product impact the marketing mix?

Apply Your Knowledge

1. In earlier chapters, you identified the product for which you are creating a marketing plan. What is the good or service you will be marketing? Is it for the B2C or B2B market?
2. If you are marketing a good, there are three product elements on which you will focus: features, usage, and protection. Create a chart for two of the goods you are marketing and define each one of the product elements as they pertain to the good. If you are marketing a service, create a chart for each service that describes its characteristics of intangible, inseparable, variable, and perishable.
3. Assume your business will offer a product warranty or guarantee. Describe the protection that is offered for your good or service. Create a document for the warranty or guarantee.
4. Write a set of directions or instructions on how to use your product.
5. Describe the packaging for your product and explain why it is important.
6. What elements of your product's packaging relate to marketing the product?
7. Describe the product mix and product line for your business. Explain how you think this product mix will meet customer expectations.
8. Evaluate your company's product offerings. Do you see any gaps in product lines? Are the product offerings competitive? What can you do to address these issues?
9. Think of a new service your company might offer and explain the need or want it fulfills. Design a chart illustrating the key new-product development steps for this new service.
10. Name a product that your company offers that could be repositioned simply by changing the packaging. Describe the changes you would make and how the changes benefit customers.

Apply Your Math Skills

Introducing a new product can be a risky business decision and is often evaluated in terms of percentages. Apply your math skills to solve the following problems.

1. To generate new product ideas, a marketing manager reviewed customer feedback in the form of product reviews on the company website. One product in particular had 280 customer reviews, of which 5 percent were negative. How many of the product reviews were negative?
2. Before opening their business to the public, the owners of a new café decide to perform a trial run to evaluate their processes and the preparedness of their staff. During the trial run, each customer was asked to complete a survey about their experience. After the trial run, the customer surveys were evaluated. Of the 300 customers served, 255 were satisfied with the goods and services. What percentage of customers surveyed were satisfied?

Communication Skills

College and Career Readiness

Reading *Skimming* means to quickly glance through an entire document. Skimming will give you a preview of the material to help your comprehension when you read the chapter. You should notice headings, key words, phrases, and visual elements. Skim this chapter. Identify the main ideas of the content.

Writing Standard English means that word choice, sentence structure, paragraphs, and the narrative follow standard conventions used by those who speak English. Well-written paragraphs are usually the product of editing. Using Standard English, write several paragraphs to describe a product you would like to buy that does not exist yet. Edit and revise your work until the ideas are refined and clear to the reader.

Speaking The way in which you communicate with others will have a significant impact on the success of the relationships you build with them. Write a speech that explains the process of developing a new product. Deliver the speech to your class. How did the style, words, phrases, and tone you used influence the way the audience responded to the speech?

Internet Research

Product Elements Visit the website of an automobile manufacturer or dealer. Select a vehicle that you would like to buy. Describe the basic product and identify the optional product elements (features, usage, and protection). How do these product features give the car a competitive edge?

New Products Conduct an Internet search for the phrase *new products* plus the current year. Identify three products from the search results that recently came on the market. Identify the products you selected as truly new-to-the-world products, minor variations of an existing product, new product lines, additions to existing product lines, repositioned products, or less expensive versions of existing products. How did you make the determination?

Product Life Cycle Fashion, entertainment, and electronics trends change regularly. Businesses watch these trends in an effort to determine the demand for products. Choose a product that was once popular but has fallen out of demand. The Tickle Me Elmo doll, portable CD players, and shoes with built-in wheels are examples of these products. Once you have selected a product, research its life cycle. Try to determine when each stage began and ended and what may have caused the product to become obsolete or fall out of demand. Create a chart showing each stage of the cycle with corresponding dates.

Teamwork

Developing a new product can be a fun and exciting activity. Working with your team, identify an example of a product that is missing from today's market. Using the idea generation step of the new-product development process, write a short description of the product and how it meets customer needs or wants. Share your ideas with your class.

Portfolio Development

College and Career Readiness

Transcripts A transcript is an official school record of the courses you have taken, the grades you received in each one, when you took them, and your grade point average (GPA). Transcripts may also include standardized test scores, your behavioral record, or honors received. This document proves your academic accomplishments.

1. Obtain your official transcripts from your school. This may require completing a form or inquiring in the school's office, so plan ahead. If you have attended more than one school, obtain your transcript from each one.
2. If you receive transcripts as a hard copy, scan the document and put it in an appropriate folder.
3. Place the hard-copy documents in the container for future reference.
4. Update your spreadsheet.

CHAPTER 12

Branding

Sections

12.1 **Product Branding**
12.2 **Brand Identity and Protection**

College and Career Readiness

Reading Prep

Before reading this chapter, read the Review Your Knowledge questions at the end of the chapter. This exercise will prepare you for the content that will be presented in this chapter. Review questions serve as a self-assessment to help you evaluate your comprehension of the material.

Check Your Marketing IQ

Before you begin the chapter, see what you already know about marketing by taking the chapter pretest. The pretest is available at www.g-wlearning.com/marketing/.

◇DECA Emerging Leaders

Buying and Merchandising Team Decision-Making Event, Part 2

Career Cluster: Marketing
Instructional Area: Product/Service Management Promotion

Procedure, Part 2

1. In the previous chapter, you studied the performance indicators for this event.
2. The event will be presented to you through your reading of the Knowledge and Skills Developed, Specific Performance Indicators, and Case Study Situation. You will have up to 30 minutes to review this information and prepare your presentation. You may make notes to use during your presentation.
3. You will have up to ten minutes to make your presentation to the judge followed by up to five minutes to answer the judge's questions. You may have more than one judge. Both members of the team must participate in the presentation, as well as answer the questions.
4. Turn in all of your notes and event materials when you have completed the event.

Case Study Situation

You are to assume the role of marketing specialists for Shopmart, a national discount retail chain. The **CEO of Shopmart (judge)** has asked you to develop a strategy to raise customer awareness of the store's private-label brand to ultimately increase sales and increase profit margins.

Shopmart is one of several large national discount retail chains across the country. The store sells a wide variety of merchandise, such as household items, clothing, health and beauty products, electronics, small furniture, and seasonal items. While merchandise sales have been steady, the past two quarters have not shown any significant increases.

The CEO of Shopmart (judge) is now focusing on the store's private label brand, Match. The Shopmart health and beauty department offers all major brand-name products consumers expect to find, plus the additional private label brand, Match. Priced from five to 20 percent less than the national brands, Match products are just as effective as national brands. Sales of Match-brand health and beauty products should be higher than what they are, given the economic conditions in the country. The CEO (judge) has asked you to develop a strategy to raise awareness of the Match brand to Shopmart customers, which will increase sales.

The CEO (judge) warns that price alone does not create customer loyalty to a brand. Please consider the following product qualities. Your strategy should:
- meet customer needs;
- exude quality; and
- deliver a positive experience.

You will explain your strategy to the CEO (judge) in a meeting to take place in the CEO's (judge's) office. The CEO (judge) will begin the meeting by greeting you and asking to hear your ideas. After you have explained your strategy and answered the CEO's (judge's) questions, the CEO (judge) will conclude the meeting by thanking you for your work.

Critical Thinking

1. How does your strategy create differentiation from the competition?
2. If successful, what other departments could use the Match brand?

Visit www.deca.org for more information.

Published by DECA Inc. Copyright © by DECA Inc. No part of this publication may be reproduced for resale without written permission from the publisher. Printed in the United States of America.

Section 12.1

Product Branding

Essential Question
How do marketers distinguish their brands from the competition?

Learning Objectives
LO 12.1-1 Describe elements of a brand.
LO 12.1-2 Define three types of product brands.

Key Terms

brand name
logo
trade character
tagline
jingle
metaphor
brand promise
perception
national brand
private-label brand
generic brand

Elements of a Brand
LO 12.1-1

An important part of product planning is branding. Recall that a *brand* is a name, term, or design that sets a product or business apart from its competition. All goods, services, and businesses have a brand. Some brands are stronger and more effective than others. The brand is a result of everything a customer sees, hears, and experiences about a company or product. A positive brand experience can ensure the success of a product. A product or business with a negative brand image has a difficult time overcoming it to remain profitable. Just as first impressions are made by people, the way a product is packaged, priced, and presented also makes a first impression. Brands are created through both tangible and intangible elements.

Tangible Brand Elements

The *tangible elements* of a brand are its name, graphic design elements, packaging, and tagline or slogan. These are the elements that can be seen and heard. Tangible brand elements are often the first experience a consumer has with a product. Each tangible element should be carefully considered to make sure it reflects the desired image.

Name

A **brand name** is the name given to a product consisting of words, numbers, or letters that can be read and spoken. Sometimes, choosing the right name for a product can guide the product strategy and other marketing mix decisions. For example, a vacation resort was developed on Hog Island in the Bahamas. However, the resort did not take off until the island name was changed to Paradise Island.

Graphic Design Elements

Some of the most powerful aspects of a brand are the graphic design elements. These elements appear in packaging, on labels, and form the logo. A **logo** is the picture, design, or graphic image that represents a brand. A logo may also be called a *brand mark*. A logo can be a graphic symbol, like the Nike swoosh or the red target symbol for Target. It may also be the name of the company or product without a symbol, such as Ray Ban and Lego.

Symbols tend to work best when they evoke some aspect of the product. Part of the reason the

The colors chosen for the graphic design elements project the desired image of the product. *In what ways does color shape your perception of a brand?*

Nike logo is so effective is that it evokes a sense of movement and power. A symbol may simply be the name with a special graphic treatment or unique typeface, such as the IBM, Citibank, and Dell logos.

The colors used in the graphic design elements for a product also contribute to the visual identity of a brand. Colors are carefully chosen to attract attention and to project the desired image. Many research studies have been conducted evaluating the impact of color on human behavior, including product perceptions and buying behavior. For example, the color red is often perceived as exciting, and blue commonly suggests dependability. Marketers purposely use color in the graphic design elements of a brand to appeal to customers and support the brand image.

Trade characters are another type of graphic design element that may be used for branding purposes. A **trade character** is an animal, a real or fictional person, or an object used to advertise a good or service. Effective trade characters symbolize the good, service, or company. These characters typically become so closely associated with the good or service that they can actually become the brand. The Jolly Green Giant and Mister Clean are successful trade characters.

Packaging

The brand takes a physical form through packaging. The graphic elements of a brand are often prominently displayed on product packaging. Packaging should reinforce the brand image with consistent use of brand colors, logos, slogans, and other elements. In a retail environment, the graphic design elements used on packaging position a product among its competition and should promote its competitive advantages.

Packaging choices that might affect buying behavior, such as design, color, and materials, are part of the marketing function. For example, using recyclable plastic containers for beverages and child-safety caps for medicines is important to many consumers.

Packaging also includes labeling. The function of label information is to describe the product and verify facts about it, such as contents, nutritional information, weight, and grade. Some packaging and labeling contain safety precautions and directions to prevent injury to the user. Special governmental agencies may be involved in packaging standards for certain products. For example, the United States Department of Agriculture (USDA) requires that safe-handling instructions appear on all packages of raw and partially cooked meat and poultry to prevent the spread of food-borne illnesses. The USDA also requires that the package states a product's *grade*, which is a rating of the quality of agricultural food products.

The Jolly Green Giant is a trade character used to advertise Green Giant vegetables. *What other examples of trade characters can you name?*

Tagline

A **tagline**, or *slogan*, is a phrase or sentence that summarizes an essential part of the product or business. A catchy phrase or memorable tagline can strengthen a brand. For example, Wheaties cereal has been "The Breakfast of Champions" since the 1930s. This tagline has appeared in every promotion and on every box of cereal along with the image of a champion athlete. It has become a strong brand identifier for the General Mills product.

A tagline or slogan set to music is called a **jingle**. Jingles are used for radio, television, and Internet advertising purposes. An example of a jingle is that of Nationwide Insurance Company, which says, "Nationwide is on your side." Companies also purchase the rights to popular songs to represent their brands. The music of the jingle or song becomes a very identifiable part of the overall brand.

Metaphors are often used in advertising as a way to enhance the perceived value of a product. *Value* is the relative worth of something to a person. A **metaphor** is a word or phrase for one thing used in reference to a very different thing in order to suggest a similarity. An example of a metaphor is describing someone as "drowning in paperwork." An advertising metaphor may also combine a phrase with an image to strengthen the message. For example, Geico Insurance advertises its services as "so easy, a caveman can do it." BMW promotes its vehicles as "the ultimate driving machine."

Intangible Brand Elements

Intangible elements of a brand include the implied promise of the brand, consistency of the brand, and customer perceptions of the brand image. Intangible elements are hard to measure because they cannot be seen or heard. Examples include customer expectations, their feelings about the brand, and their direct interactions with it. Recall that *image* is the idea that people have about someone or something. Brands can convey a variety of images, such as prestige, value, or trendiness.

Bloomicon/Shutterstock.com

Brands can convey a variety of images, such as prestige, value, or trendiness. *What brands can you identify that convey trendiness?*

Case in Point

M&M's® and State Farm

Catch phrase, tagline, slogans—all these are words used for a product line that consumers remember and connect to a particular product. An effective and memorable slogan can sell a product for years to come. However, creating a slogan that fits and sells a product is no easy feat. Some slogans have been around for years and are proof that people will remember a product with a catchy phrase.

In 1941, Mars, Inc. introduced M&M's® candy for US troops fighting World War II. The popularity of the product led to a public release of M&M's a few years later with several promotional campaigns that targeted the general public. The slogan, "Melts in your mouth, not in your hand" was created for M&M's in 1954 and has been used ever since.

In 1971, famous American songwriter Barry Manilow wrote State Farm's musical jingle, "Like a good neighbor, State Farm is there." Baby boomers related well to it, and State Farm still uses the same jingle today. Slogans create emotional buying experiences for customers that they remember. If customers can recognize a slogan or hum a jingle, branding has done its job.

Brand Promise

In its simplest form, a brand is a promise made to consumers. It may or may not be included in the graphics or tagline. A **brand promise** is a statement made by an organization to its customers that tells customers what they can expect from its products. Consumers develop expectations for a brand based on how it is promoted and priced. When customers use their hard-earned money to purchase something, they assume their expectations will be met.

Brand Consistency

Brand consistency means that the good or service is the same whenever and wherever you buy it. For example, when you go to a Best Buy store, you expect the same products, prices, décor, signage, and service at every location across the country. If a brand fails to meet consumer expectations at any time, the product or business may eventually run into problems. Customers tend to remember failed expectations and often discuss them with others.

Perceptions of Brand Image

Perception is the mental image a person has about something. Perception of a brand image includes feelings about a product or company. For example, consider your perceptions about these entirely different brands: BP, Microsoft, Levi Strauss, and Coach. Just saying their names can evoke certain feelings based on your perception of the company's image. Consumers form perceptions of brand images in three ways:
- personal experience;
- hearing the experiences of others; and
- how a company promotes the brand.

Because perception is so critical to brand success, marketers use every tool and technique they can to enhance the image of their brand.

Product Brand Types
LO 12.1-2

The brand of a product is what sets it apart from its competitors. There are three types of product brands: national, private label, and generic. Each brand type has unique qualities and market appeal.

National Brand

A **national brand** is one created by a manufacturer for its own products. It may also be called

> ### Employability Skills
>
> #### Humility
> *Humility* means to be modest and not to think one is better than other people. Possessing humility does not mean to be meek or have diminished self-esteem or self-image. Instead, it means treating people respectfully, being confident in your abilities, and behaving as a professional. When soft skills are mastered, some aspects of humility naturally happen. For example, simply saying "thank you" to someone demonstrates humility.

a *manufacturer's brand*. For example, Ritz, Cover Girl, and Ugg are all well-known national brands. National brands are probably the most familiar to consumers because they are carried by many large and small retail stores. Some manufacturers also have their own retail stores that exclusively sell their own brands.

Private-Label Brand

Private-label brands are products owned by and created specifically for large retailers. Private-label products are only sold by one retailer. For example, Abercrombie & Fitch stores only carry Abercrombie-label products. Other brands cannot be purchased at Abercrombie & Fitch; nor can you buy Abercrombie clothing at any other retailer.

Sheila Fitzgerald/Shutterstock.com

Walmart's Great Value brand is an example of a private-label brand. *How do you decide between purchasing a national brand or a generic brand?*

Generic Brand

A consumer product that lacks a widely recognized name or logo is a **generic brand**. Generic brands are not advertised, and it is not immediately obvious who manufactures them. With no promotional costs to recoup, generic brands can cost up to 50 percent less than similar brand-name products.

Many products are made and sold for less in a generic-brand format. For example, most prescription and over-the-counter medicines are also available in generic forms. Grocery stores in particular create and sell many generic brands of packaged foods and other products. Generic brands appeal to value-conscious consumers.

You Do the Math

Problem Solving and Reasoning

When solving word problems, the elements of the math problem must be identified before it can be solved. However, there must be enough information provided to solve the stated problem. If certain information is not provided, it may not be possible to determine the math problem.

Solve the following problems.

1. A business sells smartphones across the nation. Each phone comes in packaging that measures 6 inches by 4 inches by 1 inch. The products are shipped to resellers in cartons that measure 18 inches by 12 inches by 12 inches. The cartons can hold a maximum of 15 pounds. The company wants to know how much each full carton weighs. Is there enough information to solve this problem? If not, what information is missing?
2. Darren orders office supplies every Monday. This week he must order 23 reams of paper, 2,000 envelopes, and 12 boxes of tape. He wants to know how much this will cost. Is there enough information to solve this problem? If not, what information is missing?
3. Lana is a marketing manager who travels for work. On Monday, she drove 48 miles. On Tuesday, she drove 37 miles. On Thursday, she drove 76 miles. She is reimbursed for gasoline at a rate of 53 cents per mile. Lana wants to determine how many miles per gallon she averaged while traveling. Is there enough information to solve this problem? If not, what information is missing?

Section 12.1 Review

Check Your Understanding

1. What is the difference between the tangible and intangible elements of a brand?
2. Identify functions of labeling.
3. How are perceptions of brand image formed?
4. List three types of product brands.
5. Which product brand type is likely the most familiar to consumers?

Build Your Vocabulary

As you progress through this text, develop a personal glossary of key terms. This will help you build your vocabulary and prepare you for a career. Write a definition for each of the following terms and add them to your personal glossary.

brand name
brand promise
generic brand
jingle
logo
metaphor

national brand
perception
private-label brand
tagline
trade character

Section 12.2

Brand Identity and Protection

Essential Question

How can brand identity influence consumer buying decisions?

Learning Objectives

LO 12.2-1 Explain brand identity.
LO 12.2-2 Define branding strategies.
LO 12.2-3 Identify ways in which a company can protect its brand.

Key Terms

brand identity
brand equity
brand loyalty
branding strategy
brand extension
co-branding
brand licensing
intellectual property
trademark
service mark

LO 12.2-1 Brand Identity

Brand identity is the way in which a business wants to be perceived by customers. While many factors impact a customer's opinion of the brand, the brand identity is what the company wants the customer to think and the image it tries to project through its marketing efforts. Examples of the most well-known and valuable brands, listed in Figure 12-1, have strong brand identities.

The true power of a brand lies in its ability to influence purchasing behavior. **Brand equity** is the value of having a well-known brand name. The brand equity of companies like Disney and Ford is priceless. Branding helps promote products to increase sales. Marketers hope their branding efforts will achieve the following goals:
- create a unique brand identity;
- contribute to the positive image of the brand; and
- inspire brand loyalty and repeat sales.

Most Valuable Brands

Rank	Brand	Brand Value ($ billions)	Industry
1	Apple	154.1	Technology
2	Google	82.5	Technology
3	Microsoft	75.2	Technology
4	Coca-Cola	58.5	Beverages
5	Facebook	52.6	Technology
6	Toyota	42.1	Automotive
7	IBM	41.4	Technology
8	Disney	39.5	Leisure
9	McDonald's	39.1	Restaurants
10	GE	36.7	Diversified

Source: Forbes Media LLC; Goodheart-Willcox Publisher

Figure 12-1 A strong brand identity can be an invaluable asset for the success of a business.

Unique Brand

Many companies use product features to sell a product. However, product features can easily be copied by the competition and are rarely unique. Recall that a *benefit* is the ability of a product to satisfy a need. In order to make a brand stand out from the competition, it is important to learn which product benefits are valued by customers in different target markets. Marketing research plays a large part in creating unique brand identity.

The key to a unique brand is creating products and promotions that appeal to the needs and wants of the target market. For example, most computers have fast processing capabilities. That feature is common. However, some customers want fast processing for online video gaming. Other customers need a computer for word processing, creating spreadsheets, and online research. Depending on the target market, the computer promotions will focus on different benefits.

Positive Brand Image

Developing a unique brand does not always translate into a positive brand image. Recall that a positive brand image is tied directly to customer perception. Businesses want their brands perceived in a positive light in order to keep sales growing.

One way to accomplish this goal is to align the brand with a positive message. *Corporate social responsibility* is the actions of a business to further social good. It goes beyond the profit interests and legal requirements of a business. Examples include donating to nonprofits, recycling, or supporting a cause like cancer research. The brand of a company reflects its image in the community. For this reason, many companies visibly participate in community and charitable events. For example, Sony Pictures partners with nonprofits and other organizations that promote environmental causes. Among others, Sony donates to and encourages employees to participate in Habitat for Humanity, Special Olympics, and the "Arts for All" initiative.

Some large corporations buy the *naming rights* for sports stadiums, convention centers, and other public places to show their support for a community. In these cases, a corporation makes a financial investment in exchange for the privilege of having its name on a structure accessible to the public for a defined period of time. Displaying the corporation's name in this way promotes its brand as one that supports the economic well-being of the region. It is hoped that people attending events at the venue will perceive the company positively. This positive image may lead some people to think of the corporation and their products when the need arises.

Brand Loyalty

Research has shown that it costs four times as much to attract a new customer as it does to keep an existing one. **Brand loyalty** is customer dedication to a certain brand of product. If that brand is not available, the customer will search elsewhere for it or choose not to buy the product at all. Brand-loyal customers are the best customers because they make repeat purchases.

Brand loyalty occurs when a good, service, or business consistently meets customer needs and expectations. This creates a strong relationship between the customer and the brand. A unique brand with a positive image may impact brand loyalty. However, customer experience with the

Green Marketing

Sustainable Packaging

A company's brand takes physical form through product packaging. Marketers understand that packaging choices might affect consumer buying behavior. Using sustainable packaging appeals to environmentally conscious consumers and can contribute to a positive brand image. Sustainable packaging:
- is designed to reduce the amount of material used;
- uses recycled and/or recyclable materials;
- uses biodegradable and compostable materials; and
- is safe and healthy for people and the environment throughout its life cycle.

Using sustainable product packaging demonstrates a company's commitment to going green and efforts to be socially responsible.

brand is the main factor in brand loyalty. For example, some people will only buy a General Motors (GM) car because they have had a positive experience with GM vehicles. Others may never consider buying a GM car due to their own negative experiences or perceptions of GM.

If customers have any type of negative experience, the chance for a repeat purchase drops drastically. Customers who receive poor service at a certain restaurant are much less likely to return, for example. People who have had bad experiences with a product or company often discuss their dissatisfaction with other people. Negative perceptions about a brand can spread quickly through word-of-mouth, and they become hard to change. Excellent customer service is vital for brand loyalty. Any negative experiences must be turned around to keep customers satisfied.

Rob Crandall/Shutterstock.com

Whole Foods Market is an example of a company with many loyal customers. *Why might a consumer become loyal to a brand?*

LO 12.2-2 Branding Strategies

A **branding strategy** is a plan to develop a brand in a way that supports the goals of the business. A business that has developed a recognizable brand can maximize opportunity for growth by positioning its brand to create a new customer experience. Some strategies used are brand extension, co-branding, and brand licensing.

Brand Extension

Brand extension is the practice of using an established brand name on different products in a product mix. For example, Ralph Lauren was known for its Polo brand of clothing. They extended the Ralph Lauren brand to market a line of linens, including bath towels and bed sheets. The Ralph Lauren brand was already well established and successful in the clothing market. Therefore, the business expected their customers would assume the linens with the same brand would be of the same high quality as the clothing they were accustomed to buying. The strategy worked, and the Ralph Lauren brand is now on other items, such as furniture and home décor, in addition to linens.

Extending a brand creates new marketing opportunities, which can lead to higher sales and profit for the company. Customers who were not interested in the brand before might be interested in the new products. However, brand extension does come with risks. This practice may cause the brand to appear stretched too thin. Using the brand on too many products or products that are unrelated to the original can cause the brand to lose customer appeal. In addition, if a brand is extended to a new product and that product fails, the entire brand could suffer.

Co-branding

Co-branding combines the products of one or more manufacturers in the creation of a product. This strategy works well when the two companies who are introducing the co-branded product have a high level of brand recognition.

For example, the home-furnishing store Pottery Barn noticed its customers asking questions about the wall paint colors used in its advertisements. The company decided to partner with a well-known paint company, Sherwin-Williams, to market an exclusive line of paint colors that match Pottery Barn products. The paint colors carry the brand recognition of both companies. Pottery Barn customers can browse the exclusive Sherwin-Williams shades on the Pottery Barn website. At the same time, Sherwin-Williams customers can see the exclusive shades wherever Sherwin-Williams paints are sold. Pottery Barn and Sherwin-Williams have also extended this co-branding strategy to include Pottery Barn Kids, PB Teen, and West Elm, other Pottery Barn brands aimed at different target markets.

Brand Licensing

Brand licensing is the practice of leasing a brand name for use by another business under the specifications of an agreement. For example, when Apple first created the iPod, it needed accessories. Rather than create speakers and other peripherals on its own, Apple (the licensor) extended a licensing agreement to Bose (the licensee). Bose created a Bose Sound System with an iPod docking station. In return, Bose paid royalty to Apple for the use of their brand.

As with other branding strategies, extending a branding license to another company does have risks. Failure to understand the agreement or its terms can be an issue for both parties. In addition, more than one brand can give a customer a reason not to buy. In the previous example, if a customer wanted to purchase an iPod but did not want to purchase a Bose product, the customer might choose to not buy a Bose brand docking station *or* an Apple iPod.

Brand Protection
LO 12.2-3

A brand is only valuable if competitors cannot copy it. In business, a brand is considered the intellectual property of its owner and should be protected from theft. **Intellectual property** is something that comes from a person's mind, such as an idea, invention, or process. Certain intellectual-property laws protect the unique phrases, symbols, and designs associated with brands. Many companies also choose to protect their brands by registering them with the United States Patent and Trademark Office (USPTO).

Trademarks and Service Marks

A **trademark** protects taglines, names, graphics, symbols, or any unique method used to identify a product or company. A **service mark** is similar to a trademark, but it identifies a service rather than a product. Trademarks and service marks do not protect the product itself from theft. They only protect the ways in which the product is identified. The symbols ™ for trademark and ℠ for service mark can be used without USPTO registration.

Trademark Registration

Ownership of all intellectual property, including brands, is implied. However, registering the trademark or service mark with the USPTO is recommended for increased protection. Once a trademark or service mark has been registered, the symbol ® can be used with the mark, as shown in Figure 12-2. These symbols notify the public that the creator claims exclusive rights to the brand and its use.

Generic terms cannot be registered trademarks. For example, the words *disposable facial tissue* cannot be trademarked, but the brand name *Kleenex* can be. A generic phrase can be part of a trademarked name, but it cannot be the sole name. *Corn flakes* is a generic term to describe a type of breakfast cereal. The phrase *corn flakes* cannot be trademarked, but a phrase such as *Kellogg's Corn Flakes* that uses the company's name can be trademarked.

Many people use current brand names in place of generic product categories. One brand may become so powerful it replaces the generic

Social Media

Social-Media Analytics

Metrics are ways to measure the effectiveness of marketing activities. *Social-media analytics* is gathering information from social-media activities. It is important for a marketer to measure the returns from using social media as a tool. There are programs available that measure how many responses are received from an activity, how many dollars are being generated, and other important information that helps determine if the investment of time and money has been productive. Google Analytics is an example of a tool that helps measure the outcomes of social media. For example, when using this program, a marketer can view reports on who the audience is, find out how customers who interact with you on social media behave, and determine if your social-media marketing is meeting your goals.

Correct Usage of Trademark Symbols

Symbol	Meaning
™	Trademark, not registered
SM	Service mark, not registered
®	Registered trademark

Goodheart-Willcox Publisher

Figure 12-2 Graphic marks are symbols that indicate legal protection of intellectual property.

be used by anyone. Many now-familiar generic names began as trademarked brand names, such as aspirin, granola, and zipper.

Most companies want to protect their brands and the investments made in them. Losing trademark protection is not desirable. To help distinguish the brand from the generic category and maintain legal protection, marketers often use the word *brand* along with the name. For example, Band-Aid is often advertised as "Band-Aid brand bandages."

category name. The Ziploc brand name has replaced the category name *resealable storage bags*. Another example of a powerful brand is Google. Most people now refer to using an Internet search engine as *googling*. This is evidence that the company has created a very powerful brand. Other examples include Band-Aid, Styrofoam, and Xerox. The generic usage of the name attests to the popularity of the brand. This brand is sometimes said to have become *genericized*.

However, there are drawbacks to the brand name becoming a generic name for a general class of product. When this happens, the brand no longer has legal trademark protection and can

Keith Homan/Shutterstock.com

The usage of a brand name as a general product category attests to the popularity of the brand, such as Ziploc plastic bags. *Why do you think a company might not want their brand to become genericized?*

Section 12.2 Review

Check Your Understanding

1. What is the key to a unique brand?
2. How can a company develop a positive brand image?
3. What are the benefits and risks of brand extension?
4. What is the difference between a trademark and a service mark?
5. What is a benefit of registering a trademark?

Build Your Vocabulary

As you progress through this text, develop a personal glossary of key terms. This will help you build your vocabulary and prepare you for a career. Write a definition for each of the following terms and add them to your personal glossary.

brand equity
brand extension
brand identity
branding strategy
brand licensing

brand loyalty
co-branding
intellectual property
service mark
trademark

CHAPTER 12 Review and Assessment

Chapter Summary

Section 12.1 Product Branding

LO 12.1-1 Describe elements of a brand.
Brands are created through both tangible and intangible elements. Tangible elements of a brand can be seen and heard and are often the first experience a consumer has with a product. These include the product name, graphic design elements, packaging, and tagline or slogan. Intangible elements of a brand include customer expectations, their feelings about the brand, as well as their direct interactions with it. These elements include the implied promise of the brand, the consistency of the brand, and customer perceptions of the brand image.

LO 12.1-2 Describe three types of product brands.
Three types of product brands are national, private label, and generic. A national brand is created by a manufacturer for its own products. Private-label brands are products owned by and created specifically for large retailers. A generic brand is a consumer product that lacks a widely recognized name or logo.

Section 12.2 Brand Identity and Protection

LO 12.2-1 Explain brand identity.
Brand identity is the way in which a business wants to be perceived by customers. Branding efforts should create a unique brand identity, contribute to the positive image of the brand, and inspire brand loyalty and repeat sales. In developing a unique brand identity, businesses create products and promotions that appeal to the needs and wants of the target market. Aligning the brand with a positive message helps brands to be perceived in a positive light. Brand loyalty occurs when a brand consistently meets customer needs and expectations.

LO 12.2-2 Define branding strategies.
A branding strategy is a plan to develop a brand in a way that supports the goals of the business. Brand extension is the practice of using an established brand name on different products in a product mix. Co-branding combines the products of one or more manufacturers in the creation of a product. Brand licensing is the practice of leasing a brand name for use by another business under the specifications of an agreement.

LO 12.2-3 Identify ways in which a company can protect its brand.
A brand is only valuable if competitors cannot copy it. Certain intellectual-property laws protect the unique phrases, symbols, and designs associated with brands. Trademarks and service marks do not protect the product itself from theft; however, they protect the ways in which the product is identified. Many companies also choose to protect their brands by registering them with the United States Patent and Trademark Office (USPTO).

Check Your Marketing IQ

Now that you have completed the chapter, see what you have learned about marketing by taking the chapter posttest. The posttest is available at www.g-wlearning.com/marketing/.

Review Your Knowledge

1. Describe elements of a brand.
2. Explain brand promise as an intangible brand element.
3. Define three types of product brands.
4. How are generic brands different from national and private-label brands?
5. Explain brand identity.
6. What goals do marketers hope their branding efforts will achieve?

7. Define three branding strategies.
8. Identify ways in which a company can protect its brand.
9. Identify the symbols used for trademark and service mark.
10. Explain why a company would not want its brand name to become a generic term.

Apply Your Knowledge

1. Describe the tangible elements of the brand of the company you have selected, including its name, graphic design elements, packaging, and tagline or slogan.
2. Evaluate the company's packaging and labeling strategies. How do they contribute to the brand and the company image?
3. What types of branding decisions have been made for the company? Do you believe they will be effective? Do you have recommendations to improve the brand and image?
4. What is the company's brand promise? Describe what customers expect when they purchase a good or service from the company's brand.
5. Assume you are a marketer for a company that provides a consumer service. Write two metaphors for that service that could be used in promotions.
6. It is important for marketers to know the general perception of the company's brand among the customer base. How would you go about learning about the perceptions of your customers?
7. As a marketer, how could the branding of your company's products help you make decisions about the three other Ps?
8. Describe how your company uses the branding strategies of brand extension, co-branding, or brand licensing. Think of three new possible ways your company could employ these branding strategies to reach its business goals.
9. Think about the brand loyalty for the products you market. What does the company currently do to develop brand loyalty? How could you increase brand loyalty for your products?
10. Is any part of the company brand trademarked? Describe the process for trademarking a part or all of the tangible parts of your company brand.

Apply Your Math Skills

Without the expenses of branding and advertising, generic brands cost less than brand-name products and often appeal to value-conscious consumers. Apply your math skills to solve the following problems.

1. While preparing an office supply order, Curtis noticed the price difference between brand-name and generic dry-erase markers. A four pack of brand-name dry-erase markers costs $7.00, while the generic equivalent costs $4.50. Curtis ordered 10 packages of the generic dry-erase markers. How much did Curtis save by ordering 10 packages of the generic dry-erase markers instead of the brand-name product?
2. Nina is the marketing manager for a local grocery store. She regularly reviews company sales figures to evaluate the effectiveness of marketing activities. Over the last year, Nina tracked sales of generic brands and found that $450,000 of the total product revenue came from generic brands. The company's total annual product revenue is $3,000,000. What percentage of revenue can be attributed to generic brands?

Communication Skills

College and Career Readiness

Reading After you have read this chapter, determine the central idea and analyze its development over the course of the chapter. How is it shaped or refined by details? Review the major arguments or points made by the author and provide an objective summary of the chapter.

Writing Writing that is objective is free of personal feelings, prejudices, or interpretations. Write a paragraph about the importance of branding to a company's marketing strategies that only uses objective statements or language.

Listening Your purpose for listening varies depending on whether you are in a personal conversation, listening to a group discussion, or a member in a large audience. What was your purpose for listening to your instructor present this lesson today? Was it because you have to, needed to learn the material for a test, or other reasons? When you listen with purpose, you get more out of the information that is being presented.

Internet Research

History of Labeling Using the Internet, conduct a search for the phrase *history of product labeling*. Research the historical events that have brought about food and drug labeling laws in the United States and around the world. Cite examples of how and why changes have been made to product labels over the course of history.

Branding Strategies Select a brand that interests you and conduct Internet research on the company's branding strategies. How do you think the branding strategies used helped develop the image of the company or brand? Summarize your research findings.

Rebranding Using the Internet, research a product or company that was rebranded. Describe the motivation for rebranding and how the rebranding was executed. Was the outcome positive? If so, describe the positive changes that occurred. If not, is there evidence that points to why the rebranding attempt failed?

Teamwork

Working with a partner, identify brands with which you are familiar in a newspaper or magazine. Select several examples and create a poster to show how the different brands are represented. What did you learn from this experience? Share your project with the class.

Portfolio Development

College and Career Readiness

Soft Skills Employers and colleges review various qualities of candidates. For example, the ability to communicate effectively, get along with customers and coworkers, and solve problems are important skills for many jobs. These types of skills are called soft skills. Make an effort to learn about and develop the soft skills needed for your chosen career field.

1. Conduct research about soft skills and their value in helping people succeed.
2. Create a Microsoft Word document and list the soft skills important for a job or career that you currently possess. Use the heading "Soft Skills" and your name. For each soft skill, write a paragraph that describes your abilities. Provide examples to illustrate your skills. Save the document.
3. Update your master spreadsheet.

UNIT 4 Product

Building the Marketing Plan

Without products to sell, there would be no businesses. As the marketing manager for your company, you must decide not only what products or services to offer, but why yours are better than those sold by the competition. Describing your products and their competitive advantages is an important part of the marketing plan. Marketers help create solid, positive brand identities to ensure the success of the business.

Part 1 Product

Objectives

- List the products or services offered by your business.
- Complete a features and benefits chart for each one.
- Determine the unique selling proposition (USP) for each one.

Directions

In this activity, you will begin the Product Strategies portion of the Marketing Mix subsection, which appears in the Marketing Strategies section of the marketing plan. Access the *Marketing Dynamics* companion website at www.g-wlearning.com/marketing/. Download the activity file as indicated in the following instructions.

1. **Unit Activity 4-1—Product** Describe the products or services your business will offer. Discuss the features and benefits for each and write your unique selling proposition (USP).

2. Open your saved marketing plan document.

3. Locate the Marketing Mix subsection under Marketing Strategies and start the Product Strategies section. Use the suggestions and questions listed in the marketing plan template to help you generate ideas. Delete the instructions and questions when you are finished recording your responses. Proofread your document and correct any errors in keyboarding, spelling, and grammar.

4. Save your document.

Part 2 Branding

Objectives

- Describe the brand and show the tangible brand elements.
- Explain how the current branding strategy supports the products or company.
- Make recommendations for improving the branding strategy.

Directions

In this activity, you will complete the portion of the Marketing Strategies section that describes your Product Strategies. Access the *Marketing Dynamics* companion website at www.g-wlearning.com/marketing/. Download the activity file as indicated in the following instructions.

1. **Unit Activity 4-2—Branding** Analyze the branding strategies that are currently in place for your products or company, and recommend ways to improve the branding program for a stronger brand identity.

2. Open your saved marketing plan document.

3. Locate the Marketing Mix subsection under Marketing Strategies and complete the portion under Product Strategies that relates to branding. Use the suggestions and questions listed in the marketing plan template to help you generate ideas. Delete the instructions and questions when you are finished recording your responses. Proofread your document and correct any errors in keyboarding, spelling, and grammar.

4. Save your document.

UNIT 5 Price

Chapters

13 **Price**
14 **Pricing Product**

While studying, look for the activity icon ↗ for:
- Building the Marketing Plan activity files
- Pretests and posttests
- Vocabulary terms with e-flash cards and matching activities
- Self-assessment

These activities can be accessed at www.g-wlearning.com/marketing/.

Developing a Vision

Price—what does it mean? To one buyer, it may mean *value*. For other buyers, it may mean *quality*. To one seller, price may mean *profit*. To other sellers, it may mean *competition*. There is no single answer. Price has different meanings to everyone depending on their situations.

For a marketer, creating the correct pricing model that is effective for both buyers and sellers is a challenge. Marketers must study economic conditions to create realistic pricing structures. Product life cycles must be considered. Government regulations must also be followed. Pricing is a complicated task for even the most experienced marketing professionals.

Marketing Core Functions Covered in This Unit

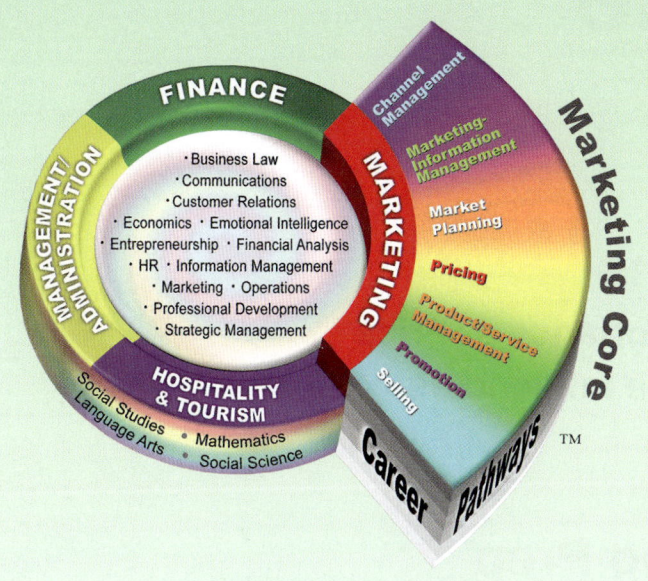

Functions of Marketing
- Market planning
- Pricing
- Selling

Copyright MBA Research, Columbus, Ohio. Used with permission.

EYE-CATCHER

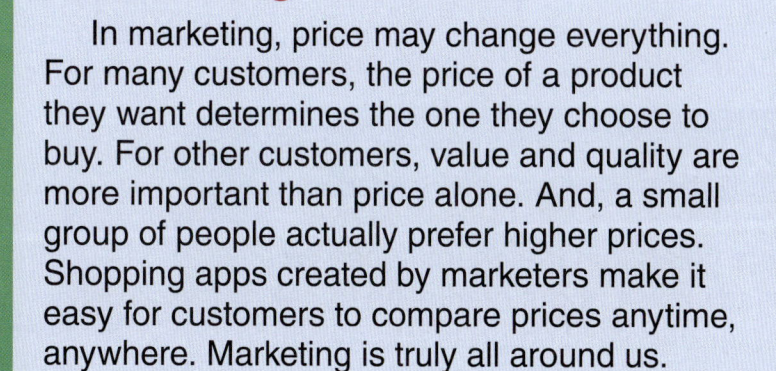

Marketing Matters

In marketing, price may change everything. For many customers, the price of a product they want determines the one they choose to buy. For other customers, value and quality are more important than price alone. And, a small group of people actually prefer higher prices. Shopping apps created by marketers make it easy for customers to compare prices anytime, anywhere. Marketing is truly all around us.

Zapp2Photo/Shutterstock.com

CHAPTER 13 Price

Sections

13.1 **Importance of Price**
13.2 **Price Influencers**

Reading Prep

College and Career Readiness

As you read this chapter, take notes on the important points you want to remember. Record key terms and important concepts. Is this helpful in understanding the material?

Check Your Marketing IQ

Before you begin the chapter, see what you already know about marketing by taking the chapter pretest. The pretest is available at www.g-wlearning.com/marketing/.

◇DECA Emerging Leaders

Food Marketing Series Event, Part 1

Career Cluster: Marketing
Career Pathway: Marketing Management
Instructional Area: Pricing

Knowledge and Skills Developed

- communication and collaboration
- creativity and innovation
- critical thinking and problem solving
- flexibility and adaptability
- information literacy
- initiative and self-direction
- leadership and responsibility
- productivity and accountability
- social and cross-cultural skills

Specific Performance Indicators

- Explain the nature and scope of the pricing function.
- Describe the role of business ethics in pricing.
- Explain the use of technology in the pricing function.
- Describe factors used by marketers to position products/businesses.
- Explain factors affecting pricing decisions.

Purpose

Designed for an individual DECA member, the event measures the member's proficiency in the knowledge, skills, and attitudes in the business administration core and appropriate career cluster and pathway of a given career in a role-play. This event consists of a 100-question, multiple-choice, cluster exam and two role-play activities in a written scenario.

Participants are not informed in advance of the performance indicators to be evaluated. For the purpose of this textbook, sample performance indicators are given so that you may practice for the competition.

For the purposes of this text, you will be presented with the material for this event in two parts. Part 1 presents the knowledge and skills assessed and an overview of the event's purpose and procedure. Part 2 presents the remaining procedures and the event situation.

Procedure, Part 1

1. For Part 1 in this text, read both Knowledge and Skills Developed and Specific Performance Indicators. Discuss these with your team members.
2. If there are any questions, ask your instructor to clarify.

Critical Thinking

1. List responses to each performance indicator. In what areas do you need additional information?
2. Anticipate the role you might assume in food marketing based on the performance indicators. What questions might be asked about pricing?
3. How will you respond to the questions?

Visit www.deca.org for more information.

Published by DECA Inc. Copyright © by DECA Inc. No part of this publication may be reproduced for resale without written permission from the publisher. Printed in the United States of America.

Section 13.1

Importance of Price

Essential Question
How does a marketer determine the price of a product?

Learning Objectives
LO 13.1-1 Explain price as one of the four Ps of marketing.
LO 13.1-2 Identify two categories of pricing objectives.

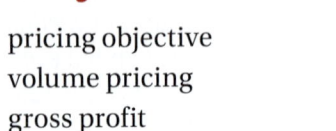

Key Terms
pricing objective
volume pricing
gross profit
return on investment (ROI)
net profit
total assets
break-even point

LO 13.1-1 Price

Price is the amount of money requested or exchanged for a product. The pricing function of marketing handles all activities involved in setting acceptable prices for product.

A primary focus of marketing is to set prices that will help the company increase sales and profits. Every business faces the challenge of correctly setting the prices of goods and services. The price of a product:
- must cover the costs of producing and selling the product;
- should generate the desired level of profit for the business; and
- must be what customers are willing to pay for the product.

As you learned earlier, the decisions marketers make about a marketing mix influence each other. When a decision is made about one of the four Ps, there is a ripple effect among the other components of the mix. Pricing decisions influence those made about product, place, and promotion. And, the decisions made about product, place, and promotion affect pricing decisions.

Syda Productions/Shutterstock.com

Price is the amount of money requested or exchanged for a product. *How do you evaluate whether the price for a product is reasonable?*

Decisions made about product, place, and promotion can be difficult to change after the marketing mix has been determined. Pricing, however, can be easily changed to meet the competition or address changes in the economy. The setting of prices typically follows the four-step pricing process in Figure 13-1.

Price-Setting Process

- Establish pricing objectives
- Determine costs
- Analyze product demand
- Evaluate the competition

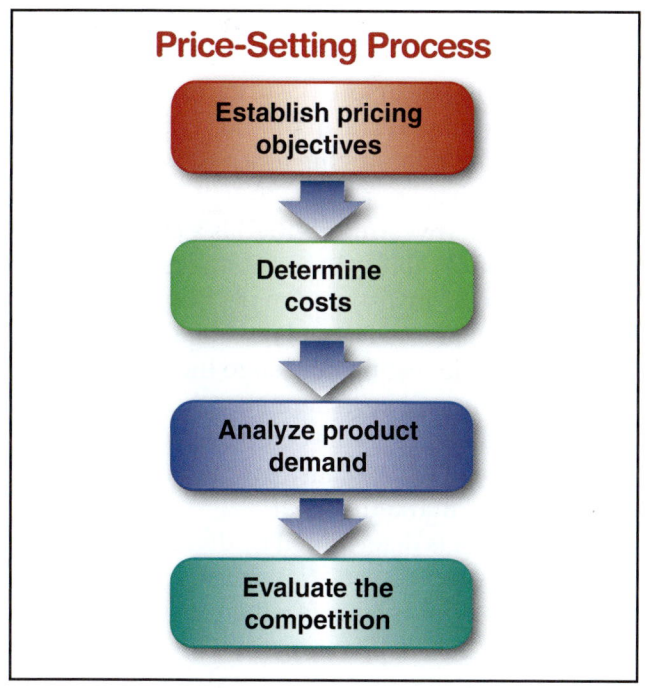

Goodheart-Willcox Publisher

Figure 13-1 Setting prices typically follows these four steps.

LO 13.1-2 Pricing Objectives

An important part of the marketing plan is to create pricing objectives. The price of a product plays a major role in determining whether both the product and the company are successful. **Pricing objectives** are goals defined in the business and marketing plans for the overall pricing policies of the company. Pricing objectives may be based on both short- and long-term company goals.

Pricing objectives often change and are revised regularly. The price must be at a level that encourages customers to purchase the product in addition to generating profits for the business. Pricing objectives typically fall under one of two categories: maximize sales or maximize profit.

Maximize Sales

Maximizing sales is a pricing objective based on offering the lowest price possible to get the

Exploring Marketing Careers

Trade Show Manager

Have you ever been to a trade show or exhibition? These huge gatherings allow companies to show the public—especially prospective customers—their latest products. Companies purchase booth space to showcase and even demonstrate their wares. Organizing these enormous events is the job of the trade show manager. Coordinating everything from the location of the event to the logistics of how to get all the companies' products into the exhibit area, a good trade show manager is critical to the success of the event. Typical job titles for these positions include *trade show manager*, *events manager*, *conference manager*, *conference planner*, and *director of events*.

Some examples of tasks that trade show managers perform include:
- Inspect the event facility to make sure it offers everything needed for the trade show
- Meet with the staff at the chosen location to work out details of the event
- Monitor event activities to make sure they comply with all applicable laws and ordinances
- Ensure the safety and security of the exhibits and all people, including participants, vendors, and the public
- Arrange for any equipment and services needed by the participants, such as electricity, monitors or other display devices, tables, and chairs

Trade show managers need excellent organizational skills. They must be able to understand the requirements for a show or event and coordinate all of the detailed tasks needed to make it successful. In addition, they must have good management skills. In most cases, a four-year bachelor degree is required to be a trade show manager, although a highly experienced applicant may be accepted without a degree. Knowledge and skills related to trade shows may also be required. On-the-job training is sometimes offered. For more information, access the *Occupational Outlook Handbook* online.

Maximizing sales is based on offering the lowest price possible to get the largest number of customers to buy a product. *What actions have you seen businesses take to try to maximize sales?*

Lutya/Shutterstock.com

largest number of customers to buy a product. There are different ways this can be accomplished. Two ways are to increase market share and establish volume pricing.

Recall that *market share* is the percentage of total sales in a market held by one business. Increasing market share by gaining more customers is one way to maximize sales. For example, a marketing goal might be to increase market share from 10 percent to 13 percent. In order to increase market share, the company has to find additional customers. A business might lower prices, offer discount coupons, or use other incentives to attract more customers.

Volume pricing is lowering the list price of a product based on a higher number of units purchased at the same time, as shown in Figure 13-2. Lower prices generally lead to increased sales. The strategy behind volume pricing is to give the buyer a price incentive to purchase more at one time and receive the per-item discount.

Maximize Profit

Gross profit is the amount of profit before subtracting the costs of doing business. Maximizing profit is a pricing objective that means generating as much revenue as possible in relation to total cost. A business charges the highest price customers will pay before the price exceeds the value for customers. The high-end jewelry industry is one in which maximizing profit per sale is the pricing objective.

Return on investment (ROI) is a common measure of profitability based on the amount earned from the investment made in the business. ROI is expressed as a percentage. The better a company is at investing in itself to increase profit, the more profit will be generated. A high ROI typically indicates a profitable company. Marketers are always aware of ROI because profitability is both a corporate and marketing goal.

Simple ROI is determined by dividing net profit after taxes by total assets. **Net profit**, sometimes called *net income*, is what is left after all company expenses are subtracted from total revenue. Everything the company owns is its **total assets**.

net profit after taxes ÷ total assets = ROI

For example, if a business has a net profit after taxes of $50,000 and assets of $150,000, the ROI is 33 percent.

$50,000 ÷ $150,000 = .33
.33 × 100 = 33%

A product starts making profit after the revenue it generates reaches the break-even point. The **break-even point** is the point at which revenue from sales equals the costs. It is often expressed as the number of items that must be sold to recover the money spent to create or buy them. When this point is reached, the company is not losing or making money, it is breaking even. Any revenue made from sales after the break-even

Volume Pricing

Price per Item	Number Purchased	Total Sale	Volume-Pricing Savings
Up to 12: $9.99	10	$99.90	0
13–36: $8.99	30	$269.70	$30.00
37–74: $7.99	50	$399.50	$100.00
75–100: $6.99	100	$699.00	$300.00

Goodheart-Willcox Publisher

Figure 13-2 Volume pricing is lowering the list price of a product based on a higher number of units purchased at the same time.

Case in Point

Microsoft

Many consumers continue to use their favorite products because the products are familiar and keep the consumers in their comfort zones. In order for a company to keep product sales up, marketers may suggest newer versions of the products. It is up to the marketers to craft campaigns that convince consumers to trade up to the newer version or model of a product they already own.

The Microsoft marketing mix is a good example of how to convince consumers it is time to switch—by making a great introductory offer. Microsoft released a new operating system, Windows 10, in July 2015. To encourage existing Windows users to upgrade right away, Microsoft offered a *promotional price* to grab the attention of PC owners. It offered free upgrade licenses for users currently operating eligible editions of Windows 7 and 8. However, the offer was available to the general public only for one year after the product release. After that time, anyone who wanted to upgrade to Windows 10 would have to pay the retail price of $119 (Home Edition). Was the promotional offer the key to success? Maybe. It was reported that after nine months of sales, Windows 10 captured 30 percent of the market.

---

point is profit. The break-even point formula is as follows.

$$\frac{\text{cost} \times \text{number of units}}{\text{selling price}} = \text{break-even point}$$

For example, a business ordered 100 units of the newest-model lawn mower to include in that product line. Each lawn mower costs the business $140. The pricing plan is to sell the mowers for $250 each. By following the formula, 56 lawn mowers would need to be sold just to reach the break-even point.

$$\frac{\$140 \text{ cost} \times 100 \text{ units}}{\$250 \text{ selling price}} = \text{56 units is the break-even point}$$

Marketers must be able to calculate the break-even point of their products in order to price them correctly, forecast sales, and estimate potential profit. A change in the selling price directly affects the forecasted sales numbers, the break-even analysis, and expected profits.

Section 13.1 Review

Check Your Understanding

1. Describe the pricing function of marketing.
2. What three goals must a price meet if it has been set correctly?
3. Name the two categories that pricing objectives typically fall under.
4. State the formula for return on investment (ROI).
5. State the formula for break-even point.

Build Your Vocabulary

As you progress through this text, develop a personal glossary of key terms. This will help you build your vocabulary and prepare you for a career. Write a definition for each of the following terms and add them to your personal glossary.

break-even point
gross profit
net profit
pricing objective
return on investment (ROI)
total assets
volume pricing

Section 13.2

Price Influencers

Essential Question
Why is it important for marketers to understand factors that influence price?

Learning Objectives

LO 13.2-1 Summarize the influence of demand on price.
LO 13.2-2 State the influence of costs on price.
LO 13.2-3 Explain the influence of competition on price.
LO 13.2-4 Discuss how customer perception and the product life cycle influence price.

Key Terms

demand-based pricing
elastic demand
marginal utility
law of diminishing marginal utility
inelastic demand
fixed expense
variable expense
cost-based pricing
markup
base price
keystone pricing
competition-based pricing

LO 13.2-1 Influence of Demand on Price

The principle of supply and demand is critical to business because it determines the price of goods and services. *Supply* is the quantity of goods available for purchase. *Demand* is the quantity of goods that consumers want to purchase.

The law of supply and demand is tied directly to price, as shown in Figure 13-3. When demand is high and the supply is low, marketers usually raise prices. Customers are willing to pay higher prices for products they really want. When demand is low and supply is high, marketers usually lower prices to increase sales. Customers are often more willing to buy a product when the price is low. *Equilibrium* is the point at which the supply equals the demand for the product.

Demand-based pricing is a pricing strategy based on the amount customers are willing to pay. It is also called *value-based pricing* and reflects customer perceptions of the value of a product. Demand-based pricing is a short-term pricing strategy. It is most effective when the product is unique in the market or the demand is high.

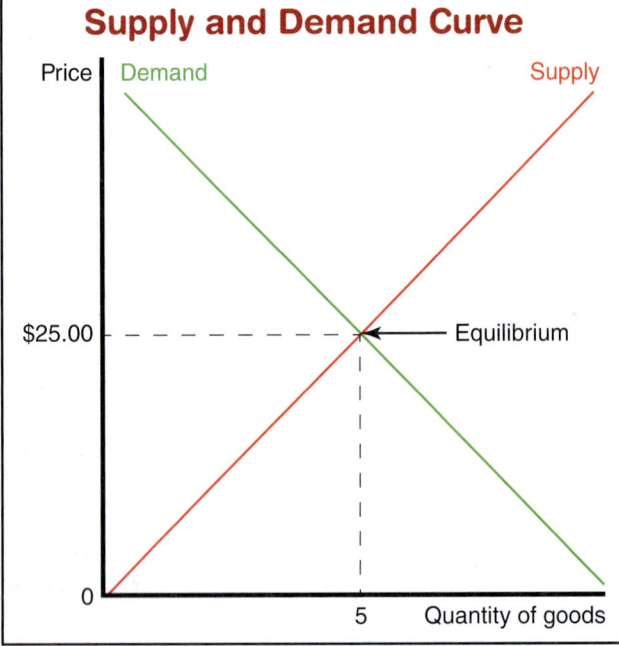

Supply and Demand Curve

Goodheart-Willcox Publisher

Figure 13-3 The principle of supply and demand is critical to business because it determines the prices of goods and services.

Employability Skills

Self-Awareness

Self-awareness is a sense of being aware of one's feelings, behaviors, needs, and other elements that make up the whole person. In order to promote yourself to others, you have to be aware of who you are and what your ultimate goal may be in the organization.

For example, perhaps a local boutique is the only business in the area selling a new line of bracelets popular with preteens. The bracelets can be ordered online for $7 plus $3 shipping for $10 total, but they would not arrive for weeks. However, the local business can charge $12 for the bracelets and earn a higher profit per sale until demand drops.

Price can also affect the demand for some products. Higher prices tend to lower the demand because fewer people can afford the product. In contrast, lower prices tend to raise the demand. For some products, demand is not affected by price. *Demand elasticity* is the degree to which price changes demand. When the demand for products is elastic, the demand changes when the price changes. However, when demand for products tends to remain constant, or is inelastic, demand does *not* change when the price changes.

Elastic Demand

Elastic demand is product demand in which the percent of change in demand is greater than the percent of change in price. Think of a rubber band. A rubber band is elastic; its size changes with the amount of pressure applied. For many products, demand is elastic like a rubber band. The higher the price, the lower the demand.

For example, if the prices of your favorite clothing brand become too high, your demand for that brand will drop. You will buy it less often or not at all. Luxury products that you do not really need tend to have elastic demand. Products that have less expensive substitutes also tend to have elastic demand. For example, if the price of beef goes up, chicken can be substituted. The demand for beef is elastic.

Similarly, when prices of products with elastic demand are lowered, the demand rises. As the price of the product falls, consumers tend to buy more of that product. However, there will come a point at which no matter how low the price, consumers will not buy any more of a product. Even at the lower price, people will not buy any more of the product because they cannot use any more.

Consumers gain satisfaction from a product when it is used. Recall that *utility* defines the characteristics of a product that satisfy human wants and needs. **Marginal utility** is the additional satisfaction gained by using one additional unit of the same product. For example, when you eat an apple, you get satisfaction, or utility. If you eat a second apple, you get a bit more satisfaction, which is its marginal utility. As you continue to eat, you begin to feel full. The second apple does not give you as much satisfaction as the first. If you

Darren Baker/Shutterstock.com

The marginal utility of each apple eaten decreases as the number of apples eaten increases. *When have you experienced the law of diminishing marginal utility?*

continue to eat more apples, each additional one gives you little or no added satisfaction. This is an example of the law of diminishing marginal utility. The **law of diminishing marginal utility** states that consuming more units of the same product decreases the marginal utility from each unit. This law limits the effects of elastic demand on consumer buying behavior.

Inelastic Demand

Inelastic demand is product demand that is *not* affected by price. The demand for certain products does not drop when the prices rise. For example, basic food products, such as milk and bread, have inelastic demand because they are necessities. Medicines also tend to have inelastic demand. People who must take a particular medication daily to stay healthy will find a way to afford the higher price. Their demand remains the same because without the medication, they would become ill. Brand loyalty also can create inelastic demand. Some consumers are loyal to a certain product brand and will not buy another brand, even if it costs less.

Elastic and Inelastic Demand

Some products have both elastic and inelastic demand depending on the situation. For example, perhaps you drive a car to school every day. If the price of gasoline doubles, you may choose to decrease your demand for gasoline by carpooling with other students. In this case, your demand for gasoline is elastic.

However, suppose that you are driving on a limited-access highway and notice that your fuel gauge is on empty. You must pull into the only gas station within 50 miles, but the price of gas at this station is double what you usually pay. You need gas in order to reach your destination and will pay the high price. In this case, your demand for gasoline is inelastic because it is a necessity.

LO 13.2-2 Influence of Costs on Price

There are expenses related to the creation, marketing, and distribution of all products. In addition, there are many costs related to the daily operations of a business. These costs influence the price set for products because a profit is made only after all of the expenses are paid. There are two basic types of expenses: fixed and variable.

A **fixed expense** is a set amount that must be paid on a regular basis, such as monthly or annually. These amounts do not change and are not

Rustic/Shutterstock.com

Basic food products, such as milk, have inelastic demand because they are necessities. *What causes a consumer to purchase an item regardless of its price?*

Marketing Ethics

Going Out of Business Sale

A going out of business sale must be an actual sale due to the fact the business is closing permanently. It is unethical for a business to advertise a going out of business sale to lure customers into their business as an advertising scheme.

affected by the number of products produced or sold. For example, fixed expenses may include rent payments, insurance premiums, and salaries. These amounts stay the same each month.

A **variable expense** is an amount that changes in both the cost and the amount of time it must be paid. These payments are based on the activities of the business. For example, variable expenses might include advertising and sales commissions that may vary month-to-month.

Pricing strategically is a balancing act because both profit and sales goals are important. In order to make a profit, prices must be set high enough to cover the costs. However, if the product is priced too high, customers and sales may be lost. If the price is set too low, the costs related to the products may not be covered, which means the company could lose money.

Cost-based pricing is a strategy that uses the cost of a product to set the selling price. The first step in cost-based pricing is to accurately determine the actual cost of the item for the business. The price of the product must cover the fixed and variable expenses related to a product in order for the company to make a profit. For manufacturers, price has to cover the cost of making goods and marketing them to customers. For retailers, the price has to cover the cost of buying goods and reselling them to consumers.

Markup is the amount added to the cost of a product to determine the base price. The **base price** of a product is the general price at which the company expects to sell the product. The following equation expresses cost-based pricing.

cost + markup = base price

Markup can be expressed as a dollar amount or as a percentage. Percentage markup, keystone pricing, and dollar-markup method are three approaches that may be used.

Percentage-Markup Method

Using a *percentage markup* is the most common way to determine a base price. Management decides the percent of profit necessary for each item. The percentage markup for each product is turned into a dollar figure and added to the cost. Most retail businesses use the percentage-markup method because it guarantees a consistent level of profit. The following formula is used to determine base price when using the percentage-markup method.

(cost × percentage of markup) + cost = base price

In the previous example, the cost for lawn mowers is $140 each. Suppose the company's business model states that it must make a 40 percent profit on all sales. To achieve a 40 percent markup, each $140 lawn mower needs to be priced at $196.

$140 cost × 40% markup = $56
$56 + $140 cost = $196 base price

Keystone-Pricing Method

Keystone pricing is a pricing method in which the total cost of a product is doubled to determine its base price. Many businesses use keystone pricing because it is an easy way to create a 100-percent markup on the cost. The formula for keystone pricing is as follows.

cost × 2 = base price

For example, using the keystone-pricing method, the base price for the $140 lawn mower is $280.

$140 cost × 2 = $280 base price

Dollar-Markup Method

Companies that use the *dollar-markup* method determine a specific dollar amount that must be made, above product costs, for each product sold.

cost + dollar markup = base price

Suppose the company decides it must make $156 after costs on each mower. Using the dollar-markup pricing method, the base price is $296.

$140 cost + $156 dollar markup = $296 base price

LO 13.2-3 Influence of Competition on Price

Researching the product pricing of competitors is an important step in remaining competitive in the market. Marketers understand that price may be the deciding factor for a customer when making a purchase. If the competition offers lower prices, a customer may buy from the competitor because price was the deciding factor. If a business wants to maintain market share, it must be aware of competitor pricing and decide what pricing strategy to use.

Competition-based pricing is a pricing strategy based primarily on what competitors charge. Competition-based pricing does not take into account the cost of producing the product and may not provide enough, or any, profit. The price may be set above, below, or at the competitor's price, depending on the pricing objective. To effectively use a competition-based pricing strategy, marketers monitor the prices of competitors often and propose price adjustments as necessary.

Businesses are always aware of the prices of the competition. A company might decide to match the competition or set prices that are higher or lower than its competitors. The prices of competitors are constantly monitored because they may change. If a competitor suddenly lowers its prices, that could negatively impact sales for the business if it does not respond in some way.

When local competitors are matching prices, sometimes a price war will begin. During a price war, one company lowers its price. When a competitor sees this, it lowers its price on the same product. The original company will then lower its price even more, and so on.

LO 13.2-4 Other Factors That Influence Price

There are many factors that influence the price of a product. Additional factors include customer perception and product life cycle.

Customer Perception

Customers generally look for prices they consider to be reasonable. However, reasonable to one person may not be reasonable to another. Some companies use price to influence customer perception. A value proposition explains the value of the product over others that are similar. Value may also be a part of the brand promise. Customers may be willing to pay more if they believe in the value of the product or service.

Customers have different perceptions when making a purchase and may perceive price to be an indicator of the quality of a product. Sometimes, customers believe that a higher price means a better-quality product, but that is not always the case. The following are three general quality levels.

- *Premium quality* is the highest level of quality available in products. Premium-quality products usually have the highest prices.
- *Moderate quality* is the middle range of product quality. These products usually combine good-quality materials with moderate prices.
- *Value quality* is an adequate level of product quality. Value-quality products are typically functional, but are not made to last a long time.

Have you ever wondered what was wrong with a product because the price was so low? If you said *yes*, then the price of a product influenced your perception of its quality. On the other hand, products also can be priced too highly. When the price of a product is too high, customers may not buy

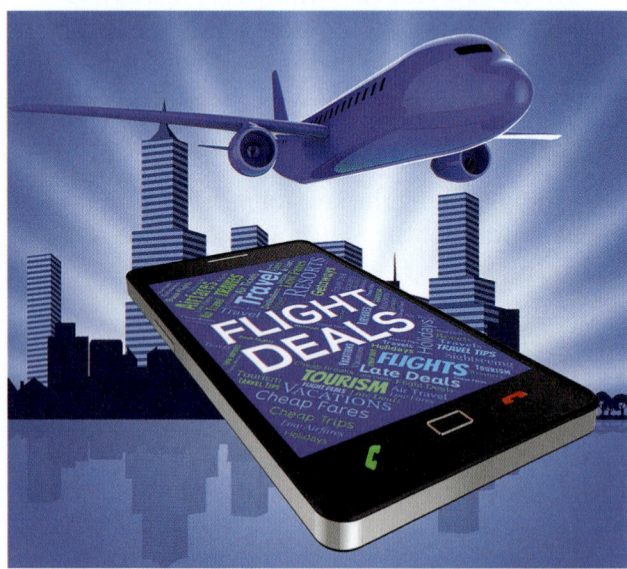

Stuart Miles/Shutterstock.com

Competition-based pricing may be set above, below, or at the competitor's price, depending on the pricing objective. *How does competition-based pricing benefit the customer?*

Chapter 13 Price

Premium quality is the highest level and usually has the highest prices. *What factors might help a customer determine a product's level of quality?*

Radu Bercan/Shutterstock.com

it. Their perception of the product is that it is not worth the money. In this situation, the marketer can lower the price to see if customers will then buy the product.

Customers also look for nonprice factors that may influence the price of a product. Special services, extended warranties, and other non-price issues can convince a customer not to pay a higher price for added amenities.

Product Life Cycle

The stage in the product life cycle affects the pricing of a product. During the introduction stage, the price of a brand-new product is often high. The manufacturer wants to recover some of the costs required to develop the new product. In addition, only one company is usually making the new product. This causes the supply to be low while demand may be high. Some companies may choose to introduce new products at very low prices so people will try the product. After sales of the new product increase, the prices are usually raised.

During the growth stage, more competitors enter the market, and the price of a high-priced, new product usually falls. This is particularly true for technology products, such as computers and smartphones.

During the maturity and decline phases of a product, prices are usually lowered even further. The lower prices help a declining product generate more sales.

You Do the Math

Exponents

Compound interest is *exponential*. This means that previously earned interest itself earns interest in the future. This can be thought of as *interest on interest*. The future value of a balance with compound interest is calculated by multiplying the present value by one plus the annual interest rate taken to the power of the number of terms.

$$FV = PV \times (1 + r)^n$$

In this equation, *FV* is the future value, *PV* is the present value, *r* is the annual interest rate, and *n* is the period of time over which interest is compounded.

Solve the following problems.
1. Susan has placed $10,000 in a certificate of deposit (CD) that earns 3.78 percent interest per year. The term of the CD is three years. How much money will she have at the end of the term?
2. A business owner has taken out a small business loan for $25,000 over a term of five years. The interest rate is 2.9 percent annually. How much interest will have been paid at the end of the loan?
3. A florist needs to purchase a new delivery van. The amount that will be financed is $36,575. The dealership is offering three financing options: 4.9 percent for 48 months, 1.9 percent for 60 months, and 0.9 percent for 72 months. Which option results in the lowest total interest paid?

Section 13.2 Review

Check Your Understanding
1. What is the difference between elastic demand and inelastic demand?
2. State the formula used to determine base price when using the percentage-markup method.
3. State the formula for the keystone-pricing method.
4. How is a price determined when using competition-based pricing?
5. Name three quality levels that are often associated with price.

Build Your Vocabulary
As you progress through this text, develop a personal glossary of key terms. This will help you build your vocabulary and prepare you for a career. Write a definition for each of the following terms and add them to your personal glossary.

base price
competition-based pricing
cost-based pricing
demand-based pricing
elastic demand
fixed expense
inelastic demand
keystone pricing
law of diminishing marginal utility
marginal utility
markup
variable expense

CHAPTER 13 Review and Assessment

Chapter Summary

Section 13.1 Importance of Price

LO 13.1-1 Explain price as one of the four Ps of marketing.
As one of the four Ps of marketing, price is the amount of money requested or exchanged for a product. As a function of marketing, businesses set prices that will help the company increase sales and profits.

LO 13.1-2 Identify two categories of pricing objectives.
Two categories of pricing objectives are to maximize sales and maximize profits. Maximizing sales means offering the lowest price possible to get the largest number of customers to buy a product. Maximizing profit means generating as much revenue as possible in relation to total cost.

Section 13.2 Price Influencers

LO 13.2-1 Summarize the influence of demand on price.
When demand is high and the supply is low, marketers usually raise prices. Customers are willing to pay higher prices for products they really want. When demand is low and supply is high, marketers usually lower prices to increase sales. Customers are often more willing to buy a product when the price is low. Demand elasticity is the degree to which price changes demand. Elastic demand changes when price changes. Inelastic demand does *not* change when the price changes.

LO 13.2-2 State the influence of costs on price.
There are expenses related to the creation, marketing, and distribution of all products. In addition, there are many costs related to the daily operations of a business. These costs influence the price that is set for that product because a profit is made only after all of the expenses are paid.

LO 13.2-3 Explain the influence of competition on price.
Researching the pricing of competitors is an important step in remaining competitive. Marketers understand that price may be the deciding factor for a customer when making a purchase. If the competition offers lower prices, a customer may buy from the competitor. If a business wants to maintain market share, it must be aware of competitor pricing and decide what pricing strategy to use.

LO 13.2-4 Discuss how customer perception and the product life cycle influence price.
Customers may perceive price to be an indicator of the quality of a product. Sometimes, customers believe that a higher price means a better-quality product, but that is not always the case. The stage in the product life cycle also affects the pricing of a product. During introduction, the price of a brand-new product is often high. During growth, more competitors enter the market, and the price usually falls. During maturity and decline, prices are usually lowered even further.

Check Your Marketing IQ

Now that you have completed the chapter, see what you have learned about marketing by taking the chapter posttest. The posttest is available at www.g-wlearning.com/marketing/.

Review Your Knowledge

1. Explain price as one of the four Ps of marketing.
2. Identify two categories of pricing objectives.
3. Summarize the influence of demand on price.
4. What is equilibrium?

5. Explain how some products have both elastic and inelastic demand.
6. State the influence of costs on price.
7. Explain the influence of competition on price.
8. Explain how customer perceptions influence price.
9. What do customers look for in addition to price when deciding what to buy?
10. Discuss how the product life cycle influences price.

Apply Your Knowledge

1. Describe how your company can utilize pricing strategies to maximize return and meet your customers' perception of value.
2. Explain how the other three Ps, product, place, and promotion, might be affected by the pricing decisions made by your business.
3. Assume your company has a pricing objective of maximizing sales by increasing market share. Describe two possible ideas for meeting this objective that relate to the pricing function.
4. Assume your company has a pricing objective of maximizing profit. Describe two possible ideas for meeting this objective that relate to the pricing function.
5. The following factors affect price: company goals, supply and demand, expenses, competition, customer perception, and product life cycle. Critique each factor and explain how you think these factors influence pricing for your products or services.
6. Make a list of the fixed and variable expenses that impact the products or services your business sells.
7. How do you think customers perceive the prices for your products? How does price contribute to your image?
8. How does marginal utility apply to your products?
9. Explain how product, place, and promotion influence the pricing of your products.
10. What nonprice factors of your good or service would entice customers to make a purchase?

Apply Your Math Skills

Emma is a farmer who has begun selling organic honey produced by bees on her farm. She used the following formulas to calculate her profitability.

Percentage-markup pricing:

(cost × percentage of markup) + cost = base price

Keystone pricing:

cost × 2 = base price

Dollar-markup pricing:

cost + dollar markup = base price

Return on investment:

net profit after taxes ÷ total assets = ROI

Break-even point:

$$\frac{\text{cost} \times \text{number of units}}{\text{selling price}} = \text{break-even point}$$

Apply your math skills to solve the following problems.

1. Emma must determine a price for the jars of honey she is going to sell. An 8-oz jar of honey costs $3 to produce, package, and market. Which pricing method would give Emma the highest price?
   A. Percentage-markup pricing with a 50-percent markup.
   B. Keystone pricing.
   C. Dollar-markup pricing with a $4 markup.
2. Emma chose to sell jars of honey using the formula with the highest price in question 1. What is the return on investment for her honey business?
3. Emma's bees made enough honey to produce 280, 8-ounce jars. Use the break-even point formula to calculate how many jars of honey she must sell in order to break even.

Communication Skills

Reading Determine the meaning of the words and phrases used to explain the concepts discussed in this chapter. Different words and phrases might have figurative, connotative, or technical meanings. Analyze the impact of the author's word choices and which ones have figurative, connotative, or technical meanings.

Writing To persuade someone is to attempt to change that person's behavior or influence a course of action. Apply your writing skills by persuading the vice president of marketing to raise the price of a product line. Write a script in a step-by-step format that presents business reasons for increasing the price.

Speaking Participate in a collaborative classroom discussion about the role of supply and demand on pricing. Ask questions as you participate in the discussion. Contribute comments that connect your ideas to the relevant evidence that has been presented by your classmates.

Internet Research

Pricing Mistakes Conduct an Internet search for *mistakes in setting prices*. Select two of the common pricing mistakes that you uncover in your research. Use what you read in this chapter to evaluate why this is a mistake and how it can be corrected.

Competitive Pricing Using the Internet, search for *how to create a competitive pricing strategy*. What kind of suggestions did you find? Write a summary of the information.

Customer Perception Theory Research *customer perception theory* using Internet resources. How can this theory be applied to pricing goals?

Teamwork

Working with a team, compare and contrast the three different pricing methods described in this chapter. Create a chart to make your comparisons. Share your chart with the class.

Portfolio Development

Hard Skills Employers review candidates for various positions and colleges are always looking for qualified applicants. When listing your qualifications, you may discuss software programs you know or machines you can operate. These abilities are often called *hard skills*. Make an effort to learn about and develop the hard skills you will need for your chosen career.

1. Conduct research about hard skills and their value in helping people succeed.
2. Create a Microsoft Word document and list the hard skills that are important for a job or career that currently you possess. Use the heading "Hard Skills" and your name. For each hard skill, write a paragraph that describes your abilities. Provide examples to illustrate your skills. Save the document.
3. Update your master spreadsheet.

CHAPTER 14

Pricing Product

Sections

14.1 **Pricing Strategies**
14.2 **Governmental Influence on Pricing**

Reading Prep

College and Career Readiness

Before reading this chapter, go to the end of the chapter and read the summary. The chapter summary highlights important information that was presented in the chapter. Did this help you prepare to understand the content?

Check Your Marketing IQ

Before you begin the chapter, see what you already know about marketing by taking the chapter pretest. The pretest is available at www.g-wlearning.com/marketing/.

DECA Emerging Leaders

Food Marketing Series Event, Part 2

Career Cluster: Marketing
Career Pathway: Marketing Management
Instructional Area: Pricing

Procedure, Part 2

1. In Chapter 13, you studied the performance indicators for this event.
2. The event will be presented to you through your reading of these instructions, including the Performance Indicators and Event Situation. You will have up to ten minutes to review this information to determine how you will handle the role-play situation and demonstrate the performance indicators of this event. During the preparation period, you may make notes to use during the role-play situation.
3. You will have up to ten minutes to role-play your situation with a judge. You may have more than one judge.
4. You will be evaluated on how well you meet the performance indicators of this event.
5. Turn in all your notes and event materials when you have completed the role-play.

Event Situation

You are to assume the position of owner/manager of a small gourmet food shop, The Brown Bag. One of your **sales associates (judge)** has asked you to discuss the shop's pricing decisions.

The Brown Bag is a specialty gourmet food shop located in a small historic town. The Brown Bag carries many unique foods that cannot be found in the local grocery stores. The town is about 25 miles from a larger metropolitan area. The population of the area is diverse. However, there are a growing number of young professionals in the community who entertain quite a bit for work and pleasure. The Brown Bag remains a favorite store for many of the residents and weekend visitors.

The shop has been open for three years and has recently undergone extensive renovations. The exterior and interior of the store have been redesigned to match the historical era of the town. A gourmet dine-in deli and café have been added. Customer service operations have also been added, including carry-out and delivery service, online ordering, and reward cards. A new computer system provides customer information and makes online and specialty ordering easier.

A recently hired sales associate (judge) has only been working at The Brown Bag for six weeks but has become a favorite with customers. The sales associate (judge) has commented that customers have asked about the high prices of some of the products. The sales associate (judge) has asked you to explain pricing so that he/she may better understand and answer customer questions.

You have asked the sales associate (judge) to meet with you in the store's office. The sales associate (judge) will begin the role-play by thanking you for taking the time to explain pricing. Once you have completed your presentation and have answered the sales associate's (judge's) questions, he or she will end the role-play by thanking you for explaining the pricing.

Critical Thinking

1. In a small town like this, do we even have to consider competition when pricing?
2. Is competitive pricing more important than other marketing functions such as customer service, promotion, and product selection?
3. Will the purchase of the new computer system affect pricing?

Visit www.deca.org for more information.

Published by DECA Inc. Copyright © by DECA Inc. No part of this publication may be reproduced for resale without written permission from the publisher. Printed in the United States of America.

Section 14.1

Pricing Strategies

Essential Question

Why do marketers use different pricing strategies?

Learning Objectives

LO 14.1-1 Cite examples of product-mix pricing strategies.
LO 14.1-2 Identify examples of psychological pricing strategies.
LO 14.1-3 List examples of B2B pricing strategies.

Key Terms

price mix
price lining
captive pricing
bundling
psychological pricing
odd pricing
even pricing
prestige pricing
buy one, get one (BOGO) pricing
manufacturer's suggested retail price (MSRP)
list price

Product-Mix Pricing Strategy
LO 14.1-1

The *base price* of a product is the general price at which a company expects to sell a product. After the base price is established, a business typically adjusts the price and applies price mix strategies to remain competitive. The **price mix** is the decisions made about pricing levels, discounts offered, and credit offered to customers. One or more strategies are often used, depending on the situation or product type.

One common strategy for adjusting price is *product-mix pricing*. Recall that a product mix is all the products a business sells. In a product mix, each product line has its own level of profitability because there are different costs for producing and marketing each one. In product-mix pricing, marketers choose to balance the overall profit of an entire product mix by applying different pricing strategies to individual lines. This is so the entire product mix can reach a profit goal rather than specific lines reaching individual goals. Three examples of product-mix pricing strategies are price lining, captive pricing, and bundling.

Price Lining

Price lining sets various prices for the same type of product to indicate different levels of quality. For example, appliance stores often use price lining. A dishwasher with three features may be priced at $350, a dishwasher with four features at $500, and a dishwasher with five or more features at $750. Price lining gives customers options and allows them to choose the features and benefits they want based on their needs and budgets.

Captive Pricing

Captive pricing sets prices low for the base product but charges high prices for other components that are needed to complete the product or service. For example, a haircut may be $10, which sounds like a deal. However, if you want to have your hair washed, dried, or styled, there are additional costs.

Bundling

Bundling combines two or more services or goods for one price. Bundling can reduce the overall price when compared to buying the items separately. For example, a clothing store might bundle a $10 hat and a $20 T-shirt for a single price of $25. This bundled price saves the customer $5. Bundling benefits the customer by saving him or her money, and it benefits the store by selling two items instead of one. Bundling conveys savings and value.

Psychological Pricing
LO 14.1-2

Psychological pricing is a pricing strategy that creates an image of a product and entices customers to buy. It is based on the assumption that some customers buy on emotions. If they think they are getting a good deal, they may purchase a product whether they need it or not. These strategies are most often used by marketers working for retail companies (B2C). Common B2C psychological pricing includes odd; even; prestige; and buy one, get one (BOGO) pricing.

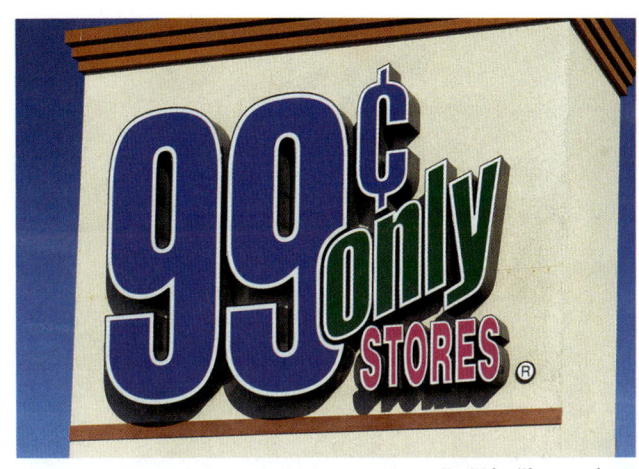

Ken Wolter/Shutterstock.com

Odd pricing sets prices to end in an odd number, such as 99 cents, and conveys an image of a bargain. *In your experience, does odd pricing convey value to you?*

Odd Pricing

Odd pricing sets prices to end in an odd number. These prices, such as $9.99 and $99.95, convey an image of a bargain. Discount-store prices and sale items usually end in odd numbers. A shopper might think of these prices as $9 and $99, even though the prices are actually closer to $10 and $100, respectively.

Even Pricing

Even pricing sets the price of a product to end in an even number, most often zero. Prices might be set at $40, $100, or $5,000. Even pricing conveys quality. Customers see the even number and think the product is better than one priced for value.

Prestige Pricing

Prestige pricing sets prices high to convey quality and status. Customers see a higher price and think the product is better than lower-priced, competing products. High-end fashion designers and car manufacturers often use prestige pricing.

Buy One, Get One Pricing

Buy one, get one (BOGO) pricing gives customers a free or reduced-price item when another is purchased at full price. Depending on the promotion, the items included may be the

Case in Point

Dollar Tree

One important responsibility of marketing is to set a pricing strategy. A price that is too high will deter customers from buying. A price that is too low will have a negative impact on profits. Sometimes, a simple pricing strategy works as well as a strategy that is more complex.

One example of simple pricing is the Dollar Tree retail chain. Products at Dollar Tree are priced at one dollar or less—even name brand items that might cost more elsewhere. The Dollar Tree brand name reflects its pricing strategy, so customers know exactly what they will spend. The four Ps are clearly defined: product, one item for a dollar; price, one dollar; place, Dollar Tree; and promotion, all products cost one dollar. Dollar Tree is a good example of a complete marketing strategy that works. In 2015, the company opened its 5,000th store. Dollar Tree continues to grow and post profits as the largest single-price-point company in North America.

Tupungato/Shutterstock.com

Payless competes with other retailers by offering BOGO sales. *When have you felt encouraged to buy more as a result of this pricing strategy?*

same or similar. The BOGO technique conveys savings and value. Some stores have *buy two, get one free* promotions and other similar offers.

B2B Discount Pricing
LO 14.1-3

Companies that sell to businesses (B2B) use different discount pricing strategies than those used for selling to the consumer market. The most popular B2B discount pricing strategies marketers use are cash discount, quantity discount, trade discount, promotional discount, and seasonal discount.

Cash Discount

A *cash discount* is a percentage deducted from the total invoice amount that is offered to encourage a customer to pay a bill early. A cash discount often shows up in a format similar to *2/10, net 30*. This means that a *2* percent discount off the invoice total applies if the customer pays the bill within *10* days. Otherwise, the customer has *30* days to pay the entire bill without receiving a penalty. Cash discounts encourage customers to pay their bill early, which helps with the cash flow of the business.

Quantity Discount

A *quantity discount* offers a reduced per-item price for larger numbers of an item purchased. This is similar to volume pricing discussed in the previous chapter. Many companies offer quantity discounts as an incentive for buying more product. The more a customer buys, the more money is saved on each item. For example, if a customer buys 48 sweatshirts, the price may be $22 per shirt. If the customer buys 96 sweatshirts, however, the price may be $18 per shirt.

Trade Discount

A *trade discount* is the way manufacturers quote prices to wholesalers and retailers. A trade discount is not applied in the same way as other traditional discounts. Some manufacturers use a **manufacturer's suggested retail price (MSRP)**, which is a price recommended for the product by

Green Marketing

Carbon Footprints

A *carbon footprint* is a measurement of how much the everyday behaviors of an individual, company, or community impact the environment. This includes the amount of carbon dioxide put into the air from the consumption of energy and fuel used in homes, for travel, and for business operations.

Online carbon footprint calculators can be used to determine areas and practices that need to change. Companies can reduce their carbon footprints by recycling, reducing waste, and using responsible energy options. For example, video communication can be used to hold marketing meetings among departments in locations across the country. This reduces the fossil fuel emissions for travel by automobile, train, or airplane.

Employability Skills

Workspaces

Employees are expected to keep company workspaces clean and in order. When using a shared copier, do not leave paper clips or other supplies behind. If you take breaks or eat lunch in the common eating area, clean up dishes, utensils, or food packaging. Keep your personal space clean and free from clutter.

the manufacturer. The MSRP is often used as a list price. The **list price** of a product is the established price printed in a catalog, on a price tag, or in a price list. The manufacturer then offers the wholesaler or retailer a percentage off the list price. A trade discount may be 20 percent or more off the list price.

Promotional Discount

A *promotional discount* is given to businesses that agree to advertise or promote a manufacturer's product. The discount may be a dollar amount or a percentage of the product order. When you see a product listed in a store's weekly sale ad, it is likely that the retail store got a promotional discount on that product.

Seasonal Discount

If retailers buy goods well in advance of the season, they are often given a *seasonal discount*. For example, buyers for goods sold during the holiday gift-giving season often place orders about 11 months before. Buying goods this far in advance allows them to take advantage of lower prices. Similarly, summer clothing orders are placed at least six months in advance of the season. Seasonal discounts help manufacturers plan production and reduce inventory.

Section 14.1 Review

Check Your Understanding

1. Why do marketers employ product-mix pricing?
2. On what assumption is psychological pricing based?
3. Name a psychological pricing strategy that conveys value or the image of a bargain.
4. What is a cash discount?
5. Why do manufacturers give businesses promotional discounts?

Build Your Vocabulary

As you progress through this text, develop a personal glossary of key terms. This will help you build your vocabulary and prepare you for a career. Write a definition for each of the following terms and add them to your personal glossary.

bundling
buy one, get one (BOGO) pricing
captive pricing
even pricing
list price
manufacturer's suggested retail price (MSRP)

odd pricing
prestige pricing
price lining
price mix
psychological pricing

Section 14.2

Governmental Influence on Pricing

Essential Question
Why does the government influence pricing?

Learning Objectives

LO 14.2-1 Cite examples of pricing practices regulated by the government.
LO 14.2-2 State examples of governmental price controls.

Key Terms

bait and switch
price discrimination
deceptive pricing
predatory pricing
unit pricing
loss leader
price ceiling
price floor

Governmental Pricing Regulations

Both businesses and consumers are affected by unfair, illegal pricing practices. Businesses that use unfair pricing practices are breaking laws in addition to being unethical. Businesses must comply with local, state, and federal laws. Part of the commitment businesses make is to operate within the legal system. Marketers who misrepresent their products risk legal consequences. Some unfair and illegal pricing activities about which marketers need to be informed are as follows.

- **Bait and switch** is the practice of advertising one product with the intent of persuading customers to buy a more expensive item when they arrive in the store.
- *Price-fixing* occurs when two or more businesses in an industry agree to sell the same product at a set price, which is usually high.
- **Price discrimination** occurs when a company sells the same product to different customers at different prices based on personal characteristics.
- **Deceptive pricing** is the practice of setting the prices of products in a way to intentionally mislead a customer.
- **Predatory pricing** is setting very low prices to remove competition, such as foreign companies that price their products below the same domestic ones to drive the domestic companies out of business.

There are both state and federal laws that regulate pricing to prevent unfair pricing policies and practices. A list of specific laws that regulate or affect pricing is presented in Figure 14-1.

Some states have laws that protect consumers from price gouging practices. *Price gouging* is the raising of prices on certain kinds of goods to an excessively high level during an emergency. The state laws consider price gouging as a form of price-fixing.

The government also prevents the forming of *monopolies*, which interfere with the workings of a market economy. Recall that a monopoly takes place when a company controls the market for a single product and is the only seller of a product or service. As a result, a monopoly usually sets high, unfair prices that hurt consumers.

Unit pricing is of particular importance to those working with items that are sold in packages, particularly grocery and personal items. **Unit pricing** is a price that allows customers to compare prices based on a standard unit of measure, such as an ounce or a pound. The unit prices are posted on shelving labels under the items. In some states, unit pricing is required by law to help consumers make smart buying decisions.

Some states have *sales-below-cost (SBC) laws* that ban loss-leader pricing. A **loss leader** is an item that is priced much lower than the current market price or the cost of the product and taking a loss on each sale. The purpose of loss leaders is

Laws That Regulate Pricing		
Law	**What It Regulates**	**When It Might Be Used**
Sherman Antitrust Act (1890)	This law regulates price-fixing.	The gasoline stations in your town all collude to charge the same price for gasoline.
Clayton Antitrust Act (1914)	Passed in 1914, this law makes price discrimination illegal.	Your school store ordered 100 widgets from a company and was charged $4.00 a widget. The school store manager finds out that another store ordered 100 widgets from the same company and was charged $3.50 a widget.
Robinson-Patman Act (1936)	This law strengthened the Clayton Act by specifically prohibiting a seller from charging different prices to different customers for the same product and same quantity.	This law helps small retailers compete against large chains. The same types of discounts, financing, etc., have to be offered to both large and small retailers.
Wheeler Lea Act (1938)	This law prohibits deceptive advertising of prices. Companies cannot advertise that their prices are lower unless they can prove it; they cannot advertise lowered prices unless the original price was higher; and list prices cannot be used in reference to a sale price unless the product was actually sold at the list price.	You see a pair of shoes on sale for $45.99; however, you were in the same store last week before the sale, and they were $45.99.
Unit-Pricing Laws	These laws vary from state to state. Retailers must display pricing that shows the price of an item per unit. Most packaged items are priced per package, which makes it hard to compare the prices of certain items, particularly grocery items.	The price of a 32-ounce bottle of shampoo is $5.99. A sign on the shelf should state that it costs 19 cents an ounce.
Minimum Price Laws or Sales-Below-Cost Laws	These laws vary from state to state. Retailers cannot sell a product for less than its cost.	A retailer buys running shoes from the manufacturer for $20; it cannot resell them for less than $20.
Federal Trade Commission Price Advertising Guidelines	Guidelines prohibit any deceptive or bait-and-switch advertising.	This law prohibits advertising that makes unsubstantial claims about health or safety, such as sunscreen that "reduces the risk of skin cancer."

Goodheart-Willcox Publisher

Figure 14-1 Both state and federal laws regulate pricing to prevent unfair pricing policies and practices.

to draw customers into a business by advertising a product for a very low price. The business hopes that once in the store, consumers will buy other products to make up for the lost profit. Some state laws consider loss-leader pricing to be a predatory and misleading pricing practice.

Governmental Price Controls
LO 14.1-2

The government may intervene in the pricing of some products in an attempt to control the economy or help consumers. *Price controls* are often set when the public becomes alarmed about a fast-growing rate of inflation. Most economists believe price controls can help suppliers and consumers. However, others think that price controls can worsen the very problems the government is trying to solve.

Price ceilings are maximum prices set by the government when it thinks certain products are being priced too high. The government may believe that consumers need some help to purchase the products. Price ceilings on some products are often set during times when there may be shortages that could drive prices unreasonably high. However, price ceilings can also cause the very shortages the government is trying to prevent. Existing businesses or producers have to accept a lower price than they would otherwise set for their goods or services, and many are likely to leave the business. For example, many urban cities establish a price ceiling for rent, known as *rent control*, in an effort to make housing more affordable. However, this can create long waiting lists for housing. In addition, landlords may choose to sell their rental properties because they cannot make enough profit.

Price floors are minimum prices set by the government for certain products that it thinks are being priced too low. Price floors are set to help the producers. However, if the price floor is set higher than the market price, a surplus situation will occur. A surplus happens because consumers will not buy the higher-priced products and many products are unsold. In some cases, a surplus situation forces the government to buy the excess inventory to prevent rampant waste.

You Do the Math

Multiplication

The number that is going to be multiplied by another number is called the *multiplicand*. The number by which the multiplicand is multiplied is called the *multiplier*. To multiply whole numbers and decimals, place the numbers, called the *factors*, in pairs in a vertical list.

Solve the following problems.
1. A local bicycle shop, Sunbeam Cycles, is comparing its sale prices to an online competitor, Express Bikes. Sunbeam Cycles has a popular bike model on sale for $265. The same model is available from Express Bikes for $220. The sales tax rate for both is 6 percent. Express Bikes charges $25 for shipping and handling. Sunbeam Cycles assembles bicycles for customers free of charge. The bicycle available online from Express Bikes is shipped unassembled. It costs $35 to have someone put it together. Which business offers a better deal?
2. A shoe retailer is evaluating its competition and recorded the following information. Store A has flip-flops on sale at two pairs for $5.50. Store B has them on sale for 25 percent off their normal price of $3.50 a pair. Store C gives you one free pair of flip-flops if you buy a pair at the regular price of $5.
   A. How much do the flip-flops cost per pair at each store?
   B. Which store has flip-flops at the lowest price per pair?
   C. Which store charges the highest price?

Social Media

Social-Media Dashboards

One of the biggest challenges with social media is managing the time it takes to monitor multiple business profiles. For example, marketers need to keep information current, interact with followers, and publish posts on a consistent basis. Social-media dashboards, such as SproutSocial, HootSuite, or Datorama, can help effectively manage the time that needs to be spent on social media. A social-media dashboard is an interactive tool, much like a car dashboard, that organizes and presents information in an easy-to-read format. A social media dashboard helps a marketer get a snapshot of all the social-media activity for the business. These tools also allow a business to schedule alerts and notifications, create groups, browse site activity, and send automatic updates or messages. While everything cannot be automated, a social-media dashboard can make the process of keeping social media updated easier and more efficient.

Section 14.2 Review

Check Your Understanding

1. Explain the difference between price-fixing and predatory pricing.
2. Why do governments prevent monopolies?
3. What type of laws ban loss-leader pricing?
4. What is the purpose of a price ceiling?
5. Are price floors set to help consumers or producers?

Build Your Vocabulary

As you progress through this text, develop a personal glossary of key terms. This will help you build your vocabulary and prepare you for a career. Write a definition for each of the following terms and add them to your personal glossary.

bait and switch	price ceiling
deceptive pricing	price discrimination
loss leader	price floor
predatory pricing	unit pricing

CHAPTER 14 Review and Assessment

Chapter Summary

Section 14.1 Pricing Strategies

LO 14.1-1 Cite examples of product-mix pricing strategies.
Three examples of product-mix pricing strategies are price lining, captive pricing, and bundling. One or more strategies are often used, depending on the situation or product type.

LO 14.1-2 Identify examples of psychological pricing strategies.
Psychological pricing creates an image of a product and entices customers to buy. It is based on the assumption that some customers buy on emotions. Common B2C psychological pricing includes odd; even; prestige; and buy one, get one (BOGO) pricing.

LO 14.1-3 List examples of B2B pricing strategies.
Companies that sell to businesses use different discount pricing strategies than those used for selling to the consumer market. The most popular B2B discount pricing strategies marketers use are cash discount, quantity discount, trade discount, promotional discount, and seasonal discount.

Section 14.2 Governmental Influence on Pricing

LO 14.2-1 Cite examples of pricing practices regulated by the government.
Some examples of pricing practices regulated by the government are bait and switch, price-fixing, price discrimination, deceptive pricing, predatory pricing, price gouging, monopolies, unit pricing, and sales-below-cost (SBC) laws. Marketers need to be informed about these pricing practices.

LO 14.2-2 State examples of governmental price controls.
The government may intervene in the pricing of some products in an attempt to control the economy or help consumers. Price controls are often set when the public becomes alarmed about a fast-growing rate of inflation. Price ceilings are maximum prices set by the government when it thinks certain products are being priced too high. Price floors are minimum prices set by the government for certain goods and services that it thinks are being priced too low.

Check Your Marketing IQ

Now that you have completed the chapter, see what you have learned about marketing by taking the chapter posttest. The posttest is available at www.g-wlearning.com/marketing/.

Review Your Knowledge

1. Cite examples of product-mix pricing strategies.
2. How does bundling benefit both the customer and the store?
3. Identify examples of psychological pricing strategies.
4. Name a psychological pricing strategy that conveys quality or status.
5. List examples of B2B pricing strategies.
6. Why do businesses offer cash discounts?
7. Explain how trade discounts are applied.
8. What is an advantage of B2B businesses buying seasonal goods in advance?
9. Cite examples of pricing practices regulated by the government.
10. State examples of governmental price controls.

Apply Your Knowledge

1. In earlier chapters, you identified the product or service for which you are creating a marketing plan. Create a chart of the major products or services that you are responsible for marketing with three columns: list price, selling price, and MSRP. Calculate the percentage of difference among each price. Is the difference a consistent percentage?
2. To be competitive, it might be necessary to offer multiple pricing options to your customers. What criteria would you consider for special pricing? Why?
3. Identify key product-mix pricing strategies used by the business you have selected.
4. Does your business use any loss leaders? If so, describe them and when they are used.
5. What is the unit price for each of your products?
6. Given the nature of your business, which pricing laws or regulations are relevant?
7. What types of discounts are offered by your company? Explain each type of discount and why it is a good pricing strategy.
8. Evaluate the pricing strategies of your business. In your opinion, do the pricing strategies help the company meet its business and marketing goals?
9. Think about the types of promotional discounts you might be able to negotiate from manufacturers or other vendors. How would they affect your company pricing policies?
10. Describe examples of psychological pricing strategies you have seen in the B2C market. Do you think these strategies are effective? Which do you think is the most effective in your market? Explain your answer.

Apply Your Math Skills

Cody owns a small convenience store. He is shopping for supplies for his business. Apply your math skills to solve the following problems.

1. A warehouse club sells large amounts of all-purpose cleaning solutions. Calculate the unit prices of each brand of cleaner. What is the lowest unit price?
   - One 210-ounce bottle of Brand A lavender-scented cleaner is $7.88
   - A two-pack of 100-ounce bottles of Brand B pine-scented cleaner is $11.18
   - A two-pack of 100-ounce bottles of Brand C lemon-scented cleaner is $9.83
2. Cody is ordering packages of food to sell in his convenience store from a supplier. The total cost of his order is $678.90. The vendor offered a cash discount with terms stated as *5/10, net 20*. What price will Cody pay for his order if he accepts the terms of the cash discount?

Communication Skills

Reading When engaging in active reading, it is important to evaluate the material as you read it. Evaluation after reading often occurs naturally without the reader realizing it. Evaluate the information as you read this chapter. Note the questions and comments that you think about as you read.

Writing Create a Venn diagram to show the relationships between pricing factors and pricing objectives. Where do the circles overlap? What do you think this overlap signifies? Write arguments to support your claims of what the overlap signifies. Use valid reasoning and sufficient evidence in your arguments.

Listening Practice active listening skills while listening to a news report on the radio, on television, or a podcast about a topic that involves pricing in some form. As you are listening, take notes on important points that you hear. When you are finished, review your notes and conclude whether you were an active listener.

Internet Research

Pricing Strategies Conduct an Internet search for *pricing strategies*. List three websites or articles that address the topic. What important advice did these sites offer?

Local Sales Use Internet resources to locate the online version of a weekly flyer or advertising circular for a local grocery store. Peruse the advertisements and make notes of the sale prices you see advertised. Identify any psychological pricing strategies used. Do these prices reflect value or prestige?

Pricing Laws Research pricing laws for your state. Identify a law that is of interest to you. Summarize the purpose it serves for businesses, customers, and the community.

Teamwork

Psychological pricing creates an image of a product and entices customers to buy. It is based on the assumption that some customers buy on emotions. With your team, develop an argument about whether psychological pricing strategies should be used by a retailer. Present the main points of your argument to the class.

Portfolio Development

College and Career Readiness

Technical Skills Your portfolio must showcase the technical skills you have. Are you exceptionally good working with computers? Do you have a talent for creating videos? Technical skills are very important for succeeding in school or at work.

1. Create a Microsoft Word document that describes the technical skills you have acquired. Use the heading "Technical Skills" and your name. Describe the skill, your level of competence, and any other information that will showcase your skill level. Save the document file.
2. Update your master spreadsheet.

UNIT 5 Price

Building the Marketing Plan

Pricing products correctly can mean the difference between success and failure for many businesses. Owners look to marketing professionals to help them with the pricing process. In your role as a marketing manager for the company you selected, you will be involved in pricing decisions. Make sure your pricing is competitive and aligns with the company's financial goals. Often a company's financial goals also help marketers to set marketing goals. You will be making decisions about markup, pricing strategies, and techniques for setting the base and final prices.

Part 1 Marketing Objectives

Objectives
- Find and list the company's financial goals.
- Determine pricing objectives for your company.
- Determine the company's marketing goals.

Directions
In this activity, you will continue writing the Marketing Strategies section of the marketing plan by developing the Marketing Goals subsection. The *marketing goals* are those a business wants to achieve during a given time, usually one year, by implementing the marketing plan. They include goals related to both finances and marketing activities. Access the *Marketing Dynamics* companion website at www.g-wlearning.com/marketing/. Download the activity file as indicated in the following instructions.

1. **Unit Activity 5-1—Marketing Goals** First, find and list the financial goals of the company for your marketing plan. Then, determine and list the company pricing objectives. Explain how the pricing objectives relate to the overall financial goals of the company. Then, list the marketing goals you wish to accomplish or begin to accomplish in the coming year.

2. Open your saved marketing plan document.

3. Locate the Marketing Goals section of the plan. Then, complete the Marketing Goals and Company Financial Goals subsections. Use the suggestions and questions listed to help you generate ideas. Delete the instructions and questions when you are finished recording your responses. Proofread your document and correct any errors in keyboarding, spelling, and grammar.

4. Save your document.

Part 2 Price

Objectives
- Determine the base price for one company product.
- Research the product prices of your competitors.
- Determine the pricing strategy and technique to set the final price.

Directions
In this activity, you will continue writing the Marketing Strategies section of the marketing plan by developing the Price Strategies subsection, which is part of the Marketing Mix. The marketing strategies are the decisions made about product, price, place, and promotion. Access the *Marketing Dynamics* companion website at www.g-wlearning.com/marketing/. Download the activity file as indicated in the following instructions.

1. **Unit Activity 5-2—Price** Select one good or service you market for your company. First, determine the cost to the company. Next, determine the markup needed to make the profit your company wants. Then, use the correct formula from Chapter 13 to set the base price. Show your math. Research and list the prices of the competition. Describe the pricing strategy and the technique to set the final price for your product or service.

2. Open your saved marketing plan document.

3. Locate the Marketing Strategies section of the plan. Complete the Price Strategies subsection under Marketing Mix. Use the suggestions and questions listed to help you generate ideas. Delete the instructions and questions when you are finished recording your responses. Proofread your document and correct any errors in keyboarding, spelling, and grammar.

4. Save your document.

UNIT 6 Place

Chapters

15 **Place**
16 **Purchasing and Inventory Control**

While studying, look for the activity icon for:
- Building the Marketing Plan activity files
- Pretests and posttests
- Vocabulary terms with e-flash cards and matching activities
- Self-assessment

These activities can be accessed at www.g-wlearning.com/marketing/.

Developing a Vision

Have you ever thought about how an iPad gets from Apple to the customer? A marketing team at Apple had a lot to do with customers getting iPads when they wanted them, in the places they wanted to buy them, and for the prices they were willing to pay. A major challenge for marketing is distribution of product. The channel of distribution is the *path* that the product takes from the producer to the end user. The supply chain is the *people* who move the goods.

Supply chain management is an important marketing activity that focuses on the marketing concept of customer satisfaction. This involves getting the product to you, the end user, as quickly and efficiently as possible.

Marketing Core Functions Covered in This Unit

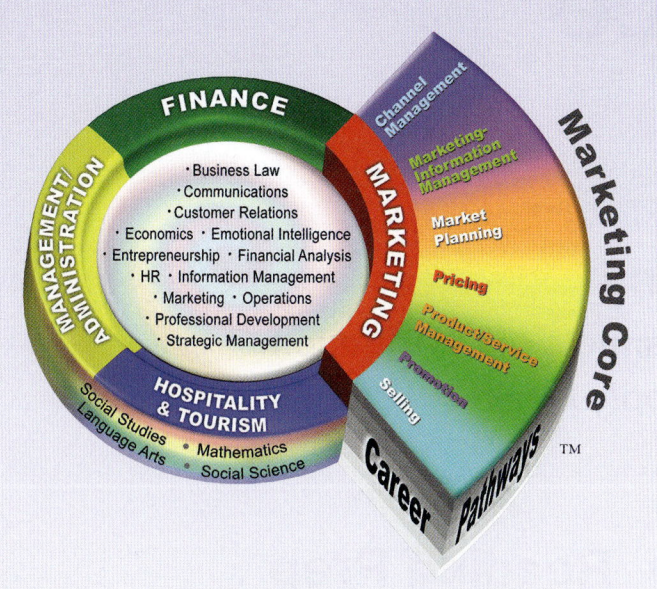

Functions of Marketing
- Channel management
- Market planning
- Pricing

Copyright MBA Research, Columbus, Ohio. Used with permission.

EYE-CATCHER

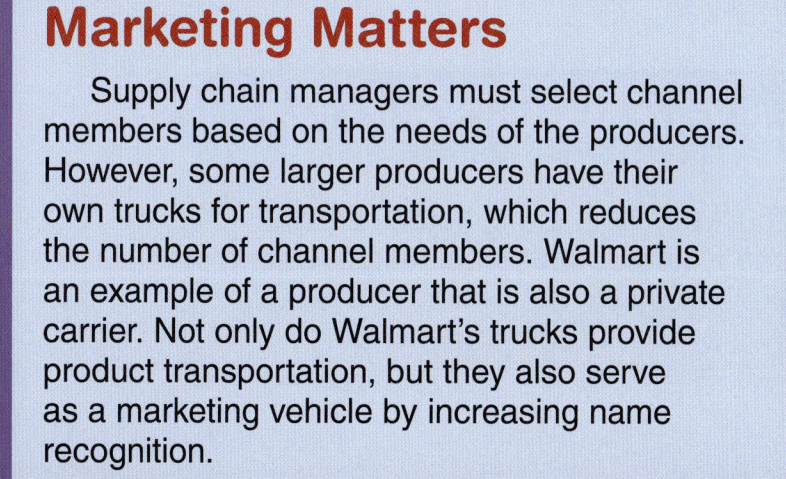

Marketing Matters

Supply chain managers must select channel members based on the needs of the producers. However, some larger producers have their own trucks for transportation, which reduces the number of channel members. Walmart is an example of a producer that is also a private carrier. Not only do Walmart's trucks provide product transportation, but they also serve as a marketing vehicle by increasing name recognition.

Frontpage/Shutterstock.com

CHAPTER 15

Place

Sections

15.1 **Channels of Distribution**

15.2 **Supply Chain**

Reading Prep

College and Career Readiness

Before reading this chapter, look at all the illustrations. Illustrations help readers visualize the concepts and topics presented in the content. What information can you deduce from the chapter illustrations?

Check Your Marketing IQ

Before you begin the chapter, see what you already know about marketing by taking the chapter pretest. The pretest is available at www.g-wlearning.com/marketing/.

◇DECA Emerging Leaders

Hospitality Services Team Decision-Making Event, Part 1

Career Cluster: Hospitality and Tourism
Instructional Area: Market Planning

Knowledge and Skills Developed

Participants will develop many 21st century skills desired by today's employers in the following categories:
- communication and collaboration
- creativity and innovation
- critical thinking and problem solving
- flexibility and adaptability
- information literacy
- initiative and self-direction
- leadership and responsibility
- productivity and accountability
- social and cross-cultural skills

Specific Performance Indicators

- Identify information monitored for marketing decision-making.
- Explain the concept of marketing strategies.
- Explain the nature of marketing plans.
- Explain the role of situational analysis in the marketing planning process.
- Describe factors used by marketers to position products/services.
- Explain the role of customer service as a component of selling relationships.
- Explain the role of ethics in human resources management.

Purpose

Designed for a team of two DECA members, the event measures the team's ability to explain core business concepts in the format of a case study in a role-play. This event consists of a 100-question, multiple-choice, cluster exam for each team member and a decision-making case study situation. The Team Decision-Making Event provides an opportunity for participants to analyze one or a combination of elements essential to the effective operation of a business in the specific career area presented as a case study.

For the purposes of this text, you will be presented with the material for this event in two parts. Part 1 presents the knowledge and skills assessed and an overview of the event's purpose and procedure. Part 2 presents the remaining procedures and the event situation.

Procedure, Part 1

1. For Part 1 in this text, read both sets of performance indicators. Discuss these with your team member.
2. If there are any questions, ask your instructor to clarify.

Critical Thinking

1. In a business, what information should be monitored for effective decision making?
2. Explain how marketing strategies and marketing plans impact marketing decisions.
3. What is the role of situational analysis in the marketing planning process?
4. Describe various factors marketers use to position products/services. Why are the factors important?
5. Discuss with your team member why performance indicators about the role of customer service and ethics might be included.

Visit www.deca.org for more information.

Published by DECA Inc. Copyright © by DECA Inc. No part of this publication may be reproduced for resale without written permission from the publisher. Printed in the United States of America.

Section 15.1

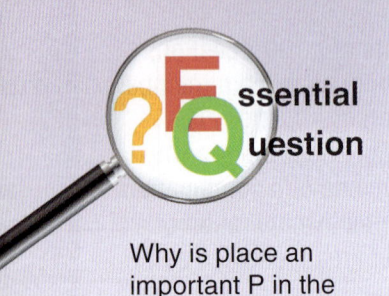

Channels of Distribution

Essential Question

Why is place an important P in the marketing mix?

Learning Objectives

LO 15.1-1 Explain place as one of the four Ps of marketing.
LO 15.1-2 Identify distribution channels for B2C and B2B markets.
LO 15.1-3 Explain how to manage the channel of distribution.

Key Terms

supply chain
channel of distribution
intermediary
bulk-breaking
nonstore retailer
e-tailer
multi-channel retailer
direct channel
indirect channel

retailer channel
wholesaler channel
agent/broker channel
industrial goods
industrial distributor channel
agent/broker industrial distributor channel
channel conflict

LO 15.1-1 Place

Place is one of the four Ps of marketing. *Place* refers to the activities involved in getting a good or service to the end user. It involves determining when, where, and how products get to customers. Place is also known as *distribution*.

A **supply chain** is the businesses, people, and activities involved in turning raw materials into products and delivering them to end users. Physical distribution is a part of the larger process of the supply chain. The supply chain can be very long for some businesses or very short for others.

A major part in the decision of place is selecting the channel of distribution. A **channel of distribution** is the *path* that goods take through the supply chain. *Channel members* are the organizations that help move products from their origination to the consumer. Channel members include producers and intermediaries.

Producers

Producers are businesses that create goods or services. They provide a specific role in the economy. In order for a business to meet consumer needs and wants, producers are needed to create

Erasmus Wolff/Shutterstock.com

Place refers to the activities involved in getting a good or service to the end user. *What companies can you name that help facilitate distribution?*

the end product. This industry creates three basic types of products: natural resources, agricultural products, and finished goods.

Natural Resources

Natural resources, such as timber, water, or minerals, are one type of product produced by the industry. Natural resources are also called *raw materials*. *Extractors* are businesses or people that take natural resources from the land.

Agricultural Products

Farmers raise crops and livestock that are sold to end users, such as consumers. These products may also be used by manufacturers to create other products.

Finished Goods

Finished goods are another type of product created by producers. *Manufacturers* are businesses that use supplies from other producers to make products. Some manufacturers use raw materials purchased from extractors. These businesses are called *raw-materials manufacturers* or *raw-materials producers*.

Manufacturers generally use assembly lines to mass produce identical products. However, there are also custom manufacturers, such as builders. A *builder* is an individual or business that contracts and supervises the construction of a building. Builders are considered manufacturers because they turn raw goods into a finished product.

Intermediaries

An **intermediary** is a business in the supply chain between the manufacturer or producer and the end users. Intermediaries serve three functions: transactional, logistical, and facilitating. These functions help make sure goods are in the right place and at the right time.

- The *transactional function* is typically the sales and marketing activities for the business. The intermediary contacts customers and provides information about the products.
- The *logistics function* is physically moving products from the manufacturers to distributors, retailers, or end users. The intermediary makes sure the product moves through the supply chain. This includes transportation, such as trucking, rail, or other shipping options.

Marketing Ethics

Collusion

It is unethical and illegal for intermediaries to participate in acts of collusion. *Collusion* occurs when channel members work together to eliminate competition by misleading supply chain managers, setting prices, or other fraudulent activities. Unethical businesses sometimes collude with other businesses so that they can dominate the marketplace. Collusion is not only unethical, it is illegal.

- The *facilitating function* is the final part of the supply chain. This involves the actual selling of the product or service to the end users. The end user could be consumers or businesses.

For example, think of an apple you ate recently. As shown in Figure 15-1, the apple was grown in an apple orchard owned by an apple farmer, the producer. The apple farmer sold the apples to an apple buyer, an intermediary. The apple buyer sold apples to the local store, another intermediary. You, a consumer, visited the store and bought the apple. You could have bought the apple directly from the apple farmer. However, the apple buyer and the store made the apple more convenient for you to buy when you wanted it.

Intermediaries are important to the supply chain process. They can add substantial value to a business by providing specialized services the business may not be able to afford. Intermediaries help to increase the number of end users a producer can reach, increase market share for the producer, and help to reduce some costs by sharing responsibilities.

One service that intermediaries can provide is bulk-breaking. **Bulk-breaking** is the process of separating a large quantity of goods into smaller quantities for resale. An intermediary buys goods in bulk and then breaks the bulk into smaller quantities of goods. For example, it is easier and cheaper to ship a bushel of apples rather than 100 separate apples. A grocery store can buy apples by the bushel and sell them to customers a few at a time.

There are several types of intermediaries, including wholesalers, retailers, and agents. Some intermediaries take ownership of the product. Other intermediaries act as facilitators and do not

Supply Chain Example

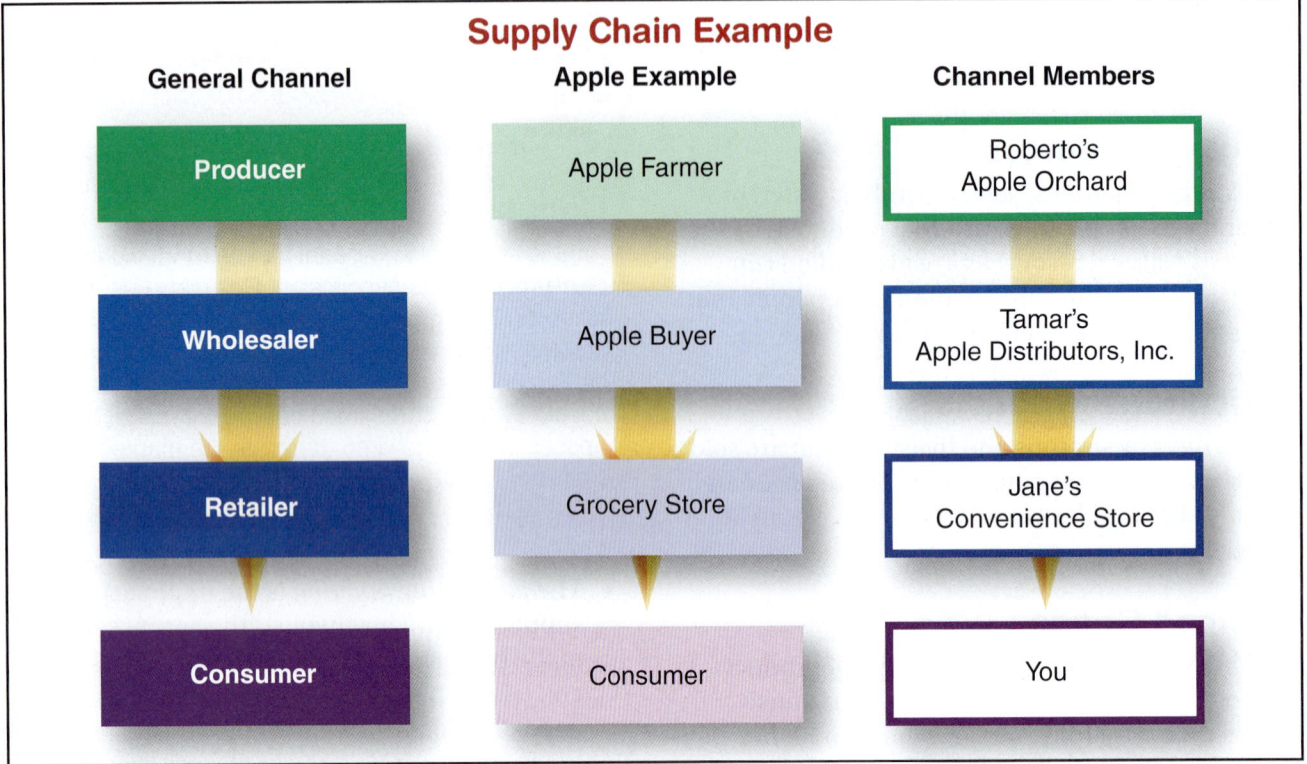

General Channel	Apple Example	Channel Members
Producer	Apple Farmer	Roberto's Apple Orchard
Wholesaler	Apple Buyer	Tamar's Apple Distributors, Inc.
Retailer	Grocery Store	Jane's Convenience Store
Consumer	Consumer	You

Goodheart-Willcox Publisher

Figure 15-1 Intermediaries are important to the supply chain.

take ownership, but rather transfer the goods to another channel member.

Wholesalers

A *wholesaler* is a middleman between the producer and a person or organization in the B2B supply chain. They are often called *distributors* in the private enterprise system because they buy products in bulk and resell them in smaller quantities to retailers. They are a type of intermediary that facilitates storage and transportation of products in addition to other services, such as marketing. Wholesalers are sometimes categorized as merchant wholesalers or manufacturers' sales branches.

Merchant wholesalers own the merchandise they sell. They purchase large amounts of goods directly from manufacturers. Some merchant wholesalers offer limited service and may or may not provide additional services to the customer, such as marketing or transportation. *Rack jobbers* are merchant wholesalers who provide full services to the retailer and set up racks, maintain stock, and other activities. They bill the retailer only for the items that are sold.

Manufacturers' sales branches are company-owned businesses that are operated by the manufacturer and sell only their merchandise at wholesale prices directly to the customer. They typically do not take ownership of stock, but only display the goods. One example is the Tandy Corporation that owned Radio Shack stores. These stores displayed and sold Tandy products and provided service and financing, but did not typically stock the merchandise.

Retailers

A *retailer* is a business that buys products from wholesalers or directly from producers and sells them to consumers to make a profit. Retailers play multiple roles in the private-enterprise system. Primarily, retailers directly provide consumers with the products that meet their needs and wants. Other functions they perform include promotion, credit, and returns. On a larger scale, retailers provide employment in communities and contribute to local economies.

Many retailers have physical brick-and-mortar stores, but some do not. A **nonstore retailer** is a business that sells directly to consumers in ways that do not involve a physical store location. Nonstore retail businesses include catalog sales, direct sales, and e-tailers.

Catalog sales generally use direct mailings. Retail businesses mail product catalogs to customers who can shop from the comfort of their

Corepics VOF/Shutterstock.com

An intermediary, like this shipper of oil, is between the manufacturer or producer and the end users in the supply chain. *What activities of intermediaries do you see in your community?*

home or office. An example of a business that uses catalog sales is L.L. Bean.

Direct sales retailers have sales representatives who approach customers outside of a fixed location. The sales representatives sell products to customers either in their homes or by telephone. For many years, businesses like Avon and Tupperware have sold products in this manner. Direct sales companies also sell products through their websites.

E-tailers are retailers that sell products through websites. Amazon is an example of an e-tailer.

Multi-channel retailers sell products through both brick-and-mortar stores and online sites. Target is an example of a multi-channel retailer because it sells products both in its physical stores and through its website.

Agents

Agents bring buyers and sellers together. They buy and sell goods for a commission and never take direct ownership of the products. An agent is someone working on the behalf of another party. Agents are also known as *brokers*. An agent may be hired by either the buyer or the seller. An example of an agent is a realtor. Realtors can be hired by property buyers to help find a property to buy, or by sellers to help facilitate a sale.

The goal of an agent is to create a favorable exchange for both the buyer and seller. Agents can be used anywhere in the supply-chain process. They are especially useful in facilitating international trade because they are often familiar with international laws, regulations, and customs that impact supply-chain transactions.

Distribution Channels

Physical distribution involves responsibilities associated with the transfer of ownership of products from the producer to the end user. The original owner is at the beginning of the distribution channel. The final owner is the end user at the end of the distribution channel.

Most, but not all, intermediaries take ownership of the product as it moves through the channel of distribution. Agents/brokers never take ownership of the products.

When ownership is transferred to intermediaries in the distribution channel, each one assumes the risk and responsibility for the product. The new owner is the one who will suffer any loss if the product is damaged or lost. For that reason, producers must use caution when hiring intermediaries to transport their products to the end user.

Distribution Channels for B2C Market

Distribution for consumer goods can be either direct or indirect, as shown in Figure 15-2. A **direct channel** is the path of selling goods or services directly from a producer or manufacturer to end users without using intermediaries. The direct channel in the B2C market is when a consumer buys goods or services directly from the producers or manufacturers. Buying a computer online from Dell is an example of a direct-channel purchase.

An **indirect channel** uses intermediaries to get the product from the producer or manufacturer to the consumer. Indirect channels include the participation of a retailer, wholesaler, or agent/broker.

Employability Skills

Polite Language

When speaking to others at work, use respectful and polite language at all times. Use polite phrases such as "please," "thank you," and "you are welcome" whenever possible. Choose words that show respect to others. Never use profane words or phrases. To do so is inappropriate and unacceptable workplace behavior.

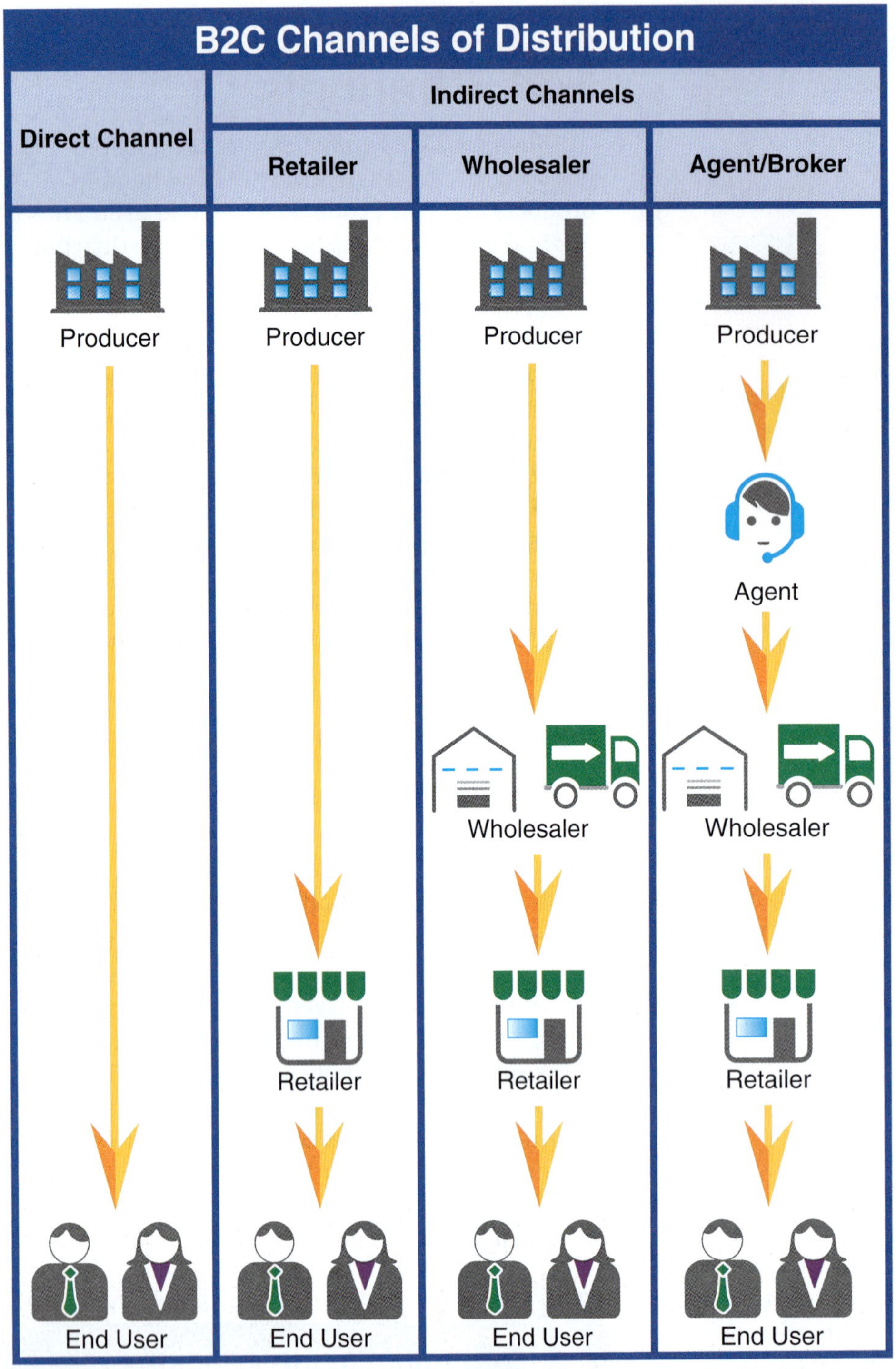

Figure 15-2 Distribution for consumer goods can be direct or indirect.

B2C Channels of Distribution

Direct Channel	Indirect Channels		
	Retailer	Wholesaler	Agent/Broker
Producer → End User	Producer → Retailer → End User	Producer → Wholesaler → Retailer → End User	Producer → Agent → Wholesaler → Retailer → End User

Goodheart-Willcox Publisher

The **retailer channel** is the path a product takes from the producer to the retailer, then from the retailer to the consumer. An example is a customer buying a product from a sporting goods store. The producer sells to the sporting goods store, which then sells to the consumer. The retailer channel is the shortest indirect channel in the B2C market.

The **wholesaler channel** is the path a product takes from the producer to a wholesaler, and then to a retailer before reaching the end user. For example, a producer manufactures athletic equipment. The producer sells the goods to a wholesaler, who in turn sells to sporting goods retailers. The retailers then put the goods in their stores and sell to consumers. The wholesaler channel is an indirect channel.

The **agent/broker channel** is the path of selling in which the producer hires an agent to sell to the wholesaler. Some producers do not want to assume the responsibility of selling or shipping products. Those producers contract with an agent to handle their goods after production. The agent never takes ownership of the goods, but facilitates the path from the producer to the wholesaler. This can include arranging transportation, scheduling shipping, and facilitating payment between the parties involved. The agent/broker channel is the longest indirect channel in the B2C market.

Distribution Channels for B2B Market

Goods used in the production of other goods or consumed by a business are called **industrial goods**. All businesses use industrial goods, either to manufacture goods or to operate the business.

Similar to consumer products, the channel to the end user may be direct or indirect, as

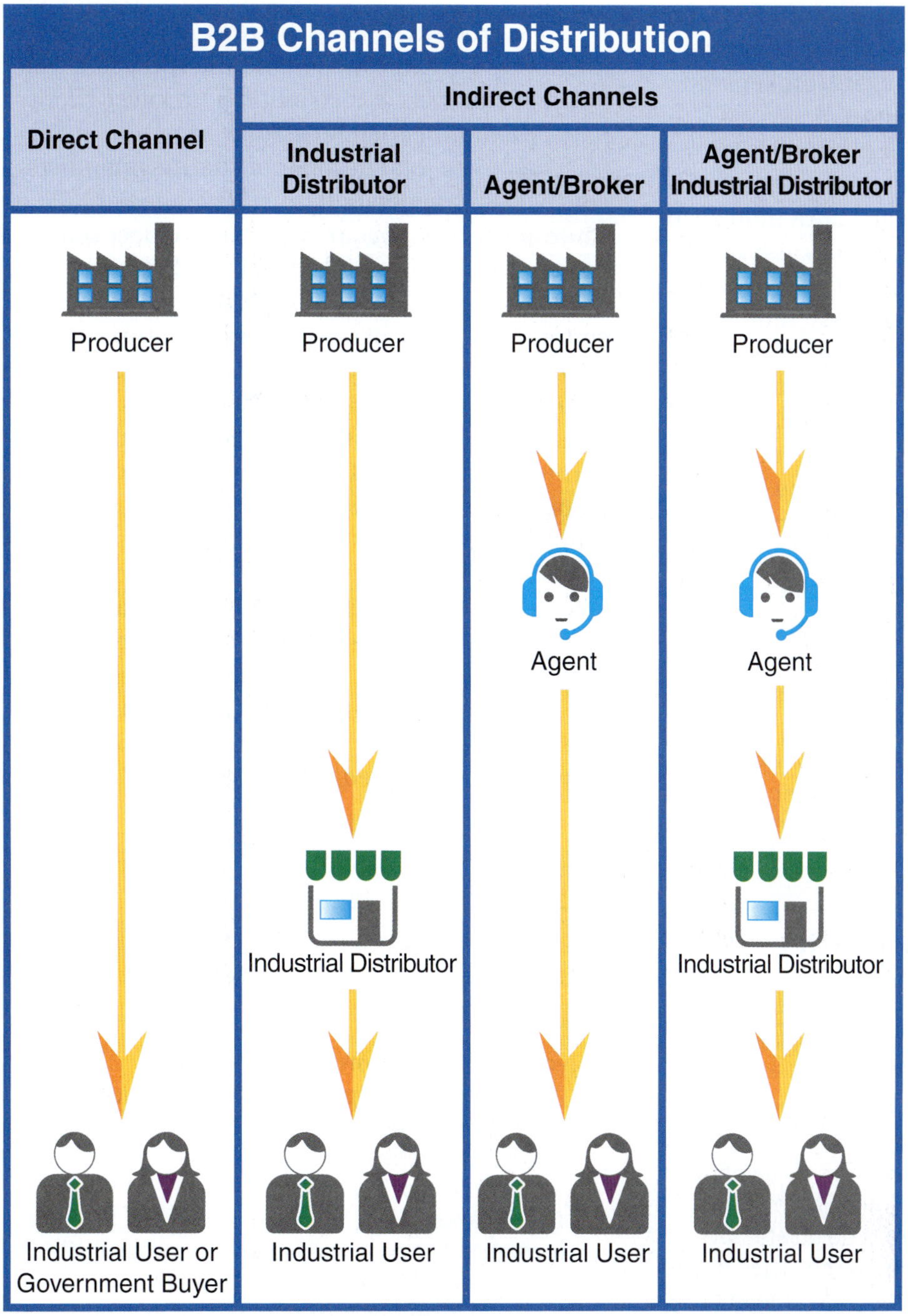

Figure 15-3 Distribution for industrial goods in the B2B market can be direct or indirect.

B2B Channels of Distribution

Direct Channel	Indirect Channels		
	Industrial Distributor	Agent/Broker	Agent/Broker Industrial Distributor
Producer → Industrial User or Government Buyer	Producer → Industrial Distributor → Industrial User	Producer → Agent → Industrial User	Producer → Agent → Industrial Distributor → Industrial User

Goodheart-Willcox Publisher

illustrated in Figure 15-3. The *direct channel* in the B2B market is getting a product from the producer to the end user, which is a business or government. No intermediaries are used. An industrial user might purchase steel from a mill to build a new headquarters for a company. A business user may purchase computers from the manufacturer to use in day-to-day operations. The direct channel of distribution is the most common method for industrial goods.

An *indirect channel* uses intermediaries to get the product from the producer or manufacturer for industrial goods in the B2B market. This channel includes industrial distributor, agent/broker, and agent/broker industrial distributor.

In the **industrial distributor channel**, a product moves from the producer to an industrial distributor, and then to the end user. An industrial distributor performs the same services as a wholesaler in the B2C market. The difference is usually in the variety of products carried. Most industrial distributors specialize in one area of products. For example, an industrial distributor may focus on aftermarket car parts or chemicals used in the production of paint. Through the industrial distributor channel, end users in the B2B market buy a producer's goods from an industrial distributor.

In the *agent/broker channel*, a producer uses an agent to assume the full responsibility of selling, storing, and shipping products. Using this channel, end users in the B2B market buy a producer's goods from an agent/broker.

The **agent/broker industrial distributor channel** combines both the agent/broker and industrial distributor channels and is the longest distribution channel. The producer first contracts with an agent/broker to find the best industrial distributors to provide selling, storage, and shipping services. In this channel, the end users in the B2B market buy the producer's goods directly from an industrial distributor.

LO 15.1-3 Channel Members

In a direct channel of distribution, the channel members are the producer and the end users. For indirect channels of distribution, however, there may be a number of intermediaries.

Due to the total number of channel members, conflict can happen and must be managed. **Channel conflict** occurs when a producer sells products directly to end users in addition to maintaining its other channels of distribution. A common example of this is a manufacturer selling its products directly to customers through an e-commerce website, while also using its traditional channels of distribution to sell its products to intermediaries and retailers. Another term for channel conflict is *disintermediation* because the producer is reducing its use of intermediaries. The result of channel conflict is that the manufacturer, intermediaries, and retailers may end up competing with one another for the same product sales.

To manage the channel of distribution and maintain efficiencies, the channel members must be selected, motivated, and evaluated.

You Do the Math

Measurement Reasoning

Three-dimensional figures have length, width, and height. In other words, they have volume. Volume is an important measurement for shipping boxes, bottles, containers, and many other items. The area of a rectangular figure is calculated by multiplying its length, height, and width. The volume of a cylinder is calculated by multiplying the area of its base by its height.

Solve the following problems.
1. The inside of a shipping container is 6 feet by 18 feet by 8 feet. If a single box is 1 foot by 2 feet by 6 inches, how many boxes can fit inside the shipping container?
2. If a rectangular box has a volume of 161.28 cubic inches and its base measures 3.5 inches by 7.2 inches, what is the height of the box?
3. If a cylindrical fuel tank is 4.25 feet tall and holds 122.6 cubic feet of fuel, what is the area of the base of the cylinder?

Select Channel Members

Once the channel of distribution is chosen, the best channel members are selected. When choosing channel members with whom to work, these factors should be reviewed:
- length of time in business;
- product lines carried;
- reputation in the industry;
- previous experience with the producer;
- financial stability; and
- quality of the sales force and customer service.

Motivate Channel Members

Once a channel member is selected, it is necessary to keep that member motivated. Producers need their channel members to promote, sell, and distribute their products in order to make a profit. To motivate channel members, producers may offer special deals, premiums, and sales contests in an effort to maintain long-term relationships.

If more than one channel member is necessary to carry out distribution, the supply chain manager is in charge of supervising them. There is always a possibility of conflict among channel members. Examples of issues include exclusive distribution rights for one intermediary and not the other, or one channel member feels another is not doing its job well. It is important that the supply chain manger maintains control and keeps all lines of communication open.

Evaluate Channel Members

After channel members are in place and performing, they should be evaluated. The supply chain manager sets measurable performance standards for evaluation. Standards may include prompt delivery, cooperative advertising, meeting sales quotas, service quality, treatment of lost or damaged goods, and overall satisfaction. Most producers review their contracts with channel members on an annual basis. They replace channel members who do not meet expectations or perform poorly. Intermediaries that have competitive pricing and meet or exceed expectations remain part of the distribution channel.

Section 15.1 Review

Check Your Understanding

1. What is a major part in the decision of place?
2. Name types of intermediaries.
3. Name two categories of wholesalers.
4. Why might some producers choose to use an agent/broker channel?
5. List examples of standards on which a channel member may be evaluated.

Build Your Vocabulary

As you progress through this text, develop a personal glossary of key terms. This will help you build your vocabulary and prepare you for a career. Write a definition for each of the following terms and add them to your personal glossary.

agent/broker channel
agent/broker industrial distributor channel
bulk-breaking
channel conflict
channel of distribution
direct channel
e-tailer
indirect channel
industrial distributor channel
industrial goods
intermediary
multi-channel retailer
nonstore retailer
retailer channel
supply chain
wholesaler channel

Section 15.2

Essential Question
Why is a supply chain important in the economy?

Supply Chain

Learning Objectives

LO 15.2-1 State various modes of transportation used by businesses.
LO 15.2-2 Identify why storage is important.
LO 15.2-3 Explain why a supply chain should be controlled by a business.
LO 15.2-4 State specific concerns related to global distribution.

Key Terms

transportation
freight forwarder
private carrier
common carrier
pipeline
private warehouse
public warehouse
supply chain management
supply chain manager
intensive distribution
selective distribution
exclusive distribution
export management company

LO 15.2-1 Transportation

Transportation is the physical movement of products through the channel of distribution. Transportation decisions impact the price of a product and the length of time it takes to reach the end user. The cost of transportation can add up to 10 percent to the price of a product.

Physical distribution is one of the most important parts of place. The selling function helps to transfer ownership to the end user. However, the physical distribution actually gives the end user possession of the goods. Physical distribution also plays a competitive role in product promotion. It makes products available where they are needed, correctly fills orders, and provides on-time delivery.

Distribution is an important component of the supply chain as it influences the final price of a product and affects company profitability. Distribution strategies include decisions about transportation, storage, and utility costs. The goal is to utilize the best distribution services for the lowest cost. Efficient distribution services help keep customer prices lower.

egd/Shutterstock.com

Transportation is the physical movement of products through the channel of distribution. *Why do you think companies choose one mode of transportation over another?*

A **freight forwarder** is a company that organizes transportation. It is not a shipper or carrier. Rather, it functions as an agent. Freight forwarders generally combine shipments from various companies. They combine the shipments and hire a transportation company to move them as one large shipment. By putting these smaller shipments together, money is saved for the companies shipping the goods.

Each type of transportation has different costs, efficiencies, and time constraints. For example, a less expensive and slower mode of transportation may be fine to ship large quantities of durable products. However, when shipping perishable goods, a more expensive and faster mode of transportation may be necessary.

There are six main methods of transportation, as shown in Figure 15-4. These transportation methods are road, rail, air, water, pipeline, and digital.

Road

Road transportation includes any motor vehicle that moves products on highways and roads. Vehicles used in road transportation are trucks, buses, vans, and automobiles.

According to the US Department of Transportation, trucking is the most common method of distribution in the United States. Trucks are a flexible mode of transportation and can be modified to carry a specific type of cargo. For example, refrigerated trucks are designed to carry products that must be kept cold. Trucks that transport canned beverages are structured to hold the cases so they will not get broken in transit. Trucks that transport cars are designed to fit as many cars as possible on one truck. Many other types of trucks are designed for the specific product they carry.

Some large companies, such as Kroger, own their trucks. Products are shipped daily from company warehouses across the country to the local stores. A **private carrier** is a company that transports its own goods. Other companies hire independent trucking firms to move their products. Independent trucking companies are called **common carriers**, or *contract carriers*.

Transportation Modes for Distribution

Mode	Advantages	Disadvantages
Road	• Can deliver door-to-door • Flexible schedules • Can be modified for specific cargo (i.e., refrigerator trucks)	• Weather delays • Traffic delays • Maintenance problems
Rail	• Sends large quantities over long distances • Inexpensive • Can carry trucks closer to the destination • Can be modified for specific cargo (i.e., flatbed railcars for intermodal containers)	• Slower method of transportation • Minimal destination flexibility • Needs a second mode of transportation to get to final destination
Air	• Fastest mode of transportation • Less chance of damage to items • Can save on warehousing as products arrive as needed	• Most expensive • Weather delays • Maintenance problems • Needs a second mode of transportation to get to final destination
Water	• Send large quantities over long distances • Can be modified for cargo (i.e., tankers for oil) • Inexpensive	• Slowest method • No destination flexibility • Needs a second mode of transportation to get to final destination
Pipeline	• Not subject to weather delays • Fewer maintenance issues • Low operating costs	• Can only carry products that flow (i.e., gasoline) • Expensive to build • Leaks linked to environmental damage • Needs a second mode of transportation to get to final destination
Digital	• Low to no operating costs • Easy access • Very fast delivery	• Only for electronic products or services

Goodheart-Willcox Publisher

Figure 15-4 Each type of transportation has different costs, efficiencies, and time constraints.

The main advantage of using motor vehicles to deliver products is door-to-door delivery. Vehicles can be scheduled to deliver products at a specific place and during a specific time period. This advantage is useful for restaurants, which must receive food products at specific times.

There are disadvantages to shipping by road. Delays caused by traffic, bad weather, or vehicle maintenance problems can impact delivery. Road transportation can also be more costly than rail or water transportation. In addition, trucks may be subject to weight limits on interstate highways.

Rail

Rail transportation is the second-most used mode of transportation in the United States based on findings from the US Department of Transportation. Rail transportation is one of the least-expensive modes and is good for long-distance shipping of large, bulky items. Shipping long distances by rail takes about the same amount of time as freight shipped by trucks.

Steel, cars, and coal are often transported by rail. Refrigerated railcars carry perishable items, such as vegetables. Tankers can be fitted on railcars to carry flammable and hazardous materials, such as chemicals or fuel.

Flatbed railcars can carry shipping containers and truck trailers. From the train, each container or trailer can be taken off and trucked to its destination. The contents of the container or truck trailer are not unloaded or reloaded. Thus, there is less chance for goods to be damaged during the train-to-truck transfer. Using the train-truck combination also combines the lower cost of train transportation with the door-to-door advantage of truck transportation.

A major disadvantage to rail is that there is no flexibility in destination. Trains can only go where there are railroad tracks, stations, and terminals. However, very few events stop or slow a train.

Air

Air transportation is the most expensive method of transporting products. Many private transportation companies offer air services, such as UPS and FedEx. High-value, low-weight items are often shipped by air. An example is emergency medicines that must arrive quickly. Air shipments are also used for some perishable goods. *Perishable goods*, such as fresh flowers, are goods that spoil quickly.

Shipping by plane is used when delivery time must be short and the higher transportation cost can be justified. For example, government contracts often have strict delivery dates for their vendors to deliver finished goods. Parts for the manufacturing of the goods must be delivered on time. Also, the finished goods must be shipped on time. Shipping costs are not spared for these business deals.

The speed of air transportation can sometimes save on inventory costs. Holding expensive or

Case in Point

Amazon Prime Air

Advances in technology impact many areas of business, including channels of distribution. Many companies are testing the use of remote-controlled drones to make product deliveries. This technology can drastically reduce the cost of delivering product on the last leg of distribution, such as from a warehouse or distribution center to the customer's door. Currently, drones are a cost-effective delivery option for packages that weigh less than five pounds and can be delivered in less than one hour, round trip.

In 2016, Amazon.com created an experimental drone-delivery service called *Prime Air*. This service automates small deliveries from Amazon facilities to customers who live nearby. The company made its first commercial drone delivery to a shopper in England in December of 2016. This initial drone flight delivered an Amazon Fire streaming video device and popcorn. The trip, from the local Amazon warehouse to the consumer's home, was two miles long and took 13 minutes. The company celebrated this event as a significant achievement in automated shipping.

As drone technology continues to develop, improvements in carrying capacity and battery life will certainly expand its applications. Increasing flight time between chargings will expand the range for deliveries. This technology has many exciting possibilities and the potential to greatly change the channels of distribution. When the implementation of drone deliveries becomes more widespread, the Federal Aviation Administration (FAA) will likely become more involved in the use of commercial drones in the United States.

Drone delivery could be a form of transportation utilized by some businesses. *What are some advantages and disadvantages of drone delivery?*

perishable goods in a warehouse is costly. Products can spoil, plus warehouse space costs money. For these reasons, the cost of air transportation is offset by the savings on inventory storage.

A disadvantage of air transportation is the high cost. Once a product arrives at an airport, it still needs to be delivered to its final destination. Road transportation companies called *air cargo companies* specialize in delivering air cargo.

Water

Water transportation includes ocean-going ships, inland ships, and coastal ships. Ships are also called *freighters*. *Ocean-going ships* transport products across the ocean, normally between countries. *Inland ships* use rivers and lakes to transport products. *Coastal ships* move products up and down the coastline of a country. In the United States, coastal ships move products up and down the Pacific and Atlantic coastlines.

Ships can be modified for the type of cargo they carry. *Tankers* are ships designed specifically for transporting petroleum oil. *Barges* are large holding vessels that are towed or pushed. *Container ships* are ships designed to hold large metal shipping containers for cargo shipped long distances. It is easier to load and unload one large metal container than many small boxes. Containers can be transferred from a ship to a truck or flatbed railcar to continue to their destinations. Containers allow large quantities of goods to travel long distances without being unpacked.

The low cost of water transportation must be weighed against the disadvantages. Water transportation is the slowest option. Hurricanes and monsoons at sea can also impact the delivery of products. In addition, products can only be shipped to a port, instead of a specific delivery address. The products delivered to a port must then be transported by another mode of transportation, usually road or rail transportation. This generally increases the final shipping cost.

Pipeline

A **pipeline** is a line of connected pipes that carry liquids and gases over a long distance. Products carried through pipelines move slowly but continuously. Pipelines are limited in what they can carry, such as liquid or oil products. However, the products are safe from damage or theft. Also, they are not subject to delivery delays due to bad weather.

Building a pipeline is expensive, but the cost to operate it is low. Leaks rarely occur. However, when there is a leak, the risk of environmental damage is great.

Digital

Digital delivery is the norm for many products such as video games, e-books, and music and movie downloads. The prevalence of Internet-connected devices, including smartphones, tablets, televisions, and gaming systems, has made digital delivery a widely used form of distribution. This form of delivery is relatively inexpensive and time-saving. The consumer can take possession of the product instantly after an order is placed.

Storage
LO 15.2-2

Storage is critical to place strategies. Products need protection from weather, theft, and damage. Retail and manufacturing businesses need areas to store physical inventory. This may increase distribution costs, which will affect the price of the final product. If a business does not have enough storage space within its facility, it will need to rent, lease, or build space. Businesses may also use wholesalers to store products until they are needed.

Products need protection from weather, theft, and damage. *How does the warehousing of products help protect them?*

Maxim Blinkov/Shutterstock.com

Private warehouses are those owned by a company for storage of its own goods. Large companies, such as Bed, Bath, and Beyond and Toys"R"Us, have their own warehouse facilities.

Smaller companies may lease storage space. A **public warehouse** is one that rents storage space to any company. Some public warehouse facilities provide delivery to the end user. By using this type of warehousing service, a business can reduce inventory-storage costs and losses due to damage or theft.

Some companies prefer not to use storage facilities, but stagger the delivery of inventory instead. By ordering a large quantity of product, they can negotiate when inventory is delivered. The manufacturer will make and hold the products in storage until the ship date.

LO 15.2-3 Supply Chain

A *supply chain* is the businesses, people, and activities involved in turning raw materials into products and delivering them to end users. **Supply chain management** is coordinating the events happening throughout the supply chain. It may also be called *channel management*.

When a business controls the supply chain, it can recognize efficiencies in time, process, and money. The supply chain is visualized vertically, with the raw material at the top and the final customer at the bottom. Products start at the top and move from link to link to reach the final customer. Effective supply chain management results in the following benefits:
- streamlined inventories;
- lower operating costs;
- timely product availability; and
- increased customer satisfaction.

Exploring Marketing Careers

Supply Chain Manager

One of the many tasks that contributes to a company's success is managing product flow. Not having enough of a product carries the risk of running out of stock. On the other hand, having too much of the product increases the need for warehousing, which in turn increases the company's costs. Forecasting managers are responsible for managing the flow of products through a company. They analyze purchasing patterns to forecast the need for specific products. Then they coordinate the activities of the production or purchasing, warehousing, and distribution departments to ensure that products flow smoothly from production or purchase through final sales and distribution. Other typical job titles for a supply chain manager are *forecasting manager*, *channel manager*, *supply chain director*, and *supply chain coordinator*.

Some examples of tasks that forecasting managers perform include:
- Analyze inventories to determine how quickly products are turned over
- Create demand and supply plans to ensure the timely availability of materials or products
- Monitor industry forecasts to identify trends that may affect the supply chain
- Coordinate purchasing, manufacturing, sales, marketing, warehousing, and distribution of products

Supply chain managers need a sound knowledge of production processes and should be able to maximize the efficient manufacture or purchase and distribution of products. They should understand transportation and distribution. In addition, they must have excellent math skills and an ability to analyze data to find purchasing trends. Most jobs in this field require a bachelor or master degree in accounting or a related field, as well as several years of experience. For more information, access the *Occupational Outlook Handbook* online.

Copyright Goodheart-Willcox Co., Inc.

These benefits directly impact the level and quality of customer service a company is able to provide. Streamlined inventories and timely product availability mean that salespeople can accurately schedule product deliveries. Lower operating costs mean that product prices are likely competitive. Satisfied customers, whether in the B2C or B2B market, are loyal customers.

The **supply chain manager** is the person who coordinates and monitors all the distribution activities, from building the product to delivery to the end user. After the product moves through the supply chain to the distribution stage, the manager makes place decisions. The supply chain manager must make choices about how to best get products to the end users. Several factors should be considered before deciding which channel of distribution to use. These factors include characteristics of the target market, distribution requirements of the product itself, impact of distribution cost on final price, and level of distribution used.

Target Market

First, objectives must be identified for the distribution channel. Answering the *who, when, where, why,* and *how* about the target market is the first step.
- Who is the target market?
- When do the customers buy?
- Where do they go to buy?
- Why do they buy?
- How do they buy?

Once these questions are answered, the supply chain manager can begin to weigh the choice of a direct channel or indirect channel to get the product to the end user.

Product

Product considerations are important when selecting the channel of distribution. The product itself will help to determine how it should be transported. If a product has a short shelf life or is perishable, it will need to be handled differently than a staple clothing item like jeans. Product life cycle is also important. Winter coats and summer bathing suits have different seasonal opportunities for selling. They must be shipped early or in the most efficient manner to get them to the final retailer on time.

Price

The method of transportation will influence the price that the end user pays for the product. If the product must be shipped quickly, transportation costs may be high. This means the final price of the product may be higher. The opposite may also be true, and prices can be kept low by using less-costly shipping options.

Levels of Distribution

The level of distribution varies depending on how intensely the products will be distributed. The level of distribution plays a role in the channel that is selected. The three levels of distribution are intensive, selective, and exclusive, as illustrated in Figure 15-5.

Intensive Distribution

Intensive distribution is when product is placed in every potential sales situation possible. This allows a manufacturer, wholesaler, or retailer to have as much exposure as possible. Producers and distributors of convenience goods often choose intensive distribution strategies. For example, consumers can find newspapers, gum, milk, and bread at many different locations.

Selective Distribution

Selective distribution is selecting only certain places the manufacturer or wholesaler wants a product to be sold. Only select channel members are used. This method is used most often with shopping goods or brands with an exclusive image. For example, Coach purses and accessories can only be found at high-end department stores or Coach retail stores.

With selective distribution, there are just enough locations selling the product in a market area to adequately serve the target market. A retailer using selective distribution might locate one store in each major shopping mall. For example, Old Navy has a selective distribution approach.

Distribution Intensity	
Intensive distribution	Product is placed in every potential sales situation possible
Selective distribution	Product is sold in certain places selected by the manufacturer or wholesaler
Exclusive distribution	Product is sold by only one distributor in a market area

Goodheart-Willcox Publisher

Figure 15-5 The level of distribution plays a role in the channel that is selected.

Exclusive Distribution

Exclusive distribution occurs when there is only one distributor of products in a market area. Exclusive distribution traditionally occurs with highly technical or complex products that are expensive. An exclusive-distribution retailer has only one store to serve the entire market area.

For example, there is only one Rolls Royce automobile dealer in the Chicago area. These retailers can use the exclusive approach because their customers are willing to travel to buy these special products.

Global Distribution
LO 15.2-4

Companies that buy, sell, or distribute products globally can have more complex, or different, place decisions than those that only sell domestically. As explained in Chapter 7, there are legal and political issues that must be considered when operating a business globally. In addition, before distributing products to foreign markets, a business plan should be created. There are many product, price, place, and promotion issues that must be addressed. Examples of issues include the following.

- Does the company or product appeal to the foreign markets that are being considered? Is this company the right choice?
- Are there any cultural or other issues that would influence consumer acceptance of the products?
- Does the foreign market have the necessary technology to make conducting business seamless?
- What are the logistics of getting the product to the foreign market?
- Does the exchange value make the product profitable to export?
- Are there labor issues in the foreign country that should be investigated?

Distribution can be a challenge as other countries may not have the same quality of transportation infrastructure, including roads and airports, that is needed. In less-developed countries, basic infrastructure services may be inadequate, such as electricity, telephone services, and Internet connectivity.

To facilitate global distribution, many US businesses use intermediaries to help with foreign trade and distribution. An **export management company** is an independent company that provides support services, such as warehousing, shipping, insuring, and billing on behalf of another business. They are also called *export trading companies*. These companies also help businesses with foreign customs offices; documentation; and sizing, weight, and measurement conversions. Export management companies can be either local or foreign-owned.

Section 15.2 Review

Check Your Understanding

1. What role does physical distribution play in product promotion?
2. What is the goal of distribution?
3. What options does a business have if it does not have enough storage space within its facility?
4. Provide an example of the benefits of effective supply chain management.
5. Explain why distribution can be a challenge when selling into other countries.

Build Your Vocabulary

As you progress through this text, develop a personal glossary of key terms. This will help you build your vocabulary and prepare you for a career. Write a definition for each of the following terms and add them to your personal glossary.

common carrier
exclusive distribution
export management company
freight forwarder
intensive distribution
pipeline
private carrier
private warehouse
public warehouse
selective distribution
supply chain management
supply chain manager
transportation

CHAPTER 15 Review and Assessment

Chapter Summary

Section 15.1 Channels of Distribution

LO 15.1-1 Explain place as one of the four Ps of marketing.
Place refers to the activities involved in getting a good or service to the end user. It is also known as distribution. A major part in the decision of place is selecting the channel of distribution. Channel members help move products from their origination to the consumer. They include producers and intermediaries.

LO 15.1-2 Identify distribution channels for B2C and B2B markets.
Distribution channels can be direct or indirect. A direct channel is from the manufacturer or producer to the end user without using intermediaries. There are indirect channels of distribution for B2C goods that include retailer, wholesaler, or agent/broker. Three channels of indirect distribution in the B2B market include industrial distributor, agent/broker, and agent/broker industrial distributor.

LO 15.1-3 Explain how to manage the channel of distribution.
To manage the channel of distribution and maintain efficiencies, channel members must be selected, motivated, and evaluated. Multiple factors should be considered when choosing channel members. Once selected, it is necessary to keep that member motivated. After channel members are in place and performing, they should be evaluated.

Section 15.2 Supply Chain

LO 15.2-1 State various modes of transportation used by businesses.
Transportation is the physical movement of products through the channel of distribution. Six main methods of transportation are road, rail, air, water, pipeline, and digital. Physical distribution gives the end user possession of the goods, plays a competitive role in product promotion, makes products available where they are needed, correctly fills orders, and provides on-time delivery.

LO 15.2-2 Identify why storage is important.
Products need protection from weather, theft, and damage. Retail and manufacturing businesses need areas to store physical inventory.

LO 15.2-3 Explain why a supply chain should be controlled by a business.
A supply chain is the businesses, people, and activities involved in turning raw materials into products and delivering them to end users. Supply chain management is coordinating the events happening throughout the supply chain. Factors to consider before deciding which channel to use are target market, distribution requirements, impact of distribution cost on final price, and level of distribution.

LO 15.2-4 State specific concerns related to global distribution.
Companies that buy, sell, or distribute products globally can have more complex, or different, place decisions than those that only sell domestically. Many product, price, place, and promotion issues must be addressed. Before distributing products to foreign markets, a business plan should be created. Distribution can be a challenge as other countries may not have the same quality of infrastructure.

Check Your Marketing IQ

Now that you have completed the chapter, see what you have learned about marketing by taking the chapter posttest. The posttest is available at www.g-wlearning.com/marketing/.

Review Your Knowledge

1. Explain place as one of the four Ps of marketing.
2. List and explain functions of intermediaries.
3. Identify distribution channels for B2C and B2B markets.
4. What is the result of channel conflict?
5. How is the channel of distribution managed to maintain efficiencies?
6. Identify various modes of transportation used by businesses.
7. Explain why storage is important.
8. Explain why a supply chain must be controlled by a business.
9. List and describe three levels of distribution.
10. State specific concerns related to global distribution.

Apply Your Knowledge

1. Does the business you selected qualify as a producer or intermediary? Describe why the business is one or the other.
2. A major part in the decision of place is selecting the channel of distribution. Review the channels of distribution described in this chapter. Which channel or channels would be the most appropriate choice for the business you have selected? Explain why.
3. Intermediaries serve three functions: transactional, logistical, and facilitating functions. Describe how your channel members serve these functions.
4. Identify the products that you will distribute as B2C or B2B. Next, create a flowchart to show the supply chain from the producer or manufacturer to the end user.
5. How would you motivate the members in your channel of distribution?
6. How would you evaluate the members in your channel of distribution?
7. Divide a sheet of paper into two columns. In the left column, list all the ways your company can move its products from a producer or manufacturer to the end user. In the right column, explain the cost of the transportation method versus the amount of control it provides your company.
8. Describe how a freight forwarder could help facilitate transportation of products for your business.
9. Storage is critical to place strategies. Explain the storage needs of the products distributed by your business.
10. What is the level of distribution in your business? Should it be changed? If so, why?

Apply Your Math Skills

A movie production company is releasing a new movie for home viewing. It costs the company $12 to produce each copy of the movie in any format. Apply your math skills to solve the following problems.

1. The consumer price for a DVD is $19.99. How much profit does the production company generate on each DVD?
2. The consumer price of a Blu-ray disc is $21.99. How much profit does the production company generate on each Blu-ray disc?
3. The consumer price of a digital download is $16.99. How much profit does the production company generate on each digital download?

Communication Skills

Reading Read about the advantages and disadvantages of different transportation modes for distribution in Figure 15-4. How does the information in this chart relate to your prior knowledge about transportation?

Writing Think about your experiences with the digital delivery of products. This may include downloading music, books, or apps. Write several paragraphs that summarize your experiences. Use well-chosen details and well-structured event sequences. Evaluate the benefits and challenges you have experienced with products that are distributed digitally.

Speaking Read the Marketing Ethics feature in this chapter. Think of a time when you used your ideals and principles to make a decision that involved ethics. In retrospect, do you think you made the correct decision? Did your decision have any consequences? Share your opinions with the class.

Internet Research

Advantages of Buying Local Using the Internet, conduct a search for *advantages of buying local*. What are the advantages to a consumer who buys locally produced products? What are the advantages to businesses with shorter channels of distribution or supply chains?

Digital Delivery Conduct Internet research on *digital delivery*. What do you think its advantages and disadvantages are? What type of business could benefit from digital delivery of products?

Global Distribution Use Internet resources to research how distribution differs in other countries compared to the United States. How has technology impacted transportation and storage overseas? Identify any distribution challenges that still exist in developing nations.

Teamwork

Working with a team, create a chart that describes the major modes of transportation and the advantages and disadvantages of each. Identify types of products that may be best suited for delivery by each mode of transportation. Analyze how each mode of transportation can affect the cost of the products you identified.

Portfolio Development

College and Career Readiness

Documents Your portfolio will include documents that you have collected as well as those you have created. Any collected documents that highlight your skills and qualifications should be included. To add these to your printed portfolio, photocopy the documents. To add to your digital portfolio, scan the items.

Decide which file formats to use for the documents that you have created. You can use the default format to save your documents. For example, use Microsoft Word format for letters and essays or the Microsoft Excel format for spreadsheets. Someone reviewing your digital portfolio will need to have the same or a compatible program to open these files. Another option is to save created documents as PDF or HTML files. Keep in mind that having all of the files in the same format can make viewing easier for others who need to review your portfolio. If you are hosting your digital portfolio online, check the website for specifications on file formats and how to upload the documents.

1. Identify documents you have *collected* that will be included in your portfolio.
2. Identify documents you have *created* that will be included in your portfolio.
3. Photocopy these for your print portfolio. Next, scan each collected document for inclusion in your digital portfolio. Save created documents in an appropriate format.

CHAPTER 16
Purchasing and Inventory Control

Sections

16.1 **Purchasing**

16.2 **Inventory Control**

Reading Prep

College and Career Readiness

Before reading this chapter, flip through the pages and make notes of the major headings. Compare these headings to the objectives. What did you discover? How will this help you prepare to read new material?

Check Your Marketing IQ

Before you begin the chapter, see what you already know about marketing by taking the chapter pretest. The pretest is available at www.g-wlearning.com/marketing/.

DECA Emerging Leaders

Hospitality Services Team Decision-Making Event, Part 2

Career Cluster: Hospitality and Tourism
Instructional Area: Market Planning

Procedure, Part 2

1. In the previous chapter, you studied the performance indicators for this event.
2. The event will be presented to you through your reading of the Knowledge and Skills Developed, Specific Performance Indicators, and Case Study Situation. You will have up to 30 minutes to review this information and prepare your presentation. You may make notes to use during your presentation.
3. Teams will meet with the judge for a 15-minute presentation. The team will spend no more than ten minutes at the beginning of the interview describing the team's analysis of the situation given. Both members of the team must participate in the presentation. The judge will spend the remaining five minutes questioning the participants. Each participant must respond to at least one question posed by the judge.
4. Turn in all your notes and event materials when you have completed the event.

Case Study Situation

You are to assume the role of a management team at White Bear Resort, an upscale resort located in a very popular tourism and recreation area. The **owner (judge)** of White Bear Resort has asked you to develop a strategy to deal with a natural disaster that occurred last week.

White Bear Resort is located on picturesque Lake Loraine. It is a destination vacation resort featuring 720 rooms, four restaurants, a 200,000-square-foot indoor water park, fitness center, spa, tennis courts, boating, Jet Skis, parasailing, rock climbing, a championship golf course, and a miniature golf course. Targeted to middle- and upper-income customers, White Bear Resort is an all-suite resort charging $325 to $475 per night during the peak summer season. The resort employs mostly part-time and seasonal employees. Only 20 percent of the employees are full time.

Located in the Loraine Valley, the region forms one of the top family vacation destinations in the United States. Loraine Valley is an enormous vacation and recreation area with three outdoor water parks, an amusement park, go-kart tracks, scenic boat tours, horseback riding, a thrill show, two shopping districts, several nightclubs, and two casinos. Yearly, the area boasts an estimated five million annual visitors who pump over $1 billion into the local economy.

Last week, a dam holding back the water to Lake Loraine burst and the entire lake emptied into local rivers—turning Lake Loraine into one giant mud hole. The lake is expected to remain empty for more than a year. News of the unusual event was widely reported on television and radio. White Bear Resort has experienced a cancellation of 30 percent of their summer reservations in less than a week.

With Lake Loraine now empty, all boating and other lake activities have been cancelled. The remainder of White Bear Resort's operation is unaffected, however. In fact, 90 percent of all Loraine Valley attractions will operate as usual this summer. Nonetheless, many visitors to White Bear Resort are canceling their upcoming summer reservations.

The owner (judge) has asked to meet with you to hear your ideas on the following:

- a plan to try to get those who have already cancelled to reconsider their cancellations; and
- a strategy that White Bear Resort can implement to reduce the number of future cancellations and draw in new customers.

If it becomes necessary to reduce the workforce, how should those decisions be made and from which areas of operation should they come? Be as complete and specific as possible.

You will present to the owner (judge) of White Bear Resort in a meeting to take place in the owner's (judge's) office. The owner (judge) will begin the meeting by greeting you and asking to hear your ideas. When you have finished your presentation and have answered the owner's (judge's) questions, he or she will conclude the meeting by thanking you for your work.

Critical Thinking

1. Other than reducing personnel, are there any other areas that White Bear Resort can look at to reduce overall expenses?
2. Should we mention the fact that Lake Loraine is currently empty in any of our advertising? Why or why not?

Visit www.deca.org for more information.

Published by DECA Inc. Copyright © by DECA Inc. No part of this publication may be reproduced for resale without written permission from the publisher. Printed in the United States of America.

Section 16.1

Purchasing

Essential Question

How do buyers decide what inventory they are going to stock?

Learning Objectives

LO 16.1-1 Discuss two types of organizational buyers.
LO 16.1-2 List steps of the purchasing process.

Key Terms

business purchasing
organizational buyer
purchasing agent
buyer
purchasing process
electronic data interchange (EDI)
bid
negotiation
economy of scale
purchase order (PO)
receiving record
marking
invoice
terms for delivery
free on board (FOB)
quality control

LO 16.1-1 Business Purchasing

Business purchasing is the activity of acquiring goods or services to accomplish the goals of an organization. Businesses buy a wide variety of goods and services depending on their different needs.

The person who handles all the purchasing duties for a business or an organization is an **organizational buyer**. There are two types of organizational buyers: purchasing agents and buyers. However, sometimes the terms *purchaser* and *buyer* are used for the same purpose.

Purchasing Agents

Purchasing agents buy goods and services the company needs internally to operate its business. The goods purchased are not resold to customers; rather, they are used within the organization. Other terms for purchasing agents include *specialized purchaser* and *purchasing manager*.

Purchasing agents often need technical knowledge about the company's products or production

Chubarov Mikhail/Shutterstock.com

Purchasing agents buy goods and services the company needs to operate its business. *What goods do you think a business would need in its day-to-day operations?*

Case in Point

Target

Successful inventory management is critical for every business. Without it, retailers would have a challenge meeting customer needs. But at times, even the best inventory management strategies do not always keep a business from running out of stock.

Target is one of the largest discount retailers in the United States. Target offers a large and varied product mix at its stores. In recent years, the retail chain's inventory was not always able to keep up with customer demands as the store increased in popularity. Stock-outs led to disappointed, frustrated customers and lost sales for the company.

In order to solve the issue, the retailer asked its employees to look closely at what was selling on store shelves to identify different products that customers were not buying. The store began eliminating these low-selling products from its product mix.

Target's solution was to actually simplify its product mix, carrying selected varieties of products—fewer sizes, brands, flavors, and colors of myriad products. Simplifying the products in its inventory allowed Target to also simplify its supply chains. This strategy helped Target forecast inventory needs to make sure the most popular products were in stock and available for purchase. The strategy worked, as Target reported a forty-percent reduction in stock-outs during the 2015 holiday shopping season.

---

processes. For example, a purchaser for a manufacturer must know a great deal about the raw materials and equipment used for producing the company's products. Purchasers must also buy the furniture, fixtures, equipment, and supplies needed to run the business. Purchasing agents research where to get the best products at the best prices.

In small businesses, it is not always clear who makes the final buying decisions. There is often more than one person involved. Written approval is generally needed to make large purchases. Sometimes, the people making the decision are obvious, such as the company president or vice president. Sometimes, they are not obvious. For example, the person who knows the department's needs best may choose which computers are purchased. That person may be a manager or an administrative assistant.

Buyers

Wholesale and retail **buyers** purchase goods for the sole purpose of reselling them to customers. They purchase products that the business will not use, but resell to customers. Other terms for buyers include *professional buyer*, *retail buyer*, and *merchandise manager*. However, sometimes the terms *purchaser* and *buyer* are used for the same purpose.

The buyer in a retail business is in a very important position. Decisions about what goods to purchase for resale have a major effect on the success of the business. Much planning goes into purchasing inventory. For example, retailers spend an average of 70 cents of every dollar made in sales on inventory. If the wrong inventory is purchased, customers may not buy enough for the business to make a profit. Depending on the type of business, inventory may be purchased daily, weekly, monthly, or even less frequently.

LO 16.1-2 Purchasing Process

The **purchasing process** is a series of steps a purchasing agent or buyer takes to buy goods and services for a business. These steps may vary depending on the business, but in general, are similar. The specific steps in the purchasing process are shown in Figure 16-1.

Much of the business purchasing process takes place electronically to maximize efficiency and easily maintain records. **Electronic data interchange (EDI)** is the standard transfer of electronic data for business transactions between organizations. Transactions can include orders, confirmations, and invoices.

Identify Inventory Needs

In a retail business, the type and quality of merchandise purchased depends on the goals

Purchasing Process

- Identify inventory needs
- Identify vendors
- Initiate bidding process
- Negotiate the purchase
- Award the contract
- Receive the order
- Pay the invoice
- Evaluate the vendor

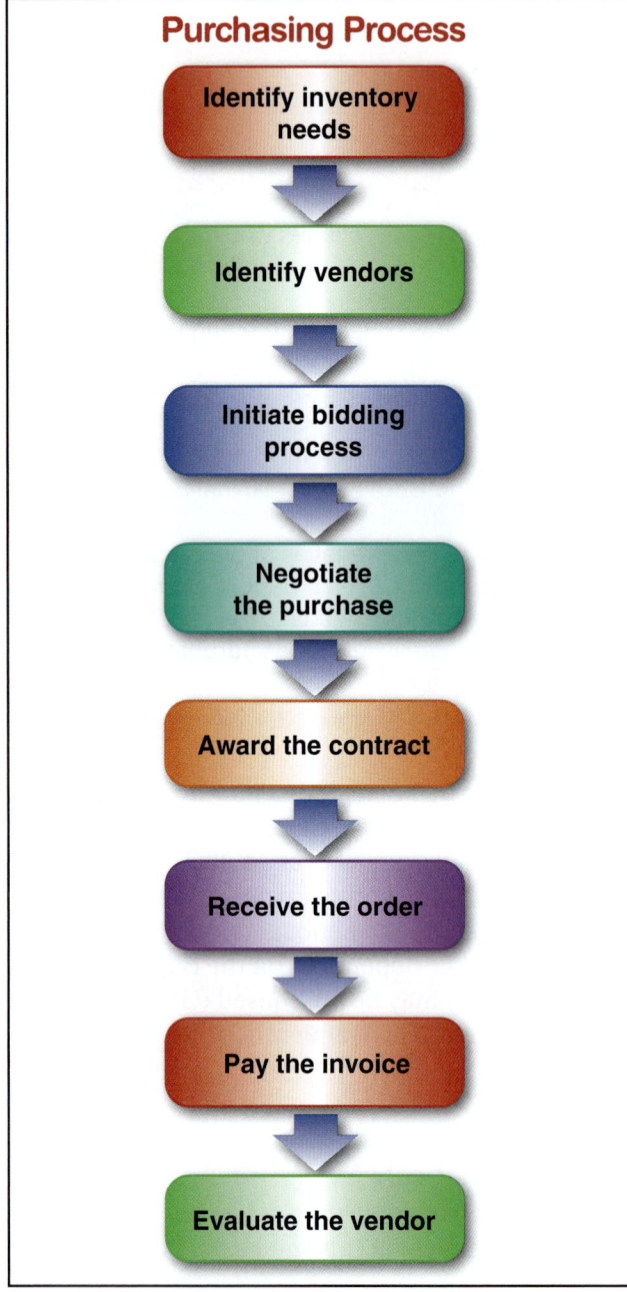

Goodheart-Willcox Publisher

Figure 16-1 The purchasing process includes these specific steps.

Identify Vendors

Vendors, also known as *suppliers*, are companies that sell products to other businesses. Depending on the products needed, there may be many vendors from which to choose. The service quality, product quality, and pricing can greatly differ by vendor. Buyers can check with other business contacts in their industry for vendor recommendations. The Better Business Bureau (BBB) also provides reports on vendor standings.

Initiate Bidding Process

Most organizations require their agents or buyers to get a number of bids from different vendors. The *bidding process* is a series of steps the buyer takes to obtain the best price for a purchase. A **bid** is a formal written proposal that lists all the goods and services that will be provided, their corresponding prices, and the timeline for delivery. After vendors have been researched and selected, an invitation to bid is extended to those who are interested in participating. Included in the invitation are the date the bid is due and specifications that the vendor must meet, such as size, colors, weight, or other important details. Interested vendors can then issue a bid.

Negotiate the Purchase

After all bids are received, the buyer determines which bid and vendor is the best for the business. The buyer makes a recommendation to the management team, who will eventually

michaeljung/Shutterstock.com

Inventory is adjusted to meet the changing needs and wants of customers. *How do you see changing customer needs and wants reflected in the products carried in local stores?*

of the business stated in the marketing plan. Retail and service businesses must be aware of the changes in customer needs and wants. In order to maintain a successful business, inventory is adjusted to meet those needs. Before placing orders for merchandise, buyers study the target market. Marketers help the buyers know which products are popular, how often are they purchased, and about new trends. This information is important because inventory is purchased before a business needs it.

Green Marketing

Ecofriendly Purchasing

A business typically chooses its vendors based on price, quality, and services offered. However, many businesses are also considering the location of vendors when making purchasing decisions. Minimizing the transportation miles required to receive inventory is an ecofriendly, energy-saving consideration in the purchasing process.

When evaluating vendor options, inquire about delivery routes and local distribution centers. Many businesses may choose to use local suppliers for materials and business services. Choosing local sources reduces the amount of travel needed, which lowers fuel consumption and emissions. Making use of local business resources has the added benefit of supporting the local economy.

---

approve the purchase. Organizations do not necessarily choose the lowest-priced bid. They take into consideration factors such as vendor quality, delivery time, and service.

Negotiation with a vendor may be necessary before making a final decision. **Negotiation** is when individuals come together in an attempt to reach an agreement. Negotiating a purchase involves getting a good price and payment schedule for the goods as well as timely delivery. It also includes confirming quality and value, as well as scale discounts.

Quality and Value

The quality of products a business can offer ranges from high-end and expensive to low-end and inexpensive. The key to negotiating for quality is to insist on *value*, or getting the highest quality for the lowest price. A business marks up the price it paid for items to earn a profit on customer sales. The choice of product quality also depends on how much the target market is willing to pay for certain items.

Buyers must understand how quality and price affect value in their industries to negotiate the best deals. Sometimes vendors offer higher-quality merchandise for very good prices to encourage a business to also buy inexpensive items. Depending on the vendor, this area is open for negotiation.

Economies of Scale

Most vendors offer *quantity discounts,* or a reduced per-item price based on the number purchased, to encourage larger orders. The greater the quantity purchased, the lower the per-unit price. It is usually more cost-effective for businesses to purchase inventory in larger quantities to obtain the lower unit prices. After markup to the list prices, the profit margin on the goods sold is greater.

Quantity discounts are based on the economy of scale. **Economy of scale** is the decrease in unit cost of a product resulting from large scale manufacturing operations. The efficiency of production increases as more of a product is made. This in turn reduces the cost per piece.

Economies of scale also occur in other business functions. For example, the per-item shipping and handling cost on larger orders may be less than when purchasing fewer products. Transportation costs can be spread over the total cost of all the products purchased and not just one item.

djordjevla/Shutterstock.com

Economies of scale can reduce shipping and handling costs on large orders. *How might a business purchasing a large quantity of a product benefit the consumer?*

Award the Contract

Once the vendor has been chosen and the details of the purchase have been negotiated, the business can award the contract to the vendor. This is done by notifying the vendor that their bid was accepted and completing a purchase order for the product. A **purchase order (PO)** is a form a buyer sends to the vendor to officially place an order. It lists the negotiated quantities, varieties, and prices for the products ordered. The purchase order includes the company information and the product, shipping, and payment details, as shown in Figure 16-2.

POs should be consecutively numbered so the recordkeeping system remains sequential. Copies of the PO are made for business records and for the vendor.

Receive the Order

Tracking purchases is an important step to make sure shipments are correct and delivered when promised. When a shipment of goods is received, it includes a *packing list*, sometimes called a *packing slip*, that lists the contents of the package. The person receiving the shipment verifies the contents by comparing items to the packing slip. The confirmation process ensures that everything received also agrees with the PO.

A **receiving record** is the form on which all merchandise received is listed as it comes into the place of business. After receiving and inspecting the shipment, the details are recorded on a receiving record and filed for future use. Sometimes the contents will not match the packing slip.

Extreme Sporting Goods
123 Main Street
Tampa, FL 33601
Phone: (813) 555-1234
Fax: (813) 555-1235

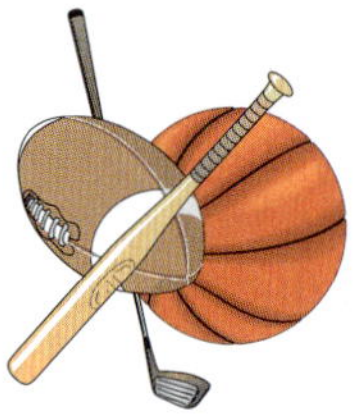

PURCHASE ORDER

PO #: 003725 | Date: 03/31/20--

Vendor Name/Address:	Vendor ID:	Customer ID:
Salt Lake Wholesale
9807 Second Avenue
Atlanta, GA 30060
(678) 555-1236	24	1068A

SHIPPING METHOD	SHIPPING TERMS	DELIVERY DATE
Ground	Received by 05/01/20--	05/01/20--

Item	Job	Description	Qty	Unit Price	Line Total
013188	12	Extreme water bottles	24	3.70	88.80
011088	12	Small camping packs	60	11.25	675.00
012488	12	12-pack DC golf balls	48	6.15	295.20

1. Please send two copies of your invoice.
2. Enter this order in accordance with the prices, terms, delivery method, and specifications listed above.
3. Please notify us immediately if you are unable to ship as specified.
4. Send all correspondence to:
   Extreme Sporting Goods
   E-mail: extremesport@esg.com
   Fax: (813) 555-1235

Subtotal		1,059.00
For resale? Yes/ No	Tax ID: 12-3456789	Sales Tax —
	Shipping	126.95
Total Net 30 days		**$1,185.95**

Authorized by: *Carl Jackson*
Date: 3/31/20--

Goodheart-Willcox Publisher

Figure 16-2 A buyer sends a purchase order (PO) to the vendor to officially place an order.

The contents of a shipment are verified by comparing items to the packing slip. *What might occur if the business does not have an employee verify the package contents?*

XiXinXing/Shutterstock.com

Or, products may have become damaged in the shipping process. In those cases, the receiving record is used to help the vendor correct an order.

Marking is the process of attaching the price to each item that will be sold. Once goods are received and checked, they are usually marked with tickets or UPC codes. These tickets record the price and also serve as inventory tracking information.

Pay the Invoice

An **invoice** is a vendor bill requesting payment for goods shipped or services provided. After an order is shipped, the vendor sends an invoice to the buyer. The invoice lists the goods purchased, amount owed, and payment terms. Before paying an invoice, the buyer makes sure that the costs and payment terms listed on the invoice match those on the PO. In addition, the buyer must verify that the receiving record matches the invoice. Large businesses often have a formal process for payment and approval of invoices that includes management. After approval, the buyer submits invoices to accounting for payment.

Discounts

Most vendors expect payment either upon receipt of goods or within 30 days. Recall that some vendors offer a cash discount to encourage businesses to pay invoices early. A *cash discount* is usually a percentage deducted from the total invoice amount offered to encourage a customer to pay a bill early. A cash discount often shows up in a format similar to *2/10, net 30*. This means that a *2* percent discount off the invoice total applies if the customer pays the bill within *10* days. Otherwise, the customer has *30* days to pay the entire bill without receiving a penalty. Cash discounts encourage customers to pay bills early, which helps the cash flow of the vendor.

Terms for Delivery

Terms for delivery are the delivery arrangements made between the buyer and seller. **Free on board (FOB)** indicates which party, the buyer or shipper, has liability for the shipment if damages are incurred and at what point ownership of the goods changes hands.

- *FOB shipping point* means the buyer is responsible and pays for shipping.
- *FOB destination point* means the seller is responsible until the shipment reaches the buyer. The seller pays the shipping.

Insurance is typically purchased by the party responsible for the shipping. By purchasing insurance, potential losses are covered.

Evaluate the Vendor

The person or department responsible for receiving shipments helps buyers to evaluate vendors. Checking the merchandise received for any damages, shortages, or overages is crucial. At this point, the business is performing quality control. **Quality control** is the activity of checking goods as they are produced or received to ensure the quality meets expectations.

A good time for a buyer to evaluate vendors is after receiving their invoices. A form similar to the one shown in Figure 16-3 can be used to monitor the track record of vendors over time. A rating scale is helpful to score the criteria. If a vendor proves to be reliable and provides value and consistent product quality, the vendor can be used again.

Vendor Evaluation Form

Vendors	Date	Availability of products	Quality	Reliability	On-time delivery	Damages or discrepancies	Service	Price
Vendor #1								
Vendor #2								
Vendor #3								
Vendor #4								

Goodheart-Willcox Publisher

Figure 16-3 A vendor evaluation form can be used to monitor the track record of vendors over time.

Section 16.1 Review

Check Your Understanding

1. Why do purchasing agents buy goods and services?
2. Why do buyers for a business purchase products?
3. What is the bidding process?
4. What does negotiating a purchase involve?
5. Explain the difference between FOB shipping point and FOB destination point.

Build Your Vocabulary

As you progress through this text, develop a personal glossary of key terms. This will help you build your vocabulary and prepare you for a career. Write a definition for each of the following terms and add them to your personal glossary.

bid	negotiation
business purchasing	organizational buyer
buyer	purchase order (PO)
economy of scale	purchasing agent
electronic data interchange (EDI)	purchasing process
free on board (FOB)	quality control
invoice	receiving record
marking	terms for delivery

Section 16.2

Essential Question
Why is it important for a business to manage its inventory?

Inventory Control

Learning Objectives

- LO 16.2-1 Explain inventory management.
- LO 16.2-2 Describe inventory-control systems.
- LO 16.2-3 Identify the role of sales forecasting in inventory management.
- LO 16.2-4 Discuss inventory shrinkage.

Key Terms

inventory management
stockout
reorder point
buffer stock
carrying costs
physical inventory
perpetual inventory-control system
manual-tag system
unit-control system

point-of-sale (POS) software
radio frequency identification (RFID)
periodic inventory-control system
just-in-time (JIT) inventory-control system
80/20 inventory rule
turnover rate
inventory shrinkage
internal theft
external theft

LO 16.2-1 Managing Inventory

Every business wants to maximize profits. Managing inventory correctly is one key factor in keeping costs down while maintaining enough products for maximum sales. **Inventory management** is ordering the goods, receiving them into stock on arrival, and paying the supplier or vendor. It also includes managing the costs of shipping, storage, and other tasks while keeping the costs associated with the inventory low. Inventory management is usually the responsibility of the supply chain manager. When managing inventory, there are three factors that need to be considered:

- lead time;
- stock needs; and
- carrying costs.

wavebreakmedia/Shutterstock.com

Inventory management is ordering goods, receiving them into stock, and paying the supplier or vendor. *Why is it important for a business to manage its inventory?*

Lead Time

It takes time for vendors to process an order and send it to the business. *Lead time* is the total time it takes from placing an order until it is received. Lead time could be days, weeks, or longer, depending on the product and vendor. The product may need to be made or assembled. The vendor may not have enough of the product in stock when the order is placed. Lead time must be taken into consideration when planning for inventory purchases.

Stock Needs

Forecasting sales is always a challenge for businesses. It can be difficult to gauge how much product is needed each day or month of a selling season. A business should avoid being out of stock of any items and missing sales opportunities. A **stockout** is running out of stock. Moreover, a business does not want to fail to meet customer needs by not having the latest products.

It is necessary to have a reorder point for each item. The **reorder point** is the point at which a business orders more of a product before the inventory gets too low. This puts a control in place to trigger placing an order before a stockout could occur. However, a business also needs to avoid purchasing too much inventory in the event projections were incorrect.

To help avoid running out of inventory, stock may be maintained as a buffer or cushion. **Buffer stock**, also known as *safety stock,* is additional stock kept above the minimum amount required to meet forecasted sales. This helps prevent the business from running out of stock. Some businesses anticipate that certain products sell more on a seasonal basis. For example, many more barbeque grills are sold in the summer than in the winter. *Anticipation stock* is the necessary extra stock of products that sell more in certain seasons.

Carrying Costs

Carrying costs are costs directly related to carrying, or holding, inventory and are part of inventory management. These are the costs that must be controlled as they directly affect profit. Carrying costs include the following.

- *Capital costs* are related to borrowing cash from lenders to purchase inventory from vendors.
- *Handling costs* are related to the physical handling of the inventory and any necessary clerical work.
- *Storage costs* are paid for renting warehouse space or building a company-owned warehouse.
- *Inventory-risk costs* include the cost of inventory shrinkage, slow-moving inventory, damaged or obsolete inventory, and nonselling merchandise that must be destroyed or donated for a tax write-off.
- *Inventory insurance costs* include premiums and taxes that are calculated as a percentage of the inventory value.

The cost of carrying inventory is often described as a percentage of the inventory value, as shown in Figure 16-4. Carrying costs can usually run between 24 percent and 48 percent of the inventory value per year. Businesses use this percentage to help them determine how much profit can be made on current inventory.

Calculating Inventory Carrying Rate and Costs

1. Add the annual inventory costs:
   Example:
   $1,500 = storage
   $2,000 = handling
   $2,500 = clerical
   $5,000 = obsolete, damaged, and dead products (markdowns and losses)
   $4,000 = theft
   $15,000 total inventory costs

2. Divide the inventory costs by the inventory value:
   Example:
   $15,000 ÷ $100,000 = 15%

3. Add the percentages for insurance and taxes:
   5% = insurance premiums as a percentage of inventory value
   6% = taxes as a percentage of inventory value
   11%

4. Add all of the percentages:
   15% + 11% = 26%
   inventory carrying rate = 26% (or .26)

5. Multiply the inventory value by the inventory carrying rate:
   carrying costs = $100,000 × .26 = $26,000

Goodheart-Willcox Publisher

Figure 16-4 The carrying cost is often described as a percentage of the inventory value.

Inventory-Control Systems

LO 16.2-2

There are three primary types of retail inventory-control systems: perpetual, periodic, and just-in-time. Every business has different inventory needs, so the supply chain manager chooses the system that best fits the goals of the company business plan.

No matter which inventory-control system a business uses, it is important to conduct a physical inventory once or twice a year. A **physical inventory** is an actual count of all items in inventory at that time. It is used to verify the inventory-control system counts. If there are differences in the counts, the physical count is considered accurate. The records of the inventory-control system must be adjusted to reflect the physical count.

Perpetual Inventory

A **perpetual inventory-control system** is a method of counting inventory that shows the quantity on hand at all times. The system records the receipt of goods into stock and all merchandise sales. There are two types of perpetual inventory systems: manual and computerized.

Manual Perpetual Inventory-Control System

In a *manual perpetual inventory-control system*, the inventory is calculated by physically counting and recording individual items. A person records each item that comes into inventory and each item that goes out of inventory as a sale or vendor return. This information is recorded on a spreadsheet or entered into a software program. The important part to note is that the inventory is done manually, *not* electronically.

One example of a manual perpetual inventory-control system is the manual-tag system that some small retailers use. A **manual-tag system** tracks sales by removing price tags when the products are sold. The retailer keeps the tags and uses them to deduct the sales from the inventory. Another example of a manual perpetual inventory-control system is the **unit-control system**, which uses a visual determination to decide when more stock is needed. This can be done by looking at the inventory to see if it looks low. It may also be done by using bin tickets. A *bin ticket* is a tiny card placed by the product. It lists the stock number, description, minimum and maximum quantities, and cost in a code known only by store employees. A set number of bin tickets are placed with the merchandise. Each time a unit is sold, a bin ticket is removed. When the supply of bin tickets gets low, it is a visual signal to order more inventory.

In both manual-tag and unit-control systems, the reorder point is determined manually. The business must then place POs and hope the lead time is acceptable. A manual perpetual inventory-control leaves a business open to human errors and can be an inefficient use of time.

You Do the Math

Unit Conversion

Different systems of measurement are used throughout the world. The United States uses a system called the US Customary System that consists of feet, pounds, and degrees Fahrenheit. However, most of the world uses a variation of the metric system called the *Système International d'Unités* (SI), or International System of Units. The SI system consists of meters, grams, and degrees Celsius. The following are some common conversions:

- To convert degrees Fahrenheit to degrees Celsius, subtract 32, multiply by 5, and divide by 9.
- One inch is equal to 25.4 millimeters.
- One pound is equal to 0.45 kilograms.

Solve the following problems.

1. If a carton ready for shipping weighs 18.7 kilograms, how many pounds does it weigh?
2. Marion must ship a temperature-sensitive good to a country that uses the metric system. The product cannot be exposed to temperatures below 0 degrees Fahrenheit. She must place a label on the package indicating this temperature in Celsius. What temperature must she write on the label?
3. Luis must order a length of specialized steel rod from a company in Germany. He needs 0.3 feet of the rod. However, the rod must be ordered in increments of 10 millimeters. What length of rod must be ordered?

Computerized Inventory-Control System

While manual systems have their place, most businesses use a *computerized inventory-control system* for more control and information. Computerized inventory-control systems are an important part of EDI. Inventory software programs track incoming inventory and sales. The software can run sales and inventory reports to track costs, track sales by salesperson or by category, and manage sales tax by state. Daily sales reports can also be generated, making it easier to balance the cash drawer. The software may also analyze profit by items sold. Some software can automatically reorder standard products.

Most retail businesses use cash registers with point-of-sale software. **Point-of-sale (POS) software** electronically records each sale when it happens by scanning product bar codes. When the product bar code is scanned, the merchandise is immediately deducted from inventory. Management always has a current inventory count.

POS software allows different reorder points to be entered for various products. Depending on the system, it automatically produces an alert when it is time to order more merchandise, or it immediately places the order. This prevents stockouts and helps the business run efficiently. POS systems also improve pricing accuracy, which eliminates the human error factor of keying information.

Another computerized inventory system is the radio frequency identification system. **Radio frequency identification (RFID)** is a system that uses computer chips attached to inventory items and radio frequency receivers to track inventory. You may be familiar with the computer chip that is placed under the skin of the family pet. This chip identifies the pet and its owner when scanned. This is a type of RFID system. Many businesses use RFID systems to track inventory as it moves within a building and while it is stored in trailers outside a manufacturing plant.

Periodic Inventory-Control System

A **periodic inventory-control system** involves taking a physical count of merchandise at regular periods, such as weekly or monthly. The business actually counts everything that is in inventory and compares those numbers to the reorder points. Taking physical inventories is time-consuming, so it is only done at intervals. Because the count is only completed at given times, the actual inventory is not accurate on a day-to-day basis. A periodic inventory-control system is typically used by small businesses or businesses without inventory software.

Just-in-Time Inventory-Control System

Carrying too much inventory can reduce the profitability of a company. The **just-in-time (JIT) inventory-control system** keeps a minimal

sirtravelalot/Shutterstock.com

When a bar code is scanned, point-of-sale software immediately deducts it from inventory. *How might a company determine the most effective method of inventory management?*

Employability Skills

Prompt Response

Every area of business operation requires that both customers and coworkers receive prompt responses to communications. When people try to reach you via phone or e-mail, respond as soon as possible. If you are not able to do what the person is asking for right away, acknowledge that you have received the call and will follow up at a later time. It is important that senders know that their calls were received and not lost in transmission.

amount of production materials or sales inventory on hand at all times. JIT was developed in Japan by Toyota to reduce the costs of carrying inventory. Manufacturing companies use JIT most often.

In a JIT system, materials are made available *just in time* for the next link in the supply chain to use them. For a JIT system to be successful, each company in the supply chain must coordinate each activity and be flexible when necessary. When JIT works well, both manufacturers and retailers can save time and money. A retail business using JIT tracks sales and only orders the least amount of stock necessary for any given point in time. A manufacturing company using JIT makes sure raw materials are delivered right before they are needed in the assembly process. Ideally, it would finish producing goods just before they are shipped to customers.

Advantages of JIT are increased efficiency, reduced waste, reduced storage space, and freed up cash for other purposes. Another advantage of a JIT system is that it reduces losses and possible damage to products sitting on shelves or with expiration dates. A disadvantage of JIT is when products arrive late, or products are not available when they should be. The lack of product on hand would mean sales could be lost. If raw materials are late in arriving for any reason, a manufacturing production line may even be shut down. For companies needing smaller amounts of goods, they may not meet the minimum order amount or shipping costs may be too high. Also, if projected sales are too low, then the advantages of JIT are not achieved.

Sales Forecasting to Manage Inventory

A business needs to determine the correct amount of money to invest in inventory each year. Sales forecasting based on previous sales history helps businesses plan for upcoming inventory needs. It is usually done a year in advance, depending on the type of business. Most businesses then review actual weekly sales and adjust the sales projections, which will also impact inventory orders.

A typical sales projection may look like the one shown in Figure 16-5 for The Computer Shack. This forecast is for the projected number of units sold per month for one year. The yearly sales projection is 16,885 laptop units and 3,380 desktop computer units. Sales forecasts after the first year in business are based on the previous sales history and current market conditions.

80/20 Inventory Rule

Many businesses use the 80/20 rule to forecast sales to have enough inventory on hand. The **80/20 inventory rule** states that 80 percent of the sales for a business come from 20 percent of its inventory. The *productive inventory* is the 20 percent of the inventory that produces the most sales. The

The Computer Shack
Unit Sales Forecast for 20--

	Jan.	Feb.	Mar.	Apr.	May	June	July	Aug.	Sep.	Oct.	Nov.	Dec.
Laptops	1,000	1,200	1,250	1,300	1,320	1,111	1,345	1,450	1,454	1,460	1,975	2,020
Desktops	300	200	210	210	225	175	200	250	250	300	500	560

Goodheart-Willcox Publisher

Figure 16-5 A typical sales projection may look like this one.

80/20 inventory rule helps a buyer determine which merchandise to keep in stock at higher levels and which products to keep at a minimum. The buyer will then need to decide how much to purchase in advance and when to place the orders.

Turnover Rate

When forecasting inventory, another factor to consider is the turnover rate of stock. A **turnover rate**, or *turnover ratio*, is the number of times inventory has been sold during a time period, usually one year. A *ratio* is a way to see how two numbers compare with each other. To calculate turnover rate, use the following formula.

$$\frac{\text{cost of goods sold}}{\text{average inventory value}} = \text{turnover rate}$$

The following shows an example of using the turnover-rate formula. A business has a cost of merchandise sold of $120,000 for the previous year. The cost of merchandise sold includes beginning inventory, plus any inventory purchased during the year, minus ending inventory. The business has stated that the average inventory of merchandise on hand at the end of the year was $50,000.

$$\frac{\$120,000}{\$50,000} = 2.4 \text{ turnover rate}$$

The turnover rate for this business is 2.4. Is that number good? It depends on the business. This ratio indicates that inventory has been turned a total of 2.4 times during the year. A turnover rate is an indicator of how effectively a business is managing its inventory. A high turnover rate generally indicates higher sales and a more productive inventory. Depending on the industry, a business may benefit from ordering high-turnover products in larger quantities to save shipping costs and lower the price per unit. Merchandise with a low-turnover rate means the inventory is sitting on the shelves longer and is nonproductive.

LO 16.2-4 Inventory Shrinkage

When the annual physical inventory is completed, the results are compared against the perpetual inventory. The two inventories are rarely exactly the same. The physical inventory usually shows fewer items in stock than the perpetual inventory indicates. The difference between the perpetual inventory and the actual physical inventory is called **inventory shrinkage**. There are three main causes for inventory shrinkage.

- Data-input errors can occur during receiving, stocking, or selling.
- Product damage, or breakage, may occur when products are being moved from receiving dock to storage to store shelves.
- Theft can be from employees or outsiders, such as customers or burglars.

Theft is the largest cause of inventory shrinkage. There are two types of theft: internal and external. **Internal theft** is committed by employees of a store, a supplier, or a delivery

Social Media

Facebook

With over a billion users, Facebook is a must for most businesses, both large and small. Businesses, organizations, and brands create pages to share their stories and connect with potential customers. Like personal time lines, a business can customize pages by adding apps, posting stories, hosting events, and more. A marketer can communicate directly with customers about products, promote a brand, and work toward other SMM goals. Facebook is also a great tool for engagement marketing, which is a strategy that encourages visitors to participate in live events.

Facebook also offers support to businesses to help guide them in making the most of this social-media tool. Analytics are available to help businesses track how many people visit the page, visitors' demographics, and other important marketing information. In addition, a business page provides marketers tips and tricks for making the most of social media to meet its business goals.

company. It is also called *employee theft*. It is the source of most inventory shrinkage. **External theft** is stealing by people who are not employed or otherwise associated with the retailer. A *shoplifter* is a person posing as a customer who takes goods from the store without paying for them.

To discourage theft, closed-circuit television (CCTV) and video-security systems may be installed. Sensing devices placed on merchandise, ringing alarms, and security guards also help to prevent theft. The obvious presence of security measures cuts down on stealing.

Section 16.2 Review

Check Your Understanding
1. What is lead time?
2. List examples of carrying costs.
3. How often should a business conduct a physical inventory?
4. State the turnover-rate formula.
5. Provide examples of how businesses might discourage theft.

Build Your Vocabulary
As you progress through this text, develop a personal glossary of key terms. This will help you build your vocabulary and prepare you for a career. Write a definition for each of the following terms and add them to your personal glossary.

80/20 inventory rule	periodic inventory-control system
buffer stock	perpetual inventory-control system
carrying costs	physical inventory
external theft	point-of-sale (POS) software
internal theft	radio frequency identification (RFID)
inventory management	reorder point
inventory shrinkage	stockout
just-in-time (JIT) inventory-control system	turnover rate
manual-tag system	unit-control system

CHAPTER 16 Review and Assessment

Chapter Summary

Section 16.1 Purchasing

LO 16.1-1 Discuss two types of organizational buyers.
Two types of organizational buyers are purchasing agents and buyers. Purchasing agents buy goods and services the company needs internally to operate its business. Wholesale and retail buyers purchase goods for the sole purpose of reselling them to customers.

LO 16.1-2 List steps of the purchasing process.
The purchasing process is a series of steps a purchasing agent or buyer takes to buy goods and services for a business. These general steps are identify inventory needs, identify vendors, initiate bidding process, negotiate the purchase, award the contract, receive the order, pay the invoice, and evaluate the vendor.

Section 16.2 Inventory Control

LO 16.2-1 Explain inventory management.
Inventory management is ordering goods, receiving them into stock, and paying the supplier or vendor. It also includes managing shipping costs, storage, and other tasks while keeping the costs associated with the inventory low. Inventory management is usually the responsibility of the supply chain manager. Three factors to be considered in inventory management are lead time, stock needs, and carrying costs.

LO 16.2-2 Describe inventory-control systems.
Three primary types of retail inventory-control systems are perpetual, periodic, and just-in-time. A perpetual inventory-control system shows the quantity on hand at all times. Two types of perpetual inventory systems are manual and computerized. A periodic inventory-control system involves taking a physical count of merchandise at regular periods. The just-in-time (JIT) inventory-control system keeps a minimal amount of production materials or sales inventory on hand at all times.

LO 16.2-3 Identify the role of sales forecasting in inventory management.
A business needs to determine the correct amount of money to invest in inventory. Sales forecasting based on previous sales history helps businesses plan for upcoming inventory needs. It is usually done a year in advance. Most businesses review actual weekly sales and adjust the sales projections, which will also impact inventory orders. Many businesses use the 80/20 rule to forecast sales.

LO 16.2-4 Discuss inventory shrinkage.
The difference between perpetual inventory and actual physical inventory is called inventory shrinkage. Main causes for inventory shrinkage include data input errors, product damage, and theft. Internal theft is committed by employees of a store, a supplier, or a delivery company. External theft is stealing by people who are not employed or otherwise associated with the retailer.

Check Your Marketing IQ

Now that you have completed the chapter, see what you have learned about marketing by taking the chapter posttest. The posttest is available at www.g-wlearning.com/marketing/.

Review Your Knowledge

1. Discuss two types of organizational buyers.
2. List the steps of the purchasing process.
3. How are bids selected?
4. Explain the receiving process.
5. Explain inventory management.

6. Describe inventory-control systems.
7. What is required for a just-in-time (JIT) inventory-control system to be successful?
8. Identify the role of sales forecasting in inventory management.
9. In the 80/20 inventory rule, which percentage represents the productive inventory?
10. Discuss inventory shrinkage.

Apply Your Knowledge

1. All businesses buy products to operate the company. What products, including both goods and services, might your business need to buy?
2. In earlier chapters, you identified the product or service for which you are creating a marketing plan. Make a list of the inventory your business carries.
3. How does the specific target market for your business impact its inventory needs?
4. In what ways might your business be able to utilize economies of scale when making business purchases?
5. A stockout can negatively impact the image of a business. How would you handle stockouts in your business as a marketing manager?
6. Compare and contrast the inventory-control systems described in this chapter and choose the one you think is most appropriate for your business. Write an argument in support of the type of inventory-control system you would use.
7. List products you think will have a low turnover rate in your business and those you think will turn over quickly.
8. As a marketer, what steps might you recommend the business take to increase stock turnover while still keeping inventory at adequate levels?
9. Describe strategies that could be used in your business to reduce internal theft.
10. What methods could your business use to reduce external theft?

Apply Your Math Skills

When forecasting inventory, the turnover rate of stock is often considered. To calculate turnover rate, use the following formula.

$$\frac{\text{cost of goods sold}}{\text{average inventory value}} = \text{turnover rate}$$

Apply your math skills to solve the following problems.

1. A business has a cost of merchandise sold of $480,000 for the previous year. The average inventory of merchandise on hand at the end of the year was $190,000. What is the turnover rate of this business?
2. A business has a cost of merchandise sold of $64,000 for the previous year. The average inventory of merchandise on hand at the end of the year was $15,000. What is the turnover rate of this business?

Communication Skills

Writing Etiquette is the art of using good manners in any situation. Etiquette is especially important when establishing and maintaining professional relationships. Create a script that you would use in accepting a vendor's bid during the bidding process. Practice your script with a classmate. How would you and your classmate rate your use of good manners?

Listening Engage in a conversation with someone you have not spoken with before. Ask the person his or her definition of a *quality product*. Actively listen to what that person shares. Build on his or her ideas by sharing your own. Try this again with other people you have not spoken to before. How clearly were the different people able to articulate themselves? How is having a conversation with someone you do not normally speak with different from a conversation with a familiar friend or family member?

Speaking It is important to be prepared when you are speaking to an individual or to an audience. Style and content influence how the listener understands your message. Create a short presentation about methods of inventory management. Make use of visuals or demonstrations to enhance the presentation. Adjust your presentation length to fit the attention of the audience.

Internet Research

Business Procurement The term *procurement* is used in business when purchasing goods and services for use in the business. Conduct Internet research on *business procurement*. Write one to two paragraphs that relate the concept of procurement to what you learned in this chapter.

Inventory Shrinkage Research the level of retail inventory shrinkage in the last year. What were the most common sources of inventory shrinkage? Identify techniques a company can use to prevent this issue.

Pareto Principle The 80/20 rule is also known as Pareto principle. Conduct an Internet search for *Pareto principle*. What did you learn about the 80/20 rule that you can apply to other parts of business, marketing, or your life?

Teamwork

Working with a teammate, select a retail business with which you are familiar. Focus on one type of product that consumers may buy from the business. Create a flowchart for the purchasing process that the business might use for that product. Use graphics to illustrate each step. Share your flowchart with the class.

Portfolio Development

College and Career Readiness

Talents You have collected documents that show your skills and qualifications. Select a book report, essay, or poem that you have written that demonstrates your writing talents. If you are an artist, include copies of your completed works. If you are a musician, create a video with segments from your performances.

1. Create a Microsoft Word document that lists your talents. Use the heading "Talents" along with your name. Next to each talent listed, write a description of an assignment or performance and explain how your talent is shown in it. If there is a video, state that it will be made available upon request or identify where it can be viewed online. Indicate that sample screenshots are attached.
2. Scan hard-copy documents related to your talents to serve as samples. Save screenshots from a video, if appropriate, in an appropriate file format. Place hard copies in the container for future reference.
3. Place the video file in an appropriate subfolder for your digital portfolio.
4. Update your master spreadsheet.

UNIT 6   Place

Building the Marketing Plan

Place decisions are some of the most important decisions marketers can help their businesses make. Place activities can affect pricing as well as how the end users receive products and experience the company. Every retail or service business has inventory it must purchase and store. The purchasing and inventory management processes directly impact the bottom line of the company. Controlling those costs is vital to making a profit.

Part 1 Supply Chain

Objectives
- Describe the supply chain for your company.
- Explain the channel of distribution as it pertains to the marketing and company goals.

Directions
In this activity, you will continue writing the Marketing Strategies section of the marketing plan. Marketing strategies are the decisions made about product, price, place, and promotion. Access the *Marketing Dynamics* companion website at www.g-wlearning.com/marketing/. Download the activity file as indicated in the following instructions.

1. **Unit Activity 6-1—Supply Chain** A supply chain is the businesses, people, and activities involved in turning raw materials into products and delivering them to end users. Show the supply chain and the distribution channel for your company. Explain how each member contributes to the marketing and company financial goals stated in the marketing plan.

2. Open your saved marketing plan document.

3. Locate the Marketing Strategies section of the plan. In the Marketing Mix subsection, start writing the Place Strategies subsection. Use the suggestions and questions listed to help you generate ideas. Delete the instructions and questions when you are finished recording your responses. Proofread your document and correct any errors in keyboarding, spelling, and grammar.

4. Save your document.

Part 2 Inventory Management

Objective
- Explain the purchasing process and inventory management systems for the business for which you are writing the marketing plan.

Directions
In this activity, you will continue writing the Marketing Strategies section of the marketing plan. Marketing strategies are the decisions made about product, price, place, and promotion. Access the *Marketing Dynamics* companion website at www.g-wlearning.com/marketing/. Download the activity file as indicated in the following instructions.

1. **Unit Activity 6-2—Purchasing and Inventory Management** Create a flowchart showing the purchasing process for your business. After performing online research, identify several computerized inventory-control systems that may work well for your particular business. List the pros and cons of each, and select the one you think is the most efficient.

2. Open your saved marketing plan document.

3. Locate the Marketing Strategies section of the plan. Complete the Place Strategies subsection. Use the suggestions and questions listed to help you generate ideas. Delete the instructions and questions when you are finished recording your responses. Proofread your document and correct any errors in keyboarding, spelling, and grammar.

4. Save your document.

UNIT 7 Promotion

Chapters

17 **Promotion**
18 **Advertising**
19 **Visual Merchandising**
20 **Personal Selling**

While studying, look for the activity icon for:
- Building the Marketing Plan activity files
- Pretests and posttests
- Vocabulary terms with e-flash cards and matching activities
- Self-assessment

These activities can be accessed at www.g-wlearning.com/marketing/.

Developing a Vision

Marketers are challenged daily to find new ways to communicate with customers. Without knowledge, customers will not know a product exists. Without customers, a business will not make money.

Customers learn about products through promotion. Product promotion informs, persuades, and reminds customers to buy a good or service. Marketers use all the promotional mix elements to give information. Advertising, sales promotions, public relations, and personal selling make up the mix. By combining these elements in a coordinated manner, marketers can push product information to customers. This is known as integrated marketing communications (IMC).

Marketing Core Functions Covered in This Unit

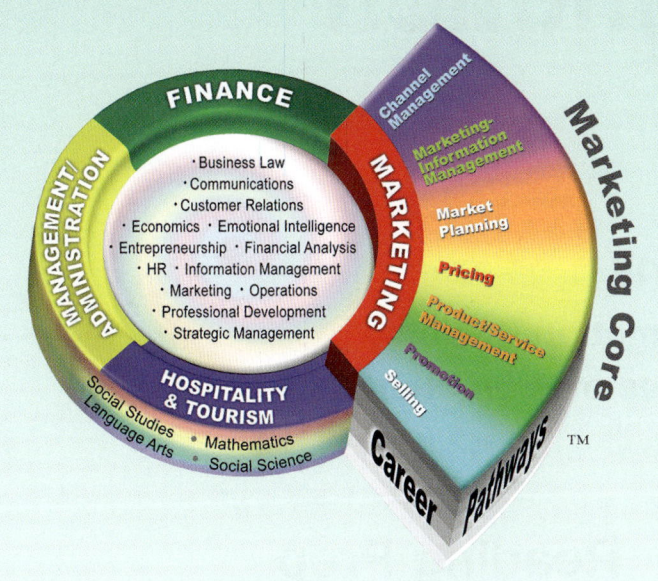

Functions of Marketing

- Market planning
- Pricing
- Promotion
- Selling

Copyright MBA Research, Columbus, Ohio. Used with permission.

EYE-CATCHER

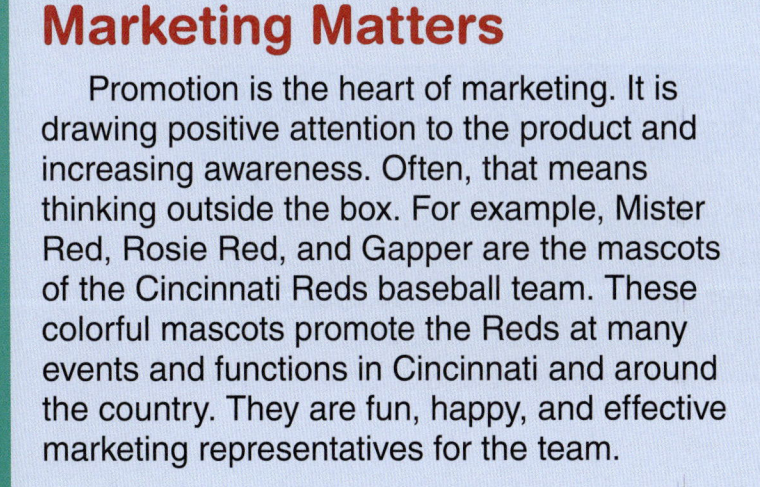

Marketing Matters

Promotion is the heart of marketing. It is drawing positive attention to the product and increasing awareness. Often, that means thinking outside the box. For example, Mister Red, Rosie Red, and Gapper are the mascots of the Cincinnati Reds baseball team. These colorful mascots promote the Reds at many events and functions in Cincinnati and around the country. They are fun, happy, and effective marketing representatives for the team.

Bill Florence/Shutterstock.com

CHAPTER 17

Promotion

Sections

17.1 **Promotion Basics**

17.2 **Types of Promotion**

Reading Prep

College and Career Readiness

Before reading the chapter, skim the photos and their captions. As you read, determine how these concepts contribute to the ideas presented in the text.

Check Your Marketing IQ

Before you begin the chapter, see what you already know about marketing by taking the chapter pretest. The pretest is available at www.g-wlearning.com/marketing/.

◇DECA Emerging Leaders

Marketing Management Team Decision-Making Event, Part 1

Career Cluster: Marketing
Instructional Area: Selling

Knowledge and Skills Developed

Participants will develop many 21st century skills desired by today's employers in the following categories:
- communication and collaboration
- creativity and innovation
- critical thinking and problem solving
- flexibility and adaptability
- information literacy
- initiative and self-direction
- leadership and responsibility
- productivity and accountability
- social and cross-cultural skills

Specific Performance Indicators

- Explain the nature of effective verbal communication.
- Employ communication styles appropriate to a target audience.
- Make oral presentations.
- Explain the nature and scope of the selling function.
- Discuss motivational theories that impact buying behavior.
- Explain the key factors in building a clientele.
- Explain the role of customer service as a component of selling relationships.

Purpose

Designed for a team of two DECA members, the events measure the team's ability to explain core business concepts in the format of a case study in a role-play. This event consists of a 100-question multiple-choice cluster exam for each team member and a decision-making case study situation. The Team Decision-Making Event provides an opportunity for participants to analyze one or a combination of elements essential to the effective operation of a business in the specific career area presented as a case study.

For the purposes of this text, you will be presented with the material for this event in two parts. Part 1 presents the knowledge and skills assessed and an overview of the event's purpose and procedure. Part 2 presents the remaining procedures and the event situation.

Procedure, Part 1

1. For Part 1 in this text, read both the knowledge and skills developed and the specific performance indicators. Discuss these with your team member.
2. If there are any questions, ask your instructor to clarify.

Critical Thinking

1. Evaluate the marketing methods used to meet customer needs.
2. How is the marketing mix achieved?

Visit www.deca.org for more information.

Published by DECA Inc. Copyright © by DECA Inc. No part of this publication may be reproduced for resale without written permission from the publisher. Printed in the United States of America.

Section 17.1

Promotion Basics

Essential Question

What does it mean to promote a product?

Learning Objectives

LO 17.1-1 Explain promotion as one of the four Ps of marketing.
LO 17.1-2 Cite examples of promotional strategies.
LO 17.1-3 Identify goals of promotion.
LO 17.1-4 Explain the purpose of a promotional plan.

Key Terms

marketing communication
product promotion
institutional promotion
integrated marketing communications (IMC)
participatory marketing
blog
viral marketing
push promotional concept
pull promotional concept
persuasion
promotional campaign
AIDA

Marketing Promotion

Promotion is one of the four Ps of marketing. It is the process of communicating with potential customers in an effort to influence their behavior or beliefs. Businesses are interested in influencing a customer's buying behavior by promoting the price of a product, its features and benefits, and the place where it is offered. If customers do not know a product exists, they *cannot* buy it. If customers do not know where to find the product, they will *not be able* to buy it. Organizations, such as charities, also conduct promotions. Their goal is often increasing public awareness or influencing the public to support a cause, frequently through financial donations.

Promotion is considered **marketing communication**, which is broadly described as communications from an organization to its customers and to the public. It is the most visible part of marketing. Because it is important to the success of a business, some organizations have a marketing communications team, often called *MarCom*, that focuses on communication for the organization.

Two basic types of promotion are product promotion and institutional promotion. A **product promotion** promotes specific products, as illustrated in Figure 17-1. Most promotional campaigns are product promotions. In contrast, an **institutional promotion** is promoting the company rather than its products, as shown in Figure 17-2. These promotions are designed to create a favorable view of the company and its

Marketing messages are often clever or humorous to draw attention to them, like this advertisement for the California Milk Advisory Board. *What types of marketing messages attract your attention?*

©California Milk Advisory Board

Product Promotion

Get your computer working like a dream.

Slowdown? Virus? Crashes? Raj's fixes every kind of computer, old or new.

Let us make your life easier!

Raj's Computer Repair
www.rajcomputerrepair.com

Goodheart-Willcox Publisher

Figure 17-1 A product promotion is for a specific product.

Institutional Promotion

Raj's supports a cleaner Detroit.

We worked with partners to recycle 200 used computers and components last year.

See us for all your computer needs!

Raj's Computer Repair
www.rajcomputerrepair.com

Goodheart-Willcox Publisher

Figure 17-2 An institutional promotion promotes the company rather than its products.

brands and increase awareness. Increased awareness will hopefully lead to increased sales.

Promotional Strategies
LO 17.1-2

Many promotional strategies can be used to promote an organization's products or brands. The *promotional mix*, shown in Figure 17-3, is a combination of the elements of advertising, sales promotion, public relations, and personal selling used to reach the target market. These elements are sometimes referred to as a *promotional channel* because each element of the mix is a channel, or method, used to communicate information. Promotional strategies involve choosing the best promotional mix for the budget. Each dollar spent on promotions should provide a return on the marketing investment.

Integrated Marketing Communications

Integrated marketing communications (IMC) is an approach to marketing that integrates all promotional efforts to deliver one message about a product using various media. Not all the pieces of the promotional mix need to be used at one time. However, when multiple components are used, they must complement each other to effectively convey a clear and consistent message. All the promotional elements used should present a unified image about the product or business. For example, Apple uses the slogan, "Think Different" on each promotional piece. If the slogan were omitted from any element, the message would be lost and money would be wasted. IMC integrates every element to convey the same story.

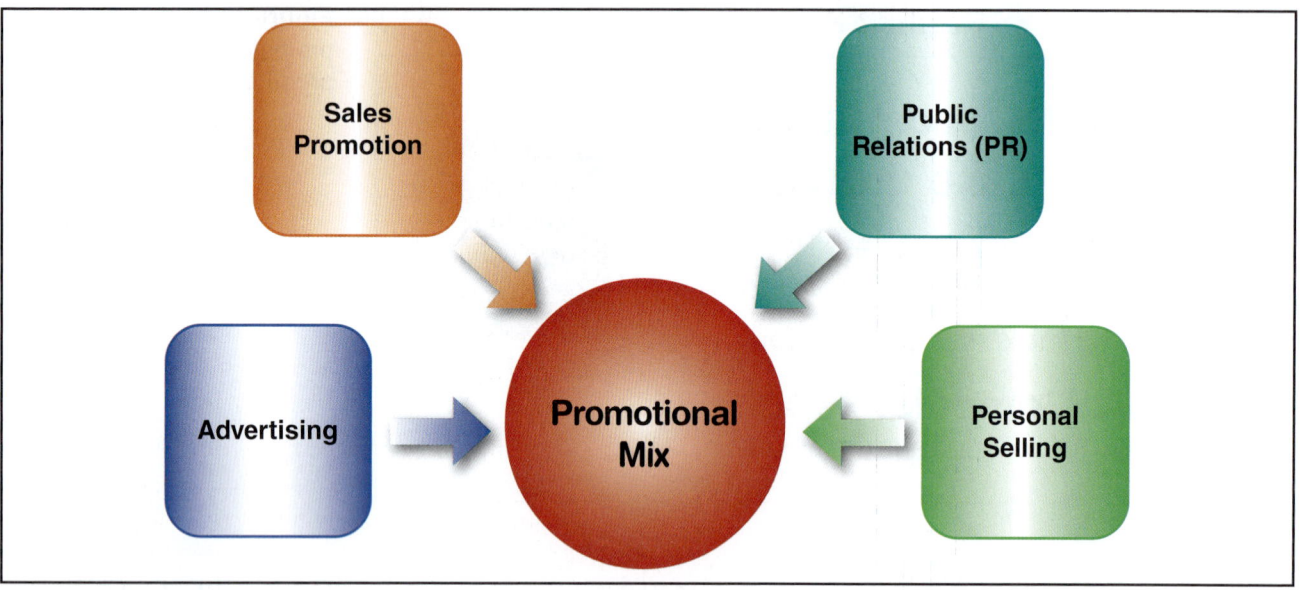

Figure 17-3 Many promotional strategies can be used to promote products and an organization's brand.

Participatory Marketing

IMC can be designed to trigger responses from an audience. **Participatory marketing** is a strategy that invites customers to participate in an element of the promotional mix through a type of response. It is also referred to as *engagement marketing* because it requires communicating *with* customers rather than *at* customers. A goal is to create a connection between a customer and the brand. It also seeks input from an audience and takes action on their feedback. This strategy works on the premise that customers will participate in promotional activities when they think they will benefit. Contests, free samples, and opportunities to voice opinions are examples of ways in which customers can participate in marketing promotions. Examples of participatory marketing include e-mail campaigns, social media, videos, and blogs.

- *E-mail campaigns* are a form of participatory marketing that is easy to implement. Organizations can push information to customers who choose to opt-in to the promotion. E-mail can be an effective tactic to provide information, new product updates, or announce sales.
- *Social-media* platforms such as Twitter, Facebook, and Instagram are used by marketers to encourage customers to participate virtually. Social media creates online communities where information, ideas, messages, and pictures can be shared. Marketers can take advantage of social media to make special offers, create dialogue about products, encourage feedback, and address other topics of interest.
- *Videos* can also be shared through social media. Marketers can post product demonstrations, creative advertisements, and other videos about a product or business that people will want to share. Viewers can leave comments, recommend products, and share links to the videos posted.
- A **blog** is a web page in a journal format created by a person or organization. A blog can be linked to the main business website or function as a stand-alone website. A marketer can make regular posts about products or services and provide the most up-to-date information.

Participatory marketing can be effective, especially when it results in viral marketing. **Viral marketing**, or *buzz marketing*, is information about products that customers or viewers feel compelled to pass along to others. Both are alternative terms for *word-of-mouth advertising*. Social media is the basis of viral marketing because sharing is built into the platforms and shows quick results.

Push and Pull Strategies

Promotional strategies take into consideration how the product travels from the manufacturer to the retailer and then to the customer. These strategies affect which element of the promotional mix is used.

The **push promotional concept** is a manufacturer *pushing a retailer* to handle that manufacturer's merchandise to sell to customers. The

Icatnews/Shutterstock.com

In a pull promotion, the manufacturer pulls customers to actively seek out that manufacturer's product. *How does the push promotional concept encourage customers to buy?*

manufacturer works directly with retailers and encourages them to carry products by offering discounts or other incentives. They may provide displays and other materials to make it easier for the retailer to reach a customer.

The **pull promotional concept** is a manufacturer *pulling customers* to actively seek out that manufacturer's product. A pull promotion for a manufacturer may be discounts and promotional items to pull customers into a store to request the item. For example, Procter & Gamble may send coupons directly to customers for a new soap product. The customer has the coupon in hand and goes to the retailer to find the product. Customer demand encourages the retailer to go the manufacturer and stock the product. The pull promotional concept takes advantage of supply and demand. If customers want a product, the retailers will stock it.

LO 17.1-3 Goals of Promotion

Promotion has three goals: to inform, persuade, or remind people about the business or its products. Some promotions do one thing, while others may do all three. Effective promotions reach the target market with a message the customer values.

Inform

Promotions that *inform* tell people something they want or need to know to make decisions. Brochures, advertisements, e-mails, and catalogs make customers aware of the latest product offerings. Businesses aim to keep current and potential customers informed about:

- existing products;
- new products;
- new features of existing products;
- how to use or assemble products;
- safety issues that may affect the use of a product;
- charities and cultural organizations the business supports; or
- events the business sponsors in the community.

Persuade

Persuasion is the use of logic to change a belief or get people to take a certain action. The end goal of most promotions is to persuade people to buy a product. Information is given about product features and consumer benefits. The target market must consider the purchase worthwhile. Otherwise, the message is not persuasive. Rebates, loyalty programs, or new product samples may persuade customers to take action.

EXTRA
30% OFF
SUMMER SALE STYLES

and an extra
50% OFF
final sale styles

PICK OUT SOMETHING NEW >

PureSolution/Shutterstock.com

The end goal of most promotions is to persuade people to buy a product. *When have you been persuaded by a promotional message?*

Marketing Ethics

Truth-in-Advertising Laws

It is unethical to take part in deceptive advertising or marketing practices. Marketers must comply with truth-in-advertising laws and make promotional messages that are truthful and not misleading. This is not only an ethical and legal consideration, but it is also considered a good business practice.

Remind

Promotions that *remind* are created to strengthen the message in a person's mind by exposing him or her to the message frequently. The first few times a person sees a message, he or she may not remember it. Reminder messages are those that appear in multiple places over a period of time. For example, when watching television, think about how many times you see the same commercial. By showing it often, the goal is to strengthen the message in the mind of the viewer.

Promotional Plan

The coordination of marketing communication to achieve a specific goal is a **promotional campaign**. It is also called a *promotional plan*. Promotional plans are designed to encourage customers to buy. Each element of the promotional mix is focused on attracting customer attention, interest, desire, and action. The acronym for these activities is **AIDA**, which is shown in Figure 17-4.

- *Attention.* Getting customers to look at the product or promotion is the first step. The design elements used should gain the attention of viewers and listeners. Customers should know exactly what the business offers.
- *Interest.* Customers must be interested in the business or product to make a purchase. The promotion should identify the features and benefits most important to the customers. It should show the business is interested in the specific needs of customers.
- *Desire.* The promotion should encourage customers to sample, use, or touch the product. This persuades customers to experience and want it. Positive experiences with the product may create desire to purchase it.
- *Action.* The promotion should explain exactly how, where, and when the product can be bought. It should be convenient for customers to buy.

AIDA integrates the different elements of the promotional mix. Following the AIDA model helps marketers focus and create effective promotional messages.

Included in a promotional plan is a detailed list of goals, dates, and other activities that are carefully researched and documented. This serves as a guideline to make sure the business can reach its goals effectively.

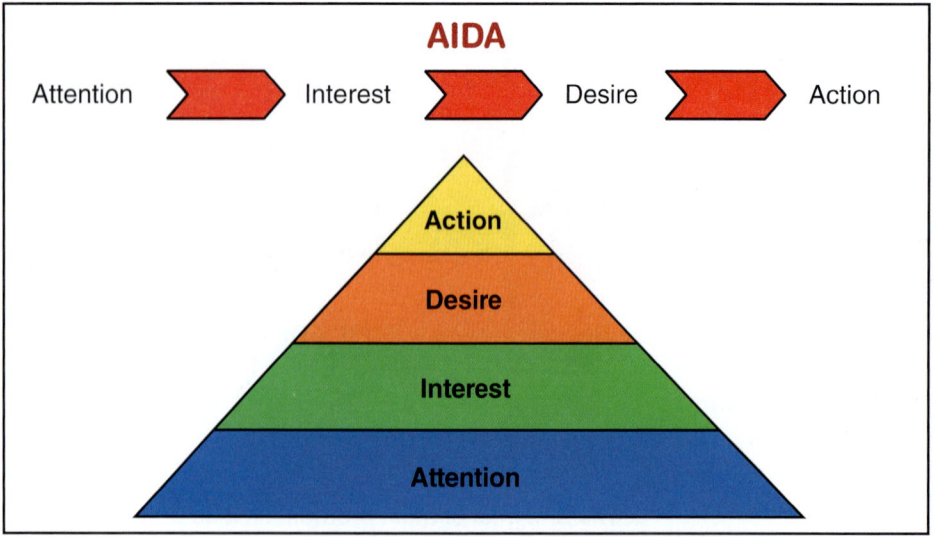

Figure 17-4 Each element of the promotional mix is focused on attracting customer attention, interest, desire, and action.

AIDA

Attention → Interest → Desire → Action

(Pyramid from bottom to top: Attention, Interest, Desire, Action)

Goodheart-Willcox Publisher

Employability Skills

Networking

Networking means talking with others and establishing relationships with people who can help you achieve career, educational, or personal goals. A professional network is a group of professionals you know and who know you. These people are supportive in your career endeavors and may or may not be social friends.

Goals

The first step in creating a promotional plan is to identify the goals for the promotion. Goals should follow the SMART goal model and be specific, measurable, attainable, realistic, and time-related. Promotional campaigns may run for a limited time or be ongoing.

Budget

The promotional budget is important to the overall success of the plan. If a company has multiple products to promote, each product will be assigned a specific budget within which the promotional plan must operate. It is important to realize that not every plan will have a large budget. Sometimes creativity is necessary when budget dollars are not as high as requested.

Target Market

A target market is the specific group of customers whose needs and wants a company will focus on satisfying. Each dollar of marketing must be spent wisely, so targeting the appropriate customer is necessary to maximize exposure of a product.

Marketing Mix

The marketing mix is the strategy for using the elements of product, price, place, and promotion. Each of these elements will influence the budget and the target market. For example:
- the *product* must be clearly defined to determine the type of promotion that is appropriate;
- the *price* of an item can determine which element of the promotional mix is needed, such as coupons or rebates, which will be influenced based on projected revenue; and
- *place* is important, especially if the product is only available online or in a store.

Promotional Mix

The promotional mix will be determined based on the goals, budget, target market, and

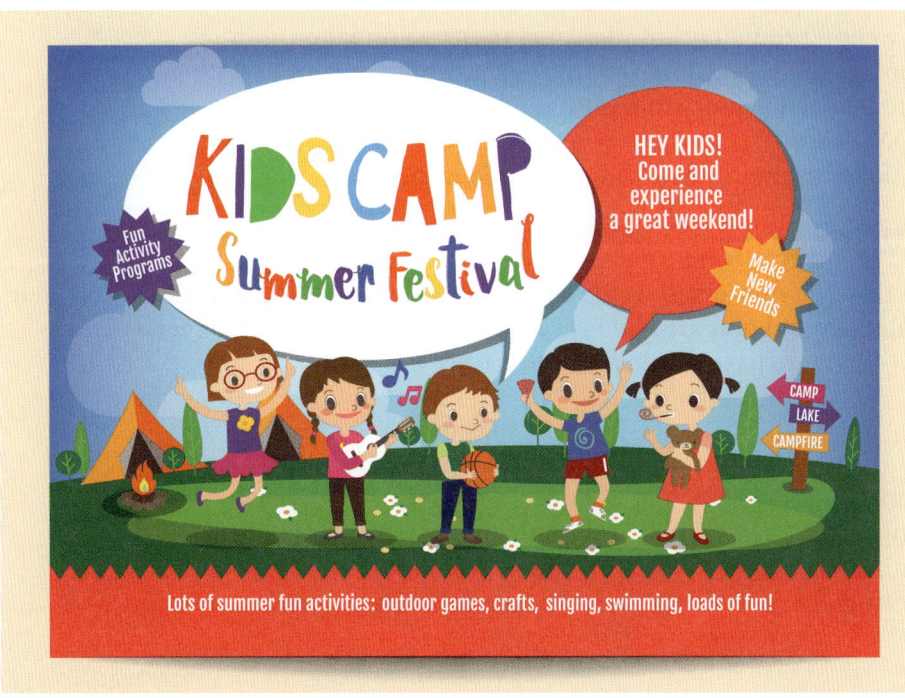

Targeting the appropriate market, such as parents of young children, can maximize the exposure of a product. *How is this promotional message appropriate for its target market?*

Kraphix/Shutterstock.com

marketing mix for the product. Decisions will be made as to which elements will be used to reach the customer in the target market. If more than one promotional element is used, IMC will be used to create a unified marketing message. This means that advertising, sales promotion, public relations, direct marketing, and personal selling must all work together to strengthen the brand and use the budget in an effective manner.

Implementation

The promotional plan is the overall strategy for the product that is being marketed. A detailed budget and schedule of execution will be created for the plan. Within the promotional plan, there may be specific plans related to individual promotional elements that were selected. For example, a separate advertising plan, including a schedule and budget, may be necessary if advertising pieces are part of a campaign. This can apply to each promotional mix element that is used.

Evaluation

Metrics are standards of measurement that determine the effectiveness of a promotion. Metrics can be basic, such as tracking the number of website visits during a promotion. They can be complex, such as tracking the number of products sold during a promotion. Each dollar spent on promotions should provide a return on the marketing investment. Sales tracking can help marketers learn which promotions influenced sales the most. Examples of metrics include the following.

- *New-customer metrics* measure market share, cost of acquiring new customers, customer awareness levels, and brand awareness.
- *Customer-retention metrics* measure customer retention and abandonment rates, brand loyalty, return visits, and the likelihood to refer a brand.
- *Product metrics* measure overall customer satisfaction, ease of learning and using a product, and first-time-user satisfaction.

Marketers choose the best metrics to meet the goals of the promotion. After evaluating the results, decisions can be made on what worked and what did not work. This helps guide decisions regarding future promotions.

Section 17.1 Review

Check Your Understanding

1. Distinguish between a product promotion and an institutional promotion.
2. Describe the concept of the promotional mix.
3. Provide examples of participatory marketing.
4. Explain the AIDA model.
5. How are promotions commonly evaluated for effectiveness?

Build Your Vocabulary

As you progress through this text, develop a personal glossary of key terms. This will help you build your vocabulary and prepare you for a career. Write a definition for each of the following terms and add them to your personal glossary.

AIDA
blog
institutional promotion
integrated marketing communications (IMC)
marketing communication
participatory marketing
persuasion
product promotion
promotional campaign
pull promotional concept
push promotional concept
viral marketing

Section 17.2

Types of Promotion

Learning Objectives

LO 17.2-1 Cite examples of media used in advertising.
LO 17.2-2 Describe direct marketing.
LO 17.2-3 Identify types of sales promotions.
LO 17.2-4 Explain two types of public relations (PR).
LO 17.2-5 Differentiate between B2C sales and B2B sales.

Key Terms

advertising
preselling
embedded marketing
direct marketing
sales promotion
event marketing
visual merchandising
public relations (PR)
press release
press kit
press conference
personal selling
business-to-consumer (B2C) selling
business-to-business (B2B) selling

Essential Question

Why would a marketer use more than one type of promotion?

Advertising

LO 17.2-1

Advertising is any nonpersonal communication paid for by an identified sponsor. It can be the key part of the promotional mix as it provides information about the features and benefits of a product, including prices and descriptions. Advertising is also a good strategy to presell products. **Preselling** is creating interest and demand for a product before it is available for sale.

Traditional advertising includes print and broadcast media. However, other media, such as outdoor signage or Internet advertisements, may be used in an advertising campaign.

- *Print media.* Print media is one of the most effective forms of advertising. It includes all tangible promotional messages used in mass communication. Newspapers, magazines, and directories are print media.
- *Broadcast media.* There are two forms of broadcast media: television and radio. Radio and television advertisements, or *commercials*, reach a large number of people daily. Although commercials are typically 15-, 30-, or 60-second messages, they can be expensive to create.
- *Outdoor media.* Outdoor media, such as billboards and transit media, can be an affordable advertising method to display promotional messages 24 hours a day. Outdoor signage can be print or electronic.
- *Internet advertising.* Internet advertising is placing advertisements on websites or sending e-mail campaigns where typical viewers are the target market.

Advertising can be used in unique ways to capture the attention of the audience. Think about a movie or television show that you have seen lately. Did you see a familiar consumer product being used by the actors, such as an automobile or food product? The actor may not have mentioned the product, but the audience recognized it and made a connection that the product was visible. This technique is known as **embedded marketing**, which is intentionally and subtly placing a branded product in a media without formally calling it to the attention of the viewer. It is also known as *product placement*. It is hoped that by viewing a famous person with or using a product, sales will be generated.

Direct Marketing

Direct marketing is a type of advertising sent directly to individual customers without the use of a third party. It includes marketing pieces such as brochures, coupons, flyers, e-mail, and postcards. When delivered by the US Postal Service, it is sometimes considered *junk mail*.

Direct marketing is a common and popular form of advertising used by marketers. It is has a distinct advantage in that it can be tracked because it is sent to individual addresses. For example, 1,000 marketing postcards or 500 e-mails may be sent to names on a mailing list. A marketer knows exactly how many adverting pieces were sent and the addresses that were used.

Direct marketing includes a call to action as part of the message. A *call to action* is a statement or request that urges the customer to do something in

DayOwl/Shutterstock.com

Billboards can be an affordable advertising method to display promotional messages 24 hours a day. *What products have you seen advertised on billboards?*

Exploring Marketing Careers

Advertising and Promotions Manager

One of the most basic needs of any company is to let the public know what it has to offer. Companies rely on advertising and promotional events to inform potential customers about their products and services. Advertising and promotions managers plan and coordinate advertising programs, promotional materials, and coupons. They also organize contests and other events to help make people aware of a company's products and services. Typical job titles for these positions include *advertising manager*, *promotions director*, *promotions manager*, *marketing and promotions manager*, and *advertising sales manager*.

Some examples of tasks that advertising and promotions managers perform include:
- Plan advertising and promotional campaigns to increase public awareness and increase sales of products or services
- Review and approve layouts and advertising copy, including audio and video scripts
- Coordinate or direct a campaign team to meet the company's campaign goals
- Prepare budgets for advertising or promotional campaigns

Advertising and promotions managers must have a strong knowledge of various types of media production and communication techniques. They must understand how to use written, oral, and visual media effectively to promote specific products and services. They should also have a basic knowledge of sales and marketing principles, including strategies and tactics for creating interest in a company's products or services. Most positions for advertising and promotions managers require a bachelor degree. Many also require experience and knowledge both in the type of product or service the company sells and in advertising or promotions techniques. For more information, access the *Occupational Outlook Handbook* online.

Case in Point

T-Mobile

Marketers have found that using different elements of the promotional mix can create successful marketing campaigns. Marketers can stretch their budgets by using both traditional methods of promotion as well as less-expensive, nontraditional methods, such as online videos. These integrated campaigns are unique and achieve desirable results by going viral. Viral videos can mean low-cost advertising for the company.

One example of a company that has successfully used nontraditional means to expand its brand is T-Mobile. Since the T-Mobile products appeal to consumers of every age, the company decided to focus on viral-video marketing efforts. At various times, the company has used surprise flash mobs and other buzz-marketing techniques on YouTube™ and Twitter to achieve that goal. Along with traditional ads, T-Mobile created entertaining viral videos that were a hit in the global marketplace. By using memorable social-media campaigns, T-Mobile conveys a clear message of its products.

---

response to a promotion. It may ask a customer to buy or sample a product, or click on a link to get more information. For that reason, it is also sometimes called *direct response marketing* because the customer is asked to respond in some manner. If a customer responds, a marketer can keep track of the response rate. Success can be measured when the customer actually reads the message and responds in some way. A metric can be established for the number of responses received and how many responses constitute various levels of success. Each direct response creates a potential lead on which a salesperson can follow up, and hopefully, close a sale.

Sales Promotion
LO 17.2-3

Sales promotion is the efforts used to encourage customers to buy a product within a specific time period, usually as soon as possible. It is common for retailers to promote special sales, such as "Fourth of July Weekend Sale" that have a specific start date and end date.

A sales promotion can include coupons, rebates, promotional items, samples, loyalty programs, contests and sweepstakes, trade shows, and displays. Advertising works with sales promotion to provide the message and design for the final product.

Coupons

A *coupon* is a printed or digital offer giving a discount on products bought before a certain

Zakharchenko Anna/Shutterstock.com

Sales promotions encourage customers to buy a product as soon as possible. *What sales promotions have you seen recently?*

date. Coupons create customer incentives to buy a new product or increase sales of current products. Because they cannot be used after the expiration date, coupons create a sense of urgency.

Rebates

A *manufacturer's rebate* is a return of a portion of the purchase price of an item. Unlike coupons, rebates are received after a product is purchased. Rebates also have expiration dates. Manufacturers offer rebates to encourage customers to purchase a product during a certain time frame. By offering rebates, manufacturers can also capture customer data for future campaigns or market research.

To receive a rebate, a customer is required to complete a form and mail it to the manufacturer. Some rebate forms are completed online. The manufacturer then sends a check for the rebate amount to the buyer. However, it may take months for the customer to receive a rebate. Because only a small percentage of rebates are actually claimed, the strategy results in most customers paying full price. This can result in a higher profit than using discounts or sales.

Promotional Items

Promotional items are given away to remind customers about a business and its products. The business name, address, phone number, and website are often printed on the items. Promotional items can include inexpensive items, such as key chains, calendars, pens, and pencils. They can also be more expensive items, such as blankets, calculators, or books. Marketers sometimes call them *marketing premiums*.

Samples

When introducing a new product, companies may offer free product samples to encourage customers to try the new items. Samples give customers the product experience; they hopefully will like the product and purchase it. Product samples are often given in stores, such as food samples in grocery stores. They may also be small, individual samples sent by direct mail, such as those sent by cosmetic companies. Some retailers offer samples from vending machines at which customers can scan their membership or loyalty cards to receive a free sample.

Loyalty Programs

Many companies reward customers for their continued business through loyalty programs. Loyalty programs can take many forms. The most common ones revolve around giving customers a free product or service after making a certain number of purchases. For example, a hair salon may give each customer a card that is punched every time he or she receives a haircut. After 12 punches, the next haircut is free. Customers like the free products, and loyalty programs often encourage repeat sales.

Contests and Sweepstakes

Contests and sweepstakes are tools that encourage people to visit a store or provide contact information. These promotional tools help marketers capture data for future campaigns or market research purposes. In *contests*, customers must do something to win, such as submit a video of themselves using the product. *Sweepstakes* are games of chance in which prizes are given to randomly selected winners from a number of entries.

Trade Shows

Many businesses exhibit at industry trade shows and conventions. Marketers attend trade shows to introduce new products or sell existing products to potential customers. Trade shows provide a face-to-face opportunity to talk with customers, gather sales leads, and give a promotional item or sample of a product or service.

Marketers often use event marketing strategies at trade shows. **Event marketing** is a promotional activity that encourages customers to participate rather than just observe. For example, conducting a cooking demonstration allows people to interact with the demonstrator and the product.

Sponsorships are another way marketers can help reach business goals at a trade show. A *sponsorship* is the support of an activity, usually financial, that can help a business meet its goals. A company might host a refreshment break for trade-show attendees or provide financial support

Alfie Photography/Shutterstock.com

Promotional items are given away to remind customers about a business and its products.

What promotional items have you received from a company?

You Do the Math

Statistical Reasoning

Qualitative data include things that can be observed, but not measured. Smell, taste, color, appearance, and texture are all examples of types of qualitative data. On the other hand, quantitative data include things that can be measured. Distance, weight, cost, speed, and temperature are all examples of types of quantitative data.

Solve the following problems.
1. The catalog description of a product reads as follows: attractive, blue product has a smooth finish, fits in a space 5 inches wide, and weighs 14 ounces. List the qualitative data and quantitative data in this description.
2. A business describes its customer service staff as follows: a staff of 17 pleasant and helpful representatives includes five certified technicians and two master technicians. List the qualitative data and quantitative data in this description.
3. Look around your classroom. Describe your classmates using only quantitative data.

---

to honor an outstanding professional at a closing show session. Sponsorships send the message that the business cares and supports customers and the organization. They can create positive brand recognition as well as goodwill.

Displays

Visual merchandising is the process of creating floor plans and displays to attract customer attention and encourage purchases. Retail stores use displays to build product awareness. Attractive visual merchandising can tempt potential customers to purchase. Many stores display merchandise at the checkout counter to increase sales. These are called *point-of-purchase (POP)* displays.

Public Relations (PR)

LO 17.2-4

Public relations (PR) consists of the marketing activities promoting goodwill between a company and the public. Unlike advertising, public relations is unpaid media coverage. Public relations can be proactive or reactive.

Proactive public relations is when the company presents itself in a positive manner to build an image. For example, companies issue PR communications to explain their contributions to the community, environment, and other socially responsible activities.

Reactive public relations is used to counteract a negative public perception about the company. Negative media publicity can be received for any number of reasons. Marketers need to take action to reestablish the positive image of the company. An example of reactive public relations is the effort by BP to clean up the *Deepwater Horizon* oil spill it caused in the Gulf of Mexico in 2010.

Established businesses may hire PR managers or specialists to coordinate media communications. In general, most public relations activities cost little or are free. It takes time to create the PR materials, but the only other cost may be printing. Some communication channels used in PR include press releases, press kits, and press conferences.

Press Release

A **press release**, or *news release*, is a story featuring useful company information written by the company PR contact. Press releases are sent to selected media that will reach the target market. Many industry associations can help guide this process. The media will only publish information in a press release if it is considered newsworthy.

Press Kit

A **press kit** is a packet of information sent to the media about a new business opening or other major business events. Press kits can include marketing materials, photos, videos, frequently-asked-questions (FAQ) sheets, and other important information. Many companies create *green press kits* that include only web-delivered information rather than printed materials to save paper.

Press Conference

A **press conference** is a meeting set by a business or organization to which the media is invited to attend. Press conferences are called to make major announcements that affect a large number of people. Large press conferences may be televised and covered by major print and broadcast media. Smaller press conferences may just include local media.

Personal Selling
LO 17.2-5

Personal selling is any direct contact between a salesperson and a customer with the objective of making a sale. Customers appreciate face-to-face interaction when making a buying decision. While the other elements of the promotional mix are important, most customers prefer personal contact. By meeting customer needs with a product, a company can grow company sales.

Business-to-consumer (B2C) selling is selling to consumers. Retail is a typical example of the B2C market. Most retail sales are made by a salesperson in the place of business. However, some retail businesses conduct the selling process via telephone. *Telemarketing* is personal selling done over the telephone.

Business-to-business (B2B) selling is a business selling to another business. B2B sales may also be called *field sales*, *industrial sales*, and *organizational sales*. Companies that sell equipment and raw materials to manufacturers are involved in B2B sales. Manufacturers that sell finished products to retailers are involved in B2B sales.

Customers appreciate face-to-face interaction when making a buying decision. *When has a salesperson helped you make a buying decision?*

Uber Images/Shutterstock.com

Section 17.2 Review

Check Your Understanding

1. Why can advertising be the key part of the promotional mix?
2. What is a call to action?
3. How are sponsorships used in sales promotion at trade shows?
4. List communication channels used in public relations (PR).
5. Provide an example of B2B sales.

Build Your Vocabulary

As you progress through this text, develop a personal glossary of key terms. This will help you build your vocabulary and prepare you for a career. Write a definition for each of the following terms and add them to your personal glossary.

advertising
business-to-business (B2B) selling
business-to-consumer (B2C) selling
direct marketing
embedded marketing
event marketing
personal selling
preselling
press conference
press kit
press release
public relations (PR)
sales promotion
visual merchandising

CHAPTER 17 Review and Assessment

Chapter Summary

Section 17.1 Promotion Basics

LO 17.1-1 Explain promotion as one of the four Ps of marketing.
Promotion is one of the four Ps of marketing. It is communicating with potential customers in an effort to influence their behavior or beliefs. Businesses are interested in influencing a customer's buying behavior by promoting the price of a product, its features and benefits, and the place where it is offered. Promotion is considered marketing communication.

LO 17.1-2 Cite examples of promotional strategies.
Many promotional strategies can be used to promote an organization's products or brands. Integrated marketing communications (IMC) integrates all promotional efforts to deliver one message about a product using various media. Participatory marketing invites customers to participate in an element of the promotional mix through a type of response. Push promotions push a retailer to handle that manufacturer's merchandise to sell to customers. Pull promotions pull customers to seek out that manufacturer's product.

LO 17.1-3 Identify goals of promotion.
Promotion has three goals: to inform, persuade, or remind people about the business or its products. Promotions inform people of something they want or need to know to make decisions. Persuasion changes a belief or gets people to take action. The end goal of most promotions is to persuade people to buy a product. Promotions that remind are created to keep the product on a person's mind.

LO 17.1-4 Explain the purpose of a promotional plan.
Promotional plans are designed to encourage customers to buy. Each element of the promotional mix is focused on attracting customer attention, interest, desire, and action. Included in a promotional plan is a detailed list of goals, dates, and other activities that are carefully researched and documented.

Section 17.2 Types of Promotion

LO 17.2-1 Cite examples of media used in advertising.
Traditional advertising includes print and broadcast media such as newspapers, magazines, directories, television, and radio. Other media, such as outdoor signage or Internet advertisements, may also be used in an advertising campaign.

LO 17.2-2 Describe direct marketing.
Direct marketing is sent directly to individual customers without the use of a third party. It is has a distinct advantage in that it can be tracked because it is sent to individual addresses. Direct marketing includes a call to action as part of the message. Success can be measured when the customer actually reads the message and responds in some way.

LO 17.2-3 Identify types of sales promotions.
Sales promotion is the efforts used to encourage customers to buy a product as soon as possible. A sales promotion can include coupons, rebates, promotional items, samples, loyalty programs, contests and sweepstakes, trade shows, and displays.

LO 17.2-4 Explain two types of public relations (PR).
Public relations (PR) consists of the marketing activities promoting goodwill between a company and the public. Proactive public relations is when the company presents itself in a positive manner to build an image. Reactive public relations is used to counteract a negative public perception about the company.

LO 17.2-5 Differentiate between B2C sales and B2B sales.
Personal selling is any direct contact between a salesperson and a customer. Business-to-consumer (B2C) selling is selling to

consumers. Business-to-business (B2B) selling is a business selling to another business.

Check Your Marketing IQ

Now that you have completed the chapter, see what you have learned about marketing by taking the chapter posttest. The posttest is available at www.g-wlearning.com/marketing/.

Review Your Knowledge

1. Explain promotion as one of the four Ps of marketing.
2. Cite examples of promotional strategies.
3. Identify goals of promotion.
4. Explain the purpose of a promotional plan.
5. Explain types of promotion.
6. Cite examples of media used in advertising.
7. Describe direct marketing.
8. Identify types of sales promotions.
9. Explain two types of PR.
10. Differentiate between B2C sales and B2B sales.

Apply Your Knowledge

1. You will be creating a promotional campaign for your chosen business. Decide if you will create an institutional promotional campaign or product promotion campaign. Describe what you need to understand to create a promotional schedule for the campaign.
2. Which promotional strategies will you use in your promotional campaign? Explain your selections.
3. Which promotional goals will your campaign seek to achieve: informing, persuading, or reminding customers of the product or brand? List the information you will need to relate to the customer in order to achieve this goal.
4. Compare and contrast elements of the promotional mix. Explain how your promotional plan will use each one in your promotional campaign.
5. To which types of promotion do you think your target market will respond? Explain your reasoning.
6. Determine which types of advertisement would reach your target market. Select at least one type of media you will use.
7. Determine which types of sales promotions would reach your target market. Select at least one type of sales promotion you will use.
8. Write a press release to inform your company's industry about your product or brand.
9. You will need to train the sales team to sell your product. Make a list of the features and benefits that you will use as part of the training script.
10. Outline a social media plan for your business.

Apply Your Math Skills

A new teen apparel company, Sasha's Threads, is implementing a promotional plan to promote the new brand. Apply your math skills to solve the following problems.

1. Sasha's Threads has a total promotional budget of $3,000. The circle graph shows the percentages of the budget spent on different types of promotions. Interpret the graph to calculate the dollar amount spent on each type of promotion.

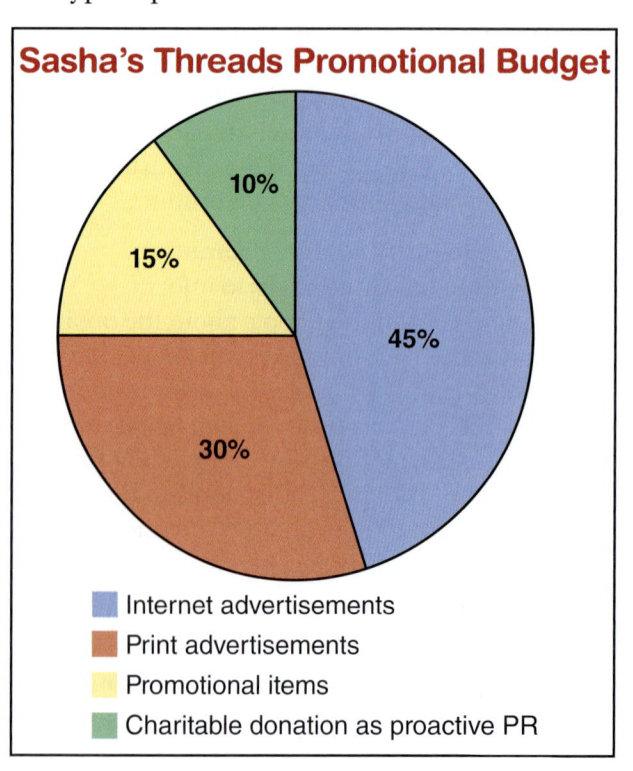

Sasha's Threads Promotional Budget

- Internet advertisements: 45%
- Print advertisements: 30%
- Promotional items: 15%
- Charitable donation as proactive PR: 10%

2. Print advertising for Sasha's Threads included an advertisement in a local magazine with a circulation of 2,000 households. The advertisement included a coupon that 80 customers redeemed. What percentage of potential customers who received the coupon actually redeemed it?

Communication Skills

Writing Revision is the key to effective writing. Write a promotional message for a new brand of toothpaste called Pearly White. Decide if the message will inform, persuade, or remind the audience. Write the first draft of the message. Refine and organize the message so it flows logically. Ask a classmate to review your work and help you use language in a more effective and precise manner.

Speaking Public relations is important for all businesses. Explain to a classmate why it is important for a business to engage in *proactive* public relations to try to decrease instances that require *reactive* public relations.

Listening Listen to your instructor as he or she presents this lesson. Listen carefully and take notes about the main points. Then, organize the key information that you heard. Were you able to effectively understand the information in this chapter?

Internet Research

Ineffective Promotions Read an online article about a sales promotion for a business or product that caused negative customer reactions. Review the conclusions made by the author. Why was the response negative? Provide a summary of your reading, making sure to incorporate the *who, what, when, where* and *how* of the situation.

Viral Marketing Use the Internet to research *best viral marketing campaigns* for the past year. Make a list of the top three promotions. Do you remember seeing any of these campaigns? If so, why did they stand out? Did any of these promotions result in you purchasing the advertised product?

Content Marketing Conduct an Internet search for the term *content marketing*. What are the benefits of using a content marketing strategy? Cite an example of content marketing you find in your research.

Teamwork

Working with your team, select a product with which you are all familiar. Create a visual representation of the product, such as a model, poster, or slide presentation. Present the team's interpretation of the product's marketing mix to the class. Include details and examples that illustrate each of the four Ps of the marketing mix (product, price, place, and promotion).

Portfolio Development

Clubs and Organizations Being involved in academic clubs or professional organizations will help you make a good impression. You can also learn a lot that will help you with your studies or your career. While in school, you may belong to clubs, such as National Honor Society and Future Business Leaders of America. When you are employed, you may belong to professional organizations related to your career area, such as American Nurses Association.

1. Identify clubs or organizations to which you belong. Create a Microsoft Word document to list the name of each organization. Use the heading "Clubs and Organizations" and your name.
2. In your document, briefly describe the organization, your level of involvement, and how long you have been a member. Save the document.
3. Update your master spreadsheet.

CHAPTER 18

Advertising

Sections

18.1 **Advertising Basics**
18.2 **Creating an Advertising Campaign**

Reading Prep

College and Career Readiness

Before you begin reading this chapter, preview the section heads and vocabulary lists. Make a list of questions that you have before reading. Search for answers to your questions as you continue reading the chapter.

Check Your Marketing IQ

Before you begin the chapter, see what you already know about marketing by taking the chapter pretest. The pretest is available at www.g-wlearning.com/marketing/.

DECA Emerging Leaders

Marketing Management Team Decision-Making Event, Part 2

Career Cluster: Marketing
Instructional Area: Communication Skills, Selling

Procedure, Part 2

In Chapter 17, you studied the performance indicators for this event.

1. The event will be presented to you through your reading of the Knowledge and Skills Developed, Specific Performance Indicators, and Case Study Situation.
2. You will have 30 minutes to review this information and prepare your presentation. You may make notes to use during your presentation.
3. You will have ten minutes to make your presentation to the judge, followed by up to five minutes to answer the judge's questions. Both members of the team must participate in the presentation, as well as answer the questions.
4. Turn in all your notes and event materials when you have completed the event.

Case Study Situation

You are to assume the role of sales team for Fit for Life, a new health club located next door to a large hospital. The **manager (judge)** of Fit for Life has called on your team to describe a sales and marketing strategy to sell memberships to the 1,000 employees who work at the hospital.

Fit for Life is a 24-hour health club equipped with a running track, racquetball and tennis courts, swimming pool, exercise equipment, and numerous fitness classes. Since Fit for Life is open 24 hours a day, seven days a week, it is highly accessible to medical employees who work any shift at the hospital.

The manager (judge) of Fit for Life wants to obtain memberships from the majority of hospital employees. The manager (judge) has asked your team to develop a sales and marketing strategy that will convince hospital employees to join the health club. Your team has been called on to describe an effective sales presentation for hospital employees. Your team must describe special incentives you will offer to encourage hospital employees to attend the sales presentation and special promotional events offered by Fit for Life to sign up new members.

Your team must describe the types of communication that will be the most effective for recruiting health club members. Your presentation should include the following topics: communication, oral presentation, building clientele, motivational theories, customer service, and product features.

You will present your sales strategy to the manager (judge) of Fit for Life in a meeting to take place in the manager's (judge's) office. The manager (judge) of Fit for Life will begin the meeting by greeting you and asking to hear your ideas. After you have presented your information about a sales strategy to sell health club memberships and have answered the manager's (judge's) questions, he or she will conclude the meeting by thanking you for your work.

Critical Thinking

1. Which features should be emphasized by Fit for Life that are attractive to hospital workers?
2. Why should Fit for Life's hours of operation be emphasized in the meetings with hospital employees?

Visit www.deca.org for more information.

Published by DECA Inc. Copyright © by DECA Inc. No part of this publication may be reproduced for resale without written permission from the publisher. Printed in the United States of America.

Section 18.1

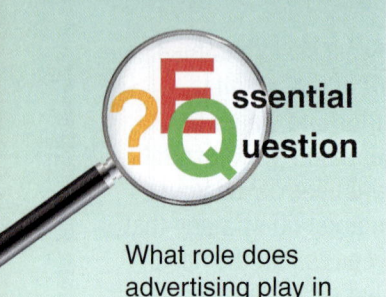

Advertising Basics

Learning Objectives

LO 18.1-1 Describe advertising as an element of the promotional mix.
LO 18.1-2 Cite common types of advertising media.
LO 18.1-3 Identify considerations in media selection.

Key Terms

search engine optimization (SEO)
media planning
advertising agency
creative plan
reach
frequency
cost per thousand (CPM)
circulation
lead time

Essential Question

What role does advertising play in promotion?

LO 18.1-1 Advertising

Advertising is one element of the promotional mix. It is any nonpersonal communication paid for by an identified sponsor. *Nonpersonal* means the message is delivered through a media channel, not in person. The message is the same for everyone who receives it.

Advertising is a daily influence in our lives. It is everywhere—on the street, on the Internet, in smartphone apps, and on television and the radio. Advertising can change people's beliefs and attitudes about products and help them make buying decisions. It may create positive or negative feelings about a product, brand, or company. The main purposes of advertising are to persuade customers to buy a product or accept an idea, inform customers about products, or remind them to take action.

Advertising and Society

While advertising clearly benefits business, it also can benefit society. Advertising can:

pxl.store/Shutterstock.com

Advertising is one element of the promotional mix and is everywhere you look. *Where do you encounter ads in your daily life?*

- inform consumers and businesses about product choices;
- encourage consumers to seek a higher standard of living;
- stimulate competition among businesses so they offer better products at lower prices;

326 Copyright Goodheart-Willcox Co., Inc.

- help increase employment needed to keep up with demand for advertised products;
- encourage acceptance of new and innovative products; and
- help people learn about health and social issues.

Advertising Law

Advertisers have legal and ethical obligations to consumers and business customers. They are responsible for providing honest, accurate information. Advertisements often make promises about product features and benefits that encourage people to buy. Misleading or false advertisements sometimes make promises that are not kept. Laws and regulations protect buyers from deceptive and improper advertising practices. These laws regulate what advertisers can and cannot say.

Information conveyed through promotional material must be factual and accurate. As you will recall from Chapter 4, advertising materials must follow federal guidelines set by the Federal Trade Commission (FTC), the main federal agency that enforces advertising laws and regulations. Under the *Federal Trade Commission Act*, federal law states the following.

- Advertising must be truthful and nondeceptive.
- Advertisers must have evidence to back up their claims.
- Advertisements cannot be unfair.

False advertising is overstating the features and benefits of goods or services or making false claims about them. It is both unethical and illegal. Businesses that misrepresent their products or services risk losing customers, at the very least.

The FTC's website provides information on advertising and marketing basics. The website should be consulted before creating advertisements to ensure that guidelines are followed.

Types of Advertising Media

LO 18.1-2

Advertising makes its way to an audience through various types of media. The types of media used can include print media, outdoor media, broadcast media, and the Internet.

Print Media

Print media is one of the most effective forms of advertising. It includes all tangible promotional messages. Print media includes newspapers, magazines, directories, and direct mail.

Newspapers

A newspaper is a daily or weekly publication printed on inexpensive paper. It is usually discarded after reading. Newspapers are bought by many different people, so they do not fit any specific target market. Consumers often rely on newspaper advertising for information on sales, new products and stores, and coupons. Although print newspaper sales have declined, newspapers are still a viable advertising medium.

Consumers often look at newspaper advertisements to learn about new products and current sales. *Coupon clippers* are people who cut out coupons to save money on products. Coupons generally have a promotion code that indicates

Social Media

Twitter

Twitter is a free microblogging service that allows its users to publish short posts called *Tweets*. Twitter can be a useful tool for conversations with customers. Businesses can connect in real time with customers who may be using a product or visiting a booth at a trade show. Customers can instantly find information about a company and its products from the Tweets posted. Marketers can see what customers are saying about the company, the industry, or a topic that helps gather intelligence about the competition.

Tweeting for marketing takes careful planning because the message is limited to 140 characters. Similar to other social media, thoughtful messages should be composed rather than responding or sending a Tweet without thought. It is better to take a few extra minutes to compose a strategic Tweet that will be effective and send a message that is appropriate.

Magazines are purchased by people in specific target markets based on their interests. *How can advertising in a magazine be tailored to a magazine's target market?*

where the coupon originally appeared. Marketers use different promotion codes to track consumer response to advertisements and coupons.

Magazines

Magazines are printed weekly, monthly, or quarterly, usually on high-quality paper. Magazines are purchased by people in specific target markets based on their interests. People tend to keep magazines longer than they keep newspapers. Therefore, magazine advertisements, just like the articles, can be repeatedly seen by readers. The value of more expensive magazine advertisements can be higher than that of newspaper advertisements, even though the circulation may be lower.

Directories

Businesses and individuals still use print telephone directories. These directories list names, addresses, and phone numbers in alphabetical order. Directories are given to all households and businesses, so they are not targeted publications. Included in most telephone directories are the yellow pages for business listings, advertisements, and coupons. Advertisements in the yellow pages can be affordable for businesses with a small promotional budget. Telephone directories are used repeatedly, so an advertisement is seen many times.

Direct Mail

Direct mail is a type of print advertisement sent directly to individual customers without the use of a third party. It includes direct marketing pieces such as brochures, coupons, flyers, and post cards.

Outdoor Media

Outdoor signs have been used as a form of advertising since the 19th century. They are placed where an audience on the move can see them. Two common forms of outdoor advertising media are billboards and transit promotion. Other forms of outdoor advertising include skywriting, blimps, and hot-air balloons.

Billboards

A *billboard* is a large outdoor sign typically placed in a high-traffic area, such as next to a highway. Billboards can be an affordable advertising method to display promotional messages 24 hours a day. The only way to target billboards is by location.

Digital billboards change images every four to ten seconds. Messages from one or more advertisers may be flashing on the same sign, which can be distracting for drivers. Some states and a number of cities have banned digital billboards.

Transit Promotion

Transit advertising is found on the outside or inside of buses, taxis, subways, trolleys, and

Billboards, including digital billboards, can be an affordable advertising method. *Where do you commonly see billboards?*

commuter trains. Transit advertisements have high visibility to a narrow market. They are generally an inexpensive way to reach an often captive audience. Putting information on company vehicles is an inexpensive way marketers can promote a business.

Broadcast Media

There are two forms of broadcast media: television and radio. Television and radio advertisements, or *commercials*, reach a large number of people daily. Commercials are short messages, typically 15, 30, or 60 seconds in length. Still, they can be costly to produce.

Television

The most expensive advertising medium is television because it reaches the most people. Similar to other forms of advertising, television commercials are designed to appeal to specific target markets. Making television commercials is much like making short movies, which makes the cost of using it for advertising high.

Commercial time can be bought on the national or local level. Local-television advertising is more affordable because it reaches only local viewers.

Infomercials are paid product demonstrations. Infomercials are longer than commercials, usually 30 minutes. This type of programming is watched by some consumers and can be a good way to sell a new product. Infomercials tend to run at times with low viewership, so the costs may be less than some commercials.

Radio

Radio is an affordable advertising option to reach local customers. Radio advertising is typically much less expensive than television. There are many radio stations. They play music or have talk programs that attract very different target markets. For example, classical music and talk radio stations tend to have older listeners. Rock and pop music stations have more listeners in the teen and young-adult markets. Radio is an effective way to reach certain groups of people.

Internet Media

Internet advertising is advertising using the Internet for promoting product. This includes advertising on a company's own website, as well as placing advertisements on the websites of other businesses. The goal is to reach typical users who are in the target market for the business or product. Internet advertising also includes e-mail campaigns and social media.

Online Advertising

Online advertising is placing advertisements on websites where typical viewers are the target market for the business. Examples of online advertising are described in Figure 18-1. Marketers must know which websites will best reach the market. It is also important to know if dollars spent on digital advertising are providing value by delivering customers.

MikeDotta/Shutterstock.com

Transit advertisements, such as those on buses, are highly visible to a narrow market. *What types of transit advertisements have you seen in your community?*

Employability Skills

Inside Voice

Be aware of the volume of your voice when speaking to a coworker or on the phone. Often, others are within earshot of your conversation. Talking in the hallways, outside an office, or in a cubicle can be disturbing to those around you. If a conversation requires more than a few words, move into a conference room or other space where a door can be closed.

Online Advertising

- **Banner advertisements** are placed at the top of a website, typically in a box, and look similar to a print advertisement.
- **Demonstration videos** are posted on free video-sharing websites.
- **Floating advertisements** float across or around the screen and disappear in seconds.
- **Pop-up advertisements** pop up when a website is clicked open; customers can typically close these on the screen or block them completely.
- **Pop-under advertisements** are similar to pop-up advertisements, but they appear after the web page is closed; customers can typically close these on the screen or block them completely.

Goodheart-Willcox Publisher

Figure 18-1 There are many types of online advertising.

Search engine optimization (SEO) is the process of indexing a website to rank it higher on the list of results that appears when a search is conducted. This process includes adding special coding and typical search terms to the website text. SEO helps increase the chances of higher rankings on any Internet search engine.

Marketers often purchase key search terms on search engines, which is called *paid SEO*. Small text advertisements show up on the side of the URL list when the purchased terms are used in a search. Advertisers are charged by the number of people who click on the small advertisement, which is a link to the main website. Most search engines have tracking metrics, such as Google AdWords for advertisements purchased on Google. The metrics provide daily reports that track how many people clicked on an advertisement or made a purchase because of an advertisement.

E-mail Campaigns

E-mail can be an effective way to reach a wide variety of customers. However, in order to abide by the spam laws, e-mail campaigns must allow the receiver the option to receive or reject the e-mail. This is known as *opt-in*, which means the receiver must be given the option to opt-in or opt-out of the e-mail campaign. Unsolicited e-mail is called *spam* and reflects poorly on any business sending it. The last thing marketers want to do is offend a customer. One way to avoid being labeled a spammer is to send e-mails only to people who give permission to use their e-mail address for promotional purposes.

Before conducting an e-mail campaign, marketers should read and understand the 2004 CAN-SPAM Act. This act is enforced by the FTC and allows individuals to report companies that send spam. Businesses that violate the CAN-SPAM Act are subject to financial penalties. Highlights of the act are shown in Figure 18-2.

Social Media

Social media is a platform that connects people with similar interests. Social-media websites create online communities where information, ideas, messages, pictures, and videos are shared. Businesses can also connect to people through social media. Marketers can take advantage of social-media websites to make special offers to different groups of people. They can also create a dialogue with people about products, suggestions, and other topics of

CAN-SPAM Act

1. E-mail header information, including the originating website or e-mail address, must identify the organization that sent the message.
2. The e-mail subject line must accurately represent the content of the e-mail message.
3. The e-mail must be identified as an advertisement or promotion.
4. The e-mail must provide a valid physical postal address for the organization.
5. Recipients must be given clear instructions on how to opt out of receiving future e-mails from the organization. The organization must ensure these opt-out requests do not get caught in its own spam filter.
6. Opt-out requests must be honored within 10 business days. Organizations cannot charge a fee or require the recipient to take any other step as a condition for honoring an opt-out request.
7. The organization cannot sell or transfer e-mail addresses of those who have opted out.
8. Even if an outside company is hired to conduct e-mail marketing, both companies are still responsible for compliance with the law.

Goodheart-Willcox Publisher

Figure 18-2 Marketers should read and understand the CAN-SPAM Act before conducting an e-mail campaign.

Chapter 18 Advertising 331

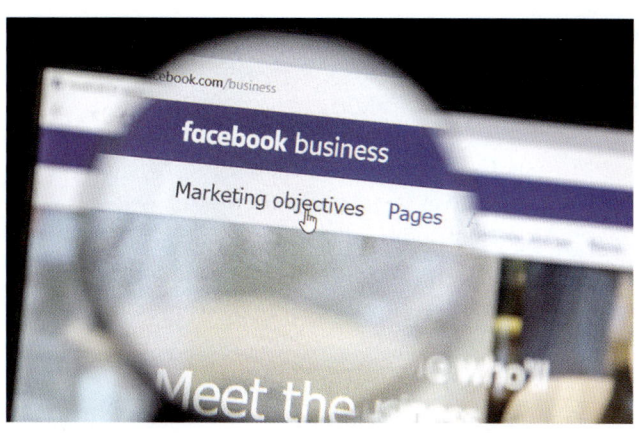

IB Photography/Shutterstock.com

Marketers use social media like Facebook to make special offers to different markets. *What is your opinion of a business using social media to advertise to potential customers?*

interest. Examples of social media include Twitter, Facebook, Instagram, Pinterest, and Snapchat.

LO 18.1-3 Media Selection

The process of determining the best media that meets a campaign's objectives is known as **media planning**. Selecting media for a campaign involves considerations of factors such as the target market and type, or types, of media that will be available in the demographic area. It also includes considering the pros and cons of each type of media, as shown in Figure 18-3, to ensure the appropriate choice is made.

Advertising is an expensive part of the promotional mix. For that reason, budgetary and scheduling considerations must be evaluated. These include the cost of creating the advertisement, cost of placement, and lead time.

Cost of Creation

Many people are involved in the development of an advertising campaign, including writing, designing, and physically creating the final pieces. Each person must be paid for his or her time and talent. Some companies have professionals on staff to create the various elements in the promotional mix. Other businesses, both large and small, may choose to use outside resources to create their promotions. For example, freelance graphic designers and copywriters may be hired to perform those services.

Some companies use an advertising agency to create promotions. An **advertising agency** is a firm that creates advertisements, commercials, and other parts of promotional campaigns for its clients. Typically, the advertising manager from the marketing team is the *client*, or primary contact, for the advertising agency. The manager works with an agency account representative to produce advertisement campaigns. The client makes agency assignments through the account representative who manages the agency staff. The staff creates and delivers the assigned creative services.

The advertising or marketing manager works closely with the account representative to develop a creative plan for the agency. A **creative plan** outlines the goals, primary message, budget, and target market for the advertising campaign.

The advertising agency will have a copywriter who writes the message. A graphic designer chooses the visual graphics and creates the overall design. A layout artist or broadcast production manager delivers the final advertisement or commercial. A media buyer purchases print advertisement space and broadcast commercial time on behalf of the client. The advertising agency bills the clients for work performed on an hourly basis.

Cost of Placement

The cost to place advertisements varies depending on a number of factors. When a single person views an advertising message, it is called an *impression*. In all types of media, the cost increases depending on the amount of exposure, or number of impressions, the ad will get.

- **Reach** is the total number of people expected to see an advertisement.
- **Frequency** refers to the number of times the advertisement appears before the customer.
- **Cost per thousand (CPM)** refers to the cost of an advertisement per one thousand impressions. The abbreviation is CPM because *mille* means *one thousand* in Latin.

In print advertising, costs are usually based on size of the advertisement, the price paid for the print space, and how many times the advertisement will be printed. Costs are also based on how many people see the advertisement based on circulation. **Circulation** is the number of copies distributed to subscribers in a defined time period. A full-page advertisement in a national magazine might be as much as $50,000. A small advertisement in a local newspaper may only cost $500 because fewer people will see it.

Running advertisements on broadcast media is even more expensive, often costing thousands, or

Pros and Cons of Advertising Media

Media Type	Medium	Pros	Cons
Print	Newspapers	• Flexible by geographic need • Provides detailed message • Short lead time	• Expensive to reach target audience • Hard to target a specific market • Print audiences declining
Print	Magazines	• High quality • Highly targeted markets • Long advertisement life • People share or give away magazines	• Advertisement clutter • Print audiences declining • High cost • Long lead time
Print	Directories	• Efficiently reach those needing the service • Kept for a year or more	• Cannot change advertisement for one year • Limited readership • May be expensive
Print	Direct Mail	• Easy to reach a target market • Easy to track and collect metrics • Flexible by geographic need • Provides detailed message	• Considered *junk mail* by many • High cost • Low response rate • Negative environmental impact
Outdoor	Billboards	• Flexible by geographic need • High frequency • Low cost	• Hard to measure demographics • Low reach • Short message
Outdoor	Transit Promotion	• Flexible by geographic need • High reach and frequency • High visibility to narrow market • Low costs	• Could become damaged by vandalism or weather • Hard to target a specific market • Space limitations
Broadcast	Television	• May impact popular culture • Messages can be entertaining • Most watched medium • Visual and audio	• Advertisement clutter • Channel surfing or skipping commercials • Fragmented audiences • Most expensive medium
Broadcast	Radio	• Highly targeted markets • Increased frequency • Relatively low costs • Short lead time	• Advertisement clutter • Difficult to achieve high reach • Channel surfing during commercials • Only audio
Internet	Online Advertising	• Changes made quickly • Cost effective • Easy to measure effectiveness • Highly targeted markets • Short lead time • Visual and audio	• Fragmented search engines • Limited Internet access for some customers • Many people install software to block ads
Internet	E-mail Campaigns	• Cost effective • Easy to measure effectiveness • Highly targeted markets • Interactivity • Short lead time	• Laws must be followed to avoid sending spam • Limited Internet access for some customers • Many people delete or filter ads without reading • Risk of hacking and/or identity theft
Internet	Social Media	• Cost effective • Easy to measure effectiveness • Highly targeted markets • Invites dialogue with customers • Short lead time	• Limited Internet access for some customers • Risk of hacking and/or identity theft

Goodheart-Willcox Publisher

Figure 18-3 There are many considerations when selecting the appropriate type of media for an advertisement.

even millions, of dollars. In broadcast media, costs depend on the length of the advertisement and how many times it will be viewed or heard. *Prime time* refers to the hours during which broadcast media consumption is at its peak. In the United States, prime time is generally considered to be 7:00 p.m. to 10:00 p.m., depending on the location. Running broadcast advertisements during prime time is more expensive than during other hours of the day. For example, a 30-second commercial during the Super Bowl can cost several million dollars because the television event takes place during prime time and draws millions of viewers.

Lead Time

Lead time is the time between reserving the advertisement space or broadcast time and when the advertisement actually runs. It is important to consider lead times when planning an advertising campaign. Consider, for example, a campaign with the goal to increase sales during the Fourth of July holiday weekend. The advertising materials must be ready for placement well before that time.

Lead time must be considered when selecting media because lead times vary by medium. The lead time to run an advertisement in a national magazine could be a month or more. The lead time to run an advertisement in the local newspaper might be only 24 hours.

Section 18.1 Review

Check Your Understanding

1. What is the main purpose of advertising?
2. Explain false advertising.
3. What is the most expensive advertising medium?
4. Name the law that is important for marketers to understand before conducting an e-mail campaign.
5. What factors can affect the cost of a print ad?

Build Your Vocabulary

As you progress through this text, develop a personal glossary of key terms. This will help you build your vocabulary and prepare you for a career. Write a definition for each of the following terms and add them to your personal glossary.

advertising agency
circulation
creative plan
cost per thousand (CPM)
frequency
lead time
media planning
reach
search engine optimization (SEO)

Section 18.2

Creating an Advertising Campaign

Essential Question: How might an advertising campaign affect the success of a product?

Learning Objectives

LO 18.2-1 Summarize how an advertising campaign is developed.
LO 18.2-2 List elements of an advertisement.

Key Terms

- advertising campaign
- headline
- copy
- action words
- typography
- typeface
- weight
- art
- layout
- white space
- signature

Developing an Advertising Campaign (LO 18.2-1)

An **advertising campaign** is a coordinated series of related advertisements with a single idea or theme. It is one piece of the overall promotional campaign.

Some media are more appropriate than others for use in a campaign. The types of media used depend on the product being advertised and the target market. There is no one medium or mix of media that is the best to use for all advertising situations. Steps for creating successful advertising campaigns are to set goals, establish a budget, brainstorm the creative concept, write the message, select the media, and evaluate the results, as shown in Figure 18-4.

Goals

The promotional plan addresses each element of the promotional mix that will be used. Since advertising is one part of the promotional mix defined in the promotional plan, advertising goals will be a part of the goals that are already established. For example, advertising goals might include reaching a specific sales goal or increasing brand awareness by 10 percent. However, these goals may be refined as the advertising plan is developed.

Budget

The advertising campaign budget must be established before media is chosen. It will be

Advertising Campaign Development
- Set campaign goals
- Establish a budget
- Brainstorm the creative concept
- Write the message
- Select the media
- Evaluate the results

Goodheart-Willcox Publisher

Figure 18-4 An advertising campaign is a coordinated series of related advertisements with a single idea or theme.

Part of concepting is brainstorming what the campaign should look like. *Why is concepting important when developing an advertising campaign?*

assigned based on the amount designated for advertising in the overall promotional budget. It is important to be clear on the amount allocated for the campaign and to understand what can be afforded. For example, a marketer may want to run television advertisements, but the budget cannot support the cost. Criteria for allocating budget dollars should be influenced by the objectives that are intended to be met.

Concept

The creative concept process, also known as *concepting,* is looking at the big picture and brainstorming what the campaign should look like. The concept may be an idea for a print advertisement, or one for a television commercial with a well-known public figure that provides entertainment value. When the concept is developed, it may be presented as a prototype or rough draft to management for approval.

Message

Effective campaigns deliver a marketing message that is valuable to the customer. The unique selling proposition (USP) should be at the heart of the campaign. The *unique selling proposition (USP)* is a statement of how the products, brand, or company are better than the competition. It explains why the customer should purchase products from your company rather than another company. For example, price, features, benefits, new items, store location, hours, and sale pricing are often included in advertising.

Case in Point

Airbnb

Airbnb is an online community that allows travelers to book accommodations in the homes of other people all over the world. Homeowners can offer just one room or their entire house, condo, or apartment. The company's goal is to provide "a sense of belonging and comfort and community" no matter where its customers may travel.

Airbnb was started in San Francisco in 2008. In just a few years, the company grew to over 1.5 million listings in more than 34,000 cities around the world. Airbnb achieved its success through careful planning and research. The company understood that social media and the Internet were the perfect media to market their new company.

The company launched the #OneLessStranger campaign and social experiment in 2015 to promote the Airbnb brand. The campaign encouraged people to do random acts of kindness for strangers and to post a picture including the hashtag. The goal of the campaign was for every participant to get to know someone new and create one less stranger in the world. Airbnb showcased the photos taken as part of this campaign on its website's map. In less than three weeks, over three million people worldwide had contributed to or were talking about the campaign. This kind of success does not happen without a detailed, well-thought-out marketing plan.

Media

An important step in planning is selecting the appropriate media for a campaign. It must be determined which media will best communicate the message. Costs and scheduling are also considered when selecting the media.

Evaluate

Marketing must evaluate whether their advertisements are seen by the expected number of people. *Reach* is total number of people expected to see an advertisement. *Frequency* is the number of times the advertisement appears before the customer. Reach and frequency numbers help to determine the cost of some media.

Reach and frequency metrics are used to measure advertisement effectiveness. The more often a person sees an advertisement, the better the chance the message will be remembered. However, viewers begin tuning out the message after seeing it too many times.

Elements of an Advertisement

LO 18.2-2

The classic structure for an advertisement has four elements:
- headline;
- copy;
- graphics; and
- signature.

wavebreakmedia/Shutterstock.com

A graphic designer at an advertising agency creates the overall design of an advertisement. *How might a marketing team benefit from hiring an advertising agency?*

Green Marketing

Ecofriendly Marketing Premiums

Many businesses advertise through marketing premiums for customers, such as pens, reusable tote bags, and other novelty items. When using these products in promotions, your company name is repeatedly seen by current and potential customers as the item is used. Consider the environmental impact of the items when planning to purchase marketing premiums. Choose promotional items made from recycled or sustainable material, and avoid unnecessary packaging. Be conscious of the sourcing and distribution practices related to the items. Using carriers with low carbon ratings can reduce the environmental impact of product distribution. Customers typically appreciate and remember environmentally responsible actions of businesses and companies.

Figure 18-5 There are no set rules for where each element of an advertisement appears. However, most advertisements begin with a headline.

These elements are identified in the Schwinn bicycle advertisement in Figure 18-5.

Headline

A **headline** is a statement designed to grab the attention of viewers so they will read the rest of the advertisement. Headlines usually appear in large type or have some other attention-getting graphic element. A general rule recommends that headlines have no more than seven words.

The headline uses words to call attention to the advertisement, much like a lure on a fishing hook. Copywriters hope that by reading the headline, a person is hooked into reading the rest of the advertisement. In fact, the aspect of an advertisement that grabs attention is often called the *hook*.

Research shows that over 80 percent of readers only read headlines. Because of this fact, many advertisers think the headline is the most important part of the advertisement.

Copy

Copy is advertisement text that provides information and sells the product. In advertising, *copy* refers to the words in the advertisement. The term *body copy* is often used to refer to the words that explain the product and give added information. The person who writes advertising copy, including the headlines, is called a *copywriter*.

The headline and body copy should work together. The headline attracts attention while the body copy presents the selling message. Body copy should be brief and clearly give reasons to purchase the product. It should provide any information needed to locate the product and make the buying decision. The most effective advertising copy does the following.

- *Creates intrigue.* Copywriters use words to arouse interest, curiosity, and desire. Words like *new, hottest, free, limited offer, sale, bonus,* and *special offer* may be intriguing to readers.
- *Appeals to the senses.* It is hard to make products seem real on a printed page. Copywriters use descriptive words so the reader can almost see, hear, taste, feel, or smell the product.
- *Sounds newsworthy.* Stating the *who, what, when, where, why,* and *how* of a product can make the copy sound newsworthy. Include data, such as statistics, performance results, case histories, comments from satisfied customers, and quotes from experts.
- *Uses action words.* **Action words** are verbs that tell the readers what to do. These call-to-action words include *save, join, get, buy, come in, visit, call, e-mail,* and *register,* to name a few. They are joined by adverbs suggesting when or how to act, such as *now, toll-free,* and *today.*

Graphics

Graphics provide visual interest. The graphics are often the first part of the advertisement a reader notices, especially when colorful or unusual. Those in the advertising industry argue about whether the graphics or the headline is most important. Actually, the two must work together to attract the reader. Graphics include typography, art, and layout.

Typography

Typography is the visual aspect of the style and arrangement of type. Choosing typography

passion artist/Shutterstock.com; MaryValery/Shutterstock.com; Top Vector Studio/Shutterstock.com; Brosko/Shutterstock.com

Typography is the visual aspect of the style and arrangement of type. *How might these typefaces be used to advertise different products?*

includes decisions about typeface, size, and weight. A **typeface** is a particular style for the printed letters of the alphabet, punctuation, and numbers. There are hundreds of typefaces from which to choose.

A second aspect of typography is size. Letters can vary in size from small to very large. Larger letters have more emphasis. Headlines are usually larger than body copy. In a long headline, some words may be larger than others. Size makes these words stand out and emphasizes the key ideas.

The third aspect of typography is weight. **Weight** in typography refers to the thickness and slant of the letters. There are three weights: regular, italic, and bold. Size and weight are both used to make some words more prominent. Headlines are usually bold and appear in the largest size.

Color may also impact headlines and advertising copy. White or yellow letters on a dark or colored background can make the words stand out. Words in red also pop out. Blue is often used to attract attention, but has a serious look and suggests reliability.

Art

Art is all the elements that illustrate the message of an advertisement. Art includes drawings, photographs, charts, and graphs. Logos, shapes behind text, and abstract images or designs are also considered art. The art used in advertising should be consistent with the brand. In fact, art sometimes helps to define a brand if it is used properly.

A product photograph is the most common type of advertising art. Grocery, fashion, and automobile advertisements use product photos to make products look attractive. Businesses that

Layout

Layout is the arrangement of the headline, copy, and art on a page. An advertisement may have a great headline and fascinating art. However, if they are not placed attractively on the page, the advertisement might be ineffective.

One of the most useful layout tools is white space. **White space** is the blank areas on a page where there is no art or copy. White space acts as a frame for the message. It can also separate the parts of an advertisement so they stand out. Advertisements with little white space appear cluttered and are hard to read. Graphic designers are tasked with creating advertisements that are easy to read.

Signature

The **signature** identifies the person or company paying for the advertisement. Signatures usually include the company name and logo. It may also include the company slogan or tagline. The advertisement signature completes an advertisement, much like a signature ends a letter. An advertisement signature may also include location and contact information, such as a website address, phone number, and street address.

paul prescott/Shutterstock.com

A product photograph is the most common type of advertising art. *When have images of a product made you want to buy the product?*

sell services also use art to convey the idea of the service. Photos may show people using the service.

Most people are attracted to photos of other people, particularly children. Celebrities, such as sports figures and actors, are often used in advertising because they are well-known. Shocking, surprising, or amazing art may also act as a hook. Well-executed drawings are often as effective as photographs.

You Do the Math

Fundamental Counting Principle

The *fundamental counting principle* is a way to calculate the sample space for multiple independent events. The *sample space* is the set of all possible outcomes when determining probability. To use the fundamental counting principle, simply multiply the total possible outcomes of all events to find the sample space.

For example, if a printing company offers five types of printed banner material in one of seven sizes and four choices of fonts:

$5 \times 7 \times 4 = 140$

There are 140 possible combinations.

Solve the following problems.

1. The owner of a construction company must purchase a new work truck. The dealership offers 3 choices for engine size, 14 choices for paint color, 2 choices for drive train, 5 choices for wheels and tires, and 3 choices for seat configuration. How many total combinations are possible for the work truck?

2. A marketing company specializes in promotional items. It offers a package in which a company's logo is printed as stickers in one of three sizes, magnets in one of five shapes, key chains in two styles, and water bottles in one of four styles. How many different packages are available?

3. Chad must price the printing of his business's annual report. The printer he has selected offers four choices of page size, three choices for binding, and nine choices for paper. How many combinations are possible?

Section 18.2 Review

Check Your Understanding

1. What is concepting?
2. Why is the unique selling proposition (USP) an important part of the advertising message?
3. What is a hook in advertising?
4. When choosing typography for an advertisement, what decisions are included?
5. What elements make up the graphics of an advertisement?

Build Your Vocabulary

As you progress through this text, develop a personal glossary of key terms. This will help you build your vocabulary and prepare you for a career. Write a definition for each of the following terms and add them to your personal glossary.

action words
advertising campaign
art
copy
headline
layout
signature
typeface
typography
weight
white space

CHAPTER 18 Review and Assessment

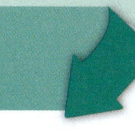

Chapter Summary

Section 18.1 Advertising Basics

LO 18.1-1 Describe advertising as an element of the promotional mix.
Advertising is any nonpersonal communication paid for by an identified sponsor. The main purposes of advertising are to persuade customers to buy a product or accept an idea, inform customers about products, or remind them to take action.

LO 18.1-2 Cite common types of advertising media.
Advertising media includes print media, outdoor media, broadcast media, and the Internet. Newspapers, magazines, and directories are print media. Outdoor media includes billboards and transit promotion. Broadcast media is television and radio. Internet advertising includes online advertising, e-mail campaigns, and social media.

LO 18.1-3 Identify considerations in media selection.
The process of determining the best media that meets a campaign's objectives is known as media planning. Considerations made when selecting the appropriate type of media for an advertisement include the costs of creation, the costs of placement, and lead time.

Section 18.2 Creating an Advertising Campaign

LO 18.2-1 Summarize how an advertising campaign is developed.
An advertising campaign is a coordinated series of related advertisements with a single idea or theme. The advertising campaign is one piece of the overall promotional campaign. Steps for creating successful advertising campaigns are to set the goals, establish a budget, brainstorm the creative concept, write the message, select the media, and evaluate the results.

LO 18.2-2 List elements of an advertisement.
The classic structure for an advertisement has four elements: headline, copy, graphics, and signature. A headline is designed to grab the attention of viewers so they will read the rest of the advertisement. Copy provides information and sells the product. Graphics provide visual interest. Graphics include typography, art, and layout. The signature identifies the person or company paying for the advertisement.

Check Your Marketing IQ

Now that you have completed the chapter, see what you have learned about marketing by taking the chapter posttest. The posttest is available at www.g-wlearning.com/marketing/.

Review Your Knowledge

1. Describe advertising as an element of the promotional mix.
2. Provide an example of how advertising benefits society.
3. List the main points of the Federal Trade Commission Act that relate to advertising.
4. Cite common types of advertising media.
5. Identify considerations to be made when selecting media.
6. Explain advertising campaigns.
7. Summarize how an advertising campaign is developed.
8. Name a metric that can be tracked to evaluate the success of an advertising campaign.
9. List the elements of an advertisement.
10. Cite examples of what the most effective advertising copy does.

Apply Your Knowledge

1. In an earlier chapter, you selected a company for which you are writing a marketing plan. Identify one product for which you will create an advertising campaign.
2. Identify the goals for your advertising campaign. What are you trying to accomplish with this element of the promotional mix?
3. Describe a segment of the target market for your product. Write a profile that describes the demographics, interests, lifestyle, and typical daily activities and purchases of your market segment.
4. List the types of media you will use in this campaign and cite the pros and cons of each one. Explain how each type of media relates to the goals of the campaign.
5. Develop a time line that could be used to deliver the advertising campaign.
6. Think about advertisements you have seen or heard in the last 24 hours. List the ones you remember. Why do you think you remembered those specific advertisements and not others? How might you repurpose the effective elements of these advertisements in your own campaign?
7. Develop a theme concept for your advertisement by brainstorming what the campaign should look like. List or illustrate two to three concepts that could potentially reach your campaign's goals. Select one concept to use for the campaign.
8. Write a headline and copy for one print advertisement for your product using the AIDA model. The features and benefits of the product should be clearly stated. Include a call to action to close the message. Contact information for your company should be provided so customers can obtain samples or information, or make a purchase.
9. Design the advertisement. Include the headline, copy, graphics, and other necessary elements of the advertisement. Ensure the headline grabs attention, the copy gives compelling reasons to buy the product, the graphics and typography are visually appealing, and the signature includes all necessary elements.
10. Identify metrics you can use to evaluate your advertising campaign. Describe how you will use these to measure responses. How will you evaluate the results?

Apply Your Math Skills

Hero's Sandwich Shoppe is a local restaurant chain. The owner of the business wants to expand to the rest of the state. To begin, the owner hired an advertising agency to launch an advertising campaign. Apply your math skills to solve the following problems.

1. A radio commercial that will air on four radio stations throughout the state cost $1,000 to produce. The air time for the 60-second commercial is $500 per radio station. What is the total cost of the radio commercial?
2. The Hero's Sandwich Shoppe website was configured for SEO. The website configuration cost $5,000. The advertising agency charges $300 per month for continuation of the SEO service. Hero's Sandwich Shoppe signed a contract to use this service for one year. What is the total cost of the SEO?
3. How much is Hero's Sandwich Shoppe paying the advertising agency for both the radio commercial and the SEO service?

Communication Skills

Reading Analyze the quality of the information presented in the visuals in this chapter. Is the information coherent? Is concrete evidence presented? Report your findings to the class.

Writing Review the list of ways advertising benefits society that appears in Section 18.1. Select one of these benefits and write several paragraphs about how advertising benefits you, including your personal life and your community.

Speaking Impromptu speaking is talking without advance notice to plan what will be said. Turn to the person next to you and ask him or her to explain what *nonpersonal* means in advertising. Were you able to hold an impromptu conversation on this topic? What did you learn from speaking with the other person?

Internet Research

Effective Campaigns   Conduct an online search for *examples of effective advertising campaigns*. Select two or three examples. Describe how these successful campaigns coordinated all the elements of the promotional mix.

E-Commerce Marketing   *E-commerce* refers to the buying and selling of goods on the Internet. Visit the website of a business that conducts e-commerce. Also conduct an online search for the name of this business. Study both the company's website and the search results to determine the role of e-commerce in this company's marketing efforts.

Social-Media Advertising   Select an online advertisement that utilizes social media. How does the company incorporate social media into the advertisement? Note any websites, social-media pages, or mobile apps used or mentioned in the advertisement. What can you deduce about the target market based on the elements of this advertisement?

Advertising Media by Generation   Your generation is called *Generation Z* or *iGeneration*, partly due to the amount of time it spends communicating on electronic devices. Conduct Internet research about the types of advertising media used to reach people in your age group. How does this differ from the best ways to reach adults in their 40s and 50s? Are there any similarities?

Teamwork

With a teammate, create a collage of advertisements you believe are excellent. Identify the headline, copy, logo, and signature on each advertisement. List all the reasons you think these advertisements are effective.

Portfolio Development

College and Career Readiness

CTSO Competitive Events   Participation in CTSO competitive events encourages leadership, teamwork, and career development. Many CTSOs, including DECA, host competitive events in which students compete against each other. These events usually require advance preparation and study.

1. Identify the CTSO events in which you have competed. Create a Microsoft Word document to list the name of each organization and title of the event. Use the heading "CTSO Competitive Events" and your name.
2. In your document, briefly describe each event, how you prepared, and the outcome of the event such as how you placed. Save the document.
3. Locate copies of the rubrics for the competitive events listed in your document. The rubric will explain how the event judges evaluated you. Include these rubrics in the portfolio along with the document you created.
4. Update your master spreadsheet.

CHAPTER 19

Visual Merchandising

Sections

19.1 **Visual Merchandising**

19.2 **Display**

Reading Prep

College and Career Readiness

As you read this chapter, stop at the Section Reviews and take time to answer the Check Your Understanding questions. Were you able to answer these without referring to the chapter content?

Check Your Marketing IQ

Before you begin the chapter, see what you already know about marketing by taking the chapter pretest. The pretest is available at www.g-wlearning.com/marketing/.

◇DECA Emerging Leaders

Professional Selling and Consulting Events, Part 1

Career Cluster: Marketing
Instructional Area: Not identified for this event.

Knowledge and Skills Developed

Participants will develop many 21st century skills desired by today's employers in the following categories:
- communication and collaboration
- creativity and innovation
- critical thinking and problem solving
- flexibility and adaptability
- information literacy
- initiative and self-direction
- leadership and responsibility
- media literacy
- productivity and accountability
- social and cross-cultural skills

Purpose

Designed for individual DECA members, the participant will organize and deliver a sales presentation for one or more products and/or services while demonstrating skills needed for a career in sales. The guidelines and evaluation form for each Professional Selling and Consulting Events career category will be exactly the same. However, each career area will deliver a sales presentation for a different product described in the Products/Services and Target Customer Descriptions section. Products, services, and target markets are identified annually.

Procedure, Part 1

1. For Part 1 in this text, read the skills assessed and purpose of the event.
2. The objective for the sales presentation or consultation is for the participant to assume the role of salesperson or consultant making a presentation to a potential **buyer (judge)**. Prior to ICDC, the participant will prepare a sales presentation or consultation presentation for the product/service and target market customers described.
3. The participant will make a 15-minute sales presentation or consultation to the judge worth 100 points.
4. The presentation begins immediately after the introduction of the participant by the adult assistant to the judge.
5. The participant will spend no more than 15 minutes setting up visual aids and delivering the sales presentation or consultation. The participant may bring presentation notes to use during the sales presentation or consultation.
6. If time remains, the judge may ask questions pertaining to the project.
7. If there are any questions, ask your instructor to clarify.

Critical Thinking

1. What role does marketing research play in the preparation?
2. Why are new products and services important to business/industry?

Visit www.deca.org for more information.

Published by DECA Inc. Copyright © by DECA Inc. No part of this publication may be reproduced for resale without written permission from the publisher. Printed in the United States of America.

Section 19.1

Visual Merchandising

Learning Objectives

LO 19.1-1 Describe visual merchandising.
LO 19.1-2 Identify four elements of visual merchandising.

Key Terms

display
store image
storefront
marquee
store layout
fixture
point-of-purchase (POP) display

Essential Question

How does visual merchandising attract customer attention?

Visual Merchandising

LO 19.1-1

Visual merchandising is the process of creating floor plans and displays to attract customer attention and encourage purchases. It is often used as the sales promotion element of the promotional mix, especially in the B2C market. Visual merchandising attracts customers and invites them to examine merchandise more closely. A **display** is a visual presentation of merchandise or ideas. Displays are designed to excite customers, motivate their interest in the merchandise, and entice them to buy.

Visual merchandising helps define the image of the store. **Store image** is created through the location, design, and décor of a business. Some words that can describe a store's image are *bargain, casual, discount, expensive, sophisticated, trendy, upscale,* and *youthful*.

In an independent store, the store owner usually establishes the store image, or *brand*. In a chain store, the image is usually established at the headquarters by the marketing department based on company goals.

Jeff Whyte/Shutterstock.com

A display is a visual presentation of merchandise or ideas designed to excite customers, motivate their interest in the merchandise, and entice them to buy. *When has a display captured your attention?*

Visual merchandising is used primarily in retail situations and at trade shows. Retail stores arrange products in small and large displays to make them more appealing. Trade shows present products in displays on the exhibit floor so customers can have a clear vision of what is being offered.

346 Copyright Goodheart-Willcox Co., Inc.

Visual merchandising is also important for other types of businesses, such as service businesses, manufacturers, and wholesalers. Service businesses, such as hair salons, may also sell hair products to customers. They create displays to promote their products. Many manufacturers of consumer products have showrooms to promote their products to retailers. Some wholesalers have showrooms with displays to show products to their buyers. For example, a business that sells and rents commercial printers and copiers may have a showroom to demonstrate different models to customers.

Elements of Visual Merchandising
LO 19.1-2

Many factors contribute to successful visual merchandising. To accomplish the goals of visual merchandising, four elements must be considered: store exterior, store layout, store interior, and interior displays.

Store Exterior

The store exterior is the first part of the store that a customer sees. The store exterior is often called the **storefront**. It often includes the store sign or logo, marquee, display windows, entrances, outdoor lighting, landscaping, and the building itself. All of these elements contribute to the store image.

The store sign is a major element of a store exterior. Many businesses develop a unique way of writing the company name, often with design elements. Businesses may also use the company logo. Often, this is the way the name is displayed on the store sign.

Another use of exterior space is a marquee. A **marquee** is an overhanging structure containing a signboard located at the entrance to the store. The advantage to using a marquee is that it displays information that can be changed and provides a way to advertise store promotions and special events.

Tupungato/Shutterstock.com

The elements of a storefront contribute to the store's image. *How do the elements of a storefront entice customers to enter?*

Case in Point

Apple

Many people have fond memories of holiday displays in windows of their favorite department stores. These displays are examples of visual merchandising. Visual merchandising plays an important role to attract customer attention and interaction.

Not just during holidays, but every day of the year, retailers are becoming more competitive and taking visual displays to all new levels. Take a look at the iconic Fifth Avenue Apple Store in New York City. The glass cube that serves as the entrance to the store is a landmark as well as a tourist destination. The store was renovated in 2011 at a cost of over $6 million. The giant glass cube is a unique structure that creates a storefront demanding attention and reflecting the Apple image. Inside the store, customers find Apple products in tastefully designed displays. They also have the opportunity to demonstrate the latest in technology. The unmistakable Apple logo is visible throughout the store in displays and as decoration. Visual merchandising—where would we be without it?

A display window shows a selection of merchandise available in the store. *How do you think visual merchandisers decide which products to display?*

Display windows are used to show a selection of merchandise available in the store. These displays often have a theme, such as a season or holiday, to attract customers' interest. Merchandise featured in the display is usually at eye level so people walking past the store will see it, and hopefully be inspired to make a purchase.

The design of a business exterior is often also part of the *place* decision. The location of the business often influences a store image. Stores located in a high-rent district create an image of upscale merchandise. Stores located in a mall may reflect family shopping and reasonable prices.

Store Layout

A **store layout** is a floor plan that shows how the space in a store will be used. A store layout is usually divided into four sections: the selling area, sales support area, storage space, and customer comfort space. Figure 19-1 shows an example of a store layout.

The *selling area* is where the merchandise is presented to the customer. This area includes shelves or racks holding merchandise, displays of merchandise, and counters with cash registers for sales transactions.

The *sales support area* contains employee areas, such as offices, lockers, and a lunchroom. Sales support areas are clearly marked so customers do not enter these areas by mistake. *Storage space* may be used to receive and store merchandise. Customers never see these areas.

An additional area is referred to as *customer comfort space*. This area contains amenities for customers, such as restrooms, lounges, and cafés. Many stores have added luxury comfort areas to appeal to customers.

Store Interior

The interior of the store must be appealing to customers. Its décor, including the colors, lighting, flooring, signage, and artwork, should reflect the preferences and taste of target market.

Signs that relay information, as well as advertising messages, are a part of a store's interior. *Men's Clothing*, *Customer Service*, and *Shoes* are examples of permanent signage that a retail store may display. Promotion or advertisements such as *Back to School Sale* and *Clearance* are examples of temporary signage that is common in most retail stores.

The interior includes permanent items, such as flooring and wall coverings, other furnishings, lighting fixtures, and display fixtures. A **fixture** is an item designed to hold something. Some fixtures are permanent, such as counters and display cases. Other fixtures are movable, such as tables, wall shelving, bins, and racks. Display fixtures are often customized to meet the needs of the particular product. For example, fixtures designed to display

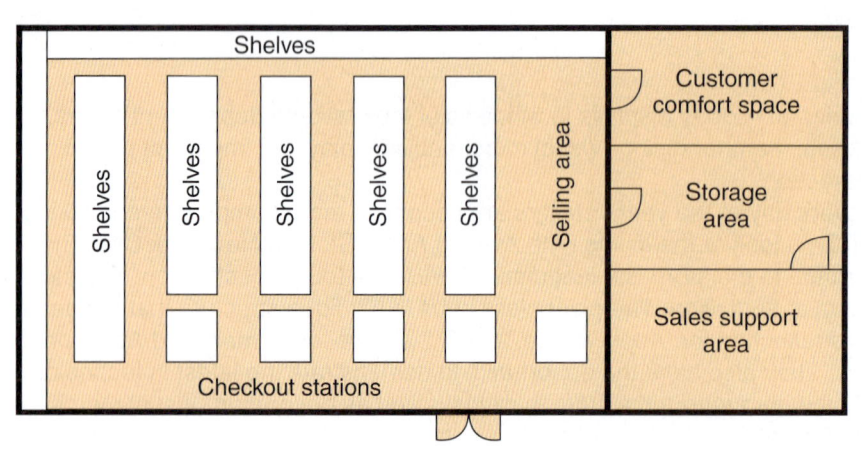

Figure 19-1 A store layout is usually divided into the selling area, sales support area, storage space, and customer comfort space.

Chapter 19 Visual Merchandising

spiphotoone/Shutterstock.com

A fixture is an item designed to hold merchandise, such as a rack that holds clothing. *Why are fixtures considered a part of visual merchandising?*

fishing rods have a different shape from fixtures designed to display shoes.

Interior Displays

An *interior display* is located inside a store. Interior displays are strategically placed to draw the attention of visitors and move traffic through the store. Common locations for interior displays include the store entrance, by elevators, at the ends of escalators, along major aisles, and near cash registers. Interior displays often provide information, such as how to wear new styles or coordinate accessories.

Displays are a critical part of visual merchandising. In fact, when people think of visual merchandising, they most often think of display creation. Five types of *merchandise presentation*, or displays, that most retailers use are point-of-purchase, open, closed, and architectural displays, plus store decorations.

Point-of-Purchase Display

A **point-of-purchase (POP) display** is a special display usually found near a cash register where goods are purchased. A point-of-purchase display is designed to increase impulse buying as customers are waiting to pay for their purchases. These displays may be developed and provided by the manufacturer. They include the display itself as well as the merchandise. A POP may be temporary or permanent, and is used to attract customers to new, special, or holiday products. An example of a POP is a gift card rack or candy display next to the sales register in a supermarket. An interactive kiosk where the customer can actually make a purchase is also a POP. Interactive kiosks are used for customer convenience.

Open Display

In an open display, the merchandise is arranged so the shopper can view and handle the products. Most retail stores have open displays because customers want to know exactly what they are buying.

You Do the Math

Area

The area of a two-dimensional shape considers measurements of its perimeter. The area of a rectangle, for example, is calculated by multiplying the length of two sides that meet at a right angle. The area of a circle is calculated by multiplying the constant *pi* (3.14) by the radius of the circle squared. To calculate the volume of a cylinder, multiply its height by the area of its base.

Solve the following problems.

1. Catalina must calculate the area of a parking lot in order to estimate the cost of repaving it. The parking lot measures 75 feet by 125 feet. What is the area of the parking lot?
2. Jean must calculate the area of her living room in order to estimate the cost of carpet. The room measures 17 feet by 23 feet. What is the area of the living room?
3. Enough plywood must be purchased to cover the floor in a space that is 12 feet by 25 feet. One sheet of plywood is 4 feet by 8 feet. How many sheets of plywood must be purchased? Round up to the nearest whole sheet.
4. Tim must order paint for his new home. The paint comes in buckets that are 12 inches in diameter and 2 feet in height. What is the volume of paint in each bucket?

Copyright Goodheart-Willcox Co., Inc.

be locked. This type of display is often used for jewelry, china, and other expensive products due to the risk of theft or breakage.

Architectural Display

An architectural display contains items that are arranged so customers can imagine how these products might look in their own homes. Examples of products used in architectural displays include cabinets and countertops. Architectural displays are found in home and furniture stores and at some trade shows.

Store Decorations

Store decorations are used for special products or occasions. Banners, signs, and other props may be used to decorate the store for holidays or special events. Decorative displays are usually seasonal, and they add to the atmosphere of the store.

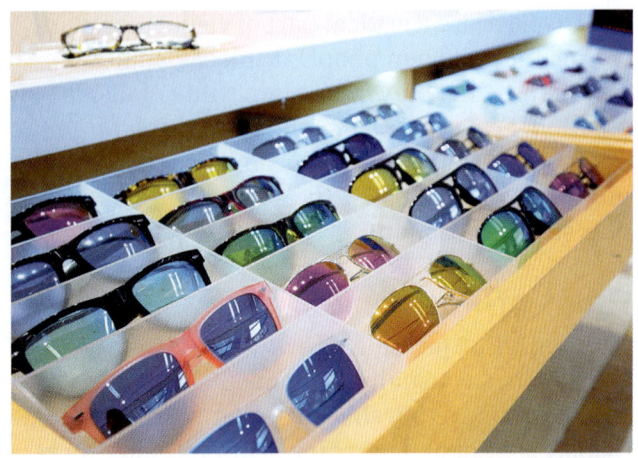

zhu difeng/Shutterstock.com

An open display allows shoppers to view and handle the products. *Why do you think open displays encourage customers to make purchases?*

Closed Display

In a closed display, the merchandise is enclosed in a display case so that the shopper cannot touch it. Closed display cases may also

Section 19.1 Review

Check Your Understanding

1. What is the purpose of visual merchandising displays?
2. List examples of words that can describe a store's image.
3. Provide examples of store exterior elements that contribute to a store's image.
4. Name four sections of a store's layout.
5. List examples of interior displays.

Build Your Vocabulary

As you progress through this text, develop a personal glossary of key terms. This will help you build your vocabulary and prepare you for a career. Write a definition for each of the following terms and add them to your personal glossary.

display
fixture
marquee
point-of-purchase (POP) display

storefront
store image
store layout

Section 19.2

Display

Essential Question: What makes visual merchandising effective?

Learning Objectives

LO 19.2-1 List elements of design.
LO 19.2-2 Describe the principles of design.
LO 19.2-3 List steps to develop a display.

Key Terms

design
color wheel
hue
value
intensity
color scheme
complementary color
triadic color
analogous color
emphasis
movement
balance
proportion
prop

LO 19.2-1 Elements of Design

Successful visual merchandising involves designing powerful and effective displays that generate sales for a business. **Design** is the purposeful arrangement of materials to produce a certain effect. *Elements of design* include color, line, shape, texture, light, and motion. They function as building blocks that can be manipulated to create visual effects in a display's design.

An effective display helps customers envision how the item can benefit them. For example, a male mannequin wearing trendy athletic clothing can influence a male shopper to buy because he thinks he will look fashionable like the display. The ultimate goal of visual merchandising is to entice a customer to buy the merchandise.

Color

Color is often the most dramatic and noticeable design element. Colors can grab attention, create a mood, or affect how someone feels.

Psychologists have studied colors and the associations people have with them. Figure 19-2 shows common responses that Americans have to some colors. Notice that the same color can have both positive and negative associations.

dimbar76/Shutterstock.com

Elements of design include color, line, shape, texture, light, and motion. *Why are the elements of design important in visual merchandising?*

Color and Emotions in US Culture

Black. Elegant, sophisticated, strong, serious, wise, mysterious, tragic, sad, old, evil, gloomy

Gray. Modest, sad, old

White. Youthful, innocent, faithful, pure, peaceful

Violet. Royal, dignified, powerful, rich, dramatic, mysterious, passionate

Blue. Peaceful, calm, restful, tranquil, truthful, serious, cool, formal, spacious, sad, depressed

Green. Cool, fresh, natural, friendly, pleasant, calm, restful, lucky, envious, immature

Yellow. Bright, sunny, cheerful, warm, prosperous, hopeful, cowardly, deceitful

Orange. Lively, energetic, cheerful, joyous, warm, hospitable

Red. Exciting, vibrant, passionate, hot, aggressive, angry, dangerous

Goodheart-Willcox Publisher

Figure 19-2 Colors can grab attention, create a mood, or affect how someone feels.

Colors have different meanings in different cultures. For example, brides in America wear white because white symbolizes purity and innocence. In China, brides wear red instead of white because red symbolizes luck and joy. White is the color of mourning in that country.

Colors can also have different meanings in different eras in the same culture. For example, the in-fashion colors change frequently. Visual merchandisers must use their artistic experience and social awareness when using color.

Color Wheel

The perception of color is individual. Whether a person likes certain colors or color combinations is very subjective. However, many people tend to agree on which color combinations are pleasing to look at. One tool that is used as a guide for developing color combinations is the color wheel. The **color wheel** is a standard arrangement of 12 colors in a wheel that shows the relationships among the colors. A color wheel is shown in Figure 19-3.

The *primary colors* are red, blue, and yellow. They are placed at equal distances on the color wheel. If equal amounts of two primary colors are mixed, the secondary colors are created. The *secondary* colors are green, violet, and orange. If equal amounts of a primary and secondary color are mixed, the intermediate colors are created. The *intermediate* colors are yellow-orange, yellow-green, blue-green, blue-violet, red-violet, and red-orange. Black, white, and gray are neutral colors.

A color has three distinct qualities: hue, value, and intensity. **Hue** is the pure color itself, for example, red. *Color* is often used as a synonym for *hue*. **Value** refers to the lightness or darkness of the color, that is, how much white or black is mixed with the hue. Hues mixed with white are called *tints*. For example, pink is a tint of red. Hues mixed with black are called *shades*. Burgundy is a shade of red. **Intensity** refers to the brightness or dullness of a color.

Color Schemes

A **color scheme** is a description of color combinations. There are many color schemes. In fact, some industries, such as the fashion industry, try to come up with new color schemes every season. However, there are six basic color schemes, as shown in Figure 19-4.

In designing a display, it is important to understand the relationships among colors. Colors found opposite to one another on a color wheel are called **complementary colors**. Using complementary

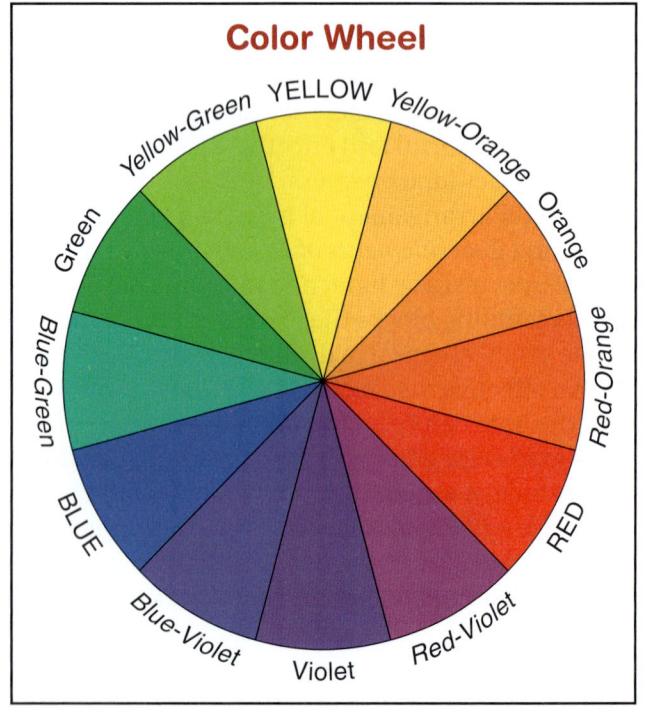

Goodheart-Willcox Publisher

Figure 19-3 A color wheel is used as a guide for developing color combinations.

Display Development

Name	Number	Location on Wheel	Examples
Monochromatic	One color	Any color plus its tints or shades	
Accented Neutral	Two colors	One neutral plus one color from anywhere	
Complementary	Two colors	Opposite each other	
Split Complementary	Three colors	Choose one color; add the two colors on either side of the complementary color	
Triad	Three colors	Equal distances from each other	
Analogous	Three colors	Next to each other	

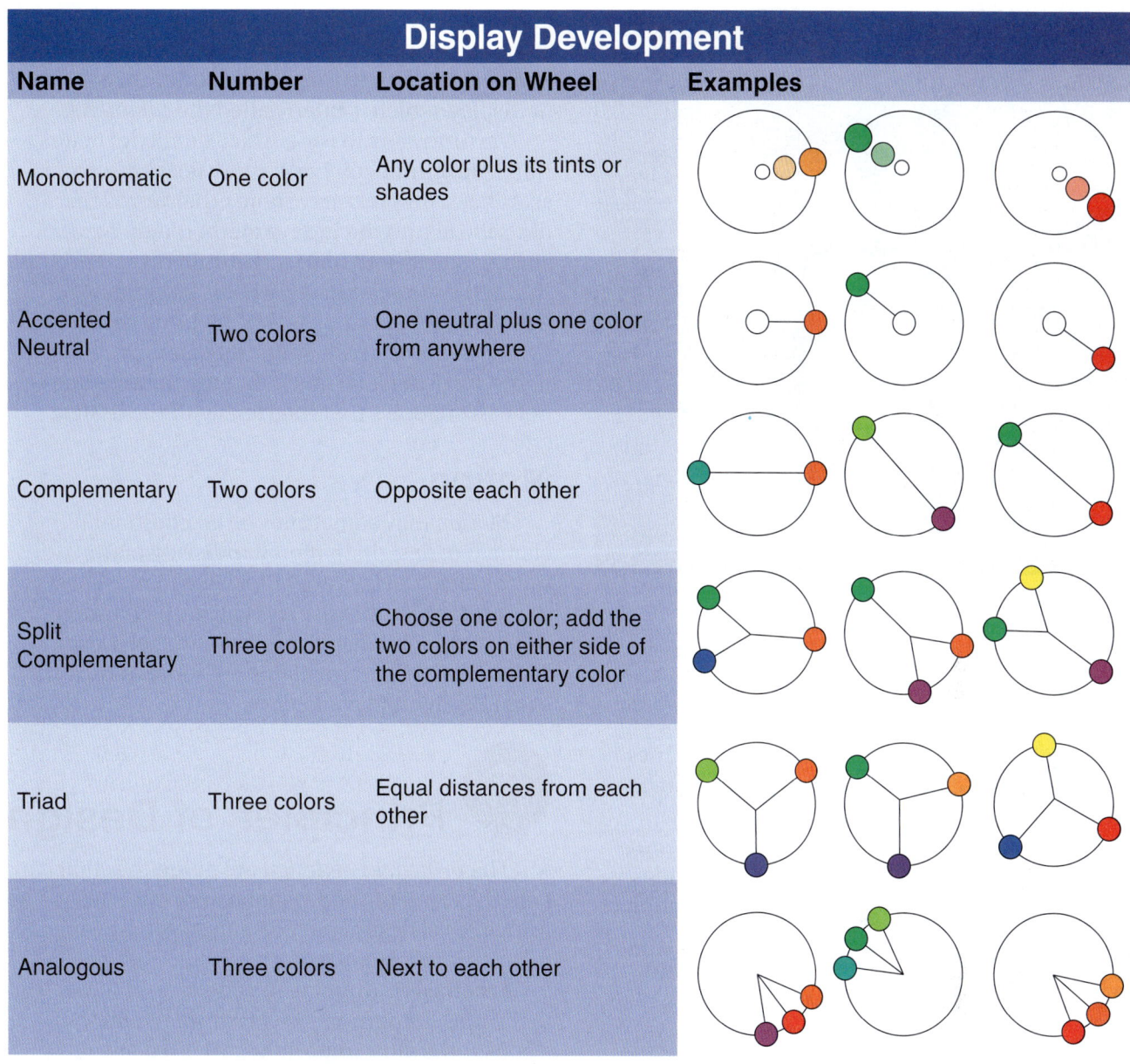

Goodheart-Willcox Publisher

Figure 19-4 It is important to understand the relationships among colors when designing a display.

colors in a display, such as purple and yellow, creates contrast. **Triadic colors** are three colors that are equally spaced on the color wheel. Examples are orange-red, blue-violet, and yellow-green. **Analogous colors** are adjacent to one another on the color wheel. Analogous colors go well together.

Line, Shape, Texture, and Light

Line refers to a one-dimensional mark that looks as if it were drawn by a pen. A line can be an actual line drawn by a pen. A line can also be a boundary, for example, where two walls meet

Vividrange/Shutterstock.com

Using complementary colors in a display, such as purple and yellow, creates contrast. *What color schemes have you seen used in displays?*

mongione/Shutterstock.com

Texture refers to the surface quality of materials, like the rough wood used as the background for this display. *How does texture help create interest in a display?*

Pavel L Photo and Video/Shutterstock.com

Elements of design include light so the viewer can see what is being displayed. *What factors should be considered when making lighting decisions for a display?*

circles, triangles, and octagons; or three-dimensional, such as spheres, cubes, and cylinders. Shape also refers to the overall outline of an item or display, which is often called the *silhouette*.

Texture refers to the surface quality of materials. Aluminum foil has a shiny texture. A wool scarf has a dull texture. Some other words that describe texture include smooth, rough, fuzzy, shaggy, sheer, soft, hard, crisp, and furry.

So the viewer can see what is being shown, *light* is necessary in a display. Lighting can be from overhead lights, track lights, table lamps, and spotlights. Care must be taken that the lighting does not cast shadows that interfere with the design.

Motion

Motion may sometimes be an additional element of design. In merchandise displays, mechanical devices are often used to move the products in the display. The most common use of motion in displays is a rotating platform. Sometimes, mechanical figures add motion, for example, in holiday displays.

Principles of Design

The *principles of design* are guidelines that can help the elements of design be used effectively. The principles of design include emphasis, movement, balance, and proportion.

Emphasis is drawing the attention of the viewer to the most important part of a display. Suppose a book is the most important part of a display. Lines can be used to point toward the book and give it emphasis. Color can be used by placing the book on a bright red cloth. Texture can be used by surrounding the book with sparkling confetti. Light can be used by pointing a spotlight on the book.

Movement refers to the way the design guides viewer eyes over an item or display. Readers of Western languages, such as English and Spanish, read from left to right. Therefore, people will tend to view windows and displays from left to right. A designer can use color, shape, line, texture, and light to direct the viewer's attention to move along a desired direction. Another technique used to direct the viewer's attention and focus is through use of mannequins or other items in a display. For example, the direction in which the mannequin looks can also direct the eyes of a viewer.

or where a seam joins two pieces of fabric. Lines can be straight, curved, or jagged. A line also has direction. A line can be *vertical* (up and down), *horizontal* (side to side, like the horizon), or *diagonal* (at an angle). The direction of a line guides the eye from one point to another. The direction of lines gives movement to a design.

Shape refers to the shapes used in a design. The shapes can be two-dimensional, such as

Exploring Marketing Careers

Graphic Designer

Advertisements for a company's products or services can take many forms, including newspaper, magazine, radio, Internet, and television ads. All of these except radio rely to some extent on graphic images to catch the eye of potential customers. The job of a graphic designer is to create graphics that present products or services in an appealing manner for packaging, logos, brochures, and other items that represent the company. Other typical job titles for a graphic designer include *graphic artist*, *creative director*, *design director*, and *desktop publisher*.

Some examples of tasks that graphic designers perform include:
- Consult the client or company executives to determine layout design
- Create designs and layouts for product packaging and company logos
- Use graphic design software to generate layouts
- Design the arrangement of illustrations and text
- Prepare final layouts for printing

Graphic designers need a solid knowledge of layout principles and design concepts, as well as artistic ability. They must also be familiar with design, illustration, photographic, and layout software. Communication skills help them understand the client's requirements and produce designs that showcase products or services effectively. Many graphic design jobs require a bachelor degree, but talented and experienced designers may be hired without a four-year degree. For more information, access the *Occupational Outlook Handbook* online.

goodcat/Shutterstock.com

A viewer's attention and focus can be directed through mannequins or other items in a display. *Do you think the use of mannequins is an effective strategy? Why or why not?*

Balance refers to the way items are placed around an imaginary centerline. *Formal balance* means that you have an object on one side of the centerline, and another object of equal size the same distance from the line on the other side. *Informal balance* means that you have a large object on one side of the line. However, on the other side, you have two smaller objects that together are about the same size as the larger object. Informal balance also occurs when you have a large pale object on one side and a smaller, but very bright object, on the other side. The small but bright object balances the larger but pale object.

Proportion refers to the size and space relationship of all items in a display to each other and to the whole display. Proportion can also be applied to a single item, for which you consider the size and space relationships of all the parts of the item to the whole item. For example, imagine a very light-colored, delicate dress; a wide, dark, heavy leather belt would be out of proportion. A narrow silver belt would look more in proportion.

pyzata/Shutterstock.com

Proportion refers to the size and space relationship of all items in a display to each other and to the whole display. *How can proportion affect the success of a display?*

Display Development
LO 19.2-3

Before a display can be constructed, it must be planned. In addition to selecting the appropriate merchandise, other considerations should be made. Most importantly, the display should appear in good taste and not be offensive to anyone who might see it. A display should not appear to project stereotyping of any form that focuses on culture, religion, gender, or age. The use of props should be appropriate and not degrade any individual. In addition, socially responsible businesses value the importance of the environment. Use of recycled materials and conservation of energy are two strategies that can be used to project an environmentally friendly display. There are six steps in the development of a display, as shown in Figure 19-5.

Set the Display Goals

First, set the goals the display will hopefully accomplish. The purpose of displays is to promote store image and sell products. Each display will have unique goals that depend on the marketing mix and the marketing plan.

Display Development
1. Set the display goals
2. Select the merchandise
3. Determine the display type
4. Choose a theme
5. Evaluate the display
6. Maintain the display

Goodheart-Willcox Publisher

Figure 19-5 There are six steps used in the development of a display.

Select the Merchandise

The first step in display development is to select the merchandise that will be featured. The merchandise should be eye-catching or notable in some way. For example, it may be a new product, a seasonal product, or one for a certain age group.

Determine the Display Type

The next step is to determine the type of display. A one-item display can be used to show just one product. Instead, a similar product display may be more appropriate. For example, the display may show only wallets, but shows multiple designer brands. Another approach is to show similar or complementary products. If the merchandise relates to another product, such as coats and scarves, the two items may be displayed together. On the other hand, a variety of products

Marcin Balcerzak/Shutterstock.com

Display merchandise should be eye-catching or notable, such as seasonal products or one for a certain age group. *What types of merchandise catch your eye when they are on display?*

Chapter 19   Visual Merchandising   357

Employability Skills

Workspace Etiquette

Whether you are in an office, a cubicle, or an open room, chances are you will have to share your workspace with others. Always allow your neighbors their privacy. Knock before entering or speaking to someone. Walk around walls or partitions to communicate; do not shout over or around them. Wait to be invited into a conversation rather than jumping in just because it is within earshot.

Kzenon/Shutterstock.com

To maintain a good image, a visual merchaniser must keep a display clean and orderly. *What message does a messy display send to customers?*

might be used to show an assortment of unrelated merchandise.

Choose a Theme

The display theme is chosen next. The theme for a display can be an artistic element, such as a color scheme. It can also be an idea, such as a beach or carnival. Often, an entire store will have a theme, such as back to school.

To complement the theme, props may be used. **Props** are objects used in a display to support the theme or to physically support the merchandise. Props can be either *decorative* or *functional*. A beach ball for a swimsuit display is a decorative prop. Mannequins in beachwear are functional props.

rolkadd/Shutterstock.com

The theme for a display can be an idea, such as the beach and use of decorative props. *What display themes might be successful for customers in your age group?*

The merchandise should be arranged in a way that attracts customers and promotes the products. Placing items at eye level makes it easy for customers to see the merchandise that is being displayed. Signs can be used to give information, such as the manufacturer or pricing. Lighting is important and should be used to spotlight specific items.

Evaluate the Display

A display should be evaluated to determine whether it is meeting these goals. These questions will help determine the quality of the display:
- Does the display fit the store image?
- Does the display grab the attention of customers?
- Does the display focus attention on the merchandise?
- Are the signs clear and easy to read?
- Is there enough light, with minimal glare and shadows?
- Is the display clean and neat?
- Does the display accomplish your goal?

To measure the success of a display, solicit feedback from coworkers or customers. Feedback can be helpful when creating future displays.

Maintain the Display

Finally, maintain the display. To maintain a good image, a display must be kept clean and orderly. Suppose you are looking at a clothing display. You notice the mannequin has a broken

Copyright Goodheart-Willcox Co., Inc.

hand, the shirts on the table are scattered about, and the bulb in the spotlight is out. What would you think? Dirty, messy displays can ruin the image of a store. The following is a guide for good display maintenance.

- Check at least once a day to make sure the display looks as clean, crisp, and fresh as when it was first completed.
- Clean the floor, table, props, and merchandise regularly.
- Replace any merchandise that has been removed or damaged.
- If merchandise has been moved, put it back where it belongs.
- Check lights and replace as necessary.

Marketing Ethics

Ethical Sales Messages

Sometimes it is necessary to write a sales message or other type of document for your organization. Even though it may be tempting to focus on sales "hype" or other persuasive techniques to convey a message, remember to keep the information honest. Embellishing a message about a product or service or intentionally misrepresenting a product or service is unethical and may be illegal. There are truth-in-advertising laws that must be followed.

Section 19.2 Review

Check Your Understanding

1. What is the ultimate goal of visual merchandising?
2. Name three distinct qualities of color.
3. What is formal balance?
4. Explain the first step in display development.
5. Why is it important to maintain a display?

Build Your Vocabulary

As you progress through this text, develop a personal glossary of key terms. This will help you build your vocabulary and prepare you for a career. Write a definition for each of the following terms and add them to your personal glossary.

analogous color	hue
balance	intensity
color scheme	movement
color wheel	prop
complementary color	proportion
design	triadic color
emphasis	value

Chapter 19 Review and Assessment

Chapter Summary

Section 19.1 Visual Merchandising

LO 19.1-1 Describe visual merchandising.
Visual merchandising is creating floor plans and displays to attract customer attention and encourage purchases. It is often used as the sales promotion element of the promotional mix. Visual merchandising attracts customers and invites them to examine merchandise more closely. It also helps to define the image of the store.

LO 19.1-2 Identify four elements of visual merchandising.
The four elements of visual merchandising are store exterior, store layout, store interior, and interior displays. The store exterior includes the store sign or logo, marquee, display windows, entrances, outdoor lighting, landscaping, and the building itself. A store layout shows how the space in a store will be used. The store interior includes the colors, lighting, flooring, signage, and artwork. Interior displays are strategically placed to draw the attention of visitors and move traffic through the store.

Section 19.2 Display

LO 19.2-1 List elements of design.
Elements of design include color, line, shape, texture, light, and motion. Color is often the most dramatic and noticeable design element. Line refers to a one-dimensional mark that looks as if it were drawn by a pen. Shape refers to the shapes used in a design. Texture refers to the surface quality of materials. So the viewer can see what is being shown, light is necessary.

LO 19.2-2 Describe the principles of design.
The principles of design are guidelines that can help the elements of design be used effectively. They include emphasis, movement, balance, and proportion. Emphasis draws attention to the most important part of a display. Movement is the way the design guides viewer eyes over an item or display. Balance is the way items are placed around an imaginary centerline. Proportion refers to the size and space relationship of all items in a display to each other and to the whole display.

LO 19.2-3 List steps to develop a display.
The first step to develop a visual display is to set goals the display will hopefully accomplish. Next, select the merchandise that will be featured. Then, determine the type of display. The display theme is chosen next. Then, the display is evaluated to measure its effectiveness. Finally, maintain the display.

Check Your Marketing IQ

Now that you have completed the chapter, see what you have learned about marketing by taking the chapter posttest. The posttest is available at www.g-wlearning.com/marketing/.

Review Your Knowledge

1. Describe visual merchandising.
2. How is store image created?
3. Identify four elements of visual merchandising.
4. Explain the purpose of display windows.
5. List elements of design.
6. What are the three distinct qualities of a color?
7. Describe the principles of design.
8. Explain how the elements and principles of design function in visual merchandising.
9. List steps to develop a display.
10. Provide examples of ways a display should be maintained.

Apply Your Knowledge

1. Recall the last time you went to a mall. Why did you walk into one store, but pass by another? Describe how visual merchandising enticed you to enter a store.
2. In your marketing plan, you will describe the image of your business. What image does your business project to customers?
3. Draw a store layout for your business using graph paper or other materials. Include each of the four sections of a store's layout.
4. List both the permanent and temporary fixtures that are used in visual merchandising displays by your business.
5. Management has requested you create new displays for a major product. Select two of the types of displays described in this chapter and explain why these could work well for your business.
6. Describe two elements of design that will help you in creating a visual display.
7. Describe two principles of design that are needed to create a visual display for your merchandise.
8. List the steps you will take to create your merchandise display.
9. Create a checklist you can use to evaluate whether your display meets your goals.
10. Create a checklist you can use to maintain your display.

Apply Your Math Skills

Terrence is a visual merchandise manager at a store in the United States. The company's corporate headquarters are in Canada. Terrence is preparing new visual displays for the store but the instructions from corporate are provided in metric units. The units can be converted as follows.
1 inch = 2.54 centimeters
1 foot = 0.30 meters
Apply your math skills to solve the following problems.

1. Terrence needs to install hooks to hang products on a wall. The instructions from corporate state the fixtures should be placed 40 centimeters apart. How many inches apart should Terrence place the hooks? Round to the nearest inch.
2. Next, Terrence needs to hang a set of promotional signs from the ceiling of the store. The instructions from corporate state the signs should hang 3.5 meters apart. How many feet apart should Terrence hang the signs? Round to the nearest foot.

Communication Skills

College and Career Readiness

Writing It is important to use critical thinking skills to make sense of challenges you will face as a marketing professional. Suppose a customer has submitted a complaint stating that a visual-merchandising display was offensive. Write a letter from the position of marketing manager addressing the customer's complaint.

Listening In order to be effective, product displays must attract customers and invite them to examine merchandise more closely. Ask a friend, classmate, or family member to recall a recent shopping experience. What displays did they see? What enticed them to buy or convinced them to not make a purchase? As you listen, note which elements of the display were successful in gaining their attention and which were not.

Speaking Locate a display in your school building, such as a display of athletic trophies or student artwork. Analyze how elements and principles of art are used in the display. Deliver an informal presentation to your class to share your analysis.

Internet Research

Successful Visual Merchandising Use Internet resources to locate real-world examples of successful visual merchandising. Select one example that interests you. Describe how visual merchandising techniques may have led to increased sales for this company.

Elements of Visual Merchandising Conduct an Internet search for *most important elements of visual merchandising*. Select one or two articles from the search results. Which elements did these articles list? How can these elements be applied to visual merchandising displays?

Store Image Using the Internet, locate pictures of the interior and exterior of a business at which you would like to shop. One resource may be the company's website. Describe the elements of visual merchandising shown in the photos. How do they contribute to the store image?

Teamwork

Working with your team, combine elements of advertising and visual merchandising to develop a display for DECA products. Follow the steps described in this chapter. Select the merchandise that will be featured and determine the type of display. Choose a display theme and set goals for the display. Create the display. Write a list of steps that could be taken to maintain the display.

Portfolio Development

College and Career Readiness

Community Service Community service is an important quality to show in a portfolio. Serving the community shows that a candidate is well rounded and socially aware. In this activity, you will create a list of your contributions to nonprofit organizations. Many opportunities are available for young people to serve the community. You might volunteer for a park clean-up project. Perhaps you might enjoy reading to residents in a senior-living facility. Maybe raising money for a pet shelter appeals to you. Whatever your interests, there is sure to be a related service project.

1. Create a Microsoft Word document that lists service projects or volunteer activities in which you have taken part. Use the heading "Community Service" on the document along with your name. List the name of the organization or person you helped, the date(s) of service, and the activities that you performed. If you received an award related to this service, mention it here.
2. Save the document in an appropriate folder.
3. Update your spreadsheet to reflect the inclusion of this Community Service document.

CHAPTER 20

Personal Selling

Sections

20.1 **Role of Sales**
20.2 **Selling**
20.3 **Customer Service**

Reading Prep

College and Career Readiness

After reading each section, stop and write a three- to four-sentence summary of what you just read. Be sure to paraphrase and use your own words.

Check Your Marketing IQ

Before you begin the chapter, see what you already know about marketing by taking the chapter pretest. The pretest is available at www.g-wlearning.com/marketing/.

DECA Emerging Leaders

Professional Selling and Consulting Event, Part 2

Career Cluster: Marketing
Instructional Area: Not identified for this event.

Procedure, Part 2

In the previous chapter, you studied the skills developed and procedures for this event.

1. The participants may use the following items during the oral presentation:
   - visual aids appropriate for an actual sales presentation
   - no more than three standard-sized posters not to exceed 22 1/2 inches by 30 1/2 inches each. Participants may use both sides of the posters, but all attachments must fit within the poster dimensions.
   - one standard-sized presentation display board not to exceed 36 1/2 inches by 48 1/2 inches
   - one desktop flip chart presentation easel, 12 inches by 10 inches (dimensions of the page)
   - one personal laptop computer
   - cell phones, smartphones, iPods, MP3 players, iPads, tablets, or any type of a handheld, information-sharing device will be allowed in written events *if* applicable to the presentation
   - sound, as long as the volume is kept at a conversational level
2. Only visual aids that can be easily carried to the presentation by the actual participant will be permitted, and the participant must set up the visuals by himself or herself. No set-up time will be allowed. The participant must furnish his or her own materials and equipment. No electrical power will be supplied.
3. Materials appropriate to the situation may be handed to or left with judges in all competitive events. Items of monetary value may be handed to but may not be left with judges. Items such as flyers, brochures, pamphlets, and business cards may be handed to or left with the judge. No food or drinks are allowed.
4. If any of these rules are violated, the adult assistant must be notified by the judge.

Products/Services and Target Customer Description

For this event, you will assume the role of sales representative for a company that manufactures bicycle tires. A major bicycle manufacturer is taking meetings with tire manufacturers to hear their sales pitches to be the tire supplier for the company's new entry-level mountain bike. You have a meeting scheduled with the bicycle manufacturer's supply chain manager to pitch your company's products and price points.

Critical Thinking

1. What key points will you include in your presentation?
2. Based on your presentation, what visual aids will you bring? How will you use them?

Visit www.deca.org for more information.

Published by DECA Inc. Copyright © by DECA Inc. No part of this publication may be reproduced for resale without written permission from the publisher. Printed in the United States of America.

Section 20.1

Essential Question
Why is personal selling important to the marketing mix?

Role of Sales

Learning Objectives
LO 20.1-1　Explain the value of personal selling.
LO 20.1-2　Describe skills needed for a career in sales.

Key Terms
relationship selling
call center
customer service
customer-service mindset
quality service
presentation
master slide
visual aid

Value of Personal Selling

Personal selling is any direct contact between a salesperson and a customer with the objective of making a sale. It is an important component of the promotional element of the marketing mix. Without the sales function, it would be difficult for a company to generate revenue. For this reason, companies have teams that perform personal selling.

As with other components of promotion, selling applies the marketing concept of customer satisfaction. By meeting customer needs with a product or service, a company can grow its sales.

A salesperson adds value to the promotional mix. Personal selling provides information that a marketing brochure or website cannot provide. A salesperson can persuade a customer to make a decision about how to meet a need or want. Customers can give feedback to the salesperson that may help product development meet customer needs. People like to have personal contact when making a buying decision. While other parts of the promotional mix are important, personal contact is at the top of the customer list. Personal selling is important for both business-to-business (B2B) and business-to-consumer (B2C) sales.

Kzenon/Shutterstock.com

Personal selling is direct contact between a salesperson and a customer with the objective of making a sale. *In what ways does selling add value to a business?*

364　　Copyright Goodheart-Willcox Co., Inc.

Business-to-Business (B2B) Selling

Business-to-business (B2B) selling is a business selling to another business. In this type of sale, the salesperson usually goes to the customer's place of business. Companies that sell equipment and raw materials to manufacturers are involved in B2B sales. Manufacturers that sell finished products to retailers are involved in B2B sales, too.

The term *B2B sales* often includes governmental and institutional sales. When a business sells to a government, it is referred to as *government sales*. When a business sells to a nonprofit organization, such as a school or hospital, it is called *institutional sales*.

There are typically two types of sales positions for B2B sales, inside sales and outside sales. An *inside salesperson* communicates with customers via phone or e-mail from inside the company's place of business. The salesperson typically does not have face-to-face contact with a customer. An *outside salesperson* visits with the customer at his or her place of business. Some communication will be via phone or e-mail, but the primary contact is face-to-face and relationship selling. **Relationship selling** focuses on building long-term relationships with customers.

Business-to-Consumer (B2C) Selling

Business-to-consumer (B2C) selling is selling to consumers. Retail is a typical example of B2C sales. Most B2C sales are made by a salesperson in the place of business, such as a retail store.

michaeljung/Shutterstock.com

B2C sales are often made in the place of business, such as a retail store. *How do you think a salesperson convinces a customer to buy?*

However, some retail businesses conduct the selling process via telephone. *Telemarketing* is personal selling done over the telephone. Many larger retailers have call centers for the telemarketing function. A **call center** is an office that is set up for the purpose of receiving and making customer calls for an organization. Each telemarketer usually has a telephone headset so he or she can record orders on a computer. Some call centers specialize in *inbound* calls, or customers calling into the center. For example, Lands' End is a company that sells clothing, luggage, and home products. When customers order items from Lands' End over the telephone, their call goes to an inbound call center.

Other call centers specialize in *outbound* calls, or salespeople making customer calls. For example, a local newspaper might have a telemarketer. This salesperson might call local businesses to ask them to advertise in the newspaper. Many nonprofit organizations use outbound call centers to raise money for their organizations. The people who make these calls are usually called *fund-raisers*, but their tasks are very similar to a telemarketer.

The Internet is also used for personal selling. Many websites have a *live chat* feature that allows customers to interact with a salesperson in real time. If the customer visits a website and does *not* interact with a salesperson in real time, it is not considered a personal-selling situation.

LO 20.1-2 Career in Sales

Look anywhere job openings are posted and you will see a large number of advertisements for salespeople. Most businesses need someone to sell their products. Think of any good, service, or idea that interests you. You can probably find a job selling that product. Careers in sales provide great opportunities for career success. Many corporations are headed by people who began their careers in sales.

Sales can be a rewarding career. Some people have a natural talent for sales. However, most people can learn the skills and develop the qualities of a successful salesperson. Community, technical, business, and four-year colleges provide courses in sales. Many businesses provide sales training for their employees. You can also learn about sales through experiences with student organizations, such as DECA.

People who are successful in sales must have excellent work habits and be goal oriented. Personal traits needed for the position include an eagerness to learn, initiative, and persistence. Most salaries include a commission or bonus for reaching sales goals, so hard work and determination is critical.

Strong ethics are important for successful long-term relationships that lead to repeat sales. This includes the qualities of honesty, integrity, and confidentiality. *Honesty* is the quality of being fair and truthful. *Integrity* means adhering to moral or ethical values. *Confidentiality* is the ability to keep information secret. Salespeople usually know secret company information, such as new products in development, as well as private information about customers. It is important for them to keep this information confidential.

Sales positions are generally independent and require minimal day-to-day supervision. A salesperson must be able to work a full day without clocking in or being constantly supervised. Salespeople must be *responsible*, which means they are accountable for their actions, accepting when they make good decisions or bad decisions.

In addition, working in sales requires that a person have excellent customer service skills. It also requires that person to be able to make presentations that are clear, concise, and persuasive.

Customer Service Skills

Personal selling requires customer service skills. **Customer service** is the way in which a business provides services before, during, and after a purchase. Good customer service should be provided by all employees in a company as a part of the marketing concept. *Company image* is often projected through employee interactions with the public. Whenever any employee has direct or indirect contact with a customer, customer service is provided in some form. It could be as simple as answering a question or saying *hello* when someone enters a store.

Exceptional customer service meets or exceeds customer needs. The phrase *going above and beyond* is often used to refer to exceptional customer service. Every business can provide exceptional customer service. Businesses committed to the marketing concept focus their energies on the customer and providing exceptional customer service. Businesses that succeed at this develop a customer-service mindset in all

imtmphoto/Shutterstock.com

A customer-service mindset is the attitude that customer satisfaction always comes first. *Why is this mindset important to the success of a salesperson?*

their employees. A **customer-service mindset** is the attitude that customer satisfaction always comes first.

The sales team is the first line of contact with a customer. For example, a salesperson in a retail store or a restaurant probably has the first encounter with the customer. A successful business expects quality service from its sales team. **Quality service** meets customer needs as well as the standards for customer service set by the company. The difference between poor service and quality service is the difference between a sullen salesperson and a smiling salesperson. It is the difference between rushing customers to make a decision, and giving them enough time and information to be comfortable and make a satisfying choice. It is the difference between a salesperson irritably saying, "No, we don't do that," and a salesperson cheerfully saying, "Let me see what I can do for you."

External customers are the people and businesses who purchase product from an organization. *Internal customers* are the coworkers within the business with whom each employee works and collaborates. It is necessary for salespeople to apply relationship building with both types of customers.

Listening to customers, hearing their concerns, and meeting their needs are necessary for a company to exist and be profitable. Learning how to resolve complaints from external customers can help ensure that product is sold and customers return for future transactions. Understanding and collaborating with internal customers helps a business create product that meets customer needs and generates profits. Both types of customers are necessary for a successful business.

Presentation Skills

Working in sales requires an individual to possess presentation skills. A **presentation** is a prepared speech that delivers information to an audience. The audience may be one person or several. Sales presentations have the added goal of persuading people to make a purchase.

A *slide presentation* is an effective visual aid that is commonly used when presenting to an audience. A professional-looking slide presentation can easily be created by using software such as Microsoft PowerPoint, Google Slides, and Prezi. If the end product needs to be a presentation with text and some visuals, a slideshow will be adequate.

Three important elements of a slide presentation are the master slides, the content, and visual aids.

- A **master slide** is one containing design elements that are applied to a particular set of slides or all slides in a presentation. If you need to make a design change, simply change the master slide and it is reapplied to all associated slides.
- The most important feature of a presentation is the content. When creating slides, focus on the important points of your speech. The slides are not intended for you to read each line to the audience. Instead, they should be talking points to help you stay on track with the presentation. Slides also help the audience stay on track with what you are saying. Keep the sentences short and do not crowd the space with too many words.
- A **visual aid** is an object that is used to clarify an idea, concept, or process. They are effective when used appropriately in a slide presentation. Tasteful and appropriate visual aids can emphasize key points and add variety and interest to a presentation. In a sales presentation, the product being sold can be demonstrated. Slides that include charts, tables, and diagrams can also be used. These add interest and help the audience interpret data. As with content, do not overuse or crowd too many items on a screen. Overuse of visuals can disengage the audience and lead to an unsuccessful presentation. The rule of "less is more" applies here.

Many elements go into a successful presentation. It is critical to hold the attention and interest of an audience.

Section 20.1 Review

Check Your Understanding

1. How does selling add value to a business?
2. What is another name for B2B sales?
3. Where are most B2C sales made?
4. What is the difference between external and internal customers?
5. Who is typically the first line of contact with a customer?

Build Your Vocabulary

As you progress through this text, develop a personal glossary of key terms. This will help you build your vocabulary and prepare you for a career. Write a definition for each of the following terms and add them to your personal glossary.

call center
customer service
customer-service mindset
master slide
presentation
quality service
relationship selling
visual aid

Section 20.2

Selling

Essential Question

How do salespeople prepare to sell?

Learning Objectives

LO 20.2-1 Summarize tasks to complete when preparing to sell.
LO 20.2-2 List steps in the sales process.
LO 20.2-3 Identify options for completing sales transactions in B2B and B2C sales.
LO 20.2-4 Explain how a lost sale can be a learning experience.

Key Terms

preapproach
feature-benefit selling
certification
lead
cold calling
sales process
approach
service approach
greeting approach
merchandise approach
substitute selling
objection
excuse
empathy
close
buying signal
overselling
suggestion selling

LO 20.2-1 Preparing to Sell

A salesperson does not just go out and start selling. There are specific tasks that must be completed before making contact with the customer. The **preapproach** consists of tasks that are performed before contact is made with a customer. These tasks include understanding company selling policies, participating in product training, and learning how to identify potential customers.

Selling Policies

Before product training begins, a salesperson must understand selling policies that have been established by the business. *Selling policies* are guidelines that explain how interactions with customers should be made. Specific policies include how to approach customers, determine discounts, handle returns, and resolve customer service issues.

Companies need guidelines to protect them legally. By setting clear guidelines, a business can be assured that all customers are being treated fairly and that business is being conducted in an approved manner.

Product Training

Product training is the first step to becoming successful in a sales role. A salesperson must be confident that he or she understands the product so customer questions can be answered accurately. Product training is generally a joint effort of the sales and marketing teams. The marketing manager or product trainer typically conducts training for new salespeople on how to use and sell the product. Ongoing training is usually provided throughout the year for the entire sales team. Many companies hold sales meetings on a regular basis to introduce new products and for the teams to exchange selling tips.

The marketing team provides catalogs, brochures, and other materials that present the features and benefits of the products. They also provide a competitive analysis that illustrates how the company's products compare with the competition. The **feature-benefit selling** approach is the method of showing the major selling features of the product and how it benefits the customer. This is also known as *solution selling*. It is vital that the salesperson can convey how the product satisfies the needs of customers and makes their lives better or easier.

The product itself can be the best source of information. If the product is consumable, such as food, tasting the item may be helpful in understanding how to sell it to a customer. If the product is a piece of equipment, such as a lawn mower, using the product is a good learning strategy. First-hand experience makes it easier to sell and demonstrate the product to a customer.

Product training also includes strategy about product pricing so customer questions can be answered. Many companies have specific pricing levels that may vary depending on the customer, amount purchased, and other factors. Pricing is a very important part of the sale.

For some products, informal product training on an individual level is necessary. A salesperson will study and become familiar with information about how to use the product in the catalog, in brochures, and on the website. Most products are sold with printed information, such as care tags, content labels, and user manuals. Other sources may include publications from manufacturers, consumer publications, and trade publications. Manufacturers often provide videos, booklets, and samples of their products.

In some situations, informal product training may not be sufficient to prepare a person to sell.

Kobby Dagan/Shutterstock.com

Sales training may include experiencing the product in order to understand how to best demonstrate it to a customer. *How does first-hand experience make it easier to sell a product?*

Some products require formal training or certification to sell, such as financial investments. **Certification** is a professional status earned by an individual after passing an exam focused on a specific body of knowledge. To become certified, aspiring salespeople may be required to take accredited classes at a local university or pass a certification exam. This training may take weeks or months to complete.

Other types of formal training may be provided by the company in a class or workshop format. A product expert may offer classes on a product, such as a piece of equipment, to illustrate how the product works. The marketing manager may follow this training with how to sell the features and benefits of the product.

Case in Point

IBM

One important goal of most successful companies is to employ sales representatives who are *solution providers* for the customer. Simply closing sales is not enough. These companies want the best and brightest sales representation that meets customer and business needs. To turn this goal into a reality, many companies provide their own training for sales representatives to ensure selling excellence.

IBM is one example of a company that has a well-organized sales training program. The IBM program has multiple offerings to fit the needs of individual sales employees, which also fulfill the needs of the company. Through live classroom instruction or virtual learning, participants can learn solution-based selling techniques. Classes are aimed at specific groups of employees to customize learning for the skills needed in their particular sales positions. These classes offer instruction not only on how to sell, but how to provide client satisfaction after the sale.

A company is only as successful as its sales team. As IBM has found, dedicating a large part of its resources for sales training is a win for everyone.

Identify Potential Customers

The next step in the preapproach stage of selling is identifying potential customers. A **lead** is a potential customer. They are also called *prospects*. For a salesperson in a retail situation, potential customers may walk into the store. However, for salespeople who need to call on customers, they must start with a list of contacts.

Identifying sales leads is most common in B2B sales. They are generated in a variety of ways.

- Customers visiting a trade show may ask for someone to contact them about more information.
- People who visit a website or call customer support may ask for a salesperson to call them.
- A dedicated sales staff may generate leads.
- Lists of names of potential customers can be purchased.

Once a sales lead is identified, additional information about the lead must be gathered. Before making contact, a salesperson should know as much as possible about the company. Learning about the customer is called *qualifying the lead*. The buyer or decision-maker within that organization should be identified. Information about the company such as size, the current supplier for the product being sold, and the purchasing practices should be known before making a call.

Cold calling is the process of making contact with people who are not expecting a sales contact. A customer's and salesperson's time is valuable. Calling on people who are not interested in buying a product may not be a productive use of time. It is important to know the lead is qualified and may generate a sale. However, cold calling is another way to generate sales prospects.

Most sales forces use a *customer-relationship management (CRM)* system in which customer information is entered on a regular basis. The CRM system will have a list of potential customers whom a salesperson may contact. A CRM system typically includes profile information about customers that includes contact information, product preferences, and buying habits. Each sale is noted along with prices paid and whether the sale was made through a physical visit with the customer, a telephone call, or online. In addition, it is usually noted if the sale was a result of a catalog mailing, coupon, social-media promotion, or other marketing campaign.

The amount of information captured varies according to the CRM software used. However, the end goal generally revolves around personalizing the customer experience, determining value-added services to offer, improving customer satisfaction, and building product loyalty.

LO 20.2-2 Sales Process

The **sales process** is a series of steps a salesperson goes through to help the customer make a satisfying buying decision. There are generally six steps in the process, as shown in Figure 20-1.

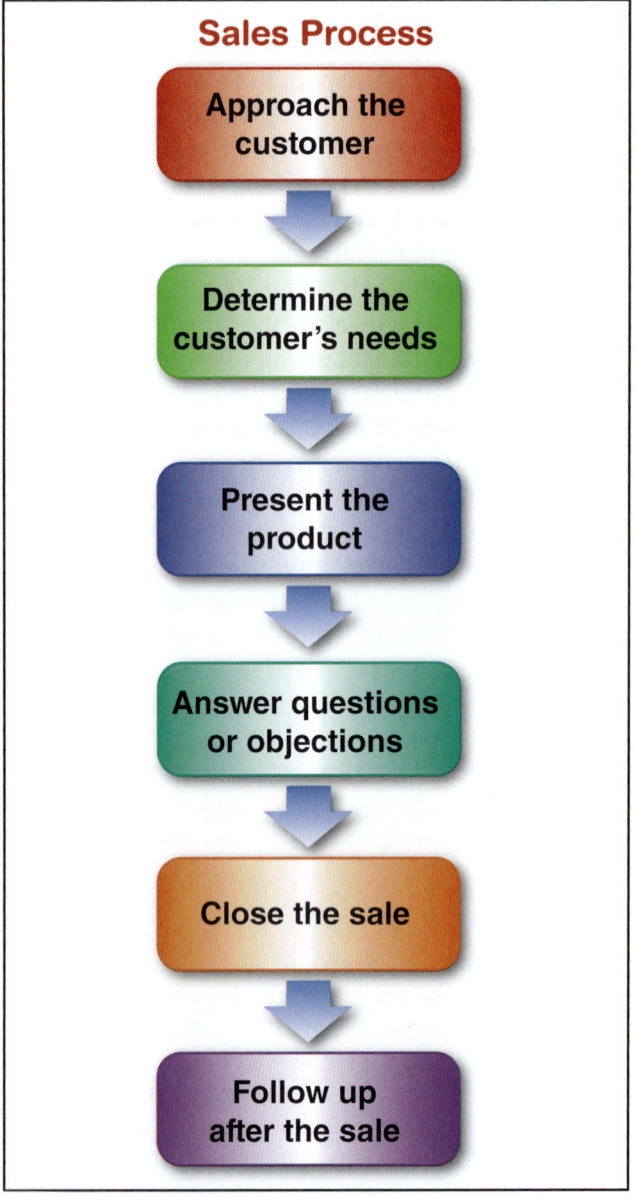

Sales Process

- Approach the customer
- Determine the customer's needs
- Present the product
- Answer questions or objections
- Close the sale
- Follow up after the sale

Goodheart-Willcox Publisher

Figure 20-1 Salespeople generally use six steps to help customers make buying decisions.

Employability Skills

Workplace Attire

The workplace requires appropriate dress. Most businesses have a dress code that employees are required to follow. Some jobs require uniforms or protective clothing. If your company requires business attire, clarify with your manager what is expected. Remember that "business casual" does not typically mean jeans or shorts. Always dress appropriately and do not push the limits on the appearance that is expected of you.

Approach the Customer

The **approach** is the first in-person contact a salesperson makes with a potential customer. The first contact is important to a successful sale. A salesperson should always:
- lead with a handshake;
- be appropriately dressed;
- have good posture;
- smile;
- have pleasant tone of voice and clear speech;
- make direct eye contact; and
- focus on the customer.

Researchers say strangers form an opinion of another person within seconds of meeting. Many sales experts say customers decide within four minutes whether they want to continue working with a salesperson. In those four minutes, a salesperson must:
- get the customer's attention;
- project a positive, professional image of himself or herself, and the products;
- show true concern and interest in the needs of the customer;
- show that he or she is trustworthy and honest; and
- make the customer feel comfortable.

Business-to-Business (B2B) Sales

In B2B sales, a salesperson will typically make an appointment so the customer is expecting the visit. It is important for a salesperson to be on time and prepared to present the product, leave brochures, and answer any questions the customer may have. A business card should be offered to the customer. B2B sales are often based on relationship selling, so it is acceptable to talk about current events or use other conversation starters.

Business-to-Consumer (B2C) Sales

B2C sales will typically be in a retail situation. Usually, in a typical retail setting, business cards are not offered by members of the sales staff. However, if the person is selling large-ticket items such as appliances or automobiles, a business card should be offered to the customer. Three types of approaches are often used in this setting: the service approach, the greeting approach, and the merchandise approach.

The **service approach** starts with the phrase, "May I help you?" It is the most common sales approach and works well in many situations. Another wording for the service approach is, "What can I help you with today?" This question might lead to a fuller response from the customer instead of, "No, thanks." However, the customer might still say, "Nothing" or, "I'm just browsing." A good reply to a "No, thanks" response is, "If you need anything, let me know."

The **greeting approach** consists of a friendly welcome to the store or department. Words such as "hi," "hello," or "good afternoon" should be used. A genuine smile and eye contact help make a positive impression.

If a salesperson knows the customer, that person can be approached with a personal

Syda Productions/Shutterstock.com

An outside B2B salesperson visits with the customer at his or her place of business. *Why is the first contact with the customer important to making a sale?*

A genuine smile and eye contact help make a positive impression on a customer. *What else can a salesperson do to make a positive impression?*

greeting. Calling customers by name when they enter the store is especially effective because it makes that person feel important. If a salesperson does not personally know the customer, that person can be made to feel comfortable by making a comment on something that can be observed. For example, if the customer is wearing a sports team T-shirt, a remark can be made on the standing of the team. A compliment can also be a good way to make a connection.

In the **merchandise approach**, a conversation with a customer starts with a comment about a product. This approach works well when a salesperson takes notice which product the customer is considering. For example, a customer in a shoe store is holding a dress shoe. A salesperson might walk up to the customer and say, "That shoe is on sale today for half price." The customer is provided with a money-saving tip, which can establish immediate rapport. Product features are also used in the merchandise approach. Details such as availability, color, dependability, material content, newness, price, quality, size, special features, style, and warranty can be good conversation starters.

Often a combination approach works best. For example, a customer in a sporting goods store is holding a fishing rod. A comment such as, "Hi, Mr. Campos. Those fishing poles just arrived today and are selling like crazy" combines the greeting and merchandise approaches. A salesperson made the customer feel welcome and provided information that might help sell the product.

Determine the Customer's Needs

The marketing concept of meeting customer needs is very important in the selling process. In B2B selling, the needs may be defined during the qualifying process. In B2C selling, the needs will probably be determined during the approach.

There are many reasons why customers buy a product. *Rational buying motives* are based on reason. For example, in a B2B sale, the customer knows certain merchandise must be purchased for inventory so the business can resell the products. *Emotional buying motives* are based more on feelings than reason. For example, in a B2C sale, the customer may struggle over selecting a blue or red car. *Loyalty buying motives* are based on customer loyalty to a company with which they always do business. It is important that a salesperson understands the customer and the specific needs to be met.

There are three ways to determine customer needs and wants: observation, questioning, and listening. All three of these skills intersect, as shown in Figure 20-2.

Observation is the first step in learning about the customer. Much can be learned through nonverbal communication. Facial expressions, raising an eyebrow, or the shrugging of shoulders can tell a salesperson about what the customer is thinking.

Figure 20-2 Salespeople observe, question, and listen to customers to determine their needs.

Green Marketing

Customer Incentives

Marketing can help shape customer behavior. Giving customers incentive to adopt environmentally friendly products and behaviors can help your business *go green*. Offer coupons or other benefits to encourage customers to make green choices. For example, a business could offer 25-percent-off coupons to customers who participate in the town's *Clean up the Parks* event. Some businesses may designate parking spaces for hybrid cars and equip those spaces with charging stations. Many retailers give customers a small discount for bringing in their own reusable shopping bags. There are many ways businesses can support the environmentally friendly choices and activities of their customers.

The goal of *questioning* is to learn about the different needs and wants of different customers. Salespeople will use the answers to determine which products to offer to satisfy those needs and wants. Four types of questions are useful.

- *Yes/no questions* require a response of only *yes* or *no*.
- *Choice questions* offer the customer choices and request the customer to select one.
- *Clarifying questions* request the customer to provide more details about the product he or she wants; for example, "What size do you need?"
- *Open-ended questions* request the customer to describe his or her wants and needs and often begin with one of the five Ws: *who, what, when, where,* and *why*.

After you have identified what the customer is looking for, your questions can be more refined. You can then learn more about the details of the product solution. However, it is important not to ask any embarrassing questions or too many questions.

Listening combines hearing with evaluating and often leads to learning more information. Questioning is useless if a salesperson does not listen to the response. A salesperson must carefully listen to what the customer does and does not say in order to improve sales and customer satisfaction.

Present the Product

The product presentation stage is the heart of the sales process. This is where desire is created for the product. It is a chance to tell the customer about the product, show how that product meets needs, and answer any questions or objections. It is the main opportunity for a salesperson to influence the customer to buy the product. Making a sales presentation is similar to an actor on a stage. The performance should be professional and polished. An unprofessional or unprepared presentation may lose a sale.

The sales presentation demonstrates and reinforces the brand promise. Recall that a *brand promise* is a statement made by an organization to its customers that tells customers what they can expect from its products. Consumers develop expectations for a brand based on how it is promoted and priced. When customers use their hard-earned money to make a purchase, they assume their expectations will be met.

Select the Product

One of the keys to successful selling is to select the appropriate products to show the customer. Knowing which products to show requires careful listening and extensive product knowledge on the part of a salesperson. Experience helps salespeople select appropriate products, as shown in Figure 20-3.

Substitute Sell

Sometimes, a customer may be looking for a specific brand that is not carried or is out of stock. **Substitute selling** is the technique of showing products that are different from the originally requested product. The goal is to get the customer to buy a different product that will still fit the need. It is important to not pressure the customer into buying something he or she does not really want.

Presenting Products to Customers

- If the customer requests a specific product, show that product first.
- If no specific request is made, show the product that seems most likely to fit the customer's needs.
- If it is not apparent which product will fit the customer's needs, show the most popular product or recently advertised product.
- If the product is available in a variety of price ranges, show a product in the middle price range.
- Show only two or three items at a time.
- Remove products that the customer has rejected as quickly as possible.

Goodheart-Willcox Publisher

Figure 20-3 Successful salespeople select the appropriate products to show the customer.

The customer must believe that the substitution is acceptable and that it will satisfy the original need.

Prepare the Presentation

In B2B sales, a salesperson often makes a formal presentation to a group of customers. Sales presentations are sometimes created by the marketing team. The presentation can then be customized for different sales opportunities.

Feature-benefit selling techniques that were learned in product-training sessions are used. Many times a *script* is provided so the presenter knows what to say in each part of the presentation. A formal presentation may include an electronic slide show or short video focusing on the features and benefits of the product. Product samples or promotional items, such as key chains, may be offered. Marketing materials such as a catalog, brochure, or sales sheet may be distributed.

A demonstration of the product or a website may also be appropriate. Demonstrations are most effective when the customer can actually try the product. While trying out the product, customers often sell themselves on its benefits.

It is often effective to create a product display similar to, but smaller than, the one used for a trade show. Customers appreciate browsing the products the company offers. Having the opportunity to touch the product and get a firsthand look is beneficial to the sales process.

In B2C sales, product presentations are usually informal. For example, in a retail store, the presentation may be showing an item off a rack and giving the price. Alternatively, for an automobile dealer, it might involve offering a test-drive and providing printed materials describing the features and benefits of the car.

Answer Questions or Objections

During and after the presentation, the customer should be asked for comments and questions. Customers need to know why they should buy the product. It is important to reinforce the features and benefits of the product and how the purchase will make the individual's life easier or better.

Create Objections Grid

Preparing for objections and excuses makes it easier to overcome them. **Objections** are concerns or other reasons a customer has for not making a purchase. **Excuses** are personal reasons not to buy.

One way to be prepared is to create a grid that shows common objections and excuses with responses to each. The marketing team may already have created this tool for the sales team to use. This grid is not for the customer to have, but to be used as a reference for a salesperson.

Handle Objections

Objections give insight into a customer's concerns. They also provide an opportunity to give information specific to that customer's needs.

It is important to listen, observe body language, and maintain eye contact. The customer should be allowed enough time to express the objection. Then, pause to show respect for the

Andrey_Popov/Shutterstock.com

During and after the presentation, the customer should be asked for comments and questions. *How might this help the salesperson close the sale?*

customer and the objection. This gives time to consider the objection and compose a response that meets this particular customer's needs.

The best way to show understanding of an objection is to show empathy. Having **empathy** is understanding or being sensitive to the thoughts and feelings of others. People who have empathy see things from another person's point of view. To *empathize* means to show that you understand another person's feelings. The following statements work well.
- "I know how you feel."
- "I'm glad you asked that question."
- "I understand your concern."
- "You've made a good point."

Making these statements using a sincere tone of voice will encourage trust in a salesperson and help the customer communicate more freely.

Sometimes, restating the customer's objection is helpful. This shows that the customer's point of view is appreciated and understood. Specific product features or benefits can be restated that answer the objection. Then ask, "Have I answered your question?"

There is no right or wrong way to handle objections as long as courtesy and respect to the customer are given. Experience is the best teacher for deciding how to respond to a customer.

Close the Sale

The goal of all sales activities is to close the sale. The **close** is the moment when a customer agrees to buy a product. It can occur at any point during the sales process. Some customers make decisions quickly and will decide to make a purchase soon after the approach or during a presentation. They might say, "I'll take it!" Giving the customer an opportunity to buy during the presentation is known as a *trial close*.

Other customers may be ready to buy, but they do not initiate the close. A salesperson's job is to determine when the customer is ready to buy and then close the sale. **Buying signals** are verbal or nonverbal signs that a customer is ready to purchase. Buying signals include comments, facial expressions, and actions. Buying signals often indicate *mental ownership*. Mental ownership has occurred when the customer acts and speaks as if the product is already his or hers. For example, the customer might say, "I have the perfect place for that in my living room." Evidence of mental ownership is an indication of readiness to buy.

Other customers require more time to make a decision. For those customers, there are different approaches to help them make the purchase, as shown in Figure 20-4.
- The *assumption close* is used when it is assumed a customer is going to purchase the product. "Mr. Wainwright, I will have the equipment delivered Thursday morning. Does that fit into your schedule?"
- The *bonus close* provides an additional *bonus*, such as a free item or a second item at a reduced cost. Examples are buy one, get one free; or buy one, get one half off. "Cynthia, if you purchase the mattress set today, the bed frame is included."
- The *choice close* provides the customer with choices between two or three different products. The number of items to choose should be limited or the customer may become confused. "Mr. Lee, after looking at both smartphones, do you prefer the black one or the silver one?"
- The *satisfaction close* guarantees the customer will like the product. "Mrs. Miller, you can try this

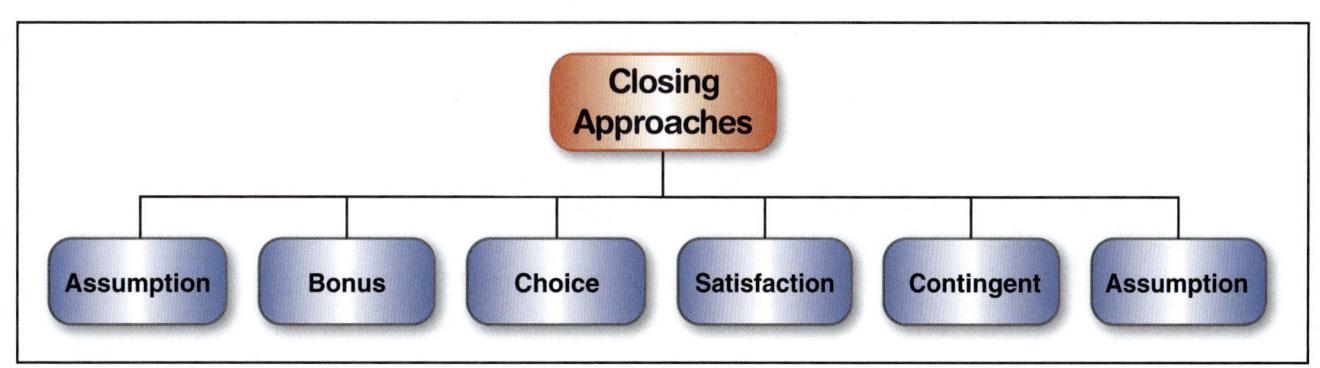

Closing Approaches

- Assumption
- Bonus
- Choice
- Satisfaction
- Contingent
- Assumption

Goodheart-Willcox Publisher

Figure 20-4 Different closing approaches can help customers make a purchase.

worry-free for 60 days. If you aren't completely satisfied, you can return it for a full refund."
- A *contingent close* is dependent on fulfilling a specific condition. "Mr. Stanis, if I can have the office furniture delivered and installed on Monday, will that be soon enough for you?"
- The *direct close* is just that—asking the customer to buy. "Ms. Clarkston, would you like me to finance the Ford Focus through Ford Credit?" is a direct close statement. This can sometimes be the best approach.

There are many ways to close a sale. However, salespeople should always avoid overselling. **Overselling** is promising more than the product or the business can deliver. This is unethical. The result might be a returned product, a customer who will never buy from the company again, or a lawsuit.

After the sale is closed, a salesperson may use suggestion selling. **Suggestion selling** is the technique of suggesting additional items or optional features to go with merchandise requested by a customer. It is sometimes referred to as *upselling*. Suggestion selling most often occurs after the customer has made a choice to purchase a specific item or items. For example, if a man buys a suit, a salesperson might recommend a shirt, tie, and belt that go well with it. Often, the suggested item is something the customer needs but would have forgotten to buy. Sometimes, suggestion selling is for optional features that increase the value of the sale. An example of this is an automobile salesperson who suggests a customer purchase the vehicle model with leather seats. Customers are usually very appreciative when a salesperson knows enough to suggest appropriate merchandise.

Follow Up After the Sale

After the transaction is complete, it is important for a salesperson to follow up with the customer. The purpose of following up after a sale is to ensure customer satisfaction. Following up also helps maintain selling relationships. Customers have a large number of product choices and places to buy them. Research has shown that it is much more costly to find new customers than to keep current ones. One way to keep customers coming back is to follow up with them after a sale to make sure they are satisfied. Following up is part of relationship selling. Relationship selling sees the customer relationship as starting at the approach, continuing indefinitely, and including many purchases.

Was the Order Received?

After the sale is complete, the product is transferred to the customer. In a retail situation, the customer typically leaves with the purchase. In a B2B sale, it will involve a purchase order and delivery arrangements.

A *transaction* is the exchange of payment and product. In retail sales, the transaction happens immediately. It is important that the merchandise is packed carefully. In a B2C sale, the customer will pay with cash, check, credit card, or debit card. For larger sales, such as an automobile, a loan may be obtained by the customer. Exceptional customer service is essential both during and after the sale to make sure the order is received.

In B2B sales, the customer will typically issue a purchase order and pay later with a check. Shipping will be arranged and any specific directions will be given. The transaction includes taking and processing the order, plus arranging for shipment and payment. Courtesy and efficiency are important in this step. Paperwork must be handled quickly and accurately. An error made in a product number or price will create problems for the customer.

Is the Customer Satisfied?

Confirmation includes contacting the customer after the sale to make sure he or she is satisfied. This gives the salesperson the opportunity to solve any problems that might have occurred and

Dragon Images/Shutterstock.com

The goal of all sales activities is to close the sale.
Which closing approach do you think is the best way to close a sale?

You Do the Math

Slope

Slope is the angle of a line measured in relation to a horizontal axis. It is the ratio of rise over run (rise/run). The *rise* is the distance of a line above or below the horizontal axis. The *run* is the length of a line measured along the horizontal axis. The greater the slope, the steeper the line. Two lines are parallel if their slopes are identical. If the slopes are not identical, the lines will intersect.

Solve the following problems.
1. Line A has a run of 2 inches and a rise of 1 inch. Line B has a run of 12 inches and a rise of 6 inches. Are these parallel or intersecting lines?
2. The roof on house A has a slope of 4/12. What is the rise of this roof? What is the run?
3. Hill A has a slope of 8/4. Hill B has a slope of 8/6. Which hill is steeper?

---

increases customer satisfaction with the product and the company. For example, a customer bought a bicycle that required assembly. The salesperson would check with the maintenance department to make sure the assembly was completed. Next, the salesperson would check to see if the customer picked up the assembled bicycle. Finally, the salesperson would call the customer to make sure the assembly was satisfactory.

Many salespeople send personal thank-you messages after the sale. This not only thanks the customer but also invites him or her to purchase additional products. It is appropriate to include a business card and an update on new products or sales.

Sometimes, salespeople make a thank-you phone call and use it as an opportunity to determine customer satisfaction. If there are problems, the salesperson can then take steps to correct them.

LO 20.2-3 Sales Transactions

Once a sale is closed, the sales transaction must be completed. A salesperson will perform calculations in order to tell the customer the correct amount and complete a sales transaction.

When a customer purchases multiple items, the costs of these items are added together. For example, a customer purchased three items. The individual cost for each item was $125, $75, and $100. The costs of the three items are added together.

item one + item two + item three = sales price

$125 + $75 + $100 = $300

Any discounts are then subtracted from the sales price. Assume the salesperson was authorized to give the customer a 20 percent discount on the entire purchase. In order to make the calculation, 20 percent must be converted to a decimal (0.2) and multiplied by the sales price.

sales price × discount percentage = discount

$300 × 0.2 = $60

The dollar amount of the discount is $60. This amount is subtracted from the total sales price to find the sales price after the discount.

sales price − discount = sales price after discount

$300 − $60 = $240

Sales tax is a tax collected on the selling price of a product. The sales tax rate is usually expressed as a percentage of the selling price. Sales tax is calculated by multiplying the sales price by the tax rate. Suppose the sales tax rate is 8 percent. The 8 percent tax rate must be converted to a decimal (0.08) and multiplied by the sales price.

sales price × sales tax rate percentage = sales tax

$240 × 0.08 = $19.20

The amount of the sales tax is then added to the sales price of the items purchased.

sale price + sales tax amount = total price

$240 + $19.20 = $259.20

In addition, there may be fees associated with a customer's purchase, such as shipping charges. Taxes are not paid on shipping charges, so they are

Social Media

YouTube

YouTube is a video sharing website that allows users to upload videos they have created and watch videos posted by other users. YouTube videos can actively engage viewers, which is good for business. Users are able to talk about videos by asking questions, giving comments, sharing, and requesting additional information from the content creator. For example, you can include links, Q&As, or comments associated with precise moments in the video. Viewers can also share a YouTube video on other social-media sites. Plus, on YouTube, businesses can buy pay-per-click advertising to promote their videos. This option can help videos become recognized by a specific target audience.

Videos are a great way to position the company as a go-to expert in the industry. When something important happens, such as new technology is invented or new products are introduced, a video can offer the latest information or advice. People will be searching for content on that topic, so your video can take advantage of the interest.

---

not included as part of the sales tax calculation. They are added after the total price is calculated. Assume the items purchased for $259.20 must be shipped. Shipping costs are $8.99.

total price + shipping = final price

$259.20 + $8.99 = $268.19

The final price the customer must pay is $268.19.

It is important and ethical for the salesperson to make sure customers understand the final cost of items purchased. When customers know the final price to pay, the sales transaction can be processed.

B2B Sales

In B2B sales transactions, a salesperson will request the billing department to create an invoice to be sent to the customer. As you will recall from Chapter 16, an *invoice* is a bill requesting payment for goods shipped or services provided. The invoice will show details of the sale and terms of payment. Most B2B customers pay invoices by check or credit card.

B2C Sales

B2C sales transactions usually occur in a retail situation. These sales are completed by the use of cash, credit cards, or debit cards.

Cash Transaction

A *cash transaction* is a sale for which a customer pays with cash or a check. If a check is used for payment, the salesperson will ask for identification before accepting the check. Each business has policies on accepting checks, so the salesperson must understand proper procedures. If the check is accepted, the purchase is recorded as cash. The salesperson will then provide the customer with a receipt for the transaction.

If cash is used for payment, the salesperson will accept the money and give correct change. When the amount of cash received from the customer is entered in the register, the amount of money to be returned is indicated. It is the salesperson's responsibility to count the change correctly and give it to the customer.

In the previous example, a customer purchased items that totaled $268.19, including tax and shipping. Assume the customer gave the salesperson three one-hundred-dollar bills. The cash register shows the customer should receive $31.81 in cash. The following bills and coins will be given to the customer:
- one twenty-dollar bill;
- one ten-dollar bill;
- one one-dollar bill;
- three quarters;
- one nickel; and
- one penny.

Finally, the salesperson provides the customer with a receipt for the merchandise purchased.

Credit and Debit Card Transactions

A *credit card transaction* is a purchase for which the customer pays for goods or services with a credit card. Banks and credit unions offer credit cards, such as MasterCard or Visa. Some retail businesses, such as Macy's and Home Depot, offer *proprietary credit cards* that can only be used with the merchant issuing the card.

When a credit card is used to make a purchase, either the salesperson or customer swipes the card at a card terminal. The amount is immediately relayed to the bank or merchant that issued the card. If the sale is approved, the customer signs to authorize the sale. The salesperson then accepts the sale on the cash register and a receipt is produced.

A *debit card transaction* allows the cardholder to make a purchase by electronically accessing funds in his or her bank account. The debit card is swiped at a card terminal, and a personal identification (PIN) is usually required to authorize the transaction. The salesperson then accepts the sale on the cash register and a receipt is produced.

LO 20.2-4 Lost Sales

Not every sales opportunity actually closes. Even the experienced salesperson who executes the sales process perfectly may not be able to convince the customer to buy.

It is necessary to evaluate lost sales and determine exactly why the sale was not closed. Customer feedback may provide reasons the purchase was not made. It could be due to factors beyond the control of the salesperson, such as price, wrong product selection, or delivery options.

Feedback from coworkers or supervisors on the execution of the sales process may also be helpful. An impartial observer may be able to point out something that went wrong in the sales process. For example, perhaps the salesperson was not working with the proper decision-maker in the company. Maybe the customer wanted accurate pricing information that the salesperson could not provide.

The most important thing to remember is that keeping a good attitude is important to succeed in a sales career. Rejection is part of the process. Learning from experiences, both good and bad, will help close future sales.

Section 20.2 Review

Check Your Understanding

1. Name tasks included in the preapproach.
2. List examples of ways sales leads are generated.
3. What are three types of approaches a salesperson can use in a B2C environment?
4. Why is the product presentation stage the heart of the sales process?
5. How is sales tax calculated?

Build Your Vocabulary

As you progress through this text, develop a personal glossary of key terms. This will help you build your vocabulary and prepare you for a career. Write a definition for each of the following terms and add them to your personal glossary.

approach
buying signal
certification
close
cold calling
empathy
excuse
feature-benefit selling
greeting approach
lead
merchandise approach
objection
overselling
preapproach
sales process
service approach
substitute selling
suggestion selling

Section 20.3

Customer Service

Essential Question

How does providing customer service benefit a business?

Learning Objectives

LO 20.3-1 Define *customer support team*.
LO 20.3-2 List types of online customer support.
LO 20.3-3 Identify the importance of handling customer complaints.

Key Terms

customer support team
frequently asked questions (FAQ) page

Customer Support Team
LO 23.3-1

While customer service is provided by all employees, an organized customer support team is usually a part of the sales and marketing team. The **customer support team** consists of the employees who assist customers, take orders, or answer questions coming into the company via phone or website.

Marketing plays an important role by providing product information and training to the customer support team. Information about features and benefits, pricing, and other vital information is usually provided by marketing. Catalogs, brochures, and other marketing materials are sent to the customer support team so they are aware of the information customers receive.

Receiving information from the customer is as equally important as giving information to them. Customer support training usually includes suggestions on how specific feedback can be gained from customers. For example, the customer may be asked how he or she learned about a product that is being ordered. This information can then be sent to marketing to track metrics to evaluate the success of a marketing campaign.

A customer support employee may also ask for feedback on a product that a customer purchased. Questions about likes and dislikes or what could be improved about the product can be asked. This information may be useful to the product-development team to help create better products.

Online Support
LO 23.3-2

Many organizations provide constant customer support online. Online support can take several different forms and provide many types of information. This support is usually through the company's website or social media pages. Online support gives customers the option to use the type of support with which they are most comfortable. Some company websites offer all forms of online customer support. Other organizations can only offer one or two. Online support is convenient for customers because they can find answers when they are needed.

Frequently Asked Questions (FAQ) Pages

A **frequently asked questions (FAQ) page** is the part of a website that gives detailed answers to questions or issues that show up most often. FAQ pages are effective in answering customer questions quickly without taking the time of a support person. If new questions or issues are raised through e-mail or by phone, they can be added to the FAQ page.

E-mail Support

Many issues can be solved through e-mail, which is a fast and efficient online support option. However, when using e-mail support, the turnaround time to answer customer inquiries and issues is critical. A business must have sufficient personnel to respond to customer questions.

Product Tracking

Customers appreciate being able to track their orders. When orders are placed, the tracking information and link is sent to the customers via e-mail. The link provides a way to check the shipping progress at any time.

Online Chat

A popular form of online customer support is the ability for customers to chat live online with a member of the customer support team. Customers interact with staff dedicated to answering their questions and problem solving. One advantage to this type of customer support is the responses are immediate so problems can usually be solved quickly.

Social Media

Social media is a great way to address customer issues directly. Facebook and Twitter allow customers to post both positive and negative feedback. The person in charge of monitoring the company's social media pages can immediately address any questions or solve problems.

Discussion Boards

Discussion boards are public. Any customer or product user can answer the questions other customers might have. Discussion boards free the support staff to work with other customers. Discussion boards can also be used to post timely announcements, much like using social media.

LO 23.3-1 Handling Customer Complaints

Communication with customers presents many opportunities. Customers create new opportunities when they disagree with store policies or make demands. Common customer service problems include:
- a product is out of stock;
- a store does not have the right size or color;
- a salesperson does not speak the customer's language;
- a customer becomes angry or upset over a store policy; and
- there is not enough staff available to efficiently help customers.

Customer service representatives are trained to be polite and communicate with customers in a professional manner. If a customer service

OPOLJA/Shutterstock.com

Customer service representatives are trained to be polite and communicate with customers in a professional manner. *How might this training contribute to the customer-service mindset?*

representative is unable to resolve a customer issue, the call will probably be transferred to a supervisor. A supervisor may have more options to offer the customer a solution. There will be company policies on how to address specific customer complaints.

Handling customer complaints appropriately is a courtesy that encourages repeat business. When customers feel like their voices were heard and their problems were resolved, they often continue to give the company their business.

Section 20.3 Review

Check Your Understanding

1. What role does marketing play in customer support?
2. Why is online support convenient for customers?
3. Explain why a customer support employee may ask for customer feedback.
4. What is an advantage of online chat as a form of customer support?
5. Why are customer service calls sometimes transferred to supervisors?

Build Your Vocabulary

As you progress through this text, develop a personal glossary of key terms. This will help you build your vocabulary and prepare you for a career. Write a definition for each of the following terms and add them to your personal glossary.

customer support team

frequently asked questions (FAQ) page

CHAPTER 20 Review and Assessment

Chapter Summary

Section 20.1 Role of Sales

LO 20.1-1   Explain the value of personal selling.
Personal selling is any direct contact between a salesperson and a customer with the objective of making a sale. Without the sales function, it would be difficult for a company to generate revenue. Personal selling provides information and persuades customers to make a decision about how to meet a need or want. Personal selling is important for both business-to-business (B2B) and business-to-consumer (B2C) sales.

LO 20.1-2   Describe skills needed for a career in sales.
People who are successful in sales must have excellent work habits and be goal oriented. Strong ethics of honesty, integrity, and confidentiality are important for successful long-term relationships that lead to repeat sales. Sales positions are generally independent and require minimal day-to-day supervision, requiring that salespeople are responsible. In addition, working in sales requires that a person have excellent customer-service skills. It also requires that a person be able to make presentations that are clear, concise, and persuasive.

Section 20.2 Selling

LO 20.2-1   Summarize tasks to complete when preparing to sell.
The preapproach consists of tasks that are performed before contact is made with a customer. These include understanding company selling policies, participating in product training, and learning how to identify potential customers.

LO 20.2-2   List steps in the sales process.
The sales process is a series of steps a salesperson goes through to help the customer make a satisfying buying decision. There are generally six steps in the process: approach the customer, determine the customer's needs, present the product, answer questions or objections, close the sale, and follow-up after the sale.

LO 20.2-3   Identify options for completing sales transactions in B2B and B2C sales.
Once a sale is closed, the customer is informed of the final price they will need to pay. In B2B sales, a salesperson will request an invoice be sent to the customer. Most B2B customers pay invoices by check or credit card. B2C sales transactions usually transpire in a retail situation and are completed by the use of cash, credit cards, or debit cards.

LO 20.2-4   Explain how a lost sale can be a learning experience.
Not every sales opportunity actually closes. Customer feedback may provide reasons the purchase was not made. Feedback from coworkers or supervisors on the execution of the sales process may also be helpful. An impartial observer may be able to point out something that went wrong. Keeping a good attitude is important to do well in a sales career. Learning from experiences, both good and bad, will help close future sales.

Section 20.3 Customer Service

LO 20.3-1   Define *customer support team*.
A customer support team consists of the employees who assist customers, take orders, or answer questions coming into the company via phone or website.

LO 20.3-2   List types of online customer support.
Online support can take several different forms, including frequently asked questions (FAQ) pages, e-mail support, product tracking, online chat, social media, and discussion boards.

LO 20.3-3   Identify the importance of handling customer complaints.
Handling customer complaints appropriately is a courtesy that encourages repeat business. When customers feel like their voice was heard and their problems were resolved, they often continue to give the company their business.

Copyright Goodheart-Willcox Co., Inc.

Check Your Marketing IQ

Now that you have completed the chapter, see what you have learned about marketing by taking the chapter posttest. The posttest is available at www.g-wlearning.com/marketing/.

Review Your Knowledge

1. Explain the value of personal selling.
2. Name and describe two types of salespeople for B2B sales.
3. Describe skills needed for a career in sales.
4. Summarize tasks to complete when preparing to sell.
5. List steps in the sales process.
6. Identify options for completing sales transactions in B2B and B2C sales.
7. Explain how a lost sale can be a learning experience.
8. Describe the role of a customer support team.
9. List types of online customer support.
10. Identify the importance of handling customer complaints.

Apply Your Knowledge

1. Identify the role of the sales force in the company for which you are writing a marketing plan. Is the sales force selling mostly to the B2B or B2C market?
2. Think about the two types of sales positions: B2B and B2C. Which type of position would fit your personality better? Explain your choice.
3. Write one to two paragraphs about why a career in sales would or would not be a suitable choice for you.
4. Explain concepts and techniques of selling that could be used by a salesperson in your company.
5. Draft a plan for maintaining or strengthening your company's relationship with its customers. Describe how often customers should be contacted and by what methods, including any social-media marketing. Identify ways your company can add value to the customer experience by increasing services offered. Note activities the company can use to improve customer satisfaction, loyalty, and advocacy.
6. Assume the sales team of your company will need product training for new products and existing products. List the types of training you anticipate they will need.
7. Analyze information about the product or products your company sells. Identify and list the features and benefits of the main product or products the sales team will be selling.
8. Draw a flowchart for the sales process for your sales team. Include each of the six steps described in this chapter.
9. Which types of online customer service does your company offer? Which do you think customers use most often? Should any new types be added?
10. Describe how excellent customer service can help resolve conflicts and foster positive relationships with customers to enhance the company's image and encourage repeat business.

Apply Your Math Skills

Quentin is a salesperson at a furniture warehouse. He made the following sales and needs to find the final price each customer must pay. Apply your math skills to solve the following problems.

1. Smith Insurance Company remodeled its small office. The company is purchasing the following items. Sales tax is six percent. Shipping and assembly is an additional $200. What is the total cost of the new office furniture?

Item	Quantity	Price
Corner desk	6	$339
Executive desk	2	$275
Two-drawer file cabinet	8	$190
Adjustable desk chair	8	$149

2. The Hernandez family has moved into a new home and must buy new furniture for their living room. Sales tax is six percent. Quentin was able to give the Hernandezes a $50 discount on shipping and assembly, which normally costs $200. What is the total cost of the new furniture?

Item	Quantity	Price
Sofa and love seat set	1	$999
End table	2	$100
8' x 10' accent rug	1	$215
70" television stand	1	$500

Communication Skills

Reading In order to retain information, it is necessary to focus and read with a purpose. The Green Marketing feature in this chapter discusses customer incentives for making green choices. Read the feature with the intention of focusing on each word that is written. After you have finished, close the text. Can you remember what you read?

Speaking Create a sales script for employing steps in the sales process to sell a computer to an adult consumer. The script should be clear and developed so it is appropriate to the task of selling to the target audience. Select a member of your class to whom you will make the presentation.

Listening Deliberative listening is determining the quality or validity of what is being said. Volunteer to listen to a sales script created by a classmate for the last activity from the perspective of the customer. Listen to the sales presentation carefully using deliberative listening. Cite which points the person made that would convince you to purchase the product.

Internet Research

Selling Policies Conduct an Internet search on *company selling policies*. What information is typically included in these types of policies? How does this information relate to responding to questions asked by customers?

Relationship Selling Research the Internet for information on relationship selling. Identify sales processes and techniques that can be used in relationship selling to enhance customer relationships and increase the likelihood of making sales.

Customer Service Customer service is an important asset for all businesses. Conduct an Internet search for *customer service stories*. List examples of creative solutions for handling customer complaints or problems that some companies used to win customers.

Teamwork

Working with a team, create a sales presentation for a product. The presentation should focus on attracting customer attention, interest, desire, and action (AIDA). Analyze the features and benefits of the product. Determine if there are any accompanying products that could be suggested to the customer. Use slide presentation software or another medium to prepare visual aids that will enhance the oral presentation and sustain listener attention and interest. Deliver the presentation to your class. Respond to any questions or objections from the audience.

Portfolio Development

Foreign Language Skills As part of an interview with an organization, you may be asked about your ability to speak multiple languages or experience with people who speak a language other than your own. People who speak more than one language and have traveled, studied, or worked in other countries can be valuable assets to an organization. A candidate who notes multilingual skills may be considered to have a competitive edge over other candidates. By being proactive and noting any experiences you have in working with people in other cultures, you may catch the eye of the interviewer even before the interviewing process begins.

1. If you are fluent in another language, create a document that describes the language in which you are proficient, where you received your training, and your level of fluency. Use the heading "Languages Spoken" and your name.
2. If you have limited language proficiency, create a document that says "Limited Language Proficiency" and list each language and your ability to communicate using it.
3. Place a printed copy in the container for future reference.

UNIT 7 Promotion

Building the Marketing Plan

Promotion may be one of the most important functions of marketing. It is the job of marketers to communicate with potential customers about what products are available and why people should buy those products. It is said that without products, there would be no businesses. However, without promotion, there would not be enough sales to keep the businesses profitable. The most effective form of promotion is through integrated marketing communications (IMC), or using elements of the promotional mix in a coordinated way.

Part 1 Promotional Strategies

Objective
- Write promotional strategies for the elements of the promotional mix.

Directions
In this activity, you will complete the Marketing Strategies section of the marketing plan. The marketing strategies are the decisions made about product, price, place, and promotion. Access the *Marketing Dynamics* companion website at www.g-wlearning.com/marketing/. Download the activity files as indicated in the following instructions.

1. **Unit Activity 7-1—Promotional Plan Goals** Each product may require its own individual promotion plan that will be included in the overall marketing plan. Write the goals for your promotional plan.

2. **Unit Activity 7-2—Promotional Mix** List each element of the promotional mix for your campaign. Describe the strategies for each one: advertising, public relations, sales promotions, and personal selling. Include the job title of the team member responsible for managing or completing each activity. This information will be included in the final action plan.

3. Open your saved marketing plan document. Locate the Marketing Strategies section of the plan, followed by the Marketing Mix subsection. Write the Promotional Strategies section. Use the suggestions and questions listed to help you generate ideas. Delete the instructions and questions when you are finished recording your responses. Proofread your document and correct any errors in keyboarding, spelling, and grammar.

4. Save your document.

Part 2 Action Plan

Objective
- Create an action plan for your promotional plan.

Directions
In this activity, you will complete the Action Plan section of the marketing plan. The Action Plan explains the specific activities that will be used to carry out the promotional strategies. The action plan includes a time line that identifies the person responsible for each task, detailed budget, and the metrics used to evaluate the effectiveness of the campaigns in the promotional plan. You will combine the necessary information from Unit Activities 7-2 through 7-5 to create the action plan. Access the *Marketing Dynamics* companion website at www.g-wlearning.com/marketing/. Download the activity files as indicated in the following instructions.

1. **Unit Activity 7-3—Budget** You have identified the campaign and promotional elements for your promotional plan. Now, create the budget using spreadsheet software. You will place the final detailed budget spreadsheet in the Appendices.

2. **Unit Activity 7-4—Timeline** Next, you will create the timeline for the promotional activities using spreadsheet software. List each promotional activity in the order it will be performed. Next to each activity should be the job title of the person responsible, date to begin creating the marketing piece, and date each marketing piece must be finished or delivered. If it is a form of advertising, the start and end dates of the advertising campaign must also be listed. You will place the final detailed timeline spreadsheet in the Appendices.

3. **Unit Activity 7-5—Metrics** Next, you will determine the metrics that will be used to evaluate the success of your promotional plan. Describe how metrics will be used to measure each promotional activity. Explain how you plan to calculate return on investment (ROI) and measure the effectiveness of the campaigns.

4. Open your saved marketing plan document. Locate the Action Plan section. Write a paragraph that introduces the action plan and its components. Note the elements that will be located in the Appendices. Use the suggestions and questions listed to help you generate ideas for explaining your budget, time line, and metrics. Delete the instructions and questions when you are finished recording your responses. Proofread your document and correct any errors in keyboarding, spelling, and grammar.

5. Save your document.

UNIT 8 Management

Chapters

21 **Marketing Management**
22 **Soft Skills**
23 **Communication in the Workplace**

While studying, look for the activity icon for:
- Building the Marketing Plan activity files
- Pretests and posttests
- Vocabulary terms with e-flash cards and matching activities
- Self-assessment

These activities can be accessed at www.g-wlearning.com/marketing/.

Developing a Vision

All employees are managers in some sense of the word. *Management* is the process of controlling and making decisions about a business. Managers can manage people, projects, or both.

Management skills take time and patience to develop. Successful managers develop job-specific skills, which are necessary to perform the required work-related tasks of a position. Job-specific skills are acquired through work experience and education or training. Managers also spend time developing soft skills. *Soft skills* are the group of skills that enable a person to interact with others in a positive way. Possessing soft skills helps workers interact effectively with supervisors, peers, customers, and vendors.

Effective communication skills are equally important for a manager to master. Communication skills affect a person's ability to understand others, establish positive relationships, and perform in most situations. Communication is a soft skill that is essential to career success.

Marketing Core Functions Covered in This Unit

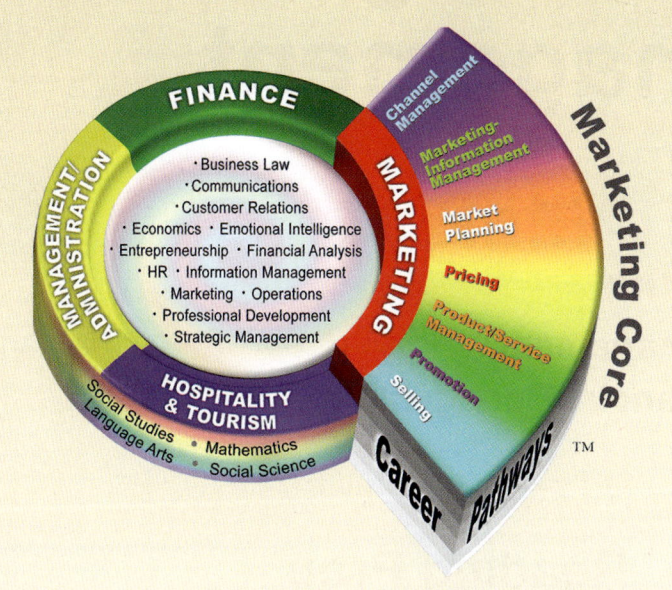

Copyright MBA Research, Columbus, Ohio. Used with permission.

Functions of Marketing

- Marketing-information management
- Market planning

EYE-CATCHER

Marketing Matters

Many products are created for use in the world of work. For those products, savvy marketers advertise where working people can see the product, hopefully use it, and experience its features and benefits. For example, Oracle exhibits at a technology conference in hopes of attracting new customers who may be looking for computer hardware or software for their businesses. Useful products reflect the marketing concept of customer satisfaction and lead to increased sales.

Adriano Castelli/Shutterstock.com

CHAPTER 21
Marketing Management

Sections

21.1 **Management**
21.2 **Financial Management**

Reading Prep

College and Career Readiness

Before reading this chapter, look at the chapter title. What can you predict will be presented?

Check Your Marketing IQ

Before you begin the chapter, see what you already know about marketing by taking the chapter pretest. The pretest is available at www.g-wlearning.com/marketing/.

DECA Emerging Leaders

Principles of Marketing Event

Career Cluster: Marketing
Instructional Area: Economics

Knowledge and Skills Developed

Participants will develop many 21st century skills desired by today's employers in the following categories:
- communication and collaboration
- creativity and innovation
- critical thinking and problem solving
- flexibility and adaptability
- information literacy
- initiative and self-direction
- leadership and responsibility
- productivity and accountability
- social and cross-cultural skills

Performance Indicators
- Describe marketing functions and related activities.
- Explain the role of business in society.
- Explain the concept of private enterprise.
- Describe types of business activities.

Purpose

Designed for first-year DECA members who are enrolled in introductory-level principles of marketing/business courses, this event measures the student's proficiency in those knowledge and skills identified by career practitioners as common academic and technical content in marketing. This event consists of a 100-question, multiple-choice, business administration core exam and a business situation role-play with a business executive. Participants are not informed in advance of the performance indicators to be evaluated.

Procedure

1. The event will be presented to you through your reading of these instructions, including the Performance Indicators and Business Situation. You will have ten minutes to review this information to determine how you will handle the role-play and demonstrate the performance indicators of this event. During the preparation period, you may make notes to use during the role-play.
2. You will have up to ten minutes to role-play your situation with the judge. You may have more than one judge.
3. You will be evaluated on how well you meet the performance indicators of this event. Turn in all your notes and event materials when you have completed the interview.

Business Situation

You are to assume the role of customer-service representative in the public relations department at Southwest Oil, a large energy company involved in the refining and distribution of gasoline and petroleum products. You have been invited to a meeting with the **public information director (judge)** to discuss the important role that business plays in society.

The public relations department of Southwest Oil administers and communicates all civic and charitable contributions the company makes. In the first part of the meeting, you will explain how the company's charitable contribution program benefits society and the role it plays in the overall marketing efforts of Southwest Oil. Your presentation must also include the additional performance indicators listed at the beginning of this event. Following your explanation, the public information director (judge) will ask you to respond to additional questions.

The meeting will take place in the public information director's (judge's) office. The public information director (judge) will begin the meeting by greeting you and asking to hear your explanation on the role of business in society. After you have provided your explanation and have answered the director's (judge's) questions, the public information director (judge) will conclude the meeting by thanking you for your presentation.

Critical Thinking

1. How does a company decide which civic or charitable causes deserve its financial support?
2. Do charitable donations produce higher sales for a business?
3. Is it better for a company to support one charity with one large contribution or to make smaller contributions to many charitable organizations?

Visit www.deca.org for more information.

Published by DECA Inc. Copyright © by DECA Inc. No part of this publication may be reproduced for resale without written permission from the publisher. Printed in the United States of America.

Section 21.1

Essential Question
Why is effective management important for business success?

Management

Learning Objectives
LO 21.1-1 Describe the role of a manager.
LO 21.1-2 List five elements of the management function.
LO 21.1-3 Describe effective management styles.

Key Terms
manager
strategic planning
tactical planning
operational planning
organizational chart
staffing
leader
control
democratic management style
autocratic management style
consulting management style
laissez-faire management style

Managers

Among the many skills a marketer needs are management skills. *Management* is the process of controlling and making decisions about the business. When a marketer adds employees to the team, he or she becomes a manager. A **manager** is an employee who directs the work of others and is responsible for carrying out the goals of a department.

The manager of a marketing team could be a person in one of a variety of positions. Examples of such positions are *marketing manager, communications manager, director of marketing,* or *vice president of marketing.* One common task of marketing managers is to create and execute the marketing plan. Another is to train individual team members to perform specific job duties. Still another is to monitor the performance of individual team members. Managers are responsible for making sure that all marketing tasks are completed.

Managers may also be responsible for working with customer service representatives and providing product training. Providing excellent

Stephen Coburn/Shutterstock.com

The management function of business controls and makes decisions about a business. *Why is the role of a manager important?*

service is vitally important to maintaining customer satisfaction and the marketing concept. The image of a company is positively reinforced through exceptional customer service.

There are three levels of management: upper, middle, and supervisory. Smaller companies may have only two levels: upper and supervisory. Large companies may have several levels of management in the middle.

Upper management is the top level of management. Upper management develops goals for the entire company and the strategies to meet those goals. The next level of managers reports to the upper management. *Middle management* consists of one or more levels of management between the top level and the supervisory level. They usually manage a group of supervisors in a particular region or area. *Supervisory management* is the level of management closest to the workers. Supervisors are usually responsible for a group of workers in a specific department.

Management Function

The management function of business controls and makes decisions about a business. It includes all the activities required to plan, coordinate, and monitor a business. The five elements of the management function are plan, organize, staff, lead, and control. The five elements are shown in Figure 21-1.

Plan

Marketing managers are responsible for the success of the marketing team. During marketing planning, managers set goals and plans for the entire team.

Strategic planning is setting long-term marketing goals for the company. Long-term goals are usually achieved over a period of three to five years. The senior management team sets the long-term goals for the company. Marketing then determines specific long-term marketing goals to help reach company goals.

Tactical planning is setting short-term marketing goals for the company. Short-term goals are typically set for the next six to 24 months. Marketing managers work with the sales team to set specific marketing goals and determine how to reach each goal.

Operational planning is setting day-to-day goals for the company. Marketing can refine those goals to reflect monthly, weekly, or daily tasks.

Organize

To *organize* is to coordinate the efforts of a team to reach its goals. A marketing manager organizes the marketing team by giving specific jobs or assignments to individuals.

The *chain of command* is the structure in a company from the highest to the lowest levels of authority. The chain of command is important so employees know to whom various positions report in the operation of the business. Most businesses create an organizational chart to show the chain of command. An **organizational chart** is a diagram of employee positions showing how the positions interact within the chain of command. An example of an organizational chart for a marketing team is shown in Figure 21-2.

Staff

Marketing managers must find the right employees to fill positions on the team. **Staffing** is the process of hiring people and matching them to the best position for their talents. Staffing

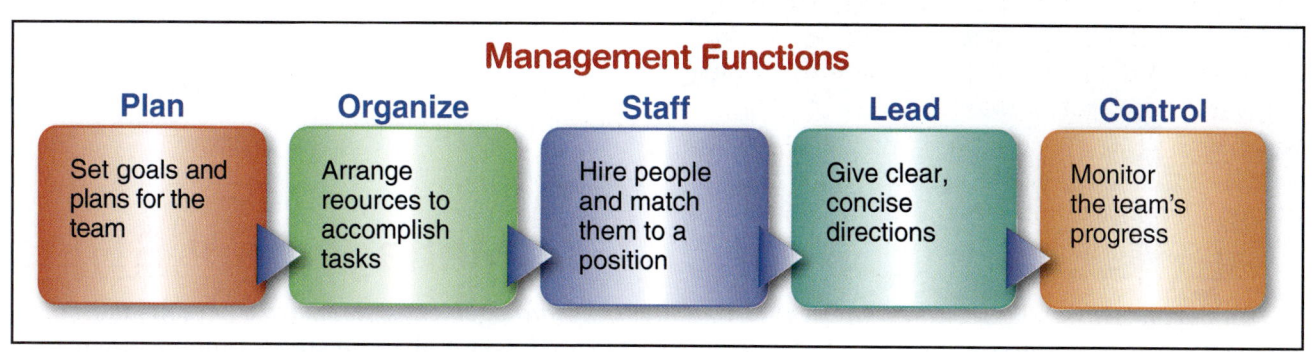

Management Functions

Plan	Organize	Staff	Lead	Control
Set goals and plans for the team	Arrange reources to accomplish tasks	Hire people and match them to a position	Give clear, concise directions	Monitor the team's progress

Goodheart-Willcox Publisher

Figure 21-1 There are five elements of the management function.

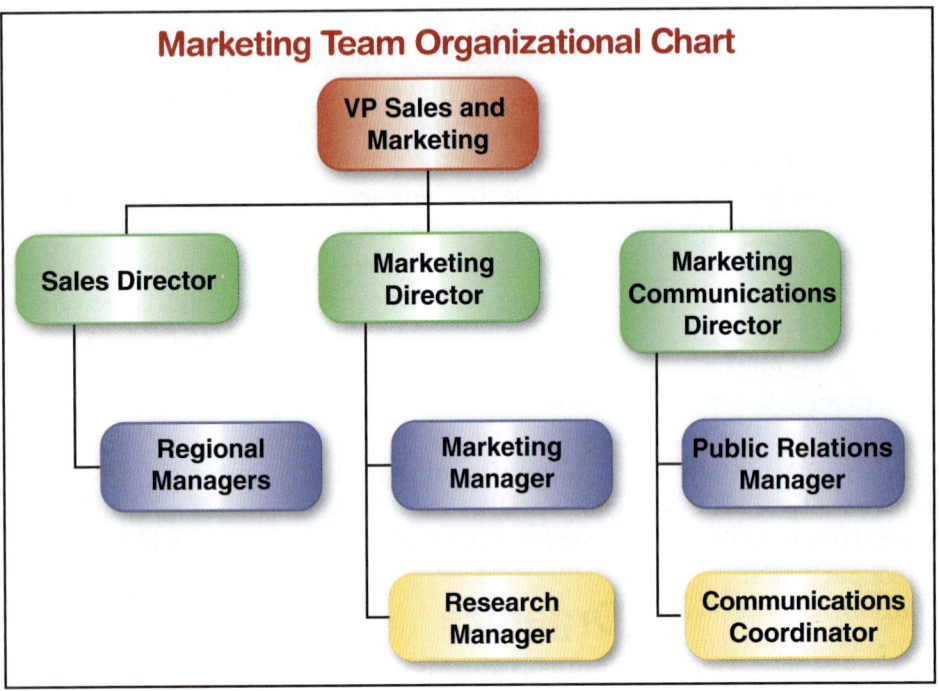

Figure 21-2 An organizational chart is a diagram of employee positions showing how the positions interact within the chain of command.

Marketing Team Organizational Chart

- VP Sales and Marketing
  - Sales Director
    - Regional Managers
  - Marketing Director
    - Marketing Manager
    - Research Manager
  - Marketing Communications Director
    - Public Relations Manager
    - Communications Coordinator

Goodheart-Willcox Publisher

is a challenging responsibility for all managers. *Human resources (HR)* are the employees who work for a company. In larger companies, the *human resources (HR) department* helps determine the human resources needs for a department or company. The HR department also helps find and hire the right employees for open positions.

Lead

Successful marketing managers lead their teams by giving clear, concise directions. A person who guides others to a goal is a **leader**. Leaders must be ethical and lead by example. Successful managers recognize the work of others and reward positive performances.

Soft skills are skills used to help an individual find a job, perform in the workplace, and gain success in a job or career. Managers must possess soft skills, such as a positive attitude, respectfulness, a sense of humor, and trustworthiness, among others. *Self-management skills* are the skills that help an individual be productive and successful in the workplace. These skills include time management, problem solving, critical thinking, and stress management.

Control

To **control** is to monitor the progress of the team to meet its goals. Actual performance is compared to stated business goals. If the team is missing its goals, the manager must take corrective action and make adjustments. Employee evaluation also falls under this managerial function. In addition, marketing managers are responsible for controlling marketing costs.

Pressmaster/Shutterstock.com

A person who guides others to a goal is a leader. *How do you think leadership and management are related?*

LO 21.1-3 Management Styles

A *management style* is how a person leads a team. In general, there are four management styles.

Case in Point

Enterprise Holdings

Successful businesses realize the importance of the management function within the organization. They also understand the value of focused management training according to company standards. For example, Enterprise Holdings, which owns the Enterprise, Alamo, and National brands of car-rental services, has a management-training program. This program focuses on collaborative hands-on training. Future managers learn to work with customers and apply the company's values of hard work, exceptional customer service, honesty, integrity, and social responsibility.

At Enterprise, management trainees are taught the skills necessary to excel in their role and learn the company's business model. Trainees focus on the importance of customer service and exceeding customer expectations. Sales and marketing strategies, finance concepts like profit and loss statements, and operations are also taught.

Enterprise values performance and maintains a policy of promoting employees from within. The company helps management trainees gain the ability to manage their own stores and attain success. Management trainees are the future of their company. Just ask Andrew C. Taylor, CEO. He, too, started his career as a manager in training.

- In the **democratic management style**, the leader encourages team members to participate and share ideas equally. This style is often called the *participatory style*.
- In the **autocratic management style**, the leader makes all decisions without input from others. This is also known as *top-down management*.
- The **consulting management style** is a combination of the democratic and autocratic management styles. The leader makes the final decision, but only after considering input from the team.
- In the **laissez-faire management style**, a leader allows employees to make their own decisions about how to complete tasks. There is little involvement from the leader.

Regardless of the style, effective managers are also delegators, motivators, and are fair to all employees. They learn from their mistakes and can manage stressful situations well. Managing by example is important for all people in leadership positions, especially marketers.

Section 21.1 Review

Check Your Understanding

1. What is management?
2. List three levels of management.
3. Which type of planning involves setting day-to-day goals for the company?
4. What is the chain of command?
5. What is a management style?

Build Your Vocabulary

As you progress through this text, develop a personal glossary of key terms. This will help you build your vocabulary and prepare you for a career. Write a definition for each of the following terms and add them to your personal glossary.

autocratic management style
consulting management style
control
democratic management style
laissez-faire management style
leader
manager
operational planning
organizational chart
staffing
strategic planning
tactical planning

Section 21.2

Financial Management

Learning Objectives

LO 21.2-1 Explain financial planning.
LO 21.2-2 Discuss the concept of a budget.
LO 21.2-3 List and explain financial reports used in business.

Key Terms

financial planning
revenue
sales forecast
sales-increase factor
cost control
balance sheet
asset
liability
income statement

Essential Question

How does financial planning help a manager make decisions?

Financial Planning

Financial planning is the process of setting financial goals and developing methods for reaching them. Most businesses set yearly goals and develop plans to achieve them. One of the most important business goals is usually to earn a specific amount of revenue. **Revenue** is the money that a business makes for the products or services it sells. Revenue is also called *income* or *sales*.

Sales and marketing teams work with senior management to help define specific revenue goals for the company. The process begins with creating a sales forecast. A **sales forecast** is a prediction of future sales based on past sales and a market analysis for a specific time period. Historical sales figures are evaluated, marketing plan successes and failures are reviewed, and external and internal factors are considered. External factors are those things that are beyond company control, such as the economy or political events. Internal factors are events, such as changes in the distribution channel or labor problems.

By evaluating past performance, future performance can be predicted. A sales forecast helps define actions the sales and marketing team will take to meet those revenue goals. The formula for a *sales forecast* is as follows.

previous-year sales dollars +
forecasted sales-increase dollars =
forecasted sales-dollar goal

Employability Skills

Respect

If your workplace provides a parking facility, respect what has been provided for the employees. Cars should only be parked in designated parking spots. Handicapped spaces should only be used by people who need them. A handicapped placard is *not* a parking pass. Misuse of a handicapped permit is unethical, as well as illegal, and subject to penalty.

Exploring Marketing Careers

Community Affairs

Presenting a positive image to customers and others can be important to the success of an organization. People who work in community affairs help businesses and other organizations make a favorable impression with the public. Typical job titles for these positions include *community affairs manager*, *public relations director*, *communications specialist*, and *press secretary*. Community affairs professionals may work for businesses, government agencies, or other organizations.

Some examples of tasks that community affairs professionals perform include:
- Work with others to promote an organization's image, activities, or product brands
- Prepare press releases, write newsletters, maintain blogs, give presentations, and answer questions from the media or the public
- Arrange for company executives to give speeches or presentations
- Work with community groups or charities which the organization helps sponsor

Community affairs professionals need strong communication and human relations skills. Computer skills in areas such as word processing, desktop publishing, and web page creation are also needed. A bachelor degree in communications, public relations, marketing, or related studies is required for many jobs in this field. Managers and directors may be required to have several years of work experience in community affairs. For more information, access the *Occupational Outlook Handbook* online.

In this example, the sales forecast for the year is $96,000 based on an expected $16,000 increase sales goal.

$80,000 + $16,000 = $96,000

Sales forecasts may be *quantitative*, or based on facts and figures. Quantitative data includes past sales history, market share, and the disposable income of the target market. One way to complete a quantitative sales forecast is to use the previous sales dollar amount and add a sales-increase factor. A **sales-increase factor** is the percentage of expected increase in sales. Many companies set sales goals based on a percentage of increase from the previous year. The formula for *forecasted sales dollar increase* is as follows.

previous-year sales dollars ×
sales-increase factor percentage =
forecasted sales-increase dollars

For example, perhaps a company had a sales goal of a 20-percent increase in sales from year one to year two. If year-one sales were $80,000, the expected amount of sales increase is $16,000.

$80,000 × 20% = $16,000

Sales forecasts may also be *qualitative*, or based on judgment. Qualitative sales forecasts are most often used when a new business is opening or a new product is being introduced. In order to remain profitable, it is important for a company to constantly monitor its sales forecasts and make changes as necessary.

LO 21.2-2 Budget

A *budget* is a financial plan for a fixed period of time that reflects anticipated revenue and shows how it will be allocated in the operation of the business. Budgets are often used during financial planning.

Marketing Ethics

Expense Accounts

Marketing professionals may have an expense account at their disposal through their employer. An expense account is to be used when it is necessary to buy a meal for a client or for other business expenses related to the functions stated in your job description. Personal expenses should *not* be charged against a business expense account. It is unethical to charge your employer for expenses that are not related to company business.

The marketing budget may be divided into two parts: operations and marketing activities. The operations budget includes payroll and other operating expenses for the marketing team. The marketing activities budget includes amounts for advertising and other marketing activities.

Managers must determine which expenses and other costs are necessary to keep the business operating successfully. **Cost control** means monitoring costs to stay within a planned budget. At year-end, managers compare the actual income, expenses, and other costs with the budgeted amounts. This comparison provides management with a tool for future planning.

Financial Reports

Financial reports reflect how a business is doing at a given time. It is important that all managers understand the financial statements for the business. Two of the main financial reports used in business are the balance sheet and the income statement.

Balance Sheet

A **balance sheet** is a financial report that reports the assets, liabilities, and owner's equity. Owners' equity reflects the net worth of a business. A balance sheet is like a snapshot that shows the value of the business on a specific date. Figure 21-3 shows an example of a balance sheet.

kurhan/Shutterstock.com

Managers compare actual income, expenses, and other costs with budgeted amounts to use as a tool for future planning. *How might a budget be useful in your own financial planning?*

Typically, each department in a company has a yearly budget, and the company has an overall budget. Budgets can be prepared for one month, one quarter, six months, or one year.

Figure 21-3 This financial statement is an example of a balance sheet.

Cook's Computer Warehouse
Balance Sheet
December 31, 20--

ASSETS		
Cash	$36,000	
Accounts Receivable	22,000	
Equipment	15,000	
Total Assets		$73,000
LIABILITIES		
Accounts Payable	$24,000	
Notes Payable	18,000	
Total Liabilities		$42,000
OWNER'S EQUITY		
David Cook, Capital		31,000
Total Liabilities and Owner's Equity		$73,000

Goodheart-Willcox Publisher

You Do the Math

Algebraic Reasoning

In algebra, letters stand in place of unknown numbers. These letters are called *variables*. When a variable appears with numbers and signs for adding, subtracting, multiplying, or dividing, the expression is called a *variable expression*. For example, $x + 5$ is a variable expression.

Solve the following problems.

1. Lucy budgets $25 a week for office refreshments. Sometimes, the amount she spends each week is less than $25. Write a variable expression to calculate the amount of money left over after a given week.
2. Travis sells advertising space in the local newspaper. The price for an advertisement is based on how many inches of vertical space it fills. The rate for advertisement space is $2.37 per inch. Write a variable expression to calculate the price of advertisement space.
3. A business orders $350 worth of office equipment from a single supplier each month. Payment for the order is made in a single payment or is sometimes divided into equal smaller payments. Write a variable expression to calculate equal payment amounts for the office equipment order.

A balance sheet lists the assets and liabilities of a company. An **asset** is property or item of value owned by a business. A **liability** is a debt of a business. A balance sheet is based on the following accounting equation:

assets = liabilities + owners' equity

A balance sheet is useful to marketing for several reasons. By reviewing inventory on the balance sheet, a marketing manager can evaluate how effectively he or she projected inventory needs. By reviewing accounts receivable, a marketing manager can determine how much customers still owe to the business.

A marketing manager does not have to be an accountant. However, understanding basic accounting activities is important for effective management.

Income Statement

An **income statement** is a financial report that shows the revenue and expenses for a business during a specific period of time. An example of a company income statement is shown in Figure 21-4.

If the amount of income is larger than the amount of expenses, the result is a positive

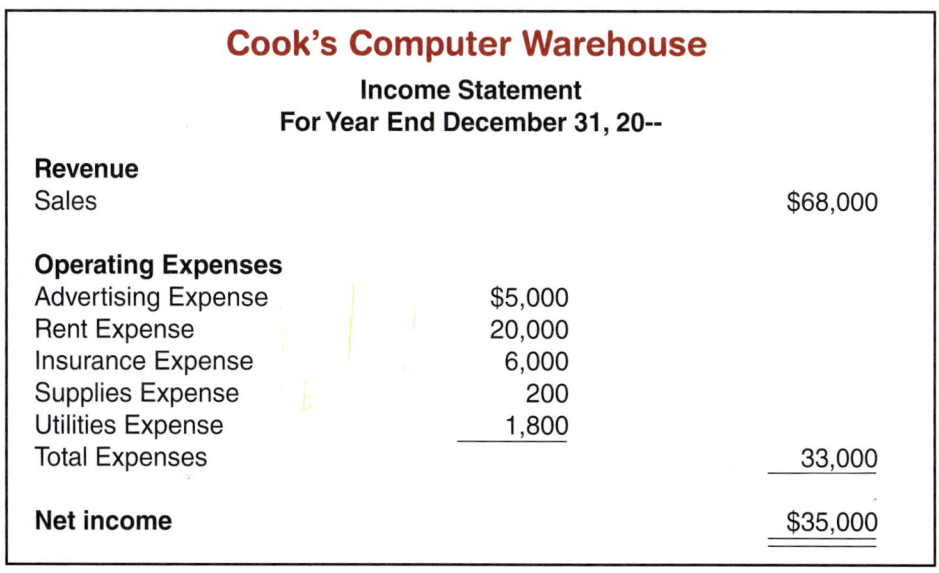

Figure 21-4 This financial statement is an example of an income statement.

Cook's Computer Warehouse
Income Statement
For Year End December 31, 20--

Revenue		
Sales		$68,000
Operating Expenses		
Advertising Expense	$5,000	
Rent Expense	20,000	
Insurance Expense	6,000	
Supplies Expense	200	
Utilities Expense	1,800	
Total Expenses		33,000
Net income		$35,000

Goodheart-Willcox Publisher

number. A positive result is referred to as *net income* or *profit*. If expenses are larger than income, the result is a negative number. A negative result is referred to as a *loss*. In accounting, a loss is indicated by placing the number in parentheses.

An income statement may be created for specific departments within the business. Each department can then evaluate its contribution to the overall profit for the company. This is especially useful for marketing, since its contribution to the bottom line is directly related to marketing activities.

Section 21.2 Review

Check Your Understanding

1. State the formula used to calculate a sales forecast.
2. State the formula used to calculate forecasted sales dollar increase.
3. What is a budget?
4. Explain the difference between assets and liabilities.
5. What is a positive result on an income statement called?

Build Your Vocabulary

As you progress through this text, develop a personal glossary of key terms. This will help you build your vocabulary and prepare you for a career. Write a definition for each of the following terms and add them to your personal glossary.

asset
balance sheet
cost control
financial planning
income statement
liability
revenue
sales forecast
sales-increase factor

CHAPTER 21 Review and Assessment

Chapter Summary

Section 21.1 Management

LO 21.1-1 Describe the role of a manager.
A manager directs the work of others and is responsible for carrying out the goals of a department. Managers are responsible for making sure that all marketing tasks are completed. Three levels of management are upper, middle, and supervisory.

LO 21.1-2 List five elements of the management function.
The management function of business controls and makes decisions about a business. The five elements of the management function are plan, organize, staff, lead, and control.

LO 21.1-2 Describe effective management styles.
In the democratic management style, the leader encourages team members to participate and share ideas equally. In the autocratic management style, the leader makes decisions without input from others. The consulting management style is a combination of the democratic and autocratic management styles. In the laissez-faire management style, a leader allows employees to make their own decisions about how to complete tasks.

Section 21.2 Financial Management

LO 21.2-1 Explain financial planning.
Financial planning is setting financial goals and developing methods for reaching them. A sales forecast helps define actions that the sales and marketing team will put into motion to meet those revenue goals. In order to remain profitable, it is important for a company to constantly monitor its sales forecasts and make changes as necessary.

LO 21.2-2 Discuss the concept of a budget.
A budget is a financial plan for a fixed period of time that reflects anticipated revenue and shows how it will be allocated in the operation of the business. Typically, each department in a company has a yearly budget, and the company has an overall budget. Budgets can be prepared for one month, one quarter, six months, or one year.

LO 21.2-3 List and explain financial reports used in business.
Two of the main financial reports are the balance sheet and the income statement. A balance sheet is a financial report that reports the assets, liabilities, and owner's equity. An income statement is a financial report that shows the revenue and expenses for a business during a specific period of time.

Check Your Marketing IQ

Now that you have completed the chapter, see what you have learned about marketing by taking the chapter posttest. The posttest is available at www.g-wlearning.com/marketing/.

Review Your Knowledge

1. Describe the role of a manager.
2. List five elements of the management function.
3. List and describe types of planning done by managers.
4. Why is an organizational chart used?
5. Describe different management styles.
6. Explain financial planning.
7. What external and internal factors must be considered when creating a sales forecast?
8. Discuss the concept of a budget.
9. List and explain financial reports used in business.
10. State the accounting equation.

Apply Your Knowledge

1. Which of the five functions of management do you think you would excel at the most? Explain why this function might come easily to you.
2. Which of the five functions of management do you think you would struggle with the most? Explain why this function might be difficult for you.
3. Explain why strategic, tactical, and operational planning are each important for successfully marketing your business.
4. Create an organizational plan that could be used by the marketing department of your company.
5. Which leadership style best motivates you to do your best work? Why?
6. Compare and contrast the four different management styles. Which management style do you think you would adopt as a manager? Explain your answer.
7. As the marketing manager for your company, write a short report about how you propose to control marketing expenses.
8. Based on the sales goals in your marketing plans, calculate the overall sales forecast for your business.
9. Examine the balance sheet in the business plan you are using to write the marketing plan for your company. Write a short explanation of what the balance sheet tells readers about the business.
10. Examine the income statement in the business plan you are using to write the marketing plan for your company. Write a short explanation of what the income statement tells readers about the business.

Apply Your Math Skills

Dakota is a marketing manager making financial plans for the upcoming year. She is using the following formulas to prepare her financial documents.

Forecasted sales dollar increase:

> previous-year sales dollars × sales-increase factor percentage = forecasted sales-increase dollars

Sales forecast:

> previous-year sales dollars + forecasted sales-increase dollars = forecasted sales-dollar goal

Apply your math skills to solve the following problems.

1. Dakota's company has a sales goal of a 15-percent increase in sales from this year to next year. This year's sales were $46,740. What is the expected amount of sales increase in dollars?
2. What is the sales forecast for next year based on the expected 15-percent increase sales goal?

Communication Skills

Reading Managers may need to engage in professional networking to further a career. Read the Portfolio Development activity about networking that appears in this chapter. Identify and analyze the audience, purpose, and message of the author's writing.

Speaking Marketing managers are required to make presentations to the management team for various reports such as budgets, organization charts, etc. Present the organizational chart in Figure 21-2 to your class as if this were the organizational chart for your employer. Speak clearly and prepare for questions from the audience.

Writing Sales forecasting is a combination of applying quantitative data and qualitative information to determine projected sales. What would happen to a sales forecast if it was done using only quantitative data or using only qualitative information? Write a paragraph to summarize your opinion.

Internet Research

Management Structure Management structures have different names depending on the specific company. Using the Internet, conduct a search for *types of organizational structure in management*. Select two types of structures that interest you and compare and contrast them. Write a brief summary of a management structure you would recommend to someone who is in the process of creating a management team.

Empathy in the Workplace Using the Internet, research *empathy in the workplace*. What is the role of this soft skill in the workplace? List ways an employee can show empathy to coworkers, supervisors, and customers.

Marketing Budget Templates Conduct an online search for *marketing budget template*. Review three of the ones you find that can be downloaded at no charge. Which template do you like best? Why?

Teamwork

Working with your team, create a one-page handout that lists each type of management style. Under each style, make a list of bullets that describe the characteristics of that type of manager. Duplicate enough of these handouts to distribute to your classmates. Ask if they will participate in an anonymous survey and select the characteristics that apply to him or her. Tally the votes. Which style was most dominant in your class?

Portfolio Development

College and Career Readiness

Networking Networking means talking with others and establishing relationships with people who can help you achieve career, educational, or personal goals. You have probably already begun to build one, even if you have not thought of it in these terms. People in your network include your instructors, employers, coworkers, or counselors who know about your skills and interests. Those who participate with you in volunteer efforts, clubs, or other organizations can also be part of your network. These people may help you learn about open positions and may be able to provide you with information that will help you get a position.

1. Identify people who are part of your network.
2. Create a spreadsheet that includes information about each person. Include each person's name, contact information, and relationship to you. For example, the person might be a coworker, employer, or fellow club member. Save the file. This will be used for your personal use and not included in your portfolio.

CHAPTER 22

Soft Skills

Sections

22.1 **Skills for Managers**
22.2 **Teams in the Workplace**

Reading Prep

College and Career Readiness

As you read the chapter, determine the point of view or purpose of the author. What aspects of the text help establish the purpose or point of view?

Check Your Marketing IQ

Before you begin the chapter, see what you already know about marketing by taking the chapter pretest. The pretest is available at www.g-wlearning.com/marketing/.

DECA Emerging Leaders

Marketing Management Team Decision-Making Event, Part 1

Career Cluster: Marketing
Instructional Area: Selling

Knowledge and Skills Developed

Participants will develop many 21st century skills desired by today's employers in the following categories:
- communication and collaboration
- creativity and innovation
- critical thinking and problem solving
- flexibility and adaptability
- information literacy
- initiative and self-direction
- leadership and responsibility
- productivity and accountability
- social and cross-cultural skills

Specific Performance Indicators

- Explain the nature of effective verbal communications.
- Employ communication styles appropriate to a target audience.
- Make oral presentations.
- Explain the nature and scope of the selling function.
- Discuss motivational theories that impact buying behavior.
- Explain the key factors in building a clientele.
- Explain the role of customer service as a component of selling relationships.

Purpose

Designed for a team of two DECA members, the events measure the team's ability to explain core business concepts in the format of a case study in a role-play. This event consists of a 100-question multiple-choice cluster exam for each team member and a decision-making case study situation. The Team Decision-Making Event provides an opportunity for participants to analyze one or a combination of elements essential to the effective operation of a business in the specific career area presented as a case study.

For the purposes of this text, you will be presented with the material for this event in two parts. Part 1 presents the knowledge and skills assessed and an overview of the event's purpose and procedure. Part 2 presents the remaining procedures and the event situation.

Procedure, Part 1

1. For Part 1 in this text, read both the Knowledge and Skills Developed and the Specific Performance Indicators. Discuss these with your team members.
2. If there are any questions, ask your instructor to clarify.

Critical Thinking

1. Evaluate the marketing methods used to meet customer needs.
2. How is the marketing mix achieved?

Visit www.deca.org for more information.

Published by DECA Inc. Copyright © by DECA Inc. No part of this publication may be reproduced for resale without written permission from the publisher. Printed in the United States of America.

Section 22.1

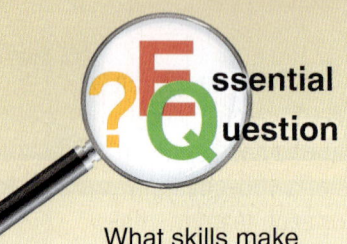

Skills for Managers

Essential Question
What skills make an employee successful?

Learning Objectives

LO 22.1-1 Define *soft skills*.
LO 22.1-2 Cite examples of self-management skills.
LO 22.1-3 Explain the role of ethics in the workplace.

Key Terms

soft skills
professionalism
work ethic
adaptability
etiquette
time management
work-life balance
problem solving

critical thinking
stress
stress management
stereotyping
proprietary information
conflict of interest
insider trading

Soft Skills Basics

Successful managers possess well-developed soft skills. **Soft skills** are skills used to help an individual find a job, perform in the workplace, and gain success in a job or career. They are also known as *interpersonal skills*, *people skills*, and *transferrable skills*. These are the group of skills that enable a person to interact with others in a positive way. Possessing soft skills helps workers interact effectively with supervisors, peers, customers, and vendors. Examples of soft skills are shown in Figure 22-1. Important soft skills for workplace success include professionalism, positive attitude, respectfulness, trustworthiness, and etiquette.

Professionalism

Conducting one's self as a professional is a soft skill that is important for workplace success. **Professionalism** is the act of exhibiting appropriate character, judgment, and behavior by a person who is trained to perform a job. It is knowing how to interact with others in a manner that makes it conducive for everyone to be successful in their responsibilities. Employers expect professionalism in their employees so that positive, effective workplace relationships can develop. This includes relationships with peers, supervisors, and customers.

Professionals have *initiative*, which means to take the first step and take charge. When they see a task to be done or a decision to be made, they are comfortable making the first move to find a solution. They are also *responsible*, which means they are accountable for their actions, accepting when they make good decisions or bad decisions.

Professionalism is a soft skill that can be demonstrated in many ways, such as respecting the workspaces of coworkers, dressing in appropriate clothing for the job, and showing responsibility for proper behavior in the workplace. This includes having a strong work ethic. **Work ethic** is the belief that honest work is a reward on its own. It is a soft skill that can help a person be successful in the workplace. Coming to work on time and respecting employer and coworkers are ways to demonstrate a professional work ethic.

Soft Skills			
adaptability	digital citizenship	negotiation	responsibility
assertiveness	emotional control	open-mindedness	self-confidence
collaboration	etiquette	optimism	self-control
communication	flexibility	patience	self-motivation
conflict resolution	goal setting	perseverance	sense of humor
courtesy	honesty	positive attitude	speaking
creativity	independence	problem solving	stress management
credibility	initiative	professionalism	time management
critical thinking	integrity	reading	trustworthiness
decision making	leadership	reliability	work ethic
dependability	listening	respectfulness	writing

Goodheart-Willcox Publisher

Figure 22-1 Successful managers possess well-developed soft skills.

Professionalism is exhibiting appropriate character, judgment, and behavior by a person who is trained to perform a job. *How can a student prepare to become a professional?*

Blend Images/Shutterstock.com

Positive Attitude

Employers, customers, and coworkers want to be around people with positive attitudes. A person's *attitude* is how he or she feels about something. Attitude affects the way a person looks at the world and responds to events. A person with a positive attitude exhibits the following traits.

- *Optimism* is the expectation that things will turn out well. Optimism helps people persevere when things do not go as planned. *Perseverance* is continued effort to achieve a goal despite difficulties.
- **Adaptability** is the ability to make changes to better match, or fit, in new situations. An adaptable person can adjust to changes and new conditions smoothly and with a positive attitude.
- *Flexibility* is being able to adjust to when situations change. A person who is flexible has an *open mind*, or is willing to consider a point of view different from his or her own.

Respectfulness

Being respectful to those with whom you work is important to workplace success. Always consider the point of view of others, listen to what they are saying, and be courteous. Doing so makes others feel important and valued. It also encourages them to show you respect and courtesy in return. Respect is especially important when you disagree with someone. It shows you are listening to what they have to say.

You Do the Math

Solution Accuracy

In business and at home, you may be tasked with checking the work of others. When the work includes figures, it is often a good idea to check the solution for accuracy and effectiveness. For example, a business calculates the fuel economy of its delivery truck to be 19 miles per gallon. However, the fuel used on a 20-mile delivery run is four gallons. This either means the calculation is incorrect or the reported usage is incorrect.

Solve the following problems.
1. A business sells 387 units of product for an average of $27.48 each. It reports the gross sales are $10,634.78. Is the reported sales figure correct?
2. Harris drives 687 miles in 16 hours. He uses 18.5 gallons of gasoline. He states that his car gets 47 miles to the gallon. Is he correct?
3. A business spent a total of $43.87 on office supplies in one month and has decided to wait one month to pay the charge. The credit account charges 19.7 percent on outstanding balances. The business estimates the finance charge will be $2.25. Is this correct?

Trustworthiness

Positive workplace relationships develop when people trust each other. A trustworthy person keeps promises and deals fairly with others. He or she acts with honesty and integrity in all situations. *Honesty* is the quality of being fair and truthful. *Integrity* means adhering to moral or ethical values. Having high moral standards and refraining from lying, stealing, and cheating are examples of traits of a trustworthy professional.

Trustworthy people are dependable. *Dependability* is the ability to be relied upon in any given situation. Dependable people follow through on their responsibilities and establish credibility. *Credibility* is established when a person says or does what he or she has promised to do.

Etiquette

Etiquette is the art of using good manners in any situation. *Professional etiquette* is using good manners in a professional or business setting. It means to be courteous as well as acting and speaking appropriately in all situations. Examples of professional etiquette are shown in Figure 22-2.

Self-Management Skills
LO 22.1-2

Self-management skills help an individual be productive and successful in the workplace. Possessing these soft skills helps employees communicate with customers, peers, and supervisors. Examples of self-management skills are time management, problem solving, critical thinking, and stress management.

Time Management

Time management is the practice of organizing time and work assignments to increase personal

Professional Etiquette

- Dress appropriately for your job
- Address people you meet by name
- Be courteous with those with whom you come in contact
- Respect the workspace of others
- Use professional language and avoid slang, jargon, or words that are condescending
- Say "please" and "thank-you" to others when appropriate
- Turn your cell phone to silent during meetings or conversations
- Avoid being a part of conversations that include gossip
- Apply social manners when attending a business meeting or dinner

Goodheart-Willcox Publisher

Figure 22-2 Professional etiquette is using good manners in a professional or business setting.

Andrey_Popov/Shutterstock.com

Time-management skills help people work efficiently, meet deadlines, and keep appointments. *What strategies do you use for time management?*

efficiency. Time-management skills help people work efficiently, meet deadlines, and keep appointments.

Time management starts with creating to-do lists. A *master to-do list* is a list of the things you need to do in a week or other period of time. A *daily to-do list* is the activities that you intend to accomplish in a day. Items on these lists can be added on your calendar along with other appointments. You can use the calendar on your digital device to note all weekly, monthly, and annual appointments, meetings, and obligations.

A major challenge to managing time at work is handling customer e-mails, coworker inquiries, and marketing files. A key to being organized is to handle each piece of communication only once, and do one of three things:
- act on it;
- file it; or
- recycle or delete it.

If a piece of communication needs to be maintained, creating a system of folders can help for both paper and electronic documents. Label the folders so communication on each subject can be easily found.

In order to manage time each day, it may be necessary to multitask. *Multitasking* is performing several tasks at the same time. However, attempting to do too many complex tasks at a time can cause managers to be less efficient and productive. For projects that require deep concentration and high accuracy, it is best to focus on only one task at a time.

An important rule of time management is to avoid procrastination. *Procrastination* is the delay of doing something that should be done immediately. Procrastination can become a serious barrier to work success when it results in missed deadlines or substandard work. It is best to start assigned tasks right away. The longer you put off a task, the more anxious and worried you are likely to become.

Time management can help in your professional life as well as help you maintain work-life balance. **Work-life balance** is the amount of time an individual spends working compared to the amount of time spent in a personal life. By managing your time

Case in Point

Cisco

As a world leader in networking, Cisco provides services to business customers, including corporations and governments. Cisco provides limited products, such as Wi-Fi routers, to the consumer market. Its largest market, by far, is selling to resellers who sell or provide services to end users. Like other B2B companies, Cisco has been very successful marketing to the business customer. That is why they are known as the market leader in networking.

However, Cisco has taken networking a step further. The company wants to make sure their business customers know how to resell the Cisco product lines. Cisco holds an annual Cisco Partner Summit to share product information, offer education opportunities, and provide marketing direction. Cisco also offers eLearning courses and proficiency certification to empower their resellers and help them be successful using Cisco tools. Topics addressed include marketing fundamentals, marketing with Cisco, revenue marketing, and digital marketing. The company also hosts a convention that is entirely focused on marketing called Cisco Marketing Velocity. The goal of this event is to help partners learn to use the latest marketing tactics to engage with customers. Cisco understands the marketing concept of customer satisfaction.

wavebreakmedia/Shutterstock.com

Problem solving is choosing a course of action after evaluating information that is available. *Describe a recent problem for which you applied problem-solving skills.*

at work, you may have more time at home to spend the way you want to spend it.

Problem Solving

Problem solving is a process of choosing a course of action after evaluating available info and weighing the costs, benefits, and consequences of alternative actions. It is the process of choosing a course of action after evaluating information that is available. Using a systematic decision-making process, shown in Figure 22-3, is a good tool to use when solving a problem.

Critical Thinking

An important component of self-management is the ability to apply analysis and logic in the workplace. **Critical thinking** is the process of interpreting and making reasonable judgments and decisions by analyzing a situation. Developing critical thinking skills allows individuals to see how things are connected, such as ideas, problems, or cause-and-effect situations.

A critical thinker is an active participant in learning and making decisions, rather than simply receiving information. Because thinking takes places in a person's mind, no one can monitor or control the critical thinking of another person. A critical thinker removes personal thoughts, feelings, and opinions from the situation and focuses on the situation at hand. Critical-thinking skills allow individuals to find solutions to complicated problems.

Two types of critical thinking are deductive reasoning and inductive reasoning. *Deductive reasoning* uses logic to form a conclusion or opinion about a situation. When using deductive reasoning, the information already known is evaluated. Afterward, more information is sought to explain what is already known and reach a conclusion. *Inductive reasoning* uses many facts or examples to form a general conclusion. When using inductive reasoning, the facts or examples observed are considered to be evidence of a conclusion. Both deductive and inductive reasoning can be applied in the workplace to solve problems.

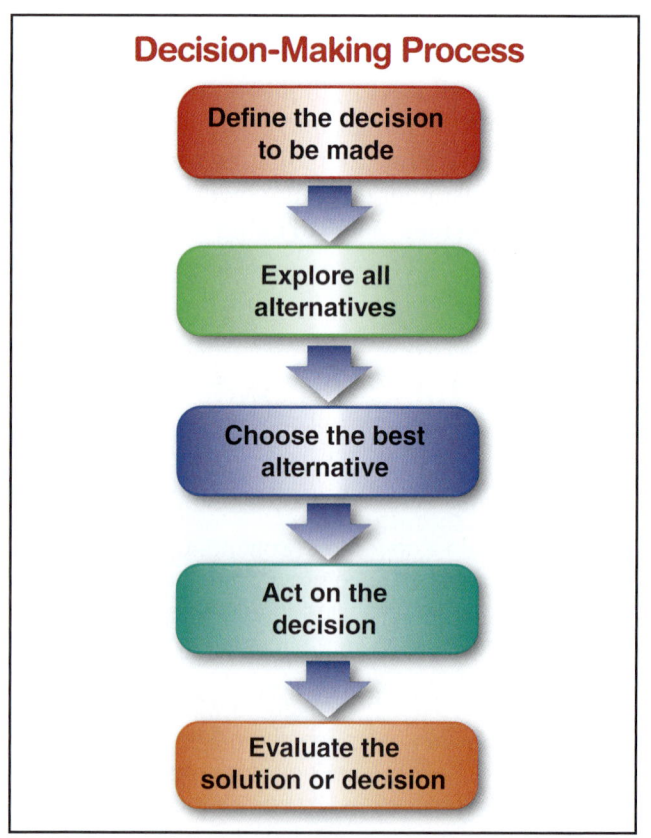

Decision-Making Process

- Define the decision to be made
- Explore all alternatives
- Choose the best alternative
- Act on the decision
- Evaluate the solution or decision

Goodheart-Willcox Publisher

Figure 22-3 The systematic decision-making process is a five-step process.

Stress is the body's reaction to increased challenges, pressures, or dangerous situations. *What do you do to manage your personal stress level?*

Dean Drobot/Shutterstock.com

Stress Management

Stress is the body's reaction to increased challenges, pressures, or dangerous situations. A person experiences stress when he or she becomes unable to cope with life's demands. A *stressor* is something that causes stress.

Stressors can be positive or negative. Positive stressors create positive stress, or *eustress*. Starting a new job, getting a promotion, and planning a vacation can cause positive stress. Negative stressors create negative stress, or *distress*. Losing a job and conflict with another person are examples of negative stress. Distress often lasts longer than eustress and can impact a person's life more. Having multiple stressors can cause overall stress levels to increase.

Stress can also be internal or external. *Internal stressors* come from a person's own goals, standards, and expectations of himself or herself. Setting a personal goal and not reaching it is an example of an internal stressor. *External stressors* are outside factors that cause stress, such as work demands, relationships, and finances. An example of an external stressor common in the workplace is information overload. *Information overload* occurs when the amount of information available exceeds the ability of the brain to process it.

Stress management is the practice of reducing and effectively handling stress. People often have more control over their stress levels than they realize. The Mayo Clinic's *four As of stress management* are strategies that can be used to manage stress.

- *Avoid*. Stay away from the source of the stress on purpose. Plan in advance, rearrange your schedule, or do whatever is necessary to not come in contact with the stressor.
- *Alter*. Change your behavior in order to change the situations that cause stress.
- *Adapt*. Modify your standards or expectations in order to adapt to the source of the stress. Changing the way you perceive the stressor can reduce the stress it causes.
- *Accept*. Some stressors cannot be avoided, altered, or adapted to, and must be accepted as they are. Develop a positive attitude about these stressors in order to reduce your personal stress level.

Figure 22-4 lists additional ways to reduce and manage stress.

LO 22.1-3 Ethical Behavior

Ethics are the set of moral values that guide a person's behavior. *Morals* are an individual's ideas of what is right and wrong. Ethics help people determine the most appropriate behavior for situations in both their personal and professional lives.

Ethical behavior refers to actions that adhere to a person's ethical standards. Examples of ethical behavior include respecting diversity, keeping proprietary information confidential, avoiding conflicts of interest, and avoiding participation in insider trading.

Stress-Management Techniques
- Accept that you cannot control everything
- Eat a healthy diet
- Exercise regularly
- Get enough sleep
- Have a positive attitude
- Learn what your stressors are
- Slowly count to ten
- Take a deep breath
- Talk with a friend
- Try to do your best, rather than try to be perfect

Source: Anxiety and Depression Association of America; Goodheart-Willcox Publisher

Figure 22-4 The practice of reducing and effectively handling stress is stress management.

Diversity

Ethical people respect the diversity of their coworkers and customers. Recall that *diversity* means having representatives from different backgrounds, cultures, or demographics in a group. It includes age, race, nationality, gender, mental ability, physical ability, and other qualities that make an individual unique.

Ethical people refrain from stereotyping others. **Stereotyping** is a belief or generalization about a group of people with a given set of characteristics. It is not acceptable to stereotype.

Proprietary Information

People who work in marketing are often exposed to important company information. New products in development, competitive data, and other valuable information are handled by marketing. Employees are required to keep company information private. **Proprietary information**, sometimes referred to as *trade secrets*, is information a company wishes to keep private. Proprietary information can include many things, such as product formulas, customer lists, or manufacturing processes. All employees must understand the importance of keeping company information confidential. The code of conduct should explain that company information may only be shared with permission. Employees who share proprietary information with outsiders are behaving unethically and, possibly, illegally.

Before hiring an employee for its marketing team, a company may require the person to sign a confidentiality agreement, as shown in Figure 22-5. A *confidentiality agreement* typically states that the employee will not share any company information with outsiders. A confidentiality agreement is especially important for a team that might have product information that could benefit competitors. These agreements can also prevent former employees from working for a competitor for a certain period of time.

Conflict of Interest

A **conflict of interest** exists when an employee has competing interests or loyalties. For example, an employee tells you about a great opportunity to buy marketing promotional items at a low price. The employee convinces you that the items will be a big hit for the marketing team, and the cost of carrying the product will be low. What the employee did *not* tell you is that he or she gets a percentage of every sale made from the manufacturer. This is known as a kickback. A *kickback* is an amount of money given to someone in return for

---

Confidentiality Agreement

THIS AGREEMENT made on _____, 20_____, between Yours in Retro, a place of business at 101 Main Street, Anytown, IL, and _____, an employee of Yours in Retro.

As an employee of Yours in Retro, we require nondisclosure of any proprietary information about our products, employees, or business plans. This confidential information may include, but is not limited to, patents, trademarks, research, market analyses, or any other information concerning Yours in Retro.

All work contributed by the employee as part of the employee's paid position remains the property of Yours in Retro.

The obligations of this agreement shall continue two (2) years after employee leaves Yours in Retro.

Goodheart-Willcox Publisher

Figure 22-5 A confidentiality agreement typically states that the employee will not share any company information with outsiders.

Employability Skills

Telephone Etiquette

Telephone etiquette is using good manners when speaking on the telephone. Always be courteous to the person on the other end of the call. Be aware of the volume and tone of your voice. Smile when you are talking on the phone; it will make your voice sound more pleasant.

providing help in a business deal. This is clearly a conflict of interest.

Conflicts of interest can take many forms and harm a business. Some are illegal; others are unethical, yet still legal. Be aware of how specific conflicts of interest could negatively affect your company. These situations should be addressed in the code of conduct.

Insider Trading

Insider trading is when an employee uses private company information to purchase company stock or other securities for personal gain. Using company information for personal gain is both unethical and illegal. Sometimes, marketers help to develop new products or learn other information that could affect the price of company stock before it is made public. While it may be hard to control information, marketers and other employees should know the legal consequences of insider trading.

Section 22.1 Review

Check Your Understanding

1. List examples of soft skills that can aid with workplace success.
2. What is perseverance?
3. Why are time-management skills important?
4. Name two types of critical thinking.
5. What is a kickback?

Build Your Vocabulary

As you progress through this text, develop a personal glossary of key terms. This will help you build your vocabulary and prepare you for a career. Write a definition for each of the following terms and add them to your personal glossary.

adaptability
conflict of interest
critical thinking
etiquette
insider trading
problem solving
professionalism
proprietary information
soft skills
stereotyping
stress
stress management
time management
work ethic
work-life balance

Section 22.2

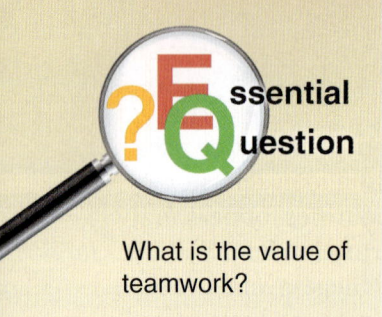

Teams in the Workplace

Essential Question

What is the value of teamwork?

Learning Objectives

LO 22.2-1 Discuss teams in the workplace.
LO 22.2-2 Describe skills required for team success.

Key Terms

team
teamwork
leadership
collaboration
constructive criticism
destructive criticism
conflict resolution

LO 22.2-1 Teams

A **team** consists of two or more people working together to achieve a common goal. Work teams have much in common with sports teams. In both situations, all members of the team must work together in order to achieve success. Teams can be beneficial in the workplace in the following ways.

- Being a part of a work team helps build relationships in the workplace.
- Teams involve more people in the decision making, so the decisions are more likely to be implemented.
- Team members continually learn from each other.
- Discussions among team members often generate new ideas.
- A group of people in a team has more knowledge and resources than an individual.
- Teams are more likely to find and correct mistakes.
- Teams are usually more productive than individuals.

Effective teams usually take the actions described in Figure 22-6.

There are two basic types of teams: functional and cross-functional. In a *functional team*, each member has basically the same skills and qualifications. The purpose of a functional team is to come together for a specific purpose. For example, sales teams are usually functional teams. All of the members of the team are salespeople.

wavebreakmedia/Shutterstock.com

A team consists of two or more people working together to achieve a common goal. *Describe what you think are important responsibilities for team members.*

Effective Teams

Share in Leadership	➤	Team members take turns leading the team
Rotate Roles	➤	Teams usually need people to act as leader, encourager, taskmaster, critic, and recorder; successful teams rotate the roles among all team members
Work Together for the Common Good	➤	Team members agree on their goals and help each other achieve them
Focus on the Goals	➤	Teams work to help each other accomplish goals and reduce distractions
Value Team Productivity	➤	Effective teams produce more work and meet their goals faster than ineffective teams

Goodheart-Willcox Publisher

Figure 22-6 Effective teams usually take the actions shown in this table.

In a *cross-functional team*, the members have different skills. A cross-functional team is often brought together to solve a specific problem. For example, a product-development team might be composed of a marketer, a design expert, an engineer, the production manager, and a salesperson.

LO 22.2-2 Teamwork

An effective team is one that accomplishes its goals. **Teamwork** is the cooperative efforts by individual team members to achieve a goal. Team members must possess soft skills in order for a team to work together and be successful. Leadership, collaboration, and conflict resolution are some of the skills that contribute to a successful team. Career and technical student organizations (CTSOs), such as DECA, Future Business Leaders of America (FBLA), Business Professionals of America (BPA), and SkillsUSA, provide many opportunities for working in teams and learning team skills.

Leadership

Leadership is the ability of a person to guide others to a goal. A person who guides others to a goal is a *leader*. Leaders influence others and inspire excellence. They are *assertive*, which means to be self-assured and confident. Leading others requires that an individual take charge and get a job done.

Leadership skills are necessary for success in the workplace. They are also valuable in other areas of life, such as in school, government, and civic organizations. Some people are natural leaders, but most people can develop the skills that make a leader successful. Skills often associated with successful leaders are self-confidence, communication, dependability, enthusiasm, flexibility, the ability to set goals, and the ability to inspire others.

Green Marketing

Green Team

The managers of ecofriendly businesses plan their operations with the goal of being a greener business. Assembling an employee green team is a good place to start going green in the workplace. Most green teams begin by addressing employee habits in the workplace, such as implementing a recycling program and eliminating the use of disposable plastic water bottles.

Green teams may also look for ways to make the operations of the business more environmentally friendly. Companies can improve shipping routes to consume less fuel, implement online systems that replace paper forms, and replace traditional office lighting with low-voltage bulbs. Some green teams offer tips to help employees make environmentally friendly decisions in their personal lives, as well.

Social Media

LinkedIn

LinkedIn is a professional social-media networking website. By creating a LinkedIn Company Page, a marketer can build brand recognition for the business. The page provides space for information to be posted about the company, its brand, and other content that would be helpful to someone wanting to learn more about the business. There is also an opportunity to connect and invite a target audience to follow and be a part of the community. An analytics tool helps a marketer understand who is following and the market that is being reached.

For a fee, businesses can post open jobs on the site that are available for any LinkedIn member to search for and apply. Creating a professional network helps businesses recruit candidates as well as obtain referrals for open positions.

LinkedIn offers other professional services that provide an opportunity to market a company without a major financial investment. The site offers solutions and tips to help employers make the most of the vehicle as well as other support.

Collaboration

Teams must be able to collaborate in order to be successful. **Collaboration** is working with others to achieve a common goal. Collaboration includes cooperation, sharing ideas and responsibilities, and compromising when necessary.

- *Cooperation* is the willingness to do what it takes to get the job done. A cooperative worker follows instructions and asks questions when he or she does not understand what to do.
- Sharing ideas and responsibilities includes risk. *Risk* is the possibility of something unpleasant happening, such as a team member disagreeing with your ideas or not completing his or her share of the work. However, it is important for members of a team to express their ideas without fear of rejection. The entire team benefits from everyone sharing his or her unique perspective.
- When people *compromise*, each person gives up a little of what he or she thinks is important so the group can come to a decision or solve a problem.

Conflict Resolution

When people work together, there is likely to be some conflict. A *conflict* is a strong disagreement between two or more people or a difference that prevents agreement. Conflict can be positive when people disagree respectfully and learn from the disagreements. Positive solutions can result when conflict is handled in a proper manner.

Conflict can be the result of many situations, including criticism from team members. When everyone speaks his or her mind and offers new ideas, other members of the team may offer criticism. **Constructive criticism** is a well-reasoned opinion about the ideas or work of another. **Destructive criticism** is a judgment about the ideas or work of another given with the intention

Solomia Malovana/Shutterstock.com

A conflict is a strong disagreement between two or more people or a difference that prevents agreement. *How do you think conflicts should be handled at work?*

of harming or offending someone. This behavior is unproductive for the workplace.

Conflict resolution is the process of recognizing and resolving disputes. Following a conflict-resolution model, as shown in Figure 22-7, can help a team work toward a resolution when disagreements arise. Conflict resolution requires that each party involved exhibits *self-control*. This means each person directs his or her feelings and reactions toward a desirable result that is socially acceptable. Yelling or losing emotional control will not be helpful in resolving an issue. Listening to each other without interruption is necessary to resolve the conflict. Speaking clearly and in a calm manner is required to keep the communication lines open. Effective listening and speaking skills will be covered in more detail in Chapter 23.

Consensus building is a way to solve a problem and resolve conflicts by coming to a decision that all stakeholders can live with. A *stakeholder* is a person that has an issue to be resolved. Consensus building is not the same as majority rules. During the majority-rules process, the winners may be happy, but the losers may be very unhappy and could undermine management's efforts to resolve the issue. The goal of building a consensus is to have all stakeholders agree on a unanimous solution. *Unanimous* means to be of one mind.

Formal methods of conflict resolution, such as negotiation, may be required in extenuating circumstances. Recall that *negotiation* is when individuals come together in an attempt to reach an agreement. Negotiation requires that each party is willing to compromise by giving something up and meeting the other party in the middle. Mediation is sometimes necessary during negotiation. *Mediation* is the inclusion of a neutral person, called a *mediator*, to help the conflicting parties resolve their dispute and reach an agreement.

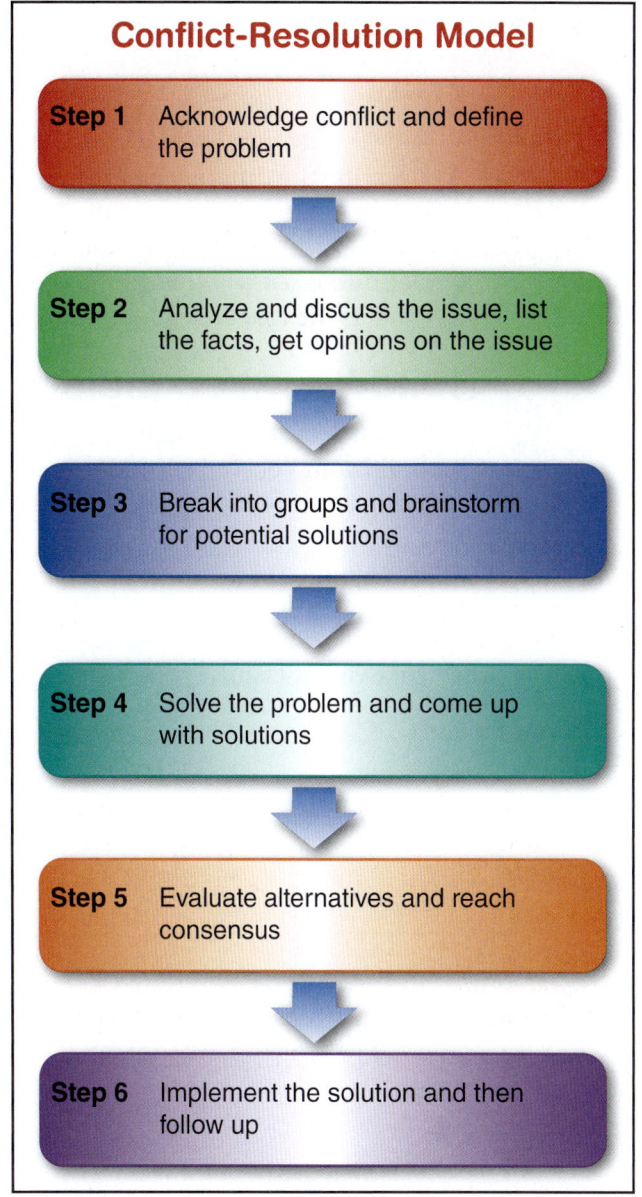

Conflict-Resolution Model

Step 1 Acknowledge conflict and define the problem

Step 2 Analyze and discuss the issue, list the facts, get opinions on the issue

Step 3 Break into groups and brainstorm for potential solutions

Step 4 Solve the problem and come up with solutions

Step 5 Evaluate alternatives and reach consensus

Step 6 Implement the solution and then follow up

Goodheart-Willcox Publisher

Figure 22-7 The process of recognizing and resolving disputes is conflict resolution.

Section 22.2 Review

Check Your Understanding

1. Describe the difference between a functional team and a cross-functional team.
2. Why must leaders be assertive?
3. Why is it important to practice self-control during a conflict?
4. Define *consensus building*.
5. What is the role of negotiation in conflict resolution?

Build Your Vocabulary

As you progress through this text, develop a personal glossary of key terms. This will help you build your vocabulary and prepare you for a career. Write a definition for each of the following terms and add them to your personal glossary.

collaboration	leadership
conflict resolution	team
constructive criticism	teamwork
destructive criticism	

CHAPTER 22 Review and Assessment

Chapter Summary

Section 22.1 Skills for Managers

LO 22.1-1 Define *soft skills*.
Soft skills help an individual find a job, perform in the workplace, and gain success in a job or career. These skills enable a person to interact with others in a positive way. Important soft skills include professionalism, positive attitude, respectfulness, trustworthiness, and etiquette.

LO 22.1-2 Cite examples of self-management skills.
Self-management skills help an individual be productive and successful in the workplace. Possessing these skills help employees communicate with customers, peers, and supervisors. Examples are time management, problem solving, critical thinking, and stress management.

LO 22.1-3 Explain the role of ethics in the workplace.
Ethics are the set of moral values that guide a person's behavior. Ethical behavior refers to actions that adhere to a person's ethical standards. Examples include respecting diversity, keeping proprietary information confidential, avoiding conflicts of interest, and avoiding participation in insider trading.

Section 22.2 Teams in the Workplace

LO 22.2-1 Discuss teams in the workplace.
A team consists of two or more people working together to achieve a common goal. In a functional team, each member has similar skills and qualifications. In a cross-functional team, the members have different skills.

LO 22.2-2 Describe skills required for team success.
Leadership, collaboration, and conflict resolution are some of the skills that contribute to a successful team. Leadership is the ability of a person to guide others to a goal. Collaboration is working with others to achieve a common goal. Conflict resolution is the process of recognizing and resolving disputes.

Check Your Marketing IQ

Now that you have completed the chapter, see what you have learned about marketing by taking the chapter posttest. The posttest is available at www.g-wlearning.com/marketing/.

Review Your Knowledge

1. Define *soft skills*.
2. Why do employers expect professionalism in their employees?
3. Cite examples of self-management skills.
4. Explain why procrastination should be avoided.
5. Name and describe the Mayo Clinic's four As of stress management.
6. List examples of ethical behaviors expected in the workplace.
7. Discuss teams in the workplace.
8. Describe skills required for team success.
9. Explain the difference between constructive criticism and destructive criticism.
10. Why is consensus building not the same as majority rules?

Apply Your Knowledge

1. Refer to the list of soft skills in Figure 22-1. List those soft skills in which you excel and explain why you excel in them.
2. Which one of the soft skills in Figure 22-1 is the most important to you? Make your own list of soft skills in the order of their importance. Explain the reasoning for your order.
3. Professionals take initiative in the workplace. Describe a time you took initiative in school or at work. What was your motivation for doing so?
4. Individuals with a positive attitude exhibit optimism, adaptability, and flexibility. How can each of these traits contribute to your interpersonal relationships?
5. Do you consider yourself to be organized? Why or why not? What can you do to improve your time-management skills?
6. Do you consider yourself to be a critical thinker? Why or why not?
7. Look at the list of stress-management techniques in Figure 22-4. Identify the ones you practice on a regular basis and the ones you need to improve.
8. Write a paragraph on your opinion of the role of teams in business when interacting with coworkers, supervisors, or employees.
9. Describe a time you acted as a leader in a team or a group.
10. Describe a conflict in which you were involved. Using the conflict-resolution model in Figure 22-7, make a list of actions that could have helped resolve the conflict.

Apply Your Math Skills

Often, managers must keep track of sales during a specific period of time. It is one step in determining if a business is making a profit. Apply your math skills to solve the following problems.

1. A sporting goods store had sales in the following departments during the month of March. Calculate the total sales for the month.
   - sporting equipment: $5,280
   - footwear: $3,260
   - apparel: $4,752
   - accessories: $283
   - fan shop: $6,770
   - clearance: $1,298.
2. Expenses for the sporting goods store totaled $19,678. Did the store show a profit or loss for the month of March? How much was the profit or loss?

Communication Skills

Reading *Scanning* is done when you know the information you need is in a document, you just have to find it. Scan this chapter for the Employability Skills feature. Did scanning work for you? How long did it take you to find it?

Writing It is important to have a positive attitude in the workplace when interacting with customers, coworkers, or supervisors. Create a list of ways a person can maintain a positive attitude in the workplace with all individuals.

Speaking Learning to behave in a professional manner is important to success in a career. Share your opinions about professionalism by making an informal speech to your class. Emphasize what you think professionalism involves and how you and your classmate can start developing these behaviors while you are still a student.

Internet Research

Negotiation Skills Negotiation is a soft skill needed to build good relationships. Using the Internet, research the phrase *negotiation skills*. List strategies you think are important when negotiating with others. How do you think negotiation skills help build positive workplace relationships?

Respecting Diversity Conduct an Internet search for *respecting diversity*. Read the strategies presented in your findings for how diversity can be respected. List the behaviors described that you already employ. Note new behaviors you may need to adopt in order to respect diversity more fully.

Self-Management Skills Research the term *self-management skills* and compare your results with the self-management skills listed in this chapter (time management, problem solving, critical thinking, and stress management). List five self-management skills you think are important for the workplace and explain why they are needed. Evaluate your level of mastery of each of the skills you listed.

Teamwork

Working with a teammate, practice using the conflict-resolution model in Figure 22-7 for managing conflict. Create a scenario that includes a conflict arising between two or more students. Discuss with your team how each step of the conflict-resolution model could be applied to resolve the conflict in your team's scenario.

Portfolio Development

College and Career Readiness

Reference An important part of any portfolio is a list of references. A *reference* is a person who knows your skills, talents, or personal traits and is willing to recommend you. References will probably be someone from your network. These individuals can be someone for whom you worked or with whom you provided community service. Someone you know from your personal life, such as a youth group leader, can also be a reference. However, you should not list relatives as references. Consider which references can best recommend you for the position for which you are applying. Always get permission from the person before using his or her name as a reference.

1. Ask several people from your network if they are willing to serve as a reference for you.
2. Create a Microsoft Word document with the names and contact information for your references. Use the heading "References" and your name. Save the document.
3. Update your master spreadsheet.

CHAPTER 23
Communication in the Workplace

Sections

23.1 **Communication Basics**
23.2 **Communication Skills**

Reading Prep

College and Career Readiness

Before you begin reading this chapter, preview the section heads and vocabulary lists. Make a list of questions that you have before reading. Search for answers to your questions as you continue reading the chapter.

Check Your Marketing IQ

Before you begin the chapter, see what you already know about marketing by taking the chapter pretest. The pretest is available at www.g-wlearning.com/marketing/.

DECA Emerging Leaders

Marketing Management Team Decision-Making Event, Part 2

Career Cluster: Marketing
Instructional Area: Selling

Procedure, Part 2

1. In the previous chapter, you studied the performance indicators for this event.
2. The event will be presented to you through your reading of the Knowledge and Skills Developed, Specific Performance Indicators, and Case Study Situation. You will have up to 30 minutes to review this information and prepare your presentation. You may make notes to use during your presentation.
3. You will have up to ten minutes to make your presentation to the judge followed by up to five minutes to answer the judge's questions. You may have more than one judge. All members of the team must participate in the presentation, as well as answer the questions.
4. Turn in all your notes and event materials when you have completed the event.

Case Study Situation

You are to assume the role of the marketing team for Dress to Impress, a large nonprofit organization that supports underprivileged teenagers. The **executive director (judge)** of Dress to Impress has called on your team to describe a sales and marketing strategy to overcome recent negative publicity.

The primary goal of Dress to Impress is to minimize the economic challenges encountered by teens. Each summer, Dress to Impress holds a month-long campaign in over 500 communities throughout the United States and Canada. The international campaign asks community members to donate new articles of clothing for teenage youth and bring them to the local drop-off location. At the end of the month-long campaign, Dress to Impress is able to award thousands of brand-new clothing to underprivileged teenagers in the community, just in time for fall. Dress to Impress is recognized as the best youth charity in North America. Dress to Impress has full-time staff located at the organization's headquarters and hires temporary workers in each Dress to Impress community to work during the month-long campaign. Dress to Impress has several corporate partners that help promote the campaign and donate funds and clothing for the event.

Dress to Impress has recently encountered negative publicity. A Dress to Impress temporary worker in a mid-sized city was arrested on theft charges after being caught with stolen goods. The temporary worker had 20 brand-new clothing items, meant for donation, for sale on an Internet auction site. Upon further investigation, the temporary worker had already sold close to 50 articles of clothing meant for the charity. While this is a local occurrence, it has put the entire Dress to Impress organization in the spotlight. People across North America are now leery of donating clothing for fear they will not end up with the intended recipients.

The executive director (judge) of Dress to Impress wants a marketing strategy to prevent negative publicity when conducting organizational campaigns. Your team must describe special procedures you will offer to prevent negative publicity when conducting organizational campaigns. Your team must describe the types of communication that will be the most effective for assuring donors their efforts are not in vain.

You will present your marketing strategy to the executive director (judge) of Dress to Impress in a meeting to take place in the executive director's (judge's) office. The executive director (judge) of Dress to Impress will begin the meeting by greeting you and asking to hear your ideas. After you have presented your information about a marketing strategy to prevent negative publicity when conducting organizational campaigns, the executive director (judge) of Dress to Impress will conclude the meeting by thanking you for your work.

Critical Thinking

1. Which promotion activities are identified in the case study?
2. Which promotion activities focus on the company?
3. When is it appropriate to use items donated for charity as personal profit?
4. Provide recommendations with supportive rationale on how Dress to Impress should respond to this incident.

Visit www.deca.org for more information.

Published by DECA Inc. Copyright © by DECA Inc. No part of this publication may be reproduced for resale without written permission from the publisher. Printed in the United States of America.

Section 23.1

Communication Basics

Essential Question
How does the *way* in which a person communicates affect *what* is communicated?

Learning Objectives

LO 23.1-1 Define *communication*.
LO 23.1-2 Identify types of communication.
LO 23.1-3 Describe barriers to effective communication.
LO 23.1-4 Explain communication ethics.

Key Terms

communication process
channel
feedback
interpersonal communication
small-group communication
public communication
Standard English
jargon
barrier
intercultural communication

Communication (LO 23.1-1)

Communication is the sending and receiving of messages that convey information, ideas, feelings, and beliefs. Communication skills affect a person's ability to understand others, establish positive relationships, and perform in most situations. Communication is a soft skill that is essential to career success.

The **communication process** is a series of actions on the part of the sender and the receiver of the message and the path the message follows. The six elements of the communication process are sender, message, channel, receiver, translation, and feedback, as shown in Figure 23-1.

- The person who has a message to communicate is called the *sender*.
- The sender creates the *message*, which is the information to be conveyed. *Encoding* is the process of turning the idea for a message into symbols that can be communicated.
- The **channel** is how the message is transmitted, such as face-to-face conversation, telephone, text, or another method that is appropriate for the situation.
- The *receiver* is the person who reads, hears, or sees the message.

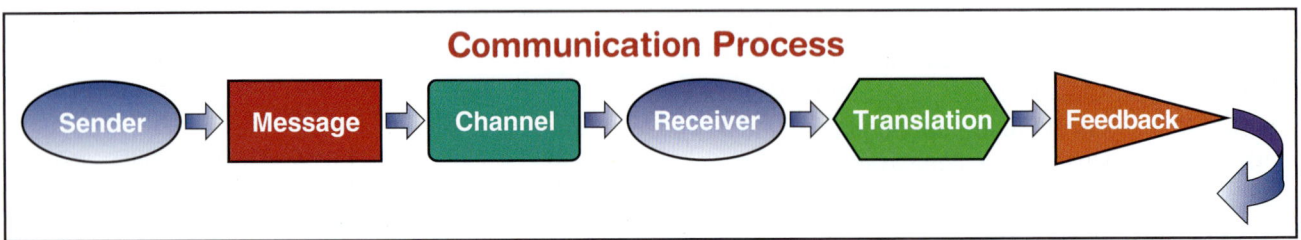

Communication Process

Sender → Message → Channel → Receiver → Translation → Feedback

Goodheart-Willcox Publisher

Figure 23-1 The communication process is a series of actions on the part of the sender and the receiver of the message and the path the message follows.

424 Copyright Goodheart-Willcox Co., Inc.

- Once the message is received, it is decoded. *Decoding* is the translation of a message into terms that the receiver can understand.
- **Feedback** is the receiver's response to the sender and concludes the communication process.

The communication process can occur with any number of people, from one coworker to the thousands of people who see a television commercial. **Interpersonal communication** is communication that occurs between the sender and one other person. When communication takes place with a *peer*, or someone of the same standing or rank, it is called *peer-to-peer communication*. Peer-to-peer communication is often informal and progresses naturally.

Small-group communication is communication that occurs with three to 20 people. **Public communication** is communicating with a group larger than 20 people. Public communication may also be referred to as *large-group communication*.

In contrast to peer-to-peer communication, small-group and public communication is generally presentation-style communication. *Presentation-style communication* requires preparation and practice. The speaker must plan what is going to be said and often has a specific outcome of the conversation in mind.

All communication has a purpose. When people communicate, there is a specific reason for doing so. This reason will usually fall into one of these categories.

- *Inform*. A message that informs provides information or education.
- *Persuade*. A message that persuades attempts to change the behavior of the receiver.
- *Instruct*. A message that instructs others attempts to provide direction or guidance.
- *Make a request*. A message that makes a request asks a question or for an action to occur.
- *Respond to a request*. Alternatively to making a request, there will be times you must respond to a request that has been made of you.

LO 23.1-2 Types of Communication

Communication is generally classified as four different types. It includes written, visual, verbal, and nonverbal communication.

Written Communication

Written communication is recording words through writing to communicate. It takes many forms and can have an impact on the reputation of a business. Business communication represents you as a professional as well as the company.

Business writing requires the use of Standard English. **Standard English** refers to English language usage that follows accepted rules for spelling, grammar, and punctuation. Words are the tools of all written communication. How well these tools are used affects the success of the message.

Business writing may require the use of jargon in order to communicate effectively with an audience. **Jargon** is language specific to a line of work or area of expertise. Some industries have specific words and phrases familiar to their customers. For example, stockbrokers talk about bull and bear markets. These would be appropriate words to use in a message that is going to professionals in the investment field.

When someone sends a message, language is selected and sentences are constructed in a way that will achieve a specific purpose. The form that the message will take is also chosen. Communication could be a promotional piece to send to customers or a letter sent to a supplier. In some organizations, text-messaging is an approved form of written communication. If texting is used for business purposes, Standard English should be

a katz/Shutterstock.com

Public communication is communicating with a group larger than 20 people. *Describe soft skills you think are important when engaging in public communication.*

Case in Point

Fisher-Price

Marketers focus on the importance of communication and the success of a business. Clear, concise, accurate product information is important for each piece of communication that reaches the customer. However, information sent out is not always good news. For example, product recalls can damage the reputation that marketers work so hard to build. In addition, product recalls can be time-consuming.

In 2016, Fisher-Price issued a voluntary recall of three models of its Cradle 'n Swing™ due to the risk of infant injuries. The company received two reports of a peg coming out of the infant swing seat, which caused the seat to fall. While no injuries were reported, the potential was too great. The marketers posted recall information on social media. The Fisher-Price website also keeps an updated webpage dedicated to *Recalls & Safety Alerts* where all product recall information is listed.

Companies are socially and legally responsible for communicating information about products that have been placed on the Consumer Product Safety Commission (CPSC) Recall List by the US government. All marketing efforts should consider the best interests of customers and follow consumer-protection laws.

---

used. Slang and abbreviations typically used for social correspondence should be avoided.

Visual Communication

Visual communication is using visual aids or graphics to communicate an idea or concept. It may or may not accompany written communication. Visuals add clarity, understanding, and interest to attract and maintain the attention of the audience. Visual communication is an important part of a marketing message.

Verbal Communication

Verbal communication is speaking words to communicate. In the course of a workday, most people spend some portion of their time talking with coworkers, supervisors, managers, or customers. This communication involves a variety of situations, such as conversations about work tasks, asking and answering questions, giving information, and participating in meetings. *Verbal skills* enable a person to communicate effectively using spoken words. They are also known as *speaking skills*.

Nonverbal Communication

Nonverbal communication is the actions, as opposed to words, that send messages. When you speak, nonverbal messages are sent through gestures, facial expressions, posture, and other actions. Individuals representing a business must be very aware of what their nonverbal communications are telling receivers. If the message is positive, but the tone or mannerisms are negative, the entire message may be lost.

Nonverbal skills enable a person to communicate effectively using body language, eye contact, touch, personal space, behavior, and attitude. Nonverbal skills can be used to send messages. *Body language* is nonverbal communication through facial expressions, gestures, body movements, and posture. Facial expressions include smiles, frowns, raised eyebrows, and eye contact. *Eye contact* occurs when two people look directly into each other's eyes. Gestures include

michaeljung/Shutterstock.com

Body language includes facial expressions, gestures, body movements, and posture. *How might body language impact a message?*

handshakes, waving, pointing, or a shoulder shrug. Body movements include trembling, stepping closer, and turning around. Posture includes standing straight, leaning back in a chair, and slouching.

LO 23.1-3 Barriers to Effective Communication

A **barrier** is anything that prevents clear, effective communication. Another word for a barrier is an *obstacle*. They may occur with all types of communication. Barriers can arise from many situations in the workplace. The *situation*, or setting, is all the facts, conditions, and events that affect the message.

It is important not to let diversity be the cause of communication issues. Special training may be required for employees to learn how to communicate in a diverse workplace. Employees may have to adjust their way of thinking and daily habits to work with a diverse population.

In order to understand and embrace diversity, culture must be understood. *Culture* is the shared beliefs, customs, practices, and social behavior of a particular group or nation. Culture influences how people respond to the communication and behavior of individuals and organizations. It affects how people think, work, and interact with others.

Intercultural communication is the process of sending and receiving messages between people of various cultures. Not understanding another person's culture may result in the misinterpretation of verbal and nonverbal communication. For example, in the United States, a topic is "tabled" if it is put off for another time. In contrast, the same phrase in Great Britain means to "bring it to the table" for discussion. Professional etiquette should always be applied in intercultural communication.

Sending Barriers

A *sending barrier* can occur when the sender says or does something that causes the receiver to stop listening. This can happen when the receiver simply does not understand what the sender is saying. The words used may not be clear to the receiver. Such misunderstandings cause problems ranging from minor events to serious, costly errors. Sending barriers for written and visual communication may include:

- using poor grammar or spelling;
- overlooking typographical and formatting errors;

Exploring Marketing Careers

Copywriter

Have you ever wondered how the people who do radio, television, or other live advertisements think of what to say? Actually, they rarely have to think about it. A company's image is too important to allow the people who make those commercials to say whatever pops into their heads. The job of a copywriter is to write the advertisements a company uses to promote its goods or services. A good copywriter presents the company's products in the best possible way, encourages people to buy them, and uses a "hook"—an angle or scenario that helps people remember the company. Other typical job titles for a copywriter include *account executive*, *advertising copywriter*, *advertising writer*, *advertising associate*, and *content writer*.

Some examples of tasks that copywriters perform include:
- Consult with experts in the company to learn about the product or service to be advertised
- Write advertising copy for use in written publications, broadcast media, or Internet media
- Present drafts to clients or company executives
- Edit copy based on feedback received from the company
- Work with the company's art department or director to develop visuals

Copywriters must have an excellent knowledge of the English language and must understand how to use language to persuade people to purchase products. They must have good communication skills to get information about the product or service and to present the information in an appealing way. They should also have a sound understanding of principles of sales and marketing. Most copywriting jobs require a bachelor degree. For more information, access the *Occupational Outlook Handbook* online.

- presenting visually unattractive text or inappropriate graphics;
- assuming too much or too little about what the receiver already knows; and
- using inappropriate language.

Nonverbal communication that causes barriers includes:
- distracting mannerisms;
- facial expressions that conflict with the words being said;
- inappropriate dress or demeanor;
- sarcastic or angry tone of voice; and
- speaking too softly or too loudly.

In these situations, the sender's written or verbal message may be lost or undermined by competing nonverbal messages. The sender who does not have a good grasp of the purpose for communicating is likely to relay a confused and ineffective message.

The sender has a responsibility to the receiver to make sure the message is clear and understood. The appropriate format for the message should be selected based on the situation, such as an e-mail or a phone call. The sender should not assume too much or too little about what the receiver already knows. Ask for feedback from the receiver to see if the message came across clearly.

For written documents, the rules of writing, grammar, and formatting documents should be followed. A well-written and properly formatted document will send a positive message. For face-to-face communication, positive body language and behavior should be maintained. Keep in mind that speaking loudly does not overcome communication barriers.

Receiving Barriers

A *receiving barrier* can occur when the receiver says or does something that causes the sender's message not to be received. These barriers can be just as harmful to the communication process as sending barriers. The receiver has a responsibility to give attention and respect to the sender. Most receiving barriers can be overcome with a little self-awareness.

The receiver of a message should give feedback to let the sender know the message was received. This can be done by asking questions or giving information if needed. The receiver should take responsibility for getting clarification if the message is not understood.

Monkey Business Images/Shutterstock.com

While *hearing* is physical ability, *listening* is a conscious action. *How does listening to messages affect your understanding of them?*

While *hearing* is physical ability, *listening* is a conscious action. Although senders are responsible for sending clear messages, listeners should be ready to recognize unclear messages. A listener who is willing to accept responsibility for getting clarification will be a more effective communicator.

LO 23.1-4 Communication Ethics

Ethical communication is applying ethics to make sure all communication is honest and respectful. It is every employee's responsibility to be ethical in communication that represents an employer.

Many companies have a communication plan in place to identify how ethical communication about the company is provided to the public. This communication plan provides an outline of the appropriate channels of communication for the company. It also includes an analysis of how communication for the company should occur. When creating messages that represent your organization, ask the following questions to analyze if the information is ethical.
- Has confidentiality been honored?
- Has the privacy of the company been protected?
- Is the information factual and honest?

- Has appropriate credit been given to contributors of the communication?
- Has copyrighted material been used appropriately?

This communication plan may be part of the company's code of ethics.

Carefully consider the impact company communication has on the public. It may be tempting for those writing messages or representing the business to get caught up in exaggerations or inaccurate claims about the company. The point of view presented should be honest. Marketing messages that persuade the reader to buy or respond to the message must be written according to laws.

Section 23.1 Review

Check Your Understanding

1. List the steps in the communication process.
2. Contrast peer-to-peer communication with presentation-style communication.
3. What is eye contact?
4. How do sending and receiving barriers occur?
5. What is ethical communication?

Build Your Vocabulary

As you progress through this text, develop a personal glossary of key terms. This will help you build your vocabulary and prepare you for a career. Write a definition for each of the following terms and add them to your personal glossary.

barrier
channel
communication process
feedback
intercultural communication

interpersonal communication
jargon
public communication
small-group communication
Standard English

Section 23.2

Communication Skills

Essential Question

Why is it important for a marketing manager to master basic communication skills?

Learning Objectives

LO 23.2-1 Explain how writing is used for marketing purposes.
LO 23.2-2 Identify common speaking situations in the workplace.
LO 23.2-3 Describe listening skills.
LO 23.2-4 Identify strategies for improving reading comprehension.

Key Terms

writing style
tone
memo
parliamentary procedure
motion
listening
active listening
passive listening
emotional intelligence
prejudice
active reading

Writing for Marketing Purposes

LO 23.2-1

Promotion is marketing communications, so it is required that marketing managers develop writing skills. Marketing managers write marketing plans, promotion pieces, and many other forms of communication in the course of a day. These communications represent the company. The ability to write clear, concise, and well-written messages is a necessary soft skill for marketing careers.

Promotions

Words carry most of the information in marketing communication. Imagine watching a television commercial without sound or seeing a print ad without any words. Very few images are strong enough to carry a marketing message without words. Those that can, such as the apple icon used by Apple, Inc., are strong in part due to the advertising words that have preceded them.

Marketers write copy for each element in the promotional mix. These promotions include advertising pieces, items for sales promotions, press releases, media kits, sales brochures, social media posts, and scripts for personal selling.

Developing messages for promotions is an important part of a marketing manager's responsibilities. Many decisions must be made when

Mladen Mitrinovic/Shutterstock.com

Developing promotional messages is part of a marketing manager's responsibilities. *How do you think the tone of a promotional message affects the way customers perceive it?*

430 Copyright Goodheart-Willcox Co., Inc.

developing a written message. **Writing style** is the way in which a writer uses language to convey an idea. The words chosen depend on the target market, purpose of the message, and desired response from the receivers.

Writing style is the most important tool in written communication because it creates the tone of the message. **Tone** is an impression of the overall content of the message. It can be friendly or hostile, courteous or demanding, sensitive or insensitive, as shown in Figure 23-2.

The personal pronoun *you* is often used in marketing pieces. This is known as using the "you" attitude. Statements such as, "we look forward to hearing from you," influence the reader to connect to the sender. The message sounds more personal, helpful, and friendly.

The quality of written communication can be improved through revising and editing. *Revising* is the process of rewriting paragraphs and sentences to improve organization and content. It also involves checking the structure of the document as a whole. Many writers need to go through several revisions of the first draft before achieving an acceptable final draft.

Editing is a more-refined form of revising. It is focused on sentence construction, wording, and clarity of ideas. Headings should be checked for consistency and adherence to style. Sentences must be checked for correct grammar, mechanics, spelling, and word usage.

Words are very powerful. Think of the effect of the word "SALE" posted in the window of a store. That one word will cause people to enter the store, look at merchandise, and possibly make a purchase.

A good way to begin writing is to use the journalistic approach. The *journalistic approach* to writing is asking *who, what, where, when, why,* and *how* questions. Answering these basic questions will help gather information. Journalists use the approach as a formula for getting a complete story.

- *Who is the target audience?* The audience is the person or group to whom the message is directed. Determine whether the individuals are internal or external to the organization.
- *What do you want to communicate?* Knowing what ideas to communicate helps focus the purpose of the message. The *scope* is the guideline of how much information will be included. When you want the reader to do something in response to the message, be specific about the expectations.
- *Where is the information?* The topic dictates where to look for source material. Be prepared to track down what is needed in a timely manner so that you can write a message with substance while meeting the deadline.
- *When is the deadline?* Deadlines will be established in the promotional plan. Missing deadlines can cost the company revenue.
- *Why are you writing?* Recall that the goals of promotions are to inform, persuade, and remind. It is important to identify the primary purpose of the message before you begin writing. A clear and concise message will help the receiver understand what is expected as a response or feedback.
- *How should the information be organized?* Decide on the order in which the information will be presented.

Employability Skills

Listening

Listening requires discipline. Companies lose millions of dollars every year because employees are not listening to what is being said by customers, managers, or peers. Paying attention is important in the workplace. Not learning how to listen effectively can cost you your job.

Reports

A *report* is a longer discussion of a topic presented in a structured format. Reports often include references to research. The marketing plan is an example of a report. Reports are often written

Tone in Writing

Example	Tone
We look forward to your response to our inquiry.	Friendly, courteous
You must respond immediately.	Hostile, demanding

Goodheart-Willcox Publisher

Figure 23-2 Tone can be friendly or hostile, demanding or courteous, sensitive or insensitive.

to present new ideas, propose solutions to problems, or summarize work completed.

The specific format and length depends on the type of report, its purpose, and the receivers. Many departments submit reports at regular time intervals, such as weekly, monthly, or quarterly.

Business Correspondence

All professionals write a variety of correspondence that represents the business. Common forms of correspondence include letters, e-mail, and memos.

Letters

Letters are messages printed on stationery and should conform to workplace communication standards. Standard business communication is often printed on letterhead. *Letterhead stationery* is high-quality paper that includes preprinted information about an organization such as its name, address, contact information, and logo. A sample business letter is shown in Figure 23-3. The standard business letter has eight parts:

- date: date the letter was written;
- inside address: name, title, and address of the receiver;
- salutation: greeting;
- body: message;
- complimentary close: closing lines;
- signature block: name and title of sender;
- notation: may indicate initials of the person who keyed the letter, if other than the writer; and
- enclosure notation: to note additional information is included.

E-mail

E-mail often takes the place of letters and routine telephone conversations with both

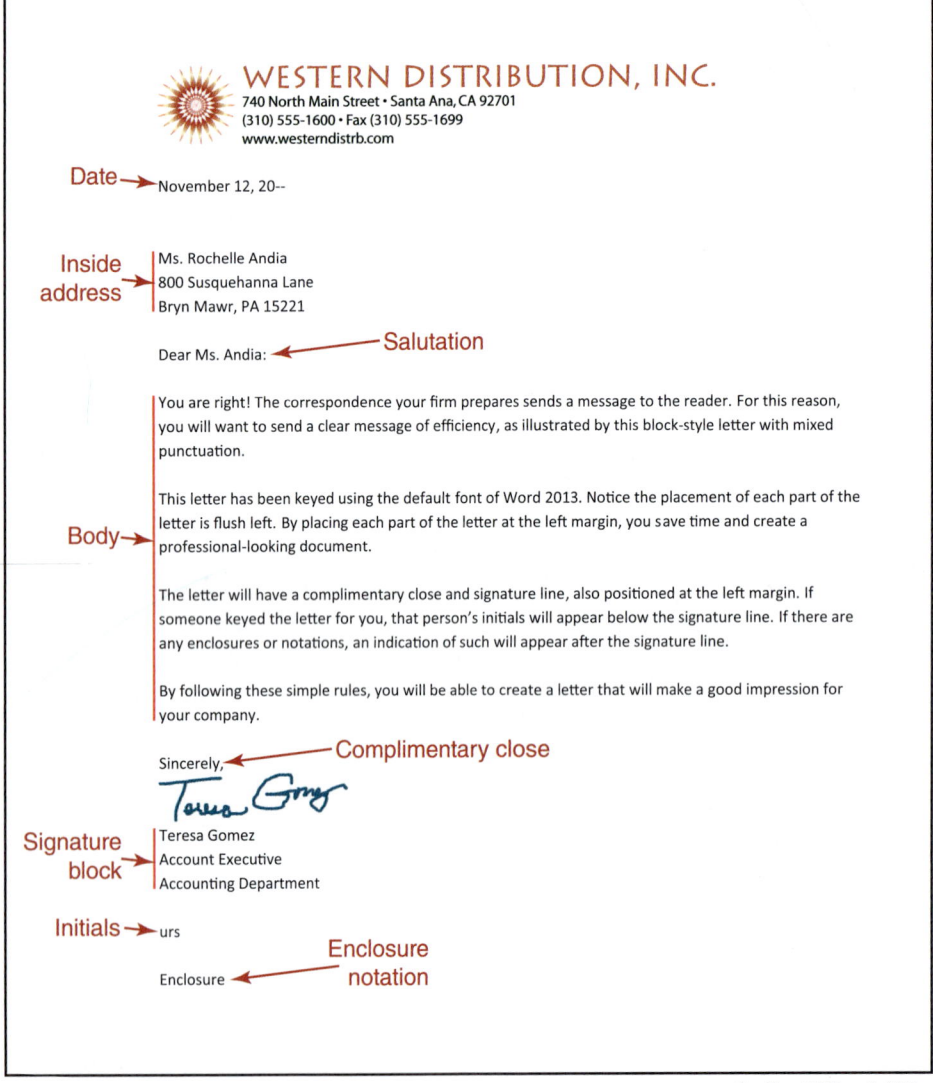

Figure 23-3 This is a sample of a business letter.

coworkers and customers. However, when sent in place of a letter, an e-mail is usually more informal in tone. Most professionals address each other by first name in e-mail correspondence. Some companies adopt a style of addressing customers by first name as well. The standard parts of an e-mail include:

- to: name of recipients from whom you want a response or who have a primary interest in the topic;
- copy *or* cc: names of those who are receiving the information as secondary recipients; a reply is not normally expected from those who are copied;
- blind copy *or* bcc: names of those who are receiving the information without the primary recipients' knowledge; for an e-mail sent to a large number of people outside of an organization, it is courteous to use the blind copy function to ensure the e-mail addresses of the recipients remain private;
- subject: the topic of the e-mail clearly and concisely stated;
- attachments: indicates whether any files were sent as attachments to the recipients;
- salutation: greeting;
- body: message;
- complimentary close: closing lines; and
- signature block: name and title of sender;

E-mail programs automatically supply certain information when an e-mail is sent, including the sender's name and e-mail address and the date the e-mail was sent. Figure 23-4 shows an example of an appropriately formatted e-mail.

The subject line of an e-mail is critical. E-mail etiquette suggests the company name appear in the subject line if the e-mail is being sent to a customer. It is important to know some words trigger filters that automatically send e-mails with those words to spam folders. Words like *free, act now, offer,* or *credit* will almost always trigger spam filters.

Keep the e-mail message short and to the point. When a customer opens an e-mail, it should take no more than 15–20 seconds to understand it. Avoid too many graphics or other elements that may cause the e-mail to open slowly.

When corresponding via e-mail, it is important to include a complimentary close, just as in a printed letter. Communication sent via e-mail

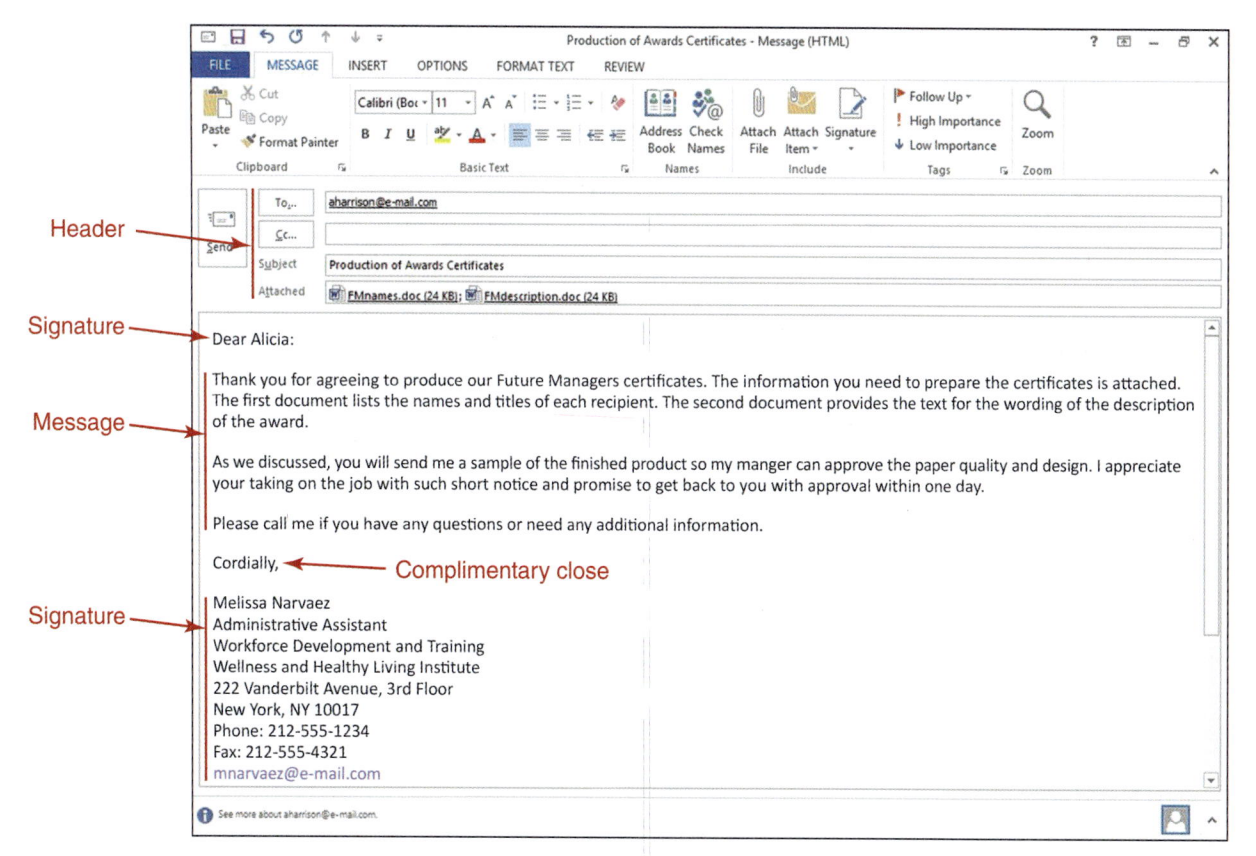

Goodheart-Willcox Publisher

Figure 23-4 This sample e-mail is formatted appropriately.

should always be professional and appropriate for the workplace. A courteous thank-you at the end of the message is usually appropriate. It is standard to include your full name and contact information at the bottom of the e-mail for the convenience of the reader.

Memos

A **memo** is a brief message sent to someone within an organization. A memo usually deals with only one topic or issue. The term "memo" is short for "memorandum." Memos usually have a standard format, shown in Figure 23-5. "Memo" or "memorandum" appears at the top of the page. The parts of a memo include:
- to: person or persons who will receive the memo;
- from: sender name;
- date: date the memo was written;
- subject: brief description of the topic;
- body: the message; and
- notations: indicate specifics to the reader, such as who was copied on the memo, and if there are any attachments.

Speaking
(LO 23.2-2)

Verbal communication is speaking words to communicate. Marketing professionals are expected to have speaking skills. *Tone of speech* refers to the feeling conveyed to the receiver from the way words are spoken. Tone can vary from warm to cold, friendly to hostile, humorous to serious, casual to professional, formal to informal. Words carry with them emotional value. Both the words and the tone chosen should convey the message and emotion you want.

Telephone Calls

Appropriate telephone skills are important to master for effective communication. Knowing techniques for making introductions and learning how to lead a meeting are also essential in the professional world.

The telephone, including landlines and cell phones, is one of the major vehicles of communication at work. Marketing employees will commonly need to make telephone calls for a variety of reasons. Telephone skills are essential for success in marketing. When making and receiving calls, *telephone etiquette*, which is using good manners on the telephone, is important. Telephone etiquette includes the following.
- Return phone calls promptly.
- Smile when answering the phone because it makes the voice sound more pleasant.
- Speak clearly and in a normal tone of voice; avoid using a speaker phone when others are present.
- Use the greeting specified by the company.
- When making a call, plan the message in advance.
- Have paper and a pen available for taking notes.

Telephone etiquette should be applied during every phone call, including conference calls and unsolicited calls. A *conference call* is when a person speaks on the telephone with two or more

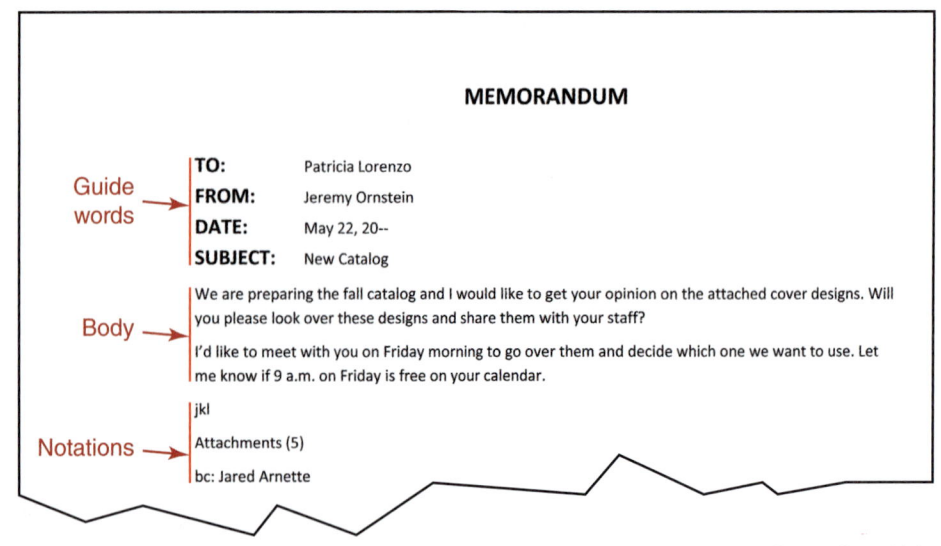

Figure 23-5 This sample memo is properly formatted.

MEMORANDUM

Guide words →
TO: Patricia Lorenzo
FROM: Jeremy Ornstein
DATE: May 22, 20--
SUBJECT: New Catalog

Body →
We are preparing the fall catalog and I would like to get your opinion on the attached cover designs. Will you please look over these designs and share them with your staff?
I'd like to meet with you on Friday morning to go over them and decide which one we want to use. Let me know if 9 a.m. on Friday is free on your calendar.

Notations →
jkl
Attachments (5)
bc: Jared Arnette

Goodheart-Willcox Publisher

additional people. An *unsolicited call* is one that is unexpected.

A *voice mail greeting* is necessary for times when the phone cannot be answered. The greeting should include your name, your company, and a specific message to tell the caller a return call can be expected.

Placing a Telephone Call

Making telephone calls for business purposes is a common task for most employees. Any time there are a number of issues to discuss, questions to ask, or items of information to provide, develop a list ahead of time. The goal is to be friendly and achieve the purpose in an efficient amount of time. Guidelines for making telephone calls are shown in Figure 23-6.

Leaving a Voice Mail Message

Voice mail is an important part of professional communication. Before making a call, think about what to say if a voice mail message must be left. If you want the call returned, specify a time you will be available. Speak slowly and pronounce each word clearly. Give the phone number at the beginning of the message and again at the end. Say the numbers distinctly. When leaving your name, spell it in full. The guidelines in Figure 23-7 will help you prepare to leave a voice mail message.

Making Telephone Calls

- Prepare notes to use for the call.
- If the call will be lengthy, make an appointment in advance.
- When the telephone is answered, state your name, job title, and company.
- Speak clearly and in a normal tone of voice.
- Avoid using the speakerphone feature unless other people are in the room with you.
- At the end of the call, summarize any important points or decisions.
- If follow-up action is required, summarize what each person will do and when.
- Thank the person you called for his or her time, information, or assistance.

Goodheart-Willcox Publisher

Figure 23-6 Follow these guidelines when placing telephone calls.

Leaving Voice Mail Messages

- Speak clearly and at a pace that can be easily understood.
- State your name, company, your position or department, and your telephone number.
- If your name is unfamiliar or difficult to understand, clearly spell it.
- Leave a brief message stating the purpose of the call and when you will be available to receive a return call.
- If your call is urgent, say when you need a response.

Goodheart-Willcox Publisher

Figure 23-7 These are guidelines for leaving voice mail messages.

Receiving Telephone Calls

Employees receive calls from colleagues and customers. The telephone should be answered on the first or second ring. Identify yourself when you answer stating your name and your company.

Making Introductions

An *introduction* is making a person known to someone else by sharing the person's name and other relevant information. Introductions are often made the first time people meet one another, such as at business events or when someone new is hired.

Common reasons for making introductions include introducing yourself, introducing others, and introducing speakers. Coworkers, managers, and customers may need to be introduced to each other or to other people in the company. On occasion, a formal introduction may be required when a person is a speaker at an event. Occasions such as these may require the person making the introduction to appear on stage and use a microphone. An introduction can contribute to whether a person makes a positive first impression on others.

Introducing Yourself

In the workplace, you will need to introduce yourself to new people. Introducing yourself exhibits friendliness and confidence. A firm handshake is customary when meeting people for the first time. Make eye contact and leave an appropriate amount of personal space between yourself and the other person. Tell the person your full name and your role in the company. For example, a person might introduce herself by saying, "Hello, my name is Madison Gomez. I am the marketing manager."

When the other party gives his or her name, repeat the person's name as you greet him or her. Using a title like "Mr." or "Ms." may be appropriate. "It is great to meet you, Mr. Alexander," is a polite way to respond when being introduced to someone. Saying a person's name after being introduced will help you remember it.

When you approach someone whom you may have met before but do not know well, introduce yourself again. This saves embarrassment for all parties if names have been forgotten. Doing so puts everyone at ease and shows professionalism.

Introducing Others

When introducing two people to each other, say each person's full name clearly. Introduce the lower-ranking person to the higher-ranking person first. For example, when introducing a new employee to an executive, say, "Tyler, this is Ms. Anita Ogawa, vice president. Anita, this is Tyler Lombard. Tyler is our new marketing associate." Try to offer more information to help the two people easily make conversation. For example, say, "Clark Morgan, I would like to introduce you to Olivia Price. Olivia is a set designer for the local theater. She has a great idea about how we can improve our merchandise displays."

Introducing Speakers

Many individuals become nervous when called on a stage to make introductions using a microphone. The person making the introduction should remain calm, project his or her voice, and show enthusiasm.

If you are introducing yourself, give a brief background of who you are and why you are making a presentation. Keep it short and interesting. Do not use the time as a bragging session.

If you are introducing another person as a speaker, request information in advance. Be specific with what you would like to convey to the audience. For example, say what city the person is from or where he or she went to college. Select information from the speaker's notes that will complement the presentation to be made. Write the information down so it is not forgotten on stage.

Leading a Meeting

Meetings are a fact of life in the business world. Meetings are also important in government and civic organizations. If you are a member of student government, a club, or a CTSO, you have probably attended meetings. The general purpose of meetings is to make decisions or solve problems. A meeting is required when more than one person is needed to make a decision or solve a problem. Business meetings can take place in person or virtually, such as with a video conferencing service.

Many meetings in the workplace are informal. During an *informal meeting*, a group of workers may discuss a problem or coordinate their work. For example, some teams have weekly meetings. At these meetings, each person reports on the work that he or she has done during the preceding week. Any problems or projects that need input from other team members are discussed.

Sometimes, meetings are formal. *Formal meetings* are usually run according to parliamentary procedure. **Parliamentary procedure** is a process for conducting a meeting so that the meeting is orderly and democratic. Parliamentary procedure is based on the guidelines in *Robert's Rules of Order*. The central process of parliamentary procedure is proposing, discussing, and voting on motions. A **motion** is a recommendation for action to be taken by the group. Parliamentary procedure aids in facilitating discussions during meetings and closing them when they end.

Monkey Business Images/Shutterstock.com

A meeting is required when more than one person is needed to make a decision or solve a problem. *Describe speaking skills that a person may need to use when leading a meeting.*

Formal meetings require an agenda and someone to lead the meeting. An *agenda* is the list of topics to be discussed, decisions to be made, or other goals for a meeting.

Occasionally, meetings may require the use of visual aids. A slide presentation is an example of a visual aid that is commonly used in meetings. Visual aids can be used to emphasize key points during a meeting.

LO 23.2-3 Listening

Hearing is a physical process. **Listening** is an intellectual process that combines hearing with evaluation. *Listening skills* are the ability of an individual to not only hear what a person says, but also understand the message. Listening is required for all positive communication.

Effective listening is an active process, as shown in Figure 23-8. **Active listening** is fully participating as you process what a person says. It takes place when the listener is focused on what is being said. Active listeners usually give nonverbal or verbal feedback to the speaker. For example, when a listener smiles, nods, makes eye contact, or says, "I see," a speaker knows the message is received. Active listening is essential in business.

The opposite of active listening is passive listening. **Passive listening** is casually listening to someone talk. It takes place when the listener hears the message, but does not pay attention to what is being said. The passive listener lets the words wash over him or her without catching the meaning. A careless listener pays attention only to part of what is being said. This type of selective listening leads to misunderstandings or words being taken out of context. Narrow-minded listeners pay attention only to the messages that match their preconceived ideas. They ignore other messages. Defensive listeners hear a hostile or negative message in what is being said.

Professionals learn how to listen to customers and vendors and interpret the communication. Two important listening skills to learn are showing empathy and overcoming barriers to listening.

Show Empathy

Having *empathy* is understanding or being sensitive to the thoughts and feelings of others. People who are empathetic can see things from the point of view of another person. Empathy enables people to understand how someone is feeling, even when they do not have the same feelings. It is a key to effective listening.

For example, suppose a customer is angry because a product did not work as expected. An empathetic salesperson understands the anger of a customer, even though the salesperson is not angry. The effective salesperson lets the customer know that he or she empathizes with the situation. The salesperson may nod and say, "I can see why you are so angry," or similar words. This small act of understanding helps the customer to know he or she is heard and will receive help.

A person's **emotional intelligence** is his or her ability to perceive emotions in one's self and in others and use this information to guide behavior. Having empathy for others is an important component of emotional intelligence.

Barriers to Listening

When a receiver says or does something that causes a message to not be received as intended, a receiving barrier occurs. There are many receiving barriers that interfere with listening and keep

Becoming an Active Listener
- Think about the purpose of a presentation before, during, and after it.
- Evaluate what you hear by relating the information to what you already know, or your prior knowledge.
- Take notes when necessary.
- If possible, make eye contact with the speaker to show attention.
- Ask relevant questions and make comments when appropriate.
- At formal presentations, sit close to the speaker, such as in the front of the room.
- Fight distractions; never engage in texting or answering a phone call when listening to another person.
- Concentrate on the speaker.

Goodheart-Willcox Publisher

Figure 23-8 Active listening is fully participating as you process what a person says.

receivers from understanding spoken messages. Interruptions, assumptions, prejudice, and planning a response are some forms of interference that may occur at work.

Interruptions

Interruptions can come from anyone during a conversation. They may come from an outside source or from either participant. When they happen, it is likely that both the listener and the speaker will lose their trains of thought.

Assumptions

Sometimes, people assume they know what a speaker will say. As a result, they do not pay attention to what the speaker actually says. When not paying close attention, listeners can miss part or all of a message. For this reason, assumptions can be a problem in the communication process. For example, it is possible that someone has changed his or her viewpoint since your last conversation.

Prejudice

Prejudice is an opinion that is formed without sufficient knowledge. It often appears as a feeling of like or dislike for someone, especially when the feeling is not reasonable or logical. For a variety of reasons, a listener may be prejudiced for or against a speaker. Prejudice interferes with the communication process because it generally means an opinion was formed before the communication

ESB Basic/Shutterstock.com

When listening, focus on the speaker, listen carefully, and then plan your response after he or she finishes. *How have receiving barriers affected you?*

was over. It is a good idea to work on keeping an open mind while listening to any speaker, especially customers. Be able to defend your ideas objectively and without prejudice.

Planning a Response

Many people find themselves planning a response while the speaker is still speaking. When this happens, the mind is taken away from the speaker. Several of his or her points are likely to be missed. When listening, focus on the speaker and plan your response after he or she finishes. For example, salespeople may lose sales if they are too busy planning their responses instead of listening to customer needs.

LO 23.2-4 Reading

Reading is one of the main ways to learn new information. An essential part of reading is comprehension. It is important to comprehend what is being read. **Active reading** is processing the words, phrases, and sentences you read. It is as important as active listening. Active reading takes place when the reader is thinking about what he or she is reading. Active reading is a learned skill that takes practice to perfect. The following strategies can help improve reading comprehension.

Marketing Ethics

Communication

Ethical communication is very important in both the business and personal life of marketers. Distorting information for your own gain is an unethical practice. Honesty, accuracy, and truthfulness should guide all communications. Ethically, communication must be presented in an unbiased manner. Facts should be given without distortion. If the information is an opinion, label it as such. Do not take credit for ideas that belong to someone else; always credit sources appropriately.

You Do the Math

Using a Calculator

Using a calculator enables you to apply math concepts as you learn financial responsibility. The calculator on your computer or smartphone will help increase your accuracy when used properly. The Math Skills Handbook at the end of this textbook illustrates proper calculator use.

Solve the following problems.
Balance a checking account that recorded the following activity since the last statement. How much is in the account?
- Deposits: $25 and $120
- Checks: $25.00, $8.50, and $98.00
- ATM withdrawals: $20
- Bank fee: $3 for using an ATM outside the bank's network
- Balance on the last statement: $250

Have a Purpose

It often helps to frame your purpose for reading as a question. Think about what question this particular material will answer for you. You will have better comprehension if you know why you are reading. For example, you may be reading a research document to learn why consumers view one product as better than another.

Skim, Scan, or Read for Detail

Skimming is quickly glancing over the entire document to identify the main ideas. Start by reading the headings and captions and looking at any pictures. People often skim when they have a limited amount of time to read a lot of material.

Scanning is moving the eyes quickly down the page to find specific words and phrases. Usually, scanning is done when the reader is looking for a certain topic. If more details are needed, read the material more carefully.

Reading for detail involves reading all of the words and phrases and considering their meanings. Reading for detail takes much longer than skimming or scanning.

Focus on the Words

Focusing on the words and their meanings helps to keep distracting thoughts out of your mind. Try to see in your mind's eye what the words are describing. Look up unfamiliar words in a dictionary.

Read for Meaning

As you read, make sure you understand what you are reading. Review the concepts in your mind. Take notes. If possible, highlight key concepts. Evaluate what you have read to make sure you understand the content.

Section 23.2 Review

Check Your Understanding

1. List examples of documents that marketing professionals may need to write.
2. What is tone of speech?
3. Name workplace situations in which speaking skills are important.
4. What is the difference between hearing and listening?
5. Why is active reading important?

Build Your Vocabulary

As you progress through this text, develop a personal glossary of key terms. This will help you build your vocabulary and prepare you for a career. Write a definition for each of the following terms and add them to your personal glossary.

active listening
active reading
emotional intelligence
listening
memo
motion
parliamentary procedure
passive listening
prejudice
tone
writing style

CHAPTER 23 Review and Assessment

Chapter Summary

Section 23.1 Communication Basics

LO 23.1-1 Define *communication*.
Communication is sending and receiving messages that convey information, ideas, feelings, and beliefs. The communication process is a series of actions on the part of the sender and the receiver of the message and the path the message follows. The six elements of the communication process are sender, message, channel, receiver, translation, and feedback.

LO 23.1-2 Identify types of communication.
Communication includes written, visual, verbal, and nonverbal communication. Written communication is recording words through writing to communicate. Visual communication is using visual aids or graphics to communicate an idea or concept. Verbal communication is speaking words to communicate. Nonverbal communication is the actions that send messages.

LO 23.1-3 Describe barriers to effective communication.
A barrier is anything that prevents clear, effective communication. Barriers may occur in all types of communication. A sending barrier can occur when the sender says or does something that causes the receiver to stop listening. A receiving barrier can occur when the receiver says or does something that causes the sender's message to not be received.

LO 23.1-4 Explain communication ethics.
Ethical communication is applying ethics to make sure all communication is honest and respectful. It is every employee's responsibility to maintain ethical behavior in communication that represents his or her employer.

Section 23.2 Communication Skills

LO 23.2-1 Explain how writing is used for marketing purposes.
Marketing managers write marketing plans, promotion pieces, and many other forms of communication in the course of a day. These communications represent the company. The ability to write clear, concise, and well-written messages is a necessary soft skill for marketing careers.

LO 23.2-2 Identify common speaking situations in the workplace.
Marketing professionals are expected to have verbal communication skills. Appropriate telephone skills are important to master effective communication. Knowing techniques for making introductions and learning how to lead a meeting are also essential in the professional world.

LO 23.2-3 Describe listening skills.
Listening is an intellectual process that combines hearing with evaluation. Listening skills are the ability of an individual to not only hear what a person says, but also understand the message. Listening is required for all positive communication. Active listening is fully participating as you process what a person says.

LO 23.2-4 Identify strategies for improving reading comprehension.
Reading is one of the main ways to learn new information. An essential part of reading is comprehension. Active reading is processing the words, phrases, and sentences you read. Having a purpose; skimming, scanning, or reading for detail; focusing on the words; and reading for meaning can all contribute to reading comprehension.

Check Your Marketing IQ

Now that you have completed the chapter, see what you have learned about marketing by taking the chapter posttest. The posttest is available at www.g-wlearning.com/marketing/.

Review Your Knowledge

1. Define *communication*.
2. Name and describe five purposes of communication.
3. Identify types of communication.
4. Describe barriers to effective communication.
5. Explain communication ethics.
6. Explain how writing is used for marketing purposes.
7. What is the journalistic approach to writing?
8. Identify common speaking situations in the workplace.
9. Describe listening skills.
10. Identify strategies for improving reading comprehension.

Apply Your Knowledge

1. Refer to the communication process as illustrated in Figure 23-1. Describe how each step could be applied in the following situations.
    A. Manager verbally directing an employee to stock shelves.
    B. Company president requesting a meeting with a manager via e-mail.
    C. Manager posting a memo on a bulletin board that explains new employee break policies.
    D. Employee placing a telephone call to a customer about a special order.
    E. Introducing yourself to your new supervisor.
2. Think about how you communicate with your friends. What communication skills do you use? Now think about the people with whom you have more formal relationships, such as instructors or coaches. How does your communication style differ with your friends compared to people who are your professional contacts?
3. Identifying appropriate channels of communication is an important skill. Sometimes it is also important that a record of communication is made. Other times, documenting information is not necessary. Identify which channel of communication should be used for the following situations (letter, formal e-mail, casual e-mail, text, memo, or phone call). Provide a reason for your answer.
    A. Asking a colleague where to find information about a company organizational chart.
    B. Confirming a meeting time for a presentation.
    C. Summary of minutes from a marketing meeting.
    D. Telling someone to meet you at the front door in five minutes.
    E. Forwarding product information to a client via e-mail.
4. Assume you are on the marketing team of medium-sized company. You have been asked give a short speech at a company meeting in which you attempt to persuade every employee, including your coworkers and supervisors, to complete a survey. Draft a short speech for this purpose and demonstrate your ability to speak effectively to coworkers and supervisors by delivering this speech using appropriate grammar and terminology.
5. Written communication requires the use of Standard English. Create a list of at least 20 words or phrases in texting language. For each, write the correct form in Standard English. Are any of these words or phrases appropriate in work texting? Why or why not?
6. Analyze your listening skills. Write a list of the things you do well when listening to someone. Write a list of the things you do while listening that may create receiving barriers. What did you learn from this exercise?

7. In an earlier unit, you selected a company for which you are creating a marketing plan. Assume you are a marketing manager planning to exhibit your company's products at a trade show in the local mall. Write a letter to the mall manager to convey your interest in exhibiting and obtain information about how to secure a spot.

8. The marketing team is sometimes responsible for creating the script that the company employees use when they answer the phone. Sometimes it is as simple as directing the person to state his or her name. Write the script that your company should use when answering the telephone that uses appropriate grammar and terminology.

9. Explain how a marketing professional could use empathy when listening to a customer complaint.

10. You have just hired a marketing coordinator for your team. Write a draft of a professional e-mail to this new coworker in which you explain the importance of mastering effective communication.

Apply Your Math Skills

A marketing manager decided to send six employees to a seminar presented by a nationally renowned expert on workplace communication. Apply your math skills to solve the following problems.

1. Expenses per person include the following. How much will the manager need to budget to send the six employees?
    - registration: $200
    - overnight hotel stay: $168
    - meal package: $150

2. The manager has already set aside $400 to cover the cost of mileage for each of these six employees. The number of miles round trip to the conference is 203 miles. Using the IRS mileage reimbursement rate of $0.535 per mile, calculate the total amount needed to reimburse all six employees for mileage. Was enough budgeted to cover the reimbursement? Why or why not?

Communication Skills

Reading Read about the purposes of communication described in Section 23.1. Recall the three goals of promotion described in Section 17.1: inform, persuade, remind. How do the purposes of personal communication relate to the goals of marketing promotion? Draw conclusions about the information.

Writing Record four important soft skills you learned about in this chapter. Write a paragraph for each one about how you can use this information to improve your personal communication skills as well as in communicating your message as a marketer.

Listening Empathetic listening occurs when you attempt to put yourself in the speaker's place and understand how he or she feels. How can you demonstrate empathetic listening when a classmate is asking for your opinion on a situation they are sharing with you?

Internet Research

Nonverbal Communication Nonverbal communication is necessary in the workplace. Conduct an Internet search for *nonverbal communication*. Cite five examples of situations in which nonverbal communication could influence a decision you make as a marketing professional.

Emotional Intelligence Managers who understand how other people feel can manage relationships effectively. Conduct a search for *evaluating emotional intelligence*. How would you evaluate your emotional intelligence?

Cultural Differences Research *respecting cultural differences in the workplace*. Select and read one or two articles from your search results. What advice is given? How might you implement this advice in a marketing career?

Annotation Techniques Using the Internet, research different ways to annotate, or make notes as you read. Which techniques are commonly used? Did you learn any new ones? Write a brief summary of the techniques you researched. Then, create a system for annotating works, such as color coding, a symbol system, or listing topics of importance.

Teamwork

With your teammates, describe a recent situation where each of you observed or created a sending barrier and a receiving barrier. Ask your teammates questions and listen to their feedback. Facilitate a discussion about what caused the barrier and what you could have done differently to avoid it. Respectfully close the discussion of each person's barrier before moving on to the next person.

Portfolio Development

College and Career Readiness

Letter of Recommendation

A letter of recommendation is a letter in which a person in your network assesses your qualities and abilities to perform in a specific capacity. It highlights your achievements in your academic or professional career and is usually written by an instructor, supervisor, or someone else who is familiar with your qualifications for a given job or application. The purpose of the letter is to advocate for you as a candidate for a position.

1. Ask someone in your network if they are willing to write you a letter of recommendation. Writing the letter can take time, so plan in advance.

2. If you receive a hard copy, scan the letter. If you receive an electronic file, save the file. Name the file appropriately and save in a folder or subfolder.

3. Place a hard copy of the letter in a container for future reference.

4. Update your master spreadsheet.

UNIT 8 Management

Building the Marketing Plan

Just like every function of business, marketing activities need to be managed properly to produce the desired results. Probably the biggest function of marketing management is to help the company increase sales, which will contribute to increased profits. Before a company can determine its sales goals, previous actual sales must be analyzed along with the current economic environment. This exercise also helps marketers identify which marketing strategies and tactics are best to achieve those goals.

Sales Analysis

Objectives
- Create a sales forecast for your business.
- Create a best-opportunities list for the sales and marketing team.

Directions

In this activity, you will complete the Sales Analysis section of the marketing plan. This section involves analyzing the previous-year actual sales and applying the sales goals to create a sales forecast for the upcoming year. A best-opportunities list will help the sales and marketing teams focus on where to spend the marketing budget effectively. Access the *Marketing Dynamics* companion website at www.g-wlearning.com/marketing/. Download the activity files as indicated in the following instructions.

1. **Unit Activity 8-1—Sales Forecast** Study the business plan for your company. Locate the previous-year sales figures and the sales goals for the business. Based on the information, determine the forecasted sales by product for the upcoming year.

2. **Unit Activity 8-2—Best Opportunities** Based on your knowledge of the target market, competition, and customer profile, determine the top-ten best sales opportunities for the company in the coming year.

3. Open your saved marketing plan document.

4. Locate the Sales Analysis section of the plan. Use the suggestions and questions listed to help you generate ideas. Delete the instructions and questions when you are finished recording your responses. Proofread your document and correct any errors in keyboarding, spelling, and grammar.

5. Save your document.

UNIT 9
Entrepreneurship

Chapters

24 **Entrepreneurship**
25 **Risk Management**
26 **Business Funding**

While studying, look for the activity icon for:
- Building the Marketing Plan activity files
- Pretests and posttests
- Vocabulary terms with e-flash cards and matching activities
- Self-assessment

These activities can be accessed at www.g-wlearning.com/marketing/.

Developing a Vision

You may already know that you want to start your own business someday. Your career plan may be to gain marketing and business experience first, then pursue your own dreams of starting a business. Real-world experience is a teacher that can prepare you to become an entrepreneur.

Entrepreneurs are people who have ideas, are creative, and figure out how to finance their ideas. They are risk-takers who learn how to manage risks. They are persistent and will not take no for an answer. Studying this unit may help you decide if becoming an entrepreneur is in your future.

Marketing Core Functions Covered in This Unit

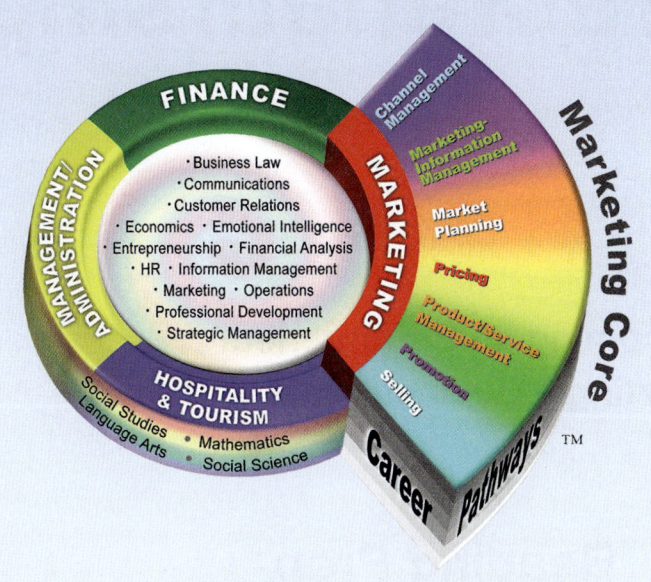

Functions of Marketing

- Marketing-information management
- Pricing
- Promotion
- Selling

Copyright MBA Research, Columbus, Ohio. Used with permission.

EYE-CATCHER

Marketing Matters

You are surrounded by marketing messages. Sometimes you may not even realize it. For example, the Petco mascot, Red Ruff, appears at functions to call attention to the efforts of Petco and its nonprofit organization, the Petco Foundation. As a socially responsible company, Petco and its nonprofit organization work together to promote and improve the welfare of pets. They support thousands of animal welfare groups around the United States, as well as host adoption events to find homes for pets in need. Communities around the country benefit from Petco's socially responsible marketing efforts. In turn, Petco benefits as a business by increasing awareness of its brand. Marketing does matter.

a katz/Shutterstock.com

CHAPTER 24

Entrepreneurship

Sections

24.1 **Becoming an Entrepreneur**

24.2 **Starting a Business**

Reading Prep

College and Career Readiness

Before reading this chapter, read the opening pages for this unit and review the chapter titles. These can help prepare you for the topics that will be presented in the unit. What does this tell you about what you will be learning?

Check Your Marketing IQ

Before you begin the chapter, see what you already know about marketing by taking the chapter pretest. The pretest is available at www.g-wlearning.com/marketing/.

◆DECA Emerging Leaders

Business Services Marketing Series Event, Part 1

Career Cluster: Marketing
Career Pathway: Marketing Management
Instructional Area: Product/Service Management

Knowledge and Skills Developed

- communication and collaboration
- creativity and innovation
- critical thinking and problem solving
- flexibility and adaptability
- information literacy
- initiative and self-direction
- leadership and responsibility
- productivity and accountability
- social and cross-cultural skills

Specific Performance Indicators

- Describe factors used by businesses to position corporate brands.
- Explain the nature of marketing management.
- Explain the impact of product life cycles on marketing decisions.
- Describe the use of technology in the product/service management function.
- Describe word-of-mouth channels used to communicate with targeted audiences.

Purpose

Designed for an individual DECA member, the event measures the member's proficiency in the knowledge, skills, and attitudes in the business administration core and appropriate career cluster and pathway of a given career in a role-play. This event consists of a 100-question, multiple-choice, cluster exam and two role-play activities in a written scenario.

Participants are not informed in advance of the performance indicators to be evaluated. For the purpose of this text, sample performance indicators are given so that you may practice for the competition. You will be presented with the material for this event in two parts. Part 1 presents the knowledge and skills assessed and an overview of the event's purpose and procedures. Part 2 presents the remaining procedures and the event situation.

Procedure, Part 1

1. For Part 1 in this text, read both Knowledge and Skills Developed and Specific Performance Indicators. Discuss these with your team members.
2. If there are any questions, ask your instructor to clarify.

Critical Thinking

1. Based on the performance indicators, what functions and tasks might be involved in the situation?
2. For each specific performance indicator, provide responses.
3. Explain the relationship between the Knowledge and Skills Developed and Specific Performance Indicators.

Visit www.deca.org for more information.

Published by DECA Inc. Copyright © by DECA Inc. No part of this publication may be reproduced for resale without written permission from the publisher. Printed in the United States of America.

Section 24.1

Becoming an Entrepreneur

Essential Question

What are common elements of success in entrepreneurship?

Learning Objectives

LO 24.1-1 Explain what it means to be an entrepreneur.
LO 24.1-2 Identify examples of traits and skills necessary to become an entrepreneur.
LO 24.1-3 List and explain ownership options for starting a business.

Key Terms

- entrepreneur
- self-assessment
- hard skills
- liability
- DBA license
- unlimited liability
- partnership agreement
- general partnership
- limited partnership (LP)
- limited liability
- stock
- stockholders
- corporate formalities

Entrepreneurs

LO 24.1-1

Have you ever had the goal of owning your own business and being your own boss? Are you creative? Do you have an idea about a product or service that could make money? Recall that *entrepreneurship* is the willingness and ability to start a new business. An **entrepreneur** is a person who starts a new business.

Small businesses are the backbone of the US economy. While each individual business may be small, the impact on the overall economy is significant. According to the Small Business Administration (SBA), there are 28 million small businesses operating in the United States. These businesses account for over half of all sales in the United States.

Entrepreneurs continue to be more important than ever. Carl Schramm, former president and CEO of the Kauffman Foundation, said, "Americans in big numbers are looking to entrepreneurs to rally the economy. More than 70 percent of voters say the health of the economy depends on the success of entrepreneurs. And a full 80 percent want to see the government use its resources to actively encourage entrepreneurship in America."

The reasons for starting a business are countless. Controlling your destiny is an exciting reason to be an entrepreneur. Other rewards include the following.

Monkey Business Images/Shutterstock.com

Small businesses are the backbone of the US economy. *How does your community benefit from small businesses?*

- *Being your own boss.* An entrepreneur can determine his or her own work schedule, set prices for products, and see the hard work pay off.
- *Taking advantage of your earning potential.* An entrepreneur does not depend on someone else for an income.
- *Enjoying your career.* As an entrepreneur, you can do something you truly like, are good at, and believe in; you can apply your creativity with no limits.
- *Making a difference in the world.* Most entrepreneurs do not start a business solely for the potential profit. They start a business because they are passionate about what they are doing.

Every new venture comes with risks. Generally, the higher the risk, the greater potential for both reward and loss. Being aware of the risks makes a person better prepared for a career as an entrepreneur. Risks of entrepreneurship can include the following.

- *Being responsible for the success or failure of the business.* An entrepreneur takes responsibility for both the good and bad decisions he or she might make. This can mean a successful business that makes money, or a failing business that loses money.
- *Working long hours.* An owner of a new business will probably work long days that can put stress on personal health and emotions as well as affect the family.
- *Risking personal finances.* Start-up costs and expenses may need to come from the entrepreneur's personal funds. New businesses often do not make a profit for several months to several years. This can mean the business owner may not make a regular income. It is important to be financially prepared because an uncertain income may be a hardship for an owner.

Many marketing professionals become entrepreneurs. Marketing exposes employees to business activities that other employees may never see. Marketers participate in business and market planning, interact with customers, and work with sales teams. These experiences mean that marketing professionals are also involved in the fundamental practices of business. Many marketers enjoy these activities and use those experiences to create their own businesses. Your marketing studies and experiences may lead you to becoming a business owner sometime in your future.

Traits and Skills of Successful Entrepreneurs

LO 24.1-2

There are many traits that entrepreneurs have in common. *Traits* are behavioral and emotional characteristics that make each person unique. *Personality traits* are qualities related to a person's mind or character. Personality traits include the *five Ps of entrepreneurship*: passion, perseverance, persistence, planning, and problem solving, as shown in Figure 24-1.

Entrepreneurs do not need to be at work 24 hours a day, 7 days a week. However, they do need to enjoy their work and have the ability to sell their products. It is important to evaluate your own personal traits as you consider starting a business. One way to evaluate this is by completing a self-assessment. **Self-assessment** is the process of an individual evaluating his or her aptitudes, abilities, values, interests, and personality. The goal is to use that personal information when making your career decisions. There are many self-assessment tools available from your counselors and on the Internet.

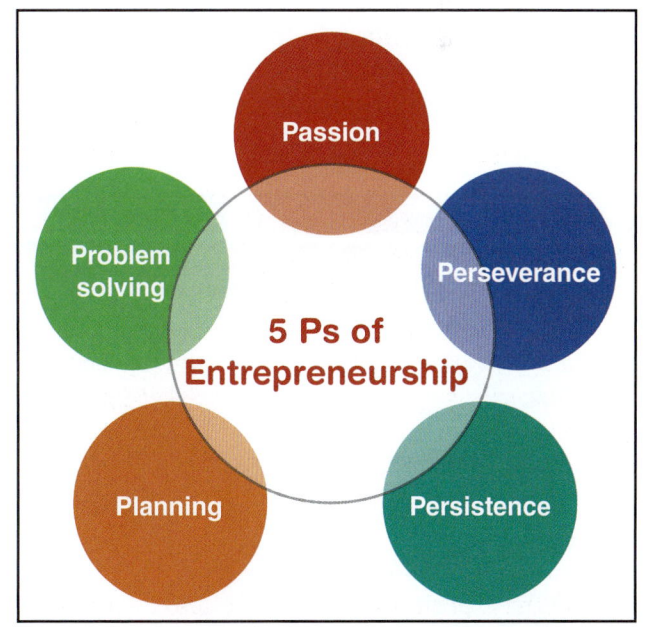

Goodheart-Willcox Publisher

Figure 24-1 The five Ps of entrepreneurship are passion, perseverance, persistence, planning, and problem solving.

Figure 24-2 lists effective entrepreneurship traits and skills, although there are many more. How many of the traits and skills do you possess?

Hard Skills

Hard skills are the critical skills necessary to perform the required work-related tasks of a position. They are also known as *job-specific skills*. Job-specific skills, like many entrepreneurial skills, are acquired through experience and education or training. Without them, a worker would be unlikely to perform a job successfully.

For example, math skills are hard skills needed to calculate start-up costs, monitor sales and profits, and prepare financial statements and tax returns. Inventory management and product pricing also require good math skills.

Some entrepreneurs start their businesses without much business knowledge or experience. However, they quickly learn they need to know about the economy, accounting, financing, marketing, and business management. Both high school and college courses, continuing education courses, and books help entrepreneurs gain business skills. A mentor or business consultant can also provide business knowledge and expertise.

Soft Skills

Entrepreneurs also need soft skills. *Soft skills* are used to perform in the workplace and gain success in a job or career. Reading, writing, listening, and speaking are essential soft skills. All

ESB Basic/Shutterstock.com

Entrepreneurs need soft skills to interact with others in a positive way. *What soft skills do you possess that might help you become an entrepreneur?*

entrepreneurs will need to write business plans, promote their products to customers, work with suppliers, and organize their businesses. Entrepreneurs will also need to explain their business ideas to banks in order to receive business funding. Each of these activities requires soft skills.

Entrepreneurs need to be able to get along with others, encourage cooperation, and persuade people to understand their point of view. Entrepreneurs also need to know how to negotiate fairly and honestly.

Problem solving and decision making are two soft skills that work together. Entrepreneurs confront many new situations and problems when starting a business. They need to be able to

Entrepreneurial Traits and Skills

Personality Traits	Hard Skills	Soft Skills
competitiveness	accounting	accountability
creativity	business analysis	adaptability
energy	computer skills	discipline
intuition	data analysis	empathy
motivation	foreign language(s)	honesty
passion	math skills	independence
positivity	organization	open-mindedness
risk-tolerance	planning	perseverance
self-confidence	software	vision

Goodheart-Willcox Publisher

Figure 24-2 These are effective entrepreneurship traits and skills.

Chapter 24　Entrepreneurship　　453

Case in Point

method®

Successful entrepreneurs often look at existing products for their next great idea. Often, these ideas can be turned into business opportunities. Cleaning products have been on the market for generations. However, consumers have increasingly demanded products that are socially responsible and ecofriendly. Entrepreneurs Adam Lowry and Eric Ryan knew that being ethically and socially responsible can influence the success of a business. Their company, method®, makes nontoxic cleaning products that are free of harsh chemicals and packaged in 100-percent-recycled plastic bottles. In addition, the company promotes the practice of using only one bottle and refilling it with the lower-cost method® product refills.

Lowry and Ryan started method® after being exposed to harmful toxins in standard cleaning products. They began producing several environmentally friendly cleaners that also smelled good. They first sold four cleaning-spray products to one local store in California. By 2010, the company had gone global. It is honored by many organizations for its commitment to social responsibility. The company opened the industry's first LEED platinum-certified soap factory in 2015. The facility includes wind turbines, greenhouses, and solar panels that track the sun to maximize the generation of solar power. Today, method® is one of the fastest-growing private American companies. Being a socially responsible business creates loyal customers who will continue to purchase your products, and more importantly, tell others about them.

analyze a problem, brainstorm and research solutions, and then decide on the best course of action.

Forms of Business Ownership
LO 24.1-3

When starting a new business, an entrepreneur must decide on the form of business ownership. The three basic forms of ownership are sole proprietorship, partnership, and corporation, as shown in Figure 24-3. There are advantages and disadvantages to each type of ownership structure. It is wise to seek professional advice before signing any ownership documents.

Sole Proprietorship

A *sole proprietorship* is a business owned by one person. A sole proprietor is the person who owns the business and is personally responsible for all its debts. He or she has total responsibility for the business and receives all the profits. **Liability** means legal responsibility.

Depending on the specific business, licenses or permits may be required. Many counties and states require sole proprietors to apply for a DBA

Forms of Business Ownership

Sole Proprietorship	Partnership	Corporation
One owner	Two or more owners	Many owners

Nevena Radonja/Shutterstock.com; Goodheart-Willcox Publisher

Figure 24-3　The three basic forms of ownership are sole proprietorship, partnership, and corporation.

Copyright Goodheart-Willcox Co., Inc.

license before starting a new business. A **DBA license**, or a *doing business as* license, is needed to register a business under a name other than the name of the business owner. In some states, a DBA license is known as a *fictitious name registration*. For example, Spencer Jones may wish to do business as Soapy Suds Car Wash rather than as his own name. Some types of businesses also require a specific license or permit for a service business, such as a hair salon or dental practice.

Sole proprietorships are the easiest to start. If the business is a home- or Internet-based business, it might not need a large amount of money to operate. Many home-based businesses are sole proprietorships. Examples include dog walking, website development, and marketing consulting.

However, operating as a sole proprietorship has its drawbacks. As a sole proprietor, you must raise all the money to start the business. You personally bear all of the risk involved in the business. A sole proprietor has unlimited liability in the business. **Unlimited liability** means the business owner is responsible for all risks. If you are sued and lose, you alone must pay the damages. Figure 24-4 shows some of the advantages and disadvantages of a sole proprietorship.

Partnership

A *partnership* is the relationship between two or more people who join to create a business. Each person involved in owning a partnership is a partner. The partners share the legal and financial responsibilities as well as the profits.

Those who want to form a partnership should hire an experienced lawyer to draw up the partnership agreement. The **partnership agreement**

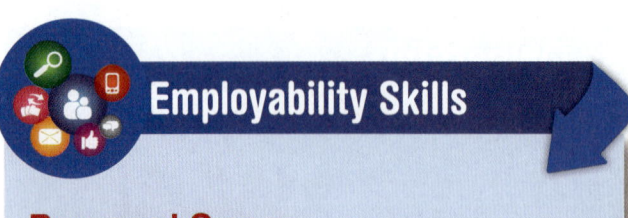

Advantages and Disadvantages of a Sole Proprietorship

Advantages	Disadvantages
• Complete control of business	• Unlimited liability
• Keep 100 percent of the profits	• Assume 100 percent of the losses
• Easy to create	• Sole responsibility
• Possible tax benefits	• May need other professional expertise

Goodheart-Willcox Publisher

Figure 24-4 There are advantages and disadvantages of being a sole proprietor.

is a document that details how much each partner will invest, each partner's responsibilities, and how profits are to be shared. All partners must agree to the terms of the agreement because it is a legal document.

The main advantage of a partnership is that two or more people are giving ideas, sharing the work, and sharing the responsibility. Two or more people can generate more excitement and motivation. Partners can keep each other going during the rough times. A partnership can often be more creative in problem solving and decision making. Partnerships can often gather more money to start the business.

However, the advantage of shared control and responsibility is often the main disadvantage of the partnership. Partners may disagree about how the business should be operated and how much of the profits each partner should receive. Each partner in the business is responsible for the decisions made by the other partners. Suppose one partner decides to sign a contract to buy a building for the business. All the other partners are bound by that contract. Figure 24-5 shows some of the advantages and disadvantages of a partnership.

Two types of partnerships are general partnerships and limited partnerships (LP). A **general partnership** is a business structure in which all partners have unlimited liability. The personal assets of each partner, including savings, investments, and homes, can be used to pay the debts of the business. This is the most common type of business partnership.

The second type is a limited partnership. In a **limited partnership (LP)**, there is one managing partner and at least one limited partner. Limited partners have limited liability. **Limited liability**

Employability Skills

Personal Space

Personal space is the physical space between two individuals. It is an aspect of body language. How you identify your personal space and the judgment you apply to the space of others are important to communication success. Be aware that the workplace has its own unwritten rules, so make sure that you respect the personal space of others.

Advantages and Disadvantages of a Partnership

Advantages	Disadvantages
• Individual strengths • Shared risk; limited liability for limited partners • Ease of setup • More financial resources • Tax benefits	• Personality conflicts • Unlimited liability for general partners • Share profits and losses • Obtaining loans more difficult • Bound by the agreement

Goodheart-Willcox Publisher

Figure 24-5 There are advantages and disadvantages of being a partner in a business.

means that a partner or owner cannot lose more than the amount originally invested by that person. They are not personally liable for the debts of the business.

Corporation

A *corporation* is a business that is legally separate from its owners and has most of the legal rights of an actual person. It is the most complicated form of ownership. A corporation is considered to be a legal entity and is considered a person in the eyes of the law. As a legal entity, a corporation can perform all business activities. A corporation can buy and own property, run a business, manufacture products, earn money, pay taxes, sue, and be sued. A corporation can even buy businesses and other corporations.

Owners of a corporation buy **stock**, or a percentage of ownership in the corporation. They receive one or more certificates stating the number of shares they own based on how much they invested in the corporation. Owners are also called **stockholders** because they hold stock in the corporation. The stockholders then receive the profits of the corporation based on the number of shares they own.

In order for a corporation to be established, a *charter* or *certificate of incorporation* is needed. The people who want to start the corporation apply for this legal document from a state government. There are both advantages and disadvantages to incorporating as illustrated in Figure 24-6.

Because a corporation is considered a legal entity, if a shareholder sells stock, the company continues to exist, which is called *perpetual life*. In addition, stockholders have limited liability for the corporation. Corporations sell stock to raise investment funds. Having the notation "Inc.," which stands for "incorporated," at the end of a company name adds credibility for many potential customers. However, forming a corporation is also the most expensive and complicated form of business ownership. In some types of corporations, both the individual stockholders and the corporation's profits are taxed. This is called *double taxation* and is seen as a disadvantage to many business founders.

Corporate formalities are the records and procedures that corporations are required by law to complete. If the corporation fails to meet any of the formalities, the business may lose the limited liability protection of being a corporation.

Alternative Forms of Ownership

Two alternative forms of ownership resemble both a partnership and a corporation: *limited liability company (LLC)* and *limited liability partnership (LLP)*. Both of these limit the personal liability of the owners and can provide tax benefits.

The owners of an LLC are called members. LLCs can have any organizational structure agreed upon by its members. One disadvantage of the LLC is limited life. The business ends on the retirement or death of one member. It also ends if a member decides to leave the business. LLCs are more expensive to form than sole proprietorships and partnerships. They are also subject to more state and federal regulations.

The owners of an LLP are called partners. The LLP has a similar business structure to a limited

Advantages and Disadvantages of a Corporation

Advantages	Disadvantages
• Perpetual life • Investors raise capital • Credibility • Limited liability for owners	• Double taxation • Cost of entry • Corporate formalities

Goodheart-Willcox Publisher

Figure 24-6 There are advantages and disadvantages of ownership in a corporation.

partnership (LP) but has no managing partner. All the partners have limited personal liability. LLPs are an attractive partnership option because no partner wants to be liable for another's mistakes.

Profits from LLCs and LLPs are reported on personal tax returns. There is limited liability, less paperwork, and owners can share the profits however they choose. In addition, there is no limit to how many stockholders can be a part of the business.

LLPs and LLCs are not permitted in all states. Each state allowing LLPs determines the amount of limited liability for the partners, which can make it less desirable. Most states require LLPs to carry liability insurance and register with the state.

Green Marketing

Sustainability Training

Business owners lead by example. This is true in all areas of their businesses, including ecofriendly activities and considerations in the workplace. It is important to train and educate employees on sustainable business practices. Through sustainability training, employees learn the importance of *going green* at work and the best practices to reduce waste and lower energy consumption.

Training employees in green company procedures can help save the environment and also save the company money. Employees should be instructed to make small changes in their daily habits. Turning lights off when exiting a room and shutting down computer equipment over the weekend can make a big difference. Companies that work toward sustainability are socially responsible and create goodwill.

Section 24.1 Review

Check Your Understanding

1. List reasons a person may want to start a business.
2. What are the five Ps of entrepreneurship?
3. Name three common types of business ownership.
4. What is the purpose of a DBA license?
5. Identify alternative forms of business ownership.

Build Your Vocabulary

As you progress through this text, develop a personal glossary of key terms. This will help you build your vocabulary and prepare you for a career. Write a definition for each of the following terms and add them to your personal glossary.

corporate formalities
DBA license
entrepreneur
general partnership
hard skills
liability
limited liability

limited partnership (LP)
partnership agreement
self-assessment
stock
stockholders
unlimited liability

Section 24.2

Essential Question

Why is planning important when starting a business?

Starting a Business

Learning Objectives

LO 24.2-1 Discuss the process of creating a business.
LO 24.2-2 Identify three options for creating a business.
LO 24.2-3 Explain a business plan.

Key Terms

entrepreneurial discovery process
business operations
franchisor
franchisee
franchise agreement
franchise fee

LO 24.2-1 Creating a Business

Entrepreneurs are always thinking about new and innovative uses for existing products and creating ideas for brand-new ones. *Business opportunities* are ideas that have potential to become successful commercial ventures. Many people have good ideas, but most do not turn into businesses. Finding business opportunities requires that you actively engage with other people and organizations. Before starting a new business, entrepreneurs must go through a discovery process and then determine if the new business is feasible.

Entrepreneurial Discovery Process

In its simplest form, the **entrepreneurial discovery process** is the process of finding a need for a product. The entrepreneurial discovery process consists of two parts: the recognition of a need or want that is not being met and the willingness to take advantage of the opportunity.

Vasin Lee/Shutterstock.com

Entrepreneurs are willing to risk their time, energy, and money to pursue business opportunities. *What might you consider risking in order to become an entrepreneur?*

Recall that a *need* is something necessary for survival, such as food, clothing, and shelter. A need can also be defined as something necessary to function in society, such as schoolbooks, transportation, and electricity. A *want* is something that a person desires, but could function without, such as a new cell phone or a vacation.

Copyright Goodheart-Willcox Co., Inc.

Being an entrepreneur requires risk. Entrepreneurs are willing to risk their time, energy, and money to pursue opportunities to create a new product, improve our world, and find new uses for existing items.

Feasibility

One of the biggest challenges an entrepreneur will face is determining the feasibility of a business idea. *Feasible* means it is possible for something to be done successfully. Successful entrepreneurs and businesses conduct some form of feasibility analysis, often called a *feasibility study*, before starting a new business. The analysis helps determine if the new product idea is worth pursuing. Research may be needed to determine whether customers will buy the product and if investors would be likely to fund the business. Feasibility studies must be based on reality, not theory.

Many sources of information can be used when evaluating the feasibility of a business idea. These include chambers of commerce, industry organizations, and government resources, such as the Small Business Administration (SBA). Through SBA, you can reach out to the Service Corps of Retired Executives (SCORE). The members of SCORE are retired executives who volunteer their time to help new entrepreneurs develop their business plans and run new businesses. Other governmental sources of information include Small Business Investment Companies (SBIC), Minority Enterprise Small Business Investment Companies (MESBICS), the Economic Development Administration (EDA), and state and local governments. Local and large-market newspapers can also be useful sources of information to find statistics about the industry, good business locations, and potential target markets.

Only a small percentage of business ideas and new products achieve long-term success. Failure rates are high for new businesses. Some of those failures could have been prevented if the owners had studied the feasibility of their businesses *before* starting them.

LO 24.2-2 Business Options

You may opt for a brand-new business that you start from the ground up. Or, you may decide to buy an existing business. Another option is to buy into a franchise. The choice is yours.

Start a New Business

Many entrepreneurs decide to start their businesses totally on their own. Doing this gives you the opportunity to develop the business the way you want. You can take your own ideas and turn

---

You Do the Math

Probability

Probability is the likelihood of an event occurring. In general, probability is stated as the number of ways an event can happen over the total number of outcomes. Flipping a coin, for example, can result in either heads or tails. The probability of the result being heads is one in two (1/2). There is only one side of the coin with heads, and there are two total possible outcomes. Probability can be expressed as a percentage. In the case of a flipped coin: 1/2 = .5 × 100 = 50 percent chance of being heads.

Solve the following problems.

1. A local office-supply store offers a random discount to its regular customers. The discount may be 2 percent, 4 percent, 6 percent, or 25 percent. The discount is randomly selected by the cash register computer. What is the probability that a customer will receive the 25 percent discount?
2. Of 100 patients that a nurse treated in one week, 20 of them had the flu. What is the probability percentage that the next patient treated by the nurse will *not* have the flu?
3. The manager in a shoe store has observed that of 100 pairs sold, 42 were blue. What is the probability percentage that the next customer will buy shoes in a color other than blue?
4. At a combination supermarket and retail store, 47 customers purchased only groceries, 13 customers purchased groceries and items from the retail area, and 62 customers purchased items only from the retail area. What is the probability that a customer will purchase groceries?

them into reality. A new business could be a storefront for providing existing products or services to consumers. Examples of this type of business include a day spa, car-repair garage, or restaurant. Another alternative is to create a new product or service that does not exist yet. Research the ideas, get a patent to protect the ownership, manufacture it, and sell it.

Buy an Existing Business

From time to time, a business is offered for sale. There are websites that specialize in listing businesses for sale. These sites often list advertising agencies and other marketing businesses for sale, as well as many consumer businesses.

There are many advantages to buying an existing business. The business already has customers, employees, a location, business equipment, and working business operations. **Business operations** are the day-to-day activities necessary to keep a business up and running. An existing business also has records that describe its financial history. In addition, the person selling the business may be willing to act as a consultant to help you get started.

The main disadvantage of buying an existing business is that you might be buying problems. The most important question to ask when buying an existing business is, "Why is this business being sold?" Many are sold because they are not making a profit. However, some businesses are sold because the owner is ready to retire. Such a business might be an excellent choice.

Diego Cervo/Shutterstock.com

Many types of businesses can be started from home to save on start-up costs, such as this fashion designer's business. *What methods would you choose to start a new business?*

Buy a Franchise

A *franchise* is the right to sell a company's goods or services in a specific area in return for royalty fees. Many franchises have well-known names, such as H&R Block or Subway. The company or person who owns the business and the brand is called the **franchisor**. The person who buys the rights to sell the brand products is the **franchisee**.

The legal document that sets up a franchise is called a **franchise agreement**. It includes the rules and standards the franchisee must follow in running the business. While the franchisee owns the franchise business, it is legally connected to the franchisor by the franchise agreement. A franchise agreement also states the franchise fee. The **franchise fee** is the money that the franchisee pays the franchisor for the rights to use the business brand name and sell its products.

There are many advantages to buying a franchise. One advantage is an established product or service with a known reputation. In addition, the franchisor provides assistance for new franchisees with many aspects of starting and running the business.

However, there are some disadvantages to owning a franchise. The franchisor makes many of the product and marketing decisions. The franchisee must follow the rules and requirements set by the franchisor. From the beginning, the franchisor will set certain requirements that must be met in order to be considered for buying a franchise.

The initial cost to buy the franchise can be large. Initial franchise fees vary, but fees for well-known and successful franchises are often in the $20,000 to $75,000 range, or more. In addition, franchisees usually have to pay an ongoing monthly franchise fee, often called a *royalty fee*. Typically, the franchisor can terminate the franchise agreement for any number of reasons. If this happens, the franchisee may lose all of his or her investment.

LO 24.2-3

Business Plan

A *business plan* is a document that describes a business, how it operates, and how it makes a profit. A business plan is a required part of a business loan application. Writing a business plan is also a valuable planning tool. Researching and writing a business plan will help you figure out how to start and run your business successfully. Creating a thorough business plan will also identify the risks of the business so you can overcome them.

There are many ways to lay out a business plan. A well-written business plan will have the sections shown in Figure 24-7. Once a business plan is written and the loan is obtained, the business plan can be used as an operating guide. Business plans should be reviewed and updated regularly to take advantage of new business opportunities and any economic changes.

Title Page

All formal reports include a title page that shows the name of the company, owner, and date the plan is presented. The title page makes the first impression of what will follow in the business plan.

Table of Contents

The table of contents is a map to the information contained within a document. A table of contents is a necessary part of the business plan so the reader knows what will be included in the plan and the exact page number where each section is located. The table of contents is prepared after the business plan is completed.

Executive Summary

The executive summary is the first part of a business plan, but it is usually the last part written. In it, you should present the key points in a way that makes the reader excited about your business and its potential for success. The executive summary is the first thing that the lenders will read. If they are not impressed with the summary, they might not bother to read the rest of the business plan.

Business Description

The description of the business should include the business' concept, goals, products, and ownership structure. Emphasize what is unique about the business and what will make it successful.

The business description should also explain the type of business. Your business may be one of the following.

- A *manufacturer* turns raw materials from natural resources into new products for sale.
- A *wholesaler* purchases large amounts of goods directly from the manufacturer. The wholesaler then sells those products to retailers.
- The *retailer* buys products and resells to the consumer.
- A *service business* earns money by providing services and expertise to businesses or consumers.
- A *nonprofit* is an organization that exists to serve some public purpose. Any profit it makes goes to support the nonprofit goal.

Market Evaluation

This section describes the current state of the industry and economy in the area where you want to start your business. Include a description of the competitors and an analysis of the need for the business. Describe the competitive edge the business will have over its competitors. Customers are crucial to the success of your business, so describe the target market. Estimate how many customers you expect to have and how much they might spend at your business.

Operations

This section covers the proposed organizational chart and operations procedures. It also includes the necessary material resources, technology, human resources, and the staffing plan. In this section, detail how you will tell your customers about your business and convince them to buy your products and services. Describe what kind of advertising you will plan and whether you will have a sales force. You will also need to

Sections of a Business Plan
- Title page
- Table of contents
- Executive summary
- Business description
- Market evaluation
- Operations
- Financial plan
- Conclusion
- Bibliography
- Appendices

Goodheart-Willcox Publisher

Figure 24-7 A business plan typically includes common basic sections.

Social Media

Blogs

Web logs, or *blogs* as they are commonly known, are websites maintained by an individual who posts topics or opinions. Blogs typically provide information or news about subjects that the owner of the site chooses to discuss. The entries are posted in reverse chronological order, so the line of communication is easy to follow. Some blogs are written on a daily basis, while others are updated less frequently. People who want to follow a blog can usually subscribe to be notified of updates. A blog's followers may also comment on any posts.

Business blogs are generally used to share information with current or potential customers. There is no maximum word count, so blogs allow your customers, and you, to communicate freely. Many people follow blogs to look for product information, seek employment, or learn more about a company. Blogs are indexed on search engines, which is great for business promotion. And, as an added benefit, the messages are permanently posted, so readers can go back at any time to review information.

estimate your marketing budget and plan a time line for the initial marketing program.

Financial Plan

The financial plan describes how you plan to fund the business and expect to make a profit. First, present the start-up costs. Next, describe how you will get the money to cover the start-up costs. Include how much of your own money you plan to use and the amount and sources of any loans. When discussing the loans, explain how you will repay them. Also present anticipated sales and profits. This section will include many financial documents, such as budgets, cash flow analysis, profit and loss statement, and balance sheet.

Conclusion

The conclusion summarizes why your business will be successful and ends with a specific request for financing. The conclusion should be written so it is easy to read and highlights all the points important to potential investors and lenders.

Bibliography

The bibliography lists all of the resources used to develop the business plan. This might include interviews you conducted; books, periodicals, and websites cited; or other information you gathered while researching your business plan. The bibliography is an important record of the sources used to write the business plan.

Appendices

An *appendix* is a section of a document that contains additional information that would be helpful to the reader, but is not necessary to know. In a business plan, this may include résumés, financial statements, promotional plans, and other documents that support your plan. An appendix is an optional section of the business plan.

Section 24.2 Review

Check Your Understanding

1. Define *business opportunities*.
2. What purpose does a feasibility analysis serve?
3. What are some advantages of buying an existing business?
4. Explain why a franchise agreement is important to both the franchisor and franchisee.
5. List sections of a business plan.

Build Your Vocabulary

As you progress through this text, develop a personal glossary of key terms. This will help you build your vocabulary and prepare you for a career. Write a definition for each of the following terms and add them to your personal glossary.

business operations
entrepreneurial discovery process
franchise agreement
franchise fee
franchisee
franchisor

CHAPTER 24 Review and Assessment

Chapter Summary

Section 24.1 Becoming an Entrepreneur

LO 24.1-1 Explain what it means to be an entrepreneur.
An entrepreneur is a person who starts a new business. Reasons for starting a business include being your own boss, taking advantage of your earning potential, enjoying your career, and making a difference in the world. Risks of entrepreneurship can include being responsible for the success or failure of the business, working long hours, and risking personal finances.

LO 24.1-2 Identify examples of the traits and skills necessary to become an entrepreneur.
Many traits and skills are necessary to become an entrepreneur. Personality traits include the five Ps of entrepreneurship: passion, perseverance, persistence, planning, and problem solving. Entrepreneurial skills include communication, math, business, computers, and soft skills including problem solving and decision making.

LO 24.1-3 List and explain ownership options for starting a business.
Three forms of ownership are sole proprietorship, partnership, and corporation. A sole proprietorship is a business owned by one person. A partnership is the relationship between two or more people who join to create a business. A corporation is a business that is legally separate from its owners and has most of the legal rights of an actual person.

Section 24.2 Starting a Business

LO 24.2-1 Discuss the process of creating a business.
The entrepreneurial discovery process is the process of finding a need for a product. It consists of two parts: the recognition of a need or want that is not being met and the willingness to take advantage of the opportunity. Successful entrepreneurs and businesses conduct a feasibility study to determine if the new product idea is worth pursuing.

LO 24.2-2 Identify three options for creating a business.
As a new business owner, you can start a new business, purchase an existing business, or buy into a franchise.

LO 24.2-3 Explain a business plan.
A business plan is a written document that describes a new business, how it will operate, and how it will make a profit. A business plan is a required part of a business loan application. Writing a business plan is also a valuable planning tool.

Check Your Marketing IQ

Now that you have completed the chapter, see what you have learned about marketing by taking the chapter posttest. The posttest is available at www.g-wlearning.com/marketing/.

Review Your Knowledge

1. Explain what it means to be an entrepreneur.
2. Identify examples of the traits and skills necessary to become an entrepreneur.
3. List and explain ownership options for starting a business.
4. How does a limited partnership differ from a general partnership?
5. Explain double taxation.

6. Discuss the process of creating a business.
7. Identify three options for creating a business.
8. Explain a business plan.
9. What is the purpose of the executive summary of a business plan?
10. What information is contained in the financial plan section of a business plan?

Apply Your Knowledge

1. How could your high school classes help you decide whether to become an entrepreneur? Explain your answer.
2. What traits and skills do you think are most important for an entrepreneur to be successful?
3. Could you be an entrepreneur? Which entrepreneurial traits and skills do you possess?
4. Think about the activities that you enjoy most. Take time to observe needs in the community that also tie into your favorite activities. This could lead to potential entrepreneurial ideas. List four of your favorite activities and how they might become business ideas.
5. Select one of the business ideas you thought of for the previous question. Is it a new business, established business you would purchase, a franchise, or is there a product you want to invent?
6. List franchise businesses in your community. Which would you consider for a business opportunity? Explain your reasoning for each.
7. Which form of ownership would you prefer: sole proprietorship, partnership, or corporation? Defend your decision.
8. What are some of the risks you might face as an entrepreneur? Brainstorm ways you could overcome each risk.
9. What research would you do to make sure your idea for a business is feasible? How could you ensure that your business will not fail?
10. List experts or people from whom you would want help if you were to start a business tomorrow. Explain why you would need each.

Apply Your Math Skills

Marius is an entrepreneur who operates a brick-and-mortar business. The following graph shows the income of his business over the last five years. Interpret the graph and apply your math skills to solve the problems that follow.

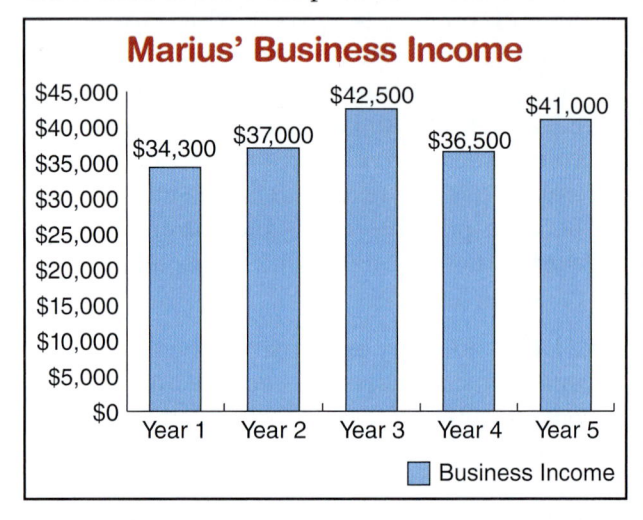

Marius' Business Income

Year	Income
Year 1	$34,300
Year 2	$37,000
Year 3	$42,500
Year 4	$36,500
Year 5	$41,000

1. In which year did the business have the highest profit?
2. In which year did the business lose money?
3. After Year 1, in which year did the business have the largest gain in income?
4. Marius' business expenses are $30,000 annually. Calculate the amount of money he was able to take as payment for each of the five years.
5. Marius expects his business expenses to increase by $3,000 next year due to new marketing efforts. However, he also expects income to increase by $4,500 as a result of the increased marketing. How much money would Marius make as income if his prediction is correct?

Communication Skills

Reading When engaging in active reading, it is important to relate what you are reading to prior knowledge, or what you already know. This helps readers evaluate information as they read to ensure understanding and form judgments. Select one of the sections of this chapter to read again. As you read, make notes about your prior knowledge that relates to the content. Evaluate whether your prior knowledge helped you understand the content.

Listening Reflective listening occurs when the listener demonstrates an understanding of what was said. Engage in a conversation with a classmate about a topic covered in this chapter. After the conversation, use active listening skills to restate what your classmate said. How much did you recall?

Speaking This chapter discussed different ways to start a business. Plan and deliver a speech to a group of classmates about an idea you have for a new business. Be clear in your perspective for the business idea and demonstrate solid reasoning for why you think the business can be successful.

Internet Research

Entrepreneurs Research a well-known entrepreneur or one whom you know personally. List the person's name, business, and when the business was organized. Cite evidence that supports that person's entrepreneurial spirit.

Chamber of Commerce Search the Internet for your local chamber of commerce. How does the chamber of commerce help entrepreneurs in your community? How would you use the chamber of commerce if you were starting a local business?

Small Business Administration The Small Business Administration (SBA) has many resources for people interested in entrepreneurship. Visit the site and explore the information it presents. List five topics or articles you think would be useful if you were starting a business.

Teamwork

Working with a teammate, make a list of personality traits that you observe in that person. Then, have your teammate make a list of your personality traits. Discuss your opinions with each other. What did you learn from this experience?

Portfolio Development

Personal Photo A personal photo will help the person who reviews your portfolio remember who you are. Employers review hundreds of applications and portfolios each year. Use your annual school photo, or dress professionally and have a friend take your photo. Photos that show your head and shoulders, called a headshot, can work well for this purpose.

1. Print the photo on high-quality paper for a print portfolio.
2. Save the file as a digital copy for your electronic portfolio.
3. Update your master spreadsheet.

CHAPTER 25

Risk Management

Sections

25.1 **Identify Risk**

25.2 **Manage Risk**

Reading Prep

College and Career Readiness

Before reading this chapter, review the key terms and definitions to preview the new content. Building a marketing vocabulary is an important activity to broadening your understanding of new material.

Check Your Marketing IQ

Before you begin the chapter, see what you already know about marketing by taking the chapter pretest. The pretest is available at www.g-wlearning.com/marketing/.

DECA Emerging Leaders

Business Services Marketing Series Event, Part 2

Career Cluster: Marketing
Career Pathway: Marketing Management
Instructional Area: Product/Service Management

Procedure, Part 2

1. In the previous chapter, you studied the performance indicators for this event.
2. You will have up to 10 minutes to review this information to determine how you will handle the event situation. You may make notes to use during the role-play situation.
3. You will have up to 10 minutes to role-play your situation with a judge. You may have more than one judge.
4. Turn in all your notes and event materials when you have completed the role-play.

Event Situations

You are to assume the role of manager at JS Solutions, a software-development company. The **company owner (judge)** has asked you to make recommendations, which will increase brand awareness and company revenue.

JS Solutions is a relatively new company that develops and markets business software. Begun just eight months ago, the company was founded on the strength of its four employees who possess years of practical business experience. When combined with the two-member software development team, business customers of JS Solutions have quickly discovered that the company's slogan, *Do It Better*, will do just that for them.

All JS Solutions' company operations exist only online at the company's website. All prospecting, marketing, and selling are done through the company website. To date, JS Solutions has developed six different business-software programs. But, its most complex and expensive product is *Locate*, a warehouse management program. *Locate* is targeted to midsized warehouses looking to increase employee productivity, improve inventory accuracy, and reduce shipping errors.

As with any new business, having customers find you and accept your products as legitimate is a challenge—especially when selling computer software online. The company's software sales have not met initial forecast levels, but it is believed that the program with the greatest potential is *Locate*. According to the company, *Locate* is at the forefront of the next generation of warehouse-management software. Competitors' software clearly lags behind *Locate* when considering function and overall benefit for the customer. For now, the owner would like to see most of the company's marketing efforts directed to *Locate*.

The owner (judge) of JS Solutions has requested a meeting with you to obtain your analysis and recommendations to increase brand awareness and to increase revenue. Specifically:

- list and explain strategies that would increase the customer confidence level in new products being developed and marketed by JS Solutions;
- identify and explain strategies that will help increase the sales revenue for *Locate* as well as for other JS Solutions software; and
- state one strategy that could be implemented immediately to address a company's needs and be cost effective at the same time.

You will present your analysis to the company owner (judge) in a role-play to take place in the owner's (judge's) office. The owner (judge) will begin the role-play by greeting you and asking to hear your ideas. After you have presented your analysis and have answered the owner's (judge's) questions, the owner (judge) will conclude the role-play by thanking you for your work.

Critical Thinking

1. What are the advantages for the company not having an actual brick-and-mortar location?
2. In addition to selling online, identify another possible distribution channel for JS Solutions.

Visit www.deca.org for more information.

Published by DECA Inc. Copyright © by DECA Inc. No part of this publication may be reproduced for resale without written permission from the publisher. Printed in the United States of America.

Section 25.1

Essential Question
What risks does a business face?

Identify Risk

Learning Objectives
LO 25.1-1 Explain the nature of risk.
LO 25.1-2 Describe four types of business risk.

Key Terms

- risk
- risk management
- controllable risk
- insurance
- uncontrollable risk
- natural risk
- economic risk
- market risk
- planned obsolescence
- human risk
- burglary
- robbery
- embezzlement
- fraud

LO 25.1-1 Nature of Risk

A **risk** is the possibility of loss, damage, or injury. *Business risk* is the possibility of loss or injury that might occur in a business. Businesses must plan for the unexpected and identify possible risks. They must also assess the seriousness of the risks and the likelihood of loss. **Risk management** is the process of measuring risk and finding ways to minimize or manage loss.

Risks can be categorized as controllable or uncontrollable. A **controllable risk** is one that cannot be avoided, but can be minimized by purchasing insurance or implementing a risk management plan. **Insurance** is a financial service used to protect individuals and businesses against financial loss. For example, the risk of fire is controllable because it is covered by insurance.

Uncontrollable risk is a situation that cannot be predicted or covered by purchasing insurance. For example, a price war started by competitors is an example of an uncontrollable risk. There are no insurance plans to cover this type of financial loss.

Risk can also be categorized as speculative or pure. A *speculative risk* carries with it the chance of a profit or loss. For example, starting a business is a speculative risk because the business may or may not be successful. A *pure risk* is the threat of loss with no chance for profit. For example, if a natural disaster happens, there is no possibility of gain from this event. Some pure-risk events can also be considered liability risks. A *liability risk* is one that has the possibility of losing money or other property as a result of legal proceedings.

LO 25.1-2 Types of Business Risk

There are four basic types of business risk: natural, economic, market, and human. Each can cost a business money should they happen. These risks are shown in Figure 25-1.

Natural Risks

Natural risk is a situation caused by acts of nature. Tornadoes, hurricanes, floods, and

468 Copyright Goodheart-Willcox Co., Inc.

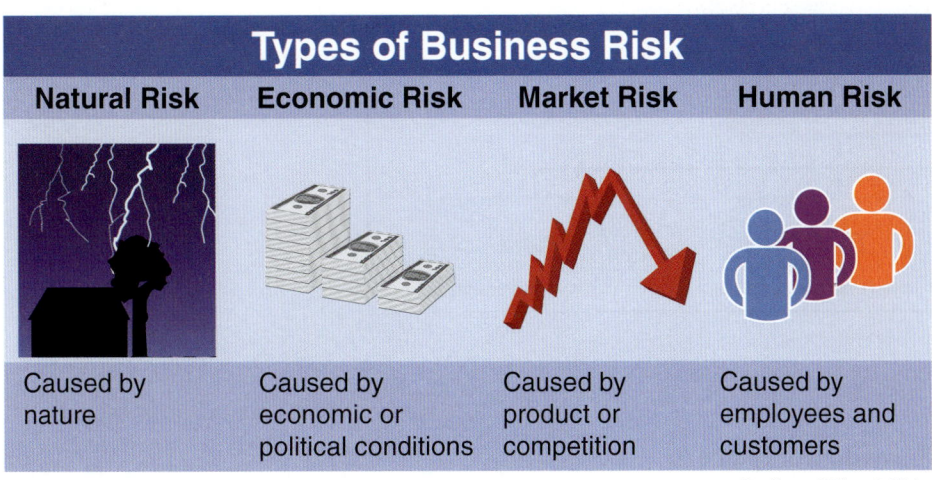

Figure 25-1 Four basic types of business risk are natural, economic, market, and human.

earthquakes are examples. Natural risks are considered controllable risks. Insurance can help recover the losses from damage caused by a natural risk.

Economic Risks

Economic risk is a situation that occurs when the economy suffers due to negative business conditions in the United States or the world. Local, national, and world economic and political conditions can affect the success of a business. Economic risk is hard to predict and is uncontrollable. For example, during times of recession, many people lose their jobs. As a result, people stop spending on luxuries, which puts businesses at risk. Political conditions can create risks for companies engaged in business globally.

kyrien/Shutterstock.com

Flooding is an example of a natural risk that can strike at any time. *What other natural risks can you think of that might impact a business?*

Market Risks

Market risk is the potential that the target market for new products or services is much less than originally thought. The market for many products is very unpredictable. Introducing a new product is especially risky. Will customers be willing to buy it? Will they be happy with it? Research shows that most new products fail in their first year on the market.

Another market risk is competition. Just because your product is currently successful does not mean that it will always be successful. Competitors might enter your market with an improved product or a new, better product. Customers might prefer products from the competition. As a result, your business might lose sales and earn less revenue.

A related market risk is product obsolescence. Some products have short life cycles. In the event of *product obsolescence*, a product becomes outdated over time. Product obsolescence is a major problem for fashion and technology businesses. Many types of clothing go out of style very quickly. People often do not want to buy last year's fashions. In technology, faster products with newer features make the older ones obsolete. This obsolescence is particularly obvious in products such as cell phones and computers. **Planned obsolescence** is evaluating and updating current products or adding new ones to replace older ones.

Human Risks

Human risk is a negative situation caused by human actions. Employees and customers pose potential human risks of accidental injury, theft, or fraud, as shown in Figure 25-2.

Figure 25-2 Human risks include accidental injury, theft, or fraud.

Accidents

Accidents can happen easily in the workplace. Employees and customers run the risk of falling or becoming involved in situations that lead to injury. For example, a customer may break a leg by tripping over a bucket left in an aisle. An employee may be injured while using heavy equipment. In such cases, the business is responsible for all associated costs of injuries that occur on the premises. The business may even face a negligence lawsuit.

Theft

Two types of theft are external theft and internal theft. *External theft* is stealing by people who are not employed or otherwise associated with the retailer. Examples of external theft include shoplifting, burglary, and robbery.

- A *shoplifter* is a person posing as a customer who takes goods from a store without paying for them. Small, high-priced goods like jewelry and electronics are common targets for shoplifting because these are easy to take from stores. They also receive cash when sold illegally by the shoplifter. Shoplifting has increased because there are fewer salespeople in stores. Plus, more organized, professional shoplifting is taking place than ever before. Shoplifting is a serious crime that is punishable by fines or time in prison.
- A **burglary** occurs when a person breaks into a business to steal merchandise, money, valuable equipment, or confidential information. Burglars can enter a business in several ways. Breaking the glass on a window or a door, picking locks, using a stolen key, and even hiding inside the business until it closes are all ways burglars might enter.
- A **robbery** is a theft involving another person, often by using force or with the threat of violence.

You Do the Math

Problem Solving and Reasoning

Insurance is a financial service used to protect against loss. The insurance company charges its customers to assume their risk. The charge is called a *premium*. When a claim is made, the policyholder is responsible to pay a certain amount toward the loss before the insurance company begins to pay. This amount is called a *deductible*. Once the deductible is met, the insurance company begins to pay for covered losses above the deductible amount.

Solve the following problems.

1. Scott's auto insurance has a deductible of $500. Scott is in an accident that affects only his car and requires $3,000 worth of repairs. How much will both he and the insurance company pay toward the repairs?
2. Angela's business policy premium is $1,500 annually. She wants to increase the business property coverage limit from $150,000 to $250,000. Her insurance agent says this change will raise her premium by 6 percent. How much is Angela's new annual premium for this policy? How much more will Angela pay each month with her new premium?
3. Ahmed's car insurance premium is $1,889.50. He is eligible for a 15 percent discount. After the discount is applied, how much will Ahmed's premium be?

Theft is a human risk that can cause a business to suffer a loss in profit. *How does theft hurt a business?*

Internal theft is committed by employees of a store, supplier, or delivery company. It is also called *employee theft*. Internal theft costs businesses thousands of dollars each year. **Embezzlement** occurs when an employee steals either money or goods entrusted to him or her. Employees who handle money have many opportunities to take cash from a business. They can overcharge customers, steal gift cards, and commit a variety of other activities to take cash from the business. Anyone with a record of shoplifting should not be employed in retail stores.

Fraud

Fraud is cheating or deceiving a business out of money or property. Employees, vendors, and customers can commit fraud. Examples of fraud include the following.

- *Vendor theft* occurs when dishonest vendors deliver less than what was ordered but charge for the full order.
- *Bad checks* are fake or stolen checks written by dishonest customers. They may also write checks that have no money in the bank to cover the purchase.
- *Expired or stolen credit cards* have no value when used by dishonest customers.
- *Counterfeit money* is fake money that is not legal tender.
- *Data fraud* occurs when hackers steal sensitive customer and credit card information from vulnerable businesses that use e-commerce.

Section 25.1 Review

Check Your Understanding

1. What is business risk?
2. Provide examples of ways risk is often categorized.
3. What is a liability risk?
4. Identify types of human risks.
5. List examples of external theft.

Build Your Vocabulary

As you progress through this text, develop a personal glossary of key terms. This will help you build your vocabulary and prepare you for a career. Write a definition for each of the following terms and add them to your personal glossary.

burglary
controllable risk
economic risk
embezzlement
fraud
human risk
insurance
market risk
natural risk
planned obsolescence
risk
risk management
robbery
uncontrollable risk

Section 25.2

Manage Risk

Essential Question

In what ways can risk management contribute to business success?

Learning Objectives

LO 25.2-1 Summarize risk management.
LO 25.2-2 Explain ways risk can be avoided or reduced.
LO 25.2-3 Identify how risk can be transferred.
LO 25.2-4 Describe how risk is assumed.

Key Terms

lawsuit
risk assessment
loss prevention
security
surveillance
hazard
emergency
insurance premium
uninsurable risk

Risk Management

LO 25.2-1

Risk management is the process of measuring risk and finding ways to minimize or manage loss. Four common ways to manage business risks are to avoid, reduce, transfer, or assume the risk, as shown in Figure 25-3.

Businesses and individuals are liable for their risks. Recall that the *liability* means legal responsibility for actions and costs. A **lawsuit** is the process of bringing a complaint to a court for resolution. The purpose of a lawsuit is to have an impartial party, such as a judge or jury, determine who is liable for the costs of the damage or injury. For example, a customer might become injured after slipping and falling on the ice in front of a business entrance. The customer may try to hold the business liable for injuries and related medical costs.

Individuals and businesses handle potential liability by assessing the risks. **Risk assessment** is the process of analyzing a situation for possible risks. Risk assessments should be done on a regular basis as risks may change over time.

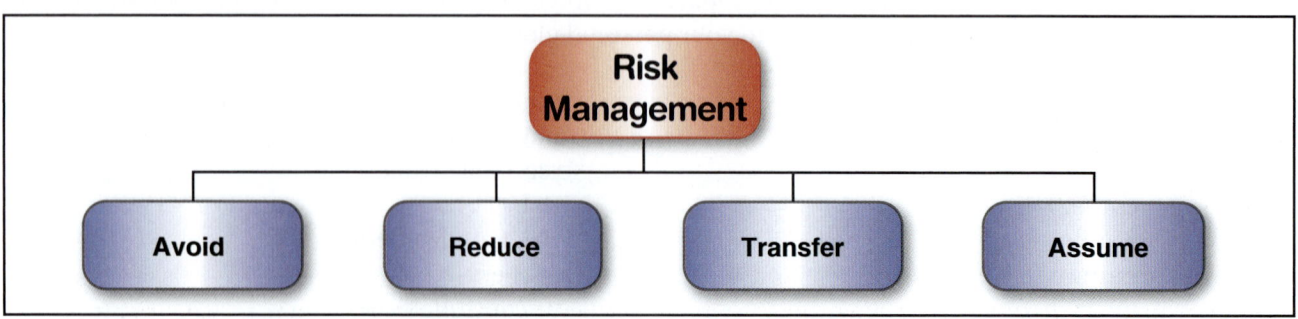

```
                    Risk
                 Management
        ┌───────────┬──────────┬──────────┐
      Avoid       Reduce    Transfer    Assume
```

Goodheart-Willcox Publisher

Figure 25-3 Four common ways to manage business risks are to avoid, reduce, transfer, or assume the risk.

Case in Point

Gillinder Glass

Good business is not all about making money. It also involves being prepared in case of a disaster. Businesses of all types must try to predict potential risks and develop plans to manage them.

Gillinder Glass is an industrial glass manufacturer located in Port Jervis, New York, and has been in business for over 150 years. The company was one of the countless businesses devastated by Hurricane Sandy, which struck the eastern United States in 2012. The hurricane caused Gillinder's factory to lose electricity for two days. Furnaces in the factory kept glass continuously molten at a temperature of 2,500° Fahrenheit, ready to be manufactured at any time. Without electricity, the molten glass hardened and became unusable. This halted operations for several days and damaged the furnaces, causing the company to lose over $150,000.

The company's insurance policy only covered $50,000, or one-third of its losses. To avoid future losses in the event of another natural disaster, the company has since spent tens of thousands of dollars to upgrade its operations, including the installation of backup generators. "We will always be somewhat susceptible to Mother Nature's fury…but the upgrades we have made will allow us to recover more quickly and reduce the financial impact," said CFO Fred Harding. Successful risk management includes not only purchasing insurance, but planning ahead and preparing for the unexpected.

Avoid or Reduce the Risk

LO 25.2-2

One of the first steps in risk management is to assess those risks that can be avoided or reduced. Risks can be *avoided* by taking steps to eliminate the risk. Risks can also be *reduced* by creating a plan to minimize risks that cannot be totally avoided. Often, one risk management technique is used more frequently for certain types of risks. Market risks and human risks are examples of risks that are commonly avoided or reduced.

Market Risk

Business success depends on selling products. Which products will sell well? If a product is selling well now, will it continue to sell well? Businesses use marketing research to answer these questions. One of the purposes of marketing research is to prevent losses from marketing mistakes. Marketing research will help avoid or reduce risk.

Human Risks

By putting safeguards in place, some human risks can be avoided. Many business losses are caused by people who steal, damage property, or harm employees and customers. Retail stores are crime targets. This is due partly because they have easy public access, available cash, and are open after dark. Often, the few employees on duty in the store are busy in different locations. **Loss prevention** is the term used for programs designed to prevent loss of assets, such as merchandise, money, or other property. Such programs help businesses recognize, prevent, and monitor theft problems.

Businesses often use multiple loss-prevention strategies. **Security** consists of actions taken to prevent crime and protect the safety of people and property. Security personnel, such as guards, are often part of the loss prevention program. To discourage crime, closed circuit television and video security systems may be installed. Sensing devices placed on merchandise and ringing alarms also help prevent external and internal theft. The obvious presence of security measures cuts down on stealing.

External Theft

To avoid external theft, security precautions are needed. Security activities can be classified as structural security, surveillance, and security policies.

Structural security consists of security features in a building, such as lights, alarms, locks, and computerized security systems. Valuable merchandise is often displayed in locked display cases. Retailers may attach security tags to their merchandise. Security tag detectors are then placed at the exits of the store. When a customer buys an item, the security tag is removed. If a person tries to walk out of the store without paying, the security tag on the item will set off the security tag detector and alarms.

Many businesses, especially retailers, use security tags such as this RFID hard tag to prevent thefts. *What loss-prevention strategies have you seen at local retailers?*

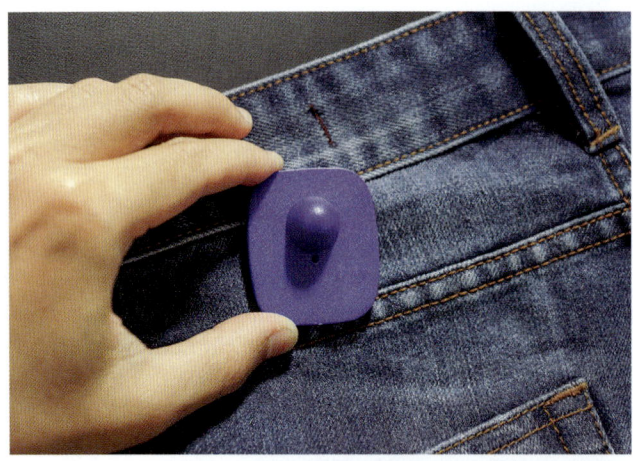

wk1003mike/Shutterstock.com

Surveillance is the process of closely observing what is going on in order to prevent crimes. Many businesses hire security guards to provide surveillance. Video and closed-circuit TV (CCTV) cameras are also used for observation.

Security policies are rules that employees must follow to ensure security. There may be security policies for handling money, locking the building, and obtaining supplies. Keeping careful inventory records is also a security measure. Inventory records can show if items are missing. If items are missing, someone may have stolen them. Sales associates learn what to do during a robbery and how to recognize shoplifters. Cashiers receive training on how to identify counterfeit money. Cashiers also learn the proper techniques for accepting checks and credit cards.

Internal Theft

Retailers and other businesses also have problems with internal theft. Theft is usually grounds for immediate dismissal and possibly prosecution. In order to reduce employee theft, employers use a variety of methods of prevention, including:

- require background checks of job applicants;
- hire honest, reliable employees;
- train employees to be aware of theft risks and active in theft prevention;
- place surveillance cameras and devices at cash registers and in receiving docks, warehouses, and back rooms;
- use a computerized accounting system to keep close track of cash register transactions; and
- use computerized inventory systems to keep track of inventory.

Accidents

Health and safety procedures are the actions taken to prevent illness and injury. Businesses are responsible for the health and safety of customers

Exploring Marketing Careers

Outside Sales Representative

To sell their products, wholesale companies and manufacturers need people to present the products to potential buyers in a positive way. Outside sales representatives present, demonstrate, and sell the company's products to both businesses and individuals. Other typical job titles for an outside sales representative are *marketing associate*, *field representative*, *field marketing representative*, *account manager*, and *sales executive*.

Some examples of tasks that outside sales representatives perform include:
- Identify potential customers by following leads, attending trade shows and conferences, and using business directories
- Monitor competitors' products, prices, and sales statistics
- Determine which products to recommend, based on customer needs and interests
- Demonstrate products and explain their features
- Provide price quotes, terms, warranties, and potential delivery dates

Outside sales representatives usually have a specific territory, which may or may not require frequent traveling to maintain. They must have an excellent knowledge not only of their own products, but also of competitors' products, and should understand the principles of promoting and selling products. Because almost 100 percent of their job involves working with people, sales representatives should enjoy working with people and should have good communication skills. Most jobs in this field require on-the-job experience, training in a vocational school, or an associate degree. For more information, access the *Occupational Outlook Handbook* online.

Employability Skills

Paralanguage

Paralanguage is the attitude you project with the tone and pitch of your voice. It is reflected in speech as a sharp or soft tone, raising or lowering of the voice, speaking quickly or slowly, and the general quality of the voice. It reflects your true attitude, so it is important to be aware of it when communicating with others.

while they are on company property. Most businesses have procedures to try to prevent hazards. A **hazard** is a situation that could result in injury or damage. For example, water on the floor is a hazard that might cause a customer to slip and fall. If floors become wet, signs are posted to warn that floors may be slippery. Improperly prepared food is a health hazard. Meeting governmental regulations regarding food preparation and sanitation standards can avoid or reduce this risk.

Businesses are also responsible for the health and safety of employees. Most businesses have rules for office, warehouse, and store accident prevention. In an office, file drawers must be closed when not in use, and electric cords must be kept out of the way. In a warehouse, workers must wear protective clothing. In a retail store, merchandise must be displayed in a safe manner.

To encourage employers to make the workplace safe, the Occupational Safety and Health Act was passed in 1970. This act requires employers to make the workplace free of hazards that might cause injury or death to employees. The act also established the Occupational Safety and Health Administration (OSHA). OSHA develops and enforces job safety and health standards.

Many businesses provide safety training for employees. Safety training should cover three areas: general safety rules, job-related safety training, and a safety attitude. *General safety rules* apply to everyone in the business. Topics include hazards, safe lifting, and emergency procedures. *Job-related safety training* should be tailored to each specific job. For example, warehouse workers need special training in the equipment they use to move heavy loads. A *safety attitude* is a positive attitude toward safety. A safety attitude is important and must be promoted in the workplace. Employees should be made aware of how important safety is to their well-being and continued employment.

Emergencies can occur at any time and in any place. An **emergency** is an unforeseen event that can cause harm to people and property. One of the goals of safety training is to help employees keep minor emergencies from becoming major emergencies. Employees must know when and how to call for help. In many companies, employees must report any accident, large or small, to their supervisors. *Emergency procedures* are a series of actions taken to minimize risks in the event of an emergency. These procedures describe what to do in case of fires or other disasters. A major component of emergency procedures is an evacuation plan to safely get every person out of the building if necessary.

LO 25.2-3 Transfer the Risk

To *transfer* risk is to shift the risk to another person or business. Many risks can be transferred by purchasing insurance to cover different risk events. The cost of an insurance policy is a payment, usually made monthly, called an **insurance premium**. In exchange for the premium, the insurance company agrees to pay the costs in case of a specific list of damages. The cost of insurance depends on how likely the buyer is to use the insurance. When the possibility of using insurance is high, the premium is usually more expensive. There are three basic types of insurance for businesses: property, liability, and crime.

- *Property insurance* pays for loss or damage of property owned by the business. It usually covers losses due to fires, tornadoes, hail, accidents, burglary, and arson.

zhu difeng/Shutterstock.com

A hazard is a situation that could result in injury or damage, such as a wet floor. *How do health and safety procedures protect a business?*

Marketing Ethics

Tax Returns

It is unethical to file a fraudulent tax return. In a fraudulent tax return, a person deliberately reports information that is not correct. A person who intentionally files a tax return that is not accurate may be subject to penalties, interest, and possible prison time.

- *Liability insurance* provides payment if the business is sued and the court determines that the business is liable. Customers and employees might sue if they are injured at the business. Customers might also sue if an item they purchase causes injury. If the court determines that the business is liable, then it usually requires the business to pay money to the victim. Liability insurance will cover the cost to pay the victim. *Professional liability insurance* protects against losses caused by negligent acts of a professional, such as an attorney.
- *Crime insurance* pays for losses due to crimes, such as theft, arson, forgery, and embezzlement. This form of insurance is important for any type of business.

A *surety bond* is a document signed by a contractor to fulfill a service agreed upon by the parties. A surety bond company issues the bond. If the contractor fails to perform, monetary compensation is made to the person to which the services are owed.

LO 25.2-4 Assume the Risk

Unfortunately, insurance may not be available for all the risks that need to be covered. These risks are uninsurable and must be assumed. An **uninsurable risk** is one that an insurance company will not cover. In these situations, a business must assume the full risk and be responsible for losses associated with uninsurable risks. To *assume* the risk means to make financial preparations for the possibility of future loss. For example, no insurance will cover economic or market risks.

A business may choose to assume a risk and *self-insure* by saving money to cover some risks should they happen. One way to self-insure is by depositing money in a designated bank account each month to cover a future loss instead of paying a premium to an insurance company. The difference is that the premium is paid to the business, and the business assumes 100 percent of the risk. If the business suffers a loss, self-insurance money is available to cover the losses. State regulations may require a business to prove it can finance self-insurance before allowing it to use this strategy.

Section 25.2 Review

Check Your Understanding

1. Identify four techniques for risk management.
2. How is a risk avoided?
3. Name the governmental organization that enforces job safety.
4. Explain emergency procedures.
5. What does it mean to self-insure?

Build Your Vocabulary

As you progress through this text, develop a personal glossary of key terms. This will help you build your vocabulary and prepare you for a career. Write a definition for each of the following terms and add them to your personal glossary.

emergency	lawsuit	security
hazard	loss prevention	surveillance
insurance premium	risk assessment	uninsurable risk

CHAPTER 25 Review and Assessment

Chapter Summary

Section 25.1 Identify Risk

LO 25.1-1 Explain the nature of risk.
A risk is the possibility of loss, damage, or injury. Business risk is the possibility of loss or injury that might occur in a business. Controllable risk is one that cannot be avoided, but can be minimized by purchasing insurance or implementing a risk plan. Uncontrollable risk is a situation that cannot be predicted or covered by purchasing insurance.

LO 25.1-2 Describe four types of business risk.
Several types of risk with which an individual or business needs to be concerned include natural risk, economic risk, market risk, and human risk. Natural risk is caused by acts of nature. Economic risk occurs when the economy suffers due to negative business conditions in the United States or the world. Market risk is the potential that the target market for new products or services is less than originally thought. Human risk is caused by human actions.

Section 25.2 Manage Risk

LO 25.2-1 Summarize risk management.
Risk management is the process of measuring risk and finding ways to minimize or manage loss. Risk assessment is the process of analyzing a situation for possible risks. Through proper risk management, risks may be avoided, reduced, transferred, or assumed.

LO 25.2-2 Explain ways risk can be avoided or reduced.
One of the first steps in risk management is to assess those risks that can be avoided or reduced. Marketing research can avoid or reduce market risk by helping to prevent losses from marketing mistakes. By putting safeguards in place, some human risks can be avoided. Security consists of actions taken to prevent crime and protect the safety of people and property.

LO 25.2-3 Identify how risk can be transferred.
Many risks can be transferred by purchasing insurance. In exchange for the premium, the insurance company agrees to pay the costs in case of a specific list of damages. For a business, there are three basic types of insurance: property, liability, and crime.

LO 25.2-4 Describe how risk is assumed.
An uninsurable risk is one that an insurance company will not cover. All businesses must assume the full risk and be responsible for losses associated with those risks that cannot be avoided or insured. A business may choose to assume a risk and *self-insure* by saving money to cover some risks should they happen.

Check Your Marketing IQ

Now that you have completed the chapter, see what you have learned about marketing by taking the chapter posttest. The posttest is available at www.g-wlearning.com/marketing/.

Review Your Knowledge

1. Explain the nature of risk.
2. What is the difference between speculative risk and pure risk?
3. Describe the four types of business risk.
4. Which of the four categories of risk are considered uncontrollable risks?
5. Provide examples of fraud.
6. Summarize risk management.
7. Explain ways risk can be avoided or reduced.
8. What is structural security?
9. Identify how risk can be transferred.
10. Describe how risk is assumed.

Apply Your Knowledge

1. Identify specifics risk the business for which you are writing your marketing plan might encounter. Label each as controllable or uncontrollable.
2. List examples of the natural risks your business might face.
3. Considering the current economy, which specific economic and political risks might be challenging for your business?
4. Considering the current economy, describe specific market risks your business might face. As a marketing professional, how can you help your company reduce those risks?
5. List examples of human risks your business might face.
6. List examples of both speculative risks and pure risks your business might face.
7. Describe a plan for reducing risks that pertains to the employees in your business.
8. Describe a plan for reducing risks from burglary or robbery in your company.
9. How will you protect your company's technology assets from risks?
10. Describe a plan for transferring risks in your business. Describe the types of insurance your company should have and why they are necessary.

Apply Your Math Skills

Hannah is an entrepreneur who owns a small catering business. Apply your math skills to solve the following problems.

1. Hannah currently pays $510 annually for business insurance premiums. What is the monthly cost of this insurance policy?
2. Hannah's business is growing, so she wants to increase her insurance coverage. Instead of the policy described in question 1, she wants to purchase two separate policies:
   - policy A: $25 per month
   - policy B: $45 per month

   What is the total annual cost of the two insurance policies together?

Communication Skills

Reading Figurative language is used to describe something by comparing it with something else. Locate an advertisement for insurance services. Scan the information for figurative language about the product. Compare this with a description using literal language. Did the use of literal or figurative language influence your opinion of the services? Did the advertisement help you understand the service or company?

Listening Engage in a conversation with someone about risk. Ask the person how he or she manages risk in personal circumstances and more formal circumstances such as at school or a job. Actively listen to what that person is sharing. Next, summarize and retell what the person conveyed in conversation to you. Did you really hear what was being said?

Speaking The way you communicate with others will have a significant impact on the success of the relationships you build with them. Create a speech that explains methods of risk management. Deliver the speech to your class. How did the style, words, phrases, and tone you used influence the way the audience responded to the speech?

Internet Research

Natural Risks Research the most common natural risks for your city or state. Find out how often these risks usually occur and what they cost both individuals and businesses. What recommendations are made by the government and insurance companies to manage these risks? Present your findings to the class.

Filing an Insurance Claim Use the Internet to locate instructions on how to file an insurance claim. What specific information is needed to file the claim? What did you learn from the information that was given to you?

Marketing Risk Management Research *how to prevent shoplifting* using online resources. Take notes of the information you learn and its source. Then, write a two-page report to summarize your findings. Cite your sources at the end of the report.

Teamwork

Working with your team, identify examples of natural, economic, market, and human risks a business might face. How might a business manage each? Share your opinions with the class.

Portfolio Development

Introduction As you assemble your final portfolio, compose an introduction that provides an overall snapshot of who you are. This will be the first page of the portfolio that sets the stage for your presentation, so you want to make a good impression.

College and Career Readiness

1. Create a Microsoft Word document that will serve as your introduction. Use the heading "Introduction" and your name.
2. Tell the reader who you are, your goals, and any biographical information that is relevant. Highlight information by making references to sections or page numbers.
3. If applicable, direct the reader to the website or other electronic storage medium that contains examples or documents of importance.
4. Save the document.
5. Place a printed copy in the container for future reference.
6. Update your master spreadsheet.

CHAPTER 26

Business Funding

Sections

26.1 **Options for Funding**

26.2 **Apply for Financing**

Reading Prep

College and Career Readiness

Skim the chapter by reading the first sentence of each paragraph. Use this information to create an outline for the chapter before you read it.

Check Your Marketing IQ

Before you begin the chapter, see what you already know about marketing by taking the chapter pretest. The pretest is available at www.g-wlearning.com/marketing/.

DECA Emerging Leaders

Business Growth Plan Event

Career Cluster and **Instructional Area** are not identified for this event.

Knowledge and Skills Developed

Participants will develop many 21st century skills desired by today's employers in the following categories:
- communication and collaboration
- creativity and innovation
- critical thinking and problem solving
- flexibility and adaptabilty
- information literacy
- initiative and self-direction
- leadership and responsibility
- media literacy
- productivity and accountability
- social and cross-cultural skills

Purpose

Designed for one to three chapter members, the plan involves strategy development needed to grow an existing business owned by a current DECA member. Participants will analyze their current business operations and identify opportunities to grow and expand the business. **All participants must be documented owners/operators of the business.** A parent's business does not qualify. The Business Growth Plan Event consists of two major parts: the written document and the oral presentation by the participants.

Procedure

1. The written document will account for 60 points, and the oral presentation will account for the remaining 40 of the total 100 points. The body of the written entry must be limited to 30 numbered pages, including the appendix (if an appendix is attached), but excluding the title page and the table of contents. Prior to the presentation, the judge will evaluate the written portion of the entry. The major emphasis of the written entry is on the content. Drawings, illustrations, and graphic presentations (where allowed) will be judged for clarity.
2. The oral presentation may be a maximum 15 minutes in length including time for judge's questions worth 40 points. The presentation begins immediately after the introduction of participants to the judge by the adult assistant. Each participant must take part in the presentation. If time remains, the judge may ask questions pertaining to the proposal. Each participant may bring a copy of the written entry or note cards pertaining to the written entry and use these as a reference during the presentation. Each participant must respond to at least one question posed by the judge. Review Written Entry Format Guidelines and Checklist Standards in the DECA Guide.

Project

The business expansion may include franchising, expanding into new markets, opening a second location, licensing agreements, merging with or acquiring another business, diversifying product lines, forming strategic alliances with other businesses, expanding to the Internet, etc.

Critical Thinking

1. What existing business will you expand?
2. How will you expand the business?
3. What is the rationale for selecting this growth and expansion?

Visit www.deca.org for more information.

Published by DECA Inc. Copyright © by DECA Inc. No part of this publication may be reproduced for resale without written permission from the publisher. Printed in the United States of America.

Section 26.1

Options for Funding

Essential Question: How do entrepreneurs obtain enough money to begin operations?

Learning Objectives

LO 26.1-1 Explain the concept of bootstrapping for entrepreneurs.
LO 26.1-2 Describe common sources of business financing.
LO 26.1-3 Identify considerations owners have when starting a new business.

Key Terms

- bootstrapping
- start-up capital
- equity
- equity financing
- angel investor
- venture capitalist
- debt financing
- collateral
- line of credit
- peer-to-peer lending
- start-up cost
- operating expense

Bootstrapping
LO 26.1-1

Entrepreneurs need to create strategies for funding their new businesses. However, before seeking funds from outside sources, they often evaluate alternative strategies for getting the business off the ground.

When starting a new business, most entrepreneurs practice the art of bootstrapping. **Bootstrapping** is cutting all unnecessary expenses and operating on as little cash as possible. In your personal life, you may have used bootstrapping practices without realizing it. Perhaps you reduced extra spending to save for a vacation, buy a car, or get a new phone. There are many ways to practice bootstrapping when starting a business. Some ways to bootstrap are use free resources, use personal assets, negotiate, monitor expenses, and barter, as shown in Figure 26-1.

Use Free Resources

There will be many times when you need professional advice on starting a business. Before hiring someone to advise you, look for free services. There are many professional resources and services available at no cost to business owners. SCORE, the SBA, and state websites offer advice and other resources at no charge. Social media is also a free resource to use as a marketing tool.

Use Personal Assets

Many entrepreneurs start businesses from home to save on start-up and operating costs. They use their own equipment, such as a computer, phone, and printer. If additional equipment is

Bootstrapping Techniques

- Use free resources
- Use personal assets
- Negotiate
- Monitor expenses
- Barter

Goodheart-Willcox Publisher

Figure 26-1 Cutting all unnecessary expenses and operating on as little cash as possible is bootstrapping.

Many entrepreneurs start businesses from home to save on start-up and operating costs. *What personal assets could you use to start a business?*

needed, leasing instead of buying will help to save the up-front costs.

Negotiate

Many vendors are willing to offer better terms than what they advertise. Some of them began as small business owners and are willing to help new entrepreneurs. They may not negotiate on price, but might be willing to negotiate terms. Instead of a payment due in 30 days, ask if the vendor will give you a 45- or 60-day payment window.

Monitor Expenses

Create a budget and monitor your personal expenses. This will free up additional funds for your business expenses. Some ways to do this are to cut back on utilities and unnecessary spending. You might also switch to less-expensive utilities or rent a smaller space. There are many more ways to conserve cash.

Barter

Bartering is the exchange of goods or services for other goods or services. No money changes hands. Rather than pay for professional services, try bartering. For example, perhaps a person is opening a catering business and is in need of an accountant. The accountant needs a catering service for a client meeting. The two entrepreneurs can exchange catering services for accounting services. No money is exchanged, but both parties provide a service needed by the other business.

Start-Up Capital

As an entrepreneur, you will need cash to get a business up and running. **Start-up capital** is the cash used to start the business. Very few people have enough cash on hand to completely fund a business. Therefore, many entrepreneurs must look for other sources of start-up capital. Two common sources of financing are equity financing and debt financing, as shown in Figure 26-2.

Equity Financing

Equity is the amount of ownership a person has in a business. If an entrepreneur starts a business using only his or her own funds, he or she would have 100 percent equity in that business. This is called *self-funding*.

Equity financing is raising money for a business in exchange for a percentage of the ownership. For example, selling stock to raise money is really selling a percentage of ownership in the company. Many entrepreneurs use a combination of self-funding and equity financing.

Personal Funds

Many entrepreneurs use their own money as equity capital. This can include money from savings accounts, selling stock, cash in a retirement fund, or other personal resources.

Family and Friends

Sometimes entrepreneurs ask people they know to help fund a business. However, before asking family and friends to invest in the company,

Sources of Start-Up Capital

Equity Financing	Debt Financing
• Personal savings	• Banks and credit unions
• Family and friends	• Peer-to-peer/social lending
• Partners	• SBA-assisted loans
• Angel investors	• Retirement accounts
• Venture capitalists	• Family and friends
	• Trade credit

Figure 26-2 There are many sources of start-up capital to fund a new business.

Case in Point

Warby Parker

Friends Neil Blumenthal, David Gilboa, Andrew Hunt, and Jeffrey Raider were consumers frustrated by the high cost of designer eyeglasses. One pair of designer frames can cost as much as $500 or more, not including the additional costs for the lenses that go in the frames. These friends knew that glasses frames are often marked up two to three times.

As a result, the four friends developed a business idea. They decided to start a business, Warby Parker, to sell designer-style prescription glasses for under $100. In addition, for each pair the company sells, Warby Parker helps a person in need buy one pair of glasses. In order to fund the business idea, the group turned to some famous angel investors, including the former CEO of Tommy Hilfiger, actor Ashton Kutcher, and singer Lady Gaga's manager Troy Carter. More recently, a venture capital firm helped Warby Parker raise $12 million from Tiger Global, Menlo Talent Fund, and existing investors. This is an example of entrepreneurs creating a successful business as well as demonstrating social responsibility.

---

think about what could happen to the relationships should something go wrong with the business. Other alternatives may be better suited to the situation.

Partners

Another option for raising equity capital is to take on partners in the business. Partners can contribute to the start-up funding and share in responsibility and operations of the business. Like other equity options, a formal partnership agreement is necessary.

Angel Investors

Angel investors, or *angels*, are private investors who are interested in funding promising start-up businesses. An angel often has business experience that will help the new company. He or she is interested in adding value as well as making a return on the investment.

Some angels actively participate in the business to protect their investment. They may charge a monthly management fee. Others do not choose active participation in the operation. However, they are part owners in the company and expect a good return on the money invested.

Venture Capitalists

Venture capitalists, or *VCs*, are professional investors or investing groups that fund new start-ups or expansions of existing companies. *Venture capital* is the money invested in businesses by venture capitalists. VCs manage large investment funds and are always looking for suitable investment opportunities. They are willing to invest more money than angels in riskier start-ups to earn a high rate of return on the investment. Most VCs require 25 percent or more equity in the company.

VCs usually prefer investing in start-ups run by experienced entrepreneurs. They often fund new or expanding high-tech or other successful companies. Less than 1 percent of all businesses are funded by VCs.

Unlike angels, VCs rarely have personal experience in the industries in which they invest. Many have general management experience and want to remain involved in the business to protect the investment. Like some angels, there are also VCs who leave the daily business operations to the experts.

Rawpixel.com/Shutterstock.com

Debt financing is borrowing money for business purposes. *In what ways might the advantages of debt financing outweigh the disadvantages?*

Employability Skills

Shared Workspaces

Whether you are in an office, a cubicle, or an open room, chances are you will have to share your workspace with others. Always allow your neighbors their privacy. Knock before entering a room or speaking to someone. Walk around walls or partitions to communicate; do not shout over or around them. Wait to be invited into a conversation rather than jumping in just because it is within earshot.

Debt Financing

Debt financing is borrowing money for business purposes. Debt financing is one way to start or expand a business. One advantage is that the entrepreneur remains the business owner. One disadvantage is that the loan must be repaid plus interest, just like credit card debt. For those with poor credit, the interest rates can be higher.

To obtain debt financing, an application process is required. Like other types of loans, it is important to have a good credit rating. Some larger loans require collateral. **Collateral** is an asset pledged that will be claimed by the lender if the loan is not repaid. Loans that require collateral are known as *secured loans*. Examples of collateral for a loan can include a home, vehicle, or retirement savings.

Loans that do not require collateral are known as *unsecured loans*. Similar to credit cards, the loan can be granted on a signature rather than property. Sources for debt financing include banks and credit unions, peer-to-peer loans, SBA-assisted loans, retirement accounts, family and friends, or trade credit.

Banks and Credit Unions

The traditional way to obtain start-up capital is to obtain a loan through a bank or credit union. After a business is established and has a good credit history, a bank or credit union may extend a line of credit. A **line of credit** is a specific dollar amount that a business can draw against as needed. The business accesses money from the line of credit and pays it back on a regular basis, usually monthly.

Banks and credit unions might also extend credit to an established company through an overdraft agreement. An *overdraft agreement* allows a business to write checks for more than what is in the checking account. The institution pays the check through a line of credit and charges the company a fee for the overdraft protection.

Peer-to-Peer Lending

Peer-to-peer lending is a form of debt financing without the use of a financial institution. It is also known as *social lending*. With this type of loan, there is no lending institution. Peer-to-peer lending finds lenders who are willing to make loans to prospective borrowers. The loans are typically made via websites like Kickstarter.com. The advantages of peer-to-peer loans include potentially lower interest rates and shorter repayment time frames than traditional bank loans. Disadvantages include up-front fees, having personal information posted on a public website, and low loan amounts.

SBA-Assisted Loans

The SBA does not directly lend money, but it works closely with banks to provide small business loans through its Small Loan Advantage program. To qualify, a business owner must personally guarantee the loan by showing sufficient cash available for repayment. There are a number of different types of SBA-assisted lending programs for small business funding.

Retirement Accounts

Many people do not realize they can borrow from their retirement accounts, such as an individual retirement account (IRA) or 401(k). An individual retirement account (IRA) is a personal account for setting money aside for retirement. A 401(k) plan is an employer-sponsored account that an individual to deposit money for retirement. Caution should be used when borrowing from retirement accounts. There are very strict federal laws about how loans from retirement accounts can be used and repaid. There may also be tax consequences for borrowing from an IRA.

Money can be borrowed from an IRA interest-free for 60 days, which might be helpful to get through a short-term cash flow problem. Some 401(k) plans permit borrowing for any reason, but most allow loans only for specifically defined reasons outlined in the plan. A person may borrow up to $50,000 from a 401(k), but must pay interest along with the repayment of the loan.

Family and Friends

You may decide to ask for a loan from a relative or friend to help fund the business. One advantage to getting a loan from someone you know is the possibility of negotiating a lower interest rate. A family member or friend may also give you a better repayment schedule than a bank or credit union. It is important to sign a formal agreement with *any* lender, even ones you already know, so there are no misunderstandings. This also provides some legal protection for both parties.

Trade Credit

Trade credit is when one business grants a line of credit to another business for a short period of time to purchase its goods and services. The line of credit is most often 30 or 60 days. This makes it possible to make an interest-free purchase for 30 or 60 days. Payment is due in full at the end of the time period.

For example, a business that sells footwear and accessories might purchase a large quantity of socks from a clothing manufacturer on trade credit. The goal of the footwear retailer is to sell the socks within the 30- or 60-day time period. This would allow the retailer to repay the manufacturer with the profits made by selling the socks to customers.

The real benefit of trade credit is that you get products interest free for 30 or 60 days. Trade credit is most often used by established businesses. While most new businesses may have difficulty getting trade credit initially, it never hurts to ask.

LO 26.1-3 Starting the Business

New business owners must plan for a number of considerations before actually opening the doors. It is important for business owners to project the start-up costs and operating expenses, budget for owner cash withdrawal, and price products correctly.

Project Start-Up Costs and Operating Expenses

Start-up costs are the initial expenses necessary to begin operating a business. While identifying the exact start-up costs for a business, determine whether each expense is essential. For example, if your current computer is adequate, do not include the purchase of a new one in the start-up budget.

Some expenses will be one-time costs, such as equipment, filing a DBA license, utility deposits, and initial inventory. Typical one-time start-up costs are similar to those in Figure 26-3.

One-Time Start-Up Costs

- Down payment or rental deposit
- Furniture and fixtures
- Initial product inventory
- Office equipment
- Property improvements
- Utility deposits

Goodheart-Willcox Publisher

Figure 26-3 Entrepreneurs think of ways to save money on one-time start-up costs.

Other start-up costs are recurring operating expenses. **Operating expenses** are the ongoing expenses that keep a company functioning. Examples include rent payments and utilities. Operating expenses are classified as fixed or variable. A *fixed expense* is the same every month, such as mortgage payments and insurance premiums. A *variable expense* can change on a monthly basis. They include the cost of advertising, fees, and utilities, as shown in Figure 26-4.

According to Hiscox USA research, 20 percent of small business owners underestimate their start-up costs. The same study shows that over one-third of small business owners underestimate their operating expenses. For many business owners, underestimating start-up costs and operating expenses can mean the end of the business.

Monthly Operating Expenses

Fixed Expenses	Variable Expenses
• Insurance premiums • Mortgage or rent payment • Telephone bill	• Advertising • Fees • Office supplies • Utilities

Goodheart-Willcox Publisher

Figure 26-4 Be realistic when estimating ongoing operating expenses.

Social Media

Hashtags

Many social media platforms, including Twitter, Facebook, and Instagram, can convert a word with a hashtag in front of it into a searchable term. Any word can be turned into a hashtag by adding the pound symbol (#) immediately before the word with no space between the symbol and the word. A string of words can also be turned into a hashtag using the same process. To make multiple words into a hashtag, precede the phrase with the pound symbol and remove spaces between each word.

For example, if a business wants to promote its new product called OrcaWater, #OrcaWater would be placed in every post to create a searchable stream of relevant information about that product. Anyone searching on social media for that term can find all posts containing the hashtag in a single location.

Follow the *rule of two*: expect everything to cost twice as much and take twice as long as you think it will. Project exactly what the business can afford before incurring expenses. Review financial reports from other companies in the industry to learn types of operating expenses.

Ask area business owners who are not direct competitors about their typical operating expenses. Use a start-up cost calculator on the Internet to help estimate start-up costs. A SCORE mentor may be able to help set realistic amounts for start-up costs and operating expenses. Consider working with an accounting professional to help guide you through this process.

Budget for Owner Cash Withdrawal

A business owner does not receive a salary from his or her own business. Salaries are compensation for employees, not the owner. However, an owner may withdraw cash or assets from the business for personal use. It is very common for owners to make a cash withdrawal from the business, called a *draw*, to cover personal expenses.

Price Products and Services Correctly

Accurate pricing of products is crucial to business success. Conduct research and seek professional advice to help set prices. Pricing must be competitive and allow the business to make a profit.

Profit margin is the amount by which product sales exceed the cost of producing or selling the product. Profit margin is typically shown as a percentage. Each industry has acceptable profit-margin guidelines for pricing purposes. Some businesses calculate the cost of creating the product and then double that amount to set the price. Other businesses add a percentage of desired profit to the cost of creating the product. The industry and competition will dictate what is acceptable.

Forecast Sales Accurately

Sales forecasting is a complicated part of the business plan. The goal of the sales forecast is to not only project revenue but to also make sure the business has enough products to sell. Accurate sales forecasts are necessary to predict revenue and profits. Follow the rule of two by cutting your

mangostock/Shutterstock.com

New business owners must plan for a number of things before actually opening the doors. *How does careful planning lead to business success?*

Green Marketing

Paper Consumption

In our "paperless society," the average office worker in the United States will use approximately 10,000 sheets of paper in a year according to the EPA. Consider how much paper, ink, toner, and electricity is needed to print those pages. Businesses can reduce the consumption of paper and other resources by adopting a few simple practices.

Using digital forms and records cuts down on both costs and waste by reducing the amount of paper used. Transmitting digital forms via e-mail or file transfer network and using electronic signatures further lower the costs for a business by reducing the amount of time employees spend preparing and handling paperwork. Implementing digital alternatives to paper use whenever practical increases the efficiency of most business processes, in addition to saving natural resources.

---

best sales estimate in half. It is better to underestimate potential revenue than to overestimate it and come up short on revenue. Sales forecasting should be done in dollars as well as number of units that are projected to be sold.

There are multiple methods used to forecast sales. Use a sales-forecasting worksheet for your projections. You can find samples at the SCORE or SBA websites. Sales forecasts are usually done for monthly, quarterly, and yearly time periods.

Calculate the Break-Even Point

The *break-even point* is the amount of revenue a business must generate in order to equal its expenses. It is only after the break-even point is reached that profits are earned. Do not assume profits will increase by selling more products or services. This may happen over time. However, variable expenses may also initially increase and actually reduce the profit margin. Many entrepreneurs do not know their break-even points and end up running out of cash before making a profit.

First, estimate total costs by adding the fixed and variable expenses. Then, project sales for a year. Plot the sales and expenses on a graph, as shown in Figure 26-5. The break-even point is where the two lines intersect.

After reaching the break-even point, evaluate the marginal benefit and cost to producing various

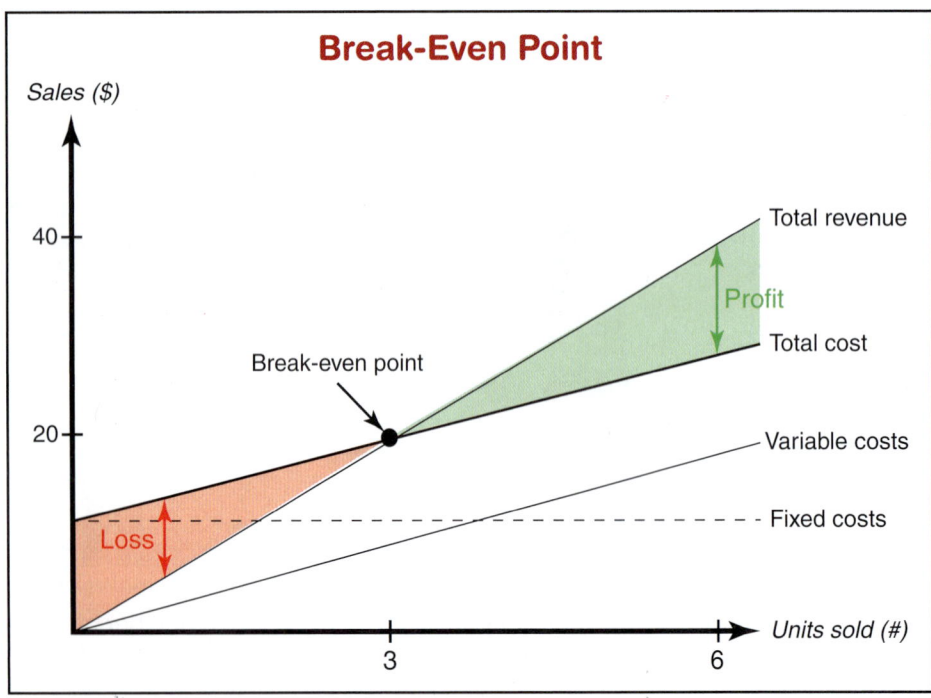

Figure 26-5 After finding the break-even point, assume it will take more sales than you project to reach that point.

Goodheart-Willcox Publisher

quantities of additional products. *Marginal benefit* measures the potential gains of producing more products that sell because the profit margin is higher. *Marginal cost* measures the potential losses from producing more products that might not sell. While the products may cost less to make, there is also the risk they will not sell and will decrease profits.

You Do the Math

Interpreting Circle Graphs

Graphs are used to illustrate data in a picture-like format. Many times, it is easier to understand the data if they are shown in a graphical form instead of a numerical form.

A circle graph looks like a divided circle and shows how a whole object is cut up into parts. Circle graphs are also called *pie charts* and are often used to illustrate percentages.

Monthly Expenses
- Gasoline 21%
- Meals 17%
- Entertainment 12%
- Rent 25%
- Savings 25%

Solve the following problems using the circle graph.
1. How much of the monthly expenses are for meals?
2. How much of the monthly expenses are spent on entertainment?
3. What accounts for the highest monthly expenses?
4. Determine the difference between the percentage of money spent on gasoline and the percentage spent on meals.

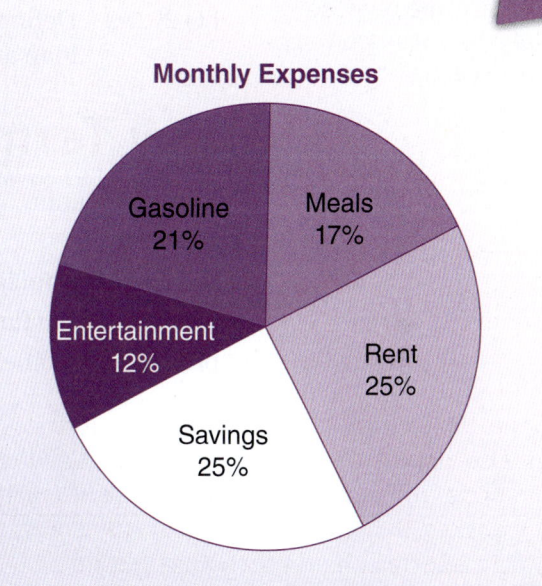

Section 26.1 Review

Check Your Understanding
1. What is bartering?
2. Name sources of equity financing.
3. What is the difference between a fixed expense and a variable expense?
4. Explain the rule of two.
5. How does the break-even point relate to profit?

Build Your Vocabulary

As you progress through this text, develop a personal glossary of key terms. This will help you build your vocabulary and prepare you for a career. Write a definition for each of the following terms and add them to your personal glossary.

angel investor
bootstrapping
collateral
debt financing
equity
equity financing
line of credit
operating expense
peer-to-peer lending
start-up capital
start-up cost
venture capitalist

Section 26.2

Apply for Financing

Essential Question
What is the purpose of a business loan application?

Learning Objectives

LO 26.2-1 Describe the business loan application process.
LO 26.2-2 Define three pro forma statements that accompany a business loan application.

Key Terms

loan application
cosigner
pro forma financial statement
pro forma cash flow statement
pro forma income statement
pro forma balance sheet
fixed asset
liquid asset
accounts payable
owner's equity

Business Loan Application Process
LO 26.2-1

Applying for a business loan is a complex process. A bank or credit union may be more likely to lend to existing customers with other accounts. However, there is no guarantee any customer will be granted a loan. It may be necessary to apply for a loan multiple times until the application is approved.

What Lenders Require

All lenders require the completion of a loan application. A **loan application** is a form with spaces for entry of financial and other information about the borrower. The application will ask for detailed information. It is important to take your time and complete the application form fully and accurately. Education, experience, past jobs, current debt, and the business projections all help the lender evaluate the application.

When applying for equity or debt financing, applicants are asked to provide documentation proving they are good credit risks. Items that are typically required for any small business loan application are shown in Figure 26-6.

It is important for all owners to provide résumés. Most lenders require applicants to have some management or business experience, especially for start-up businesses. Many loan programs require owners with more than 20-percent ownership in a business to submit signed personal financial statements. This is true for sole proprietorships, partnerships, and corporations.

All business loan programs require a sound business plan to be submitted with the loan application. The financial plans section of the business plan includes details about raising capital and future plans for the business. It also contains the

Loan Application Documents

- Bank statements
- Business plan with pro forma financial statements
- Collateral documentation, if necessary
- Income tax returns
- Personal financial statements
- Résumé(s)

Goodheart-Willcox Publisher

Figure 26-6 The quality of these documents may be the deciding factor in getting a business off the ground.

pro forma cash flow, income, and balance sheet financial statements. In addition, the following items may be requested, which are included in the business plan appendices:
- DBA, licenses, and registrations required to conduct business;
- partnership agreement or Articles of Incorporation;
- copies of supplier contracts;
- franchise agreement; or
- commercial lease.

Most business-loan programs require applicants to submit personal and, if possible, business income tax returns for the previous three years. Many also require one year of personal and business bank statements.

Collateral requirements vary greatly, often depending on the requested loan amount and degree of risk. It is a good idea to prepare a document describing the cost and value of any collateral used to secure a loan.

How Lenders Evaluate Applicants

Lenders making personal loans evaluate applicants on character, capacity, and capital, which are known as the *three Cs of credit*. However, when applying for a business loan, the criteria are somewhat different. This criteria is known as the *five Cs of banking*. The five Cs of banking include character, cash flow, capital, collateral, and conditions, as shown in Figure 26-7.

Character

All lenders run a credit report to learn an applicant's history of creating and paying debt. The report will come from a credit bureau that tracks individuals and their debt. Each consumer is rated according to the types of debt they have, on-time payments, and how quickly debt is repaid. The higher a credit score, the better the rating. Credit scores play a part in the ability to get a loan. Also, having very good credit may qualify you for a lower interest rate.

Cash Flow

Lenders want to know a business can generate enough cash flow to repay a loan on time. Sometimes, lenders ask for a cosigner on the loan. A **cosigner** is a person who signs a loan with the applicant and takes on equal responsibility for repaying

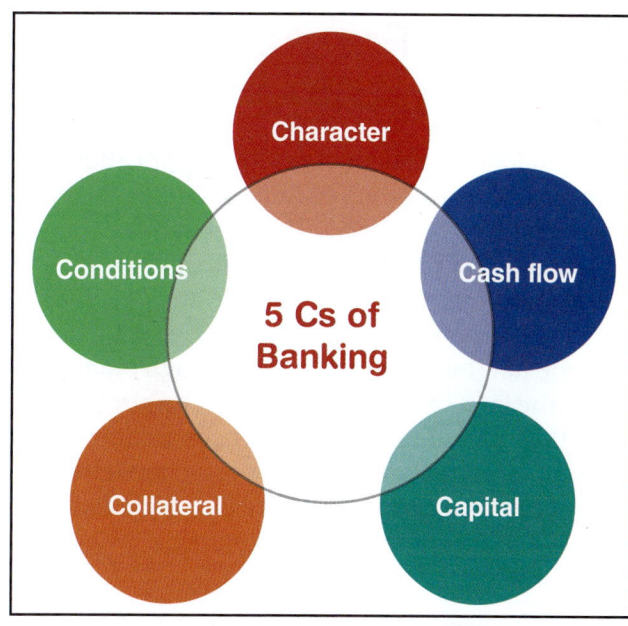

Figure 26-7 Lenders making business loans evaluate applicants on the five Cs of banking.

it. The cosigner usually has a better-established financial history than the primary applicant.

Capital

Applicants are asked about the amount of personal resources invested in the business and how they were obtained. It is important that there are enough assets in the business to keep it operating.

Collateral

If the loan is large enough, lenders require collateral to secure it. Collateral comes in many forms and is valued by lenders in different ways. For example, an entrepreneur may use the equity in his or her house as collateral for a loan.

Conditions

Lenders assess the economic conditions of the business' industry, the potential for the business to grow, and the form of ownership. They also consider the business location, competition, and applicant's insurance coverage. Given the conditions they find, the lender defines the terms under which a loan would be given. These terms may be as simple as the owner buying insurance for the business, or they may be more complex.

Pro Forma Financial Statements

LO 26.2-2

A major component of the loan application process is the pro forma financial statements that support the business plan. **Pro forma financial statements** are financial statements based on the best estimate of future revenue and expenses for a new business. Lenders need to see evidence that the new business will make enough money to repay the loan in a timely manner. The pro forma cash flow statement, pro forma income statement, and pro forma balance sheet will be completed as part of the application. They are also included in the Appendices of the business plan.

Pro Forma Cash Flow Statement

A **pro forma cash flow statement** reports the anticipated flow of cash into and out of the business. An example of projected cash flow for a service business is shown in Figure 26-8.

To prepare a pro forma cash flow statement, project the amount of sales, or *cash in*, expected for the first 12 months. Next, project the expenses, or *cash out*, for the same time period. If the business projects receiving more cash from sales than is spent on expenses, the cash flow is *positive*. If the business projects spending more than the amount of cash taken in, the cash flow is *negative*. It is a good idea to project several levels of sales to understand the best and worst scenarios.

Pro Forma Income Statement

A **pro forma income statement** projects the financial progress of the business. The two main sections of a pro forma income statement are projected revenue and projected expenses. A lender or investor may require a forecast for one year or multiple years. An example of a pro forma income statement for a three-year period is shown in Figure 26-9.

Pro Forma Balance Sheet

The **pro forma balance sheet** reports the assets, liabilities, and owner's equity for a proposed business. An example of a pro forma balance sheet is shown in Figure 26-10.

Sophia's Web Design Co.
Pro Forma Income Statement
Year Ended December, 20--

	Year 1	Year 2	Year 3
Revenue			
Sales	$76,500	$81,500	$92,000
Expenses			
Advertising Expense	15,000	16,000	18,000
Rent Expense	48,000	48,000	48,000
Insurance Expense	600	700	800
Supplies Expense	750	900	1,200
Utilities Expense	1,800	2,000	2,100
Total Expenses	66,150	67,600	70,100
Net Income	$10,350	$13,900	$21,900

Goodheart-Willcox Publisher

Figure 26-9 The pro forma income statement is used to project net income over a period of time.

Sophia's Web Design Co.
Pro Forma Cash Flow Statement
Year Ended December, 20--

	Jan.	Feb.	Mar.	Apr.	May	June	July	Aug.	Sept.	Oct.	Nov.	Dec.
Cash Receipts	$2,000	$3,500	$4,000	$4,200	$5,600	$8,200	$8,500	$8,600	$9,000	$9,100	$9,200	$9,600
Cash Disbursements												
Advertising	200	200	200	200	200	300	200	200	200	200	200	200
Rent	400	400	400	400	400	400	400	400	400	400	400	400
Insurance	50	50	50	50	50	50	50	50	50	50	50	50
Supplies	100	100	50	50	50	75	25	25	200	25	25	25
Utilities	150	150	150	150	150	150	150	150	150	150	150	150
Total	900	900	850	850	850	975	825	825	1,000	825	825	825
Net Cash Flow	$1,100	$2,600	$3,150	$3,350	$4,750	$7,225	$7,675	$7,775	$8,000	$8,275	$8,375	$8,775

Goodheart-Willcox Publisher

Figure 26-8 Use a pro forma cash flow statement to predict the best and worst outcomes.

Sophia's Web Design Co.
Pro Forma Balance Sheet
Year Ended December, 20--

Assets		
Cash	$5,000	
Accounts Receivable	9,600	
Equipment	32,000	
Total Assets		46,600
Liabilities		
Accounts Payable	$12,000	
Notes Payable	10,000	
Total Liabilities		22,000
Owner's Equity		
Sophia Nguyen, Capital		24,600
Total Liabilities and Owner's Equity		$46,600

Goodheart-Willcox Publisher

Figure 26-10 This pro forma balance sheet provides a snapshot of a business' financial position at the time of the loan application.

Assets are the property or items of value owned by a business. Assets may be fixed or liquid. A **fixed asset** is an item of value that may take time to sell. A building or heavy equipment is a fixed asset. A **liquid asset** is cash or the items a business owns that can be easily turned into cash. A checking account and accounts receivables are considered liquid assets. *Accounts receivable* is amounts owed to a company by its customers. Often, it is money owed for goods or services delivered. In accounting, accounts receivable are considered an asset.

Liabilities are the debts of a business. Liabilities may be short-term or long-term. *Short-term liabilities* are those expected to be paid within the current year. This includes salaries and accounts payable. **Accounts payable** is the money a business owes to its suppliers for goods or services received. In accounting, accounts payable are considered a liability. *Long-term liabilities* are debts that extend beyond the current year. Long-term liabilities can include repayment of a bank loan and rent.

The difference between a business' assets and its liabilities is called **owner's equity**. Owner's equity is also known as the owner's *net worth*. This information on a balance sheet is expressed as the *accounting equation*:

$$\text{assets} = \text{liabilities} + \text{owner's equity}$$

A lender may also ask for personal financial statements showing assets and liabilities unrelated to the business. The personal financial status of the business owner or owners will be reviewed along with the financial status of the business.

Section 26.2 Review

Check Your Understanding

1. Provide examples of documents lenders require in a business loan application.
2. List the five Cs of banking.
3. Why are pro forma financial statements required for a business loan application?
4. Name the two main sections of a pro forma income statement.
5. Explain the difference between fixed assets and liquid assets.

Build Your Vocabulary

As you progress through this text, develop a personal glossary of key terms. This will help you build your vocabulary and prepare you for a career. Write a definition for each of the following terms and add them to your personal glossary.

accounts payable
cosigner
fixed asset
liquid asset
loan application
owner's equity
pro forma balance sheet
pro forma cash flow statement
pro forma financial statement
pro forma income statement

Chapter 26 Review and Assessment

Chapter Summary

Section 26.1 Options for Funding

LO 26.1-1 Explain the concept of bootstrapping for entrepreneurs.
Bootstrapping is cutting all unnecessary expenses and operating on as little cash as possible. Some ways to bootstrap are use free resources, use personal assets, negotiate, monitor expenses, and barter.

LO 26.1-2 Describe common sources of business financing.
Two common sources of financing are equity financing and debt financing. Equity financing is raising money for a business in exchange for a percentage of the ownership. Debt financing is borrowing money for business purposes.

LO 26.1-3 Identify considerations owners have when starting a new business.
Business owners must plan for a number of considerations before starting a new business. It is important for owners to project the start-up costs and operating expenses, budget for owner cash withdrawal, and price products correctly.

Section 26.2 Apply for Financing

LO 26.2-1 Describe the business loan application process.
All lenders require a loan application, résumés, a sound business plan, income tax returns, and a description of any collateral that is required. Lenders making business loans evaluate applicants on the five Cs of banking: character, cash flow, capital, collateral, and conditions.

LO 26.2-2 Define three pro forma statements that accompany a business loan application.
The loan application requires pro forma financial statements that support the business plan. A pro forma cash flow statement reports the anticipated flow of cash into and out of the business. A pro forma income statement projects the financial progress of the business. The pro forma balance sheet reports the assets, liabilities, and owner's equity for a proposed business.

Check Your Marketing IQ

Now that you have completed the chapter, see what you have learned about marketing by taking the chapter posttest. The posttest is available at www.g-wlearning.com/marketing/.

Review Your Knowledge

1. Explain the concept of bootstrapping for entrepreneurs.
2. What types of free resources of advice are available to entrepreneurs?
3. Describe common sources of business financing.
4. Name sources of debt financing.
5. Identify considerations owners have when starting a new business.
6. Describe the business loan application process.
7. Why might a loan applicant need a cosigner?
8. Define three pro forma statements that accompany a business loan application.
9. What causes a business to project a positive cash flow?
10. Explain the difference between short-term liabilities and long-term liabilities.

Apply Your Knowledge

1. What challenges might you face as an entrepreneur when looking for ways to finance a new business?

2. Create a chart that shows ways to bootstrap your business. Write a description of how you could use each method of bootstrapping to help fund your business.

3. Create a chart that shows equity financing options for your business. Write a description of how you could use each method of equity financing to fund your business.

4. Create a chart that shows debt financing options for your business. Write a description of how you could use each method of debt financing to fund your business.

5. List all the potential start-up costs you might have for your business. Categorize each one as either a fixed expense or a variable expense.

6. Use the five Cs of banking to evaluate yourself as a business loan applicant.

7. List items you could use as collateral for a business loan.

8. Create a sample pro forma cash flow statement for three months of business operations. Use Figure 26-8 as a guide.

9. Create a sample pro forma cash income statement for one year of business operations. Use Figure 26-9 as a guide.

10. Create a sample pro forma balance sheet of your assets, liabilities, and owner's equity.

Apply Your Math Skills

Jeremiah wants to open a bait and tackle shop in a popular vacation destination. He is preparing pro forma financial statements in order to apply for a business loan. Apply your math skills to solve the following problems.

1. Jeremiah's cash flow statement shows the following information for the month of August. What is his expected net cash flow for August?
   - cash receipts: $3,000
   - advertising: $500
   - mortgage payment: $825
   - insurance: $60
   - supplies: $300
   - utilities: $75

2. In September, fishing season ends and many vacationers leave the town. Jeremiah plans to reduce his advertising and supplies expenses by half. He also expects to have half the amount in cash receipts. What is his expected net cash flow for September?

3. Jeremiah is unsatisfied with the amount of expected net cash flow in September. If he chooses to rent a business space for $500 a month instead of purchasing a building and having a mortgage payment, what would his new expected net cash flow be for August and September?

Communication Skills

Reading Select several chapters of this textbook. Identify two features that are used in each chapter selected. Compare and contrast how each feature is used. Why do you think the author chose those particular features to apply in multiple chapters?

Writing It is important for an employee to apply both technical and academic skills in the workplace. Understanding basic financial information is a workplace skill that is applied each day in personal and work life. Write a paragraph describing why understanding finance is considered a workplace skill for marketers. How do you think understanding finance will help you in your professional career?

Listening Critical listening occurs when specific information or instructions are needed. When your instructor provides instructions to the class, use your critical listening skills to understand the message. How can critical listening help you follow instructions and accomplish tasks?

Internet Research

SCORE Visit the website for SCORE. The SCORE website has many resources for business owners. Select an article from SCORE's library of business articles. Write a list of the main points of the article you choose.

Start-Up Costs Research typical start-up costs for a business in your industry. Were there any surprises as to the investment required? Next, use the Internet to locate a business start-up cost calculator. Use the calculator to predict what start-up costs will be for your business. Were the costs affordable?

Crowdfunding Peer-to-peer lending is a form of debt financing without the use of a financial institution. A popular example of this is called *crowdfunding*, in which entrepreneurs solicit small donations of just a few dollars from a large number of investors through social media. Search the Internet for *crowdfunding success stories* and read several. Did any of these stories surprise you?

Small Business Loan Application Form Research *small business loan applications* on the Internet. You may find these posted on the websites of financial institutions. Select an application form and review the information for which the form is asking. Then, complete it to the best of your ability. How long did it take you to complete the form? What did you learn from this exercise?

Teamwork

This chapter discusses the process for funding a start-up business. Working with your team, evaluate the ways to obtain debt financing. Rank these alternatives in the order that your team thinks is the most desirable financing choice for a new business owner and why. Present your opinions to the class.

Portfolio Development

College and Career Readiness

Organizing Your Portfolio You have collected various items for your portfolio and tracked them in your master spreadsheet. Now is the time to organize the contents. Review the items and select the ones you want to include in your final portfolio. There may be documents that you decide not to use. Next, create a flow chart to determine the organization for your portfolio. Your instructor may have specific guidelines for you to follow.

1. Review the documents you have collected. Select the items you want to include in your portfolio. Make copies of certificates, diplomas, and other important documents. Keep the originals in a safe place.

2. Check the quality of each item in your folders. Make sure that the documents you scanned are clear. Do a final check of the documents you created to make sure they are high quality in form and format.

3. Create the flow chart. Revise until you have an order that is appropriate for the purpose of the portfolio.

UNIT 9 Entrepreneurship

Building the Marketing Plan

Entrepreneurs are also marketers. After creating an idea for a new business, they must *sell* the idea to a great many people before actually beginning operations. Most entrepreneurs need some form of start-up capital from lenders or investors. In order to obtain necessary funding, the people who can grant that funding must want or believe in the new business.

The features and benefits of the business must be clear in a business plan. It is important to give customers or people granting business funding a reason to believe in the new product. It is important to give the reader of a marketing (or business) plan a way to quickly learn about what the plan contains and where to find what they are looking for. This takes place in the Executive Summary and the Table of Contents. The bibliography and appendices are important so that all the resources, research, financials, and other information is shown to be accurate and reasonable.

Part 1 Executive Summary

Objective
- Write the Executive Summary.

Directions
In this activity, you will write the Executive Summary for your marketing plan. An executive summary provides the overview of the marketing plan by highlighting the critical points of the plan. It should be written last because it reflects the entire plan you have spent so much time researching and writing. Access the *Marketing Dynamics* companion website at www.g-wlearning.com/marketing/. Download the activity file as indicated in the following instructions.

1. **Unit Activity 9-1—Executive Summary** Download the file for Unit Activity 9-1. Start the Executive Summary with an introductory paragraph designed to entice the reader to review the entire document. Finally, give an overview of the topics the marketing plan addresses. This section should be no longer than two pages.
2. Open your saved marketing plan document.
3. Locate the Executive Summary section of the marketing plan and write the Executive Summary. Delete the instructions and questions when you are finished recording your responses.
4. Save your document.

Part 2 Bibliography, Appendices, and Table of Contents

Objectives
- Create the Bibliography.
- Collect documents for the Appendices.
- Create the Table of Contents.

Directions
In this activity, you will write the Bibliography, assemble the Appendices, and create the Table of Contents. Access the *Marketing Dynamics* companion website at www.g-wlearning.com/marketing/. Download the activity files as indicated in the following instructions.

1. **Unit Activity 9-2—Bibliography** The Bibliography might include interviews, books, periodicals, websites cited, or other information you gathered while researching your marketing plan.
2. **Unit Activity 9-3—Appendices** List every document that you refer to in the plan in a logical order. The Appendices will be composed of these documents, which reinforce the information presented in the plan.
3. Open your saved marketing plan document.
4. Locate the Bibliography section of the marketing plan and list every source.
5. Locate the Appendices page in your marketing plan document.
6. Locate the Table of Contents and insert the final page numbers for each part of the plan.
7. Proofread your entire marketing plan. Make any final additions or corrections.
8. Save and print your document. Assemble and bind it in a professional manner.

UNIT 10
Preparing for a Career

Chapters

27 **Planning for Success**
28 **Preparing for Your Career**
29 **Digital Citizenship**

While studying, look for the activity icon for:
- Building the Marketing Plan activity files
- Pretests and posttests
- Vocabulary terms with e-flash cards and matching activities
- Self-assessment

These activities can be accessed at www.g-wlearning.com/marketing/.

Developing a Vision

Marketing yourself is one of the most important challenges you will face in your career. Create the image you want to project and begin focusing on your talents and strengths. It is never too early to begin marketing your own personal brand.

To compete in today's fast-paced economy, it will be important to know who you are and the goals you want to pursue. Creating a plan for your future will help guide you through endless personal and professional decisions. You may want a career in marketing or prefer one in a completely different field. Regardless of the direction you choose, this unit will walk you through the basic steps of planning for success.

Marketing Core Functions Covered in This Unit

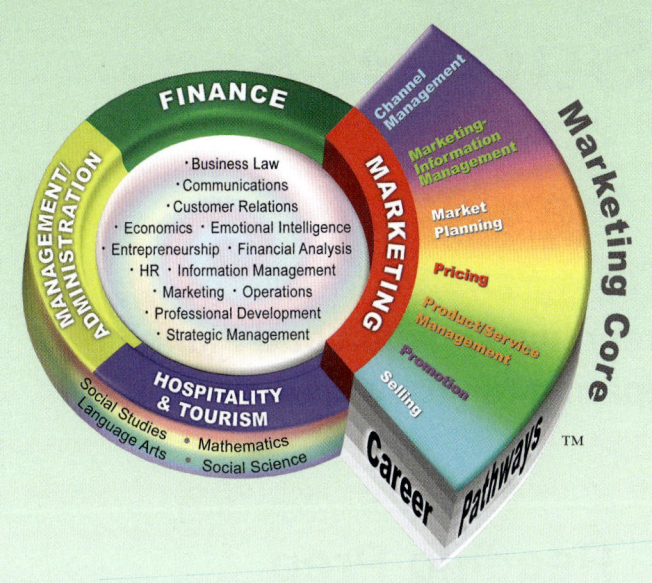

Functions of Marketing
- Promotion
- Selling

Copyright MBA Research, Columbus, Ohio. Used with permission.

EYE-CATCHER

Marketing Matters

As you begin looking for your first job, you may choose to use an online job-search service. Monster.com is one service that uses integrated marketing communications to appeal to its customers, who are both job seekers and employers. One strategy was the company's "Find Better" campaign. The multimedia campaign used the company website, mobile app, videos, multiple social media platforms, and the #FindBetter hashtag to reposition Monster.com. The company wanted to be seen as a solutions provider that young job seekers could turn to when searching for their first job or changing jobs for the first time.

dennizn/Shutterstock.com

CHAPTER 27
Planning for Success

Sections

27.1 **Career Investigation and Planning**
27.2 **Preparing for Your Education**

Reading Prep

College and Career Readiness

Before reading this chapter, go to the Review Your Knowledge section at the end of the chapter and read the questions. This exercise will prepare you for the content that will be presented in this chapter. Review questions at the end of the chapter to serve as a self-assessment to help you evaluate your comprehension of the material.

Check Your Marketing IQ

Before you begin the chapter, see what you already know about marketing by taking the chapter pretest. The pretest is available at www.g-wlearning.com/marketing/.

◆DECA Emerging Leaders

Principles of Hospitality and Tourism Event

Career Cluster: Hospitality and Tourism
Instructional Area: Economics

Performance Indicators
- Explain the principles of supply and demand.
- Describe the functions of prices in markets.
- Explain the concept of economic resources.
- Identify factors affecting a business's profit.

Purpose
Designed for first-year DECA members who are enrolled in introductory-level principles of marketing/business courses, the event measures the student's proficiency in those knowledge and skills identified by career practitioners as common academic and technical content in hospitality and tourism. This event consists of a 100-question, multiple-choice, business administration core exam and a business situation role-play with a business executive. Participants are not informed in advance of the performance indicators to be evaluated.

Procedure
1. The event will be presented to you through your reading of these instructions, including the Performance Indicators and Business Situation. You will have ten minutes to review this information to determine how you will handle the role-play and demonstrate the performance indicators of this event. During the preparation period, you may make notes to use during the role-play.
2. You will have up to ten minutes to role-play your situation with a judge. You may have more than one judge.
3. You will be evaluated on how well you meet the performance indicators of this event.
4. Turn in all your notes and event materials when you have completed the role-play.

Business Situation
You are to assume the role of business operations manager at the Plaza Hotel, a 500-room hotel located five blocks from the site of the upcoming Super Bowl. You have been invited to meet with the **chief revenue officer (judge)**. The chief revenue officer (judge) wants to make sure he or she understands economic concepts necessary for setting prices and profit goals.

You will explain the principles of supply and demand, pricing implications for hospitality and tourism-related businesses, and the additional performance indicators listed for this event. Following your explanation, the chief revenue officer (judge) will ask you to respond to additional concerns.

The meeting will take place in the hotel's small conference room. The chief revenue officer (judge) will begin the meeting by greeting you and asking to hear your explanation of economic concepts necessary to set prices and profit goals. After you have provided your explanation and have answered the chief revenue officer's (judge's) questions, he or she will conclude the meeting by thanking you for your presentation.

Critical Thinking
1. How are hotel prices impacted by a city hosting the Super Bowl?
2. Why should the hotel monitor the prices charged by competing hotels for the Super Bowl?

Visit www.deca.org for more information.

Published by DECA Inc. Copyright © by DECA Inc. No part of this publication may be reproduced for resale without written permission from the publisher. Printed in the United States of America.

Section 27.1

Essential Question

How are research and planning activities beneficial when making career decisions?

Career Investigation and Planning

Learning Objectives

LO 27.1-1 Describe the difference between a job and a career.
LO 27.1-2 Discuss the career planning process.
LO 27.1-3 List ways to research a marketing career.

Key Terms

job
career
profession
occupation
career clusters
career pathway
self-esteem
aptitude
ability

work values
interest
short-term goal
long-term goal
career plan
career ladder
internship
cooperative education program
employment trend

Exploring Career Options
LO 27.1-1

The average worker spends 37 percent of his or her day working, as shown in Figure 27-1. This means the choice of a career is one of the most important decisions a person will make.

In the world of work, the word *job* has two meanings. A **job** is the work a person does regularly in order to earn money. For example, a job may be a part-time position you work after school. A *job* is also a specific task done by a worker. A person can have a job as a retail sales associate for a local department store. On that job, the sales associate has the job, or *task*, of restocking the shelves as products are sold.

A **career**, on the other hand, is a series of related jobs in the same profession. **Profession** is the term used for jobs in a business field requiring similar education, training, or skills. A career is a

Time Use on an Average Workday

- Working and related activities 37%
- Sleeping 32%
- Leisure and sports 11%
- Household activities 4%
- Eating and drinking 4%
- Caring for others 5%
- Other 7%

Note: Data include employed persons on days they worked, ages 25–54, who lived in households with children under 18. Data include non-holiday weekdays and are annual averages for 2014. Data include related travel for each activity.

Source: US Department of Labor; Goodheart-Willcox Publisher

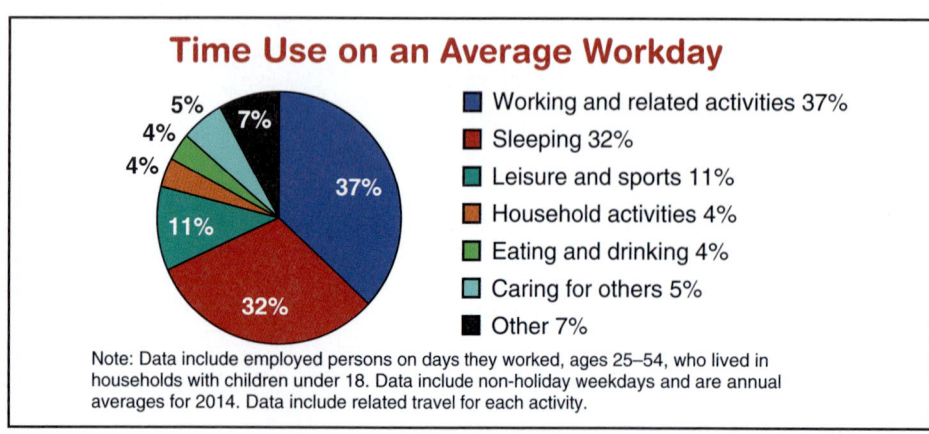

Figure 27-1 A person will spend many hours of his or her life at work.

position for which you prepare by attending school or completing specialized training. Over time, a job can turn into a career. **Occupation** is the term used for a specific career area, such as advertising. With each job, a worker usually gains greater knowledge and expertise. The series of jobs held often leads a person to greater responsibility and higher income. Getting a job is often a short-term goal. Building a career is a long-term goal.

With so many options available, researching a career can seem overwhelming. Studying the career clusters is a good starting point to determine where your interests lie. The **career clusters**, shown in Figure 27-2, are 16 groups of

The 16 Career Clusters

Careers involving the production, processing, marketing, distribution, financing, and development of agricultural commodities and resources.	Agriculture, Food & Natural Resources	Careers involving management, marketing, and operations of foodservice, lodging, and recreational businesses.	Hospitality & Tourism
Careers involving the design, planning, managing, building, and maintaining of buildings and structures.	Architecture & Construction	Careers involving family and human needs.	Human Services
Careers involving the design, production, exhibition, performance, writing, and publishing of visual and performing arts.	Arts, A/V Technology & Communications	Careers involving the design, development, support, and management of software, hardware, and other technology-related materials.	Information Technology
Careers involving the planning, organizing, directing, and evaluation of functions essential to business operations.	Business Management & Administration	Careers involving the planning, management, and providing of legal services, public safety, protective services, and homeland security.	Law, Public Safety, Corrections & Security
Careers involving the planning, management, and providing of training services.	Education & Training	Careers involving the planning, management, and processing of materials to create completed products.	Manufacturing
Careers involving the planning and providing of banking, insurance, and other financial-business services.	Finance	Careers involving the planning, management, and performance of marketing and sales activities.	Marketing
Careers involving governance, national security, foreign service, revenue and taxation, regulation, and management and administration.	Government & Public Administration	Careers involving the planning, management, and providing of scientific research and technical services.	Science, Technology, Engineering & Mathematics
Careers involving planning, managing, and providing health services, health information, and research and development.	Health Science	Careers involving the planning, management, and movement of people, materials, and goods.	Transportation, Distribution & Logistics

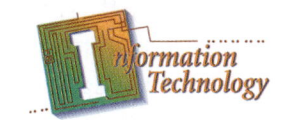

Source: States' Career Clusters Initiative 2008; Goodheart-Willcox Publisher

Figure 27-2 Each of the 16 career clusters contains multiple career pathways.

Case in Point

Walt Disney

Success is not always reached on the first attempt to meet your goal. As the old saying goes, "try, try, again." Walt Disney had that attitude. People think of Disney as a businessman who seemed to have been successful throughout his whole career. The truth is, he had many false starts as well as failures.

At age 16, he was rejected by the Army, so he joined the Red Cross and went to Europe and drove an ambulance. After returning home at age 21, Disney tried to get work at the *Kansas City Star* newspaper as a cartoonist, clerk, and even a truck driver. But the newspaper turned him down for each position.

However, drawing was his true calling. With family encouragement, Disney pursued a career in animation and started his own company. At first, he was mildly successful, but he ran out of money and went bankrupt. Eventually, he moved to Hollywood and continued to have some failures as well as great successes. Disney went on to lead one of the best-known and loved corporations in the world. Determination and motivation can help you reach your goals.

---

occupational and career specialties that share common knowledge and skills.

Within each of the clusters are multiple career pathways. A **career pathway** is a subgroup within a career cluster that reflects occupations requiring similar knowledge and skills. In these pathways, or *career areas*, you will find careers ranging from entry-level to those requiring advanced college degrees and years of experience. The careers within any given pathway share a common foundation of knowledge and skills.

No matter which career you choose, education and training will be necessary for success. Strengthen the skills you have and set a goal to improve those that need additional work. For example, if you need to improve your writing skills, consider taking a writing course. If you are a strong leader, look for additional opportunities to lead. Consider running for president of a career and technical student organization (CTSO) chapter or volunteer to chair a school or work event.

The career opportunities in marketing are endless. Remember that careers are constantly changing. By the time you finish school, there will be new careers and job titles that do not exist today.

Career Planning
LO 27.1-2

Success is a lifelong journey. When you read about an overnight success, you usually discover that person has been working hard for many years. Successful people often have a long-term goal and a detailed plan for achieving that goal.

Now is the perfect time to start thinking about your future. Planning can help you become successful in all areas of your life and help assure your career success. Career planning includes conducting a self-assessment, setting goals, and creating a career plan.

Conducting a Self-Assessment

Making personal decisions can be challenging. Decisions about your future should be based on your personal qualities and goals. Recall that *self-assessment* is the process of an individual evaluating his or her aptitudes, abilities, values, interests, and personality. Consider writing what you learn about yourself in a journal to help analyze your findings. Then, you can make decisions based on what you learned. You will likely change and grow as you learn more about the world of work and yourself. Your journal can be used to record and monitor these changes. This information can provide the basis for future decisions.

The way you feel about yourself can influence your self-assessment. **Self-esteem** is the confidence and satisfaction you have in yourself. The importance of self-esteem in the workplace is profound. People with positive self-esteem work well with others and tend to be encouraging. They want everyone to succeed. When facing difficult challenges or failures, people with positive self-esteem keep moving forward and still strive for excellence. They value themselves and their contributions to the workplace. Figure 27-3 provides strategies for building positive self-esteem.

Building Positive Self-Esteem
• Celebrate your achievements, no matter how big or small.
• Focus on the positive by turning negative thoughts into positive ones. For example, turn "I always make mistakes" into "I do many things well."
• Help someone else. It is amazing how your self-esteem grows when you put the needs of others first.
• Take good care of yourself by eating healthful foods, exercising, and taking the time to do things you enjoy.

Goodheart-Willcox Publisher

Figure 27-3 Individuals with positive self-esteem value themselves and their contributions.

Aptitudes

An **aptitude** is a characteristic that an individual has developed naturally. Aptitudes are also called *talents*. If you have an aptitude for something, you can do it or learn it easily. For example, some people have an aptitude for working with numbers. They can easily learn the mathematics required for a career as a market-research analyst. People usually have increased job satisfaction when they are able to use their aptitudes. Aptitude tests available through school counselors can help you discover natural strengths and weaknesses.

Abilities

An **ability** is the mastery of a skill or the capacity to do something. Having ability often involves learning a skill or a set of skills. Abilities affect your career choices by determining what you are able to do. While a person is born with aptitudes, abilities can be acquired. Often, it is easier to develop abilities that match your natural aptitudes. For example, a market-research analyst who does not have a natural aptitude for mathematics can learn how to do the equations, but it may take some time and practice. This person might not enjoy being a market-research analyst as much as other careers, since that job requires using mathematics and statistics.

Values

Recall that the principles and beliefs an individual considers important are *values*. They are developed as people mature and learn. Your values influence how you relate to other people and make decisions about your education and career.

Career counselors have discovered that people often have increased job satisfaction when their job matches their values. For example, some people value working outdoors. Such people are not usually happy in office jobs. They would probably be happier in an outside sales job than an inside telemarketer job.

Work values are the aspects of work that are most important to a person. Work values represent what you want from a job or career. Some work values may not be discovered until you have experience in the workplace, such as flexibility and time off, as they relate to family responsibilities and personal priorities. These can affect career choices.

A *work-life balance* is the amount of time spent at work compared to the amount of time spent with family and friends and engaged in leisure activities. For example, if you expect to have a family, you may decide that free time is a family responsibility. You may want to spend as much time as possible with your children as they grow. This may mean choosing a career that does not typically require travel or working long hours. On the other hand, it may be important to you to live in an expensive house and drive an expensive car. This personal priority will require a career with an income level that supports these choices.

Other work values may include the following.
- *Activity level.* Some jobs require a higher level of physical activity and stamina than others. Positions in sales, warehousing, and teaching typically involve a great deal of movement and

goodluz/Shutterstock.com

Self-assessment is an individual evaluating his or her aptitudes, abilities, values, interests, and personality. *What do you think a self-assessment might reveal about you?*

Marketing Ethics

Copyrights

It is unethical and illegal to use something created or written by another person without the permission to do so. Under copyright law, as soon as something is in tangible form, it is automatically copyrighted. Anything in print, including music, in TV or movies, or on the Internet is copyrighted. If any material is copied or used without permission by the owner, a theft has occurred. It is critical for a marketing professional to *not* use copyrighted material in promotions without permission from the owner.

Personality

Personality looks at an individual's traits and attitudes. *Traits* are behavioral and emotional characteristics that make each person unique. A variety of personal traits may affect your career decisions, including physical traits and personality traits.

- *Physical traits* are qualities related to a person's body, including levels of energy and stamina. For example, many sales and athletic coaching jobs require a great deal of physical stamina.
- *Personality traits* are qualities related to a person's mind or character. Personality traits include friendliness and creativity. Friendliness is important for certain jobs in the marketing career area, such as a sales associate. For other marketing jobs, such as copywriter or art director, creativity is more important.

Setting Goals

A *goal* is something you want to achieve in a specified time period. Areas in which people have goals include personal growth, finances, possessions, education, career, relationships, family, and community. For example, a personal-growth goal might be to run a marathon. An educational goal

physical activity throughout the day. Jobs in telemarketing, graphic arts, writing, and marketing research usually involve less activity.

- *Control*. Amount of control refers to how much workers control what they do on the job. Some jobs require employees to follow very strict and precise procedures, such as telemarketers who are required to read a set script to customers over the phone. Other jobs may offer workers more control in deciding how a job gets done. For example, an advertising sales representative may decide which clients to visit on which days and can develop his or her own sales approach.
- *Reward*. Rewards are related to the satisfaction workers get from a job. One form of reward is the money paid to do a job. There are other forms of rewards in the workplace in addition to salary, such as promotions, opportunities for increased responsibility, and recognition among coworkers.

Interests

An **interest** is a feeling of wanting to learn more about a topic or to be involved in an activity. Interests are those things that capture your attention and you are willing to spend time doing. What do you enjoy doing during your spare time? What hobbies do you have? In which classes are you most alert? How do you feel after participating in a sport or committee meeting? Do you participate in the activities of any organizations? There is a good chance a career exists that will allow you to do what you enjoy as a profession.

Sergey Nivens/Shutterstock.com

Interests are those things that capture your attention and you are willing to spend time doing. *How might your interests lead you to a career?*

You Do the Math

Functions

A function involves relating an input to an output. Each value in a *discrete function* is one of a specified set, usually a whole number. For example, the number of children in a family must be a whole number, so the function for how many children are in a family is a discrete function. The values in a *continuous function* do not have to be one of a specific set; they can include fractions, decimals, or irrational values. For example, the average age of students in a class does not need to be a whole number, so the function for average age is a continuous function.

Solve the following problems.
1. The number of marketing research participants needed for a representative sample. Is this a discrete or continuous function?
2. The amount a vendor charges for product delivery. Is this a discrete or continuous function?
3. The average income of a target market. Is this a discrete or continuous function?
4. The time required to create a marketing plan. Is this a discrete or continuous function?

---

might be to earn a college degree. The goals you set for yourself have to make sense to you. Your goals must be based on your personal characteristics, strengths, interests, and what you want in life.

One advantage of having goals is that they help you organize activities in order to more efficiently achieve them. Setting a goal is like having a target market. Once you know your goal, you can make decisions to help reach it. Not having a goal is like being in an airport and taking the first plane you see. You may or may not like your destination. Instead, if you know where you want to go before you get to the airport, you will buy the proper ticket and get there on time. Planning ensures that you will arrive at your chosen destination. You may have delays along the way, but you are more likely to get to the destination you chose.

There are two basic types of goals: short-term and long-term. A **short-term goal** is a goal that can be achieved in less than one year. A **long-term goal** is a goal that will take a longer time to achieve, usually longer than one year. *Goal setting* is a process of deciding what a person wants to achieve.

When setting career goals, it is important to make sure they are well defined. Recall that a *SMART goal* is specific, measurable, attainable, realistic, and timely.

Specific

A goal should be specifically defined and stated. For example, "I want to work in marketing" is not a specific goal. Instead, you might say, "I want to have a career as a marketing director."

Measurable

How will you know if you have reached your career goal? To be measurable, the progress toward achieving a goal should be able to be tracked. For example, "I want to earn a bachelor degree in business" is a measurable goal. The requirements of the school's business program allow you to track progress toward earning the degree.

Attainable

Is the goal actually attainable? For example, a student may want to be a marketing research analyst. However, this position requires strong math skills and knowledge of data management, in addition to marketing education. The goal becomes more attainable with a plan to obtain the necessary education and skills.

Realistic

For a goal to be realistic, it must also be practical. Sometimes, several shorter, more realistic goals are necessary to reach a final goal. For example, your ultimate goal may be to own a clothing store. Your first goal might be to get a job as a salesperson in a retail store. Then, set a goal to become a manager in the store. After learning how to manage that store, perhaps the next goal could be to obtain a position at the store's corporate headquarters and work your way into a position in the marketing department. Ambitious goals can be achieved if a person is highly motivated and has a plan to achieve them.

Timely

Setting a time for achieving a goal is the step most often overlooked. A goal needs an end date in order for progress to stay on track. For example, you may have a goal to find a summer job. If you do not set a firm date to achieve that goal, you may not have any job prospects by the time summer begins. However, if you establish that you will have a job by May 31, you can plan to achieve your goal by applying to three businesses every week. Setting an end date helps you remain motivated to reach your goal on time.

Creating a Career Plan

A **career plan** is a list of steps on a timeline an individual can follow to reach career goals. It is also known as a *postsecondary plan*. Figure 27-4 shows action items for a career plan for a student who wants to be a marketing director of a nonprofit organization.

A career plan is like a map used to guide a person to a career goal. There is no set format for writing one. Many people can have the same career goal, but each person develops a unique way to achieve the goal. In addition, a career plan is never final. It may change as you continue learning and gain experience in your career.

The challenge is to choose a career that matches your aptitudes, abilities, values, interests, and personality. The career choice you make now is not necessarily permanent. People often change careers over the course of their working lives. However, making a career choice and setting a career goal in high school can be very beneficial. By committing to a chosen career, you will learn a great deal about that career and yourself. You will also have a solid plan for a way to earn a living.

Before you match yourself to a career, learn about the careers you are considering. Narrow your choice to a career that really suits you. As you work on your self-assessment and evaluate careers, the career clusters become an important tool. While researching different careers, identify the training, education, and certification requirements for the occupations you might choose. You will need this information when creating your career plan.

Career planning is a lifelong process. Making a career plan now points you in a direction that enables you to gain experience and expertise in a particular area. If you know yourself well and form a good plan, your future career will have a solid foundation. As you pursue a specific career goal through planning, you learn a great deal about yourself and the career.

Once you have a career, you can always make changes along the way. People change careers because the world of work keeps changing. New technology leads to changes in job requirements. Changes in local and world economies also result in changes in jobs. People who are able to assess their skills and update their career plans are in the best position to continually find gainful employment.

In the process of working through your career plan, you might discover the career is not right for

Action Items for a Career Plan: Marketing Director of a Nonprofit Organization

	Education and Training	Job Experience	Extracurricular and Volunteer Activities
During Middle School	Enroll in a career exploration course	Summer camp counselor-in-training	Volunteer at animal shelter
During High School	Enroll in a college preparatory program and marketing courses	Co-op job, summer job as camp counselor, summer job as cashier	Join DECA, run for DECA officer, volunteer at animal shelter
During College	Study to earn a college degree in marketing	Internship in public relations at local hospital	Volunteer to do marketing for a nonprofit
After College	Attend a seminar in grant writing	Find a job in the marketing or fund-raising department of a nonprofit	Join the Association of Fundraising Professionals

Goodheart-Willcox Publisher

Figure 27-4 A career plan can be changed and updated as a person gains more experience in a chosen field.

you. You will not have wasted your time pursuing the career, though. The experience will have allowed you to gather important information about yourself and the world of work to develop your next career goal and plan.

LO 27.1-3 Researching a Marketing Career

Are you always coming up with new ideas? Are you a person who is creative? *Creativity* is inventing an original idea or thought. Many people in marketing careers are able to use their creativity every day. Recall that *marketing professionals* help determine the marketing needs of a business, develop and implement marketing plans, and focus on customer satisfaction.

Marketers take on both the risks and responsibilities of persuading others to buy products. Activities involved in marketing include:
- determining what customer research is needed;
- deciding how to get products to customers;
- pricing, promoting, and selling products; and
- deciding how to manage data and information.

There are many marketing careers that fit different interests, skills, and abilities. Students who are good at math may consider a career as a market researcher. Those that enjoy and have a talent for art may consider a career in advertising or graphic design. If you enjoy meeting and interacting with new people, a career as a professional salesperson may be perfect for you. Marketing professionals work for institutions, nonprofits, small companies, and large companies. They work in large cities and small towns. Opportunities are all around.

Careers related to marketing appear in every pathway in the career clusters. However, the career pathways that fall specifically in the Marketing career cluster include: *Marketing Management*, *Professional Sales*, *Merchandising*, *Marketing Communications*, and *Marketing Research*. Selected careers from each Marketing pathway are listed in Figure 27-5.

Work Focus

There are many ways to analyze employment opportunities. One of the most useful ways is to determine whether the job focuses more on people, objects, or data. When researching a marketing career, consider the work focus of the career.
- *People-focused jobs* center on working with people, usually helping them in some way. Sales jobs and teaching jobs are examples of people-focused jobs.
- *Objects-focused jobs* involve working with objects to build or create things. For example, visual merchandising is an objects-focused job because visual merchandisers arrange items to create a display.
- *Data-focused jobs* work with data, such as numbers, words, and information. A data-focused job can involve researching, accounting, or writing. Market-research analyst and inventory management are data-focused jobs. Figure 27-6 shows some general characteristics of people who succeed in each work focus area.

Careers within the Marketing Career Pathways

Marketing Management	Professional Sales	Merchandising	Marketing Communications	Marketing Research
• Chief executive officer • Entrepreneur • Inventory clerk • Shipping/receiving manager • Small business owner	• Account executive • Broker • Regional sales manager • Sales executive • Technical sales specialist	• Department manager • Merchandise buyer • Retail marketing coordinator • Sales associate • Store manager	• Advertising manager • Creative director • Interactive media specialist • Public relations manager • Sales representative	• Brand manager • Market-development director • Product planner • Research associate • Research specialist

Goodheart-Willcox Publisher

Figure 27-5 There are many career opportunities in the Marketing career pathways.

Work Focus

People Focus	Objects Focus	Data Focus
• Enjoy being in groups • Belong to one or more organizations • Volunteer to help others • Outgoing and friendly	• Enjoy working alone • Like to build, cook, sew, paint • Good at building or repairing things • Collect things	• Enjoy working alone • Like to write or work with numbers and computers • Enjoy research and learning • Read many books

Goodheart-Willcox Publisher

Figure 27-6 Most jobs have a people focus, an objects focus, or a data focus.

Supervisory or management roles usually have a people focus plus one other focus, objects or data. Their major responsibility is to work with employees and maintain productivity. However, supervisors also need strong data skills because they usually are responsible for planning and organizing.

Career Ladder

Some marketing careers require more education, training, and experience than others. A **career ladder** is a series of jobs organized in order of education and experience requirements. Often, each job in a person's career path requires more education and experience than the previous one.

The steps on the career ladder are called *career levels*. In each career area, there are multiple opportunities for employment on each level.

The positions are generally grouped by skill levels or education. Each higher level on the career ladder requires more education, more experience, or both. Advancing a level also tends to involve more responsibility, but usually offers higher pay. Figure 27-7 shows an example of a corporate career ladder. Career ladders vary within specific career areas and among companies.

The first job on a career ladder is an *entry-level job*. Entry-level jobs require the least amount of education and experience. These first-level jobs are called "entry-level" because they are the jobs through which a person enters the career. Some

Career Ladder

Career Level	Description	Minimum Education or Experience Requirements	Relative Wages or Salary
Entry level	First job in the career area; worker must be trained and supervised	No experience or specific education required; high school diploma often preferred	$
Career level	Knows job well and can perform it with little supervision; levels and titles for these positions vary	One year or more experience usually required; high school diploma preferred	$$
Specialist level	Specialized skills and knowledge for the job are mastered; levels and titles for these positions vary	Two or more years of experience or a two-year college degree and one or more years of experience usually required	$$$
Supervisory level	Responsible for operating a department, including hiring employees and fiscal budgets	Two-year college degree and two or more years of supervisory experience; a four-year college degree often preferred	$$$$
Executive level	Responsible for operating a corporate division	Four-year college degree and ten or more years of management experience usually required; graduate degree (MBA) often preferred	$$$$$

Goodheart-Willcox Publisher

Figure 27-7 Every career has a ladder of jobs with increasing pay and responsibilities.

sirtravelalot/Shutterstock.com

First-level jobs are called "entry-level" because they are the jobs through which a person enters the career. *How might an entry-level job help you reach your career goals in the future?*

entry-level jobs have no education or experience requirements. Examples include cashiers, some sales jobs, and stock handler jobs. Other entry-level jobs may require a four-year college degree, such as jobs in advertising, public relations, and marketing research.

Not everyone wants to climb the career ladder. Many people are happy in their first-level jobs. These jobs suit their personalities, income requirements, and other needs. A person can turn an entry-level job into a career. For example, many retail sales associates make a career of retail sales.

Some people are interested in moving up the career ladder. For these people, an entry-level job is usually considered a stepping-stone to a higher-level job. A *career-level* position requires employees to have the skills and knowledge for continued employment and advancement in a field. Career-level positions in marketing include sales promotion coordinator, marketing specialist, customer-insights analyst, and buyer trainee.

A *specialist-level* position requires specialized knowledge and skills in a specific field of study. Specialist-level positions in marketing include public relations specialist, industrial sales agent, merchandiser, and assistant product analyst.

A *supervisory-level* position requires specialized knowledge and skills and has management responsibility over other employees. Supervisory-level managers direct the work of others, make decisions, and are usually responsible for a group of workers in a specific department. Supervisory-level positions in marketing include public relations manager, product manager, marketing-research supervisor, merchandise manager, and national sales manager.

An *executive-level* position is the highest level position responsible for the planning, organizing, and management of a company. Positions at this level typically develop goals for the entire company and the strategies to meet those goals. Executive-level positions in marketing include vice president of marketing, vice president of merchandising, and vice president of sales.

Career and Technical Student Organizations

A *career and technical student organization (CTSO)* is an organization for high school students interested in a particular career area, such as DECA for marketing students. CTSOs are national student organizations with local school chapters related to career and technical education (CTE) courses. Participation in CTSOs helps students learn about themselves and their interests. Work experiences may also be a part of the CTSO experience. CTSOs can help prepare high school graduates for their next step, whether it is college or entering the workforce.

CTSO Goals

The goal of CTSOs is to help students acquire knowledge and skills in different career and technical areas. This includes developing leadership skills and gaining work experience for professional development. CTSOs guide students to become competent, successful members of the workforce. Support for local CTSO chapters is often coordinated through each state's education department. Local chapters elect officers and establish a program of work. The CTSO advisors help students run the organization and identify the best programs to meet the goals of the educational area.

CTSO Opportunities

Competitive events are a main feature of most CTSOs. Competing in various events enables students to show mastery of specific content. These events also measure the use of decision-making, problem-solving, and leadership skills. Students may receive awards for participating

Employability Skills

Punctuality

Employees are expected to be on time to begin work each day. You should be at your workstation ready to work when you are to begin your day. It is not acceptable to arrive at your starting time, hang up your coat, talk to your coworkers, and then go to your workstation. If your starting time is 8:00 a.m., you should begin working at 8:00 a.m., rather than 8:15 a.m. It is equally important to be on time to meetings scheduled throughout the day.

in events. In some cases, scholarships may be awarded if students win at state- and national-level competitions.

Participating in a CTSO can promote a lifelong interest in community service and professional and career development. Student achievement in specific areas, such as leadership or patriotism, is recognized with certificates or awards. Other professional development opportunities may include:

- completing a school or community project related to the field of study;
- training in the career area;
- supporting a local or national philanthropic organization; and
- attending CTSO state meetings.

Informational Interviewing

Another way to learn about a marketing career is to talk to a marketing professional. *Informational interviewing* is talking with a professional to ask for advice and direction, rather than asking for a job opportunity. Suppose you are interested in becoming an advertising copywriter. You could enlist the help of your teacher or guidance counselor to arrange an informational interview with a professional copywriter to learn more about the position, requirements, opportunities, and daily tasks.

Before an informational interview, develop a list of questions. They should cover what you most want to know about the career. Figure 27-8 shows some examples of questions a student might ask during an informational interview.

Job Shadowing

Watching someone at his or her place of employment is also a way to learn about a career. *Job shadowing* is following a person while he or she works. For example, if you are interested in becoming a hotel manager, call the manager of a nearby hotel and explain your interest in becoming a hotel manager. Ask if you could shadow him or her for a few hours.

On-the-Job Experience

An excellent way to learn about an industry is to actually work in the industry. Students typically have several opportunities to gain work experience in marketing. For example, you could get a part-time or a summer job at a retail business. Your school may offer an internship or cooperative education program.

An **internship** is a short-term position with a sponsoring organization that provides an opportunity to gain on-the-job experience in a certain field of study or occupation. In an internship, students prepare for an occupation through actual job experience. Internships may be paid or unpaid.

In a **cooperative education program**, or *co-op*, students prepare for an occupation through a paid job while taking classes that are related in subject matter to the job. In these programs, your school helps you find the part-time job. The job becomes part of your educational experience and is usually considered equal to your classroom studies. Many schools also run school stores where marketing students have an opportunity to learn a variety of marketing and business skills.

Informational Interview Questions

- What do you like most about your job?
- How many hours do you work each day?
- What do you like least about your job?
- What was your first job?
- Which jobs and experiences were the most helpful in reaching your career goal?
- In what area should I focus my education?
- How much education should I complete?
- Do you have any advice for me?

Goodheart-Willcox Publisher

Figure 27-8 Develop a list of questions before an informational interview to cover what you most want to know about the career.

Sergey Nivens/Shutterstock.com

A way to learn about a career is to talk with a career professional in an informational interview. *What questions would you ask in an informational interview?*

Employment Trends

An **employment trend** is the direction of change in the number of jobs within a particular career. Are the number of jobs increasing or decreasing in the career you are considering? It is always a good idea to look for a job in a career that is growing. For the near future, many occupations in marketing are growing. According to the US Department of Labor's Bureau of Labor Statistics, jobs in sales and related occupations are projected to grow more than 5 percent from 2014 to 2024, resulting in hundreds of thousands of new jobs.

There are two points to keep in mind about employment trends. First, employment trends can change quickly. There can be unexpected changes in the national or global economy. If the economy begins to contract, jobs in many sectors may be lost. In addition, unexpected political events, such as war, can also affect employment. Second, the economic environment of the city in which you are looking for a job may be different than the reported national trends.

Many occupations that are not growing still need a large number of people each year because people retire or change jobs. Sources of information on employment trends include the US Department of Labor (DOL), industry-specific professional associations or organizations, and professional publications. You can also ask friends, family, and professionals you know for their experience and guidance.

US Department of Labor

The DOL sponsors the *Occupational Information Network (O*NET) OnLine*, an interactive career resource. This website enables you to research careers, read their descriptions, and match your skills to a career.

Another online resource sponsored by the DOL is CareerOneStop. It operates as a federal-state partnership and is a collection of online tools to help job seekers find jobs and employers find workers. It includes links to state job banks that list open jobs for each participating state. The Toolkit on the website includes information for making smart career decisions, such as how to find schools and scholarships.

The US Department of Labor's Bureau of Labor Statistics (BLS) compiles and publishes a great deal of information on occupations, industries, and jobs in the United States. One of the most useful documents is the *Occupational Outlook Handbook*. The publication is available at most libraries and online. It provides information and statistics on occupations and individual jobs. The information is revised every two years.

Another useful publication is the *Career Outlook*, a website maintained by the BLS. It covers a variety of topics on job searching and career development, as well as ideas and information about specific careers. An online version is also available.

Professional Associations and Organizations

Professional associations and organizations often provide continuing education, training seminars, and networking opportunities for people in different industries. They may also be called *trade associations*. Many associations have regular meetings and events and often provide information about the industry and specific jobs within it. These groups may have a division or services specifically for students and others interested in the occupation. Some may even provide scholarships.

One of the largest associations for marketing professionals is the American Marketing Association (AMA). Many marketing occupations have their own professional associations. For example, the National Retail Federation and the National Automobile Dealers Association serve occupations in sales. In advertising, there is the American Association of Advertising Agencies. The National Association of Wholesale Distributors applies to the wholesale trade. A listing of professional associations can be found in the *Occupational Outlook Handbook*.

Professional Publications

There are many marketing-related newspapers, magazines, journals, and books. Several marketing associations have publications in their marketing area. These are often available online. Some are available only to members, while others are more widely available. *The Wall Street Journal* is an excellent source for financial, business, and marketing news. The AMA publishes a variety of newspapers and journals, including *Marketing News*. Crain Communications, Inc. publishes various newspapers and magazines, including *Advertising Age* and *B2B*. VNU Business Publication publishes *Adweek*, *Brandweek*, and *Sales and Marketing*, among others.

Section 27.1 Review

Check Your Understanding

1. How does a career differ from a job?
2. What three steps are part of career planning?
3. Cite examples of the attributes a student might examine when conducting a self-assessment.
4. What is the goal of CTSOs?
5. What are entry-level jobs?

Build Your Vocabulary

As you progress through this course, develop a personal glossary of key terms and add it to your portfolio. This will help you build your vocabulary and prepare you for a career. Write a definition for each of the following terms, and add it to your personal glossary.

ability
aptitude
career
career clusters
career ladder
career pathway
career plan
cooperative education program
employment trend
interest
internship
job
long-term goal
occupation
profession
self-esteem
short-term goal
work values

Section 27.2

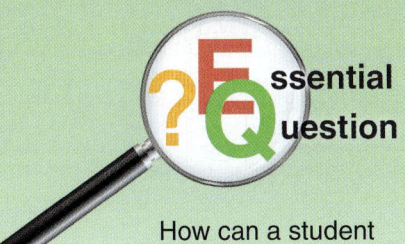

Preparing for Your Education

Essential Question

How can a student prepare for his or her education and training after high school?

Learning Objectives

LO 27.2-1 Describe the role of education, training, and certification in career choices.
LO 27.2-2 Cite factors that indicate the quality of an education investment.
LO 27.2-3 Explain the term *college access*.
LO 27.2-4 Identify sources of funding for pursuing an education.

Key Terms

education
formal education
tech prep
postsecondary education
not-for-profit school
for-profit school
graduate education
postgraduate education
occupational training
apprenticeship
college access
529 plan
grant
scholarship
work-study program
need-based award

Education, Training, and Certification (LO 27.2-1)

There are many steps you will take as you plan your career. Your educational needs will depend on your career interests and goals. Some careers require a high school diploma followed by technical training or a bachelor degree. Others require a master or doctorate degree. Many may also require professional certification. Early career planning can help you make decisions about your education. Investigating the opportunities and costs of future education, training, and certification is an investment in your future.

Education, training, and certification have a direct effect on income and career potential. Some employers pay higher salaries to those individuals who continue training in their positions and become more skilled in their areas. Certain positions may require additional training in order to advance career potential.

Education

Education is the general process of acquiring knowledge and skills. Education can occur anywhere and continues throughout your life. **Formal education** is the education received in a school, college, or university. Most careers require a college degree. However, for an entry-level position, a high school diploma may get you in the door. Jobs higher up the career ladder often require additional, formal education. Figure 27-9 shows the general order of degrees.

High School

The minimum educational requirement for most entry-level jobs is a high school diploma. During high school, a variety of subjects are covered. This gives students a well-rounded education to serve as a foundation for continued learning. To an employer, a diploma indicates that you have basic reading, writing, and math skills.

Educational Degrees

Degree	Institution of Higher Learning	Career Examples
High school diploma • Four years to complete	• Public or private high school	• Entry-level sales • Retail supervisor
Certificate • Usually complete in one year or less • High school diploma prerequisite	• Career center • Vocational-technical school • Career school • Community college • Professional organization	• Real estate broker • Security officer • Cosmetologist
Associate degree • Generally a two-year program • High school diploma prerequisite	• Community college • Vocational-technical school • Career school	• Retail management trainee • Technical sales representative • Web designer
Bachelor degree • Generally a four-year program (two if an associate degree is held) • High school diploma prerequisite	• Four-year college or university	• Advertising account representative • Public relations • Warehouse manager
Master degree • Generally a two-year program • Bachelor degree prerequisite	• Four-year college or university	• Marketing manager • Database administrator • Senior project manager
Doctorate degree • Completion time varies depending on course of study • Bachelor or master degree prerequisite	• Four-year college or university	• Director of research • Chief executive officer • University professor

Goodheart-Willcox Publisher

Figure 27-9 Different careers require different levels of formal education.

totojang1977/Shutterstock.com

Formal education is the education received in a school, college, or university. *How much formal education do your career goals require?*

A type of career preparation program for high school students is tech prep. **Tech prep** is a career preparation program that combines the last two years of high school with two years of postsecondary education. However, it does not include on-the-job experience. Tech prep programs are also called *2+2 programs* because they include two years of high school coursework plus two years of postsecondary classes. The postsecondary classes are often taken at a community college or a career school. At the end of the program, the student has a high school diploma and an associate degree or a technical certificate. The student is prepared to enter the workforce or continue his or her education at a four-year college.

Postsecondary Education

Postsecondary education is any education achieved after high school. This includes all two- and four-year colleges and universities. Common postsecondary degrees are an associate degree and a bachelor degree. An associate degree is a two-year degree. A bachelor degree is a four-year degree.

Area of Study Students in postsecondary schools choose an area of study that interests them or meets a career goal. This is referred to as a *major area of study* or *major*. For example, a student who wants to become a market-research analyst may major in statistics or business.

When considering a major, research the income potential of various related careers. Some careers start at a low salary and steadily increase over the course of the career. Other careers may start high and continue to increase. Also look into the number of jobs available in the career area, both for new graduates and for those with experience.

In addition to major areas of study, postsecondary students are typically required to take a wide variety of classes in other subjects. These courses are referred to as *general education* courses. They cover many of the same subject areas as high school courses. The courses also cover subjects not often offered at the high school level, such as political science and psychology.

Not-for-Profit and For-Profit Schools A postsecondary school may be either a not-for-profit school or a for-profit school. A **not-for-profit school** is one that returns the money it earns back into the school. These schools receive funding from student tuition and fees, donations, and governmental programs. A not-for-profit school is what most people think of as "college." It may be a public school, such as a state university, or a private college or a university. Not-for-profit schools tend to encourage academic exploration and personal growth beyond the specific requirements of a student's major.

A **for-profit school** is one that is set up to earn money for investors. It sells a product, which is education. In return for providing education, for-profit schools receive money from their customers, who are students. For-profit schools are also known as *proprietary schools*. They tend to focus on specific skills and do not require general education courses. They typically offer a two-year degree specialized in a field or trade, such as automotive repair or cosmetology. Some for-profit schools offer bachelor degree programs.

Requirements and Costs When considering a college or university, be aware of what is needed to apply. Requirements may include:
- official transcripts;
- college exam test scores;
- essays; and
- interviews.

For all requirements, be sure to know the deadlines for completing and submitting the information. Missing a deadline can mean not being accepted to the school.

The costs of a postsecondary education must be considered. In addition to tuition, there are fees for many classes. Some majors include many laboratory classes that can have more fees than other courses. Living expenses must also be included as part of the cost of a postsecondary education.

Graduate and Postgraduate Education

Education received after an individual has earned a bachelor degree is **graduate education**. Master degrees are graduate degrees. Education beyond a master degree is called **postgraduate education**. Doctorate degrees are postgraduate degrees.

Graduate study often builds on the same subject area, or a closely related subject, in which the bachelor degree was earned. For example, a student who earned a Bachelor of Science in Marketing may pursue a Master of Business Administration (MBA) degree.

Continuing Your Education

In order to advance in your career, you must continually improve your job skills. Some

AN NGUYEN/Shutterstock.com

A not-for-profit school may be a public school, such as a state university, or a private college or a university. *Which type of school will help you achieve your career goals?*

Exploring Marketing Careers

Interactive Media Specialist

Everyone enjoys a good computer game, and in general, the better the graphics, the more enjoyable the game can be. An interactive media specialist creates the graphics, animations, 3D art, and special effects needed for computer games. They also provide graphics and animated sequences for music videos, films, commercials, and even full-length movies. Other typical job titles for an interactive media specialist are *animator*, *3D artist*, *animation director,* and *creative director*.

Some examples of tasks that interactive media specialists perform include:
- Create storyboards to show the intended animation of key scenes and characters
- Provide designs, drawings, and illustrations for multimedia presentations
- Create 2D and 3D images and animations using computer modeling and animation programs
- Write scripts for animated sequences
- Create interactive sequences and animations for computer games and web pages

Interactive media specialists need both artistic ability and creative vision. They must be skilled in using computer illustration, modeling, and animation software. Because they generally work under tight deadlines, media specialists also need to be able to work well under pressure. A little more than half of the jobs in this field require a bachelor degree, usually in commercial arts or a related field. A well-developed portfolio to showcase graphics and animation skills is also helpful. For more information, access the *Occupational Outlook Handbook* online.

employers will pay for classes at a college or professional school if the classes are related to your job. Many professional organizations offer classes, workshops, and certification programs.

Some careers that have professional licenses require *continuing education classes*. These classes are completed to maintain the license and enhance opportunities for career advancement. Completing these classes earns the student *continuing education units (CEUs)*. If you are a teacher, for example, your school system may require that you earn a specified number of CEUs every year.

Another form of continuing education is more commonly called *adult education* or *adult ed*. These classes are for people age 18 or older and traditionally focus on basic skills. Classes are offered in a variety of topics ranging from learning computer skills to the English language.

Lifelong learning is the voluntary attainment of knowledge throughout life. It typically refers to adults who are learning for the sake of learning in a variety of situations. Lifelong learning often relates to hobbies and interests, including art, cooking, foreign languages, outdoor recreation, and physical fitness. Continuing to learn throughout your life has numerous benefits, such as maintaining communication and social skills, expanding your interests, and mental acuity.

Training

A college degree is not necessary for all career paths. Before taking on the expense of college classes, decide if college is right for you and your goals. There are many options for career training, including occupational training, internships, apprenticeships, and military service.

Occupational Training

Training for a specific career can be an option for many technical, trade, and technology fields. **Occupational training** is education that prepares an individual for a specific type of work. This type of training typically costs less than a traditional college education. It may also be completed in less time.

Internships

An *internship* provides the opportunity to gain on-the-job experience in a certain field of study or occupation. Internships may be paid or unpaid. High schools, colleges, and universities often award school credit for completing internships.

GaudiLab/Shutterstock.com

Internships allow students to gain work experience while completing their education. *How might an internship fit into your career plan?*

Internships allow students to gain work experience while completing their education.

Apprenticeships

An **apprenticeship** is a combination of on-the-job training, work experience, and classroom instruction. Apprenticeships are typically available to those who want to learn a trade or technical skill. The apprentice works on mastering the skills required to work in the trade or field under the supervision of a skilled tradesperson.

Military Service

Service in the military can provide opportunities to receive skilled training, often in highly specialized technical areas. In addition to receiving this training, often it can be translated into college credit or professional credentials. After completing military service, there are many benefits available to veterans. For example, the GI Bill is a law that provides financial assistance to veterans pursuing education or training. Other forms of tuition assistance are also available.

Some people choose to enter the armed forces through the *Reserve Officers' Training Corps (ROTC)*. Each branch of the military has an ROTC program at selected colleges and universities. Some high schools have Junior ROTC programs. The purpose of the ROTC program is to train commissioned officers for the armed forces. It can provide tuition assistance in exchange for a commitment to military service. Students enrolled in this program take classes just like other college students. The program is considered an elective. However, students also receive basic military and officer training. Information is available on the Today's Military website sponsored by the US Department of Defense. Opportunities available in the armed forces are also outlined in the *Occupational Outlook Handbook*.

Professional Certification

Some careers require a professional certification. *Certification* is a professional status earned by an individual after passing an exam focused on a specific body of knowledge. The individual usually prepares for the exam by taking classes and studying content that will be tested. Certification requirements should be considered when creating a career plan.

There are many types of certifications in most industries and trades. For example, a financial planning firm might require a financial planner to be certified as a qualification for the job. Other employers may prefer, but not require, certification.

Some certifications must be renewed on a regular basis. For example, many certifications sponsored by Microsoft are only valid for a specific version of software. When the next version is released, another exam must be taken to be certified for the update. Other certifications require regular continuing education classes to ensure individuals are knowledgeable on current information in the profession.

Some certifications are not subject-specific. Instead, they verify that an individual has employability skills. These certifications confirm a person possesses the skills to be a contributing employee. The focus of these certifications is on soft skills. Individuals who earn this type of certification have demonstrated they possess the qualities necessary to become effective employees.

Quality of Education
LO 27.2-2

Colleges, universities, and training programs can vary significantly in the quality and type of education offered. There are many websites available that rank schools and provide other tools to help you evaluate an institution.

As you begin making decisions about your postsecondary education, analyze the quality of the education that institutions offer. Doing so can ensure that the education you receive will be well worth the investments of both time and money. The academic reputation, credentials of faculty, graduation statistics, and potential earning power of graduates should be reviewed.

Academic Reputation

When selecting an institution, consider its academic reputation. Research and confirm that it offers areas of study in which you are interested and is accredited in those areas. *Accreditation* is a process that assures the college or university meets standards for their curriculum established by national or regional organizations. Accreditation is especially important if your career plan includes earning multiple degrees. Some schools may not consider an associate or a bachelor degree from a nonaccredited school to be legitimate.

Some schools may rank higher than others for certain areas of study or may specialize in a specific field. For example, there are colleges that are well known for the education they offer to those who want to become teachers, doctors, or information technology (IT) professionals. Consider your career goals and evaluate how well the school of your choice can help you achieve them.

Faculty

Consider the experience and reputation of faculty. The institution's website may post biographies of faculty members, which will enable you to learn more about their qualifications. Visit the campus and talk with professors and counselors to learn about their credentials and the qualifications necessary for employment at the school. Investigate how many instructors are full time versus how many are adjunct in your area of interest.

Review the ratio of teachers to students. General education classes are typically large, sometimes having more than a hundred students at larger universities. In contrast, some schools advertise small class sizes as an attractive feature. Research the typical class size of the courses in your major. Evaluate whether you feel the class size is appropriate for your learning style. The number of students in a class and the amount of individual attention from an instructor can influence your learning.

stock_photo_world/Shutterstock.com

The number of students in a class and the amount of individual attention from an instructor can influence your learning. *Would you learn better in a classroom or a lecture hall? Explain why.*

Acceptance Standards

Review the standards for acceptance into the school of your choice. Often, those with stricter entrance standards maintain a higher reputation of academic quality. Are certain grade point averages or other standards required for admission to a specific degree program? A school may have relaxed entrance standards, but certain degree programs within the school are harder to get into.

The number of students accepted to a school or degree program per academic year can affect how strict the acceptance standards are. When there are more applicants than available spots, prospective students often get put on a *wait list*. In this case, the maximum number of students have been accepted into the program, but in the event one of those students chooses another major or decides to attend a different school, a spot will be available for someone on the wait list.

Graduation Statistics

The graduation statistics for both the institution as a whole and within your planned degree program should be researched. Find the number of students who entered the institution during a recent year and the number of students who actually graduated. Compare the two figures, which many institutions express as a percentage. How many students stayed with the program? How many dropped out? What is the likelihood of starting and finishing a program of study?

Monkey Business Images/Shutterstock.com

College access refers to building awareness about college opportunities, providing guidance regarding college admissions, and identifying ways to pay for college. *How can your school's guidance counselor help you with college access?*

Statistics about those who graduated and earned degrees within the last few years should be reviewed. Evaluate the reported starting salaries of students who graduated, which degrees they earned, their programs of study, and the number of years required to reach graduation.

Other Considerations

There are several additional considerations when selecting a postsecondary institution. The years spent on your education can be impacted significantly by where you choose to attend school and your experiences while there. Consider where you plan to live, such as in a student dorm, an apartment, or at home.

College is often a time to explore new interests, develop friendships, and broaden your horizons while earning a degree. Check out the campus life, sports, and other social activities to see if they meet your expectations. Many schools have student groups centered on interests like sports, religion, recreational games, and taking trips on weekends and school breaks.

Some students want or need to hold a job while also getting an education. Consider the jobs that are available to students on campus and in the surrounding community. Investigate any student work programs available through the school.

You will be spending a lot of time on the school's campus, so try to visit the campus to experience it firsthand. Is it small enough to walk to everything, or will a vehicle be required to get from place to place? Look for cafeterias and restaurants to determine on-campus food options. Does the campus offer a variety of areas to study or relax between classes? Make sure the campus is safe and offers its students security.

These are just some of the factors to consider when choosing a postsecondary institution. Use the resources available to you, such as the Internet, your guidance counselor, and friends and family, to find out all you can about the schools that interest you.

College Access

LO 27.2-3

College access refers to building awareness about college opportunities, providing guidance regarding college admissions, and identifying ways to pay for college. College access encompasses access to many types of postsecondary institutions, including colleges, universities, and trade schools. Attending a postsecondary school to further your education can be a critical step in your career plan. However, preparing to go to college can present challenges to students and families, both academically and financially. The sooner you begin planning, the better. It is never too early.

Academic preparation includes taking the right classes and doing your best. If you have always been a good student, keep up the good work and habits. If you have not been performing to your potential, demonstrate your abilities and commitment by showing improvement. Along with strong academics, involvement in organizations at your high school or within your community will also provide greater access to college. Most schools look for well-rounded individuals. As you plan for your education, learn as much as possible about what it takes to be admitted to the college of your choice.

Many websites provide information to help you gain access to college. You can begin by searching the Internet for resources offered in your state. Search using the term *college access* plus the name of your state. If you have already been thinking about a specific school, visit its official website to learn about admission requirements and to find out what financial help might be available to you. The US Department of Education, the College Board, and the National College Access Network have websites that include a wealth of information about college access. Topics include applying to college and paying for college. If you have not already done so, talk to your family, friends, and guidance counselor today for information to begin planning for college.

LO 27.2-4 Funding Your Education

As you make decisions about your education, you will need to create a financial plan for paying for your education. Whether you attend a trade school, community college, or university, someone has to pay the cost of your education. Funds to pay for education can come from a variety of sources. Each student's financial situation is different. Many online college-cost calculators can help estimate how much money you will need to fund your education. Once you have an idea of how much it will cost to go to college, you will need to figure out how to pay for it.

Some families can afford to pay for college with current income, savings, or investments. If your parents or other family members are able and willing to pay for a college education for you, take advantage of their generosity. Thank them by studying hard and earning your degree.

Saving money for a college education is an investment strategy for the future. Someone in your family may have established a 529 plan to fund your college education. A **529 plan** is a savings plan for education operated by a state or educational institution. These plans are tax-advantaged savings plans and encourage families to set aside college funds for their children. These funds may be used for qualified colleges across the nation. Each state now has at least one 529 plan available. Plans vary from state to state because every state sets up its own plan. There are restrictions on how this money can be used, so make sure you understand how the plan works. There are penalties if money invested in a 529 plan is used for anything other than college expenses.

Even if your family has a 529 plan, the amount saved might not be enough to pay for all your college expenses. Many families pay for college using savings, current income, and loans. Parents, other family members, and students often work together to cover the cost of college. You might contribute money you have saved, money you earn if you work while attending school, and money received through loans you will have to repay. More than half of students attending college get some form of financial aid. Figure 27-10 shows potential sources of funding for your education.

Financial aid is available from the federal government, as well as from nonfederal agencies. Some states also offer money toward tuition to attend a state school, if you have good grades in high school. There is more than $100 billion in grants, scholarships, work-study, need-based awards, and loans available each year.

A **grant** is a financial award that does not have to be repaid and is typically provided by a nonprofit organization. Grants are generally need-based and usually tax exempt. A Federal Pell Grant is an example of a government grant.

A **scholarship** is financial aid that may be based on financial need or some type of merit or accomplishment. There are scholarships based on standardized test scores, grades, extracurricular activities, athletics, and music. There are also scholarships available for leadership, service, and other interests, abilities, and talents.

It is surprising how many scholarships and grants go unused because no one has applied for them. Do not fail to apply for help just because you do not want to write the essay or fill out the application. Talk to your school counselor. Be persistent if you think you might qualify for a scholarship.

Work-study programs are part-time jobs on a college campus. They are subsidized by the government. Wages earned at a work-study job go toward paying for tuition and other college expenses, such as dormitory expenses and purchasing books.

Need-based awards are financial-aid awards available for students and families who meet certain economic requirements. Income and other demographics are used to determine if a student qualifies for this assistance.

The *Free Application for Federal Student Aid (FAFSA)* is the application form used to determine your eligibility for federal financial aid. Many institutions require the FAFSA form if you are applying for any type of financial aid. You can file your application online at the Federal Student Aid website, which is an office of the US Department of Education. In addition to the financial aid application, the FAFSA website has resources to help you plan for college.

Potential Sources of Funding a College Education

Source	Brief Description	Repayment
529 Plan	Tax-advantage savings plan designed to encourage saving for future college costs. Plans are sponsored by states, state agencies, and educational institutions.	No repayment.
Grants	Money to pay for college provided by government agencies, corporations, states, and other organizations. Most grants are based on need and some have other requirements.	No repayment.
Scholarships	Money to pay for college based on specific qualifications including academics, sports, music, leadership, and service. Criteria for scholarships vary widely.	No repayment.
Work-study	Paid part-time jobs for students with financial need. Work-study programs are typically backed by government agencies.	No repayment.
Need-based awards	Aid for students who demonstrate financial need.	No repayment.
Government education loans	Loans made to students to help pay for college. Interest rates are lower than bank loans.	Repayment is required. Repayment may be postponed until you begin your career.
Private education loans	Loans made to students to help pay for college. Interest rates are higher than government education loans.	Repayment is required.
Internships	Career-based work experience. Some internships are paid and some are not. In addition to experience, you will likely earn college credit.	No repayment.
Military benefits	The US military offers several ways to help pay for education. It provides education and training opportunities while serving and also provides access to funding for veterans. The US Reserve Officers' Training Corps (ROTC) programs and the military service academies are other options to consider.	No repayment; however, a service commitment is required.

Goodheart-Willcox Publisher

Figure 27-10 There are many options for funding a college education.

Section 27.2 Review

Check Your Understanding

1. Provide examples of ways an individual can meet his or her educational needs for a career.
2. List examples of career training opportunities.
3. Why is it important to evaluate the quality of an educational investment?
4. How can a student learn more about college access?
5. Identify the document that must be submitted by a student in order to determine the student's eligibility for federal financial aid.

Build Your Vocabulary

As you progress through this course, develop a personal glossary of key terms and add it to your portfolio. This will help you build your vocabulary and prepare you for a career. Write a definition for each of the following terms, and add it to your personal glossary.

529 plan	need-based award
apprenticeship	not-for-profit school
college access	occupational training
education	postgraduate education
formal education	postsecondary education
for-profit school	scholarship
graduate education	tech prep
grant	work-study program

CHAPTER 27 Review and Assessment

Chapter Summary

Section 27.1 Career Investigation and Planning

LO 27.1-1 Describe the difference between a job and a career.
A job is the work a person does regularly in order to earn money. A career is a series of related jobs in the same profession. Over time, a job can turn into a career. Getting a job is often a short-term goal. Building a career is a long-term goal.

LO 27.1-2 Discuss the career planning process.
Creating a career plan will help you reach your goals. Conducting a self-assessment is the first step to discover who you are and what your interests are. Next, setting SMART goals will help you as you write your career plan. The third step is creating a career plan that will lead you to achieve your goals.

LO 27.1-3 List ways to research a marketing career.
There are many marketing careers that fit different interests, skills, and abilities. Career and technical student organizations, informational interviewing, job shadowing, on-the-job experience, and examining employment trends are ways to research marketing careers.

Section 27.2 Preparing for Your Education

LO 27.2-1 Describe the role of education, training, and certification in career choices.
Your educational needs will depend on your career interests and goals. Most careers require a college education. However, there are many options for career training, including occupational training, internships, and apprenticeships. The military is also a career option. Some careers require a professional certification.

LO 27.2-2 Cite factors that indicate the quality of an education investment.
Colleges, universities, and training programs can vary significantly in the quality and type of education offered. Analyze the quality of the education that an institution offers. Factors that may indicate the quality of an educational investment include academic reputation, faculty, acceptance standards, and graduation statistics.

LO 27.2-3 Explain the term *college access*.
College access refers to building awareness about college opportunities, providing guidance regarding college admissions, and identifying ways to pay for college. It includes access to many types of postsecondary institutions, including colleges, universities, and trade schools.

LO 27.2-4 Identify sources of funding for pursuing an education.
It is important for students to create a financial plan for paying educational costs. A 529 plan is a savings plan and is one way to pay for an education. There are also grants, scholarships, work-study programs, need-based awards, and loans available to help students and their families with this financial obligation.

Check Your Marketing IQ

Now that you have completed the chapter, see what you have learned about marketing by taking the chapter posttest. The posttest is available at www.g-wlearning.com/marketing/.

Review Your Knowledge

1. Describe the difference between a job and a career.
2. List the five levels of careers.
3. Discuss the career planning process.
4. Summarize the process of conducting a self-assessment.

5. List ways to research a marketing career.
6. Describe the role of education, training, and certification in career choices.
7. What kinds of training do students receive in JROTC and ROTC programs?
8. Cite factors that indicate the quality of an education investment.
9. Explain what is meant by *college access*.
10. Identify sources of funding for pursuing an education.

Apply Your Knowledge

1. Examine the career clusters chart shown in Figure 27-2. Which career cluster interests you the most? Which one would be your second choice?
2. Each individual has a personal idea of success. What is your definition of success?
3. Conduct an informal self-assessment by determining your aptitudes, abilities, values, interests, and personal traits. Use this list as a source of information when you create a career plan.
4. Consider how your values might influence the type of career you would pursue. List values that could influence your plans for a future career and explain how each one might impact your choices.
5. Marketing professionals are typically creative people. How creative are you? Write several paragraphs that describe your level of creativity and how this would help you in a marketing career.
6. Write three of your career goals as SMART goals. Specify how each of these goals is specific, measurable, attainable, realistic, and time related.
7. Write a list of action items that could appear on a career plan you might create for the next five years. Use Figure 27-4 as an example. Include your career objectives and the strategies you will use to accomplish your goals.
8. Refer to the Marketing career pathways in Figure 27-5. How are the different careers within the Marketing cluster related to one another?
9. Would you prefer to have a people career, a data career, or an objects career? Why? Explain how this preference might influence your future career choices.
10. Discuss the key advantages and disadvantages of going from high school to each of the following: college, occupational training, an internship, an apprenticeship, the military.

Apply Your Math Skills

1. Wesley was accepted to two different postsecondary schools. One is a state university, and the other is a private, liberal-arts college. The state university costs $32,518 per year. The private college costs $64,020 per year. He estimates his books will cost around $1,200 each year at either school. How much would Wesley's tuition and books cost over four years at each school?
2. Bella's parents have set aside $10,000 for her college expenses. She is eligible for a $10,000 scholarship for the academic year. Tuition is $1,750 per credit hour. Bella will enroll as a full-time student at 12 credit hours per semester. How much additional money will she need for her tuition this year?

Communication Skills

College and Career Readiness

Reading Review the vocabulary list at the beginning of this chapter. *Sight words* are those words that you recognize automatically. Identify the sight words with which you are familiar. For those words that are unfamiliar, write context clues that will help you decide the meaning of those words.

Writing Successful career planning requires individuals to continually evaluate a career. Write several paragraphs to explain why it is necessary to continually investigate career information both when planning a career and when a person is working in a career.

Speaking A presentation is usually a speech given to a group of people. This chapter discussed careers and career planning. Plan and deliver a speech to your peers about ways to start planning for a career. Be clear in your perspective for the idea and demonstrate solid reasoning.

Internet Research

Self-Assessment Conduct an Internet search for *self-assessment tools for students*. Select one that appeals to you and complete it. What did you find out about yourself?

Aptitude Testing Using independent research, write a short report to analyze and describe the use of aptitude tests such as the SAT, ACT, ACCUPLACER, and ASVAB. Why do these tests play such an important role in the post-high school plans of students? Cite specific evidence from the text and your research to support your understanding of this issue.

Career Plan It is important that you take ownership of a career plan that matches your interests and skills. Using the Internet, research how to create a career plan. Select a template that meets your needs. List any education, application, testing, or credentialing requirements. State the potential beginning earnings and expected future earnings, and any other information that will help you create a viable postsecondary plan. Using your list of SMART goals, create a career plan for the next five years that aligns a career pathway to your educational goals.

Teamwork

Work with your team to create a list of the CTSOs available at your school. Do these organizations provide any leadership activities for students? Do they provide professional development activities? Describe each of these activities. How can your school's CTSOs help you prepare for adult life? Share your findings with the class.

Portfolio Development

College and Career Readiness

Presenting Your Digital Portfolio You have organized the components of the portfolio. Now, you will create the final product. Start with the flowchart to recall the order of your documents. After you have sorted through the documents that you want to include, ensure that each one is in the appropriate file format you will need.

Your instructor may have examples of print and digital portfolios you can review for ideas. There may be an occasion where a print portfolio is required rather than a digital one. The organization processes are similar. Search the Internet for articles about how to organize a print or digital portfolio.

1. Review the documents you have collected. Select the items you want to include in your portfolio.
2. Create the slide show, web pages, or other medium for presenting your portfolio.
3. View the completed digital portfolio to check the appearance.
4. Present the portfolio to your instructor, counselor, or other person who can provide constructive feedback.
5. Review the feedback you received. Make necessary adjustments and revisions.

CHAPTER 28
Preparing for Your Career

Sections

28.1 **Finding and Applying for Employment**

28.2 **Interviewing and the Employment Process**

Reading Prep

College and Career Readiness

Before reading this chapter, flip through the pages and make notes of the major headings. Compare these headings to the objectives. What did you discover? How will this help you prepare to read new material?

Check Your Marketing IQ

Before you begin the chapter, see what you already know about marketing by taking the chapter pretest. The pretest is available at www.g-wlearning.com/marketing/.

DECA Emerging Leaders

Business Operations Research Events, Part 1

Career Cluster and **Instructional Area** are not identified for this event.

Knowledge and Skills Developed

Participants will develop many 21st century skills desired by today's employers in the following categories:
- communication and collaboration
- creativity and innovation
- critical thinking and problem solving
- flexibility and adaptability
- information literacy
- initiative and self-direction
- leadership and responsibility
- media literacy
- productivity and accountability
- social and cross-cultural skills

Purpose

Designed for a team of one to three DECA members, the Business Operations Research Events provide an opportunity for participants to demonstrate skills needed by management personnel. The Business Operations Research Events consist of two major parts: the written document and the oral presentation by the participants. The guidelines for each of the Business Operations Research Events will be exactly the same in each career category. However, each area will be treated separately as a competitive event.

For the purposes of this text, you will be presented with the material for this event in two parts. Part 1 presents an overview of the event's purpose and procedure. Part 2 presents the remaining procedures and the research topic.

Procedure, Part 1

1. For Part 1 in this text, read the skills developed and purpose of the event. Discuss these with your team members.
2. The written document will account for 60 points and the oral presentation will account for the remaining 40 of the total 100 points.
3. The body of the written entry must be limited to 30 numbered pages, including the appendix (if an appendix is attached), but excluding the title page and the table of contents.
4. The Written Event Statement of Assurances and Academic Integrity must be signed and submitted with the entry. Do not include it in the page numbering.
5. If there are any questions, ask your instructor to clarify.

Critical Thinking

1. Identify the various activities or careers addressed by each Business Operations Research Event. How do they connect to career clusters?
2. What are the benefits of learning to conduct research pertaining to business operations in different career areas?

Visit www.deca.org for more information.

Published by DECA Inc. Copyright © by DECA Inc. No part of this publication may be reproduced for resale without written permission from the publisher. Printed in the United States of America.

Section 28.1

Finding and Applying for Employment

Essential Question

How can marketing concepts be used to market yourself as a potential employee?

Learning Objectives

LO 28.1-1 Explain ways to market yourself during a job search.
LO 28.1-2 Cite sources of job leads.
LO 28.1-3 Identify documents needed to apply for a job.
LO 28.1-4 Describe the process of applying for employment.

Key Terms

personal brand
job lead
networking
résumé
career objective
chronological résumé
keyword
reference
cover message
portfolio
job application

LO 28.1-1 Marketing Yourself

You have learned several marketing strategies throughout this text. Many of the same marketing strategies used to market products can be applied to your job search. Imagine you as a product, your name as the brand, and potential employers as your target market. Your **personal brand** is the sum of the differences between you and those around you.

The easiest way to understand the concept of personal branding is through celebrities. Celebrities are defined by what people think about them. These perceptions are based on how they look, their behaviors, and what causes they support. In effect, the celebrity becomes a unique brand. Celebrities are often hired by a company to help endorse its brand. The celebrity chosen usually has a personal brand with which the company wants to be associated. Examples of this include Sofia Vergara for Head & Shoulders shampoo and Jim Parsons for Intel.

The purpose of developing your own personal brand is the same as the purpose of a product

Phase4Studios/Shutterstock.com

Imagine you as a product, your name as the brand, and potential employers as your target market. *How can you develop a personal brand?*

brand. Your brand should positively distinguish you from the rest of the competition. In the competitive world of job searching, the concept of personal branding is very important. It should persuade a potential employer to buy your product by hiring you.

First, make sure that you are the right product. *Self-awareness* is a sense of being aware of one's feelings, behaviors, needs, and other elements that make up the whole person. In order to promote yourself to an employer, you must be aware of who you are. Analyze whether you meet the requirements for the positions you seek. Match your skills, talents, and other qualities with the needs of the right employer.

Next, think about the marketing concept. One of the major aspects of the marketing concept is meeting the needs of the customer. When you apply for a job, think in terms of what the employer needs and how you can fulfill those needs. What specific needs does the employer advertise? How can you meet those needs? How can you contribute to making the business successful?

Finally, actively market yourself to the employer and launch an organized promotional campaign. The campaign can include items such as a résumé, portfolio, and eventually an interview. Make sure you are appropriately packaged. Everything about the way you dress, speak, and act should be targeted toward the position you are seeking. Most job seekers have profiles on professional networking sites like LinkedIn. Many also have personal websites to display their résumés, portfolios, and other accomplishments. How you look and sound online determines your personal brand even before participating in an interview.

You are now ready to market yourself and find the first job on your career plan. Keep the marketing concept in mind during your job search as you follow these four steps: finding job leads, applying for jobs, interviewing, and following up.

LO 28.1-2 Finding Job Leads

A **job lead** is information that leads a person to a job opening. Job leads are all around, if you know where to look. The most common ways of finding job leads are through online resources, networking, and newspapers. Other potential sources include career placement offices and career fairs.

Online Resources

Numerous online resources exist for those searching for jobs. Most are free to applicants. *Online job boards* are websites that host job postings for employers and enable applicants to apply for jobs. Employment websites like Monster, Indeed, CareerBuilder, and SimplyHired are well-known job boards for finding open positions. These sites give job seekers the ability to upload their résumés and apply directly for listed positions.

Twitter and Facebook are examples of free social media tools that businesses use for recruiting purposes. Social media sites for professionals, such as LinkedIn, list open job positions that may be found nowhere else.

Job openings are also generally posted on company websites. If there is a company for which you would like to work, it may be beneficial to check their website instead of searching through a job board or social media.

Networking

Networking means talking with others and establishing relationships with people who can help you achieve career, educational, or personal goals. You have probably already begun to build a network, even if you have not thought of it as one. People in your network include your instructors, employers, coworkers, and counselors who know about your skills and interests. Those who participate with you in volunteer efforts, clubs, or other

ESTUDI M6/Shutterstock.com

People in your network, such as your instructors, may help you learn about open positions. *Who is in your professional network?*

Social Media

Ethical Social Media Use

Most social media platforms are readily available and easy to use. Businesses and organizations commonly used them to reach out to current customers, as well as to find new ones. Marketers have a responsibility to use social media in an ethical manner.

All social-media communication on behalf of the company must be ethical. This means that information about company, brand, or product must be truthful. Embellishing or intentionally misrepresenting information is unacceptable—and may be illegal. The messages must also be in good taste, which means not offensive to individuals or groups. Use bias-free language in all communications, no matter the platform, to show respect for those with whom you come in contact. In addition, it is unethical to capitalize on a negative situation to gain brand equity.

---

organizations can also be part of your network. These people may help you learn about open positions and may be able to give you information that will help you get a position.

Governmental Resources

The US Department of Labor (DOL) sponsors CareerOneStop, a federal-state partnership to help job seekers find jobs and employers find workers. CareerOneStop offers online resources in addition to office locations with career counselors and other support services. An important feature of these career centers is the ability to match applicants with jobs nationwide, not just within one geographical area. CareerOneStop also offers a wide variety of career counseling services to help you find the job that is right for you.

*Occupational Information Network (O*NET) OnLine* is a valuable resource for career information that was also created by the DOL. O*NET OnLine contains a comprehensive database of occupational information that can be searched by career cluster. This website contains data on salary, growth, openings, education requirements, skills and abilities, work tasks, and related occupations for more than 1,000 careers.

Recall that the US Department of Labor's Bureau of Labor Statistics (BLS) publishes information on occupations, industries, and jobs in the United States. Both the *Occupational Outlook Handbook* and *Career Outlook* are produced by the BLS.

Private Employment Agencies

A *private employment agency* is a business that matches job applicants with employers who are looking to fill open positions. These agencies charge either employers or the job seekers a fee for their job matching services. The fees charged can be substantial, so an employment agency is generally used by professionals with specific career opportunities that are not normally publicly or widely advertised.

Newspapers

The traditional place to start looking for a job is in the newspaper want ads in a print or online edition. A *classified ad* is a written advertisement for a job placed by the company that needs the worker. Reading the classified ads can give a job seeker a good idea of the types of jobs available and which companies are hiring.

Career Placement Offices and Career Fairs

Career and technical centers, colleges, and universities operate career placement offices as a free service for students. The placement offices encourage businesses to post job openings that fit the skills of enrolled students.

Educational institutions often sponsor *career fairs* to help students gather information on their areas of career interest. Companies from various industries typically attend and offer information about their businesses. These events are a great way to meet potential employers in person. Job seekers visit the booths to discuss job opportunities, submit résumés, and complete job applications.

LO 28.1-3 Preparing to Apply

Before applying for a job, you will need to prepare several documents. These documents include a résumé, cover message, and references list. It is often valuable to prepare a portfolio as well.

Résumé

When looking for employment, you must sell your talents and skills to a potential employer. A job applicant must persuade the hiring manager that his or her traits, skills, and experience match the qualifications of the job being sought. A **résumé** is a document that profiles a person's career goals, education, and work history. Think of a résumé as a snapshot that shows who you are and why you would be an asset as an employee.

A résumé is the first impression that potential employers will have of you. It must be well-written and free of errors. A résumé that contains typographical errors or poor grammar reflects negatively on the applicant. The *four Cs of communication* should be applied when writing for employment: clarity, conciseness, courtesy, and correctness. Take the time to proofread your documents and check each line for correct grammar, vocabulary, and punctuation.

A general rule of thumb is that a résumé should be one page. Résumés have standard parts that employers expect to see. A typical résumé is shown in Figure 28-1. In this example, the student is applying for a job as a customer service representative.

Name and Personal Information

The top of the résumé should present your name, address, telephone number, and e-mail address. Use an e-mail address that is your real name, or at least a portion of it. E-mail addresses that use nicknames or screen names do not make a professional impression. Before you begin applying for jobs via e-mail, set up an e-mail address that you will use only for professional purposes.

Career Objective

A **career objective** is a summary of the type of job for which the applicant is looking. An example of an objective is, "To gain industry experience as a sales associate while earning my business degree." The career objective should match or be related to the position for which you are applying.

Experience

The experience section of a résumé includes details about the jobs you have held in the past, as well as your current job. The information in this section is typically the main focus of an employer's attention.

As you begin composing this section, list your current or most recent employer first. This format is known as a chronological résumé. A **chronological résumé** lists information in reverse chronological order, with the most recent information listed first.

Case in Point

TaskRabbit

Marketing yourself as the right person for an employer takes not only planning, but creativity also. Spencer Bryan from TaskRabbit can attest to this. TaskRabbit is a website that connects individuals with people in their neighborhoods who run errands and complete other tasks for a fee.

Spencer Bryan, then a Tuck Business School student at Dartmouth, liked the concept and became interested in working at TaskRabbit. However, writing a résumé and completing an application was not in Spencer's approach to getting an interview. Instead, just like any other person wanting to use the site, Spencer created a task on TaskRabbit. It was not for someone to mow the lawn or pick up groceries, though. Spencer's task requested that someone at TaskRabbit meet him in person. Brian Rothenberg, the director of TaskRabbit, saw the posted task and accepted it. He thought Spencer was very creative, met him for an interview, and within a week, offered him a job. Remember, marketing yourself may take more than just a well-written résumé. It may require some creative ideas to get the job you really want.

Robert Jefferies
123 Eastwood Terrace
Saratoga Springs, NY 60123
123-555-9715
rjefferies@e-mail.edu

OBJECTIVE
To obtain a customer service representative position to apply my strong people skills, organizational skills, and educational background and help customers find the information and products they seek.

EXPERIENCE
September 2017 to Present: Customer Service Assistant
Saratoga Springs City Hall, Saratoga Springs, NY
- Assist clients as they enter the office and over the phone.
- Perform filing, data management, and drafting and editing short office communications.
- Assist with all other office administrative duties.

September 2016 to September 2017: Office Assistant
Hunter High School, Saratoga Springs, NY
- Inputting data, running office errands, providing internship and alumni updates.
- Scheduling appointments and assisting students to register and find information.

EDUCATION
Hunter High School, Saratoga Springs, NY
Expected graduation date: May 2019
Relevant coursework: Bookkeeping, Public Speaking, Psychology, Job Skills, and Practical Math

HONORS
- Hunter High School Honor Roll, 8 quarters
- Outstanding French Student, 2016
- Volunteer of the Year, 2015

ACTIVITIES
- National Honor Society (2016 to present)
- French Club (2015 to present)
- Cross Country (2015 to present)

Goodheart-Willcox Publisher

Figure 28-1 A résumé provides a potential employer with a snapshot of your educational background and work experience.

For each work experience entry, include the company name, your job title, and the duration of time you worked in that position. List the responsibilities and details about the position you held. Do not list the addresses or telephone numbers of previous employers. This information will be provided on a job application.

Volunteer work may also be listed as work experience. Employers are typically interested in community-oriented applicants who do volunteer work. Be certain to list any volunteer activities and the length of time you have participated in the activities.

Employers often scan résumés for keywords. A **keyword** is a word that specifically relates to the functions of the position for which the employer is hiring. They are typically nouns rather than verbs. To identify keywords to use in your résumé, review the job advertisement and underline the keywords. If you have the relevant experience, use the same words to describe it in your résumé. Remember to be truthful.

Education

The education section should list the name of your high school and where it is located. Indicate the year in which you will graduate. Briefly describe any courses you have taken that are relevant to the job for which you are applying. List any certifications you have earned, special courses or training programs completed, and any other educational achievements related to the job you are seeking.

Honors, Activities, and Publications

Employers look for well-rounded individuals. Include information on your résumé that shows your involvement in activities outside of work or school. List applicable honors, activities, and publications with the corresponding year in which each occurred. If you have been a leader in an organization, note that experience. If you are a member of a career and technical student organization (CTSO), include the name of the organization and number of years you have been a member.

References

A **reference** is a person who can comment on the qualifications, work ethic, personal qualities, and work-related aspects of another person. Your list of references should include three or four people for whom you have worked and one person who knows you socially. Do not include relatives. Ask permission from the people you intend to use as references. Include each person's name, title, and contact information.

It is customary for references to be provided only when requested by the employer. For that reason, references should not be included on your résumé. Instead, create a separate document for your list of references.

To be prepared, bring copies of your list of references to job interviews. Employers who require references in advance usually indicate this in the job advertisement. Otherwise, you will be told during the interview process when references are needed.

Cover Message

A **cover message**, sometimes called a *cover letter* or *letter of application*, is a letter or e-mail sent with a résumé to introduce the applicant and summarize his or her reasons for applying for a job. It is a sales message written to persuade the reader to grant an interview. A cover message provides an opportunity to focus a potential employer's attention on your background, skills, and work experience that match the job you are seeking. Writing a cover message is an important part of applying for a job because it sets the tone for the résumé that follows. Figure 28-2 shows an example of a cover letter sent by e-mail.

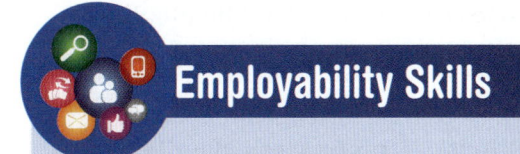

Employability Skills

Out-of-Office Notice

If you are going to be out of the office for a significant period of time, such as for an afternoon off or a week of vacation, notify your coworkers in advance. Remind others of your absence by setting up an automatic e-mail reply and a voicemail greeting that states you are out of the office and when you will return. Doing so helps people remember you are unavailable, not simply avoiding them.

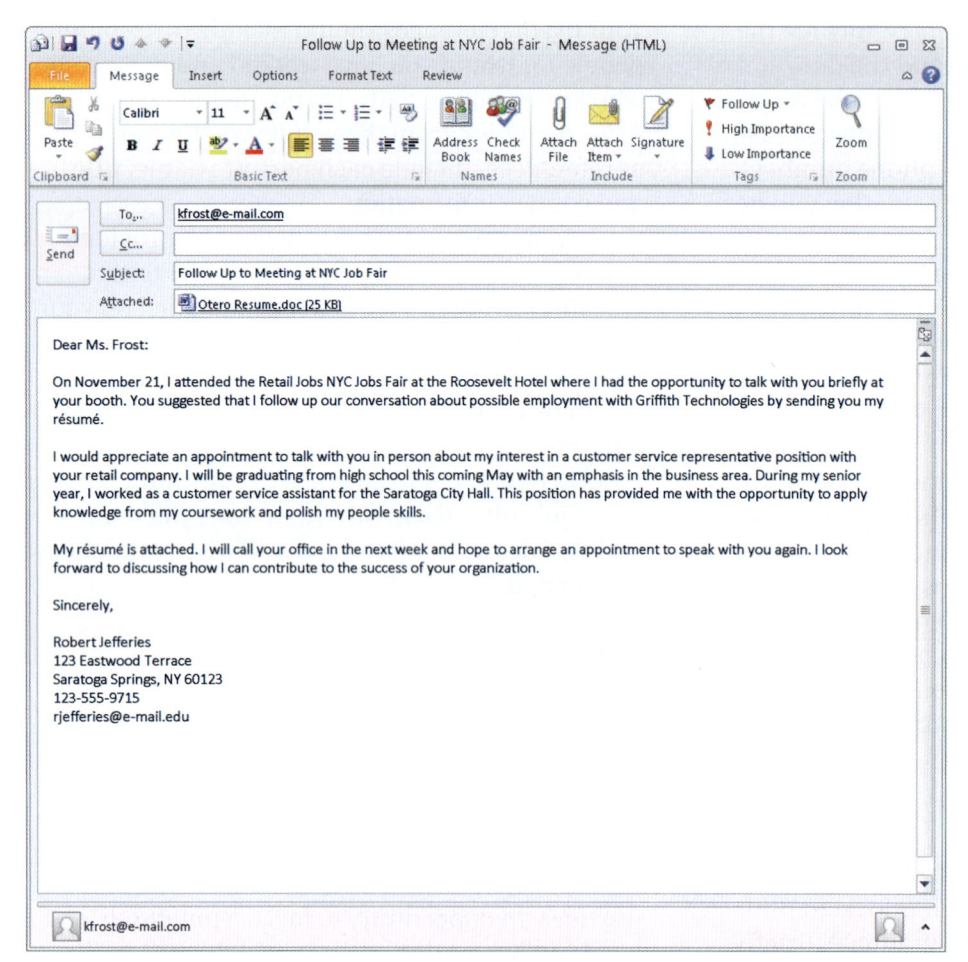

Figure 28-2 A cover message should focus attention on the most relevant points of your résumé.

> Dear Ms. Frost:
>
> On November 21, I attended the Retail Jobs NYC Jobs Fair at the Roosevelt Hotel where I had the opportunity to talk with you briefly at your booth. You suggested that I follow up our conversation about possible employment with Griffith Technologies by sending you my résumé.
>
> I would appreciate an appointment to talk with you in person about my interest in a customer service representative position with your retail company. I will be graduating from high school this coming May with an emphasis in the business area. During my senior year, I worked as a customer service assistant for the Saratoga City Hall. This position has provided me with the opportunity to apply knowledge from my coursework and polish my people skills.
>
> My résumé is attached. I will call your office in the next week and hope to arrange an appointment to speak with you again. I look forward to discussing how I can contribute to the success of your organization.
>
> Sincerely,
>
> Robert Jefferies
> 123 Eastwood Terrace
> Saratoga Springs, NY 60123
> 123-555-9715
> rjefferies@e-mail.edu

Goodheart-Willcox Publisher

Introduction

The cover message should begin with an introduction. The introduction should tell the employer who you are and why you are applying. If applying for a specific position, state the title of the position.

If responding to an advertisement, mention where you found it. For example, you might be responding to a posting on the company's website. Mention this in the introduction.

If sending a general letter of application, explain in specific terms how you identified the company and why you are interested in working there. If someone gave you the name of the employer to contact, mention the person and his or her connection to the company.

Body

In the body of the cover message, demonstrate your positive work behaviors and the qualities that make you employable. This may include illustrating your ambition, determination, and skills. Examine the job description for the position and identify the positive traits and skills the employer seeks. Then, focus on these traits and skills. Describe your personal strengths that relate to the job. Explain why you are qualified and how your skills and experience make you the best candidate for the job.

Conclusion

The cover message should end with a conclusion. The conclusion has two purposes: to request an interview, and to make it easy for the reader to grant an interview. Leave no doubt in the reader's mind about your desire to be contacted for an interview. Specifically request an interview. State how and when you can be reached to schedule an interview. Provide the information necessary to arrange an interview. You may also state how and when you will follow up to schedule an interview.

Portfolio

A **portfolio** is a selection of materials that a person collects and organizes to show his or her

Green Marketing

Green Job Search

Technology has made finding employment a greener process than ever before. Before the widespread availability of the Internet, applicants needed to either mail their résumés or travel to multiple businesses to complete job applications. This required the consumption of a great deal of resources, such as paper and fuel.

Using the Internet, job seekers can now locate and apply for open positions online by electronically submitting résumés and application forms in response to a job posting. Some companies even conduct online interviews using Skype or similar technology. This saves on travel costs and fuel consumption. Searching and applying for jobs electronically saves employers and job seekers time and money.

qualifications, skills, and talents. When you apply for a job, community service position, or to college, you will need a working portfolio to showcase your qualifications. A portfolio is usually shown during an interview, not sent in before the meeting. However, some job advertisements might request candidates to submit a portfolio as part of the application process.

Choose items for your portfolio that show the skills and abilities valuable to the job you want. Only your best, most impressive work should be selected. Figure 28-3 lists some examples of items that might be included in a portfolio.

There are two types of portfolios: a print portfolio and a digital portfolio. A digital portfolio may also be called an *electronic portfolio*, or *e-portfolio*. In a print portfolio, place each item in a plastic sleeve, and then place the items in a binder. Each item should have a caption or brief paragraph explaining why it is included in the portfolio and what it shows about your abilities. In a digital portfolio, you may create a website or a digital binder stored on a disc or USB drive. It is important to identify each item that you include.

LO 28.1-4 Applying for Employment

The process of applying for employment typically involves completing a job application form along with submitting a résumé and cover message. A **job application** is a form with spaces for entry of contact information, education, and work experience.

In today's market, the job application process is typically completed online. However, there are some employers who require applicants to physically visit the human resources department and apply in person.

Before applying for a position, confirm the application process described in the job advertisement. A call to the company's human resources department can also help clarify what is expected by the employer.

Applying Online

The first step in applying online may be to complete an application. Next, you may be required to upload a résumé, copy and paste résumé information into a form on the website, or send it as an e-mail attachment. Do not omit a cover message just because you are applying online.

Be aware that copying and pasting text into a form usually strips out formatting, such as tabs, indentations, and bold type. Avoid pasting text that

Portfolio Components

- Copy of diplomas, certificates, and degrees
- Final school transcripts
- Awards
- Job evaluations
- Samples of original written, artistic, or photographic work
- List of volunteer work
- List of memberships to organizations

Goodheart-Willcox Publisher

Figure 28-3 Items chosen for your portfolio should show the skills and abilities valuable to the job you want.

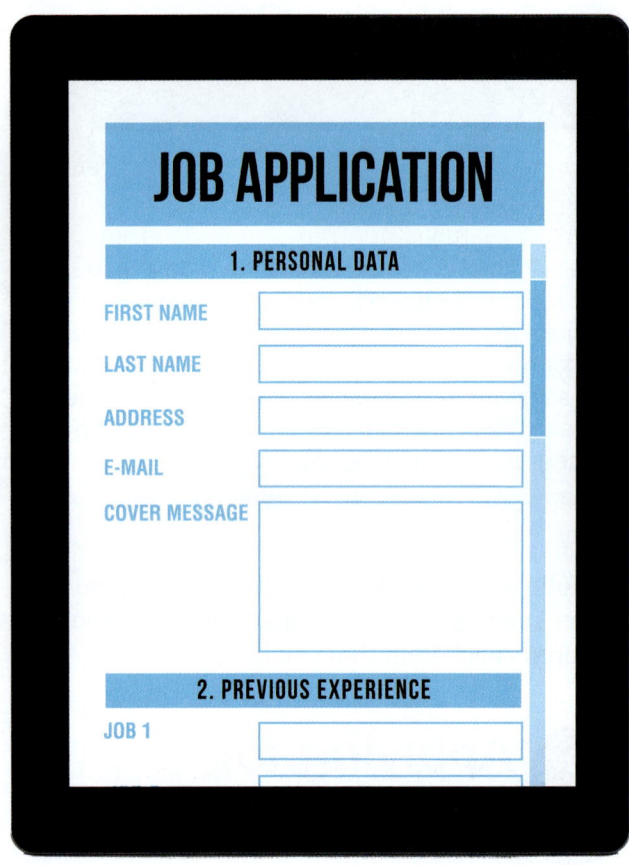

The first step in applying online may be to complete an application. *Why do you think many companies prefer online job applications?*

is formatted in any way. Even if the formatting is retained, it can make the information difficult to read when the employer accesses the application. Some guidelines to follow for preparing a résumé that will be submitted online follow.
- Use a one-column format.
- Avoid horizontal lines, boxes, or shading to set off sections.
- Avoid asterisks, dashes, parentheses, and brackets.
- Use all capital letters for headings.
- Do not use italics, underlining, or graphics.
- Insert a blank line between each section.

You may need to adjust the layout of your résumé after uploading it or pasting it into an online application form.

Alternatively, you may need to send your résumé as an e-mail attachment. In these cases, your résumé should be formatted in the file just as if it were printed. Use common fonts, such as Arial or Times New Roman. If you use a font the reader does not have, a font substitution is automatically made when the file is opened. This substitution may drastically change the formatting of the file.

Carefully review everything before submitting. Remember to follow proper spelling, grammar, and usage rules when applying online. Your application materials will be the employer's first impression of you. Submitting an application with misspellings or other errors may persuade an employer to eliminate you as a serious candidate.

There may be an opportunity to include a cover letter and portfolio with your application. Follow the directions on the website for attaching additional employment materials.

Applying in Person

The traditional way of applying for employment is to visit the human resources office of the company to which you are applying. When you arrive, be prepared to complete a job application. It is useful to compile a *personal fact sheet* that contains any information an employer may request on the application. It is especially helpful to include information that you might forget or do not currently know. Write neatly and use blue or black ink. Like a résumé or cover message, an employment application needs to be free of spelling, grammar, and usage errors. Carefully review the form before submitting it.

Bring a copy of your résumé, cover message, and portfolio when applying in person. All documents should be printed on the same high-quality, white or off-white paper using a laser printer. Do not fold or staple the documents. Instead, use a large envelope, file folder, or paper clip to keep the pages together. If using an envelope or folder, print your name on the outside and list the components included.

Managing the Job Search

It is helpful to keep track of information related to your job search. Record basic information about each application you submit, including the following.
- Name, address, phone number, and e-mail address of the company
- Title of the position for which you applied
- Name and title of the company contact
- How you found out about the job

Make note of all contact you have with the company. For example, if you send a résumé, note the date that you sent it. In addition, if you have a print advertisement or other information from the Internet, file the information in an orderly way. Many personal information management (PIM) systems have features to keep track of this type of information.

Once you have applied for a job, you must wait for a response. If you do not hear back within a week or two, call the company to find out whether the job was filled. If the job is not yet filled, express your interest and desire for an interview. Ask if there is any additional information you could send the hiring manager about your qualifications.

Section 28.1 Review

Check Your Understanding

1. List the steps required to market yourself for employment.
2. What are online job boards?
3. Describe the purpose of a résumé.
4. What information is contained in the body of a cover letter?
5. What does the process of applying for employment typically involve?

Build Your Vocabulary

As you progress through this text, develop a personal glossary of key terms. This will help you build your vocabulary and prepare you for a career. Write a definition for each of the following terms and add them to your personal glossary.

career objective
chronological résumé
cover message
job application
job lead
keyword
networking
personal brand
portfolio
reference
résumé

Section 28.2

Interviewing and the Employment Process

Essential Question

How can you prepare for a job interview?

Learning Objectives

LO 28.2-1   Discuss how to prepare for a job interview.
LO 28.2-2   Describe the employment process.

Key Terms

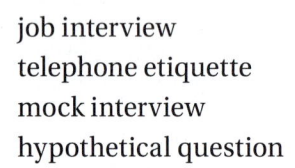

job interview
telephone etiquette
mock interview
hypothetical question
behavioral question
employment verification
background check
digital footprint
resign

LO 28.2-1 Interviewing

A **job interview** is a meeting in which an applicant and an employer discuss the job and the candidate's skills and qualifications. The purpose of the interview for the employer is to decide which candidate will be the best for the job. Being invited to a company for an interview is an important accomplishment. It means the employer is interested in your résumé or application and wants to learn more about you. Many companies conduct phone interviews before inviting job candidates to the business for an in-person interview.

In an interview, the job applicant wants to impress the employer and learn about the job. The employer wants to learn about the job applicant and decide whether to offer the applicant the position. Usually, the employer interviews several candidates for the same job before choosing whom to hire.

Preparing for the Interview

When preparing for a job interview, learn as much as you can about the position and the company. There are several ways to do this. If the company has a website, thoroughly study the site. Pay special attention to the *About Us* section for an overview of the company. Look for press releases,

michaeljung/Shutterstock.com

Being invited for an interview means the employer is interested in your résumé or application and wants to learn more about you. *What would you do to prepare for a job interview?*

annual reports, and information on its goods or services.

While a company website can be a valuable source of information, do not limit your research to just the company site. Use your network of friends and relatives to find people who are familiar with the employer. Get as much information as you can from them.

Call the company's human resources department. The human resources department often has materials specifically for potential employees. Use your best telephone etiquette while speaking with the person who answers the phone. Recall that *etiquette* is the art of using good manners in any situation. **Telephone etiquette** is using good manners while speaking on the telephone. Introduce yourself, state your purpose for calling, and be prepared with a list of questions to ask. Be polite and say "please" and "thank you" when speaking with each person so that you project a positive impression.

Depending on the position, there may be a performance test as part of the interview. For example, a graphic artist may be asked to create a simple design using the software the company utilizes. This will test not only the person's design abilities, but also his or her proficiency with the software. Be prepared to take a performance test if needed.

Place of Interview

Make sure you know where the interview will take place, exactly how to get there, and the time needed for travel. If you are unfamiliar with the location, make a trial run before the interview. Try to plan your time so that you arrive a few minutes early, allowing time for travel and parking. It is generally not appropriate to bring anyone with you to an interview. If someone must drive you, have that person wait for you in the car or at a nearby location.

Introduction

Know the name and title of the person who will interview you. Prepare a few sentences of introduction. Practice speaking slowly and clearly. Practice your handshake. Use your right hand to grasp the other person's hand firmly. A common rule of thumb is to break a handshake after three seconds.

The way in which you greet the interviewer makes a strong impression. Stand tall, speak clearly, and use Standard English. Smile, maintain eye contact, and give the interviewer a firm handshake. Use the interviewer's name in the greeting. For example, "Hello, Ms. Reed. My name is Casey Shamoun. I am here to interview for the management trainee position."

Dressing for the Interview

A face-to-face interview is typically the first time you are seen by a company representative. First impressions are important, so dress appropriately. You should be well groomed and professionally dressed. Your appearance communicates certain qualities about you to the interviewer. When dressing for an interview, consider how you are marketing yourself and what you wish to communicate about yourself with your appearance.

The easiest rule to follow is to dress in a way that shows you understand the work environment and know what attire is appropriate. It is better to dress more conservatively than to dress in trendy clothing. Employers understand that interviewees want to put their best foot forward. Dressing more conservatively than needed is not likely to be viewed as a disadvantage. However, dressing too casually, too trendy, or wearing inappropriate clothing is likely to cost you the job. Figure 28-4 provides general guidelines for dressing for an interview.

Preparing for Interview Questions

Interview questions are intended to assess your skills and abilities and to explore your personality. Your answers to these questions will help determine whether you will fit in with the company team and the manager's leadership style. Interviewers also want to assess your critical-thinking skills. They may ask you to cite specific examples of projects you have completed or problems you have solved.

During the interview, your communication skills will be observed. Communicate as clearly and effectively as possible.

Common Questions

Before the interview, try to anticipate questions the interviewer is likely to ask you. The following are some common interview questions.
- What are your strengths?
- What are your weaknesses?

Appropriate Attire for an Interview

Women
- Wear a suit or a dress of a conservative length
- Choose solid colors over prints
- Wear pumps with a moderate heel or flats
- Keep any jewelry small
- Have a well-groomed hairstyle
- Use little makeup
- Avoid perfume or apply it very lightly
- Nails should be manicured and of moderate length without decals
- Cover all tattoos

Men
- Wear a conservative suit of a solid color
- Wear a long-sleeved shirt, either white or a light color
- Choose a tie that is a solid color or conservative print
- Wear loafers or lace-up shoes with dark socks
- Avoid wearing jewelry
- Have a well-groomed hairstyle
- Avoid cologne
- Nails should be neatly trimmed
- Cover all tattoos

Viorel Sima/Shutterstock.com; YURALAITS ALBERT/Shutterstock.com; Goodheart-Willcox Publisher

Figure 28-4 Dress to show you understand the work environment and know what attire is appropriate.

- What about this position interests you?
- What do you plan to be doing five years from now?
- Why do you want to work for this organization?

Write down your answers to these questions. Practice answering the questions in front of a mirror.

Another way to prepare for an interview is to conduct a mock interview with a friend or instructor. A **mock interview** is a practice interview conducted with another person. Practice until you can give your planned responses naturally. The more prepared you are, the more relaxed, organized, competent, and professional you will appear to the interviewer.

Hypothetical Questions

Interviewers may also ask candidates hypothetical questions. **Hypothetical questions** require a person to imagine a situation and describe how he or she would act. Frequent topics of hypothetical questions relate to working with and getting along with coworkers. For example, "How would you handle a disagreement with a coworker?" You cannot prepare specific answers to these questions, so you need to rely on the ability to think on your feet.

For this type of question, the interviewer is aware that you are being put on the spot. In addition to what you say, he or she considers other aspects of your answer as well. Body language is first and foremost. Avoid fidgeting and looking at the ceiling while thinking of your answer. Instead, look at the interviewer and calmly take a moment to compose your thoughts. Keep your answer brief. If your answer runs on too long, you risk losing your train of thought. Try to relate the question to something that is familiar to you and answer honestly.

Do not try to figure out what the interviewer wants you to say. Showing that you can remain poised and project confidence carries a lot of weight, even if your answer is not ideal. In many cases, the interviewer is not as interested in *what* your response is as much as *how* you responded. Was your response quick and thoughtful? Did you ramble? Did you stare blankly at the reviewer before responding?

Behavioral Questions

Interviewers may ask behavioral questions. **Behavioral questions** are questions that draw on an individual's previous experiences and decisions. Your answers to this type of question indicate past behavior, which may be used to predict future behavior and success in a position. The following are some examples of behavioral questions.

- Tell me about a time when you needed to assume a leadership position in a group. What were the challenges, and how did you help the group meet its goals?
- Describe a situation in which you needed to be creative in order to help a client with a problem.
- Describe a mistake that you made. How did you correct the mistake and what measures did you put in place to ensure it did not happen a second time?

Again, you cannot prepare specific answers to these questions. Remain poised, answer honestly, and keep your answers focused on the question. Making direct eye contact with the interviewer can project a positive impression.

Questions Interviewers Should Not Ask

State and federal laws prohibit employers from asking questions on certain topics. These laws protect you from discrimination during the hiring process. It is illegal for employers to ask questions about a job candidate's religion, national origin, gender, or disability. Questions about age can only be asked if a minimum age is required by law for a job. Figure 28-5 provides examples of illegal questions.

Illegal Interview Questions

- What is the name of your spouse?
- What is the occupation of your spouse?
- Have you ever filed a workers' compensation claim or been injured on the job?
- Do you have any physical impairments?
- Have you ever been arrested?
- What is your height or weight?
- Have you ever been hospitalized? If so, for what condition?
- Have you ever been treated by a psychiatrist or psychologist?
- How many days were you absent from work last year due to illness?
- Are you taking any prescribed drugs?
- Have you ever been treated for drug addiction or alcoholism?

Goodheart-Willcox Publisher

Figure 28-5 It is illegal for an employer to discriminate based on race, color, religion, national origin, sex, age, and disability.

If you are presented with any such questions during an interview, remain professional. You are not obligated to provide an answer. You may choose to calmly respond by saying, "Please explain how that relates to the job," or, "I would rather not answer personal questions."

Questions to Ask the Interviewer

It is a good idea to prepare a list of questions to ask the interviewer. Consider asking about the position, the job responsibilities, and the company. Keep in mind the questions you ask reveal details about your personality. Asking questions can make a positive impression. Questions can show you are interested and aware. Good questions cover the duties and responsibilities of the position. Be aware of how you word questions.

In the early stages of the interview process, your questions should demonstrate your value as an employee and interest in the company. The following are some questions you may want to ask.

- What are the specific duties of this position?
- What is company policy or criteria for employee promotions?
- Do you have a policy for providing on-the-job training?
- When do you expect to make your hiring decision?
- What is the anticipated start date?

Some questions are not appropriate until after you have been offered the job. Usually, questions related to pay and benefits, such as vacation time, should not be asked in the interview unless the employer brings them up. These can be asked after an offer of employment is made to you.

Sometimes, however, an interviewer asks about the salary you want or expect. It is also common for salary requirements to be requested in the job posting, in which case you would need to address that in your cover message. Prepare for questions about salary by researching the industry. If you are unsure, you can simply tell the interviewer that the salary is negotiable.

Writing Follow-Up Messages

After an interview, you should always write a *thank-you message* to each person who interviewed you. A thank-you may be in the form of a printed letter sent through the mail or an e-mail. An example of a thank-you message is shown in Figure 28-6.

> Dear Ms. Cary:
>
> Thank you for the opportunity to discuss the position of sales associate.
>
> I am very excited about the possibility of working for Ellsworth Electronics. The job is exactly the sort of challenging opportunity I had hoped to find. I believe my educational background will enable me to make a contribution, while also learning and growing on the job.
>
> Please contact me if you need any additional information. I look forward to hearing from you.
>
> Sincerely,
>
> Joseph Carmichael

Figure 28-6 A thank-you message shows you are sincerely interested in the position and helps you to stand out from other candidates.

The message can be brief. Thank the interviewer for his or her time and interest. If you are interested in the job, say a few words expressing your interest and your strongest qualifications for the job. Sending a thank-you message shows you are sincerely interested in the position and helps you to stand out from other candidates who did not send thank-you letters.

Employment decisions can take a long time. Some companies notify all applicants when a decision has been made, but some do not. If you have not heard anything after a week or two, it is appropriate to send a brief follow-up message. Simply restate your interest in the job and politely inquire whether a decision has been made.

Evaluating the Interview

Evaluate your interview performance as soon as you can after it is completed. Asking yourself the following questions can help evaluate your performance.
- Was I adequately prepared with knowledge about the company and the position?
- Did I remember to bring copies of my résumé, list of references, portfolio, and any other requested documents to the interview?
- Was I on time for the interview?
- Did I talk too much or too little?
- Did I honestly and completely answer the interviewer's questions?
- Did I dress appropriately?
- Did I display nervous behavior, such as fidgeting, or forget things I wanted to say?
- Did I come across as composed and confident?
- Which questions could I have handled better?

Every job interview is an opportunity to practice. If you discover that you are not interested in the job, do not feel as though your time was wasted. List the things you feel you did right to help you stay motivated to continue your job search. Identify things you would do differently in the next interview to improve your performance.

LO 28.2-2 Employment Process

The employment process can take a substantial amount of time. There are tasks that the employer completes to make sure a candidate is a fit for the position. In addition, there are forms that the employee must complete before starting a position.

Employment Verification

The employer will complete an employment verification using the information on your application or résumé. **Employment verification** is a process through which the information provided on an applicant's résumé is checked to verify it is correct. A person's past employers typically verify only the dates of employment, position title, and other objective data. Most companies will not provide opinions about employees, such as whether he or she was considered a good worker.

Another important component of the employment verification process is a background check.

A **background check** is an investigation into personal data about a job applicant. This information is available from governmental records and other sources, including public information on the Internet. The employer must inform you that a background check will be conducted, and you must grant permission before the employer can perform the check. Sometimes employers also run a check of your credit. Employers must have your permission to conduct this check as well.

Many employers use Internet search engines, such as Google, to search for your name. Employers may also check social networking websites, such as Facebook and Twitter. Be aware of this before posting any personal information or photos. These checks might work to your advantage or against you, depending on what the employer finds. It is up to you to ensure that the image you project on social networking sites is not embarrassing or, more importantly, does not prevent you from achieving your career goals.

Andrey_Popov/Shutterstock.com

An offer of employment is the stage of the hiring process in which salary, benefits, and other details are discussed. *What criteria might you use to evaluate an offer?*

A **digital footprint** is a data history of all an individual's online activities. What you post on the Internet never really goes away.

Evaluating an Offer

If the employment checks on an applicant are successful, the employer will typically make a job offer. An initial offer may be extended via mail, e-mail, or telephone. This is the stage of the hiring process in which salary, benefits, and other details of the position are discussed between the employer and applicant. Evaluate the offer in terms of your expectations and career goals. Consider the position and whether it is right for you. Compare the salary and benefits offered to similar companies in the area and within the industry. Be sure to understand the demands that will be placed on you if you accept the position.

If both parties accept the terms of the offer, a formal job offer will be made as a written, legal document. Once you receive the job offer document, you will be requested to sign, date, and return it in a timely manner. It is customary to include a letter of acceptance to accompany the job offer document. If you decide to decline the offer for some reason, return the job offer document and include a letter of refusal stating that you are declining the position. It is not necessary to go into detail explaining why you are rejecting the offer. However, your letter should express appreciation for the consideration, and provide reason for declining. A professional statement of refusal is shown in Figure 28-7.

Employment Forms

The first day on the job, you will spend a considerable amount of time in the human resources department completing necessary forms for your employment. Come prepared with the personal information required for the many forms you will need to complete. You will need your social security number, contact information for emergencies, and other personal information.

Form I-9

A *Form I-9 Employment Eligibility Verification* is used to verify an employee's identity and that he or she is authorized to work in the United States. This form is from the US Citizen and Immigration Services, a governmental agency within the US Department of Homeland Security. Both

Statement of Refusal

Dear Ms. Cary:

I received your job offer for assistant marketing manager. I appreciate the time you have spent discussing the position with me. However, I must decline the offer at this time. After careful consideration, I have decided to accept a position at another company.

Thank you again for the opportunity.

Sincerely,

Joseph Carmichael

Goodheart-Willcox Publisher

Figure 28-7 A statement of refusal may be brief and should express appreciation for the job offer.

---

citizens and noncitizens are required to complete this form. An example of a Form I-9 is shown in Figure 28-8.

The Form I-9 must be signed in the presence of an authorized representative of the human resources department. Documentation of identity must be presented at the time the form is signed. Acceptable documentation commonly used includes a valid driver's license, a state-issued photo ID, or a passport.

Employment Eligibility Verification
Department of Homeland Security
U.S. Citizenship and Immigration Services

USCIS
Form I-9
OMB No. 1615-0047
Expires 03/31/20XX

▶ **START HERE.** Read instructions carefully before completing this form. The instructions must be available during completion of this form.
ANTI-DISCRIMINATION NOTICE. It is illegal to discriminate against work-authorized individuals. Employers **CANNOT** specify which document(s) they will accept from an employee. The refusal to hire an individual because the documentation presented has a future expiration date may also constitute illegal discrimination.

Section 1. Employee Information and Attestation *(Employees must complete and sign Section 1 of Form I-9 no later than the **first day of employment**, but not before accepting a job offer.)*

Last Name (Family Name)	First Name (Given Name)	Middle Initial	Other Names Used (if any)
Address (Street Number and Name)	Apt. Number	City or Town	State	Zip Code
Date of Birth (mm/dd/yyyy)	U.S. Social Security Number	E-mail Address	Telephone Number

I am aware that federal law provides for imprisonment and/or fines for false statements or use of false documents in connection with the completion of this form.

I attest, under penalty of perjury, that I am (check one of the following):

☐ A citizen of the United States
☐ A noncitizen national of the United States *(See instructions)*
☐ A lawful permanent resident (Alien Registration Number/USCIS Number): _____
☐ An alien authorized to work until (expiration date, if applicable, mm/dd/yy) _____. Some aliens may write "NA" in this field. *(See instructions)*

For aliens authorized to work, provide your Alien Registration Number/USCIS Number **OR** Form I-94 Admission Number:

US Department of Homeland Security

Figure 28-8 The Form I-9 Employment Eligibility Verification confirms an employee's identity.

You Do the Math

Multiplication

To multiply whole numbers and decimals, place the numbers, called the *factors*, in pairs in a vertical list. When multiplying a percentage, move the decimal two places to the left. To find the number of decimal places needed in the final product, add the number of places in each number. Two decimal places plus three decimal places means the product must have five decimal places.

Solve the following problems.

1. Shelia earns $12 an hour and earns time and a half (1.5 ×) for hours over 40. Last week, she worked a total of 42 hours. What is her gross pay? (Alternative problem format: Shelia earns $12 an hour and is covered by the Fair Labor Standard Act. Last week, Shelia worked a total of 42 hours. What is her gross pay?)
2. Your business must pay a 2 percent fee on all credit card transactions. What is the total fee for all of these transactions: $24.76, $52.76, and $29.35?
3. You live in an area that has a general sales tax rate of 8.5 percent on most purchases. How much sales tax would you pay for the following goods and services from area stores?
   A. $150 jacket
   B. $30 haircut
   C. $2 magazine

The tax rate in a neighboring county is 7 percent. How much can you save on each item by crossing the county line to do your shopping?

Form W-4

A *Form W-4 Employee's Withholding Allowance Certificate* is used by the employer to determine the appropriate amount of taxes to be withheld from an employee's paycheck. Withholdings are based on marital status and the number of dependents claimed, including the employee. The amounts withheld are forwarded to the appropriate governmental agency.

At the end of the year, the employer sends the employee a *Form W-2 Wage and Tax Statement* to use when filing income tax returns. This form summarizes all wages and deductions for the year for an individual employee.

Benefits Forms

The human resources department will provide a variety of forms that are specific to the compensation package offered by the employer. Health insurance forms will need to be completed. If the position involves driving, you may need to fill out additional forms related to your driving record. Other benefits offered by the employer may also have forms that need to be completed.

Changing Jobs

In order to achieve your career goals, you may have an opportunity to move up the career ladder with your current employer. Some companies automatically promote employees when they believe that a promotion has been earned. Other companies post job openings and urge internal candidates to apply. There may be times when your current employer does not offer new job opportunities for you and you decide to seek employment elsewhere. When looking for a new job while still in your old job, maintain a sense of integrity. Continue to fulfill all your obligations to your current employer. Avoid carrying out any job-hunting activities at your current place of work. If you need time to interview, take a personal day or vacation time.

Once you have obtained a new job, be professional about leaving your old job. Most businesses require that you give at least a *two-week notice* before leaving a job. To *give notice* means to notify a supervisor of your intention to leave a job. Usually, this is done by writing a *letter of resignation*. To **resign** means to voluntarily leave an employment position. The letter should express appreciation for the time you have spent with the company, express regrets about leaving, and give the date of your last day on the job. This letter should be addressed to your supervisor. Then, take the letter with you when you tell your supervisor in person that you are leaving. Politely explain why you are leaving the company, express appropriate appreciation, and leave the letter with your supervisor.

The two-week notice gives the employer time to find someone to take your place. It also gives you time to finish up your projects and leave instructions for the next person. Be cautious of changing companies too often because it can seem like job hopping. Employers look for people who will commit to the company for some time.

Section 28.2 Review

Check Your Understanding

1. State the purpose of a job interview.
2. Why is an employer's first impression of a job candidate important?
3. Explain the difference between hypothetical questions and behavioral questions.
4. Provide examples of employment forms a new hire may be required to complete.
5. What does it mean to give notice on a job?

Build Your Vocabulary

As you progress through this text, develop a personal glossary of key terms. This will help you build your vocabulary and prepare you for a career. Write a definition for each of the following terms and add them to your personal glossary.

background check
behavioral question
digital footprint
employment verification
hypothetical question

job interview
mock interview
resign
telephone etiquette

CHAPTER 28 Review and Assessment

Chapter Summary

Section 28.1 Finding and Applying for Employment

LO 28.1-1 Explain ways to market yourself during a job search.
First, make sure that you are the right product. Conduct marketing research on jobs and employers and match your skills and qualities with the needs of the right employer. Next, think about the marketing concept in terms of what you can do for the employer. Finally, actively market yourself to the employer. Everything about the way you dress, speak, and act should be targeted toward the position you are seeking.

LO 28.1-2 Cite sources of job leads.
A job lead is information that leads you to a job opening. The most common ways of finding job leads are online resources such as job boards, social media, and company websites; networking; and newspapers. Other potential places include career and college placement offices, and job fairs. Want ads appear in a variety of places.

LO 28.1-3 Identify documents needed to apply for a job.
A job applicant will need to prepare several documents before sending in an application. These include a personal fact sheet, résumé, cover message, and references list. For many marketing jobs, it is often valuable to prepare a portfolio.

LO 28.1-4 Describe the process of applying for employment.
Most applicants apply for positions online. This includes an online job application, résumé, cover message, and potentially a portfolio. The traditional way to apply for a job is to visit the human resources department of a company, complete a job application in person, and submit the application documents in printed form.

Section 28.2 Interviewing and the Employment Process

LO 28.2-1 Discuss how to prepare for a job interview.
The job interview is your opportunity to sell yourself. To prepare for the interview, rehearse answers to questions likely to be asked. At the interview, it is important to dress appropriately and professionally. Immediately after, follow up with a thank-you letter or e-mail to the person who interviewed you.

LO 28.2-2 Describe the employment process.
The employment process can take a substantial amount of time. Employers must conduct employment verification and a background check to make sure the candidate is qualified for the position. In addition, employment forms must be completed by an employee when beginning a new job.

Check Your Marketing IQ

Now that you have completed the chapter, see what you have learned about marketing by taking the chapter posttest. The posttest is available at www.g-wlearning.com/marketing/.

Review Your Knowledge

1. Explain ways to market yourself during a job search.
2. Cite sources of job leads.
3. Identify employment documents necessary for a job search.
4. What information appears on a personal fact sheet?
5. Describe the process of applying for employment.
6. Name two methods of applying for a job.
7. Discuss how to prepare for a job interview.
8. How should a job applicant respond to illegal interview questions?
9. Describe the employment process.
10. Summarize how to appropriately resign from a job.

Apply Your Knowledge

1. Describe your personal brand. Explain how you can apply marketing strategies and concepts to your own job search to market yourself.
2. Describe how you can use multiple sources of leads for your own job search.
3. Prepare to write a draft of a personal résumé for a marketing position of your choice. Make a list of all your past work experiences. Write a brief description of your job responsibilities to demonstrate the positive work behaviors and qualities that make you employable. If you have any special licenses or certifications, note them. List your educational background and any other information you think should be included on your résumé.
4. Write a draft of your résumé. After the draft is complete, format the document. Using Figure 28-1 as an example, create your final résumé. Be sure to use formatting that is appropriate for submitting the résumé electronically. Check the final document for accuracy and truthfulness, as well as spelling, grammar, and formatting errors.
5. Write a cover message you would submit with your résumé if you were applying for a marketing position. Use Figure 28-2 as an example. Explain how your positive work behaviors and other qualities make you employable. Mention any special licenses or certifications you have earned. Note that your professional portfolio will contain samples of your work. Check the final document for spelling, grammar, and formatting errors.
6. Write an answer for each of the following potential interview questions.
   A. What makes you a good employee?
   B. What are your strengths?
   C. What are your weaknesses?
7. List five questions you might ask during a job interview. Be aware of how you word questions to make the best impression.
8. Assume you have recently been interviewed for the position of salesperson. Write a thank-you message to the interviewer.
9. Assume you have been offered the position of salesperson after the interview in the previous question. Write a message to the interviewer to state that you will be accepting the offer. Then, write a message to state that you will be refusing the offer.
10. Assume you have decided to change jobs in order to achieve your career goals. Write a letter to your supervisor giving notice that you will be leaving the company. Express appreciation for the time you have spent with the company, express regrets about leaving, and give the date of your last day on the job.

Apply Your Math Skills

There are a variety of positions to consider within the marketing field when choosing a career. Wages are an important factor to evaluate when researching career opportunities at various levels. Interpret the table below by answering the questions that follow.

Hourly and Annual Wages in Marketing Careers (in dollars)

Position	Annual Median	Hourly Median
Cashier	$19,310	$9.28
Market research analyst	$62,150	$29.88
Marketing manager	$128,750	$61.90
Telemarketer	$23,530	$11.31
Visual merchandiser	$26,870	$12.92

Source: O*Net OnLine

1. Which marketing career earns the highest wages?
2. What is the highest hourly wage represented in the chart?
3. What is the hourly wage of the marketing career that earns the least?
4. What is the annual median wage of a telemarketer?

Communication Skills

Reading Now that you have completed reading multiple chapters in this text, analyze the themes and structures that the author used. Create a concept map that illustrates how the themes of this text are related.

Writing Using the information in this chapter and other sources, prepare a brief paper on how to prepare for an interview. Include information on appropriate dress, grooming, and behavior; commonly asked questions; and how to follow up after the interview. Use this information as a resource when preparing for the Teamwork activity that follows.

Speaking Applying for a marketing career will require that individuals be able to stay motivated throughout a job search. Prepare a one- to two-minute speech that you might deliver to a friend who is becoming discouraged during the search for a marketing job. Deliver the speech to a classmate, using note cards if necessary. Practice correct pronunciation and grammar.

Internet Research

Marketing Yourself You have learned about marketing a product. Now it is time to market yourself as a potential employee. Conduct an online search for the phrase *marketing yourself*. Make notes on ideas that the article provided to help you learn how to present yourself as a potential employee.

Personal Branding Conduct an Internet search for *personal branding*. Determine the central ideas the author explored about the importance of branding yourself when looking for a position. Summarize the key supporting details and ideas.

Online Job Search Using the Internet, conduct a job search for a marketing position that interests you. Select two positions that are currently being advertised. Create a Venn diagram to compare and contrast the qualifications and requirements of each position. Consider the responsibilities of each job. Which job would you prefer?

Job Application Form Use the Internet to locate a sample job application form. Practice completing the form. If you are able to complete the form electronically, key your responses in the spaces provided. If you complete the form by hand, use your best handwriting and blue or black ink. Submit the completed form to your instructor.

Teamwork

Working with a teammate, conduct a mock job interview. Both students should dress appropriately for an interview. One team member should act as the employer and the other team member as the person being interviewed. Model an appropriate personal introduction at the beginning of the interview including an appropriate hand shake, personal space, and eye contact. Each student should prepare a completed application form, letter of application, and résumé. Practice interviewing techniques and rotate roles of employer and interviewee. Working together, create a thank-you letter for the interview.

Portfolio Development

College and Career Readiness

Presenting Your Printed Portfolio There may be an occasion where a print portfolio is required rather than a digital one. The organization process is similar to the digital version. Start with the flowchart to recall the order of your documents. After you have sorted through the documents that you want to include, print a copy of each. Next, prepare a table of contents for the items. This will help the person reviewing the portfolio locate each item and give a professional appearance to your portfolio. Consider adding title pages to each section of the printed portfolio to aid organization.

Your instructor may have examples of printed portfolios that you can review for ideas. You can also search the Internet for articles about how to organize a printed portfolio.

1. Review the documents you have collected. Select the items you want to include in your portfolio. Make copies of certificates, diplomas, and other important documents. Keep the originals in a safe place.

2. Place the items in a binder, folder, or other container.

3. Give the portfolio to your instructor, counselor, or other person who can provide constructive feedback.

4. Review the feedback you received. Make necessary adjustments and revisions.

CHAPTER 29
Digital Citizenship

Sections

29.1 **Communicating in a Digital Society**
29.2 **Internet Use in the Workplace**

College and Career Readiness

Reading Prep
Before reading this chapter, go to the end of the chapter and read the summary. The chapter summary highlights important information presented in the chapter. Did this exercise help you prepare to understand the content?

Check Your Marketing IQ

Before you begin the chapter, see what you already know about marketing by taking the chapter pretest. The pretest is available at www.g-wlearning.com/marketing/.

◇DECA Emerging Leaders

Business Operations Research Events, Part 2

Career Cluster and **Instructional Area** are not identified for this event.

Procedure, Part 2

1. In Chapter 28, you studied the skills assessed and procedures for this event.
2. For the purposes of this text, this event will be presented to you as a written activity that will be created and submitted at the time of the event. This event provides an opportunity for participants to demonstrate knowledge and skills needed by management personnel through a presentation based on the results of the research study (written activity). For the presentation, the participants are to assume the role of hired consultants. The judge will assume the role of owner/manager of the business/organization. He or she will evaluate the presentation, focusing on the effectiveness of public speaking and presentation skills and how well the participants respond to questions that the judge may ask during the presentation.
3. The oral presentation may be a maximum 15 minutes in length including time for the judge's questions.
4. The participants will bring all visual aids to the event briefing. Only approved visual aids may be used during the presentation.

Research Topic

Although the research topic is the same for each career category, the topic for the Business Operations Research Events changes each year. The topic allows DECA members to conduct research in current areas of business operations, analyze the research study results, develop a strategic plan based on the research, and propose a solution or business practices to improve the business operations. Students enter an event based on the company/organization in which they conduct research.

Critical Thinking

1. Anticipating questions is a strategy presenters use to deliver effective presentations. Brainstorm questions your team may be asked during your presentation on the following:
   - participants' research methods;
   - details of the participants' findings and conclusions; and
   - participants' proposed plan.
2. Discuss your answers to the anticipated questions.

Visit www.deca.org for more information.

Published by DECA Inc. Copyright © by DECA Inc. No part of this publication may be reproduced for resale without written permission from the publisher. Printed in the United States of America.

Section 29.1

Communicating in a Digital Society

Essential Question
What implications does digital citizenship have for society as a whole?

Learning Objectives

LO 29.1-1 Describe the elements of digital communication.
LO 29.1-2 Explain intellectual property and what it includes.
LO 29.1-3 Discuss the importance of the Electronic User's Bill of Rights.

Key Terms

digital communication
digital literacy
digital citizenship
cyberbullying
netiquette
slander
libel
plagiarism
piracy
infringement
public domain
open source

Digital Communication

LO 29.1-1

Digital communication is the exchange of information through electronic means. Using technology to communicate in the workplace, as well as in one's personal life, requires users to be responsible. This requires the knowledge and skills to successfully navigate the Internet to interact with individuals and organizations. Digital communication is composed of digital literacy and digital citizenship.

Digital Literacy

Digital literacy is the ability to use technology to locate, evaluate, communicate, and create information. Digital communication requires digital literacy skills. According to the US federal government, digital literacy skills include:

- using a computer or mobile device, including the mouse, keyboard, icons, and folders;
- using software and applications to complete tasks, such as word processing and creating spreadsheets, tables, and databases;
- using the Internet to conduct searches, access e-mail, and register on a website;
- communicating online, including sharing photos and videos, using social media, and learning to be an informed digital citizen; and
- helping children learn to be responsible and make informed decisions online.

StockLite/Shutterstock.com

Digital literacy skills are necessary when working in a business environment. *How would you rate your level of digital literacy?*

To learn more about digital literacy skills, visit the federal Digital Literacy website for information, resources, and tools. This website is supported by various departments of the US government.

Digital Citizenship

Digital citizenship is the standard of appropriate behavior when using technology to communicate. Good digital citizenship focuses on using technology in a positive manner rather than using it for negative or illegal purposes. People who participate in the digital society have a legal responsibility for their online actions, be they ethical or unethical. *Ethics* are the principles of what is right and wrong that help people make decisions. Ethical actions are those that apply ethics and moral behavior. Unethical actions involve immoral behavior, crime, or theft. These actions can be punishable by law.

It is important to understand the difference between ethical and unethical electronic activities. For example, it is sometimes difficult for a reader to know where joking stops and bullying starts. **Cyberbullying** is using the Internet to harass or threaten an individual. It includes using social media, text messages, or e-mails to harass or scare a person with hurtful words or pictures. A victim of cyberbullying cannot be physically seen or touched by the bully. However, this does not mean the person cannot be harmed by his or her actions. Cyberbullying is unethical and can be prosecuted.

Other unacceptable behaviors include flaming and spamming. *Flaming* is purposefully insulting someone and inciting an argument on social media. *Spamming* is sending unwanted mass e-mails or intentionally flooding an individual's social media site or e-mail inbox with unwanted messages. Spamming is equally unethical.

Etiquette is the art of using good manners in any situation. **Netiquette** is etiquette used when communicating electronically. It is also known as *digital etiquette*. Netiquette includes accepted social and professional guidelines for Internet-based communication. These guidelines apply to e-mails, social networking, and other contact with customers and peers via the Internet. For example, using all capital letters in a message, which has the effect of yelling, is not acceptable. Always use correct capitalization, spelling, and grammar.

Having poor netiquette can also have legal ramifications. **Slander** is speaking a false statement about someone that causes others to have a bad opinion of him or her. **Libel** is publishing a false statement about someone that causes others to have a bad or untrue opinion of him or her. Slander and libel can be considered crimes of defamation. It is important to choose words carefully when making comments about others, whether online or in person.

wavebreakmedia/Shutterstock.com

Good digital citizens only use office equipment for business purposes. *How does this show respect to an employer?*

What you post on the Internet never really goes away. A *digital footprint* is a data history of all an individual's online activities. Even if you delete something you have posted on the Internet, it still impacts your digital footprint. Always think before posting to social media sites or sending an e-mail. What you post online today could risk your future college and job opportunities.

Intellectual Property
LO 29.1-2

The Internet provides countless sources for obtaining text, images, video, audio, and software. Even though this material is easily obtainable, this does not mean it is available for you to use any way you choose. Laws exist to govern the use of media and creative works. The creators or owners of this material have certain legal rights. Recall that *intellectual property* is something that comes from a person's mind, such as an idea, invention, or process. Intellectual property laws protect a person's or a company's inventions, artistic works, and other intellectual property.

Plagiarism is claiming another person's material as your own, which is both unethical and

Case in Point

Hyatt

Happy customers are generally repeat customers. Companies looking to provide superior customer service often go the extra mile for their customers. However, employees of any business are only human, and sometimes even the best employees can make mistakes. The most important thing for continued success is to acknowledge a mistake when it happens and attempt to correct it.

One Hyatt hotel even took advantage of the Twitter to raise customer service to a new level. A Hyatt guest had an unfortunate experience when entering the room that had been previously booked. When the guest opened the in-room refrigerator, the last guest's food was still there. The hotel's housekeeping department had forgotten to clean the refrigerator.

The customer took a picture of the food in the dirty refrigerator and tweeted it to @HyattConcierge. Within a matter of hours, the guest received a phone call from Hyatt management apologizing for the inconvenience. The situation was fixed immediately, and a handwritten note and gift were also sent to his room. The Hyatt staff turned a potentially damaging tweet into an opportunity for exemplary customer service.

---

illegal. If you must refer to someone else's work, follow intellectual property laws to ethically acquire the information. Use standard methods of citing sources. Citation guidelines in *The Chicago Manual of Style* and the *MLA Style Manual and Guide to Scholarly Publishing* can be helpful.

Piracy is the unethical and illegal copying or downloading of software, files, and other protected material. Examples of protected material include images, movies, and music. Piracy carries a heavy penalty, including fines and incarceration.

Copyright

A *copyright* acknowledges ownership of a work and specifies that only the owner has the right to sell the work, use it, or give permission for someone else to sell or use it. Any use of copyrighted material without permission is called **infringement**. Copyright laws cover all original work, whether it is in print, on the Internet, or in any other form of media. Scanning a document does not make the content yours.

All original material is automatically copyrighted as soon as it is in a tangible form. This means that an essay is copyrighted as soon as it is written and saved or printed. Similarly, a photograph is copyrighted as soon as it is taken. Copyrighted material that is published is often indicated by the © symbol or the statement "copyright by." Lack of the symbol or statement does not mean the material is not copyrighted. An idea cannot be copyrighted. A copyright can be registered with the US Copyright Office, which is part of the Library of Congress. However, original material is still legally protected whether or not the copyright is registered.

Marketers rely heavily on the Internet to perform many job duties, including marketing research, monitoring the competition, and creating marketing materials. Most information on the Internet is copyrighted, whether it is text, graphics, illustrations, or digital media. This means it cannot be reused without obtaining permission from the owner. Sometimes, the owner

lightpoet/Shutterstock.com

Reusing material without permission, such as photocopying pages out of a textbook, is unethical. *How would you react if someone used your original material without permission?*

of the material places the material on the Internet for others to reuse.

However, if this is not explicitly stated, assume the material is copyrighted and cannot be freely used. Plagiarism is a form of copyright infringement. Therefore, marketers should never copy something from the Internet and use it without permission.

Many websites list rules, called the *terms of use* or *terms of service,* that must be followed for downloaded files. The terms of use agreement may come up automatically, for example, if you are downloading a file or software application. If, however, you are copying an image or a portion of text from a website, you will need to look for the terms of use information.

Fair use doctrine allows individuals to use copyrighted works without permission in limited situations under very strict guidelines. Fair use doctrine allows copyrighted material to be used for the purpose of describing or reviewing the work. A student writing about the material in an original report is an example of fair use. Another example is a product-review website providing editorial comment. Fair use doctrine does not change the copyright or ownership of the material used under the doctrine.

In some cases, individuals or organizations may wish to allow others to use their intellectual property without needing permission. This type of use assignment may be called *copy left,* which is a play on the word *copyright.*

One popular method of allowing use of intellectual property is a Creative Commons license. A *Creative Commons (CC) license* is a specialized copyright license that allows free distribution of copyrighted work. Figure 29-1 shows the Creative Commons symbol that often appears on material bearing this license. If the creator of the work wants to give the public the ability to use, share, or advance his or her original work, a Creative Commons license provides that flexibility. The creator maintains the copyright and can specify how the copyrighted work can be used. For example, one type of Creative Commons license prohibits commercial use.

Public domain refers to material that is not owned by anybody and can be used without permission. Material can enter the public domain when a copyright expires and is not renewed. Much of the material created by federal, state, or local governments is often in the public domain.

Creative Commons

Figure 29-1 The Creative Commons (CC) license allows free sharing of intellectual property.

This is because taxpayer money was used to create it. Additionally, the owner of the material may choose to give up ownership and place the material in the public domain.

Patent

A *patent* gives a person or company the right to be the sole producer of a product for a defined period of time. Patents protect an invention that is functional or mechanical. The invention must be considered useful and inoffensive, and it must be operational. This means an idea may not be patented. A process can be patented under certain conditions. The process must be related to a particular machine or transform a substance or item into a different state or thing. In the United States, patents are granted by the US Patent and Trademark Office (USPTO).

Marketing Ethics

Online Merchandise

When merchandising online, businesses should display all the information the customer needs. Details such as fabric content, size charts, and shipping dates should all be easily accessible and visible. Withholding any information will leave the customer uninformed and untrusting of your company. This may be considered unethical if the customer has not been properly informed.

Most brand logos, such as those seen on social media websites, are trademarks. *Why is it important for a company to protect a trademark?*

Trademark

A *trademark* protects taglines, slogans, names, symbols, and any unique method to identify a product or company. A *service mark* is similar to a trademark, but it identifies a service rather than a product. The term "trademark" is often used to refer to both trademarks and service marks. These marks do not protect a work or product, only the way in which the product is described. Trademarks never expire. Just as with patents, trademarks and service marks are registered with the USPTO.

The symbols used to indicate a trademark or service mark are called *graphic marks*. Some graphic marks can be used without being formally registered.

Licensing Agreement

A *licensing agreement* is a contract that gives one party permission to market, produce, or use the product or service owned by another party. The agreement grants a license in return for a fee or royalty payment. For example, Disney may give a clothing manufacturer permission to print the image of Mickey Mouse on T-shirts.

When buying software, the purchaser agrees to follow the terms of a license. A *license* is the legal permission to use a software program. All software has terms of use that explain how and when the software may be used. Figure 29-2 explains the characteristics of different software licensing.

Alternative usage rights for software programs are typically covered by the *GNU General Public License (GNU GPL)*. The GNU GPL guarantees all users the freedom to use, study, share, and modify the software. The term **open source** applies to software that has had its source code made available to the public at no charge. Open-source software can be downloaded and used for free and can be modified and distributed by anyone. However, part or all of the code of open-source software may be owned by an individual or organization.

LO 29.1-3 Electronic User's Bill of Rights

The *Electronic User's Bill of Rights* details the rights and responsibilities of both individuals and institutions regarding the treatment of digital information. It was originally proposed in 1993 by Frank W. Connolly of American University. It is modeled after the original United States Bill of Rights, although it contains only four articles. The articles are not legally binding, but contain guidelines for the appropriate use of digital information. The articles in the Electronic User's Bill of Rights are as follows.

- Article I: Individual Rights
- Article II: Individual Responsibilities
- Article III: Rights of Educational Institutions
- Article IV: Institutional Responsibilities

Software Type			
Characteristics	**For-Purchase**	**Freeware**	**Shareware**
Cost	• Must be purchased to use • Demo may be available	• Never have to pay for it	• Free to try • Pay to upgrade to full functionality
Features	• Full functionality	• Full functionality	• Limited functionality without upgrade

Goodheart-Willcox Publisher

Figure 29-2 Each type of software has specific licensing permissions.

Article I: Individual Rights

Article I: Individual Rights focuses on the rights and freedoms of the users of computers and the Internet. It states "citizens of the electronic community of learners" have the right to access computers and informational resources. They should be informed when their personal information is being collected. They have the right to review and correct the information that has been collected. Users should have freedom of speech and rights of ownership for their intellectual property.

Article II: Individual Responsibilities

Article II: Individual Responsibilities focuses on the responsibilities that come with those rights outlined in Article I. A digital citizen is responsible for seeking information and using it effectively. It is also the individual's responsibility to honor the intellectual property of others. This includes verifying the accuracy of information obtained electronically. A digital citizen is expected to respect the privacy of others and use electronic resources wisely.

Article III: Rights of Educational Institutions

Article III: Rights of Educational Institutions states the right of educational institutions to access computers and informational resources. Like individuals, an educational institution retains ownership of its intellectual property. Each institution has the right to use its resources as it sees fit.

Article IV: Institutional Responsibilities

Article IV: Institutional Responsibilities focuses on the responsibilities that come with the rights granted in Article III. Educational institutions are held accountable for the information they use and provide. Institutions are responsible for creating and maintaining "an environment wherein trust and intellectual freedom are the foundation for individual and institutional growth and success."

Section 29.1 Review

Check Your Understanding

1. Explain the importance of digital citizenship.
2. What actions are considered cyberbullying?
3. Name two unethical uses of another person's intellectual property.
4. What does a licensing agreement allow?
5. List the articles of the Electronic User's Bill of Rights.

Build Your Vocabulary

As you progress through this course, develop a personal glossary of key terms and add it to your portfolio. This will help you build your vocabulary and prepare you for a career. Write a definition for each of the following terms, and add it to your personal glossary.

cyberbullying
digital citizenship
digital communication
digital literacy
infringement
libel

netiquette
open source
piracy
plagiarism
public domain
slander

Section 29.2

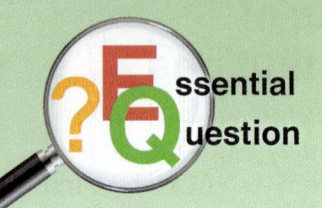

Internet Use in the Workplace

Essential Question

How can unacceptable Internet use by an employee affect a company as a whole?

Learning Objectives

LO 29.2-1 Explain how employers ensure appropriate Internet use in the workplace.
LO 29.2-2 List examples of ways to practice digital security.

Key Terms

acceptable use policy
cloud computing
Internet protocol address
hacking
cookies
phishing
malware
spyware
software virus
ransomware
identity theft
firewall

LO 29.2-1 Internet Use

An important aspect of digital citizenship is respecting your employer's electronic resources and time spent using them. Marketers use computers, printers, and other office equipment to complete their daily job duties and responsibilities. Company equipment is for performing business-related functions, such as sending electronic ad campaigns, updating social media, or managing time and resources. Using company equipment for personal tasks is unethical. Some personal uses of company equipment add costs; others may take time away from job duties. The code of conduct should outline expected employee behavior while at work.

Internet access provided by the company should be used for business purposes only. For example, checking personal e-mail or playing a game online is not acceptable. Most companies have an established acceptable use policy. An **acceptable use policy** is a set of rules that explains what is and is not acceptable use of company-owned and company-operated equipment and networks. Employees are typically made aware of acceptable use policies during training, before they are allowed access to the company's computers and network. Many codes of conduct also have guidelines for visiting websites and rules for downloading to company computers. These rules protect the business' computer system and its private information.

It is common for companies and schools to use *filters* that prevent unauthorized Internet surfing

Employability Skills

Prompt Response

Business requires prompt responses to customers and coworkers. When people try to reach you via telephone or e-mail, respond as soon as possible. If you are not able to do what the person is asking you right away, acknowledge that you have received the call and will follow up at a later time. It is important that the sender knows the call was received and not lost in transmission.

or visiting selected websites during working hours. *Censorship* is the practice of examining material, such as online content, and blocking or deleting anything considered inappropriate. Employers are legally allowed to censor information that employees read on the Internet accessed through company computers during work hours.

Many organizations allow cloud computing to support collaboration and working remotely. **Cloud computing** is using Internet-based resources to store and access data rather than on a personal computer or local server. This allows users to access personal content, such as saved files, from anywhere with an Internet connection. Cloud computing makes private digital information accessible from any Internet-enabled device.

Whether at work or home, each time you access a search engine or visit a web page, the computer's identity is revealed. The **Internet protocol address**, known as the *IP address*, is a unique number used to identify an electronic device connected to the Internet. While your personal information cannot be easily discovered, an IP address can reveal your approximate geographic location. Any e-mails you send from your computer or mobile devices have an IP address attached to them.

One way to protect yourself online is to ensure that you are transmitting data over a secure connection. When transmitting private information to a website, check that the site is secure. A secure address begins with https. The s stands for *secure*. This is not 100 percent foolproof, but generally is a sign of protection. If the connection is secure, the browser will also display an icon somewhere, usually in the address bar, to indicate the communication is secure. Be wary of providing personal information to sites that are not secure. Public Wi-Fi hotspots should be avoided. While convenient, these networks are generally not secure and put your devices at risk of inadvertently exposing data.

One definition of **hacking** is illegally accessing or altering digital devices, software, or networks. Hackers may create illicit hotspots in locations where free or paid public Wi-Fi exists. Users unknowingly connect to the incorrect network, which allows the hacker access to any data being transmitted over that connection. The signal with the best strength may not always be the legitimate hotspot. An easy way to avoid illicit hotspots is to check with an employee of the business providing the Wi-Fi access. Ask the employee for the name of the network and the access key. If a Wi-Fi authentication screen asks for credit card information, confirm that the Wi-Fi connection is legitimate before providing a credit card number.

Cookies

Cookies are bits of data stored on your computer that record information about the websites you have visited. Cookies may also

Exploring Marketing Careers

Webmaster

Most companies today have a website through which they do at least some of their marketing and selling. Logically, a website that looks interesting and is easy to use will be more successful than one that is poorly designed. A webmaster manages web design and development and maintains the site after it becomes active. Other typical job titles for webmasters include *website manager* and *corporate webmaster*.

Some examples of tasks that webmasters perform include:
- Work with web development teams to provide an easy-to-use interface and solve usability issues
- Install updates and upgrades as needed
- Troubleshoot web page and server problems, keeping downtime to a minimum
- Implement and monitor firewalls and other security measures
- Update content and links as requested or needed by the company

Webmasters must be proficient in application server software, graphics software, and web page creation software. They need a good understanding of graphic design and web design. If the website is used for sales, they must also be familiar with the company's products or services, as well as electronic payment software and techniques. Most jobs in this field require an associate's degree in web design or a related field, or training in a vocational school. Related job experience is also helpful. For more information, access the *Occupational Outlook Handbook* online.

contain the personal information you enter on a website. Most cookies are from legitimate websites and will not harm your computer. Some advertisers place them onto your computer without your knowledge or consent. Marketers use the information for research and selling purposes. However, if a hacker gains access to your cookies, you are at risk. The cookies can be used to steal personal information you have entered on a website. Cookies also can be used to target you for a scam based on your Internet history.

As a precaution, there are ways to protect your computer from cookies. One way is to prevent them from being accepted by the browser. Most Internet browsers allow you to set a preference to never accept cookies. Check your browser for specific instructions. Another way to protect your computer is to delete cookies on a regular basis. Cookies can also be removed by running a disk cleanup utility.

Phishing

Phishing is the use of fraudulent e-mails and copies of valid websites to trick people into providing private and confidential data. A common form of phishing is sending a fraudulent e-mail that appears to be from a legitimate source, such as a bank. The e-mail asks for certain information, such as a Social Security number or bank account number. Sometimes it provides a link to a web page. The linked web page looks real, but its sole purpose is to collect private information that will be used to commit fraud.

Most legitimate organizations do not use e-mail to request this type of information. Never provide confidential information in response to an unsolicited e-mail. Avoid clicking a link to a website in an e-mail. It is better to manually enter the website URL into a web browser. Never open an e-mail attachment that you are not expecting.

Malware

Malware, short for *malicious software*, is a term given to software programs that are intended to damage, destroy, or steal data. Beware of an invitation to click on a website link for more information about an advertisement, as the link may trigger malware. One click can activate a code, and your computer could be hacked or infected. Any person who purposefully introduces malware to a computer or network has broken the law. Malware comes in many forms, including spyware, Trojan horses, worms, viruses, and ransomware.

Spyware is software that spies on a computer. It can capture private information, such as e-mail messages, usernames, passwords, bank account information, and credit card information. Often, affected users are not aware that spyware is on their computer.

A *Trojan horse* is malware usually disguised to appear as a useful or common application in order to convince people to download and use the program. However, the Trojan horse performs malicious actions on the user's computer, such as destroying data or stealing information. Trojan horses do not self-replicate, nor do they infect other files.

Worms are similar to Trojan horses, except they self-replicate. This allows them to infect other computers and devices. Like Trojan horses, worms do not infect other files.

A **software virus** is a computer program designed to negatively impact a computer system by infecting other files. A virus may destroy data on the computer, cause programs to malfunction, bring harm to a network, or steal information. Viruses can be introduced to a computer in many ways, such as by downloading infected files from an e-mail or website.

Ransomware is a type of malware that seizes control of your computer and demands payment to unlock it. This type of malware encrypts all files on the computer, which makes them unusable. If the ransom is paid, the criminals will—hopefully—unlock the computer by decrypting the files. Always report a ransomware attack to law enforcement officials. Do not pay to unlock the computer without first consulting experts.

Kues/Shutterstock.com

A security plan includes storing backup of important digital files in a fireproof container. *Do you have a security plan for your digital files?*

Digital Security

LO 29.2-2

Digital security refers to staying safe and protecting yourself on the Internet. Ways you can practice digital security for yourself and your employer include using common sense, avoiding identity theft, and creating a security plan.

Use Common Sense

Do not be lulled into a false sense of security when communicating with others online. Be especially careful with those whom you do not personally know. Avoid opening e-mails that look suspicious. Use common sense when deciding what personal details you share, especially your address and Social Security number. Resist the urge to share too much information, which could be stolen.

If you have any suspicions about communicating with someone or giving your information via a website, do not proceed. Investigate the person or the company with whom you are dealing. You may be able to avoid a scam before it is too late.

Avoid Identity Theft

Identity theft is an illegal act that involves stealing someone's personal information and using it to commit theft or fraud. There are many ways that your personal information can be stolen without your knowing. A lost credit card or driver's license can provide thieves with the information they need to steal a person's identity. Be wary of how much information you share on social networking websites. Criminals also steal physical mail to commit identity theft. This method is often called *dumpster diving*. However, computer technology has made identity theft through digital means the most prevalent.

If you suspect your identity has been stolen, visit the identity theft website provided by the Federal Trade Commission (FTC) for resources and guidance. Time is of the essence, so if this unfortunate situation happens to you, act immediately.

Create a Security Plan

A security plan should be in place for your computer in general, any databases you maintain, and any mobile devices you have. Your employer will assist in creating a plan for your workplace equipment.

Consider downloading and running antivirus software for your mobile device, especially if you rely on it to complete daily tasks. It is important to guard mobile devices against viruses that would disrupt a primary means of communication and expose personal data.

You must also plan to protect your mobile devices from theft. If you become careless and leave your smartphone or other device in an unexpected location, your identity can be stolen. You may also be stuck with a large bill. If it is an employer-issued device, you may be responsible for replacing it using your personal funds. To protect your mobile device from use by a thief, create a password to lock it. Have the number of your mobile device in a safe place so that if the unexpected happens, you can contact your service provider.

You Do the Math

Units

When solving an equation, it is important to make sure the units match. For example, when calculating fuel economy in miles per gallon (MPG), the final unit must be miles over gallons. So, the equation must be the number of miles *divided* by the number of gallons. If the equation is incorrectly expressed as the number of miles *times* the number of gallons, the final unit would be mile-gallons, not miles/gallon.

Solve the following problems.

1. A business must calculate the number of sales dollars generated per sales representative ($/rep). Is the following equation correct for this calculation: dollars × reps? If this is not the correct equation, what is?
2. A shipping box is rated to hold 65 pounds. The company ships products that weigh 1.3 pounds each. It uses the following formula to determine how many products can be placed in one box: pounds per product × pounds per box. Is this the correct equation? If this is not the correct equation, what is?
3. What is the final unit for this equation: 12.8 feet × 3.6 feet ÷ 7.6 seconds?

Virus-protection software helps safeguard a computer against malware and should be used on any computer or electronic device that is connected to the Internet or any type of network. This software is also referred to as *antivirus* or *antimalware* software.

A firewall should also be used. A **firewall** is a program that monitors information coming into a computer. It helps ensure that only safe information gets through.

Secure Passwords

Unfortunately, many people have weak passwords for even their most important accounts, such as banking or credit card accounts. To help ensure your digital security, create passwords that are secure and change them regularly. When creating new passwords, use the tips shown in Figure 29-3. Your employer will have guidelines for creating passwords for work accounts.

Security Settings

Become familiar with the security settings and features of your Internet browser. Change your settings to protect your computer and your information. Enabling a *pop-up blocker* prevents your browser from allowing you to see pop-up ads, which can contain malware.

Back Up Your Computer

An important part of a security plan is backing up the data on your computer. If a virus invades your computer or the hard disk crashes, it may be too late to retrieve your files and computer programs.

Your employer will request regular backups of files on your work computer. For your personal computer, put a plan in place to perform regular backups. Decide on a storage device and method for backing up your files. Place the backup in a fireproof container and store it at a location other than your home, such as a safety deposit box at a bank.

Secure Passwords

- Do not be careless or in a hurry.
- Do not use passwords that contain easily guessed information.
- Do not use the same passwords for multiple accounts or profiles.
- Do change your passwords often.
- Do record your passwords on a dedicated and secure hard-copy doccument.

Goodheart-Willcox Publisher

Figure 29-3 Use these tips to create safe, secure passwords.

Section 29.2 Review

Check Your Understanding

1. What is the purpose of an acceptable use policy in the workplace?
2. A secure address begins with https. What does the s stand for?
3. What is the difference between spyware and a software virus?
4. How can a mobile device be protected from theft?
5. Why should a computer be backed up on a regular basis?

Build Your Vocabulary

As you progress through this course, develop a personal glossary of key terms and add it to your portfolio. This will help you build your vocabulary and prepare you for a career. Write a definition for each of the following terms, and add it to your personal glossary.

acceptable use policy	Internet protocol address
cloud computing	malware
cookies	phishing
firewall	ransomware
hacking	software virus
identity theft	spyware

CHAPTER 29 Review and Assessment

Chapter Summary

Section 29.1 Communicating in a Digital Society

LO 29.1-1 Describe the elements of digital communication.
Digital communication is the exchange of information through electronic means. It requires digital literacy skills and appropriate digital citizenship behavior.

LO 29.1-2 Explain intellectual property and what it includes.
Intellectual property comes from a person's mind, such as an idea, invention, or process. Copyrights, patents, and trademarks can protect intellectual property rights. Material in the public domain refers to material that is not owned by anyone and can be used without permission. Products can be protected by issuing a licensing agreement.

LO 29.1-3 Discuss the importance of the Electronic User's Bill of Rights.
The Electronic User's Bill of Rights details the rights and responsibilities of both individuals and institutions regarding the treatment of digital information. Its four articles contain guidelines for the appropriate use of digital information.

Section 29.2 Internet Use in the Workplace

LO 29.2-1 Explain how employers ensure appropriate Internet use in the workplace.
Internet access provided by a company should be used only for business purposes. Most companies have an acceptable use policy that explains what is and is not acceptable use of company-owned and company-operated equipment.

LO 29.2-2 List examples of ways to practice digital security.
Digital security refers to staying safe and protecting yourself on the Internet. Ways you can practice digital security for yourself and your employer include using common sense, avoiding identity theft, and creating a security plan.

Check Your Marketing IQ

Now that you have completed the chapter, see what you have learned about marketing by taking the chapter posttest. The posttest is available at www.g-wlearning.com/marketing/.

Review Your Knowledge

1. Describe the elements of digital communication.
2. Provide two examples of digital literacy skills.
3. Explain what intellectual property is and what it includes.
4. What is fair use doctrine?
5. Discuss the importance of the Electronic User's Bill of Rights.
6. Explain how employers ensure appropriate Internet use in the workplace.
7. How can a digital citizen protect his or her computer from cookies?
8. Describe the most common form of phishing.
9. List examples of ways to practice digital security.
10. Why is it important to back up a computer?

Apply Your Knowledge

1. Create a list of behaviors that are considered to be examples of proper netiquette. Next to each, explain why these behaviors are necessary in a digital society.

2. Select a topic related to digital citizenship, such as social media use or identity theft. Explain the implications of your topic on individuals, society, and businesses.

3. Your digital footprint is important to your personal life as well as your future professional career. List activities that may have a negative impact on your life if you posted about them on social media. After putting these actions in writing, will you think more seriously about what you post? Explain your answer.

4. Analyze the legal and ethical responsibilities required in the workplace. List the responsibilities you think you may be faced with in your career.

5. Photocopying copyrighted material is illegal and unethical. What is your opinion of a friend photocopying a textbook chapter instead of buying the textbook? Do you think that duplicating copyrighted materials is illegal, unethical, or both? Do you think the fair use doctrine would apply in this situation? Explain your positions.

6. Professional marketing communication regularly involves persuasive messages. Advertisements that claim weight loss overnight or white teeth in four hours attempt to persuade the audience to purchase a product. How do these communication messages impact society? Does the advertiser's point of view sway the audience? What social responsibilities does marketing have to society? Write several paragraphs discussing your opinion.

7. When shopping online, you may notice that with each new site you browse, you see advertisements for previous sites and products that you have searched. This is due to the presence of cookies on your computer. Marketers use this information for selling purposes. That is why you are likely to see those products appear repeatedly when shopping online. Is this an ethical practice? Explain why or why not.

8. Locate your school or district's policy on acceptable Internet use. This is often located in the student handbook. What policies does your school have in place regarding appropriate Internet use? How are these policies enforced?

9. Secure passwords are crucial to digital security. Describe your experiences creating passwords for various online accounts or electronic devices, such as an e-mail account, social media website, or cell phone. What were the requirements for these passwords? How do you keep track of them?

10. Create your own digital security plan. Make a list of the actions you will take to protect your online identity as well as your private information.

Apply Your Math Skills

1. Spencer is purchasing antivirus software for his laptop computer. Antivirus A costs $7.49 per month for the duration of a two-year contract. Antivirus B costs $79.99 for a one-year subscription. Which antivirus software is less expensive to purchase for two years of virus protection?

2. Alexandria has been the victim of identity theft. She has the following charges on her monthly credit card statement: $48.75 for utilities; $74.80 for groceries; $376.30 at a department store; and $94.55 at an online retailer. She never shopped at the department store or the online retailer. What percentage of her total credit card bill is for charges she did not make? Round your answer to the nearest percentage.

Communication Skills

Reading Most people use technology on a daily basis. Using technology in the workplace can help employees be more productive. In other instances, technology can be a distraction. Read about types of technology and how people can use each to be more productive in the workplace. What did you learn?

College and Career Readiness

Speaking What role do you think ethics and integrity have in decision-making in the workplace? Think of a time when your ideals and principles helped you make a decision. How did they influence your decision? In retrospect, do you think you made the correct decision? Make an informal presentation to your class to share your thoughts about how your decision was influenced by ethics and integrity, and whether it was the right decision.

Writing Most people in the United States act as responsible and contributing citizens. How can a person demonstrate social and ethical responsibility in a digital society? Can you think of ways that are not discussed in this chapter? List your ideas on how a person can demonstrate responsibility in a digital society. Use this list to write a brief code of conduct for a digital citizen.

Internet Research

Copyright Copyright laws protect intellectual property. Conduct an Internet search for *copyright law violation example*. Select an example and discuss the law and how it was violated. What copyright issues were at stake? Write your findings and cite your sources using *The Chicago Manual of Style* or your choice of style guide.

Malware Select one of the types of malware described in this chapter. Use the Internet to find a recent case of malware reported. How did the type of malware affect people or businesses? What actions were recommended if a computer or network became infected?

Password Strength Use the Internet to locate a password strength meter. Test the passwords that you use for your online accounts. How strong are your passwords? What strategies can you apply to make your passwords stronger?

Teamwork

Working with your team, identify and analyze examples of ethical responsibilities that a professional person in business has to society. Make a list of applicable rules your team thinks are appropriate for professional conduct. How can a professional exhibit ethical conduct?

Portfolio Development

College and Career Readiness

Evaluating Your Portfolio A portfolio can be used for many purposes both in school and in the professional world. Ensure that your portfolio represents you in the way you desire by evaluating it periodically. Keep the contents and documents up-to-date to reflect your most recent accomplishments. Remove any information or documents that are no longer relevant.

As your goals progress, the purpose of the portfolio may change. It is important to check that the documents collected in the portfolio reflect the goal you want to achieve. Documents that are not relevant can be stored in a separate place if you may need them again later.

1. Review the documents you have collected. Determine if the portfolio reflects your current accomplishments and goals.
2. Determine if any documents need to be added, removed, or updated. If necessary, create a new flowchart to determine the organization of your updated portfolio.
3. Make the necessary changes.
4. Give the portfolio to your instructor, counselor, or other person who can provide constructive feedback on your updated portfolio.
5. Review the feedback you received. Make necessary adjustments and revisions.
6. Set a reminder to evaluate the portfolio again in the future, such as in six months or one year.

UNIT 10 Preparing for a Career

Building the Marketing Plan

In the last Building the Marketing Plan activity in Unit 9, you finalized and printed your marketing plan. Now it is time to develop a presentation to present your marketing plan to management. Presenting a marketing plan is similar to selling a product. You must convince the audience that your plan is viable.

Part 1 Develop the Presentation

Objectives
- Organize the presentation with an outline.
- Write the content of the presentation.
- Create a slide show to deliver the presentation.

Directions

1. Develop an outline for your presentation. An *outline* is a guideline that helps identify the information to be presented and its proper sequence. Consider using your Table of Contents as a starting point. Select the main points you want to present. Under each item, list its supporting points and any necessary details.

2. Write the introduction. The introduction should introduce the marketing plan and preview the main points. In other words, "tell them what you are going to tell them." Your goal is to sell the audience on your marketing plan so it gets approval and funding.

3. A slide presentation is an effective tool for presenting to an audience. Create a slide presentation using software such as Microsoft PowerPoint, Google Slides, or Prezi. When creating slides, focus on the important points. Slides are not intended to be read to the audience. Keep sentences short and do not crowd the space with too many words. A common rule of thumb is the *4 × 5 rule*, which states no more than four points per slide each with no more than five words per point.

4. Consider adding visuals to the presentation, such as tables and figures. These will add interest and help the audience interpret any marketing research or other data being presented.

5. Write the conclusion of the presentation. In other words, "tell them what you said," and restate the main points. Be prepared to request a call to action and ask management if they will accept your plan and provide funding.

6. Prepare for audience questions during and after the presentation. Many presenters invite audience questions by announcing that the time has come for them. Having time for questions helps engage the audience with the presentation. It also allows the audience to get clarification on any points they did not understand.

7. Develop a set of presentation notes to use during the presentation. These will help you keep your place and to remind yourself of points should you forget anything. To create the notes, begin with the outline for the presentation. Write down a few words for each point that remind you of what you want to say. If you are using Microsoft PowerPoint to create a slideshow for your presentation, you can make use of the notes feature. Some presenters prefer to use index cards.

Part 2 Deliver the Presentation

Objectives
- Practice the presentation.
- Prepare for the presentation.
- Deliver the presentation.

Directions

1. Once the presentation is developed, practice is essential. Become familiar with the sequence of the topics and practice the key points over and over. Practice transitions between points. Do not read your presentation word-for-word even when you are practicing. Commit important points to memory so you can look at your audience and move with ease. Use your voice, body movements, or visual

aids in addition to words to tell the audience you are introducing a new thought. Use the presentation notes as reference to keep you on topic.

2. Time your practice presentations. It is essential to control the length of the presentation.

3. As a marketing manager, you will probably be a part of a marketing team. Coordinate your team members to assist in the presentation. It is most efficient if roles are assigned to make sure all tasks are completed. For example, one person may be assigned the task of printing and collating copies of the presentation for the members of the audience. This should also include distributing them at the meeting. Another person may be in charge of creating the slide show, while still another team member may be responsible for reserving and setting up the conference room.

4. Arrive early for your presentation. Make one final check of the room arrangement and equipment. Set up the computer and launch your presentation to make sure everything is working.

Congratulations! You have finished presenting your marketing plan.

Math Skills Handbook

Table of Contents

Getting Started — 571
Using a Calculator 571
Solving Word Problems 571
Number Sense 571

Numbers and Quantity — 572
Whole Numbers 572
   Place Value 572
   Addition 572
   Subtraction 572
   Multiplication 572
   Division 572
Decimals 572
   Place Value 573
   Addition 573
   Subtraction 573
   Multiplication 573
   Division 573
Rounding 574
Fractions 574
   Proper 574
   Improper 574
   Mixed 574
   Reducing 574
   Addition 575
   Subtraction 575
   Multiplication 575
   Division 575
Negative Numbers 576
   Addition 576
   Subtraction 576
   Multiplication 576
   Division 576
Percentages 576
   Representing Percentages as Decimals .. 576
   Representing Fractions as Percentages .. 577
   Calculating a Percentage 577
Ratio 577

Measurement — 577
US Customary Measurement 577
Metric Conversion 578
Estimating 578
Accuracy and Precision 578

Algebra — 578
Solving Equations with Variables 578
Order of Operations 579
Recursive Formulas 579

Geometry — 579
Parallelograms 579
Circles and Half Circles 580
Triangles 580
Perimeter 580
Area 581
Surface Area 581
Volume 582

Data Analysis and Statistics — 583

Math Models for Business and Retail — 583
Markup 583
Percentage Markup to Determine Selling Price 584
Markdown 584
Gross Profit 585
Net Income or Loss 585
Break-Even Point 585
Sales Tax 585
Return on Investment 585

Getting Started

Math skills are needed in everyday life. You will need to be able to estimate your purchases at a grocery store, calculate sales tax, or divide a recipe in half. This section is designed to help develop your math proficiency for better understanding of the concepts presented in the textbook. Using the information presented in the Math Skills Handbook will help you understand basic math concepts and their application to the real world.

Using a Calculator

There are many different types of calculators. Some are simple and only perform basic math operations. Become familiar with the keys and operating instructions of your calculator so calculations can be made quickly and correctly.

Shown below is a scientific calculator that comes standard with the Windows 8 operating system. To display this version, select the **View** pull-down menu and click **Scientific** in the menu.

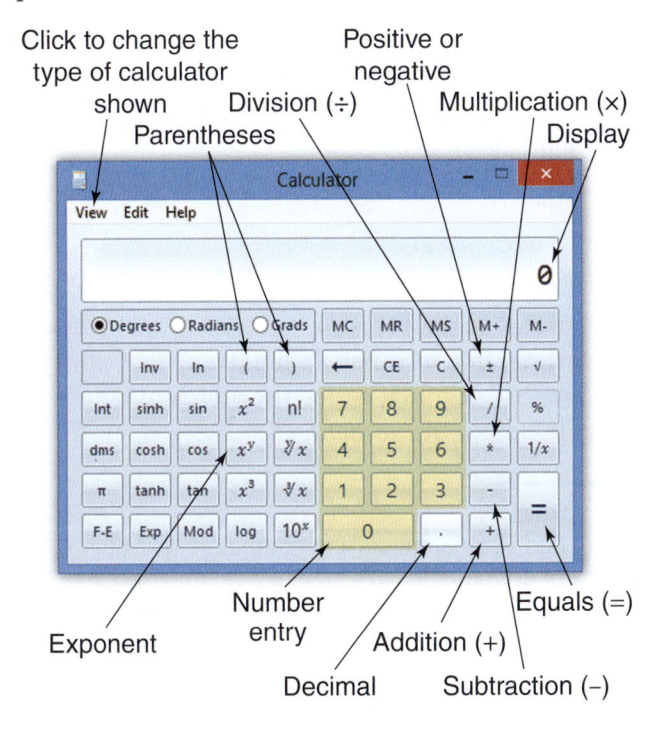

Solving Word Problems

Word problems are exercises in which the problem is set up in text, rather than presented in mathematical notation. Many word problems tell a story. You must identify the elements of the math problem and solve it.

Strategy	How to Apply
List or table	Identify information in the problem and organize it into a table to identify patterns.
Work backward	When an end result is provided, work backward from that to find the requested information.
Guess, check, revise	Start with a reasonable guess at the answer, check to see if it is correct, and revise the guess as needed until the solution is found.
Substitute simpler information	Use different numbers to simplify the problem and solve it, then solve the problem using the provided numbers.

There are many strategies for solving word problems. Some common strategies include making a list or table; working backward; guessing, checking, and revising; and substituting simpler numbers to solve the problem.

Number Sense

Number sense is an ability to use and understand numbers to make judgments and solve problems. Someone with good number sense also understands when his or her computations are reasonable in the context of a problem.

> **Example**
> Suppose you want to add three basketball scores: 35, 21, and 18.
> - First, add 30 + 20 + 10 = 60.
> - Then, add 5 + 1 + 8 = 14.
> - Finally, combine these two sums to find the answer: 60 + 14 = 74.

> **Example**
> Suppose your brother is 72 inches tall and you want to convert this measurement from inches to feet. Suppose you use a calculator to divide 72 by 12 (number of inches in a foot) and the answer is displayed as 864. You recognize immediately that your brother cannot be 864 feet tall and realize you must have miscalculated. In this case, you incorrectly entered a multiplication operation instead of a division operation. The correct answer is 6.

Numbers and Quantity

Numbers are more than just items in a series. Each number has a distinct value relative to all other numbers. They are used to perform mathematical operations from the simplest addition to finding square roots. There are whole numbers, fractions, decimals, exponents, and square roots.

Whole Numbers

A whole number, or integer, is any positive number or zero that has no fractional part. It can be a single digit from 0 to 9, or may contain multiple digits, such as 38.

Place Value

A digit's position in a number determines its *place value*. The digit, or numeral, in the place farthest to the right before the decimal point is in the *ones position*. The next digit to the left is in the *tens position*, followed by the next digit in the *hundreds position*. As you continue to move left, the place values increase to thousands, ten thousands, and so forth.

> **Example**
> Suppose you win the lottery and receive a check for $23,152,679. Your total prize would be *twenty-three million, one hundred fifty-two thousand, six hundred seventy-nine dollars*.

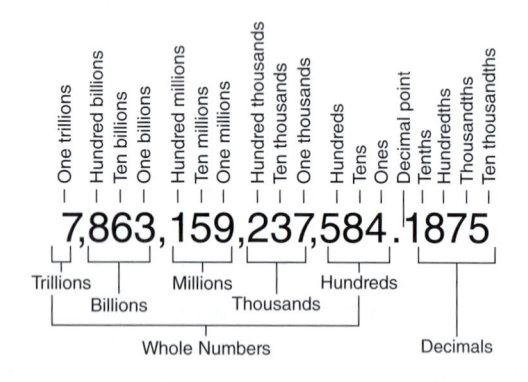

Place value chart: 7,863,159,237,584.1875 — with positions labeled One trillions, Hundred billions, Ten billions, One billions, Hundred millions, Ten millions, One millions, Hundred thousands, Ten thousands, One thousands, Hundreds, Tens, Ones, Decimal point, Tenths, Hundredths, Thousandths, Ten thousandths. Grouped as Trillions, Billions, Millions, Thousands, Hundreds (Whole Numbers) and Decimals.

Addition

Addition is the process of combining two or more numbers. The result is called the *sum*.

> **Example**
> A plumber installs six faucets on his first job and three faucets on his second job. How many faucets does he install in total?
>
> 6 + 3 = 9

Subtraction

Subtraction is the process of finding the *difference* between two numbers.

> **Example**
> A plumber installs six faucets on her first job and three faucets on her second job. How many more faucets did she install on the first job than the second? Subtract 3 from 6 to find the answer.
>
> 6 − 3 = 3

Multiplication

Multiplication is a method of adding a number to itself a given number of times. The multiplied numbers are called *factors*, and the result is called the *product*.

> **Example**
> Suppose you are installing computers and need to purchase four adaptors. If the adaptors are $6 each, what is the total cost of the adaptors? The answer can be found by adding $6 four times:
>
> $6 + $6 + $6 + $6 = $24
>
> However, the same answer is found more quickly by multiplying $6 times 4.
>
> $6 × 4 = $24

Division

Division is the process of determining how many times one number, called the *divisor*, goes into another number, called the *dividend*. The result is called the *quotient*.

> **Example**
> Suppose you are installing computers and buy a box of adaptors for $24. There are four adaptors in the box. What is the cost of each adaptor? The answer is found by dividing $24 by 4:
>
> $24 ÷ 4 = $6

Decimals

A decimal is a kind of fraction with a denominator that is either ten, one hundred, one thousand, or some power of ten. Every decimal has three parts: a whole number (sometimes zero), followed by a decimal point, and one or more whole numbers.

Math Skills Handbook

Place Value

The numbers to the right of the decimal point indicate the amount of the fraction. The first place to the right of a decimal point is the tenths place. The second place to the right of the decimal point is the hundredths place. As you continue to the right, the place values move to the thousandths place, the ten thousandths place, and so on.

> **Example**
> A machinist is required to produce an airplane part to a very precise measurement of 36.876 inches. This measurement is *thirty-six and eight hundred seventy-six thousandths* inches.
>
> 36.876

Addition

To add decimals, place each number in a vertical list and align the decimal points. Then add the numbers in each column starting with the column on the right and working to the left. The decimal point in the answer drops down into the same location.

> **Example**
> A landscaper spreads 4.3 pounds of fertilizer in the front yard of a house and 1.2 pounds in the backyard. How many pounds of fertilizer did the landscaper spread in total?
>
> ```
>    4.3
> + 1.2
>   ---
>    5.5
> ```

Subtraction

To subtract decimals, place each number in a vertical list and align the decimal points. Then subtract the numbers in each column, starting with the column on the right and working to the left. The decimal point in the answer drops down into the same location.

> **Example**
> A landscaper spreads 4.3 pounds of fertilizer in the front yard of a house and 1.2 pounds in the backyard. How many more pounds were spread in the front yard than in the backyard?
>
> ```
>    4.3
> − 1.2
>   ---
>    3.1
> ```

Multiplication

To multiply decimals, place the numbers in a vertical list. Then multiply each digit of the top number by the right-hand bottom number. Multiply each digit of the top number by the bottom number in the tens position. Place the result on a second line and add a zero to the end of the number. Add the total number of decimal places in both numbers you are multiplying. This will be the number of decimal places in your answer.

> **Example**
> An artist orders 13 brushes priced at $3.20 each. What is the total cost of the order? The answer can be found by multiplying $3.20 by 13.
>
> ```
>      $3.20
>   ×     13
>   -------
>        960
> +     3200
>   -------
>     $41.60
> ```

Division

To divide decimals, the dividend is placed under the division symbol, the divisor is placed to the left of the division symbol, and the quotient is placed above the division symbol. Start from the *left* of the dividend and determine how many times the divisor goes into the first number. Continue this until the quotient is found. Add the dollar sign to the final answer.

```
      3.2 0
   3)9.6 0
     9↓      Product of 3 × 3
     ---
     0 6↓    Bring down the 6
       6↓    Product of 2 × 3
       ---
         0   No remainder
```

> **Example**
> An artist buys a package of three brushes for $9.60. What is the cost of each brush? The quotient is found by dividing $9.60 by 3.
>
> ```
>      3.2 0
>   3)9.6 0
>    −9↓
>    ---
>     0 6↓
>     ---
>       0 0
> ```

Rounding

When a number is rounded, some of the digits are changed, removed, or changed to zero so the number is easier to work with. Rounding is often used when precise calculations or measurements are not needed. For example, if you are calculating millions of dollars, it might not be important to know the amount down to the dollar or cent. Instead, you might *round* the amount to the nearest ten thousand or even hundred thousand dollars. Also, when working with decimals, the final answer might have several more decimal places than needed.

To round a number, follow these steps. First, underline the digit in the place to which you are rounding. Second, if the digit to the *right* of this place is 5 or greater, add 1 to the underlined digit. If the digit to the right is less than 5, do not change the underlined digit. Third, change all the digits to right of the underlined digit to zero. In the case of decimals, the digits to the right of the underlined digit are removed.

> **Example**
> A company's utility expense last year was $32,678.53. The owner of the company is preparing a budget for next year and wants to round this amount to the nearest 1,000.
> **Step 1:** Underline the digit in the 1,000 place.
> $3**2**,678
> **Step 2:** The digit to the right of 2 is greater than 5, so add 1.
> 2 + 1 = 3
> **Step 3:** Change the digits to the right of the underlined digit to zero.
> $33,000

Fractions

A fraction is a part of a whole. It is made up by a numerator that is divided by a denominator.

$$\frac{\text{numerator}}{\text{denominator}}$$

The *numerator* specifies the number of these equal parts that are in the fraction. The *denominator* shows how many equal parts make up the whole.

Proper

In a *proper fraction*, the numerator is less than the denominator.

> **Example**
> A lumber yard worker cuts a sheet of plywood into four equal pieces and sells three of them to a carpenter. The carpenter now has 3/4 of the original sheet. The lumber yard has 1/4 of the sheet remaining.

Improper

An *improper fraction* is a fraction where the numerator is equal to or greater than the denominator.

> **Example**
> A chef uses a chili recipe which calls for 1/2 cup of chili sauce. However, the chef makes an extra-large batch that will serve three times as many people and uses three of the 1/2 cup measures. The improper fraction in this example is 3/2 cups of chili sauce.

Mixed

A mixed number contains a whole number and a fraction. It is another way of writing an improper fraction.

> **Example**
> A chef uses a chili recipe that calls for 1/2 cup of chili sauce. However, the chef makes an extra-large batch that will serve three times as many people and uses three of the 1/2 cup measures. The improper fraction in this example is 3/2 cups of chili sauce. This can be converted to a mixed number by dividing the numerator by the denominator:
>
> The remainder is 1, which is 1 over 2. So, the mixed number is 1 1/2 cups.
>
> $$2\overline{)3}$$
> $$\underline{-2}$$
> $$1$$

Reducing

Fractions are reduced to make them easier to work with. Reducing a fraction means writing it with smaller numbers, in *lowest terms*. Reducing a fraction does not change its value.

Math Skills Handbook

To find the lowest terms, determine the largest number that *evenly* divides both the numerator and denominator so there is no remainder. Then use this number to divide both the numerator and denominator.

> **Example**
> The owner of a hair salon asks ten customers if they were satisfied with the service they recently received. Eight customers said they were satisfied, so the fraction of satisfied customers is 8/10. The largest number that evenly divides both the numerator and denominator is 2. The fraction is reduced to its lowest terms as follows.
>
> $$\frac{8}{10} = \frac{8 \div 2}{10 \div 2} = \frac{4}{5}$$

Addition

To add fractions, the numerators are combined and the denominator stays the same. However, fractions can only be added when they have a *common denominator*. The *least common denominator* is the smallest number to which each denominator can be converted.

> **Example**
> A snack food company makes a bag of trail mix by combining 3/8 pound of nuts with 1/8 pound of dried fruit. What is the total weight of each bag? The fractions have common denominators, so the total weight is determined by adding the fractions.
>
> $$\frac{3}{8} + \frac{1}{8} = \frac{4}{8}$$
>
> This answer can be reduced from 4/8 to 1/2.

> **Example**
> Suppose the company combines 1/4 pound of nuts with 1/8 cup of dried fruit. To add these fractions, the denominators must be made equal. In this case, the least common denominator is 8 because 4 × 2 = 8. Convert 1/4 to its equivalent of 2/8 by multiplying both numerator and denominator by 2. Then the fractions can be added as follows.
>
> $$\frac{2}{8} + \frac{1}{8} = \frac{3}{8}$$
>
> This answer cannot be reduced because 3 and 8 have no common factors.

Subtraction

To subtract fractions, the second numerator is subtracted from the first numerator. The denominators stay the same. However, fractions can only be subtracted when they have a *common denominator*.

> **Example**
> A snack food company makes a bag of trail mix by combining 3/8 pound of nuts with 1/8 pound of dried fruit. How much more do the nuts weigh than the dried fruit? The fractions have common denominators, so the difference can be determined by subtracting the fractions.
>
> $$\frac{3}{8} - \frac{1}{8} = \frac{2}{8}$$
>
> This answer can be reduced from 2/8 to 1/4.

> **Example**
> Suppose the company combines 1/4 pound of nuts with 1/8 cup of dried fruit. How much more do the nuts weigh than the dried fruit? To subtract these fractions, the denominators must be made equal. The least common denominator is 8, so convert 1/4 to its equivalent of 2/8. Then the fractions can be subtracted as follows.
>
> $$\frac{2}{8} - \frac{1}{8} = \frac{1}{8}$$
>
> This answer cannot be reduced.

Multiplication

Common denominators are not necessary to multiply fractions. Multiply all of the numerators and multiply all of the denominators. Reduce the resulting fraction as needed.

> **Example**
> A lab technician makes a saline solution by mixing 3/4 cup of salt with one gallon of water. How much salt should the technician mix if only 1/2 gallon of water is used? Multiply 3/4 by 1/2:
>
> $$\frac{3}{4} \times \frac{1}{2} = \frac{3}{8}$$

Division

To divide one fraction by a second fraction, multiply the first fraction by the reciprocal of the second fraction. The *reciprocal* of a fraction is created by switching the numerator and denominator.

> **Example**
> A cabinet maker has 3/4 gallon of wood stain. Each cabinet requires 1/8 gallon of stain to finish. How many cabinets can be finished? To find the answer, divide 3/4 by 1/8, which means multiplying 3/4 by the reciprocal of 1/8.
>
> $$\frac{3}{4} \div \frac{1}{8} = \frac{3}{4} \times \frac{8}{1} = \frac{24}{4} = 6$$

Negative Numbers

Negative numbers are those less than zero. They are written with a minus sign in front of the number.

> **Example**
> The number −34,687,295 is read as *negative thirty-four million, six hundred eighty-seven thousand, two hundred ninety-five.*

Addition

Adding a negative number is the same as subtracting a positive number.

> **Example**
> A football player gains nine yards on his first running play (+9) and loses four yards (−4) on his second play. The two plays combined result in a five yard gain.
>
> $$9 + (-4) = 9 - 4 = 5$$
>
> Suppose this player loses five yards on his first running play (−5) and loses four yards (−4) on his second play. The two plays combined result in a nine yard loss.
>
> $$-5 + (-4) = -5 - 4 = -9$$

Subtraction

Subtracting a negative number is the same as adding a positive number.

> **Example**
> Suppose you receive a $100 traffic ticket. This will result in a −$100 change to your cash balance. However, you explain the circumstance to a traffic court judge, and she reduces the fine by $60. The effect is to subtract −$60 from −$100 change to your cash balance. The final result is a −$40 change.
>
> $$-\$100 - (-\$60) = -\$100 + \$60 = -\$40$$

Multiplication

Multiplication of an odd number of negative numbers results in a *negative* product. Multiplication of an even number of negative numbers results in a *positive* product.

> **Example**
> If you lose two pounds per week, this will result in a −2 pound weekly change in your weight. After five weeks, there will be a −10 pound change to your weight.
>
> $$5 \times (-2) = -10$$
>
> Suppose you have been losing two pounds per week. Five weeks ago (−5) your weight was 10 pounds higher.
>
> $$(-5) \times (-2) = 10$$

Division

Division of an odd number of negative numbers results in a *negative* quotient. Division of an even number of negative numbers results in a *positive* quotient.

> **Example**
> Suppose you lost 10 pounds, which is a −10 pound change in your weight. How many pounds on average did you lose each week if it took five weeks to lose the weight? Divide −10 by 5 to find the answer.
>
> $$-10 \div 5 = -2$$
>
> Suppose you lost 10 pounds. How many weeks did this take if you lost two pounds each week? Divide −10 by −2 to find the answer.
>
> $$-10 \div -2 = 5$$

Percentages

A percentage (%) means a part of 100. It is the same as a fraction or decimal.

Representing Percentages as Decimals

To change a percentage to a decimal, move the decimal point two places to the left. For example, 1% is the same as 1/100 or 0.01; 10% is the same as 10/100 or 0.10; and 100% is the same as 100/100 or 1.0.

Math Skills Handbook

> **Example**
> A high school cafeteria estimates that 30% of the students prefer sesame seeds on hamburger buns. To convert this percentage to a decimal, move the decimal point two places to the left.
>
> $$30\% = 0.30$$

Representing Fractions as Percentages

To change a fraction to a percentage, first convert the fraction to a decimal by dividing the numerator by the denominator. Then convert the decimal to a percentage by moving the decimal point two places to the right.

> **Example**
> A high school cafeteria conducts a survey and finds that three of every ten students prefer sesame seeds on hamburger buns. To change this fraction to a percentage, divide 3 by 10, and move the decimal two places to the right.
>
> $$3 \div 10 = 0.30 = 30\%$$

Calculating a Percentage

To calculate the percentage of a number, change the percentage to a decimal and multiply by the number.

> **Example**
> A car dealer sold ten cars last week, of which 70% were sold to women. How many cars did women buy? Change 70% to a decimal by dividing 70 by 100, which equals 0.70. Then multiply by the total number (10).
>
> $$0.70 \times 10 = 7$$

To determine what percentage one number is of another, divide the first number by the second. Then convert the quotient into a percentage by moving the decimal point two places to the right.

> **Example**
> A car dealer sold 10 cars last week, of which seven were sold to women. What percentage of the cars were purchased by women? Divide 7 by 10 and then convert to a percentage.
>
> $$7 \div 10 = 0.70$$
>
> $$0.70 = 70\%$$

Ratio

A ratio compares two numbers through division. Ratios are often expressed as a fraction, but can also be written with a colon (:) or the word *to*.

> **Example**
> A drugstore's cost for a bottle of vitamins is $2.00, which it sells for $3.00. The ratio of the selling price to the cost can be expressed as follows.
>
> $$\frac{\$3.00}{\$2.00} = \frac{3}{2}$$
>
> $$\$3.00 : \$2.00 = 3:2$$
>
> $$\$3.00 \text{ to } \$2.00 = 3 \text{ to } 2$$

Measurement

The official system of measurement in the United States for length, volume, and weight is the US Customary system of measurement. The metric system of measurement is used by most other countries.

US Customary Measurement

The following are the most commonly used units of length in the US Customary system of measurement.

- 1 inch
- 1 foot = 12 inches
- 1 yard = 3 feet
- 1 mile = 5,280 feet

> **Example**
> An interior designer measures the length and width of a room when ordering new floor tiles. The length is measured at 12 feet 4 inches (12′ 4″). The width is measured at 8 feet 7 inches (8′ 7″).

> **Example**
> Taxi cab fares are usually determined by measuring distance in miles. A recent cab rate in Chicago was $3.25 for the first 1/9 mile or less, and $0.20 for each additional 1/9 mile.

Metric Conversion

The metric system of measurement is convenient to use because units can be converted by multiplying or dividing by multiples of 10. The following are the commonly used units of length in the metric system of measurement.
- 1 millimeter
- 1 centimeter = 10 millimeters
- 1 meter = 100 centimeters
- 1 kilometer = 1,000 meters

The following are conversions from the US Customary system to the metric system.
- 1 inch = 25.4 millimeters = 2.54 centimeters
- 1 foot = 30.48 centimeters = 0.3048 meters
- 1 yard = 0.9144 meters
- 1 mile = 1.6093 kilometers

Example
A salesperson from the United States is traveling abroad and needs to drive 100 kilometers to meet a customer. How many miles is this trip? Divide 100 kilometers by 1.6093 and round to the hundredth place.

```
              62.138
     1.6093 ) 100.0000000
              −96558
               34420
              −32186
               22340
              −16093
               62470
              −48279
              141910
             −128744
               13169
```

Estimating

Estimating is finding an *approximate* answer and often involves using rounded numbers. It is often quicker to add rounded numbers, for example, than it is to add the precise numbers.

Example
Estimate the total miles a delivery truck will travel along the following three segments of a route.
- Detroit to Chicago: 278 miles
- Chicago to St. Louis: 297 miles
- St. Louis to Wichita: 436 miles

The mileage can be estimated by rounding each segment to the nearest 100 miles.
- Detroit to Chicago: 300 miles
- Chicago to St. Louis: 300 miles
- St. Louis to Wichita: 400 miles

Add the rounded segments to estimate the total miles.

$$300 + 300 + 400 = 1,000 \text{ miles}$$

Accuracy and Precision

Accuracy and precision mean slightly different things. *Accuracy* is the closeness of a measured value to its actual or true value. *Precision* is how close measured values are to each other.

Example
A machine is designed to fill jars with 16 ounces of peanut butter. The machine is considered accurate if the actual amount of peanut butter in a jar is within 0.05 ounces of the target, which is a range of 15.95 to 16.05 ounces. A machine operator tests a jar and measures the weight to be 16.01 ounces. The machine is accurate.

Suppose a machine operator tests 10 jars of peanut butter and finds the weight of each jar to be 15.4 ounces. The machine is considered precise because it fills every jar with exactly the same amount. However, it is not accurate because the amount differs too much from the target.

Algebra

An *equation* is a mathematical statement that has an equal sign (=). An *algebraic* equation is an equation that includes at least one variable. A *variable* is an unknown quantity.

Solving Equations with Variables

Solving an algebraic equation means finding the value of the variable that will make the equation a true statement. To solve a simple equation, perform inverse operations on both sides and isolate the variable.

Math Skills Handbook

> **Example**
> A computer consultant has sales of $1,000. After deducting $600 in expenses, her profit equals $400. This is expressed with the following equation.
>
> sales − expenses = profit
>
> $1,000 − $600 = $400

> **Example**
> A computer consultant has expenses of $600 and $400 in profit. What are her sales? An equation can be written in which sales are the unknown quantity, or variable.
>
> sales − expenses = profit
>
> sales − $600 = $400

> **Example**
> To find the value for sales, perform inverse operations on both sides and isolate the variable.
>
> sales − $600 = $400
>   + $600 + $600
> sales   = $1,000

Order of Operations

The order of operations is a set of rules stating which operations in an equation are performed first. The order of operations is often stated using the acronym *PEMDAS*. PEMDAS stands for parentheses, exponents, multiplication and division, and addition and subtraction. This means anything inside parentheses is computed first. Exponents are computed next. Then, any multiplication and division operations are computed. Finally, any addition and subtraction operations are computed to find the final answer to the problem. The equation is solved from left to right by applying PEMDAS.

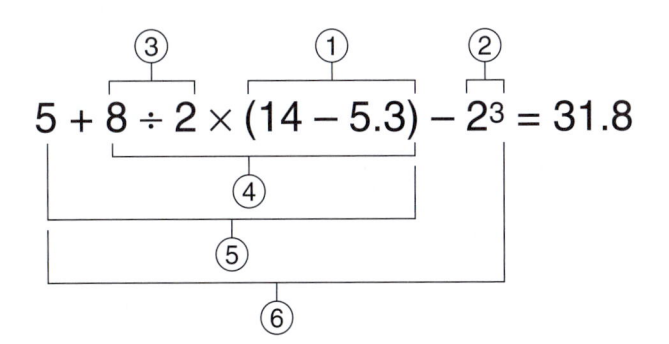

$$5 + 8 \div 2 \times (14 - 5.3) - 2^3 = 31.8$$

Recursive Formulas

A *recursive formula* is used to determine the next term of a sequence, using one or more of the preceding terms. The terms of a sequence are often expressed with a variable and subscript. For example, a sequence might be written as a_1, a_2, a_3, a_4, a_5, and so on. The subscript is essentially the place in line for each term. A recursive formula has two parts. The first is a starting point or seed value (a_1). The second is an equation for another number in the sequence (a_n). The second part of the formula is a function of the prior term (a_{n-1}).

> **Example**
> Suppose you buy a car for $10,000. Assume the car declines in value 10% each year. In the second year, the car will be worth 90% of $10,000, which is $9,000. The following year it will be worth 90% of $9,000, which is $8,100. What will the car be worth in the fifth year? Use the following recursive equation to find the answer.
>
> $$a_n = a_{n-1} \times 0.90$$
>
> where $a_1 = \$10,000$
>
> a_n = value of car in the nth year

Year	Value of Car
n = 1	$a_1 = \$10,000$
n = 2	$a_2 = a_{2-1} \times 0.90 = a_1 \times 0.90 = \$10,000 \times 0.90 = \$9,000$
n = 3	$a_3 = a_{3-1} \times 0.90 = a_2 \times 0.90 = \$9,000 \times 0.90 = \$8,100$
n = 4	$a_4 = a_{4-1} \times 0.90 = a_3 \times 0.90 = \$8,100 \times 0.90 = \$7,290$
n = 5	$a_5 = a_{5-1} \times 0.90 = a_4 \times 0.90 = \$7,290 \times 0.90 = \$6,561$

Geometry

Geometry is a field of mathematics that deals with shapes, such as circles and polygons. A *polygon* is any shape whose sides are straight. Every polygon has three or more sides.

Parallelograms

A *parallelogram* is a four-sided figure with two pairs of parallel sides. A *rectangle* is a type of parallelogram with four right angles. A *square* is a special type of parallelogram with four right angles (90 degrees) and four equal sides.

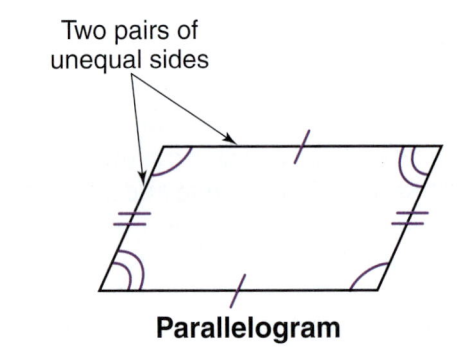

Triangles

A three-sided polygon is called a *triangle*. The following are four types of triangles, which are classified according to their sides and angles.
- *Equilateral:* Three equal sides and three equal angles.
- *Isosceles:* Two equal sides and two equal angles.
- *Scalene:* Three unequal sides and three unequal angles.
- *Right:* One right angle; may be isosceles or scalene.

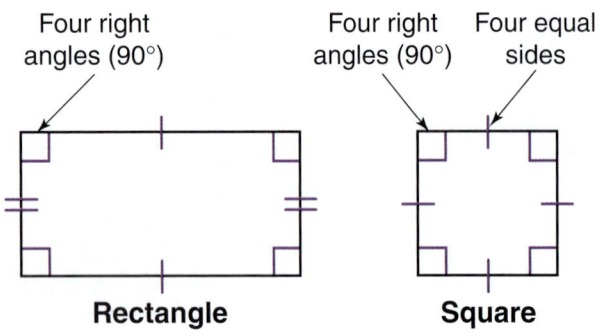

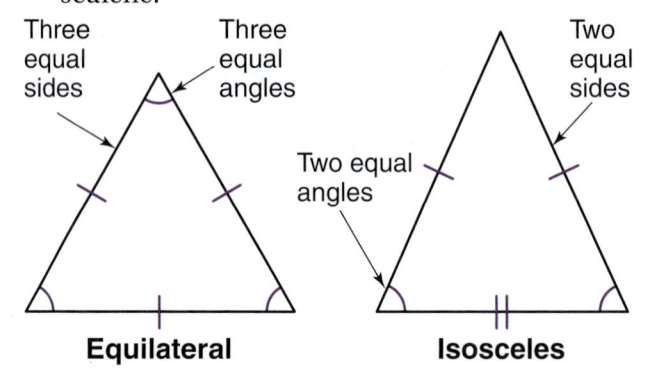

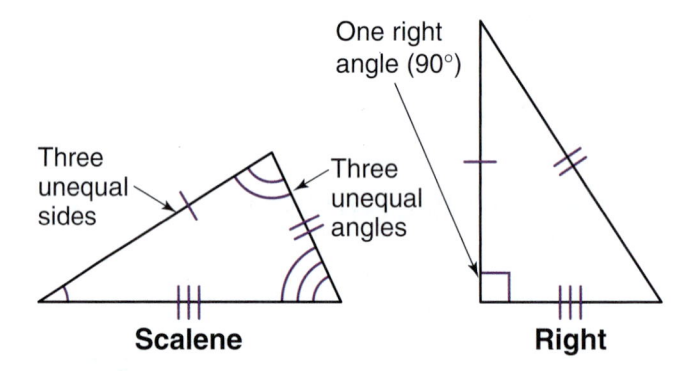

Example
Real-life examples of squares include ceramic floor and wall tiles, and each side of a die. Real-life examples of a rectangle include a football field, pool table, and most doors.

Circles and Half Circles

A *circle* is a figure in which every point is the same distance from the center. The distance from the center to a point on the circle is called the *radius*. The distance across the circle through the center is the *diameter*. A half circle is formed by dividing a whole circle along the diameter.

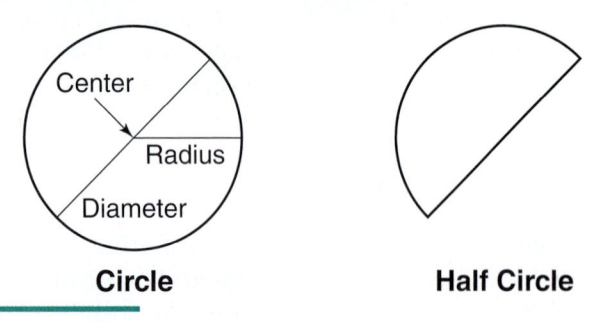

Example
Real life examples of circles include wheels of all sizes.

Example
Real-life examples of equilateral triangles are the sides of a classical Egyptian pyramid.

Perimeter

A *perimeter* is a measure of length around a figure. Add the length of each side to measure the perimeter of any figure whose sides are all line segments, such as a parallelogram or triangle. The perimeter of a circle is called the *circumference*. To measure the perimeter, multiply the diameter

Math Skills Handbook

by pi (π). Pi is approximately equal to 3.14. The following formulas can be used to calculate the perimeters of various figures.

Figure	Perimeter
parallelogram	2 × width + 2 × length
square	4 × side
rectangle	2 × width + 2 × length
triangle	side + side + side
circle	π × diameter

Example
A professional basketball court is a rectangle 94 feet long and 50 feet wide. The perimeter of the court is calculated as follows.

2 × 94 feet + 2 × 50 feet = 288 feet

Example
A tractor tire has a 43 inch diameter. The circumference of the tire is calculated as follows.

43 inches × 3.14 = 135 inches

Area

Area is a measure of the amount of surface within the perimeter of a flat figure. Area is measured in square units, such as square inches, square feet, or square miles. The areas of the following figures are calculated using the corresponding formulas.

Figure	Area
parallelogram	base × height
square	side × side
rectangle	length × width
triangle	1/2 × base × height
circle	π × radius^2 = π × radius × radius

Example
An interior designer needs to order decorative tiles to fill the following spaces. Measure the area of each space in square feet.

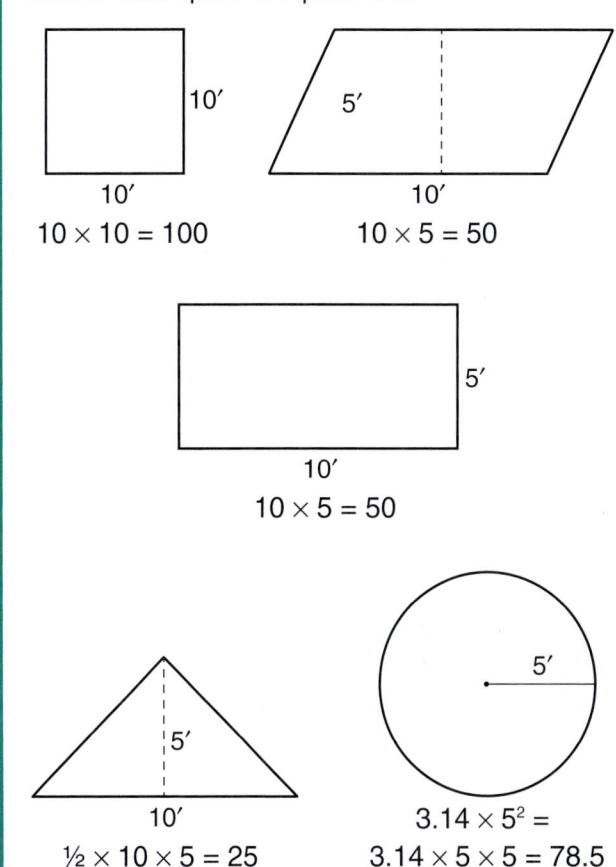

10 × 10 = 100

10 × 5 = 50

10 × 5 = 50

½ × 10 × 5 = 25

3.14 × 5^2 =
3.14 × 5 × 5 = 78.5

Surface Area

Surface area is the total area of the surface of a figure occupying three-dimensional space, such as a cube or prism. A *cube* is a solid figure that has six identical square faces. A *prism* has bases or ends which have the same size and shape and are parallel to each other, and each of whose sides is a parallelogram. The following are the formulas to find the surface area of a cube and a prism.

Object	Surface Area
cube	6 × side × side
prism	2 × [(length × width) + (width × height) + (length × height)]

Example
A manufacturer of cardboard boxes wants to determine how much cardboard is needed to make the following size boxes. Calculate the surface area of each in square inches.

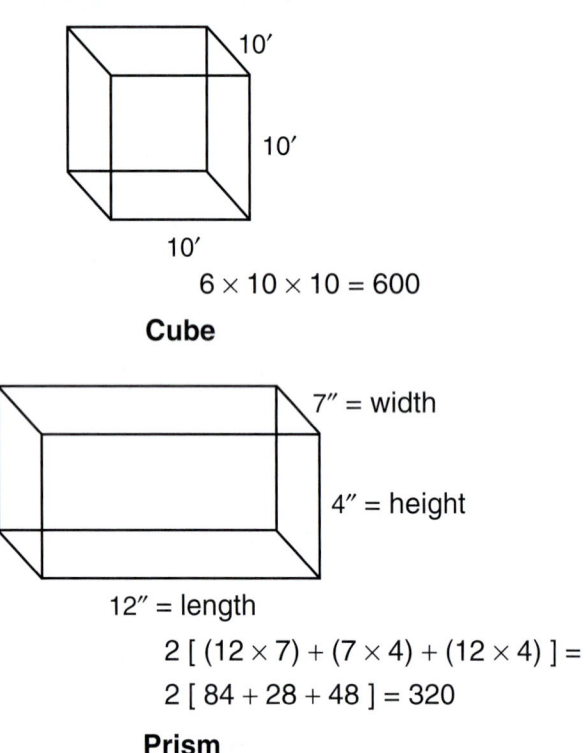

$6 \times 10 \times 10 = 600$

Cube

$2 [(12 \times 7) + (7 \times 4) + (12 \times 4)] =$
$2 [84 + 28 + 48] = 320$

Prism

Volume

Volume is the three-dimensional space occupied by a figure and is measured in cubic units, such as cubic inches or cubic feet. The volumes of the following figures are calculated using the corresponding formulas.

Solid Figure	Volume
cube	side^3 = side × side × side
prism	length × width × height
cylinder	π × radius^2 × height = π × radius × radius × height
sphere	4/3 × π × radius^3 = 4/3 × π × radius × radius × radius

Example
Find the volume of packing material needed to fill the following boxes. Measure the volume of each in cubic inches.

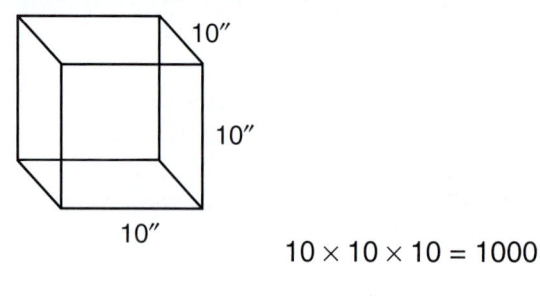

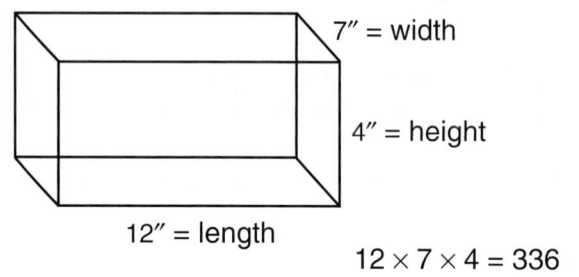

$10 \times 10 \times 10 = 1000$

$12 \times 7 \times 4 = 336$

Example
Find the volume of grain that will fill the following cylindrical silo. Measure the volume in cubic feet.

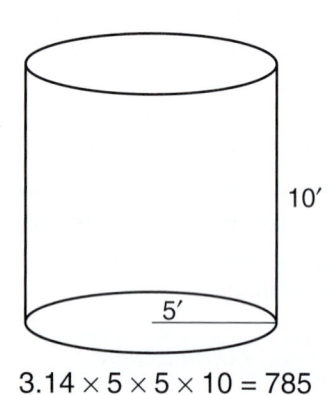

$3.14 \times 5 \times 5 \times 10 = 785$

Example
A manufacturer of pool toys wants to stuff soft material into a ball with a 3 inch radius. Find the cubic inches of material that will fit into the ball.

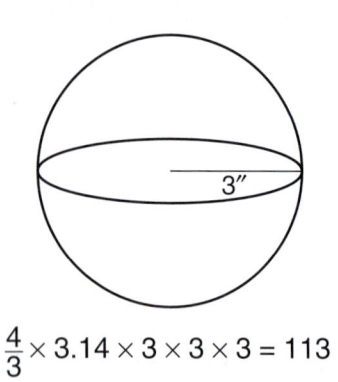

$\frac{4}{3} \times 3.14 \times 3 \times 3 \times 3 = 113$

Math Skills Handbook

Data Analysis and Statistics

Graphs are used to illustrate data in a picture-like format. It is often easier to understand data when they are shown in a graphical form instead of a numerical form in a table. Common types of graphs are bar graphs, line graphs, and circle graphs.

A *bar graph* organizes information along a vertical axis and horizontal axis. The vertical axis runs up and down one side; the horizontal axis runs along the bottom.

A *line graph* also organizes information on vertical and horizontal axes; however, data are graphed as a continuous line rather than a set of bars. Line graphs are often used to show trends over a period of time.

A *circle graph* looks like a divided circle and shows how a whole object is cut up into parts. Circle graphs are also called *pie charts* and are often used to illustrate percentages.

Example
A business shows the following balances in its cash account for the months of March through July. These data are illustrated below in bar and line graphs.

Month	Account Balance	Month	Account Balance
March	$400	June	$800
April	$600	July	$900
May	$500		

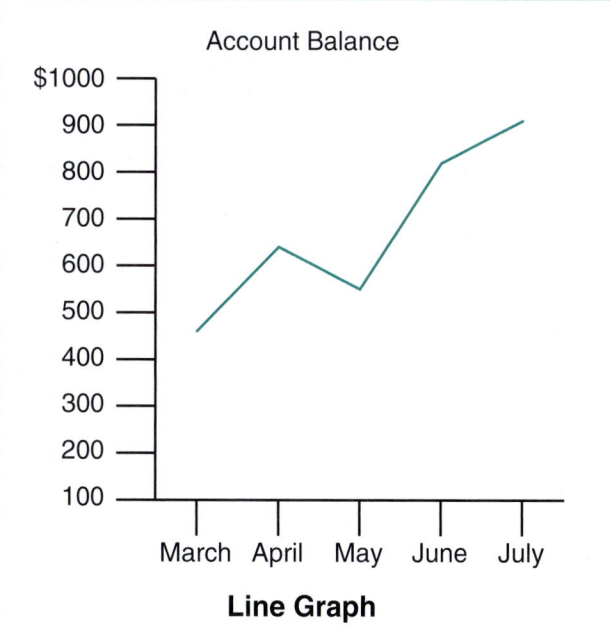

Line Graph

Example
A business lists the percentage of its expenses in the following categories. These data are displayed in the following circle graph.

Expenses	Percentage
Cost of goods	25
Salaries	25
Rent	21
Utilities	17
Advertising	12

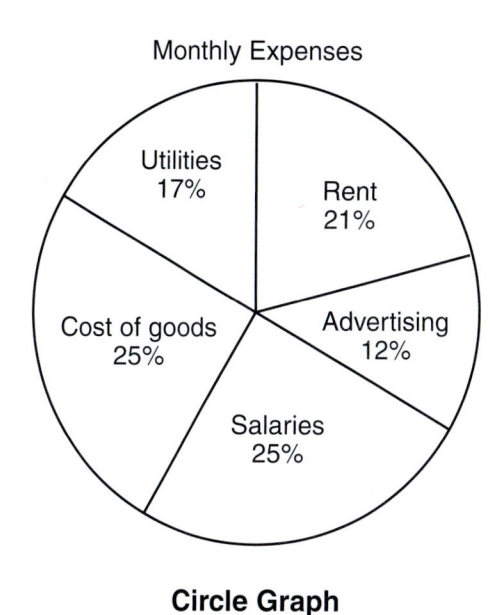

Monthly Expenses

Circle Graph

Math Models for Business and Retail

Math skills used in business and retail are the same math skills required in everyday life. The ability to add, subtract, multiply, and divide different types of numbers is very important. However, this type of math is often focused on prices, taxes, profits, and losses.

Markup

Markup is a retailing term for the amount by which price exceeds the cost. One way to express markup is in dollars. Another way to express markup is percentage. The *markup percentage* is the amount of the markup as a percentage of the cost.

Example
A retailer pays $4 for a pair of athletic socks and prices them for sale at $7. The dollar markup is $3.

selling price − cost = dollar markup

$7 − $4 = $3

Example
A pair of athletic socks, which cost $4, is priced at $7. The dollar markup is $3. To find the markup percentage, divide $3 by $4. The markup percentage is 75%.

markup dollars ÷ cost = markup percentage

$3 ÷ $4 = 0.75 = 75%

Percentage Markup to Determine Selling Price

The selling price of an item can be determined if you know the markup percentage and the cost. First, convert the markup percentage to a decimal. Next multiply the cost by the decimal. Then, add the markup dollars to the cost to determine the selling price. Another way to find the selling price is to convert the markup percentage to a decimal and add 1.0. Then multiply this amount by the cost.

Example
A pair of athletic socks costs $4, which the retailer marks up by 75%. Find the selling price.

1. Convert the markup percentage to a decimal.

   75% = 0.75

2. Multiply the cost by the markup.

   cost × markup = dollar markup

   $4 × 0.75 = $3

3. Add the $3 markup to the $4 cost to find the selling price. The selling price is $7.

   $4 + $3 = $7

Example
A pair of athletic socks costs $4, which the retailer marks up by 75%. Find the selling price.

1. Convert the 75% markup percentage to 0.75 and add 1.0.

   0.75 + 1.0 = 1.75

2. Multiply 1.75 by the $4 cost to find the selling price.

   $4 × 1.75 = $7

Markdown

A *markdown* is the amount by which the selling price of an item is reduced. Sometimes a markdown is also called a *discount*. To find the amount of a markdown, subtract the new or discounted price from the original price. A markdown can also be expressed as a percentage of the original price. Sometimes this is called a *percentage discount*.

Example
A package of meat at a supermarket is originally priced at $10. However, the meat has not sold and is nearing its expiration date. The supermarket wants to sell it quickly, so it reduces the price to $6. This is a markdown of $4.

selling price − discounted price = dollar markdown

$10 − $6 = $4

Example
A package of meat at a supermarket is originally priced at $10. However, the meat has not sold and is nearing its expiration date. The supermarket wants to sell it quickly, so it marks down the price by $4. The markdown percentage is determined by dividing the $4 markdown by the original $10 price.

markdown ÷ selling price = markdown percentage

$4 ÷ $10 = 40%

Math Skills Handbook

Gross Profit

Gross profit is a company's net sales minus the cost of goods sold. Gross margin is often expressed as a percentage of revenue.

Example
A wristband manufacturer generated net sales of $100,000 last year. The cost of goods sold for the wristbands was $30,000. The net sales of $100,000 minus the $30,000 cost of goods sold leaves a gross profit of $70,000.

net sales − cost of goods sold = gross profit

$100,000 − $30,000 = $70,000

Example
The gross profit of $70,000 divided by the net sales of $100,000 is 0.70, or 70%.

gross profit ÷ net sales = gross margin percentage

$70,000 ÷ $100,000 = 0.70 = 70%

Net Income or Loss

Net income or loss is a company's revenue after total expenses are deducted from gross profit. Total expenses include marketing, administration, interest, and taxes. A company earns a *net income* when gross profit exceeds expenses. A *net loss* is incurred when expenses exceed gross profit.

Example
A wristband manufacturer had a gross profit of $70,000. In addition, expenses for marketing, administration, interest, and taxes were $50,000. Net profit is calculated by subtracting the total expenses of $50,000 from the gross profit of $70,000. The net profit was $20,000.

gross profit on sales − total expenses = net income or loss

$70,000 − $50,000 = $20,000

Break-Even Point

A *break-even point* is the number of units a company must sell to cover its costs and expenses and earn a zero profit. Use the following formula to find a company's break-even point.

total costs ÷ selling price = break-even point

Sales Tax

Sales tax is a tax collected on the selling price of a good or service. The sales tax rate is usually expressed as a percentage of the selling price. Sales tax is calculated by multiplying the sale price by the tax rate.

Example
Suppose you buy a T-shirt for $10.00. How much is the sales tax if the tax rate is 5%? Convert 5% to a decimal (.05) and multiply it by the sale price.

sale price × sales tax rate percentage = sales tax

$10 × 0.05 = $0.50

Return on Investment

Return on investment (ROI) is a calculation of a company's net profit as a percentage of the owner's investment. One way to determine ROI is to divide net profit by the owner's investment.

Example
Suppose you start a dry-cleaning business with a $100,000 investment, and you earn a $20,000 net profit during the first year. Divide $20,000 by $100,000, which equals a 20% return on your investment.

net income ÷ owner's investment = return on investment (ROI)

$20,000 ÷ $100,000 = 0.20 = 20%

Glossary

529 plan Savings plan for education operated by a state or educational institution. (27)

80/20 inventory rule 80 percent of the sales for a business comes from 20 percent of its inventory. (16)

A

ability Mastery of a skill or the capacity to do something. (27)

absolute advantage Exists when a country can produce goods more efficiently and at a lower cost than another country. (7)

acceptable use policy Set of rules that explains what is and is not acceptable use of company-owned and company-operated equipment and networks. (29)

accounts payable Money a business owes to its suppliers for goods or services received. (26)

accounts receivable Amounts owed to a company by its customers. (10)

accounts receivable aging report Shows when accounts receivables are due, as well as the length of time accounts have been outstanding. (10)

action plan List of the marketing tactics with details about how to execute each tactic. (2)

action words Verbs that tell the readers what to do. (18)

active listening Fully participating as you process what a person says. (23)

active reading Processing the words, phrases, and sentences you read. (23)

adaptability Ability to make changes to be a better match, or fit, in new situations. (22)

adaptation Changing the marketing strategies to meet the preferences and demands of customers in a specific market. (7)

advertising Any nonpersonal communication paid for by an identified sponsor. (17)

advertising agency Firm that creates advertisements, commercials, and other parts of promotional campaigns for its clients. (18)

advertising campaign Coordinated series of related advertisements with a single idea or theme. (18)

agent/broker channel Path of selling in which the producer hires an agent to sell to the wholesaler. (15)

agent/broker industrial distributor channel Combines both of the agent/broker and industrial distributor channels and is the longest distribution channel. (15)

AIDA Acronym for each element of the promotional mix focused on attracting customer attention, interest, desire, and action. (17)

analogous color Adjacent to one another on the color wheel. (19)

angel investor Private investors who are interested in funding promising start-up businesses; also called an *angel*. (26)

antitrust law Law that promotes fair trade, open markets, and competition among businesses. (3)

appendix Section of a document that contains additional information that would be helpful to the reader, but is not necessary to know. (24)

apprenticeship Combination of on-the-job training, work experience, and classroom instruction. (27)

approach First in-person contact a salesperson makes with a potential customer. (20)

aptitude Characteristic that an individual has developed naturally. (27)

art All the elements that illustrate the message of an advertisement. (18)

asset Property or items of value owned by a business. (21)

attitude How a person feels about something. (9)

Note: The number in parentheses following each definition indicates the chapter in which the term can be found.

autocratic management style Leader makes all decisions without input from others; also called *top-down management*. (21)

B

background check Investigation into personal data about a job applicant. (28)

bait and switch Advertising one product with the intent of persuading customers to buy a more expensive item when they arrive in the store. (14)

balance Way items are placed around an imaginary centerline. (19)

balance of payments Total amount of money that comes in to a country, minus the total amount of money that goes out for a specific period of time. (7)

balance of trade Difference between a nation's exports and its imports. (7)

balance sheet Financial report that reports the assets, liabilities, and owner's equity. (21)

bankruptcy Legal process that allows a company to reorganize or go out of business when it runs out of funding. (3)

barrier Anything that prevents clear, effective communication. (23)

base price General price at which the company expects to sell the product. (13)

behavioral question Questions that draw on an individual's previous experiences and decisions. (28)

behavioral segmentation Divides a market by the relationships between customers and a good or service. (9)

benefit Trait of a product that serves as an advantage for the customer. (9)

bibliography Lists all of the resources used to develop the business plan. (24)

bid Formal written proposal that lists all the goods and services that will be provided, their corresponding prices, and the timeline for delivery. (16)

blog Web page in a journal format created by a person or organization. (17)

body language Nonverbal communication through facial expressions, gestures, body movements, and posture. (23)

bootstrapping Cutting all unnecessary expenses and operating on as little cash as possible. (26)

brand Name, term, or design that sets a product or business apart from its competition. (11)

brand equity Value of having a well-known brand name. (12)

brand extension Practice of using an established brand name on different products in a product mix. (12)

brand identity Way in which a business wants to be perceived by customers. (12)

branding strategy Plan to develop a brand in a way that supports the goals of the business. (12)

brand licensing Practice of leasing a brand name for use by another business under the specifications of an agreement. (12)

brand loyalty Customer dedication to a certain brand of product. (12)

brand mark See *logo*.

brand name Name given to a product consisting of words, numbers, or letters that can be read and spoken. (12)

brand promise Statement made by an organization to its customers that tells customers what they can expect from its products. (12)

break-even point Point at which revenue from sales equals the costs. (13)

budget Financial plan for a fixed period of time that reflects anticipated revenue and shows how it will be allocated in the operation of the business. (2)

buffer stock Additional stock kept above the minimum amount required to meet forecasted sales; also called *safety stock*. (16)

bulk-breaking Process of separating a large quantity of goods into smaller quantities for resale. (15)

bundling Combines two or more services or goods for one price. (14)

burglary Occurs when a person breaks into a business to steal merchandise, money, valuable equipment, or confidential information. (25)

business Activities involved in developing and exchanging goods and services. (3)

business cycle Alternating periods of expansion and contraction in the economy. (6)

business ethics Rules for professional conduct and integrity in all areas of business. (4)

business operations Day-to-day activities necessary to keep a business up and running. (24)

business plan Document that describes a business, how it operates, and how it makes a profit. (2)

business purchasing Acquiring goods or services to accomplish the goals of an organization. (16)

business-to-business (B2B) market Consists of customers who buy products for use in a business rather than for personal use. (1)

business-to-business (B2B) selling Business selling to another business. (17)

business-to-consumer (B2C) market Consists of customers who buy products for their own use. (1)

business-to-consumer (B2C) selling Business selling to consumers. (17)

buyer Person who purchases goods for the sole purpose of reselling them to customers; also called *professional buyer, retail buyer, merchandise manager* or *organizational buyer*. (16)

buying motive Reason a consumer seeks and buys a good or service. (10)

buying signal Verbal or nonverbal signs that a customer is ready to purchase. (20)

buying status Describes when a customer will buy a good or service. (9)

buy one, get one (BOGO) pricing Gives customers a free or reduced-price item when another is purchased at full price. (14)

buzz marketing See *viral marketing*.

C

call center Office that is set up for the purpose of receiving and making customer calls for an organization. (20)

capital Tools and machinery used to produce goods or provide services. (5)

capital goods Products businesses use to produce other goods. (5)

captive pricing Sets prices low for the base product but charges high prices for other components that are needed to complete the product or service. (14)

career Series of related jobs in the same profession. (27)

career clusters Sixteen groups of occupational and career specialties that share common knowledge and skills. (27)

career ladder Series of jobs organized in order of education and experience requirements. (27)

career objective Summary of the type of job for which the applicant is looking. (28)

career pathway Subgroup within a career cluster that reflects occupations requiring similar knowledge and skills. (27)

career plan List of steps on a timeline an individual can follow to reach career goals; also called *postsecondary plan*. (27)

carrying costs Costs directly related to carrying, or holding, inventory and are part of inventory management. (16)

category manager Marketing professional who performs the same functions as a product manager for an entire category of products. (11)

cause marketing Cause marketing is a type of marketing in which a for-profit business and a nonprofit organization or charity work together for mutual benefit. (4)

certification Professional status earned by an individual after passing an exam focused on a specific body of knowledge. (20)

channel In distribution, route a product takes from a producer to a customer. (1) In communication, how the message is transmitted, such as face-to-face conversation, telephone, text, or another method that is appropriate for the situation. (23)

channel conflict Producer selling products directly to end users in addition to maintaining other channels of distribution. (15)

channel management Handling the activities involved in getting products through the different routes from producers to customers; also called *supply chain management*. (1)

channel of distribution Path goods take through the supply chain. (15)

chart Shows a process or hierarchy. (8)

chronological résumé Lists information in reverse chronological order, with the most recent information listed first. (28)

circulation Number of copies distributed to subscribers in a defined time period. (18)

Glossary

close Moment when a customer agrees to buy a product. (20)

cloud computing Using Internet-based resources to store and access data rather than on a personal computer or local server. (29)

co-branding Combines the products of one or more manufacturers in the creation of a product. (12)

code of conduct Document that identifies the manner in which employees should behave while at work or when representing the company. (4)

code of ethics Document that dictates how business should be conducted; also referred to as a *statement of ethics*. (4)

cold calling Process of making contact with people who are not expecting a sales contact. (20)

collaboration Working with others to achieve a common goal. (22)

collateral Asset pledged that will be claimed by the lender if the loan is not repaid. (26)

collection agency Company that collects past-due bills for a fee. (10)

college access Building awareness about college opportunities, providing guidance regarding college admissions, and identifying ways to pay for college. (27)

collusion When two or more businesses work together to remove their competition, set prices, and control distribution. (6)

color scheme Description of color combinations. (19)

color wheel Standard arrangement of 12 colors in a wheel that shows the relationships among the colors. (19)

command economy Economy in which the government makes all economic decisions for its citizens. (5)

common carrier Independent trucking company; also called *contract carrier*. (15)

communication process Series of actions on the part of the sender and the receiver of the message and the path the message follows. (23)

comparative advantage Exists when a country specializes in products that it can produce efficiently. (7)

competition Two or more businesses attempting to attract the same customers. (2)

competition-based pricing Pricing strategy based primarily on what competitors charge. (13)

competitive advantage Offering better value, features, or service than the competition. (9)

competitive analysis Tool used to compare the strengths and weaknesses of a product or company that competes with a business. (2)

complementary color Color found opposite to another on a color wheel. (19)

conclusion Summarizes why your business will be successful and ends with a specific request for financing. (24)

conflict of interest Employee has competing interests or loyalties. (22)

conflict resolution Process of recognizing and resolving disputes. (22)

constructive criticism Giving well-reasoned opinions about the ideas or work of others. (22)

consulting management style Combination of the democratic and autocratic styles. (21)

consumer Customer who buys a product for his or her own use. (1)

consumer behavior Behavior and actions taken by people to satisfy their needs and wants, including what they buy. (10)

consumer credit Credit granted to an individual consumer by a retail business. (10)

consumer decision-making process Series of steps people take when making buying decisions. (10)

consumer price index (CPI) Measure of the average change in the prices paid by consumers for typical consumer goods and services over time. (6)

contract carrier See *common carrier*.

contract manufacturing Transferring production work to another company; also known as *outsourcing*. (7)

control Monitor the progress of the team to meet its goals. (21)

controllable risk One that cannot be avoided, but can be minimized by purchasing insurance or implementing a risk management plan. (25)

cookies Bits of data stored on your computer that record information about the websites you have visited. (29)

cooperative education program Students prepare for an occupation through a paid job while taking classes that are related in subject matter to the job; also called *co-op*. (27)

copy Advertisement text that provides information and sells the product. (18)

corporate formalities Records and procedures that corporations are required by law to complete. (24)

corporate social responsibility (CSR) Actions a business takes to further social good. (4)

corporation Business that is legally separate from its owners and has most of the legal rights of an actual person. (3)

cosigner Person who signs a loan with the applicant and takes on equal responsibility for repaying it. (26)

cost-based pricing Strategy that uses the cost of a product to set the selling price. (13)

cost control Monitoring costs to stay within a planned budget. (21)

cost per thousand (CPM) Cost of an advertisement per one thousand impressions. (18)

cover letter See *cover message*.

cover message Letter or e-mail sent with a résumé to introduce the applicant and summarize his or her reasons for applying for a job; also called *cover letter* or *letter of application*. (28)

creative plan Outlines the goals, primary message, budget, and target market for the advertising campaign. (18)

credit Agreement or contract to receive goods or services before actually paying for them. (10)

credit bureau Private firm that maintains consumer-credit data and provides credit information to businesses for a fee. (10)

credit report Record of a business' or person's credit history and financial behavior. (10)

credit risk Potential for financial loss due to credit not being repaid. (10)

creditor Individual or business to whom money is owed for goods or services provided. (10)

critical thinking Process of interpreting and making reasonable judgments and decisions by analyzing a situation. (22)

culture Beliefs, customs, practices, and social behavior of a particular group or nation. (7)

customer loyalty Continued and regular patronage of a business even when there are other places to purchase the same or similar products. (10)

customer profile Detailed description of the typical consumer in a market segment. (9)

customer-relationship management (CRM) System to track contact information and other information for current and potential customers. (4)

customer service Way in which a business provides services before, during, and after a purchase. (20)

customer-service mindset Attitude that customer satisfaction always comes first. (20)

customer support team Employees who assist customers, take orders, or answer questions coming into the company via phone or website. (20)

cyberbullying Using the Internet to harass or threaten an individual. (29)

D

data Pieces of information gained through research. (8)

database Organized collection of data in digital form. (8)

database marketing Consists of gathering, storing, and using customer data for marketing directly to customers based on their histories. (8)

data mining Searching through large amounts of digital data to find useful patterns or trends. (8)

DBA license Needed to register a business under a name other than the name of the business owner; also called *fictitious name registration*. (24)

debt financing Borrowing money for business purposes. (26)

debtor Individual or business who owes money for goods or services received. (10)

deceptive pricing Setting the prices of products in a way to intentionally mislead a customer. (14)

decline stage Stage in which product sales begin to decrease. (11)

decoding Translation of a message into terms that the receiver can understand. (23)

deflation General decline in prices throughout an economy. (6)

demand-based pricing Pricing strategy based on the amount that customers are willing to pay. (13)

democratic management style Leader encourages team members to participate and share ideas equally; also called *participatory style*. (21)

demographics Qualities of a specific group of people including age, gender, income, ethnicity, education level, occupation, marital status, and family size. (7)

demographic segmentation Dividing the market of potential customers by their personal statistics. (9)

depression Period of economic contraction that is severe and lasts a long time. (6)

design Purposeful arrangement of materials to produce a certain effect. (19)

destructive criticism Judgment given with the intention of harming or offending someone. (22)

digital citizenship Standards of appropriate behavior when using technology to communicate. (29)

digital communication Exchange of information through electronic means. (29)

digital etiquette See *netiquette*.

digital footprint Data history of all an individual's online activities. (28)

digital literacy Ability to use technology to locate, evaluate, communicate, and create information. (29)

direct channel Path of selling goods or services directly from a producer or manufacturer to end users without using intermediaries. (15)

direct competitor Company that sells identical or very similar goods or services. (9)

direct marketing Type of advertising sent directly to individual customers without the use of a third party; also called *direct response marketing*. (17)

discretionary income Remaining take-home pay after life necessities are paid for. (9)

display Visual presentation of merchandise or ideas. (19)

disposable income Take-home pay a person has available to spend. (9)

distribution See *place*.

diversity Having representatives from different backgrounds, cultures, or demographics in a group. (7)

E

economic input Resources used to make products. (5)

economic output Goods and services produced by an economic system during a specific time. (5)

economic risk Situation that occurs when the economy suffers due to negative business conditions in the United States or the world. (25)

economics Science that examines how goods and services are produced, sold, and used. (5)

economic system Organized way in which a nation chooses to use its limited resources to create goods and services that answer the three economic questions. (5)

economy of scale Decrease in unit cost of a product resulting from large scale manufacturing operations. (16)

education General process of acquiring knowledge and skills. (27)

elastic demand Product demand in which the percent of change in demand is greater than the percent of change in price. (13)

electronic data interchange (EDI) Standard transfer of electronic data for business transactions between organizations. (16)

embargo Governmental order that prohibits trade with a foreign country. (7)

embedded marketing Intentionally and subtly placing a branded product in a media without formally calling it to the attention of the viewer; also known as *product placement*. (17)

embezzlement Occurs when an employee steals either money or goods entrusted to him or her. (25)

emergency Unforeseen event that can cause harm to people and property. (25)

emotional intelligence Ability to perceive emotions in one's self and in others and use this information to guide behavior. (23)

empathy Understanding or being sensitive to the thoughts and feelings of others. (20)

emphasis Drawing the attention of the viewer to the most important part of a display. (19)

employment trend Direction of change in the number of jobs within a particular career. (27)

employment verification Process through which the information provided on an applicant's résumé is checked to verify it is correct. (28)

encoding Process of turning the idea for a message into symbols that can be communicated. (23)

endorsement Advertising message that a person, business, or other organization is paid by another party to give. (3)

entrepreneur Person who starts a new business. (24)

entrepreneurial discovery process Process of finding a need for a product. (24)

entrepreneurship Willingness and ability to start a new business. (24)

environmental scan Analysis of the external factors that affect the success of business. (2)

equilibrium Point at which the supply equals the demand for a product. (5)

equity Amount of ownership a person has in a business. (26)

equity financing Raising money for a business in exchange for a percentage of the ownership. (26)

e-tailer Retailer that sells products through its website. (15)

ethics Set of moral values that guide a person's behavior. (4)

etiquette Art of using good manners in any situation. (22)

even pricing Sets the price of a product to end in an even number. (14)

event marketing Promotional activity that encourages customers to participate rather than just observe. (17)

exclusive distribution Occurs when there is only one distributor of products in a market area. (15)

excuse Personal reasons not to buy. (20)

expansion Period in which the economy is growing and the GDP is rising. (6)

export Product that is produced within a country's borders and sold in another country. (7)

export management company Independent company that provides support services, such as warehousing, shipping, insuring, and billing, on behalf of another business; also called *export trading company*. (15)

export trading company See *export management company*.

extensive buying decision Purchase involving a great deal of research and planning. (10)

external influence Motivator or change factor from outside the business. (10)

externality Something that is not directly connected to an economic activity, but that affects people. (6)

external theft Stealing by people who are not employed or otherwise associated with the retailer. (16)

F

factors of production Economic resources a nation uses to make goods and supply services for its population. (5)

false advertising Overstating the features and benefits of products or services or making false claims about them. (3)

feature Facts about a product. (9)

feature-benefit selling Method of showing the major selling features of the product and how it benefits the customer; also called *solution selling*. (20)

Federal Reserve System Central bank of the United States created by Congress in 1913. (6)

Federal Trade Commission (FTC) Federal agency that was created to protect consumers and promote business competition. (3)

feedback Receiver's response to the sender and concludes the communication process. (23)

fictitious name registration See *DBA license*.

field sales See *business-to-business (B2B) selling*.

financial planning Process of setting financial goals and developing methods for reaching them. (21)

firewall Program that monitors information coming into a computer. (29)

fiscal policy Tax spending decisions made by the president and Congress. (6)

fixed asset Item of value that may take time to sell. (26)

fixed expense Set amount that must be paid on a regular basis, such as monthly or annually. (13)

fixture Item designed to hold something. (19)

floating currency One with an exchange rate that is set by the market forces of supply and demand in the foreign exchange market. (7)

focus group Group of people brought together to discuss a specific topic. (8)

foreign exchange rate Cost to convert one currency into another. (7)

formal education Education received in a school, college, or university. (27)

for-profit school One that is set up to earn money for investors. (27)

franchise Right to sell a company's goods or services in a specific area in return for royalty fees. (7)

franchise agreement Legal document that sets up a franchise. (24)

franchisee Person who buys the rights to sell the brand products. (24)

franchise fee Money that the franchisee pays the franchisor for the rights to use the business brand name and sell its products. (24)

franchisor Company or person who owns the business and the brand. (24)

fraud Cheating or deceiving a business out of money or property. (25)

free on board (FOB) Indicates which party, the buyer or shipper, has liability for the shipment if damages are incurred and at what point ownership of the goods changes hands. (16)

freight forwarder Company that organizes transportation. (15)

frequency Number of times an advertisement will be shown to an audience. (18)

frequently asked questions (FAQ) page Part of a website that gives detailed answers to questions or issues that show up the most often. (20)

G

general partnership Business structure in which all partners have unlimited liability. (24)

generation Group of people who were born and lived during the same time period. (9)

generic brand Consumer product that lacks a widely recognized name or logo. (12)

geographic segmentation Segmenting a market based on where customers live. (9)

globalization Connection made among nations worldwide when economies freely move goods, labor, and money across borders. (7)

global marketing Consists of dynamic activities that identify, anticipate, and satisfy customer demand for products in countries worldwide while making a profit for the business. (7)

good Physical item that can be touched. (1)

goodwill Goodwill is the advantage a business has due to its positive reputation. (4)

government market Market that includes national, state, and local governmental offices and agencies. (10)

graduate education Education received after an individual has earned a bachelor degree. (27)

grant Financial award that does not have to be repaid and is typically provided by a nonprofit organization. (27)

graph Depicts information through the use of lines, bars, or other symbols. (8)

green marketing Green marketing is producing and promoting products using methods and practices that emphasize environmental conservation. (4)

greeting approach Friendly welcome to the store or department. (20)

gross domestic product (GDP) Market value of all final products produced in a country during a specific time period. (6)

gross profit Amount of profit before subtracting the costs of doing business. (13)

growth stage Stage in which product sales increase rapidly. (11)

guarantee Promise that a product has a certain quality or will perform in a specific way. (11)

H

hacking Illegally accessing or altering digital devices, software, or networks. (29)

hard skills Critical skills necessary to perform the required work-related tasks of a position; also called *job-specific skills*. (24)

hazard Situation that could result in injury or damage. (25)

headline Statement designed to grab the attention of viewers so they will read the rest of the advertisement. (18)

hierarchy of needs Order in which certain needs are satisfied before others. (10)

hue Pure color itself. (19)

human risk Negative situation caused by human actions. (25)

hypothesis Statement that can be tested and proved to be either true or false. (8)

hypothetical question Require a person to imagine a situation and describe how he or she would act. (28)

I

idea Concept, cause, issue, image, or philosophy. (1)

identity theft Illegal act that involves stealing someone's personal information and using that information to commit theft or fraud. (29)

image Idea that people have about someone or something. (11)

imperfect competition See *monopolistic competition*.

import Product that is brought into a country from outside its borders. (7)

impulse buying decision Purchase made without any planning or research. (10)

income See *revenue*.

income statement Financial report that shows the revenue and expenses for a business during a specific period of time. (21)

indirect channel Uses intermediaries to get the product from the producer or manufacturer to the consumer. (15)

indirect competitor Company that offers different, but similar, goods or services that meet customer needs. (9)

industrial distributor channel Product moves from the producer to an industrial distributor, and then to the end user. (15)

industrial goods Goods used in the production of other goods or consumed by a business. (15)

industrial sales See *business-to-business (B2B) selling*.

inelastic demand Product demand that is not affected by price. (13)

inflation General rise in prices throughout an economy. (6)

inflation rate Calculated as the rate of change in prices over a period of time, usually monthly or yearly, and expressed as a percent. (6)

infrastructure Transportation systems and utilities necessary in a modern economy. (5)

infringement Any use of copyrighted material without permission. (29)

insider trading Employee uses private company information to purchase company stock or other securities for personal gain. (22)

installment loan Loan for a specific amount of money that is repaid in regular payments, or *installments*, with interest until the loan is paid in full; also called *secured loan*. (10)

institution Established public or private organization. (10)

institutional promotion Promoting the company rather than its products. (17)

insurance Financial service used to protect individuals and businesses against financial loss. (25)

insurance premium Cost of an insurance policy, usually made monthly. (25)

integrated marketing communications (IMC) Approach to marketing that integrates all promotional efforts to deliver one message about a product using various media. (17)

intellectual property Something that comes from a person's mind, such as an idea, invention, or process. (12)

intensity Brightness or dullness of a color. (19)

intensive distribution Product is placed in every potential sales situation possible. (15)

intercultural communication Process of sending and receiving messages between people of various cultures. (23)

interest In finance, amount a borrower pays to a lender for a loan. (6) In career planning, feeling of wanting to learn more about a topic or to be involved in an activity. (27)

interest rate Represents the cost of a loan and is expressed as a percent of the amount borrowed. (6)

intermediary Business in the supply chain between the manufacturer or producer and the end users. (15)

internal influence Motivator or change factor that comes from within the business itself. (10)

internal theft Committed by employees of a store, a supplier, or a delivery company. (16)

international trade Buying and selling of goods and services between two or more specific nations rather than all nations in the world. (7)

Internet protocol address Number used to identify an electronic device connected to the Internet; also known as an *IP address*. (29)

internship Short-term position with a sponsoring organization that provides an opportunity to gain on-the-job experience in a certain field of study or occupation. (27)

interpersonal communication Communication that occurs between the sender and one other person. (23)

introduction stage Stage when a new product is first brought to the market. (11)

inventory management Ordering the goods, receiving them into stock on arrival, and paying the supplier or vendor. (16)

inventory shrinkage Difference between perpetual inventory and actual physical inventory. (16)

invoice Vendor bill requesting payment for goods shipped or services provided. (16)

IP address See *Internet protocol address*.

J

jingle Tagline or slogan set to music. (12)

job Work a person does regularly in order to earn money. (27)

job application Form with spaces for entry of contact information, education, and work experience. (28)

job interview Meeting in which an applicant and an employer discuss the job and the candidate's skills and qualifications. (28)

job lead Information that leads a person to a job opening. (28)

job-specific skills See *hard skills*.

joint venture Partnership of two or more companies that work together for a specific business purpose. (7)

junk mail See *direct marketing*.

just-in-time (JIT) inventory-control system Keeps a minimal amount of production materials or sales inventory on hand at all times. (16)

K

keystone pricing Pricing method in which the total cost of a product is doubled to determine its base price. (13)

keyword Word that specifically relates to the functions of the position for which the employer is hiring. (28)

L

labor Work performed by people in businesses. (5)

labor force All the people in a nation who are capable of working and want to work. (6)

laissez-faire management style Manager allows employees to make their own decisions about how to complete tasks. (21)

large-group communication See *public communication*.

law of diminishing marginal utility States that consuming more units of the same product decreases the marginal utility from each unit. (13)

law of supply and demand Price of a product is determined by the relationship between the supply of a product and the demand for the product. (5)

lawsuit Process of bringing a complaint to a court for resolution. (25)

layout Arrangement of the headline, copy, and art on a page. (18)

lead Potential customer. (20)

leader A person who guides others to a goal. (21)

leadership Ability of a person to guide others to a goal. (22)

lead time Time between reserving the advertisement space or broadcast time and when the advertisement actually runs. (18)

letter of application See *cover message*.

liability Debt of a business (21) or legal responsibility (24).

libel Publishing a false statement about someone that causes others to have a bad opinion of him or her. (29)

licensing When a business sells the right to manufacture its products or use its trademark. (7)

Likert scale Asks survey respondents how strongly they agree or disagree with a given statement. (9)

limited buying decision Purchase requiring some amount of research and planning. (10)

limited liability Partner or owner cannot lose more than the amount originally invested by that person. (24)

limited partnership (LP) One managing partner and at least one limited partner. (24)

line of credit Specific dollar amount that a business can draw against as needed. (26)

liquid asset Cash or the items a business owns that can be easily turned into cash. (26)

listening Intellectual process that combines hearing with evaluation. (23)

list price Established price printed in a catalog, on a price tag, or in a price list. (14)

logo Picture, design, or graphic image that represents a brand; also known as *brand mark*. (12)

long-term goal Goal that will take a longer time to achieve, usually longer than one year. (27)

loss leader Item that is priced much lower than the current market price or the cost of the product and taking a loss on each sale. (14)

loss prevention Term used for programs designed to prevent loss of assets such as merchandise, money, or other property. (25)

M

macroeconomics Branch of economics that studies human behavior and choices that relate to the entire economy of a nation. (5)

malware Term given to software programs that are intended to damage, destroy, or steal data; short for *malicious software*. (29)

management Function of business that controls and makes decisions about a business. (3)

manager Employee who directs the work of others and is responsible for carrying out the goals of a department. (3)

manual-tag system Tracks sales by removing price tags when the products are sold. (16)

manufacturer Type of producer that uses raw materials from other producers and converts them into finished goods; also called *producer*. (3)

manufacturer's brand See *national brand*.

manufacturer's suggested retail price (MSRP) Price recommended for the product by the manufacturer. (14)

MarCom See *marketing communication*.

marginal utility Additional satisfaction gained by using one additional unit of the same product. (13)

market Anywhere a buyer and a seller convene to buy and sell goods. (1)

market economy Economy in which individuals and businesses are free to make their own economic decisions with limited governmental involvement. (5)

market forces Economic factors that affect the price, demand, and availability of a product or service. (5)

marketing Dynamic activities that identify, anticipate, and satisfy customer demand while making a profit. (1)

marketing communication Communications from an organization to its customers and to the public; often called *MarCom*. (17)

marketing concept Approach to business that focuses on satisfying customer needs and wants while achieving profit goals for the company. (1)

marketing-information management (MIM) Gathering and analyzing information about markets, customers, industry trends, new technology, and competing businesses; also called *marketing research*. (1)

marketing-information system (MkIS) Organized system of gathering, sorting, analyzing, evaluating, distributing, and storing information for marketing purposes. (8)

marketing mix Strategy for using the elements of product, price, place, and promotion. (1)

marketing plan Document that describes business and marketing goals and the strategies and tactics that will be used to achieve them. (2)

marketing professional Person who helps determine the marketing needs of a company, develops and implements marketing plans, and focuses on customer satisfaction. (1)

marketing research Gathering and analyzing information to help make sound marketing decisions. (8)

marketing strategy Decision made to execute the marketing plan and meet the goals of the business. (2)

marketing tactic Specific activity implemented to carry out the marketing strategies. (2)

marketing trend Pattern of change in consumer behavior that leads to changes in the marketing mix. (8)

market planning Analyzing the potential of different marketplaces in order to create strategies to target a specific market. (1)

market potential Maximum number of customers and amount of sales that can be generated from a specific segment in a defined time period. (2)

market risk Potential that the target market for new products or services is much less than originally thought. (25)

market segmentation Process of dividing a large market into smaller groups. (2)

market share Percentage of total sales in a market that is held by one business. (2)

market-share leader Company with the largest combined market share. (9)

market size Total sales per year for a specific product held by all the competing businesses. (2)

market structure How a market is organized based on the number of businesses competing for sales in an industry. (6)

marking Process of attaching the price to each item that will be sold. (16)

markup Amount added to the cost of a product to determine the base price. (13)

marquee Overhanging structure containing a signboard located at the entrance to the store. (19)

mass market Overall group of people who might buy a good or service. (9)

maturity stage Stage that occurs when product sales are stable. (11)

media planning Process of determining the best media that meets a campaign's objectives. (18)

medium of exchange Item that is accepted in exchange for goods and services. (3)

memo Brief message sent to someone within an organization; short for *memorandum*. (23)

merchandise approach Conversation starts with a comment about the product. (20)

merchandise manager See *buyer*.

metaphor Word or phrase for one thing used in reference to a very different thing in order to suggest a similarity. (12)

metrics Standards of measurement. (2)

microeconomics Branch of economics that studies human behavior and choices that relate to the economic decisions of individuals and businesses. (5)

mission statement Company message to customers about why the business exists. (2)

mixed economy Economy in which both the government and individuals make decisions about economic resources. (5)

mock interview Practice interview conducted with another person. (28)

monetary policy Policy that regulates the supply of money and interest rates by a central bank in an economy. (6)

money Anything of value that is accepted in return for goods or services. (3)

money supply Total money circulating at any one time in a country. (6)

monopolistic competition Large number of businesses selling similar, but not the same, products and at different prices; also known as *imperfect competition*. (6)

monopoly Occurs when one business has complete control of a market's entire supply of goods or services. (3) Market structure with one business that has complete control of a market's entire supply of a product. (6)

morals Individual's ideas of what is right and wrong. (4)

motion Recommendation for action to be taken by the group. (23)

motive Internal push that causes a person to act. (10)

movement Way the design guides viewer eyes over an item or display. (19)

multi-channel retailer Business that sells products through both brick-and-mortar stores and online sites. (15)

multinational corporation Business that operates in more than one country. (7)

N

national brand Brand created by a manufacturer for its own products; also called *manufacturer's brand*. (12)

natural risk Situation caused by acts of nature. (25)

need Something necessary for survival, such as food, clothing, and shelter. (1)

need-based award Financial-aid awards available for students and families who meet certain economic requirements. (27)

negotiation When individuals come together in an attempt to reach an agreement. (16)

net income See *net profit*.

net profit What is left after all company expenses are subtracted from total revenue; sometimes called *net income*. (13)

netiquette Etiquette used when communicating electronically; also known as *digital etiquette*. (29)

networking Talking with others and establishing relationships with people who can help you achieve career, educational, or personal goals. (28)

new product Product that is different in some way from existing products. (11)

news release See *press release*.

niche market Portion of a market segment that is very narrow and specific. (9)

nonprice competition When strategies other than price are used to attract customers. (6)

nonprofit organization Entity that exists to serve some public purpose. (3)

nonstore retailer Business that sells directly to consumers in ways that does not involve a physical store location. (15)

North American Industry Classification System (NAICS) Numerical system used to classify businesses and collect economic statistics. (10)

not-for-profit school One that returns the money it earns back into the school. (27)

O

objection Concerns or other reasons a customer has for not making a purchase. (20)

occupation Specific career area, such as advertising. (27)

occupational training Education that prepares an individual for a specific type of work. (27)

odd pricing Sets prices to end in an odd number. (14)

offshoring Moving sections of a business to another country. (7)

oligopoly Market structure with a small number of businesses selling the same or similar products. (6)

open source Applies to software that has source code freely available to the public. (29)

operating expense Ongoing expenses that keep a company functioning. (26)

operational planning Setting day-to-day goals for the company. (21)

opportunity cost Value of the next-best option that was not selected. (5)

order bias Skewing of results caused by the order in which questions are placed in a survey. (8)

organizational buyer Person who handles all the purchasing duties for a business or an organization; also called *purchaser* or *buyer*. (16)

organizational chart Diagram of employee positions showing how the positions interact within the chain of command. (21)

organizational sales See *business-to-business (B2B) selling*.

outsourcing See *contract manufacturing*.

overselling Promising more than the product or the business can deliver. (20)

owner's equity Difference between a business' assets and its liabilities. (26)

P

packaging Protects products until customers are ready to use them. (11)

parliamentary procedure Process for conducting a meeting so that the meeting is orderly and democratic. (23)

participatory marketing Strategy that invites customers to participate in an element of the promotional mix through a type of response. (17)

participatory style See *democratic management style*.

partnership Relationship between two or more people who join to create a business. (3)

partnership agreement Document that details how much each partner will invest, each partner's responsibilities, and how profits are to be shared. (24)

passive listening Casually listening to someone talk. (23)

peak Highest point in the business cycle and marks the end of expansion. (6)

peer-to-peer lending Form of debt financing without the use of a financial institution. (26)

perception Mental image a person has about something. (12)

perfect competition Characterized by a large number of businesses selling the same product at the same prices. (6)

periodic inventory-control system Taking a physical count of merchandise at regular periods. (16)

perpetual inventory-control system Method of counting inventory that shows the quantity on hand at all times. (16)

personal brand Sum of the differences between you and those around you. (28)

personal selling Any direct contact between a salesperson and a customer with the objective of making a sale. (17)

persuasion Use of logic to change a belief or get people to take a certain action. (17)

PEST analysis Evaluation of the political, economic, social, and technological factors in a certain market or geographic region that may impact the success of a business. (2)

philanthropy Philanthropy is promoting the welfare of others, usually through donating time, property, or money. (4)

phishing Use of fraudulent e-mails and copies of valid websites to trick people in to providing private and confidential data. (29)

physical inventory Actual count of all items in inventory at that time. (16)

pipeline Line of connected pipes that carry liquids and gases over a long distance. (15)

piracy Illegal copying or downloading of software, files, or other protected material, including images, movies, and music. (29)

place Activities involved in getting a product or service to the end users; also known as *distribution*. (1)

plagiarism Unethical and illegal practice of claiming another person's material as one's own. (29)

planned obsolescence Evaluating and updating current products or adding new ones to replace older ones. (25)

point-of-purchase (POP) display Special display usually found near a cash register where goods are purchased. (19)

point-of-sale (POS) software Electronically records each sale when it happens by scanning product bar codes. (16)

portfolio Selection of materials that a person collects and organizes to show his or her qualifications, skills, and talents. (28)

postgraduate education Education beyond a master degree. (27)

postsecondary education Any education achieved after high school. (27)

postsecondary plan See *career plan*.

preapproach Tasks that are performed before contact is made with a customer. (20)

predatory pricing Setting very low prices to remove competition. (14)

prejudice Opinion that is formed without sufficient knowledge. (23)

preselling   Creating interest and demand for a product before it is available for sale. (17)

presentation   Prepared speech that delivers information to an audience. (20)

press conference   Meeting set by a business or organization in which the media is invited to attend. (17)

press kit   Packet of information sent to the media about a new business opening or other major business events. (17)

press release   A story featuring useful company information written by the company PR contact; also called *news release*. (17)

prestige pricing   Sets prices high to convey quality and status. (14)

price   Amount of money requested or exchanged for a product. (1)

price ceiling   Maximum price set by the government when it thinks certain products are being priced too high. (14)

price competition   When a lower price is the main reason for customers to buy from one business over another. (6)

price discrimination   Selling the same product to different customers at different prices based on personal characteristics. (14)

price-fixing   Occurs when two or more businesses in an industry agree to sell the same product at a set price. (6)

price floor   Minimum price set by the government for certain goods and services that it thinks are being priced too low. (14)

price lining   Sets various prices for the same type of product to indicate different levels of quality. (14)

price mix   Decisions made about pricing levels, discounts offered, and credit offered to customers. (14)

pricing   Activities involved in setting prices for products. (1)

pricing objective   Goal defined in the business and marketing plans for the overall pricing policies of the company. (13)

primary data   Pieces of information collected directly by an individual or organization. (8)

private carrier   Company that transports its own goods. (15)

private-label brand   Products owned by and created specifically for large retailers. (12)

private warehouse   Those owned by a company for storage of its own goods. (15)

pro forma balance sheet   Reports the assets, liabilities, and owner's equity for a proposed business. (26)

pro forma cash flow statement   Reports the anticipated flow of cash into and out of the business. (26)

pro forma financial statement   Financial statement based on the best estimate of future revenue and expenses for a new business. (26)

pro forma income statement   Projects the financial progress of the business. (26)

problem solving   Process of choosing a course of action after evaluating available info and weighing the costs, benefits, and consequences of alternative actions. (22)

producer   Business that creates goods and services; also called *manufacturer*. (3)

product   Good, service, or idea. (1)

product depth   Number of product items within a product line. (11)

production   Activity related to making a product, which can be a good, a service, or an idea. (3)

product item   Specific model, color, or size of products in a line. (11)

productivity   Amount of work a person can do in a specific amount of time, usually an hour. (5)

product life cycle   Stages a product or a product category goes through from its beginning to end. (11)

product line   Group of closely related products within the product mix. (11)

product manager   Marketing professional who guides the selection of products and oversees the marketing and sales of those products. (11)

product mix   All the goods and services a business sells. (11)

product mix strategy   Process of planning which goods or services the business will support. (11)

product obsolescence   Occurs when a product becomes outdated. (11)

product placement See *embedded marketing*.

product planning Process of making decisions about features and benefits that will help a product be successful and about managing the product throughout its life cycle. (11)

product positioning Process used to influence the customer's perception of a brand or product in relation to the competition. (2)

product promotion Promotes specific products. (17)

product/service management Determining which products a business should offer to meet customer needs. (1)

product width Number of product lines a company offers. (11)

profession Jobs in a business field requiring similar education, training, or skills. (27)

professional buyer See *buyer*.

professionalism Act of exhibiting appropriate character, judgment, and behavior by a person who is trained to perform a job. (22)

profit Difference between the income earned and expenses incurred by a business during a specific period of time. (1)

promotion Process of communicating with potential customers in an effort to influence their buying behavior. (1)

promotional campaign The coordination of marketing communications to achieve a specific goal; also called *promotional plan*. (17)

promotional mix Combination of the elements used in a promotional campaign and includes personal selling, advertising, sales promotion, and public relations. (1)

promotional plan See *promotional campaign*.

prop Objects used in a display to support the theme or to physically support the merchandise. (19)

proportion Size and space relationship of all items in a display to each other and to the whole display. (19)

proprietary information Information a company wishes to keep private; also called *trade secrets*. (22)

prospect See *lead*.

protectionism Policy of protecting a country's domestic industries by enforcing trade regulations on foreign competitors. (7)

prototype Working model of a new product for testing purposes. (11)

psychographics Data about the preferences or choices of a group of people. (9)

psychographic segmentation Dividing the market by certain preferences or lifestyle choices. (9)

psychological influence Influence that comes from within a person and explains why a person has certain needs and wants. (10)

psychological pricing Pricing strategy that creates an image of a product and entices customers to buy. (14)

public communication Communicating with a group larger than 20 people; also called *large-group communication*. (23)

public domain Refers to material that is not owned by anybody and can be used without permission. (29)

public relations (PR) Marketing activities promoting goodwill between a company and the public. (17)

public warehouse Rents storage space to any company. (15)

pull promotional concept Manufacturer pulling customers to actively seek out that manufacturer's product. (17)

purchase order (PO) Form a buyer sends to the vendor to officially place an order. (16)

purchaser See *organizational buyer*.

purchasing agent Person who buys goods and services the company needs internally to operate its business; also called *specialized purchaser* or *purchasing manager*. (16)

purchasing manager See *purchasing agent*.

purchasing process Series of steps a purchasing agent or buyer takes to buy goods and services for a business. (16)

push promotional concept Manufacturer pushing a retailer to handle that manufacturer's merchandise to sell to customers. (17)

Q

qualitative data Provides insight into what people think about a topic. (8)

quantitative data Facts and figures from which conclusions can be drawn. (8)

quality control Checking goods as they are produced or received to ensure the quality meets expectations. (16)

quota Limit on the amount of a product imported into a country during a specific period of time. (7)

R

radio frequency identification (RFID) System that uses computer chips attached to inventory items and radio frequency receivers to track inventory. (16)

ransomware Malware that locks a computer and demands payment to unlock it. (29)

raw data Research that has not yet been analyzed. (8)

reach Total number of people expected to see an advertisement. (18)

receiving record Form on which all merchandise received is listed as it comes into the place of business. (16)

recession Period of significant decline in the total output, income, employment, and trade in an economy. (6)

recycling Reprocessing of resources so they can be used again. (4)

reference Person who can comment on the qualifications, work ethic, personal qualities, and work-related aspects of another person. (28)

reference group Specific group of people that influences our attitudes, beliefs, and behavior. (10)

relationship selling Focuses on building long-term relationships with customers. (20)

reliability Quality of providing consistent and dependable measurement and results. (8)

reorder point Point at which a business orders more of a product before the inventory gets too low. (16)

repackaging Using new packaging on an existing product. (11)

repositioning Changing the marketing strategy used to influence consumer perception of a product in comparison to the competition with the goal of increasing sales. (9)

representative sampling Group that includes a cross section of the entire population that is targeted. (8)

reseller Business that buys finished products to resell to consumers. (10)

resign Voluntarily leave an employment position. (28)

résumé Document that profiles a person's career goals, education, and work history. (28)

retail buyer See *buyer*.

retailer channel Path a product takes from the producer to the retailer, then from the retailer to the consumer. (15)

return on investment (ROI) Measure of profitability based on the amount earned from the investment made in the business. (13)

revenue Money that a business makes for the products or services it sells; also called *income* or *sales*. (21)

reverse engineering Taking apart an object to see how it was made in order to produce something similar. (11)

risk Possibility of loss, damage, or injury. (25)

risk assessment Process of analyzing a situation for possible risks. (25)

risk management Process of measuring risk and finding ways to minimize or manage loss. (25)

robbery Theft involving another person, often by using force or with the threat of violence. (25)

routine buying decision Purchase made quickly and with little thought. (10)

S

safety stock See *buffer stock*.

sales See *revenue*.

sales forecast Prediction of future sales based on past sales and a market analysis for a specific time period. (21)

sales-increase factor Percentage of expected increase in sales. (21)

Glossary

sales process Series of steps a salesperson goes through to help the customer make a satisfying buying decision. (20)

sales promotion Efforts used to encourage customers to buy a product within a specific time period, usually as soon as possible. (17)

saturated market One in which most of the potential customers who need, want, and can afford a product have bought it. (11)

scarcity When demand is higher than the available resources. (5)

scholarship Financial aid that may be based on financial need or some type of merit or accomplishment. (27)

search engine optimization (SEO) Process of indexing a website to rank it higher on the list of results that appears when a search is conducted. (18)

secondary data Information, statistics, or other type of data that already exists. (8)

secured loan See *installment loan*.

security Actions taken to prevent crime and protect the safety of people and property. (25)

selective distribution Selecting only certain places the manufacturer or wholesaler wants a product to be sold. (15)

self-actualization Expression of a person's true self through reaching personal goals and helping others. (10)

self-assessment Process of an individual evaluating his or her aptitudes, abilities, values, interests, and personality. (24)

self-esteem Confidence and satisfaction you have in yourself. (27)

self-management skills Skills that help an individual be productive and successful in the workplace. (22)

selling Personal communications with customers. (1)

service Action that is done for you, usually for a fee. (1)

service approach Starts with the phrase, "May I help you?" (20)

service business Business that provides services. (10)

service mark Similar to a trademark, but it identifies a service rather than a product. (12)

short-term goal Goal that can be achieved in less than one year. (27)

signature Identifies the person or company paying for the advertisement. (18)

situational influence Influence that comes from the environment. (10)

situation analysis Snapshot of the environment in which a business has been operating over a given period of time, usually the last 12 to 16 months. (2)

slander Speaking a false statement about someone that causes others to have a bad opinion of him or her. (29)

slogan See *tagline*.

small-group communication Communication that occurs with three to 20 people. (23)

SMART goal Goal that is specific, measurable, attainable, realistic, and timely. (2)

social environment Aggregate of the groups that make up the surroundings in which people live and interact. (10)

socially responsible marketing Socially responsible marketing is a belief that a company's marketing approach should consider the benefit to and betterment of society as a whole. (4)

social responsibility Social responsibility is behaving with sensitivity toward social, economic, and environmental issues. (4)

social trend Pattern of change in society as a whole. (8)

soft skills Skills used to help an individual find a job, perform in the workplace, and gain success in a job or career. (22)

software virus Computer program designed to negatively impact a computer system by infecting other files. (29)

sole proprietorship Business owned by one person. (3)

solution selling See *feature-benefit selling*.

spam Electronic messages sent in bulk to people who did not give a company permission to e-mail them. (4)

specialization Focusing on the production of specific goods so more products can be produced with the same amount of labor. (6)

specialized purchaser See *purchasing agent*.

603

spyware Software that spies on a computer. (29)

staffing Process of hiring people and matching them to the best position for their talents. (21)

Standard English English language usage that follows accepted rules for spelling, grammar, and punctuation. (23)

standardization Applying consistent promotion strategies to the marketing of a product regardless of the specific market. (7)

standard of living Financial well-being of the average person in a country. (6)

start-up capital Cash used to start the business. (26)

start-up cost Initial expenses necessary to begin operating a business. (26)

statement of ethics See *code of ethics*.

stereotyping Belief or generalization about a group of people with a given set of characteristics. (22)

stock Percentage of ownership in a corporation. (24)

stockholders Hold stock in the corporation. (24)

stock market System and marketplace for buying and selling stocks. (6)

stockout Running out of stock. (16)

storefront Store exterior. (19)

store image Created through the location, design, and décor of a business. (19)

store layout Floor plan that shows how the space in a store will be used. (19)

store of value Something that can be saved or stored and used at a later date. (3)

strategic planning Setting long-term marketing goals for the company. (21)

stress Body's reaction to increased challenges, pressures, or dangerous situations. (22)

stress management Practice of reducing and effectively handling stress. (22)

substitute selling Technique of showing products that are different from the originally requested product. (20)

suggestion selling Technique of suggesting additional items to go with merchandise requested by a customer. (20)

supply chain Businesses, people, and activities involved in turning raw materials into products and delivering them to end users. (15)

supply chain management Coordinating the events happening throughout the supply chain; also called *channel management*. (15)

supply chain manager Person who coordinates and monitors all the distribution activities. (15)

surveillance Process of closely observing what is going on in order to prevent crimes. (25)

survey Set of questions posed to a group of people to determine how that group thinks, feels, or acts. (8)

sustainability Sustainability is creating and maintaining conditions under which humans and nature can coexist both now and in the future. (4)

SWOT analysis Strengths, weaknesses, opportunities, and threats the business faces. (2)

systematic decision-making Process of choosing an option after evaluating the available information and weighing the costs and benefits of the alternatives. (5)

T

table Visual that displays information in columns and rows and is often used to compare data. (8)

tactical planning Setting short-term marketing goals for the company. (21)

tagline Phrase or sentence that summarizes an essential part of the product or business; also known as *slogan*. (12)

target market Specific group of customers whose needs and wants a company will focus on satisfying. (1)

tariff Governmental tax on imported goods. (7)

team Two or more people working together to achieve a common goal. (22)

teamwork Cooperative efforts by individual team members to achieve a goal. (22)

technology Use of science to invent useful things or to solve problems. (5)

tech prep Career preparation program that combines the last two years of high school with two years of postsecondary education. (27)

telemarketing Personal selling done over the telephone. (3)

telephone etiquette Using good manners while speaking on the telephone. (28)

terms for delivery Delivery arrangements made between the buyer and seller. (16)

test marketing Process of introducing a new product to a small portion of the target market to learn how it will sell. (11)

time management Practice of organizing time and work assignments to increase personal efficiency. (22)

time value of money Idea that money decreases in value over time. (3)

tone Impression of the overall content of the message. (23)

top-down management See *autocratic management style*.

total assets Everything the company owns. (13)

trade agreement Document listing the conditions and terms for importing and exporting products between countries. (7)

trade barrier Any governmental action taken to control or limit the amount of imports. (7)

trade character Animal, a real or fictional person, or an object used to advertise a good or service. (12)

trade credit Granting a line of credit to a business for a short period of time to purchase its goods and services. (10)

trademark Protects taglines, names, graphics, symbols, or any unique method used to identify a product or company. (12)

trade-off When something is given up in order to gain something else. (5)

trade policy Body of laws related to the exchange of goods and services for international trade. (7)

trade sanction Embargo that affects only certain goods. (7)

trade secrets See *proprietary information*.

trade show Large gathering of businesses for the purpose of displaying products for sale. (9)

trading bloc Group of countries that has joined together to trade as if they were a single country. (7)

traditional economy Economy in which economic decisions are based primarily on a society's values, culture, and customs. (5)

transportation Physical movement of products through the channel of distribution. (15)

triadic color Three colors that are equally spaced on the color wheel. (19)

trial run Testing a service on a few select customers to make sure that everything runs smoothly. (11)

trough Lowest stage of a business cycle and marks the end of a recession. (6)

turnover rate Number of times inventory has been sold during a time period, usually one year; also called *turnover ratio*. (16)

turnover ratio See *turnover rate*.

typeface Particular style for the printed letters of the alphabet, punctuation, and numbers. (18)

typography Visual aspect of the style and arrangement of type. (18)

U

uncontrollable risk Situation that cannot be predicted or covered by purchasing insurance. (25)

unemployment rate Percentage of the civilian labor force that is unemployed. (6)

uninsurable risk One that an insurance company will not cover. (25)

unique selling proposition (USP) Statement that summarizes the special features or benefits of a product or business. (9)

unit-control system Uses a visual determination to decide when more stock is needed. (16)

unit of value Common measure of what something is worth or what something costs. (3)

unit pricing Allows customers to compare prices based on a standard unit of measure. (14)

unlimited liability Business owner is responsible for all risks. (24)

usage rate How often a customer buys or uses a good or service. (9)

utility Characteristics of a product that satisfies human wants and needs. (1)

V

validity Extent to which questions address the intended marketing research topic. (8)

value Relative worth of something. (10) In art, lightness or darkness of the color. (19)

values Principles and beliefs that an individual considers important. (9)

variable Something that changes or can be changed. (8)

variable expense Amount that changes in both the cost and the amount of time it must be paid. (13)

venture capitalist Professional investor or investing group who funds new start-ups or expansions of existing companies; also called *VC*. (26)

viral marketing Information about products that customers or viewers feel compelled to pass along to others; also called *buzz marketing* or *word-of-mouth advertising*. (17)

virtual test markets Computer simulations of products and shopping environments. (11)

vision statement What the business aspires to accomplish. (2)

visual aid Object that is used to clarify an idea, concept, or process. (20)

visual merchandising Process of creating floor plans and displays to attract customer attention and encourage purchases. (17)

volume pricing Lowering the list price of a product based on the higher number of units purchased at the same time. (13)

W

want Something that a person desires, but could live without. (1)

warranty Document that states the quality of a product with a promise to correct certain problems that might occur. (11)

weight Thickness and slant of the letters. (18)

white space Blank areas on a page where there is no art or copy. (18)

wholesaler channel Path a product takes from the producer to a wholesaler, and then to a retailer before reaching the end user. (15)

word-of-mouth advertising See *viral marketing*.

work ethic Principle that honest work is a reward on its own. (22)

work-life balance Amount of time an individual spends working compared to the amount of time spent in a personal life. (22)

work-study program Part-time jobs on a college campus. (27)

work values Aspects of work that are most important to a person. (27)

writing style Way in which a writer uses language to convey an idea. (23)

Index

3D artist. *See* interactive media specialist
529 plan, 522
80/20 rule, 150, 297

A

ability, 505
absolute advantage, 109
academic sources of secondary data, 134
acceptable use policy, 560
accident, 470
    preventing, 474–475
account executive. *See* copywriter
accounting, 41
accounting equation, 493
account manager. *See* outside sales representative
account service representative. *See* customer service representative
accounts payable, 493
accounts receivable, 183, 493
    accounts receivable aging report, 183
accreditation, 520
action plan, 31
    budget, 31–32
    metrics, 32
    timeline, 31
action word, 338
active listening, 437
active reading, 438
adaptability, 407
adaptation, 119
adding value, 14
adult education (adult ed), 518
advertisement elements, 336–339
advertising, 326
    basics, 326–333
    benefits to society, 326–327
    cost of creation, 331
    cost of placement, 331, 333
    developing a campaign, 334–339
    laws governing, 327
    media selection, 331, 333
    media types used, 315, 327–331
    truth in advertising laws, 312
Advertising Age, 514
advertising agency, 331
advertising and promotions manager, 316
advertising associate. *See* copywriter
advertising campaign, 334
    advertisement elements, 336–339
    budget, 334–335
    concepting, 335
    developing, 334–336
    goals, 334
    message, 335
advertising copywriter. *See* copywriter
advertising laws, 43–45
advertising manager. *See* advertising and promotions manager
advertising sales manager. *See* advertising and promotions manager
advertising writer. *See* copywriter
Adweek, 514
age, as segmentation variable, 151
agenda, 437
agent, 269
agent/broker channel, 270, 272
agent/broker industrial distributor channel, 272
AIDA, 312
Airbnb, 335
air cargo company, 277
air transportation, 276–277
algebraic reasoning, 399
AMA. *See* American Marketing Association
Amazon.com, 61
    Prime Air, 276
American Marketing Association (AMA), 56, 513
    marketing plan templates, 23
Amtrak, 74
analogous color, 353
analytics, 224
angel investor (angel), 484
animation director. *See* interactive media specialist
animator. *See* interactive media specialist
anticipation stock, 294
antimalware software, 564
antitrust laws, 45, 102
antivirus software, 564
appendices, 28, 460
Apple, 224, 347

application. *See* job application; loan application
apprenticeship, 519
approach, 370–372
aptitude, 505
architectural display, 350
area, 349
Arm & Hammer baking soda, 209
art, 338
assertive, 415
assets, 399, 493
associations, professional, 513
assuming risk, 476
assumptions, 438
attention, interest, desire, action. *See* AIDA
attire
    for a job interview, 541
    for workplace, 371
attitude, 150, 152–153, 407
autocratic management style, 395
avoiding risk, 473–475

B

B2B. *See* business-to-business
B2C. *See* business-to-consumer
background check, 545
bait and switch, 254
balance, 355
balance of payments, 109
balance of trade, 109
balance sheet, 398–399
bank cards, 181
bankruptcy, 46
bankruptcy laws, 46
barrier, 427
bartering, 39, 483
base price, 241, 250
Basics for Industry guides, 48
BBB. *See* Better Business Bureau
B corporation. *See* benefit corporation
behavioral questions, 542–543
behavioral segmentation, 153–154
benefit, 157
benefit corporation, 182
benefits forms (employment), 547
Better Business Bureau (BBB), 56
    Business Partner Code of Conduct, 56
    vendor reports, 288

bibliography, 23, 460
bid, 288
bidding process, 288
billboard, 328
bin ticket, 295
blog, 310, 461
BLS (Bureau of Labor Statistics), 513, 532
body copy, 338
body language, 426
BOGO (buy one, get one) pricing, 251
bond, 95
bootstrapping, 482–483
Bose, 224
BrainReserve, 135
brainstorming, 203
brand, 205
brand consistency, 219
brand equity, 221
brand extension, 223
brand identity, 221–223
brand image, 219, 222
branding, 216–225
    elements, 216–219
    identity, 221–223
    protection, 224–225
    strategies, 223–224
    types, 219–220
branding strategy, 223
brand licensing, 224
brand loyalty, 154, 222–223
brand manager. *See* marketing manager
brand mark. *See* logo
brand name, 216
    versus generic term, 224–225
brand promise, 219
brand protection, 224–225
Brandweek, 514
break-even point, 236–237, 488–489
broadcast media, 329
broker. *See* agent
budget, 31–32, 41, 397–398
buffer stock, 294
builder, 267
Building the Marketing Plan
    action plan, 386–387
    activity files
        1-1—Research Company, 66
        2-1—Research Economic Conditions, 123
        3-1—Competition Research, 188
        3-2—Competitive Analysis, 188
        3-3—Company Assessment, 188
        3-4—SWOT Analysis, 188
        3-5—Environmental Scan, 188
        3-6—PEST Analysis, 188
        3-7—Global Environmental Scan, 188
        3-8—Target Market Analysis, 188
        3-9—Customer Profile, 188
        4-1—Product, 229
        4-2—Branding, 229
        5-1—Marketing Goals, 261
        5-2—Price, 261
        6-1—Supply Chain, 303
        6-2—Purchasing and Inventory Management, 303
        7-1—Promotional Plan Goals, 386
        7-2—Promotional Mix, 386
        7-3—Budget, 386
        7-4—Timeline, 386
        7-5—Metrics, 387
        8-1—Sales Forecast, 445
        8-2—Best Opportunities, 445
        9-1—Executive Summary, 497
        9-2—Bibliography, 497
        9-3—Appendices, 497
    bibliography, appendices, and table of contents, 497
    branding, 229
    complete a customer profile, 188
    complete SWOT and PEST analyses, 188
    deliver the presentation, 568
    determine the target market, 188
    develop the presentation, 568
    economic conditions, 123
    executive summary, 497
    identify your company, 66
    introduction, 66
    inventory management, 303
    marketing objectives, 261
    price, 261
    product, 229
    promotional strategies, 386
    research the competition, 188
    sales analysis, 445
    supply chain, 303
bulk-breaking, 267
bundling, 250–251
Bureau of Competition, 45
Bureau of Consumer Protection, 47
Bureau of Labor Statistics (BLS), 513, 532
burglary, 470
business
    basic concepts, 38–48
    definition, 38–39
    forms of ownership, 42, 453–456
    functions, 39–42
    laws and regulations, 43–48
business analysis, 204–205
business correspondence, 432
business cycle, 95–98
    expansion, 96
    peak, 96
    recession, 96
    relationship with economic indicators, 97–98
    trough, 97
business description, 27, 460
    company goals, 28
    mission statement, 28
    vision statement, 28
business development specialist. *See* market analyst
business ethics, 10, 54–58
    employee conduct, 54–56
    marketing practices, 56–58
business functions, 39–42
    finance, 40–41
    management, 41–42
    marketing, 41
    production, 40
business loan. *See* loan application
business market. *See* business-to-business
business operations, 459
business opportunities, 457–459
    existing, 459
    feasibility, 458
    financing, 482–493
    franchise, 459
    new, 458–459
    operating expenses, 486–487
    start-up costs, 486
business ownership, 42
    alternative forms, 455–456
    forms, 453–456
business plan, 27
    sections, 459–461
business product, 195–196
business protocol, 133
business purchasing, 286
business risk, 468–471
business spending, 91
business-to-business (B2B), 175
    channel of distribution examples, 271–272
    customers. *See* clients
    market, 10
    selling, 320, 365
business-to-consumer (B2C), 168
    channel of distribution examples, 269–271
    customers. *See* consumers

Index

market, 10
selling, 320, 365
buyer, 287
See also product manager
buying motive, 170–171
buying signal, 375
buying status, 154
buy one, get one (BOGO) pricing, 251
buzz marketing. *See* viral marketing

C

calculator use, 439
call center, 365
call center representative. *See* customer service representative
call to action, 316
CAN-SPAM Act (2004), 330
capital, 74–75
capital good, 74
capitalism. *See* market economy
captive pricing, 250
carbon footprint, 252
career
    differs from job, 502
    education level affects, 515
    options available, 502–504
    planning, 504–509
    researching, 509–514
career and technical student organizations (CTSOs), 511–512
career area. *See* career pathway
career clusters, 503
career fair, 532
career ladder, 510–511
career-level position, 511
career levels, 510–511
career objective, 533
Career Outlook website, 513, 532
career pathway, 504
career plan, 508–509
career planning, 504–509
    career plan, 508–509
    goals, 506–508
    self-assessment, 504–506
CareerOneStop, 513, 532
careers in marketing and sales
    advertising and promotions manager, 316
    copywriter, 338, 427
    customer service representative, 115
    ethics important, 366
    graphic designer, 355
    interactive media specialist, 518
    market analyst, 149
    marketing manager, 10
    outside sales representative, 474

product manager, 199, 200
qualities necessary, 366
sales manager, 47
sales positions, 365–367
skills required, 366–367
supply chain manager, 278
telemarketer, 79
trade show manager, 235
webmaster, 561
carrying costs, 294
cash discount, 252
cash transaction, 378
catalog sales, 268
category manager, 200
cause marketing, 61–62
CC (Creative Commons) license, 557
censorship, 561
census, 150
centrally planned economy. *See* command economy
certificate of incorporation, 455
certification, 369, 519
CEUs (continuing education units), 518
chain of command, 393
chamber of commerce, 134
channel (communication), 424
channel (distribution), 13
channel conflict, 272
channel management. *See* supply chain management
channel manager. *See* supply chain manager
channel members, 266
    intermediaries, 267–269
    producers, 266–267
channel of distribution, 266
    B2B market examples, 271–272
    B2C market examples, 269–271
    managing, 272–273
    members, 266–269
chart, 140
charter, 455
children, laws for marketing to, 43
Children's Online Privacy Protection Act (COPPA), 43
chronological résumé, 533
circle graphs, 489
circulation, 331
Cisco, 409
citation guidelines, 556
civil laws, 101
classified ad, 532
Clayton Antitrust Act, 45, 102
clients, 10, 175–179, 195
    influences, 177–178
    levels of buying decisions, 178–179
    market segments, 175

segmentation variables, 175–177
close, 375
closed display, 350
closing a sale, 375–376
cloud computing, 561
coastal ships, 277
co-branding, 223
code of conduct, 54–55
code of ethics, 46, 55–56
cohorts, 151
coincident indicator, 97
cold calling, 370
collaboration, 416
collateral, 181, 485
collection agency, 181
college access, 521–522
collusion, 102, 267
color, 351–353
color scheme, 352
color wheel, 352
command economy, 80
commercialization. *See* introduction stage
commercial lines manager. *See* marketing manager
commercial, 315, 329
common carrier, 276
common interview questions, 541–542
communication, 424
    barriers, 427–428
    ethics, 428–429
    listening, 437–438
    nonverbal, 426
    process, 424–425
    purpose, 425
    social-media company posts, 532
    speaking, 434–437
    types, 425–427
    verbal, 426
    visual, 426
    written, 425–426, 430–434
communication process, 424–425
company image, 366
comparative advantage, 109
comparative reference group, 170
competition, 26, 83, 99–100, 102, 156–162
    direct versus indirect, 156
    influence on price, 242
    market analysis, 157–159
    price versus nonprice, 157
    product positioning, 160
    sales analysis, 161–162
competition-based pricing, 242
competitive advantage, 158
competitive analysis, 26, 157–158
complaints, handling, 381–382
complementary colors, 352

compound interest, 243
compromise, 416
computer
　security settings, 564
　backing up data, 564
computerized inventory-control system, 296
concepting, 335
conference call, 434
conference manager. *See* trade show manager
conference planner. *See* trade show manager
confidentiality, 366
confidentiality agreement, 412
conflict, 416
conflict of interest, 412–413
conflict resolution, 416–417
consensus building, 416
constructive criticism, 416
consulting management style, 395
consumer behavior, 168–169
Consumer Bill of Rights, 47
consumer credit, 181
consumer decision-making process, 171–173
consumer economy. *See* market economy
consumer market. *See* business-to-consumer
consumer price index (CPI), 93
consumer products, 195
Consumer Product Safety Act, 47
Consumer Product Safety Commission (CPSC), 47
consumer protection laws, 46–48
consumers, 7, 10, 195
　behavior, 168–169
　decision-making process, 171–173
　influences, 169–170
　levels of buying decisions, 173–174
　motives, 170–171
consumer spending, 91
container ships, 277
content marketing, 136
content writer. *See* copywriter
contests, 318
continuing education classes, 518
continuing education units (CEUs), 518
continuous function, 507
continuum, 194
contract carrier. *See* common carrier
contraction, 96
contract manufacturing, 115
control, 394
controllable risk, 468

cookies, 561–562
co-op, 512
cooperation, 416
cooperative education program, 512
COPPA (Children's Online Privacy Protection Act), 43
copy, 338
copy left, 557
copyright, 556–557
copyrighted material, ethical use, 506
copywriter, 338, 427
corporate formalities, 455
corporate social responsibility (CSR), 59, 222
　environmentally sustainable practices, 60
　philanthropy, 59–60
　socially responsible marketing, 60–62
　support of local economy, 60
corporate webmaster, 561
corporation, 42, 455
　multinational, 115
correspondence, 432
cosigner, 491
cost-based pricing, 241
cost per thousand (CPM), 331
costs, influence on price, 240–241
coupon, 317
coupon clippers, 327
cover letter, 535–536
cover message, 535–536
CPI (consumer price index), 93
CPM (cost per thousand), 331
CPSC (Consumer Product Safety Commission), 47
Crain Communications, Inc., 514
Creative Commons (CC) license, 557
creative director. *See* graphic designer; interactive media specialist
creative plan, 331
creativity, 509
credibility, 408
credit, 180
　consumer, 181
　reducing risks, 182
　rewards of extending, 181
　risks of extending, 181–182
　role, 180–183
　trade, 181
credit application, 182
credit bureau, 182
credit card transaction, 379
credit policy, 182
credit report, 182
credit risk, 181
crime insurance, 476

criminal laws, 101
critical thinking, 410
CRM. *See* customer relationship management
cross-functional team, 414
CSR. *See* corporate social responsibility
CTSOs (career and technical student organizations), 511–512
Cuisinart, 41
culture, 117, 427
currency, 109–110
　conversion, 116
　see also money
customer comfort space, 348
customer database, 129
customer feedback, 203
customer incentives, 373
customer information, responsible use, 152
customer loyalty, 181
　programs, 318
customer privacy, 56
customer profile, 154
customer relationship management (CRM), 56, 370
　responsible use of information, 152
customers. *See* consumers
customer satisfaction, 10
customer service, 366, 380–382
　complaint handling, 381–382
　online support, 380–381
　support team, 380
customer-service mindset, 366
customer service representative, 115
customer service specialist. *See* customer service representative
customer support team, 380
customs broker, 114
customs duty. *See* tariff
cyberbullying, 555

D

Daisy® Brand sour cream, 202
dashboards, 257
data, 129
　backing up computer, 564
　primary, 129–133
　raw, 140
　secondary, 133–135
data analysis, 140, 141
database, 129
database marketing, 136
data-focused jobs, 509
data mining, 140
DBA license, 454

debit card transaction, 379
debt financing, 485–486
debtor, 180
debtor-creditor relationship, 180
DECA Emerging Leaders, 5, 21, 37, 53, 71, 89, 107, 127, 147, 167, 193, 215, 233, 249, 265, 285, 307, 325, 345, 363, 391, 405, 423, 439, 467, 481, 501, 529, 553
deceptive pricing, 254
decimals, 97
decision-making, systematic, 76–77
decline stage, 209
decoding, 425
deductive reasoning, 410
deflation, 93
demand, 82, 238
    influence on price, 238–240
demand-based pricing, 238
demand curve, 83
demand elasticity, 239–240
democratic management style, 395
demographics, 117, 135, 150
demographic segmentation, 150–152
demographic trends, 135–136
dependability, 408
depression, 96
design, 351
    elements and principles, 351–355
design director. *See* graphic designer
desktop publisher. *See* graphic designer
destructive criticism, 416
diary, 132
digital billboard, 328
digital citizenship, 555
digital communication, 554–564
    digital citizenship, 555
    digital literacy, 554–555
    Electronic User's Bill of Rights, 558–559
    intellectual property, 555–558
    security practices, 563–564
    workplace Internet use, 560–563
digital delivery, 277
digital etiquette. *See* netiquette
digital footprint, 545, 555
digital literacy, 554–555
digital revolution, 151
digital security, 563–564
    common-sense measures, 563
    computer and browser settings, 564
    identity theft, 563
    password strength, 564
    plan, 563
digital technology, 75
direct channel, 269, 272
direct competitors, 156

direct mail, 328
direct marketing, 316–317
directories, 328
director of events. *See* trade show manager
director of sales. *See* sales manager
direct response marketing. *See* direct marketing
direct sales retailers, 269
discrete function, 507
discretion, 152
discretionary income, 152
discussion boards, 381
disintermediation, 272
Disney, Walt, 504
displays, 319, 346
    development and maintenance, 355–358
    elements and principles of design, 351–355
    interior, 349–350
    merchandise presentation, 349–350
display windows, 348
disposable income, 152
distress, 411
distribution. *See* place
distributors. *See* wholesalers
diversity, 117, 412
documents needed for job search, 533–537
    portfolio, 536–537
    résumé, 533, 535
doing business as. *See* DBA license
DOL (US Department of Labor), 45, 513, 532
dollar-markup method, 241
Dollar Tree, 251
double-digit inflation, 93
double taxation, 455
draw, 486
drone delivery, 276
dumpster diving, 563
duty. *See* tariff

E

Eataly, 7
ecofriendly promotional items, 336
ecofriendly purchasing, 289
economic activity, 90
    measuring, 90–98
economic factors, 25, 116–117
economic growth rate, 91–92
economic indicators, 90–95, 97–98, 117
    bond market, 95
    gross domestic product (GDP), 90–92

    inflation, 92–93
    interest rates, 93
    labor, 93–95
    relationships with business cycle, 97–98
    stock market, 95
economic input, 78
economic output, 78. *See also* gross domestic product
economic problem, 75
economic recovery, 97
economic risk, 469
economics
    economic problem, 75
    factors of production, 73–75
    global business, 113–119
    governmental role in United States, 100–102
    international trade, 108–112
    macroeconomics, 72
    market forces, 82–83
    market structure, 99–100
    measuring activity, 90–98
    microeconomics, 72–73
    systems, 78–82
economic systems, 78–82
economic utility, 14–15
economy
    command, 80
    effort to support local, 60
    governmental role in United States, 100–102
    market, 80–81
    mixed, 82
    traditional, 79–80
economy of scale, 289
EDI (electronic data interchange), 287
editing, 431
education, 515–522
    certification, 519
    college access, 521–522
    direct effect on income and career potential, 515
    formal, 515–518
    funding options, 522
    quality of institution, 519–521
    training, 518–519
education level, as segmentation variable, 152
EEOC (Equal Employment Opportunity Commission), 45
elastic demand, 239–240
electronic data interchange (EDI), 287
elements of design, 351
e-mail, 432–434
    advertising, 330
    customer service support, 381

embargo, 111
embedded marketing, 315
embezzlement, 471
emergency, 475
emergency procedures, 475
emotional buying motives, 171, 372
emotional control, 92
emotional intelligence, 437
empathy, 375, 437
emphasis, 354
employed, 94
Employee's Withholding Allowance Certificate (Form W-4), 547
employee theft. *See* internal theft
Employment Eligibility Verification (Form I-9), 545–546
employment forms, 545–547
employment laws, 45
employment process, 544–548
    changing jobs, 547–548
    employment and benefits forms, 545–547
    employment verification, 544–545
    evaluating an offer, 545
    see also job application; job interview; job search
employment trends, 513
employment verification, 544–545
encoding, 424
endorsements, 43–44
Enforcement Policy Statement on US Origin Claims, 44
engagement marketing. *See* participatory marketing
Enterprise Holdings, 395
entrepreneur, 450
entrepreneurial discovery process, 457–458
entrepreneurship, 75, 450–461
    business opportunities, 457–459
    business plan, 459–461
    financing options, 482–486
    forms of business ownership, 453–456
    loan application process, 490–493
    new business considerations, 486–489
    rewards and risks, 450–451
    traits and skills needed, 451–453
entry-level job, 510
Environmental Protection Agency (EPA), 58, 61
environmental responsibility, truthfulness of marketing claims, 44
environmental scan, 24–25, 159
    global, 115–118
EPA (Environmental Protection Agency), 58, 61

Equal Employment Opportunity Commission (EEOC), 45
equilibrium, 82, 238
equity, 483
equity financing, 483–484
error, 141
    margin of, 139
e-tailer, 269
ethical communication, 438
ethics, 54, 411–413, 555
    business, 10, 54–58
    code of ethics, 46, 55–56
    collusion, 267
    communication, 428–429, 438
    copyrighted material, 506
    customer information, 152
    expense accounts, 397
    going out of business sale, 241
    integrity, 75
    online merchandise, 557
    proprietary information, 195, 412
    sales careers, 366
    sales messages, 358
    social-media company communications, 532
    sourcing, 110
    tax returns, 476
    truth-in-advertising laws, 312
ethnicity, as segmentation variable, 152
etiquette, 60, 408, 541, 555
    netiquette, 555
    professional, 60, 408
    telephone, 413, 434, 541
    workspace, 357
European Union (EU), 112
eustress, 411
evaluation, 207
even pricing, 251
event marketing, 318
events manager. *See* trade show manager
exceptional customer service, 366
exclusive distribution, 280
excuse, 374
executive-level position, 511
executive summary, 27, 460
existing business, buying, 459
expansion, 96
expense account, 397
experiment, 133
exponential, 243
exponent, 243
export, 109, 113
    net exports, 91
export management company, 280
export trading company. *See* export management company
extended product feature, 197

extensive buying decision, 174
external customer, 366
external influence, 177–178
externality, 102
external stressor, 411
external theft, 299, 470
    avoiding or reducing, 473–474
extractor, 267
eye contact, 426

F

Facebook, 298
factors of production, 73–75
fad, 135
FAFSA (Free Application for Federal Student Aid), 522
fair use doctrine, 557
false advertising, 43, 57, 327
family size, as segmentation variable, 152
FAQ (frequently asked questions) page, 381
FDA. *See* Food and Drug Administration
feasibility, 458
feasibility study, 458
feasible, 458
feature, 157, 197
feature-benefit selling, 369
Fed. *See* Federal Reserve System
Federal Emergency Management Agency (FEMA), 101
Federal Reserve System, 100
Federal Trade Commission (FTC), 43, 57, 102
    Bureau of Competition, 45
    Bureau of Consumer Protection, 47
    CAN-SPAM Act (2004), 330
    Enforcement Policy Statement on US Origin Claims, 44
    Green Guides, 44, 94
    Guides Concerning Use of Endorsements and Testimonials in Advertising, 44
    Telemarketing Sales Rule, 45
Federal Trade Commission Act (1914), 43, 57, 102
feedback, 425
FEMA (Federal Emergency Management Agency), 101
fictitious name registration. *See* DBA license
field marketing representative. *See* outside sales representative
field representative. *See* outside sales representative

Index

field sales. *See* business-to-business
filter, 560
finance, 40–41
finance laws, 45–46
financial management, 396–400
    budget, 397–398
    financial planning, 396–397
    reports, 398–400
financial planning, 396–397
financial report, 398–400
financial service, 181
financing, 482–493
    debt, 485–486
    equity, 483–484
    loan application process, 490–493
    options, 482–486
firewall, 564
fiscal policy, 100
Fisher-Price, 426
five Cs of banking, 491
five Ps of entrepreneurship, 451
fixed asset, 493
fixed expense, 240, 486
fixture, 348
flaming, 555
flexibility, 407
floating currency, 110
flowchart, 140
FOB (free on board), 291
focus group, 131
following up after a sale, 376–377
follow-up messages, 543–544
Food and Drug Administration (FDA), 47
    Basics for Industry guides, 48
forced-choice format, 132
forecasted sales dollar increase, 397
forecasting manager. *See* supply chain manager
foreign exchange market (FOREX), 110
foreign exchange rate, 109, 116
FOREX (foreign exchange market), 110
formal balance, 355
formal education, 515–518
    graduate, 517
    high school, 515–516
    postgraduate, 517
    postsecondary, 516–517
formal meeting, 436
formal research, 138
Form I-9 Employment Eligibility Verification, 545–546
forms
    benefits, 547
    employment, 545–547
form utility, 14

Form W-2 Wage and Tax Statement, 547
Form W-4 Employee's Withholding Allowance Certificate, 547
for-profit school, 517
four As of stress management, 411
four Cs of communication, 533
four Ps of marketing, 11–12, 118–119
franchise, 114, 459
franchise agreement, 459
franchisee, 114, 459
franchise fee, 459
franchisor, 114, 459
fraud, 471
Free Application for Federal Student Aid (FAFSA), 522
free enterprise. *See* market economy
free on board (FOB), 291
free-trade zone, 112
freighter. *See* water transportation
freight forwarder, 274
frequency, 331, 336
frequently asked questions (FAQ) page, 381
FTC. *See* Federal Trade Commission
full employment, 94
function, 507
functional team, 414
functions of marketing, 12–14
fundamental counting principle, 339
funding
    business opportunities. *See* financing
    college education, 522

G

GDP. *See* gross domestic product
gender, as segmentation variable, 151–152
general education courses, 517
general partnership, 455
general safety rules, 475
generation, 151
generic brand, 220
genericized, 225
generic term, versus brand name, 224–225
geographic segmentation, 150
Gillinder Glass, 473
Give Back Box, 61
giving notice, 547
global business
    environmental scan, 115–118
    marketing strategies, 118–119
    marketplace, 113–119
    ways to enter, 113–115
    see also international trade

global dependency, 109
global distribution, 280
global environmental scan, 115–118
globalization, 108
global marketing, 118–119
global marketplace. *See* global business
Global Public-Private Partnership for Handwashing (PPPHW), 131
global trade. *See* international trade
GNU General Public License (GNU GPL), 558
goals, 506–508
    advertising campaign, 334
    company, 28
    long-term, 507
    marketing, 30, 172
    promotional, 313
    sales, 29
    setting, 507
    short-term, 507
    SMART, 29, 172, 313, 507–508
goal setting, 507
going green, 31
going out of business sale, 241
goods, 6
    public, 101
goodwill, 59
Goodwill Industries, 61
government
    price laws and controls, 254–256
    role in international trade, 110–112
    role in US economy, 100–102
governmental agencies, secondary data source, 134
government market, 175
government sales, 365
government spending, 91
graduate education, 517
grant, 522
graph, 82, 140
    circle, 489
    line, 84
graphic artist. *See* graphic designer
graphic designer, 355
graphic marks, 558
graphics, 338
green business, 58
Green Guides, 44, 94
green marketing, 31, 61
    benefit corporation, 182
    carbon footprint, 252
    customer incentives, 373
    Environmental Protection Agency (EPA), 58
    Green Guides, 44, 94
    green job-search process, 537
    green team, 415

greenwashing, 94
  Lifestyles of Health and Sustainability (LOHAS), 130
  packaging, 222
  paper consumption, 488
  promotional items, 336
  purchasing, 289
  sustainability training, 456
  truthfulness of claims, 44
green press kit, 319
green team, 415
greenwashing, 94
greeting approach, 371
gross domestic product (GDP), 90–92
  coincident indicator, 97
  growth rate, 91–92
  measuring, 91
gross profit, 236
growth rate, economic, 91–92
growth stage, 208
guarantee, 198
Guides Concerning Use of Endorsements and Testimonials in Advertising, 44
gut feeling, 141

H

hacking, 561
handwashing, 131
hard metrics, 32
hard skill, 452
Harry Potter and the Deathly Hallows, 207
hashtag, 487
hazard, 475
headline, 337
health-related advertising, truthfulness of claims, 44
healthy economy, 90
hearing, 428, 437
hierarchy of needs, 168–169
honesty, 366, 408
hook, 337
HR (human resources) department, 394
hub associate. *See* customer service representative
hue, 352
human resources. *See* labor
human resources (HR) department, 394
human risk, 469–470
  avoiding or reducing, 473
humility, 219
Hyatt, 556
hyperinflation, 93
hypothesis, 139
hypothetical questions, 542
Hyundai, 100

I

I-9 (Employment Eligibility Verification form), 545–546
IBM, 389
idea, 6
idea generation, 203
idea screening, 204
identity theft, 563
image, 205, 218
  professional, 25
IMC (integrated marketing communications), 309
imperfect competition. *See* monopolistic competition
import, 109, 113–114
import duty. *See* tariff
impression, 331
improved product, 202
impulse buying decision, 173
incentives, customer, 373
income
  business. *See* revenue
  education level affects, 515
  segmentation variable, 152
income statement, 399–400
indicator, economic, 90–95, 97–98, 117
indirect channel, 269, 272
indirect competitor, 156
inductive reasoning, 410
industrial distributor channel, 272
industrial goods, 271
industrial sales. *See* business-to-business
industrial technology, 75
industry, 176
industry publications, 135
inelastic demand, 240
inflation, 92–93
inflation rate, 93
  coincident indicator, 97
infomercial, 329
inform, 311
informal balance, 355
informal meeting, 436
informal research, 138
informational interviewing, 512
information overload, 411
information utility, 15
infrastructure, 74, 116
infringement, 556
initiative, 406
in-person job application, 538
input, economic, 78

insider trading, 413
inside salesperson, 365
inside voice, 329
installation, 198
installment loan, 181, 485
installments, 181
institution, 175
institutional promotion, 308
institutional sales, 365
instructions, 198
insurance, 468
  types for businesses, 475–476
insurance premium, 475
intangible elements, 218–219
integrated marketing communications (IMC), 309
integrity, 75, 366, 408
intellectual property, 224, 555
  copyright, 556–557
  licensing agreement, 558
  patent, 557
  trademark, 558
intensity, 352
intensive distribution, 279
interactive media specialist, 518
intercultural communication, 427
interest, 93
interest, as related to career planning, 506
interest rate, 93
intermediary, 267–269
intermediate colors, 352
internal customer, 366
internal influence, 177
internal stressor, 411
internal theft, 298, 471
  avoiding or reducing, 474
International Business Machines. *See* IBM
international trade, 108–112
  agreement, 111
  currency, 109–110
  governmental role, 110–112
  policy, 111
  regulation, 111
  see also global business
Internet
  browser settings, 564
  cookies, 561–562
  malware, 562
  phishing, 562
  source of secondary data, 135
  workplace use, 560–563
Internet advertising, 329–331
Internet protocol (IP) address, 561
internship, 512, 518–519
interpersonal communication, 425
interpersonal skill. *See* soft skill
interruption, 438

interview
    data collection, 131
    employment. *See* job interview
introduction, 435–436
introduction stage, 207, 208
inventory, 177
inventory-control systems, 295–297
inventory management, 293
    control systems, 295–297
    shrinkage, 298–299
    using sales forecasting, 297–298
inventory shrinkage, 298–299
investment spending. *See* business spending
invoice, 291
IP (Internet protocol) address, 561

J

Jaguar X-Type, 205
jargon, 426
jingle, 218
JIT (just-in-time) inventory control system, 296
job, 502
    changing, 547–548
job application, 537
    in-person, 538
    online, 537–538
job interview, 540
    behavioral questions, 542–543
    common questions, 541–542
    follow-up messages, 543–544
    hypothetical questions, 542
    post-interview evaluation, 544
    preparation, 540–542
    prohibited questions, 543
    proper attire, 541
    questions interviewees may ask, 543
job lead, 531–532
job offer, evaluating, 545
job-related safety training, 475
job search
    application process, 537–538
    documents needed, 533–537
    finding leads, 531–532
    green process, 537
    managing, 538–539
    marketing oneself, 530–531
job shadowing, 512
job-specific skill. *See* hard skill
joint venture, 115
journalistic approach, 431
junk mail, 316
just-in-time (JIT) inventory control system, 296

K

keystone pricing, 241
keyword, 535
kickback, 412
Kleenex, 202

L

labor, 74, 93–95, 116–117
labor force, 93
labor laws, 45
lagging indicator, 97
laissez-faire management style, 395
land, 73–74
language, polite, 269
large-group communication. *See* public communication
law of diminishing marginal utility, 240
law of supply and demand, 82
laws
    advertising, 43–45
    antitrust, 45, 102
    bankruptcy, 46
    civil, 101
    consumer protection, 46–48
    criminal, 101
    employment, 45
    finance, 45–46
    labor, 45
    marketing, 43–45
    pricing, 254–256
    securities, 46
    truth-in-advertising, 312
lawsuit, 472
layout, 339
lead, 370, 394
leader, 394, 415
leadership, 415
leading indicator, 97
lead time, 294, 333
letter, 432
letterhead stationery, 432
letter of application. *See* cover message
letter of resignation, 547
liability, 399, 453, 493
liability insurance, 476
liability risk, 468
libel, 555
license, 558
licensee, 114
licensing, 114
licensing agreement, 558
licensor, 114
lifelong learning, 518

Lifestyles of Health and Sustainability (LOHAS), 130
light, 354
Likert scale, 153
limited buying decision, 174
limited liability, 454
limited liability company (LLC), 455–456
limited liability partnership (LLP), 455–456
limited partnership (LP), 454
line, 353–354
line graph, 84
line of credit, 485
LinkedIn, 416
liquid asset, 493
listening, 373, 428, 431, 437–438
    barriers, 437–438
    skills, 437
list price, 253
L.L. Bean, 197
LLC (limited liability company), 455–456
LLP (limited liability partnership), 455–456
loan application, 490
    applicant evaluation criteria, 491
    process, 490–493
    pro forma financial statements, 492–493
    required documents, 490–491
local economy, effort to support, 60
logo, 216
LOHAS (Lifestyles of Health and Sustainability), 130
long-term goal, 507
long-term liabilities, 493
loss, 400
loss leader, 255
loss prevention, 473
lost sales opportunities, 379
loyalty buying motives, 372
loyalty programs, 318
LP (limited partnership), 454

M

M&Ms®, 218
macroeconomics, 72
Made in the USA claims, 44
magazines, 328
major area of study, 517
malware (malicious software), 562
management, 41–42, 392
    ethics, 411–413
    financial, 396–400
    function, 393–394

managers, 392–393
    roles, 392–393
    skills needed, 406–411
    styles, 394–395
management function, 393–394
management styles, 394–395
manager, 41, 392–393
manual perpetual inventory-control system, 295
manual-tag system, 295
manufacturer. *See* producer
manufacturer's brand. *See* national brand
manufacturer's rebate, 318
manufacturers' sales branches, 268
manufacturer's suggested retail price (MSRP), 252
MarCom. *See* marketing communication
marginal benefit, 489
marginal cost, 489
marginal utility, 239
margin of error, 139
marital status, segmentation variable, 152
market, 148
market analysis, 28, 157–159
market analyst, 149
market economy, 80–81
market forces, 82–83
    competition, 83
    profit motive, 83
    supply and demand, 82
market identification, 10
marketing, 6, 41
    basics, 9–16
    benefits, 15–16
    economic utility, 14–15
    ethical practices, 56–57
    expert definitions, 7
    functions, 12–14
    laws, 43–45
    more than advertising, 6–7
    oneself, 7–8, 530–531
    through social media, 29
    why to study, 7–8
marketing and promotions manager. *See* advertising and promotions manager
marketing associate. *See* outside sales representative
marketing communication, 308
marketing concept, 9–11
marketing coordinator. *See* marketing manager
marketing director. *See* marketing manager
marketing goals, 30, 172

marketing-information management (MIM), 13, 128–141
    data, 128–135
    reliability, 141
    research process, 138–141
    systems, 136–137
    trend research, 135–136
marketing-information system (MkIS), 136–137
marketing manager, 10
marketing mix, 11–12, 30, 118
    product life cycle's impact, 209
Marketing News, 514
marketing plan, 22–32
    action plan, 31–32
    analysis section, 28–29
    business description, 27–28
    competitive analysis, 26
    executive summary, 27
    marketing strategies, 29–31
    overview, 22–23
    situation analysis, 24–25
    target market, 25–26
marketing premium. *See* promotional item
marketing professional, 7, 509
marketing research. *See* marketing-information management (MIM)
marketing research database, 129
marketing strategies, 29–31
    goals, 30
    marketing mix, 30
    product positioning, 31
    target market, 30
marketing tactic, 31
marketing trend, 135
market planning, 13
market potential, 26, 161
market price, 82
market research analyst. *See* market analyst
market research consultant. *See* market analyst
market risk, 469
    avoiding or reducing, 473
market segment, 25–26
market segmentation, 25, 149–154
    behavioral, 153–154
    demographic, 150–152
    geographic, 150
    psychographic, 152–153
market share, 26, 161–162, 236
market-share leader, 162
market size, 26, 161
market structure, 99–100
marking, 291
markup, 241

marquee, 347
Maslow, Abraham, 168–169
Maslow's Hierarchy of Needs, 168–169
mass market, 148
    versus target market, 148–149
mass marketing, 148
master slide, 367
Mattel, Inc., 114
maturity stage, 209
mean, 160
measurement reasoning, 272
median, 160
media planning, 331
mediation, 417
mediator, 417
medium of exchange, 39
meetings, leading, 436–437
memos, 434
mental ownership, 375
merchandise approach, 372
merchandise manager. *See* buyer
merchandise presentation, 349–350
merchandiser. *See* product manager
merchandising manager. *See* product manager
merchant wholesalers, 268
message, 424
metaphor, 218
method®, 453
metrics, 32, 314
microeconomics, 72–73
Microsoft, 237
middle management, 393
military service, 519
Millennial generation, 151
MIM. *See* marketing-information management
mission statement, 28
mixed economy, 81–82
MkIS (marketing-information system), 136–137
mock interview, 542
mode, 160
modified purchase, 179
monetary policy, 100–101
money
    functions and properties, 39
    supply, 101
monopolistic competition, 100
monopoly, 45, 100, 254
morals, 54, 411
motion (element of design), 354
motion (parliamentary procedure), 436
motivate, 170
motive, 170
movement, 354

Index

MSRP (manufacturer's suggested retail price), 252
multi-channel retailer, 269
multigenerational population, 151
multinational corporation, 115
multiplication, 256, 547
multitasking, 409

N

NAFTA (North American Free Trade Agreement), 112
NAICS (North American Industry Classification System), 176
naming rights, 222
national brand, 219
National Do Not Call Registry, 45
National Retail Federation (NRF), 135
natural resources, 73–74, 267
natural risk, 468–469
need-based awards, 522
needs, 6, 457
    determining customer's, 372–373
    hierarchy of, 168–169
negotiation, 288–289, 417
net exports, 91
net income, 400
netiquette, 555
net profit, 236
networking, 313, 531–532
net worth. See owner's equity
new business
    considerations, 486–489
    starting, 458–459
new product, 201
new-product development, 201–207
    categories, 201–203
    steps, 203–207
new purchase, 179
newspaper, 327–328, 532
news release. See press release
new-to-the-world product, 201
niche market, 150
nonprice competition, 101, 157
nonprofit organization (nonprofit), 42
nonstore retailer, 268
nonverbal communication, 426
nonverbal skills, 426
normative reference group, 169
North American Free Trade Agreement (NAFTA), 112
North American Industry Classification System (NAICS), 176
not-for-profit organization. See nonprofit organizations
not-for-profit school, 517
NRF (National Retail Federation), 135

number sense, 44

O

objection, 374–375
objectivity, 131
objects-focused job, 509
observation, 130–131, 203, 372
occupation, 503
Occupational Information Network (O*NET) OnLine, 513, 532
Occupational Outlook Handbook, 513, 532
Occupational Safety and Health Act (1970), 475
Occupational Safety and Health Administration (OSHA), 45, 475
occupational training, 518
ocean-going ship, 277
odd pricing, 251
offshoring, 115
oligopoly, 100
O*NET (Occupational Information Network) OnLine, 513, 532
online advertising. See Internet advertising
online customer service support, 380–381
online job application, 537–538
online job boards, 531
online merchandise, 557
on-the-job experience, 512
open display, 349
open-response format, 132
open source, 558
operating expenses, 486–487
operational planning, 393
opportunities, 24
opportunity cost, 76
optimism, 407
opt-in, 330
option, 197
optional feature, 197
order bias, 141
order of operations, 32
organizational buyers, 286–287
organizational chart, 393
organizational sales. See business-to-business
organizations, professional, 513
organize, 393
OSHA (Occupational Safety and Health Administration), 45, 475
outdoor media, 328–329
out-of-office notice, 535

output, economic, 78
outside salesperson, 365
outside sales representative, 474
outsourcing. See contract manufacturing
overdraft agreement, 485
overselling, 376
owner's equity, 493

P

packaging, 199, 217
    sustainable, 222
packing list, 290
packing slip, 290
paid SEO, 330
paper consumption, 488
paralanguage, 475
parliamentary procedure, 436
participatory marketing, 310
participatory style. See democratic management style
partnership, 42, 454–455
partnership agreement, 455
passive listening, 437
password strength, 564
patent, 557
patronage buying motive, 171
peak, 96
peer-to-peer communication, 425
peer-to-peer lending, 485
PEMDAS (order of math operations), 32
people-focused job, 509
people skill. See soft skill
per capita GDP, 90
percentage markup, 241
percentage, 55
perception, 219
    influence on price, 242–243
perfect competition, 100
periodic inventory-control system, 296
perishable good, 276
perpetual inventory-control system, 295
perseverance, 407
personal brand, 530–531
personal fact sheet, 538
personality, 170, 506
personality trait, 451
personal selling, 320, 364–365
personal space, 454
persuade, 311
persuasion, 311
PEST analysis, 24–25, 115–118, 159, 178

philanthropy, 59–60
phishing, 562
physical distribution, 269
physical inventory, 295
pie chart. *See* circle graph
pipeline, 277
piracy, 556
place, 12, 118
    channel of distribution, 266–273
    one of four Ps of marketing, 266
    supply chain, 274–280
place strategies, 30
place utility, 14
plagiarism, 555
plan, 393
planned obsolescence, 469
PO (purchase order), 290
point-of-purchase (POP) displays, 319, 349
point-of-sale (POS) software, 296
policy
    fiscal, 100
    monetary, 100–101
polite language, 269
political factors, 24, 116
Popcorn, Faith, 135
POP (point-of-purchase) displays, 319, 349
population, 129
pop-up blocker, 564
portfolio, 536–537
positive attitude, 150, 407
possession utility, 15
POS (point-of-sale) software, 296
postgraduate education, 517
postsecondary education, 516–517
postsecondary plan. *See* career plan
Pottery Barn, 223
PPPHW (Global Public-Private Partnership for Handwashing), 131
PR (public relations), 319–320
preapproach, 368–370
predatory pricing, 254
prejudice, 438
premium, 470
preselling, 315
presentation, 367
presentation skills, 367
presentation-style communication, 425
press conference, 320
press kit, 319
press release, 319
prestige pricing, 251
price, 12, 118, 234–243
    government laws and controls, 254–256
    influencers, 238–243

objectives, 235–237
one of four Ps of marketing, 234
strategies, 30, 250–253
price ceiling, 256
price competition, 101, 157
price controls, 256
price discrimination, 254
price-fixing, 102, 254
price floor, 256
price gouging, 254
price lining, 250
price mix, 250
price stability, 93
pricing, 13
    ethical practices, 57–58
    objectives, 235–237
    strategies, 30, 250–253
primary color, 352
primary data, 129–133
    diary, 132
    experiment, 133
    interview, 131
    observation, 130–131
    survey, 131–132
primary research, 129
prime time, 333
principles of design, 354
print media, 327–328
Prius, 205
private carrier, 275
private employment agency, 532
private enterprise. *See* market economy
private-label brand, 219
private warehouse, 278
pro forma balance sheet, 492–493
pro forma cash flow statement, 492
pro forma financial statements, 492–493
pro forma income statement, 492
proactive public relations, 319
probability, 458
problem solving, 220, 410, 470
procrastination, 409
Procter & Gamble, 202
procurement specialist. *See* product manager
producer, 40, 175, 177, 266–267
product, 6, 12, 118
    one of the four Ps of marketing, 194
product adaptation, 118
product depth, 197
product design, 205–206
production, 40
    factors of, 73–75
product item, 197
productive inventory, 297
productivity, 74, 94
product life cycle, 208–209

impact on marketing mix, 209
influence on price, 243
product line, 196
product manager, 199, 200
product mix, 196
product-mix pricing, 250–251
product mix strategy, 197
product obsolescence, 202, 469
product placement. *See* embedded marketing
product planning, 196–199
product positioning, 31, 160
product presentation, 373–374
product promotion, 308
product, 194–209
    branding, 216–225
    business, 195–196
    consumer, 195
    features, 197–198
    goods and services, 194
    importance of pricing correctly, 487
    life cycle, 208–209
    new-product development, 201–207
    planning, 196–199
    pricing, 250–257
    protection, 198–199
    usage, 198
product/service management, 14, 199–200, 209
product strategies, 30, 197
product tracking, 381
product training, 368–369
product trend, 135–136
product width, 197
profession, 502
professional associations and organizations, 513
professional buyer. *See* buyer
professional etiquette, 60, 408
professionalism, 25, 43, 406
professional liability insurance, 476
professional publications, 514
profit, 11, 38, 83, 400
    maximizing, 236–237
profit margin, 487
profit motive, 83
promotion, 12, 14, 118–119, 308–320
    basics, 308–314
    goals, 311–312
    one of four Ps of marketing, 308
    plan, 312–314
    strategies, 30, 308–311
    types, 315–320
    writing, 430–431
promotional campaign, 312
promotional channel. *See* promotional mix

Index

promotional discount, 253
promotional item, 319
    ecofriendly, 336
promotional mix, 12, 30, 309
promotional plan, 312–314
promotional price, 237
promotional strategies, 30, 308–311
promotions director. *See* advertising and promotions manager
promotions manager. *See* advertising and promotions manager
prop, 357
property insurance, 475
proportion, 355
proprietary credit card, 181, 379
proprietary information, 195, 412
proprietary school. *See* for-profit school
prospect. *See* lead
prosperity, 96
protectionism, 111
protocol, 133
prototype, 205
provider, 100
psychographics, 152
psychographic segmentation, 152
psychological influence, 170
psychological pricing, 251–252
publications, professional, 514
public communication, 425
public domain, 557
public goods and services, 101
public relations (PR), 319–320
public warehouse, 278
pull promotional concept, 311
punctuality, 512
purchase order (PO), 290
purchasing, 286–299
    ecofriendly, 289
    organizational buyer, 286–287
    process, 287–291
purchasing agent, 286–287
purchasing manager. *See* product manager; purchasing agent
purchasing process, 287–291
pure risk, 468
push promotional concept, 310

Q

qualitative data, 130
quality control, 291
quality service, 366
quantitative data, 130
quantity discounts, 89, 252
questioning, 373
questions
    behavioral, 542–543
    common, 541–542
    hypothetical, 542
    interview, 541–543
    prohibited in job interview, 543
    those interviewees may ask, 543
quota, 111

R

rack jobber, 268
radio, 329
radio frequency identification (RFID), 296
rail transportation, 276
Ralph Lauren, 223
ransomware, 562
rational buying motive, 171, 372
raw data, 140
raw materials. *See* natural resources
raw-materials manufacturer, 267
raw-materials producer, 267
reach, 331, 336
reactive public relations, 319
reading, improving comprehension, 438–439
real numbers, 97
reasoning, 220, 470
rebates, 318
receiver, 424
receiving barrier, 428
receiving record, 290
recession, 96
recycling, 60
reducing risk, 473–475
reference, 535
reference group, 169
regulations. *See* laws
regulator, 100
relationship selling, 178, 365
reliability, 141
remind, 311
rent control, 256
reorder point, 294
repackaging, 202
repeat purchase, 179
reporting error, 141
report, writing, 160, 431–432
repositioning, 202
representative sampling, 129
research firm, secondary data source, 134
researching a marketing career, 509–514
    employment trends, 513
    career and technical student organizations (CTSOs), 511–512
    informational interviewing, 512
    job shadowing, 512
    on-the-job experience, 512
research process, 138–141
reseller, 175
Reserve Officers' Training Corps (ROTC), 519
resign, 547
resilience, 112
resources, natural, 73–74, 267
respect, 396, 407
responsible, 266, 406
responsiveness, 297, 560
résumé, 533, 535
retail buyer. *See* buyer
retailer, 268–269
retailer channel, 270
return on investment (ROI), 236
revenue, 396
reverse engineering, 207
revised product, 202
revising writing, 431
RFID (radio frequency identification), 296
rise, 377
risk, 416, 468
    assuming, 476
    avoiding, 473–475
    business, 468–471
    categories, 468
    management, 472–476
    reducing, 473–475
    transferring, 475–476
risk assessment, 472
risk management, 468, 472–476
road transportation, 275–276
robbery, 470
Robert's Rules of Order, 436
robocalling, 45
ROI (return on investment), 236
ROTC (Reserve Officers' Training Corps), 519
rounding, 177
routine buying decision, 173–174
royalty, 114
royalty fee. *See* franchise fee
rule of two, 486
run, 377
rural, 150

S

safety, 475
safety stock. *See* buffer stock
sales, 364–382
    business-to-business (B2B), 365
    business-to-consumer (B2C), 365
    careers, 365–367
    customer service, 380–382

leads, 370
lost opportunities, 379
maximizing, 235–236
preapproach, 368–370
process, 370–377
role and value, 364–365
transaction, 377–379
sales analysis, 161–162
best opportunities, 29
goals, 29
history and projections, 29
Sales and Marketing, 514
sales-below-cost laws, 255
sales executive. *See* sales manager
sales forecast, 396–397
sales forecasting, 487–488
use in inventory management, 297–298
sales-increase factor, 397
sales manager, 47
sales messages, ethical, 358
sales process, 370–377
answering questions or objections, 374–375
approach, 370–372
closing, 375–376
determining customer needs and wants, 372–373
following up, 376–377
presenting product, 373–374
sales promotion, 317–319
sales representative. *See* outside sales representative
sales supervisor. *See* sales manager
sales support area, 348
sales tax, 377
samples, 318
sample size, 129
factor in reliability of research, 141
Sarbanes-Oxley Act (2002), 46
saturated market, 209
SBA (Small Business Association), 485
SBI (Strategic Business Insights), 153
scanning, 439
scarcity, 75
scholarship, 522
Scholastic, Inc., 207
schools, for-profit and not-for-profit, 517
script, 374
search engine optimization (SEO), 330
seasonal discount, 253
SEC (US Securities and Exchange Commission), 46
secondary color, 352
secondary data, 133–135

secondary research, 133
secret shopper, 130
secured loan. *See* installment loan
securities, 46
securities laws, 46
security, 473
security plan, 563
security policies, 474
selective distribution, 279
self-actualization, 168
self-assessment, 451, 504–506
self-awareness, 239, 531
self-confidence, 174
self-control, 416
self-esteem, 202, 504
self-funding, 483
self-insure, 476
self-management skills, 76, 394, 408–411
selling, 14
ethical practices, 58
selling area, 348
selling policies, 368
sender, 424
sending barrier, 427
SEO (search engine optimization), 330
service approach, 371
service business, 175
service mark, 224, 558
services, 6
importance of pricing correctly, 487
public, 101
shades, 352
shape, 354
share, 95
shared workspace, 485
shareholder, 95
Sherman Antitrust Act, 45, 102
Sherwin-Williams, 223
ship. *See* water transportation
shoplifter, 299, 470
shortage, 83
short-term goal, 507
short-term liabilities, 493
signature, 339
silhouette, 355
situational influence, 170, 178
situation analysis, 24–25
skill
hard, 452
listening, 437
nonverbal, 426
presentation, 367
self-management, 394, 408–411
soft, 15, 394, 406–408, 452–453
speaking, 426
teamwork, 415–417

verbal, 426
skimming, 439
slander, 555
slide presentation, 367
slogan. *See* tagline
slope, 377
Small Business Association (SBA), 485
small-group communication, 425
Small Loan Advantage program, 485
SMART goal, 29, 172, 313, 507–508
SMM. *See* social media marketing
social environment, 169–170
social factor, 25, 117–118
social lending. *See* peer-to-peer lending
socially responsible marketing, 60–62
social media, 330–331
analytics, 224
blogs, 461
content marketing, 136
customer service avenue, 381
dashboards, 257
ethical company communications, 532
Facebook, 298
hashtags, 487
LinkedIn, 416
marketing tool, 29
Twitter, 327
YouTube, 378
social-media analytics, 224
social-media dashboards, 257
social-media marketing (SMM), 60
goals, 172
terms, 100
social needs, 168
social responsibility. *See* corporate social responsibility (CSR)
social trend, 135
soft metrics, 32
soft skill, 15, 394, 406–408, 452–453
software virus, 562
sole proprietorship, 42, 453–454
solution accuracy, 408
solution selling. *See* feature-benefit selling
sourcing, ethical, 110
spam, 57, 330
spamming, 555
Spanish-language television, 153
speaking
introductions, 435–436
meetings, 436–437
telephone calls, 434–435
speaking skills, 426
specialist-level position, 511
specialization, 94

Index

specialized purchaser. *See* purchasing agent
speculative risk, 468
sponsorship, 318
spyware, 562
staff, 393
staffing, 393
stakeholder, 416
Standard English, 425
standardization, 118
standard of living, 90, 117
start-up capital, 483–486
start-up costs, 486
State Farm, 218
statement of ethics. *See* code of ethics
statistical reasoning, 319
stereotyping, 412
sticky, 60
stock, 95, 455
stockholders, 95, 455
stock market, 95
    leading indicator, 98
stockout, 294
storage, 277–278
store exterior, 347–348
storefront, 347–348
store image, 346
store interior, 348–349
store layout, 348
store manager. *See* sales manager
store of value, 39
STORES Magazine, 135
Strategic Business Insights (SBI), 153
strategic planning, 393
strengths, 24
stress, 411
stress management, 411
structural security, 473
substitute selling, 373
suburban, 150
suggestion selling, 376
supervisory-level position, 511
supervisory management, 393
supplier. *See* vendor
supply, 82, 238
supply chain, 118, 266, 274–280
    global distribution considerations, 280
    management, 278–280
    storage, 277–278
    transportation, 274–277
supply chain coordinator. *See* supply chain manager
supply chain director. *See* supply chain manager
supply chain management, 13, 278–280
supply chain manager, 278, 279
supply curve, 82
surety bond, 476

surplus, 83
surveillance, 474
survey, 131–132
sustainability, 60
sustainability training, 456
sustainable packaging, 222
sweepstakes, 318
SWOT analysis, 24, 159
system, 78
systematic decision-making, 76–77

T

table, 140
tactical planning, 393
tagline, 218
talent. *See* aptitude
tangible elements, 216–218
tanker, 277
Target, 287
target market, 25–26, 30, 148
    versus mass market, 148–149
tariff, 111
task. *See* job
TaskRabbit, 533
tax returns, 476
teamwork, 415
    skills needed, 415–417
technical support, 198
technological factor, 25, 118
technology, 75
tech prep, 516
telemarketer, 79
telemarketing, 45, 320, 365
telemarketing sales representative. *See* telemarketer
Telemarketing Sales Rule, 45
telephone etiquette, 413, 434, 541
telephone sales representative. *See* telemarketer
telesales specialist. *See* telemarketer
television, 329
    Spanish-language, 153
templates, marketing plan, 23
terms for delivery, 291
terms of service, 557
terms of use, 557
testimonials. *See* endorsements
test marketing, 206–207
texture, 354
thank-you message, 543
theft, 470–471
threat, 24
three Cs of credit, 183, 491
Tide purclean™, 202
timeline, 31
time management, 408–410
time utility, 15

time value of money, 39
tint, 352
T-Mobile, 317
to-do list, 409
tone
    of speech, 434
    written, 431
top-down management. *See* autocratic management style
total assets, 236
total company approach, 11
total embargo, 111
Toyota Prius, 205
trade agreement, 111
trade association, 513
    secondary data source, 134–135
trade barrier, 111
trade character, 217
trade credit, 181, 486
trade deficit, 109
trade discount, 252
trade journal, 135
trademark, 224, 558
trade-off, 76
trade policy, 111
trade regulation, 111
trade sanction, 111
trade secrets. *See* proprietary information
trade show, 158, 207, 318–319
trade show manager, 235
trade surplus, 109
trading, 95
trading bloc, 112
tradition, 79
traditional economy, 79–80
training, 198, 518–519
trait, 451
transaction, 377–379
transferrable skill. *See* soft skill
transferring risk, 475–476
transit advertising, 328
transportation, 274–277
transportation infrastructure, 74
trend, 135
trend research, 135–136, 203
triadic color, 353
trial close, 375
trial run, 207
Trojan horse, 562
trough, 97
trustworthiness, 408
truth-in-advertising laws, 312
Truth in Lending Act, 183
turnover rate, 298
Twitter, 327
two-week notice, 547
typeface, 338
typography, 338

U

uncontrollable risk, 468
unemployed, 94
unemployment rate, 94
    lagging indicator, 97
uninsurable risk, 476
unique brand, 222
unique selling proposition (USP), 157, 335
unit-control system, 295
unit conversion, 295
United Parcel Service. *See* UPS
unit of value, 39
unit pricing, 255
units, 563
unlimited liability, 454
unsecured loan, 485
unsolicited call, 434
upper management, 393
UPS, 178
upselling. *See* suggestion selling
urban, 150
usage, 198
usage rate, 154
US Department of Labor (DOL), 45, 513, 532
USP (unique selling proposition), 157, 335
US Securities and Exchange Commission (SEC), 46
utility, 14
utility infrastructure, 74

V

validity, 141
VALS™ survey, 153
value, 76, 172, 218
    adding, 14
value (color component), 352
value-based pricing. *See* demand-based pricing
values, 152–153, 505–506
variable, 133
variable expense, 241, 486
VC (venture capitalist), 484
vendor, 177, 288
    evaluation, 291
venture capital, 484
venture capitalist (VC), 484
verbal communication, 426, 434
verbal skills, 426
viral marketing, 60, 310
virtual test market, 206
virus. *See* software virus
vision statement, 28
visual aid, 367
visual communication, 426
visual merchandising, 319, 346–358
    design elements and principles, 351–355
    display development and maintenance, 355–358
    elements, 347–350
    interior displays, 349–350
    store exterior, 347–348
    store interior, 348–349
    store layout, 348
VNU Business Publication, 514
voice mail, 435
volume pricing, 236

W

W-2 (Wage and Tax Statement form), 547
W-4 (Employee's Withholding Allowance Certificate form), 547
wage, 38
Wage and Tax Statement (Form W-2), 547
wait list, 520
wants, 6, 457
    determining customer's, 372–373
Warby Parker, 484
warehouse, 278
warranty, 197
water transportation, 277
weaknesses, 24
webmaster, 561
website manager. *See* webmaster
weight, 338
white space, 339
whole number, 97
wholesaler, 268
wholesaler channel, 270
word-of-mouth advertising. *See* viral marketing
word problem, 206
work ethic, 406
work focus, 509
work-life balance, 409, 505
workplace attire, 371
workplace bullying, 55
workplace Internet use, 560–563
workspace etiquette, 357
workspaces, 253, 485
work-study programs, 522
work values, 505
World Trade Organization (WTO), 111
worms, 562
written communication, 425–426
    for marketing purposes, 430–434
    writing style, 431
WTO (World Trade Organization), 111

X

X-Type, 205

Y

YouTube, 378

Z

Zappos, 28